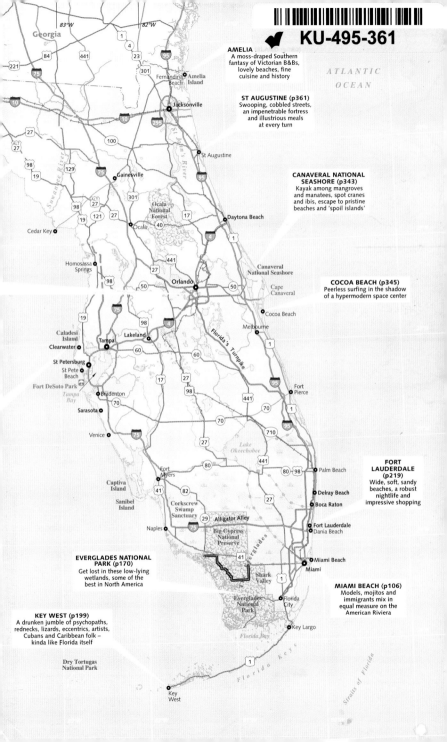

KU-495-361

AMELIA
A moss-draped Southern fantasy of Victorian B&Bs, lovely beaches, fine cuisine and history

ST AUGUSTINE (p361)
Swooping, cobbled streets, an impenetrable fortress and illustrious meals at every turn

CANAVERAL NATIONAL SEASHORE (p343)
Kayak among mangroves and manatees, spot cranes and ibis, escape to pristine beaches and 'spoil islands'

COCOA BEACH (p345)
Peerless surfing in the shadow of a hypermodern space center

FORT LAUDERDALE (p219)
Wide, soft, sandy beaches, a robust nightlife and impressive shopping

EVERGLADES NATIONAL PARK (p170)
Get lost in these low-lying wetlands, some of the best in North America

MIAMI BEACH (p106)
Models, mojitos and immigrants mix in equal measure on the American Riviera

KEY WEST (p199)
A drunken jumble of psychopaths, rednecks, lizards, eccentrics, artists, Cubans and Caribbean folk – kinda like Florida itself

Georgia

ATLANTIC OCEAN

Jacksonville

St Augustine

Gainesville

Ocala National Forest

Cedar Key

Homosassa Springs

Orlando

Cape Canaveral

Canaveral National Seashore

Daytona Beach

Cocoa Beach

Melbourne

Caladesi Island

Clearwater

Tampa

Lakeland

St Petersburg

St Pete Beach

Fort DeSoto Park

Tampa Bay

Bradenton

Sarasota

Venice

Florida's Turnpike

Fort Pierce

Lake Okeechobee

Palm Beach

Delray Beach

Boca Raton

Fort Lauderdale

Dania Beach

Miami Beach

Miami

Captiva Island

Fort Myers

Sanibel Island

Corkscrew Swamp Sanctuary

Alligator Alley

Naples

Big Cypress National Preserve

Everglades

Shark Valley

Everglades National Park

Florida City

Key Largo

Dry Tortugas National Park

Florida Bay

Florida Keys

Key West

Straits of Florida

On the Road

JEFF CAMPBELL
Coordinating Author
Like generations of Campbell men, here I am teaching my son how to build sandcastles at Daytona Beach. When our efforts succumbed to the feet of my nephews, we hopped in an ATV to admire the undemolished sand creations of others further up the beach.

ADAM KARLIN Here I am in my old stomping grounds in the Florida Keys – specifically, Anne's Beach in Islamorada. The sun and the sea have vanished into each other, the mud is cool between my toes, the water is teal, and all is well on this perfect Florida day.

WILLY VOLK At Sangrias in St Augustine I inhaled white sangria (or 'Sangri-La') and devoured a tapas trio. At the intersection of St George and Hypolita, up on the 2nd floor, I soon learned that this was the best seat in town for sunsets and people-watching.

BECCA BLOND It's an absolutely gorgeous day on St Pete's Pass-a-Grille Beach and I'm taking a couple of hours off work to relax, read on the beach and swim in the Gulf of Mexico's warm water with my fiancé, Aaron. After hanging out for a while, we head to the rooftop bar across the street for frozen cocktails and a fantastic southwest Florida sunset.

BETH GREENFIELD On my way up north from the Emerald Coast, I took a little detour on the advice of a really friendly guy who worked at the Sundog Bookstore in Seaside. He sent me to Eden Gardens State Park, where I strolled the grounds of the impressive estate but then made a beeline for this lone, skinny dock, which beckoned me out over Choctawhatchee Bay. I sat there for nearly half an hour, though I had a lot more exploring to do. The sun was delicious.

JENNIFER DENNISTON My husband and girls tagged along for some of my Disney research, and I'm incredibly lucky to be able to incorporate their perspectives and insight into my writing. We flew to Orlando from Iowa, and headed straight from the airport to Disney's Pirate Princess Party. Here, we're collapsing on the curb for the parade.

For full author biographies see p528.

C700632591

 South Lanarkshire Libraries

This book is to be returned on or before
the last date stamped below or may be
renewed by telephone or online.

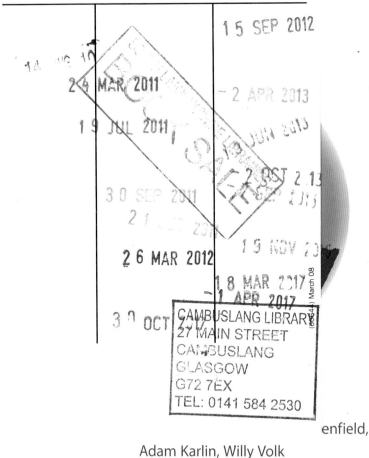
enfield,

Adam Karlin, Willy Volk

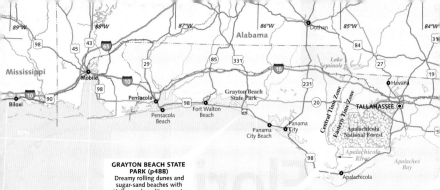

GRAYTON BEACH STATE PARK (p488)
Dreamy rolling dunes and sugar-sand beaches with Hollywood-quality sunsets

SUWANNEE RIVER (p477)
Lazy river paddles among sparkling freshwater springs, folk music and Southern hospitality

APALACHICOLA NATIONAL FOREST (p474)
Hike and bike this otherworldly forest of cypress hammocks, dunes, swamps, sinks and karst terrain

WALT DISNEY WORLD (p290)
A sentimental favorite, the granddaddy of theme parks enchants even the most cynical travelers

GULF OF

MEXICO

CALADESI ISLAND (p430)
Canoe to secluded island beaches that are considered to be some of the USA's finest

ELEVATION

500ft

0

LEGEND

Tollway
Freeway
Primary Road
Secondary Road
Tertiary Road
Unsealed Road

0 — 100 km
0 — 60 miles

Florida Highlights

Ah, the Sunshine State. Where else do wild alligators, art-deco masterpieces, raucous theme parks, idyllic beaches and sleepy small towns peacefully coexist? The USA's subtropical paradise offers subcultures that will surprise and delight even the most discerning traveler. Whether you're looking for a slick city getaway in steamy Miami or want to waste away 'Margaritaville'-style in the Keys, Florida's hyperbolic extremes are ripe for the picking. Bring your sense of adventure and fasten your mouse ears. We're goin' in.

RICHARD I'ANSON

① DRIVING IN MIAMI

Driving in Miami (p83) is either the most frustrating or exhilarating experience in the automotive world. On a bad day, it's hell's own traffic: cars crammed up your tailpipe, jerks in Hummers cutting you off and honking in your face, and a stream of Spanish curses flying between you and every other driver in South Florida. But on a good day, it's the breeze in your face, teal water to either side, palm trees over your head and the spell of the Magic City cast endlessly over the city skyline.

Adam Karlin, author, USA

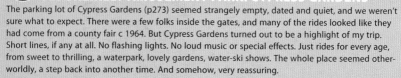

©JEFF GREENBERG / WORLD OF STC

② AN UNLIKELY AMUSEMENT PARK: CYPRESS GARDENS

The parking lot of Cypress Gardens (p273) seemed strangely empty, dated and quiet, and we weren't sure what to expect. There were a few folks inside the gates, and many of the rides looked like they had come from a county fair c 1964. But Cypress Gardens turned out to be a highlight of my trip. Short lines, if any at all. No flashing lights. No loud music or special effects. Just rides for every age, from sweet to thrilling, a waterpark, lovely gardens, water-ski shows. The whole place seemed other-worldly, a step back into another time. And somehow, very reassuring.

Jennifer Denniston, author, USA

MARK NEWMA

③ GETTING UP CLOSE & PERSONAL WITH ALLIGATORS, EVERGLADES NATIONAL PARK

Seeing 12 – no, 15 – no, 20 – no…well, a lot of pairs of alligator eyes winking at me from across the still waters of Everglades National Park (p170). And then eating them. Alright, not 'them' per se, but I had some alligator tail and frog's legs in Everglades City afterwards, and you know what? Those alligators should fear me, because they were delicious.

Adam Karlin, author, USA

NIGHTLIFE IN DOWNTOWN ORLANDO

Downtown Orlando is one of my favorite spots for nightlife (p281) in the country – it sports a concentration of bars on par or better than almost any US city. Recent investment and construction have remade the downtown area into a vibrant and safe social mecca for Central Florida. Located around Orange Ave and Central Blvd, off the beaten path of amusement parks and tourist traps, the area is overrun on weekends with local hipsters and the like getting their drink/dance on. Pedicabs swarm the streets at 2am for those too soused to drive or walk home.

Todd Grisar, Lonely Planet staff member, USA

WILLY VOLK

RAY LASKOWITZ

4

CENTRAL FLORIDA'S COUNTRY ROADS

Sunny, warm afternoon. Blue, cloudless sky. Top on the red convertible down. Tom Petty blaring through the speakers. No one else on the country roads as I whizz and bank among lemon-yellow wildflowers, bawk-bawking wild turkeys and hulking trees thick with Spanish moss. Central Florida (p385) feels deliciously far from anywhere else in the state.

Willy Volk, author, USA

5

6

© STEPHEN FRINK COLLECTION / ALAMY

SNORKELING AT BAHIA HONDA STATE PARK

Snorkeling near the channel at Bahia Honda State Park (p196) tests your nerve. I was once quietly trailing a shark who was cruising the grassy bottom, when I looked up to find myself almost nose to nose with a barracuda. Seeing all those teeth close up, I panicked and flippered back to shore as fast as I could. I stuck to shallow coral reefs after that.

Jeff Campbell, author, USA

MICHAEL

7 MANATEE SPOTTING, CRYSTAL RIVER

I love to just throw my kayak up on the roof of the SUV and drive to Crystal River (p460), north of Tampa. The river is absolutely clear, and somewhat of a sanctuary from the fast boats of the Gulf, so if you are lucky, you might get to gaze into the wonderful eyes of a manatee.

Stephanie Costa, traveler, USA

EDDIE BRA

8 SUNSET ON THE MATANZAS RIVER

The sun slid slowly down the sky that evening, inching to a mangrove-lined horizon. While much of Florida's sunset spots are besmirched with condos and storefronts, the westward view over the Matanzas River in northeast Florida (p351) was unobstructed, and brushed with lilac, periwinkle and peach. The river was smooth as a tabletop. The frosted mug in my hand stuck to my fingers. My wife was seated next to me, smelling sweet and smiling sweeter.

Willy Volk, author, USA

Contents

Regional Map Contents

THE PANHANDLE
(pp462-3)

NORTHEAST
FLORIDA
(p352)

ORLANDO &
WALT DISNEY
WORLD
(p262)

THE SPACE
COAST
(p336)

TAMPA BAY &
SOUTHWEST
FLORIDA
(p404)

SOUTHEAST
FLORIDA
(p216)

THE EVERGLADES
(pp168-9)

MIAMI
(pp86-7)

FLORIDA KEYS
& KEY WEST
(pp184-5)

Destination Florida

Walt Disney was right: Florida is a place that captures the imagination. The landscape is exaggerated and invites exaggeration. Spanish explorers saw manatees and imagined they were mermaids; Ponce de León saw a crystal-clear spring and imagined it was a fountain of youth. Developers saw swamps and sold them as paradise, but if they are, there's plenty of the devil in them. In its history, Florida has inspired as much madness and murder as it has fantasies of a magical kingdom where dreams really do come true.

If you're coming to Florida for a simple beach vacation, this might all sound beside the point. With a looping coil of coastline containing over 650 miles of sandy beaches, Florida knows what side its bread is buttered on. Indeed, the state is organized chiefly to satisfy the singular human desire for a clean room, a cold beer, a quiet beach with gently lapping waves, a palm tree and a rose-tinged sunset.

That's the postcard, anyway. If the actual scene doesn't always materialize – if, say, another condo tower now blocks said view, or the beach is too crowded with others seeking the same reverie – it still happens often and regularly enough to keep people coming. And that is very much the point, from Florida's perspective.

And that's OK. The vision of a seaside paradise can falter, as can the mechanical magic of Florida's phantasmagorical theme parks, and the land – the watery, swampy, humid, shimmering, creature-filled peninsula – remains. In the end, it's this unstable, ever-shifting landscape that never fails to overwhelm and that works its way indelibly inside, never to be forgotten. And it does so both in that grand, uplifting, aching-beauty-of-nature kind of way, and in that fetid, surreal, alligators-in-the-swamp-snakes-in-the-trees-get-me-outta-here kind of way.

Florida, more civilized than it once was, is still seductively and unnervingly fluid. Miami continues to be washed with wave after wave of Latin immigrants, and the city vibrates with energy and culture and change. The Deep South of northern Florida lovingly tends its memories, even as old ways fade or are simply paved over. And just off the coast, another hurricane is always brewing.

So come for the beaches and Mickey Mouse, come for the people and the Everglades, come for the nightlife and the kayaking and the manatees and the gators. But make sure to come. Because Florida is always stranger than you imagine, and it never holds still.

Getting Started

Florida makes its living from tourism, so it's always eager and ready to welcome you. Getting here, renting a car, finding a hotel, a meal, a drink, the beach – Florida makes these details easy, and relatively affordable, so that you can focus solely on having a great time, which ideally inspires you to return again and again.

So far, anyway, that formula has worked pretty well. And it means that you, the visitor, need only decide what you want to do and when you want to do it. The only hitch is that Florida, being so attractive and welcoming and popular, can also get insanely crowded. Advance planning is essential, because like the Magic Kingdom, Florida is all about crowd management: savvy travelers know the best rides fill up fast, and beating those inevitable, growing, snaking lines sometimes requires perfect timing.

WHEN TO GO

Unfortunately (or not), Florida has no single perfect season. The best time to go depends entirely on your agenda.

Always consider the weather first. Similar to the tropics, Florida has essentially two seasons: wet and dry. Winter, Florida's dry season, is from roughly November through April. Temperatures are lower, there's less humidity and rain, and it's the ideal time to hike, canoe and explore nature, particularly in South Florida. Snowbirds (northerners who winter in Florida) love winter because sunny 70°F days mean no snow, ever.

Summer is the 'wet season': from May to October, it's hot, sticky and rainstorms deluge many an afternoon. This is also roughly hurricane season, which peaks in September (for more on hurricanes, see p507).

See Climate Charts (p505) for more information.

All this would seem to make winter the best time to come, and it often is; particularly in Miami and South Florida, winter is high season, bringing with it higher prices and more crowds. But in northern Florida, the ocean is a little too cold for swimming in winter, so the Panhandle, St Augustine and others boom in summer.

Orlando's high season is year-round. Here, theme-park lines respond more to school vacations and holidays than to weather. Also, those who brave summer's heat and mosquitoes often find that its dreaded rains can blow through quickly; duck inside for an hour, and it's over before you know it.

Finally, wildlife keeps its own schedule: migrating birds, manatees, sea turtles, whales – all come at different times, so if you're set on seeing a particular animal, find out when it's visiting (see p71 for more on parks and wildlife).

COSTS & MONEY

The rich and famous adore Florida, but you don't need be either to enjoy its sunny climes. In this guide, we emphasize the middle ground, while providing plenty of choices for travelers to splash out or conserve their pennies as they like.

How low can you go? If you're camping and making most of your own meals, you could spend under $50 a day. If you're two people staying in budget motels and eating out (even cheaply), budget $100 a day per person. Whether you rent a car is the real wild card; without one, your expenses plummet; with one, that's a base of at least $40 to $50 a day (depending on insurance and gas). However, unless you're staying in one spot, you'll probably want a car, as public-transportation networks do not stretch to all locations in Florida.

DON'T LEAVE HOME WITHOUT...

▪ strong sunscreen, high-quality sunglasses and a wide-brimmed hat

▪ a bathing suit

▪ binoculars for wildlife- and bird-watching

▪ a great road map

▪ your mp3 player loaded with great beach tunes

▪ leaving half of what you think you'll need at home

▪ a spiffy black outfit if you're heading to Miami

▪ a copy of your passport, driver's license and 800 numbers for your credit cards

---

For comfortable midrange travel, budget $150 to $200 per person a day. 'Comfort' is relative, but with this budget, expect to mix up a nicer B&B with a budget hotel and to balance days at expensive destinations (Miami and Orlando theme parks) with days at free ones (the beach and state parks). Going in a destination's high season also significantly affects your costs, particularly in beach-resort towns like Sanibel and Amelia Islands. And of course, if you spend all your time in Miami's art-deco hotels and nightclubs, or bounce from theme park to theme park, the sky is very nearly the limit.

One thing in the traveler's favor is the intense competition for business in Florida, which generally keeps prices lower, and which inspires a blizzard of promotions, deals and discounts. If you plan ahead, check the web, call and ask, and are a little flexible, you'll find numerous opportunities to trim your costs here and there.

HOW MUCH?

Canoe rental per half/full day $25/35

Disney one-day adult admission $71

Everglades frog legs $15

Daytona Beach ATV rental per hour $25

South Beach art-deco hotel room $150 to $300

TRAVELING RESPONSIBLY

Like Hawaii, Florida is a uniquely beautiful and even rare place that is constantly in danger of being loved to death. And like Hawaii, Florida's record of caring for itself is spotty (to put it mildly). This means that, perhaps more than elsewhere, visitors to Florida need to travel with an awareness of their impact.

In fact, there is very little agreement among Floridians about the environmental, ecological and cultural impacts of many popular activities. For instance, are Everglades airboats terrible or no big deal? It depends on who you ask, and even the authors of this book disagree. So, throughout this guide, we have tried to highlight issues and provide information so travelers can make their own informed decisions.

One resource is the 'GreenDex,' p548, which is an index of what we consider environmentally friendly businesses included in this guide. For more on specific activities, begin with the boxed texts, p75 and p56. If you prefer farmers markets to supermarkets, visit www.florida-agriculture .com for a statewide list.

Established in 2004, Florida's **Department of Environmental Protection** (www .dep.state.fl.us) tackles the state's ecological and sustainability issues head-on and provides a wealth of practical information. In particular, check out **Green Lodging Program** (www.dep.state.fl.us/greenlodging).

TRAVEL LITERATURE

What is Florida really like? We are so glad you asked.

In *Dream State* (2004), bawdy, gimlet-eyed journalist Diane Roberts weaves her family's biography with Florida's history to create a compelling,

TOP PICKS

FLORIDA
Gulf of Mexico
Miami

FOLK ART & ODDITIES

With its kitschy billboards and quaint postcards, Florida pioneered the very idea of the roadside attraction. Here are a few worth stopping for, though not all are along the road.

- Coral Castle (p174) – this quintessential roadside attraction is a modern-day Stonehenge commemorating a scorned groom's grief.
- Pelicans in Paradise, Pensacola (p492) – colorful fiberglass pelicans waddle downtown.
- Dog Wall, Grayton Beach (p488) – a community mural on which local dog owners paint portraits of their canines.
- Venetian Pool, Coral Gables (p116) – the world's most beautiful swimming hole, this 820,000-gallon, spring-fed pool was formed from a coral rock quarry.

- Bahama Village, Key West (p206) – though not what it once was when Hemingway loved it, Key West's old Bahamian district still has a colorful Caribbean flair.
- Ochopee post office (p171) – this former tool shed is the nation's smallest postal facility.
- Christ of the Abyss (p186) – glass-bottom boat tours sail over this bronze statue at the John Pennekamp Coral Reef State Park.
- Vehicle Assembly Building (p341) – the place where the Space Shuttle is assembled is so big that it makes its own weather.

TACKIEST SOUVENIRS

Nothing says Florida like a tacky souvenir, but some scream this could *only* be from Florida. Here are some we found and couldn't pass up.

- 'Fidel es Muerto' champagne and 'Burn in Hell, Fidel' hot sauce, Little Havana
- Velvet paintings of sad-eyed manatees, St Augustine
- Photo T-shirt of yourself 'riding' a real-live 12ft alligator, Gatorland, Orlando

- Pirate-emblazoned bongs, Fort Lauderdale
- Mickey Mouse ears, Walt Disney World, Orlando
- 'I Love to Fart' T-shirt, Key West
- Henry Flagler action doll (just kidding, but we'd love one!)

CLAIMS TO FAME

Florida has never been shy, and a number of Florida towns make grandiose self-congratulatory claims that at times we find a touch, well…dubious. Here then is Florida's gallery of famous, almost-famous, and we-really-hope-no-one-Googles-this titles.

- Miami: 'Capital of Latin America'
- Key West: 'Southernmost City'
- Daytona: 'World Center of Racing'
- Orlando: 'Theme Park Capital of the World'
- Florida: 'Fishing Capital of the World'
- Stuart: 'Sailfish Capital of the World'
- Palatka: 'Bass Capital of the World'
- Destin: 'World's Luckiest Fishing Village'

- Ocala: 'Horse Capital of the World'
- Ybor City: 'Cigar Capital of the US'
- Panama City Beach: 'Wreck Capital of the South'
- Deland: 'Athens of Florida'
- Winter Park: 'Venice of the US'
- Venice: 'Shark's Tooth Capital of Florida'
- High Springs: 'Friendliest Town in Florida'

And the historic award goes to…1920s Miami, which adopted the slogan: 'The Most Richly Blessed Community of the Bountifully Endowed State of the Most Highly Enterprising People of the Universe.'

unique, hilarious masterpiece: Roberts is like the troublemaking cousin at Florida's family reunion, bumming cigarettes and dishing the dirt everyone else is too polite to discuss.

A St Petersburg journalist, Jeff Klinkenberg excels at bringing to life the people who make Florida what it is: in *Seasons of Real Florida* (2004) and *Pilgrim in the Land of the Alligators* (2008), Klinkenberg interviews Marjory Stoneman Douglas, the Coppertone girl, the original *Creature from the Black Lagoon* creature, the inventor of the Everglades skiff, and a host of other intriguing natives.

Few writers are as inextricably linked to Florida as Carl Hiaasen. Most know him for his fictional thrillers, but he found his material and honed his outrageous, biting sarcasm as a *Miami Herald* columnist. For a piquant taste, pick up *Paradise Screwed* (2001).

Another mystery writer, James W Hall collected meditative essays on his favorite state and the writer's life in *Hot Damn!* (2002).

Naturalist Doug Alderson helped create the Big Bend Paddling Trail, and in *Waters Less Traveled* (2005) he describes his adventures: dodging pygmy rattlesnakes, meeting Shitty Bill, discussing Kemp's ridley turtles and pondering manatee farts.

When former *David Letterman* writer Rodney Rothman burned out, he decided to test drive 'retirement' in Boca Raton – at age 28. A good Jewish boy who went south too soon, Rothman crafts a very personal anthropological study of the unsentimental world of Florida retirees in *Early Bird: A Memoir of Premature Retirement* (2005). You'll chuckle on the beach all day.

Tim Hollis' *Glass Bottom Boats & Mermaid Tails* (2006) is an openly nostalgic history of Florida's first tourist attractions: the 'Big Five' springs. It's chock-full of postcards, billboards and photos from the era when the Weeki Wachee mermaid's 'adagio' was the pinnacle of entertainment.

For a list of great Florida crime fiction, see the boxed text, p44, and for more great books, see p44.

INTERNET RESOURCES

Florida Smart (www.floridasmart.com) Your one-stop shop for links to everything you ever wanted to know about Florida, from history to hurricanes to phone numbers.

Florida State Parks (www.floridastateparks.org) A wonderful resource serving the nation's best state-park system.

Lonely Planet (www.lonelyplanet.com) Get fellow travelers' advice, post questions and much more.

Miami Herald (www.miamiherald.com) Find out what's happening from one of the state's major daily newspapers.

My Florida (www.myflorida.com) Florida's official web portal for all government services, with comprehensive links to parks, travel information and media.

Roadside America (www.roadsideamerica.com) For per-capita wackiness, does any state top Florida?

Visit Florida (www.visitflorida.com) The state's official tourism commission, with 'experts' dispensing travel advice.

Events Calendar

Florida throws some of the biggest, weirdest, loudest, most delicious, most stylish, most crowded parties in the country. Whether you fly a freak flag, a pirate flag or a Confederate flag, and whether you prefer wine by the glass or beer by the keg, Florida has a festival that speaks your language.

JANUARY–FEBRUARY

ORANGE BOWL early Jan
One of Florida's biggest sporting events of the year is the Orange Bowl (p127), which often crowns the collegiate champion. It's held at Miami's Dolphin Stadium.

**FLORIDA CITRUS
FESTIVAL** 11 days in late Jan
Winter Haven hosts a well-attended 'state fair'–like celebration of Florida's citrus, with carnival rides, a beauty pageant and livestock shows (p61).

**EDISON FESTIVAL OF
LIGHT** late Jan–early Feb
Fort Myers celebrates the inventor Thomas Edison with a block party (p445), concerts, and a huge science fair. Events culminate on February 11, Edison's birthday, with an incredible Parade of Light.

SPEED WEEKS 1st 2 weeks in Feb
Several hundred thousand folks get their motors running (p358) in Daytona for lots of high-octane partying, a great deal of revving of engines and several big car races.

GARLIC FEST 3 days in mid-Feb
For a decade, Delray Beach (p234) has held an annual three-day salute to the stinking rose. Modeled after California's Gilroy Garlic Festival, Delray has the same orgy of pungent gourmet cuisine (featuring garlic ice cream, naturally) and several cooking contests.

FLORIDA STATE FAIR 2 weeks in mid-Feb
For over a century, the Florida State Fair (p412) has been a classic, drawing Floridians from around the state for its livestock shows, greasy food, loud music and old-fashioned carnival rides and games.

**SOUTH BEACH WINE
& FOOD FESTIVAL** late Feb
This is not your typical paper-plate grub-fest, but a celebration of fine dining and gourmet cuisine, sponsored by the Food Network and *Food & Wine* magazine. South Florida's celebrity chefs headline the show (p128).

MARDI GRAS late Feb or early Mar
Fat Tuesday inspires a smattering of celebrations around the state, but Pensacola Beach (p497), closest to New Orleans, is Florida's best.

MARCH–APRIL

CARNAVAL MIAMI 9 days in early Mar
Miami's premiere Latin festival (p128) hits a lot of high notes: there's a Latin drag-queen show, an in-line-skate competition, a domino tournament, the immense Calle Ocho street festival, a cooking contest, crowning of Miss Carnaval Miami, an 8km marathon, and generally, all-around good times.

BIKE WEEK 10 days in early Mar
Half a million bikers come to Daytona Beach for Bike Week (p358), which, similar to Speed Weeks, involves admiring a lot of internal-combustion engines, drinking, racing said machinery, and more drinking, not necessarily in that order.

SPRING BREAK Mar-Apr
Have you heard? When US colleges release their students for a one-week 'break' in March or April, many of those coeds gather on Florida beaches to drink and drink and drink, sometimes losing their clothes in the process (thank goodness no one ever *records* these embarrassing slips…). Some towns, like Fort Lauderdale (p219) and Daytona (p353), have clamped down on the debauchery, which simply moves to new beaches, like Hollywood (p217) and Panama City Beach (p484). You've been warned.

**EPCOT INTERNATIONAL FLOWER AND
GARDEN FESTIVAL** Mar-May
Amazing topiaries and flowers from around the world fuse Disney characters with Epcot's World Showcase (p305).

PET PARADE Mar
In Palm Beach (p240), old ladies dress their dogs like humans and flaunt them on Worth Ave, Florida's answer to Rodeo Drive.

FLORIDA FILM FESTIVAL Mar
Held at the wonderfully quirky Enzian Theater (p286) in Winter Park, near Orlando, this celebration of independent films is fast becoming one of the largest in the southeast.

ART IN THE PARK Mar
In Winter Park (p284), meander among local art and linger over a glass of wine at one of this quintessential small town's many sidewalk cafés and wine bars.

CAPTAIN ROBERT SEARLE'S RAID Mar
Jamaican pirate Robert Searle pillaged St Augustine in memorable fashion in 1668, and St Augustine (p363) makes sure no one forgets with a meticulous re-enactment in authentic period garb.

ST PATRICK'S DAY Mar 17
The patron saint of Ireland is honored with more fanfare elsewhere in the US, but in Miami (p128), a sizeable contingent of loyal folks raise a pint (or three) on St Patty's Day.

WINTER MUSIC CONFERENCE 5 days in late Mar
DJs, musicians, promoters and music-industry execs converge on Miami to rub elbows, strike deals, listen to new dance music, and ooh and aah over the latest technology. These folks also know how to throw a party (p128).

INTERSTATE MULLET TOSS late Apr
On Perdido Key, near Pensacola, locals have become famous for their annual ritual of tossing dead fish over the Florida–Alabama state line (p501). Distance trumps style, but some have quite a bit of style.

MAY–JUNE

ISLE OF EIGHT FLAGS SHRIMP FESTIVAL 1st weekend in May
This three-day festival on Amelia Island (p380) takes its shrimp and juried art show seriously, but when the pirates invade, everyone gets downright silly and lets loose their inner 'aaaarrrgh!'

SUNFEST 5 days in early May
A quarter of a million folks gather in West Palm Beach for South Florida's largest waterfront music and arts festival (p251).

MEMORIAL DAY CIRCUIT PARTY Memorial Day weekend
For late May's Memorial Day weekend, Pensacola (p493) becomes one massive three-day gay party, with lots of DJs, dancing and drinking.

SEASIDE JAZZ FESTIVAL Memorial Day weekend
Quaint, pastel-colored Seaside (p488) makes a delightful venue for two days of top-flight jazz.

PALATKA BLUE CRAB FESTIVAL Memorial Day weekend
For four heady late-May days in Palatka (p389), not only can you stuff yourself with as much blue crab as you can handle, but this festival hosts the state championship for chowder and gumbo. Yum.

GAY DAYS ORLANDO 1 week in early Jun
Upwards of 40,000 gay and lesbians don red shirts and gather at the Magic Kingdom on the first Saturday of June for Gay Day at Walt Disney World (p306). Begun in 1991, this event now inaugurates a week's worth of gay celebrations in other parks, hotels and clubs in Orlando.

GOOMBAY FESTIVAL early Jun
In Miami's Coconut Grove, this massive street party (p128) draws more than 300,000 to celebrate the city's Bahamian culture. One of the nation's largest black-culture festivals, it features Caribbean music and dancing troupes, with the highlight being the 55-member Royal Bahamas Police Band.

SIR FRANCIS DRAKE'S RAID Jun
The same folks who re-enact Searle's Raid in St Augustine in March switch their clothes to recreate Drake's 1586 sacking of the town (p363). Volunteers are welcome!

JULY–AUGUST

FOURTH OF JULY Jul 4
Independence Day for the US is the cause for parades and fireworks, large and small, across the state. Miami does the day justice, with an excellent fireworks show (p128).

STEINHATCHEE SCALLOP
SEASON
Jul to Sep

The opening day of scallop season in Steinhatchee (p476) can draw a thousand folks, who take to the waters to harvest by hand this delectable bivalve. It's like a two-month treasure hunt, and anyone can join in.

MIAMI SPICE RESTAURANT
MONTH
Aug

Most Floridians do nothing but hunker next to the air-con during the year's hottest month. To draw them out, Miami's restaurants join together in August to offer prix-fixe lunches and dinners (p128).

SEPTEMBER–OCTOBER

MICKEY'S NOT-SO-SCARY
HALLOWEEN PARTY
Sep-Oct

On select evenings over two months at Disney World, kids can trick-or-treat in the shadow of Cinderella's Castle, with costumed Disney favorites and a Halloween-themed parade (p296).

EPCOT FOOD & WINE
FESTIVAL
Oct

As you would expect from Disney's Epcot (p303), this is a wide-ranging international celebration of food and wine. Its 'Eat to the Beat' music series features national acts.

FANTASY FEST
last week of Oct

Key West pulls out all the stops, and pulls the stopper out of every bottle, for this weeklong costumed extravaganza (p207) culminating in Halloween. Everyone's even more crazy than usual, and Key West's own Goombay Festival competes for attention the same week. Bring plenty of aspirin.

MOONFEST
late Oct

West Palm Beach (p245) throws a rocking, riproaring, riotous block party for Halloween. Guests are encouraged to come in costume (the top prize is $1000!), and dozens of the best local bands play for free.

NOVEMBER–DECEMBER

FLORIDA SEAFOOD
FESTIVAL
2 days in early Nov

Apalachicola (p481) hosts one of Florida's oldest seafood festivals, and the local specialty – oysters – is celebrated in numerous ways, such as with oyster-shucking and -eating contests and the annual blessing of the fleet.

TAMPA CIGAR HERITAGE
FESTIVAL
mid-Nov

Tampa's Ybor City has a long history as the cigar-making capital of the US. That heritage, and the cigars themselves, are celebrated in this one-day festival (p412).

ST ARRRGUSTINE PIRATE
GATHERING
3 days in mid-Nov

Put on an eye patch and dust off your pirate lingo for this hokey celebration of scurvy dogs and seafaring rascals (p363).

WHITE PARTY
1 week in late Nov

A raucous gay and lesbian celebration (and HIV/AIDS fundraiser), White Party (p129) is a series of parties and nightclub events in and around Miami Beach and Fort Lauderdale. Yes, wear white.

ART BASEL
MIAMI BEACH
4 days in early Dec

Very simply, this is one of the biggest international art shows in the US, with more than 150 art galleries and over 2000 artists from around the world involved (p129).

VICTORIAN CHRISTMAS
STROLL
3 weeks in early Dec

The landmark 1891 Tampa Bay Hotel (now a museum) is given over to Christmas, Victorian style, for three weeks in December, with folks in period costume acting out fairy tales (p412).

KING MANGO STRUT
late Dec

Miami's Coconut Grove has held this wacky, after-Christmas parade, which spoofs current events and local politics, for over 20 years. It's a light-hearted, freak-alicious way to ring in the new year (p129).

Itineraries
CLASSIC ROUTES

MIAMI TO KEY WEST
10 Days

Start in **Miami** (p83) for three solid days of arts and culture, fine eats, hedonistic nightlife, South Beach sunning and, of course, serious shopping! On the fourth day, put on your grubby duds for a visit to **Everglades National Park** (p170). Take the low road, from **Homestead** (p173) to the area around **Flamingo** (p175), from where you can explore mangroves, go kayaking and watch the sunset.

Now backtrack and head for the **Upper Keys** (p183). At **Key Largo** (p183), enjoy snorkeling and beachside camping at **John Pennekamp Coral Reef State Park** (p183). For the next day or two, slowly key-hop along: ride a bike around the Keys; swim with the dolphins at the **Dolphin Research Center** (p192) in Grassy Key; fish from **Old Seven Mile Bridge** (p195) in Marathon; and sun and snorkel at **Bahia Honda State Park** (p196). Finally, get thyself to **Key West** (p199) to spend the remainder of your vacation saluting the sunset – or stay active (and sober) and trip out to **Dry Tortugas National Park** (p213).

Is it possible to see more in under 300 miles? From urban, Latin, pastel-hued Miami – both caliente and cool – to the prehistoric swamps and leathery beasts of the Everglades. And thence, past teeming coral reefs to devil-may-care Key West, always lifting a glass to the sunset.

ATLANTIC COAST   **Two Weeks**

Florida's Atlantic Coast is a symphony of beaches and barrier islands, of mangroves and sea turtles, of nostalgic 'Old Florida' and happening 'new' Florida. With three driving routes to choose from (I-95, Hwy 1 and A1A), pick scenic A1A as often as possible.

Start in **Jacksonville** (p370); take in bustling downtown, a football game and the beaches. Hop a ferry for kayaking at **Fort George Island** (p379), and then it's a scenic drive through the **Talbot Islands State Park** (p380) to pretty-as-a-picture **Amelia Island** (p380) for a moonlight horse ride on the beach.

Heading south, 'Old Florida' doesn't get older than **St Augustine** (p361), with its romantic hostelries and historic lanes. Keep zooming along Hwy A1A to the 'birthplace of speed,' **Daytona Beach** (p353): drive on the Speedway *and* the sand!

Get back to nature with a canoe trip among manatees and mangroves in **Mosquito Lagoon** (p343) in the **Canaveral National Seashore** (p343). Explore the wonders of space at the **Kennedy Space Center** (p337). Learn how to surf at **Cocoa Beach** (p345) and enjoy an evening cocktail at its **Sunset Waterfront Grill** (p347).

Drop a line in the water at **Sebastian Inlet State Park** (p349), or book a sailfishing charter in **Stuart** (p255). Near Jupiter, take a memorable kayak trip on the **Loxahatchee River** (p254), and make sure to visit the windswept dunes of **Hutchinson Island** (p256). Put on dress clothes and stroll posh **Palm Beach** (p240); work on your tan at **Delray Beach** (p234); and join the party at **Fort Lauderdale** (p219). Finally, hit **Miami** (p83), for Latin culture and cuisine, and for the ultimate cruise, take Ocean Dr, which is the strutting, sexy, art-deco belly of the beast that is South Beach.

Cruise 400 miles down the Atlantic Coast, trailing your hand in the water the whole way. It's the full Florida buffet: kayak among mangroves, stroll Spanish forts, lunch with astronauts, learn to surf, sunbathe next to celebrities, sweat to Cuban hip-hop in Miami nightclubs and more.

CINDERELLA TO THE SWAMP:
ORLANDO & THE GULF COAST   Two Weeks

Let yourself be seduced by the mouse: start this trip in Orlando with several days at **Walt Disney World Resort** (p290), for the magic and mayhem of Earth's most popular tourist attraction. Worth a day as well are the thrill-a-minute theme-park rides at the **Universal Orlando Resort** (p319), the animal shows and roller coasters of **SeaWorld** (p328), a dolphin swim at **Discovery Cove** (p332), and Florida's original theme park, **Cypress Gardens** (p273), with its Southern belles and water-ski shows.

In between all that silliness, chill out in a kayak in nearby **Wekiwa Springs State Park** (p274), and when you've had enough theme-park fun, head west on I-4 to **Tampa** (p405). Enjoy Ybor City and its Cuban history, gourmet eats and nightlife.

In **St Petersburg** (p418) cool off in the surreal Salvador Dalí Museum and unwind on one of Florida's best beaches: **Fort DeSoto Beach** (p428).

Enjoy more museums and fine dining in **Sarasota** (p433) and more wild nature in **Myakka River State Park** (p442). Beach-combing doesn't get any finer than at seashell-littered **Sanibel Island** (p451), nor wildlife-watching any better than at **JN 'Ding' Darling National Wildlife Refuge** (p452) in Sanibel.

After a classy meal at upscale **Naples** (p454), go the other extreme: sample some deep-fried alligator in **Everglades City** (p172) before dipping a paddle among live gators with a kayak trip in the Everglades' **10,000 Islands** (p174). Then enjoy the 'Old Florida' tourist traps of the **Tamiami Trail** (p170) on the way to an Everglades tram tour at **Shark Valley** (p171).

This 370-mile trip bookends two overwhelming, creature-filled worlds, one fake, one real: from Orlando's cartoon-filled theme parks, you take in the beauty and culture of Gulf Coast cities and beaches until you reach the Everglades and its decidedly less-cuddly alligator- and snake-filled swamps.

NORTH FLORIDA BACKROADS & BYWAYS   Two to Three Weeks

There's a lot of spectacular natural beauty and good ol' warm Southern hospitality to experience in northern Florida and the Panhandle, most of it tucked away along meandering backroads. **Jacksonville** (p370) makes a good arrival point. Spend a few days visiting Jacksonville's museums, Fort Caroline, then Timucuan sites on **Fort George Island Cultural State Park** (p379), and of course, relaxing on gorgeous **Amelia Island** (p380).

Go south, following St John's River to **Blue Springs State Park** (p386), where you can cruise alongside manatees. Visit the nearby Spiritualist community of **Cassadaga** (p386) and explore **Ocala National Forest's** (p392) moss-draped trails.

In **Ocala** (p390), get yourself cleaned up and catch its drag-racing shrines, Don Garlits Museums, and the original glass-bottom boats of Silver Springs.

North, Tom Petty's hometown of **Gainesville** (p394) is still a great place to hear live rock and punk and to experience Florida college football. A side trip to **Micanopy** (p401), an 'Old Florida' time capsule, is a must.

Now, shoot southwest to take in beautiful, isolated **Cedar Key** (p478), shuffle up to **Ichetucknee Springs State Park** (p401) for some lazy tubing, then go for a paddle in the **Suwannee River** (p477).

The state capital, **Tallahassee** (p464), makes another good rest stop before more hiking in the atmospheric **Apalachicola National Forest** (p474).

Take Hwy 98 west along the Gulf Coast, be sure to visit **St George Island** (p483), have some fresh-shucked oysters in **Apalachicola** (p481) and lounge on exceedingly picturesque sugar-sand **Grayton Beach State Park** (p488).

Pensacola (p492) and its gorgeous shoreline are a good deal more attractive than its nickname, the 'Redneck Riviera,' suggests. Go diving, go fishing, and go out in Southern style.

There's no hurry along this winding, 700-mile-or-so journey through the mossy forests and towns of Old Florida. Just remember: the seafood is often fried, the springs always 72°F, the drawl Southern, the rivers lazy, the beaches sugar-bright, and the music loud, but it'll be fun.

TAILORED TRIPS

KIDDING AROUND

If you have kids, yes, yes of course, please, by all means take them to Orlando's **Walt Disney World Resort** (p290). This is what parents do, and it's something children never forget – particularly sitting curbside as Disney characters parade by, then watching fireworks explode over **Cinderella's Castle** (p300).

And while you're in Orlando, enjoy the thrill rides of **Universal Orlando Resort** (p319) and watch Shamu jump and splash at **SeaWorld** (p328). But then, show them something else.

Take a canoe ride down the **Suwannee River** (p477), stopping at freshwater springs for rope swings and cannonballs. At **Daytona Beach** (p353), build sandcastles and ride all-terrain vehicles (ATVs) along the beach. Take a glass-bottom boat ride in **John Pennekamp Coral Reef State Park** (p183), snorkel the coral reef or perhaps swim with dolphins, if your kids are older, then help them understand what they've just seen at the **Florida Keys Eco-Discovery Center** (p201) in Key West.

The **Kennedy Space Center** (p337) has exhibits appealing to all ages that capture the wonder of space and the exhilaration of space flight. **The Everglades** (p164) offers easy boardwalks and accessible canoe trails into its fantastical world. And **Miami** (p83) shouldn't be overlooked: it certainly has great zoos and children's museums, but the city itself will be a memorable experience for all but the youngest. For much more, see Florida for Kids (p63).

SECLUDED STRANDS

For a list of some of Florida's best beaches, see p50. But what if you want a quiet patch of sandy real estate to get *away* from everyone else? Here are a few choices. Some take a little more work to get to, but then that's how you escape all the toddlers, cooler-dragging coeds and four-wheelers, isn't it?

On the Atlantic Coast, a short trek from West Palm Beach, **Singer Island** (p252) is a great place to spread your towel. Near Stuart, aim for **Hutchinson Island** (p256), which gets more secluded as you go north. You really can't go wrong with any of the beaches along the **Canaveral National Seashore** (p344).

Escape the buzz of Daytona at **Flagler Beach** (p361), 30 miles north. Around St Augustine, ditch the tourist hordes at **Anastasia Island** (p366). Finally, near Jacksonville, head for **Atlantic Beach** (p377), and then get in your kayak and paddle for **Little Talbot & Big Talbot Islands** (p380).

On the Panhandle, get yourself out to **St George Island State Park** (p483). Near Tampa, take a boat to **Honeymoon Island State Recreation Area** (p430) and look for shark's teeth on **Venice beaches** (p441). Near Fort Myers, work on your tan on **Lover's Key** (p447) and **Cayo Costa Island** (p450).

Really serious about alone time? Go to the **Dry Tortugas** (p213).

OLD FLORIDA

Maybe it's something in the aquifer, but all Floridians, even those who arrived yesterday, are afflicted by a strong sentimental attachment to 'Old Florida' – which is whatever the state used to be 50, 100, even 300 years ago (for more, see above). Rhapsodies about 'Real Florida' often mourn for disappearing Deep South towns dripping in Spanish moss like **Micanopy** (p401), aka 'the town that time forgot' and home to **Marjorie Kinnan Rawlings Historic State Park** (p402). Other places where the Cracker spirit lives on include **Everglades City** (p172) and **Homosassa Springs** (p460).

'Old Florida' can mean tourist attractions from before the Disney era: the swamp buggy tours, BBQ pits, and gambling halls of the **Tamiami Trail** (p170); the moody cypress and glass-bottom boats of **Wakulla Springs State Park** (p473); the topiary and Southern belles of Orlando's **Cypress Gardens** (p273); and the alligator wrestling of **Gatorland** (p269).

In **Miami** (p83), 'Old Florida' means smoking cigars and betting on jai alai and sleeping in the candy-colored art-deco district.

The entire Florida Keys qualifies, but here, the heart of 'Old Florida' is **Key West** (p199), where you will find Hemingway House and the Wreckers' Museums.

Then there's the oldest 'Old Florida' of all: **St Augustine** (p361), whose houses and Spanish fort, Castillo de San Marcos, are centuries-old, as is Tallahassee's evocative Spanish relic, the 17th-century **Mission San Luis** (p467).

WHAT'S COOKIN'?

Yes, it's easy to eat badly in Florida, but it's just as easy to eat very, very well. Any culinary tour of the Sunshine State begins (and could deliciously end) in **Miami** (p138), where you can sample Cuban, Nicaraguan, Haitian, Caribbean and Floribbean cuisines, to name a few. Celebrity chefs hold court here, and you can also toodle up to **Palm Beach** (p243) for gourmet plates.

From here, it's easy to go chasing the perfect Key lime pie and conch fritters through the Florida Keys to **Key West** (p210), where you can also get toasted toasting the setting sun.

Everglades City (p172) is a good place for adventure: try some deep-fried alligator and frog's legs. Further up the Gulf Coast, we seem to remember somebody saying something about a place with good cheeseburgers – follow your nose to **Cabbage Key** (p450).

Great restaurants are a calling card of both **Sarasota** (p438) and Ybor City in **Tampa** (p407).

In the Panhandle, **Apalachicola** (p481) is famous for its oysters and **Steinhatchee** (p476) for its scallops. More fresh Gulf seafood and Southern specialities are served in **Destin** (p491) and **Pensacola** (p499). Really like Cracker cooking? Grab a seat at **Yearling Restaurant** (p402) in Micanopy.

Meanwhile, **Amelia Island** (p384) is a beautiful place to be, and local eateries maintain the delightful mood.

WEIRD FLORIDA

Alligator wrestling, mermaids, the fountain of youth: so much of Florida is given over to weirdness, it's hard to know where to begin. As a matter of fact, Florida has not one but several 'Fountains of Youth.' The **Fountain of Youth** (p364) in St Augustine is the original, the one Ponce de León himself probably drank from. Have a cup, then search for St Augustine's **ghosts** (p366) while wielding your own 'electromagnetic-field meter.'

Or let ghosts and the dead come to you: have a reading with a Spiritualist medium at **Cassadaga** (p386). Or creep yourself out among the dead in the bizarre **cemetery** (p205) in Key West. Or forget the dead and help search for UFOs and **alien life** (p498) near Pensacola.

Florida's perpetually flowing, crystalline springs are surreal in themselves, but add seductive mermaids and you've really got something: **mermaid shows** (p459) in Weeki Wachee still defy logic. Or, make like a mermaid yourself and sleep underwater in **Jules' Undersea Lodge** (p188) in Key Largo.

Think Florida doesn't mess with your head? Check out **Coral Castle** (p174), a stone monument to unrequited love, and stop off at **Robert Is Here** (p177) in Homestead, one man's kitschy plea for attention.

In itself, **the Everglades** (p164) pretty much embodies everything strange about nature, and in the Panhandle, go underground for more at **Florida Caverns State Park** (p487).

LATIN FLORIDA

Florida has always enjoyed a close relationship with its Latin and Caribbean neighbors, and particularly in South Florida, the mix of cultures and cuisines makes for a dish that is *muy caliente* (very hot).

When you're dubbed the 'Capital of Latin America,' it's a lot to live up to. **Miami** (p83) earns it, though, and a good place to begin is the Cuban exile community of **Little Havana** (p113), strolling Calle Ocho and Máximo Gómez Park for chess and dominoes. But if anything, **Hialeah Park** (p118) is more Cuban than Little Havana.

Visit Miami Beach's **Normandy Isle** (p106) for a meet-and-greet with the city's South American contingent: Argentinians, Brazilians, Uruguayans, Colombians and more. Fix up your mojo with a *botanica* visit in **Little Haiti** (p111). After dark, of course, Miami sizzles with **Latin food** (p138) and spicy **nightlife** (p150).

Next, tramp out to **Key West** (p199), historically a major immigration point for Latin America that pulses with a distinctly Bahamian vibe. **Ybor City** (p407) in Tampa is less Latin than it once was, but its famous Cuban cigar district is a pungent reminder. In nearby St Petersburg, the **Salvador Dalí Museum** (p421) is surrealist Latin.

Finally, hit the button on the way-back machine and experience the original Spanish Florida in **St Augustine** (p361).

PLAY BALL!

Florida is home to two major-league baseball teams: the **Florida Marlins** (p158) in Miami and the **Tampa Bay Devil Rays** (p426), whose field is in St Petersburg. But in March and April, many pro teams hold their spring training games in Florida; these provide a much more relaxed, intimate atmosphere to watch the pros. Then, during summer, most of these stadiums host minor-league baseball, where you can see future big leaguers in action.

Roger Dean Stadium (p254) in Jupiter is home to minor-league affiliates of the Marlins and the St Louis Cardinals. **Jackie Robinson Ballpark** (p357) near Daytona Beach hosts the Chicago Cubs affiliate.

Around **Orlando** (p283), Atlanta Braves' spring training is at Disney's Wide World of Sports, for the Cleveland Indians at Chain of Lakes Park in Winter Haven, and the Houston Astros at Osceola County Stadium in Kissimmee.

The New York Yankees host spring training and minor-league games at **Legends Field** (p416) in Tampa; the field is modeled after the 'House that Ruth Built.' The Devil Rays play spring-training games at **Progress Energy Park** (p426) in St Petersburg.

In Fort Myers, the Boston Red Sox play at **City of Palms Park** (p446), and the Minnesota Twins play at **Lee County Sports Complex** (p446).

There's more, but that's certainly enough to…*play ball!*

THRILL RIDES & ROLLER COASTERS

Pretty much the whole point of Florida theme parks is to provide you with that three-second shot of adrenalin when the whole world goes whoooosh. So where do you get the best bang for your buck?

Walt Disney World Resort in Orlando is not a mecca for pure thrill-seekers, but **Space Mountain** (p299) is a classic roller coaster that still delivers, and the **Twilight Zone Tower of Terror** (p302) is certainly one heart-stopping elevator ride.

Universal Orlando knows what you want: in Islands of Adventure, make for the **Incredible Hulk** (p324) and **Dueling Dragons** (p326), and do not miss the scare-tastic **Revenge of the Mummy** (p323) in Universal Studios.

Also in Orlando, SeaWorld rates five out of five screams with **Kraken** (p329), as does the 120ft free-fall of the **Skycoaster** (p272).

Busch Gardens (p418) represents for Tampa with the dive coaster SkeiKra and the looping, looping, looping Kumba.

Prefer speeding the old-fashioned way – in a car? Strap yourself into the **Richard Petty Driving Experience** (p356) in Daytona Beach and ride shotgun on the Daytona Speedway.

Want to rocket into space? Well, you can't do that, but the Kennedy Space Center mimics an astronaut's ultimate thrill ride in the **Shuttle Launch Simulator** (p337).

Finally, in Jacksonville, find out how Oz works his magic by taking a behind-the-scenes tour at the **Sally Corporation** (p374), maker of animatronics and 'dark rides.'

History

Florida has many histories, myths, legends and oversized personalities, each one caught in the watery peninsula's dreamlike spell. At times, they collide and intersect, but they don't make for a singular tale. Here, then, are some of the numerous stories of Florida.

FIRST INHABITANTS & SEMINOLES

No one quite knows when or how humans first got to Florida. Unlike the bone-dry southwest, Florida's fecund swamps quickly swallow evidence of human passing. Most likely, the humans who crossed the Bering Strait from Siberia to Alaska beginning around 60,000 BC were the first to reach Florida, in around 10,000 BC.

Over the next 11,500 years they prospered, splitting into numerous small chiefdoms or villages, but never organizing into large, cohesive tribes. The Apalachee occupied Florida's Panhandle; with the best soil, they developed the most complex agriculture- and village-based society. The Timucua occupied northern Florida (and Georgia); in their agricultural, matrilineal society, both men and women could be chiefs.

Further south, Florida's indigenous peoples were more nomadic and warlike. The Tequesta lived along the central Atlantic Coast, a host of groups encircled Tampa Bay, and the fierce Calusa hunted and gathered in southern Florida. Because of them, no European settlements appeared on this coastline, and legends say it was a Calusa arrow that killed Ponce de León.

The most striking evidence of these early cultures are shell mounds or middens – great heaping piles of conch, oysters, mussels and snails. Florida's ancestral peoples ate well, to the point where discarded shells reached 30ft high and themselves became the foundations of villages, as at Mound Key.

In 1513, when Ponce de León arrived, the indigenous population numbered perhaps 250,000. Over the next 200 years, European diseases killed 80% of them. The rest were killed by war or sold into slavery, so that by the mid-1700s, virtually none of Florida's original inhabitants were left.

However, as the 18th century unfolded, Creeks and other tribes from the north migrated into Florida, driven by or enlisted in the partisan European feuds for New World territory. These tribes intermingled and intermarried, and in the late 1700s they were joined by numerous runaway black slaves, whom they welcomed into their society.

At some point, these uncooperative, fugitive, mixed peoples occupying Florida's interior were dubbed 'Seminoles,' a corruption of the Spanish word *cimarrones,* meaning 'free people' or 'wild ones.' Defying European rule and ethnic category, they were, ironically enough, considered too

Heritage of the Ancient Ones (HOTAO, www
.ancientnative.org) is a nonprofit organization preserving Florida's Indian history and culture. Its website tells the story of pre-Columbian Florida life.

The Enduring Seminoles (1998) by Patsy West is the unexpected story of how Florida's proud, resourceful Seminoles went from utter destitution to tourist attraction to flourishing culture in 150 very strange years.

TIMELINE

10,000 BC	AD 500	1513
First humans arrive in Florida, hunting mastodon and saber-toothed tigers, at the end of the last Ice Age.	Indigenous peoples settle in year-round villages and begin farming, cultivating the 'three sisters' of corn, beans and squash, plus pumpkins, lemons and sunflowers.	Ponce de León discovers Florida, landing south of Cape Canaveral and believing it an island. Since it's around Easter, he names it La Florida, 'The Flowery Land' or 'Feast of Flowers.'

THE UNCONQUERED SEMINOLES

The US waged war on Florida's Seminoles three times. The First Seminole War, from 1817 to 1818, was instigated by Andrew Jackson when he attacked the Seminoles in Spanish-controlled Florida as punishment for sheltering runaway slaves and attacking US settlers.

Jackson was ruthless; he took Pensacola and was ready to take all of Florida. Though Spain protested this foreign military incursion, they negotiated immediately afterward for the US to take Florida, please.

In 1930, 'Old Hickory,' now President Andrew Jackson, passed the Indian Removal Act, which aimed to move every single American Indian west of the Mississippi River. Some Seminoles agreed to give up their lands and move to reservations, but not all of them. In 1835, US troops arrived to enforce agreements, and Osceola, a Seminole leader, attacked an army detachment, triggering the Second Seminole War.

The war was fought guerrilla-style by 2000 or so Seminoles in swamps and hammocks, and it's considered one of the most deadly and costly Indian wars in US history. In October 1837, Osceola was captured under a flag of truce and later died in captivity, but the Seminoles kept fighting. In 1842 the US finally called off its army, having spent $20 million and seen the deaths of 1500 US soldiers.

Thousands of Seminoles had been killed or marched to reservations, but hundreds survived and took refuge in the Everglades. In 1855 a US army survey team went looking for them, but the Seminoles found and killed them first. The resulting backlash turned into the Third Seminole War, which ended after Chief Billy Bowlegs was paid to go west in 1858.

But 200 to 300 Seminoles refused to sign a peace treaty and slipped away again into the Everglades. Technically, these Seminoles never surrendered and remain the only 'unconquered' American Indian tribe.

In the 1910s, brutally impoverished, the Seminoles discovered that tourists would pay to watch them in their temporary camps, and soon 'Seminole villages' were a mainstay of Florida tourist attractions; alligator wrestling and Seminole weddings aside, they were remarkably authentic.

In 1957, the US officially recognized the **Seminole Tribe** (www.semtribe.com), and in 1962, they recognized the separate **Miccosukee Tribe** (www.miccosukee.com). Both tribes now operate casinos and make millions doing so. For more history, visit the Ah-Tah-Thi-Ki Museum (p172).

free for the newly independent United States, who soon brought war to them (see above).

FIVE FLAGS: FLORIDA GETS PASSED AROUND

All Florida schoolchildren are taught that Florida has been ruled by five flags: those of Spain, France, Britain, the US and the Confederacy. Like a rare bird, Florida has been highly sought but hard to hold.

Spain claimed Florida in 1513 – when explorer Ponce de León arrived. Spanish slave traders from Cuba probably beat him here, spreading tall tales of 'rejuvenating waters' (ie Florida's springs). Ponce's ensuing mythic

1539	1565	1702
Hernando de Soto arrives in Florida with 800 men, seeking rumored cities of gold. He fights Indians with every step, camps near Tallahassee, but finding no precious metals, keeps marching west.	Pedro Menéndez de Aviles founds St Augustine, which becomes the first permanent European settlement in the New World and is the oldest city in the continental US.	In their ongoing struggle with Spain and France over New World colonies, the British burn St Augustine to the ground; two years later they destroy 13 Spanish missions in Florida.

quest for the everlasting 'fountain of youth' has, under many guises, plagued Florida ever since.

Spain couldn't do much with Florida. Five more Spanish expeditions followed (and one French, raising their flag on the St Johns River), and nothing stuck until 1565, when St Augustine was settled. A malarial, easily pillaged outpost that produced little income, St Augustine truly succeeded at only one thing: spreading the Catholic religion. Spanish missionaries founded 31 missions across Florida, converting and educating Indians, occasionally with notable civility.

In 1698 Spain established a permanent military fort at Pensacola, which was thence variously captured and recaptured by the Spanish, French, English and North Americans for a century.

During the 1754–63 French and Indian War, Spain sided with France in its battle with England over the US. When France lost, Spain bartered with the English, giving them Florida in return for the captured Havana. Almost immediately, the 3000 or so Spaniards in Florida gratefully boarded boats for Cuba.

The British held Florida for 20 years and did marginally well with it, producing indigo, rice, oranges and timber. But in 1783, as Britain and the US were tidying up accounts after the close of the American Revolution, Britain handed Florida back to Spain – which had supported the US in its war for independence.

The second Spanish period, from 1783 to 1819, was marked by one colossal misjudgment. Spain needed settlers, and quickly, so they vigorously promoted immigration to Florida, but this backfired when, by 1810, those immigrants (mainly North American settlers) started demanding 'independence' from Spain. Within a decade, Spain threw up its hands. They gave Florida back to the US for cash in a treaty formalized in 1822. In 1845 Florida became the 27th state of the US, but in 16 short years, it would reconsider that relationship and raise its fifth flag.

FROM CIVIL WAR TO CIVIL RIGHTS

In 1838 the Florida territory was home to about 48,000 people, of whom 21,000 were black slaves. By 1860, 15 years after statehood, Florida's population was 140,000, of whom 40% were slaves, most of them working on highly profitable cotton plantations.

Thus, unsurprisingly, when Abraham Lincoln was elected president on a platform to curtail slavery's expansion, Florida joined the Confederacy of southern states that seceded from the Union in 1861. During the ensuing Civil War, which lasted until 1865, only moderate fighting occurred in Florida.

Afterward, from 1865 to 1877, the US government used federal troops to impose 'Reconstruction,' which protected the rights of freed blacks, on all ex-Confederate states. As a result, during this period, 19 blacks were elected

Michael Gannon's excellent *The New History of Florida* (1996) provides a comprehensive, definitive Florida overview, but if you want to know something - but not that much! - pick up his compact, fun *Florida: A Short History* (2003).

The Florida State Archives website (www.florida memory.com) presents a fascinating collection of historical documents (including a 1586 map of St Augustine and Civil War letters), plus oodles of great photos, both historic and modern.

1776	1823	1835
The American Revolution begins, but Florida's two colonies don't rebel. They remain loyal to the British crown, and soon English Tories flood south into Florida to escape the fighting.	Tallahassee is established as Florida's territorial capital because it's halfway between Pensacola and St Augustine. Later, politicians try to move the state capital to someplace more fun, but fail.	In attacks coordinated by Seminole leader Osceola, Seminoles destroy five sugar plantations on Christmas Day and soon after kill 100 US soldiers marching near Tampa, launching the Second Seminole War.

to Florida's state congress, but the radical social and political upheaval this represented was too much for most white Floridians.

When federal troops finally left, Florida 'unreconstructed' in a hurry, adopting a series of Jim Crow laws that segregated and disenfranchised blacks in every sphere of life – in restaurants and parks, on beaches, buses and golf courses – while a poll tax kept blacks and the poor from voting. From then until the 1950s, black field hands in turpentine camps and cane fields worked under a forced-labor 'peonage' system, in which they couldn't leave till their wages paid off their debts, which of course never happened.

The Ku Klux Klan thrived, its popularity peaking in the 1920s, when Florida led the country in lynchings. Racial hysteria and violence were commonplace; even massacres, such as the one in Rosewood in 1923 (p480), went unpunished.

In 1954 the US Supreme Court ended legal segregation in the US with Brown vs Board of Education, but in 1957 Florida's Supreme Court rejected this decision, declaring it 'null and void.' This sparked protests but little change until 1964, when a series of race riots and demonstrations, some led by Martin Luther King Jr, rocked St Augustine and helped spur passage of the national Civil Rights Act of 1964.

More race riots blazed across Florida cities in 1967 and 1968, after which racial conflict eased as Florida belatedly and begrudgingly desegregated itself. Florida's racial wounds healed equally slowly – as evidenced by more race riots in the early 1980s. Today, despite much progress and the fact that Florida is one of the nation's most ethnically diverse states, these wounds haven't completely healed yet.

DRAINING SWAMPS & LAYING RAIL

Everyone, even Ponce de León, who has seen Florida has thought: 'Paradise!'. But as a place to actually live? Well, the phrases 'fixer-upper' and 'tremendous potential' spring to mind.

By the middle of the 19th century, the top half of Florida was reasonably well explored, but South Florida was still an oozing, mosquito-plagued swamp. So, in the 1870s, Florida inaugurated its first building boom by adopting laissez-faire economic policies centered on three things: unrestricted private development, minimal taxes, and land grants for railroads. Florida's politicians have sung variations of that tune ever since.

In 10 years, from 1881 to 1891, Florida's railroad miles quintupled, from 550 to 2566. Most of this track crisscrossed northern and central Florida, where the people were, but one rail line went south to nowhere. In 1886, railroad magnate Henry Flagler started building a railroad down the coast on the spectacular gamble that once he built it, people would come.

In 1896 Flagler's line stopped at the squalid village of Fort Dallas, which incorporated as the city of Miami that same year. Then, people did come,

Dreamers, Schemers & Scalawags: The Florida Chronicles (1994) by Stuart McIver gives the lowdown on the mobsters, millionaires, movie stars and visionaries who influenced Florida's colorful history.

1845	**1861**	**1912**
Florida is admitted to the Union as the 27th state. Since it is a slave state, it's admission is balanced by that of Iowa, a free state.	On a vote of 62-7, Florida secedes from the United States, raising its fifth flag, the stars-and-bars of the Confederacy. Florida's farms and cattle provide vital Confederate supplies during the ensuing Civil War.	'Flagler's Folly,' Henry Flagler's 128-mile overseas railroad connecting the Florida Keys, reaches Key West. Upon completion, it's hailed as the 'Eighth Wonder of the World,' but is destroyed by a 1935 hurricane.

and kept coming, and Flagler is largely credited with founding every town from West Palm Beach to Miami.

It's hard to do justice to what happened next, but it was madness, pure and simple – far crazier than Ponce's dream of eternal waters. Why, all South Florida needed was to get rid of that pesky *swamp,* and then it really *would* be paradise: a land of eternal sunshine and profit.

In 1900 Governor Napoleon Bonaparte Broward envisioned creating an 'Empire of the Everglades,' and he set in motion a frenzy of canal building that over the next 70 years etched over 1800 miles of canals and levees across Florida's porous limestone. These earthworks successfully drained about half the Everglades (about 1.5 million acres) below Lake Okeechobee, replacing it with vegetable farms, cattle ranches, orange groves, sugarcane fields and suburbs.

From 1920 to 1925, the South Florida land boom swept the nation. In 1915, Miami Beach was a sand bar; by 1925, it had 56 hotels, 178 apartment buildings, and three golf courses. In 1920, Miami had one skyscraper; by 1925, 30 were under construction. In 1925 alone, 2.5 million people moved to Florida. Real-estate speculators sold undeveloped land, undredged land, and then just the airy paper promises of land. Everything went like hotcakes.

Then, two hurricanes struck, in 1926 and 1928, and the party ended. The coup de grâce was the October 1929 stock-market crash, which took everyone's money. Like the nation, Florida plunged into the Depression, though the state rode it out better than most due to New Deal public works, tourism, and a highly profitable new crop: liquor.

At the height of the industry in the 1940s, Florida's sugarcane fields produced one of every five teaspoons of sugar consumed in the US.

THE BLACK MARKET: RUMRUNNERS, SMUGGLERS & FUGITIVES

Ironically, Florida was mostly dry, alcoholically speaking, when the US passed the 18th Amendment in 1919, making liquor illegal and inaugurating Prohibition. But from that moment on, Florida became 'wet as a frog.'

Florida had already proven a good place to hide: black slaves, Seminoles and British Tories, all had escaped the government in Florida's marshes. Now, fleets of ships and airplanes brought Cuban and Jamaican rum into hidden coves for dispersal nationwide. Florida rumrunning became a free-flowing tap run mostly by local 'mom-and-pop' operations, not the mob, despite the occasional presence of vacationing mobsters like Al Capone.

According to legend, the phrase 'the real McCoy' was originally a reference to famous Florida rumrunner William McCoy, who claimed he never cut his rum with industrial alcohol or water.

More significantly, however, Prohibition really drove home the benefits of a thriving black market. When times were good, as in the early 1920s, all that (illicit) money got launder-...um...pumped into real estate, making the good times unbelievably great! When times were hard, as in the 1930s, out-of-work farmers and mechanics could make bathtub gin and still pay the bills. Because of this often-explicit understanding, in 1920s Miami, bars served drinks with impunity, in plain view of the police, who simply kept walking.

1926	1933–40	1935
A major hurricane flattens and floods South Florida. Nearly 400 people die, most drowning when Lake Okeechobee bursts its dike. Over 18,000 are homeless. Two years later, another hurricane exacts five times that death toll.	New Deal public-works projects employ 40,000 Floridians and help save Florida from the Depression. The most notable construction project is the Overseas Highway through the Keys, which replaces Flagler's railroad.	'Swami of the Swamp' Dick Pope opens Cypress Gardens, the first theme park in the US, with water-ski stunts, opulent gardens, topiary and pretty Southern belles. Allegedly, this inspires Walt Disney to create Disneyland in California.

In the 1960s and '70s, the story was repeated with marijuana. Down-on-their-luck commercial fisherman made a mint smuggling plastic-wrapped bails of pot, and suddenly Florida was asking, 'Recession? What recession?' West Florida experienced a condo boom.

In the 1980s, cocaine became the drug of choice. But this time the smugglers were Colombian cartels, and as the saying went, they did business with a gun, not a handshake. Bloody shootouts on Miami streets shocked Floridians (and inspired the *Miami Vice* TV show), but it didn't slow the estimated $10 billion drug business – and did you notice Miami's new skyline? In the 1980s, so much cash choked Miami banks that smuggling currency itself became an industry – along with smuggling out guns to Latin American countries and smuggling in rare birds, flowers, and of course, Cuban cigars.

By the 1990s the cartels were finished and banking laws were stricter, but some still believed that smuggling remained Florida's number-one industry.

PEDDLING PARADISE: TIN CAN TOURISTS, RETIREES & A BIG-EARED MOUSE

For the record, tourism is Florida's number-one industry, and this doesn't count retirees – the tourists who never leave.

Tourism didn't become a force in Florida until the 1890s, when Flagler built his coastal railroad and his hoity-toity Miami Beach resorts. In the 1920s, middle class 'tin can tourists' arrived via the new Dixie Hwy – driving Model Ts, sleeping in campers and bringing their own food.

In the 1930s, savvy promoters, realizing tourists don't spend money sunning themselves, created the first 'theme parks': Cypress Gardens and Silver Springs. But it wasn't until after WWII that Florida tourism exploded. During the war, Miami was a major military training ground, and afterward, many of those GIs returned with their families to enjoy Florida's sandy beaches at leisure.

Additionally, the advent of effective bug spray and affordable air-conditioning did wonders for the tourism industry. Only widespread after the war, these two technological advancements finally made Florida's subtropical climate safe for delicate Yankee skin.

And so, as Social Security kicked in, the nation's aging middle class migrated south to enjoy their first taste of retirement. As old folks will, they came slowly but steadily, at a rate of a thousand a week, till they numbered in the hundreds of thousands and then millions. Many came from the East Coast, and quite a few were Jewish: by 1960, Miami Beach was 80% Jewish, creating an ethnic enclave so rich it even had its own gangster, 'kosher nostra' boss Meyer Lansky.

Then one day in 1963, so the story goes, Walt Disney flew over central Florida, spotted the intersection of I-4 and the Florida Turnpike, and said,

Parrots, caviar, human skulls and gorillas all make appearances in *A History of Smuggling in Florida* (2006) by Stan Zimmerman, a wry, rollicking look at Florida's favorite pastime.

1941–45	1942	1946
US enters WWII. Two million men and women receive basic training in South Florida, including 25% of all Air Force officers. At one point, the army commandeers 85% of Miami Beach hotels to house personnel.	From January to August, German U-boats sink over two dozen tankers and ships off Florida's coast. By war's end, Florida holds nearly 3000 German POWs in 15 labor camps.	Frozen concentrated orange juice is invented. As the nation's top orange producer, this event leads to Florida's orange boom and gives birth to the orange millionaires of the '50s and '60s.

NEFARIOUS, NOTORIOUS FLORIDIANS QUIZ

Can you match these famous Floridians with their crime? The crimes and Floridians are listed below, but are all mixed up. Your job is to match each name with the correct crime, eg 1. John Smith matches crime D.

We've cross-referenced to answers on other pages so you can find out more information, and the answers are listed below, but come on – no peeking first!

Famous Floridian	Crime
1. EJ Watson	A. Attacked and killed Seminoles in Florida swamps, and transformed American Indians by 'removing' them (p29).
2. Ed Ball	B. Pillaged St Augustine and burned it to the ground, drank rum, hijacked Spanish ships, and was an occasional slave-trader (p363).
3. Katherine Harris	C. Transformed central Florida into a personal fantasy, and in doing so, hijacked the dreams of children and the vacations of parents everywhere (p33).
4. Walt Disney	D. Plume-hunter and alligator-skinner in the Everglades who killed people who worked for him; later murdered by townsfolk (p45).
5. Meyer Lansky	E. Mistakenly purged thousands of legitimate voters from voter roles in Florida during the 2000 election of George W Bush (p37).
6. Sir Francis Drake	F. Transformed Cuban music with disco and inspired everyone in Miami to dance the conga (p47).
7. Gianni Versace	G. Attacked and killed humans in Florida swamps, transforming the Everglades into own personal lunch counter and wrestling humans for entertainment (p77).
8. American alligator	H. Ran the 'kosher nostra' gambling syndicate and was an ardent Zionist; later retired in Miami Beach and died of old age (p33).
9. Gloria Estefan	I. Resurrected South Beach by renovating a home; transformed women into own personal fantasy and was gunned down by a stalker (p105).
10. Andrew Jackson	J. Bought Florida land for cents on the dollar, became a politically powerful timber baron, drank bourbon and ran a company that transformed the Panhandle into a suburban fantasy (p79).

Answers: 1, D; 2, J; 3, E; 4, C; 5, H; 6, B; 7, I; 8, G; 9, F; 10, A.

'That's it.' In secret, he bought 43 sq miles of Orlando-area wetlands. Afterward, like an expert alligator wrestler, Disney rubbed the belly of the Florida legislature till it went still and quiet with the promise of untold tourist dollars, and they gave him what amounted to sovereign powers to build his world.

Exempt from a host of state laws and building codes, largely self-governing, Disney World opened in 1971. How big was it? In 1950, Florida

1947	1961	1969
Everglades National Park is established, successfully culminating a 19-year effort, led by Ernest Coe and Marjorie Stoneman Douglas, to protect the Everglades from the harm done by dredging and draining.	Brigade 2506, a 1300-strong volunteer army, invades Cuba's Bay of Pigs on April 16. To avoid the appearance of US sponsorship, President Kennedy withholds air support, leading to Brigade 2506's immediate defeat and capture by Fidel Castro.	On July 16, *Apollo 11* lifts off from Cape Canaveral and four days later lands on the moon, winning the space race with the Russians. Floridians would watch five more lunar-bound rockets take off until 1972.

received 4.5 million tourists, not quite twice its population. In 1971, 10 million came to see Disney World alone, and by the 1980s, Disney was drawing 40 million visitors a year, or four times the state population.

Disney had the Midas touch. In the shadow of the Magic Kingdom, Florida's old-school attractions – Weeki Wachee, Seminole Village, Busch Gardens; all the places made famous through billboards and postcards – seemed hokey, small-time. The rules of tourism had changed forever, and you either emulated the big mouse or you died.

VIVA CUBA LIBRE!

South Florida could often be described as having a more intimate relationship with Cuba than with the rest of the US. Spain originally ruled Florida from Havana, and in the 20th century, so many Cuban exiles sought refuge in Miami, they dubbed it the 'Exile Capital.' Later, as immigration expanded, Miami simply became the 'Capital of Latin America.'

During Cuba's long struggle for independence from Spain, from 1868 to 1902 (when José Martí's revolution declared victory), Cuban exiles settled in Key West and Tampa, giving birth to Ybor City and its cigar-rolling industry (p407).

After independence, many Cubans returned home, but the economic ties they'd forged remained. Then, in 1959, Fidel Castro led a rag-tag revolution (plotted in part in Miami hotels) that overthrew the Batista dictatorship. This triggered a several-year exodus of over 600,000 Cubans to Miami, most of them white, wealthy, educated professionals.

In April 1961, Castro declared Cuba a Communist nation, and himself dictator, and this set the course for US–Cuban relations to the present day. The next day, President Kennedy approved the ill-fated Bay of Pigs invasion, which buffoonishly failed to overthrow Castro, and in October 1962, Kennedy blockaded Cuba to protest the presence of Russian nuclear missiles. Khrushchev famously 'blinked' and removed the missiles, but not before the US secretly agreed never to invade Cuba again.

None of these events and tactics sat well with Miami's Cuban exiles, who agitated for the USA to free Cuba (chanting '*Viva Cuba libre*': long live free Cuba). Between 1960 and 1980, a million Cubans emigrated, or 10% of the island's population; by 1980, 60% of Miami was Cuban. Meanwhile, the USA and Cuba wielded immigration policies like cudgels to kneecap each other.

Unlike most immigrant groups, Cuban exiles disparaged assimilation (and sometimes the US), because the dream of return animated their lives. Miami became two parallel cities, Cuban and North American, that rarely spoke each other's language.

In the 1980s and 1990s, poorer immigrants flooded Miami from all over the Latin world – particularly El Salvador, Nicaragua, Mexico, Colombia,

Joan Didion's *Miami* (1987) is a period piece of mid-1980s Miami/Cuban society and US politics; Didion's meticulous prose insightfully distills Miami's contradictory, enticing, easily riled personality into one very dry martini.

1971	**May 1980**	**1980**
Walt Disney World in Orlando opens and around 10,000 people arrive on the first day. The park attracts 10 million visitors by the end of first year.	In the McDuffie police brutality trial, white cops are acquitted of wrongdoing in the death of a black man, igniting racial tensions that devolve into Miami's Liberty City riots, in which 18 people are killed.	Responding to Cuban demonstrations, Castro 'opens the floodgates,' dumping felons, the poor, and the mentally ill onto US-bound boats. In the Mariel Boatlift, the US rescues 125,000 *Marielitos*, who then face intense discrimination in Miami.

Venezuela, the Dominican Republic and Haiti. These groups did not always mix easily or embrace each other, but they found success in a city that already conducted business in Spanish. By the mid-1990s, South Florida was exporting $25 billion in goods to Latin America, and Miami's Cubans were more economically powerful than Cuba itself.

Now firmly entrenched, Miami's Cubans had a shockingly muted reaction when Fidel finally stepped down from power in 2008 (p115), a clear signal that the younger generation of Cubans are no longer exiles, but residents.

SEEKING BALANCE

Like tourists who'd taken Mr Toad's Wild Ride one too many times, the 1990s left Florida feeling bruised and queasy (perhaps this was why Disney World retired the ride in 1998).

In 1992 Hurricane Andrew ripped across South Florida, leaving a wake of destruction and mangled buildings that stunned the state and the nation (p175). Mounting evidence of rampant pollution – fish kills, dying mangroves, murky bays – appeared like the bill for a century of unchecked sprawl and industrial nonchalance.

Florida had sold itself too well, and newcomers were trampling what they were coming for. From 1930 to 1980, Florida's population growth rate was 564%. Florida had gone from the least-populated to the fourth-most-populated state, and its infrastructure was woefully inadequate: there were too few police, overcrowded prisons, traffic jams, broken roads, ugly condos and strip malls, and some of the nation's worst schools. In the 1990s, South Florida's rising cost of living even started driving residents away (p182).

In particular, saving the Everglades became more than another environmental crusade. It was a moral test: would Florida really squander one of Earth's wonders over subdivisions and a quick buck? Commissions were held and, remarkably, actual legislation emerged: the Florida Forever Act and the Comprehensive Everglades Restoration Plan (p166) were both signed into law in 2000.

However, the year 2000 also contained a reminder of 'old' Florida: the Bush/Gore presidential-election voting fiasco. Election results were marred by numerous 'irregularities': defective punch cards left 'hanging chads' and unclear votes, and 'butterfly ballots' confused voters. Election-day roadblocks kept some from the polls, as did voter rolls that mistakenly denied some eligible voters the right to vote. Florida's vote made the difference in who was elected president – Democrat Al Gore or Republican George W Bush – and after months of lawsuits and calls for recounts, Bush was eventually declared the winner by 537 votes.

And so the ups and downs for Florida have continued since. In the last eight years, the Everglades restoration efforts have been increasingly criticized

It's all too easy to mock Florida for its bumbling 2000 presidential vote, but the HBO movie *Recount* (2008) doesn't. Instead, it cogently shows what happened and unearths the political grudges that shadowed an honest recount.

1984	1992	1999
The ground-breaking *Miami Vice* TV show debuts, combining music-video sensibilities, pastel fashions, blighted South Beach locations and cynical undercover cops battling gun-wielding Miami cocaine cartels.	On August 24, Hurricane Andrew devastates Dade County, leaving 41 people dead, over 200,000 homeless, and causing about $15.5 billion in damage, then the costliest natural disaster in US history.	On Thanksgiving Day, five-year-old Elián Gonzalez is rescued at sea, his Cuban mother having died trying to reach the US. Despite wild protests by Miami's Cuban exiles, the US agrees to return Elián to his father in Cuba.

for (and hampered by) a lack of funding, and then in 2008 Florida's 44th governor, Charlie Crist, unveiled a truly stunning conservation coup: a state plan to buy and convert 300 sq miles of Lake Okeechobee sugarcane fields into wetlands. Then, hoping to gain more influence in the presidential election, Florida improperly moved its Democratic primary to January 2008. Consequently, the Democratic party stripped Florida of its delegates, so its votes do not count.

Thus, taken together, all these events gave ammunition to skeptics and optimists alike – Florida entered the 21st century sincerely trying to develop a more balanced, sustainable way of life, but like an alligator 'sleeping' on the bank, its uneasy past could lash out and bite at any moment.

The Everglades: River of Grass (1947) by Marjory Stoneman Douglas makes the compelling case that the history of the Everglades *is* the history of Florida, and both shine vividly in this elegant, celebrated telling.

2000	2004	2008
Before the 2000 presidential election, Florida's Secretary of State Katherine Harris mistakenly purges thousands of legitimate voters from voter roles. George W Bush then narrowly defeats Al Gore by 537 votes in Florida to win the presidency.	Florida records its worst hurricane season ever, when four storms – Charley, Frances, Ivan and Jeanne – strike Florida over two months, causing 130 deaths and $22 billion in damage.	Wanting greater influence in the Democratic presidential nomination, Florida improperly moves up its primary to January 29. As punishment, the Democratic party strips Florida of its delegates, so its votes do not count.

The Culture

Most visitors, when asked why they visited Florida, mention the beaches, the beaches, a prehistoric swamp, a bevy of hyperactive theme parks, and oh right, the beaches. Florida's people, if they make the list, are an afterthought. And Florida culture? Are you kidding?

In fact, Florida's people and culture are a compelling mix of accents and rhythms, of pastel colors and Caribbean spices. They make Florida one of the USA's most unique and fascinating states, and they would be worth visiting even if Florida had no beaches. Thankfully, Florida is truly 'paradise' because visitors get both.

A rich oral history, *Voices of the Apalachicola* (2006) by Faith Eidse sits you down with former sharecroppers, turpentine workers, beekeepers, Creeks and environmentalists, who spin tales of a fast-changing land.

REGIONAL IDENTITY

Florida is far too watery to ever be pinned down. In fact, it's so complex, so constantly evolving and brand new, that Florida frequently questions its sense of self like a hormonal teenager – is it too weird, too boring, too sweaty?

That is, when Florida isn't acting the self-satisfied beauty queen: smiling graciously, knowing how popular it is, always pretty, always desired.

For instance, is Florida most like the South, the East, the West or the Midwest? It depends where you stand. As everyone likes to say, north is South in Florida. In the Panhandle and northern regions, folks is folks, and they speak with that distinctive Southern drawl, serve sweet tea as a matter of course, and have long, long memories. The Civil War still matters, as do your manners.

Why were white Florida pioneers called 'Crackers'? Some say it was for the cracking of the whip during cattle drives; others for the cracking of corn to make cornmeal, grits or moonshine.

But central Florida and the Gulf Coast were frequently settled by Midwesterners, and here you often find a plainspoken, Protestant worker-bee sobriety. East Coast Yankees, often mocked as willing dupes for any old piece of swamp, have nevertheless carved a definable presence on the southern Atlantic Coast – such as in Jewish retirement communities and calloused, sophisticated Miami.

Finally, Florida was the western frontier of the US after the West was won. It was the last place where pioneers could simply arrive, plant stakes and make a life. These pioneers became Florida's 'Crackers,' the poor rural farmers and cowhands and outlaws who traded life's comforts for independence on their

FROM THE NORTHERN CAPITAL OF THE LATIN WORLD...

Welcome to Latin America.

Hip, urban-tropical Miami is so unlike the rest of Florida that it's like being in another country. Once a nexus for New York retirees, Miami-Dade County now has a Hispanic majority; you're as likely to hear Spanish as English on the streets and on the airwaves. The feel and flavor are distinctly tropical and exotic. Even the air smells different – spicier, richer.

Miami is called the northern capital of Latin America with good reason: it's where US and Latin commerce and politics come together. Cubans – prosperous, Catholic and politically conservative – are the city's dominant Latin group and have a strong influence on commerce and local and national politics. More than 500 US corporations have their Latin offices here and two of the largest Latin TV broadcasters are here as well. Miami also hosts the annual Billboard Latin Music Awards; see p128.

Visitors, even those from other parts of Florida, can be forgiven for thinking they're in Buenos Aires, Rio or the Havana of the pre-Castro days. It's best to make like a local: sit back, listen up, sip your mojito and go with the flow.

…TO THE REDNECK RIVIERA

If Miami resembles Latin America, the rest of Florida more closely resembles the Deep South or parts of the Midwest.

In Florida, in fact, the further north you go (and the further from the city limits), the further South you get. Central Florida and Orlando, largely agricultural till 50 or 60 years ago, are more Southern than Miami and Fort Lauderdale, but not nearly as Southern as Jacksonville and the Panhandle. Parts of north Florida have more in common historically, culturally and politically with Alabama and Georgia than they do with South Florida.

This is the land of beer-drinking, and Nascar-loving rednecks who drive trucks with Confederate-flag bumper stickers and don't apologize for it. 'Redneck Riviera' beach towns in the Panhandle attract family crowds that prize fishing and fried seafood while eschewing models, celebrities and martini-drinkers. Panama City and Daytona have their own version of wildlife, however – Spring Break, when thousands of college students descend to drink and party.

---

terms. Sometimes any Florida pioneer is called a Cracker, but that's not quite right: the original Crackers scratched out a living in the backwoods (Conchs are Crackers in the Keys). They were migrant field hands, not plantation owners, and with their lawless squatting, make-do creativity, vagrancy and carousing, they weren't regarded kindly by respectable townsfolk. But today, all native Floridians like to feel they too share that same streak of fierce, undomesticated self-reliance.

Then again, stand in parts of Tampa, Miami or South Florida, and you won't feel like you're in the US at all. The air is filled with Spanish, and the politics of Cuba, Haiti or Colombia animate conversations. You might find Cuban lawyers more politically conservative than redneck construction workers, and fixed-income retirees in gated communities more liberal than well-off gay South Beach restaurateurs. Or not. Florida satisfies and defies expectations all at once.

Or, to put it another way: in Florida, nearly everyone is from someplace else. Nearly everyone is a newcomer, and like good 'got miners' one and all, they wholeheartedly agree on two things: more newcomers are going to ruin Florida, and isn't it great to live here?

Cracker: The Cracker Culture in Florida History (1998) by Dana Ste Claire is an eclectic, affectionate, witty look at what makes a Cracker a Cracker. He talks to alligator poachers and teaches you all about grits.

LIFESTYLE

Florida's diverse population means an equal diversity of lifestyles and attitudes (for more, see p42).

First things first: Florida is indeed the nation's oldest state; it has the most people over 65, which pulls the state's median age up to 39.6, or three years higher than the national average. In fact, ever since WWII, South Florida has been 'God's waiting room' – the land of the retiree.

But those averages hide a complex picture. Actually, most immigrants to the state are aged 20 to 30, and they don't come for the shuffleboard. They come because of Florida's historically low cost of living and its usually robust job and real-estate markets.

What they find is that, if they can own one of those new-built condos or tract homes, they're money ahead, as Florida home-values outpace the nation's by $50,000. But wages are lower than average because Florida's tourist and service jobs don't pay that much, and its construction jobs boom and bust with the yo-yo real-estate market. Thus, those 20- to 30-year-olds also leave the state in the highest numbers.

Florida's urban and rural divides are also pretty extreme. Urban sprawl, particularly around Miami, Orlando and Tampa, is universally loathed – because who likes traffic jams and cookie-cutter sameness? – but it's nearly unavoidable: 80% of Floridians live within 10 miles of the coast because that's why everyone came here – the beach.

So, along the peninsula's urbanized edges, everyone lives on top of each other, and to a great degree, puts up with each other: the racial and ethnic tensions that once defined the state certainly haven't disappeared, but they have calmed tremendously. Tolerance of gays is the norm (when not a cause for celebration, as in Miami, Fort Lauderdale and Key West). And tolerance of visitors is the rule. After all, they pay the bills.

But wilderness and rural life define much of interior and northern Florida: here, small working-class towns can be as white, old-fashioned and conservative as Miami is ethnic, fashion-conscious and permissive. This is one reason why it's so hard to predict Florida elections, and why sometimes they turn on a handful of votes.

The Museum (www
.flamuseum.com),
existing only online, is
devoted to the life and
culture of Muskogee
Creeks, who live in Florida's Apalachicola region;
it shares myths, tall tales,
history, language and
much more.

ECONOMY

Florida is a boom-and-bust place. People find something they can get rich with – oranges, real estate, tourists – and they ride it into the sky until nature, the stock market or their own exuberance sends them tumbling back to earth.

For example, between 2002 and 2006, skyrocketing real-estate prices sparked a huge construction boom and growth soared, leading to Florida's highest levels of immigration in 30 years. Then, with 2007's national home-mortgage crisis and real-estate collapse, Florida construction and home prices went bust, growth flatlined, and Florida immigration sunk to its lowest point in 30 years.

With a state gross domestic product of $734 billion in 2007, Florida is the nation's fourth-largest economy, and tourism is its number-one industry. Together, tourism and real estate drive the bulk of state job growth, which outpaces the national average. Orlando, for instance, has oodles of full-time jobs, but they are mostly low-wage, low-skill positions as maids, waiters and theme-park 'hosts.'

Agriculture is the second-largest industry, with Florida growing most of the nation's citrus and a wealth of other crops, like sugarcane. But as with phosphate mining, another major industry, agriculture has serious environmental impacts, which the state has yet to solve.

Two important industries the state would like to keep growing are high-tech aerospace jobs – which stretch along 'Silicon Beach,' from Cape Canaveral to Miami – and bio-tech, medical and health-care jobs. And actually, Florida's health-care professions are feeling robust, mostly because the Baby Boomer population bubble is reaching retirement age right about now.

POPULATION

For the last 70 years, the story of Florida has been population growth, which has been driven almost entirely by immigration. Before WWII, Florida was the least populated state (with under two million), and by the 1990s, it was the fourth most populated (with nearly 13 million). In 2008 the estimated population was 18.3 million, and by 2030, Florida is expected to add another 10 million newcomers.

Florida's growth rate has been astonishing – it was 44% for the 1970s – but it's been steadily declining. In 2008, due to the slumping economy, population growth slowed to a trickle, but no one expects that to last. From 2000 to 2007 it was 14%, still twice the national average.

Immigrants to Florida come mainly from elsewhere in the US, the Caribbean and Latin America, and the state's demographics reflect this. About 61% of residents are white, and about 20% are Hispanic – a percentage that's growing, and is 5% above the national average. Black residents make up 15.4%, and foreign-born residents make up 19% – meaning *one in five* Floridians was born elsewhere. Asians are 2% and American Indians (mostly Seminoles) 4%, which are both half the national average.

SPORTS

Floridians are passionate about sports. If you let them, they'll fervently talk baseball, football, basketball and Nascar through dinner, dessert and drinks on the porch.

Florida has two pro basketball teams, the Orlando Magic (p283) and Miami Heat (p158). The state also boasts three pro football teams: the Miami Dolphins (p158), Tampa Bay Buccaneers (p416) and Jacksonville Jaguars (p376). But really, college football is the true religion: for more on this particular madness, see below.

Baseball's major-league Florida Marlins play in Miami (p158), while the Tampa Bay Devil Rays play in St Petersburg (p426). Many major-league teams hold their spring training in Florida, and these intimate, relaxed preseason games are their own annual ritual (see p27). In addition, minor-league teams inspire considerable loyalty across the state.

The Stanley Cup–winning Tampa Bay Lightning (p416) is one of several pro and semi-pro hockey teams in the state, including the Miami-based Florida Panthers.

Nascar originated among liquor bootleggers who needed fast cars to escape the law – and who later raced them against each other. Fast outgrowing its Southern redneck roots to become popular across the US, Nascar (for more, see p356) is near and dear to Floridians.

THE CHOKE AT THE DOAK

Everyone who doesn't understand that reference, listen up: Florida has three of the best college football programs in the country, and they are, you might say, a little competitive with each other. In fact, the teams and their rivalries have become an indelible part of Florida life and lore. Here's a quick primer:

The teams are the University of Miami Hurricanes (p158), the University of Florida Gators (in Gainesville, p400), and the Florida State University Seminoles (in Tallahassee, p471). The Miami Hurricanes have won the most national championships (five, versus two apiece for the Florida Gators and the FSU Seminoles), but in Florida, bragging rights are about more than mere championships.

Since 2002, when all three teams play each other in a season, the team with the best head-to-head record wins the 'Florida Cup.' It's happened three times so far, and Miami has won all three.

Miami's rivalry with the Gators began in 1938, and when they play each other, it's for the 'War Canoe Trophy,' a hand-carved Seminole canoe. Miami *hates* the Florida Gators, and while Miami's rivalry with the Seminoles has, if anything, affected the outcome of more national championships, the emotions don't run quite as high.

But the Florida Gators and the FSU Seminoles *hate* each other as well, and their rivalry may be even more fierce. Since 1977, they have played each other on the season's last game, and it's no exaggeration to say that, for many fans, winning this game is more important than winning any of the others.

Naturally, some of these games are legendary, such as the one in 1994 when the Florida Gators were crushing the FSU Seminoles 31-3 (at Doak Campbell Stadium). Then in the fourth quarter FSU scored 28 unanswered points, and the game ended tied 31-31, ruining Florida's chance to be number one that year. This epic collapse, the source of real tears and everlasting taunts, is the 'Choke at the Doak.'

One unusual sport is jai alai, a dangerous Basque game in which players hurl a pelota – a very hard ball – at more than 150mph. In South Florida, jai alai remains popular with cigar-smoking wagering types and is fascinating to watch (see p124).

MULTICULTURALISM

Like Texas and California, modern Florida has been largely redefined by successive waves of Hispanic immigrants from Latin America. What sets Florida apart is the teeming diversity of its Latinos and their self-sufficient, economically powerful, politicized, Spanish-speaking presence.

How pervasive is Spanish? One in four Floridians speak a language other than English at home, and three-quarters of these speak Spanish. Further, nearly half of these Spanish-speakers admit they don't speak English very well – because they don't need to. This is a sore point with some Anglo Floridians, perhaps because it's incontrovertible evidence that Florida's Latinos are enjoying the capitalism of the US without necessarily having to adopt its culture or language.

Florida's Cuban exile community (concentrated in Little Havana, p113, and Hialeah Park, p118) began arriving in Miami in the 1960s following Castro's Cuban revolution (see p35), and they created this community from the start. Educated and wealthy, these Cubans ran their own businesses, published their own newspapers, and developed a Spanish-speaking city within a city. Their success aggravated Florida's black population, who, at the moment the civil-rights movement was opening the doors to economic opportunity, found themselves outmaneuvered for jobs by Hispanic newcomers.

Then Latinos kept arriving, nonstop, ranging from the very poorest to the wealthiest, and evincing the entire ethnic palette. In Miami they found a Spanish-speaking infrastructure to help them, while sometimes being shunned by the insular Cuban exiles who preceded them.

A true story, *The Orchid Thief* (1998) by Susan Orlean is an only-in-Florida mix of religious fervor, strange botany, illegal profits, megalomania, hallucinatory dreams and everyday smuggling, and its seductive power over one Yankee journalist.

CELEBRATING FLORIDA HERITAGE & CULTURE

Florida's diversity really comes alive in its many cultural festivals. In fact, there are simply too many to keep up with. So here we highlight a handful worth planning a trip around. For more, see p17.

- **Zora! Festival** (www.zoranealehurstonfestival.com; Eatonville; 1 week in late Jan–early Feb) For 20 years, Zora Neale Hurston's hometown has honored her with this African American cultural festival. A series of lectures and discussions culminates in a lively three-day street fair with lots of music, crafts, art and food.

- **Carnaval Miami** (www.carnavalmiami.com; Miami; 9 days in early Mar) The Calle Ocho festival in Little Havana may be the biggest Hispanic street fair in the US, but there are also domino tournaments, cooking contests, Latin music concerts and much more.

- **Florida Folk Festival** (www.floridastateparks.org/folkfest; White Springs; Memorial Day weekend) Since 1953, the Stephen Foster State Folk Cultural Center (p477) has held this enormous heritage festival, with hundreds of Florida musicians – from gospel singers to banjo pickers – plus storytellers and Seminole craft demonstrations.

- **Miami Goombay Festival** (www.goombayfestivalcoconutgrove.com; Coconut Grove; 1 week in early Jun) One of the nation's largest black-culture festivals celebrates Miami's Bahamian immigrants with tons of Caribbean music, dancing and food.

- **Barberville Jamboree** (www.pioneersettlement.org; Barberville; 1st weekend of Nov) The Pioneer Settlement for the Creative Arts hosts Florida's best pioneer-heritage festival, with authentic demonstrations of pioneer and Cracker life (such as grinding grits and cutting timbers) and wonderful folk music.

Today, every Latin American country is represented in South Florida. Nicaraguans arrived in the 1980s, fleeing war in their country, and now number over 100,000. Miami's Little Haiti (p111) is home to over 70,000 Haitians, the largest community in the US. There are 80,000 Brazilians, and large communities of Mexicans, Venezuelans, Colombians, Peruvians, Salvadorans, Jamaicans, Bahamians and more. This has led to significant in-migration around South Florida, as groups displace each other and shift to more fertile ground.

The children of Cuban exiles are now called YUCAs, 'young urban Cuban Americans,' while the next generation of Latinos has been dubbed Generation Ñ (pronounced enyey), embodying a hybrid culture. For instance, the traditional Cuban *quinceañera*, or *quince,* celebrating a girl's coming of age at 15, is still celebrated in Miami, but instead of a community-wide party, kids now plan trips. With each other, young Latinos slip seamlessly between English and Spanish, typically within the same sentence, reverting to English in front of Anglos and to Spanish or old-school *cubano* in front of relatives (for more, see p84).

Florida has also welcomed smaller waves of Asian immigrants from China, Indonesia, Thailand and Vietnam. And, of course, South Florida is famous for its Jewish immigrants, not all of whom are over 65 or even from the US. There is a distinctly Latin flavor to South Florida Judaism, as Cuban and Latin Jews have joined those from the US East Coast, Europe and Russia. Overall, Florida is home to 850,000 Jews, with two-thirds in the greater Miami area. Like Cuban exiles, Jewish communities were originally insular re-creations of their previous homes, but this has become less pronounced with each generation.

Cuban Miami (2000) by Robert Levine and Moisés Asís is a wonderful, intimate portrait of Miami's Cuban exile community, packed with photos like a family album.

MEDIA

Florida has hundreds of newspapers, with three highly regarded major city dailies: the *Miami Herald, Orlando Sentinel* and *St Petersburg Times.* Each has a national reputation, great columnists and numerous prizes to its credit.

The *Miami Herald* publishes a separate Spanish-language version, *El Nuevo Herald.* This is more than a translation; it's different news aimed at Miami's Cuban and Latin citizens. The same is true for Spanish-language magazines and radio stations, which treat events in Cuba or Latin America with the same urgency English-language media give to Washington.

For a comprehensive list, with links to Florida newspapers, TV stations, radio stations and magazines, see www.floridasmart.com/news.

RELIGION

Florida is not just another notch in the South's Evangelical Bible Belt. It's actually considerably more diverse religiously than its neighboring states.

In Florida, religious affiliations split less along urban/rural lines than along northern/southern ones. About 40% of Florida is Protestant, and about 25% of Protestants are Evangelicals, who tend to be supporters of the religious right. However, these conservative Protestants are much more concentrated in northern Florida, nearer their Southern neighbors.

To find the majority of the state's Roman Catholics, who make up 26%, and Jews, who make up 3%, head to South Florida. In South Florida, Jews make up 12% of the population, which is the second-highest percentage after the New York metro area. The high Catholic population is due mainly to South Florida's wealth of Latin American immigrants.

South Florida also has a growing Muslim population, and it has a noticeable number of adherents of Santeria, a mix of West African and Catholic beliefs, and *vodou* (voodoo), mainly practiced by Haitians. Santeria and

Boca Raton is more than a Seinfeld punchline, and the collection of essays in *Jews of South Florida* (2005) by Andrea Greenbaum brings the vast and varied history of Florida's Jewish community to life.

voodoo both involve animal sacrifice, and in Miami, it's not entirely unusual to find the remains of such rituals.

Further, about 16% of Floridians say that they have no religious affiliation. That doesn't mean they lack spiritual beliefs; it just means their beliefs don't fit census categories. Florida has long sheltered those who don't fit census categories, but in terms of religion, one of Florida's most famous religious communities is Cassadaga (p386), a home for Spiritualists for over 100 years.

You can count among Florida's snowbirds some of the USA's best writers, like Robert Frost, Isaac Bashevis Singer and Annie Dillard, and every January, the literati of the US hold court at the Annual Key West Literary Seminar (p208).

ARTS

Floridians have an inferiority complex about their culture. Developing so much later than New York or California, Florida hasn't been known as a mecca for world-class museums or a leader of art movements. No, Florida has the reputation of being decidedly low-brow, a mangy mutt of Nascar-loving metalheads, trashy noir fiction and ironic retro pop. This is certainly true, but it's not the whole story, either of the past or of what Florida is becoming – that is, almost respectable.

Literature

Beginning in the 1930s, Florida cleared its throat and developed its own bona-fide literary voice, courtesy mainly of three writers. The most famous was Ernest Hemingway, who settled in Key West (see p201) to drink, fish and write, pretty much in that order. However, 'Papa' only set one novel in Florida, *To Have and Have Not* (1937), thus making his life far more Floridian than his writing.

FLORIDA PULP

Mystery and crime writers love to tickle the swampy underbelly of the Sunshine State. Grab one from this list (which focuses on the early novels of famous series) and hit the beach for another murderous day in paradise.

- *Rum Punch* (Elmore Leonard, 1992) Leonard is the undisputed master of intricate plots, crackling dialogue and terrific bad guys. This one's set in Miami, and it inspired Tarantino's movie *Jackie Brown*.

- *Double Whammy* (Carl Hiaasen, 1987) Hiaasen perfected his absurdist, black-comic rage in his second novel. Bass tournament murders lead to riotous consequences; you'll laugh till you cry.

- *Girl in the Plain Brown Wrapper* (John D MacDonald, 1968) The godfather of Florida crime fiction introduces us to Travis McGee, who saves a girl from suicide and gets only trouble as thanks.

- *Sanibel Flats* (Randy Wayne White, 1990) Oh, White can turn a phrase. Here he introduces his much-beloved 'retired' NSA agent Doc Ford.

- *Miami Blues* (Charles Willeford, 1984) Willeford first made it big with this addictive novel about a denture-wearing detective's chase after a cold, quirky criminal.

- *Cold Case Squad* (Edna Buchanan, 2004) Miami police sergeant Craig Burch leads the cold-case squad after killers whose 'trails vanished long ago like footprints on a sea-washed beach.'

- *Torpedo Juice* (Tim Dorsey, 2005) Zany Serge A Storm only kills people who really deserve it – people who don't respect Florida – as he searches for love in the Keys.

- *Tropical Depression* (Laurence Shames, 1996) Shames is off-the-wall silly. Here, an inept Jersey bra magnate seeks to find himself in Key West. Yeah, right.

The honor of 'most Floridian writer' is generally bestowed on Marjorie Kinnan Rawlings, who lived in Cross Creek between Gainesville and Ocala. She turned her sympathetic, keen eye on Florida's pioneers – the Crackers who populated 'the invisible Florida' – and on the elemental beauty of the state's swampy wilderness. Her novel *The Yearling* (1938) won the Pulitzer Prize, and *Cross Creek* (1942) is a much-lauded autobiographical novel. Her original homestead is now a museum (p402).

Rounding out the trio is Zora Neale Hurston, an African-American writer who was born in all-black Eatonville, near Orlando. Hurston became a major figure in New York's Harlem renaissance of the 1930s, and her most famous novel, *Their Eyes Were Watching God* (1937), evokes the suffering of Florida's rural blacks, particularly women. Controversial in her time, Hurston died in obscurity and poverty.

Among contemporary novels, Patrick Smith's *A Land Remembered* (1984) is a sprawling, multigenerational saga of Florida's settlers that highlights the Civil War. One of the most brilliant renditions of backwoods Cracker life is *Killing Mister Watson* (1991) by Peter Matthiessen. It fictionalizes the true story of EJ Watson, a turn-of-the-century Everglades plume hunter who murdered his employees, and who in turn was murdered by the townsfolk.

As a genre, Florida crime fiction is its own wacky branch of hard-boiled noir. Stories frequently revel in the absurd, and plots are often thinly disguised environmentalism, in which the bad guys are developers and their true crimes are against nature. Some of the most popular names are Carl Hiaasen, Randy Wayne White, John D Macdonald and James W Hall; for some recommended reads, see opposite.

For more great Florida books, see p14.

Cinema & Television

Get this: Jacksonville almost became Hollywood. In the 1910s, Jacksonville had 30 production companies – far more than Hollywood – who were using its palm tree–lined beaches as 'exotic' backdrops for 120 silent films. Yet, even as Laurel and Hardy were becoming famous in one-reeler slapstick comedies, religiously conservative Jacksonville decided to run those wild movie types out of town. Then Florida's 1926 real-estate bust (and the talkies) killed what Florida moviemaking remained.

Still, it was a close call, and you can see why: Florida, like California, has always fostered dreams and fantasies. Only Florida's are now 3-D, and they're called theme parks.

Actually, Hollywood has returned to Florida time and again to film both TV shows and movies, and Florida has learned to court both by providing the necessary production infrastructure and politicians willing to stop traffic according to the day's shooting schedule.

Hundreds of major motion pictures have been shot in Florida, and for a list of top Florida-themed films, see p46. Other notable, popular movies include *There's Something About Mary, Donnie Brasco, Monster, Caddyshack, Ace Ventura: Pet Detective, True Lies, Get Shorty, Cocoon, Edward Scissorhands, Hoot* and *Miami Blues*.

Florida, as setting, has been a main character in a number of TV shows. In the 1960s, the most famous were *Flipper*, about a boy and his dolphin, and *I Dream of Jeannie*. Set in Cocoa Beach, *Jeannie* was Florida all over: an astronaut discovers a pinup-gorgeous female genie in a bottle, only she never quite fulfills his wishes like he wants.

In the 1980s, Miami was never the same after *Miami Vice* hit the air, a groundbreaking cop drama that made it OK to wear sport coats over T-shirts and which helped inspire the renovation of South Beach's then-dilapidated

Immigrants arrive in Florida daily to start over, and Russell Banks' novel *Continental Drift* (1985) powerfully evokes the tragic intersection of two: a burned-out New Hampshire man and a Haitian woman in unforgiving Miami.

Two of the best film festivals in the US are the Miami International Film Festival (www .miamifestival.com; March), a showcase for Latin cinema, and the up-and-coming Florida Film Festival (www .floridafilmfestival.com; April) in Orlando.

FLORIDA ON FILM

Florida, always fertile ground for delusions and fantasies, has been a goldmine for Hollywood, providing surreal stories and exotic settings.

■ *Cocoanuts* (1929) In this Marx Bros farce about the 1920s Florida land boom, Groucho famously quips: 'You can even get stucco! Oh boy, can you get stucco…'

■ *Key Largo* (1948) John Huston directed Humphrey Bogart, Lauren Bacall and Edward G Robinson in this noir classic involving ruthless gangsters and an unstoppable hurricane.

■ *Creature from the Black Lagoon* (1954) Some call it the best rubber-suit-monster movie ever made, with Wakulla Springs standing in for the Amazon.

■ *Scarface* (1983) 'Say hello to my little…' Oh, you know the line. Al Pacino, as Cuban immigrant Tony Montana, guns his way to the top of Miami's decadent cocaine-fueled underworld.

■ *The Birdcage* (1996) Meanwhile, on Miami's farce side, a gay South Beach cabaret owner and his drag-queen lover must act 'straight' for their son's future in-laws. It works out very, very well.

■ *Ulee's Gold* (1997) Peter Fonda nearly won an Oscar for his moving portrayal of a 'Wewa' beekeeper (from Wewahitchka, Florida) who risks everything to help his estranged son. The 'gold' is tupelo honey.

■ *The Truman Show* (1998) Real-life Seaside proved the perfect town for a movie in which an ordinary man slowly realizes that his idyllically ordinary life is a fake, a sham, nothing, in fact, but a TV show.

■ *Sunshine State* (2002) John Sayles pits Florida developers against a coastal town and an ex–Weeki Wachee mermaid over whether 'progress' means more or fewer condos.

■ *Adaptation* (2002) What's real, and what isn't, in Florida's swamps? Susan Orleans' *The Orchid Thief* inspired Charlie Kaufman to pen the most perfectly surreal, strangely accurate portrait of Florida ever made.

historic district. Today's popular *CSI: Miami* owes a debt to actor Don Johnson and *Miami Vice* it can never repay.

Music

Florida's got a syncopated Latin rhythm, a thumping bass line, some sweet acoustic guitar and one helluva drum kit. In other words, Florida's musical heritage is as rich and satisfying as its cuisine.

It's illegal to sing while wearing a bathing suit in Sarasota.

Folk and blues are deep-running currents in Florida music, and pioneers Ray Charles and Cannonball Adderley both hailed from the state. For folk, visit the **Spirit of the Suwannee Music Park** (www.musicliveshere.com), near Suwannee River State Park (p477), while Tallahassee has a notable blues scene (p470).

Florida's state song, 'Old Folks at Home,' was written by Stephen Foster in 1851. Best known for the refrain 'Waaaay down upon the Suwannee River…,' it is the lament of a displaced slave for the plantation. In recent decades, Florida has sought to modernize the lyrics, so that the song's sentimental paean to Old Florida is sanitized of racism, but some argue it should be retired nonetheless.

Florida definitely knows how to rock. Tom Petty, Lynyrd Skynyrd, the Allman Brothers, Matchbox Twenty and Dashboard Confessional all got their start in Florida. Tampa is the home to both punk and 'death metal.' Plus, as any parrothead knows, Jimmy Buffet found his 'Cheeseburger in Paradise' on Cabbage Key near Fort Myers (p450); Buffet's heart, though, remains in Key West, wherever his band may roam.

Rap and hip-hop have flourished in Tampa and Miami, most notoriously with 2 Live Crew, while Orlando (by way of mogul and now jailbird

YOUR FLORIDA PLAYLIST

So much good music has come out of Florida, or been made by Floridians, that some want to create a **Florida Music Hall of Fame** (www.floridahof.com). We hope they do. In the meantime, here's a small sampling of some of Florida's iconic music and musicians.

- 'Conga' Gloria Estefan and the Miami Sound Machine: Miami
- 'Cheeseburger in Paradise' Jimmy Buffet: Key West
- 'Me So Horny' 2 Live Crew: Miami
- 'I Want It That Way' Backstreet Boys: Orlando
- 'Rebels' Tom Petty: Gainesville
- 'Swamp Music' Lynyrd Skynyrd: Jacksonville
- 'Miami Vice theme' Jan Hammer: Miami
- 'Eslow Motion' Los Primeros: Miami
- 'Smooth' Matchbox Twenty: Orlando
- 'Mercy, Mercy, Mercy' Cannonball Adderley: Tampa

Lou Pearlman) bestowed to the world with the boy bands N Sync and Backstreet Boys.

Miami is a tasty mélange of Cuban salsa, Jamaican reggae, Dominican merengue, and Spanish flamenco, plus mambo, rumba, cha-cha, calypso and more. Gloria Estefan and the Miami Sound Machine launched a revival of Cuban music in the 1970s, when they mixed Latin beats with disco. Since then, disco has thankfully waned, but Latin music has not, and Miami is awash in great Latin nightclubs. The best times to see ensemble Cuban bands – often with up to 20 musicians and singers – is during celebrations like Carnaval Miami (p17).

For a short list of essential Florida songs, see above.

Architecture

Just like its literature, Florida's architecture has some distinctive strains. These run from the old, such as the Spanish-Colonial and Revival styles of St Augustine (p361), to the modern, such as the 'New Urbanism' of quaint Seaside (p488).

At the turn of the century, Henry Flagler was instrumental in promoting a particularly Floridian Spanish-Moorish fantasia, which, as historian Michael Gannon writes, combined 'the stately architecture of Rome, the tiled rooftops of Spain, the dreamy beauty of Venice, [and] the tropical casualness of Algiers.' The monumental Ponce de León in St Augustine (now Flagler College, p365) is a prime example, but also see Flagler's Whitehall Mansion in Palm Beach (now Flagler Museum, p240) and the awesome, George Merrick–designed Coral Gables (p116).

Miami Beach got swept up in the art-deco movement in the 1920s and '30s (which Florida technically transformed into 'tropical deco'), and today it has the largest collection of art-deco buildings in the US. However, these languished until the mid-1980s, when their rounded corners and glass bricks were dusted off and spruced up with new coats of pastel pink and aquamarine paint. The best examples are the hotels along South Beach (see p103 and p125).

Florida's vernacular architecture is the oft-maligned 'Cracker house.' However, these pioneer homesteads were cleverly designed to maximize comfort in a pre-air-conditioning, subtropical climate. Raised off the ground, with windows and doors positioned for cross-ventilation, extra-wide gables and porches for shade, and metal roofs reflecting the sun. They weren't pretty, but they worked. And they're vanishing; a great example is Marjorie Kinnan Rawlings' home in Cross Creek (p402).

Painting, Sculpture & Visual Arts

Florida has an affinity for Modern art, and Modern artists find Florida allows them to indulge their inner pink. In 1983, Bulgarian artist Christo 'wrapped' eleven islands in Biscayne Bay in flamingo-colored fabric, so that they floated in the water like giant discarded flowers, dwarfing the urban skyline.

Everyone loved it; it was so Miami.

Today, everyone loves Brazilian émigré Romero Britto for the same reason: his sunshiny colors splash and swoop in silly-happy grandeur. Among several examples, see his Miami Children's Museum mural (p119). More public art is scattered throughout the Miami region, much of it aimed to make you smile.

Some say the trend started with the Florida **Highwaymen** (www.highway menartist.com). In the 1960s, these self-taught African American painters created vivid, super-saturated 'Florida-scapes' on canvas-board and masonite, which they sold from the trunks of their cars. Their style became a home-grown phenomenon.

And Florida does not lack for high-quality museums, though they don't match the depth and breadth of Chicago or New York. In Miami, top destinations include the Lowe Art Museum (p117), the Miami Art Museum (in new digs in 2010; p108), the Bass Museum of Art (p104), and ArtCenter/South Florida (p104).

St Petersburg has two worthy stops: the wild Salvador Dalí Museum (p421) and the St Petersburg Museum of Fine Arts (p421). In Fort Lauderdale, the Museum of Art (p219) is a standout for Latin art, and West Palm Beach's Norton Museum of Art (p245) is the state's largest museum.

Naturally, the Miami art-gallery scene is quite lively (visit the Design District, p110), but Sarasota also has a thriving art community (p437).

Florida's Division of Cultural Affairs (www .florida-arts.org) lists arts organizations, museums, theaters and local art agencies.

Theater & Dance

Florida is not a cutting-edge destination for theater or dance, but those who like to mix sunshine with the symphony won't go away empty-handed. Florida has a good mix of respected theater, dance, opera and classical-music venues.

Miami leads the way. The Miami City Ballet (p157), a Balanchine company, is one of the largest in the nation. The statewide **Florida Dance Association** (www.floridadanceassociation.org) promotes dance performances and education. Miami's latest showstopper is the Adrienne Arsht Center for the Performing Arts (p107), containing the opera house and concert hall.

For theater, Miami has several professional stages and a decent scene. Shakespeare gets his due in Orlando (p269), while the Tampa Bay Performing Arts Center (p415) is a huge five-theater venue that hosts touring Broadway shows, concerts and more.

Florida
Outdoors

Florida doesn't have mountains. It doesn't have big waves. It doesn't have granite cliffs. It doesn't have rivers churning with rapids. It doesn't have snow.

Now that that's out of the way, what *does* Florida have?

For starters, Florida has water, lots and lots of water – freshwater, saltwater, rainwater, spring water, swamp water. Florida's signature peninsula bends with over 1350 miles of coastline, which includes over 660 miles of the best beaches in the US. Stretch that sand out, and you could walk from New York to Detroit without ever touching pavement. For most visitors (and residents, frankly), that's all they need to know.

But consider: under the ocean is the largest coral reef system in North America, while the peninsula is crisscrossed with 50,000 miles of lazy rivers and streams and dotted with some 700 springs, which bubble up like champagne. And Florida's prehistoric swamps are teeming with Ice Age flora and dinosaur-era beasts.

Because of this surreal, watery landscape, Florida is legendary for its swimming, snorkeling, diving, hiking, paddling, fishing, sailing, windsurfing, and wildlife watching. Florida is a bird-watcher's paradise, and who leaves before seeking out the local megafauna – alligators, sea turtles and manatees? (For more on viewing wildlife, see p71.)

Some people stopped reading at 'beaches,' and we can't blame them. But get off your towel and you'll experience one of the greatest shows on Earth.

HIKING & CAMPING

In Florida, one thing hikers never have to worry about is elevation gain. But the weather more than makes up for it. Particularly if your destination is South Florida, hike and camp in winter, from November through March. This is Florida's 'dry season,' when rain, temperature, humidity and mosquitos decrease to tolerable levels. In summer, make sure to hike first thing, before noon, to avoid the heat of the day and the typical afternoon thundershowers.

Florida National Scenic Trail (FSNT; wwwflorida trail.org) is one of just eight national scenic

top ten

BEACHES

Choosing Florida's top beaches is like trying to pick Manhattan's best pizza – you're doomed from the start. See the Florida's Parks & Beaches map (Map pp72–3) for the whole pie. Still, a few slices *do* stand out. For a list based on 'science,' consult Dr Beach (www.drbeach.org). Here are our favorites, in order of preference:

Caladesi Island State Park p430)
Tampa Bay

Siesta Key Beach (p436)
Tampa Bay

Grayton Beach State Park (p488)
Panhandle

Fort DeSoto Park (p428)
Tampa Bay

Canaveral National Seashore (p344)
Space Coast

St George Island State Park (p483)
Panhandle

Bahia Honda (p196)
Florida Keys

Sanibel Island p451
Tampa Bay

Bill Baggs Cape Florida State Recreation Area p112)
Miami

Naples Beach p455)
Tampa Bay

trails and covers 1400 not-yet-contiguous miles. It runs north from the swamps of **Big Cypress National Preserve** (p171); around Lake Okeechobee; through the **Ocala National Forest** (p392); and then west to the **Gulf Islands National Seashore** (p497) near Pensacola. All sections are highly recommended.

Other prime hiking areas include the remote pine wilderness, karst terrain and limestone sinkholes of **Apalachicola National Forest** (p474) and **Paynes Prairie Preserve State Park** (p402). **Wekiwa Springs State Park** (p274) rewards hikers, paddlers and snorkelers.

Hiking in the verdant Ocala National Forest (p393)

© M. TIMOTHY O'KEEFE / ALAMY

Top camping spots include the shady riverside at **Stephen Foster Folk Culture Center State Park** (p477); the **Ocala National Forest** (p392); the Panhandle's **St Joseph State Park** (p484); and the **Florida Keys** (p195).

For reservations, hiking organizations and statewide trail information, see p505.

CANOEING & KAYAKING

Hiking only gets you so far in Florida. To really experience its swamps and rivers, its estuaries and inlets, its lagoons and barrier islands, you need watercraft, preferably the kind you paddle. The intimate quiet of dipping among mangroves, startling gators and ibis, stirs wonder in the soul.

As with hiking, winter is best for paddling season, as you avoid the worst of the rain, heat and humidity. If it's summer, aim to canoe near cool freshwater springs and swimming beaches, 'cause you'll be dreaming about them.

...ayaking the grassy waters of Everglades National Park (p172)

MARK NEWMAN

GET YOUR BOARD ON

Eight-time world champion surfer Kelly Slater is from Cocoa Beach, and four-time women's champion Lisa Anderson is from Ormond Beach. Both first learned how to carve in Space Coast waves, in the shadow of rockets, and Slater honed his aerials at Sebastian Inlet.

All of which is to say that while Florida's surf may be considered 'small' by Californian and Hawaiian standards, Florida's surfing community and history are not. Plus, Florida makes up in wave quantity what it may lack in wave size.

Nearly the entire Atlantic Coast has rideable waves, but the best spots are indeed gathered along the Space Coast, which has lessons, rentals and popular competitions: shoot for **Cocoa Beach** (p346), **Indialantic**, **Sebastian Inlet**, and **Playalinda Beach** (p344). However, you'll find good waves from **Fort Lauderdale** (p222) down to Miami's **South Beach** (p123).

Florida's northern Atlantic Coast is less attractive, partly due to chilly winter water, but consistent, 2ft to 3ft surf can be had at **Daytona Beach** (p357); from **Flagler Beach** (p361) up to **St Augustine** (p366); and around **Amelia Island** (p380).

Surf's up: Florida's excellent beaches and warm climate are perfect for a spot of wave-riding

RICHARD CUMMINS

In terms of rivers, the 207-mile **Suwannee River** is quintessential Florida: a meandering, muddy ribbon decorated with 60 clear-blue springs that runs from Georgia's Okefeno-kee Swamp to the Gulf of Mexico. About 170 miles are an official **Wilderness Trail** (www.floridastateparks.org/wilderness; p477), and the section near Big Shoals State Park actually has some Class III rapids – woohoo!

Other unforgettable rivers include: the Atlantic Coast's 'Wild and Scenic' **Loxahatchee River** (p254); Orlando's 'Wild and Scenic' **Wekiva River** (p274); and the Tampa region's jade-green **Hillsborough River** (p417) and **Myakka River** (p442).

You'll tell your grandchildren about kayaking **Everglades National Park** (p170); **Hell's Bay paddling trail** (p177) is heavenly. The nearby **10,000 Islands** (p174) are just as amazing, and nothing beats sleeping in the Everglades in a chickee (wooden platform above the waterline; p178).

And with all that, we've hardly touched the coasts. You'll kick yourself if you don't kayak Miami's **Bill Baggs Cape Florida State Recreation Area** (p112); Tampa Bay's **Caladesi and Honeymoon Islands** (p430); Sanibel Island's **JN 'Ding' Darling National Wildlife Refuge** (p452); and the Big Bend's **Cedar Key** (p478).

Plus, on Florida's Atlantic Coast, more mangroves, waterbirds, dolphins and manatees await in **Mosquito Lagoon** (p343), the **Canaveral National Seashore** (p343), and the Intercoastal Waterway near **Sebastian Inlet** (p349). We've left out a bunch, but that should get you started.

For paddling organizations, see p504.

DIVING & SNORKELING

For diving and snorkeling, Florida collapses with superlatives. Florida's limestone has more holes than Swiss cheese, and so many are beneath freshwater springs, making northern Florida the 'Cave Diving Capital of the US.'

Many spots line the Suwannee River: try **Peacock Springs State Park** (www.floridastateparks.org/peacocksprings), one of the continent's largest underwater cave systems; **Troy Spring State Park** (www.floridastateparks.org/troyspring); and **Manatee Springs State Park** (p477). Another fun dive is **Blue Spring**

SWIMMING WITH THE FISHES

Between Florida's lakes, rivers, springs and ocean beaches – not to mention hotel pools – you're probably never more than 10ft from a swimmable body of water. By the time you're packing your bathing suit to leave, you might feel a bit amphibious.

As for saltwater, see the Florida's Parks & Beaches map (Map pp72–3) for an overview and Top 10 Beaches (p50) for highlights. You can swim in the ocean year-round in South Florida, while the north gets chilly in winter.

Florida's 700 freshwater springs (this chapter mentions some great ones) are each one a goose-bump-inducing 72°F and, when healthy, clear as glass. If you're certified, (see above), don't miss the unforgettable experience of divingthese springs, where, as William Bartram once wrote, 'the trout swims by the very nose of the alligator and laughs in his face.'

Some swimming options in Florida are not for the feint of heart. Alligators also enjoy springs, and sharks, barracuda and jellyfish like coastal waters; in all cases, actual danger is minimal, and the only real protection is alertness (see p348). Swim where there are lifeguards to avoid surprises.

Florida's beaches are uniformly calm, relatively safe places to swim, but rip tides and undertows do occur. If you get caught in either, don't fight it; go with the flow until the current subsides and you can swim back to safety. The most dangerous surf will occur just before and after a storm.

A school of tropical fish brighten up a diver's day in John Pennekamp Coral Reef State Park (p183)

© STEPHEN FRINK/C

State Park (p386), near Orlando. Note that you need to be cavern certified to dive a spring (an open-water certification won't do), and solo diving is usually not allowed. But local dive shops can help with both (for dive organizations and resources, see p504).

Every Florida spring is a prime snorkeling spot. At times, the clarity of the water is disconcerting, as if you were flying, not floating; every creature and school of fish all the way to the bottom feels just out of reach.

If your idea of diving and snorkeling is coral reefs teeming with rainbow-bright tropical fish, you just may be in luck...Florida has the continent's largest coral reef system. Aim for the Florida Keys, where **John Pennekamp Coral Reef State Park** (p183) is prime, but you won't be disappointed at **Bahia Honda State Park** (p196) or at **Biscayne National Park** (p177).

Meanwhile, so many Spanish galleons sank off the Emerald Coast (near **Panama City Beach**, p486) that it's dubbed the 'Wreck Capital of the South,' and more sunken ships await off the 'Treasure Coast,' near **Sebastian Inlet State Park** (p349).

Named for its abundant sea turtles, the **Dry Tortugas** (p213) rewards visitors who make the effort to reach them.

TOP FIVE 'GREEN' GOLF COURSES

Florida has a wealth of perfectly manicured golf greens. Here, we present five of the best courses that combine world-class golf with the highest standards of environmental and wildlife conservation (as certified by the Audubon Cooperative Sanctuary Program, www.auduboninter national.org/programs/acss/golf.htm). For a comprehensive list of Florida courses, see **Florida Golf** (www.fgolf.com).

- Old Corkscrew Golf Club (www.oldcorkscrew.com), Estero, near Fort Myers (p442)
- Pelican Preserve (www.pelicanpreservelifestyles.com), Fort Myers (p442)
- Raptor Bay Golf Club (www.raptorbaygolfclub.com), Bonita Springs, near Naples (p454)
- St James Bay Golf Course (www.stjamesbay.com), Carrabelle, on the Panhandle's Gulf Coast (p480)
- Venetian Golf & River Club (www.venetiangolfandriverclub.com), Venice (p441)

BIKING

Florida is too flat for mountain biking, but there are plenty of off-road opportunities to get your tires muddy, along with hundreds of miles of paved trails for those who prefer to keep their ride clean. As with hiking, avoid biking in summer, unless you like getting hot and sweaty.

Top off-roading spots include **Big Shoals State Park** (www.floridastateparks.org/bigshoals), with 25 miles of trails along and around the Suwannee River, and **Paynes Prairie Preserve State Park** (p402), with 20 miles of trails through its bizarre landscape. Also recommended are the **Ocala National Forest** (p392) and the **Apalachicola National Forest** (p474), particularly the sandy Munson Hills Loop.

With so many paved cycling trails, it's hard to choose. To dip among the Panhandle's sugar-sand beaches, take the 19-mile **Timpoochee Trail** (p489), which parallels Hwy 30A. In Tallahassee, the 16-mile **Tallahassee–St Marks Historic Railroad State Trail** (p467) shoots you right to the Gulf. Both paved and off-road trails encircle **Lake Okeechobee**, which is a great way to take in the lake and the surrounding countryside. The 15-mile, paved **Shark Valley Tram Road Trail** (p171) gets you and your bike into the gator-infested Everglades.

Two more don't-miss bike trails are the **Florida Keys Overland Heritage Trail** (p189), which mirrors the Keys Highway for 61 noncontiguous miles, though eventually it will connect for the entire 106 miles through the Keys. Then, the urban-and-coastal **Pinellas Trail** (p423) goes 43 miles from St Petersburg to Tarpon Springs, facilitating car-free explorations. For more trails and advice, see p504.

family chooses peddle-power to tour the Shark Valley (p171)

© PATRICK WARD/CORBIS

FISHING

The world may contain seven seas, but there's only one Fishing Capital of the World: Florida. Sure, dismiss it as typically overwrought Floridian hype, but be prepared for arguments from the world's fishermen. Then again, who needs that? Just grab a pole and charter a boat.

In Florida's abundant rivers and lakes, largemouth bass are the main prize. Prime spots, with good access and facilities, are **Lake Manatee State Park** (www.floridastateparks.org/lakemanatee), south of St Peterburg; fly-fishing at **Myakka River State Park** (p442); and **Jacksonville** (p375), which has charters to the St Johns River and Lake George for freshwater fishing, to the bay for ocean fishing, plus kayak fishing.

Near-shore saltwater fishing means redfish and mighty tarpon, snook, spotted seatrout and much more, up and down both coasts. The jetties at **Sebastian Inlet** (p349) are a mecca for shore anglers on the Atlantic Coast, while on the Gulf, Tampa's **Skyway Fishing Pier** (p427) is dubbed the world's longest fishing pier – and it's lit at night.

In the Keys, **Bahia Honda** (p196) and **Old Seven Mile Bridge** (p195) are other shore-fishing highlights.

However, as 'Papa' Hemingway would tell you, the real fishing is offshore, where majestic sailfish leap and thrash. Bluefish and mahimahi are other popular deep-water fish. For offshore charters, aim for **Stuart** (p255), **Destin** (p491), **Steinhatchee** (p476), and **Miami** (p122). The best strategy is to walk the harbor, talking with captains, till you find one who speaks to your experience and interests.

Note that you usually need a license to fish, and there are a slew of regulations about what you can catch; see p505 for fishing organizations and details.

SAILING

If you prefer the wind in your sails and your hand on the tiller, Florida is your place. **Miami** (p121) is a sailing sweet spot, with plenty of marinas for renting or berthing your own boat – **Key Biscayne** (p112) is a particular gem. **Fort Lauderdale** (p223) is chockful of boating options. In **Key West** (p206), sail on a schooner with real cannons, though tour operators are plentiful throughout the Keys. To learn how to sail, check out the Pensacola's **Lanier Sailing Academy** (p498), and for a taste of what it's like to be yacht deckhand, see the boxed text, p223.

TREAD LIGHTLY, EXPLORE SAFELY

These days, it should go without saying that any wilderness, even a swamp, is a fragile place. Whether hiking, biking, paddling, or snorkeling, always practice 'Leave No Trace' ethics (see Leave No Trace at www.lnt.org, for comprehensive advice). In short, this boils down to staying on the trail, cleaning up your own mess, and observing nature rather than plucking or feeding it. See also the boxed text, A Kinder, Gentler Wilderness Encounter, p75.

As you enjoy Florida's natural bounty, watch out for yourself, too. In particular, carry lots of water, up to a gallon per person per day, and always be prepared for rain. Line backpacks with plastic bags, and carry rain gear and extra clothes for when (not if) you get soaked. Reid Tillery's *Surviving the Wilds of Florida* will help you do just that, while Tillery's website **Florida Adventuring** (www.floridaadventuring.com) covers backcountry essentials.

Food & Drink

Imagine you're driving down the highway and spot a restaurant: non-descript, large parking lot, weathered teal exterior and a sputtering neon sign announcing 'Real Florida Cuisine!' You're skeptical. You've passed a dozen restaurants with similar come-ons in as many miles. But you're hungry, you can't bear to stop at another one of those flavor-free, squeaky-clean corporate eateries, so you shrug, pull over, and brave the creaking front door's air-conditioned blast.

What do you find? A bewildering warren of dimly lit, paneled rooms, holding piles of deep-fried alligator, iced oysters on the half shell, succulent stone crab, grilled Cuban sandwiches, mountainous reubens, Haitian *griot* (fried, spicy pork), bubbling gumbo, chilled gazpacho, hushpuppies, Key lime pie, ceviche, delicate saffron-infused pastas – and then it hits you. A Florida meal doesn't *have* to be boring. Instead, culinary explorers willing to push past the thicket of homogenized restaurants are rewarded with a bountiful, sublime feast of land and sea that mixes rustic traditions, gourmet inventions and a hemisphere's-worth of cultures.

> In *The Florida Cookbook: From Gulf Coast Gumbo to Key Lime Pie*, celebrated food writer Jeanne Voltz, with Caroline Stuart, explores centuries of Florida culture through venerated, classic recipes.

STAPLES & SPECIALTIES

As with Florida's peoples, so with its cuisine: the north is home to traditional Southern food and fryers full of fatty goodness, while in the south, the influences of Cuba, the Caribbean, and Latin America expand the spice rack and often glam up the menu. Gourmands looking to notch one-of-a-kind experiences will only be held back by their nerve: boiled peanuts, frog's legs, snake, alligator, chitlins (hog intestines) – how far will you go? Truculent gourmets should stick to the greater Miami monstropolis, while making targeted forays to other urban centers and tourist enclaves. Tarpon Springs is known for its Greek cuisine (p458), and Jewish Miami Beach for its kosher delis (p142). Of course, be aware that some towns seem to have but one special – the early bird.

Seafood & Shellfish

Florida has always fed itself from the sea, which lies within arm's reach from nearly every point. If it swims or crawls in the ocean, you can bet some enterprising local has shelled or scaled it, battered it, dropped it in a fryer and put it on a menu.

> Forget that toothsome grin - alligator is actually healthier than chicken, with as much protein but half the fat, fewer calories and less cholesterol. But once you drop it in a fryer…

Grouper is far and away the most popular fish – hunting the perfect blackened grouper sandwich and the most tender deep-fried grouper nuggets (in a basket or po' boy) is an obsessive Floridian quest. Of course, Floridians occasionally use grills and ovens to cook fish too, and other popular species include snapper (with dozens of varieties), mahimahi (still sometimes called dolphin, but it's the fish, not the mammal) and catfish.

Food in Florida really shines when it comes to crustaceans: try pink shrimp and rock shrimp, and don't miss soft-shell blue crab – Florida is the only place with blue-crab hatcheries, making them available fresh year-round. Winter (October to April) is the season for Florida spiny lobster and stone crab (out of season, both will be frozen). Florida lobster is all tail, without the large claws of its Maine cousin, and stone crab is simply heaven, served steamed with butter or the ubiquitous mustard sauce.

Finally, the Keys popularized conch (a giant sea snail); now fished out, most conch is from the Bahamas. From July to September, Steinhatchee

FLORIBBEAN CUISENE

Okay, somebody worked hard to come up with 'Floribbean' – a term for Florida's tantalizing gourmet mélange of just-caught seafood, tropical fruits and eye-watering peppers, all dressed up with some combination of Nicaraguan, Salvadoran, Caribbean, Haitian, Cajun, Cuban and even Southern influences. Some still call it 'fusion' or 'Nuevo Latino,' but we call it delicious. You'll find it mainly in Miami, and it could refer to anything from a ceviche of lime, conch, sweet peppers and scotch bonnets to grilled fish with mango, adobo and fried plantains.

(p476) is the place for fresh scallops, and in fall/winter, Apalachicola Bay (p481) produces 90% of Florida's small but flavorful oysters.

Fruits & Vegetables

You will have heard of Florida citrus, and that's because Florida is the nation's largest producer of oranges, grapefruits, tangerines and limes, not to mention mangoes and sugar cane. Scads of bananas, strawberries, coconuts, avocados (once called 'alligator pears'), and the gamut of tropical fruits and vegetables are also grown in Florida. The major agricultural region is around Lake Okeechobee, with field upon field, and grove upon grove, as far as the eye can see.

Heart of palm, or 'swamp cabbage,' is the heart of the sabal palm, Florida's state tree, and it was a mainstay for Florida pioneers. Try it if you can find it served fresh (don't bother if it's canned; it's not from Florida) – it has a delicate, sweet crunch.

If you love farmers markets, visit www.florida-agriculture.com and click on 'Info for Consumers' and 'Community Farmers' Markets' to find a statewide list.

Coinciding with modern refrigeration, frozen concentrated orange juice was invented in Florida in 1946: this popularized orange juice as a year-round drink and created a generation of 'orange millionaires.'

Southern Cooking

The further north you travel, the more Southern the cooking, which makes up in fat what it may lack in refinement. 'Meat and three' is Southern restaurant lingo for a main meat (like fried chicken, catfish, barbecued ribs or steak) and three sides: perhaps some combination of hushpuppies, cheese grits, cornbread, coleslaw, mashed potatoes, black-eyed peas, collard greens or buttery corn. End with pecan pie, and that's living.

Meanwhile, Cracker cooking is a rough-and-tumble Southern variation but with more reptiles and amphibians.

Southern Floridian cooking is epitomized by writer Marjorie Kinnan Rawlings' famous cookbook *Cross Creek Cookery*. Near Rawlings' former home in Micanopy, the Yearling Restaurant (p402) is a good place to try Southern Floridian food.

A slim, personal collection of recipes and memories, *Florida Bounty* by Eric and Sandra Jacobs covers sweet tea and tailgating, gator chili and crab bisque, and their one-of-a-kind heart-of-palm dip.

Cuban

Cuban food, once considered 'exotic,' is a mix of Caribbean, African and Latin American influences, and in Tampa and Miami, it's now a staple of everyday life. Sidle up to a Cuban *loncheria* (snack bar) and order a *pan cubano*: a buttered, grilled baguette stuffed with ham, roast pork, cheese, mustard and pickles (see also p147).

Integral to many Cuban dishes are *mojo* (a garlicky vinaigrette, sprinkled on sandwiches), *adobo* (a meat marinade of garlic, salt, cumin, oregano and sour orange juice) and *sofrito* (a stew-starter mix of garlic, onion and chili peppers). Main-course meats are typically accompanied by fried plantains, and rice and beans.

DRINKS
Florida's spirited mix of people has stirred up a rather tasty selection of spirits and cocktails, juices and caffeinated pick-me-ups.

Alcoholic Drinks
Is it the humidity? With the exception of the occasional teetotaling dry town, Florida's embrace of liquor is prodigious, even epic. And as you ponder this legacy – from Prohibition-era rumrunners, Spring Break hedonists and drive-thru liquor stores, to Ernest Hemingway and Jimmy Buffet – you realize quantity trumps quality most of the time.

This is particularly true for beer, which runs from bland to blander to blandest; Anheuser-Busch has a Jacksonville brewery (p374) that will never go out of business. Cuban bartenders, though, became celebrities in the 1920s for what they did with all that sugar cane and all those limes: the two classics are the *Cuba libre* (rum, lime and cola) and the mojito (rum, sugar, mint, lemon and club soda), traditionally served with *chicharrónes* (deep-fried pork rinds). Today, Miami bartenders keep the cutting edge of mixology nicely honed.

Hemingway? He favored piña coladas, lots of them. Jimmy Buffet memorialized the margarita – so that now every sweaty beach bar along the peninsula claims to make the 'best.' Go ahead, *you* try them all and decide.

Nonalcoholic Drinks
Ice tea is so ubiquitous it's called the 'wine of the South,' but watch out for 'sweet tea,' which is an almost entirely different Southern drink – tea so sugary your eyes will cross. Cuban coffee, also known as *café cubano* or *cortadito,* is one of Miami's signature drinks; this hot shot of liquid gold is essentially sweetened espresso, while *café con leche* is just *café au lait* with a different accent: equal parts coffee and hot milk.

Another Cuban treat is *guarapo,* or fresh-squeezed sugar-cane juice. Cuban snack bars serve the greenish liquid straight or poured over crushed ice, and it's essential to an authentic mojito. It also sometimes finds its way into *batidos,* a milky, refreshing Latin American fruit smoothie.

Steve Raichlen mixes up Cuban, Caribbean and Latin American flavors in *Miami Spice: The New Florida Cuisine.* With wit and verve, he covers everything from *mojo* to mojitos, from Key limes to carambolas.

CELEBRATIONS
With such an abundance of raw materials and such a rich mix of ethnicities, Florida abounds with food-focused festivals and celebrations; for highlights, see boxed text Sunshine State Food Festivals, p61.

Florida is also awash in all kinds of everyday community events centered on eating. For instance, 'tailgating' in parking lots before football games is

---

MIXING THE PERFECT MOJITO

In fashionable foodie circles, today's mojitos are yesterday's cosmopolitans. A bartender's stock, especially in places like South Beach, tends to rise and fall with their creative riffs on a theme. Although mojito recipes vary widely, they still define cool bar culture. A standard (heaven forbid!) blend might go something like this:

Juice half a lime into an 8oz glass. Add a teaspoon of sugar and three sprigs of mint. Bruise the mint into the sugar and stir it into the lime juice. Fill the glass with shaved ice. Add 2oz of light Puerto Rican rum and a dash of dark rum. Add a dash of club soda. Garnish with (unbruised) mint.

Derivations (not trademarked by any trendy high priestesses of pouring that we know of) include floating the dark rum on the top, or making it with lemon juice, rather than lime.

EXPLORING FLORIDA, ONE DISH AT A TIME

From north to south, here's a list of dishes strange and sublime, but 100% Florida; try not to leave without trying them at least once.

- **Boiled peanuts** In rural north Florida, they take green or immature peanuts and boil them until they're nice and mushy, sometimes spicing them up with Cajun or other seasonings. Sure, they feel weird in the mouth, but they're surprisingly addictive.

- **Tarpon Springs Greek salad** Please don't ask why, but in Tarpon Springs, Greek restaurants started hiding a dollop of potato salad inside a regulation Greek salad – now you can find this odd combination throughout central Florida.

- **Alligator** The meat comes from the tail, and even at its best, it's chewy. Alligator tastes like a cross between fish and pork, and is usually served as deep-fried nuggets, which overwhelms the delicate flavor. Try it grilled. Most alligator is legally harvested on farms and is common enough to be found in grocery stores.

- **Frog's legs** Those who know say the 'best' legs come from the Everglades; definitely ask, since you want to avoid imported ones from India, which are smaller and disparaged as 'flavorless.' What do flavorful Glade's legs taste like? Well…like chicken, sort of, only not.

- **Stone crabs** The first recycled crustacean: only one claw is taken from a stone crab – the rest is tossed back in the sea (the claw regrows in 12 to 18 months, and crabs plucked again are called 'retreads'). The claws are so perishable that they're always cooked before selling. October through April is less a 'season' than a stone-crab frenzy. Joe Weiss of Miami Beach is credited with starting it all, and his claws, cakes and bisque can still be had at Joe's Stone Crab Restaurant (p140).

- **Griots** This Haitian fried specialty is tops: pork cubes marinated in garlic and sour orange juice, then fried. Find it by following your nose in Miami's Little Haiti.

- **Key lime pie** Key limes are yellow, and that's the color of an authentic Key lime pie, which is nothing more than a custard of Key lime juice, sweetened condensed milk and egg yolks in a cracker crust, then topped with meringue or whipped cream. If your pie is green, or stands ramrod straight when cut, then just push it back. The extra-tart Key lime matches well with the oversweet milk, which nicely captures the personality of Key West Conchs. See the boxed text, p211.

popular: a movable feast of barbecue grills and sizzling meats that's sometimes more fun than the game itself.

In the Panhandle and north Atlantic Coast, you can also still stumble across old-fashioned communal fry fests, U-peel shrimp feasts (an echo of Louisiana's crawfish boils) and even oyster roasts.

WHERE TO EAT & DRINK

Despite its rich culinary heritage, Florida wasn't known as a place for good restaurants until the 1990s, when a wave of gourmet chefs arrived. Today, more than ever, restaurants are highlighting local ingredients and traditions. Of course, sophisticated palates are best served in the major cities and upscale tourist destinations: think Miami, Miami Beach, Palm Beach, Tampa, Key West, Amelia Island and so on.

If you're traveling with kids, see p66 for advice on mealtimes. Florida contains every type of restaurant imaginable: from all-night diners to fast-food chains to generic, family-style restaurants to humble local joints to overpriced seaside tourist traps. Outside of touristy beaches, prices tend to be reasonable, while along touristy beaches, prices can be high for the quality you get. In general, a budget meal will be under $12, a midrange option around $12 to $25, and a top-end meal will set you back over $25. As a rule, tip 15% to 20% of the total bill.

Restaurant hours are also variable: some serve continuously all day, others are only open for certain meals. General opening and closing hours are as follows: breakfast 6:30am to 11am; lunch 11am to 2:30pm; dinner 5pm to 10pm. It's a good idea to make dinner reservations for popular and/or high-end restaurants.

Quick Eats

Miami and Tampa are home to Cuban snack bars called *loncherias*, where you can get good Latin food for cheap, but all of Florida's cities have the typical array of lunch counters and street vendors. Key West specializes in conch fritters and sausage stands; in the Panhandle, roadside produce stands sell boiled peanuts for snacking; and snack trucks are fairly common all over (especially along crowded beaches like Daytona), typically focusing on either tacos and empanadas, or the classic trio of hot dogs, hamburgers and fries. And while you might go broke, you will never go hungry in Florida's theme parks: they gleefully gouge their captive audience with a wide array of get-and-go sandwiches and grill fare.

In Miami, you can find classic Cuban brands that are no longer sold in Cuba itself - like Hatuey beer, La Llave coffee and Gilda crackers.

VEGETARIANS & VEGANS

When it comes to cooking, Florida has long had a reputation for being unkind to vegetables: boiling them to a mealy mush and relegating them to 'side' status. This is changing, thankfully, but gradually and not universally. Southern and Latin American cuisines glorify meats and seafood, so even Florida's regional highlights don't put vegetables front and center. Also, vegetable dishes may be cooked with animal fat or bits of pork, so always ask. Honestly, with the

---

SUNSHINE STATE FOOD FESTIVALS

Many of Florida's food festivals have the tumultuous air of county fairs, with carnival rides, music, parades, pageants and any number of wacky, only-in-Florida happenings.

Florida Agriculture maintains a good list of festivals at www.florida-agriculture.com/consumers /fairs.htm. *Food Fest!* by Joan Steinbacher is the definitive guide; her companion website (www .foodfestguide.com) lists festivals for the coming week.

Florida Citrus Festival (www.citrusfestival.com) Winter Haven; 11 days, late January. Begun in 1924, this citrus celebration has a beauty pageant, livestock show and carnival rides.

Everglades Seafood Festival (www.evergladesseafoodfestival.com) Everglades City; three-day weekend, early February. Not just seafood, but gator, frog's legs and snakes, oh my!

Swamp Cabbage Festival (www.swampcabbagefestival.org) La Belle; three-day weekend, late February. Armadillo races and crowning of the Miss Swamp Cabbage Queen.

Grant Seafood Festival (www.grantseafoodfestival.com) Grant; two-day weekend, February. This small Space Coast town throws one of Florida's biggest seafood parties.

Florida Strawberry Festival (www.flstrawberryfestival.com) Plant City; 11 days, early March. Since 1930, over half a million folks come annually to pluck, eat and honor the mighty berry.

Carnaval Miami (www.carnaval-miami.org) Miami; nine days, early March. Negotiate drag queens and in-line skaters to reach the Cuban Calle Ocho food booths.

Isle of Eight Flags Shrimp Festival (www.shrimpfestival.com) Amelia Island; three-day weekend, early May. Avast, you scurvy dog! Pirates invade for shrimp and a juried art show.

Palatka Blue Crab Festival (www.bluecrabfestival.com) Palatka; four-day Memorial Day weekend. Hosts the state championship for chowder and gumbo. Yes, it's that good.

Florida Seafood Festival (www.floridaseafoodfestival.com) Apalachicola; two days, early November. Stand way, way back at their signature oyster shucking and eating contests.

Ribfest (www.ribfest.org) St Petersburg; three days, mid-November. Three words: ribs, rock, Harleys.

FLORIDA MENU DECODER

Florida menus have both a Southern twang and Spanish accent.

Arroz Rice; *arroz con leche* – rice pudding.

Batido Latin milkshake or smoothie: fruit, ice, sweetened condensed milk and sometimes sugar.

Ceviche Raw, lime-marinated seafood and fish.

Cornpone Cornmeal pancake fried in a skillet; also called johnnycake.

Empanada Latin American savory turnover.

Frijoles Beans.

Fritters Anything mixed or dipped in batter and deep-fried – from corn to conch to alligator.

Gallo pinto Central American red beans and rice.

Grits Coarsely ground white corn (a cousin to polenta); a Southern staple, served with cheese or gravy.

Hushpuppies Deep-fried cornbread nuggets.

Jerk A Caribbean seasoning and marinade – for pork, chicken or beef.

Moros y cristianos Cuban rice and beans (literally Moors and Christians – blacks and whites); also called *congri*.

Plantains Like bananas, but starchier and less sweet; served fried with Cuban meats.

Po' boy The South's answer to the Yankee hoagie or sub sandwich.

Sour orange An ugly orange that tastes like a lime, and is a major component of Cuban cuisine; *naranja agria* in Spanish.

Tres leches Nicaraguan 'three milks' cake; a sponge cake full of creamy syrup and topped with meringue.

---

exception of Miami and a few vacation spots, being a vegetarian in Florida can take work and get very boring (a conveyor belt of pastas and iceberg-lettuce salads) unless you do some shopping and cooking yourself.

HABITS & CUSTOMS

Floridians are typical North Americans when it comes to eating habits, etiquette and dining customs. In traditional Southern towns, 'dinner' may be the afternoon meal. In small towns or retirement communities, restaurants might close earlier than you expect, since everyone left once the early-bird specials (typically served from 4pm to 6pm) ended. Also, order conservatively, as portions can be generous.

If you are invited for a meal at someone's home, it's considered polite but not required to bring a bottle of wine or some small token, like a baked item or cookies (from a store is fine). People in the US tend to be very relaxed around the table, so you never need to worry about what fork to use, so long as you use one.

Allen Susser, aka Chef Allen, was a trailblazer in the Miami food renaissance in the late 1980s, and he shares his 'palm tree cuisine' philosophy and recipes online at www.chefallens.com.

Florida for Kids

Florida for kids? It's a no-brainer, right? Pony up the cash, bop around Orlando's theme parks for one exhilarating wild ride, wipe off their sticky hands, faces and legs, collapse on the flight home, and forever after be the hero with the ultimate bargaining chip ('Remember, young man, I was the one who took you to Disney World…').

And yes, sometimes it's that easy. Your only worries are how to beat the lines for the best rides, where to find your favorite cartoon characters for a high five and a photo op and which shows you should see before the meter runs out and time's up.

But, and we suspect this won't come as a complete shock, it doesn't always turn out that way. Indulging in theme parks for a week can be like a straight diet of cotton candy – it sounds better than it feels. Another staple of Florida family vacations is the week at the beach, and here again, it can be a no-brainer: pick a beach, pick a hotel, done. And yet: when everyone's overbaked, sand-chafed and sick of crowds, even the eternal charms of sandcastles and putt-putt golf can wear thin.

It certainly doesn't always happen that way, but we mention these unfortunate outcomes to make the point that sometimes the obvious choices for a Florida vacation are most enjoyable in measured doses. Florida has *so much more* for families and kids, and this chapter is devoted to presenting the range of options and offering practical suggestions for creating a satisfying trip that *everyone* remembers fondly.

For kid-sized portions of Florida history and culture, visit Florida Kids (www.flheritage.com/kids), which includes a list of every Florida governor!

PLANNING YOUR TRIP

Let's be honest: family trips rarely happen the way we expect. No matter how dutifully we anticipate and plan for every eventuality, there are so many variables at play that without serendipity and on-the-fly improvisation, disaster often results.

But one day's disaster can often be turned into tomorrow's success, if we're flexible enough to adjust. The biggest variable is our children. They grow up fast (to our amazement and delight), and they are continually moving from one stage to the next. When they travel, they confront unfamiliar challenges and strange situations: at times they mature before our eyes, handling stuff we'd never expect. Or they frustrate us by changing their minds (hadn't we noticed they weren't *two* anymore?), or they become insecure and cling to us in ways we thought they'd outgrown.

For general travel advice (and overviews of Fort Lauderdale and Sea-World), visit Travel With Your Kids.com (www.travelwithyourkids.com), which provides unvarnished tips 'by parents, for parents.'

This is important to remember. Successful family trips depend less on choosing the perfect destination than on how you get there, and it's worth having backup plans should the destination you choose not turn out as you'd hoped.

One strategy is to enlist your children's help with planning: let them make some choices about what to see and do. Talk to them in detail about what they'll see. This sets their expectations and provides a feeling of control, and both help kids when they travel.

If you want to stay in only one place, top picks are Orlando, Miami, Space Coast beaches, Tampa–St Petersburg, Fort Myers–area beaches, Jacksonville, and Key West.

Another excellent approach is to pick two (or maybe three) places to visit that have enough variety to satisfy multiple agendas and avoid boredom: good examples are going from Miami to the Florida Keys, from Orlando to Canaveral National Seashore, from Orlando to the Suwannee River, or from Tampa to the Everglades. These trips involve some car time, but just a minimum.

The classic road trip – moving every day or two and covering long distances – has several risks: first, can your kids handle long drives (will they nap, read or go insane)? Second, staying on the move, constantly packing and unpacking, requires extra 'transition time' with kids – time you could be relaxing. And three, it risks succumbing to the number one mistake parents make: trying to do too much. Kids are never in a hurry, and if they're having fun, nothing will convince them that even more fun waits two hours down the road. Tear up any itineraries that require constant motion or daily wake-up calls to stay on schedule; they're doomed from the start.

In fact, once you arrive, consider your itinerary a *suggestion*. If you can allow the rhythm of each day to unfold as it will, regardless of plans, you'll have the most fun. Often, this means doing less and more mundane things than you thought. But why shouldn't playing catch-and-release with sand crabs and practicing cannonballs in the pool be the highlights of your trip?

What Did I Forget?

Your kids will not care what you bring. They care only about what you forget. And in the frenzy of last-minute packing and getting everyone out the door before the plane leaves without you, parents typically overlook the important stuff, the things kids actually care about: their stuffed animals, dolls, superheroes, trains, books, video games, pillows – whatever.

Remember, 90% of what's in your suitcase is sold in Florida, from clothes to sandals to diapers to sunscreen. The state is extremely well stocked with baby supplies and every other item families and kids need. But it cannot replace Grandma's handknit blanket or your toddler's favorite binky. Before you leave, ask your children to help make a list of what *they* want to bring, then copy that list and tape it to the steering wheel. If your children say 'nothing,' do not believe them. Make certain to bring whatever soothes them at night, preferably several things. Kids need a bit of home on the road.

That said, consider sleeping arrangements: bring a portable playpen for infants and a sleeping bag or inflatable mattress for older kids. Hotel bed configurations may not work as planned; with these, you can make do anywhere. If you have a baby in diapers or child who is potty training, bring a waterproof pad to place under them on hotel beds. With schedules disrupted, be prepared for accidents.

Consider mealtimes: bring a range of sippy cups and water bottles; plastic bowls, plates and utensils; paper towels and washcloths; and lots of zip-able plastic bags (to handle snacks, half-eaten apples, dirty cutlery, wet washcloths – almost anything!). Bring a collapsible cooler and ice packs (which you can freeze in hotel refrigerators). The more self-sufficient you are, the more flexibility you'll have over where, when and what you eat.

Consider the weather and the outdoors: bring light rain gear and umbrellas for sudden downpours. Bring a range of footwear, particularly water sandals, that can get wet. Bring lightweight umbrella strollers and/or front-facing

Kid rock is its own genre, and two musicians who pass the 'play it again' test with flying colors are Justin Roberts and Ralph Covert of Ralph's World. They make music that kids and parents love singing along to.

TIP: SURPRISE THEM!

On every trip, there comes a moment when you need something extra, a little additional mojo to get through a meal, an unexpected flight delay, a traffic jam. Bring a surprise present (or two), and in a tight spot, spring it on the kids. Promising a reward later is nothing compared to the effect of a new present *right now* (and establishing that surprises can happen aids later negotiations). Besides, it's a vacation – surprises are fun!

HIKING WITH KIDS

Rare is the child who lights up at the mention of a hike. No, the key to successful hiking is always how well you sell the destination and downplay the mode of travel. Get kids excited enough about what they'll see – alligators! snakes! pink birds! seashells! – and they might forget they have to walk to get there. Also, hike crowded trails: when kids hook up with other kids, they start *running* instead of moping.

Then, be prepared and realistic: bring tons of water and snacks, start early to avoid the heat, bring carriers for little ones, and don't try to go far. With luck, your kids will become fascinated with every bizarre swampy thing they see, and going half a mile could take an hour. But it'll be a good hour, and it *might* convince them that the next hike won't be so bad.

---

baby carriers (or backpacks); theme parks involve a lot of walking, which means a lot of carrying. Bring mosquito repellent and full sun protection: sunscreen, hats, sunglasses, UV-protective swim shirts etc.

Finally, put together a fairly comprehensive first-aid kit: cough and antihistamine medicine, children's acetaminophen or ibuprofen, thermometer, Calamine (or similar anti-itch preparation), antibiotic ointment or spray, Band-aids (sticking plasters) and tweezers. You can get all this in Florida, but the moment you need it is typically not the best time to run to the store.

TRAVELING WITH KIDS
Surviving the Friendly Skies

Children under two who ride on a parent's lap usually fly for free, but it's prudent to bring a copy of the child's birth certificate, on the rare chance you get challenged. Cheaper fares for children in their own seats have nearly vanished.

Make sure to reserve your seats when you book. Otherwise you might not get seats together, and other passengers may or may not be willing to switch seats with you.

Surviving the flight itself usually boils down to distraction, distraction, distraction. Portable DVD players can be a lifesaver (you may not like the movie the airline is showing). Pack a lunchbox full of portable toys, and bring snacks galore. Bring a pillow too: if your child actually naps, it'll save your arm or their necks (airplane pillows stink).

Road Tripping

If you'll be spending any time driving, bring plenty of snacks, toys, books, music CDs and books on tape (Dr Seuss was a genius). If you're doing a real road trip, dedicate a map to plotting your course, on which you or your kids can highlight your progress, and keep a journal: each evening, spend time remembering what everyone saw and did and write it down. This helps foster fun, on-the-road games. (How many animals today? How many beaches?)

Be prepared for lots of stops: a good rule of thumb is that you should stop for half as long as you drive. If you drive for four hours, a two-hour break fully refreshes everyone. Also, plan to arrive at your final destination in the afternoon, at least an hour before your usual dinnertime, so you can unwind in the hotel room before braving a restaurant with starving kids.

Florida car-seat laws require that children under three must be in a car seat, and children under five in at least a booster seat (unless they are over 80lb and 4ft 9in tall, allowing seat belts to be positioned properly). Rental-car companies are legally required to provide child seats, but *only if you reserve them in advance*; they typically charge $10-15 extra. You avoid surprises by bringing your own.

Mealtime

Maybe a handful of restaurants in all of Florida would be flustered or annoyed by having to serve children. You really don't need to worry about bringing your kids into any restaurant, nor about finding a restaurant. If restaurants don't have a kids' menu, they will usually accommodate special requests for simple things (spaghetti with butter, steamed broccoli, grilled chicken without sauce). If you want to go to a 'nice' place, go early in the dinner service; it's less crowded, and waitstaff are less busy (and will be friendlier).

Also, you remembered to bring your own supplies, right? If nothing on a menu satisfies your finicky eater, or it's taking forever for the food to come, having drinks/fruit/sandwiches/string cheese on hand can save the day.

Bedtime

As with restaurants, the vast majority of Florida hotels stand ready to aid families: they have cribs and rollaway beds (perhaps charging extra); they have refrigerators and microwaves (but ask to confirm); and they have adjoining rooms and suites. Particularly in beach towns, large hotels and resorts can go toe-to-toe with condos for amenities, including partial or full kitchens, laundry facilities, pools and barbecues, and various activities.

The only places that would discourage young kids (they aren't allowed to discriminate) are certain romantic B&Bs and inns. If you're unsure, ask, and they'll tell you what minimum age they'd prefer.

Child Care

If you're in the Orlando, Miami or Tampa areas, you'll find numerous childcare services catering to visitors. Most offer in-hotel babysitting by certified sitters; a few run their own drop-off centers. Rates vary based on the number of children, and typically a four-hour minimum is required. Hourly rates generally range from $12 to $20.

Two Florida-wide agencies are **Sittercity** (www.sittercity.com) and **Sunshine Babysitting** (www.sunshinebabysitting.com). More agencies serve just **Orlando** (p265), **Walt Disney World** (p291), and **Universal Orlando** (p319), plus see other recommendations throughout this guide.

If you're visiting Miami, Orlando or Tampa, get more family-friendly advice from Go City Kids (www.gocitykids .com), which covers a wide range of needs and interests.

ITINERARIES

So, whatta ya gonna do? There is far too much great kid stuff in Florida to cover it all in a single chapter. These are just the highlights. For more recommendations, see the destination chapters, and check out 'Kidding Around' (p24) and 'Thrill Rides & Roller Coasters' (p27) in the Itineraries chapter.

Miami, the Everglades & the Keys

So many places in Florida are geared primarily to families that Miami can seem, at first glance, like the opposite: a city to avoid with kids. That's not the case at all, and skipping Miami just because you have kids would be to miss some wonderful experiences. If parents are comfortable negotiating a city, then Miami won't be a problem.

Older kids (say, from seven and up) will find **Little Havana** (p113) and the *botanicas* of **Little Haiti** (p111) quite fascinating. Miami also has delightful beaches: the skimpy suits along the **South Beach Promenade** (p104) might open young eyes, but try the more family-friendly beaches north of 21st St (particularly at 53rd St) and visit the **Bill Baggs Recreation Area** (p112) on Key Biscayne. The best only-in-Miami swim, though, is at the **Venetian Pool** (p116) in Coral Gables.

TOP SOUTH FLORIDA ANIMAL ENCOUNTERS

- Alligators near the Royal Palm Visitor Center, the Everglades (p175)
- Tropical fish at John Pennekamp State Park, Key Largo (p183)
- Sea turtles at the Turtle Hospital, Marathon (p194)
- Key deer on Big Pine Key (p197)
- Dolphins at the Dolphin Research Center, Grassy Key (p192)
- Monkeys at Monkey Jungle, Miami (p120)

Miami's newest museum is in fact the **Miami Children's Museum** (p119), which is the typically wonderful, hands-on modern playhouse, but with two-story sandcastles and exhibits emphasizing Miami neighborhoods and cultures and the Everglades.

Miami has several great animal encounters: kids aren't likely to forget walking along caged pathways while monkeys swing freely all around at **Monkey Jungle** (p120). Also worthwhile are Key Biscayne's **Miami Seaquarium** (p112) and the **Metrozoo** (p120). For more, see the boxed text Miami for Children, p126.

Miami is one of the more expensive places for families to stay, so you might as well be comfortably stylish: in South Beach, the **Greenview Map** (p133) and the **Surfcomber** (p133) are good choices, and in Northern Miami Beach, try the **Fontainebleau Hilton** (p136).

There are two very easy ways to see wild alligators and the **Everglades** (p164): drive the Tamiami Trail to **Shark Valley** (p171) and ride the tram. Or drive to the southern entrance past Homestead, stopping for milkshakes and the petting zoo at the funky **Robert Is Here** (p177), then continue to the **Royal Palm Visitor Center** (p175), where two short trails get you quickly into the gator-full swamp.

The Florida Keys have a wealth of accessible wildlife adventures. Definitely stop at **John Pennekamp Coral Reef State Park** (p183) to snorkel or take a glass-bottom boat tour over the teeming reef. On Islamadora, feed enormous tarpon from **Robbie's Marina** (p189), a fun rest stop, and on Grassy Key see a dolphin show and then get in the water and hug them yourself at the **Dolphin Research Center** (p192). On Marathon, up the aww-factor by visiting rehabilitating sea turtles at the **Turtle Hospital** (p194). **Bahia Honda** (p196) has a great beach and snorkeling (best for older kids), and on Big Pine Key, go looking for Bambi's little siblings at the **National Key Deer Refuge** (p197).

Key West certainly facilitates a party atmosphere, but this is actually fairly easy to avoid: just call it a day after sunset. During the day, the town is perfectly family friendly. Two don't-miss sights are the **Florida Keys Eco Discovery Center** (p201) and the **Key West Butterfly & Nature Conservatory** (p204). For more, see the boxed text Keys for Kids, p207.

Disney is fun, but it sure ain't cheap. Find deals and discounts for tickets, shows, packages and more at Mousesavers (www.mousesavers .com), a motherlode of pennywise advice.

Walt Disney World & Orlando Theme Parks

Seven of the top 10 theme parks in the US are in Orlando: five are in Disney World, and the other two are at Universal. They are quite literally their own worlds, and you cannot see them all in one trip. Nor, might we add, would you want to. If you love theme parks, consider Orlando a multi-trip destination: that way, you can enjoy the rides and shows you get to without stressing about the hundreds of attractions you don't.

The Orlando & Walt Disney World chapter (p260) has comprehensive ride and attraction descriptions of all the major theme parks; we highlight some of the most adrenaline-pumping rides in 'Thrill Rides & Roller Coasters,' p27. For winning theme-park strategies, see boxed text Four Golden Rules for Visiting Theme Parks, below.

Here is a more high-level comparison of the parks:

For sheer heartwarming nostalgia, nothing can match the myth of Disney, and the **Magic Kingdom** (p297) is Disney at its finest: it makes a magical first impression. Everyone, from toddlers to grandparents, knows and loves all the characters; no one beats Disney's parades and fireworks; and the staff, despite dealing daily with masses of people, are unfailingly friendly and kind. For kids two to nine, this is the best park.

That said, Disney can get a little too self-satisfied and not try as hard as it might. There's a lot of junk mixed in with great stuff, so it pays to target what you want. In particular, **Hollywood Studios** (p301) is a mixed bag and not the best park for the under-10 set. Its handful of highlights will delight pre-teens but be too scary for little ones, and the characters are modern (ie *High School Musical,* not Snow White).

Green, garden-filled, relaxing **Epcot** (p303) is a favorite; ignore those who say it's disappointing. Actually, you'll realize just how much the crowded, hyperactive atmosphere of other theme parks raises stress levels and agitates moods. Kids love poking through the different countries, and the shows Soarin' and Talk to Crush are absolute highlights with everyone.

Another bit of common wisdom to ignore is that **Universal Orlando** (p319) isn't good for little kids. Actually, **Islands of Adventure** (p324) is probably the best park for parents with three-year-olds pulling one way and 10-year-olds pulling the other, with great areas for everyone. Older kids tend to prefer Universal's superheroes over Disney's dwarfs.

Disney's **Typhoon Lagoon** (p310) is the best of Orlando's water parks, but **SeaWorld** (p328) has the best animal shows. However, for a bit of Old Florida fun, don't miss **Gatorland** (p269), an extravaganza of alligators.

Perhaps the most overlooked park is **Cypress Gardens** (p273); it's a fantastic respite from Orlando's cacophony. The water-park and water-ski shows are great, and its old-school amusement rides don't try to overpower you: they're just fun, and with fewer people, you can ride them over and over.

Of course, nearly every Orlando hotel and restaurant pitches itself as 'child-friendly,' but be wary. After a long day of pint-sized chaotic overstimulation,

The best free activity in Orlando? Become Duckmaster for the march of the Peabody Ducks (p278).

FOUR GOLDEN RULES FOR VISITING THEME PARKS

Hoping for a magical time? Follow these golden theme-park rules:

- Less is more: several half-days are more enjoyable than an all-day blowout. Resist the temptation to ride one more ride and 'get your money's worth.' Be flexible, and when kids start to melt down, take a break. Spend the afternoon cooling off at the hotel pool and return later for the parade and fireworks.

- Arrive early: come when the parks open and leave by lunch, when crowds get bad. You'll see more in less time and avoid wilting in long lines in the heat of the day.

- Pack a lunch: nothing kills time like a sit-down meal, and theme-park fast food is disappointing and overpriced. Bring a soft cooler with nonperishables and snack constantly to keep everyone's energy up.

- Factor travel time: book a hotel as close as possible to the parks you'll be visiting, and when planning each day, carefully consider travel within the parks. The logistics of getting around can be a nightmare and waste hours of your day.

MOST OVERRATED DISNEY ATTRACTIONS

Here they are – the things you can skip:

- **Swiss Family Treehouse** One hundred and sixteen steps to boredom
- **Tom Sawyer Island Boat** Ride to, essentially, a playground
- **Country Bear Jamboree** Dated, dusty and painfully corny
- **Donald's Boat & Toon Park** Sadly showing its age
- **Stitch's Great Escape** Sit in the dark and be confused
- **Muppet Vision 3-D** Ho-hum special effects; for Muppet fanatics only
- **Honey, I Shrunk the Audience** Another tarted-up playground
- **Sounds Dangerous – Starring Drew Carey** Disney's worst attraction. Sit in the dark, and listen…
- **Festival of the Lion King show** Pretty but empty theatrics

---

do you really want more? Good, low-key accommodation choices are **Perri House** (p314) and **Celebration Hotel** (p287), and a nice place to eat is **Gargi's Lakeside** (p281); on the patio by a lake and playground, you can watch your kids run around while you eat.

Atlantic Coast

If you want to do a big road trip, the Atlantic Coast might be your best bet. Great sights, beaches and tourist-ready towns are strung consistently the whole length, making it easy to go as slow and stop as often as you wish. These highlights go south to north.

In Hollywood, **Wannado City** (p218) is an indoor, role-playing theme park, in which kids (best for five and up) put on costumes and act out 'fantasy jobs,' like doctor and pilot. Also in Hollywood, the **Flying Trapeze School** (p217) gives kids (three and up) the chance to act out their high-flying circus dreams.

Fort Lauderdale (p219) is a great family-friendly beach town, and nearby is **Butterfly World** (p229), with thousands of fluttering critters.

Near Boca Raton, take a kid-friendly airboat ride into the Everglades with Wild Lyle and his **Loxahatchee Everglades Tours** (p232). **West Palm Beach** (p245) is another a good beach town, and its **Lion Country Safari** (p247) gets you face to face with some very non-Floridian wildlife.

Older kids will enjoy surf lessons in **Cocoa Beach** (p345). Likewise, **Kennedy Space Center** (p337) is great for ages eight and up, for whom lunch with an astronaut, IMAX movies, interactive science exhibits and the Shuttle Launch Simulator will make the biggest impact.

The beaches of **Cape Canaveral Seashore** (p343) are quiet getaways, and if your kids are old enough to be in a canoe, there's hardly a better place than among the lagoons, mangroves and dolphins here.

Daytona Beach (p353) is the quintessential 'week at the beach' town, with huge family resorts; its long, wide beach is great for cruising in all sorts of rentable all-terrain vehicles (ATVs), bikes and trikes. Also, a quick inland detour is **De Leon Springs** (p388): this natural spring is the perfect swimming hole with nice facilities.

Jacksonville (p370) makes a great base for families exploring northeast Florida. The four-to-eight set will love Metropolitan Park's **Kids Kampus** (p374), which recreates a city kids can ride bikes through. Kids eight and up might freak out over visiting **Sally Corporation** (p374), which makes interactive theme-park rides.

Tampa Bay, the Gulf Coast & the Panhandle

Tampa (p405) is another top spot for families, with world-class beaches, theme parks, and children's museums, and numerous day-trip possibilities. If you're not going to Disney World, you *might* make up for it by going to **Busch Gardens** (p418), which has great animal shows and encounters and, for older kids, some of the state's wildest roller coasters. **Adventure Island** (p411) is the area's best water park, but the real highlight is the **Florida Aquarium** (p410). In addition to seeing lots of fish, kids six and up (who can swim) can don gear and go into a huge reef tank *with* the fish. In Tampa, a good hotel for families is the **Westin Tampa Harbour Island** (p413), a lovely oasis.

In St Petersburg, baseball fans will like tours of **Tropicana Field** (p426), where the Devil Rays play, while further south in Sarasota, the circus is the draw. Older kids will enjoy the **Ringling Bros Circus Museum** (p434), while all ages have fun at the **PAL Sailor Circus** (p440), performed entirely by student acrobats.

Fort Myers (p442) and **Fort Myers Beach** (p447) are particularly family-friendly places. If you've been looking for a kid-welcoming B&B, try **Hibiscus House Bed & Breakfast** (p445); a child-friendly resort is **Lighthouse Resort Inn & Suites** (p448); and if you'd like a little extended parental R&R, Sanibel Island's **Sundial Beach & Gulf Resort** (p453) runs a kids' camp. Oh, and if your kids like seashells, **Sanibel Island** (p451) has scads – it might be their favorite interactive entertainment the whole trip.

Just north of Tampa, little girls in particular are likely to go gaga over the mermaids of **Weeki Wachee Springs** (p459), but really, the kitschy shows are fascinating no matter what your age. Nearby is also **Homosassa Springs** (p460), where manatees (the original mermaids) like to congregate.

Moving north, kids seven and up who can swim are likely to love tubing at **Ichetucknee Springs State Park** (p401) and easy canoeing along the **Suwannee River** (p477) to more swimming holes with rope swings.

In the **Panhandle** (p461), the barrier island beaches are some of the best Florida offers, kids or no. But **Panama City Beach** (p484) is famous for its seaside amusements, miniature golf, wacky museums and the like. It's very Old Florida, and very fun. **Pensacola** (p493) is a good place to base yourself for Panhandle explorations, and they have a decent **zoo** (p497) to boot.

A wonderful book (and also movie) for young readers (age eight and up) is *Because of Winn-Dixie* (2000) by Kate DiCamillo, about a girl and her dog (Winn-Dixie) struggling to adapt to a lonely Florida town.

Environment

Naturalist Marjory Stoneman Douglas called Florida 'a long pointed spoon' that is as 'familiar as the map of North America itself.' On that map, the shapely Floridian peninsula is the continent's panhandle, and it represents one of the most unique, ecologically diverse regions in the world.

It all began when, over millions of years, a thick layer of limestone was created as shells and bones drifted to the bottom of an ancient sea. Then, as Earth's tectonic plates shifted, North America rose up, slipped away from Africa, and left an ocean between them. The bit of limestone that would become Florida settled just north of the Tropic of Cancer, and this confluence of porous rock and climate gave rise to a watery world of uncommon abundance. One that is, of course, so fragile that it threatens to be undone by human hands in the geological blink of an eye.

THE LAND

Florida is many things, but it's also flat as a pancake, or as Douglas says, like a spoon of freshwater resting delicately in a bowl of saltwater – a spongy brick of limestone hugged by the Atlantic Ocean and the Gulf of Mexico. The highest point, the Panhandle's Britton Hill, has to stretch to reach 350ft, which isn't half as tall as downtown Miami. This makes Florida officially the nation's flattest state, despite being 22nd in total area with 58,560 sq miles.

However, over 4000 of those square miles are water; lakes pepper the map as if it were a bullet-ridden road sign. That shotgun-size hole in the south is Lake Okeechobee, which is the second-largest freshwater lake in North America. Sounds impressive, but the bottom of the lake is only a few feet above sea level, and it's so shallow you can practically wade across.

Lake Okeechobee ever so gently floods the southern tip of the peninsula (or it wants to; canals divert much of the flow). From here, the land inclines about 6in every 6 miles until finally Florida can't keep its head above water anymore, petering out into the 10,000 Islands and the Florida Keys, which end with a flourish in the Gulf of Mexico. Key West, the last in the chain, is the southernmost point in the continental US.

What really sets Florida apart, though, is that it occupies a subtropical transition zone between northern temperate and southern tropical climates. This is key to the coast's florid coral-reef system, the largest in North America, and to Florida's attention-getting collection of surreal swamps, botanical oddities, and monstrous critters. The Everglades gets the most press, and as an International Biosphere, World Heritage Site, and National Park, this 'river of grass' deserves it. For more, see p165.

But the Panhandle's Apalachicola River basin has been called a 'Garden of Eden,' in which Ice Age plants survive in lost ravines, and where more species of amphibians and reptiles hop and slither than anywhere else in the US. The Indian River Lagoon estuary, stretching 156 miles along the Atlantic Coast, is the most diverse on the continent. And across north Florida, the pockmarked and honeycombed limestone (called karst terrain) holds the Florida Aquifer, which is fed solely by rain and which bubbles up like liquid diamonds in over 700 freshwater springs.

WILDLIFE

Considering Mother Nature's effusive display in Florida, it's a wonder any theme park survives. Talk about gilding the lily. With swamps full of gators, rivers full of snakes, manatees in mangroves, sea turtles on beaches, and

Crisply written and richly detailed, *The Swamp* (2006) by Michael Grunwald is an up-to-date, avowedly political history of the Everglades, South Florida development, and current efforts to reweave the swamp's unraveling tapestry.

FLORIDA'S BEACHES & PARKS

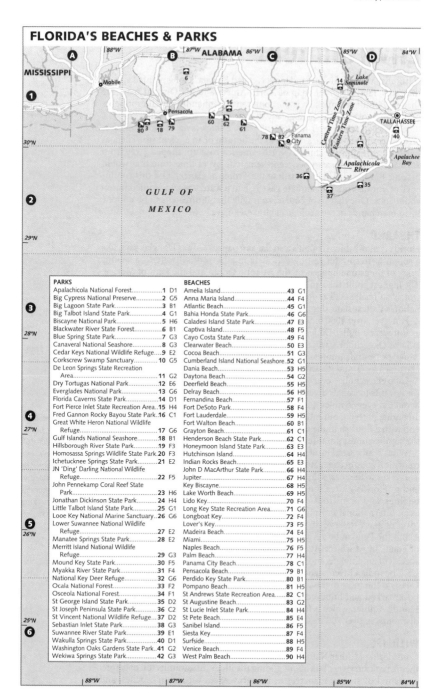

PARKS

Apalachicola National Forest	**1** D1
Big Cypress National Preserve	**2** G5
Big Lagoon State Park	**3** B1
Big Talbot Island State Park	**4** G1
Biscayne National Park	**5** H6
Blackwater River State Forest	**6** B1
Blue Spring State Park	**7** G3
Canaveral National Seashore	**8** G3
Cedar Keys National Wildlife Refuge	**9** E2
Corkscrew Swamp Sanctuary	**10** G5
De Leon Springs State Recreation Area	**11** G2
Dry Tortugas National Park	**12** E6
Everglades National Park	**13** G6
Florida Caverns State Park	**14** D1
Fort Pierce Inlet State Recreation Area	**15** H4
Fred Gannon Rocky Bayou State Park	**16** C1
Great White Heron National Wildlife Refuge	**17** G6
Gulf Islands National Seashore	**18** B1
Hillsborough River State Park	**19** F3
Homosassa Springs Wildlife State Park	**20** F3
Ichetucknee Springs State Park	**21** E2
JN 'Ding' Darling National Wildlife Refuge	**22** F5
John Pennekamp Coral Reef State Park	**23** H6
Jonathan Dickinson State Park	**24** H4
Little Talbot Island State Park	**25** G1
Looe Key National Marine Sanctuary	**26** G6
Lower Suwannee National Wildlife Refuge	**27** E2
Manatee Springs State Park	**28** E2
Merritt Island National Wildlife Refuge	**29** G3
Mound Key State Park	**30** F5
Myakka River State Park	**31** F4
National Key Deer Refuge	**32** G6
Ocala National Forest	**33** F2
Osceola National Forest	**34** F1
St George Island State Park	**35** D2
St Joseph Peninsula State Park	**36** C2
St Vincent National Wildlife Refuge	**37** D2
Sebastian Inlet State Park	**38** G3
Suwannee River State Park	**39** E1
Wakulla Springs State Park	**40** D1
Washington Oaks Gardens State Park	**41** G2
Wekiwa Springs State Park	**42** G3

BEACHES

Amelia Island	**43** G1
Anna Maria Island	**44** F4
Atlantic Beach	**45** G1
Bahia Honda State Park	**46** G6
Caladesi Island State Park	**47** E3
Captiva Island	**48** F5
Cayo Costa State Park	**49** F4
Clearwater Beach	**50** E3
Cocoa Beach	**51** G3
Cumberland Island National Seashore	**52** G1
Dania Beach	**53** H5
Daytona Beach	**54** G2
Deerfield Beach	**55** H5
Delray Beach	**56** H5
Fernandina Beach	**57** F1
Fort DeSoto Park	**58** F4
Fort Lauderdale	**59** H5
Fort Walton Beach	**60** B1
Grayton Beach	**61** C1
Henderson Beach State Park	**62** C1
Honeymoon Island State Park	**63** E3
Hutchinson Island	**64** H4
Indian Rocks Beach	**65** E3
John D MacArthur State Park	**66** H4
Jupiter	**67** H4
Key Biscayne	**68** H5
Lake Worth Beach	**69** H5
Lido Key	**70** F4
Long Key State Recreation Area	**71** G6
Longboat Key	**72** F4
Lover's Key	**73** F5
Madeira Beach	**74** E4
Miami	**75** H5
Naples Beach	**76** F5
Palm Beach	**77** H4
Panama City Beach	**78** C1
Pensacola Beach	**79** B1
Perdido Key State Park	**80** B1
Pompano Beach	**81** H5
St Andrews State Recreation Area	**82** C1
St Augustine Beach	**83** G2
St Lucie Inlet State Park	**84** H4
St Pete Beach	**85** E4
Sanibel Island	**86** F5
Siesta Key	**87** F4
Surfside	**88** H5
Venice Beach	**89** F4
West Palm Beach	**90** H4

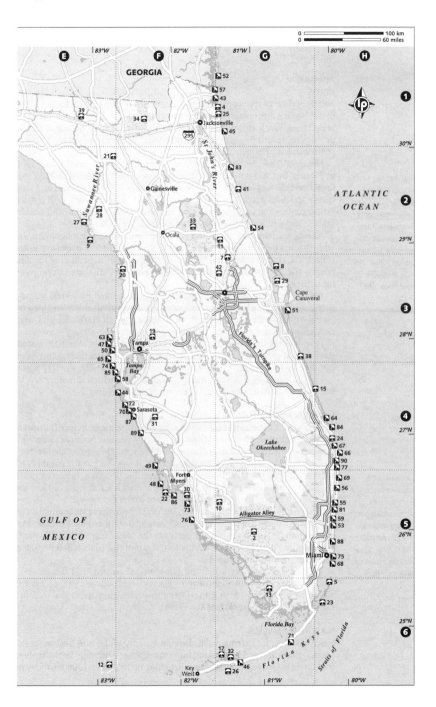

giant flocks of ancient seabirds taking wing at once, as if they would lift the land with them, how is it, again, that a squeaky-voiced mouse became the headliner?

Animals

BIRDS

Nearly 500 avian species have been documented in the state, including some of the world's most magnificent migratory waterbirds: ibis, herons, pelicans and cranes. While this makes Florida the ultimate birder's paradise, what's perhaps more amazing is that, by some estimates, Florida gets only a fraction of the birds it originally did.

Nearly 350 species spend time in the Everglades, the prime birding spot in Florida. But you don't have to brave the swamp. Completed in 2006, the **Great Florida Birding Trail** (http://floridabirdingtrail.com) runs 2000 miles and includes nearly 500 bird-watching sites. Nine of these are 'gateway' sites, with staffed visitor centers and free 'loaner' binoculars; see the website for downloadable guides, and when driving, look for brown road signs.

Among the largest birds, white pelicans arrive in winter (October to April), while brown pelicans, the only pelican to dive for its food, lives here year-round. To see the striking pale-pink roseate spoonbill, a member of the ibis family, visit **JN 'Ding' Darling National Wildlife Refuge** (p452), the wintering site for a third of the US population.

About 5000 nonmigratory sandhill cranes are joined by 25,000 migratory cousins each winter. White whooping cranes, at 4ft the tallest bird in North America, are nearly extinct; about 100 winter on Florida's Gulf Coast near Homosassa.

Florida skies are streaked with raptors too. The state has over 1000 mated pairs of bald eagles, the most in the southern US, and peregrine falcons, who can dive up to 150mph, migrate through in spring and fall.

Florida's state bird is the northern mockingbird, which is neither exotic nor endangered and can be found everywhere all the time.

LAND MAMMALS

Florida's most endangered mammal is the Florida panther. Before European contact, perhaps 1500 roamed the state. The first panther bounty ($5 a scalp) was passed in 1832, and over the next 130 years they were hunted relentlessly. Though hunting was stopped in 1958, it was too late for panthers to survive on their own. Without a captive breeding program, begun in 1991, the Florida panther would now be extinct, and with fewer than 100 known to exist (for more, see p176), they're not out of the swamp yet.

You're not likely to see a panther, but black bears have recovered to the point where they've become an occasional road hazard around Ocala and in the Panhandle. However, since forests are the black bear's natural habitat, and these are endangered in Florida too, it's doubtful bears will repopulate the entire state as they once did.

White-tailed deer are a definite Florida road hazard, and this all-too-common species troubles landscaping everywhere. Endemic to the Keys are Key deer, a Honey-I-Shrunk-the-Deer subspecies: they stand less than 3ft tall and live mostly on **Big Pine Key** (p196).

MARINE MAMMALS

Once mistaken for mermaids, the lovable manatee glides into freshwater estuaries, rivers and springs looking for warmer water beginning in November. By March, they return to the ocean. Reaching up to 13ft and 3000lb, they are

Florida is aflutter with birding festivals year-round. The Space Coast is home to two: April's Welcome Back Songbirds Festival (www.florida conservation.org) and November's Space Coast Birding and Wildlife Festival (www.nbbd .com/fly).

To learn about the incredible efforts to save the whooping crane, visit Operation Migration (www.operationmigration.org), a nonprofit run by Bill Lishman, whose techniques inspired the film *Fly Away Home*.

A KINDER, GENTLER WILDERNESS ENCOUNTER

Florida tourism was founded on the idea that you could make a killing if you just repackaged nature into a thrilling, but safe, backdrop for entertainment. While yesterday's glass-bottom boats and alligator wrestling have evolved into today's swamp buggy rides and dolphin encounters, the question remains: just because you *can* do something, does it mean you *should*? What are the impacts, and what are the best ways to experience nature without harming it in the process?

We've wrestled with this dilemma throughout this book. For many activities, there isn't a single clear answer. However, there *are* a few clear guidelines, which we highlight here. In general, Florida has become a test case in whether humans can restore ecosystems and yet still live comfortably with the increasing fauna that result – just ask the duffers playing past golf-course water hazards full of snoozing gators.

For more advice on responsible travel, see p14.

- **Airboats and swamp buggies** While airboats are far better than buggies (see p167), both are still motorized and thus have a larger impact than canoes for exploring wetlands. As a rule, choose nonmotorized activities to lighten your footprint.
- **Dolphin encounters** Captive dolphins are typically rescued animals already acclimated to humans. Some love dolphin swims; some discourage them (for both arguments, see p193). However, this is entirely different from encountering wild dolphins in the ocean, where federal law makes it illegal to feed, approach, or touch them. Habituating wild animals to humans frequently leads to the animals' deaths because they learn to approach humans, leading to conflicts and accidents (as with boats). As with bears, human interaction also sometimes brings the danger of an animal attack.
- **Coral-reef etiquette** When snorkeling or diving, never touch the coral reef. It's that simple. Coral polyps are living organisms, not rock, so oil from fingers and broken pieces create wounds and openings for infection and disease.
- **Cars on beaches** Floridians have driven cars on certain beaches like Daytona ever since there were cars to drive. However, this does not mean that *every* beach is open to cars. Don't blaze a trail.
- **Sea-turtle nesting sites** As with dolphins, it's a federal crime to approach nesting sea turtles or hatchling runs. Plus, from May to October, most beaches have a nighttime 'lights out' policy. If you encounter turtles on the beach, keep your distance and no flash photos. Better yet, join a sanctioned turtle watch, p76.
- **Manatees** If these curious 'sea cows' approach *you* in the water, simply remain still. But never feed or approach them, as boat collisions are becoming epidemic.

For more advice on ecofriendly Florida travel, visit the EcoFlorida website (www.ecofloridamag .com), which is packed with info, and see the GreenDex listings at the back of this book (p548).

solitary, gentle, curious and playful, and have been known to 'surf' waves. How to protect the manatee is a hot-button topic, as perhaps a third of manatee deaths are from boat-related collisions, which are becoming more frequent. Manatees live year-round at **Homosassa Springs** (p460), and wintering sites include **Manatee Springs State Park** (p477) and **Fort Pierce** (p258). For more on manatees, see p179.

Several species of dolphin frequent Florida's coastal waters, but the most common is the bottlenose dolphin, which is the one most often seen in captivity. To see them in the wild, try the Tampa Bay barrier islands, such as **Honeymoon** and **Caladesi Islands** (p430), and **Canaveral National Seashore** (p343), which is chockful of wildlife.

THE TRUE STORY OF FLORIDA'S PINK FLAMINGOS

The bird perhaps most associated with Florida is the shockingly pink flamingo, but in typical Floridian fashion, most flamingos today are actually semi-wild, non-native fugitives. That's right: flamingos are just another Florida outlaw.

When Europeans first arrived, a small breeding population lived at Florida's southern tip, but the flamingo's range shrank, and no flamingos breed in Florida anymore. Instead, flamingos in the wild are either Chilean 'vagrants' who got lost on their way to Mexico, or they are escapees from Florida wildlife parks.

Flamingos aren't the only animal ex-cons, either. In addition to old-fashioned jail breaks, exotic and non-native species get sprung whenever severe hurricanes blow through and tear apart enclosures. Bright flocks of chattering parrots, rhesus monkeys at Silver Springs, Burmese pythons in the Everglades: all are quite happy now in Florida's wilderness.

And of course, that *other* Florida icon – the plastic pink flamingo, the one stabbed into front lawns everywhere as an ironic, kitschy paean to trash culture and the Sunshine State – is the product of a Yankee and is now itself threatened with extinction. Massachusetts native Don Featherstone (really, we aren't making this up!) created the plastic pink flamingo in 1957, for which he won the 1996 Ig Nobel parody award. But in 2006, the company that manufactures it went bankrupt, a year shy of the plastic pink flamingo's 50th anniversary.

The North Atlantic population of about 300 right whales come to winter calving grounds off the Atlantic Coast near **Jacksonville** (p370). These giant animals can be over 50ft long, and they are the most endangered species of whale.

REPTILES

Florida's reptiles evoke a primal shudder; they are Earth's dinosaur descendents in the flesh. For Florida's poster species, the American alligator, see the boxed text, opposite.

Florida is also home to the only North American population of American crocodile. Florida's crocs number fewer than 2000; they prefer saltwater, and to distinguish them from gators, check their smile – a croc's snout is more tapered and its teeth stick out.

Florida is home to 44 species of snakes, and to reassure visitors, Floridian promoters emphasize that only six species are poisonous, and only four of those are common. Feel better? Of the baddies, three are rattlesnakes (diamondback, pygmy, canebrake), plus copperheads, cottonmouths, and coral snakes. The diamondback is the biggest (up to 7ft), most aggressive and most dangerous. Cottonmouths live in and around water (though *most* Florida water snakes are not cottonmouths, so no worries!). And the coral snake has the most deadly venom. What about those non-native Burmese pythons loose in the Everglades? Oh, well, never mind about those.

Audubon of Florida (www.audubonofflorida .org) is perhaps Florida's leading conservation organization. It has tons of birding and ecological information, and it publishes *Florida Naturalist* magazine.

SEA TURTLES

Most sea turtle nesting in the continental US occurs in Florida. Five species create 40,000 to 80,000 nests annually, mostly on Atlantic Coast beaches and the **Gulf Islands National Seashore** (p497). All five species are endangered or threatened: they are the hawksbill, Kemp's ridley, loggerhead, leatherback, and green sea turtles. The leatherback is the biggest, growing up to 8ft long and 1300lb.

During the May to October nesting season, sea turtles deposit from 70 to 120 eggs in each nest. The eggs incubate for about two months, and then the hatchlings emerge all at once and make for the ocean. Contrary to myth, hatchlings don't need the moon to find their way.

However, they do have to dodge hungry birds and not become hopelessly confused by the lights and sounds of a human audience. To join a sanctioned turtle watch, which provides the best experience for you and the turtles, visit http://myfwc.com/seaturtle, then click on 'Education and Information' and 'Public Turtle Watches.'

Plants

The diversity of the peninsula's flora, including over 4000 species of plants, is unmatched in the continental US. This is due mainly to the fact that Florida contains the southern extent of temperate ecosystems and the northern extent of tropical ones, which blend and merge in a bewildering, fluid taxonomy of environments. Interestingly enough, spin the globe and you find that most of the world at this latitude is a desert, which is one of the few environments (along with mountains) Florida definitely does not contain.

In Florida, even the plants bite: the Panhandle has the most species of carnivorous plants in the US, the result of its nutrient-poor sandy soil.

WETLANDS & SWAMPS

It takes special kinds of plants to thrive in the humid, water-logged, sometimes salty marshes, sloughs, swales, seeps, basins, marl prairies and swamps of Florida, and several hundred specialized native plants evolved to do so. Much of the Everglades is dominated by vast expanses of sawgrass, which is actually a sedge with fine toothlike edges that can reach 10ft high. South Florida is a symphony of sedges, grasses and rushes. These hardy water-tolerant species (some dominated when dinosaurs roamed) provide abundant seeds to feed birds and animals, protect fish in shallow water, and pad wetlands for birds and alligators.

Visit the Florida Native Plant Society (www .fnps.org), a nonprofit conservation organization, for updates on preservation issues and invasive species and for a nice overview of Florida's native plants and ecosystems.

The strangest plants are the submerged and immersed species that grow in, under and out of the water. Free-floating species include bladderwort and coontail, a species that lives, flowers and is pollinated entirely underwater. Yet Florida's swamps are much more abundant in rooted plants with floating leaves, like the pretty American lotus, water lilies and spatterdock (if you love names, you'll love Florida botany!). Two other common immersed plants are cat-tails and bur marigolds, which can paint whole prairies yellow.

KEEPERS OF THE EVERGLADES

Anyone who has ever dipped a paddle among the sawgrass and hardwood hammocks of Everglades National Park wouldn't quibble with the American alligator's Florida sobriquet, 'Keepers of the Everglades.' With snout, eyeballs, and pebbled back so still they hardly ripple the water's surface, alligators are everywhere and ever-watchful, both for a meal and for the swamps they've occupied for over 200 million years, long before humans learned to fear their toothy grin.

It's impossible to count the wild alligators in Florida, but estimates are that 1.25 million lumber among the state's lakes, rivers and golf courses. They are no longer officially endangered, but they remain protected because they look like the still-endangered American crocodile. Alligator served in restaurants typically comes from licensed alligator farms, though since 1988, Florida has conducted an annual alligator harvest, open to nonresidents, that allows two alligators per person.

Alligators are alpha predators who keep the rest of the food chain in check, and their 'gator holes' become vital water cups in the dry season and during droughts, aiding the entire wetlands ecosystem. Alligators, who live about 30 years, can grow up to 14ft long and weigh 1000lb.

Alligators hunt in water, often close to shore; typically, they run on land to flee, not to chase. In Florida, there are an estimated 15 to 20 nonfatal attacks on humans each year, and there have been 13 fatal attacks since 1948.

Apparently, no one has clocked an alligator's top land speed, but it's a myth that you must zigzag to avoid them. The best advice is to run in a straight line as fast as your little legs can go.

Across Florida, whenever the land rises enough to create drier islands, tracts, hills and hillocks, dense tree-filled hammocks occur. These go by many names depending on their location and type. Tropical hammocks typically mix tropical hardwoods and palms with semideciduous and evergreen trees like live oak.

David W Nellis' *Seashore Plants of South Florida & the Caribbean* (1994) is filled with color photos, good descriptions and medicinal uses for local flora.

Another dramatic, beautiful tree common to Florida's swamps is the bald cypress, which is the most flood-tolerant tree. It can grow 150ft tall, with buttressed, wide trunks and roots with 'knees' that poke above the drenched soil. Cypress domes are a particular kind of swamp when a watery depression occurs in a pine flatwood.

FORESTS, SCRUBS & FLATWOODS

Florida's northern forests, particularly in the Panhandle, are an epicenter of plant and animal biodiversity, as much or moreso than South Florida's swamps. Here, the continent's temperate forests of hickory, elm, ash, maple, magnolia, and locust combine with the various pine, gum and oak trees that are common throughout Florida along with the sawgrass, cypress and cabbage palms of southern Florida. The wet but temperate Apalachicola forest supports 40 kinds of trees and more insect species than scientists have been able to count.

Central and northern Florida were once covered in longleaf and slash pine forests. These pines were prized for timber and pine gum, and today, due to logging, only 2% of old-growth longleaf forests remain. Slash pine is much faster growing, and it has now largely replaced longleaf pine in Florida's second-growth forests.

Scrubs are found throughout Florida, and they are typically old dunes with well-drained sandy soil. In central Florida (along the Lake Wales Ridge), scrubs are the oldest plant communities, with the highest number of endemic and rare species. Sand pines, scrub oak, rosemary and lichens predominate.

GHOST HUNTERS

Florida has more species of orchids than any other state in the US, and orchids are themselves the largest family of flowering plants in the world, with perhaps 25,000 species. On the dial of botanical fascination, orchids go well past 11, and the Florida species that inspires the most intense devotion is the extremely rare ghost orchid.

This bizarre epiphytic flower has no leaves and usually only one bloom, which is of course deathly white with two long thin drooping petals that curl like a handlebar mustache. The ghost orchid is pollinated by the giant sphinx moth, which is the only insect with a proboscis long enough to reach down the ghost orchid's 5in-long nectar spur and who arrives in the dead of night.

In 2007 a new species was discovered, the Corkscrew Swamp Ghost Orchid, which has been called a 'superghost' because it can produce up to 20 flowers in a season. The exact locations of ghost orchids are usually kept secret for fear of poachers, who, as Susan Orlean's book *The Orchid Thief* made clear, are a real threat to their survival.

But the flower's general whereabouts are common knowledge: the approximately 1200 ghost orchids known to exist are almost all in Big Cypress National Preserve (p171) and **Fakahatchee Strand Preserve State Park** (www.floridastateparks.org/fakahatcheestrand). Of course, these parks are home to a great many other wild orchids, as are Everglades National Park (p170), Myakka River State Park (p442) and Corkscrew Swamp Sanctuary (p458).

To learn more, and perhaps become a (photographic) orchid hunter yourself, visit **Florida Native Orchids** (www.flnativeorchids.com) and **Ghost Orchid.info** (www.ghostorchid.info), and also visit Sarasota's Selby Botanical Gardens (p436), which displays a truly astonishing collection of 6000 orchid species.

THE ST JOE COMPANY: DISNEY IN REAL LIFE

In the 1920s, the St Joe Paper Company started harvesting Florida Panhandle slash pines, turning them into pulp at their mills in Panama City and Port St Joe. The company was led for over 50 years by the pugnacious Ed Ball, who became the most powerful businessman of the most powerful company in Florida. Ball could make or break politicians (such as when he scuttled Florida Senator Claude Pepper's reelection in 1950), and he famously ended each day with a bourbon and the toast: 'Confusion to the enemy!'

Flash forward to 1997: through Ball's efforts (he died in 1981), St Joe was now the state's largest private landowner, with about one million acres (or 3% of state lands), of which 90% were in the Panhandle. But the virgin forests were kaput, and pulp didn't smell like the future. So St Joe made the classic Florida shift: they decided to become real-estate developers, and they hired ex-Disney execs to run the show.

St Joe's first planned community, WaterColor, broke ground in 1999, and the next, WaterSound, got underway in 2002, the first in a wave of pastel-perfect, upscale new towns that may forever change the Panhandle's working-class 'Redneck Riviera' reputation. WaterColor and WaterSound were inspired by their neighbor, Seaside – which has been lauded as a model of 'New Urban' planning, one that weaves pretty suburban homes with pleasant stretches of nature in hopefully sustainable harmony.

At the same time, St Joe has been selling land to the state for conservation and, by most accounts, accommodating local concerns. Controversially, they're also angling to move US 98 inland to accommodate more coastal developments and a new airport, and the Florida Department of Environmental Protection granted them exemptions to the usual permit process to develop wetlands.

Overall, given Florida's checkered history of development, political commentators have expressed skepticism about the impact and scope of St Joe's plans. After all, Seaside was the setting for *The Truman Show,* a movie about a man who does not realize that his perfect town and his perfect life were nothing but a TV show.

Scrubs often blend into sandy pine flatwoods, which typically have a sparse longleaf or slash-pine overstory and an understory of grasses and/or saw palmetto. Saw palmetto is a vital Florida plant: its fruit is an important food for bears and deer (and an herbal medicine that's believed to help prevent cancer), it provides shelter for panthers and snakes, and its flower is an important source of honey. It's named for its sharp saw-toothed leaf stems, and it also enjoys coastal dunes and marshes.

MANGROVES & COASTAL DUNES

Where not lined with smooth beaches, southern Florida's coastline is often covered with mangroves like a three-day stubble. Mangroves are not a single species; the name refers to all tropical trees and shrubs that have adapted to loose wet soil, saltwater, and periodic root submergence. Mangroves also developed 'live birth,' that is, they germinate their seeds while they're still attached to the parent tree. There are over 50 species of mangroves worldwide, but only three predominate in Florida: red, black and white. For more on these species, see p199.

Mangroves play a vital role on the peninsula, and their destruction usually sets off a domino-effect of ecological damage. Mangroves 'stabilize' coastal land, trapping sand, silt and sediment. As this builds up, new land is created, which ironically strangles the mangroves themselves. Mangroves mitigate the storm surge and damaging winds of hurricanes, and they anchor tidal and estuary communities, providing habitats for numerous species, including sea turtles, crocodiles, eagles and falcons. Mangroves extend into central Florida, but 90% are in southern Florida.

In *Green Empire* (2004), Kathryn Ziewitz and June Wiaz are evenhanded in their cautionary tale of the St Joe Company, which is single-handedly remaking the Panhandle into 'Florida's Great Northwest,' a fantasia of upscale development.

Coastal dunes are typically home to grasses and shrubs, saw palmetto and occasionally pines and cabbage palm (or sabal palm, the Florida state tree). Sea oats, with large plumes that trap wind-blown sand, are important for stabilizing dunes, while coastal hammocks welcome the wiggly gumbo-limbo tree, whose red peeling bark has earned it the nickname the 'tourist tree.'

NATIONAL, STATE & REGIONAL PARKS

About 26% of Florida's land lies in public hands, which breaks down to three national forests, 11 national parks, 28 national wildlife refuges (including the first, Pelican Island), and 160 state parks. Overall, attendance is up, with over 19 million folks visiting state parks annually and over a million getting to the Everglades. Florida's state parks have twice been voted the nation's best.

Plus, Florida has what you might call a well-established tourist infrastructure that makes these parks easy to explore. For more information on what to do, and where best to do it, see Florida Outdoors (p49), as well as

NATIONAL, STATE & REGIONAL PARKS IN FLORIDA

Major Park or Natural Area	Features	Activities	Best Time to Visit	Page
Apalachicola National Forest	938 sq miles of lowlands, pine, cypress, hammocks, wildlife galore, miles of trails	hiking, cycling, horseback riding, canoeing, kayaking	summer	p474
Bahia Honda State Park	trails, white-sand beaches	camping, swimming, hiking, water sports	winter	p196
Big Cypress National Preserve	1139 sq miles of mangrove, hammocks, pine, prairie, marshes, all loaded with wildlife, including panthers	hiking, camping	winter & spring	p171
Biscayne National Park	300-sq-mile park that's 95% underwater; clear water, sandy beaches, coral reefs	canoeing, kayaking, boat tours, swimming, snorkeling, diving, camping	winter	p177
Blue Spring State Park	tranquil waters, ranger guides, hiking trails	manatee-viewing, swimming, diving, snorkeling, canoeing, nature tours, hiking, camping	Nov-Mar	p386
Canaveral National Seashore	beaches, trails, wildlife-viewing programs, thousands of wading birds	big-time migratory-bird watching, sea-turtle watching, surfing, swimming, camping, walking	Mar-Sep, bird migrations Oct-May, sea-turtle nesting Jun & Jul	p343
Corkscrew Swamp Sanctuary	crown jewel of Audubon's national holdings, a pristine swamp & jungle forest teeming with endangered wildlife	wildlife-watching with virtually no mosquitos!	year-round	p458
Dry Tortugas National Park	turtles, turtles & more turtles, lighthouse, old fort	camping, snorkeling, diving, boating	winter	p213
Everglades National Park	land & water trails, including the 10,000 Island Wilderness Waterway	hiking, cycling, canoeing, airboating, swamp buggying, kayaking, camping	winter & spring	p170

listings throughout this guide. For specific park information, here are the main organizations:

Florida State Parks (☎ 850-245-2157; www.floridastateparks.org)
National Forests, Florida (☎ 850-523-8500; www.fs.fed.us/r8/florida)
National Park Service (NPS; www.nps.gov, reservations http://reservations.nps.gov)
National Wildlife Refuges, Florida (NWR; www.fws.gov/southeast/maps/fl.html)
Reserve USA (☎ 877-444-6777; www.reserveusa.com) National forest campground reservations.

In addition, the **Florida Fish & Wildlife Commission** (http://myfwc.com) manages Florida's mostly undeveloped Wildlife Management Areas (WMA), and has information about boating, hunting, fishing and permits, as well as great advice on the best places to view wildlife.

Florida's Department of Environmental Protection (www.dep.state.fl.us) features environmentally friendly places to stay, as well as a kids' page.

ENVIRONMENTAL ISSUES

Historically speaking, Florida has treated its land like a cash machine. While it is far from alone in this, the consequences for the state have been vast, multifaceted and possibly overwhelming; they include erosion of wetlands,

Major Park or Natural Area	Features	Activities	Best Time to Visit	Page
Gulf Islands National Seashore	gorgeous barrier islands, white-sand beaches, historic fort, sea-turtle nesting	hiking, cycling, canoeing, boating, snorkeling, fishing camping, wildlife-watching	year-round	p497
Gumbo Limbo Nature Center	saltwater tanks with critters, dunes, hammocks, a butterfly garden, mangroves	hiking, sea-turtle nesting	mid-May–mid-Jul for observing turtles	p230
John D MacArthur State Park	spectacular 1600ft boardwalk over mangroves, dunes	excellent turtle observation program, nature walks, kayak tours	winter	p252
John Pennekamp Coral Reef State Park	75 sq miles, mostly underwater with coral reefs, nature trails, canoe trails, an aquarium, excellent ranger programs	snorkeling, diving, kayaking, canoeing, camping	winter	p183
Myakka River State Park	Florida's largest park with 38 miles of boardwalks and trails, airboat & tram tours	bird- & alligator-watching, walking, hiking, canoeing, kayaking, camping	year-round	p442
Ocala National Forest	400,000-acre network of springs & biomes with endangered flora & fauna	camping, boating, swimming, hiking, cycling, horseback riding, canoeing, bird- & wildlife-watching	spring & fall	p392
Sebastian Inlet State Park	narrow chain of barrier islands	diving & snorkeling among sunken Spanish galleons; digging clams, surfing, camping, fishing	year-round	p349
Wakulla Springs State Park	timeless natural area with a 125ft-deep natural spring and 15 miles of underwater caves	great wildlife-watching, glass-bottom boat tours, river cruises	summer	p473
Wekiwa Springs State Park	palmetto wilderness, clear springs	horseback riding, canoeing, hiking trails, snorkeling, camping	summer	p274

depletion of the aquifer, rampant pollution (particularly of waters), invasive species, endangered species, and habitat destruction. Nearly every issue revolves around development, which is spurred by the state's galloping population growth.

The problem, of course, is that a warm winter day in Florida always tops the same day in Chicago or Iowa or New Jersey.

To help fix the sins of the past, the state passed the **Florida Forever Act** (www.supportfloridaforever.org) in 2000, a 10-year, $3 billion conservation program that in 2008 was renewed another 10 years, until 2020. Along with the multibillion-dollar **Comprehensive Everglades Restoration Plan** (CERP; www.evergladesplan.org). For more on Everglades restoration, see p165), Florida is making significant conservation efforts and, in some cases, progress.

For instance, phosphorous levels in the Everglades have been seriously reduced in recent years, and the Kissimmee River is a model of restoration: within a few years of backfilling the canal that had restricted its flow, the river's floodplain is again a humid marsh full of waterbirds and alligators. All these programs are being studied avidly for their applications worldwide.

Also, in 2008, the state unveiled a six-year, $1.75 billion plan to buy 300 sq miles of Lake Okeechobee sugarcane fields from US Sugar, and convert them back to swamp so the lake can once again water the Glades.

And yet, it's so far not enough. Funding lags, costs rise, and some say Florida's destruction has merely been slowed, not stopped or reversed.

Lake Okeechobee, imprisoned by Hoover Dike since 1928, is full of toxic sludge, which gets stirred up during hurricanes and causes 'red tides,' or algae blooms that kill fish. Red tides occur naturally, but they are also sparked by pollution and unnatural water flows, and they have become big problems along the Gulf Coast and in the Indian River Lagoon.

Studies have found that half of the state's lakes and waterways are too polluted for fishing. Though industrial pollution has been curtailed, pollution from residential development (sewage, fertilizer runoff) more than compensates. This is distressing Florida's freshwater springs, which are turning green or brown with algae. Plus, as the groundwater gets pumped out to slake homeowners' thirsts, the springs are shrinking and the drying limestone honeycomb underfoot sometimes collapses, causing sinkholes that swallow cars and homes.

Meanwhile, the Miami–Fort Lauderdale–West Palm Beach corridor is the sixth-largest urban area in the US. As the developers say, southeast Florida is essentially 'built out,' having squeezed the Everglades as much as current political sensibilities will allow. So, the St Joe Company is aiming to inspire the next Florida land rush in the Panhandle (p79). Projections for the next 50 years show unrelenting urban sprawl up and down both coasts (where 80% of the population currently lives) and painted across central Florida.

And then there's the coming apocalypse: rising seas due to global warming. Almost no one disputes it will happen. The only question is will it be 6in, 1ft, or 3ft in the next 50 years? Rising seas will swallow Florida's coastline, intrude on wetlands, taint drinking water, and lead to unprecedented hurricane storm surges.

As some have quipped, Florida is poised to become a modern-day Atlantis, with its most expensive real estate underwater.

The Florida chapter of the Nature Conservancy (www.nature.org) has been instrumental in the Florida Forever legislation. Check the web for updates and conservation issues.

How do Floridians feel when their landscapes and history are paved over for quick riches? Read Bill Belleville's personalized, compellingly angry tale *Losing It All to Sprawl: How Progress Ate My Cracker Landscape* (2006).

Miami

Cruise down I-95 from the northeast corridor and at some point, near Richmond, you cross an invisible line separating the north from the south. Now go further, all the way to the USA's tip.

Somewhere around Orlando, you crossed another line, separating the rest of Florida from reality.

Welcome to Miami: the Magic City, *caliente* (hot) capital of *cubanos* (Cuban sandwiches) and quirkiness. What was once a little citrus town is now a pan-American mosaic, the most Latin city in the world north of Mexico. Throw in enterprising Caribbean immigrants, Jewish Holocaust survivors and their children, a fantabulous gay party scene, mad rednecks, the cast-off spawn of the dinosaur age cruising local waterways, and a South Beach celebrity scene that would make *OK!* magazine wee itself in joy, and, well…

Look guys: it's *weird* here.

And beautiful. Think of those clean lines slimming down a deco hotel on Miami Beach, or the model checking into said hotel, or the white sand she poses on. Even the day-to-day edges of this town have a tropical grace, glimpsed in slammed shots of *cortadito* (Cuban coffee) as laborers head to work, and the bright wrap of a Haitian mother walking her children to school.

Modern Miami has its problems. Economic inequality is rampant, and the gulf between the haves and have-nots seems vast. But that shimmering mirage of wealth and sex is also what makes this town so fun and fast. So come on down. The air feels like a silk kiss, and the beach smells like lotion and hormones. Welcome to Miami. The party started five minutes ago.

You gonna dance?

HIGHLIGHTS

- Take the quintessential Miami drive along the **A1A** (p103) from downtown's glittering skyline, over baby-blue Biscayne Bay right into the sexy solar plexus of South Beach

- Go for **Design District drinks** (p155) and enjoy free art, free drinks and a free walking (well, stumbling) tour of Miami's artsy enclaves

- Cigar smoke, dominoes and *guayaberas* (linen dress shirts); say *bienvenido a* Little Havana in **Máximo Gómez Park** (p114)

- If you can't get to Port-au-Prince, pay a *vodou* (voodoo) priest a visit in **Little Haiti** (p111)

- Smoked fish, beer, Laz-E-Boys and a mangrove swamp – aw yeah – get to **Jimbo's** (p113)

★A1A

Design District, Little Haiti ★

Máximo ★ Gómez Park   ★Jimbo's

MIAMI

HISTORY

It's always been the weather that's attracted Miami's two most prominent species: developers and tourists. But it wasn't the sun per se that got people moving here – it was an ice storm. The great Florida freeze of 1895 wiped out the state's citrus industry; at the same time widowed Julia Tuttle bought out parcels of land that would become modern Miami, and Henry Flagler was building his Florida East Coast Railroad. Tuttle offered to split her land with Flagler if he extended the railway to Miami, but the train man didn't pay her any heed until north Florida froze over and Tuttle sent him an 'I-told-you-so' message: an orange blossom clipped from her Miami garden.

The rest is a history of boom, bust, dreamers and opportunists. Generally, Miami has grown in leaps and bounds following major world events and natural disasters. Hurricanes (particularly the deadly Great Miami Hurricane of 1926) have wiped away the town, but it just keeps bouncing and building back better than before. In the late 19th and early 20th centuries, Miami earned a reputation for attracting design and city-planning mavericks like George Merrick, who fashioned the artful Mediterranean village of Coral Gables, and James Deering, designer of the fairy-tale Vizcaya mansion.

Miami Beach blossomed in the early 20th century when Jewish developers recognized the potential American Riviera in their midst. Those hoteliers started building resorts that were branded with a distinct art-deco facade by daring architects willing to buck the more staid aesthetics of the northeast. The world wars brought soldiers who were stationed near local naval facilities, many of whom liked the sun and decided to stay. Latin American and Caribbean revolutions introduced immigrants from the other direction, most famously Cubans, who have arrived in two waves: the

---

NORTHERN CAPITAL OF THE LATIN WORLD

Miami may technically be part of the USA, but it's widely touted as the 'capital of the Americas' and the 'center of the New World.' That's a coup when it comes to marketing Miami to the rest of the world, and especially to the USA, where Latinos are now the largest minority. Miami's pan-Latin mixture makes it more ethnically diverse than any Latin American city. At the turn of the century, the western suburbs of Hialeah and Hialeah Gardens were numbers two and one respectively on the list of US areas where Spanish is spoken as a first language (over 90% of the population).

How did this happen? Many of Miami's Latinos arrived in this geographically convenient city as political refugees – Cubans fleeing Castro starting around the '60s, Venezuelans fleeing President Hugo Chávez (or his predecessors), Brazilians and Argentines running from economic woes, Mexicans and Guatemalans arriving to find work. And gringos, long fascinated with Latin American flavors, can now visit Miami to get a taste of the pan-Latin stew without having to leave the country.

This has all led to the growth of Latin American businesses in Miami, which has boosted the local economy. Miami is the US headquarters of many Latin companies, including LanChile, a Chilean airline; Televisa, a Mexican TV conglomerate; and Embraer, a Brazilian aircraft manufacturer. Miami is also home to Telemundo, one of the biggest Spanish-language broadcasters in the US, as well as MTV Networks Latin America and the Latin branch of the Universal Music Group. Miami is the host city of the annual Billboard Latin Music Conference and Awards.

Cubans still lead the pack of Latinos in Miami, and Cubans have a strong influence on local and international politics. Conservative exile groups have often been characterized as extremists; many refused to visit Cuba while Castro was in power. A newer generation, however – often referred to as the 'YUCAs' (Young Urban Cuban Americans) – are more willing to see both sides of issues in Cuba and are not as caught up in ending Cuba's current way of life as their parents are.

While many of the subtleties may escape you as a Miami visitor, one thing is obvious: the Latino influence, which you can experience by seeking it out or waiting for it to fall in your lap. Whether you're dining out, listening to live music, overhearing Spanish conversations, visiting Little Havana or Little Buenos Aires, or simply sipping a chilled mojito at the edge of your hotel pool, the Latin American energy is palpable, beautiful and everywhere you go.

stridently anti-Castro types of the '60s, and those looking for a better life since the late 1970s, such as the arrivals on the 1980 Mariel Boatlift during a Cuban economic crisis. The glam and over-consumption of the 1980s, personified in *Scarface* and *Miami Beach,* attracted a certain breed of the rich and beautiful, and their associated models, designers, hoteliers and socialites, all of whom transformed South Beach into the beautiful beast she is today.

Today, Miami feels like a city on the edge. Political changes in Latin America continue to have repercussions in this most Latin of cities – as mayor Manny Diaz likes to say, 'When Venezuela or Argentina sneezes, Miami catches a cold.' Economically, as housing prices soar and families move to more distant suburbs like Kendall, it seems Miami will either become a town split between patricians and poverty, or a first-class city that lets its own citizens in on the good life it promises to the rest of the world.

ORIENTATION

Two things divide Miami: water and income. Canals, lakes, bays and bank accounts are the geographic, spatial and social boundaries of this city. Rivers and roads cut design districts from drug dens, and *botanicas* (*vodou* shops) from investment banks. Of course, the great water that divides here is Biscayne Bay, holding apart the city of Miami from its preening sibling, Miami Beach. *Never* forget (many tourists do) that Miami Beach is not Miami's beach, but its own distinct town.

Maps

McNally, AAA and Dolph's all make great maps of the Miami area. The best free map is from the **Greater Miami & the Beaches Convention & Visitor's Bureau** (Map pp92-3; ☎ 305-539-3000, 800-933-8448; www.miamiandbeaches.com; 701 Brickell Ave; ☽ 8:30am-5pm Mon-Fri).

South Beach

The southern part of the city of Miami Beach refers to the region below 21st St (though realtors and hoteliers alike have been known to push that border up as high as 40th St and on our maps it is the area below 23rd St). It encompasses the widest section of the island, with streets running east–west and avenues north–south. Major arteries – Washington Ave, Collins Ave, Alton Rd and Ocean Dr – are named rather than numbered.

Washington Ave is the bustling main drag, functioning as the main commercial artery and least trendy strip; Collins Ave is famous for its long string of art-deco hotels. The chic outdoor cafés and restaurants along Ocean Dr (which only goes as high as 15th St) overlook the wide Atlantic shorefront. Alton Rd is the utilitarian main drag on the west side, more for driving than strolling, while Lincoln Rd is pedestrian-only between Alton Rd and Washington Ave.

Northern Miami Beach

Maps refer to the swath just above South Beach as, simply, Miami Beach, but know that locals use the jargon Mid-Beach (around the 40s) and North Beach (the 70s and above), depending on how high up they're talking about (and on our maps it is just Northern Miami Beach). Two northern Miami Beach communities, Surfside (up in the 90s) and Bal Harbour (though this is technically just above Miami Beach proper), and higher up Sunny Isles and Aventura, are usually included in spirit. Indian Creek waterway separates Collins Ave, which is almost exclusively lined with high-rise condos and luxury hotels, from the residential districts in the west. Alton Rd winds through an exclusive neighborhood that sits in the shadow of Mt Sinai Medical Center and La Gorce Country Club, and connects with Collins Ave at W 63rd St. Keep in mind the separate city of North Miami Beach (as opposed to the *region* of Northern Miami Beach) is not, technically, on the spit of land known as Miami Beach – it's on the mainland. And yes, we'd like to sucker punch the city planners who devised all of the above too.

Downtown Miami

Downtown Miami is a fairly normal grid, with Flagler St one of the main east–west drags and 2nd Ave serving as a major north–south conduit. An international financial and banking center, Brickell Ave runs south to Coconut Grove along the water, and boasts new condos and high-rise luxury hotels including the Four Seasons and the Conrad (it also leads to exclusive Brickell Key, home to the Mandarin Oriental Miami). The lazy, gritty Miami River divides downtown into north and south, and is crossed by the Brickell Ave Bridge. Biscayne Blvd runs north from the river and Brickell Ave runs south of it; both are on the eastern side of the district.

(Continued on page 99)

MIAMI

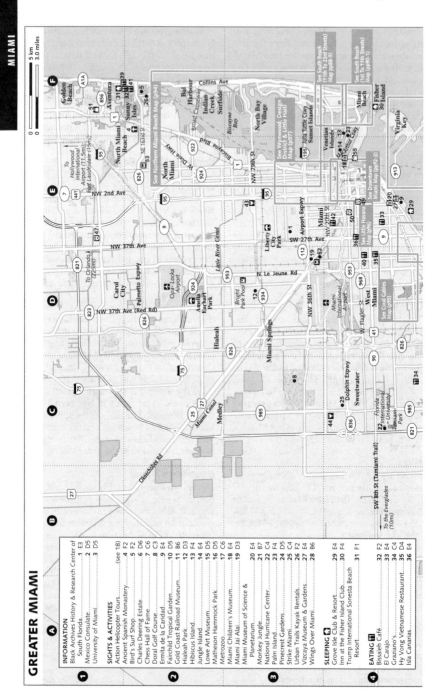

GREATER MIAMI

INFORMATION
Black Archives History & Research Center of
  South Florida..1 E3
Mexico Consulate...2 D5
University of Miami..3 D5

SIGHTS & ACTIVITIES
Action Helicopter Tours............................(see 18)
Ancient Spanish Monastery............................4 F2
Bird's Surf Shop...5 F2
Charles Deering Estate...................................6 D6
Chess Hall of Fame..7 C6
Doral Golf Course..8 C3
Ermita de la Caridad......................................9 E4
Fairchild Tropical Garden.............................10 D5
Gold Coast Railroad Museum.......................11 B6
Hialeah Park...12 D3
Hibiscus Island..13 F4
Jungle Island...14 E4
Lowe Art Museum.......................................15 D5
Matheson Hammock Park.............................16 D5
Metrozoo...17 C6
Miami Children's Museum............................18 E4
Miami Jai Alai..19 D3
Miami Museum of Science &
  Planetarium...20 E4
Monkey Jungle...21 B7
National Hurricane Center............................22 D4
Palm Island..23 F4
Pinecrest Gardens..24 D5
Strike Miami...25 C4
Urban Trails Kayak Rentals...........................26 F2
Vizcaya Museum & Gardens.........................27 E4
Wings Over Miami.......................................28 B6

SLEEPING
Grove Isle Club & Resort..............................29 E4
Inn at the Fisher Island Club.........................30 F4
Trump International Sonesta Beach
  Resort..31 F1

EATING
Bissaleh Café...32 F2
El Carajo..33 E4
Graziano's...34 C4
Hy Vong Vietnamese Restaurant...................35 D4
Isla Canarias..36 E4

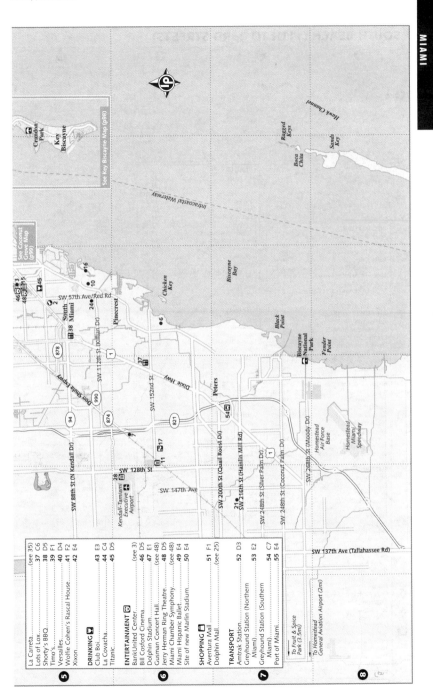

La Carreta	(see 35)
Lots of Lox	37 C6
Shorty's BBQ	38 D5
Timo's	39 F1
Versailles	40 D4
Wolfie Cohen's Rascal House	41 F2
Xixon	42 E4

DRINKING
Club Boi	43 E3
La Covacha	44 C4
Titanic	45 D5

ENTERTAINMENT
BankUnited Center	(see 3)
Bill Cosford Cinema	46 D5
Dolphin Stadium	47 E1
Gusman Concert Hall	(see 48)
Jerry Herman Ring Theatre	48 D5
Miami Chamber Symphony	49 E4
Miami Hispanic Ballet	50 E4
Site of new Marlin Stadium	

SHOPPING
Aventura Mall	51 F1
Dolphin Mall	(see 25)

TRANSPORT
Amtrak Station	52 D3
Greyhound Station (Northern Miami)	53 E2
Greyhound Station (Southern Miami)	54 C7
Port of Miami	55 E4

MIAMI

SOUTH BEACH (11TH TO 23RD STREETS)

Biscayne
Bay

Number 2

Sunset Islands

Number 3

W 24th St

See Northern Miami Beach Map (p94)

Number 4

INFORMATION
Beach Dental Center.....................1 E4
Books & Books.............................2 E4
Eckerd Drugs...............................3 D5
Kafka Kafe.................................4 F5
Miami Beach Chamber of Commerce.5 E3
Miami-Dade Public Library..........6 G2
Post Office.................................7 F6
South Beach Languages Center.....8 G6

SIGHTS & ACTIVITIES
Agua Bathhouse Spa.................(see 28)
ArtCenter/South Florida...............9 E4
Bass Museum of Art...................10 G2
Crunch.....................................11 F6
David Barton Gym....................(see 28)
Fritz's Skate Shop......................12 E4
Gold's Gym South Beach.............13 D5
Holocaust Memorial....................14 E3
Idol's Gym................................15 E4
Miami Beach Botanical Garden......16 F3
Miami Duck Tours......................17 F4
Miami Yogashala.......................18 G2
Post Office...............................(see 7)
South Beach Ironworks...............19 D4
Spa at the Setai.......................(see 38)
Synergy Center for Yoga and the Healing
  Arts....................................20 F5
Temple Emanu El........................21 F3
World Erotic Art Museum.............22 F6

SLEEPING
Aqua Hotel...............................23 G5
Beachcomber Hotel....................24 G6
Cardozo Hotel...........................25 G6
Cavalier Hotel..........................(see 25)
Clay Hotel & Miami Beach International
  Hostel..................................26 F5
De Soleil.................................27 G5
Delano Hotel.............................28 G4
Gansevoort...............................29 H1
Greenview................................30 F4
Hotel Impala.............................31 G5
Loews Miami Beach....................32 G4
Marlin Hotel.............................33 G4
National Hotel...........................34 G4
Raleigh Hotel............................35 G3
Royal Palm Hotel.......................36 G5
Sagamore................................37 G4
Setai......................................38 G3
Shore Club...............................39 G3
Standard.................................40 B4
Surfcomber..............................41 G3
Tides.....................................42 G6
Townhouse Hotel.......................43 G3
Tropics Hotel & Hostel................44 G5
W Hotel..................................45 G2
Winter Haven...........................46 G5

EATING
A La Folie...............................47 F5
Balans...................................48 E4
Blue Door..............................(see 28)
Café Papillon...........................49 F4
Casa Tua................................50 G3
CJ's Crab Shack........................51 G6
Escopazzo...............................52 F6
Flamingo Restaurant...................53 F5
Front Porch Café.......................54 G5
Gelateria Parmalat.....................55 F4
Grillfish..................................56 G5
Guru.....................................57 G6
Jerry's Famous Deli....................58 G5
Le Sandwicherie........................59 G5
Miss Yip................................(see 83)
Osteria del Teatro......................60 F5
Pasha's..................................61 E4
Pizza Rustica............................62 F5
Presto Pizza.............................63 G4
San Loco................................64 G5
Table 8.................................(see 27)
Tapas y Tintos..........................65 F5
Van Dyke Café..........................66 F4
Yuca.....................................67 F4

Belle
Isle

Island
View
Park

DRINKING
Abbey Brewery..........................68 D4
Automatic Slims.........................69 F6
Bond Street Lounge...................(see 43)
Buck 15................................(see 83)
Cameo..................................70 F5
Florida Room at the Delano.........(see 28)
Jazid.....................................71 F6
Laundry Bar.............................72 E4
Lost Weekend...........................73 G5
Mac's Club Deuce Bar..................74 G5
Mansion.................................75 F6
Mynt....................................76 G3
Raleigh Hotel Bar.....................(see 35)
Sagamore Bar.........................(see 38)
Score....................................77 E4
Skybar.................................(see 39)
Table 8 Bar............................(see 27)
Touch....................................78 E4

ENTERTAINMENT
Colony Theatre..........................79 D4
Jackie Gleason Theater of the Performing
  Arts....................................80 F3
Lincoln Theatre.........................81 F4
Miami City Ballet........................82 G2
New World Symphony.................(see 81)

SHOPPING
En Avance................................83 E4
Epicure Market...........................84 D4
Española Way Art Center..............85 F5
Scoop...................................(see 39)
Sofi Swimwear...........................86 F5

Sunset Dr

N Bay Rd

20th St

19th St

West Ave

Alton Rd

18th St

Sheridan Ave

Bay Rd

Sun Trust
Bank

Lincoln Rd

Lincoln Rd Mall

Lenox Ave

16th St

15th Tce

15th St

Flamingo Way

14th Ct

West Ave

Alton Ln

Lincoln La S

14th St

13th Tce

13th St

Alton Rd

Alton Ct

11th St

N Chase Ave

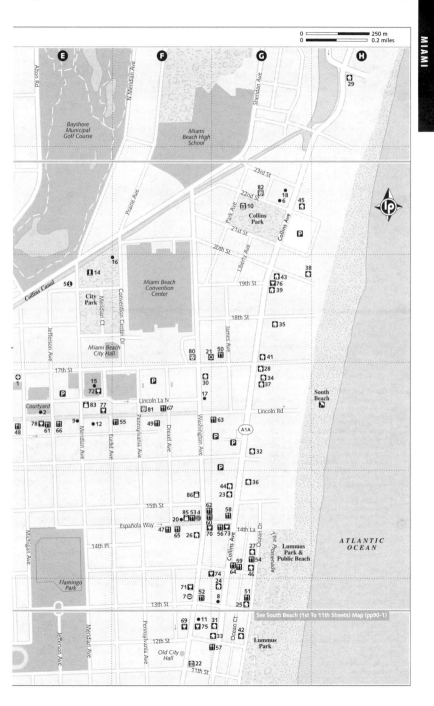

See South Beach (1st To 11th Streets) Map (pp90-1)

SOUTH BEACH (1ST TO 11TH STREETS)

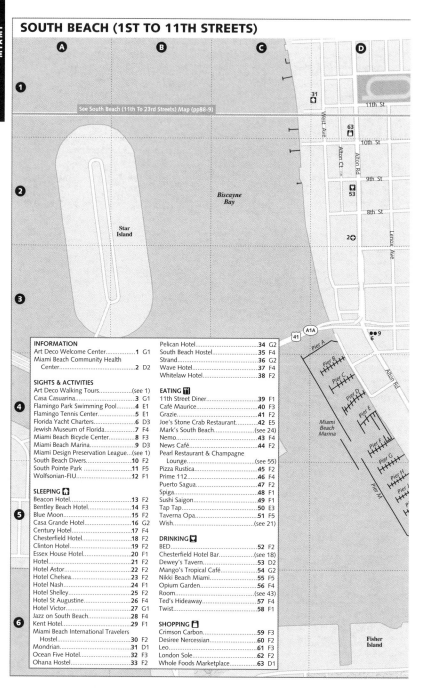

See South Beach (11th To 23rd Streets) Map (pp88-9)

Biscayne Bay

Star Island

Miami Beach Marina

Fisher Island

INFORMATION
Art Deco Welcome Center...............**1** G1
Miami Beach Community Health
   Center...**2** D2

SIGHTS & ACTIVITIES
Art Deco Walking Tours...................(see 1)
Casa Casuarina.................................**3** G1
Flamingo Park Swimming Pool..........**4** E1
Flamingo Tennis Center....................**5** E1
Florida Yacht Charters.....................**6** D3
Jewish Museum of Florida.................**7** F4
Miami Beach Bicycle Center.............**8** F3
Miami Beach Marina..........................**9** D3
Miami Design Preservation League...(see 1)
South Beach Divers...........................**10** F2
South Pointe Park **11** F5
Wolfsonian-FIU.................................**12** F1

SLEEPING
Beacon Hotel....................................**13** F2
Bentley Beach Hotel.........................**14** F3
Blue Moon.......................................**15** F2
Casa Grande Hotel...........................**16** G2
Century Hotel...................................**17** F4
Chesterfield Hotel............................**18** F2
Clinton Hotel...................................**19** F2
Essex House Hotel............................**20** F1
Hotel...**21** F2
Hotel Astor......................................**22** F2
Hotel Chelsea..................................**23** F2
Hotel Nash.......................................**24** F1
Hotel Shelley....................................**25** F2
Hotel St Augustine...........................**26** F4
Hotel Victor.....................................**27** G1
Jazz on South Beach.........................**28** F4
Kent Hotel.......................................**29** F1
Miami Beach International Travelers
   Hostel...**30** F2
Mondrian...**31** D1
Ocean Five Hotel..............................**32** F3
Ohana Hostel...................................**33** F2

Pelican Hotel....................................**34** G2
South Beach Hostel..........................**35** F4
Strand..**36** G2
Wave Hotel......................................**37** F4
Whitelaw Hotel................................**38** F2

EATING
11th Street Diner..............................**39** F1
Café Maurice....................................**40** F3
Grazie..**41** F2
Joe's Stone Crab Restaurant.............**42** E5
Mark's South Beach.........................(see 24)
Nemo...**43** F4
News Café..**44** F2
Pearl Restaurant & Champagne
   Lounge...(see 55)
Pizza Rustica....................................**45** F2
Prime 112...**46** F4
Puerto Sagua....................................**47** F2
Spiga..**48** F1
Sushi Saigon.....................................**49** F1
Tap Tap..**50** E3
Taverna Opa.....................................**51** F5
Wish...(see 21)

DRINKING
BED..**52** F2
Chesterfield Hotel Bar......................(see 18)
Dewey's Tavern................................**53** D2
Mango's Tropical Café......................**54** G2
Nikki Beach Miami............................**55** F5
Opium Garden..................................**56** F5
Room..(see 43)
Ted's Hideaway................................**57** F4
Twist...**58** F1

SHOPPING
Crimson Carbon................................**59** F3
Desiree Nercessian...........................**60** F2
Leo...**61** F3
London Sole.....................................**62** F2
Whole Foods Marketplace................**63** D1

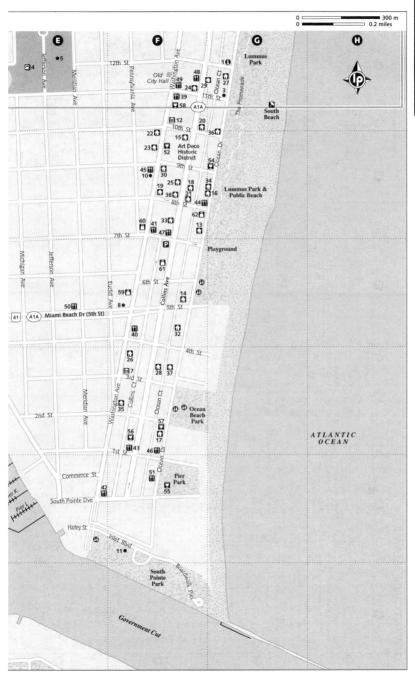

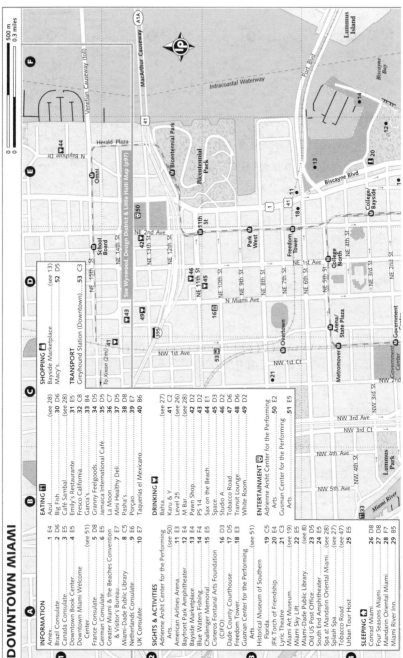

DOWNTOWN MIAMI

INFORMATION
Amex	1 E4
Brazil Consulate	2 D6
Canada Consulate	3 E5
Downtown Book Center	4 E5
Downtown Miami Welcome Center	(see 51)
France Consulate	5 D8
German Consulate	6 E5
Greater Miami & the Beaches Convention & Visitor's Bureau	7 E7
Miami-Dade Public Library	8 C5
Netherlands Consulate	9 E6
UK Consulate	10 E7

SIGHTS & ACTIVITIES
Adrienne Arsht Center for the Performing Arts	(see 50)
American Airlines Arena	11 E3
Bayfront Park Amphitheater	12 E4
Bayside Marketplace	13 E4
Blue Waters Fishing	14 F4
Challenger Memorial	15 F5
Cisneros Fontanal Arts Foundation (CIFO)	16 D3
Dade County Courthouse	17 D5
Freedom Tower	18 E3
Gusman Center for the Performing Arts	(see 51)
Historical Museum of Southern Florida	19 C5
JFK Torch of Friendship	20 E4
Lyric Theatre	21 C3
Miami Art Museum	(see 19)
Miami Sky Lift	22 E5
Miami-Dade Public Library	23 D5
Old US Post Office	24 E5
South End Amphitheater	(see 27)
Spa at Mandarin Oriental Miami	(see 28)
Splash Spa	(see 47)
Tobacco Road	(see 47)
Urban Tour Host	25 E5

SLEEPING
Conrad Miami	26 D8
Four Seasons Miami	27 D8
Mandarin Oriental Miami	28 F7
Miami River Inn	29 B5

EATING
Azul	(see 28)
Big Fish	30 D6
Café Sambal	(see 28)
Emily's Restaurante	31 E5
Fresco California	32 C8
Garcia's	33 B4
Granny Feelgoods	34 D5
Jamaica International Café	35 D5
La Moon	36 C7
Mini Healthy Deli	37 D5
Pasha's	38 D8
Porção	39 E7
Taquerías el Mexicano	40 B6

DRINKING
Bahia	(see 27)
Karu & Y	41 C2
Level 25	(see 26)
M Bar	(see 28)
Pawn Shop	42 D2
PS 14	43 D2
Sax on the Beach	44 E1
Space	45 D3
Studio A	46 D2
Tobacco Road	47 D6
Transit Lounge	48 D6
White Room	49 D2

ENTERTAINMENT
Adrienne Arsht Center for the Performing Arts	50 E2
Gusman Center for the Performing Arts	51 E5

SHOPPING
Bayside Marketplace	(see 13)
Macy's	52 D5

TRANSPORT
Greyhound Station (Downtown)	53 C3

See Wynwood, Design District & Little Haiti Map (p97)

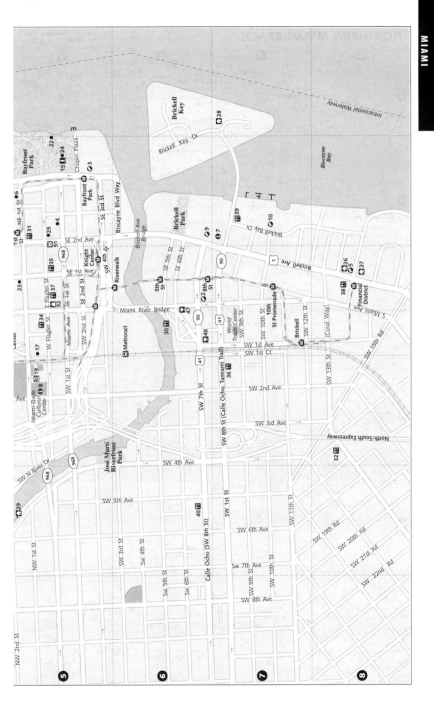

NORTHERN MIAMI BEACH

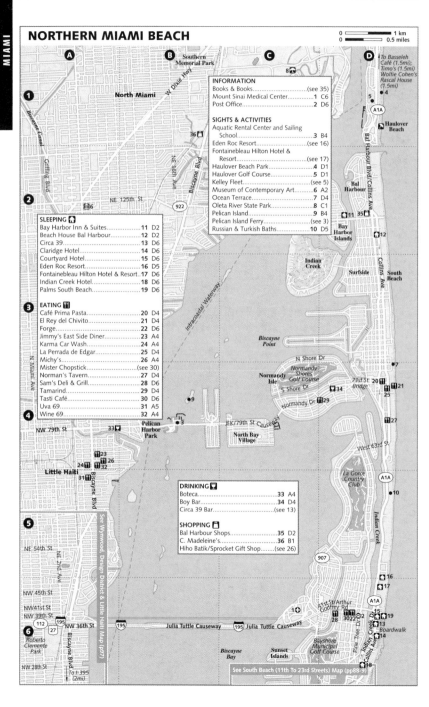

| 0 | 1 km |
| 0 | 0.5 miles |

INFORMATION
Books & Books.................................(see 35)
Mount Sinai Medical Center.............**1** C6
Post Office.......................................**2** D6

SIGHTS & ACTIVITIES
Aquatic Rental Center and Sailing
  School..**3** B4
Eden Roc Resort............................(see 16)
Fontainebleau Hilton Hotel &
  Resort...(see 17)
Haulover Beach Park.......................**4** D1
Haulover Golf Course......................**5** D1
Kelley Fleet....................................(see 5)
Museum of Contemporary Art.........**6** A2
Ocean Terrace.................................**7** D4
Oleta River State Park.....................**8** C1
Pelican Island.................................**9** B4
Pelican Island Ferry........................(see 3)
Russian & Turkish Baths.................**10** D5

SLEEPING 🛏
Bay Harbor Inn & Suites................**11** D2
Beach House Bal Harbour................**12** D2
Circa 39..**13** D6
Claridge Hotel...............................**14** D6
Courtyard Hotel.............................**15** D6
Eden Roc Resort............................**16** D5
Fontainebleau Hilton Hotel & Resort..**17** D6
Indian Creek Hotel.........................**18** D6
Palms South Beach.........................**19** D6

EATING 🍴
Café Prima Pasta............................**20** D4
El Rey del Chivito...........................**21** D4
Forge..**22** D6
Jimmy's East Side Diner..................**23** A4
Karma Car Wash.............................**24** A4
La Perrada de Edgar........................**25** D4
Michy's...**26** A4
Mister Chopstick..........................(see 30)
Norman's Tavern............................**27** D6
Sam's Deli & Grill...........................**28** D6
Tamarind.......................................**29** D6
Tasti Café......................................**30** D6
Uva 69..**31** A5
Wine 69...**32** A4

DRINKING 🍷
Boteca..**33** A4
Boy Bar...**34** D4
Circa 39 Bar.................................(see 13)

SHOPPING 🛍
Bal Harbour Shops.........................**35** D2
C. Madeleine's...............................**36** B1
Hiho Batik/Sprocket Gift Shop......(see 26)

To Basseleh
Café (1.5mi);
Timo's (1.5mi);
Wolfie Cohen's
Rascal House
(1.5mi)

North Miami
W Dixie Hwy
Southern
Memorial Park
Biscayne Canal
Griffing Blvd
NE 16th Ave
Biscayne Blvd
NE 125th St
Haulover
Beach
Bal Harbour Blvd/Collins Ave
Bal Harbour
Bay Harbour Islands
Collins Ave
South Beach
Surfside
Indian Creek
Biscayne Point
N Shore Dr
Normandy Shores
Golf Course
Normandy Isle
Normandy Dr
S Shore Dr
71st St
71st St Bridge
JFK/79th St Causeway
Pelican Harbor Park
NW 79th St
North Bay Village
West 63rd St
La Gorce Country Club
Intracoastal Waterway
N Miami Ave
NE 2nd Ave
Little Haiti
NE 54th St
NW 45th St
NW 41st St
NW 39th St
NW 36th St
Julia Tuttle Causeway
Roberto Clemente Park
NW 28th St
To I-395 (2mi)
41st St/Arthur Godfrey Rd
Indian Creek
Pine Tree Dr
Collins Ave
Boardwalk
Bayshore Municipal Golf Course
Biscayne Bay
Sunset Islands
Indian Creek Blvd
See Wynwood Design District & Little Haiti Map (p97)
See South Beach (11th To 23rd Streets) Map (pp88-9)

CORAL GABLES

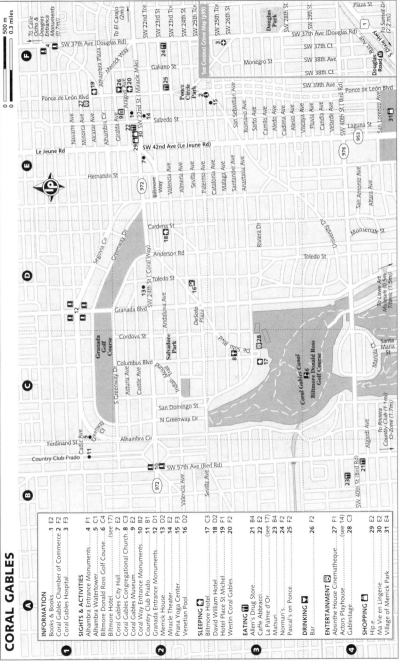

MIAMI

LITTLE HAVANA

0 ——————— 500 m
0 ——————— 0.3 miles

To Isla Canarias (0.5mi)
To Hy Vong Vietnamese
    Restaurant (1mi);
    La Carreta (1mi);
    Versailles (1mi)

WYNWOOD, DESIGN DISTRICT & LITTLE HAITI

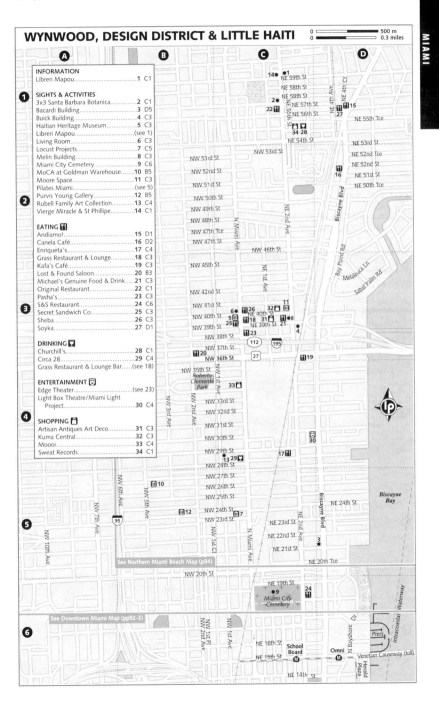

0 — 500 m
0 — 0.3 miles

INFORMATION	
Libreri Mapou	**1** C1

SIGHTS & ACTIVITIES	
3x3 Santa Barbara Botanica	**2** C1
Bacardi Building	**3** D5
Buick Building	**4** C3
Haitian Heritage Museum	**5** C3
Libreri Mapou	(see 1)
Living Room	**6** C3
Locust Projects	**7** C5
Melin Building	**8** C3
Miami City Cemetery	**9** C6
MoCA at Goldman Warehouse	**10** B5
Moore Space	**11** C3
Pilates Miami	(see 5)
Purvis Young Gallery	**12** B5
Rubell Family Art Collection	**13** C4
Vierge Miracle & St Phillipe	**14** C1

EATING 🍴	
Andiamo!	**15** D1
Canela Café	**16** D2
Enriqueta's	**17** C4
Grass Restaurant & Lounge	**18** C3
Kafa's Café	**19** C3
Lost & Found Saloon	**20** B3
Michael's Genuine Food & Drink	**21** C3
Original Restaurant	**22** C1
Pasha's	**23** C3
S&S Restaurant	**24** C6
Secret Sandwich Co	**25** C3
Sheba	**26** C3
Soyka	**27** D1

DRINKING 🍷	
Churchill's	**28** C1
Circa 28	**29** C4
Grass Restaurant & Lounge Bar	(see 18)

ENTERTAINMENT 🎭	
Edge Theater	(see 23)
Light Box Theatre/Miami Light Project	**30** C4

SHOPPING 🛍	
Artisan Antiques Art Deco	**31** C3
Kuma Central	**32** C3
Moooi	**33** C4
Sweat Records	**34** C1

MIAMI

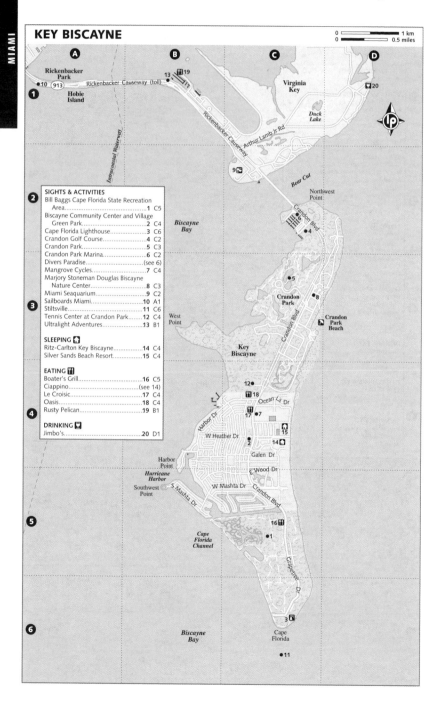

KEY BISCAYNE

0   1 km
0   0.5 miles

SIGHTS & ACTIVITIES

Bill Baggs Cape Florida State Recreation
    Area...**1** C5
Biscayne Community Center and Village
    Green Park...................................**2** C4
Cape Florida Lighthouse......................**3** C6
Crandon Golf Course............................**4** C2
Crandon Park...**5** C3
Crandon Park Marina............................**6** C2
Divers Paradise.................................(see **6**)
Mangrove Cycles...................................**7** C4
Marjory Stoneman Douglas Biscayne
    Nature Center................................**8** C3
Miami Seaquarium................................**9** C2
Sailboards Miami.................................**10** A1
Stiltsville...**11** C6
Tennis Center at Crandon Park.......**12** C4
Ultralight Adventures.......................**13** B1

SLEEPING

Ritz-Carlton Key Biscayne.................**14** C4
Silver Sands Beach Resort................**15** C4

EATING

Boater's Grill......................................**16** C5
Ciappino...(see **14**)
Le Croisic..**17** C4
Oasis..**18** C4
Rusty Pelican......................................**19** B1

DRINKING

Jimbo's..**20** D1

Rickenbacker
Park
Hobie
Island
Rickenbacker Causeway (toll)

Intracoastal Waterway

Rickenbacker Causeway Arthur Lamb Jr Rd

Virginia
Key

Duck
Lake

Bear Cut

Northwest
Point

Crandon Blvd

Biscayne
Bay

West
Point

Crandon
Park

Crandon Blvd

Crandon
Park
Beach

Key
Biscayne

Ocean La Dr

Harbor Dr

W Heather Dr

Galen Dr

Wood Dr

W Mashta Dr

Crandon Blvd

Harbor
Point
Hurricane
Harbor
Southwest
Point

S Mashta Dr

Cape
Florida
Channel

Crandon Dr

Biscayne
Bay

Cape
Florida

(Continued from page 85)

Wynwood, Design District & Little Haiti

There is something quite odd about Wynwood and the Design District, Miami's official arts neighborhoods. Come in from I-95 and you land in the heart of the art-studio spaces. 'Oh honey, look at the galleries.' But come

north on US 1, or from the side, and you'll see the jagged edges of the working-class Puerto Rican neighborhood that Wynwood once was.

All three areas are just north of downtown. While Wynwood is sort of loosely defined as being west of Biscayne Blvd and east of I-95, between 17th St and 35th St, the Design

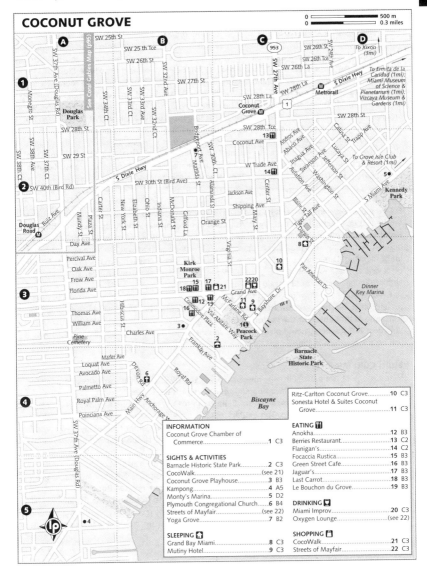

COCONUT GROVE

INFORMATION
Coconut Grove Chamber of
  Commerce..1 C3

SIGHTS & ACTIVITIES
Barnacle Historic State Park...............2 C3
CocoWalk..(see 21)
Coconut Grove Playhouse.................3 B3
Kampong...4 A5
Monty's Marina................................5 D2
Plymouth Congregational Church......6 B4
Streets of Mayfair............................(see 22)
Yoga Grove......................................7 B2

SLEEPING
Grand Bay Miami..............................8 C3
Mutiny Hotel....................................9 C3

Ritz-Carlton Coconut Grove.............10 C3
Sonesta Hotel & Suites Coconut
  Grove..11 C3

EATING
Anokha...12 B3
Berries Restaurant...........................13 C2
Flanigan's..14 C2
Focaccia Rustica..............................15 B3
Green Street Cafe............................16 B3
Jaguar's..17 B3
Last Carrot.......................................18 B3
Le Bouchon du Grove......................19 B3

DRINKING
Miami Improv...................................20 C3
Oxygen Lounge..............................(see 22)

SHOPPING
CocoWalk..21 C3
Streets of Mayfair............................22 C3

District is a small, neat grid: between NE 38th St and NE 41st St, and NE 2nd Ave and N Miami Ave. North of all three of these regions is a rapidly gentrifying neighborhood, which is known locally as the Upper East Side.

Little Haiti, which sits just above the Design District, falls loosely between NE 4th Ave to the east and I-95 to the west. Little Haiti's southern boundary is I-395, and its northern is at NW 79th St.

MIAMI IN...

Two Days

There's way more to Miami than South Beach, but we're assuming you're starting – and sleeping – here. Have breakfast at **Puerto Sagua** (p139) and, gorged, waddle to the **Wolfsonian-FIU** (p104) to get some background on the surrounding art deco. Now stroll around **Lincoln Road** (p104), hotel spot on Collins Ave or check out the Hermitage-meets-slick-design-spread-chic of South Beach's most flamboyant structures, like **Delano Hotel** (p134), **Tides** (p134) and the **Shore Club** (p134).

Get in beach time and, as evening sets in, consider an excellent deco district tour with the **Art Deco Welcome Center** (p102). For a nice dinner try **Osteria del Teatro** (p141; classy Italian) or **Tap Tap** (p139; psychedelic Haitian). When you're ready to hit the town (and the rails), we suggest early cocktails in the **Whitelaw Hotel** (p130) lobby, going buck wild at **Buck 15** (p152) and 24-hour soak-up grub at the **11th Street Diner** (p138).

Check out either **Little Haiti** (p110) or **Little Havana** (p113) the next day and potter around these excellent ethnic enclaves before dining in the trendy **Design District** (p110). End your trip rocking out in one of downtown's excellent little live venues like **PS 14** (p154) or **Transit Lounge** (p154) before scarfing scary Colombian hot dogs at **La Moon** (p144).

Four Days

Follow the two-day itinerary and go to whichever one of the 'Littles' (Haiti or Havana) you missed on the first go 'round. If you can, try to visit Coral Gables, making sure not to miss the **Biltmore Hotel** (p116), the **Venetian Pool** (p116) and a shopping stroll down Miracle Mile. If all that isn't opulent enough for you, see what happens when Mediterranean revival, Baroque stylings and a lot of money gets mashed together at the **Vizcaya Museum & Gardens** (p115). Afterwards, top off a visit to these elegant manses with dinner at one of the best restaurants in Miami in – no kidding – a gas station at **El Carajo** (p149).

On day four, head downtown and take a long ride on the free **Metromover** (p108), hopping on and off to see the excellent **Historical Museum of South Florida** (p107) and the gorgeous **Adrienne Arsht Center for the Performing Arts** (p107). Have your last meal at **Michy's** (p143) on emergent N Biscayne Blvd and please, before you leave, guzzle a beer and pick at some smoked fish on the couches of **Jimbo's** (p113).

Multi-Culti Miami

Miami is one of the most culturally diverse cities in the USA, and while you'll need to drive (or hire a taxi) for this ethnic-enclave-hopping tour, it's worth the hassle.

Start in Little Havana and meander up **Calle Ocho** (p113), then to the **Bay of Pigs Museum & Library** (p114) and **Máximo Gómez Park** (p114). Little Havana is the place to learn about pre-revolutionary, anti-Castro, exiled Cuba, one of the most important (and easily stereotyped) communities in Miami. Also, notice how even in Little 'Havana,' Nicaraguan and Salvadoran immigrants are taking the Cubans' place in the new-arrival stakes.

Get the city's best bento box in **Matsuri** (p149), where pretty much all of Miami's small Japanese community eats lunch. Then drive to Little Haiti and pay a visit to a *botanica*, or *vodou*, shop, such as **Vierge Miracle & St Phillipe** (p112), before having a caipirinha at **Boteca** (p153), where Miami's Brazilians let their hair down. Cross the 71st St bridge to **Normandy Isle** (p106) and chill with Argentines, Colombians, Uruguayans, Venezuelans and the rest of sexy South America, and finish this 'round-the-world-in-one-city tour eating some of Miami's best deli for dinner in the Jewish heart of Miami: **Arthur Godfrey Road** (p106).

Key Biscayne

The Rickenbacker Causeway, the eastern extension of 26th Rd, leads first to small Virginia Key, and then over to Key Biscayne, an island that's just 7 miles long. It turns into Crandon Blvd, the key's only real main road, which runs all the way to the southernmost tip and the Cape Florida Lighthouse.

Little Havana

Calle Ocho, or SW 8th St, doesn't just cut through the heart of the neighborhood, it *is* the heart of the neighborhood. For the purposes of our exploration, the neighborhood extends roughly from W Flagler St to below SW 8th St and from SW 11th Ave to SW 24th Ave. The Miami River separates Little Havana from downtown on the northeast border.

Coconut Grove

The Grove, the epicenter of middle class, mall-and-Gap yuppie Miami, unfolds along S Bayshore Dr (south of the Rickenbacker Causeway). S Bayshore hugs the shoreline and becomes McFarlane Rd as you approach the main part of town, where it then becomes Main Hwy and eventually leads to Douglas Rd (SW 37th Ave), Ingraham Hwy, Old Cutler Rd and attractions in South Dade. US Hwy 1 (S Dixie Hwy) acts as the northern boundary for the Grove.

Coral Gables

The lovely Mediterranean-style city of Coral Gables is essentially bordered by Calle Ocho to the north, Sunset Dr (SW 72nd St/Hwy 986) to the south, Ponce de León Blvd to the east and Red Rd (SW 57th Ave/Hwy 959) to the west. US Hwy 1 slashes through at a 45° angle from northeast to southwest. The main campus of the University of Miami is located just south of the enormous Coral Gables Biltmore Golf Course, northwest of US Hwy 1. Avenues here run east–west, while streets run north–south, the opposite of the rest of Miami. The main pedestrian drag here is Miracle Mile, which is heaven for the shopping-obsessed.

INFORMATION

There are over 400,000 people living in the city of Miami and 5.4 million in the greater Miami metropolitan area. When making phone calls, the area code for Miami is ☎ 305.

Bookstores

Books & Books (www.booksandbooks.com) Bal Harbour (Map p94; ☎ 305-864-4241; 9700 Collins Ave, Bal Harbour; 10am-9pm Mon-Sat, midday-6pm Sun); Coral Gables (Map p95; ☎ 305-442-4408; 265 Aragon Ave; 9am-11pm); South Beach (Map pp88-9; ☎ 305-532-3222; 933 Lincoln Rd; 10am-11pm Sun-Thu, 10am-midnight Fri & Sat) The undisputed king of Miami's indie bookshop scene has works by local authors and great readings, too.

Downtown Book Center (Map pp92-3; ☎ 305-377-9939; 247 SE 1st St, Downtown; 9am-5pm Mon-Fri, 9am-2pm Sat) Your best book bet downtown.

Kafka Kafe (Map pp88-9; ☎ 305-673-9669; 1464 Washington Ave, South Beach; 8am-midnight) Used books and internet café.

Libreri Mapou (Map p97; ☎ 305-757-9922; 5919 NE 2nd Ave, Little Haiti; 10am-6pm) Haitian bookshop that specializes in English, French and Creole titles and periodicals.

Emergency

Ambulance (☎ 911)
Beach Patrol (☎ 305-673-7714)
Coast Guard Search (☎ 305-535-4314)
Hurricane Hotline (☎ 305-229-4483)
Poison Information Center (☎ 800-282-3171)
Rape Hotline (☎ 305-585-7273)
Suicide Intervention (☎ 305-358-4357)

Internet Access

Most hostels have computers with internet connections for a minimal fee. You can also find plenty of strong connections at **public libraries** (☎ 305-375-2665; www.mdpls.org) and internet cafés. Wi-fi hotspots are becoming quite commonplace for folks traveling with a laptop; for a list of hotspots visit www.wi-fihotspotlist .com and click on Miami. Alternatively, check out **Kafka Kafe** (Map pp88-9; ☎ 305-673-9669; 1464 Washington Ave, South Beach) for internet access.

Internet Resources

Art Circuits (www.artcircuits.com) The best insider info on art events; includes excellent neighborhood-by-neighborhood gallery maps.

City Search (www.miami.citysearch.com) Particularly useful for finding detailed nightlife and dining reviews, often with photos.

Cool Junkie (www.cooljunkie.com/miami) A must for trendies, with info on nightclubs, fashion and more.

Mango & Lime (www.mangoandlime.net) The best local food blog is always ahead of the curve on eating events in the Magic City.

Meatless Miami (www.meatlessmiami.com) Vegetarians in need of an eating guide, look no further.

Miami Beach 411 (www.miamibeach411.com) A great guide for Miami Beach visitors, covering just about all concerns.

Miami Herald (www.herald.com) The best stop for local and regional news.

Miami New Times (www.newtimes.com) Alternative coverage with an activist bent.

Miami Nights (www.miaminights.com) Get a good, opinionated downlow on Miami's ever-shifting after-dark scene.

Miami Today News (www.miamitodaynews.com) An excellent online source for business and other daily updates.

Sun Post (www.miamisunpost.com) This new newspaper provides in-depth coverage of stories the mainstream media seems to miss.

Three Guys From Miami (www.3guysfrommiami .com) An amusing, insightful visitor's guide to Miami by, you guessed it, three local guys who offer a good Cuban-American perspective on their hometown.

Libraries

Miami-Dade Public Library (www.mdpls.org) Downtown (Map pp92-3; ☎ 305-375-2665; 101 W Flagler St; ☼ 9am-6pm Mon-Wed, Fri & Sat, 9am-9pm Thu, 1-5pm Sun); Miami Beach (Map pp88-9; ☎ 305-535-4219; 227 22nd St; ☼ 9:30am-9pm Mon-Thu, 9:30am-6pm Fri-Sat, 1-5pm Sun) The downtown branch of this beautiful library has excellent rotating exhibits and an enormous room dedicated to all things Floridian. There are branches around town, including Miami Beach.

Media

Beach Channel (www.thebeachchannel.tv) Local 24-hour TV station on channel 19, like a quirky infomercial about goings-on in Miami Beach.

Diario Las Americas (www.diariolasamericas.com) Spanish-language daily.

El Nuevo Herald (www.elnuevoherald.com) Spanish-language daily of the *Herald*.

Home Miami (www.homemia.com) Magazine about real estate and home design.

Loft Magazine for the visual-arts and design scene.

Miami Herald (www.miamiherlad.com) Major daily covering local, national and international news.

Miami New Times (www.miaminewtimes.com) Free alternative weekly paper.

Miami Sun Post (www.miamisubpost.com) In-depth news and lifestyle coverage.

ML: Miami Living Magazine (www.miamiliving.com) Glossy magazine filled with quirky features and excellent listings.

Sun-Sentinel (www.sun-sentinel.com) Daily covering South Florida.

WLRN (www.wlrn.org) Local National Public Radio affiliate, at 91.3FM on the dial.

Medical Services

Beach Dental Center (Map pp88-9; ☎ 305-532-3300; 1680 Michigan Ave, South Beach) For dental needs.

Coral Gables Hospital (Map p95; ☎ 305-445-8461; 3100 Douglas Rd, Coral Gables) A community-based facility with many bilingual doctors.

Eckerd Drugs (Map pp88-9; ☎ 305-538-1571; 1421 Alton Rd, South Beach; ☼ 24hr) One of many 24-hour Eckerd pharmacies.

Miami Beach Community Health Center (Map pp90-1; ☎ 305-538-8835; 710 Alton Rd, South Beach) Walk-in clinic with long lines.

Mount Sinai Medical Center (Map p94; ☎ 305-674-2121; 4300 Alton Rd, Miami Beach) The area's best emergency room. Beware that you must eventually pay, and fees are high.

Visitor's Medical Line (☎ 305-674-2222; ☼ 24hr) For physician referrals.

Money

Bank of America has branch offices all over Miami and Miami Beach. To get currency exchanged you can go to **Amex** (Map pp92-3; ☎ 305-358-7350; www.amex.com; 100 N Biscayne Blvd, downtown Miami; ☼ Mon-Fri 9am-5pm).

Post

The following branches have hours extended until evening thanks to self-serve machines in the lobbies:

Post Office Mid-Beach (Map p94; 445 W 40th St; ☼ 8am-5pm Mon-Fri, 8:30am-2pm Sat); South Beach (Map pp88-9; 1300 Washington Ave; ☼ 8am-5pm Mon-Fri, 8:30am-2pm Sat)

Toilets

There are public toilets at several spots on South Beach (South Pointe Park, Art Deco Welcome Center), but the area doesn't offer much in the way of public facilities. Restaurants may allow you to use their toilets if you're reasonably presentable and ask politely. Bars and Starbucks are a good bet; just walk to the back as if you're a customer. Libraries are a sure thing, but the hands-down best toilets around (and generally, no questions are asked) are those in the lobbies of big hotels.

Tourist Information

Art Deco Welcome Center (Map pp90-1; ☎ 305-672-2014; www.mdpl.org; 1001 Ocean Dr, South Beach; ☼ 10am-7:30pm Mon-Sat, to 6pm Sun) Run by the Miami

Design Preservation League (MDPL), has tons of art-deco district information and organizes excellent walking tours.

Black Archives History & Research Center of South Florida (Map pp86-7; ☎ 305-636-2390; www .theblackarchives.org; 5400 NW 22nd Ave, Suite 101, Liberty City) Information about black culture.

Coconut Grove Chamber of Commerce (Map p99; ☎ 305-444-7270; www.coconutgrove.com; 2820 McFarlane Rd, Coconut Grove; ☽ 9am-5pm Mon-Fri)

Coral Gables Chamber of Commerce (Map p95; ☎ 305-446-1657; www.coralgableschamber.org; Omni Colonnade Hotel, 2333 Ponce de León Blvd, Suite 650, Coral Gables; ☽ 9am-5pm Mon-Fri)

Downtown Miami Welcome Center (Map pp92-3; ☎ 305-379-7070; Gusman Center for the Performing Arts, 174 E Flagler St; ☽ 9am-5pm Mon-Fri) Provides maps, brochures and tour information for the downtown area.

Greater Miami & the Beaches Convention & Visitor's Bureau (Map pp92-3; ☎ 305-539-3000, 800-933-8448; www.miamiandbeaches.com; 701 Brickell Ave; ☽ 8:30am-5pm Mon-Fri) Located in an oddly intimidating high-rise building.

Miami Beach Chamber of Commerce (Map pp88-9; ☎ 305-672-1270; www.miamibeachchamber.com; 1920 Meridian Ave, South Beach; ☽ 9am-5pm Mon-Fri)

DANGERS & ANNOYANCES

There are a few areas considered by locals to be dangerous: Liberty City, in northwest Miami; Overtown, from 14th St to 20th St; Little Haiti and stretches of the Miami riverfront; and newly gentrified Biscayne Blvd (after dark) north of the Design District. Obviously, in these and other reputedly 'bad' areas, you should avoid walking around alone late at night, use common sense and travel in groups.

Deserted areas below 5th St in South Beach are more dangerous at night, but your main concerns are probably aggressive drunks or the occasional strung-out druggie, rather than muggers. In downtown Miami, use particular caution near the Greyhound station and around causeways, bridges and overpasses where homeless people and some refugees have set up shantytowns.

Natural dangers include the strong sun (use a high SPF sunscreen), mosquitoes (use a spray-on repellent) and hurricanes (between June and November). There's a **hurricane hotline** (☎ 305-229-4483), which will give you information about approaching storms, storm tracks, warnings, estimated time until touchdown – all the things you will need to make a decision about if and when to leave.

SIGHTS

Miami's 'major sights' are not really concentrated into one neighborhood; rather, there is something for everyone just about everywhere. The most frequently visited area is South Beach, home to hot nightlife, beautiful beaches and art-deco hotels. But you'll find historic sites and museums downtown, art galleries in Wynwood and the Design District, old-fashioned hotels and eateries in Mid-Beach (in Miami Beach), more beaches on Key Biscayne, and peaceful neighborhood attractions in Coral Gables and Coconut Grove.

South Beach
A1A

'Beachfront Avenue!' Driving the **A1A** (Map pp88–9) causeway between Miami and Miami Beach, over the glittering turquoise of Biscayne Bay, with a setting sun behind you, enormous cruise ships to the side, the palms swaying in the ocean breeze and, let's just say 'Your Love' by the Outfield on the radio, is basically the essence of Miami. Just try it, and trust us.

ART DECO HISTORIC DISTRICT

South Beach's heart is its Art Deco Historic District, from 18th St and south along Ocean Dr and Collins Ave. It's (deliciously) ironic that in a city built on fast real estate, the main engine of urban renewal has been the preservation of a unique architectural heritage. All those beautiful hotels, with their tropical-Americana facades, scream 'Miami.' They screamed it so loud when they were preserved they gave this city a brand, and this neighborhood a new lease on life. Back in the day South Beach was a cracked-out ghetto of vagrants, druggies and retirees. Then it became one of the largest areas in the USA on the National Register of Historic Places, and *then* it attracted models, photographers, hoteliers, chefs and…well, today it's a pastel medina of cruisers, Euro-fashionistas, the occasional glimpsed celebrity, and Stan and Fran from Indian(a) who just stepped off the Carnival Cruise Line.

Your first stop here should be the **Art Deco Welcome Center** (Map pp90-1; ☎ 305-531-3484; 1200 Ocean Dr; ☽ 10am-7:30pm Mon-Sat, to 6pm Sun). To be honest, it's a bit of a tatty gift shop, but it's located in the old beach-patrol headquarters, one of the best deco buildings out there. You can book some excellent $20 guided walking tours, which are some of the best introductions to the layout and history of South Beach on offer.

OCEAN DRIVE

Yar, here be the belly of the South Beach beast. It's just a road, right? No, it's the great **cruising strip** (Map pp90–1) of the US; an endless parade of classic cars, testosterone-sweating young men, peacock-y young women, street performers, vendors, those guys who yell unintelligible crap at everyone, celebrities pretending to be tourists, tourists who want to play celebrity, beautiful people, ugly people, people people and the best ribbon of deco preservation on the beach. Say 'Miami.' That image in your head? Probably the Drive.

LINCOLN ROAD MALL

Calling **Lincoln Rd** (Map pp88-9; Lincoln Rd) a mall is like calling Big Ben a clock: it's technically accurate but misses the point. Yes, you can shop, and shop very well here. But this outdoor pedestrian thoroughfare between Alton Rd and Washington Ave is really about seeing and being seen, and there are few better places in Greater Miami for all of the above. Morris Lapidus, one of the founders of the loopy, neo-Baroque Miami-Beach style, designed several buildings on the mall, including the **Lincoln Theatre** (555 Lincoln Rd), **Sterling Building** (927 Lincoln Rd) and **Colony Theater** (1040 Lincoln Rd), which looks like the sort of place where gangsters go to watch *Hamlet*. One standout for art lovers is the **ArtCenter/South Florida** (Map pp88-9; ☎ 305-674-8278; www.artcentersf.org; 800 Lincoln Rd). Established in 1984 by a small but forward-thinking group of artists, this compound is the creative heart of South Beach. In addition to its 52 artists' studios (many of which are open to the public), ArtCenter offers an exciting lineup of classes and lectures. There's also an excellent **farmers market** (9am-6pm Sun) and an **Antiques & Collectibles Market** (9am-5pm, 2nd & 4th Sun of the month), both held along Lincoln Rd.

THE PROMENADE

This beach **promenade** (Map pp90-1; Ocean Ave), a wavy ribbon sandwiched between the beach and Ocean Dr, extends from 5th St to 15th St. A popular location for photo shoots, especially during crowd-free early mornings, it's also a breezy, palm tree–lined conduit for in-line skaters, cyclists, volleyball players (there's a net at 11th St), dog walkers, yahoos, locals

and tourists. The beach that it edges, called Lummus Park, sports six floridly colored lifeguard stands. There's a public bathroom at 11th St; heads up, the sinks are a popular place for homeless bathing.

WOLFSONIAN-FIU

Even folks bored stiff by rooms full of furniture will want to cultivate some aesthetic space after visiting this excellent **design museum** (Map pp90-1; ☎ 305-531-1001; www.wolfsonian.org; 1001 Washington Ave; adult/child under 12yr/student/senior $5/3.50/3.50/3.50; ☺ 11am-9pm Thu, 11am-6pm Fri & Sat, noon-5pm Sun). The Wolfsonian manages to chronicle the interior evolution of everyday life, which is architecturally manifested by the Sobe's (South Beach's) exterior deco. Which reminds us of the Wolfsonian's own noteworthy, unique facade. Remember the gothic-futurist apartment complex–cum–temple of evil in *Ghostbusters*? Well, this imposing structure, with its grandiose 'frozen fountain' and lion head–studded grand elevator, could serve as a stand-in for that set.

POST OFFICE

Make it a point to mail a postcard from this 1937 deco gem of a **post office** (Map pp88-9; ☎ 305-531-3763; 1300 Washington Ave), the very first South Beach renovation project tackled by preservationists in the '70s. This Depression moderne building in the 'stripped classic' style was constructed under President Roosevelt's reign and funded by the Works Progress Administration (WPA) initiative, which supported artists who were out of work during the Great Depression. On the exterior, note the bald eagle and the turret with iron railings, and inside, a large wall mural of the Seminole's Florida invasion.

BASS MUSEUM OF ART

The best art **museum** (Map pp88-9; ☎ 305-673-7530; www.bassmuseum.org; 2121 Park Ave; adult/student/senior $8/6/6; ☺ 10am-5pm Tue, Wed, Fri & Sat, 10am-9pm Thu, 11am-5pm Sun) in Miami Beach has a playfully futurist facade, a crisp interplay of lines and bright, white wall space – like an Orthodox church on a space-age Greek isle. All designed, by the way, in 1930 by Russell Pancoast (grandson of John A Collins, who lent his name to Collins Ave). The collection isn't shabby either: permanent highlights range from 16th-century European religious works to northern European and Renaissance paintings. The Bass forms one

point of the **Collins Park Cultural Center** triangle, which also includes the three-story **Miami City Ballet** and the lovingly inviting **Miami Beach Regional Library**, which is a great place to pick up free wi-fi.

HOLOCAUST MEMORIAL

Holocaust memorials (Map pp88-9; ☎ 305-538-1663; www.holocaustmmb.com; cnr Meridian Ave & Dade Blvd) tend to be somber, but this one, dedicated to the six million Jews killed during the *shoah*, is particularly grim, and doesn't seem to offer any sort of hopeful end note; the theme is one of relentless sadness, betrayal and loss. The light from a Star of David is blotted by the racist meme of 'Jude'; a family surrounded by a hopeful Anne Frank quote is later shown murdered, framed by another Frank quote on the death of ideals and dreams. The memorial was created in 1984 through the efforts of Miami Beach Holocaust survivors and sculptor Kenneth Treister. There are several key pieces, with the *Sculpture of Love and Anguish* the most visible to passersby. The sculpture's enormous, oxidized bronze arm bears an Auschwitz tattooed number – chosen because it was never issued at the camp – and terrified camp prisoners scale the sides of the arm.

MIAMI BEACH BOTANICAL GARDEN

For more contemplation space, head across the street to the **botanical garden** (Map pp88-9; ☎ 305-673-7256; www.mbgarden.org; 2000 Convention Center Dr; admission free; ☺ 9am-5pm); a secret garden in the city. This lush but little-known 4.5 acres of plantings is operated by the Miami Beach Garden Conservancy, and is an oasis of palm trees, flowering hibiscus trees and glassy ponds.

CASA CASUARINA

Perhaps more widely known as the Versace Mansion, **Casa Casuarina** (Map pp90-1; 1114 Ocean Dr; ☺ closed to the public) was the residence of late fashion designer Gianni Versace. Long before Versace, however, the 1930 building was known as the Amsterdam Palace. A Mediterranean Revival house constructed partially of coral and featuring exposed timbers, the three-story palace was modeled after the Governor's House in Santo Domingo (where Christopher Columbus' son laid his head). When Versace purchased the property in the early 1980s, he locked horns with local pres-

ervationists after announcing plans to tear down a neighboring hotel so he could build a pool. After a battle, the moneyed designer won – but also struck a deal that would allow for law changes, saving more than 200 other historic hotels in the process.

None of it mattered in 1997, when the stalking Andrew Cunanan gunned Versace down in front of the beloved mansion. Ironically, the death of this European fashion guru attracted lots of, well, European fashion gurus. Tourists still shuffle by, armed with morbid curiosity and a thirst for celebrity-related photos of any kind. Today, Casa Casuarina is a members-only club with dining options, a day spa and private beach–cabana service.

JEWISH MUSEUM OF FLORIDA

Housed in a 1936 Orthodox synagogue that served Miami's first congregation, this small **museum** (Map pp90-1; ☎ 305-672-5044; www.jewishmuseum.com; 301 Washington Ave; adult/student/senior $6/5/5, Sat admission free; ☺ 10am-5pm Tue-Sun, closed Jewish holidays) chronicles the rather big contribution Jews have made to the state of Florida, especially this corner. After all, while Cubans made Miami, Jews made Miami Beach, both physically (in a developer's sense) and culturally (in an 'anyone is welcome' attitude). Yet there were times when Jews were barred from the American Riviera they carved out of the sand, and this museum tells that story, along with some amusing anecdotes (like seashell Purim dresses). The mainstay is *Mosaic: Jewish Life in Florida*, a mosaic (imagine that) of photographs and historical bric-a-brac. Also notable is the complete whitewash the museum makes of gangster Meyer Lansky – architect of the modern Mafia, who retired to Miami Beach and comes off here as a nice old guy who always donated to his synagogue.

TEMPLE EMANU EL

A deco temple? Not exactly, but the smooth, bubbly dome and sleek, almost aerodynamic profile of this Conservative **synagogue** (Map pp88-9; ☎ 305-538-2503; Washington Ave at 17th St), established in 1938, fits right in on Sobe's deco parade of moderne this and streamline that. Sabbath services are on Fridays at 6:30pm and Saturdays at 8:45am.

ESPAÑOLA WAY PROMENADE

Española Way (Map pp88-9; btwn 14th & 15th St) is an 'authentic' Spanish promenade…in the Florida theme-park spirit of authenticity. Whatever; it's a lovely, terracotta and cobbled arcade of rose pink and Spanish creamy architecture, perfect for art browsing (it was an arts colony in the 1920s), window shopping, people watching and café sippin'. A craft market operates here on weekend afternoons.

WORLD EROTIC ART MUSEUM

In a neighborhood where no behavior is too shocking, the **World Erotic Art Museum** (WEAM; Map pp88–9; ☎ 305-532-9336; www.weam.org; 1205 Washington Ave; admission $18, over 18yr only; ☼ 11am-midnight) screams, 'Hey! We have a giant golden penis!' Unfortunately, that's the problem. We'll sound like nerds if we analyze the historical merits of an old lady's smut collection (the museum was founded by 70-year-old Naomi Wilzig, who turned her 5000-piece private erotica collection into a South Beach attraction in 2005), but WEAM's exhibits lack the context to be taken seriously. There's titillation (no pun intended) without education. In a way, the place makes erotic art *less* accessible by reinforcing its giggle-provoking aspects and…you still with us? Oh fine, the big golden phallus is toward the exit.

Northern Miami Beach

ARTHUR GODFREY ROAD (41ST STREET)

If the **main shopping drag** (Map p94; 41st St) in Miami Beach were a movie, it might be titled 'Jews in Paradise.' It's no *shetl*, but Arthur Godfrey Rd is a popular thoroughfare for the Jewish population of Miami Beach, and possibly the best place outside Manhattan to enjoy a good reuben sandwich (and the only place outside Tel Aviv with kosher sushi houses). Just as Jews have shaped Miami Beach, so has the beach shaped its Jews: you can eat lox *y arroz con moros* (salmon with rice and beans) and while the Orthodox men don yarmulkes and the women wear headscarves, they've all got nice tans and drive flashy SUVs.

EDEN ROC RESORT & FONTAINEBLEAU HILTON HOTEL & RESORT

How over the top is the **Fontainebleau** (Map p94; ☎ 305-538-2000, 800-548-8886; www.fontainebleau.hilton.com; 4441 Collins Ave)? Well, when Brian De Palma needed a place to sign off *Scarface*, he decided this would be the spot for Al Pacino to snort a mountain of coke and slaughter an army of Colombians. You've gotta be grand to warrant that kind of cinematography, and this

iconic 1954 leviathan, another brainchild of Lapidus, is certainly grand. Note the spectacular trompe l'oeil mural on the southern exterior, designed by Richard Hass and painted over an eight-week period by Edwin Abreu. Check out the lagoonlike water park out back and the famous 'stairway to nowhere' in the massive lobby. The **Eden Roc Resort** (Map p94; ☎ 305-531-0000, 800-327-8337; www.edenrocresort.com; 4525 Collins Ave) was the second groundbreaking resort from Lapidus, and it's a fine example of the architecture known as MiMo (Miami Modern). It was the hangout for the 1960s Rat Pack – Sammy Davis Jr, Dean Martin, Frank Sinatra and crew – and at the time of research was undergoing a major renovation into a resort-cum–convention center.

BOARDWALK

What's trendy in beachwear this season? Seventeenth-century Polish gabardine coats, apparently. There are plenty of skimpy hotties on the Mid-Beach **boardwalk** (Map p94; 21st St to 46th St), but sometimes it feels like there are even more Orthodox Jews going about their business in the midst of gay joggers, strolling tourists and preening sunbathers. Not too much preening though; Mid-Beach is more of a 'real' beach (people swim here).

NORMANDY ISLE & OCEAN TERRACE

A few years ago **Normandy Isle** (Map p94; 71st St west of Collins Ave) was dubbed Little Argentina, and it's still one of the best places outside Mendoza to people-watch with a *cortada* (Argentine espresso) before digging into the sort of pasta and steak dishes the *gauchos* love so much. But today the Argentines compete with their neighbors, the Uruguayans, their rivals, the Brazilians, and even a big crop of Colombians, for first place in the Normandy Isle ethnic-enclave stakes. Not that there's tension; this is as prosperous and pleasant as Miami gets. On Saturday mornings the small village green hosts a lovely farmers market. Just across Collins Ave is **Ocean Terrace** (Map p94; beach btwn 73rd St & 75th St), evocative of an old-Miami main street (note the colorfully tiled facade of Walgreens) with oceanfront cafés, MiMo apartment buildings and a strong Argentine flavor.

HAULOVER BEACH PARK

Where are all those tanned men in gold chains and speedos going? That would be the clothing-optional beach in this 40-acre **park** (Map p94; ☎ 305-944-3040; 10800 Collins Ave; per car $4; ☼ sunrise-sunset) hidden from condos, highway and prying eyes by vegetation. There's more to do here than get in the buff though; most of the beach is 'normal' and is one of the nicer spots for sand in the area (also note the colorful deco-ish shower 'cones').

OLETA RIVER STATE PARK

Tequesta Indians were boating the Oleta River estuary (our favorite body of water, by the way) as early as 500 BC, so you're just following in a long tradition if you canoe or kayak in this **park** (Map p94; ☎ 305-919-1846; 3400 NE 163rd St; per person $2, per car $5; ☼ 8am-sunset). At almost 1000 acres, this is the largest urban park in the state and one of the best places in Miami to escape the maddening throng. Boat out to the local mangrove island, watch the eagles fly by, or just chill on the pretension-free beach. On-site **Blue Moon Outdoor Center** (☎ 305-957-3040) offers single kayaks ($18 per 1½ hours, $25 per three hours), tandem kayaks ($25.50 per 1½ hours, $40 per three hours) and bike rental ($18 per 1½ hours, $25 per three hours).

PELICAN ISLAND

On weekends you can take a short escape to itsy-bitsy **Pelican Island** (Map p94) on a free ferry from the JFK Causeway west of North Bay Village (about 2 miles west of 71st St in Miami Beach). It's a pleasant little place to unpack a picnic and peer at dozens of congregating pelicans, all with the long and lovely beach stretched before you.

Downtown Miami

ADRIENNE ARSHT CENTER FOR THE PERFORMING ARTS

The second largest **performing arts center** (Map pp92-3; ☎ 305-949-6722, 786-468-2000; www .arshtcenter.com; 1300 N Biscayne Blvd) in the USA is Miami's beautiful, beloved baby. It is also a major component of downtown's urban equivalent of a facelift and several regimens of botox. Designed by Cesar Pelli (the man who brought you Kuala Lumpur's Pertonas Towers), the center has two main components: the Ziff Ballet Opera House and Knight Concert Hall, which span both sides of Biscayne Blvd. The venues are connected by a thin, elegant pedestrian bridge, while inside the theaters there's a sense of ocean and land sculpted by wind; the rounded balconies

rise up in spirals that resemble a sliced-open seashell. It took five years and a *lot* of money to get the Arsht Center open and running, but now (almost) everyone loves it, including big-name performers from around the world, particularly Latin America.

BAYFRONT

You'll find many of downtown's attractions clustered around the waterfront, including **Bayfront Park** (Map pp92-3; www.bayfrontparkmiami .com; 301 N Biscayne Blvd). Few parks can claim to front such a lovely stretch of turquoise (Biscayne Bay), but Miamians are lucky like that. Lots of office workers catch quick naps under the palms at a little beach that does you the favor of setting out 'sit and chill' chairs. The beach is adjacent to the **Miami Sky Lift** (Map pp92-3; ☎ 305-444-0422; http://miamiskylift.com; adult/child $15.89/8.88; ☼ 11am-7pm, to 10pm Fri & Sat), an 'elevated viewing platform' (ie balloon) that takes up to 30 people on a 15-minute photo op over the city. Other notable park features (besides vagrants) are two performance venues: the **Bayfront Park Amphitheater** is a good spot for July 4 and New Year's Eve, while the smaller 200-seat **South End Amphitheater** hosts free springtime performances. In the southwest corner is the **Challenger Memorial**, a monument designed by Isamu Noguchi for the astronauts killed in the 1986 space-shuttle explosion. Also look north for the **JFK Torch of Friendship**, a fountain recognizing the accomplishments of longtime US congressman Claude Pepper, and for the sleek **American Airlines Arena** (Map pp92-3; 601 Biscayne Blvd). Looking like a massive spaceship that perpetually hovers at the edge of Biscayne Bay, this has been the home of the Miami Heat basketball team since 2000.

Just south of the arena is the **Bayside Marketplace** (Map pp92-3; ☎ 305-577-3344; www .baysidemarketplace.com; 401 Biscayne Blvd), packed to the gills with chain stores you could find in any other town in the Western world. It's nice, for a mall. But it's just a mall.

HISTORICAL MUSEUM OF SOUTHERN FLORIDA

It takes a special kind of history to create the idiosyncratic character of a place like South Florida, and it takes a special kind of **museum** (Map pp92-3; ☎ 305-375-1492; www.hmsf.org; 101 W Flagler St; adult/child 6-12yr/senior $8/5/7, Sun admission free; ☼ 10am-5pm Mon-Sat, noon-5pm Sun) to capture that narrative. This place, located in the

MIAMI

WE BUILT THIS CITY! (ON MUSEUMS & PARKS)

Miami's downtown has always been the ugly stepsister to the tourist-magnet beaches. Critics (with some justification) attack the sharp dichotomies between high office buildings and dead blocks of shuttered shopfronts, and say the downtown grid lacks a cohesive pedestrian-friendly center. At the same time, designers (with perhaps less justification) say the elevated Miami-Dade Cultural Center's Spanish-style compound is publicly inaccessible because of its perch on high concrete foundations.

To reverse these perceptions, the city of Miami has decided to hedge its bets on the grand reimagining, rebuilding and reopening of two of its main museums: the **Miami Art Museum** (below) and **Miami Museum of Science & Planetarium** (p115). The two institutions will occupy what is currently abandoned Bicentennial Park, turning this swath of dried-out green space into (everyone hopes) a showcase for two world-class yet distinctly Miami museums in a distinctly Miami setting.

It's an ambitious idea, but it seems worthy too; rather than using unchecked condo lots to resurrect downtown, Miami wants to let the arts and sciences take a crack at performing the facelift. Blueprints for the new art museum look incredible: a series of 'floating' exhibits, seemingly unconnected to the ground, will rise out of a tropical hammock (forest), supported by 'living pillars' – columns enveloped in local plantlife. These green supports and their shade, plus the wind off Biscayne Bay, will provide a natural cooling mechanism for museum-goers. In addition, the relocation of the museum will allow it to redefine (and expand) its permanent collection.

The whole plan sounds like it will involve a lot of money and more hope. But the Arsht Center faced the same odds. We hope, in 2010, when the new art museum is set to open (the science museum will open in 2011), we can say Miami took the right step toward revitalization when it put its money on the museums.

Miami-Dade Cultural Center, does just that, weaving together the stories of the region's successive waves of population, from American Indians to Nicaraguans. It's interesting for kids and open late (10am to 9pm) on the third Thursday of the month. Get off the Metromover at Government Center stop.

The next door **Miami-Dade Public Library** is a lovely escape from downtown's bustle. And if you've got the time, book a tour with Dr Paul George, Florida native, Historical Museum of Southern Florida historian, author and eccentric history buff, for a peek under the ultramodern skin of this city. See Al Capone's house, cruise the rumrunner routes or go back further to Tequesta times; call ☎ 305-375-1621 or email historictours@hmsf.org for more info. Tours generally run between $25 and $42.

MIAMI ART MUSEUM

Also within the Miami-Dade Cultural Center, this **museum** (MAM; Map pp92-3; ☎ 305-375-3000; www .miamiartmuseum.org; 101 W Flagler St; adult/child under 12yr/student/senior $5/free/2.50/2.50, Sun admission free; ☒ 10am-5pm Tue-Fri, noon-5pm Sat & Sun) is ensconced in spectacular Philip Johnson–designed digs. Without having a permanent collection, its fine rotating exhibits concentrate on post-WWII international art. In 2010, MAM will be moving to a new waterfront location at Bicentennial Park (above); the future of the current location is up in the air, but both the library and historical society have expressed interest in moving into the space. The museum is open late (noon to 9pm) on the third Thursday of the month.

FREEDOM TOWER

Designed by the New York architectural firm of Shultz & Weaver in 1925, this **tower** (Map pp92-3; 600 Biscayne Blvd) is one of two surviving towers modeled after the Giralda bell tower in Spain's Cathedral of Seville (the second is at the Biltmore Hotel in Coral Gables, p116). The 'Ellis Island of the South,' it served as an immigration processing center for almost half a million Cuban refugees in the 1960s. Placed on the National Register of Historic Places in 1979, it was also home to the *Miami Daily News* for 32 years.

METROMOVER

This elevated, electric **monorail** (Map pp92-3; www .miamidade.gov/transit) is hardly big enough to serve the mass transit needs of the city, and has become something of a tourist attraction and occasional commuting tool. Because it's free, Metromover has also become a hangout for the homeless, making the monorail an interesting place to gain insights into the grittier character of the city.

MIAMI RIVER

For a taste of a seedy Old Florida that reeks of Humphrey Bogart in shirt sleeves and a fedora, come to the lazy, sultry and still kinda spicy **Miami River** (Map pp92–3). Much of the shore feels abandoned, and is lined with makeshift warehouses, where you-can-only-imagine-what is loaded and unloaded onto small tugboats bound for you-can-only-imagine-where. Fisherfolk float in with their daily catch, fancy yachts 'slumming it' dock at restaurants, and nonconformists hang out on their houseboats.

OLD US POST OFFICE

Constructed in 1912, this **post office** (Map pp92-3; 100 NE 1st Ave; ☺ 9am-5pm Mon-Fri) and county courthouse served as the first federal building in Miami. The building, which features a low-pitched roof, elaborate doors and carved entryways, was purchased in 1937 to serve as the country's first savings and loan (funny, considering S&Ls helped build Miami in the 1980s). Check out Denman Fink's 1940 mural *Law Guides Florida Progress* in the main courtroom on the 2nd floor.

CISNEROS FONTANAL ARTS FOUNDATION (CIFO)

The **arts foundation** (Map pp92-3; ☎ 305-455-3380; www.cifo.org; 1018 N Miami Ave) is one of the best spots in Miami to catch the work of contemporary Latin American artists, and has a pretty impressive showroom to boot. Even the exterior blends post-industrial rawness with a lurking, natural ambience, offset by the extensive use of Bisazza tiles to create an overarching tropical motif. Similar to the Arsht Center, CIFO was built near the rattier edge of downtown with the intention of revitalizing this semi-blighted area with fresh arts spaces.

TOBACCO ROAD

Just south of the Miami River Bridge, **Tobacco Road** (Map pp92-3; ☎ 305-374-1198; 626 S Miami Ave; ☺ 11:30am-5am Mon-Sat, 1pm-5am Sun) proudly reminds you its liquor license was the first one issued in a city that loves its mojitos. Tobacco

Road has been here since the 1920s when it was a Prohibition-era speakeasy; today it's a decent (if slightly touristy) place to order a drink or listen to live music. Film buffs may recognize it as the place where Kurt Russell has a drink in *The Mean Season* (1985). Jump off the Metromover at the 8th St stop.

BRICKELL AVENUE BRIDGE & BRICKELL KEY

Crossing the Miami River, this lovely **bridge** (Map pp92-3; Brickell Ave) between SE 4th St and SE 5th St was made wider and higher several years ago, which was convenient for the speedboat-driving drug runners being chased by Drug Enforcement Administration agents on the day of the bridge's grand reopening! Note the 17ft bronze statue by Cuban-born sculptor Manuel Carbonell of a Tequesta warrior and his family, which sits perched atop the towering Pillar of History column. It can be tough to appreciate the bridge from your car; you may want to walk here to get a sense of the sculptures.

Nearby **Brickell Key** (Map pp92-3; at SW 8th St) looks like a floating porcupine with condos for quills, and is worth visiting to get a scary glimpse of a world where real-estate barons rule unopposed. To live the life of Miami glitterati, come here, pretend you belong, and head into a patrician hangout like the Mandarin Oriental Miami hotel, where the lobby and intimate lounges afford sweeping views of Biscayne Bay.

DADE COUNTY COURTHOUSE

If you end up on trial here, at least you'll get a free tour of one of the most imposing **courthouses** (Map pp92-3; 73 W Flagler St) in the USA. When Miami outgrew its first courthouse it moved legal proceedings to this neoclassical icon, built between 1925 and 1929 for $4 million. It's a very…appropriate building; if structures were people, the courthouse would *definitely* be a judge. Some useless trivia: back in the day, the top nine floors served as a 'secure' prison, from which more than 70 prisoners escaped.

GUSMAN CENTER FOR THE PERFORMING ARTS

The Arsht Center is modernly pretty, but the Olympia Theater at **Gusman Center for the Performing Arts** (Map pp92-3; 174 E Flagler St) is a one-of-a-kind classic. You know how the kids in Hogwarts can see the sky through

MIAMI

their dininghall roof? Well the Olympia recreates the whole effect sans Dumbledore, using 246 twinkling stars and clouds cast over an indigo-deep, sensual shade of a ceiling. The theater first opened in 1925; today the lobby serves as the Downtown Miami Welcome Center (p103), doling out helpful visitor information and organizing tours of the historic district; at night you can still catch theater and music performances.

LYRIC THEATRE

Hallowed names such as Duke Ellington and Ella Fitzgerald walked across the **Lyric** (Map pp92-3; ☎ 305-358-1146; 819 NW 2nd Ave) stage when it was a major stop on the 'Chitlin' Circuit' – the black live-entertainment trail of pre-integration USA. But as years passed both the theater and the neighborhood it served, Overtown, fell into dysfunctional disuse. Then the Black Archives History & Research Center of South Florida (p103) kicked in $1.5 million for renovations and overhauled everything. The phoenix reopened its doors in 1999 to appreciative neighbors, civic leaders and entertainers alike. A 2003 expansion feels a little too modern when juxtaposed with the Lyric's elegant early-20th-century exterior, but it's shiny, we guess.

Wynwood, Design District & Little Haiti
MOCA AT GOLDMAN WAREHOUSE

Thank God the **Museum of Contemporary Art** (MoCA; Map p97; ☎ 305-573-5411; www.mocanomi .org/warehouse; 404 NW 26th St; ☺ noon-5pm Wed-Sat) expanded into this Wynwood satellite; the main exhibit, while worth the drive, is a ways away (see p118). In the meantime, the MoCA at Goldman has dibs on this space through 2009; it's a good, downtown-adjacent spot to see some of the highlights of the MoCA's excellent collection. Open until 7pm on the second Saturday of every month.

RUBELL FAMILY ART COLLECTION

The Rubell family – specifically, the niece and nephew of the late Steve, better known as Ian Schrager's Studio 54 partner – operates some top-end hotels in Miami Beach, but they've also amassed an impressive **contemporary art collection** (Map p97; ☎ 305-573-6090; www.rubellfamily collection.com; 95 NW 29th St, Wynwood; adult/student/senior $10/5/5; ☺ 10am-6pm Wed-Sat Dec-May) that spans the last 30 years. The most admirable quality of this collection is its commitment to not just displaying one or two of its artists' pieces;

rather, the aim is to focus on a contributor's entire career.

MIAMI CITY CEMETERY

Fast fact: the first person buried in Miami was black. Depressing addendum: the first *recorded* burial in Miami was of a white guy. The long narrative of this troubled, diverse city is in its bones, and dem bones are concentrated in this eerie, quiet **graveyard** (Map p97; ☎ 305-579-6938; 1800 NE 2nd Ave; admission free; ☺ 7am-3:30pm Mon-Fri, 8am-4:30pm Sat & Sun). The dichotomy of history and modernity gets a nice visual representation in the form of looming condos shadowing the last abode of the Magic City's late, great ones. More than 9000 graves are divided into separate white, black and Jewish sections. Buried here are mayors, veterans (including about 90 Confederate soldiers) and the godmother of South Florida, Julia Tuttle herself.

HAITIAN HERITAGE MUSEUM

Miami has the largest community of *Ayisens* (Haitians) in the world outside Haiti; come to this **museum** (Map p97; ☎ 305-371-5988; 3940 N Miami Ave; ☺ by appointment) to learn their story. The museum aims to be a comprehensive mosaic of Miami's Haitian community and draws off the collection in the Diaspora Vibe Gallery, which hosts consistently excellent Caribbean and Latin American artists. At the time of research, you needed to call ahead to get inside, so make an appointment before you visit.

MAJOR ART SPACES

The galleries and design showcases in the Design District are of course multitudinous, but starting with some must-sees is a good way to stay focused.

The experimental gallery called the **Moore Space** (Map p97; ☎ 305-438-1163; www.themoorespace .org; 4040 NE 2nd Ave; ☺ 10am-5pm Wed-Sat) stands apart for a few simple reasons – its large size, historic structure (the 1920s Moore Furniture Company building) and extensive programming. Conceived in response to the first Art Basel Miami Beach, exhibits are hit 'n' miss, but always interesting – when we stopped in, one of the pieces was a looped video of a French guy crushing a coke can with his foot. Deep, man.

One great, small art and design 'mall,' for lack of a better word, is the **Melin Building** (Map p97; 3930 NE 2nd Ave), which is centered upon a shoe fetishist's most lurid fantasy – *Gondola Shoe* by Antoni Miralda, a one-story high…well, shoe.

Other stops in Melin include the Kartell design store. Call ahead as opening hours vary.

The **Buick Building** (Map p97; ☎ 305-573-8116; 3841 NE 2nd Ave; ☉ by appointment), meanwhile, has been known to exhibit some outstanding installation shows, but it's known as the gateway of the Design District because of its striking mural facade. Done on canvas in bright yellow and black, the images of Roman mythological figures were painted in 2000 by the married artist team of Roberto Behar and Rosario Marquardt (see the *Living Room*, below).

There are commercial galleries galore here; these are two favorites. Look for the squat black building emblazoned with the slogan 'I [Heart] New Art' and you'll have found **Locust Projects** (Map p97; ☎ 305-576-8570; www.locustprojects .org; 105 NW 23rd St; ☉ noon-5pm Thu-Sat), widely regarded as one of the edgier art spaces in the district (which can be a compliment or insult depending on your tastes).

Vagrant, convict and creator, Purvis Young (1943–) is Overtown's favorite native son. Although the work in his **gallery** (Map p97; ☎ 305-785-8833; 1753 NE 2nd Ave) is dubbed 'outsider' or 'folk' art (ie he didn't go to art school), we'd just classify it as good. His paintings, often done on pieces of wood and carpet samples, portray ink-blotty mothers, horses, angels, African idols and people striving for freedom from an ambiguous captivity – a poignant and well-realized message in studio spaces that abut Miami's poorest neighborhoods.

LIVING ROOM
Just to remind you that you're entering the Design District is a big, honking, public art **installation** (Map p97; cnr NW 40th St & N Miami Ave) of, yep, a living room, just the sort of thing you're supposed to shop for while you're here. Actually this Living Room, by Argentine husband-and-wife team Roberto Behar and Rosario Marquardt, is an 'urban intervention' meant to be a criticism of the disappearance of public space, but we think it serves as a nice metaphor for the Design District as a whole: a contemporary interior plopped into the middle of urban decay.

BACARDI BUILDING
You don't need to down 151 to appreciate the striking Miami headquarters of the world's largest family-owned spirits company, **Bacardi** (Map p97; ☎ 305-573-8511; 2100 Biscayne Blvd; admission free; ☉ 9am-3:30pm or 4pm Mon-Fri). The main event is a beautifully decorated tower that looks like the mosaic pattern of a tropical bathhouse on steroids; inside is a small art gallery and museum dedicated to the famously anti-Castro Bacardis (think about what 'Cuba Libre' actually means the next time you order one).

LITTLE HAITI CULTURAL STOPS
If you haven't been to Port-au-Prince, then Little Haiti (La Petite Haïti), one of the most evocative neighborhoods in Miami, is the next best thing. Young men in tank tops listen to Francophone rap, while broad-necked women wearing bright wraps gossip in front of the *botanicas* – which, by the way, are not selling plants. A *botanica* here is a *vodou* shop.

The storefronts promise to help in matters of love, work and sometimes 'immigration services,' but trust us, there are no marriage

---

PAPA LEIDER ANDRE

We spoke to Papa Leider Andre, a *vodou* priest in Little Haiti, about the intricacies of his religion.

Who do vodou worshipers pray to? One God. Only one God. Priests talk to God, and the *loa*.

Who are the loa? There are many *loa*. Dambala is one, Papa Legba. They go between. You talk to God first. The *loa* is second. First to God and then to the spirit.

What's your role in the community? If you go to the doctor and the doctor can say nothing, I can. *Houngan* (priests) and *mambos* (priestesses) are here to make you feel good. I learned (to be a priest) from my godmother and I've taught my children.

How do you communicate with God? You pray to God. You address God, and take a few minutes to take His power.

Does anyone ask you to hurt people? No, if you want to help yourself, I'm here for you. I don't hurt people. (Pauses) But I can refer you.

Papa Leider Andre is a vodou priest in Little Haiti who runs 3x3 Santa Barbara Botanica
(☎ 786-262-7895; 5700 NE 2nd Ave).

counselors or INS guys in here. As you enter *botanicas* you'll probably get a funny look, but be courteous, curious and respectful, and you should be welcomed. Before you browse, forget your stereotypes about pins and dolls. Like many traditional religions, *vodou* recognizes supernatural forces in everyday objects, and powers that are both distinct and part of one overarching deity. Ergo, you'll see shrines to Jesus next to altars to traditional *vodou* deities. Notice the large statues of what look like people; these actually represent *loa* (pronounced lwa), intermediary spirits that form a pantheon below God in the *vodou* religious hierarchy. Drop a coin into a *loa* offering bowl before you leave, especially to Papa Legba, spirit of crossroads and, by our reckoning, travelers. Two good *botanicas* are **Vierge Miracle & St Phillipe** (Map p97; 5910 NE 2nd Ave) and **3x3 Santa Barbara Botanica** (Map p97; ☎ 786-262-7895; 5700 NE 2nd Ave). Also see the boxed text, p111.

LIBRERI MAPOU
For another taste of Haitian culture, peruse the shelves at this **bookstore** (Map p97; ☎ 305-757-9922; 5919 NE 2nd Ave), bursting with 3000 titles (including periodicals) in English, French and Creole, as well as crafts and recorded music.

Key Biscayne
BILL BAGGS CAPE FLORIDA STATE RECREATION AREA
If you don't make it to the Florida Keys, come to this **park** (Map p98; ☎ 305-361-5811; www.florida stateparks.org/capeflorida; 1200 S Crandon Blvd; per person $2, per car $4, pedestrian $1; ☼ 8am-sunset) for a taste of their unique island ecosystem. The 494-acre space is a tangled clot of tropical fauna and dark mangroves – look for the 'snorkel' roots that provide air for half-submerged mangrove trees – all interconnected by sandy trails and wooden boardwalks, and surrounded by miles of pale ocean. A concession shack rents kayaks, bikes, rollerblades, beach chairs and umbrellas.

MIAMI SEAQUARIUM
This 38-acre marine-life **park** (Map p98; ☎ 305-361-5705; www.miamiseaquarium.com; 4400 Rickenbacker Causeway; adult/child $31.95/25.95; ☼ 9:30am-6pm, last entry 4:30pm) excels in preserving, protecting and educating about aquatic creatures, and was one of the country's first places dedicated to sea life. There are dozens of shows and exhibits, including a tropical reef; the Shark Channel,

with feeding presentations; and Discovery Bay, a natural mangrove habitat that serves as a refuge for rehabilitating rescued sea turtles. Check out the Pacific white-sided dolphins or West Indian manatees being nursed back to health; some are released. Frequent shows put gorgeous animals on display for the audience's amusement; shows include a massive killer whale, and some precious dolphins and sea lions. The Seaquarium's newly opened Dolphin Harbor is an especially fun venue for watching marine mammals play and show off; it also offers swim-with-the-cetacean fun via its Encounter (adult/child five to nine years $139/99) and Odyssey ($199). Note that children under five cannot participate in the Encounter, people under 5ft 2in cannot participate in the Odyssey and children under three cannot enter the observation area. Read up about the pros and cons of swimming with dolphins (see boxed text, p193) before committing to these programs.

CRANDON PARK
This 1200-acre park boasts Crandon Park Beach, a glorious but crowded beach that stretches for 3 miles. Much of the park consists of a dense coastal hammock (hardwood forest) and mangrove swamps. Then there's the wonderful **Marjory Stoneman Douglas Biscayne Nature Center** (Map p98; ☎ 305-361-6767; www.biscaynenaturecenter.org; Crandon Park, 6767 Crandon Blvd; admission free; ☼ 10am-4pm). Marjory Stoneman Douglas was a beloved environmental crusader (see boxed text, p166); the nature center is a perfect little introduction and exploration of the continental USA's own subtropical ecosystem: South Florida. There are weekend hikes and nature lessons (including programs for tots) that let kids wade into the water with nets and try to catch sea horses, sponges and other marine life (released after a short lesson).

CAPE FLORIDA LIGHTHOUSE
At the state recreation area's southernmost tip, the 1845 brick **lighthouse** (Map p98; ☎ 305-361-8779; Bill Baggs Cape Florida State Recreation Area) is the oldest structure in Florida (it replaced another lighthouse that was severely damaged in 1836 by attacking Seminole Indians). You can tour it for free at 10am and 1pm daily. Tours are limited to 12 people, so put your name on a sign-up list at least 30 minutes prior to the tour.

JIMBO'S: THE HAPPIEST PLACE ON EARTH

It's the simple things that make life worth living, and sometimes their simplicity is even more elegant in the face of life's complexity. To wit: come to **Jimbo's** (Map p98; ☎ 305-361-7026; www .jimbosplace.com; Duck Lake Rd) in Virginia Key. In a city of unfettered development, this bar…no, shrimp shack…no, smoked fish house…no, 24-hour trailer park bonfire…well, whatever. A series of dilapidated river shacks (and a bocce court) has been, for decades, its own version of everything that once was right in Florida. Of course, even here the vibe is a little artificial; all those rotting fish houses were set pieces for the 1980 horror movie *Island Claws*. Other flicks filmed here include *Ace Ventura, True Lies* and the cinematic masterpiece, *Porky's 2*. But today the shacks have been claimed as the set pieces of the Jimbo show. The point is, this place is unique, and artificial, and authentic, or all of the above; you just gotta drop in. To find Jimbo's go to the end of Arthur Lamb Jr Rd.

BISCAYNE COMMUNITY CENTER & VILLAGE GREEN PARK

A fantastic **park** (Map p98; ☎ 305-365-8900; http:// keybiscayne.fl.gov/pr; Village Green Way, off Crandon Blvd; ☺ Community Center 6am-10pm Mon-Fri, 6am-8pm Sat & Sun) for the kids; there's a swimming pool, a park full of jungle gyms, an activity room with a playset out of a child's happiest fantasies and an African Balboa tree that's over a century old and teeming with tropical birdlife. Did we mention it's free? The unmissable park and community center are west of Crandon Blvd.

STILTSVILLE

This collection of **seven houses** (Map p98; www .stiltsville.org) that stand on pilings out in Biscayne Bay has been around since the early '30s. You can view them, way out in the distance, from the southern shore of the Bill Baggs park, or take a **boat tour** (☎ 305-375-1621; $44) out there with the illustrious historian Dr Paul George. In 2003, the nonprofit Stiltsville Trust was set up by the National Parks Service to rehabilitate the buildings into as-yet-unknown facilities; proposals include a National Parks Service visitor center, artist-in-residence colony or community center. For updates, call the Stiltsville Trust on ☎ 305-443-2266.

Little Havana

MONUMENTS

The two blocks of SW 13th Ave south of Calle Ocho contain a series of monuments to Cuban patriots and freedom fighters, including those that died in the Cuban independence struggle and anti-Castro conflicts. The memorials include the **Eternal Torch in Honor of the 2506th Brigade** (Map p96) for the exiles who died during the botched Bay of Pigs invasion; a huge **Cuba brass relief** (Map p96) depicting a map of Cuba, dedicated to the 'ideals of people who will never forget the pledge of making their Fatherland free'; a **José Martí memorial** (Map p96); and a **Madonna statue** (Map p96), which is supposedly illuminated by a shaft of holy light every afternoon. Bursting out of the island in the center of the boulevard is a massive ceiba tree, revered by followers of *Santeria* (Cuban *vodou*). The tree is an unofficial reminder of the poorer *Marielitos* (those who fled Cuba in the 1980 Mariel Boatlift) and successive waves of desperate-for-work Cubans, many of whom are *Santeros* (*Santeria* practitioners) who have come to Miami since the 1980s.

Just a bit away from the main drag are a fountain and monument, collectively entitled **La Plaza de la Cubanidad** (Map p96; cnr W Flagler St & NW 17th Ave). It's a tribute both to the Cuban provinces and to the people who were drowned by Castro's forces while trying to escape from Cuba in 1994 on a ship, *13 de Mayo*, which was sunk just off the coast.

CALLE OCHO

Little Havana's main thoroughfare is SW 8th St, better know by its Spanish name of **Calle Ocho** (Map p96). In a lot of ways, it's every immigrant enclave in the USA, full of foreign restaurants, mom-and-pop convenience shops and cheap phonecard sales. But it's also the public face that Miami's Cubans – many of whom have made their fortune and left this neighborhood – present to the world. Thus, the Cubaness of Calle Ocho is slightly exaggerated for visitors. On the other hand, this is a real street serving real people, and past the embellishment there is a real community going about their lives.

MIAMI

MÁXIMO GÓMEZ PARK

Little Havana's most evocative reminder of Old Cuba is **Máximo Gómez Park** (Map p96; SW 8th St at SW 15th Ave; ☺ 9am-6pm), or 'Domino Park,' where the sound of elderly men trash-talking over games of chess is harmonized by the quick clak-clak of slapping dominoes. The jarring backtrack, plus the heavy smell of cigars and a sunrise-bright mural of the 1993 Summit of the Americas, combine to make Máximo Gómez one of the most sensory sites in Miami.

BAY OF PIGS MUSEUM & LIBRARY

This small **museum** (Map p96; ☎ 305-649-4719; 1821 SW 9th St; admission free; ☺ 10am-5pm Mon-Fri) is more of a memorial to the 2506th Brigade, otherwise known as the crew of the ill-fated Bay of Pigs invasion. Whatever your thoughts on Fidel Castro and Cuban-Americans, pay a visit here to flesh out one side of this contentious story. You'll likely chat with survivors of the Bay of Pigs, who like to hang out here surrounded by pictures of comrades who never made it back to the USA.

LITTLE HAVANA ART DISTRICT

OK, it's not Wynwood. In fact, it's more an 'Art Block' than **district** (Map p96; SW 8th St, btwn SW 15th Ave & SW 17th Ave). But this little strip of galleries and studios does house one of the best concentrations of Latin American art (particularly from Cuba) in Miami. Any one of the studios is worth a stop and a browse; check out the Cuban art in **Latin Art Core/Maxoly** (Map p96; ☎ 305-631-0025; 1600 SW 8th St).

TOWER THEATER

This recently renovated 1926 landmark **theater** (Map p96; ☎ 305-649-2960; 1508 SW 8th St) has a proud deco facade and a newly done interior, thanks to recent support from the Miami-Dade Community College the space has been brought back to life with frequent Spanish-language films and varied art exhibits in the lobby.

CASA ELIÁN

The surreal **house of Elián Gonzales** (Map p96; 2319 NW 2nd St; admission by donation; ☺ 10am-6pm), the subject of one of the most bitter international

---

FELIX RODRIGUEZ

We spoke with Felix Rodriguez, a Cuban resident of Miami who captured Che Guevera in Bolivia.

Can you describe how the operation to capture Che occurred? In 1967 the CIA sent me to Bolivia to help the Bolivian army capture Che. He was down to a few followers by then. He's the only guerilla I know of who couldn't recruit a single farmer. Most people claim we had electronic surveillance and satellites and stuff. Bullshit. We had a man who spoke Quechua who spoke to a farmer who said he heard noises where there should be none. When we finally found Che, he said, 'Don't shoot! I'm Che Guevera.' And then we confirmed it was 'The Foreigner' (the codename for Che).

What happened then? He didn't know I was Cuban at first. Then he said, 'You're Puerto Rican. Or Cuban. And I would guess Cuban.' And I said, 'I am a Cuban, and I was at the Bay of Pigs.'

How did he die? As far as the US government was concerned, we wanted him alive. We wanted to win him over because we knew he had fallen out with Castro. Then an execution order came over the phone (from the Bolivian military). We tried to change their minds. A woman came with a radio and said, 'Why don't you kill him? On the radio they say he died of combat wounds.' Then I knew there was no other way. I told Che, 'I'm sorry.' He turned white and said, 'It's better this way. I should never have been captured alive.' Then he said sarcastically, 'Tell Fidel he can expect a successful revolution in the Americas.' And added, sincerely, 'Tell my wife to be happy and remarry.' I left and told the executor to shoot him below the neck, because he was supposed to have died of combat wounds.

What do you think of the cult of personality that has evolved around Che? I knew a woman in Cuba who had a 15-year-old son who wrote some anti-Castro graffiti. This lady went to Che to personally appeal for her son. He said, 'What is your son's name?' And when she told him, he said, 'Execute so-and-so so his mother does not have to wait.' Instead of inspiring respect, Che inspired fear.

Felix Rodriguez is an ex-CIA officer.

ADIOS, FIDEL?

In the past, rumors of Fidel's ill health have set off street carnivals in Little Havana. Hostility is so strong, that when Rafael Del Pino, a Cuban defector, recently suggested some détente with his motherland, a caller to Radio Mambi commented that he should be lynched.

So in 2008, when Castro finally announced his intent to step down from power, surely a party must have broken out? At least a handover-of-power mojito? Nope. The reaction among Cuban exiles never topped cautious optimism. Will Fidel's brother and successor Raul be a reformer? Delfin Gonzalez, uncle of the famous Elián, told us: 'Fidel, Raul – they have the same mother.' The newest wave of Cuban immigrants – the working class who've been coming to the US since the late '70s – defined the public face of the community response. They have little love of Castro, but are more concerned with making a better life for themselves than settling political scores.

One Cuban waitress tersely reacted to the news of Castro's departure with these these words: 'I don't have time for the news.' Then she went back to work.

---

custody battles of the 1990s, is a shrine, time capsule and exercise in public iconography. Since 2001, the house has been a temple of anti-Castro, Cuban-exile symbology. The little property is scattered with homages to Jesus, US flags and images of Elián himself, who is all but explicitly labeled a little saint of his people. Elián's great-uncle Delfin bought the house in late 2000, then froze time inside: Elian's clothes hang in the closet, the inner tube that saved his life at sea hangs on the wall, and his Spiderman pajamas are laid out on the bed. And then there's the life-sized enlargement of the Pulitzer Prize–winning photograph of Elián hiding in the closet and being seized by federal border-patrol agents at gunpoint. When we came, Delfin seemed surprised to see us, and we assume visitors have slacked off as memory of the Elián affair has faded.

Coconut Grove

VIZCAYA MUSEUM & GARDENS

They call Miami the Magic City, and if it is, this Italian **villa** (Map pp86-7; ☎ 305-250-9133; www .vizcayamuseum.com; 3251 S Miami Ave; adult/child $12/5; ⌚ museum 9:30am-5pm, last admission 4:30pm, gardens 9:30am-5:30pm), the housing equivalent of a Fabergé egg, is its most fairy-tale residence. In 1916, industrialist James Deering started a long and storied Miami tradition by making a ton of money and building some ridiculously grandiose digs. James Deering employed 1000 people (then 10% of the local population) for four years to fulfill his desire for a pad that looked centuries old. He was so obsessed with creating an atmosphere of old money that he had the house stuffed with 15th- to 19th-century furniture, tapestries, paintings and decorative arts; had a monogram fashioned

for himself; and even had paintings of fake ancestors commissioned. The 30-acre grounds are full of splendid gardens and Florentine gazebos, and both the house and gardens are used for the display of rotating contemporary-art exhibits.

COCOWALK & STREETS OF MAYFAIR

Credited for reviving Coconut Grove during the 1990s, **CocoWalk** (Map p99; ☎ 305-444-0777; 3015 Grand Ave) and **Streets of Mayfair** (Map p99; ☎ 305-448-1700; 2911 Grand Ave), a pair of alfresco malls housing ubiquitous chain stores, are perhaps (inexplicably) the Grove's biggest tourist drawcard. Go and see them for yourself if you must, but it's really just a big, bustling collection of the usual suspects.

BARNACLE HISTORIC STATE PARK

In the center of the village is the 1891, 5-acre **pioneer residence** (Map p99; ☎ 305-448-9445; 3485 Main Hwy; admission $1; ⌚ park 9am-4pm Fri-Mon, house tours 10am, 11:30am, 1pm, 2:30pm Fri-Mon) of Ralph Monroe, Miami's first honorable snowbird. The house is open for guided tours, led by folks who are quite knowledgeable and enthusiastic about the park – which is, by the way, a lovely, shady oasis for strolling. Barnacle hosts frequent (and lovely) moonlight concerts, from jazz to classical.

MIAMI MUSEUM OF SCIENCE & PLANETARIUM

This Smithsonian-affiliated **museum** (Map pp86-7; ☎ 305-646-4200; www.miamisci.org; 3280 S Miami Ave; adult/child/student/senior $10/6/8/8; ⌚ 10am-6pm) has an incredible range of great hands-on, creative exhibits. The exhibits range from weather phenomena to creepy crawlies, coral reefs and vital-microbe displays. The planetarium hosts space lessons and telescope-viewing sessions, as well as old-school laser shows with trippy flashes set to the Beatles and Pink Floyd. Kids especially love the outdoor Wildlife Center, with its dangerous animals of South Florida and exotic birds of prey.

COCONUT GROVE PLAYHOUSE

Miami's oldest **theater** (Map p99; www.cpgplayhouse .org; 3500 Main Hwy) premiered Samuel Beckett's *Waiting for Godot* in 1956 (the show was apparently a disaster), but was shut down during its 50th-anniversary season due to major debt issues. Now the board of the theater, in conjunction with Miami-Dade's Department of Cultural Affairs, is trying to resurrect this grande dame; check the theater website for updates.

PLYMOUTH CONGREGATIONAL CHURCH

This 1917 coral Mission-style **church** (Map p99; ☎ 305-444-6521; 3400 Devon Rd; ☒ 8:30am-4:30pm Mon-Fri) is striking, from its solid masonry to a hand-carved door from a Pyrenees monastery, which looks like it should be kicked in by Antonio Banderas carrying a guitar case full of explosives and Salma Hayek on his arm.

ERMITA DE LA CARIDAD

The Catholic diocese purchased some of the bayfront land from Deering's Villa Vizcaya estate and built a **shrine** (Map pp86-7; ☎ 305-854-2404; 3609 S Miami Ave) here for its displaced Cuban parishioners. Symbolizing a beacon, it faces the homeland, exactly 290 miles due south; there is also a mural that depicts Cuban history. After visiting Vizcaya or the science museum, consider picnicking at this quiet sanctuary on the water's edge.

KAMPONG

If you speak Malay or Indonesian, yes, the **Kampong** (Map p99; 4013 Douglas Rd; tours by appointment only Mon-Fri) is named for the Bahasa word for village. David Fairchild, Indiana Jones of the botanical world and founder of Fairchild Tropical Gardens (p118), came up with the title, undoubtedly after a long Javanese jaunt. This was where the adventurer would rest in-between journeys in search of beautiful and economically viable plant life. Today it's listed on the National Register of Historic Places and the lovely grounds serve as a classroom for the National Tropical Botanical Garden, but tours are available by appointment.

Coral Gables

BILTMORE HOTEL

In the most opulent neighborhood of one of the showiest cities in the world, the **Biltmore** (Map p95; ☎ 305-445-1926, 800-727-1926; www.biltmore hotel.com; 1200 Anastasia Ave) peers down her nose and says, 'Hrmph.' It's one of the greatest of the grand hotels of the American Jazz Age, and if this joint was a fictional character from a novel, it'd be, without question, Jay Gatsby.

The history of this landmark reads like an Agatha Christie novel on speed. Al Capone had a speakeasy on-site, and the Capone Suite is still haunted by the spirit of Fats Walsh, murdered here (for more ghost details, join in the weekly storytelling in the lobby, 7pm Thursday). Back in the day, imported gondolas transported celebrity guests like Judy Garland and the Vanderbilts around because, of course, there was a private canal system out the back. It's gone now, but the largest hotel pool in the continental USA, which resembles a sultan's water garden from *One Thousand & One Nights*, is still here. The lobby is the real kicker: grand, gorgeous, yet surprisingly ungaudy, it's like a child's fantasy of an Arab castle crossed with a Medici villa. Outside, the palatial grounds are popular spots for *quincenera* shoots, when 15-year-old Latino girls get to play princess for a day. For a wonderful overview, whether you're staying here or not, call **Dade Heritage Trust** (☎ 305-445-1926; tours free; ☒ tours 1:30pm, 2:30pm & 3:30pm Sun).

VENETIAN POOL

The prettiest public **pool** (Map p95; ☎ 305-460-5306; 2701 De Soto Blvd; adult/child Nov-Mar $6.75/5.50, Apr-Oct $10/6.75; ☒ 11am-5pm) in the US is this incredible grotto, which happens to be an excellent, rare example of public planning gone very…*right*. Just imagine: it's 1923; tons of rock have been quarried for one of the most beautiful neighborhoods in Miami, but now an ugly gash sits in the middle of the village. What to do? How about pump the irregular hole full of water, mosaic-and-tile up the whole affair, and make it look like a Roman emperor's aquatic playground? Result: one of the few pools listed on the National Register of Historic Places, a spring-fed wonderland of coral rock caves, cascading waterfalls, a palm-fringed island and Venetian-style moorings. You can get romantic under the big waterfall, drop the tykes in the kiddie area (toddlers must be over 38in tall or a parent must have proof they're at least three years old), do laps or take in the view, which is highly recommended for those who don't swim. Those who do get wet are following in the tradition of stars such as Esther Williams and Johnny 'Tarzan' Weissmuller. Opening hours vary depending on the season, so call ahead for details.

MERRICK HOUSE

It's fun to imagine this simple **homestead** (Map p95; ☎ 305-460-5361; 907 Coral Way; admission $5; ◷ 1pm, 2pm & 3pm Sun & Wed), with its little hints of Med-style, as the core of what would eventually become the gaudy Gables. When George Merrick's father purchased this plot, site unseen, for $1100, it was all dirt, rock and guavas. The property is now used for meetings and receptions, and you can tour both the house and its pretty organic garden. Today the modest family residence looks as it did in 1925, outfitted with family photos, furniture and artwork.

ENTRANCES & WATERTOWER

Coral Gables–designer George Merrick planned a series of elaborate entry gates to the city, but the real-estate bust meant that projects went unfinished. Among the completed gates worth seeing are the **Country Club Prado** (Map p95; Country Club Prado); the **Douglas Entrance** (off Map p95; cnr SW 8th St & Douglas Rd); the **Granada Entrance** (Map p95; cnr Alhambra Circle & Granada Blvd); the **Alhambra Entrance** (Map p95; cnr Alhambra Circle & Douglas Rd) and the **Coral Way Entrance** (Map p95; cnr Red Rd & Coral Way). The **Alhambra Watertower** (Map p95; Alhambra Circle), where Greenway Ct and Ferdinand St meet Alhambra Circle, resembles a Moorish lighthouse.

CORAL GABLES CITY HALL

This grand **building** (Map p95; 405 Biltmore Way) has housed boring city-commission meetings since it opened in 1928. It's impressive from any angle, certainly befitting its importance as a central government building. Check out Denman Fink's *Four Seasons* ceiling painting in the tower, as well as his framed, untitled painting of the underwater world on the 2nd-floor landing. There's a small farmers market on-site from 8am to 1pm, January to March.

CORAL GABLES CONGREGATIONAL CHURCH

George Merrick's father was a New England Congregational minister, so perhaps that accounts for him donating the land for the city's first **church** (Map p95; ☎ 305-448-7421; www .coralgablescongregational.org; 3010 De Soto Blvd). Built in 1924 as a replica of a church in Costa Rica, the yellow-walled, red-roofed exterior is as far removed from New England as…well, Miami. The interior is graced with a beautiful sanctuary and the grounds are landscaped with stately palms.

CORAL GABLES MUSEUM

Set to open in late 2009, this **museum** (Map p95; ☎ 305-460-5090; www.coralgables.com/cgweb/museum.org; 285 Aragon Ave), based on its sample exhibition, should be an excellent, well-plotted introduction to the oddball narrative of the founding and growth of the City Beautiful (Coral Gables). The collection will include historic artifacts and mementos from succeeding generations in this tight-knit, eccentric little village.

MIRACLE THEATER

This gorgeous, 80-year-old **theater** (Map p95; ☎ 305-444-9293; www.actorsplayhouse.org; 280 Miracle Mile) is one of the best bits of deco anywhere off the Beach. Today, the Actors' Playhouse company puts on productions in the three performance spaces – the 600-seat main-stage auditorium, a smaller children's theater and a black box for cutting-edge works – although the theater is nice to visit whether you've got tickets or not.

LOWE ART MUSEUM

Your love of the **Lowe** (Map pp86-7; ☎ 305-284-3535; www.lowemuseum.org, 1301 Stanford Dr; adult/student $7/5; ◷ 10am-5pm Tue, Wed, Fri & Sat, noon-7pm Thu, to 5pm Sun) depends on your taste in art. If you're into modern and contemporary works, it's good. If you're into the art and archaeology of cultures from Asia, Africa and the South Pacific, it's great. And if you're into pre-Columbian and Mesoamerican art, it's simply fantastic; the artifacts are stunning and thoughtfully strung out along an easy-to-follow narrative thread. That isn't to discount the lovely permanent collection of Renaissance and Baroque art, Western sculpture from the 18th to 20th centuries, and paintings by Gauguin, Picasso and Monet; they're also gorgeous.

Greater Miami

NORTH
Ancient Spanish Monastery

The Episcopal Church of St Bernard de Clairvaux is a stunning early Gothic and

Romanesque **building** (Map pp86-7; ☎ 305-945-1461; www.spanishmonastery.com; 16711 W Dixie Hwy; adult/child $5/2; ⏱ 9am-5pm Mon-Sat, 2-5pm Sun). Constructed in 1141 in Segovia, Spain, it was converted to a granary 700 years later, and eventually bought by newspaper tycoon William Randolph Hearst. He had it dismantled and shipped to the USA in more than 10,000 crates, intending to reconstruct it at his sprawling California estate. But construction was never approved by the government, and the stones sat in boxes until 1954, when a group of Miami developers purchased the dismantled monastery from Hearst and re-assembled it here. Now it's a lovely, albeit popular (especially for weddings, so call before going), oasis, and allegedly the oldest building in the western hemisphere. Church services are held at 8am, 10:30am and noon on Sunday, and a healing service is held at 10am on Wednesday.

Black Heritage Museum
This roving **museum** (☎ 305-252-3535) presents rotating exhibits in many areas of Miami, Chapman and Deering. It is the brainchild of teachers Priscilla S Kruize, Dr Paul Cadby and Dr Earl Wells; the three set out in 1987 to establish a center that celebrates the cultures of African Americans, Bahamians, Haitians and other black cultures in Dade County.

Hialeah Park
Hialeah is more Havanan than Little Havana (more than 90% of the population speak Spanish as a first language), and the symbol and center of this working-class Cuban community is this grand but endangered **former race track** (Map pp86-7; ☎ 305-885-8000; 2200 E 4th Ave; ⏱ 9am-5pm Mon-Fri). Although Seabiscuit and Seattle Slew once raced here, the last race was held in 2001, and since then a fight has been raging to keep this gem from being paved over. The track was even the subject of a pop-culture protest in the form of the song 'Save Hialeah Park' by Los Primeros, a Hialeah-based Latin boy band in 2008. A walk through the grounds is recommended, if just to gaze at the grand staircases and pastel-painted concourse, and imaging the thunder of racing hooves. Look for the caps, boots and saddle carved into the window below the administration building, and the oft-photographed central fountain.

Museum of Contemporary Art
Located up in North Miami, a rapidly evolving neighborhood and real-estate magnet for hipsters (especially gay men) who have tired of the South Beach scene, the **Museum Of Contemporary Art** (MoCA; Map p94; ☎ 305-893-6211; www.moca nomi.org; 770 NE 125th St; adult/student/senior $5/3/3; ⏱ 11am-5pm Tue-Sat, noon-5pm Sun) has long been a reason to hike up to this stretch of Miami. Its galleries feature excellent rotating exhibitions of contemporary art by local, national and international artists. Open late on the last Friday of every month (7pm to 10pm).

SOUTH
Fairchild Tropical Garden
If you need to escape Miami drivers, consider a green day in the country's largest tropical **botanical garden** (Map pp86-7; ☎ 305-667-1651; www .ftg.org; 10901 Old Cutler Rd; adult/child $10/5; ⏱ 9:30am-4:30pm). A butterfly grove, jungle biospheres, and gentle vistas of marsh and Keys habitats, plus frequent art installations from folks like Roy Lichtenstein, are all relaxingly stunning. In addition to easy-to-follow self-guided walking tours, a (perhaps overly long) free 40-minute tram tours the entire park on the hour from 10am to 3pm.

Matheson Hammock Park
This 100-acre county **park** (Map pp86-7; ☎ 305-665-5475; 9610 Old Cutler Rd; per car $4; ⏱ 6am-sunset) is the city's oldest and one of its most scenic. It offers good swimming for children in an enclosed tidal pool, lots of hungry raccoons, dense mangrove swamps, and (pretty rare) crocodile-spotting.

Fisher Island
One day Carl Fisher purchased this little **island** (Map pp86–7) and planned on dying here. But as is wont to happen, the millionaire got bored. When William K Vanderbilt II fell in love with the place, Fisher traded the island for Vanderbilt's 250ft yacht and its crew. Things were like that in those days. Vanderbilt proceeded to build a splendiferous Spanish-Mediterranean-style mansion, with guesthouses, studios, tennis courts and a golf course.

Today, this exclusive resort is accessible only by air and private ferry. The condominiums that line the mile-long private beach range from little $1-million hovels to a

$7-million-plus pad then-President Bill Clinton once borrowed. It's said the sun shines over the island even when it's raining on Miami Beach; maybe when you play with nature by importing boatloads of sugary white sand from the Bahamas you have sway over the weather, too. Moneyed readers can overnight on Fisher Island at the Inn at the Fisher Island Club (p137). The island is usually open only to paying guests and residents, but you can arrange a tour with hotel staff if you're especially persistent.

Hibiscus, Palm & Star Islands
Somewhere in the midrange of Miami island exclusivity, **Hibiscus Island** (Map pp86–7), **Palm Island** (Map pp86–7) and **Star Island** (Map pp90–1) are little floating Primrose Hills. They're at least accessible by car, unlike Fisher Island. There aren't many famous people living here – just rich ones – although Star Island is home to Gloria Estefan, and for a short time Al Capone lived (and died) on Palm Island. The islands' drives are guarded by a security booth, but the roads are public, so if you ask politely and don't look sketchy, you can get in. Star Island is little more than one elliptical road lined with royal palms, sculpted ficus hedges and fancy gates guarding houses you can't see.

Charles Deering Estate
The **Deering estate** (Map pp86–7; ☎ 305-235-1668; www.deeringestate.org; 16701 SW 72nd Ave; adult/child under 14yr $7/5; ☼ 10am-5pm, last tickets sold at 4pm) is sort of Vizcaya lite, which makes sense as it was built by Charles, brother of James Deering (of Vizcaya fame). The 150-acre grounds are awash in tropical growth, an animal-fossil pit of bones dating back 50,000 years and the prehistoric remains of American Indians who lived here 2000 years ago. Much of what was appropriate for display can be found in places like the Historical Museum of Southern Florida (p107), but some artifacts are on display here. There's a free tour of the grounds included in admission, and the estate often hosts jazz evenings under the stars.

Chess Hall of Fame
You'd think chess fanatics would have orderly minds and be good at scheduling, but this **museum** (Map pp86–7; ☎ 786-242-4255; www.chess museum.org; 13755 SW 119th Ave; suggested donation adult/child $5/3; ☼ 10:30am-5pm) was closed both times we visited, despite coming during regular hours. So we can only tell you that the Chess HoF is located in a big, white rooklike structure with a sword-in-the-stone out front (seriously), and is apparently filled with paraphernalia such as Bobby Fischer's table and ancient chess accoutrement.

Fruit & Spice Park
Been Lonely Planet-ing around Australia, Africa or Southeast Asia? Welcome back. Set just on the edge of the Everglades, this 35-acre tropical public **park** (Map pp86–7; ☎ 305-247-5727; 24801 SW 187th Ave; adult/child $6/1.50; ☼ 10am-5pm) grows all those great tropical fruits you usually have to contract dysentery to enjoy. The park is divided into 'continents' (Africa, Asia etc) and admission to the pretty grounds includes a free tour; you can't pick the fruit, but you can eat anything that falls to the ground. If you're coming down this far, you may want to consider taking a day trip into Everglades National Park.

Gold Coast Railroad Museum
South Florida would still be a swamp today without the introduction of train services. Primarily of interest to serious train buffs (but also fun for kids), this **museum** (Map pp86–7; ☎ 305-253-0063; www.goldcoast-railroad.org; 12450 SW 152nd St; adult/child 3-11yr $5/3; ☼ 11am-3pm Mon-Fri, to 4pm Sat & Sun) was set up in the 1950s by the Miami Railroad Historical Society. It displays more than 30 antique railway cars, including the Ferdinand Magellan presidential car, where President Harry Truman famously brandished a newspaper with the famously erroneous headline 'Dewey Defeats Truman.' The car was also used by US presidents Roosevelt, Eisenhower and Ronald Reagan (for whom it was outfitted with 3in-thick glass windows and armor plating).

Miami Children's Museum
Miami's newest **museum** (Map pp86–7; ☎ 305-373-5437; www.miamichildrensmuseum.org; 980 MacArthur Causeway, Watson Island; admission $8; ☼ 10am-6pm), located between South Beach and downtown Miami, isn't exactly a museum. It feels more like a glorified playhouse, with areas for kids to practice all sorts of adult activities – banking and food shopping (in models of corporate giants Bank of America and

Publics), caring for pets, reporting scoops as a TV news anchor in a studio, and acting as a local cop or firefighter. And, to be fair, there are some educational displays about subjects ranging from Miami architecture to Brazilian culture. Be forewarned: this place is a zoo on rainy days.

Metrozoo

This **zoo** (Map pp86-7; ☎ 305-251-0400; www.miami metrozoo.com; 12400 SW 152nd St; adult/child $11.50/6.75; ☼ 9:30am-5:30pm, last admission 4pm) boasts 900 animals from more than 200 species. Look for Asian and African elephants, rare and regal Bengal tigers (including a gorgeous white tiger) prowling an evocative Hindu temple, pygmy hippos, Andean condors, cute koalas, coleus monkeys, black rhinoceroses and a pair of Komodo dragons from Indonesia. Fewer than half of the 740 acres are developed, so you'll see plenty of natural habitats. And keep your eyes peeled for informative zookeeper talks in front of some exhibits.

For a quick overview (and because the zoo is so big), hop on the Safari Monorail; it departs every 20 minutes. There's a glut of grounds tours available, and kids will love feeding the Samburu giraffes ($2).

Monkey Jungle

The **Monkey Jungle** (Map pp86-7; ☎ 305-235-1611; www.monkeyjungle.com; 14805 SW 216th St; adult/child $25.95/19.95; ☼ 9:30am-5pm, last admission 4pm) brochures have a tag line: 'Where humans are caged and monkeys run free.' And, indeed, you'll be walking through screened-in trails, with primates swinging freely, screeching and chattering all around you. It's actually incredibly fun, and just a bit odorous, especially on warm days (well, most days).

In 1933, animal behaviorist Joseph du Mond released six monkeys into the wild. Today, their descendants live here with orangutans, chimpanzees and the lowland gorilla. The tropical hardwood hammock contains plants collected in South America and feels like the Amazonian ecosystem. The big show of the day takes place at feeding time, when crab-eating monkeys and Southeast Asian macaques dive into the pool for fruit and other treats.

Jungle Island

They call it **Jungle Island** (Map pp86-7; ☎ 305-666-7834; www.parrotjungle.com; 1111 Parrot Jungle Trail, off MacArthur Causeway, Watson Island; adult/child $27.95/22.95; ☼ 10am-6pm) now, but it was formerly Parrot Jungle – a glorious homage to tourism kitsch. These days the island is a bit sleeker and this is one of those places kids beg to go, so just give up and prepare for some bright-feathered, bird-poopie-scented fun in this artificial, self-contained jungle. Actually, the 18-acre waterfront facility, lushly landscaped and using a minimum of pesticides, is pretty impressive, thanks in part to the parrots, macaws, flamingos and cockatoos flying about in outdoor aviaries. The Cape Penguin colony is especially cute. Parking costs $6.

Pinecrest Gardens

When Parrot Jungle flew the coop for the big city, the village of Pinecrest, which is the community that hosted the Jungle's former location, purchased the lovely property in order to keep it as a municipal **park** (Map pp86-7; ☎ 305-669-6942; www.pinecrest-fl.gov/gardens; 11000 SW 57th Ave; admission $5; ☼ 8am-sunset). It's now a quiet oasis with some of the best tropical gardens this side of the Gulf of Mexico, there are also playgrounds, and classrooms that house a bevy of adult-education culture and arts classes.

National Hurricane Center

Florida and hurricanes go together like peanut butter and destructive jelly, and this fascinating **center** (Map pp86-7; ☎ 305-229-4404; www .nhc.noaa.gov; 11691 SW 17th St; ☼ hurricane off-season, generally late Jan-May) on the campus of Florida International University (FIU) is the first line of defense against these devastating storms. Free 40-minute tours are available by appointment only, and document both the drama of hurricanes and the intricacies of storm-tracking.

Wings Over Miami

Plane-spotters will be delighted by this Kendall-Tamiami Executive Airport **museum** (Map pp86-7; ☎ 305-233-5197; www.wingsovermiami .com; Kendall-Tamiami Executive Airport, 14710 SW 128th St; adult/child under 13yr/senior $9.95/5.95/5.95; ☼ 10am-5:30pm Thu-Sun), which chronicles the history of aviation. Highlights include a propeller collection, a J47 jet engine, a Soviet bomber from Smolensk and the nose section of *Fertile Myrtle*, the aircraft used to drop atomic bombs on Hiroshima and Nagasaki. An impressive exhibit on the Tuskeegee Airmen features videos of the black pilots telling their own stories. Historic bombers and other aircrafts drop in for occasional visits, so you can never be sure what you'll see.

ACTIVITIES
Biking
Miami-Dade County Parks & Recreation Department (☎ 305-755-7800; www.miamidade.gov/parks) is helpful when it comes to cycling around the city. It leads frequent eco-bike tours through parklands and along waterfront paths, and offers a list of traffic-free cycling paths on its website. Try the Old Cutler Bike Path, which starts at the end of Sunset Dr in Coral Gables and leads to Matheson Hammock Park and Fairchild Tropical Garden; or the Rickenbacker Causeway, taking you up and over the bridge to Key Biscayne for an excellent workout combined with gorgeous water views. Pedaling to the end of the Key is a lovely way to spend the afternoon.

Oleta River State Park (Map p94; ☎ 305-919-1846; 3400 NE 163rd St) has a challenging dirt trail with hills for off-road adventures. For less strenuous rides, try the side roads of South Beach or the shady streets of Coral Gables and Coconut Grove. Places that rent bicycles include, **Mangrove Cycles** (Map p98; ☎ 305-361-5555; 260 Crandon Blvd, Key Biscayne; ☺ 9am-6pm Tue-Sat, 10am-5pm Sun; per 2hr/day/week $10/15/45) and **Miami Beach Bicycle Center** (Map pp90-1; ☎ 305-674-0150; 601 5th St, South Beach; per hr/day/week $8/20/70; ☺ 10am-7pm Mon-Sat, to 5pm Sun).

Boating & Kayaking
Kayaking through mangroves, one of the coolest ecosystems on Earth (see the boxed text, p199), is magical: all those slender roots kiss the water while the ocean breeze cools your flanks. In the USA, this sort of experience is pretty much uniquely available in places like **Haulover Beach Park** (Map p94; ☎ 305-944-3040; 10800 Collins Ave) or **Bill Baggs Cape Florida State Recreation Area** (Map p98; ☎ 305-361-5811; www.floridastateparks.org /capeflorida; 1200 S Crandon Blvd). Equipment rental is cheap, and you won't even need lessons to make the boat go where you want it to. Also, check out **Oleta River State Park** (Map p94; ☎ 305-919-1846; 3400 NE 163rd St), with various grove channels on the Intracoastal Waterway that are perfect for a kayak or paddleboat (both of which are available for rental here).

At **Urban Trails Kayak Rentals** (Map pp86-7; ☎ 305-947-0302; www.salimiami.com; 3400 NE 163rd St, Bal Harbour,

North Miami Beach) you can take out a canoe or kayak for solo exploration, or join one of the company's excellent guided expeditions of the Oleta River or the Everglades. Their website is a good information clearing house on local boating services, fishing conditions, crew postings and marine directories. Check out p174 for information on canoeing in the Everglades.

Sailboards Miami (Map p98; ☎ 305-361-7245; 1 Rickenbacker Causeway; per hr single/tandem $15/20) also rents kayaks. You can purchase 10-hours worth of kayaking for $90. To get some lower body exercise, you could try renting water bikes, which sit in a kayak-type boat; water-bike rental costs about the same as kayak rental. In either case, if you're goal-oriented and need a destination, head for the little offshore sandbar.

If you've got money to spend and want to buzz down to the Keys or get yourself to the Bahamas, try **Florida Yacht Charters** (Map pp90-1; ☎ 305-532-8600, 800-537-0050; 930 Alton Rd, South Beach; ☺ 9am-5:30pm), which rents yachts with and without captains (as long as you can pass a practical test) from the Miami Beach Marina.

If you're a bona-fide seaworthy sailor, the **Aquatic Rental Center and Sailing School** (Map p94; ☎ day 305-751-7514, evening 305-279-7424; 1275 NE 79th St; sailboat rental per 2hr/3hr/4hr/day $80/115/135/195, sailing courses $350) will rent you a vessel. If you're not, they'll teach you how to operate one.

Bowling
Strike Miami (Map pp86-7; ☎ 305-594-0200; before/after 5pm per hr $27/39) in the Dolphin Mall is a good example of what happens when Miami's talent for glitz and glamour meets some humble ten-pins.

Cricket
Really? Yup. Don't forget there's a huge West Indian and Jamaican community in South Florida. The **South Florida Cricket Alliance** (☎ 305-606-7603; www.southfloridacricket.com) is one of the largest cricket clubs in the US, the **Cricket Council of the USA** (www.cricketcouncilusa.com) is based in Boca Raton, and the first dedicated cricket pitch in the country opened in Lauderhill (where the population is 25% West Indian), west of Fort Lauderdale, in 2008. Contact any of the above if you'd like to watch a test or join a team.

Day Spas
As you may have guessed, Miami offers plenty of places to get pampered. Some of

the most luxurious spas in town are found at the high-end hotels, where you can expect to pay around $300 to $400 for a massage and/or acupressure, and $200 for a body wrap. Most notable are **Splash Spa** (Map pp92-3; ☎ 305-458-3535; www.fourseasons.com/miami; Four Seasons Miami, 1435 Brickell Ave), a sprawling, 50,000-sq-ft palace of massages and body wraps; the **Spa at Mandarin Oriental Miami** (Map pp92-3; ☎ 305-913-8332; www .mandarinoriental.com; Mandarin Oriental Miami, 500 Brickell Key Dr), featuring 17 private treatment rooms and several suites that overlook Biscayne Bay; **Agua Bathhouse Spa** (Map pp88-9; ☎ 305-674-6100; www.delano-hotel.com; Delano Hotel, 1685 Collins Ave), on the penthouse of Ian Schrager's original cool school; and the **Spa at the Setai** (Map pp88-9; ☎ 305-520-6000; www.setai.com; Setai, 101 20th St), a silky Balinese haven in South Beach's most expensive hotel.

But just because you enjoy a good back rub doesn't mean you want the glitziest place in town, right? Long a favorite 'hot' spot among folks who want a spa experience without the glamour, the **Russian & Turkish Baths** (Map p94; ☎ 305-867-8316; Castillo del Mar, 5445 Collins Ave) was undergoing a renovation during our visit, but should be reopened by the time you read this. The baths have a reputation for providing laid-back service, along with soothing saunas, steam rooms and whirlpools.

Diving & Snorkeling

It's better to head down to the Keys for great diving, but between offshore wrecks and the introduction of artificial coral reefs, there's still plenty to look at in Miami if you can part the waters and scratch beneath the surface. Go on a calm day with a group; try **Divers Paradise** (Map p98; ☎ 305-361-3483; 4000 Crandon Blvd; dive trip $60) of Key Biscayne, which is a good option. **South Beach Divers** (Map pp90-1; ☎ 305-531-6110; www.south beachdivers.com; 850 Washington Ave, South Beach; dive trip $100) runs regular excursions to Key Largo and around Miami, plus offers three-day classes. Or make the very worthy drive to **Biscayne National Park** (p177), in the southeastern corner of the county, a huge park that contains the northern tip of the world's third-longest coral reef. Of the park's 173,000 acres, about 95% of them are underwater. Go to www.nps.gov/bisc for more information on the park.

Fishing

Rent a pricey charter (around $800 per day), hop aboard a 'head boat' with 100 or so other fisherfolk (boats are rarely full, and it's only about $30), or cast a line off numerous piers or bridges. You don't need a license if you're fishing from shore or from a bridge or pier (just check for signs, which declare some bridges off-limits). On your own, drop a line at **South Pointe Park** (Map pp90–1), or off the **Rickenbacker Causeway** (Map p98) or any **Key Biscayne beach** (Map p98), or from **Haulover Beach Park** (Map p94; ☎ 305-944-3040; 10800 Collins Ave, Bal Harbour). To go on a fishing charter boat, try **Crandon Park Marina** (Map p98; ☎ 305-361-1281; 4000 Crandon Blvd, Key Biscayne) or **Blue Waters Fishing** (Map pp92-3; ☎ 305-373-5016; www.fishingmiami.net; Bayside Marketplace, 401 Biscayne Blvd, Downtown Miami). Alternatively, catch a group-fishing party boat with the **Kelley Fleet** (Map p94; ☎ 305-945-3801; Haulover Beach Park, 10800 Collins Ave, Bal Harbour).

Golf

At high-end resorts, expect to pay between $150 and $350 to tee off, depending on the season and time of day (it's more expensive in winter and daylight hours). Check out the lovely 1925 **Biltmore Donald Ross Golf Course** (Map p95; ☎ 305-460-5364; 1210 Anastasia Ave, Coral Gables), designed by the golfer of that name, which boasts the company of the Biltmore Hotel. **Doral Golf Course** (Map pp86-7; ☎ 305-592-2000; 4400 NW 87th Ave) is highly rated, which may explain why it's difficult to get in and also why it's the home of the PGA Ford Championship. The wealthy can blow their wad here on golf courses that follow in the path of (literally) the Masters. For easier access, try the **Crandon Golf Course** (Map p98; ☎ 305-361-9129; 6700 Crandon Blvd, Key Biscayne; daylight Dec-Apr $140, twilight May-Nov $30), overlooking the bay from its perch on Key Biscayne; or the **Haulover Golf Course** (Map p94; ☎ 305-940-6719; 10800 Collins Ave, Bal Harbour; $21-43), a nine-hole, par-three course that's great for beginners.

Gyms

Everyone else here has the body of a freakin' Greek god, so why don't you join the club? Besides, working out is one of Miami's favorite forms of people-watching and people-meeting and, you, engaged traveler, surely want to do a bit of both. **Crunch** (Map pp88-9; ☎ 305-674-8222; www.crunch.com; 1259 Washington Ave; per day/week $21/88), a branch of the New York fave, has great workout equipment, a cool attitude and a slew of classes, from 'Cardio Striptease' to 'Belly Moves.' **David Barton Gym**

(Map pp88-9; ☎ 305-534-9777; www.davidbartongym
.com; Delano Hotel, 1685 Collins Ave; per day/week $20/75, 10-
visit pass $150), another branch from a New York
base, is the nightclub of health clubs, where
striking poses with your already-in-shape bod
is the hottest activity of all. But you will find
top-notch equipment, along with loud club
music and dim (flattering) lighting. Your
workout pass gets you into the pool.

Gold's Gym South Beach (Map pp88-9; ☎ 305-538-
4653; www.goldsgymsouthbeach; 1400 Alton Rd; per day/
week $20/90), an outpost of the world's larg-
est gym chain, is a 20,000-sq-ft 'super-fit-
ness complex,' featuring cardio machines,
free weights, an outdoor patio and tons of
classes. Rounding out the sweat stakes is **Idol's
Gym** (Map pp88-9; ☎ 305-532-0089; 715 Lincoln Lane; per
3 days/week $25/50), a small but hip and hottie-
filled workout den that's walled with a glass
storefront, and **South Beach Ironworks** (Map pp88-9;
☎ 305-531-4743; www.southbeachironworks.com; 1676
Alton Rd; per day/3 days/week $15/25/56), popular with
locals for its yoga and aerobics classes and
array of workout equipment.

In-Line Skating

Serious crowds have turned promenades into
obstacle courses for anyone crazy enough to
strap on some blades. Leave the crowded strips
to experts and try the ocean side of Ocean Ave,
or Lincoln Rd before the shoppers descend.

Rent your wheels from **Fritz's Skate Shop**
(Map pp88-9; ☎ 305-532-1954; 730 Lincoln Rd; per hr/day
$7.50/22; ☺ 10am-10pm), which also offers free
lessons on Sunday at 10:30am – just about
the only time there's ever room on the
mall anymore.

Running

Running is quite popular, and the beach is
very good for jogging, as it's flat, wide and
hard-packed (apparently with amazingly
hot joggers). The **Promenade** (Map pp90-1; Ocean
Ave) in South Beach is the stylish place for
a run, as is the **boardwalk** (Map p94; 21st St to
46th St), which shoots north from 21st St on
Mid-Beach and offers great people-watching
and scenery as you move along. But more
serious runners may appreciate the **Flamingo
Park running track** (Map pp88-9), just east of
Alton Rd between 11th St and 12th St; the
entrance is on the 12th St side at the east end
of the fence. Elsewhere around the city, running is good along **S Bayshore Dr** (Map p99)
in Coconut Grove, around the **Riviera Country

Club** (off Map p95) in Coral Gables and anywhere on **Key Biscayne** (Map p98). Or try the
jogging path that runs along the beach in **Bal
Harbour** (Map p94), made of hard-packed sand
and gravel, and stretching from the southern
boundary of town to the Haulover Cut pas-
sageway. A great resource for races, special
events and other locations is the **Miami Runners
Club** (☎ 305-227-1500).

Surfing & Windsurfing

We can't say it enough: offshore Miami bears
no resemblance to the Banzai Pipeline. If you
see someone walking around South Beach
with a board under their arm, they are undoubtedly, in the industry parlance, a 'po-
seur.' If you must ride waves here, the best
surfing is just north of **South Pointe Park** (Map
pp90–1), with 2ft to 5ft waves and a nice,
sandy bottom. Unfortunately, there are a few
drawbacks: it's usually closer to 2ft than 5ft
(except, of course, before storms); it can get
a little mushy (so longboards are the way to
go); and it's swamped with weekend swimmers and surfers. It's better further north
near **Haulover Beach Park** (Map p94; ☎ 305-944-3040;
10800 Collins Ave, Bal Harbour) or anywhere north
of, say, 70th St. **Sunny Isles Beach** (Map pp86-7;
Sunny Isles Causeway), north of Bal Harbour, is
also favored by surfers. Call the recorded **surf
report** (☎ 305-534-7873) for daily conditions or
check in with the popular **Bird's Surf Shop** (Map
pp86-7; ☎ 305-940-0929, surf line 305-947-7170; 250 Sunny
Isles Blvd).

Swimming

Some folks in Miami *actually* swim in the
gorgeous pools around town that serve as
backdrops for the cocktail-swilling set. If a
bit of freestyle or breaststroke is how you like
to get your workout, fear not: there are places
for you, even if you're not lucky enough to
be staying at a hotel with an excellent swimming hole – among the best of these are the
Delano Hotel (p134), Shore Club (p134),
Biltmore Hotel (p116), Raleigh Hotel (p134)
and Fontainebleau Hilton Hotel & Resort
(p136). In Coral Gables, the famous **Venetian
Pool** (Map p95; ☎ 305-460-5306; 2701 De Soto Blvd; adult/
child Nov-Mar $6.75/5.50, Apr-Oct $10/6.75; ☺ 11am-5pm),
known more as a pretty place in which to
play and float and gawk, has lap-swimming
hours several times a week; call for details,
which change often. Other options include
the **Flamingo Park Swimming Pool** (Map pp90-1;

☎ 305-673-7730; 999 11th St, South Beach), which has a swimming pool with lap lanes.

Tennis

Key Biscayne's **Tennis Center at Crandon Park** (Map p98; ☎ 305-365-2300; 7300 Crandon Blvd, Key Biscayne; per daytime hr $3, per evening hr $5) is best known for its annual 10-day Nasdaq 100 Tennis Open, which draws star players each March. But you too can play here; choose from two grass, eight clay and 17 hard courts. The **Flamingo Tennis Center** (Map pp90-1; ☎ 305-673-7761; 1000 12th St, South Beach; per hr $8) has 19 clay courts that are open to the public. All courts around town tend to get crowded.

Ultimate Frisbee

Ultimate players have a lot of love for each other all over the world, and here they can express that emotion on miles of white-sand beach. Check www.miamiultimatefrisbee.org for more details; free-to-join beach games are currently held at 6:30pm and 7:00pm (arrive at 6:15pm) on the beach (right) side of Miami Beach, between 14th Ave and 15th Ave. Bring a white and a dark shirt to play.

Ultralights

Miami is an aviation center, and the skies are filled with hundreds of planes, including ultralights, which are regulated small aircrafts that you don't need a pilot's license to fly (scarily enough). Get a taste of the ultralight experience at the **Homestead General Aviation Airport**

(Map pp86-7; ☎ 305-247-4883; 28700 SW 217th Ave), not quite in Miami, but close enough if you're really jazzed about getting up in the air. It's a field specifically for these tiny planes; call for rates, which vary. Or try **Ultralight Adventures** (Map p98; ☎ 305-361-3909; Rickenbacker Causeway, Key Biscayne; sightseeing flights $100-200) where you can get lessons or a sightseeing flight.

Yoga & Pilates

The beach is definitely not the only place to salute the sun in Miami. At **Miami Yogashala** (Map pp88-9; ☎ 305-534-0784; www.miamiyoga.com; 210a 23rd St, South Beach), you'll find a range of classes in guided ashtanga, vinyasa and power yoga, plus private sessions, a yoga boutique selling an array of yogic items and frequent workshops. In Coral Gables, **Prana Yoga Center** (Map p95; ☎ 305-567-9812; www.pranayogamiami .com; 247 Malaga Ave, Coral Gables; 1/5 class pass $16/70) offers classes in ashtanga, prana, vinyasa, hatha, kundalini and guided meditation, while Coconut Groves' **Yoga Grove** (Map p99; ☎ 305-448-3332; www.yogagrove.com; 3100 S Dixie Hwy, Coconut Grove; 1/5 class pass $15/65) is dedicated to the ashtanga-vinyasa system made popular in Mysore, India. Other classes at the center include power yoga and the new Afroyoga, a blend of yoga and African dance.

To get your poses in without missing a single minute at the beach, there's **Synergy Center for Yoga and the Healing Arts** (Map pp88-9; ☎ 305-538-7073; www.synergyyoga.org; 435 Española Way, South Beach; beach/studio class $5/14), which offers fabulous

---

MIAMI JAI ALAI

Jai alai (pronounced high aligh), which roughly translates from Spanish as 'merry festival,' is a fascinating and dangerous game. Something of a cross between racquetball and lacrosse, it originated in the Basque region of the Pyrenees in the 17th century and was introduced to Miami in 1924. The *fronton* (arena) where the games are held is the oldest in the US, having been built just two years after the game was introduced. How is it played? Well, players hurl a *pelota* (a small ball of virgin rubber that's wrapped in goat skin and so powerful it can shatter bullet-proof glass) at more than 170mph to their opponents, who try to catch it with the *cesta* – a woven basket that's custom-made from Spanish chestnut and reeds from the Pyrenees – that's attached to their glove. The object is to toss the *pelota* against the front wall of the court with so much speed that the opposition cannot catch it or return it in the fly or first bounce. While the game is supposedly the fastest on Earth, the crowds watching it are kinda…slow. Which is to say matches are basically gambling affairs attended by chain-smoking retirees. It's cool for that Old (and we mean 'old') Florida vibe.

Catch the action for yourself at **Miami Jai Alai** (Map pp86-7; ☎ 305-633-6400; 3500 NW 37th Ave; admission $1-5; ☖ matches noon-5pm Wed-Mon, 7pm-midnight Mon, Fri & Sat). Even though the crowd is making petty bets and nipping off for a smoke – it's great fun to watch these guys whack around their *pelota* at lightning speed.

yoga classes in the sand. They also offer a selection of studio sessions in ashtanga, basic, gentle iyengar, jivamukti and pilates. Finally, **Pilates Miami** (Map p97; ☎ 305-573-4430; www.pilatesmiami.com; 3936 N Miami Ave; private/small group/mat $68/41/15) focuses solely on pilates, with a Design District loft space that offers both machine training sessions and group mat classes.

ART DECO MIAMI WALKING TOUR

The best place to start is at the **Art Deco Welcome Center** (**1**; p102), at the corner of Ocean Dr and 10th St – named Barbara Capitman Way at this stretch, after the preservationist who founded the Miami Design Preservation League in 1976. Step inside for a permanent exhibit on deco style, then head outside and go north along colorful Ocean Dr; between 12th St and 14th St you'll see three classic examples of deco hotels: the **Leslie (2)**, a typically boxy shape with eyebrows (cantilevered sun shades) wrapped around the side of the building; the **Carlyle (3)**, featured in the film *The Birdcage* and boasting modernistic styling; and the graceful **Cardozo Hotel** (**4**; p133), built by Henry Hohauser, owned by Gloria Estefan and featuring sleek, rounded edges. At 14th St, peek inside the sun-drenched **Winter Haven Hotel (5)** to see its fabulous floors of ubiquitous terrazzo, made of stone chips set in mortar that is polished when dry. Turn left and head down 14th St to Washington Ave and the **US Post Office** (**6**; p104), at 13th St. A curvy block of white deco in the 'stripped classic' style, this was the first restoration project for South Beach's revitalization group in the 1970s. Step inside to admire the Works Progress Administration project wall mural, domed ceiling and marble stamp tables. Next stop for lunch at the **11th Street Diner** (**7**; p138), a gleaming aluminum Pullman car that was imported in 1992 from Wilkes-Barre, Pennsylvania. Get a window seat and gaze across the avenue to the corner of 10th St and the stunningly restored **Hotel Astor** (**8**; p131), which was designed in 1936 by T Hunter Henderson. After your meal, walk half a block east to the imposing **Wolfsonian-FIU** (**9**; p104), an excellent museum of design that was formerly the Washington Storage Company, where wealthy snowbirds of the '30s safely stashed their pricey belongings before heading back up north. Continue walking Washington Ave and turn left on 7th St

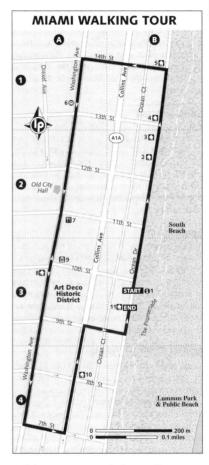

WALK FACTS

Start Art Deco Welcome Center
Finish Edison Hotel
Distance one mile
Duration one hour

and then continue north along Collins Ave to the **Hotel** (**10**; p131), featuring an interior and roof deck by Todd Oldham. L Murray Dixon designed the Hotel as the Tiffany Hotel, with a proud deco spire, in 1939. Turn right on 9th St and go two blocks to Ocean Dr, where you'll spy nonstop deco beauties, such as the 1935 **Edison Hotel (11)**, another beautiful creation of deco legend Henry Hohauser.

COURSES

It never hurts to learn a thing or two while you're on vacation – especially if it's a skill that could come in particularly handy while you're here. For up-to-date listings of general classes, seminars and lectures on a variety of topics, visit www.miamiintelligence.com.

Cooking

You can learn how to fix up some fusion and Floribbean from local celeb chefs at restaurants like **Wish** (Map pp90-1; Hotel, 801 Collins Ave; ☎ 305-674-9474; course $175) and **Azul** (Map pp92-3; Mandarin Oriental Miami, 500 Brickell Key Dr; ☎ 305-913-8358; course $175).

Salsa Dancing

Going out to a Latin club and being a wallflower feels awful. Drop into a class or two at **Salsa Mia** (☎ 305-987-3033; www.salsamia.com; 1/2/5-night pass $40/50/100) or **Latin Heat Salsa Studio** (☎ 305-868-9418; www.latin-heat.com; per class $10); both studios have a few locations around South and Miami Beach – check their websites for details.

Spanish

Take a crash course with one of the monthly classes at **South Beach Languages Center** (Map pp88-9; ☎ 305-531-5331; www.miamispanishclasses.com; 227 13th St), or try a seven-day intensive at the **University of Miami** (Map pp86-7; ☎ 305-284-4727; www.miami .edu/fastspanish). Unfortunately, there were no tourist-oriented Creole classes available at the time of research.

MIAMI FOR CHILDREN

Well, really: it's Florida, folks. Your kids will be catered to here. Many of the attractions here run toward animal experiences, starting with the **Miami Seaquarium** (p112), boasting a large collection of crocodiles, dolphins, sea lions and a killer whale, most of whom perform. Next comes the **Metrozoo** (p120), a 740-acre zoo with plenty of natural habitats (thank you tropical weather). Should your little ones like colorful animal shows, the outdoors and the smell of animal poo in all its myriad varieties, Miami shall not disappoint. **Monkey Jungle** (p120), which acts as a habitat for endangered species, is everything you'd expect: screeching primates, covered pathways and a grand finale show of Java monkeys diving for crabs. **Jungle Island** (p120), on the other hand, tends to entertain with brilliant bird shows.

Next door is the new **Miami Children's Museum** (p119), an indoor playland where youngsters can try out the roles of TV anchor, banker and supermarket customer, among others. Although adults can probably find a way to enjoy the Pink Floyd–accompanied light show at the **Miami Museum of Science & Planetarium** (p115), it's certainly good fun for the kids. Coral Gables draws the water-wise to its way-fun, lagoonlike **Venetian Pool** (p116) – as does the water park at **Fontainebleau Hilton Hotel & Resort** (p106). This, by the way, is a most excellent place for families to bunk down. Also, consider taking your kids to a **Little Haitian botanica** (p112). We're not trying to encourage more needlessly exotic stereotypes of *vodou*, but the dark, smoky spell shops are a treat for a certain kind of curious kid.

Child Care

When it's time to head out for some adult time, check with your hotel, as many offer child-care services – especially the big resorts, including the Four Seasons Miami (p136), Loews Miami Beach (p134), Conrad Miami (p136) and the Fontainebleau Hilton Hotel & Resort (p136). Or call the local **Nanny Poppinz** (☎ 305-607-1170; www.nannypoppinz.com). For more information, advice and anecdotes, read *South Florida Parenting Magazine*, available at major booksellers, and Lonely Planet's *Travel with Children* by Cathy Lanigan.

TOURS
Walking Tours

Art Deco Welcome Center (Map pp90-1; ☎ 305-531-3484; 1001 Ocean Dr, South Beach; guided tour per adult/child/senior $20/free/15, self-guided tour per adult/senior $15/10; ☼ 10:30am Wed, Fri & Sat, 6:30pm Thu) tells the fascinating stories and history behind the art-deco hotels in the South Beach historic district, either with a lively guide from the Miami Design Preservation League, or with a well-presented recording and map for self-guided walks (try to go with the guides). Tours last 90 minutes. The league also leads architectural walks of North Beach, and 'Deco Underworld' tours about the Prohibition era in Miami Beach.

For a great perspective on many different aspects of the city, call the lively Dr Paul George (☎ 305-375-1621; tours $25-42; ☼ 10am Sat, 11am Sun), historian for the Historical Museum of Southern Florida (p107). George leads several popular tours – including those that focus on Stiltsville, Miami crime, Little Havana and Coral Gables at twilight – between September and late June. Dr George also offers private tours by appointment.

Downtown Miami Welcome Center (Map pp92-3; ☎ 305-379-7070; Gusman Center for the Performing Arts, 174 E Flagler St; tours $10; ☒ 10:30am Sat) can help you to see beyond the construction sites and crumbling facades of downtown Miami to provide an explanation of historic sites from the original Burdines (now Macy's on E Flagler St) to the Gesu Church, dating from 1925. The tours are by group only, and run by the Welcome Center, which is housed in the historic Olympia Theater in Gusman Center for the Performing Arts (p109).

Urban Tour Host (Map pp92-3; ☎ 305-416-6868; www.miamiculturaltours.com; 25 SE 2nd Ave, Suite 1048; tours from $20) has a rich program of custom tours that provide face-to-face interaction in all of Miami's neighborhoods. A deluxe city tour includes Coral Gables, South Beach, downtown Miami and Coconut Grove. The new downtown Miami interactive walking tour, on Wednesday and Saturday from 10am to noon, includes sampling local restaurants and patronizing businesses that then channel profits into urban-development programs.

Other Tours

Action Helicopter Tours (Map pp86-7; ☎ 305-358-4723; Watson Island; tours $69-149) runs 12- to 35-minute jaunts above South Beach, Fisher Island, the Port of Miami, Bayside Marketplace, Coconut Grove and the houses of the rich and famous.

Bayside Marketplace (Map pp92-3; ☎ 305-379-5119; 401 Biscayne Blvd; adult/child $14/7; ☒ 11am-7pm) runs boat tours. For harbor tours, head downtown and hop aboard the *Island Queen*, Captain Jimmy's Fiesta Cruises or the smaller speedboat *Bayside Blaster*. All boats depart hourly.

The Dade County parks system leads frequent bike tours through peaceful areas of Miami and Miami Beach, including along beaches and on Key Biscayne. Times vary; call **Eco-adventure Bike Tours** (☎ 305-365-3018; www .miamidade.gov/parks; tours $25) for details.

Is it a bus, or is it a boat? No, you won't look too cool gliding through South Beach on this bus/boat hybrid, but the wacky vehicle run by **Miami Duck Tours** (Map pp88-9; ☎ 877-3825-849, 786-276-8300; 1665 Washington Ave; adult/child/senior $32/18/26; ☒ 10am-6pm) does provide a nice, high

perspective (and amusing commentary) of South Beach and downtown Miami sites, and, when it enters the water, the moneyed homes of Biscayne Bay shores. Tours depart hourly and last 90 minutes.

The well-established **Miami Nice Tours** (☎ 305-949-9180; www.miaminicetours.com; tours $36-70) has a wide range of guided bus excursions to the Everglades, the Keys and Fort Lauderdale, as well as trips around Miami, some including stops at the Miami Seaquarium, Bayside Marketplace and Jungle Island.

FESTIVALS & EVENTS

There's something special happening year-round in Miami, with well-touted events bringing in niche groups from serious DJs (Winter Music Conference) to obsessed foodies (Miami Spice Restaurant Month).

January

The beginning of the new year also happens to be the height of the tourist season in these parts. Expect fair weather, crowds of visitors, higher prices than usual and a slew of special events. New Year's Eve brings fireworks and festivals to South Beach and Downtown Miami's bayfront.

Fedex Orange Bowl football game (☎ 305-341-4700; www.orangebowl.org; Dolphin Stadium, 2269 NW 199th St, Opa-Locka) In early January flocks of football fanatics descend on Pro Player Stadium in Opa-Locka for the Orange Bowl, the Super Bowl of college football.

Art Deco Weekend (☎ 305-672-2014; www.art decoweekend.com; Ocean Dr btwn 1st St & 23rd St) This weekend fair featuring guided tours, concerts, classic-auto shows, sidewalk cafés, and vendors of arts and antiques is held in mid-January.

Key Biscayne Art Festival (☎ 305-361-0049; Crandon Blvd, Key Biscayne) Held in late January since the early 1960s, this is a showcase of more than 150 local artists, from painters to glass blowers.

Miami Jewish Film Festival (☎ 305-573-7304; www .caje-miami.org; 4200 Biscayne Blvd, Key Biscayne) There are few better chances to kvetch with one of the biggest Jewish communities in the USA.

February

The last hurrah for northerners needing to escape the harsh winter, February brings arts festivals and street parties, as well as warm days and cool nights. February 14 is Valentine's Day, when lovers celebrate their amour.

Miami International Film Festival (☎ 305-377-3456; www.miamifilmfestival.com) This early-February (sometimes late-January) event, which is sponsored by Miami-Dade College, is a two-week festival showcasing documentaries and features from all over the world.

Coconut Grove Arts Festival (☎ 305-447-0401; www.coconutgroveartsfest.com; Biscayne Blvd btwn NE 1st St & 5th St, Coconut Grove) One of the most prestigious arts festivals in the country, this late-February fair features more than 300 artists.

Miami International Boat Show & Strictly Sail (☎ 305-531-8410; www.discoverboating.com/miami; Miami Beach Convention Center, South Beach) With more than 250,000 attendees, this late-February event is a serious water-lovers' extravaganza and one of the largest new-boat shows in the world.

Miami Beach Festival of the Arts (☎ 305-865-4147; http://gonorthbeach.com; Ocean Tce) Expect some 30,000 visitors to descend on over 100 artists at this two-day, family-friendly festival. The action is east of Collins Ave on 73rd St and 75th St.

South Beach Wine & Food Festival (☎ 305-460-6563; www.sobewineandfoodfest.com) In late February, *Food & Wine* magazine and the Food Network present this fest of fine dining and sipping to promote South Florida's culinary image. Expect star-studded brunches, dinners and barbecues.

March

Spring arrives, bringing warmer weather, world-class golf and tennis tournaments, outdoor festivals and the Irish party holiday of St Patrick's Day, on March 17. Expect some Spring Breakers to behave badly on the beach.

Miami International Film Festival (☎ 305-237-3456; www.miamifilmfestival.com) Dubbed 'The Cannes of the Americas' by the *New York Times,* this one-week festival (usually held in early March) includes Encuentros, a showcase of some of the best new cinematic talent in Spain and Latin America.

Carnaval Miami (☎ 305-644-8888; www.carnaval miami.com) In early to mid-March, this is a nine-day party of festivals, concerts, a beauty contest, an in-line skating contest, a Latin drag-queen show and a Calle Ocho cooking contest.

Miami Orchid Show (☎ 305-261-3800; Coconut Grove Exhibition Center, 2700 S Bayshore Dr, Coconut Grove) Held since the mid-1940s, this annual mid-month show of flowers comes from statewide growers.

Miami-Dade County Fair (☎ 305-223-7060; www .fairexpo.com) The fair goes off in either late March or early April, and is one of the largest county fairs in the USA. Pet the livestock, ride the rides and have a go at the carnies.

Winter Music Conference (☎ 954-563-4444; www .wmcon.com) Party promoters, DJs, producers and revelers come from around the globe to hear new artists, catch up on technology and party the nights away.

Winter Party Week (☎ 305-572-1841; www.winter party.com) The gay-circuit party bonanza in mid-March benefits gay-rights organizations, including the National Gay & Lesbian Task Force.

April

Welcome to the shoulder season, bringing quieter days, lower prices, balmier temperatures and a few choice events. The religious holidays of Easter and Passover fall in April, as does the final of the Nasdaq 100 Tennis Tournament.

Nasdaq 100 Tennis Tournament (☎ 305-230-7223; Tennis Center at Crandon Park, 7300 Crandon Blvd, Key Biscayne) In late March to April, and formerly known as the Lipton and Ericsson Open, top-ranked tennis pros play for hordes of spectators.

Billboard Latin Music Awards (☎ 646-654-4660; www.billboardevents.com) This prestigious awards show in late April draws top industry execs, star performers and a slew of Latin music fans.

Miami Gay & Lesbian Film Festival (☎ 305-534-9924; www.mglff.com) Held in late April to early May, this annual event features shorts, feature films and documentaries screened at various South Beach theaters.

May & June

May and June boast increased heat, fewer visitors and several cultural events. Memorial Day is the official start of summer, bringing a beach-oriented three-day weekend.

Fashion Week of the Americas (☎ 305-604-1000; www.fashionweekamericas.com) This annual May showcase features runway shows from Latin, Caribbean, American and European designers.

Goombay Festival (☎ 305-567-1399) A massive fest, held on the first week of June, that celebrates Bahamian culture.

Florida Dance Festival (☎ 305-674-6575; www .floridadanceassociation.org/dance_festival) In mid-June, this festival brings performances, classes, workshops and seminars on dance to Miami.

July & August

The most beastly, humidity-drenched days are during these months, when locals either vacation elsewhere or spend their days melting on the beach. Official celebrations are few and far between.

Independence Day Celebration (☎ 305-358-7550; Bayfront Park, downtown Miami) July 4 features an excellent fireworks and laser show with live music that draws more than 100,000 people to breezy Bayfront Park.

Miami Spice Restaurant Month (☎ 305-358-7550; www.miamirestaurantmonth.com) Top restaurants around

Miami offer prix-fixe lunches and dinners to try to lure folks out during the heat wave.

September & October

In September the days and nights are still steamy and the start of school brings back college students. There are just a couple of tourist-oriented events in September, but they're followed by a slew of cultural offerings come October.

South Florida Dragon Boat Festival (☎ 305-633-0168; www.miamidragonboat.com; Haulover Beach Park, Bal Harbour) This new event in early to mid-October brings thousands for Chinese food, a crafts fair and the main event: festive dragon-boat races along the Florida East Coast Canal, accompanied by dramatic drumming.

Hispanic Heritage Festival (☎ 305-541-5023; www.hispanicfestival.com) Held in late October, it's one of the largest festivals in the country, commemorating the discovery of the Americas with concerts, food, games and folkloric groups.

November

Tourist season kicks off at the end of the month, bringing more crowds and slightly cooler, more bearable days. Thanksgiving falls on the last Thursday of the month.

Rasin (☎ 305-751-3740) This annual Haitian cultural festival hits in early November with music, food, crafts and more.

International Caribbean Music Festival (☎ 305-654-9991; Bayfront Park, downtown Miami) It's been one of the largest reggae events in the country since it was established in the 1980s.

Miami Book Fair International (☎ 305-237-3258; www.miamibookfair.com) Occurring in mid- to late November, this is among the most important and well-attended book fairs in the USA. Hundreds of nationally known writers join hundreds of publishers, and hundreds of thousands of visitors.

White Party (☎ 305-667-9296; www.whiteparty.net) If you're gay and not here, there's a problem. This weeklong extravaganza draws more than 15,000 gay men and women for nonstop partying at clubs and venues all over town.

December

Tourist season is in full swing, with northerners escaping south and booking rooms so they can bask in sunshine and be here for Christmas holiday festivities.

Art Miami (☎ 866-727-7953; www.art-miami.com) Held in January or December, this massive fair displays modern and contemporary works from more than 100 galleries and international artists.

Art Basel Miami Beach (☎ 305-674-1292; www.artbasel.com/miami_beach) Occurring in early December, this is one of the most important international art shows in the US, with works from more than 150 galleries and a slew of trendy parties and events.

King Mango Strut (☎ 305-401-1171; Main Ave & Grand Ave, Coconut Grove) Held each year just after Christmas, this quirky 24-year-old Coconut Grove parade is a politically charged, fun freak that began as a spoof on current events and the now-defunct Orange Bowl Parade.

SLEEPING

It's in this category, more than any other, where all the hype surrounding Miami, and particularly South Beach, is justified. Lots of places are packed with high-quality resorts and boutique sleeping spots. But what sets South Beach apart – what defines it as a travel destination – is the deco district, and the deco district's backbone is hotels. A five-minute jaunt takes you past as many sleeping spots here, all with lovingly crafted distinct personalities. And the Beach's glam only grows with every new accommodation lauded by the travel glossies, which brings the designers, which brings the fashionistas, which brings the models, which brings the tourists, which brings the chefs and…well, you get the idea. Elsewhere in Miami, accommodations are more pedestrian – a few private islands, B&Bs and lots of big-box corporate resorts (although the latter have upped the bar thanks to the Sobe competition).

You can have attitude if you want it. But there's too much competition around for owners to totally act the snob, and you'll find happy hours in local lounges more about breaking the ice and having fun than seeing and being seen. Mostly.

South Beach (1st to 11th Streets)

BUDGET

Miami Beach International Travelers Hostel (Map pp90–1; ☎ 305-534-0268, 800-978-6787; www.hostelmiamibeach.com; 236 9th St; dm $29-44, r $59-159; 🖳) The rooms are a tad worn, but security is good, the staff friendly and the lobby cheerful. Half the 100 rooms are private; the others are four-bed dorms. Strictly speaking, to get a room you'll need an out-of-state university ID, HI card, and a US or foreign passport with a recent entry stamp or an onward ticket, but these rules are only enforced when it's crowded.

 South Beach Hostel (Map pp90–1; ☎ 305-534-6669; www.thesouthbeachhostel.com; 235 Washington Ave; dm $20-28, r $60-174; 🖳) On a quiet end of Sofi (the area south of 5th St, South Beach), this relatively new hostel has a happening common area and simple, spartan rooms. It's not too flashy, but staff are friendly and the on-site bar (open till 5am) seems to stay busy. The property is split between six-bed dorms and private rooms; regarding the latter, couples are probably better off in midrange hotel rooms elsewhere, which are probably twice as nice for the same price.

Ohana Hostel (Map pp90-1; ☎ 305-534-2650; 750 Collins Ave; dm $33, r $156; 🖵) Seriously, does the same brusque French guy work the counter of every hostel in the USA? We're just sayin'. When we visited, he was definitely in this pleasant, unsigned hostel, tucked next to a surf shop. The rooms are kept sparkly clean, an international crowd chills in the lounge, and all is basically well in this corner of the budget-travel world.

Whitelaw Hotel (Map pp88-9; www.whitelawhotel .com; 855 Collins Ave; r low season $95-130, Nov-Apr $125-210; 🅿 🖵) The Whitelaw is the punky middle brother of its boutique-hotel siblings. Surreal murals wrap around a graphic designer's dream of a lounge that's constantly kicking to hot rock (and hosting hotter guests). After the white Belgian sheets, white robes, billowy white curtains and white floors, the sea-blue bathrooms come as a welcome shock (to be fair, the blinds are chrome). Parking costs $30 per day.

Hotel Chelsea (Map pp90-1; ☎ 305-534-4069; www .thehotelchelsea.com; 944 Washington Ave; r $110-205; 🅿 🖵) When you walk into the Chelsea's stylish lobby, you're greeted by a sultry, black and yellow floral pattern that feels like it's been lifted from a lingerie catalogue. The motif carries on into the dimly lit, yet sumptuous vintage rooms – which should really be called boudoirs – where the shaded chandeliers provide just the right glow. Parking costs $30 per day.

Hotel Shelley (Map pp90-1; ☎ 305-531-3341; www .hotelshelley.com; 844 Collins Ave; r low season $95-165, high season $105-260; 🖵) Gossamer curtains, a lively lounge and a sublimely relaxing violet-and-blue color scheme combine with orblike lamps that look like bunched-up glass spiderwebs. The rooms are as affordably stylish as the rest of the offerings in the South Beach Group selection of hotels (see www.southbeachgroup.com).

This place opened past our research deadline, but a new hostel in the popular 'Jazz on' chain, **Jazz on South Beach** (☎ 305-672-2137; www .jazzhotels.com/jazzsouthbeach; 321 Collins Ave), is now servicing the expanding Sobe backpacker scene. Travelers give it good reviews.

MIDRANGE

Hotel St Augustine (Map pp90-1; ☎ 305-532-0570, 800-310-7717; www.hotelstaugustine.com; 347 Washington Ave; r $120-280; 🅿 🖵) Wood that's blonder than Barbie and a crisp-and-clean deco theme combine to create one of Sofi's most elegant yet stunningly modern sleeps. The familiar, warm service is the cherry on top for this hip-and-homey standout, although the soothing lighting and glass showers – that turn into personal steam rooms at the flick of a switch – are pretty appealing too. Parking costs $15 per day.

Ocean Five Hotel (Map pp90-1; ☎ 305-532-7093; www.oceanfive.com; 436 Ocean Dr; r & ste $150-250; 🅿) This boutique hotel is all pumpkin-bright, deco-dressed-up on the outside, with cozy, quiet rooms that reveal a maritime-meets-vintage theme on the inside, with a dash of Old West ambience on top. Think mermaid murals on pale stucco walls. There are no balconies here, but the attached restaurant is a warm, friendly spot to cop a drink and a fine Italian meal before strolling up Ocean Dr. Parking is $25 per day.

Essex House Hotel (Map pp90-1; ☎ 305-534-2700, 800-553-7739; www.essexhotel.com; 1001 Collins Ave; r low season $89-325, ste $129-349; 🖵 🛎) When you gaze at this lobby, one of the best preserved interiors in the deco district, you're getting a glimpse of South Beach's glorious gangster heyday. Beyond that the Essex has helpful staff, rooms furnished with soft, subdued colors and a side veranda filled with rattan furnishings that's a particularly pleasant people-watching perch.

Chesterfield Hotel (pp90-1; ☎ 305-531-5831; www .southbeachgroup.com; 855 Collins Ave; r $130-195, ste $170-330; 🅿 🖵) Hip-hop gets jiggy with zebra-stripes on the curtains and cushions in the small lobby, which turns into one of the hoppin'-est happy hours on Collins when the sun goes down. Leave a tip for the giant African statue while you're draining that mojito. The Chesterfield is part of the ubiquitous South Beach Group, which tries to be hip, hot and affordable. Parking costs $30 per day.

Wave Hotel (Map pp90-1; ☎ 305-673-0401, 800-501-0401; www.wavehotel.com; 350 Ocean Dr; r $159-259; 🅿 🖵) Dark blue, plush molded furniture and curving, cool lines give the lobby a sense of tidal momentum. There's a space-race theme (as in '50s Sputnik-era retro chic) going on in the rooms; you gotta love the lamps, which look like cartoon bubble helmets from Buck Rogers. Parking costs $20 per day.

Blue Moon (Map pp90–1; ☎ 305-673-2262, 800-553-7739; www.bluemoonhotel.com; 944 Collins Ave; r low season $95-220, late Dec–Mar $173-279; P 🖳) The service here couldn't be friendlier, and while the hotel isn't technically deco, it's not too shabby either. The rooms are crisp and clean, and a kitschy, unpretentious atmosphere of tropical twee dominates throughout. Parking is $25 per day.

Hotel Astor (Map pp90–1; ☎ 305-531-8081, 800-270-4981; www.hotelastor.com; 956 Washington Ave; r $125-290; P 🖳 ⚽) They lay the retro-punk on thick in the Astor lobby, glamorizing and exaggerating the Age of Transportation into a hip caricature of itself: a gigantic industrial fan blows over a ceiling studded with psychedelic 'lamp balls,' all suspended over a fanciful daydream of an old-school pilot's club. The earth-toned rooms are relaxing, and the small pool gets covered at night to make room for club-goers who bop on the back-patio lounge. Parking costs $25 per day.

Kent Hotel (Map pp90–1; ☎ 305-604-5068; www.thekenthotel.com; 1131 Collins Ave; r low season $79-350; P 🖳) Young party types will probably get a kick out of this lobby, filled with fuchsia and electric-orange geometric furniture plus bright Lucite toy blocks, which makes for an aggressively playful welcome. The special Lucite Suite is almost entirely constructed of the see-through material, giving it an icy playground feel. Take refuge in a side garden with Indonesian-style tables, bamboo and hammocks. Parking costs $20 per day.

Bentley Beach Hotel (Map pp90–1; ☎ 305-938-4600; www.bentleybeachhotel.com; 101 Ocean Dr; r $175-349; P 🖳 ⚽) You like the word 'mahogany?' Reeks of dark, old-school sexy ambience, right? The folks here agree, and their lobby is a tobacco-brown exemplar of mahogany style – not the wood, per se, but its classy connotations. Shell lamps line the walls and a rooftop pool and Jacuzzi shimmer under the stars. The raised bed in the two-bedroom suite is the coolest sleeping nook in this contender. Parking costs $25 per day.

Strand (Map pp90–1; ☎ 305-538-9830; www.thestrandoceandrive.com; 1052 Ocean Dr; r $170-315; P 🖳 ⚽) Lying in the low-slung, high-threadcount beds feels like swimming in silk, while en-suite bucket chairs were just made for your fine booty. Porthole mirrors on the outside path leading into the crisp lobby remind you you're going on a voyage: namely, to getting-spoiled town. Parking is $35 per day.

Clinton Hotel (Map pp90–1; ☎ 305-938-4040; www.clintonsouthbeach.com; 825 Washington Ave; r $140-396; P 🖳 ⚽) Washington Ave is the quietest of the three main drags in Sobe, but the Clinton doesn't mind. This joint knows it would be the hottest girl in the most crowded party, with her blue velveteen banquettes and uber-contemporary metal ceiling fans. The tiny sun porches in the Zen rooms are perfect for breakfast or an evening cocktail. Parking is $27 per day.

Century Hotel (Map pp90–1; ☎ 305-674-8855, 888-982-3688; www.centurysouthbeach.com; 140 Ocean Dr; r $120-465, ste $145-515; P 🖳) The Century, dating back to 1939, is one of the best-preserved deco spots on the strip. It quietly gleams at the far-south, sedate end of Ocean Dr, its wood floors and white walls combining for a starkly sumptuous sleeping experience, setting the perfect balance of sleekness and warmth. Parking is approximately $27 per day.

ourpick Pelican Hotel (Map pp90–1; ☎ 305-673-3373, 800-773-5422; www.pelicanhotel.com; 826 Ocean Dr; r low season $165-500, high season $240-700; 🖳) When the owners of Diesel jeans purchased the Pelican in 1999, they started scouring garage sales for just the right ingredients to fuel a mad experiment: 30 theme rooms that come off like a fantasy-suite hotel dipped in hip. From the funky blue ambience of 'Some Like It Wet' to the warm 'Cubarean Islands' lovefest and playfully perverted 'Best Whorehouse,' all of the rooms are completely different (although all have beautiful recycled-oak floors), fun and even come with their own 'suggested soundtrack.'

TOP END

Hotel (Map pp90–1; ☎ 305-531-2222; 801 Collins Ave; www.thehotelofsouthbeach.com; r low season $235-295, Jan-May $250-425; P 🖳 ⚽) This place is stylin' – and why shouldn't it be, when Todd Oldham designed the boldly beautiful rooms? The theme palette of 'sand, sea and sky' adds a dash of eye candy to the furnishings, as do the mosaic doorknobs and brushed-steel sinks. Many say the Hotel boasts the best rooftop pool in South Beach, overshadowed only by a lovely deco spire (which says 'Tiffany,' because that was the name of this place before the blue-box jewelry chain threatened a lawsuit). Parking costs $25 per day.

Casa Grande Hotel (Map pp90–1; ☎ 866-420-2272; www.casagrandesuitehotel.com; 834 Ocean Dr; r & ste low season $215-475, Oct-May $315-575; P 🖳) Fall colors and a splash of bright citrus start the show in the lobby, but the main event is the snow-white elegance of the 35 so-chic rooms, each one an ultramodern Scandinavian designer's dream – although we've gotta say the big, marble Virgin Mary in the room we visited was waaaaaay out of place. We do like the flowers on the pillow though; nice touch, guys. Parking is $30 per day.

Beacon Hotel (Map pp90-1; ☎ 305-674-8200; www .beacon-hotel.com; 720 Ocean Dr; r low season $150-369, Nov-May $302-619; **P** 🖳) Overlooking a truly bumpin' slice of Ocean Dr real estate, the Beacon has a grand dame of a deco lobby and friendly service, but the rooms are kind of plain. They're nice, no doubt, with shiny marble floors and warm wood furnishings, but the bar is set high here and the Beacon is still reaching. Parking costs $20 per day.

Hotel Nash (Map pp90-1; ☎ 305-674-7800; www .hotelnash.com; 1120 Collins Ave; r $159-300, ste $545-855; **P** 🖳 🕿) The modern interior of the Nash is beige and white hot. Or is that cool? Whatever. This quiet, elegant inn has an expansive marble lobby leading to 54 rooms that are cozy while chic and suitably sleek. Parking is $25 per day.

Hotel Victor (Map pp90-1; ☎ 305-428-1234; www .hotelvictorsouthbeach.com; 1144 Ocean Dr; r $489-1595; **P** 🖳 🕿) The Victor wins – the hot design stakes, that is. And the fish tanks full of jellyfish competition. And the 'damn-that-room-is-fly' pageant too. Designed by L Murray Dixon in 1938, the redone Victor was opened in 2005 to much acclaim; these days, Shaquille O'Neal is famous for throwing parties in the $6000-a-night penthouse. Parking costs $32 per day.

Mondrian (Map pp90-1; ☎ 305-672-2662, 877-809-0007; www.mondriansouthbeach.com; 1100 West Ave) 'The idea at the Mondrian,' says this condotel's PR flack, 'is to take the concept of the Delano and the Shore Club to the next level.' The *next* level? Weren't the other two opulent enough? Guess not. Morgan Hotel Group has hired Dutch design-star Marcel Wanders (whose name they'll drop till it falls through the floor) to basically crank it up to 11. The theme is inspired by Alice in Wonderland (if penned by Crockett from *Miami Vice*) – columns carved like giant table legs, chandelier showerheads, imported Delft tiles with beach scenes instead of windmills, and magic walls with morphing celebrity faces (perhaps because the morphing nature of celebrity is what fuels South Beach's glamour?). Oh, and it'll have a private island (natch). It's on South Beach's bayside. With

the Mondrian on one side and the Delano on the other; you can just imagine a Morgan Group pincer of gentrification squeezing out what's left of the normal neighborhood in a few years.

South Beach (11th to 23rd Streets)

BUDGET

Tropics Hotel & Hostel (Map pp88-9; ☎ 305-531-0361; www.tropicshotel.com; 1550 Collins Ave; dm $27, r $100-135; 🕿) The surprisingly nice Tropics (which looks a bit skeezy from the outside) sports a big swimming pool and a patio area that seems consistently packed with chatting travelers. The clean four-bed dorms have attached bathrooms; private rooms are basic and serviceable.

Clay Hotel & Miami Beach International Hostel (Map pp88-9; ☎ 305-534-2988, 800-379-2529; www .clayhotel.com; 1438 Washington Ave; dm $25-29, r $60-260; 🖳) How many HI hostels are located in a 100-year-old Spanish-style villa? The Clay has clean and comfortable rooms, from single-sex, four-to eight-bed dorms to decent private rooms, many of which are located in a medinalike maze of adjacent buildings. Staff are harassed due to sheer volume, but are friendly and helpful. This is yet another Miami place where Al Capone got some shut-eye.

Beachcomber Hotel (Map pp88-9; ☎ 305-531-3755, 888-305-4683; www.beachcombermiami.com; 1340 Collins Ave; r $89-189; 🖳) Green sets the stage at this deco classic, with a green-banana-colored facade, a soothing, mint-green lobby, green-flecked terrazzo floor, seafoam-green couches and a chartreuse bar, all floating beneath sleek aluminum ceiling fans. The rooms, while not quite as seductive as the entrance, are basic, cozy and clean.

MIDRANGE

Aqua Hotel (Map pp88-9; ☎ 305-538-4361; www.aqua miami.com; 1530 Collins Ave; r & ste $142-282; **P** 🖳 🕿) A front desk made of shiny surfboard sets the mellow tone at this former motel – the old, family kind where the rooms are set around a pool. That old-school vibe barely survives under the soft glare of aqua (imagine that) spotlights and an alfresco lounging area, popular with the mostly gay clientele. The sleekness of the rooms is offset by quirky furniture, like a sumptuous chair made of spotted cowhide. Parking costs $35 per day.

Cavalier Hotel (Map pp88-9; ☎ 305-531-3555, 800-688-7678; www.cavaliermiami.com; 1320 Ocean Dr; low season r $99-129, ste $199, Oct-May r $129-155, ste $229; (P)(icon)) The exterior is a rare Ocean Dr example of the Mayan/Incan inspiration that graced some deco facades (look for Mesoamerican details like the step pattern on the sides of the building). Inside? The Cavalier sacrifices ultrahip for Old Florida casualness, which is frankly kinda refreshing. We love the earthy touches in the rooms, like batik fabrics in tones of brown and beige.

Townhouse Hotel (Map pp88-9; (icon) 305-534-3800, 800-688-7678; www.townhousehotel.com; 150 20th St at Collins Ave; r $105-195, ste $395-450; (icon)(icon)) You'd think the Townhouse was designed by the guy who styled the Ipod, but no it was Jonathan Morr and India Mahdavi, who have fashioned a cool white lobby and igloolike rooms with random scarlet accents and a breezy rooftop lounge. Who needs mints on pillows when the Townhouse provides beach balls? Parking costs $25 per day.

Greenview (Map pp88-9; (icon) 305-531-6588, 877-782-3557; www.greenviewhotel.com; 1671 Washington Ave; low season r $95-150, ste $175-230, high season r/ste $160/260) Aw, the Greenview is so cozy and sweet – like a hotel run by your grandma. Seriously, the staff will probably bake cookies if you ask nicely. Furnishings are spare, with sisal rugs and bamboo lamps, plus black-and-white photos on the walls – grandma again.

Winter Haven (Map pp88-9; (icon) 305-531-5571, 800-395-2322; www.winterhavenhotelsobe.com; 1400 Ocean Dr; r low season $119-199, high season $149-259; (P)(icon)(icon)) Al Capone used to stay here; maybe he liked the deco ceiling lamps in the lobby, with their sharp, retro-sci-fi lines and grand-Gothic proportions, and the oddly placed oriental mirrors (which have nothing to do with deco whatsoever). A young but laid-back crowd hangs at the Haven, which sits on the pretty-people end of Ocean Dr. Parking is $25 per day.

Surfcomber (Map pp88-9; (icon) 305-532-7715; www.surfcomber.com; 1717 Collins Ave; r $190-260; (P)(icon)(icon)) Simply one of the best classical deco structures in Miami, the Surfcomber is (shhhh) actually owned by Doubletree. Well, more power to 'em; the chain has renovated this property into an immaculate state. Note the movement-suggestive lines on the exterior and semicircular, shade-providing 'eyebrows' that jut out of the windows. Also especially note the lobby – the rounded, aeronautic feel of the space suggests you're entering a 1930s airline lounge, but no, you're just going to your room. Parking is $39 per day.

TOP END

(our pick) **Standard** (Map pp88-9; (icon) 305-673-1717; 40 Island Ave; r & ste $195-750; (P)(icon)(icon)) Look for the upside down 'Standard' sign on the old Lido building on Belle Island (between South Beach and downtown Miami) and you'll find the Standard – which is anything but. This excellent boutique blends hipster funk with South Beach sex, and the result is a '50s motel gone glam. There are organic wooden floors, raised white beds, and gossamer curtains, which open onto a courtyard of earthly delights, including a heated *hammam* (Turkish bath). The crowd, which feels like the Delano kids with a bit more maturity, gathers to flirt and gawk. Shuttles ferry you to the Sagamore every 30 minutes, so you're never too isolated from the scene – unless you want to be, and given the grace of this place, we'd totally understand why. Parking costs $10 per day.

Hotel Impala (Map pp88-9; (icon) 305-673-2021, 800-646-7252; www.hotelimpalamiamibeach.com; 1228 Collins Ave; low season r $145-225, ste $225-325, high season r $195-245, ste $345-425; (P)(icon)) The Italianate courtyard – and Italian food available at on-site Spiga (p139) – plus the marbled, plush white rooms, will make you feel like Maximus Luxurious presiding over his realm. Rooms are spacious and decked out in typically South Beach fashion: glamorous but stripped down in an ultra-modern, lots of white (sheets, curtains etc) look. The front desk is very helpful, as befits your royal status. Parking costs $25 per day

(our pick) **Cardozo Hotel** (Map pp88-9; (icon) 305-535-6500, 800-782-6500; www.cardozohotel.com; 1300 Ocean Dr; r & ste low season $227-454, Nov-May $287-487; (P)(icon)) The Cardozo and its neighbor, the Carlyle, were the first deco hotels saved by the Miami Design Preservation League, and in the case of the Cardozo, we think they saved the best first. Owner Gloria Estefan, whose videos are looped on flat-screen mini-TVs in the lobby, likely agrees. It's the combination of the usual contemporary sexiness (white walls, hardwood floors, high-threadcount sheets) and playful embellishments: leopard-skin details, handmade furniture and a general sense that, yes, you are cool if you stay here, but you don't have to flaunt it. Oh – remember the 'hair gel' scene in *There's Something About Mary*? Filmed here. Parking costs $27 per day.

National Hotel (Map pp88-9; (icon) 305-532-2311, 800-327-8370; www.nationalhotel.com; 1677 Collins Ave; r $269-509; (P)(icon)(icon)) The lobby looks like a 1920s speakeasy married to 21st-century interior design, while outside, the loooooooooooong pool seems to double as a red (well, teal) carpet for beach royalty; a carpet that runs right up to this deco landmark and back to a busy tiki bar. Rooms can't match the pool or lobby's preening good looks, but they are extremely ritzy. Parking costs $37 per day.

Royal Palm Hotel (Map pp88-9; ☎ 305-604-5700; www.royalpalmmiamibeach.com; 1545 Collins Ave; low season r $169-369, ste $299-559, high season r $189-429, ste $389-689; P ▣ ▣) Even the trolleys here have a touch of curvy deco flair, to say nothing of the chunky staircase and mezzanine, which are the best South Beach examples of the building-as-cruise-liner deco theme. Note the porthole windows, wire railings and a general sense of oceanic space; you can almost hear waves slapping the side of the building. There's a glut of Britto art in the lobby (and even a Britto-themed restaurant), and rooms are suitably luxurious. Parking costs $39 per day.

Tides (Map pp88-9; 305-604-5070, 800-688-7678; www.thetideshotel.com; 1220 Ocean Dr; r $550-850; P ▣ ▣) The 50 ocean-fronting rooms are icy cool, with their jumbled vintage, ocean organic and indie vibe. The pure, white bedding is overlaid by beige, tan and shell, and offset with cream accents. Rooms come with telescopes for planetary (or Hollywood) stargazing, and the lobby, decked with nautical embellishments, looks like a modern sea god's palace. You can't miss this place; it's one of the biggest buildings fronting Ocean Dr. Parking costs $35 per day.

Raleigh Hotel (Map pp88-9; ☎ 305-534-6300, 800-848-1775; www.raleighhotel.com; 1775 Collins Ave; r $295-395, ste $425-850; P ▣ ▣) While everyone else was trying to get all modern, the Raleigh painstakingly tried to restore itself to prewar glory. It succeeded in a big way. Celebrity hotelier André Balazs managed to capture a tobacco-and-dark-wood men's club ambience and old-school elegance while simultaneously sneaking in modern design elements and amenities. Have a swim in the stunning pool; Esther Williams used to. Parking costs $30 per day.

Marlin Hotel (Map pp88-9; ☎ 305-604-5000, 800-688-7678; 1200 Collins Ave; r & ste $325-895) Rock star. Live it. Love it. Be it. That's the fantasy you get to play out here, where the deep purple walls are smeared with club sweat, the 12 individualized rooms look like party penthouses, and an on-site studio pulls in bands from Aerosmith to U2.

Sagamore (Map pp88-9; ☎ 305-535-8088; www.sagamorehotel.com; 1671 Collins Ave; r & ste $305-1050; P ▣ ▣) Spencer Tunick got 600 people to pose nude in massive structured photo shoots set all around the Sagamore in 2007. Nude art installation – that's hot, but also expected at this hotel-cum–exhibition space, which likes to blur the boundaries between interior decor, art and conventional hotel aesthetics. For instance, rows of plaster death masks line the area around the bar – TGI Friday's, take note! – and even the rooms double as art galleries, thanks to a talented curator and an impressive roster of contributing artists. Parking costs $35 per day.

Loews Miami Beach (Map pp88-9; ☎ 305-604-1601, 800-235-6397; www.loewshotels.com; 1601 Collins Ave; r $339-1075; P ▣ ▣) If for some reason you're missing big, conventioneer-style boxes, come to Loews. There are 800 lovely (if identikit) rooms, a fitness center, pool, private beachfront, *six* restaurants (including the popular Emeril's) and endless meeting rooms. Parking costs $33 per day.

De Soleil (Map pp88-9; ☎ 305-672-4554; www.preferredboutique.com; 1458 Ocean Dr; r $330-750, ste $915-1475; P ▣ ▣) There are some hotties working the desk at De Soleil, which has large, gray-black-and-white super suites and the best bathrooms on South Beach, plus metal-grille balconies overlooking a lovely courtyard, and rooftop lounges worthy of Hugh Hefner. Govind Armstrong's deservedly lauded Table 8 (p141) is on-site. Parking costs $32 per day.

our pick Shore Club (Map pp88-9; ☎ 305-695-3100; www.shoreclub.com; 1901 Collins Ave; r & ste $295-1550; P ▣ ▣) Imagine a Zen ink-brush painting. What's beautiful isn't what's there, but what gets left out. If you could turn that sort of art into a hotel room, it might look like the stripped-down yet serene digs of the Shore Club. Yeah, yeah: it's got the 400-threadcount Egyptian cotton sheets, Mexican sandstone floors etc; a lot of hotels in Sobe lay claim to similar luxury lists. What the Shore Club does like no other hotel is arrange these elements into a greater whole that's impressive in its understatement; the aesthetic is compelling because it comes across as an afterthought. For those who thrive on aristocratic appeal, Miami's Nobu branch is here, as is the impossibly exclusive Moroccan-themed Skybar (p151). Parking costs $42 per day.

Delano Hotel (Map pp88-9; ☎ 305-672-2000, 800-555-5001; 1685 Collins Ave; r & ste low season $330-815, Jan-

Apr $405-1750; (**P** 🖵 🔊) The Delano opened in the 1990s and immediately started ruling the South Beach roost. Today, spoiled teen princesses want their rooms to be converted into Delano-esque, ultrawhite fairy-tale sleeping nooks on MTV's *Super Sweet 16*. Is this a reminder of the hotel's pop-culture cred, or a sign the coolest cat on the block is getting passé? Decide for yourself. Because if there's a quintessential 'I'm-too-sexy-for-this-song' South Beach moment, it's when you walk into the Delano's lobby, which has all the excess of an over-budgeted theater set. 'Magic mirrors' in the halls disclose weather info, tide charts, even inspirational quotes. The pool area resembles the courtyard of a Disney princess' palace and includes a giant chess set; there are floor-to-ridiculously-high-ceiling curtains in the two-story waterfront rooms; and the bedouin tent cabanas are outfitted with flat-screen TVs. Parking costs $37 per day.

Setai (Map pp88-9; ☎ 305-520-6000; www.setai.com; 101 20th St; r & ste $900-6000; (**P** 🖵 🔊) There's a linga in the lobby – nothing says high-end luxury like a Hindu phallus. It's all part of the aesthetic at Miami's most expensive sleep, where a well-realized theme mixes Southeast Asian temple architecture, Chinese furniture, contemporary luxury and conceptual atmosphere. Each floor is staffed by teams of 24-hour butlers, while rooms are decked out in chocolate teak wood, clean lines, and Chinese and Khmer embellishments. Note: the studio is small for four figures. Service is outstanding and surprisingly down-to-earth. Parking costs $34 per day.

In addition, the satellites of two huge condotel complexes, the **W Hotel** (Map pp88-9; www.wsouthbeachresidences.com; 2201 Collins Ave) and the **Gansevoort** (Map pp88-9; www.gansevoortsouth.com; 2399 Collins Ave), should be open by the time you read this. These guys want to compete with the Delano and its Morgan Group buddies, so expect completely-over-the-top opulence and resort-level rates.

Northern Miami Beach
BUDGET & MIDRANGE

Indian Creek Hotel (Map p94; ☎ 305-531-2727, 800-491-2772; www.indiancreekhotel.com; 2727 Indian Creek Dr; r $90-279; 🔊) Get your room key – attached to a plastic alligator – and walk through the old Miami lobby, spruced up with souvenir-stand schlock, to your comfortable, earthy-warm digs. Or wander out to the surprisingly mod-

ern pool, where happy, sexy people are ready to have a good time. Mix in a friendly staff and an easy walk to the boardwalk, and you've got a perfect little boutique hotel.

Bay Harbor Inn & Suites (Map p94; ☎ 305-868-4141; www.bayharborinn.com; 9660 E Bay Harbor Dr; r $150-210; (**P** 🖵 🔊) Operated by earnest Johnson & Wales University students as an integral part of their hands-on hospitality training, this upscale small hotel has a warmer, more country feel than the sleek spaces you get used to seeing in Miami.

Beach House Bal Harbour (Map p94; ☎ 305-535-8600, 877-782-3557; 9449 Collins Ave; r $105-267; 🖵 🔊) The Beach House is a down-to-earth inn with a Keys-y feel, complete with wainscoting, conch shells and fresh-looking, blue sheets in every room. The Bal Harbour Shops across the street will keep you anchored in Miami-glitz reality.

Claridge Hotel (Map p94; ☎ 305-604-8485, 888-422-9111; www.claridgefl.com; 3500 Collins Ave; r $120-280; 🖵 🔊) This 1928 Mediterranean palace feels like a (admittedly Americanized) Tuscan villa, with a sunny honey-stone courtyard enclosing a sparkling pool, framed by palms, frescoed walls and gleaming stone floors. The soothing, old-world rooms are set off by rich earth tones, and staff are eager to please.

our pick Circa 39 (Map p94; ☎ 305-538-3900, 877-824-7223; www.circa39.com; 3900 Collins Ave; r $122-279; 🖵 🔊) If you love South Beach style but loathe South Beach attitude, Circa has got your back. The lobby, with its multicolored light board, molded furniture and wacky embellishments, is one of the funkiest in Miami. The hallways are low-lit under sexy red lamps and the icy-blue-and-white rooms are hip enough for the most exclusive scenesters (although Circa frowns on folks who act snobby). Be you a family, a gay person or just someone who loves laid-back fun, this hotel welcomes all.

Palms South Beach (Map p94; ☎ 305-534-3119; www.thepalmshotel.com; 3025 Collins Ave; r & ste $140-400; (**P** 🖵 🔊) The lobby of the Palms manages to be imposing and comfortable all at once; the soaring ceiling, cooled by slow-spinning giant rattan fans, makes for a colonial-villa-on-convention-center-steroids vibe. Upstairs the rooms are perfectly fine, if a tad bland.

TOP END
Courtyard Hotel (Map p94; ☎ 305-538-3373; www.miamicourtyard.com; 3952 Collins Ave; r high season $249-454, low season $170-400; (**P** 🖵 🔊) Look for the big,

beautiful deco facade of the Cadillac building and you've found the Marriott-owned Courtyard, which tries valiantly to be a cut above the corporate chain it is. With its excellent exterior, cushy mattresses and free *Newsweeks*, this is probably the best of the large-scale chains lining Collins Ave. Parking costs $24 per day.

Fontainebleau Hilton Hotel & Resort (Map p94; ☎ 305-538-2000, 800-548-8886; www.fontainebleau .hilton.com; 4441 Collins Ave; low season r from $369, late Dec–May $469; **P** **🖳** **🏊**) Probably Miami Beach's most recognizable landmark, the 1200-room Fontainebleau opened in 1954, when it became a celeb sunning spot and set of many a Hollywood production (including *Goldfinger*, *The Bellboy* and *Scarface*). A 2003 renovation added every conceivable amenity, including beachside cabanas, seven tennis courts, grand ballroom, shopping mall and an ab-fab swimming pool. Throw in the towering condotels of the Fontainebleau II and III and you've got one of the grandest lodgings in Miami. Parking costs $30 per day.

Eden Roc Resort (Map p94; ☎ 305-531-0000, 800-327-8337; www.edenrocresort.com; 4525 Collins Ave) The Roc, set to reopen after a renovation in 2008, is the rival grand dame to the next door Fontainebleau. The big overhaul aims to turn this venerated resort into a combination of large-scale convention center and northern colony of Sobe cool. At the time of writing the new room rates had not been announced.

Downtown Miami

Miami River Inn (Map pp92-3; ☎ 305-325-0045, 800-468-3589; www.miamiriverinn.com; 119 SW South River Dr; r $69-199; **P** **🖳** **🏊**) Cute mom-and-pop B&Bs stuffed full of antique furniture, pretty-as-lace gardens and a general 'Aw, thanks for breakfast' vibe are comparatively rare here. The River Inn, listed on the National Register of Historic Places, bucks this trend, with charming New England–style rooms, friendly service and one of the best libraries of Miami literature in the city. In a place where every hotel can feel like a loud experiment in graphic design, this relaxing watercolor invites you onto the back porch.

Conrad Miami (Map pp92-3; ☎ 305-503-6500; www .conradhotels.com; 1395 Brickell Ave; r & ste $169-1225; **P** **🖳** **🏊**) Conrad is trying to slide bits of South Beach celebrity into its gray-suited facade via hot promo parties and cool lizard-lounges, but really, this is a 36-story tower of glass, steel and business-traveler amenities. Don't be ashamed Conrad: you're a credit to the genre, from the 25th-floor power-broker sky lobby to a location in the heart of Brickell's flash and finance. Parking costs $33 per day.

Four Seasons Miami (Map pp92-3; ☎ 305-358-3535; www.fourseasons.com/miami; 1435 Brickell Ave; r & ste $275-1400; **P** **🖳** **🏊**) The marble common areas double as an art gallery, a massive spa caters to corporate types and there are sweeping, could-have-been-a-panning-shot-from-*Miami-Vice* views over Biscayne Bay in some rooms. The 7th-floor terrace bar Bahia is pure mojito-laced, Latin-loved swankiness, especially on Thursdays and Fridays from 6pm to 8pm, when ladies drink free. Parking costs $33 per day.

Mandarin Oriental Miami (Map pp92-3; ☎ 305-913-8288, 866-888-6780; www.mandarinoriental.com; 500 Brickell Key Dr; r & ste $395-5000; **P** **🖳** **🏊**) The Mandarin shimmers on Brickell Key, which is actually annoying – you're a little isolated from the city out here. Not that it matters; there's a luxurious world within a world inside this exclusive compound, from swank restaurants to a private beach and skyline views that look back at Miami from the far side of Biscayne Bay. Rooms are good in a luxury-chain kind of way, but nothing sets them apart from other sleeps in this price range. Parking costs $26 per day.

Key Biscayne

Silver Sands Beach Resort (Map p98; ☎ 305-361-5441; www.key-biscayne/silversands.com; 301 Ocean Dr; r $129-189, cottage $279-329; **P** **🏊**) Silver Sands: aren't you cute, with your one-story, stucco tropical tweeness? How this little, Old Florida–style independent resort has survived amid the corporate competition is beyond us, but it's definitely a warm, homey spot for those seeking some intimate, individual attention – to say nothing of the sunny courtyard, garden area and outdoor pool.

Ritz-Carlton Key Biscayne (Map p98; ☎ 305-365-4500, 800-241-3333; www.ritzcarlton.com; 455 Grand Bay Dr; r & ste $215-3000; **P** **🖳** **🏊**) Sure, it's 'just' another Ritz-Carlton. But it's also pretty unique. There's the magnificent lobby, vaulted by four giant columns lifted from a Cecil B DeMille set – hell, the whole hotel is lifted from a DeMille set. Tinkling fountains, the view of the bay and the marble grandeur speak less of a chain hotel and more of early-20th-century glamour. Rooms and amenities are predictably excellent. Parking costs $30 per day.

Coconut Grove

MIDRANGE

Mutiny Hotel (Map p99; ☎ 305-441-2100, 888-868-8469; www.mutinyhotel.com; 2951 S Bayshore Dr; ste $119-259; P ☐ ☲) This small luxury bayfront hotel, with 120 one- and two-bedroom suites, featuring balconies, boasts an indulgent staff, high-end bedding, gracious appointments, fine amenities and a small heated pool. Although it's on a busy street, you won't hear the traffic once inside. Parking costs $24 per day.

Grand Bay Miami (Map p99; ☎ 305-858-9600, 800-433-4555; www.grandbaymiami.com; 2669 S Bayshore Dr; r $109-239, ste $159-859; P ☐ ☲) Thirteen-stories tall and tucked in opposite the bay, this waterfront resort occupies the upscale middle ground between mall shopping and sea breezes. Rooms are pretty, if predictable. Parking costs $24 per day.

TOP END

Ritz-Carlton Coconut Grove (Map p99; ☎ 305-644-4680, 800-241-3333; www.ritzcarlton.com; 3300 SW 27th Ave; r & ste $189-399; P ☐ ☲) The third of a power troika of Ritz-Carltons in Miami, this one overlooks the bay, has totally rich rooms and offers butlers for every need, from shopping and web surfing to dog walking and bathing. The massive spa is stupendous. Parking is $30 per day.

Sonesta Hotel & Suites Coconut Grove (Map p99; ☎ 305-529-2828; 2889 McFarlane Rd; r $165-500; P ☐ ☲) The Coco Grove outpost of this luxury chain of hotels has decked its rooms out in almost-all-white with a splash of color (South Beach style). The posh amenities, from flat-screen TVs to mini-kitchenettes, add a layer of luxury on this surprisingly hip big-box. Parking costs $23 per day.

Grove Isle Club & Resort (Map pp86-7; ☎ 305-858-8300, 800-884-7683; www.groveisle.com; 4 Grove Isle Dr; r $219-529, ste $389-879; P ☐ ☲) One of those 'I've got my own little island' type places, Grove Island is off the coast of Coconut Grove (just northeast of our neighborhood boundary). This stunning boutique hotel has got colonial elegance, lush tropical gardens, sunset views over Biscayne Bay, amenities galore and the cachet of staying in your own floating temple of exclusivity.

Coral Gables

Hotel Place St Michel (Map p95; ☎ 305-444-1666; www.hotelplacestmichel.com; 162 Alcazar Ave; r $125-245; P ☐) The Michel is more Metropole than

Miami, and we mean that as a compliment. The old-world wooden fixtures, refined sense of tweedy style and dinner-jacket ambience don't get in the way of friendly service. The lovely restaurant and cool bar-lounge are as elegant as the hotel they occupy. Parking is $9 a day.

David William Hotel (Map p95; ☎ 305-445-7821; www.davidwilliamhotel.com; 700 Biltmore Way; r $109-299; P ☐ ☲) It looks like a big box on the outside, but inside, the lobby is a head rush of chandeliers and pink-champagne marble. Staff are very helpful and rooms are big and beautiful (though not particularly interesting); you could probably swim laps across the huge mattresses.

Westin Coral Gables (Map p95; ☎ 305-441-2600; www.starwoodhotels.com; 180 Aragon Ave; r $195-295, ste $235-425; P ☐ ☲) Here's another surprisingly independent outpost of a luxury chain. From the colonnaded building, with its 1920s-meets-Mediterranean-Revival wonderland of marble columns and shiny stone floors, to little touches like towels twisted to look like kissing swans, this Westin has a warm, idiosyncratic touch of character and class. Parking costs $12 per day.

Biltmore Hotel (Map p95; ☎ 305-445-1926, 800-727-1926; www.biltmorehotel.com; 1200 Anastasia Ave; r & ste $219-2500; P ☐ ☲) The Biltmore is such an iconic piece of architecture that it's easy to forget its original purpose: a hotel. Though the standard rooms can be small, a stay here is a chance to sleep in one of the great laps of US luxury. Make sure to catch a ghost tour with the Dade Heritage Trust (see p116) and take a dip in the largest hotel pool in the continental USA. Parking costs $25 per day.

Greater Miami

Trump International Sonesta Beach Resort (Map pp86-7; ☎ 305-692-5600, 800-766-3782; www.trumpsonesta.com; 18001 Collins Ave; r & ste $169-889; P ☐ ☲) Located up in Sunny Isles, Trump's take on Miami is just as you'd expect: 32 stories of ocean views, a ballroom and luxury rooms, along with a spa and extensive kids' program. The lagoon pool is full of waterfalls and palm trees, and there are four on-site restaurants. Parking costs $24 per day.

Inn at the Fisher Island Club (Map pp86-7; ☎ 305-535-6080, 800-537-3708; www.fisherisland.com; r $600-2250; ☐ ☲) If you're not Jeb Bush, the only way to glimpse Fisher Island is to stay at this luxurious resort. Whether in 'simple' rooms or

Vanderbilt-era cottages, your money will be well spent: one of the best-rated spas in the country is here, as well as eight restaurants (this seems like overkill given the size of the island) and enough royal perks to please an Egyptian pharaoh.

EATING

Miami is a major immigrant entrepôt, and the great thing about immigrants – besides being the backbone of the country – is A) their delicious old country cuisines and B) their preference for excessive (USA size) portions. Ever tried Cuban cuisine in Cuba? Screw those skimpy commie rations – there's no such moderation in Miami. Break a $10 bill here and the payoff is a steaming surfeit of *ropa vieja* (shredded beef), rice and beans, and the sweetest fried plantains to ever kiss your lips.

On top of that, South Florida has always loved showing off. Locals put a lot of emphasis on style and name dropping, and despite the occasional silliness of the four-star scene, a lot of substance breaks through style's excess at the high end of the Miami dining scale.

Thus: three sides to the Miami eating scene. First: Boring Americana chain sameness – bland, blah, blech. If you eat at TGI Friday's here, frankly, you deserve food poisoning.

Next comes the ethnic eateries: Jewish delis, Japanese sushi stands, Florida stone-crab shacks and more Cuban sandwich stalls than you can shake an anti-Castro mural at. You won't find a better city in the US for Brazilian, Argentinean, Venezuelan,

Dominican or any other variation of Latin and Caribbean cuisine.

Finally comes the haute dining, as fine as the hostess seating you at your nuevo-fusioned-pan-Americo-Asian-Carribean shrine to pretension. Expect some clientele to be more interested in the name of a celebrity chef than the food said chef prepares. Also expect, more often than not, an eating experience that will pretty much blow your mind to new levels of gastronomic enlightenment.

South Beach (1st to 11th Streets)
BUDGET

Pizza Rustica (Map pp90-1; ☎ 305-674-8244; 863 Washington Ave; slices $2.50-3.50; ☼ lunch & dinner) South Beach's favorite pizza place has two locations to satisfy the demand for crusty Roman-style slices topped with an array of exotic offerings. A slice is a meal unto itself. The second branch is further north, at 1447 Washington Ave (see Map pp88–9).

11th Street Diner (Map pp90-1; ☎ 305-534-6373; 1065 Washington Ave; mains $8-15; ☼ 24hr) You've seen the art-deco landmarks. Now eat in one: a Pullman-car diner trucked down from Wilkes-Barre, Pennsylvania, as sure a slice of Americana as a *Leave it to Beaver* marathon. If you've been drinking all night, we'll split a three-egg omelette with you and the other drunkies at 6am. Dude. The bathroom's in the back. *Not on my leg!*

News Café (Map pp90-1; ☎ 305-538-6397; 800 Ocean Dr; mains $8-17; ☼ 24hr) Some kind of lodestone attracts every tourist in South Beach to this Ocean Dr landmark. Frankly, we don't get it,

---

PAULA NINO

We talked to local foodie Paula Nino about the treats and temptations on local plates.

What's the geography of the Miami eating scene? What's blowing up? First, a lot of chefs from outside Miami have moved here, especially in 2007. And local chefs are moving out of South Beach and into the neighborhoods. You could say those areas are hip, not South Beach. There's a guy opening a restaurant on Biscayne Blvd in a shady area next to a strip club, and everyone's excited. People want good food outside South Beach.

Do Miamians have distinct tastes? Do they like to go out? They like to go out. I don't know about a distinct taste. Some people are afraid to try new things.

So are chefs shaping the industry, or consumers? Oh, consumers. But it's still in-between. I think Miami wants to be a foodie city, but it's still in the learning phases.

OK, hypothetically, you're going to be executed tomorrow and you get one last Miami meal – unlimited budget. Where do you eat? I'd want to try La Palme d'Or (p149) at the Biltmore and splurge on dinner. And for lunch, I'd go to La Moon (p144) for some homey, cheap, greasy Colombian fare; I'd like to feel the comfort of home in my belly on my last day.

Colombian-American Paula Nino is the founder and editor of Miami food blog http://mangoandlime.net.

but thousands of travelers do and you may as well. So take a perch, eat some over-the-average but not-too-special food and enjoy the anthropological study that is South Beach as she rollerblades, salsas and otherwise shambles by.

Puerto Sagua (Map pp90-1; ☎ 305-673-1115; 700 Collins Ave; mains $6-25; ⏰ breakfast, lunch, dinner & late) There's a secret colony of older working-class Cubans and construction workers hidden among South Beach's sex-and-flash, and evidently, they eat here (next to a Benetton, natch). Puerto Sagua challenges the US diner with this reminder: Cubans can greasy-spoon with the best of them. Portions of favorites such as *picadillo* (spiced ground beef with rice, beans and plantains) are stupidly enormous.

Tap Tap (Map pp90-1; ☎ 305-672-2898; 819 5th St; mains $9-20; ⏰ dinner) In Haiti, tap-taps are brightly colored pickup trucks turned public taxis, and their tropi-psychedelic paint scheme inspires the decor at this excellent Haitian eatery. 'Um, what do Haitians eat?' Meals are a happy marriage of West Africa, France and the Caribbean: spicy pumpkin soup, grilled snapper with lime sauce and oh-God-yes curried goat. If you need some liquid courage, shoot some Barbancourt rum, available in several grades (all strong).

MIDRANGE
Taverna Opa (Map pp90-1; ☎ 305-673-6730; www.tavernaoparestaurant.com; 36 Ocean Dr; mains $11-23; ⏰ dinner & late) Cross Coyote Ugly Saloon with a big fat Greek wedding and you get this tourist-oriented restaurant and ouzo fest, where the meze (appetizers) are decent and the vibe resembles something like a Hellenic frat party. By the end of the night, table dancing is pretty much mandatory.

Café Maurice (Map pp90-1; ☎ 305-674-1277; 419 Washington Ave; mains $14-28; ⏰ dinner & late) Postwar Paris meets US theme restaurant at this dark red, playfully fun French bistro. The menu focuses on favorites *a la française* (the French way): *magret du canard* (duck breast), goat-cheese salad and duck shepherd's pie. Stick around for late-night gypsy dancing after you've gorged.

Sushi Saigon (Map pp88-9; ☎ 305-604-0599; www.sushisaigon.com; 1131 Washington Ave; mains $13-29; ⏰ lunch & dinner) The stark simplicity of Japanese cuisine and the colorful (and delicious) energy of Vietnamese are an odd marriage, but this menu basically splits rather than combines

the flavors, which is probably a good idea. Black-and-white photos from the two parent cuisine countries cram the walls and create a nice, Old-Asia atmosphere.

Spiga (Map pp90-1; ☎ 305-534-0079; Impala Hotel, 1228 Collins Ave; mains $15-26; ⏰ dinner) This romantic nook is a perfect place to bring your partner and gaze longingly over candlelight, before you both snap out of it and start digging into excellent traditional Italian such as lamb in olive oil and rosemary, and baby clams over linguine.

TOP END
Grazie (Map pp90-1; ☎ 305-673-1312; 702 Washington Ave; mains $18-34; ⏰ 6-11pm Sun-Thu, 6pm-midnight Fri & Sat) Thanks indeed: Grazie is top class and comfortably old-school Northern Italian. There's a distinct lack of gorgeous, clueless waitstaff and unwise menu experimentation. Instead: attentive service, solid and delicious mains, and extremely decent prices given the quality of the dining and high-end nature of the location.

Mark's South Beach (Map pp90-1; ☎ 305-604-9050; Hotel Nash, 1120 Collins Ave; mains $26-41; ⏰ lunch & dinner) Rejoice: Mark's is excellent New American cuisine, and it is good. Better than good, actually. The menu changes daily based on whatever excellent ingredients the kitchen can procure, the subterranean dining room is cozy and elegant, staff helpful and assured, and appreciative foodies outnumber posing status-seekers – a nice touch.

Nemo (Map pp90-1; ☎ 305-532-4550; www.nemorestaurant.com; 100 Collins Ave; mains $29-44; ⏰ lunch & dinner Mon-Fri, dinner Sat & Sun, brunch Sun) Raw bars and warm, copper sconces are a good sign. That nudge into greatness comes when Asian elegance graces Latin-American exuberance: fish with chimichurri sauce and kiss-the-grill nori-dusted tuna are a few jewels plucked off this fusion gem mine.

Wish (Map pp90-1; ☎ 305-531-2222; Hotel, 801 Collins Ave; mains $31-44; ⏰ breakfast & lunch daily, dinner Tue-Sun) Lots of words like 'aioli' and 'foam' get thrown around at Wish, which likes to take run-of-the-mill classics and evolve them beyond all expectations. Aged-cheddar spaetzle mac 'n' cheese and a 'PB Jay' of dark chocolate, raspberry jam and peanut-butter gelato make this a great place for the unadventurous to try some innovative (and delicious) haute cuisine.

Prime 112 (Map pp90-1; ☎ 305-532-8112; www.prime112.com; 112 Ocean Dr; mains $29-54; ⏰ dinner)

Sometimes, you need a steak: well aged, juicy, marbled with the right bit of fat, served in a spot where the walls sweat testosterone, the bar serves Manhattans and the hostesses are models. Chuck the above into Miami Beach's oldest inn – the beautiful 1915 Browns Hotel – and there's Prime 112. We just have to mention: during our research Enrique Iglesias, Anna Kournikova, Alonzo Mourning, LL Cool J, Mike Piazza and the King of Jordan all ate here. *On the same night.*

Joe's Stone Crab Restaurant (Map pp90-1; ☎ 305-673-0365; www.joesstonecrab.com; 11 Washington Ave; mains $20-60; ♥ dinner daily & lunch Tue-Sat mid-Oct–mid-May) Joe's is overrated. There, we said it. And yet it remains, inexplicably, Miami Beach's most famous restaurant. Look, the surf 'n' turf–style menu is good. But it's not great, and at this price, with so many options in Miami, you shouldn't settle for anything less than exceptional. Plus the line is a mile long and no reservations are accepted, so getting in can be a hassle. To top it off (we're really burning bridges here), compared to Dungeness, Alaskan King and Maryland Blue, the stone crabs are pretty bland. There it is. Sorry Joe.

South Beach (11th to 23rd Streets)
BUDGET
Presto Pizza (Map pp88-9; ☎ 305-531-5454; www .prestopizzasobe.com; 332 Lincoln Rd; pizza slices from $2.25, mains $3-11; ♥ lunch & dinner) Presto goes NYC style on the pie, and is beloved by northeasterners longing for a thin-crust slice of home. It's a good, greasy alternative to all that healthy stuff in Pizza Rustica.

Flamingo Restaurant (Map pp88-9; ☎ 305-673-4302; 1454 Washington Ave; mains $2.50-7; ♥ breakfast, lunch & dinner Mon-Sat) This tiny Nicaraguan storefront/café serves the behind-the-scenes laborers who make South Beach function. Workers devour hen soup, pepper chicken and cheap breakfasts prepared by a meticulous husband-and-wife team who like to get details (and portions) just right.

Gelateria Parmalat (Map pp88-9; ☎ 786-276-9475; 670 Lincoln Rd; mains $3.85-6; ♥ 9am-midnight Sun-Thu, to 1:30am Fri & Sat) It's hot. You've been walking all day. You need ice scream, stat. Why hello tamarind-and-passionfruit homemade gelato! This is an excellent spot for creamy, pillowy waves of European-style frozen goodness, and based on the crowds, it's the acknowledged favorite ice cream on South Beach.

Le Sandwicherie (Map pp88-9; ☎ 305-532-8934; 229 14th St; mains $5.50-8; ♥ 8:30am-5am) French for 'The Sandwicherie' (heh), the bustle-and-flow never stops as an endless stream of customers sidle up to the counter for some of the best baguettes (and other eats of a things-between-bread nature) on South Beach.

Pasha's (Map pp88-9; ☎ 305-673-3919; 900 Lincoln Rd; meals $4-12; ♥ lunch & dinner) Pasha's is a serious self-promoter judging by this place, a sleek, two-level, healthy fast-food emporium that has its name everywhere you look. No matter; the food at Pasha's rocks. Have some delicious *labneh* (thick yogurt), a plate of hummus and grilled chicken served over rice. Pasha's also has a branch on N Miami Ave in the Design District (see Map p97) and another downtown on Brickell Ave (see Map pp92–3).

San Loco (Map pp88-9; ☎ 305-538-3009; 235 14th St; mains $5-10; ♥ 11am-5am) You'd think laid-back, Latino-influenced South Beach would have more burrito places, because let's face it, nothing goes down better after a cold swim (or beer) than guac, sour cream and beans. But there was a serious shortage of this genre – and then San Loco arrived. The industrially cool interior is fun, but the burritos are better – they kick your hunger in the ass, but in an oh-so-delicious way.

A La Folie (Map pp88-9; ☎ 305-538-4484; www .alafoliecafe.com; 516 Española Way; mains $5-15; ♥ lunch & dinner) There's a distinct shortage of coffeehouses in Miami (we don't count *cortadito* counters because you can't sit there and read), but this *tres* French café bucks the trend. Plus, the waiters have great accents. Why yes, we would like, 'Zee moka.'

MIDRANGE
Jerry's Famous Deli (Map pp88-9; ☎ 305-532-8030; www.jerrysfamousdeli.com; 1450 Collins Ave; mains $10-17; ♥ 24hr) Important: Jerry's delivers. Why? Because when you've gorged out on the pastrami on rye, turkey clubs and other mile-high sandwiches at this enormous Jewish deli (housed in what used to be the Warsaw nightclub), you'll be craving more of the above 24/7.

Front Porch Café (Map pp88-9; ☎ 305-531-8300; 1418 Ocean Dr; mains $10-18; ♥ breakfast, lunch & dinner) A blue-and-white escape from the madness of the cruising scene, the Porch has been serving excellent salads, sandwiches and the like since 1990 (eons by South Beach standards). Weekend brunch is justifiably mobbed; the big omelettes are delicious, as are the fat pancakes, strong coffee and handsome servers.

Van Dyke Café (Map pp88-9; ☎ 305-534-3600; www .thevandykecafe.com; 846 Lincoln Rd; mains $10.50-20.50; ☺ 8am-2am) One of Lincoln Rd's most touristed spots, the Van Dyke is an institution akin to the News Café, serving adequate food in a primo spot for people-watching. It's usually packed and takes over half the sidewalk. Service is friendly and efficient, and you get free preening models with your burgers and eggplant parmigiana. There's also nightly jazz upstairs.

Tapas y Tintos (Map pp88-9; ☎ 305-538-8272; www .tapaytintos.com; 448 Española Way; tapas $6-25; ☺ lunch Wed-Sun, dinner daily) This dark, Nuevo-Spanish tapas bar is popular with the sort of good-looking young professionals who like their food and restaurants as pretty as they are. Try the octopus, or fried chickpeas with Spanish ham.

Café Papillon (Map pp88-9; ☎ 305-673-1139; 530 Lincoln Rd; mains $8-25; ☺ 8:30am-11pm) In a perfect world, the waitstaff here would wear stripy shirts, berets and have twirly moustaches. Alas, *non*, but there's quiche, tartines (filled with marinated artichokes or peppers in pesto sauce), crepes and wrought-iron sidewalk tables. 'Pass zee gauloise, Pierre.'

Balans (Map pp88-9; ☎ 305-534-9191; 1022 Lincoln Rd; mains $10-25; ☺ breakfast, lunch & dinner) Kensington, Chiswick…South Beach? Oi, give this Brit-owned fusion favorite a go, cobbler. Where else do veal saltimbocca and lamb jalfrezi share a menu? After you down the signature lobster club, you'll agree tired stereotypes about English cooking need to be reconsidered.

Guru (Map pp88-9; ☎ 305-534-3996; www.guru food.com; 232 12th St; mains $15-23; ☺ dinner) A sexy, soft-lit interior of blood reds and black wood sets the stage of this not-so-average Indian eatery, where local ingredients like lobster swim into the korma. Goan fish curry goes down a treat, too.

Grillfish (Map pp88-9; ☎ 305-538-9908; www .grillfish.com; 1444 Collins Ave; mains $13-22; ☺ dinner) Sometimes it's all in a name. They grill here. They grill fish. They could call it 'Grillfish Awesome' because that's what this simple yet elegant restaurant, with its cutely mismatched plates and church-pew benches, serves: fresh seafood, done artfully and simply and joyfully.

Miss Yip (Map pp88-9; ☎ 305-534-5488; www.misyip chinesecafe.com; 1661 Meridian Ave; mains $14-25; ☺ lunch & dinner) If you remember when Cantonese was the only Chinese cuisine you could find stateside and prefer it that way, meet Jenny Yip. She's got a bright-red booth and medicine jars full of God-knows-what waiting for you in this seemingly classic Chinese teahouse, which serves excellent Peking duck and *ma-po tofu* (marinated pork, black beans and bean curd).

CJ's Crab Shack (Map pp88-9; ☎ 305-534-3996; Cavalier Hotel, 1320 Ocean Dr; mains $18-30; ☺ lunch & dinner) This casual spot seems a cut above the rest of its Ocean Dr resto-siblings. As the name promises, there are lots of crustaceans served by a sassy waitstaff with complimentary dry attitude (it's endearing). Happy hour is a happy steal: $5 for a half-dozen oysters, $6 for two stone-crab claws.

TOP END

ourpick **Osteria del Teatro** (Map pp88-9; ☎ 305-538-7850; 1443 Washington Ave; mains $16-42; ☺ dinner Mon-Sat) There are few things to swear by, and the specials board of Osteria, one of the oldest and best Italian restaurants in Greater Miami, ought to be one. Actually, when you get here, let the gracious Italian waiters seat you, coddle you, and then basically order for you off the board. They never pick wrong.

Table 8 (Map pp88-9; ☎ 305-695-4114; www.table8la .com; 1458 Ocean Dr; mains $24-30; ☺ breakfast, lunch & dinner) You know what? Forget that Table 8 has *Oprah* cachet. Forget that celebrity chef Govind Armstrong is a celebrity chef. If all that wasn't so, Table 8 would *still* be one of the best high-end restaurants on South Beach, partly because it never feels too high end. That is to say, it delivers comforting innovation – duck breast with green beans and *frisée* (endive), mahimahi blue-crab chowder and kobe beef burgers – in an understated, accessible fashion. In a way, Table 8 is the opposite of the mystique that has grown around it. This isn't a spot for silly airs: it offers excellent food that anyone can appreciate. The lunch menu is fantastic value.

Yuca (Map pp88-9; ☎ 305-532-9822; 501 Lincoln Rd; mains $22-40; ☺ 11am-6am) This was one of the first Nuevo Latino hotspots in Miami, and it's still going strong, even if locals say it has lost a little luster over the years. Maybe, but the Yuca rellena (a mild chili stuffed with truffle-laced mushroom *picadillo*) and the tender guava ribs, still make our mouth water.

Casa Tua (Map pp88-9; ☎ 305-673-1010; 1700 James Ave; mains $23-55; ☺ dinner Mon-Sat) Casa Tua is way too cool to have a sign out front. You'll know it by the oh-so-fabulous crowd streaming in, the hovering limos out front and what you can see of the beautiful building itself (much of it's hidden behind a high hedgerow). If you manage to get a table in the magnificent, 1925 Mediterranean-style villa, you can linger over high-priced (but very delicious) lamb chops, steaks and pastas, in one of several classy and gentlemanly quarters.

Blue Door (Map pp88-9; 305-674-6400; Delano Hotel, 1685 Collins Ave; mains $30-46; lunch & dinner) 'Owned by Madonna' plus 'Delano' plus 'designed by Philippe Starck' equals 'this ain't McDonald's.' They've let Asia and Latin America rub a bit of French shoulder with dishes such as cold chayote soup with pan-seared scallops, and ragout of lobster in coconut-milk broth. Enjoy, and realize you live better than most.

Escopazzo (Map pp88-9; 305-674-9450; 1311 Washington Ave; mains $27-62; dinner Tue-Sun) There's a lot of mediocre Italian in Miami, and you won't find it here. The rustic, organic menu gets points for raw, vegan dishes such as nut cheese Caprese, and safer but still brilliant fare such as spaghetti with red-mullet roe, prosciutto-wrapped veal chops and excellent tasting-menus. Reservations are imperative.

Northern Miami Beach
BUDGET
La Perrada de Edgar (Map p94; 305-866-4546; 6976 Collins Ave; hot dogs $3-5; 10am-2am) Back in the day, Colombia's most (in)famous export to Miami was cocaine. But seriously, what's powder got on La Perrada and its kookily delicious hot dogs that were devised by some Dr Evil of the frankfurter world. Don't believe us? Try an *especial*, topped with plums, pineapple and whipped cream. How about shrimp and potato sticks? Apparently, these are normal hot-dog toppings in Colombia.

Tasti Café (Map p94; 305-673-5483; 4041 Royal Palm Ave; mains $4-9; breakfast, lunch & dinner Mon-Thu, breakfast & lunch Fri & Sun) The bagels at this Israeli-run, kosher café, which could have been plucked off the streets of Tel Aviv, are flown in from New York – now that's commitment to quality. If good bagels aren't your thing, pick from light veggie dishes, hearty pastas and sandwiches.

El Rey del Chivito (Map p94; 305-864-5566; www .elreydelchivito.com; 6987 Collins Ave; mains under $10; lunch & dinner, to late Fri & Sat) Heart, meet the 'King of Chivitos' and his signature dish: a sandwich of steak, ham, cheese, fried eggs and mayonnaise (there may have been lettuce, peppers and tomatoes too, but the other ingredients just laughed at them). Now run, heart, run away! That's just the basic, by the way, and it comes with fries. We've never heard of Uruguayan restaurants in the US, and now we know why: anyone who could spread the word died of a coronary long ago. El Rey also serves Uruguayan pizza; try it topped with *faina*, long strips of bread mixed with cheese and peppers.

Wolfie Cohen's Rascal House (Map pp86-7; 305-947-4581; 17190 Collins Ave; mains $7-15; breakfast, lunch & dinner) Wolfie's is more than a deli: it's also an icon. A serious battering from Hurricane Wilma in 2005 tore away one of the best roadside marquees in the USA, but the '50s-era red-vinyl booths, warm and sassy service, and ginormous deli menu remain, encapsulating a bygone era of US highway culture. And the corned beef on rye is da bomb.

Mister Chopstick (Map p94; 305-604-0555; 4020 Royal Palm Ave; mains $9-15; lunch Sun-Fri, dinner Sun-Thu & Sat) Yes: Kosher Chinese. That means the menu is short on pork but does serve lots of Chinese-American favorites – General Tso's chicken and Hawaiian duck – in what seems like a never-ending chaotic Jewish wedding.

MIDRANGE
Norman's Tavern (Map p94; 305-868-9248; 6770 Collins Ave; mains $15-25; lunch & dinner) Think Diet Forge: same great taste, less calories! Er, celebrities. Norman's eschews bling and attitude for a sort of high-end sports-bar atmosphere; the food is fancy pub fare and everyone's either shooting pool or watching the game.

Tamarind (Map p94; 305-861-6222; www .tamarindthai.us; 946 Normandy Dr; mains $12-21; lunch & dinner) No surprises here (unless you've never eaten Thai food); there's the standard array of Thai curries (red, green, yellow) and *pad*-everything. And it's excellent: food, service and setting. Sometimes, as the cooks at Tamarind happily know, you stick with the classics.

Sam's Deli & Grill (Map p94; 305-538-1616; 740 41st St; mains $10-20; breakfast, lunch & dinner Sun-Thu, breakfast & lunch Fri) 'It's good,' says the Israeli, with typical *Sabra* (Israeli Jew) understatement, walking out of what looks like a rabbi convention. Sam's holds the title for most popular deli on South Beach, evidenced by round-the-clock crowds noshing matzo ball soup, brisket and the excellent New Yorker:

NORTH BISCAYNE BOULEVARD

An incongruous glut of excellent restaurants is sprouting up along the otherwise unremarkable strip of N Biscayne Blvd. Here are some winners from this unexpected foodie find:

Karma Car Wash (Map p94; ☎ 305-759-1392; www.karmacarwash.com; 7010 Biscayne Blvd; sandwiches & tapas $4.25-8; ⏰ 8am-8pm) This ecofriendly car wash also serves soy chai lattes, organic tapas and good microbrews. The idea could be precocious in execution, but ends up being fun – more fun than your average wash 'n' wait, anyway. Of course, hybrid drivers get a 25% discount, and the bar becomes a lounge at 8pm, with DJs spinning as you wonder, 'Should I have gotten the wax finish?'

Jimmy's East Side Diner (Map p94; ☎ 305-754-3692; 7201 Biscayne Blvd; mains $5-11; ⏰ breakfast & lunch) Come to Jimmy's, a classic greasy spoon, for big cheap breakfasts of omelettes, French toast or pancakes, and turkey clubs and burgers later in the day.

Uva 69 (Map p94; ☎ 305-754-9022; 6900 Biscayne Blvd; mains $8-17; ⏰ breakfast, lunch & dinner Mon-Fri, lunch & dinner Sat) Woah – it's like a club. And a restaurant. And an Ikea showroom, all mashed up. The flavors are mixed but consistently rich, running from traditional Miami *cubanos* to flaky, buttery croissants, but damn if it isn't all satisfying and served under immaculately hip conditions.

Wine 69 (Map p94; ☎ 305-759-0122; www.wine69miami.com; 6909 Biscayne Blvd; meals $13-23; ⏰ 8am-8pm) Enter this low-slung, sexy wine bar, pick from a dozen categories of the grape, and pair up with – oh, let's see – baked Brie and caramelized onions? Or a Miami-inspired charcuterie with chorizo and Spanish ham? Tough decisions, but the helpful owners here love two things: good wine, and telling you what goes with it.

our pick **Michy's** (Map p94; ☎ 305-759-2001; 6927 Biscayne Blvd; meals $24-43; ⏰ lunch & dinner Tue-Fri, dinner Sat & Sun) Blue-and-white pop-decor. Organic, locally sourced ingredients. A stylish, fantastical bar where Alice could drink before painting Wonderland red. Welcome to Michelle 'Michy' Bernstein's culinary lovechild; one of the brightest stars in Miami's culinary constellation. The emphasis is on good food and fun. The 'half plates' concept lets you halve an order and mix up delicious gastronomic fare such as foie gras on corn cakes, chicken pot pie with wild mushrooms, white almond gazpacho, and blue-cheese croquettes.

turkey and corned beef piled on rye and dripping with Russian dressing.

Café Prima Pasta (Map p94; ☎ 305-867-0106; www .primapasta.com; 414 71st St; mains $13-24; ⏰ lunch & dinner Mon-Sat, dinner Sun) We're not sure what's better at this Argentine-Italian place: the much-touted pasta, which deserves every one of the accolades heaped on it (try the gnocchi), or the atmosphere, which captures the dignified sexiness of Buenos Aires. Actually, it's no contest: you're the winner, as long as you eat here.

Bissaleh Café (Map p86-7; ☎ 305-682-2224; www .bissaleh.com; 17,608 Collins Ave; mains $12-24; ⏰ lunch & dinner Sun-Thu, dinner Sat) Another Israeli café, Bissaleh has an extensive menu of fish and pasta, but the real draw is the signature dish, a puff pastry stuffed with cheese or olives, potatoes and spinach, plus similar Middle Eastern turnovers like *boreka* and *malawach*.

TOP END

Timo's (Map pp86-7; ☎ 305-936-1008; 17624 Collins Ave; mains $15-34; ⏰ lunch & dinner) When chef Tim Andriola left Mark's South Beach in 2003, he opened this classy bistro and brought Sobe style into a Nobe (North Beach) setting. His legend grows through dishes such as porcini-dusted veal and cheese platters topped with shaved black truffles.

Forge (Map p94; ☎ 305-538-8533; 432 41st St; mains $26-60; ⏰ 6pm-midnight Mon-Sat, brunch & dinner Sun) We've always wanted to eat next to Paris Hilton, but when we visited Forge all we got was Hillary Clinton's press spokesperson. That should give you an idea of the folks who eat at this Baroque temple to excess: important ones. Incidentally, the food is good, but you're at this A-list steakhouse to either spot celebrities or feel like one.

Downtown Miami

BUDGET

Emily's Restaurante (Map pp92-3; ☎ 305-375-0013; 204 NE 1st St; mains $2-5.50; ⏰ 7am-4:30pm) Two bucks gets you two eggs, toast and coffee here; $5 gets you one of the best buffet deals in town.

There are daily specials of Colombian, Cuban and Spanish cuisine: chicken soup, oxtail and *lengua en salsa* (marinated tongue).

Taquerías el Mexicano (Map pp92-3; ☎ 305-858-1160; 521 SW 8th St; mains $5-10; ⏰ 9am-11pm) This casual, friendly joint serves tasty and authentic Mexican food from enchiladas to chilaquiles – a breakfast dish that consists of tortilla chips simmered in green sauce, mixed with scrambled eggs, and covered with cheese and sour cream, then served with rice and beans. Wash your dinner down with a Mexican beer like Bohemia or Negra Modelo.

Jamaica International Café (Map pp92-3; ☎ 305-400-6694; 119 SE 1st Ave; mains $5.50-11; ⏰ breakfast, lunch & dinner) The menu at this excellent lunch spot has been around the world – you can go Mexican, Italian etc – but note the title and order something Jamaican: stewed oxtail with butter beans and, yes, jerk pork please.

Mini Healthy Deli (Map pp92-3; ☎ 305-523-2244; Station Mall, 48 E Flagler St; mains $6-10; ⏰ lunch) This excellent café, tucked into a half-vacant minimall, is where chef Carlos Bedoya works solo and churns out remarkably fresh and delicious specials, such as grilled tilapia, fresh salad, and rice and beans. There are only two little tables, but it's worth waiting – or standing while you eat.

La Moon (Map pp92-3; ☎ 305-860-602; 144 SW 8th St; $5-12) Nothing – and we're not necessarily saying this in a good way – soaks up the beer like a Colombian hot dog topped with eggs and potato sticks. Or fried pork belly and pudding. These delicacies are the preferred food and drink of Miami's 24-hour party people, and the best place for this wicked fare is in stumbling distance of the Transit Lounge (p154). To really fit in, order a *refajo:* Colombian beer (Aguila) with Colombian soda (preferably the red one).

Garcia's (Map pp92-3; ☎ 305-375-0765; 398 NW River Dr; mains $8-15; ⏰ lunch) Crowds of Cuban office workers lunch at Garcia's, which feels more like you're in a smugglers' seafood shack than the financial district. Expect occasionally spotty service (a bad thing), freshly caught-and-cooked fish (a good thing) and pleasantly seedy views of the Miami River (sweet).

Granny Feelgoods (Map pp92-3; ☎ 305-377-9600; 25 W Flagler St; mains $9-12; ⏰ breakfast & lunch Mon-Fri) If you need karmic balance after eating at Porçao (right), pop into this neighborhood health-food staple. Located next to the courthouse, Granny's must have the highest lawyer-to-bean-sprouts ratio in the USA; try simple vegetarian dishes such as tofu sandwiches and spinach lasagna. Carnivores are catered for too – there's turkey burger.

MIDRANGE

Fresco California (Map pp92-3; ☎ 305-858-0608; 1744 SW 3rd Ave; mains $9-15; ⏰ lunch & dinner Mon-Sat) Fresco serves all kinds of West Coast takes on the Mediterranean palate. Relax in the candlelit backyard dining room, which feels like an Italian porch in summer when the weather is right (ie almost always). Pear and walnut salad, and portabello sandwiches are lovely, while the pumpkin-stuffed ravioli is heaven on a platter. The prices are fairly low, but you'll inevitably be tempted to get wine, have multiple courses and turn a meal here into a long night out.

Big Fish (Map pp92-3; ☎ 305-373-1770; www .thebigfishmiami.com; 55 SW Miami Ave; mains $15.50-32.50; ⏰ lunch & dinner) Big Fish has a catch-the-sun color scheme, open deck and blue-water breezes – could you come closer to Mediterranean island ambience in Miami? OK, the Miami River isn't the Aegean Sea (you're almost under the Metromover), but the seafood is fresh; try anything off the fish menu, sip some wine and love life. Film buffs: Alec Baldwin shot a thief on the back patio here in the '80s cult flick *Miami Blues.*

Café Sambal (Map pp92-3; ☎ 305-913-8358; Mandarin Oriental Miami, 500 Brickell Key Dr; mains $20-40; ⏰ 6:30am-11pm) Sambal sports what we can only describe as 'Nouveau-rice-farmer-conical-hat chic' and serves intriguing pan-Asian fare in a more laid-back setting than upstairs Azul (both located in the Mandarin Oriental Miami. The just-out-of-the-ocean-fresh sushi and rice crab cakes are worth a try, as is the critically acclaimed small-plates menu.

TOP END

Azul (Map pp92-3; ☎ 305-913-8288; Mandarin Oriental Miami, 500 Brickell Key Dr; mains $30-68; ⏰ dinner daily, lunch Sun-Fri) Falling-water windows, clean metallic spaces and curving copper facades compliment one of the nicest views of the city. The Scandi-tastic decor works in harmony with a menu that marries the Mediterranean to Asia; try the oysters wrapped in beef and hamachi carpaccio.

Porçao (Map pp92-3; ☎ 305-373-2777; 801 Brickell Bay Dr; per person $44.90; ⏰ noon-midnight) What is it with South Americans and meat? We like beef, but this is a butcher with a grill; an all-you-can-eat Brazilian *churrascaria* (steakhouse) where the waiters wander around with swords – swords! – of skewered, juicy, fat-dribbling…actually, come here with that skirt steak, Sergio.

Wynwood, Design District & Little Haiti
BUDGET
S&S Restaurant (Map p97; ☎ 305-373-4291; 1757 NE 2nd Ave; mains $4-10; ☒ breakfast & lunch) Step back into the past at this classic '40s-style diner (located right across the street from the Miami city cemetery, by the way). It's popular with cops, has downright sassy service ('Keep yer shirt on, hon!') and serves great old-fashioned, comfort-food choices like burgers, meatloaf, and baked macaroni and cheese, plus more adventurous entries like shrimp Creole.

Original Restaurant (Map p97; ☎ 305-758-9400; 5650 NE 2nd Ave; mains $5-11; ☒ breakfast, lunch & dinner) Friendly, family-run, clean and bright, this Little Haiti standout serves excellent island standards such as *ragout* (cow's feet), *queu boeuf* (oxtail), *foie* (liver) and *griot* (fried spicy pork); the last is one of our favorite only-in-Miami dishes (well, unless you live in Haiti). This is a neighborhood spot, and staff might be surprised to see you, but that doesn't mean they'll be discourteous to their newfound customer.

Kafa's Café (Map p97; ☎ 305-438-0114; 3535 NE 2nd Ave; mains $5-8; ☒ breakfast & lunch Mon-Sat) New when we visited, Kafa's was a bare-bones café and pretty in that understated way bare-bones cafés can be. There's a pleasing menu of soup, salad and sandwiches, which attracts artsy types. Pity them; it must be hard to act grim and pathos-driven when you can enjoy a tuna melt under perfect Miami conditions in the sunny outdoor seating area.

Enriqueta's (Map p97; ☎ 305-573-4681; 186 NE 29th St; mains $5-8; ☒ breakfast & lunch Mon-Sat) Back in the day, Puerto Ricans, not installation artists, ruled Wynwood. Have a taste of those times in this perpetually packed roadhouse, where the Latin-diner ambience is as strong as the steaming shots of *cortadito* served at the counter. Balance the local gallery fluff with a steak-and-potato-stick sandwich.

Canela Café (Map p97; ☎ 305-756-3930; canelamiami.com; 5132 Biscayne Blvd; mains $6.25-9.25; ☒ lunch & dinner Mon-Sat) Miami loves its fusion cuisine but rarely mixes Latin diner with vegetarian fare. Canela challenges this convention;

there's meat on the menu (touted as 'Latin soul food'), as well as roasted pepper and goat-cheese sandwiches, vegetarian tapas and the trippy art you'd expect at the postpunk cousin to Miami's many Latin greasy spoons.

Lost & Found Saloon (Map p97; ☎ 305-576-1008; www.thelostandfoundsaloon-miami.com; 185 NW 36th St; mains $5.25-11.25; ☒ breakfast, lunch & dinner) The service is as friendly as the omelettes and burritos are awesome (which is to say, very) at this cute little Wynwood spot, the sort of saloon where microbrews are on tap and the wine list reads like a year abroad. Our only request: more burrito, gentlemen; portions were a little small.

Secret Sandwich Co (Map p97; ☎ 305-571-9990; www.secretsandwich.com; 3918 N Miami Ave; meals $6-11.50; ☒ lunch Mon-Fri) Spy-themed gourmet sandwiches? Hey, we can dig it, especially when the goods include the Bay of Pig (thin-sliced pork with onion and mojo marinade). That cute covert-ops gimmick runs through the menu, all the way to half-pound burgers and very fresh salads.

MIDRANGE
Sheba (Map p97; ☎ 305-573-1819; 4029 N Miami Ave; www.shebamiami.com; mains $7-15.50; ☒ dinner daily, lunch Mon-Sat) The only Ethiopian place in Miami is a godsend for vegetarians, especially vegans (although there's meat here too). If you eat here, eat right; communally. Grab a big plate of *injera* (spongy bread), which serves as plate, utensil and starch, and scoop up spicy mounds of the many delicious varieties of *wat* (Ethiopian stew).

Andiamo! (Map p97; ☎ 305-762-5751; 5600 Biscayne Blvd; pizzas $8.50-17; ☒ lunch & dinner) It looks like a '50s drive-through (it's actually an old car wash), but Andiamo! isn't old fashioned. This airy eatery breaks ground with award-winning pizza and toppings that range from goat cheese to white tuna. You can get creative or settle for excellent interpretations of classics such as the Vesuvius: salami, hot peppers and olives, mmm.

Soyka (Map p97; ☎ 305-759-3117; www.soykacafe.com; 5556 NE 4th Ct; mains $9-29; ☒ lunch & dinner Mon-Sun, brunch Sun) Mark Soyka, the man behind News Café (p138) and Van Dyke Café (p141), has got the magic touch when it comes to restaurants in Miami, and this gem is his best effort yet. It's housed in a bouncy Rococo space, and the eclectic menu jumps across several horizons of flavor, from sautéed chicken livers to sesame-seared salmon, with consistently tasty results.

TOP END

our pick Michael's Genuine Food & Drink (Map p97; ☎ 305-573-5550; www.michaelsgenuine.com; Atlas Plaza, 130 NE 40th St; mains $16-36; ☺ dinner Mon-Sat) The 'genuine' in Michael Schwartz' restaurant name refers to its use of locally sourced ingredients and healthy dose of innovation, moderated by respect for classics. Hence, pork shoulder in parsley sauce and cheese grits that taste like your grandma just became a cordon-bleu chef. The chocolate-and-red interior feels cheerful and welcoming rather than snobbish and intimidating, and that goes for the attentive waitstaff as well.

Grass Restaurant & Lounge (Map p97; ☎ 305-573-3355; www.grasslounge.com; 28 NE 40th St; mains $22-34; ☺ dinner Mon-Sat) Though this über-trendy spot could easily be seen only as a lounge – a fabulous one, where gorgeous folks get let in through a velvet rope – it does, in fact, have quite a good menu. The whole place is alfresco, on a lovely patio that's tucked away from the street, and has a combo of open-air lounging banquettes and individual tiki huts, on elevated platforms, for more intimate dinners. The menu is all over the Asia map, with dishes such as Szechuan tuna and Sumatra beef tenderloin taking center stage – next to the exquisite patrons, that is.

Key Biscayne

Oasis (Map p98; ☎ 305-361-5709; 19 Harbor Dr; mains $5-12; ☺ breakfast, lunch & dinner) This excellent Cuban café has a customer base that ranges from the working poor to city players, and the socio-economic barriers come tumbling down fast as folks sip high-octane Cuban coffee. Between the super-strong coffee and *masas de puerco* – marinated pork chunks, which go great with hot sauce – we're in hole-in-the-wall heaven.

Le Croisic (Map p98; ☎ 305-361-5888; 180 Crandon Blvd; mains $15-25; ☺ dinner) If this bistro were any cuter it would probably rub your leg and go 'meow.' As it is, Croisic entertains with the sort of old-school menu that even the French appreciate for nostalgia's sake: entrecote with béarnaise sauce, *boeuf bourguignon* (beef casserole) and *bouillabaisse* (fish stew) – ooh la la.

Boater's Grill (Map p98; ☎ 305-361-0080; 1200 S Crandon Blvd; mains $14-30; ☺ 9am-9pm) Located in Crandon Park (p112), this waterfront restaurant (actually, water below and all around) feels like a Chesapeake Bay seahouse from up north, except the menu is packed with South Florida maritime goodness: stone crabs, mahimahi and lobster paella.

Rusty Pelican (Map p98; ☎ 305-361-3818; 3201 Rickenbacker Causeway; mains $25-30; ☺ lunch & dinner) More than the fare itself, it's the panoramic skyline views, among the best in Miami, that draw the faithful and romantic to this airy, tropical restaurant. But if you do come for a sunset drink, the fresh air could certainly seduce you into staying for some of the surf 'n' turf menu, which is good enough, considering the setting and lack of options.

Ciappino (Map p98; ☎ 305-365-4500; Ritz-Carlton, 455 Grand Bay Dr; mains $18-46; ☺ lunch & dinner) This luxury hotel extravaganza gives you plenty of seating options and definitely sells a 'Sinatra in his heyday' vibe, couching your dining experience in an enormous half deco/half Baroque dining room of grand-ball proportions. The menu matches the opulence of the setting, offering such over-the-top fare as wild mushrooms and truffles stuffed into sea bass. Whatever your pleasure, you can't really go wrong.

Little Havana

BUDGET

Los Pinareños Frutería (Map p96; ☎ 305-285-1135; 1334 SW 8th St; snacks & drinks $2-4; ☺ breakfast, lunch & dinner) Nothing says refreshment on a sweat-stained Miami afternoon like a long, cool glass of fruit smoothie at this popular juice and veggie stand. The produce is pretty fresh and flavorful too.

El Rey de Las Fritas (Map p96; ☎ 305-644-6054; 1821 SW 8th St; snacks $2-3; ☺ 8am-10:30pm Mon-Sat) If you've never had a *frita*, or Cuban burger, make your peace with McDonalds and come down to El Rey with the lawyers, developers, construction workers and every other slice of Miami's Latin life. These *fritas* are big, juicy and served under a mountain of shoestring fries. Plus, the *batidos* (Latin American milkshakes) definitely bring the boys to the yard.

I Love Calle Ocho (Map p96; ☎ 305-643-3737; 1547 SW 8th St; mains $5-12; ☺ breakfast & lunch) And we love you. This eclectic café, with its bagels and chicken-salad wraps, is a good resting spot between rice and beans, although there are apparently two grandmas in the kitchen who whip up excellent Cuban fare upon request. A rainbow sticker on the door indicates gay-friendly, a bit of a rare pronouncement in these parts.

Exquisito Restaurant (Map p96; ☎ 305-643-0227; 1510 SW 8th St; mains $3-10.50; ☺ 7am-midnight) For cheap coffee, casual atmosphere and home-style food, this place is exquisite (ha ha ha). Order any combination of steak, french fries, sausage, ham, eggs, toast and *café con leche* (coffee with milk) and you're not even breaking a fiver. The full *desayuno* (breakfast) will keep you going all day.

El Cristo (Map p96; ☎ 305-261-2947; 1543 SW 8th St; mains $5-15; ☺ breakfast, lunch & dinner) A popular locals' hangout, the down-to-earth El Cristo has options from all over the Spanish-speaking world. Lots of locals say it's as good as Calle Ocho gets. The menu has daily specials, but the standout is fish: try it fried for a local version of fish 'n' chips, or take away some excellent fish empanadas and *croquetas* (deep-fried in breadcrumbs). The outdoor area is an excellent perch for enjoying 8th St eye candy.

Guayacan (Map p96; ☎ 305-649-2015; 1933 SW 8th St; mains $7-15; ☺ lunch & dinner) Nicaraguan meals served by friendly folks in a pleasantly homey atmosphere is what it's all about. Don't get us started on the roast pork – oh, alright, it's divine. All specials come loaded with sides: salad, rice and beans, plantains, french fries, corn tortillas and bread.

Hy Vong Vietnamese Restaurant (Map pp86-7; ☎ 305-446-3674; 3458 SW 8th; mains $7-19; ☺ dinner Tue-Sun, closed mid–late Aug) In a neighborhood full of exiles from a communist regime, it makes sense to find a Vietnamese restaurant. And it's telling that despite all the great Latin food around, Little Havanans still wait hours for a seat here. Why? Because this great Vietnamese

food (with little touches of Florida, like mango marinade) combines quality produce with Southeast Asian spice and a colonially inherited French penchant for rich flavors. Just be prepared to wait an hour or more for your culinary reward.

Islas Canarias (Map pp86-7; ☎ 305-649-0440; 285 NW 27th Ave; mains $8-19; ☺ breakfast, lunch & dinner) Islas may not look like much, sitting in a strip mall, but it serves some of the best Cuban in Miami. The *ropa vieja* is delicious, and there are nice Spanish touches on the menu (the owner's father is from the Canary Islands, hence the restaurant's name). Don't pass up the signature homemade chips, especially the ones cut from plantains.

MIDRANGE & TOP END

Versailles (Map pp86-7; ☎ 305-444-0240; 3555 SW 8th St; mains $5-20; ☺ breakfast, lunch & dinner) Versailles (ver-*sigh*-yay) is an institution, and a lot of younger Cubans will tell you it's an overrated one. But older Cubans and Miami's Latin political elite still love coming here, so much so that folks say CNN has reserved a parking space for the day Fidel Castro dies. The Cuban cuisine is decent and unsurprising (there's no French food to be found, incidentally) but the real draw is coming as close as most outsiders can to the city's Cuban aristocracy.

La Carreta (Map pp86-7; ☎ 305-444-7501; 3632 SW 8th St; mains $5-20; ☺ 24hr) The original link in a Cuban chain of restaurants, La Carreta features all the traditional Cuban dishes you'll find up the street at Versailles. The decor is a little less glaring and in-your-face, though no less kitschy in its country farmhouse way.

Casa Panza (Map p96; ☎ 305-643-5343; 1620 SW 8th St; mains around $20; ☺ lunch & dinner) Dark, cozy and more than a little kitschy – they might as well hang out flashing 'Ole!' signs – the nightly flamenco entertainment is as good as a glass of sherry and the chance to graze all night on tapas, which include *caldo gallego* (white-bean soup with pork sausage), *tortilla de patatas* (potato-stuffed tortilla) and *boquerones en vinagre* (fresh anchovies in vinaigrette).

Casa Juancho (Map p96; ☎ 305-446-4914; 2436 SW 8th St; mains $19-42; ☺ lunch & dinner) A massive, upscale, traditional Spanish tavern that's a bit out of the fray, this is the place to go for a special occasion or pull-out-all-the-stops evening. Join the festive mover-and-shaker crowd for updated takes on standards, including pan-seared salmon in creamy saffron-almond

---

BUILDING A CUBAN SANDWICH

The traditional Cuban sandwich, also known as a *sandwich mixto,* is not some slapdash creation. It's a craft best left to the experts – but here's some insight on how they do it. Correct bread is crucial – it should be Cuban white bread: fresh, soft and easy to press. The insides (both sides) should be buttered and layered (in the following order) with sliced pickles, slices of roast Cuban pork, ham (preferably sweet-cured ham) and baby Swiss cheese. Then it all gets pressed in a hot *plancha* (sandwich press) until the cheese melts. Mmmm.

sauce, baby lamb chops and filet mignon stuffed with goat cheese and peppers.

Coconut Grove

Foccacia Rustica (Map p99; ☎ 305-476-8292; 3111 Grand Ave; mains $4.75-8; ☒ 7am-6pm Mon, breakfast, lunch & dinner Tue-Sat, breakfast & lunch Sun) If you've been powering through a grease trap of *cubanos* and need a break, rejoice at the curry-chicken salads, croissants, lattes and assorted yuppie goodness at this inviting, continental-European-style spot.

Last Carrot (Map p99; ☎ 305-445-0805; www .thelastcarrot.com; 3133 Grand Ave; mains $6; ☒ 7am-6pm Mon, breakfast, lunch & dinner Tue-Sat, breakfast & lunch Sun) Folks of all walks, corporate suits included, come here for fresh juice, delicious wraps (veggie options are great but the tuna melt is divine) and old-Grove neighborliness. The Carrot's endurance next to massive CocoWalk is testament to the quality of its good-for-your-body food served in a good-for-your-soul setting, so come here and do something good for the world, or at least for your mouth.

Xixon (Map pp86-7; ☎ 305-854-9350; 1801 SW 22nd St; tapas $8-15; ☒ 10am-8pm Mon-Wed, to 10pm Thu-Sat) It takes a lot to stand out in Miami's crowded tapas-spot stakes. Having a Basque-country butcher-and-baker-gone-hip interior is a good start. Bread that has a crackling crust and a soft center that fluffs your tongue, and delicate explosions of *bacalao* (codfish) fritters, secures your spot as a top tapas contender. The *bocadillo* (sandwiches), with their blood-red Serrano ham and salty Manchego cheese, are great picnic fare. This place is a few miles north of the central Coconut Grove area.

Green Street Cafe (Map p99; ☎ 305-567-0662; www.greenstreet.net; 3110 Commodore Plaza; mains $5-17; ☒ breakfast, lunch & dinner) As sidewalk spots go, it doesn't get more popular (and many say delicious) than Green Street, which is now contending with a next door Senor Frogs. But the excellent mix of lamburgers with goat cheese, salmon salads, occasional art shows and general indie defiance of Grove gentrification is definitely up to the challenge.

Flanigan's (Map p99; ☎ 305-446-1114; www.flanigans .net; 2721 Bird Ave; mains $8-16; ☒ lunch, dinner & late) Flanigan's claims to have the best ribs in Miami, and they *are* good, but we're not giving more credit than that. Still, this is a pleasantly rowdy, all-American kind of joint tucked into

a liquor store (bonus), and a great spot to drink beer, eat decent grub and yell at TV sports.

Berries Restaurant (Map p99; ☎ 305-448-2111; 2884 SW 27th Ave; mains $10-25; ☒ lunch & dinner) Plenty of places have jumped on the seasonal-produce and fresh-ingredient bandwagon, and Berries, with its all-in-black ninja-clan waitstaff, makes the genre accessible and attitude-free. The enormous portions could feed two, but who could bear to share skirt steak with melted blue cheese or three-mushroom risotto, which reminds us: veggies get it good here.

Jaguar's (Map p99; ☎ 305-444-0216; www.jaguarspot .com; 3067 Grand Ave; mains $17-23, ceviche spoon $1.95; ☒ lunch & dinner) The menu spans the Latin world, but really, everyone's here for the ceviche 'spoon bar.' The idea: pick from six styles of ceviche (raw, marinated seafood), ranging from swordfish with cilantro to corvina in lime juice, and pull a culinary version of DIY. It's novel and fun, and the ceviche varieties are pretty damn delicious.

Anokha (Map p99; ☎ 786-552-1030; 3195 Commodore Plaza; mains $12-40; ☒ lunch & dinner) The general consensus is that this family-run phenom is as good as Indian gets in Miami, which is either big praise or small potatoes depending on your point of view. Our take: this place goes beyond excellent vindaloos, curries and tandooris with unique specials such as the shrimp cooked in mustard sauce, and chicken with spinach and cilantro. It's a small spot with a big legend.

Le Bouchon du Grove (Map p99; ☎ 305-448-6060; 3430 Main Hwy; mains $19.50-28.50; ☒ breakfast, lunch & dinner) The atmosphere here is authentic – tables crammed close together and walls laden with antique signs – and the staff is friendly and heavily accented. It's a cozy respite from the mall scene, and meal options, such as the beef filet in peppercorn sauce, light crepes or traditional onion soup are all scrumptious.

Coral Gables
BUDGET & MIDRANGE

Allen's Drug Store (Map p95; ☎ 305-665-6964; 4000 Red Rd; mains $5-8; ☒ breakfast, lunch & dinner) Don't worry: they do diner in the Gables. In Allen's case, they've just plopped one into a pharmacy. Don't let the proximity of Pepto Bismo and retirees put you off the meatloaf, vinyl booths or the little jukeboxes, because this is Florida. You should be eating among a bunch of seniors with walkers. It's called 'cultural immersion.'

our pick El Carajo (Map pp86-7; ☎ 305-856-2424; 2465 SW 17th Ave; tapas $3.50-15; ☺ dinner) Pass the Penzoil please…literally. We know it is cool to tuck restaurants into unassuming spots, but the Citgo station on SW 17th Ave? Really? Really: walk past the motor oil into a Granadan wine cellar, and try not to act too phased. And now, the food, *which is absolutely incredible.* Chorizo in cider blends burn, smoke and juice, frittatas are comfortably filling and *sardinas* and *boquerones*…oh God. These sardines and anchovies cooked with just a bit of salt and olive oil are dizzyingly delicious. It is tempting to keep El Carajo a secret, but not singing its praises would be lying, and we're not gonna lie: if there's one restaurant you shouldn't miss in Miami, it's this one.

Matsuri (Map p95; ☎ 305-663-1615; 5759 Bird Rd; mains $5-20; ☺ lunch & dinner Tue-Fri, dinner Sat & Sun) Note the customers: Matsuri, tucked into a nondescript shopping center, is consistently packed with Japanese people. They don't want scene; they want a taste of home – although many are South American Japanese who order *unagi* (eels) in Spanish, which is a cool dining sight in and of itself. Spicy *toro* (fatty tuna) and scallions, grilled mackerel with natural salt, and an ocean of raw fish are all *oishi* (delicious). The $8 bento lunch makes the rest of the day disappointing compared to your midday meal.

Caffe Abbracci (Map p95; ☎ 305-441-0700; 318 Aragon Ave; mains $14-24; ☺ lunch & dinner) Perfect moments in Coral Gables come easy. Here's an especially simple formula: you, a loved one, a muggy Miami evening, a sidewalk table at Abbracci, some northern Italian pasta and a glass of red.

TOP END

Pascal's on Ponce (Map p95; ☎ 305-444-2024; www .pascalmiami.com; 2611 Ponce de León Blvd; mains $26-37; ☺ lunch & dinner Mon-Fri, dinner Sat) They're fighting the good fight here: sea scallops with beef short rib, crème brûlée and other French fine-dining classics set the elegant stage at this neighborhood hangout, a favorite night out among Gables foodies who appreciate time-tested standards.

Norman's (Map p95; ☎ 305-446-6767; www.normans .com; 21 Almeria Ave; mains $28-46; ☺ dinner Mon-Sat) What, Coral Gables? You've already got some of the best tapas, sushi and French food in the city; now you get Norman Van Aiken, touted by critics as possibly the best chef in southeastern USA? The menu is a culinary mirror of the state of Florida, fusing the Caribbean to North America, and Europe to Latin America. Imagine Florida pompano with ham-cheek hash, then eat it.

La Palme d'Or (Map p95; ☎ 305-913-3201; Biltmore Hotel, 1200 Anastasia Ave; meals $42-66; ☺ dinner Tue-Sat) One of the most acclaimed French restaurants in the USA, Phillipe Ruiz' Palme is the culinary match for the Jazz Age opulence that ensconces it. With its white-gloved, old-world class and US attention to service, unmuddled by pretensions at hipness, the Palme captures, in one elegant stroke, all the exclusivity a dozen South Beach restaurants could never grasp. The menu shifts seasonally, but remains consistently magnificent at one of Miami's best splurges.

Greater Miami

Lots of Lox (Map pp86-7; ☎ 305-252-2010; 14995 S Dixie Hwy; mains $4-13; ☺ breakfast & lunch) In a city with no shortage of delis, especially in mid–Miami Beach, who would have thought some of the best chopped liver on rye could be found in this unassuming place all the way down in Palmetto Bay? It is bustling, it is friendly and the excellent lunch meats sneer at their cousins over on Arthur Godfrey Rd, secure in their dominance of Greater Miami's deli ranks.

Shorty's BBQ (Map pp86-7; ☎ 305-670-7732; 9200 S Dixie Highway; mains $6-16; ☺ lunch & dinner) If you're gonna make a mess of yourself, best do it by dribbling some smoky barbecue sauce on the long wooden picnic tables at this South Dade institution. It's not the best barbecue in the world, but for Texas-style brisket in South Florida, it's as good as life gets.

Graziano's (Map pp86-7; ☎ 305-225-0008; 9227 SW 40th St; mains $14-34; ☺ lunch & dinner) Anglos love to argue over who does the best South American steak in Miami, but among Argentinian the general consensus is this very traditional *parilla*, located on a strip of gas stations on Bird Rd. Everything is plucked out of Buenos Aires: the quebracho wood on the grill, Argentinian customers and, most of all, racks of *lomo* (steak), sweetbreads and blood sausage, gristly bits beloved by *portenos* (Buenos Aires natives), which are tough to find in more Yankee-friendly establishments.

DRINKING & NIGHTLIFE

Yes, yes, those are real people going into the club. They just look like they walked out of a magazine.

We probably don't need to tell you Miami's nightlife scene is hot. In fact, it's probably hotter than you, unless you happen to be a certain class of celebrity, in which case: we take it back, Ms Portman and Mr Pitt. A Spanish flair for all-night fun, warm weather, big beaches, skimpy clothing, perfect mojitos – yep, this isn't the place for those with Catholic guilt complexes.

Don't be intimidated. You don't need to be uberwealthy or ultra-attractive to get past the red rope here, just confident. Besides, who cares about the rope? Miami has got kick-ass rock bars, hipsters-gone-wild lounges and the best Latin music scene in the US. If you want to bump and grind, and look for celebrities who aren't there, you can do it, but Miami will love you just as much if you want to rock out with a Budweiser on a sweaty South Florida evening.

South Beach

BARS

Abbey Brewery (Map pp88–9; ☎ 305-538-8110; 1115 16th St) The only brewpub in South Beach is on the untouristed end of South Beach (near Alton Rd). It's friendly and packed with folks listening to the Grateful Dead and, of course, slinging back some excellent homebrew: give the Abbey Brown or Oatmeal Stout a shot.

Chesterfield Hotel Bar (Map pp90–1; ☎ 305-531-5831; Chesterfield Hotel, 855 Collins Ave) Perch on some prime Collins people-watching real estate and get crunk on the hip-hop-and-zebra-stripe theme they've got going. You'd think this would be a prefunk place, but the setting's so fly, folks end up stationary, sipping on mad martinis until they stumble into their rooms.

Dewey's Tavern (Map pp90–1; ☎ 305-532-9980; 852 Alton Rd) Dewey's is a deco dive (really; the exterior is a little gem of the genre) and it's as unpretentious as the best sordid watering holes get. Come here to get wasted and menace the crowds seeking serenity on quiet Alton Rd (just kidding – behave yourself!).

Mango's Tropical Café (Map pp90–1; ☎ 305-673-4422; www.mangostropicalcafe.com; 900 Ocean Dr; cover $10-20) Cuba meets Coyote Ugly Saloon in this tourist hotspot, where a staff of gorgeous and/or ripped bodies (take your pick) dances, gyrates and puts some serious booty on the floor. Of course, you're here for anthropological reasons: to study the nuances of Latin dance. Not to watch the bartender do that thing Shakira does with her butt.

The Room (Map pp90–1; ☎ 305-531-6061; www.theotheroom.com/room.html; 100 Collins Ave) The Room's a gem: a crowded, dimly lit boutique beer bar where you can guzzle the best (brew) Belgium has to offer and gawk at the best (hotties) Miami has to show off. It's hip as hell, but the attitude is as low-key as the sexy mood lighting.

Ted's Hideaway (Map pp90–1; ☎ 305-532-9869; 124 2nd St) Somewhere in the Florida panhandle is a bumpin', fabulous gay club, which clearly switched places with Ted's, a no-nonsense, pool table and sports-showin' 'lounge' smack in the middle of Sofi's elegant chicness.

Automatic Slims (Map pp88–9; ☎ 305-675-0795; www.automatic-slims.com; 1216 Washington Ave) Slim's sells itself as a seedy rock bar, but it's really a marketing consultant's idea of what a dive should be. The Harley outside, Coyote Ugly ambience and manufactured 'edge' make it the Blink 182 of Miami's nightlife universe: watered-down punk and pretty nonthreatening.

Lost Weekend (Map pp88–9; ☎ 305-672-1707; 218 Española Way) The Weekend is a grimy, sweaty, slovenly dive, filled with pool tables, cheap domestics and – hell yeah – a Golden Tee arcade game. God bless it. Popular with local waiters, kitchen staff and bartenders, so you know it's a good time.

Mac's Club Deuce Bar (Map pp88–9; ☎ 305-673-9537; 222 14th St) The oldest bar in Miami Beach (established in 1926), the Deuce is a real neighborhood bar and hype-free zone. It's just straight-up seediness, which, depending on your outlook, can actually be quite refreshing. Plan to see everyone from transgendered ladies to construction workers, and hipsters to bikers.

Raleigh Hotel Bar (Map pp88–9; ☎ 305-534-6300; Raleigh Hotel, 1775 Collins Ave) You'd best be orderin' a Manhattan if you're gonna sidle up to this cologne-and-leather bar. Like everything else in the Raleigh, this lounge evokes South Beach's good old days, when guys like Al Capone and Meyer Lansky cut deals in the corner and jazz set the soundtrack.

Sagamore Bar (Map pp88–9; ☎ 305-535-8088; Sagamore, 1671 Collins Ave) Should you need a more refined vibe than the madness at the Delano (p134), walk into this cool white lobby, sit across from the plaster death masks (there

LGBT NIGHTLIFE

In one of those odd twists of fate, the South Beach gay scene (in many ways the driving force behind the neighborhood's rise from the ashes) has become so integrated that it's almost indistinguishable from its surroundings. Today, every nightclub on the beach has a gay night, but to be honest, while the mainstreaming of the gay scene is a victory for civil rights, it has kind of watered down the party. The techno-and-house-loving boys of the South Beach saw Joe-sixpack and his pop 40, hip-hop-loving buddies on the horizon, and a lot of them headed north. These days the best gay party scene isn't in Miami; it has moved to Fort Lauderdale.

But don't worry, boys: you're still well catered for in Miami. Cruisers should hit up **Score** (p152) and its upstairs Crème Lounge, **Laundry Bar** (p152), **Twist** (p152), and the much-acclaimed Sunday night flesh fest at **Cameo** (p152). **O-Zone** (Map p95; ☎ 305-667-2888; 6620 SW 57th Ave) is wildly popular but a little more sedate than the thumpa-thumpa-hey-what's-your-sign Sobe scene. **Boy Bar** (p154) pulls in beautiful North Beach bodies and **Club Boi** (Map pp86-7; ☎ 305-836-8995; 728 NW 79th St) is a good place for folks seeking a little 'color' (it's the only black-owned gay club in Miami and attracts a huge African-American, Latino and lesbian crowd).

Speaking of lesbians, the scene's improved for the girls in the past few years. The crowds are more mixed at the big gay hangouts, and lesbians in general seem to have wrested a little more control of a generally boy-dominated scene. **Pandora Events** (☎ 305-495-6969) is a good number to call for the low down on lesbian parties in Miami. Here are two ladies-only gems that should keep you in heaven:

- **Sax on the Beach** (Map pp92-3; ☎ 305-534-0493; 1756 N Bayshore Dr) Gets the party going on Fever Fridays.
- **Score** (Map pp88-9; ☎ 305-535-1111; 727 Lincoln Rd; www.scorebar.net) Saturday-night Sapphic goodness with Siren, upstairs in Crème Lounge.

The women's events at the **White Party** (www.whiteparty.org), which is still one of the grandest gaybashes in the US, have improved by leaps and bounds over the years. See their website or www.kissthegirlproductions.com for more details. And we couldn't sign off without mentioning **Aqua Girl** (www.aquagirl.org) weekend held in May, one of the hottest seasonal all-girl parties in the USA.

For up-to-date club and event listings, check out the weekly *Express* or *Wire* newspapers or www.miamigaytravel.com.

when we visited anyways), tell 'em hello and have a nice glass of chardonnay.

Table 8 Bar (Map pp88-9; ☎ 305-695-4114; www .table8la.com; De Soleil, 1458 Ocean Dr) Before you get settled in for an excellent meal at Table 8 (p141), rock up to the bar and order the best drink in Miami: a Basil 8. It's like a mojito for grown-ups: more mature, with more bite, but still perfect on a hot day.

Touch (Map pp88-9; ☎ 305-532-8003; www.touch restaurant.com; 910 Lincoln Rd) Touch's owners turned Elizabeth Taylor's jewelry box into a lounge: a vintage-y, opulent mess of sensory glitter, gaudy overkill and refined elegance. Drink alongside a slew of Miami's hiperati at this new Lincoln Rd resto-lounge and try not to be overwhelmed.

Skybar (Map pp88-9; ☎ 305-695-3900; Shore Club, 1901 Collins Ave) We've never seen so many beautiful people packed into one place, anywhere. Skybar became the bar to beat as soon as it opened, and frankly, it remains so to this day. The three-part venue is fabulous: chill alfresco in a sultan's pleasure garden under enormous, wrought-iron Moroccan lanterns, gaze at the patricians dining in nearby Nobu, or try (and fail, if you're an unlisted travel writer) to get into the all-crimson, all-A-list Red Room.

CLUBS

BED (Map pp90-1; ☎ 305-532-9070; www.bedmiami .com; 929 Washington Ave; ۞ Wed-Sun) You probably know this drill: someone sets a bunch of beds around a DJ booth. House music ensues.

People go crazy. Except the music is *really* loud here, and you have to order bottle service to lounge, so come with cash if you want to lay down (which seems opposed to the whole, 'Let's go dance' thing, but hey).

Twist (Map pp90-1; ☎ 305-538-9478; 1057 Washington Ave) Never a cover, always a groove, and right across from the police station, this two-story gay hangout has some serious staying power and a little bit of something for everyone: six different bars; go-go dancers; drag shows; lounging areas and, oh yeah, a small dance floor.

Nikki Beach Miami (Map pp90-1; ☎ 305-538-1111; www.nikkibeach.com; 1 Ocean Dr) Get your groove on outdoors, wandering from immaculate gossamer beach cabana to cabana at Nikki's, which feels like a full moon party gone incredibly upscale. On Sunday (*Sunday*!?), starting around 4pm, it's the hottest party in town, as folks clamor to get in and relive whatever it was they did the night before. The attached Pearl Restaurant & Champagne Lounge attracts the dinner-club set. It's quite the cool-kid spot too.

Florida Room at the Delano (Map pp88-9; ☎ 305-672-2000; Delano Hotel, 1685 Collins Ave) 'Wanna buy me an eight-dollar beer?' asks an out-of-towner, gazing awestruck at the sheer mass of model-types packed into this den of iniquity. The Florida Room is as exclusive as they get, plus a popular dancehall/samba piano lounge for local scenesters who eschew the tourist trap megaclubs further down the beach. Show up before 11pm or be on the list (or be Lenny Kravitz – who helped design this place) to get in.

Opium Garden (Map pp90-1; ☎ 305-531-5535; www.theopiumgroup.com; 136 Collins Ave) It can be tough to break into this most coveted of clubs. Coveted and overrated, as far as we're concerned, but the Opium Group has a vicelike grip on the Miami Beach club scene that's hard to break. Once you're in, flash a wad to either score bottle service or buy your way into several layers of VIP-room snobbery.

our pick **Buck 15** (Map pp88-9; ☎ 305-538-3815; 707 Lincoln Lane) Located in a loft above Miss Yip (p141), B15 manages to blend everything we like about going out – kinda edgy but not scary graffiti chic, cast-off action figures, consistently awesome DJs (Did they just mix 'Your Love' by the Outfield into 'Low' by Flo-Rida? Oh yes they did), free entry, a good mix of the hip and the hot and the drunk and the folks who just don't care but definitely

wave their hands in the air – into one shot of nightlife fun.

Cameo (Map pp88-9; ☎ 305-532-2667; www.cameomiami.com; 1445 Washington Ave) This enormous, touristy club, where Gwen Stefani tracks get smooshed into Oakenfold, is where the sexy times are to be had – if by sexy time you mean thumping music, a packed crowd and sweat to slip on. Sunday's gay night (the specific party name frequently changes) is one of the best in town.

Laundry Bar (Map pp88-9; ☎ 305-531-7700; www.laundrybar.com; 721 Lincoln Lane N) You can go with coin-operated or Cointreau at this dark, groovy hybrid; as they say, 'Get sloshed while you wash.' There's a decidedly gay vibe, but Laundry Bar is relaxed and welcomes all, although you may have to step around break-dancing 'poseurs' on weekends. You really can clean your clothes here, although every couple in Miami is making out on the washer units.

Mansion (Map pp88-9; ☎ 305-532-1525; www.mansionmiami.com; 1235 Washington Ave) Every night the lines stretch around the block as plebs beg, cajole and strut in a vain attempt to get past that damned red rope. Inside? Well, they don't call it 'Mansion' for nothing. Expect megaclub grandiosity, plenty of attitude, waiting in line for hours and the chance to see Lindsay Lohan do something tabloid-worthy.

Mynt (Map pp88-9; ☎ 786-695-1705; www.myntlounge.com; 1921 Collins Ave) Join the partying stars – Justin Timberlake, Vin Diesel, Britney Spears etc – by bottle servicing yourself into the VIP section. Otherwise, make friends with the red rope until you can order a drink and then try not to spill it, which is tough in the sweaty scrum of models, Moët and mojitos.

Score (Map pp88-9; ☎ 305-535-1111; 727 Lincoln Rd; www.scorebar.net) Muscle boys with mustaches, glistening six-packs gyrating on stage, and a crowd of men who've decided shirts really aren't their thing: do we need to spell out the orientation of Score's customer base? It's still the best dedicated gay bar on the beach, and the addition of the more mature Crème Lounge upstairs will undoubtedly raise the cachet of this perennial favorite.

LOUNGES

Bond Street Lounge (Map pp88-9; ☎ 305-398-1806; Townhouse Hotel, 150 20th St) After the sushi eaters head home, a new crowd rolls in – one that prefers litchitinis (lychee martinis) over yellowtail. Throw yourself over a white couch or

GETTING PAST THE RED ROPE

If you're gonna go out in Miami, ask yourself: what do I want? Do I want to dance? Hear good tunes? Score? See celebrities? If you answered yes to the first two questions, the downtown Miami and Wynwood scene might be more to your liking (which isn't to say the beautiful people don't go out there. The scene is just less…well, scene-y). If you answered yes to the last two questions, you may want to stay in South Beach.

Also, ask yourself another question: What do I bring? If it's good looks, money or promoter connections, the world is your oyster. If you've got none of the above, you can still party, but be prepared for some ego-crushing. Best overheard conversation in the course of this research:

Guy A: [Looking at model] 'How do you approach a girl like that?'

Guy B: 'In a Mercedes.'

Here's how it breaks down: the South Beach club scene plays on the appeal of celebrity. More famous customers equal more regular customers. Eventually, a strange equilibrium works out where enough regular customers make people assume famous people are there, even if they're not. But those regular customers can't appear *too* regular. So a little social engineering is committed by club-owners and those titans of the cultural scene (ie bouncers) in the form of the red rope. How do you get by it?

- **Be polite** Don't be skittish, but don't act like you're J Lo, either. And whatever you do, don't yell at the doorman – or touch him or yank on his clothing – to try to get his attention.

- **Get guest-listed** Ask the concierge at your hotel to help you out, or simply call the club and leave your name; it's often that simple.

- **Remain confidently aloof** Don't stare at the doorman; it's pathetic. Look elsewhere – but look hot doing it.

- **Be aggressive. Failing that, be rich** If there's a clamoring crowd, standing at the back of it and hoping it'll part is about as effective as being meek when you need a seat on the New York subway. Push your way through to the front. Or order bottle service (ie an overpriced bottle of spirits), which usually guarantees you a pass to the front.

- **Come correct** For women, showing a sophisticated amount of skin is effective, although 'sophisticated' depends on the wearer. We've seen Brazilians in barely-there tops look less trashy than US natives in a standard sorority-girl-miniskirt ensemble. Men, don't wear T-shirts and jeans, unless you're one of those guys who *can* and still look put together. In which case, we're jealous, dude. Also, this is Miami; be a little more daring than button-up shirt and slacks if you want to stand out.

- **Get there early** Do you want to be cool, or do you want to get in? From 10:30pm to 11pm is a golden time for bouncer leniency, but you can't club-hop with this strategy.

- **If you're a man, bring a woman** A man alone is not worth much (unless you're at a gay club, natch); up your value by having a beautiful woman – or two or three – on your arm.

- **Be a Wilson brother** Luke! Owen! Come on in.

Though our listings represent the hottest parties as of press time, we urge you to do some follow-up research when you arrive: talk to friends, your concierge and pick up a copy of the local arts weekly, *Miami New Times,* or a free monthly such as *Miami Living Magazine* or the pint-sized *Ego Miami Magazine.*

cylindrical white ottoman, order up, sip and stare at the crowd.

Jazid (Map pp88–9; ☎ 305-673-9372; 1342 Washington Ave) While the downstairs caters to folks seeking a mellow, candlelit spot to hear live jazz, soul and funk bands, the upstairs lounge has DJs spinning soul and hip-hop to a cool,

multiculti crowd. By being cool and not trying to be, this place has remained popular while places all around it have come and gone.

Northern Miami Beach

Boteca (Map p94; ☎ 305-757-7735; 916 NE 79th St) If you're missing São Paolo, come to Boteca on

Friday evenings to see the biggest Brazilian expat reunion in Miami. *Cariocas* (Rio natives) and their countrymen flock here to listen to samba and bossa nova, and chat each other up over (obviously) the best capirinhas in town.

Boy Bar (Map p94; ☎ 305-864-2697; 1220 Normandy Dr) The North Beach boys (and just about everyone else) flock to this neighborhood cruise bar, where everyone plays pool, chills on the back porch and basically avoids indulging in too much South Beach–style madness. Which isn't to say they don't engage in a little bad behavior…

Circa 39 Bar (Map p94; ☎ 305-538-3900; Circa 39, 3900 Collins Ave) Tucked off to the back of Circa's moody front lobby, the designer dream bar has a warm, welcoming feel to it. Definitely stop in for a cosmopolitan if you're up this way, before sauntering across the street and checking out the nighttime ocean.

Downtown Miami

Tourists don't tend to make it across A1A, sticking to the well-hyped but somewhat overplayed scene in South Beach. That's their loss; to quote 'Bitch I'm From Dade County' (poetic in its prose, visionary in its themes), 'Do not be thinkin' we soft or we sweet/Come on the opposite side of the beach.' The real cutting edge of clubs, pubs and bars is concentrated here, specifically in the edgy transition area between Downtown and Overtown. The lounges here usually feature live music and often double as small clubs.

BARS

Level 25 (Map pp92-3; ☎ 305-503-6500; Conrad Miami, 1395 Brickell Ave) When Neo buys Morpheus a drink, they probably meet at this Conrad Miami spot (guess which floor), where it's all long white lines, low black couches, pin-striped gorgeousity and God's-eye views over Biscayne Bay.

M Bar (Map pp92-3; ☎ 305-695-1717; Mandarin Oriental Miami, 500 Brickell Key Dr) The high-class lobby bar here may be tiny, but its martini menu – over 250 strong – isn't. The views ain't bad either.

Tobacco Road (Map pp92-3; ☎ 305-374-1198; 626 S Miami Ave) Miami's oldest bar has been on the scene since the 1920s. These days it's a little touristy, but it has stayed in business for a reason: old wood, blue lights, cigarette smoke and sassy bartenders greet you like a buddy. Cold beers are on tap and decent live acts crank out the blues, jazz and rock.

CLUBS

Karu & Y (Map pp92-3; ☎ 305-403-7850; www.karu-y.com; 71 NW 14th St) Karu smacks of an Atlanta hip-hop megaclub in ways good and sundry. Basically, it's a bottle of iced-out Cristal given club form – there's a Dale Chiluly chandelier in the entrance, waterfall out front and restaurant (Karu; Y is the lounge) that serves foie-gras lollipops. It's all (literally) smack on the tracks that separate tatty but gentrifying downtown Miami (bling!) from Overtown's worst projects (bang!). Come here to star in your personal MTV video, and expect to pay for the privilege.

Space (Map pp92-3; ☎ 305-375-0001; www.clubspace.com; 142 NE 11th St) This multilevel warehouse is Miami's main megaclub. With 30,000 sq ft to fill, dancers have room to strut, and an around-the-clock liquor license redefines the concept of after-hours. DJs usually pump each floor with a different sound – hip-hop, Latin, heavy trance – while the infamous rooftop lounge is the place to be for sunrise.

LOUNGES

Pawn Shop (Map pp92-3; ☎ 305-373-3511; www.thepawnshoplounge.com; 1222 NE 2nd Ave) This den of hipness still has its original pawn-shop facade, with signs announcing 'We buy diamonds' and 'We buy gold.' It's all about true (but glamorous) grit here – and varying DJs who spin funky, edgy electronica.

PS 14 (Map pp92-3; ☎ 305-358-3600; 28 NW 14th St) In a city with justice, PS 14 would be packed every night of the week. Live gigs burn up the cute red-lit front room, while the back opens into a lush garden (you could almost forget you're on the edge of Overtown…) where DJs spin and folks chill if they ain't dancing, which you should be.

Studio A (Map pp92-3; ☎ 305-358-7625; www.studioamiami.com; 60 NE 11th St) Next to ginormous Space (above), Studio A is something between an edgy gig venue and mega-main-stage. It's very hit or miss; as a club it can suck, but as a concert hall it pulls in some incredible acts.

Transit Lounge (Map pp92-3; ☎ 305-377-4628; 729 SW 1st Ave) Transit exists in some perfect-bar conceptual space, possessing the everyone-knows-your-name camaraderie of a dive, cool-daddio ambience of a good jazz club, the street cred of some of Miami's hottest live acts and a welcoming but ruggedly sexy venue. When you've had enough, run, don't stumble, to nearby La Moon (p144) and soak that beer up with a hot dog smothered in mayo and potato sticks.

White Room (Map pp92-3; ☎ 305-995-5050; www .whiteroommiami.com; 1306 N Miami Ave) Miami's hipsters are so, well, Miami – artsy yet glam compared to their London and NYC counterparts. They flock here, where there's the requisite weird movies playing on open-air projectors, Lawrence of Arabia tents curving around an exposed-industrial main-stage and, according to promoters, a shared design-aesthetic-lifestyle-blah blah blah. Hot hipsters get drunk and dance with other hot hipsters. You go, White Room. The very popular Poplife party goes off here Saturdays.

Wynwood, Design District & Little Haiti

With all the gentrification occurring here, expect this neighborhood's nightlife to blow up in the near future. The Arts Walks (see below) that are run on every second Saturday attract both sophisticated and simplistic club kids from all across the city.

Circa 28 (Map p97; ☎ 305-788-1858; www.circa28.com; 2826 N Miami Ave) Miami can work its magic on anyone, even Wynwood's angst-y artists. Like Cinderella touched by a fairy godmother (or a very good DJ), they become glamorous club kids in this two-story hepcat hotspot. Circa is as sexy and gorgeous as Miami gets, but with its modish library and (semi)literati clientele, it's also intelligent enough to hold a conversation.

Churchill's (Map p97; ☎ 305-757-1807; www .churchillspub.com; 5501 NE 2nd Ave, Little Haiti; cover $10-15; ☽ 11am-3am Mon-Sat, noon-3am Sun) Only in Miami: Churchill's is a Brit-owned, East End–style pub in the midst of what could be Port-au-Prince. There's a lot of live music here, mainly punk and indie and more punk. Not insipid

modern punk either: think the Ramones meet the Sex Pistols. While everyone's getting their ya-ya's off, Haitian hustlers are lurking outside, waiting to park your car or sidle in and enjoy the gig and a beer with you. Brits, this is the place to watch your sports.

Grass Restaurant & Lounge Bar (Map p97; ☎ 305-573-3355; www.grasslounge.com; 28 NE 40th St; ☽ Tue-Sat) This Design District restaurant-cum-lounge is intimate yet alfresco. Dress your best and head to the velvet-roped entrance; inside, you can either dine on cool Asian-fusion dishes (see Grass Restaurant, p146) or simply posture, dance and watch the door (like everyone else).

Little Havana

Casa Panza Bar (Map p96; ☎ 305-643-5343; 1620 SW 8th St) It doesn't get cornier than this 'authentic' Spanish taverna (see p147) where the live shows, flamenco dancers, Spanish guitarists and audience participation reach new heights of sangria-soaked fun. Drop your cynicism, enter and enjoy.

Hoy Como Ayer (Map p96; ☎ 305-541-2631; 2212 SW 8th St; cover $8-25) This Cuban hotspot – with authentic music, unstylish wood paneling and a small dance floor – is enhanced by cigar smoke and packed with Havana transplants. Stop in nightly for *son* (a salsalike dance that originated in Oriente, Cuba), *boleros* (a Spanish dance in triple meter) and modern Cuban beats.

Coconut Grove

Everything here closes at 3am, thanks to stick-in-the-mud city officials.

Oxygen Lounge (Map p99; ☎ 305-476-0202; www .oxygenlounge.biz; Streets of Mayfair, 2911 Grand Ave) This is

---

ART WALKS: THE NEW CLUBBING?

It's hipsters gone wild! Hmm, that doesn't actually sound very fun, so we'll put it another way: it's free wine! And artsy types, and galleries open till late, and the eye candy of a club, and the drunken momentum of a pub crawl, and best of all, no red ropes. The Wynwood and Design District Arts Walk is, for our money (ie none, because it's free) one of the best nightlife experiences in Miami. And we're not (just) being cheapskates. The experience of strolling from gallery to gallery (That piece is *gorgeous*. Pour me another.), perusing the paintings (No, I don't think there's a bathroom behind the performance artist.), delving into the nuances of aesthetic styles (The wine's run out? Let's bounce.) and, erm, getting tanked is as genuinely innovative as…well, the best contemporary art. Just be careful, as a lot of galleries in Wynwood are separated by short drives (the Design District is more walkable). Arts walks go down on the second Saturday of each month, from 7pm to 10pm (some galleries stretch till 11pm); when it's all over, lots of folks repair to Circa 28 (above). Visit www.artcircuits.com for information on participating galleries.

MIAMI

in the mall underground – literally – Coconut Grove. It's an elegant, sprawling sushi bar-dance land with space-age decor and packs of Grove beauties. Theme-night parties rock your fine booty every night of the week.

Miami Improv (Map p99; ☎ 305-441-8200; www.miamiimprov.com; 3390 Mary St; tickets $10-70) Part of a national chain, this 3rd-floor club has the usual club-circuit suspects plus monthly Miami Comics, open-mic shows and Urban Nights, which feature stars from Comedy Central's Showtime, HBO's Def Comedy Jam and BET's Comic View.

Coral Gables

There's Gruppie (Gables yuppie) bars all along Miracle Mile, but these two gems will keep you above the silly fray.

The Bar (Map p95; ☎ 305-442-2730; 172 Giralda Ave) All in a name, right? Probably the best water-ing hole in the Gables, The Bar is just what the title says (which is ironic in this neighborhood of extravagant embellishment). If you're in the 'hood on Friday come here for happy hour (5pm to 8pm), when all the young Gables professionals take their ties off and basically let loose long into the night.

Titanic (Map pp86-7; ☎ 305-668-1742; www.titanic brewery.com; 5813 Ponce de León Blvd) By day, it's an All-American type bar and grill, but at night Titanic turns into a popular University of Miami watering hole. Thursdays tend to be big nights out here.

Greater Miami

La Covacha (Map pp86-7; ☎ 305-594-3717; www.la covacha.com; 10730 NW 25th St, Doral) Drive out about halfway to the Everglades (just kidding, but only just) and you'll find Covacha, the most hidden, most hip Latin scene in Miami. Actually, it's not hidden; all the young Latinos know about Covacha and love it well, and we do too. It's an excellent spot to see new bands, upcoming DJs (almost all local), an enormous crowd and pretty much no tourists.

ENTERTAINMENT

Miami's artistic merits are obvious, even from a distance. Could there be a better creative base? There's Southern homegrown talent, migratory snowbirds bringing the funding and attention of Northeastern galleries, and the immigrants, of course, from all across the Americas. All these disparate cultures com-municate their values via the language of ex-pression. Creole, Spanish and English, after all, are poor languages compared to dance, music and theater.

Cinemas

Absinthe House Cinematheque (Map p95; ☎ 305-446-7144; 235 Alcazar Ave, Coral Gables) This art house is a blend of old-fashioned and mod – it has only one screen dishing up independent and foreign films, but also a cool lounge serving as an atmospheric snack bar.

Bill Cosford Cinema (Map pp86-7; ☎ 305-284-4861; www.miami.edu/cosford; Memorial Classroom Bldg, University of Miami, University Dr) On the University of Miami campus, this renovated art house was launched in memory of the *Miami Herald* film critic. They do him justice, too, with a great lineup of first-run indie and foreign movies, plus presentations from visiting filmmakers.

Performing Arts

VENUES

Adrienne Arsht Center for the Performing Arts (Map pp92-3; ☎ 305-949-6722, 786-468-2000; www.arshtcenter.org; 1300 Biscayne Blvd) Skeptics, we're sorry, but it's clear this enormous centerpiece of north-ern downtown was worth both the wait and the expense. The magnificent venue manages to both humble and enthrall visitors who can't help but marvel at the split-shell design and the way the Arsht seizes upon and utilizes the most common natural resource in Florida: natural, golden sunlight, which comes crash-ing through huge plate-glass windows. Today the Arsht is where the biggest cultural acts in Miami come to perform; a show here is a must-see on any Miami trip. Get off the Metromover at Omni stop.

Colony Theatre (Map pp88-9; ☎ 305-674-1026; 1040 Lincoln Rd, South Beach) A stunning deco showpiece, this small 1934 performing-arts center has 465-seats and great acoustics. It's a treasure that hosts everything from movies and an oc-casional musical to theatrical dramas, ballet and off-Broadway productions.

Gusman Center for the Performing Arts (Map pp92-3; ☎ 305-374-2444; www.gusmancenter.org; 174 E Flagler St) This ornate venue, within an elegantly reno-vated 1920s movie palace, services a huge vari-ety of performing arts including film festivals, symphonies, ballets and touring shows. The acoustics are excellent and the fresco ceiling is covered in twinkling stars and clouds.

Jackie Gleason Theater of the Performing Arts (Map pp88-9; ☎ 305-673-7300; www.gleasontheater

.com; 1700 Washington Ave, South Beach) Built in 1951, South Beach's premiere showcase for touring Broadway shows, orchestras and other big musical productions has 2700 seats and excellent acoustics. Jackie Gleason chose to make the theater his home for the long-running 1960s TV show, but now you'll find an eclectic lineup of shows – Elvis Costello or Albita one night, the Dutch Philharmonic or an over-the-top musical the next.

Light Box Theatre/Miami Light Project (Map p97; ☎ 305-576-4350; www.miamilightproject.com; 3000 Biscayne Blvd) The Miami Light Project is a nonprofit cultural foundation that represents innovative shows from theater troupes and performance artists from around the world. Shows are performed across the city, but the project is housed at Light Box Studio.

THEATER

Actors Playhouse (Map p95; ☎ 305-444-9293; www .actorsplayhouse.org; Miracle Theater, 280 Miracle Mile, Coral Gables; tickets $30-40) Housed within the 1948 deco Miracle Theater, this three-theater venue stages musicals and comedies, children's theater on its kids stage and more avant-garde productions in its small experimental black-box space. Recent productions have included *Footloose* and *The Wizard of Oz* for the little ones.

Gablestage (Map p95; ☎ 305-445-1119; www.gable stage.org; 1200 Anastasia Ave, Coral Gables; tickets $15-35) Founded as the Florida Shakespeare Theatre in 1979 and now housed on the property of the Biltmore Hotel, this company still performs an occasional Shakespeare play, but mostly presents contemporary and classical pieces; recent productions have included *Frozen, Bug* and *The Retreat From Moscow*.

Jerry Herman Ring Theatre (Map pp86-7; ☎ 305-284-3355; www.miami.edu/ring; University of Miami, 1321 Miller Dr; tickets $15) This University of Miami troupe stages musicals, dramas and comedies, with recent productions including *Falsettos* and *Baby*. Alumni actors include Sylvester Stallone, Steven Bauer, Saundra Santiago and Ray Liotta.

Edge Theater (Map p97; ☎ 305-355-0976; 3825 N Miami Ave) The Edge stays true to its name (and Design District locale) by putting on consistently contemporary, artfully imagined productions on a small stage that feels like a makeshift living room filled with props.

DANCE

Ifé-Ilé Afro-Cuban Dance (☎ 305-476-0388; www .ife-ile.org) Ifé-Ilé is a nonprofit organization that promotes cultural understanding through dance, and performs in a range of styles – traditional Afro-Cuban, mambo, rumba, conga, chancleta, son, salsa and ritual pieces. Call them for further information.

Miami City Ballet (Map pp88-9; ☎ 305-929-7000; www.miamicityballet.org; 2200 Liberty Ave, South Beach) Formed in 1985, this troupe is guided by artistic director Edward Villella, who studied under the great George Balanchine at the NYC Ballet. So it's no surprise Balanchine works dominate the repertoire, with shows held at a lovely three-story headquarters designed by the famed local architectural firm Arquitectonica. The facade allows passersby to watch the dancers rehearsing through big picture windows, which kinda makes you feel like you're in a scene from *Fame*, except the weather is better and people don't spontaneously break into song.

Miami Hispanic Ballet (Map pp86-7; ☎ 305-549-7711; www.miamihispanicballet.com; 900 SW 1st St) Directed by Cuban-trained Pedro Pablo Peña, this troupe presents mainly classical ballets based out of the lovely Manuel Artime Theater, the 'largest, small venue' in the city.

Live Music

If you are interested in checking out some live jazz, rock or other contemporary music while in Miami, there are more live-music venues listed in the Drinking & Nightlife section, p150.

CLASSICAL

Concert Association of Florida (☎ 877-311-7469; www .concertfla.org; 555 17th St) Founded in 1967, this nonprofit association is run by dedicated folks who bring world-class music (and occasional dance) to various venues in Miami, particularly to the Arsht Center (p107). Past events have included the Boston Pops symphony, Itzhak Perlman, a Flamenco Festival, the Deutsche Philharmonie and Luciano Pavarotti on the beach.

Miami Chamber Symphony (Map pp86-7; ☎ 305-858-3500; Gusman Concert Hall, University of Miami, 1314 Miller Dr; tickets $15-30; ☼ performances Nov-May) Its yearly series features world-renowned soloists at shows held at the University of Miami's Gusman Concert Hall (not to be confused with the downtown Gusman Center for the Performing Arts).

New World Symphony (Map pp88-9; NWS; ☎ 305-673-3331; www.nws.org; 541 Lincoln Rd; tickets $20-70;

performances Oct-May) The deservedly heralded NWS serves as a three- to four-year preparatory program for very talented musicians who've already graduated from presti gious music schools. There are an astonishing number of inspiring and original performances (many of which are free), held at the Lincoln Theatre.

Sports

FOOTBALL

Miami Dolphins (☎ 305-620-2578; www.miamidolphins .com; Dolphin Stadium, 2269 NW 199th St, Opa-Locka; tickets $29-700; ☺ season Aug-Dec) 'Dol-fans' are respectably crazy about their team, even if a Super Bowl showing has evaded them since 1985. Games are wildly popular and the Dolphins are painfully successful, in that they always raise fans' hopes but never quite fulfill them. Super Bowl 44 will be held at Dolphin Stadium in 2010. If you're a real football fanatic, you can watch preseason practices near Fort Lauderdale. Take I-95 or Florida's Turnpike to I-595 west to the University Dr exit. Turn left at SW 30th St and make another left. The training facility is half a mile down on the right.

University of Miami Hurricanes (☎ 800-462-2637; www.hurricanesports.com; tickets $25-45; ☺ season Aug-Dec) On November 10, 2007, the 'Canes, one of the most successful college-football franchises of the past 25 years, were annihilated 48-0 by the University of Virginia, the worst home loss in the team's history. It was their last game in Orange Bowl Stadium (now the site of the new Miami Marlins stadium, see Map pp86–7), which was perhaps mercifully demolished two months later (they now play in the Dolphin

Stadium). For the Hurricanes, once titans of university football, the slow decline began in 2004, culminating in 2007's abysmal losing season. But the team's green-and-orange army isn't going to surrender any time soon, and the insane excitement of game day is still worth experiencing.

BASKETBALL

Miami Heat (☎ 786-777-4328; www.nba.com/heat; tickets $10-375; ☺ season Nov-Apr) The Heat used to be so hot (forgive us). First: Pat Riley took over coaching in 2003. Then they scored the first three draft picks of 2004–05 and, finally, won an NBA championship in 2006. Since then, the team has been trying to recapture that magic momentum by finding the perfect match to round out the driving game of Dwyane Wade and Shaquille O'Neal. The team plays at American Airlines Arena (p107).

University of Miami Hurricanes (☎ 800-462-2637; www.hurricanesports.com; tickets $20; ☺ season Nov-Apr) Catch the beloved college Hurricanes shooting hoops at the BankUnited Center at the University of Miami (Map pp86–7).

SHOPPING

Practically every part of Miami has a shopping 'area,' but to simplify matters, and make your beeline to spend simpler, we'll give you the most clear-cut, basic destinations, starting with South Beach, the best place for fashion hunting. There are two main strips in this neighborhood – Lincoln Mall, the pedestrian road between Washington Ave and Alton Rd that's lined with a great mix of indie shops and chain stores; and the southern end of Collins Ave, below 9th St. Here you'll find mostly

---

MIAMI MARLIN MADNESS

Ten Years. Ten years of backbiting, arguing, begging and cajoling, of almost losing the baseball team to San Antonio and Virginia Beach. Ten years and 70% of an optimistically projected $619 million bill has been spent. Costs will likely be covered (no matter what city officials say) by shuffling public-works funds. Put it all together and Miami will get to keep the Florida Marlins, rename them the Miami Marlins and house them in Major League Baseball's newest stadium, set to replace the vanquished Orange Bowl in Little Havana. The city of Miami is hoping the new stadium will anchor south downtown's resurgence, bring baseball fans streaming into the city, and further solidify Miami's position as capital of South Florida. Fans in Broward county, pissed off about the name change, will have to swallow their bitterness. And baseball goes on in South Florida, in a new, air-conditioned, retractable-domed 37,000-seat stadium, which, while small for a major-league venue, may be roomy considering only 375 fans (375!!) came out to a Marlins-Nationals game in September 2007.

Seriously.

chains, but high-end ones, such as A/X, Ralph Lauren and Barney's Co-op. Shooting way north of here, you'll find two extremely popular shopping malls: the **Aventura Mall** (Map pp86-7; ☎ 305-935-1110; www.shopaventuramall.com; 19501 Biscayne Blvd, Aventura), a mainstream collection including JC Penney and Bloomingdale's, and the chichi **Bal Harbour Shops** (Map p94; ☎ 305-866-0311; www.balharbourshops.com; 9700 Collins Ave, Bal Harbor), a classy scene boasting Prada, Gucci, Chanel and Saks Fifth Avenue outposts.

Move over to the mainland and find a few options, the hippest being the Design District, where you'll find a glut of design, art and homewares and just a sprinkling of clothing and accessories hawkers. Also, just south of here, along NW 6th Ave between 23rd St and 29th St, is the less fashionable 'Fashion District' (in Wynwood proper), with outlets for about 30 of the 500 or so garment manufacturers in Miami. You'll have an easier time at the touristy, chain store–drenched mainstream magnet, **Bayside Marketplace** (Map pp92-3; ☎ 305-577-3344; www.baysidemarketplace.com; 401 Biscayne Blvd), on the shores of downtown Miami. Find more outdoor malls in Coconut Grove, at the ever-popular **CocoWalk** (Map p99; ☎ 305-444-0777; 3015 Grand Ave) and **Streets of Mayfair** (Map p99; ☎ 305-448-1700; 2911 Grand Ave); Coral Gables, meanwhile, has the new **Village of Merrick Park** (Map p95; ☎ 305-529-0200; www.villageofmerrickpark.com; 358 San Lorenzo Ave) anchored by the classy department stores Neiman Marcus and Nordstrom.

Art, Furniture & Home Design

Española Way Art Center (Map pp88-9; ☎ 305-673-0946; 405 Española Way) There are three levels of studios here, plus excellent original work and prints for sale, all by local artists.

Hiho Batik/Sprocket Gift Shop (Map p94; ☎ 305-754-8890; www.hihobatik.com; 6925 Biscayne Blvd) Hiho is a neat little shop where you can design your own batik (wax-and-dyed artwork; here they usually put it on T-shirts) with a friendly staff of artsy types, or look for an out-there urban gift among the shelves of the attached Spocket's – think mature pop-up books, weird home decor and the like.

Kuma Central (Map p97; ☎ 305-573-4486; 130 NE 40th St) Another limited-edition toy shop that sells the sort of urban toys and playthings you can only find in Japan. The gidgets and gadgets and toys are all very neat, and the kids will no doubt love them (although they'd arguably be as happy with a fire truck) but it's

glaringly obvious parents are here for their own sense of cool.

Moooi (Map p97; ☎ 305-574-4045; www.moooimiami .com; 3438 N Miami Ave) They've got a great motto here: 'For design addicts, but more for design virgins.' If you've always wanted your house to look conceptual but haven't the slightest idea where to begin (or if you know exactly what you require of a room), the friendly folks at this Marcel Wanders boutique will get you on the road to a really fine interior.

Artisan Antiques Art Deco (Map p97; ☎ 305-573-5619; 110 NE 40th St) This wonderful shop houses one of the world's largest collections of French art-deco lighting, furniture and accessories, including unique pieces by Lalique Sabino and De Gue.

Clothing & Accessories

Crimson Carbon (Map pp90-1; ☎ 305-538-8262; 524 Washington Ave, Suite 101) Not only will you be hot after emerging from CC, you'll feel better about your place in the Circle of Life. The bubble shorts, California-style dresses and other chic standards this store sells are often organic, chemical-free and ecofriendly. CC carries Carilyn Vaile's green label, made from raw bamboo, and Mad Imports, which sources its accessories from a Madagascar co-op.

Leo (Map pp90-1; ☎ 305-531-6550; www.leomiami .com; 640 Collins Ave) A welcome break from Sobe's usual glam, Leo caters to the more indie-chic (or at least those who appreciate a decently witty T-shirt). The beautiful come to browse labels such as Diab'less, American Retro and Alexander Wang under a ceiling strewn with 500 lightbulbs.

En Avance (Map pp88-9; ☎ 305-534-0337; 734 Lincoln Rd) Want your shopping to be as chic as your nightclubbing? Then head here, where you'll be greeted by a velvet rope and a hot collection of high fashion once inside. The friendly staff will help you negotiate through the Rebecca Taylor, Juicy Couture, Tse and more. You'll also find Defile makeup and even designer styles for infants. Don't be surprised if you rub elbows with a celeb or two.

Scoop (Map pp88-9; ☎ 305-532-5929; www.scoop nyc.com; Shore Club, 1901 Collins Ave) If yours was the real-life story *Zoolander* was based on, you'd probably like to shop in Scoop, located in the Shore Club (p134) and full of hot-ticket fashion for models (male and female) from both its own label and others, including Juicy Couture, Paul Smith and Theory.

MIAMI

Desiree Nercessian (Map pp90-1; ☎ 305-604-0521; 710 Washington Ave) We're still not sure how to pronounce the name of this place, but we do know it sells lovely beachwear that gets you noticed without sacrificing your dignity or, for that matter, your wallet.

London Sole (Map pp90-1; ☎ 305-674-8688; www .londonsole.com; 760 Ocean Dr) North American girls have not rediscovered the ballerina flat the way their European counterparts have, but London Sole is working to change that, providing colorful, sexy shoes you can wear down the beach and out to the club, all in the course of one long, fashionable day.

Sofi Swimwear (Map pp88-9; www.sofiswimwear .com; 1522 Washington Ave) Goodness gracious glamorous. Founded by Brazilian designer Surya Oliveira, Sofi sells more elegantly subdued swimsuits than the average thong-tha-thong-thong-thong bikinis on display in these parts.

Ma Vie en Lingerie (Map p95; ☎ 305-444-1454; 325 Miracle Mile) The gorgeous lingerie at this store is extremely hot. Hot in a 'Your boyfriend will either be very uncomfortable or totally psyched to be instore with you' kinda way. Designs run the gamut from elegant to provocative to Wow.

Hip.e (Map p95; ☎ 305-445-3693; www.hip-eboutique .com; 359 Miracle Mile) A bit more hip than hippie, the clothes and jewelry here manage to mix up indie and hip-hop aesthetics in an admirably wearable way. Think Lucite bangles just slightly embellished by bling and you've got an idea of the vibe.

C Madeleine's (Map p94; ☎ 305-945-7770; http:// shop.cmadeleines.com; 13702 Biscayne Blvd) The undisputed queen of vintage Miami, C Madeleine is more than your standard used-clothes write-off. This is a serious temple to classical style, selling Yves Saint Laurent couture and classic Chanel suits. Come here for the sort of timeless looks that are as beautiful now as they were when they first appeared on the rack.

Gifts

El Crédito Cigars (Map p96; ☎ 305-858-4162; 1106 SW 8th St) In one of the most popular cigar stores in Miami, and one of the oldest in Florida, you'll be treated as a venerated member of the stogie-chomping boy's club.

La Tradición Cubana (Map p96; ☎ 305-643-4005; 1894 SW 8th St) Watch workers roll your cigars before you buy them at this little factory.

Little-Havana-To-Go (Map p96; ☎ 305-857-9720; www.littlehavanatogo.com; 1442 SW 8th St) This is Little Havana's official souvenir store, and it has some pretty cool items, from Cuban-pride T-shirts to posters, flags, paintings, photo books, cigar-box purses and authentic clothing.

Gourmet Food

Epicure Market (Map pp88-9; ☎ 305-672-1861; 1656 Alton Rd, South Beach) Whether you have cooking facilities in your inn or just want to shop for a fancy beach picnic, this is the place. You'll find an outstanding array of fresh produce, sinful baked goods, fresh flowers, premade meals (including matzo-ball soup, lasagna and salads), imported treats such as jams and tapenades, and an excellent selection of fine global wines.

Whole Foods Marketplace (Map pp90-1; ☎ 305-532-1707; www.wholefoodsmarket.com; 1020 Alton Rd, South Beach) This natural-food grocery-store chain has an excellent array of organic produce, packaged products from cereals to soaps, bulk items, organic dairy foods, prepared meals and a salad bar. You'll also find a good selection of wines, beers and fresh elixirs squeezed at the juice bar.

Music

Do Re Mi Music Center (Map p96; ☎ 305-541-3374; 1829 SW 8th St) It's Latin music in all forms – CDs, vinyl, cassettes and even a range of instruments for you to bust out on. Staff are very helpful with those tourists who don't know their samba from their salsa.

Sweat Records (Map p97; ☎ 305-758-5862; http:// sweatrecordsmiami.blogspot.com; 5505 NE 2nd Ave) Sweat's almost a stereotypical indie record store: it serves organic coffee, it has got big purple couches, it sells weird Japanese toys and there are skinny guys with thick glasses arguing over LPs you've never heard of. It feels a little out of place in hip-hop-y Latin Miami, but we're glad someone is waving the indie flag in this town.

GETTING THERE & AWAY

AIR
Airport

Miami is served by all major carriers via two main airports: Miami International Airport (MIA) and the Fort Lauderdale-Hollywood International Airport (FLL), half an hour

GETTING INTO TOWN

Miami International Airport
It's a quick cinch to get from the airport to just about anyplace in Miami, especially Mid-Beach. If you're driving, just follow Rte 112 from the airport, then go east on the Julia Tuttle Causeway, or I-195, and you will get to South Beach. Other options include the free shuttles offered by most hotels, a taxi ($26.50 flat rate to South Beach from the airport; metered, from South Beach, is only about $10). Alternatively, catch the Airport Owl night-only public bus, or the **SuperShuttle** (☎ 800-874-8885; www.supershuttle.com) shared-van service, which will cost about $14 to South Beach. Be sure to reserve a seat the day before.

Fort Lauderdale-Hollywood International Airport
Put the money you save on flights toward getting to Miami once you land; either rent a car at one of the many Fort Lauderdale agencies (see p521), or take the free shuttle from terminals 1 and 3 to the airport's **Tri-Rail** (☎ 800-874-7245; www.tri-rail.com; one-way $2-5.50) station; you can ride this commuter train into Miami. The schedule is infrequent, though, so you may want to opt for the **Bahama Link** (☎ 800-854-2182; 1-2 people $45-60) shared-van service or the cheaper **SuperShuttle** (☎ 954-764-1700; www.supershuttle.com), which will cost about $25 to South Beach.

---

north of MIA. **MIA** (Map pp86-7; ☎ 305-876-7000; www.miami-mia.com) is the third-busiest airport in the country. Just 6 miles west of downtown Miami, the airport is open 24 hours and is laid out in a horseshoe design. There are left-luggage facilities on two concourses at MIA, between B and C, and on G; prices vary according to bag size.

The **Fort Lauderdale-Hollywood International Airport** (off Map pp86-7; ☎ 954-359-1200; www.broward.org/airport; 320 Terminal Dr), about 15 miles north of Miami just off I-95, often serves as a lower-cost alternative to MIA, especially because it's serviced by popular, cut-rate flyers including Southwest Airlines and JetBlue.

BOAT
Though it's doubtful you'll be catching a steamer to make a trans-Atlantic journey, it is quite possible that you'll arrive in Miami via a cruise ship, as the **Port of Miami** (Map pp86-7; ☎ 305-371-7678; www.miamidade.gov/portofmiami), which received nearly four million passengers in 2003, is known as the 'cruise capital of the world.' Arriving in the port will put you on the edge of downtown Miami; taxis and public buses to other local points are available from nearby Biscayne Blvd. See p183 for details on the Key West Express ferry to Key West from Miami.

BUS
Greyhound (☎ 800-231-2222; www.greyhound.com) is the major carrier in and out of town. There are four major terminals: **Airport terminal** (☎ 305-871-1810; 4111 NW 27th St); **Main Downtown terminal** (Map pp92-3; ☎ 305-374-6160; 1012 NW 1st Ave); **Northern Miami terminal** (Map p94; ☎ 305-945-0801; 16560 NE 6th Ave); and the **Southern Miami terminal** (Map pp86-7; ☎ 305-296-9072; Cutler Ridge Mall, 20505 S Dixie Hwy). There are several buses daily to New York City ($115 one-way, 27 to 30 hours) and Washington, DC ($109 one-way, 23 to 25 hours); five daily to New Orleans ($95 one-way, 20 to 22 hours); and 10 daily to Atlanta ($95 one-way, 16 to 18 hours).

TRAIN
The main Miami terminal of **Amtrak** (Map pp86-7; ☎ 305-835-1222, 800-872-7245; www.amtrak.com; 8303 NW 37th Ave) connects the city with the rest of continental USA and Canada. Travel time between New York and Miami is a severe 27 to 30 hours and costs $99 to $246 one-way. The Miami Amtrak station has a left-luggage station, which costs $2 per bag.

GETTING AROUND

BICYCLE
Miami may be flat as a pancake, but it's also plagued by traffic backups and speedy thoroughfares, so judge the bike-ability of your desired route carefully. Biking is a perfectly sensible option in South Beach, though, as well as through most Miami Beach areas and, of course, on Key Biscayne. Use a sturdy D-lock, as mere chains and padlocks do not deter people in these parts.

MIAMI

Bicycles are allowed only on specific Metrorail or Tri-Rail train routes; you can also bike across the causeways.

Rental

There are several places in South Beach and on Key Biscayne to rent bicycles for a fee of about $20 a day. See p121 for info about bike rental.

BUS

The local bus system is called **Metrobus** (☎ 305-770-3131; www.miamidade.gov/transit) and, though it has an extensive route system, know that you may very well spend more time waiting for a bus than you will riding on one. Each bus route has a different schedule and routes generally run from about 5:30am to about 11pm, though some run 24 hours. Rides cost $1.25 and must be paid in exact change (in coins, or a bill and coins) or with a token. Most locals use the monthly Metropass. An easy-to-read route map is available online.

In South Beach, an excellent option is the **South Beach Local Circulator** (☎ 305-770-3131), a looping shuttle bus with disabled-rider access that operates along Washington between South Pointe Dr and 17th St and loops back around on Alton Rd on the west side of the beach. Rides cost only 25¢ and come along every 10 to 15 minutes between 7:45am and 1am Monday to Saturday, and 10am to 1am Sunday and holidays. Look for official bus stops, every couple of blocks, marked by posts with colorful Electrowave signs.

CAR & MOTORCYCLE

If you drive around Miami there are a few things to keep in mind. Miami Beach is linked to the mainland by four causeways built over Biscayne Bay. They are, from south to north: the MacArthur (also the extension of US Hwy 41 and Hwy A1A); Venetian ($1.50 toll); Julia Tuttle and John F Kennedy. The most important north–south highway is I-95, which ends at US Hwy 1 south of downtown Miami. US Hwy 1, which runs from Key West all the way north to Maine, hugs the coastline. It's called Dixie Hwy south of downtown Miami and Biscayne Blvd north of downtown Miami. The Palmetto Expressway (Hwy 826) makes a rough loop around the city and spurs off below SW 40th St to the Don Shula Expressway (Hwy 874, a toll road). Florida's

Turnpike Extension makes the most western outer loop around the city. Hwy A1A becomes Collins Ave in Miami Beach.

Miami has an annoying convention of giving major roads multiple names. So for example, Bird Rd is both SW 40th St and Hwy 976. Hwy 826 is the Palmetto Expressway. US 1 is the Dixie Hwy – except in downtown, when it becomes Biscayne Blvd. Hwy 836 is the Dolphin Expressway, while in Miami Beach 5th St becomes A1A. Calle Ocho is SW 8th St, as well as the Tamiami Trail, *and* US 41 (phew), and Hwy 959 is Red Rd, except when it's SW 57th St. Somehow, this all isn't as confusing as it reads on paper – most road signage indicates every name a route may have – but it can be frustrating to first-time Miami drivers.

Besides the causeways to Miami Beach, the major east–west roads are SW 8th St; Hwy 112 (also called Airport Expressway); and Hwy 836 (also called Dolphin Expressway), which slices through downtown Miami and connects with I-395 and the MacArthur Causeway, and which runs west to the Palmetto Expressway and Florida's Turnpike Extension.

Miami drivers are…how can we put this delicately…aggressive, tailgating jerks who'd cut off their grandmother if they could figure out how to properly change lanes. OK, now that *that's* off our chests, we are, of course, kidding. Only some Miami drivers fit the above description, but there are enough of these maniacs about to make driving here a nightmare. We blame the nouveau riche and their SUVs and Hummers, although there's a fair number of retirees plodding along and, here and there, a travel writer who read the map wrong.

Parking

Though it can get annoying (especially when you have to feed quarters into meters), parking around town is pretty straightforward. Regulations are well-signed and meters are plentiful (except perhaps on holiday-weekend evenings in South Beach). Downtown, near the Bayside Marketplace, parking is cheap but a bit confusing: you must find a place in the head-on parking lots, buy a ticket from a central machine, and display it in your windshield. Generally, finding street parking in South Beach is a nightmare, but in other parts of town it tends to be fairly hassle-free.

On South Beach there's metered street parking along Washington Ave, Collins Ave and Ocean Dr – and on most other streets (except Lincoln Rd and residential areas). Meters are enforced from 9am to midnight. Most allow you to pay for up to three hours, although some have increased that range to six hours. Many of the meter machines include a credit-card option (thank God); lacking that, you may want to purchase a Meter Card, available from the **Miami Beach City Hall** (Map pp88-9; 1st fl, 1700 Convention Center Dr); the **Miami Beach Chamber of Commerce** (Map pp88-9; 1920 Meridian Ave); any municipal parking lot or any Publix grocery store. Denominations come in $10, $20 and $25 (and meters cost $1 per hour).

There are many municipal parking garages, which are usually the easiest and cheapest option; look for giant blue 'P' signs. Find them on Collins Ave at 7th St, Collins Ave at 14th St, Washington Ave at 12th St, Washington Ave at 16th St, and 17th St across from the Jackie Gleason Theater of the Performing Arts (perfect if you're headed to Lincoln Rd). If you park illegally or if the meter runs out, parking fines are about $20, but a tow could cost $75.

TAXI

Outside of MIA and the Port of Miami where taxis buzz around like bees at a hive, you will need to use a phone to hail a cab. A consortium of drivers has banded together and formed a **Dispatch Service** (☎ 305-888-4444) for a ride. If the dispatch service is busy, try **Metro** (☎ 305-888-8888), **Sunshine** (☎ 305-445-3333) or **Yellow** (☎ 305-444-4444).

Taxis in Miami have flat and metered rates. The metered fare is $3.90 for the first mile, and $2.20 each additional mile, but given the cost of fuel in the US, this could well change by the time your read this. You will not have to pay more for luggage or extra people in the cab, though you are expected to tip an additional 10% to 15%. Add about 10% to normal taxi fares (or a dollar, whichever is greater). If you have a bad experience, get the driver's chauffeur license number, name and license-plate number and contact the **Taxi Complaints Line** (☎ 305-375-2460).

The flat rate for a taxi from the airport to Lincoln Rd/Downtown is $32/21.70. If you're stuck, try phoning the companies listed previously or one of the following:
Central Cabs (☎ 305-532-5555)
Flamingo Taxis (☎ 305-599-9999)
Miami-Dade Taxis (☎ 305-551-1111)

TRAIN

Around Miami the **Metromover** (www.miamidade .gov/transit), equal parts bus, monorail and train, is helpful for getting around the downtown Miami area. It offers visitors a great perspective on the city and a cheap – it's free! – orientation tour of the area (see p108). The one- and two-car, rubber-wheeled, computer-controlled (and therefore driverless) vehicles operate on three lines on two elevated-track 'loops,' covering downtown Miami as far south as the Financial District Station at Brickell Ave, and as far north as the School Board Station up on NE 15th St and NE 1st Ave. You can transfer to the Metrorail at Government Center. **Metrorail** (www.miamidade .gov/transit), meanwhile, is a 21-mile-long heavy rail system that has one elevated line running from Hialeah through downtown Miami and south to Kendall/Dadeland. Trains run every five to 15 minutes from 6am to midnight. The fare is $1.50, or 75¢ with a Metromover transfer. The regional **Tri-Rail** (☎ 800-874-7245; www.tri-rail.com) double-decker commuter trains run the 71 miles between Dade, Broward and Palm Beach counties. For longer trips (to Palm Beach, for instance), Tri-Rail is very inefficient. Fares are calculated on a zone basis, and the route spans six zones. The shortest distance traveled costs $4 round-trip. The most you'll ever pay is for the ride between MIA and West Palm Beach ($11 round-trip). No tickets are sold on the train, so allow time to make your purchase before boarding. All trains and stations are accessible to riders with disabilities. For a list of stations, log on to the Tri-Rail website.

The Everglades

South Florida is known for beauty. The model in her tight jeans; that renovated deco hotel; the glitter and sweep of the sun on Biscayne Bay and the city skyline.

But none of the above compares to an alligator's back breaking the blackwater. An anhinga flexing its wings before breaking into a corkscrew dive. The slow, dinosaur flap of a great blue heron gliding over its domain. Or the sun kissing miles of unbroken sawgrass as it sets behind humps of skeletal cypress domes.

No words can really seize the soft curves of this geography, the way the light attaches to water running under the grass, or the mud-and-wood smell of an eroded limestone hole sunk into a pine hammock. In a nation where natural beauty is measured by its capacity for drama, the Everglades subtly, contentedly flows on.

Forget what you've heard about airboats and swamp buggies. The Glades should be approached with the same silence and gentle persuasion it shows its inhabitants. Come by car and canoe, bike, kayak or walk around the park. To understand the way a nutrient-rich patch of water produces a mosquito that feeds a frog, who becomes lunch for a gator, who snaps up a fish that gets speared by an anhinga under these long, low marsh winds, you need to be still. In the quiet spaces, you realize that the Everglades, so often dismissed as a swamp, are more beautiful than all the sin and flash Miami can produce. South Beach changes by the day. The Glades have beautifully endured forever, and if we're very lucky, they'll last that much longer.

HIGHLIGHTS

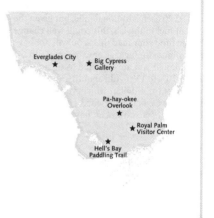

- Watching the sun set over the ingress road to **Pa-hay-okee Overlook** (p177) from the roof of your car

- Canoeing or kayaking into **Hell's Bay Paddling Trail** (p177), a tangled morass of red creeks, slow blackwater and the heavy vegetative curtain of a preserved marsh

- Checking out some of the best (and admittedly pricey) photography of the surrounding swamps, forests, beaches and sea at **Big Cypress Gallery** (p171)

- Consuming a delicious plate of gator nuggets and frog's legs at **Seafood Depot** (p173) in Everglades City

- Spotting alligators at night at the **Royal Palm Visitor Center** (p170)

Environment

It's tempting to think of the Everglades as a swamp, but 'prairie' may be a more apt description. The Glades, at the end of the day, are grasslands that happen to be flooded for most of the year: visit during the dry season (winter) and you'd be forgiven for thinking the Everglades was the Everfields.

So where's the water coming from? Look north, all the way to Lake Okeechobee and the small lakes and rivers that band together around Kissimmee. Florida dips into the Gulf of Mexico at its below-sea-level tip, which happens to be the lowest part of the state geographically *and* topographically. Run-off water from central Florida flows down the peninsula via streams and rivers, over and through the Glades, and into Florida Bay. The glacial pace of the flood means this seemingly stillest of landscapes is actually in constant motion. Small wonder the Calusa Indians called the area Pa-hay-okee (grassy water). Much beloved conservationist Marjory Stoneman Douglas (1890–1998) called it the *River of Grass;* in that book she reveals that Gerard de Brahm named the region the River Glades, which became Ever Glades on later English maps.

So what happens when nutrient-rich water creeps over a limestone shelf? The ecological equivalent of *bow-chika-bow-wow*. Beginning at the cellular level, organic material blooms in surprising ways, clumping and forming into algal beds, nutrient blooms and the ubiquitous periphyton, which are basically clusters of algae, bacteria and detritus (ie stuff). Periphyton ain't pretty: in the water it resembles puke streaks and the dried version looks like hippo turds. But you should kiss it when you see it (well, maybe not), because in the great chain of the Everglades this slop forms the base of a very tall organic totem pole. The smallest tilt in elevation alters the flow of water and hence the content of this nutrient soup, and thus the landscape itself: all those patches of cypress and hardwood hammock (not a bed for backpackers; in this case, hammock is a fancy Floridian way of saying a forest of broadleaf trees, mainly tropical or subtropical) are areas where a few inches of altitude create a world of difference between biosystems.

FIGHT FOR THE GREEN GRASSY WATERS

For years the River of Grass flowed on, concealing wading birds, fish, otters, frogs, skunks, deer, panthers and alligators. And that sound, just out of earshot? Oh, just Florida being settled by thousands of homesteaders…

Enter business, stage right. Cattle ranchers and sugar growers, attracted by mucky waters and Florida's subtropical climate (paradise for sugarcane), successfully pressured the government to make land available to them. In 1905, Florida governor Napoleon Bonaparte Broward personally dug the first shovelful of what was to become one of the most destructive diversions of water in the world. The Caloosahatchee River was diverted and connected to Lake Okeechobee. Hundreds of canals were cut through the Everglades to the coastline to 'reclaim' the land, and the flow of lake water was restricted by a series of dikes. Farmland began to claim areas previously uninhabited by humans.

Unfortunately, the whole 'River of Grass' needs, y'know, the river to survive. And besides being a pretty place to watch the birds, the Everglades acts as a hurricane barrier and kidney. Kidney? Yup: all those wetlands leeched out pollutants from the Florida Aquifer (the state's freshwater supply). But when farmland wasn't diverting the sheet flow, it was adding fertilizer-rich wastewater to it. Result? *Bow-chika-wow-chika-wow-wow-wow.* Bacteria, and eventually plant life, bloomed at a ridiculous rate (they call it fertilizer for a reason), upsetting the fragile balance of resources vital to the Glades' survival.

Enter Marjory Stoneman Douglas, stage left. Ms Douglas gets the credit for almost single-handedly pushing the now age-old Florida issue of Everglades conservation; for more on this titan of the US environmental movement, see the boxed text, p166.

Despite the tireless efforts of Douglas and other environmentalists, today the Florida Aquifer is in serious danger of being contaminated and drying up. On July 2, 2007, the water level in Okeechobee reached an all-time low of 8.82in. Mercury levels are so high fishers are warned to eat only one Everglades-caught bass per week; pregnant mothers and children should avoid bass altogether. The number of wading birds nesting has declined by 90% to 95% since the 1930s. Currently, there are 15 endangered and eight threatened animal species within the park.

It's not that agriculture and the Everglades are incompatible. The EAA (Everglades Agricultural Area) is a major state and national resource, contributing huge amounts of sugar, beef, rice and sod to the economy. But every time smart planning and wise water disposal have been forgone for quick development gains (and it happens a lot), South Florida has suffered.

The real culprit behind the demise of the Everglades has been unchecked development. This delicate ecosystem is the neighbor of one of the fastest-growing urban areas in the US. The current water-drainage system in South Florida was built to handle the needs of two million people; the local population topped six million in 2000. And while Miami can't grow north or south into Fort Lauderdale or Homestead, it can move west. Real-estate developers and local governments are hiking up property values in places like Hialeah, pushing out what developers consider economic deadweight (the working class who have already been priced out of central Miami). McMansions are being vomited all over the eastern fringes of the Glades. There's just too much money to be made from paving and

polluting up to the very edge of the wetlands, and that's why 50% of the wetlands area has vanished.

Humans are not the only enemy of the Everglades. Nature has done its share of damage to one of its best creations. During Hurricane Wilma, for example, six storm-water treatment areas (artificial wetlands that cleanse excess nutrients out of the water cycle) were lashed and heavily damaged by powerful winds. Without these natural filtration systems, the Glades are far more susceptible to nutrient blooms and external pollution.

RESTORATION OF THE EVERGLADES

Efforts to save the Everglades began in the late 1920s, but were sidelined by the Great Depression. In 1926 and 1928, two major hurricanes caused Lake Okeechobee to overflow; the resulting floods killed hundreds. So the Army Corps of Engineers did a *really* good job of damming the lake. A bit too good: the Glades were essentially cut off from their source, the Kissimmee watershed.

GLADES GUARDIAN

In a state known for eccentrics, no one can hold a candle to Marjory Stoneman Douglas. Not just for her quirks, but for her drive: a persistent, unbreakable force that fueled one of the longest conservation battles in US history.

Born in 1890, Douglas moved to Florida after her failed first marriage. She worked for the *Miami Herald* and eventually as a freelance writer, producing short stories that are notable for both the quality of the writing and their progressive themes: *Plumes* (1930) and *Wings* (1931), published in the *Saturday Evening Post,* addressed the issue of Glades bird-poaching when the business was still immensely popular (the feathers were used to decorate ladies' hats).

In the 1940s, Douglas was asked to write about the Miami River for the Rivers of America Series and promptly chucked the idea in favor of capturing the Everglades in her classic, *The Everglades: River of Grass*. Like all of Douglas' work the book is remarkable for both its exhaustive research and lyrical, rich language.

River of Grass immediately sold out of its first printing, and public perception of the Everglades shifted from 'nasty swamp' to 'national treasure.' Douglas went on to be an advocate for environmental causes ('It is a woman's business to be interested in the environment. It's an extended form of housekeeping.'), women's rights and racial equality, fighting, for example, for basic infrastructure in Miami's black Overtown.

Still, today she is remembered as Florida's favorite environmentalist. Always immaculately turned out in gloves, dress, pearls and floppy straw hat, she would bring down engineers, developers, politicians and her most hated opponents, sugar farmers ('They should go at any time, now, as far as I'm concerned. Pick up and go. Any minute. We won't miss them a bit.') by force of her oratory alone. She kept up the fight, speaking and lecturing without fail, until she died – in 1998 at the age of 108.

Today it seems every environmental institution in Florida is named for Douglas, but were she around, we doubt she'd care for those honors. She'd be too busy planting herself in the CERP office, making sure everything was moving along on schedule, and scolding like a heroic schoolmarm if it weren't.

In the meantime, conservationists began donating land for protection, starting with 1 sq mile of land donated by a garden club. The Everglades was declared a national park in 1947, the same year Marjory Stoneman Douglas' *River of Grass* was published.

By draining the wetlands, the Army Corps made huge swathes of inland Florida inhabitable, and at the same time guaranteed the entire region would one day be uninhabitable. The canal system sends, on average, 1.7 billion gallons of water into the ocean every *day*. At the same time, untreated runoff flows unfiltered into natural water supplies. Clean water is disappearing from the water cycle while South Florida's population gets bigger by the day.

Enter the **Comprehensive Everglades Restoration Project** (CERP; www.evergladesplan.org). CERP is designed to address the root of all Everglades issues: water – where to get it, how to divert it and ways to keep it clean. The plan is to unblock the Kissimmee, restoring remaining Everglades lands to predevelopment conditions while maintaining flood protection, providing freshwater for South Florida's populace and protecting earmarked regions against urban sprawl. It sounds great, but lawsuits and mistrust between developers, environmentalists and the state government have delayed the entire process. Today CERP has been implemented, but the cost of the project has bloomed from around $8 billion to $19 billion, and, as regards federal funding, 'all of that money is going to Iraq,' said one ranger (the state of Florida had, as of this writing, promised $4.5 billion). Bringing back the Everglades remains the biggest, most ambitious environmental restoration project in US history, one that combines the needs of farmers, fishers, urban residents, local governments and conservationists. The success or failure of the program will be a bellwether for the future of the US environmental movement.

Climate

During late fall and winter, the Glades can feel pleasantly cool, even dry, with temperatures averaging between 53°F and 77°F. For the rest of the year it's muggier than a coffeeshop cabinet, especially during summer: 90°F, lotsa rain (well, ideally, but it's been dry here as of late; see p165) and 90% humidity. Water – in the form of sheet flow and rainfall – is the bedrock (as it were) of the Everglades eco-

---

AIRBOATS & SWAMP BUGGIES

Airboats are flat-bottomed skiffs that use powerful fans to propel themselves through the water. Their environmental impact has not been determined, but one thing is clear: airboats can't be doing much good, which is why they're not allowed in the park.

Swamp buggies are enormous balloon-tired vehicles that can go through wetlands, creating ruts and damaging wildlife.

Airboat and swamp-buggy rides are offered all along US Hwy 41 (Tamiami Trail). Please think twice before getting on a 'nature' tour. Loud whirring fanboats and marsh jeeps are a crappy way to experience the quiet serenity of the Glades. More importantly, you may be helping to disturb the Everglades' delicate balance.

---

system, but it's in danger of vanishing from the environment; see opposite.

National, State & Regional Parks

The wetlands and prairie known as the Everglades extend outside Everglades National Park (see p170), but you'll have to enter this sprawling body of protected land at one of several entrance points to access the region (see p170 and p173). Big Cypress National Preserve encompasses similar landscapes to the above along with more traditional 'flooded forest' panoramas and runs along the Tamiami Trail (US 41) (p170). On the eastern side of Florida's southern tip is Biscayne National Park, 95% of which is underwater and packed with reefs, laser-bright marine life and great boating and diving activities (p177).

Information

The area codes used in the Everglades are ☎ 239 and ☎ 305; the population is 55,000.
Ernest Coe Visitor Center (☎ 305-242-7700; www .nps.gov/ever; Hwy 9336; ☺ 9am-5pm) Principal visitor center that's packed with excellent information and has rangers who can answer any of your questions.
Everglades Area Chamber of Commerce (☎ 239-695-3941; cnr US Hwy 41 & Hwy 29, Everglades City; ☺ 9am-5pm) General information about the region.
Everglades National Park visitor centers (☎ 305-242-7700; www.nps.gov/ever; 40001 State Rd 9336, Homestead) The main park entry points have visitor centers, where you can get maps, camping permits and ranger information. Pay the entrance fee ($10 for seven

THE EVERGLADES

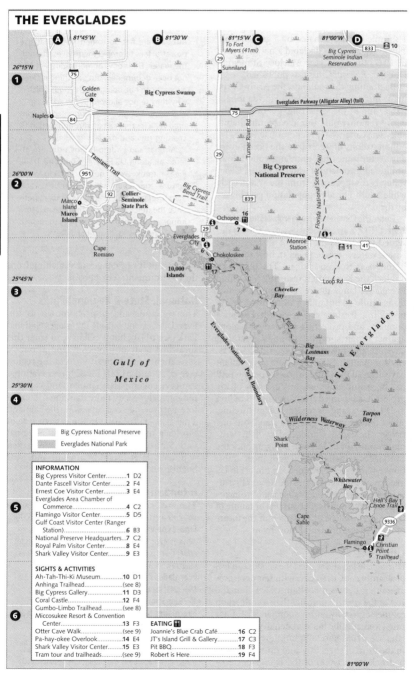

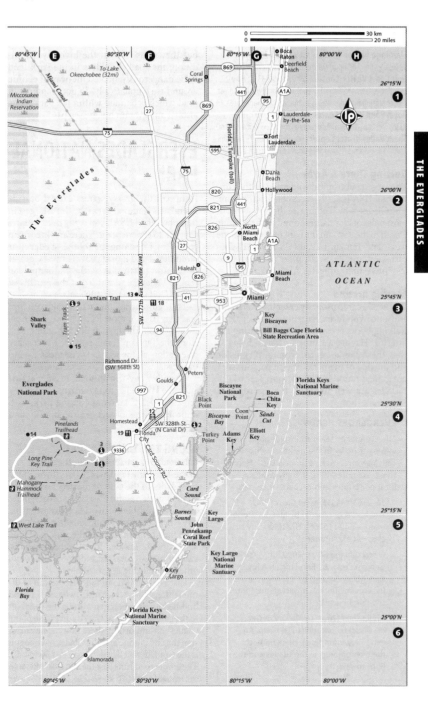

days) only once to access at all points. Fishers need a license; call ahead at ☎ 888-347-4356.

Flamingo Visitor Center (☎ 239-695-2945; Hwy 9336; ☾ 9am-4:30pm) On the park's southern coast.

Gulf Coast Visitor Center (☎ 239-695-3311; Hwy 29, Everglades City; ☾ 9am-4:30pm) This northwestern-most ranger station provides access to the 10,000 Islands area.

Royal Palm Visitor Center (☎ 305-242-7700; Hwy 9336; ☾ 8am-4:15pm) Adjacent to Ernest Coe Visitor Centre.

Shark Valley Visitor Center (☎ 305-221-8776; Tamiami Trail; ☾ 9:15am-5:15pm) Sells tickets for the tram tour.

Getting There & Away

The largest subtropical wilderness in the continental USA is easily accessible from Miami. The Glades, which comprise the 80 southernmost miles of Florida, are bound by the Atlantic Ocean to the east and the Gulf of Mexico to the west. The Tamiami Trail (US Hwy 41) goes east–west, parallel to the more northern (and less interesting) Alligator Alley (I-75).

Getting Around

You need a car to properly enter the Everglades and once you're in, wearing a good pair of walking boots is essential to penetrating the interior. Having a canoe or kayak helps as well; these can be rented from outfits inside and outside of the park, or else you can seek out guided canoe and kayak tours (see p172). Bicycles are well suited to the flat roads of

---

EVERGLADES READS

The Everglades seem to inspire good writing, particularly in the genre of what we'd call 'narrative nature journalism.' Here's three examples, all generally available in local bookstores and NPS visitor centers.

▪ *The Everglades: River of Grass* (1947, Rinehart & Company) by Marjory Stoneman Douglas (p166). The classic, by that classiest of crusaders.

▪ *Crackers in the Glade* (2000, University of Georgia Press) by Rob Storter. A lovely sketchbook/journal by a Glades native, fisherman, hunter, conservationist and self-taught artist.

▪ *Liquid Land* (2003, University of Georgia Press) by naturalist Ted Levin. An extremely informative book on both the environment of the Glades and the fight to save it.

Everglades National Park, particularly in the area between Ernest Coe and Flamingo Point, but they're useless off the highway. In addition, the road shoulders in the park tend to be dangerously small. One-way of getting around we emphatically do not recommend (and which is banned within the park) is by airboat and swamp buggy; see p167.

EVERGLADES NATIONAL PARK

Although the grassy waters extend outside Everglades National Park (the third-largest in the continental USA), you really need to enter the park to experience it. There are three main entrances: one along the southeast edge near Homestead and Florida City (Ernest Coe); at the central-north side on the Tamiami Trail (Shark Valley); and a third at the northwest shore (Gulf Coast), past Everglades City.

These entrances allow for two good road trips (easy day trips, or more leisurely two-day trips) from Miami. The first choice is heading west along the Tamiami Trail, past the Miccosukee reservation, all the way to Everglades City and the crystal waters of the 10,000 Islands.

The other day-trip option is to enter at Coe and take Hwy 9336 to Flamingo through the most 'Glades-y' landscape in the park, with unbroken vistas of wet prairie, big sky and long silences.

ALONG THE TAMIAMI TRAIL

Calle Ocho (p113) happens to be the eastern end of the Tamiami Trail, which cuts through the Everglades to the Gulf of Mexico. So go west, young traveler, along US 41, a few dozen miles and several different worlds away from the city where the heat is on. This trip leads you onto the northern edges of the park, past long landscapes of flooded forest, gambling halls, swamp-buggy tours, roadside food shacks and other Old Florida accoutrement.

Past Hialeah, Miami fades like a trail of diminishing Starbucks until…*whoosh*…it's all huddled forest, open fields and a big canal off to the side (evidence of US 41's diversion of the Glades' all-important sheet flow). The surest sign the city is gone and the Glades have begun is the Confederate flag decals on **Pit BBQ** (p172). The empty road runs past the **Miccosukee Resort & Convention Center** (☎ 305-925-2555, 877-242-6464; www

Big Cypress & Ochopee

Stay west on 41 to see Clyde Butcher's **Big Cypress Gallery** (☎ 941-695-2428; www.clydebutcher.com; Tamiami Trail; ☼ 10am-5pm Wed-Mon), a highlight of any Everglades trip. In the great tradition of Ansel Adams, Clyde's large-format black and white images elevate the swamps to a higher level. He's found a quiet spirituality in the brackish waters and you might, too, with the help of his eyes. Every Labor Day (first weekend in September) Clyde holds a gala event, which includes a fun $20 swamp walk onto his 30-acre property; the party attracts swamp-stompers from across the state.

The 1139-sq-mile **Big Cypress National Preserve** (named for the size of the park, not its trees) is the result of a compromise between environmentalists, cattle ranchers and oil-and-gas explorers. The area is integral to the Everglades' ecosystem: rains that flood the Preserve's prairies and wetlands slowly filter down through the Glades.

About 45% of the cypress swamp (actually a group of mangrove islands, hardwood hammocks, slash pine, prairie and marshes) is protected. Great bald cypress trees are nearly gone, thanks to pre-Preserve lumbering, but dwarf pond cypress trees fill the area with their own understated beauty.

Big Cypress Visitor Center (☎ 941-695-4111; 33100 Tamiami Trail E; ☼ 8:30am-4:30pm), about 20 miles west of Shark Valley, has great exhibits for the kids and an outdoor, water-filled ditch popular with alligators; or there's the **National Preserve Headquarters** (☎ 941-695-2000; ☼ 8am-4:30pm Mon-Fri), just east of Ochopee, which also has information and hosts cultural programs like artist-in-residence exhibits.

There are 31 miles of the **Florida National Scenic Trail** (FNST) within Big Cypress National Preserve. From the southern terminus, which can be accessed via Loop Rd, the trail runs 8.3 miles north to the Tamiami Trail. There are two primitive campsites with water wells along the trail; pick up a map at the visitor center. Most campsites are free, and you needn't register. **Monument Lake** (low season free, Dec 15–Apr $16) has water and toilets.

Drive to the hamlet of **Ochopee** (population about four)…no…wait…turn around, you missed it! Then pull over and break out the cameras: Ochopee's claim to fame is the country's smallest post office. It's housed in a former toolshed and set against big park skies; a friendly postal worker patiently poses for snapshots.

DETOUR: LOOP ROAD

Loop Road, off Tamiami Trail (Hwy 41), offers some unique sites. One: gambling-enriched Miccosukee (this is still their reservation), whose houses all seem to have shiny new pickup trucks parked out front. Two: great pull-offs for viewing flooded forests, where egrets that look like pterodactyls perch in the trees. Three: scary, isolated Florida types who make it very clear trespassers will be very sorry. And four: the short, pleasantly jungly **Tree Snail Hammock Nature Trail**. Be warned the Loop is a rough, unpaved road; you'll need a 4WD vehicle. True to its name, the road loops right back onto the Tamiami.

.miccosukee.com; 500 SW 177th Ave; r Nov-Apr $150), where the long-storied legacy of the nation's indigenous peoples has culminated in…slots. Lots of slots, and comatose gamblers pouring quarters into them. If the Miccosukee and Seminole are cashing in on this stuff, more power to them, but it's still depressing to watch.

The tackiness gets worse as you head west into unending swamp-tour territory. Airboat operators in these parts require three things: intimate knowledge of the backcountry, a moustache and killer tats. Rockin' out to Skynyrd doesn't hurt, either.

Shark Valley & Loop Road

After endless variations of 'Zeke's Swamp Boat Alligatorama!', Shark Valley's friendly, knowledgeable rangers feel like a gift from the heavens.

The most popular and painless way to immerse yourself in the Everglades is via the two-hour **tram tour** (☎ 305-221-8455; adult/child under 12yr/senior $13.25/8/12.25) here that runs along the 15-mile asphalt trail. If you only have time for one Everglades activity, this should be it, as guides are informative and witty, and you'll likely see gators sunning themselves on the road. Halfway along the trail is the 50ft-high **Shark Valley Observation Tower**, an ugly concrete structure that offers dramatically beautiful views of the park.

At the park entrance, the easy **Otter Cave walk** makes a boardwalk-ed loop through a thick copse of tropical hardwoods before emptying you out, disoriented, right back into the Shark Valley parking lot.

EATING

Joannie's Blue Crab Café (☎ 941-695-2682; Tamiami Trail; mains $10-13; ☺ 9am-5pm) This quintessential shack, east of Ochopee, with open rafters, shellacked picnic tables and alligator kitsch serves OK food on paper plates.

Pit BBQ (☎ 305-226-2272; 16400 SW 8th St, btwn Miami & Shark Valley; mains $4-9; ☺ 11am-11:30pm) The barbecue's decent and served on picnic tables with a side of country music and Confederate-flag accoutrement. You gotta love it (otherwise, don't stop).

Everglades City

The end of the track is an old Florida fishing village of raised houses, turquoise water and scattershot emerald-green mangrove islands. Hwy 29 runs south through town into the peaceful residential island of Chokoloskee, past a great psychedelic mural of a gator on a shed.

'What's there to do around here?' we ask our waitress.

'Eat.' Pause. 'Or go on an Everglades tour.'

North American Canoe Tours (NACT; ☎ 941-695-3299/4666; www.evergladesadventures.com; Ivey House Bed & Breakfast, 107 Camellia St; ☺ Nov–mid-Apr) rents out camping equipment and canoes for full/half-days ($35/$25) and touring kayaks ($45 to $65). You get 20% off most of these services and rentals if you're staying at the **Ivey House Bed & Breakfast** (right), which runs the tours. Tours shuttle you to places like Chokoloskee Island, Collier Seminole State Park, Rabbit Key or Tiger Key for afternoon or overnight excursions ($25 to $450).

INFORMATION

Everglades Area Chamber of Commerce (☎ 941-695-3941; cnr US Hwy 41 & Hwy 29; ☺ 9am-5pm)
Gulf Coast Visitor Center (☎ 941-695-3311; Hwy 29; ☺ 8:30am-5pm) Has loads of information on the 10,000 Islands.

SLEEPING

Ivey House Bed & Breakfast (☎ 941-695-3299; www.iveyhouse.com; 107 Camellia St; lodge $60-85, inn $85-140; P ⌨) This family-run place, with its lovely tropical inn (and somewhat less impressive lodge) serves good breakfasts in its small Ghost Orchid Grill. Plus it operates some of the best nature trips around (left).

Rod & Gun Club Lodge (☎ 941-695-2101; 200 Riverside Dr; r low season $85, mid-Jun–Jun $139; P) Built in the 1920s as a hunting lodge by Barron Collier (who needed a place to chill after watching workers dig his Tamiami Trail), this masculine place, fronted by a lovely porch, has a restaurant that serves anything that moves in them thar waters.

Parkway Motel & Marina (☎ 239-695-3261; 1180 Chokoloskee Dr; r $99-120; P) An extremely friendly owner (and an even friendlier dog) runs this veritable testament to the old-school Floridian lodge: cute small rooms and one cozy apartment in a one-story motel building.

EATING

JT's Island Grill & Gallery (☎ 239-695-3633; 238 Mamie St, Chokoloskee; mains $4-12; ☺ 11am-3pm late Oct–May) Just a mile or so past the edge of town, this awesome café-cum-art-gallery sits in a restored 1890 general store. It's outfitted with bright

---

AH-TAH-THI-KI MUSEUM

If you want to learn about Florida's American Indians, come to this **Seminole museum** (☎ 863-902-1113; www.seminoletribe.com/museum; Big Cypress Seminole Indian Reservation, Clewiston; adult/child/senior $6/4/4; ☺ 9am-5pm Tue-Sun), 17 miles north of I-75. All of the excellent educational exhibits on Seminole life, history and the tribe today were founded on gaming proceeds, which provide most of the tribe's multimillion-dollar operating budget.

The museum is good for tribal business, but the folks here really are dedicated to giving visitors a closer understanding of the Seminole and Miccosukee people. It's not the wild Glades, and there are aspects of this 60-acre cypress forest – such as alligator wrestling – that leave something to be desired, but it's a breakthrough for the tribe. Until recently, they had kept to themselves where tourism was concerned. **Seminole Safari excursions** (☎ 941-949-6101, 800-617-7516; www.seminoletours.com) offers very touristy day (adult/child $49/34) and overnight (adult/child $114/90) packages. Overnights include sleeping in a screened-in chickee (wooden platforms built above the waterline), listening to campfire storytelling, taking an airboat or swamp-buggy ride and eating local meals (catfish, fry bread, gator nuggets).

OLD FLORIDA

You hear the term 'Old Florida' thrown around a lot in these parts, but just what the heck is everyone referring to? All the retirees down in Century Village, or some such other ill-named old folks' community?

Not quite. 'Old Florida' is a term of endearment for Florida 'the way it used to be,' or at least the way a lot of people like to remember it: kitschy highway souvenir stalls; roadside motels that look quaint on the outside and, often enough, like a just-cleaned-up murder scene on the inside; clapboard gas stations rotting in the salt wind; farmers' stalls selling citrus off the highway; and fried-food shacks that combine, in the most delicious way possible, the five food groups of the Deep South (grease, cream, salt, sugar, butter).

That's the surface of Old Florida, anyways. What the term really refers to is the Florida that existed before the state – particularly South Florida – became a colony of Northeasterners on the one hand and Latino, European and Caribbean transplants on the other. From that cosmopolitan mélange a distinctive, tropical entrepôt identity has emerged. It defines Miami and that city's surrounds, but it came at the price of an older, swamp-South-and-Seminoles regional character.

Like all memories of a place, Old Florida – where plantation-style indentured labor on huge sugar and citrus farms was common and poverty was endemic – has been a bit romanticized, but it was also a time and place more in rhythm to nature, small-town hospitality and life's simple pleasures.

So where can you find authentic (but also cute and fun) Old Florida? We're tempted to say anywhere north of Orlando, particularly on the Panhandle, but you could also argue those parts of the state are too far removed from distinctively Floridian influences like the Caribbean, the Seminoles and the citrus. The 'Glades and the Keys are the best spots for accessing Old Florida in the southern half of the state. Pretty much all of the **Keys** (p180) could be included on this list, as well as much of the Everglades area cut through by the Tamiami Trail. Quiet fishing towns like **Everglades City** (opposite), fried-food stands like **Joannie's Blue Crab Café** (opposite) and little outposts of eccentricity like **Robert is Here** (p177) speak of a time long, long gone when Floridians were more into their catfish than their Roberto Cavalli.

retro furniture and piles of kitschy books, pottery, clothing and maps (all for sale). But the best part is the food (lunch only) – fresh crab cakes, salads, fish platters and veggie wraps, made with locally grown organic vegetables.

Seafood Depot (☎ 239-695-0075; 102 Collier Ave; mains $12-28; ☑ lunch & dinner) Don't totally sublimate your desire for fried food, because the gator tail and frog's legs here offer an excellent way to honor the inhabitants of the Everglades: douse them in Tabasco and devour them.

HOMESTEAD TO FLAMINGO POINT

Head south of Miami to drive into the heart of the park and the best horizons of the Everglades. Plus, there are plenty of side paths and canoe creeks to detour onto. You'll see some of the most quietly exhilarating scenery the park has to offer on this tour, and have better access to an interior network of trails for those wanting to push off the beaten track into the buggy, muggy solar plexus of the wetlands.

Homestead & Florida City

Homestead is one of the fastest-growing cities in the US, and while it isn't exactly scenic (although the 'main street' area is cute enough), it's a fair improvement from the crime-ridden strip mall it used to be. Speaking of strip, there are plenty of strip clubs on the way down here (including the excellently named 'Booby Trap'). Florida City is pretty much Homestead South. Krome Ave (Hwy 997) and Rte 1 cut through both towns.

Homestead makes a good base for exploring the Everglades, but otherwise there's not a whole lot to see here. You could pass a mildly entertaining afternoon walking around the quaintness of Homestead's 'Main Street,' which essentially comprises a couple of blocks of Krome Ave extending north and south of **Old Town Hall** (41 N Krome Ave). It's a good effort at injecting some character into a town that's otherwise been poorly planned around fast-food stops, car dealerships and gas stations.

CANOE CAMPING ON 10,000 ISLANDS

One of the best ways to experience the serenity of the Everglades – somehow desolate yet lush, tropical and foreboding – is by paddling the network of waterways that skirt the northwest portion of the park. The **10,000 Islands** consist of many (but not really 10,000) tiny islands and a mangrove swamp that hugs the southwestern-most border of Florida. The **Wilderness Waterway**, a 99-mile path between Everglades City and Flamingo, is the longest canoe trail in the area, but there are shorter trails near Flamingo.

Most islands are fringed by narrow beaches with sugar-white sand, but note that the water is brackish, and very shallow most of the time. It's not Tahiti, but it's fascinating. You can camp on your own island for up to a week.

Getting around the 10,000 Islands is pretty straightforward if you religiously adhere to National Oceanic & Atmospheric Administration (NOAA) tide and nautical charts. Going against the tides is the fastest way to make a miserable trip. The Gulf Coast Visitor Center sells nautical charts and gives out free tidal charts. You can also purchase charts prior to your visit – call ☎ 305-247-1216 and ask for chart numbers 11430, 11432 and 11433.

With that said, let us give Homestead one huge prop: it houses one of the great attractions of the US roadside.

'You will be seeing unusual accomplishment,' reads the inscription on the rough-hewn quarried wall. Oh hell yes. There is no greater temple to all that is weird and wacky about South Florida than the **Coral Castle** (☎ 305-248-6345; www.coralcastle.com; 28655 S Dixie Hwy; adult/child 7-18yr/senior/student $9.75/5/6.50/6.50; ☼ 7am-8pm). The legend: a Latvian gets snubbed at the altar. Comes to the US. Moves to Florida (of course – he's crazy). Hand carves, unseen, in the dead of night, a monument to unrequited love: a rock compound that includes a 'throne room,' a sun dial, a stone stockade (his intended's 'timeout area') and a revolving boulder gate that engineers around the world, to this day, cannot explain. Oh, and there are audio stations situated around the place that explain the site in a replicated Latvian accent, so it feels like you're getting a narrated tour by Borat.

Ah, Florida.

INFORMATION
Chamber of Commerce (☎ 305-247-2332; 43 N Krome Ave, Homestead; ☼ 9am-noon & 1-5pm Mon-Fri) Stop here for Everglades information.

SLEEPING
Everglades International Hostel (☎ 305-248-1122, 800-372-3874; www.evergladeshostel.com; 20 SW 2nd Ave, Florida City; dm $22, d $50-65; P ▣) Located in a cluttered, comfy 1930s boarding house, this friendly hostel has six-bed dorms and private doubles (and a 'semiprivate' with a window onto the dorm room) with shared

bathroom. This is a good base to meet other Glades travelers, rent gear or book park tours. A garden and high-speed internet round out the deal. Rent gear or book park tours with the environmentally minded staff, who are pretty knowledgeable about anything related to local ecotourism.

Redland Hotel (☎ 305-246-1904; 5 S Flagler Ave, Homestead; r $75-150; P ▣) This historic inn has clean individualized rooms with a distinct doily vibe. The building served as the town's first hotel, mercantile store, post office, library and boarding house (for real!) and is now favored by folks who want more of a personal touch than you can get from the chains.

Best Western Florida City/Homestead Gateway to the Keys (☎ 305-246-5100, 800-937-8376; www.bestwestern.com; 411 S Krome Ave, Florida City; r $115-158; P ▣ ▣) A standard comfy motel that's well positioned for Glades exploring.

EATING
Casita Tejas (☎ 305-248-8224; 27 N Krome Ave, Homestead; mains $6.50-11; ☼ lunch & dinner) This popular storefront eatery on the main drag has affordable, delicious Mexican lunches and dinners.

Farmers Market Restaurant (☎ 305-242-0008; 300 N Krome Ave, Florida City; lunch mains $8-10, dinner mains $12-14; ☼ 5:30am-9pm) This restaurant's as fresh and hardy as the produce in the next-door farmers market and its rural-worker clientele. It's a bit bare bones on the inside, but the food will fill you up, and nicely too.

Rosita's (☎ 305-246-3114; 199 W Palm Dr, Florida City; mains under $10; ☼ 8:30am-9pm) There's a more working-class Mexican crowd here, testament to the sheer awesomeness of the tacos and burritos. In fact, Rosita's tacos have been voted best in the Greater Miami area by the *Miami New Times* in the past; they were certainly tasty when we visited.

SHOPPING

Artsouth (☎ 305-247-9406; 240 N Krome Ave, Homestead; ◷ 10am-6pm Tue-Fri, from noon Sat & Sun) This colony of artists' studios is a good place to see local talent and pick up Glades-inspired artwork. It's also a nice sight in and of itself; outdoor exhibits make the compound feel like a dreamy sculpture garden (or at least a decent free museum), and provide a good aesthetic anchor to the north side of Homestead's main-street project.

Ernest Coe & Royal Palm to Flamingo

Drive past Florida City, through miles of paper-flat farmland and past an enormous, razor-wired jail (it seems like an escapee heads for the swamp at least once a year) and turn left when you see the signs for **Robert Is Here** (p177) – or stop in so the kids can pet a donkey.

What's up with the funny name? Well, back in the day the namesake of the stall was selling his daddy's cucumbers on this very spot, but no traffic was slowing down for the produce. So a sign was constructed that announced, in big red letters, that Robert was, in fact, here. He has been ever since, too.

Keep down this road as the farmland loses its uniformity and the flat land becomes more tangled, wild and studded with pine and cypress. After a few more miles you'll enter the park at **Ernest Coe Visitor Center** (☎ 305-242-7700; www.nps.gov/ever; Hwy 9336; ◷ 8am-5pm). Have a look at the excellent exhibits, including a diorama of 'typical' Floridians (the fisherman looks like he should join ZZ Top).

Just past here is the **Royal Palm Visitor Center** (☎ 305-242-7700; Hwy 9336; ◷ 8am-4:15pm), which offers the easiest access to the Glades in these parts. Two trails, the **Anhinga** and **Gumbo Limbo** (the latter named for the gumbo-limbo tree, also known as the 'tourist tree' because its bark peels like a sunburned Brit), take all of an hour to walk and put you face to face with a panoply of Everglades wildlife. Gators sun on the shoreline, anhinga spear their prey and wading birds stalk haughtily through the reeds. Come at night for a ranger walk on the boardwalk and shine a flashlight into the

---

HURRICANE ANDREW & HOMESTEAD

The Bush dynasty doesn't have the best record when it comes to natural-disaster relief. Most recently was George W Bush's bungled federal response to Hurricane Katrina, but back in 1992 his dad, George HW Bush, received this appeal on national TV from Dade (now Miami-Dade) County emergency-management director Kate Hale: 'Where in the hell is the cavalry on this one? They keep saying we're going to get supplies. For God's sake, where are they?'

Hale had some reason to be worked up. Federal relief was slow to materialize after Hurricane Andrew (although it quickly arrived after that sound bite) made landfall. Unlike most hurricanes, the damage done by Andrew had more to do with high-powered winds, which reached 175mph, than the resultant storm surge (generally it is the latter that causes major property damage and loss of life). Florida in general, and Homestead in particular, had essentially been flattened. Pictures and reports of the event portray a Homestead and Florida City that looked like they had been carpet bombed.

Looting was rife and the local economy was shattered. Some 100,000 residents of south Dade picked up and left, never to return. Insurance companies either went bankrupt or, in an effort to cover costs, implemented rate adjustments that, to this day, make property-owning in Florida a special kind of nightmare. Homestead Air Force base was so badly damaged it had to close and move to Italy; the grounds were later reopened as an Air Reserve Base. In addition to the human damage, some 70,000 acres of forest and hammock were wiped out, as were 33% of the reefs at Biscayne National Park.

Homestead eventually rebuilt. But the need for quick business, development and investment money, while understandable, led to strip-mall-centric planning. In the meantime, thousands of displaced people left South Dade for the Western fringes of Miami, somewhat sheltered from the raw winds of the coast and right on the edge of – you guessed it – one of the most fragile ecosystems in the US: the Everglades.

PYTHONS, GATORS & CROCS, OH MY!

Gators
Alligators are common in the park, although not so much in the 10,000 Islands, as they tend to avoid saltwater. If you do see an alligator, it probably won't bother you unless you do something overtly threatening or angle your boat between it and its young. If you hear an alligator making a loud hissing sound, get the hell out of Dodge. That's a call to other alligators when a young gator is in danger. Finally, never, ever, ever feed an alligator – it's stupid and illegal.

Crocs
Crocodiles are less common in the park, as they prefer coastal and saltwater habitats. They are more aggressive than alligators, however, so the same rules apply. With perhaps only a few hundred remaining in the USA, they are also an endangered species.

Panthers
The Florida panther is critically endangered, and although it is the state's official animal its survival in the wild is by no means assured. There are an estimated 80 to 100 panthers left in the wild, and although that number has increased from around 20 to 30 since the 1980s, it's not cause for big celebration either. As usual, humans have been the culprit behind this predator's demise. Widespread habitat reduction (ie the arrival of big subdivisions) is the major cause of concern. In the past, poor data on panther populations and the approval of developments that have been harmful to the species' survival have occurred; environmental groups contend the shoddy information was linked to financial conflicts of interest. Breeding units, which consist of one male and two to five females, require about 200 sq miles of ground to cover, and that often puts panthers in the way of one of Florida's most dangerous beasts: drivers. Fourteen panthers were killed by cars in 2007.

If you're lucky enough to see one (and you gotta be pretty damn lucky), Florida panthers are rather magnificent brown hunting cats (they are, in fact, cougars). They are extremely elusive and only inhabit 5% of their historic range. Many are relatively concentrated in **Big Cypress National Preserve** (p171).

Weather
Thunderstorms and lightning are more common in summer than in winter. But in summer the insects are so bad you won't want to be outside anyway. In emergency weather, rangers will search for registered campers, but under ordinary conditions they won't unless they receive information that someone's missing. If camping, have a friend or family member ready to contact rangers if you do not report back by a certain day.

Insects
You can't overestimate the problem of mosquito and no-see-ums (tiny biting flies) in the Everglades; they are, by far, the park's worst feature. While in most national parks there are warning signs showing the forest-fire risk, here the charts show the mosquito level (call ☎ 305-242-7700 for a report). In summer and fall, the sign almost always says 'extremely high.' You'll be set upon the second you open your car door. The only protections are 100% DEET or, even better, a pricey net suit.

Snakes in a Glade!
There are four types of poisonous snake in the Everglades: diamondback rattlesnake *(Crotalus adamanteus)*; pigmy rattlesnake *(Sistrurus miliarius)*; cottonmouth or water moccasin *(Agkistrodon piscivorus conanti)*, which swims along the surface of water; and the coral snake *(Micrurus fulvius)*. Wear long thick socks and lace-up boots – and keep the hell away from them. Oh, and now there are Burmese pythons prowling the water too. Pet owners who couldn't handle the pythons (this happens with depressing frequency) have dumped the animals into the swamp, where they've adapted like…well, a tropical snake to a subtropical forest. There's already evidence of alligators and pythons getting into rumbles, and while this is admittedly cool in a Nature's Ultimate Fighting Championship kinda way, in all seriousness the python is an invasive species that is badly mucking up the natural order of things.

water to see one of the coolest sights of your life: the glittering eyes of dozens of alligators prowling the waterways.

Rte 9336 cuts through the soft heart of the park, past long fields of marsh prairie, white, skeletal forests of bald cypress and dark clumps of mahogany hammock. There are plenty of trails to detour down; all of the following are half a mile (800m) long. **Mahogany Hammock** leads into an 'island' of hardwood forest floating on the waterlogged prairie, while the **Pinelands** takes you through a copse of rare spindly swamp pine and palmetto forest. Further on, **Pa-hay-okee Overlook** is a raised platform that peeks over one of the prettiest bends in the river of grass. The **West Lake Trail** runs through the largest protected mangrove forest in the Northern Hemisphere.

The real joy here is canoeing into the bracken heart of the swamp. There are plenty of push-off points, all with names that sound like they were read off Frodo's map to Mordor, including **Hell's Bay**, the **Nightmare**, **Snake Bight** and **Graveyard Creek**. Our favorite is Hell's Bay. 'Hell to get into and hell to get out of,' was how this sheltered launch was described by old Gladesmen, but damn if it isn't heaven inside: a capillary network of mangrove creeks, sawgrass islands and shifting mudflats, where the brambles form a green tunnel and all you can smell is sea salt and the dark organic breath of the swamp. Three chickee sites (wooden platforms built above the waterline) are spaced along the trail.

Further down you can take a good two-hour, 1.8-mile (2.9km) hike to **Christian Point**. This dramatic walk takes you through several Glades environments: under tropical forest, past columns of white cypress and over a series of mudflats (particularly attractive on grey, cloudy days), and ends with a dramatic view of the windswept shores of Florida Bay.

The area around **Flamingo Visitor Center** was damaged by Hurricane Wilma, and its restaurants and lodges were closed when we visited, but you can still rent boats or go on a backcountry boat tour with the **Pelican** (☎ 239-696-3101; adult/child $18/9; ☺ boats leave 10am, 1pm & 3pm); a 1½-hour sailing schooner tour (adult/child/sunset $22/14/33) is also available. Or rent a canoe (one hour/half-day/full day $8/22/32) or sea kayak (half-/full day $35/45) and explore the channels and islands of Florida Bay on your own. Some trails remain shut down due

to Wilma; you'll be able to access up-to-date information about what's open for exploration at the visitor center. Be careful in coastal areas here during rough weather, as storm surges can turn an attractive spread of beach into a watery stretch of danger fairly quickly.

SLEEPING & EATING

ourpick Robert Is Here (☎ 305-246-1592; 19200 SW 344th St, Homestead; ☺ 8am-7pm Nov-Aug) More than a farmer's stand, Robert's is an institution. This is redneck Florida at its kitschy best, in love with the Glades and the agriculture that surrounds it. There's a petting zoo for the kids, live music at night, plenty of homemade preserves and sauces, and while everyone goes crazy for the milkshakes – as they should – do not leave without having the fresh orange juice. It's the best in the world.

National Park Service (NPS; ☎ 800-365-2267; www .nps.gov/ever/visit/backcoun.htm; sites low season free, Nov-Apr $14) The campgrounds here are run by the NPS. None of these primitive, barely shaded sites have hookups. Depending on the time of year, cold-water showers are either bracing or a welcome relief.

Long Pine Key Campground (☎ 800-365-2267; low season free, Nov-Apr $14) This is the best bet for car campers, just west of Royal Palm Visitor Center.

BISCAYNE NATIONAL PARK

Just to the east of the Everglades is Biscayne National Park, or the 5% of it that isn't underwater. Huh? Well, a portion of the world's third-largest reef sits here off the coast of Florida (along with mangrove forests and the northernmost Florida Keys). Fortunately this unique 300-sq-mile park is easy to explore independently with a canoe or via a glass-bottom boat tour.

A bit unfairly shadowed by the Everglades, Biscayne is unique as national parks go, requiring both a little extra planning (since you can't just walk onto a reef) and a lot more reward for your effort (believe us, the reefs are worth it). The offshore keys, accessible only by boat, offer pristine opportunities for camping. Generally, summer and fall are the best times to visit the park; you'll want to snorkel when the water is calm. This is some of the best reef-viewing and snorkeling you'll find in the US, outside Hawaii (and nearby Key Largo).

Information

Dante Fascell Visitor Center (☎ 305-230-7275; www .nps.gov/bisc; 9700 SW 328th St; 🕒 8:30am-5pm) Located at Convoy Point, this center shows a great introductory film for an overview of the park and has maps, information and excellent ranger activities. The grounds around the center are a popular picnic grounds on weekends and holidays, especially for Latino families from Homestead. Also showcases local artwork. The water around Convoy Point is regarded as prime windsurfing territory.

Sights & Activities

Biscayne National Underwater Park (☎ 305-230-1100) offers canoe rentals, transportation to the keys, snorkeling and scuba-diving trips, and glass-bottom-boat viewing of the exceptional reefs. All tours require a minimum of six people, so call to make reservations. Three-hour glass-bottom-boat trips depart at 10am (adult/child $24.45/16.45) and are very popular; if you're lucky you may spot some dolphins or manatees. Canoe rentals cost $12 per hour and kayaks $16; they're rented from 9am to 3pm. Three-hour snorkeling trips (adult/child $35/30) depart at 1:15pm daily; you'll have about 1½ hours in the water. Scuba trips depart at 8:30am Friday to Sunday ($54).

Long **Elliott Key** has picnicking, camping and hiking among mangrove forests; tiny **Adams Key** has only picnicking; and equally tiny **Boca Chita Key** has an ornamental lighthouse, picnicking and camping. These little islands were settled under the Homestead Act of 1862, which gave land freely to anyone willing to take five years at turning a scratch of the tropics into a working pineapple and Key-lime farm. No-see-ums are invasive, and their bites are devastating. Make sure your tent is devoid of miniscule entry points.

Although it wasn't operating when we visited, by the time you get here the Biscayne **Maritime Heritage Trail** may be up and running. If you've ever wanted to explore a sunken ship, this may well be the best opportunity in the country. Six are located within the park 'grounds'; the 'trail' will involve taking visitors out, by boat, to the site of the wrecks where they can swim and explore among derelict vessels and clouds of fish. Five of the ships are suited for scuba divers, but one, the *Mandalay,* a lovely two-masted schooner that sank in 1966, will be (according to park officials) the rare wreck that can be accessed by snorkelers.

Boating and **fishing** are naturally very popular and often go hand in hand, but to do either you'll need to get cozy with a few reams of paperwork. Boaters will want to get tide charts from the park (or from www.nps.gov /bisc/planyourvisit/tide-predictions.htm). And make sure you comply with local slow-speed zones, designed to protect the endangered manatee (see opposite).

WILDERNESS CAMPING

Three types of backcountry campsites are available: beach sites, on coastal shell beaches and in the 10,000 Islands; ground sites, which are basically mounds of dirt built up above the mangroves; and 'chickees,' wooden platforms built above the water line where you can pitch a free-standing (no spikes) tent. Chickees, which have toilets, are the most civilized – there's a serenity found in sleeping on what feels like a raft levitating above the water. Ground sites tend to be the most bug-infested.

Warning: if you're just paddling around and see an island that looks pleasant for camping but isn't a designated campsite, beware – you may end up submerged when the tides change.

From November to April, camping permits cost $10 plus $2 per person per night; in the low season sites are free, but you must still self-register at Flamingo and Gulf Coast Visitor Centers. Some backcountry tips:

- Store food in a hand-sized, raccoon-proof container (available at gear stores).
- Bury your waste at least 10in below ground, but keep in mind some ground sites have hard turf.
- Use a backcountry stove to cook. Ground fires are only permitted at beach sites, and you can only burn dead or drowned wood.

MANATEES' BIGGEST THREAT

Manatees are shy, utterly peaceful mammals that are, for all intents, the poster children of Floridian environmentalism. They look like obese seals with vaguely elephantine noses. Back in the day sailors apparently mistook them for mermaids and sirens, which suggests these guys had been at sea for entirely too long.

Jokes aside, the manatee is a major environmental concern for Florida. Pollution is a problem to these gentle giants, but their biggest killers are boaters, and of those, the worst offenders are pleasure boaters.

Manatees seek warm shallow water and feed on vegetation. South Florida is surrounded by just such an environment, but it also has one of the highest concentrations of pleasure boats in the world. Despite pleas from environmental groups, wildlife advocates and the local, state and federal governments, which have declared many areas 'Manatee Zones,' some pleasure boaters routinely exceed speed limits and ignore simple practices that would help protect the species.

After grabbing a bite, manatees come up for air and often float just beneath the surface, chewing and hanging around. When speedboats zoom through the area, manatees are hit by the hulls and either knocked away or pushed under the boat, whose propeller then gashes the mammal as the boat passes overhead. Few manatees get through life without propeller scars, which leave slices in their bodies similar to the diagonal slices on a loaf of French bread.

There are several organizations throughout the state that rescue and rehabilitate injured manatees, but they're fighting what would appear to be a losing battle. One of the two largest is the **Miami Seaquarium** (p112). Divers, animal experts and veterinarians of Seaquarium's Marine Mammal Rescue Team patrol South Florida waters, responding to reports of stranded manatees, dolphins and whales. While the Seaquarium's program has been successful, pleasure boaters still threaten the manatees' survival. There are only between 1000 and 3000 manatees left in Florida and in 2007, 73 were killed by watercraft.

The slow zones currently extend 1000ft out from the mainland, from Black Point south to Turkey Point, and include the marinas at Black Point and Homestead Bayfront Parks. Another slow zone extends from Sands Cut to Coon Point; maps of all of the above can be obtained from rangers, and are indeed basically required before you head out on the water.

Although Biscayne is a national park, it is governed by state law when it comes to fishing, so if you want to cast a line you'll need a state license. These come in varieties many and sundry, all of which can be looked up at http://myfwc.com/license/£SWF, which also provides a list of places where licenses can be obtained. As of May 2008, nonresident seven-day salt- and freshwater fishing permits cost $30 each.

Sleeping

Primitive camping costs $10 a night; you pay on a trust system with exact change on the harbor (rangers cruise the Keys to check your receipt). Bring all supplies, including water, and carry everything out. There's no water on Boca Chita, only saltwater toilets, and since it has a deeper port, it tends to attract bigger (and louder) boaters. There are cold-water showers and potable water on Elliott, but perhaps bring your own since the generator might go out.

Getting There & Away

To get here, you'll have to drive about 9 miles east of Homestead (the way is pretty well signposted) on SW 328th St (North Canal Drive) into a long series of green-and-gold flat fields and marsh.

Florida Keys & Key West

Take: one part, rednecks. Add: snowbirds. Sprinkle with a large number of Cuban immigrants and Eastern European guest workers. Include: gay community (may consist of 'sedate partners who just bought art gallery' and 'screaming drag queens of the night'). Garnish with Bahamians. Set attitudes at 'tolerant' and 'eccentric.'

Turn up the eccentric. Finish with rum. *Lots* of rum.

Bake in searing Florida sun and serve on 45 islands scattershot over a 113-mile-long chain, connected by one long-ass road. Throw in the government of the only republic to successfully secede from the US. Yes, those Conch Republic flags say 'We Seceded Where Others Failed,' and that's the Keys in a conch shell: equal parts tacky, quirky and, damn it, alluring.

Hang out here for awhile and you start turning into a 'Freshwater Conch' – a permanent transplant – real quick. The Keys are *out there*; it's three or four hours at a good clip from Key West, at the end of the chain, back to Miami. Come out this far, and you either contract cabin fever or fall in love.

But don't just rush for Key West, because there's lots of charm and authenticity on those other islands. After all, it's these little, lovely, crazy communities that have survived hurricanes, gentrification and gouging real-estate prices to live the real American Dream – do whatever the hell you want and get away with it, an attitude that truly defines the Keys.

FLORIDA KEYS & KEY WEST

HIGHLIGHTS

- Advancing early liver failure as you down drinks at either Key West's **Green Parrot** (p211), or **The Hurricane** (p196) in Marathon
- Spotting cute Key deer while you wander the islands at the **National Key Deer Refuge** (p197)
- Watching the sun set over the ocean as you sit and take in raucous **Mallory Square** (p201) in Key West
- Feeding the fish and then strolling around the flea market and stalls for the ultimate tacky souvenir at **Robbie's Marina** (p189) in Islamorada
- Munching on pizza and striking up a conversation at Big Pine Key's **No Name Pub** (p198)

Islamorada ★
Big Pine Key ★★ ★ Marathon
★ National Key Deer Refuge
Key West

History

Calusa and Tequesta Indians plied these waters for thousands of years, but that era came to a depressingly predictable end with the arrival of the Spanish, the area's first European settlers. Upon finding American Indian burial sites, Spanish explorers named Key West Cayo Hueso (pronounced kah-ya way-so, meaning Bone Island), a title since anglicized into its current incarnation. From 1760–63, as the Spaniards transferred control of Florida to Great Britain, all of the islands' indigenous peoples were transferred to Cuba, where they either died in exile or integrated into the local ethnic mélange.

Key West itself was purchased by John Simonton in 1821, and developed as a naval base in 1822. For a long while, the area's cycle of boom and bust was tied to the military, salt manufacturing, lime production (from coral), shipwrecks (see p205) and sponges, which were harvested, dried and turned into their namesake bath product.

In the late 1800s, the area became the focus of mass immigration as Cubans fled Spanish rule and looked to form a revolutionary army. Along with them came cigar manufacturers, who turned Key West into the USA's cigar-manufacturing center. That would end when workers' demands convinced several large manufacturers, notably Vicente Martínez Ybor and Ignacio Haya, to relocate to Tampa in southwest Florida. Immigrants from the Caribbean settled in the Keys in this period, and as a result, today's local African Americans tend to be descended from Bahamian immigrants rather than Southern slaves – something of a rarity in the US.

During the Spanish-American War (1898), Key West was an important staging point for US troops, and the military presence lasted through to WWI. In the late 1910s, with Prohibition on the horizon, Key West became a bootlegging center, as people stocked up on booze (note: they've never really stopped). The Keys began to boom around 1938 when Henry Flagler constructed his Overseas Hwy, replacing the by-then defunct Overseas Railroad.

Key West has always been a place where people buck trends. A large society of artists and craftspeople congregated here at the end of the Great Depression because of cheap real estate, and that community continues to grow (despite today's pricey real estate). While gay men have long been welcomed, the gay community really picked up in earnest in the 1970s; today it's one of the most renowned and best organized in the country.

Climate

Though it's warm and tropical in the Keys, it never gets higher than about 97°F; the peak in summer is usually about 89°F, with the temperature staying a few degrees cooler than Miami because the Keys are surrounded by ocean (and refreshing ocean breezes). The coldest it gets is usually in the 50s (when some people dress like a blizzard has descended), and water temperature stays in the 80s most of the time. The thunderstorm season begins by late May, and then everyone buckles down for the feared hurricanes – if they arrive, expect them in late summer and early fall.

National, State & Regional Parks

The Keys have several top-notch parks and a fairly unique ecosystem besides, so if you're a nature lover you're in luck. Check out John Pennekamp Coral Reef State Park (p183) in Key Largo to see Florida's reef in living color; or head to Lignumvitae Key State Botanical Site (p190) by boat to bask on a 280-acre island of virgin tropical forest. The former quarry of Windley Key Fossil Reef Geologic State Park (p190) shows the history of coral and limestone formation in the Keys; Looe Key National Marine Sanctuary (p197) is a grove reef accessible by charter boat; and Long Key State Recreation Area (p192) stretches across 965 acres of Long Key. Bahia Honda State Park (p196) is a beloved stretch of white-sand beach.

Orientation

Florida's necklace of tiny islands is strung from northeast to southwest and connected

---

WHERE DID THE KEYS COME FROM?

So how'd these islands get here? Basically, they were created as coral between ice ages about 125,000 years ago. As the water level dropped during the Wisconsin Ice Age 25,000 years later, what had been living reefs emerged as low islands. Mangroves began to appear along the fringes of the islands, trapping plant matter that slowly decayed into soil. As the water level continued falling to current levels, birds and tides carried plant seeds north from the Caribbean.

UNAFFORDABLE PARADISE LOST

On October 24, 2005, Hurricane Wilma made landfall in Florida. The Keys, dangling in the ocean, bore the full brunt of the storm and – much worse – its associated storm surge. Beginning on the night of October 23 and carrying through to the next morning, two surges flooded the islands. Water levels rose as high as 8ft in Key West, where 60% of houses were flooded. Homes were ruined, boats were thrown into backyards, and cars were abandoned as useless scrap and local vegetation withered and drowned in the salt water.

In Monroe County (which encompasses the Keys), the total amount of insurance paid out from the disaster was $20 million. Beyond that, Wilma washed away the last of the affordable housing in the Keys and left a home-owner crisis that is yet to be resolved.

In truth, the crisis was preexisting. Cost of living has always been high – food and gas travels a long way to get here and is priced accordingly. But real estate is the real expense. Due to the geographic size and sensitive ecosystem, land has always been prized in the Keys. There are plenty of large resort complexes willing to pay big money for space to build on, and due to strict laws meant to protect the Keys' unique habitats, that space doesn't amount to much. A painfully complex set of rules governs what can be built where in the islands, and there are entire local law firms dedicated to navigating the byzantine Monroe County land code.

Of course, the working backbone of the islands – teachers, waiters, police and nurses – cannot afford lawyers or expensive local real estate. In Marathon, a cheap room with kitchenette, bed, and not much else – smaller than most Manhattan apartments – costs upwards of $700 a month. Tiny houses and trailer parks constitute the homes of most Keys workers.

Those residences were all but wiped out by Wilma, and many landlords decided to cash their chips in and sell to the highest bidder after the storm. For instance, post-Wilma, the Jolly Rogers trailer park, which housed hundreds of the Keys workforce, was slated for demolition. Residents were warned away with six-month eviction notices, while landlords argued – with some justification – there was no money to be made maintaining cheap housing in a storm-prone island chain.

As a result, local hotels, restaurants and bars now operate dormitory-style housing for employees. Many resort staff commute four hours to work from Homestead. In 2008, the state of Florida decided not to let Monroe County use money from resort taxes – earmarked for tourism development – to build affordable housing units. Until the crisis is resolved (and no one knows how that will happen), the Keys, once home to vagabonds, immigrants and eccentrics, will continue to morph into a series of ultrachic four-star resorts, staffed by folks who can't afford to live where they work.

---

along US Hwy 1. Also called the Overseas Hwy, US Hwy 1 is a combination of highways and causeways built on the foundations of the FEC (Florida East Coast) Railway, which was destroyed by hurricane in 1935. US Hwy 1 is the main road through to the Keys. The southernmost point in continental US (a geographic fact you will never forget after perusing Keys tourism material), Key West, is a three- to four-hour drive from Miami, depending on the traffic and season. For the record, if you come down to Key West, you're closer to Cuba than you are to the Magic City (Miami).

Keys addresses are pegged to mile markers (MM), which are small green roadside signs. On the Overseas Hwy: mile 0 (MM 0) is in Key West at the corner of Fleming St and

Whitehead St, and the final – or first, depending on where you're coming from – marker (MM 126), is 1 mile south of Florida City.

Information

The Monroe County Tourist Development Council's **Florida Keys & Key West Visitor's Bureau** (☎ 800-352-5397; www.fla-keys.com) runs an excellent website, which is packed with information on everything the Keys has to offer.

Check www.keysnews.com for good daily online news and information about the islands.

Getting There & Away

Getting here can be half the fun – or, if you're unlucky, a whopping dose of frustration. Imagine a tropical-island hop, from one bar-studded mangrove islet to the next, via one of the most unique roads in the world: the Overseas Hwy (US Hwy 1). On a good day, driving down the Overseas with the windows down, the wind in your face and the twin sisters of Florida Bay and the Atlantic stretching on either side, is the US road trip in tropical perfection. On a bad day, you end up sitting in gridlock behind some fat guy who is riding a midlife-crisis Harley.

Greyhound (☎ 800-229-9424) buses serve all Key destinations along US Hwy 1 and depart from downtown Miami and Key West; you can pick up a bus along the way by standing on the Overseas Hwy and flagging one down, Mexico-style. If you fly into Fort Lauderdale or Miami, the **Keys Shuttle** (☎ 888-765-9997) provides door-to-door service to most of the Keys ($70/80/90 to the Upper and Middle Keys/Lower Keys/Key West). Reserve at least a day in advance.

Alternatively, skip the road altogether and take a four-hour sea trip via the **Key West Express** (☎ 866-593-3779; www.seakeywestexpress.com; adult/child round-trip $106/70, one-way $53), which departs from the Miami Seaquarium (p112) daily at 9:30am (8:30am Sundays).

You can fly into one of two airports. Key West International Airport (EYW) has frequent flights from major cities – some direct, but most going through Miami – and **Marathon Airport** (☎ 305-743-2155) has less frequent, more expensive flights.

UPPER KEYS

No, really, you're in the islands!

It is a bit hard to tell when you first arrive, as the huge, rooty blanket of mangrove forest that forms the South Florida coastline spreads like a woody morass into Key Largo. In fact, the mangroves become Key Largo, which is more famous for its underwater than above-ground views. Keep heading south and the scenery becomes more archipelagically pleasant as the mangroves give way to wider stretches of road and ocean, until – bam – you're in Islamorada and the water is everywhere. If you want to avoid traffic on US 1, you can try the less trafficked FL 997 and Card Sound Rd to FL 905 (toll $1), which passes Alabama Jack's (p189).

KEY LARGO & TAVERNIER

We ain't gonna lie: Key Largo (both the name of the town and the island it's on) is slightly

underwhelming at a glance. 'Under' is the key word, as its main sights are under the water, rather than above, with a long line of low-lying hammock and strip development, which truly captivates. But that's Key Largo from the highway. Head down a side road and duck into this warm little bar, or that converted Keys plantation house, and the island idiosyncrasies become more pronounced.

The 33-mile long Largo, which starts at MM 106, is the longest island in the Keys, and those 33 miles have attracted a lot of marine life, all accessible from the biggest concentration of dive sites in the islands. The town of Tavernier (MM 93) is just south of the town of Key Largo.

Information
Key Largo Chamber of Commerce (☎ 305-451-1414, 800-822-1088; www.keylargo.org; MM 106 bayside; ☺ 9am-6pm) Helpful office; has area-wide information.
Key Largo post office (MM 100 bayside)
Mariner Hospital (☎ 305-434-3000; Tavernier, MM 91.5 bayside)
Tavernier post office (Tavernier, MM 91.5 bayside)

Sights & Activities
If you make one stop in Key Largo, make sure it's **John Pennekamp Coral Reef State Park** (☎ 305-451-1202; www.pennekamppark.com; MM 102.5 oceanside; 1/2 person $3.50/6, each additional person 50¢; ☺ 8am-sunset), the first underwater park in the USA. There's 170 acres of parkland and over 75 sq miles of ocean in this sanctuary, plus some pleasant beaches and decent nature trails. The **Mangrove Trail**, a good boardwalk introduction to this oft-maligned, ecologically awesome arboreal species (the trees, often submerged in water, breathe via long roots that act as snorkels – neat). Stick around for nightly campfire programs and ranger discussions.

The visitor center is well run and informative and has a perfectly serviceable **aquarium** (☺ to 5pm) that gives a glimpse of what's under them thar waters. But to really go beneath the surface of this park (pun intended), you should take a glass-bottom boat tour (see p186) or **snorkel-sailing tour** (adult/child $34.95/29.95), which provides over an hour of almost uniformly excellent snorkeling time. The four-hour tours are at 9am and 1:30pm; mask, fins and snorkel rental are $2 each extra. If you want to go even deeper, try straight-up **snorkeling trips** (☎ 305-451-6300; adult/child $28.95/23.95) or **diving excursions** (☎ 305-451-6300; $50). DIYers

FLORIDA KEYS

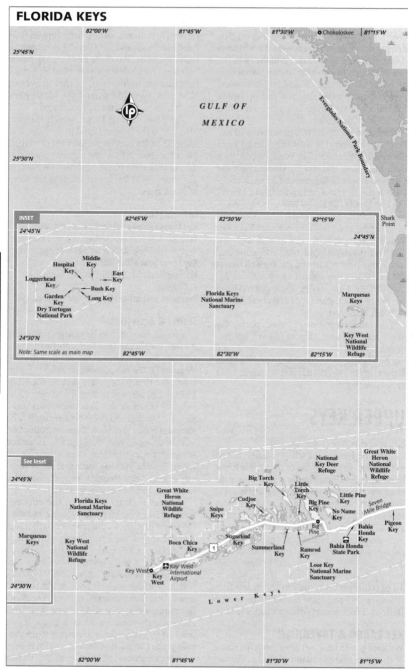

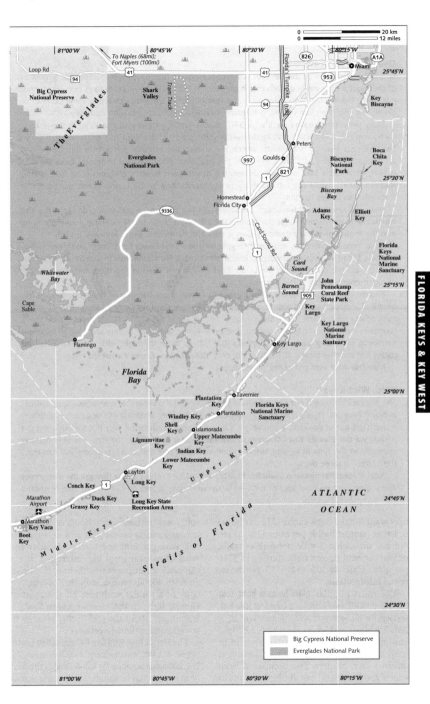

THE FLORIDA KEYS...

Overseas Pub Crawl

Lots of people come to the Keys for different reasons: to fish, to relax, to escape. But almost all of them get a little trashed. With this in mind, what follows is the ultimate Keys pub crawl – not just down Duval St, but an island to island stumble down the entire Overseas Hwy. Don't drive drunk; the trip is broken up island to island, and you can catch a cab on each Key.

Start slow at **Alabama Jack's** (p189), quintessential gateway to the Keys: a shack on a mangrove bay filled with guys in sleeveless shirts ready to get their fish on. Now head down the Overseas Hwy to Islamorada. Watch the sunset and achieve Zen with a Red Stripe and an unbeatable view of Florida Bay from the gorgeous private island of trendy **Casa Morada** (p191), then call a taxi, or find a designated driver. Even Miami's glitterati hang out at **Hog Heaven** (p191), while the full-moon party at **Morada Bay** (p191) is one of the most popular throw-downs in the islands.

Wake up, sleepyhead! Next stop: Marathon. We like the service and strong drinks at the **The Hurricane** (p196), which is, for our money, the friendliest bar in the Keys. Finish your night (long into the morning) at the satanically dive-y, dark and dangerous **Brass Monkey** (p196).

Have some herbal tea as you continue your way down the Lower Keys. There's only one watering hole today, but it's an atmospheric one: the famous **No Name Pub** (p198) on Big Pine Key. We'll bypass the other bars of the Lower Keys so you can sleep in Key West and, like a knight of old, prepare for the battle ahead.

You may be tempted to try a Duval crawl like every other frat boy in Key West, but we recommend a more nuanced approach. Start with a shot at **Captain Tony's Saloon** (p211), where Hemingway *really* drank (sorry, Sloppy Joe's), and a beer at the rockin' **Hog's Breath** (p211) for a touch of Duval vomit-on-your-neighbor ambience. Now gather your dignity and have an excellent martini at the classy jazz bar in **Virgilio's** (p212) then finish the night with a digestif – no, not really, just another beer – at the one, the only, the excellent **Green Parrot** (p211).

Now fish your liver out of the toilet, dude.

Wild, Wild Keys

The Keys are nothing if not beautiful, and you won't find a comparable mangrove island habitat in North America. Here's how you can get closer to the unique nature of the Conch Republic.

First: get out of your car. If you've got a bike and some endurance, why not try exploring the islands via the **Florida Keys Overseas Heritage Trail** (p189). While the trail was only halfway complete at the time of writing, using a combination of trail and shoulder riding you can cross the islands in three days.

Stop at **John Pennekamp Coral Reef State Park** (p183) to enjoy a walk through the mangroves and a glass-bottom boat tour of local reefs. Donate some money to our injured, fine-feathered

---

may want to take out a canoe ($12 per hour) or kayak (single/double per hour $12/$17) to journey through a 3-mile network of trails, or you can rent powerboats, starting at $210 per day. Call ☎ 305-451-6325 for boat-rental information.

The most popular **glass-bottom boat tour** (☎ 305-451-6300; John Pennekamp Coral Reef State Park, Key Largo, MM 102.5 oceanside; adult/child under 12yr $22/$15) lasts 2½ hours and leaves at 9:15am, 12:15pm and 3pm. You won't be ferried around in some rinky-dink fishing boat; you're brought out in a safe, modern 38ft catamaran from which you'll ooh and aah at filigreed flaps of

soft coral, technicolor schools of fish, dangerous-looking barracudas and massive, yet ballerina-graceful sea turtles. Besides the swirl of natural coral life, interested divers can catch a glimpse of the *Christ of the Abyss*, an 8.5ft, 4000lb bronze sculpture of Jesus – a copy of a similar sculpture off the coast of Genoa, Italy, in the Mediterranean Sea. To learn more about the reef in this area, go to www.southeastfloridareefs.net.

The **Florida Keys Wild Bird Rehabilitation Center** (☎ 305-852-4486; www.fkwbc.org; 93600 Overseas Hwy, MM 93.6; $5 donation suggested; ☽ 8am-6:30pm) is the first of many animal hospitals you'll come across friends at the **Florida Keys Wild Bird Rehabilitation Center** (opposite), one of many Keys animal hospitals and research centers. From **Robbie's Marina** (p189) in Islamorada, kayak over the waters to **Indian Key State Historic Site** (p190) or bike around the Matecumbe Keys, which offer some of the sweeping-est views of Florida Bay and the Gulf of Mexico. Nearby **Anne's Beach** (p190) is a great spot for stomping on shallow mud flats, which feel oh-so-squishy between your toes.

Crane Point Museum (p194) in Marathon is a lovely little preserve of Keys habitats and fun for the kids to boot. Just down the road, the **Turtle Hospital** (p194) is a convalescent home for injured sea turtles, a good cause, and a fun place to while away an afternoon.

Keep driving south and...ooh! Tiny deer! **Key deer** (p197) run all over Big Pine Key and No Name Key, so have a look at these cutesy dollops and visit their buddies, a pair of American alligators who like to bask at a pond known as **Blue Hole** (p197).

Key West itself isn't the best nature destination, but do spend an hour at the **Florida Keys Eco-Discovery Center** (p201), which is lovingly put together, enjoyable, educational and, unlike everything else in Key West, doesn't charge admission and has free parking.

Weird & Wonderful

What? The USA's only tropical hardwood habitat, a string of islands inhabited by alcoholic fishermen connected by some of the longest bridges and causeways in the world, isn't weird enough on its own? Fine.

Head down (and we mean down) to **Jules' Undersea Lodge** (p188), the only underwater hotel in the world, and dream happy dreams of mermaids and decompression. If you can't afford Jules', the next best thing to sleeping underwater is on it at the awesome **Key Largo House Boatel** (p188). Afterwards, have a coffee at the kitschy yet classy **Key Largo Conch House** (p189).

Feed some tarpon at **Robbie's Marina** (p189), or just enjoy watching a bunch of tourists get scared to death by the enormous fish. Did you watch *Flipper* as a kid? Want to swim with his descendants? Go to the **Dolphin Research Center** (p192), one of four (count 'em) dolphin swim sites in the islands. The **Old Seven Mile Bridge** (p195) is the 'world's largest fishing bridge' and beneath it is **Pigeon Key** (p194), a lovely old plantation island.

We know we've mentioned them already, but really: dog-sized widdle deer! You only get them at the **National Key Deer Refuge** (p197). Of course, if deer are too adorable for you, **Perky's Bat Tower** (p198) is a great place to see bats...no, wait, it isn't, because all the bats flew away as soon as they were moved in.

You could almost include the entire island of Key West in this itinerary, but there are some strange standouts from the end of the road: six-toed cats at the **Hemingway House** (p201); the tropical-Goth noir of the **Key West Cemetery** (p205); karaoke and drag queens at **801 Bourbon Bar** (p212); and the surreally hilarious 'guided tour' of **Casa Antigua** (p206) – all reminders that you have wandered into a tropical sanitarium.

built by critter-loving Samaritans throughout the Keys. This one is an alfresco bird hospital that cares for birds that have swallowed fish hooks, had wings clipped in accidents, been shot by BB pellets etc. A lovely little trail leads back to a nice vista of Florida Bay and a wading bird pond. The center is great – but it does smell like bird doo.

There are dive shops galore in Key Largo, most of which are located within Pennekamp Park. Two other recommended options are **Silent World Dive Center** (☎ 305-451-3252, 800-966-3483; www.silentworldkeylargo.com; MM 103.2 bayside) and **Amoray Dive Resort** (☎ 305-451-3595, 800-426-6729; www.amoray.com; MM 104.2 bayside), which also offers villalike accommodations.

OK movie fans, particularly Bogie buffs: here's the skinny. The **Caribbean Club Bar** (☎ 305-451-9970; MM 104 bayside) is, in fact, the only place in Key Largo where *Key Largo*, starring Humphrey Bogart and Lauren Bacall, was filmed (the rest of the island was a Hollywood soundstage). If that's not enough, the original *African Queen*, of the same-titled movie, is docked at the Holiday Inn at MM 100. Just walk around the back of the Holiday Inn or call ☎ 305-451-4655 for more info. And finally, Rick's Bar from *Casablanca* is up and running in the middle of Pennekamp State Park…just kidding.

If you approach Key Largo from FL 905, you'll be driving through **Crocodile Lake National Wildlife Refuge**, one of the last wild sanctuaries for the threatened American crocodile, indigo snake and Key Largo woodrat – the latter is an enterprising fellow who likes to build 4ft by 6ft homes out of forest debris, proving even wildlife in Florida want enormous homes. Unfortunately, this really is a refuge; the wildlife areas are closed to the public, and your chances of seeing the species we've mentioned from the road are negligible.

The Greyhound bus stops at MM 99.6 oceanside.

Sleeping

John Pennekamp Coral Reef State Park (☎ 305-451-1202, 800-326-3521; www.pennekamppark.com; MM 102.5 oceanside; per night $31.49, pavilion $32.25-53.75; **P**) You don't even have to leave Pennekamp at closing time if you opt for tent or recreational-vehicle (RV) camping, but be sure to make a reservation, as the sites fill up fast.

Key Largo House Boatel (☎ 305-766-0871; www.keylargohouseboatel.com; Shoreland Dr, MM 103.5 oceanside; small houseboat $75, large houseboat $150) If you can't afford to sleep underwater at Jules' Undersea Lodge (right), why not sleep on it here? There are three houseboats available, and more importantly, they're a steal. The largest one is incredibly spacious and fairly well decorated for the Keys, with minimal sea-themed crap and plenty of *National Geographic* issues to pass the time. The boats are right on the docks (and across from a bar), so no possibility of being isolated from land (or booze). Call ahead for directions, as the 'boatel' is a little off the beaten track.

Stone Ledge Paradise Inn (☎ 305-852-8114; http://fabulousvacations.com/stoneledgeparadiseinn; 95320 Overseas Hwy; r low season $78-98, high season $88-118, villas low season $185-250, high season $250-300; **P**) This is a pink palace (well, squat bunch of motel blocks) of old-school US seaside kitsch. The wooden fish hung on every door are only the tip of the nautical tack iceberg, but the real joy is the sweeping view over Florida Bay at the back of the property.

Largo Lodge (☎ 305-451-0424, 800-468-4378; www.largolodge.com; MM 102 bayside; low season apt $95-115, cottage $125-155, high season apt/cottage $150/195; **P**) The manager of the property couldn't be friendlier, and his six hidden cottages, tucked into a

glimmery secret tropical garden with a private swimming cove, couldn't be cozier. And, as a side note, there couldn't be more squirrels having the run of the joint.

Jules' Undersea Lodge (☎ 305-451-2353; www.jul.com; 51 Shoreland Dr, MM 103.2 oceanside; per person $375-647) Sure, you could wait for the much touted, super-luxurious Hydropolis hotel to open in Dubai. But until then, the only place you and your significant other can join the 'five-fathom club' (we're not elaborating) is tiny Jules, the world's only underwater hotel. In addition to two private guest rooms (there's just the *teensiest* nautical theme – everywhere), there are common rooms, a fully stocked kitchen/dining room, and wet room with hot showers and gear storage. Telephones and an intercom connect guests with the surface. Guests must be at least 10 years old and you gotta dive to get here – plus, there's no smoking or alcohol. If you just want to visit, sign up for a three-hour mini-adventure ($125), which also gives access to breathing hookahs (120ft-long air hoses for tankless diving). Open-water diving certification courses run through the lodge take three days and start at $495.

Kona Kai Resort & Gallery (☎ 305-852-7200, 800-365-7829; www.konakairesort.com; MM 97.8 bayside; r $211-327, ste $296-940; **P** 🖳 🖳) This intimate hideaway features 11 airy rooms and suites (with full kitchens), all warmly contemporary. It also happens to house one of the better galleries in this corner of the Keys, so pay attention artheads. There's plenty to do – from tennis, kayaking and paddleboating to lounging in one of the hammocks that dot the palm-strewn, white-sand beach.

Eating

Num Thai Restaurant & Sushi Bar (☎ 305-451-5955; 103200 Overseas Hwy; lunch mains $6-10, dinner mains $7-18; 🕑 lunch Mon-Fri, dinner daily) The whole Japanese-Thai fusion thing comes straight outta Miami and takes a trip south to this strip-mall locale. This place is bright, bouncy, and the right antidote for wasabi addicts.

DJ's Diner (☎ 305-451-2999; 99411 Overseas Hwy; mains $6-14; 🕑 breakfast, lunch & dinner) You're greeted by a mural of Humphrey Bogart, James Dean *and* Marilyn Monroe – that's a lot of Americana. It's all served with a heapin' helpin' of diner faves, vinyl-boothed ambience, and South Florida staples like *churrasco* (skirt steak) and conch.

our pick **Key Largo Conch House** (☎ 305-453-4844; www.keylargoconchhouse.com; MM 100.2 oceanside; lunch $8-14, dinner $13-25; ☺ breakfast, lunch & dinner Mon-Sat, breakfast & lunch Sun) A wi-fi hotspot, coffeehouse and innovative kitchen that likes to sex up local classics (conch in a lime and white-wine sauce, or in a vinegar sauce with capers), set in a restored old-school Keys mansion wrapped in a *Gone With the* Wind veranda? Yes please, and more of it. It's hard not to love the way the period architecture blends in seamlessly with the local tropical fauna, in contrast to the strip-mall-chic development so prevalent around the rest of the island.

Mrs Mac's Kitchen (☎ 305-451-3722; MM 99.4 bayside; breakfast & lunch $5-7, dinner $9-18; ☺ breakfast, lunch & dinner Mon-Sat) When Applebee's stuffs its wall full of license plates, it's tacky. When Mrs Mac's does it, it's homey. Plus, the food packs in the locals, tourists, their dogs and pretty much everyone else on the island.

Tugboat Restaurant (☎ 305-453-9010; 2 Seagate Blvd; mains $9-24; ☺ lunch & dinner daily, breakfast Sat & Sun) Head east from the MM 100 traffic light and you'll be grateful once you pull up to this local favorite, where the seafood is simply sumptuous. If the weather's good – and it invariably is – eat out back in the appropriately dubbed Garden of Eatin'.

Drinking & Entertainment

Alabama Jack's (☎ 305-248-8741; www.alabamajacks .com; ☺ 11am-7pm) Welcome to your first taste of the Keys: zonked out weirdos on motorcycles getting drunk on a mangrove bay. Wildlife lovers: you may spot the rare mulleted version of *Jacksonvillia Redneckus*! But seriously, everyone raves about the conch fritters, and the fact they have to close because of nightly onslaughts of mosquitoes means this place is as authentically Florida as they come. Mains are $10 to $16.

Big Fish (☎ 305-453-0820; 99010 Overseas Hwy; mains $8-17; ☺ 11:30am-4am) All-you-can-eat stone crabs? Karaoke? *And* lesbian nights? Sign us up! Look for the sea-green seafood-shack-cum-bar-cum-nightclub waiting for you off the Overseas Hwy.

Fish House Encore (☎ 305-451-0650; www.fishhouse .com; MM 102.3) A funky yet upscale addition to the Key Largo eateries, the Fish House is a piano lounge offering a nightly, festive karaoke blow-out, as well as seafood and steaks from the Fish House, served on a lovely outdoor patio.

> ### DETOUR: FLORIDA KEYS OVERSEAS HERITAGE TRAIL
>
> One of the best ways to see the Keys is by bicycle. The flat elevation and ocean breezes are perfect for cycling, and the **Florida Keys Overseas Heritage Trail** (FKOHT; www.fkoht .org), which will connect all the islands from Key Largo to Key West, is set to be complete by 2012. At the time of writing, 60 miles of this excellent trail were already paved.
>
> If you are keen to ride before 2012, it's currently possible to bike through the Keys by shoulder riding (it takes three days at a good clip). There are particularly pleasant rides around Islamorada, and if you're uncomfortable riding on the shoulder, you can contact the FKOHT through their website for recommended bike excursions.

Sushi Nami (☎ 305-453-9798; MM 99.5 bayside) Weekend evenings offer live music. You can also enjoy sushi dinners served with a flourish on the bay.

Tavernier Towne Cinemas (☎ 305-853-7003; www.taverniercinemas.com; MM 92) This multiplex, showing new releases, is a perfect rainy-day option.

ISLAMORADA

Islamorada (eye-luh-murr-*ah*-da) is also known as 'The Village of Islands.' Doesn't that sound pretty? Well, it really is. This little string of pearls (well, Keys) – Plantation, Upper and Lower Matecumbe, Shell and Lignumvitae (lignum-*vite*-ee) – shimmers as one of the prettiest stretches of the islands. This is where the scrubby mangrove is replaced by unbroken horizons of ocean and sky, one perfect shade of blue mirroring the other. Islamorada stretches across some 20 miles, from MM 90 to MM 74.

Information

Islamorada Chamber of Commerce (☎ 305-664-4503, 800-322-5397; www.islamoradachamber.com; MM 83.2 bayside; ☺ 9am-5pm Mon-Fri, 10am-3pm Sat & Sun) Located in an old caboose.

Post office (MM 82.9 oceanside)

Sights & Activities

You might think a marina makes an odd sightseeing destination, but everyone in Islamorada knows about **Robbie's Marina** (☎ 305-664-9814;

www.robbies.com; MM 77.5 bayside; ⊙ 8am-6pm), and it really is the happiest dock on Earth. More than a boat launch, Robbie's is a local flea market, tacky tourist shop (all the shells you ever wanted), sea pen for tarpons (very big-ass fish) and jump-off for excellent fishing expeditions all wrapped into one driftwood-laced compound. There's a glut of boat-rental and tour options here. The party boat (half-day/night/full-day trips $35/40/60) is just that: a chance to drink, fish and basically achieve Keys Zen. Or, for real Zen (ie the tranquil as opposed to drunken kind), take an ecotour ($39) on an electrically propelled silent boat deep into the mangroves, hammocks and lagoons. Or, if you don't want to get on the water, at least feed the freakish tarpons from the dock ($2.79 per bucket, $1 to watch).

Only accessible by boat, **Lignumvitae Key State Botanical Site** (☎ 305-664-2540) encompasses a 280-acre island of virgin tropical forest and is home to roughly a zillion jillion mosquitoes. The official attraction is the 1919 Matheson House, with its windmill and cistern; the real draw is a nice sense of shipwrecked isolation. Strangler figs, mastic, gumbo-limbo, poisonwood and lignum vitae trees form a dark canopy that feels more South Pacific than South Florida. Guided walking tours (1¼ hours) are given at 10am and 2pm Thursday to Monday. You'll have to get here via **Robbie's Marina** (p189); boats depart for the 15-minute trip (adult/child $20/12) about 30 minutes prior to each tour and reservations are recommended.

For an even greater sense of tropical timelessness, come to **Indian Key State Historic Site** (☎ 305-664-2540). In 1831, renegade wrecker (shipwreck salvager) Jacon Housman turned this quiet island into a thriving city, complete with a warehouse, docks, streets, hotel and about 40 to 50 permanent residents. By 1836, Indian Key was the first seat of Dade County, but four years later the inhabitants of the island were killed or scattered by American Indian attack during the Second Seminole War.

There's not much left at the historic site – just foundation, some cisterns, Housman's grave and jungly tangle. There are trails that follow the old layout of the city streets, and there is an observation tower, or you can walk among ruins and paddle around in utter isolation in a canoe or kayak – which, by the way, is the only way out here. Robbie's used to bring boats this way, and still does boat rental (single/double/glass-bottom kayak/canoe per

hour $20/27.50/30/30). Short of kayakers and canoeists, no-one was allowed to dock at the harbor at the time of our visit due to storm damage. You can also see the island from the water on an ecotour with Robbie's ($39).

To get his railroad built, Henry Flagler had to quarry out some sizable chunks of Key. The best evidence of those efforts can be found at **Windley Key Fossil Reef Geological State Park** (☎ 305-664-2540; MM 85.5; per vehicle $3.50). Besides having a mouthful of a name, Windley has leftover quarry machinery scattered along an 8ft former quarry wall. The wall offers a cool (and rare) public peek into the strata of coral that forms the ground in these parts. Ranger tours are offered at 10am and 2pm on Monday to Thursday for $2.50.

One of the best beaches in these parts is **Anne's Beach** (☎ 305-853-1685; MM 73 oceanside), where the sand opens up on a sky-bright stretch of tidal flats and a green tunnel of hammock and wetland. The mudflats are a joy to get stuck in, and will be much loved by the kids.

At MM 81, note the **Hurricane Memorial**, perhaps the only memorial in the US to depict a wind-blown palm tree, which commemorates the 435 victims of the great hurricane of September 2, 1935.

Area dive shops include **Holiday Isle Dive Shop** (☎ 305-664-3483, 800-327-7070; www.diveholidayisle.com; MM 84.5 oceanside) and **Ocean Quest** (☎ 305-664-4401, 800-356-8798; MM 88.5), a training facility located at the Smugglers Cove Resort.

The Greyhound bus stops at the Burger King at MM 82.5 oceanside.

Sleeping

Ragged Edge Resort (☎ 305-852-5389; www.ragged-edge.com; 243 Treasure Harbor Rd; apt $69-249; P ⊠) This low-key and popular efficiency and apartment complex, far from the maddening traffic jams, has 10 quiet units and friendly hosts. The larger studios have screened-in porches. There's no beach, but you can swim off the dock and at the pool.

La Siesta Resort & Marina (☎ 305-664-2132; www.lasiestaresort.com; MM 80.5 oceanside; ste $160-420; P ⊠) OK: the decor is a bit dated and more than a bit obsessed with the whole nautical-tropical theme (how they achieved that special shade of sea green in the carpet we cannot say). But the suites and apartments are as spacious as they get down here, service is friendly, the pool is busy and the ocean views are lovely.

Casa Morada (☎ 305-664-0044, 888-881-3030; www
.casamorada.com; 136 Madeira Rd, off MM 82.2; ste low season
$239-499, Nov-May $329-659; P ⬜ ⬜) Contemporary
chic comes to Islamorada, but it's not gentrifying away the village vibe. Rather, the Casa adds
a welcome dab of sophistication to conch chill:
a Keystone standing circle, freshwater pool,
manmade lagoon, plus a *Wallpaper* magazine–
worthy bar that overlooks Florida Bay, all make
this boutique hotel worth a reservation. It's a bit
of South Beach style over the usual Keys-style
Jimmy Buffet blah.

Cheeca Lodge & Spa (☎ 305-664-4651, 800-327-2888;
www.cheeca.com; MM 82 oceanside; r $309-810; P ⬜ ⬜)
This plush conference-style resort, recently
converted into a partial condotel property, is
for those who like to be pampered. There are
steel drums on the terrace, monkeys carved
onto the hallway lamps, and bamboo on the
wallpaper, in case you couldn't figure out the
aesthetic theme. Rooms are plush and the
spoiling never stops.

Eating

Manny & Isa's Kitchen (☎ 305-664-4757; MM 81.9 oceanside; lunch $5-8, dinner $12-22; ☯ lunch & dinner Wed-Mon)
Recently moved into some precious new digs,
this Spanish/American joint has great daily
specials, lobster enchiladas, *ropa vieja* (shred-
ded beef) and ginormous paella platters.

Bob's Bunz (☎ 305-664-8363; www.bobsbunz.com; MM
81.6 bayside; mains $6-12; ☯ breakfast & lunch) The serv-
ice at this cute café is energetic and friendly
in an only-in-America kinda way, and the
food is fine, filling and cheap. Key lime pie
(see p211) is a classic Keys dish and Key-lime
anything at this bakery is highly regarded, so
buy that souvenir pie here. A sister restaurant
that stays open for dinner (Bob's Bunz Too)
is just across the road.

Spanish Gardens Cafe (☎ 305-664-3999; MM 80.9
oceanside; mains $9.50-15; ☯ breakfast & lunch) A great
option for those sick of fried everything, this
pink, Barcelona-esque café serves sandwiches
and salads dripping with manchego cheese,
chorizo, piquillo peppers and other Iberian
foodstuffs that get foodies going.

Morada Bay (☎ 305-664-0604; www.moradabay
-restaurant.com; MM 81.6 bayside; lunch $10-15, dinner $21-
27; ☯ breakfast, lunch & dinner) If you can ignore the
overwhelmed service and awful bands that
occasionally 'headline' the lunch rush, this is
a lovely, laid-back Caribbean experience, complete with imported powder-white sandy beach,
nighttime torches, tapas and fresh seafood.

Mile Marker 88 (☎ 305-852-9315; www.marker88
.info; MM 88 bayside; mains $9-30; ☯ 5-9pm Tue-Sun, brunch
Sun) It's chef-owned, has a good view of Florida
Bay and an even better menu of surf-and-
turf faves, plus 25¢ clams and oysters during
seafood-style happy hour. Try the $140 beluga
caviar for a splurge.

Whale Harbor Buffet (☎ 305-664-9888; www
.whaleharborinn.com; MM 83.5 oceanside; adult/child
$28.95/14.95; ☯ lunch & dinner) Take every ugly
stereotype from the US obesity crisis and have
them all realized in this appropriately named
80-course buffet. It's right below Wahoo's, so
you can always get a beer after you wipe out
some small species of gulf shrimp.

Pierre's (☎ 305-664-3225; www.pierres-restaurant.com;
MM 81.6 bayside; mains $24-40; ☯ dinner) Why hello
two-story waterfront plantation – what are
you serving? Toro sashimi…good, quality
start. Oysters Rockefeller with black truffles.
Mmmm – old school with a decadent modern twist. Pan-seared duck with baby apples?
Splurge, traveler, on possibly the best food
between Miami and Key West.

Drinking & Entertainment

Loreli Restaurant & Cabana Bar (☎ 305-664-4656;
www.loraleifloridakeys.com; MM 82 bayside) Look for
the big mermaid and join the crowds for
watered-down cocktails, live music and sunset
raucousness fuelled by happy-hour specials
from 4pm to 6pm.

Hog Heaven (☎ 305-664-9669; www.hogheavensports
bar.com; MM 85 oceanside) We're tempted to place
this joint in the eating section, as the seafood
nachos are so good. But it deserves pride of
place in 'drinking' thanks to huge crowds that
trip all the way down from Fort Lauderdale
for backporch, alfresco imbibing.

Wahoo's (☎ 305-664-9888; MM 83.5 oceanside) Deep
inside every man beats the heart of a Florida
redneck. Get in touch with this inner truth
here, where guys who look like ZZ Top members clean fish on the docks during happy
hour. Trust us: fish guts make beer better.

Morada Bay (☎ 305-664-0604; MM 81.6 bayside)
In addition to its excellent food (left), the
Bay holds monthly full-moon parties that attract the entire party-people population of
the Keys.

Woody's (☎ 305-664-4335; MM 82 bayside) Sometimes you just gotta say it: this place is a strip
club. And yet it's so much more: pizza parlor,
live venue for local rockers Big Dick & the
Extenders, host of weekly James Joyce discussion

BEACHES OF THE KEYS

The Keys are not well known for their beaches. Some are plagued by sandflies, but all are lapped by calm waters. Most are really narrow ribbons of white sand that tend to be even narrower in winter because of tides. For better or worse, the water is usually very shallow close to shore. The following are good public beaches, most with picnic tables, some with grills and all with toilets.

■ **Harry Harris County Park** (MM 92.5) In Tavernier, with picnic tables, barbecues and gentle water.

■ **Anne's Beach** (MM 73) Shallow waters, boardwalk through the mangroves. See p190 for more information.

■ **Long Key** (MM 67.5) Lagoons, trails and an observation tower. See below for more information.

■ **Sombrero Beach** (MM 50) In Marathon, with a playground and wide stretch of sand. See p194 for more information.

■ **Little Duck Key Beach** (MM 38) A thin stretch for wading, just past the Seven Mile Bridge.

■ **Bahia Honda State Park** (MM 37) A favorite – with camping, swimming, trails, and rentals for water-sports equipment. See p196 for more information.

circles and…no, wait, scratch the last one. You gotta be 21 (and shorn of thy dignity) to get in.

LONG KEY

The 965-acre **Long Key State Recreation Area** (☎ 305-664-4815; MM 67.5 oceanside; per car $3.50, plus per person 50c) takes up much of Long Key. It's about 30 minutes south of Islamorada, and comprises a tropical clump of gumbo-limbo, crabwood and poisonwood trees; a picnic area fronting a long, lovely sweep of teal water; and lots of wading birds in the mangroves. Two short nature trails head through distinct plant communities. The park also has a 1.5-mile canoe trail through a saltwater tidal lagoon and rents out canoes (hour/day $5/10) and ocean-going kayaks (two/four hours $17.20/32.25).

If you want to stay here, make reservations this minute: it's tough to get one of the 60 sites at the **recreation area** (☎ 305-664-4815, reservations 800-326-3521; www.reserveamerica.com; MM 67.5 oceanside; sites $31.49; ℗). They're all waterfront, making this the cheapest (and probably most unspoiled) ocean view – short of squatting on a resort – you're likely to find in Florida.

MIDDLE KEYS

As you truck down the Keys, the bodies of water get wider until you reach the big boy: Seven Mile Bridge, one of the world's longest causeways and a natural divider between the Middle and Lower Keys. In this stretch

of islands you'll cross specks like Conch Key and Duck Key, green, quiet Grassy Key, and finally Key Vaca (MM 54 to MM 47), where Marathon, the second-largest town and most Key-sy community in the islands, is located.

GRASSY KEY

At first blush Grassy Key seems pretty sedate. Well spotted; Grassy is very much an island of few attractions and lots of RV lots and trailer parks. These little villages were once the heart of the Keys, where retirees, escapists, fishermen and the wait staff who served them lived, drank and dreamed (of a drink). Some of these communities remain, but development is relentless, and so, it seems, is the migration of the old conch trailer towns.

Sights & Activities

By far the most popular activity on this island is swimming with the descendants of Flipper at the **Dolphin Research Center** (☎ 305-289-1121; www.dolphins.org; MM 59 bayside; adult/child under 4yr/child 4-12yr/senior $19.50/free/13.50/16.50, swim program $180-650; ☉ 9am-4pm). Of all the dolphin swimming spots in the Keys we prefer this one; the dolphins are free to leave the grounds and a lot of marine-biology research goes on behind the (still pretty commercial) tourist activities, such as getting a dolphin to paint your T-shirt or playing 'trainer for a day' ($650, you better love your dolphins).

Curry Hammock State Park (☎ 305-289-2690; MM 56.2 bayside; $3.50 per vehicle; ☉ 8am-sunset) is small

but sweet and the rangers are just lovely. Like most parks in the Keys, it's a good spot for preserved tropical hardwood and mangrove habitat – a 1.5-mile hike takes you through both environments. Local waters are blissfully free of power boats, which is a blessing down here. Rent a kayak (single/double for two hours $17.20/21.50) or, when the wind is up, join the crowds of windsurfers and kiteboarders.

New and increasingly popular is the non-profit **Marathon Aqua Ranch** (☎ 305-743-6135; www .marathonaquaranch.com; MM 59 oceanside; ☾ 9am-5pm), an

alfresco…well, fish ranch. At the time of writing the facility was pretty much a small lake stuffed with all sorts of finned friends, but as it gets off the ground it wants to become a hands-on introduction to aquaculture and sustainable fishing. Activities include feeding snapper ($2) and cobia ($5), and the fun 'snorkel during a fish-feeding frenzy' option ($45).

Sleeping & Eating

Hawk's Cay Resort (☎ 305-743-9000, 800-432-2242; www .hawkscay.com; 61 Hawk's Cay Blvd, Duck Key, off MM 61 oceanside; r & ste low season $225-1105, high season $345-1545;

SHOULD YOU SWIM WITH DOLPHINS?

There are four swim-with-the-dolphin (SWTD) centers in the Keys, and many more arguments for and against the practice.

For

- While SWTD sites are commercial, they are also research entities devoted to learning more about their charges.
- The dolphins raised on-site are legally obtained and not captured from the wild.
- The dolphins are used to humans and pose a negligible danger to swimmers, especially when overseen by expert trainers.
- Dolphin swim programs increase our knowledge of dolphins and promote conservation.
- At places like the Dolphin Research Center (opposite), the dolphins can actually swim out of their pens into the open water, but choose not to.

Against

- Dolphins are social creatures that require interaction, which is impossible to provide in captivity.
- SWTD tourism encourages the capture of wild dolphins in other parts of the world.
- Dolphin behavior is never 100% predictable. Dolphins can seriously injure a human, even while playing.
- SWTD centers encourage customers to think of dolphins as anthropomorphized 'friends,' rather than wild animals.
- Dolphins never appreciate captivity. Those that voluntarily remain in SWTD sites do so to remain close to food.

If you decide to swim or see dolphins in the Keys, you can contact one of the following:

Theater of the Sea (☎ 305-664-2431; www.theaterofthesea.com; Islamorada, MM 84.5 bayside; swim programs $175; ☾ 9:30am-4pm) has been here since 1946. Structured dolphin swims and sea-lion programs ($135) include 30 minutes of instruction and a 30-minute supervised swim. You can also swim with stingrays ($55).

Dolphins Plus (☎ 305-451-1993, 866-860-7946; www.dolphinsplus.com, off MM 99.5 bayside; swim programs $165-250), a Key Largo center, specializes in recreational and educational unstructured swims. They expect you know a good deal before embarking upon the swim, even though a classroom session is included.

There is also dolphin swimming at Grassy Key's **Dolphin Research Center** (opposite) and **Hawk's Cay Resort** (above).

Ⓟ 🖥 🏊) Now, if after one dolphin swim center and fish ranch you're thinking, 'Man, I *still* want to play with some sealife…,' don't worry: Hawk's Cay Resort is there for you. The Cay is an enormous luxury compound that could well have its own zip code, and besides a series of silky-plush rooms and nicely appointed townhouses, it has more activities than you can shake a…flipper at. Which is to say, the Cay has its own dolphin pool where you can swim with the dolphins – plus a sailing school, snorkeling, tennis and boat rentals.

Rainbow Bend (☎ 305-289-1505; www.rainbowbend .com; MM 58 oceanside; r low season $165-280, high season $313-339; Ⓟ 🏊) More budget and Keys-kitsch are these big pink cabanas, where the efficiencies and suites are bright, the tiki huts are shady, the bedsheets are ghastly, the beach swing is…um, swing-y and the ocean is (splash)…right there. Half-day use of the Bend's Boston whalers (motorboats), kayaks and canoes is complimentary.

Wreck Galley & Grill (☎ 305-743-8282; MM 59 bayside; $13-20; ⏰ lunch & dinner) The Wreck doesn't offer too many surprises – fisherman types knocking back brew and feasting on wings – but it's definitely a local haunt, where island politicos like to tongue wag about the issues (fishing).

MARATHON
Marathon, the second biggest Keys' community, is trying to sell herself as Key West for families these days, but still has an edge. There are just too many pirates, fishermen, bar workers and fun-loving hotel staff here to make Marathon totally G-rated. It's an easy place to fall in love with, or fall in love on. Marathon sits right on the halfway point between Key Largo and Key West, and is a good place to stop on a lazy road trip across the islands.

Information
Fisherman's Hospital (☎ 305-743-5533; MM 48.7 oceanside) Has a major emergency room.
Food for Thought (☎ 305-743-3297; Gulfside Village Shopping Center, MM 51 bayside) A combination bookstore/health-food shop.
Marathon Visitors Center Chamber of Commerce (☎ 305-743-5417, 800-262-7284; www.floridakeys marathon.com; MM 53.5 bayside; ⏰ 9am-5pm) Sells Greyhound tickets.

Sights & Activities
We hope you're not nature-trailed out, because **Crane Point Museum** (☎ 305-743-9100; www

.cranepoint.net; MM 50.5 bayside; adult/child over 6yr/ student/senior $7.50/4/4/6; ⏰ 9am-5pm Mon-Sat, noon-5pm Sun) is one of the nicest spots on the island to stop and smell the roses. And the pinelands. And the palm hammock – a sort of palm jungle (imagine walking under giant, organic Japanese fans) that only grows between MM 47 and MM 60. There's also Adderly House, a preserved example of a Bahamian immigrant cabin (which must have *baked* in summer) and 63 acres of green goodness to stomp through. The grounds were donated by Mary and Francis Crane, the odd Florida landowners who didn't decide to pave over their backyard. This is a great spot for the kids, who'll love the pirate exhibits in an on-site museum and yet another bird hospital.

Speaking about animal safe havens, who doesn't love the **Turtle Hospital** (☎ 305-743-6509; www.theturtlehospital.org; 2396 Overseas Hwy; adult/child $15/7.50) We know, we shouldn't anthropomorphize animals, but sea turtles just seem so sweet, so it's sad and heartening to see the injured and sick ones well looked after in this motel-cum-sanctuary. The whole setup is a labor of love by Richard Moretti, who's quite the Keys character himself. Tours are educational and fun and offered at 10am, 1pm and 4pm.

Tucked away down Sombrero Beach Rd, **Sombrero Beach** (Sombrero Beach Rd, off MM 50 oceanside) is one of the few white-sand, mangrove-free beaches in the Keys. It's a good spot to lay out or swim, and it's free.

If the kids are still restless (or if you are), stop at **Marathon Community Park & Marina** (12222 Overseas Hwy), which has athletic fields and a skatepark for disaffected adolescents. The marina, better known as **Boot Key Harbor** (www .bootkeyharbor.com), is one of the best-maintained working waterfronts in the Keys, and an excellent spot to book charter-fishing and diving trips. Ask around (as players in this game change fairly frequently) and expect to burn a hole in your wallet – just fueling a boat for a day's fishing costs hundreds of dollars.

Five-acre **Pigeon Key** (☎ 305-289-0025; www .pigeonkey.net; MM 47; adult/child $11/8.50; ⏰ tours 10am, 11:30am, 1pm & 2:30pm), about 2 miles west of Marathon and basically below the Old Seven Mile Bridge, is a National Historic District. For years the island housed rail workers and maintenance men; today you can tour the Key's historic structures or just relax on the beach and get in some snorkeling. Ferries leave from Knight's Key (to the left of the

Seven Mile Bridge if you're traveling south) to Pigeon; the last one returns at 4pm. The **Old Seven Mile Bridge**, meanwhile, serves as 'the World's Longest Fishing Bridge'; park at the northeastern foot of the bridge and have a wander.

Good excursion options include **Sombrero Reef Explorers** (☎ 305-743-0536; www.sombreroreef.com; 19 Sombrero Rd, off MM 50 oceanside) and **Tilden's Scuba Center** (☎ 305-743-7255; www.tildensscubacenter.com; 4650 Overseas Hwy), both offering snorkeling and diving expeditions through nearby sections of the coral reef.

Marathon Kayak (☎ 305-743-0561; www.marathon kayak.com; 6363 Overseas Hwy) does three-hour guided mangrove ecotours (per person $45), full-day mangrove ecotours ($85), three-hour sunset tours ($45), instruction (included) and rentals (half-/full day $35/50).

The **Marathon Cinema & Community Theater** (☎ 305-743-0994; www.marathontheater.org; 5101 Overseas Hwy) is a good, old-school, single-stage theater that shows movies and plays in big reclining seats (with even bigger cupholders).

Sleeping

Knights Key Campground (☎ 305-743-4343, 800-348-2267; MM 47 oceanside; sites $35-85; **P**) On the northern end of the Seven Mile Bridge, this 200-site campground – over-developed and full of family-campground bells and whistles – has many on-water sites and some sites specifically for tenters.

Siesta Motel (☎ 305-743-5671; www.siestamotel.net; MM 51 oceanside; r $77; **P** **旦**) Head here for one of the cheapest, cleanest flops in the Keys – and it's got great service, to boot.

Anchor Inn (☎ 305-743-2213; 7931 Overseas Hwy; r $79-150; **P**) Family-owned and operated, the inn consists of seven rooms sporting a vaguely nautical theme. Loud, green, dolphin hat racks aren't the classiest touch in home furnishing, but that's kind of the point: the vibe here is island casual.

Seascape Ocean Resort (☎ 305-743-6455; 1075 75th St, off MM 50.5 oceanside; r $165-255; **P** **旦**) The classy, understated luxury in this B&B manifests in the nine rooms, which all have a different feel, from old-fashioned cottage to sleek boutique. Seascape also has a waterfront pool, kayaks for guests to use and a lovely lobby-lounge where you'll find breakfast, and afternoon wine and snack (all included).

Tranquility Bay (☎ 305-289-0888; www.tranquilitybay .com; MM 48.5 bayside; r $300-650; **P** **旦** **旦**) If you're serious about going upscale, you should be going here. Tranquility Bay is a massive condotel resort with plush townhouses, high-threadcount sheets and all-in-white chic, which houses and sleeps the endless waves of gentrifying glitterati from up north. The grounds are enormous and activity-filled; they really don't want you to leave.

Eating

Dion's (☎ 305-743-4481; MM 51 bayside; fried-chicken dinner $4-6; 24hr) Hold on – it's a gas station. Well, gas stations treated you right in Miami, didn't they (see El Carajo, p149)? Dion's does the best fried chicken in the Keys: crisp but juicy but plump but rich, and with gooey, melty mac and cheese and sweet fried-but-just-firm-enough plantains on the side…oh man, we'll be right back.

KEYS CAMPING

The cheapest way to sleep is always under the stars and in a sleeping bag. And doing so on the Keys is not only affordable, but fun, warm, beautiful – and a big relief from the commercialism that plagues much of the region. Campgrounds vary from high-tech (such as RV hook-up sites with electricity), to basic (a plot of land big enough for a tent); however, because land here is not endless, sites are in short supply. That means you need to plan ahead and reserve your spot – sometimes as much as a year in advance.

State parks offer some of the best camping options around. There's **Bahia Honda State Park Campground** (p197), with 200 bayside sites, plus 47 campsites at **John Pennekamp Coral Reef State Park** (p188), half of which are set aside for use on a first-come, first-served basis. **Long Key State Recreation Area** (p192) is secluded and shady, and fills up fast, while the **Dry Tortugas National Park** (p213), south of Key West, is secluded and not shady, and is probably the most rustic experience you'll find in these parts. For a more hotel-like camping adventure, head to the very commercial **Knights Key Campground** (above), or the **Sugarloaf Key Resort KOA** (p198), with private beaches and a beautiful, fully equipped waterfront property.

Wooden Spoon (☎ 305-743-8383; MM 51 oceanside; mains $3-9; ☺ breakfast & lunch) It's the best breakfast around, served by sweet Southern women who know their way around a diner. The biscuits are fluffy, but they drown so well in that thick, delicious sausage gravy, and the grits are the most buttery soft starch you'll ever have the pleasure of seeing beside your eggs.

Villa Blanco (☎ 305-289-7900; 2211 Overseas Hwy; mains $7-12; ☺ breakfast, lunch & dinner Mon-Sat) We're not making this statement lightly; this is South Florida after all. But the roast pork here may be the best Cuban dish we've had in Miami and outside of it. It's pillow-y soft, luscious, citrus tangy – yet comforting. It's also freakishly huge, as you will be if you eat in this friendly, barebones cafeteria too often.

Keys Fisheries (☎ 305-743-4353; www.keysfisheries .com; 3502 Gulf View Ave; mains $7-14; ☺ lunch & dinner) The lobster reuben is the stuff of legend, but you can't go wrong with any of the excellent seafood sandwiches, which are served with sass (to order you have to identify your favorite car, color, etc; a question that depends on the mood of the guy behind the counter). Expect pleasant levels of seagull harassment as you dine on a working waterfront.

Porky's (☎ 305-289-2065; 1400 Overseas Hwy; lunch $7.75-15, dinner $15-23; ☺ lunch & dinner) The barbeque is smoky and good, and only accentuated by the salt winds coming in off the docks – which are right below your feet.

Drinking

Island Fish Company (☎ 305-743-4191; www.islandfishco .com; MM 54 bayside; ☺ lunch & dinner) The Island's got friendly staff pouring strong cocktails on a sea breeze–kissed tiki island overlooking Florida Bay. Chat with your friendly Czech or Georgian bartender, tip well, and they'll top up your drinks without you realizing it. The laid-back by-the-water atmosphere is quintessentially Keys.

our pick **The Hurricane** (☎ 305-743-2200; www.the hurricanegrille.com; MM 49.5 bayside) The staff is sassy, sarcastic and warm. The drinks will kick your ass out the door and have you back begging for more. The food (mains $8 to $19) is fantastic – the mini-hamburger sliders in particular. The ambience: locals, tourists, mad fishermen, rednecks and the odd journalist saddling up for endless Jägerbombs before dancing the night away to any number of consistently good live acts. It's the best bar before Key West, and it deserves a visit from you.

Brass Monkey (☎ 305-743-4028; Marathon, MM 52) When Colonel Kurtz whispers, 'The horror, the horror,' in *Apocalypse Now* he was probably thinking about the night he got trashed in this scuzziest of dives, the preferred watering hole for off-the-clock bar and wait staff in Marathon.

Getting There & Away

You can fly into the **Marathon Airport** (☎ 305-743-2155; MM 50.5 bayside) or go Greyhound, which stops at the airport.

LOWER KEYS

The Lower Keys are fierce bastions of conch culture (although the loose zoning laws locals favor are ironically putting them square in the path of big development). Some local families have been Keys castaways for generations, and there are bits of Big Pine that feel more Florida Panhandle than Overseas Hwy. Whether or not this is a good thing is a matter of perspective, but rest assured the islands get pretty rural and redneck-y before opening into tiki-tastic Key West.

BIG PINE, BAHIA HONDA & LOOE KEY

Big Pine is home to endless stretches of quiet roads (once you leave the overdeveloped highway), Key West employees who found a way around astronomical real-estate rates, and packs of wandering Key deer. Bahia Honda has got everyone's favorite sandy beach, while Looe coral-reef system offers amazing reef-diving opportunities.

Information

All of the following are on Big Pine:
Big Pine Key public library (☎ 305-872-0992; Big Pine Shopping Center, Key Deer Blvd; ☺ 10am-6pm Wed-Sat, noon-8pm Tue) Wi-fi available.
Lower Keys Chamber of Commerce (☎ 305-872-2411; www.lowerkeyschamber.com; MM 31 oceanside; ☺ 9am-5pm Mon-Fri, 9am-3pm Sat) Stocked with brochures and tourist information.
Post office (MM 30 bayside)

Sights & Activities

Bahia Honda State Park (☎ 305-872-2353; www.bahia hondapark.com; MM 36.8 oceanside; car $3.50, plus per person 50c; ☺ 8am-sunset), with its long, white-sand (and seaweed-strewn) beach, is the big attraction in these parts. While the beach is popular with

Keys types it's a bit overrated (although it was voted 'Best Beach in Continental America' by Condé Nast…in 1992). As a tourist, the more novel experience is walking a stretch of the old Bahia Honda Rail Bridge, which offers nice views of the surrounding islands. Or check out the nature trails (ooh, butterflies!) and science center, where helpful park employees help you identify stone crabs, fireworms, horseshoe crabs and comb jellies. Ladies: no matter how far away from the crowds you hike for privacy, rangers can eject women who sunbathe topless.

Big Pine's other big attraction is the famed **Big Pine Flea Market** (MM 30.5 oceanside; ☼ 8am-sunset Sat & Sun), which probably rivals local churches for weekly attendance. You know how we keep harping on about how weird Keys residents are? Well, imagine rummaging through their closets and seeing their deepest, darkest secrets – on sale for 50¢?!

Pronounced 'Loo,' **Looe Key National Marine Sanctuary** (☎ 305-292-0311) is located off Big Pine on a 'groove and spur reef' (we're not sure what that means, but we're gonna try it next time we're at the club). It can only be visited through a specially arranged charter-boat trip. Call the sanctuary for up-to-date info on charter options, which change with the seasons. Alternatively, you can visit the area with a dive company such as **Looe Key Dive Center** (☎ 305-872-2215; snorkel/dive $40/80). The marine sanctuary is named for an English frigate that sank here in 1744, and the Looe Key reef contains the 210ft *Adolphus Busch,* which was used in the 1957 film *Fire Down Below* and then in 1998 was sunk (110ft deep) in these waters.

Now, what would make Bambi cuter? Mini Bambi. Introducing: the Key deer, an endangered subspecies of white-tailed deer that prance about primarily on Big Pine and No Name Keys. The folks at the **National Key Deer Refuge Headquarters** (☎ 305-872-0774; http://nationalkeydeer.fws.gov; Big Pine Shopping Center, MM 30.5 bayside; ☼ 8am-5pm Mon-Fri) are an incredibly helpful source of information on the deer and all things Keys. The refuge sprawls over several islands, but the sections open to the public are on Big Pine and No Name.

Once mainland dwellers, the deer were stranded during the formation of the Keys. They shrank and had single births (as opposed to large litters) to deal with reduced resources. While you won't see thundering herds of dwarf-ish deer, the little cuteballs

are pretty easy to spot if you're persistent and patient. In fact, they're so common you need to pay careful attention to the reduced speed limits. Note: speed limits drop further at night, because cars are still the biggest killer of Key deer. To visit the refuge, take Key Deer Blvd (it's a right at the lights off the Overseas Hwy at the southern end of Big Pine) north for 3.5 miles from MM 30.5.

As you travel north on Key Deer Blvd you will pass **Blue Hole**, a little pond (and former quarry) that's now the largest freshwater body in the Keys. This small park is home to turtles, fish, wading birds and two alligators, including a hefty sucker named 'Bacardi.' Apparently people have taken to (illegally) feeding the wildlife here; please don't follow in their footsteps. A quarter mile further along the same road is **Watson's Nature Trail** (less than 1 mile long) and **Watson's Hammock**.

No Name Key gets few visitors (it's basically a residential island), but it's a reliable spot for deer-watching. Go on to Watson Blvd, turn right, then left onto Wilder Blvd. Cross Bogie Bridge and you'll be on No Name.

Looe Key Reef Resort & Dive Center (☎ 305-872-2215, 800-942-5397; MM 27.5 oceanside) and **Paradise Divers** (☎ 305-872-1114; MM 38.5 bayside) rent out equipment and lead local reef dives. **Strike Zone Charters** (☎ 305-872-9863, 800-654-9560; MM 29.5 bayside) has four-hour snorkeling and diving trips aboard glass-bottom boats, in which you can explore the thousands of varieties of colorful tropical fish, coral and sea life in the Looe Key sanctuary. The Bahia Honda **park concession** (☎ 305-872-3210; MM 36.8 oceanside) offers daily snorkeling trips at 9:30am and 1:30pm. Reservations are a good idea in high season. With all that said, you can easily paddle around any of the islands in your own kayak or canoe, or snorkel at spots that catch your fancy. Some of the local inter-Keys channels are so shallow that you can walk from island to island, although we don't recommend doing so unless you're confident in your tide-chart knowledge.

Sleeping

Bahia Honda State Park Campground (☎ 305-872-2353; www.reserveamerica.com; MM 37, Bahia Honda Key; sites $31.49, cabins $136.30; P) The excellent park has six cabins, each sleeping six people, and 200 sites a short distance from the beach. Reserve well in advance.

Big Pine Key Fishing Lodge (☎ 305-872-2351; MM 33 oceanside, Big Pine Key; sites with/without electricity $40/35, motel apt $80-100; **P** ♿) This tidy canal-side spot has a loyal clientele of snowbirds who wouldn't call anywhere else their Keys home. Key deer wander the clean grounds, staff are friendly and there are plenty of activities for the kids. The lodge, geared toward fishing and diving types, does boat rental.

Looe Key Reef Resort (☎ 305-872-2215, 800-942-5397; www.diveflakeys.com; MM 27.5 oceanside, Ramrod Key; r $80-175; **P** ♿) The focus of this Ramrod Key motel is diving, so, predictably, the 20 motel rooms are basic. The thatched-roof tiki bar is a big drinking hole for Ramrod Key residents.

Parmer's Place Guesthouse (☎ 305-872-2157; www.parmersresort.com; 565 Barry Ave, Little Torch Key, off MM 28.5 bayside; r & apt $99-304; 🖥 ♿) Appearing deceptively small from the outside, this 5-acre property takes up a nice chunk of Little Torch Key and fills it with inviting rooms that overlook local cuts and channels. The rooms are spacey, although you'd be mad not to step outside them and enjoy a view of the islands from your balcony.

our pick **Deer Run Bed & Breakfast** (☎ 305-872-2015; 1997 Long Beach Dr, Big Pine Key, off MM 33 oceanside; r $175-300; **P** ♿) This state-certified green lodge and vegetarian B&B is isolated on a lonely, lovely stretch of Long Beach Dr. It's a garden of quirky delights, complemented by assorted love-the-earth paraphernalia, street signs and four simple but cozily scrumptious rooms with names such as Eden, Heaven and Utopia. The helpful owners will get you out on a boat or into the heated pool for some chillaxation, while they whip up organic, vegetarian meals, yet somehow, in the midst of all this, the vibe isn't self-righteous hippie. More like: wow, what a friendly place.

Little Palm Island Resort & Spa (☎ 305-872-2524, 800-343-8567; www.littlepalmisland.com; ste $1091-2072; 🖥 ♿) How do you get here? By boat or by plane, accompanied by a big wad of money. If you can afford to get here you can afford to spoil yourself, and this exclusive island, with its Zen gardens, blue lagoons and general Persian-empire air of decadent luxury, is very good at spoiling you.

Eating

Coco's Kitchen (☎ 305-872-4495; Big Pine Key Shopping Center, MM 30.5 bayside; breakfast mains $2-5, sandwiches & mains $2.25-6; ⏱ 7am-7:30pm Tue-Sat) Enter through the oddly mirrored storefront into this tiny luncheonette, where local fishers join shop-pers from the Winn Dixie next door for diner fare and local gossip.

Good Food Conspiracy (☎ 305-872-3945; Big Pine Key, MM 30 oceanside; mains $6.75-9; ⏱ 9:30am-7pm Mon-Sat, 9:30am-5pm Sun) This place serves pork fat and baby seal tacos. Just kidding! Rejoice, hippies: all the greens, sprouts, herbs and tofu you've been dreaming about during that long, fried food–studded drive down the Overseas are for sale in this friendly little health-food shop. Note the big pink shrimp out front, and the attractive women who love to pose beneath it.

No Name Pub (☎ 305-872-9115; www.nonamepub.com; N Watson Blvd, Big Pine Key, off MM 30.5 bayside; mains $7-18; ⏱ 11am-11pm) The No Name's one of those off-the-track places that everyone seems to know about. It feels isolated, it looks isolated, yet somehow, the tourists are all here – this doesn't detract in the slightest from the kooky ambience, friendly service, excellent locally brewed beer and primo pizzas served up at this colorful semi-dive. Note, the name of this place implies that it is located on No Name Key, but it is on Big Pine Key, just over the causeway.

SUGARLOAF & BOCA CHICA KEYS

This is the final stretch before the holy grail of Key West. There's not much going on – just a few good eats and one thoroughly batty roadside attraction.

This lowest section of the Keys goes from about MM 20 to the start of Key West.

Sights & Activities

It resembles an Aztec-inspired fire lookout, but the wooden **Perky's Bat Tower** (Sugarloaf Key, MM17) is actually one real-estate developer's vision gone utterly awry. In the 1920s Richter C Perky had the bright idea to transform this area into a vacation resort. There was just one problem: mosquitoes. His solution? Build a 35ft tower and move in a colony of bats (he'd heard they eat mosquitoes). He imported the flying mammals, but they promptly took off, leaving the tower empty. Perky never built in this area again.

Sleeping

Sugarloaf Key Resort KOA (☎ 305-745-3549, 800-562-7731; 251 County Rd, off MM 20 oceanside; tent sites $42-70, RV sites $62-105) This highly developed KOA (Kampground of America) has about 200 tent sites and 200 RV sites, with amenities includ-

GROOVY GROVES

It's easy to think of the Keys, environmentally speaking, as a little boring. The landscape isn't particularly dramatic (with the exception of those sweet sweeps of ocean visible from the Overseas Hwy); it tends toward low brush and...well, more low brush.

Hey, don't judge a book by its cover. The Keys have one of the most unique, sensitive environments in the US. The difference between ecosystems here is measured in inches, but once you learn to recognize the contrast between a hammock and a wetland, you'll see the islands in a whole new tropical light. Some of the best introductions to the natural Keys can be found at **Crane Point Museum** (p194) and the **Florida Keys Eco-Discovery Center** (p201).

But here, we want to focus on the mangroves, the coolest, if not most visually arresting habitat in the islands. They rise from the shallow shelf that surrounds the Keys (which also provides that lovely shade of Florida teal), looking like masses of spidery fingers constantly stroking the waters. Each mangrove traps the sediment that has accrued into the land your tiki barstool is perched on. That's right, no mangroves = no Jimmy Buffet.

The three different types of mangrove trees are all little miracles of adaptation. Red mangroves, which directly front the water, have aerial roots, called propagules, which allow them to 'breathe' even as they grow into the ocean. Black mangroves, which grow further inland, survive via 'snorkel' roots called pneumatophores. Resembling spongy sticks, these roots grow out from the muddy ground, gasping in fresh air. White mangroves grow furthest inland and actually sweat out the salt they absorb through air and water to keep healthy.

The other tree worth a prop here isn't a mangrove, but the lignum vitae, which is restricted to the Keys in the US, is just as cool. Its sap has long been used to treat syphilis, hence the trees' Latin name, which translates to 'tree of life.'

ing beachfront volleyball, swimming pool, minigolf and sunset cruises.

Sugarloaf Lodge (☎ 305-743-3211; Sugarloaf Key, MM 17; r $95-150; P ⓢ) The 55 motellike rooms are nothing special, though every single one has a killer bay view. There is also an on-site restaurant, a tiki bar, a marina and an airstrip, from which you can charter a seaplane tour or go skydiving.

Eating

Baby's Coffee (☎ 800-523-2326; MM 15 oceanside; ⓨ 7am-6pm Mon-Fri, 7am-5pm Sat & Sun) This very cool coffeehouse has an on-site bean-roasting plant and sells bags of the aromatic stuff along with excellent hot and cold java brews. Other essentials are sold, from yummy baked goods to Dr Brommer's liquid soap.

Sugarloaf Food Company (☎ 305-744-0631; MM 24 bayside; breakfast $2.25-4.25, lunch $5-9; ⓨ breakfast & lunch Mon-Sat) A cozy, airy alternative to fried dullness, the Food Company specializes in excellent sandwiches and salads, and hand-crafted postcards with fairies on them. Um, have a sandwich.

Mangrove Mama's (☎ 305-745-3030; MM 20 oceanside; lunch $10-15, dinner $19-25; ⓨ 11:30am-3:30pm & 5:30-10pm) This groovy roadside eatery serves

Caribbean-inspired seafood – coconut shrimp, spicy conch stew, lobster – best enjoyed on the backyard patio and accompanied by a little live reggae.

KEY WEST

If you're too weird for mainland Florida – and yes, that is a valid description for a crazy few – they ship you out to Key West, the most beautifully strange (or is it strangely beautiful?) island in the US. This place is seriously screwy, in a (mostly) good way. There's no middle separating the high and low brow, that's for sure. On one side of the road: literary festivals, Caribbean villas, tropical noir and expensive art galleries. On the other: an S&M fetishist parade, frat boys vomiting on their sorority girlfriends and 'I Love to Fart' T-shirts (seriously).

Like all good things, Key West is threatened by gentrification. Pity especially the wait- and bar-staff on Duval St, who simply cannot afford to live on the island they've made into everyone's party. But the whole funky insanity thing is stronger here than the rest of the Keys, probably because weirdness is still integral to

THE CONCH REPUBLIC: ONE HUMAN FAMILY

Conchs (pronounced 'conk' as in 'bonk,' not 'contsh' as in 'bunch') are people who were born and raised in the Keys. It's a rare title to achieve. Even transplants can only rise to the rank of 'Freshwater Conch.' You will hear reference to, and see the flag of, the Conch Republic everywhere in the islands, which brings us to an interesting tale.

In 1982 US border patrol and customs agents erected a roadblock at Key Largo to catch drug smugglers and illegal aliens. As traffic jams and anger mounted, many tourists disappeared. They decided they'd rather take the Shark Valley Tram in the Everglades, thank you very much. To voice their outrage, a bunch of fiery Conchs decided to secede from the USA. After forming the Conch Republic, they made three declarations (in this order): secede from the USA; declare war on the USA and surrender; and request $1 million in foreign aid. The roadblock was eventually lifted, and every February, Conchs celebrate the anniversary of those heady days with nonstop parties, and the slogan 'We Seceded Where Others Failed.'

Today the whole Conch Republic thing is largely a marketing gimmick, but that doesn't detract from its official motto: 'One Human Family.' This emphasis on tolerance and mutual respect has kept the Keys' head and heart in the right place, accepting gays, straights, and peoples of all colors and religions.

the Key West brand (whereas developers are happy to flatten the other islands into iden-tikit resorts). This town is still defined by its motto, which we love: One Human Family, an ideal that equals a tolerant, accepting ethos where anything goes and life is always a party (or at least a hungover day after). The color scheme: watercolor pastels cooled by breezes on a sunset-kissed Bahamian porch. Welcome to the End of the USA.

Have a drink.

ORIENTATION

The island of Key West is roughly oval-shaped, divided into Old Town and New Town. New Town is where working folks live – families with kids and hotel employees, who have been priced out of other neighborhoods. Old Town, a seriously pleasant collection of Colonial architecture, shady palms and tropical light, is where the inns and eater-ies and museums are, centering on Duval St. The north end of Old Town is a 'high street' slush of alcohol, aggression and cheap T-shirt stands. The south end caters to the gay population and tourists seeking a break from the above; restaurants, clubs and bars are interspersed with galleries and high-end boutiques. Downtown streets are laid out in a grid, with street numbers (usually painted on lamp posts) in a hundred-per-block for-mat, counting upward from Front St (100) to Truman Ave/US 1 (900) and so on. Mallory Sq is at the far northwest tip.

INFORMATION
Bookstores
For books in this very literary town, check out the following:

Flaming Maggie's (☎ 305-294-3931; 830 Fleming St; ☯ 10am-7pm) Specializes in gay books and periodicals.
Key West Island Books (☎ 305-294-2904; 513 Flem-ing St; ☯ 10am-9pm) Has an excellent selection of works by Key West writers, past and present.
Public Library (☎ 305-292-3535; 700 Fleming St) South Florida's first library. Founded in 1892.

Internet Access
Sippin' (☎ 305-293-0555; 424 Eaton St; per min 20¢; ☯ 7am-11pm) Near the center of town.

Media
Keeping up with local goings-on is easy, as this well-read town has nearly 10 newspapers (though some are entertainment-only rags):
Citizen (www.keysnews.com) A well-written, oft-amusing daily.
Key West Keynoter (www.keynoter.com) A *Miami Herald*–owned weekly.
National Public Radio (NPR) Tune into 91.3FM.
Solares Hill (www.solareshill.com) Slightly activist take on community interests.

Medical Services
The following are Key West's most accessible medical services:
Lower Keys Medical Center (☎ 305-294-5531, 800-233-3119; 5900 College Rd, Stock Island, MM 5) Has a 24-hour emergency room.

South Med (☎ 305-295-3838; 3138 Northside Dr) Dr
Scott Hall caters especially to the gay community, but also
serves visitors.
Truman Medical Center (☎ 305-296-4399; 540
Truman Ave; ☷ 9am-4:45pm Mon-Fri, 9:30am-noon Sat)
Come here for less-critical problems.

Money

Bank of America (☎ 305-296-1204; 510 Southard St,
Key West)

Post

Post office (400 Whitehead St; ☷ 8:30am-9pm Mon-
Fri, 9:30am-noon Sat)

Tourist Information

Key West Chamber of Commerce (☎ 305-294-
2587; www.keywestchamber.org; 402 Wall St, Mallory Sq;
☷ 8:30am-6:30pm Mon-Sat, until 6pm Sun) An excellent
source of information.
Key West Welcome Center (☎ 305-296-4444,
800-284-4482; 3840 N Roosevelt Blvd; ☷ 8am-7:30pm
Mon-Sat, 9am-6pm Sun) Sells discounted attraction tickets
and helps with accommodations.

SIGHTS
Mallory Square

Take all those energies, subcultures and oddities of Keys life – the hippies, the rednecks, the
foreign types and, of course, the tourists – and
focus them into one torchlit, family-friendly
(but playfully edgy), sunset-enriched street
party. The child of all these raucous forces
is Mallory Sq, one of the greatest shows on
Earth. It all begins as the sun starts to set, a
sign for the madness that it's OK to break out.
Watch a dog walk a tightrope, a man swallow
fire, British acrobats tumble and sass each
other. Have a beer. And a conch fritter. And
wait for the sun to dip behind the ocean and
the carnival to really get going.

Duval Street

Key West locals have a love–hate relationship
with the most famous road in Key West (if not
the Keys). Duval, Old Town's main drag, is a
miracle mile of booze, tacky everything and
awful behavior (and not awful in an awfully
good way either. More like awful in a loud,
belligerently drunk, seriously-dude-yelling-
curse-words-and-vomiting-on-the-sidewalk-
won't-attract-women kinda way). But it's
fun. The 'Duval Crawl' is one of the best pub
crawls in the country. The mix of live music

drink-o-ramas, T-shirt kitsch, local theaters,
art studios and boutiques is more charming
than jarring. And the experience is quintessentially Key West. Have some perspective,
have a laugh, and appreciate Duval for her
pimples-and-all, to see why this street continues to be the island's tipsy heart.

Hemingway House

Key West's biggest darling, Ernest Hemingway,
lived in this gorgeous Spanish-Colonial **house**
(☎ 305-294-1575; www.hemingwayhome.com; 907
Whitehead St; adult/child 6-12yr $11/6; ☷ 9am-5pm) from
1931 to 1940. Poppa moved here in his early
30s with wife No 2, a *Vogue* fashion editor and
(former) friend of wife No 1. *The Short Happy
Life of Francis Macomber* and *The Green Hills
of Africa* were produced here, but Hemingway
didn't just work; like all writers he wasted a lot
of time, specifically by installing Key West's
first saltwater swimming pool. The construction project set him back so badly he pressed
his 'last penny' into the cement on the pool's
deck. It's still there today, along with the evil
descendants of his famous six-toed cat, who
basically rule the house and grounds. The
author's old studio is preserved as he left it –
when he ran off in 1940 with wife No 3.

Florida Keys Eco-Discovery Center

So: you've been making your way down the
Keys, visiting all these lovely state parks and
nature reserves, thinking, 'Gosh, could there
be a place that ties all the knowledge of this
unique ecological phenomenon into one fun,
well-put-together educational exhibit?' OK,
maybe those weren't your exact thoughts, but
this is exactly what you get at this excellent
center (☎ 305-809-4750; 35 East Quay Rd, Truman Annex;
admission free; ☷ 9am-4pm Tue-Sat). This place does
a marvelous job of filling in all the wild details
of the natural Keys. The kids love it here, and
by the way, it's free *and* has free parking, an
abnormality around here.

Fort Zachary Taylor Historic State Park

'America's Southernmost State Park' (we
get it, Keys Chamber of Commerce – Key
West is southern), this **park** (☎ 305-292-6713;
Truman Annex; per vehicle $3.50; ☷ 8am-sunset) is oft-
neglected by authorities and visitors, which
is a shame as it's a nice place to while away a
quiet afternoon. The actual fort walls are still
standing, and within the compound those

KEY WEST

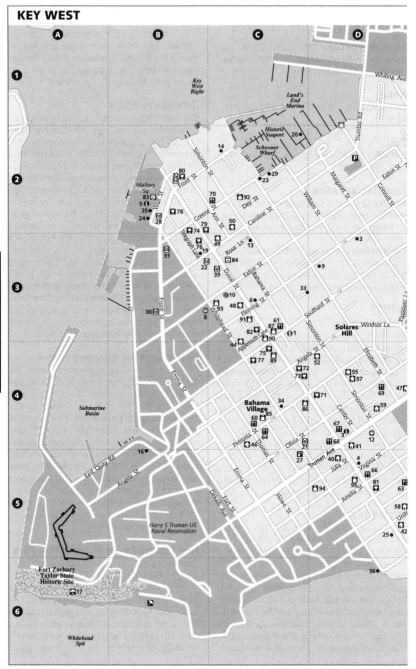

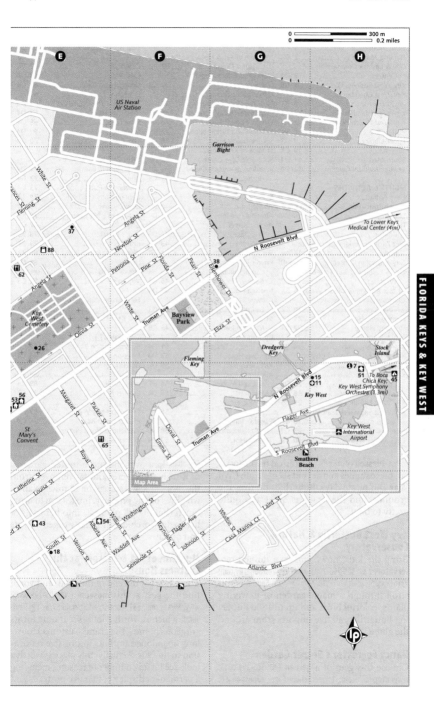

INFORMATION
- Bank of America 1 C3
- Flaming Maggie's 2 D3
- Gay & Lesbian Community Center 3 D4
- Key West Business Guild 4 D5
- Key West Chamber of Commerce 5 B2
- Key West Island Books 6 C3
- Key West Welcome Center 7 H4
- Post Office 8 B3
- Public Library 9 D3
- Sippin' 10 C3
- South Med 11 H4
- Truman Medical Center 12 D4

SIGHTS & ACTIVITIES
- Casa Antigua 13 C3
- Conch Tour Train 14 C2
- Dive Key West 15 H4
- Florida Keys Eco-Discovery Center 16 B5
- Fort Zachary Taylor Historic State Park 17 A6
- Gay & Lesbian Center (see 4)
- Gay & Lesbian Trolley Tour of Key West 18 E5
- Ghosts & Legends of Key West 19 B3
- Glass Bottom Boat Discovery Tours 20 C2
- Hemingway House 21 C4
- Heritage House 22 B3
- Jolly II Roger 23 C2
- Key West Aquarium 24 B2
- Key West Association of Dive Operators (see 15)
- Key West Butterfly & Nature Conservatory 25 D5
- Key West Cemetery 26 E3
- Key West Lighthouse 27 C5
- Key West Shipwreck Historeum Museum 28 B2
- Liberty Clipper 29 C2
- Little White House 30 B3
- Mel Fisher Maritime Heritage Museum 31 B3
- Museum of Art & History at the Customs House 32 B2
- Nancy Forrester's Secret Garden 33 C3
- Office of the Secretary General of the Conch Republic 34 C4
- Old Town Trolley Tours 35 B2
- Original Ghost Tours (see 48)
- Pelican Poop Gift Shoppe (see 13)
- Southernmost Point 36 D6
- Studios of Key West 37 E2
- Subtropic Dive Center 38 G3
- Wreckers' Museum/Oldest House 39 C3

SLEEPING
- Abaco Inn 40 D5
- Almond Tree Inn 41 D4
- Avalon Bed & Breakfast 42 D5
- Best Western Hibiscus 43 E5
- Big Ruby's Guesthouse 44 C4
- Boyd's Key West Campground 45 H4
- Caribbean House 46 C4
- Chelsea House 47 D4
- Crowne Plaza La Concha 48 C3
- Curry Mansion Inn 49 C3
- Cypress House 50 C2
- Days Inn 51 H4
- Gardens Hotel 52 D4
- Key Lime Inn 53 E4
- Key West Youth Hostel & Seashell Motel 54 E5
- Merlin Inn 55 D4
- Mermaid & Alligator 56 E4
- Paradise Inn 57 D4
- Pearl's Rainbow 58 D5
- Truman Hotel 59 D4

EATING
- Blue Heaven 60 C4
- Café 61 C3
- Café Solé 62 E3
- Camille's 63 D5
- Conch Town Café 64 C4
- El Siboney 65 E4
- Flamingo Crossing Ice Cream 66 D5
- Nine One Five 67 D4
- Salsa Loca 68 D4
- Seven Fish 69 D4
- Thai Cuisine 70 C2

DRINKING
- 801 Bourbon Bar 71 D4
- Aqua 72 C4
- Bourbon St Pub 73 C4
- Captain Tony's Saloon 74 B2
- Cowboy Bills 75 C4
- Garden of Eden Bar 76 B3
- Green Parrot 77 C4
- Hog's Breath 78 B2
- Irish Kevin's 79 B2
- Island Dogs Bar 80 B2
- La Te Da 81 D5
- Pearl's Rainbow (see 58)
- Virgilio's 82 C3

ENTERTAINMENT
- Key West Players 83 B2
- Red Barn Theatre 84 C3

SHOPPING
- Bésame Mucho 85 C4
- Dogs on Duval 86 C4
- Garcia Cigars 87 C3
- Haitian Art Co 88 E2
- Island Style 89 C4
- Leather Master 90 C3
- Montage 91 C3
- Peppers of Key West 92 C2
- Project Lighthouse 93 C3
- Whitehead Street Pottery 94 D5
- Wishbliss Boutique 95 D5

most-blessed of nerds – historical reenactors – put on costumes and act out scenes from Civil War and pirate days. Butterflies flit over the grounds, and the beach is quiet and quite pretty to boot.

Key West Butterfly & Nature Conservatory

Bring the kids, now. This vast domed **conservatory** (☎ 305-296-2988; www.keywestbutterfly.com; 1316 Duval St; adult/child $10/7.50; 9am-5pm) lets you stroll through a magic garden of flowering plants, colorful birds and up to 1800 fluttering butterflies, all live imports from around the globe.

Nancy Forrester's Secret Garden

Choose this gem of a **garden** (☎ 305-294-0015; www.nfsgarden.com; 1 Free School Lane; admission $6; 10am-5pm) over the more-touted gardens, as it truly feels secret and far removed from the more raucous goings-on in town. Nancy, who lives on the property, invites you to bring lunch (but no cell phones!) into her oasis of lush palms, orchids, and chatty caged parrots and macaws.

Museum of Art & History at the Customs House

There is art at the end of the road, and you'll find the best at this **museum** (☎ 305-295-6616; www.kwahs.com; 281 Front St; adult/child $7/5; 9am-5pm), which is worth a look-see if only for its gorgeous home – the grand Customs House, long abandoned until its impressive renovation in the '90s. Actually, this place is worth a look-see for any number of reasons, including a permanent display of massive portraits and some of the best showcases of international (particularly Caribbean) art in the region.

Key West Cemetery

A darkly alluring Gothic labyrinth beckons (rather incongruously) at the center of this pastel town. Built in 1847, the cemetery crowns Solares Hill, the highest point on the island (with an elevation of all of 16ft). Some of the oldest families in the Keys rest in peace – and close proximity – here. With body space at a premium, the mausoleums stand practically shoulder to shoulder. Island quirkiness penetrates the gloom: seashells and green macramé adorn headstones with inscriptions like, 'I told you I was sick.' Get chaperoned by George Born, of the **Historic Florida Keys Foundation** (☎ 305-292-6718), who gives guided tours for $10 per person at 9:30am on Tuesday and Thursday; departs from the main gate at Margaret and Angela Sts.

Southernmost Point

There's no way we're going to dissuade you from having your picture taken at this red-and-black buoy at the corner of South and Whitehead Sts, which isn't even the southernmost point (that's in the off-limits naval base around the corner). But we'll say it anyways: this is the most overrated attraction in Key West.

Key West Lighthouse

You can climb up 88 steps to the top of this **lighthouse** (☎ 305-294-0012; www.kwahs.com; 938 Whitehead St; adult/student over 7yr/senior $8/4/6; 🕙 9:30am-4:30pm), built in 1846, for a decent view. But honestly, it's just as enjoyable to gaze up at the tower from the leafy street below.

Little White House

President Harry S Truman – the one who came after Franklin Roosevelt? Marshall Plan? Helped start the Cold War? Never mind – used to vacation at this **house** (☎ 305-294-9911; 111 Front St; adult/child 5-12yr $11/6; 🕙 9am-4:30pm). It is as lushly luxurious as you'd expect and open only for guided tours (though the two rooms of the Harry S Truman Annex, with displays on political and presidential trivia, are free). Plenty of Truman's possessions are scattered about, but the real draw is the guides, who are intensely intelligent, quirky and helpful.

Heritage House

Of all the many historic Key West homes open to visitors, this Caribbean–Colonial **house** (☎ 305-296-3573; www.heritagehousemuseum .org; 410 Caroline St; admission $5; 🕙 10am-4pm Mon-Sat) is among the most wonderful to walk through. That's because it's rarely crowded, has passionate guides, and contains original furnishings and antiques, from a piano from

WRECKERS' MUSEUMS

Key West's economy was once built on wrecking – salvaging sunken ships and their treasures. It was a potentially dangerous and extremely profitable business that attracted a fair number of cut-throats, villains and fortune-hunters to the Keys (in other words, not a lot has changed). Proximity to busy and treacherous shipping lanes, which attracted plenty of pirates, made wrecking so lucrative that by the mid-19th century Key West was the biggest town in Florida and had the highest per-capita income in the USA. All that history of underwater exploration and rum-and-blood soaked poop decks made for plenty of 'yaar' moments in the island's history, and today, as in the past, wrecking is a backbone of Key West's industry – in this case the tourism industry. There are three local wrecking museums:

▪ The home of Confederate blockade-runner Francis B Watlington, the **Wreckers' Museum/ Oldest House** (☎ 305-294-9502; 322 Duval St; adult/child $5/1; 🕙 10am-4pm) is filled with period antiques and has enjoyable, volunteer-led tours.

▪ The **Key West Shipwreck Historeum Museum** (☎ 305-292-8990; www.shipwreckhistoreum.com; 1 Whitehead St; adult/child 4-12yr $9/4.50; 🕙 9:45am-4:45pm) is a bit more lively, with a cast of actors taking you back to 1856, when the *Isaac Allerton* was destroyed by a hurricane in the Saddlebunch Keys.

▪ The **Mel Fisher Maritime Heritage Museum** (☎ 305-294-2633; 200 Greene St; adult/child $10/6; 🕙 9:30am-5:30pm) presents an impressive number of artifacts salvaged by Fisher in 1985, along with a world map showing shipping routes taken by the Spanish ships he discovered.

the court of Marie Antoinette to a set of dining chairs from the 1600s. All have been collected and preserved by seven generations of a local family. The Robert Frost Cottage, where the poet stayed for 16 winters, is out back, along with another wonderful garden.

Bahama Village

Bahama Village was the old Bahamian district of the island, and in days past it had a colorful Caribbean feel about it – which is resurrected a bit during the **Goombay Festival** (opposite). But today the village is pretty gentrified, and those areas that haven't been swallowed into a sort of pseudo-Duval periphery zone are, if not rough, not exactly great for a tourist stroll either. At 405 Petronia St is the Office of the Secretary General of the Conch Republic, where you can see all manner of Conch Republic tat.

Casa Antigua

This was technically Hemingway's first house in Key West and the spot where he wrote *A Farewell to Arms*, but it isn't all that notable except for a lush garden in the back and one of the kitschiest 'guided tours' in the US. Here's how it breaks down: go to the **Pelican Poop Gift Shoppe** (☎ 305-296-3887; www.pelicanpoop .com; 314 Simonton St), which now occupies the Casa, pay the $2 garden entrance fee and let the kitsch begin! Go into the peaceful green area out the back, then a recorded tape plays at the volume God uses whenever he says anything that begins with 'Let there be…' At this ear-splitting volume, a man with a voice that can only be described as Big Gay Al raised in Dixie, lays down the history of the Casa for you. It's gloriously hilarious.

The Studios of Key West

This new nonprofit showcases about a dozen artists' studios in a **gallery space** (☎ 305-296-0458; www.tskw.org; 600 White St; ❂ 10am-6pm) located in the old Armory building, which includes a lovely sculpture garden. Besides its public visual-arts displays, TSKW hosts readings by local authors like Robert Stone, literary and visual workshops, concerts, lectures and community discussion groups. Essentially, it has become the accessible heart of this city's enormous arts movement, and offers a good point-of-entry for visitors who want to engage in Key West's creative scene but don't have a clue where to start.

ACTIVITIES
Beach-Going

Key West is *not* about beach-going. In fact, for true sun 'n' surf, locals go to Bahia Honda (p196) whenever possible. Still, the three city beaches on the southern side of the island are lovely and narrow, with calm and clear water. **South Beach** is at the end of Simonton St. **Higgs Beach**, at the end of Reynolds St and Casa Marina Ct, has barbecue grills, picnic tables, and a big crowd of gay sunbathers and Key West's Eastern European seasonal workforce. **Smathers Beach**, further east off S Roosevelt Blvd, is more popular with jet-skiers, parasailers, teens and college students. The best local beach, though, is at **Fort Zachary Taylor** (p201); it's worth the admission to enjoy the white sand and relative calm.

Boating

You'll find plenty of folks hawking sails and other boat rides. The **Jolly II Rover** (☎ 305-304-2235; www.schoonerjollyrover.com; cnr Greene & Elizabeth Sts, Schooner Wharf; cruise $35) is a gorgeous tanbark (reddish-brown) 80ft schooner that embarks on daily sunset cruises under sail. It looks like a pirate ship and has the cannons to back the image up. **Liberty Clipper** (☎ 305-292-0332; www .libertyfleet.com; William St, Schooner Wharf) is a 125-footer modeled after the biggest sailing craft of the 19th century. Dinner cruises (adult/child $79/55) and sunset sails (adult/child $65/45) are both magical ways of getting the salt and sea in your face.

Diving & Snorkeling

Because of pollution and activity, there's no snorkeling to speak of on Key West beaches, so most dive companies take you off-island. At some dive sites, nondivers can go along and snorkel. Dive companies set up at kiosks around Mallory Sq and other places in town, notably the corner of Truman Ave and Duval St. Check out these well-established places: **Subtropic Dive Center** (☎ 305-296-9914, 800-853-3483; www.subtropic.com; 1605 N Roosevelt Blvd) and **Dive Key West** (☎ 305-296-3823, 800-426-0707; www.divekeywest .com; 3128 N Roosevelt Blvd). In addition, the **Key West Association of Dive Operators** (http://divekeys.com; 3128 N Roosevelt Blvd) website is a clearing house for information on diving opportunities in the islands; they also work on enhancing local sustainable underwater activities by creating artificial reefs and encouraging safe boating and diving practices.

KEYS FOR KIDS

Check out some of the following options to entertain the kids:

- **Key West Aquarium** (☎ 305-296-2051; www.keywestaquarium.com; 1 Whitehead St, Mallory Sq; adult/child $9/4.50; ☼ 10am-6pm) Gaze at marine life.
- **Florida Keys Eco-Discovery Center** (p201) Get an understanding of the region's environment.
- **Glass-bottom boat tours at John Pennekamp Coral Reef State Park** (p186) Your own window to the underwater world.
- **Key West Butterfly & Nature Conservatory** (p204) Pretty flying things.
- **Turtle Hospital** (p194) Save (or watch) the turtles.
- **Conch Tour Train** (below) Kitschy, corny, enjoyable tour.
- **Ghost tours** (below) Only slightly spooky; younger kids may find this one a bit scary.
- **Key-deer spotting** (p197) Kids go crazy for cute mini-deer.
- **Key West Cemetery** (p205) Get Gothic with these often silly tombs.
- **Robbie's Marina** (p189) All sorts of activities, including the ever-popular tarpon (giant fish) feeding frenzy.

TOURS

Old Town Trolley Tours (☎ 305-296-6688; www.trolleytours.com/key-west; adult/child $27/13) are a great introduction to the city. The 90-minute, hop-on, hop-off narrated tram tour starts at Mallory Sq and makes a large, lazy loop around the whole city, with nine stops along the way. Trolleys depart every 15 to 30 minutes from 9am to 4:30pm daily. The narration is hokey, but you'll get a good overview of Key West, its history, and gossipy dirt about local issues and people in the news.

Conch Tour Train (☎ 305-294-5161; www.conchtourtrain.com; adult/child $27/13; ☼ 9am-4:30pm) is run by the same company as trolley tours, though this one seats you in breezier linked train cars with no on/off option.

Glass Bottom Boat Discovery Tours (☎ 305-293-0099; www.discoveryunderseatours.com; foot of Margaret St, Historic Seaport; adult/child under 5yr/child 6-11yr $40/free/16) depart daily in summer at 11:30am, 2:30pm and sunset, and in winter at 10:30am, 1:30pm and sunset. In Key West style, the sunset cruise includes a complimentary glass of bubbly.

The Orchid Lady (☎ 877-747-2718; www.eorchidlady.com/tours.php) provides a thoroughly unique Key West experience, with guided walk-throughs of three lush, orchid-filled gardens with Orchid Lady Bobbi Mazer. Tours are 9:30am, 11am and in the afternoon by appointment (per person $25).

Also worth noting is *Sharon Wells' Walking & Biking Guide to Historic Key West*, a booklet of self-guided walks available for free at inns and businesses around town, written by a local. See www.seekeywest.com.

There are a couple of ghost tours in town, which you'll either find frightening or corny; either way they're fun. **Original Ghost Tours** (☎ 305-294-9255; from Crowne Plaza La Concha Hotel; adult/child $15/10; ☼ 8pm & 9pm) features stories about souls who inhabit locations including the Hard Rock Café, of all places; and **Ghosts & Legends of Key West** (☎ 305-294-1713; Porter House Mansion, 429 Caroline St; adult/child $18/10; ☼ 7pm & 9pm) promises to take you 'off the beaten track' to places 'only a Conch could show you,' including the old city morgue and a small cemetery. Reservations are recommended for both tours.

FESTIVALS & EVENTS

You gotta see **Fantasy Fest**, held throughout the week leading up to Halloween in late October. It's when all the inns get competitive about decorating their properties, and everyone gets decked out in the most outrageous costumes they can cobble together (or decked down in daring body paint). The **Goombay Festival** (www.goombay-keywest.org), held during the same out-of-control week, is a Bahamian celebration of food, crafts and culture. The **Annual Key West Literary Seminar** (http://keywestliteraryseminar.org/lit), now in its 23rd year, draws top writers from around the country each January (although it costs hundreds of dollars to attend); while the **Hemingway Days** festival, held in late

---

LITERARY KEY WEST

Key West is a tropical blend of weird personalities, excellent restaurants, diverse sexual mores and free-flowing alcohol, which makes it just about perfect for writers. Ernest Hemingway was the most famous, but plenty of other scribes have set up shop on the island. Pulitzer Prize–winning poets like James Merrill, Robert Frost and Richard Wilbur (the latter two were also US poet laureates), novelists like Alison Lurie (Pulitzer), Robert Stone (National Book Award) and essayist/author Annie Dillard (Pulitzer again!) have all worked here at one point or another.

As well as the elements listed above, Key West's tropi-Gothic architecture, funny wildlife (why is it that lizards are so inspiring?) and weather (same goes for ceiling fans) just seem to get the creative juices going.

Plenty of authors, who often tread the literary circuit in the educated northeast and New England, especially love coming here for seminars and readings during the winter. Local intelligentsia have seized on this phenomenon and squeeze quite a bit of cash out of those who want to attend the Annual Key West Literary Seminar (p207). There's no doubt the seminar consistently attracts amazing authors, but fair warning: there tends to be more established talent than hungry ambition at these things. The affair pretty much consists of big names telling aspiring names how they got to where they are; some find this inspiring, others find it annoying. The point is, literary Key West, by dint of its costs, is more a posh writer's retreat than a ramshackle Left Bank. Then again, where else are you likely to see a Nobel laureate for literature stumble into the toilets of a dive like the Green Parrot?

July, brings parties, a 5km run and an Ernest look-alike contest. Nothing says dignified sexiness like **WomenFest** (www.womenfest.com), in early September, which attracts thousands of lesbians who just want to party; November's **Parrot Heads in Paradise Convention** (www.phip.com /motm.asp) is for, you guessed it, Jimmy Buffet fans (rabid ones only, natch). Contact the **Key West Art & Historical Society** (☎ 305-295-6616; www.kwahs.com) to get the skinny on upcoming studio shows, literary readings, film festivals and the like, such as the annual **Robert Frost Poetry Festival** (www.robertfrostpoetryfestival.com) held in April.

SLEEPING

There's a glut of boutique hotels, cozy B&Bs and four-star resorts here at the end of the USA, so sleepers won't want for accommodations. Although we've labeled some options as more 'central' than others, the fact is that any hotel in Old Town will put you within walking distance of all the action.

Though all people, gay and straight, will be welcome just about anywhere, there are some exclusively gay inns, noted here. Except campgrounds, all of the following properties have air-conditioning. Lodgings have higher rates during the high season (mid-December to April). In addition, many properties add a 'shoulder' (mid-season) that runs from late spring to early fall; rates may fall somewhere

between low and high during mid-season. Many hotels (especially smaller properties) enforce two-night minimum stays. Expect rates to be extremely high during events like New Year's and Fantasy Fest, when some places enforce up to seven-night minimum stays.

Historic Key West Inns (☎ 800-549-4430; www .historickeywestinns.com) is an excellent grouping of six boutique properties, most of which are listed here. Chain hotels include **Best Western Hibiscus** (☎ 305-294-3763; 1313 Simonton St); **Days Inn** (☎ 305-294-3742; 3852 N Roosevelt Blvd), one of the cheapest places in town; and **Crowne Plaza La Concha** (☎ 305-296-2991; 430 Duval St), which has a top-floor bar and observatory open to nonguests (though you'll mainly gaze at unexciting rooftops).

Budget & Midrange

Boyd's Key West Campground (☎ 305-293-9301; www.boydscampground.com; 6401 Maloney Ave; tent sites low season nonwaterfront/waterfront $50/60, mid-Nov–mid-Apr $60/70, water & electricity $75-110; **P**) Just outside town on Stock Island (turn south at MM 5), Boyd's has upwards of 300 sites. There's a bus stop for downtown practically at their front door.

Key West Youth Hostel & Seashell Motel (☎ 305-296-5719; www.keywesthostel.com; 718 South St; dm members/nonmembers $25/28, motel r low season $75, high season $110-150; **P**) They've improved this place over the past few years – it's not quite as mildew-y and the common area feels more like a youth hostel and less skeezy. The dorms are still the cheapest sleeping option in town (although you get what you pay for). Motel rooms aren't worth the cost, given what you can get at a similar rate around the way.

Caribbean House (☎ 305-296-0999; www.caribbean housekeywest.com; 226 Petronia St; r low season $55, high season $75; P ⌨) This is a cute, canary-yellow Caribbean cottage in the heart of Bahama Village. The 10 small, brightly colored guest rooms aren't too fancy, but it's a happy, cozy bargain – with free breakfast, no less.

Abaco Inn (☎ 305-292-4040; http://abaco-inn.com; 415 Julia St; r $119-189; ⌨) This intimate gem, tucked away on a quiet and diverse residential block, has three simple, airy and stylish rooms, all with wood floors and ceiling fans. There's no breakfast, but there is a small, shaded garden and a couple of warm, knowledgeable hosts. An excellent find.

Avalon Bed & Breakfast (☎ 305-294-8233; www .avalonbnb.com; 1317 Duval St; r low season $89-169, high season $169-289; ⌨ ⌨) A cute, restored Victorian house on the quiet end of Duval blends attentive service with stately old ceiling fans, tropical lounge-room rugs, and black-and-white photos of olde-timey Key West. Music the cat likes to greet guests at reception.

Chelsea House (☎ 305-296-2211; www.chelseahouse kw.com; 707 Truman Ave; r low season $120-180, high season $200-290; P ⌨ ⌨) This perfect pair of Victorian mansions beckons with large vaulted rooms and big comfy beds, with the whole shebang done out in floral, but not dated, chic. The old-school villa ambience clashes – in a nice way – with the happy vibe of the guests and the folks at reception.

Key Lime Inn (☎ 800-559-4430; 725 Truman Ave; r $99-289, ste $109-329; P ⌨ ⌨) These cozy cottages are all scattered around a tropical hardwood backdrop. Inside, the blissfully cool rooms are greener than a jade mine, with wicker furniture and tiny flat-screens on hand to keep you from ever leaving.

Mermaid & Alligator (☎ 305-294-1894, 800-773-1894; www.kwmermaid.com; 729 Truman Ave; r low season $148-198, high season $218-298; P ⌨ ⌨) It takes a real gem to stand out amid the jewelry store of Keys hotels, but this place, located in a 1904 mansion, more than pulls off the job. Each of the nine rooms is individually designed with a great mix of modern comfort, Keys Colonial ambience and playful laughs. The treetop suite, with its exposed beams and alcoved bed and bathroom, is our pick of this idiosyncratic litter.

Merlin Inn (☎ 305-296-3336, 800-642-4753; 811 Simonton St; low season $89-225, high season $135-300; P ⌨ ⌨) Set in a secluded garden with a pool and elevated walkways, everything here is made from bamboo, rattan and wood. Throw in the rooms' high ceilings and exposed rafters, and this hotel oozes Colonial-tropical atmosphere. Unfortunately, the sheets on some of the beds bring granny's house to mind.

Top End

Pearl's Rainbow (☎ 305-292-1450, 800-749-6696; www .pearlsrainbow.com; 525 United St; r & ste low season $120-199, high season $209-399; P ⌨ ⌨) Key West's sole women-only place is one of the best low-key lesbian resorts in the country, an intimate garden of tropical relaxation and enticing rooms scattered across a few cottages. A clothing-optional backyard pool bar is the perfect spot for alfresco happy hour, or to enjoy your free brekkie.

Almond Tree Inn (☎ 800-311-4292, 305-296-5415; www.almondtreeinn.com; 512 Truman Ave; r $159-399; P ⌨ ⌨) Palm-lined pool. Palm-tree lamps. Palm-engraved headboard. Plus wicker dressers and sea-green walls. Sure, the tropical theme is laid on thick, but hey, it's the Keys, and besides, they've got 5pm to 7pm happy hour by the pool.

Truman Hotel (☎ 305-296-6700; www.trumanhotel .com; 611 Truman Ave; r low season $195-285, high season $240-365; P ⌨ ⌨) Close to the main downtown drag, these teal-and-teak rooms have huge flat-screen TVs, kitchenettes and bouncy fluff-erific beds that'll serve you well after the inevitable Duval Crawl (which is only steps from your door).

Cypress House (☎ 800-525-2488, 305-294-6969; www .cypresshousekw.com; 601 Caroline St; r & ste low season $135-330, high season $159-380; P ⌨ ⌨) This plantationlike getaway has wraparound porches, leafy grounds, a secluded swimming pool and spacious, individually designed bedrooms with four-poster beds. It's lazy, lovely luxury in the heart of Old Town, although we'd recommend rooms in the Main House and Simonton House over the blander guest studios. Parking costs $10 per day.

Curry Mansion Inn (☎ 800-253-3466, 305-294-5349; http://currymansion.com; 511 Caroline St; r low season $195-285, high season $240-365; P ⌨ ⌨) In a city full of stately 19th-century homes, the Curry Mansion is especially handsome. All the elements of an aristocratic American home come together here, from plantation-era Southern colonnades to a New England–style widow's walk and, of course, bright Floridian rooms with canopied beds. Enjoy bougainvillea and breezes on the veranda.

Big Ruby's Guesthouse (☎ 305-296-2323, 800-477-7829; www.bigrubys.com; 409 Applerouth Lane; r low season $119-191, mid-Dec–Mar $315-599; P 🖳 🏊) This gay-only place looks like a refined Conch mansion on the outside, but once you get to your room you'll see it's all contemporary, white and sleeker than a designer's decadent dreams. The clothing-optional lagoon pool is capped by a treetop walkway, elegant decking and tropical palms; plus there are fine linens and lots of privacy.

Paradise Inn (☎ 305-293-8007, 800-888-9648; http://theparadiseinn.com; 819 Simonton St; r & ste low season $169-369, high season $269-599; P 🖳 🏊) Another winner from Historic Key West Inns, this friendly compound houses some simple but elegant rooms, suites and cottages. The suites are highly recommended: classy but not stodgy, breezy enough for a tropical idyll but not so laid-back that they're tacky. Although the cottages, with their Jacuzzi-jet bathtubs, aren't so bad either…

Gardens Hotel (☎ 305-294-2661, 800-526-2664; www.gardenshotel.com; 526 Angela St; r & ste low season $200-435, high season $325-645; P 🖳 🏊) Would we be stating the obvious if we mentioned this place has really nice gardens? In fact, the 17 rooms are located in the Peggy Mills Botanical Gardens, which is a longish way of saying 'tropical paradise.' Inside, Caribbean accents mesh with the fine design to create a sense of green-and-white-and-wood space that never stops massaging your eyes.

EATING

There's a great concentration of restaurants, from greasy diners to high-end fusion-concept cuisine, in this relatively small town. When it comes to eating, sticking to Duval St isn't a bad idea, although there are some real gems down those side streets as well.

Flamingo Crossing Ice Cream (☎ 305-296-6124; 1107 Duval St; ice cream $3.50-6; ⊙ to 11pm) It's fresh, it's homemade, it's the best damn 'scream on the island. The butter pecan and mint chocolate-chip (together – trust us) are almost as nice as the impeccable service.

Conch Town Café (☎ 305-294-6545; 801 Thomas St; mains $5-14; ⊙ 11:30am-7:30pm) Too many people ignore this walk-up/carry-out, with its plastic patio furniture and scruffy island vibe. It's a shame, as it serves conch – good for more than listening to the ocean – deliciously 'cracked' (deep-fried) with a lip-puckeringly sour-lime marinade. You'll be tempted to wash it down with the homemade smoothies, but be warned: they're more milky than refreshing.

Café (☎ 305-296-5515; 509 Southard St; mains $7-13; ⊙ 11am-10pm Mon-Sat) The Café is the only place in Key West that exclusively caters to herbivores. By day, it's a cute, sunny, earthy-crunchy luncheonette; by night, with flickering votive candles and a classy main dish (grilled, blackened tofu and polenta cakes), it's a sultry-but-healthy dining destination.

El Siboney (☎ 305-296-4184; www.elsiboneyrestaurant.com; 900 Catherine St; mains $9.50-16; ⊙ 11am-9:30pm) This is a rough-and-ready Cuban joint where the portions are big and there's no screwing around with either high-end embellishment or bells and whistles. It's rice, it's beans, it's cooked with a craftman's pride, and it's good.

Salsa Loca (☎ 305-292-1865; http://salsalocakeywest.com; 918 Duval St; mains $11-16; ⊙ 11am-10pm Tue-Thu, 11am-11pm Fri & Sat, noon-10pm Sun) Across the Keys, everyone from bartenders to developers to fishermen is swearing by the Mexican food at this colorful spot, with its tropical-night-and-tequila-scented backyard patio. Of course, the bucket-deep margaritas probably improve everyone's impression of the place.

Thai Cuisine (☎ 305-294-9424; www.keywestthaicuisine.com; 513 Greene St; lunch $10-12, dinner $15-24; ⊙ lunch Mon-Fri, dinner daily) There's surprisingly good Thai to be had here near the top of Duval. It's not Bangkok, but the weather's just as nice and there are no tuk-tuk drivers or ladyboys interrupting your meal.

Camille's (☎ 305-296-4811; www.camilleskeywest.com; 1202 Simonton St; breakfast $3-13, lunch $4-13, dinner $14-25; ⊙ breakfast, lunch & dinner) This healthy and tasty neighborhood joint is the kind of place where players on the Key West High School softball team are served by friends from their science class, and the hostess is the pitcher's mom. But it's also the kind of place where the homey facade conceals a sharp kitchen that makes a mean chicken-salad sandwich.

Seven Fish (☎ 305-296-2777; www.7fish.com; 632 Olivia St; mains $15-26; ⊙ dinner) This simple yet elegant tucked-away storefront is the perfect place for a romantic feast of homemade gnocchi or sublime banana chicken. The dining room might be the Zen-est interior in the islands.

KEY LIME PIE

Many places claim to serve the original Key lime pie, but no one knows who discovered the tart treat. Types of crust vary, and whether or not the pie should be topped with meringue is debated. However, the color of Key lime pie is not open to question. Beware of places serving green Key lime pie: Key limes are yellow, not green. Restaurants that add green food coloring say that tourists expect it to be green. Steer clear.

---

ourpick Café Solé (☎ 305-294-0230; www.cafesole .com; 1029 Southard St; lunch $5-11, dinner $25-32; ⊗ lunch & dinner) Conch carpaccio with capers? Yellowtail fillet and foie gras? Oh yes. This locally and critically acclaimed venue is known for its cozy back-porch ambience and innovative menus, cobbled together by a chef trained in southern French techniques who works with island ingredients. The memory of the anchovies on crostini makes us smile as we type. It's simple – fish on toast! – but it's the sort of simple yet delicious that makes you feel like mom's whipped up something special for Sunday dinner.

Nine One Five (☎ 305-296-0669; www.915duval.com; 915 Duval St; mains $16-34; ⊗ 6pm-midnight) There is a war being waged for Duval's identity. On the one side: an army of alcoholic aggression and tribal band tattoos. On the other: this immaculate, modern and elegant eating experience, with its creative, New American-dips-into-Asia menu. Korean ribs over pad thai show Eastern promise, but scallops sizzling in black-truffle butter are deliriously French. The excellent interior artwork is a nice touch.

Blue Heaven (☎ 305-296-8666; http://blueheavenkw .homestead.com; 729 Thomas St; dinner mains $19-$38; ⊗ dinner daily, breakfast & lunch Mon-Sat, brunch Sun) Proof that location is *nearly* everything, this is one of the quirkiest venues on an island of oddities. Customers and a local chicken flock dine in the spacious courtyard where Hemingway once officiated boxing matches; restrooms are in the adjacent former brothel. But Blue Heaven may have become a victim of its own success – it's sometimes uncomfortably crowded, and the food is hit or miss, even on basics as simple as cornbread.

DRINKING
Basically, Key West is a floating bar. 'No, no, it's a nuanced, multilayered island with a proud nautical and multicultural histo--' *bzzzt*! Floating bar. Make your memories (or lack thereof) at one of the following. Bars close at 3am; for gay venues, see p212.

Captain Tony's Saloon (☎ 305-294-1838; 428 Greene St) Propagandists would have you believe the nearby mega-bar complex of Sloppy Joe's was Hemingway's original bar, but the physical place where the old man drank was right here, the original Sloppy Joe's location (before it was moved onto Duval St and into frat-boy hell). Hemingway's third wife (a journalist sent to profile Poppa) seduced him in this very bar, wallpapered with business cards from around the world (including this travel writer's).

Cowboy Bills (☎ 305-295-6226; 618 Duval St) Do your best bow-legged saunter here for some (very) over-the-top country 'n' western vibe, live honky tonk and weekly 'sexy bull-riding' competitions. If you just spilled your Miller High Life in excitement, turn off *Blue Collar Comedy Tour* and git on down here.

Garden of Eden Bar (☎ 305-296-4565; 224 Duval St) Go to the top of this building and discover Key West's own clothing-optional drinking patio. Lest you get too excited, cameras aren't allowed, most people come clothed, and those who do elect to flaunt their birthday suits are often…erm…older.

ourpick Green Parrot (☎ 305-294-6133; 601 Whitehead St) The oldest bar on an island of bars, this rogue's cantina opened in the late 19th century and hasn't closed yet. The owner tells you the parachute on the ceiling is 'weighed down with termite turds,' while a blues band howls through clouds of smoke. Defunct business signs and local artwork litter the walls and, yes, that's the city attorney showing off her new tattoo at the pool table. Men: check out the Hieronymus Bosch–like painting *Proverbidioms* in the restroom, surely the most entertaining urinal talk-piece on the island.

Hog's Breath (☎ 305-292-2032; 400 Front St) A good place to start the infamous Duval Pub Crawl, the Hog's Breath is a rockin' outdoor bar with good live bands and better cold Coronas.

Island Dogs Bar (☎ 305-295-0501; 505 Front St) 'Come as you are,' reads the sign, and as it is written, so it goes in this hip (for Key West) joint, which seems to attract a younger crowd of drinkers.

Irish Kevin's (☎ 305-292-1262; 211 Duval St) One of the most popular megabars on Duval, Kevin's has a pretty good entertainment formula pinned down: nightly live acts that are a

---

GAY & LESBIAN KEY WEST

Key West's position at the edge of the USA has always attracted artists and eccentrics, and with them a refreshing dose of tolerance. The island had one of the earliest 'out' communities in the USA, and though less true than in the past, visiting Key West is a rite of passage for many LGBT (lesbian, gay, bisexual and transgender) Americans. In turn, this community has had a major impact on the local culture. Just as there is a straight trolley tour, you can hop aboard the **Gay & Lesbian Trolley Tour of Key West** (☎ 305-294-4603; $20), departing from the corner of South St and Simonton St at 11am on Saturday. The tour provides commentary on local gay lore and businesses (you'll also see the sites of the infamous Monster club). It's organized by the **Key West Business Guild**, which represents many gay-owned businesses; the guild is housed at the **Gay & Lesbian Community Center** (☎ 305-292-3223; www.glcckeywest.org; 513 Truman Ave), where you can access free internet on one of the few computers, plus pick up loads of information about local gay life. For details on gay parties and events, log onto www.gaykeywestfl.com.

Gay nightlife, in many cases, blends into mainstream nightlife, with everybody kind of going everywhere these days. But the backbone of the gay bar scene can be found in a pair of cruisey watering holes that sit across the street from one another, **Bourbon St Pub** (724 Duval St) and **801 Bourbon Bar** (801 Duval St), which can be summed up in five words: drag queen–led karaoke night. For a peppier scene that includes dancing and occasional drag shows, men and women should head to **Aqua** (☎ 305-294-0555; 711 Duval St), while women will enjoy the backyard pool bar at the women's inn **Pearl's Rainbow** (☎ 305-292-1450; 525 United St).

---

cross between a folk singer, radio shock jock and pep-rally cheerleader. The crowd consistently goes ape-poo for acoustic covers of '80s favorites. Basically, this is a good place to see 50 women from New Jersey do tequila shots, scream 'Livin' On a Prayer' at the top of their lungs and then inexplicably sob into their Michelob. It's more fun than it sounds.

La Te Da (☎ 305-296-6706; www.lateda.com; 1125 Duval St) While the outside bar is where locals gather for mellow chats over beer, you can catch high-quality drag acts – big names come here from around the country – upstairs at the fabulous Crystal Room on weekends. More low-key cabaret acts grace the downstairs lounge.

Virgilio's (☎ 305-296-1075; 524 Duval St, enter on Appelrouth Lane) This bar/stage is as un-Keys as they come, and frankly, thank God for a little variety. This town needs a dark, candlelit martini lounge where you can chill to jazz and get down with some salsa, and Virgilio's handsomely provides.

ENTERTAINMENT

Key West Players (☎ 305-294-5105; www.waterfrontplayhouse.com; Waterfront Playhouse, Mallory Sq) Catch high-quality musicals and dramas from the oldest-running theater troupe in Florida. The season runs November through April.

Key West Symphony Orchestra (☎ 305-292-1774; www.keywestsymphony.com; Tennessee Williams Theatre, 5901 Collage Rd) Key West's critically acclaimed

orchestra performs classics from Debussy, Beethoven and Mendelssohn from December through April.

Red Barn Theatre (☎ 305-296-9911; www.redbarntheatre.org; 319 Duval St) An occasionally edgy and always fun, cozy little local playhouse.

SHOPPING

Bright and breezy art galleries, excellent cigars, leather fetish gear and offensive T-shirts – Key West, what don't you sell?

Bésame Mucho (☎ 305-294-1928; 315 Petronia St) This place is well stocked with high-end beauty products, eclectic jewelry, clothing and housewares.

Dogs on Duval (☎ 305-296-8008; 800 Duval St) Pet accoutrement, like university sports jerseys for dogs, is on the rack behind – puppies! Heart-wrenchingly cute puppies. What, you don't like puppies? Don't talk to us.

Garcia Cigars (☎ 305-293-0214; 629 Duval St) There are plenty of cigar shops in Key West, but our favorite is this shackfront, where a sweet Cuban woman sells handrolled goods while she quotes and constantly reads the Bible, all in the face of the drunken screams of hundreds of horny frat boys.

Leather Master (☎ 305-292-5051; 415 Appelrouth Lane) Besides the gladiator outfits, studded jockstraps and S&M masks, they do very nice bags and shoes here. Which is what you came for, right?

Island Style (☎ 305-292-7800; 620 Duval St) You'll either love or loathe these pastel-and-tropical bright knick-knacks, furniture sets and homewares, but do visit, because the island's aesthetic is heavily influenced by this sort of place.

Montage (☎ 305-295-9101; 512 Duval St) Had a great meal or wild night at some bar or restaurant in the Keys? Well, this store probably sells the sign of the place (along with lots of Conch Republic tat), which makes for a nice souvenir.

Peppers of Key West (☎ 305-295-9333; 602 Greene St) For a downright shopping party, you should bring your favorite six-pack with you into this store and settle in at the tasting bar,

where the entertaining owners use double entendres to hawk seriously mouth-burning hot sauces like their own Right Wing Sauce (use Liberally).

Project Lighthouse (☎ 305-292-0999; 418 Eaton St) Lighthouse is a community organization that runs programs for street kids (Key West is a popular runaway destination); it partly supports itself by selling arts and crafts made by its charges.

Wishbliss Boutique (☎ 305-294-6336; 1102 Duval St) Tasteful, vintage-y, hip-to-almost-hippie clothes on Duval's south end.

Whitehead Street Pottery (☎ 305-294-5067; 322 Julia St) and the **Haitian Art Co** (☎ 305-296-8932; 600 Frances St) are excellent art-gallery shops.

DETOUR: DRY TORTUGAS NATIONAL PARK

After all those Keys, connected by all that convenient road, the nicest islands in the archipelago require a little extra effort. Ponce de León named them Las Tortugas (The Turtles) for the sea turtles that roamed here. A lack of fresh water led sailors to add a 'dry.' Today the Dry Tortugas are a national park under the control of the **Everglades National Park Office** (☎ 305-242-7700; www.nps.gov/drto) and are accessible by boat or plane.

Originally the Tortugas were the US's naval perch into the Gulf of Mexico. But by the Civil War, Fort Jefferson, the main structure on the islands, had become a prison for Union deserters and at least four people, among them Dr Samuel Mudd, who had been arrested for complicity in the assassination of Abraham Lincoln. Hence, a new nickname: Devil's Island. The name was prophetic; in 1867 a yellow-fever outbreak killed 38 people, and after an 1873 hurricane the fort was abandoned. It reopened in 1886 as a quarantine station for smallpox and cholera victims, was declared a national monument in 1935 by President Franklin D Roosevelt, and was upped to national-park status in 1992 by George Bush Sr.

The park is open for day trips and overnight camping, which provides a rare phenomenon: a quiet Florida beach. Garden Key has 13 campsites ($3 per person, per night), which are given out on a first-come, first-served basis. Reserve early by calling the Everglades National Park office. There are toilets, but no freshwater showers or drinking water; bring everything you'll need. The sparkling waters offer excellent snorkeling and diving opportunities. A visitor center is located within fascinating Fort Jefferson.

If you're hungry, watch for Cuban-American fishing boats trolling the waters. They'll happily trade for lobster, crab and shrimp; you'll have the most leverage trading beverages. Just paddle up and bargain for your supper. In March and April, there is stupendous bird-watching, including aerial fighting. Star-gazing is mind-blowing any time of the year.

Getting There

If you have your own boat, the Dry Tortugas are covered under National Ocean Survey chart No 11438. Otherwise, the **Yankee Freedom II** (☎ 305-294-7009, 800-634-0939; www.yankeefreedom .com; Historic Seaport) operates a fast ferry between Garden Key and the Historic Seaport (at the northern end of Margaret St). Round-trip fares cost $124/109 per adult/child. Reservations are recommended. Continental breakfast, a picnic lunch, snorkeling gear and a 45-minute tour of the fort are all included.

Seaplanes of Key West (☎ 305-294-0709; www.seaplanesofkeywest.com) can take up to 10 passengers (flight time 40 minutes each way). A four-hour trip costs $229/free/149/179 per adult/ child under two years/child two to six years/child under 12 years; an eight-hour trip costs $405/ free/270/325. Again, reserve at least a week in advance.

GETTING THERE & AROUND

Key West International Airport (EYW) is off S Roosevelt Blvd on the east side of the island. You can fly into Key West from some major US cities such as Miami or New York. Flights from Los Angeles and San Francisco usually have to stop in Tampa, Orlando or Miami first. **American Airlines** (☎ 800-433-7300) and **US Airways** (☎ 800-428-4322) have several flights a day. **Cape Air** (☎ 305-352-0714, 800-352-0714; www.flycapeair.com) flies between Key West and Naples. From the Key West airport, a quick and easy taxi ride into Old Town will cost about $10.

Greyhound (☎ 305-296-9072; www.greyhound.com; 3535 S Roosevelt Blvd) has two buses daily between Key West and downtown Miami. Buses leave Miami for the 4¼-hour journey at 12:35pm and 6:50pm ($38.50 to $44 one-way), and Key West at 8:55am and 5:45pm going the other way.

You can boat from Miami to the Keys on the **Key West Express** (☎ 866-593-3779; www.seakeywest express.com; adult/child round-trip $106/70, one-way $53), which departs from the Miami Seaquarium (p112) daily at 9:30am (8:30am Sundays) and does a four-hour cruise to Key West; call ahead as the boat only runs during a yet-to-be defined season. Returning boats depart the seaport at 6:30pm (5:30pm Sunday). Boats also run year-long to Fort Meyers (adult/child round-trip $129/68, one-way $73/53); boats leave Fort Meyers beach at 8:30am and Key West at 6pm.

Once you're in Key West, the best way to get around is by bicycle (rentals from the Duval St area, hotels and hostels are about $10 a day). Other options include the **City Transit System** (☎ 305-292-8160; tickets 75¢), with color-coded buses running about every 15 minutes; the convenient **Bone Island Shuttle** (☎ 305-293-8710; 3-day pass $7, child free), which makes frequent loops around both New and Old Town; mopeds, which generally rent for $30 for four hours ($35 for a six-hour day); or the ridiculous electric tourist cars, or 'Conch cruisers,' which travel at 35mph and cost about $30/170 per hour/day. As far as regular rental cars go, don't even bother in Key West.

Southeast Florida

Zooming north from Miami's seductive clutches, you'll find an endearing collection of beach towns – some classy, others quirky, all unique. From activity-packed, gay- and family-friendly Fort Lauderdale to quiet, exclusive, semireclusive Palm Beach; from laid-back Lauderdale-by-the-Sea to the rugged coast of Jupiter, you'll find more culture and nightlife than you can handle. For those looking for a more peaceful setting, the region's numerous natural gems – shady parklands dotting the shore, many with windswept dunes fending off the waves – will surely satisfy your demands for down-to-earth, outdoorsy pleasures.

Pristine wilderness awaits in state parks and the Hobe Sound National Wildlife Refuge between Stuart and northern Palm Beach. Thick with mangroves and loaded with wildlife, the area aches for exploration. Alternatively, you can kayak the coffee-colored waters of the 'wild and scenic' Loxahatchee River or camp in secluded islands that haven't seen visitors in…well, who knows how long.

Don't forget West Palm Beach and Delray Beach: vibrant, diverse communities boasting wonderful cuisines, cultural dynamos, shopping galore and robust nightlife.

But the beaches are the real reason you're here. All along the coast, dozens of public beaches will give you the chance to soak up the rays. Ranging from Lauderdale's sparkling-white but jam-packed sands (especially across from Las Olas Blvd), to Lake Worth's sparse but surfable waves off Lake Ave, this stretch of sand is, really, the USA's sandbox.

So whatever you do, don't skip over this region on your journey from Miami to Disney World.

HIGHLIGHTS

- Enjoy West Palm Beach's **Clematis By Night** (p251), a free event held every Thursday under the stars, featuring national and local musicians and a host of tasty street food

- Glide through Fort Lauderdale on an authentic **gondola ride** (p224), and discover some of the 300 miles of navigable inland waterways in 'the Venice of America'

- Take a swing on the rig of the **Flying Trapeze School** (p217) in Hollywood

- Press the shutter at sunrise as the tide rushes in at **Blowing Rocks Preserve** (p253), Jupiter Island

- Kayak Jupiter's 'Wild and Scenic' **Loxahatchee River** (p254), for close-up views of cypress knees, mangrove forests and sunning alligators

★ Jupiter Island
Loxahatchee ★
River ★ Jupiter

★ West Palm Beach

★ Fort Lauderdale
★ Hollywood & Dania

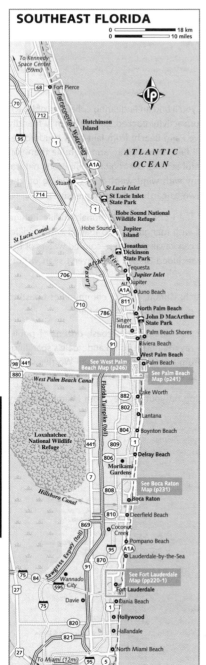

SOUTHEAST FLORIDA

History

Two words: Henry Flagler. If it weren't for this deep-pocketed visionary, southeast Florida may still be overrun with cabbage palms, bloodthirsty mosquitos and territorial gators snapping at trembling canoers. After transforming northeastern Florida into a winter wonderland in the 1870s, Flagler set his sights further south, and by the mid-1890s had already completed two world-class hotels (including the 1100-room Royal Poinciana Hotel in Lake Worth, at the time the largest wooden structure in the world), established both Palm Beach and West Palm Beach and began pushing on to Miami and the Keys.

Climate

Like the rest of South Florida, southeast Florida boasts warm temperatures year-round: 60°F on average in winter, high 70s or 80s in spring and summer. Spring, and May especially, gets the highest rainfall at around 15in.

National, State & Regional Parks

There is no shortage of parks in this region – sandy, waterfront, shady, inland or flat. Dania's John U Lloyd Beach State Park (opposite) has miles of shallow, coastal mangroves, while tiny Peanut Island (p248) in West Palm Beach delivers big fun to boaters, campers and day-trippers. When the tide's rushing in, Jupiter's Blowing Rocks Preserve (p253) stages the most dramatic show in the region, but for sheer emptiness, the windswept dunes in north Hutchinson Island (p256) win the award for Most Remote.

Information

Palm Beach Post online (www.palmbeachpost.com) A great source for all sorts of regional info.
Southeast and Florida Keys Information Pages (www.i75online.com/flse.html) A website devoted to Southeast Florida visitor information, from weather reports to activity guides.

Getting There & Around

Southeast Florida is easy to navigate – and it's a good thing, considering all the folks who want to visit. With two airports – Fort Lauderdale's big, shiny one and West Palm Beach's intimate but growing option – and plenty of easy-to-follow interstates, you can't really go wrong. Car rentals are also cheap and plentiful here.

GOLD COAST

Though the 70-or-so miles of sparkling Atlantic shoreline from Hollywood to Jupiter earned its nickname from the gold salvaged from area shipwrecks, it could easily have come from the mix of sapphire skies, cinnamon sands and wealthy residents bejeweling the region.

Here, the coastline has a split personality. First, there's slow-going, ocean-fronting Rte 1, a pleasant drive revealing infinite vistas and unspoiled beaches…though occasionally it feels like driving through the valley of a high-rise condo-canyon. Second, there's wizened, wrinkled Dixie Hwy, running parallel to Rte 1 but further inland, past dive bars, hole-in-the-wall eateries and diverse, working-class communities that sometimes forget the ocean's just a shell's throw away. Drive both stretches; each is rich with divergent offerings.

HOLLYWOOD & DANIA BEACH

☎ 954 / Hollywood pop 146,000 / Dania Beach pop 29,000

Two 'suburban Fort Lauderdale' communities have managed to make names for themselves. Hollywood, a bustling, varied waterfront town that positions itself as a gateway to Fort Lauderdale, has earned a sizable wedge of the Spring Break market since Lauderdale gave revelers the boot. The resulting influx brings with it concerts in the sand, beach-volleyball tourneys and assorted debauchery each March.

In contrast, Dania remains a mellow little town, with a fledgling antiques district and a breezy fishing pier.

Orientation & Information

Dania (dane-ya) Beach, 5 miles south of Fort Lauderdale, is mainly inland, but its small beach is delightful. Dania Beach Blvd runs between the beach/fishing pier and S Federal Hwy (US Hwy 1); its antique district goes two blocks north and south of Dania Beach Blvd along S Federal Hwy. Though it occupies just 8.5 sq miles, Dania's home to nine parks. Hollywood is just south of Dania, also mostly inland, but with a popular and bustling stretch of beach.

Greater Dania Beach Chamber of Commerce
(☎ 954-926-2323; www.greaterdania.org; 102 W Dania Beach Blvd; ☺ 9am-5pm) Lots of local info.

Hollywood Office of Tourism (☎ 954-924-2981; www.visithollywood.org; 101 N Ocean, Suite 204; ☺ 9am-5pm) Info. And some more info.

Sights & Activities

DANIA PIER

The beach action is centered on this **pier** (☎ 954-367-4423; cnr E Dania Beach Blvd & N Beach Rd; sightseeing/fishing $1/3; ☺ 24hr), which stretches almost 900ft into the Atlantic, where coral reefs begin. The pier and tackle shop are open 24/7, rod rental and bait are available for around $10, and aerated saltwater tanks along the pier keep your catch swimming while you hunt down their friends.

HOLLYWOOD BEACH & BROADWALK

Reminiscent of California's Venice Beach, the characters roaming the **beach & broadwalk** (☎ 954-921-3334) along the stretch between Sheridan St and Georgia St include local hipsters, fanny pack–wearing tourists and regular folk just trying to get to work. Standing guard over the walk are tacky T-shirt shops, ice-cream vendors, snack shacks and bars. The Broadwalk itself is a 2.2-mile, six-person-wide cement path hosting its fair share of strollers, rollerbladers, cyclists and reveling locals. If you feel like rolling along it, **Bike Shack** (☎ 954-925-2453; 101 N Ocean Dr; daily $30) offers rentals on everything from fat-tire cruisers to multi-speed racers. The beach is wi-fi enabled.

KAYAKING

Once an important stop for Prohibition-era bootleggers, lush Whiskey Creek (get it?), nestled inside **John U Lloyd Beach State Park** (☎ 954-923-2833; www.floridastateparks.org/lloydbeach; ☺ 8am-sundown), is now a kayaking hotspot. The dense mangrove-lined route, roughly 2.5 miles long, is shallow, calm, ideal for beginners and just 15 minutes from downtown Dania. **Full Moon Kayak Co** (☎ 954-328-5231; www.fullmoonkayak.com; adult/child under 14 yr $65/25; ☺ 10am-6pm Mon-Sat) runs day trips here, which average three hours. No guarantees but they have spotted manatees.

FLYING TRAPEZE

Fly through the air with the greatest of ease at the **Flying Trapeze School** (☎ 954-873-7056; www.flyinggaonastrapeze.com; 1800 Hollywood Blvd; ☺ 4:30pm-10pm Wed & Thu, noon-7:30pm Sat, 2:30pm-8pm Sun), whose rig winters at Young Circle Park (at the intersection of Hollywood Blvd and US 1. Sign up for a single class, which teaches the basics of soaring through South Florida's breezes, or schedule a series of classes and

SOUTHEAST FLORIDA

really get your swing on. Just curious? A try-out swing is $10.

Sleeping

There's an abundance of chain hotels in Hollywood and Dania, but you can find some unique options among them.

our pick Hollywood by the Sea (☎ 954-927-5301; www.hollywoodbytheseabandb.com; 301 Jackson St, Hollywood; r from $129; 🖳) Twenty steps from the beach, this homey, eight-room B&B boasts vaulted ceilings, wood floors and a fun pool area (with lots of shade if you need it).

Desoto (☎ 954-923-7210; www.thedesoto.com; 315 DeSoto St, Dania; studios $150-175, r $175-250; P 🖳) The six lovingly remodeled apartments feature Italian-tile bathrooms, granite countertops and stainless-steel cookware. The eight studio-efficiencies are small but very clean and bright. Right on the beach, all the units are only a sandy half-mile stroll to the pier.

Westin Diplomat Resort & Spa (☎ 954-602-600; 3555 S Ocean Dr, Hollywood; r & ste $215-395; P 🖳 🛉) The old Hollywood Diplomat was a grand dame in its day; the renovated palace, the result of a 2002 makeover, is a diva today. It's got more than 1000 rooms, a glass-bottom swimming pool flowing into a separate 240ft lagoon pool below, palm trees in the lobby and a day spa all overlooking a private beach.

Seminole Hard Rock Hotel & Casino (☎ 866-502-7529; www.seminolehardrockhollywood.com; 1 Seminole Way, Hollywood; r from $239; P 🖳 🛉) This Mediterranean-style monster provides everything you'd ever need under one massive roof. In this case, it's casinos, eateries, theaters, a day spa, 500 swank guest rooms and some of the most alluring concert bills in the state. It's all very Vegas. Except for the 4.5-acre lagoon-style pool totally surrounding a bar – *that's* out of this world.

Eating

Coral Rose Café (☎ 954-925-4414; 1840 Harrison St, Hollywood; mains $4-9; 🕑 7am-3pm Mon-Fri, from 8am Sat & Sun) Homemade breads (and cinnamon rolls), build-your-own eggs benedict and zero attitude, this local fave is off the southwest edge of Young Circle Park.

Jaxson's Ice Cream Parlor (☎ 954-923-4445; www.jaxsonsicecream.com; mains from $4; 128 S Federal Hwy, Dania; 🕑 noon-midnight) Originally opened in 1956, this place has 80-plus flavors of homemade ice cream. Come hungry and try one of their signature gourmet concoctions like the meant-to-be-shared Kitchen Sink – several *gallons* of ice cream served in a real kitchen sink!

our pick LeTub (☎ 954-931-9425; www.theletub.com; 1100 N Ocean Dr, Hollywood; mains $9-27; 🕑 noon-4am) Decorated exclusively with flotsam collected over four years of daybreak jogs along Hollywood Beach, this quirky spot features outdoor seating, plus bathtubs and toilet bowls sprouting lush plants. Oh, and their sirloin burger was recently named the best hamburger in the US. You know, for whatever that's worth.

Taverna Opa (☎ 954-929-4010; www.tavernaoparestaurant.com; 410 N Ocean Dr, Hollywood; mains $11-33) Thoroughly Greek (ie exuberant) and thoroughly great (ie garlicky), this place will have you shouting 'Opa!' and throwing your napkin (they don't allow you to smash your plate) before the night's out. Start with mouthwatering mezes like spanakopita and feta plates, then move on to Mediterranean dishes like barbounia (imported red mullet, pan-fried) or pastitsio (Greek lasagna).

Shopping

Josh's Organic Garden (☎ 954-456-3276; crn Harrison & S Boardwalk, Hollywood; 🕑 9am-5:30pm Sun) Under tents overlooking the ocean, Josh sells 100%

DETOUR: WANNADO CITY

Sunrise, home to the colossal Sawgrass Mills Mall (opposite) is also home to imagination-fueling **Wannado City** (☎ 954-838-7100; www.wannadocity.com; Purple Parrot Way, Sawgrass Mills Mall; over/under 14yr $7/$29.95; 🕑 variable), an enormous indoor, role-playing theme park, which asks children aged four to 11 'Whatchya wanna do?' and then lets them do it. Wearing costumes that fit their role and carrying the tools of their trade, kids can try their hands at all manner of real-life jobs, including crime-scene investigator, pilot, archaeologist, doctor – even travel writer (kidding!). Wannado doesn't just provide a reality-escape for kids, though. It also teaches them about fitness (in the co-branded Ringling Brothers wing), math (while measuring ingredients in the restaurant-style kitchen) and finance: each kidizen is provided some Wongas, the city's official currency, spendable throughout the park.

certified organic fruits, veggies, nuts and juices in PLA cups (made from corn, so it's compostable, like the bags he provides). Buy lots, because it's good for you, but don't feel compelled to spend: whatever remains is donated to a homeless shelter.

Sawgrass Mills Mall (12801 W Sunrise Blvd, Sunrise; ☉ 10am-9:30pm Mon-Sat, 11am-8pm Sun) Florida's largest retail and entertainment center, Sawgrass features 350-plus name-brand stores and outlets, so budget a whole day. From Dania or Hollywood, take I-95 north to I-595 W, follow it about 10 miles, turn right onto NW 124th Ave (S Flamingo Rd), left onto W Sunrise Blvd and right onto Purple Parrot Pl.

Getting There & Around

Hollywood has two main bus-transfer points: at Young Circle at US Hwy 1, and on Hollywood Blvd, further west at the city center. From **Broward Central Terminal** (☎ 954-357-8400) take Broward County Transit (BCt) bus 1 or 9 to Young Circle, then transfer to bus 6 or 7 to Hollywood or to Hollywood Beach.

By car, take US Hwy 1 (pretty but slow), Hwy A1A or I-95 (fast but ugly).

In Dania, the BCt bus 1 runs from Broward Central Terminal to Dania Beach Blvd. An eastbound bus 7 goes from there to the beach every 20 minutes on weekdays and every 30 to 40 minutes on weekends. If you're driving, turn east down Dania Beach Blvd and follow it to the end. Metered parking is available at the beach.

From either city, get to the Fort Lauderdale/Hollywood Airport (BCt Bus 1 takes you) and jump on **Tri-Rail** (☎ 954-359-1200; www.tri-rail.com; 200 Terminal Dr), which'll shoot you north to West Palm Beach or south to Miami.

FORT LAUDERDALE
☎ 954 / pop 165,000

For years Fort Lauderdale was known as *the* destination for beer-swilling college students on raucous Spring Breaks: drunk 19-year-old girls in wet T-shirt contests, hordes of sun-burned boys chugging beer beachside, all of them obediently standing a 24-hour keg-side vigil. Ah, those were the days. However, in the mid-1980s, the city decided to outlaw activities leading to alcohol-fueled bacchanalia. Since then, Fort Lauderdale has been angling for more mature and sophisticated visitors with its myriad offerings (though there's still plenty

of carrying-on within the confines of area bars and nightclubs). The city's Port Everglades is even the winter home to the swanky *Queen Mary II* cruise ship, for heaven's sake.

Few visitors venture far inland – except maybe to dine and shop along Las Olas Blvd; most spend the bulk of their time on the coast, frolicking at water's edge. It's understandable. Truly, it's hard to compete with beautiful beaches, a system of Venicelike waterways, an international yachting scene, spiffy new hotels, top-notch restaurants and gay hotspots.

Orientation

Fort Lauderdale, 40 miles north of Miami, is set out in a grid, though the canals sometimes interrupt what would otherwise be a straight shot. It's divided into three chunks: the beach, east of the Intracoastal Waterway; downtown, on the mainland; and Port Everglades, the cruise port south of the city. US Hwy 1 (also called Federal Hwy) cuts through downtown, while Hwy A1A runs along the ocean and may also go by several other names, depending if you're north of Sunrise Blvd (expect to see N Atlantic Blvd or Ocean Blvd) or south of it (look for N Fort Lauderdale Beach Blvd). The major roads leading to downtown and the beach are Sunrise Blvd to the north, Las Olas Blvd in the center and 17th St to the south.

Information

Clark's Out of Town News (☎ 954-467-1543; 303 S Andrews Ave, Downtown) For both local and foreign newspapers. Pick up a copy of the alternative weekly *New Times* to get the scoop on eating, arts and nightlife.
Convention & Visitors Bureau (☎ 954-765-4466; www.sunny.org; 100 E Broward Blvd, Suite 200) Has an excellent array of visitor information about hotels and attractions in the greater Fort Lauderdale region.
Post office (☎ 954-764-6501; 1404 E Las Olas Blvd, Suite B) Not the main one, but well located.

Sights & Activities
MUSEUM OF ART
Vigorously reinventing itself, this curvaceous **museum** (☎ 954-525-5500; www.moafl.org; 1 E Las Olas Blvd; adult/senior/child 6-17yr $10/7/7; ☉ 11am-7pm Wed-Mon) is one of Florida's standouts. The impressive permanent collection includes works by Picasso, Matisse, Dalí and Warhol, plus a growing and impressive collection of Cuban, African and South American art. Moreover, its exhibitions are becoming increasingly

FORT LAUDERDALE

INFORMATION
Clark's Out of Town News........1 F8
Greater Fort Lauderdale Convention &
  Visitors Bureau....................2 A3
Post Office...............................3 C4

SIGHTS & ACTIVITIES
Best Boat Club..........................4 F5
Bonnet House...........................5 F1
Carrie B...................................6 B4
Fish Culture..............................7 F5
Fort Lauderdale Ghost Tours...(see 12)
Fort Lauderdale Parasail..............8 F5
Gondola Rides...........................9 C4
IMAX...................................(see 13)
Jungle Queen Riverboat..............10 F5
Las Olas Riverfront....................11 E8
Museum of Art.........................12 F8
Museum of Discovery & Science..13 D8
Sea Experience.........................14 F5
Stranahan House........................15 B4
Trolley Stop.............................16 F3

SLEEPING
Lago Mar Resort.......................17 F7
Pillars....................................18 F3
Pineapple Point........................19 C3
Riverside Hotel........................20 B4

St Regis Resort and Spa...............21 F3
Schubert Resort.........................22 D2
Seaside Motel...........................23 F3
Sheraton Yankee Clipper............24 F5
Silver Seas Beach Club...............25 F3
Tropi Rock Resort......................26 F2

EATING
Canyon Southwest Café..............27 D1
Casablanca Café........................28 F3
Ciao Café................................29 F4
Lester's Diner...........................30 B8
Primanti Brothers.....................31 F1
Seasons 52..............................32 E1
Shula's...................................33 F3
Stork's Bakery..........................34 C4
Timpano's...............................35 B4

DRINKING
Dicey Riley's.............................36 E8
Elbo Room...............................37 F4
Lulu's Bait Shack......................38 F3
Poor House..............................39 E8

ENTERTAINMENT
Copa.......................................40 B8
Golden Lyon Bar...................(see 20)
Voodoo Lounge........................41 E8

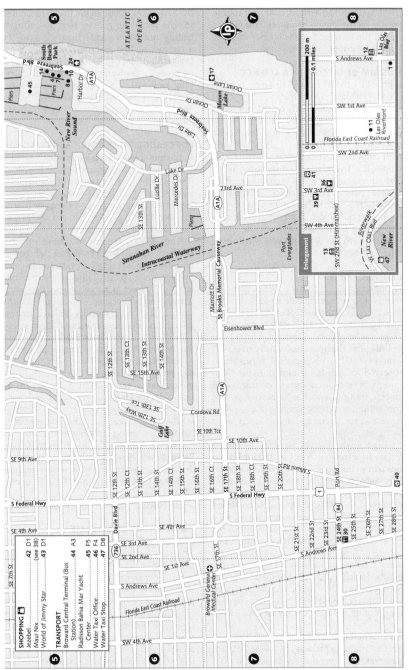

challenging and powerful…or at least appealing: the recent 'Tutankhamun and the Golden Age of the Pharaohs' made history as South Florida's most popular exhibition ever.

MUSEUM OF DISCOVERY & SCIENCE

Fronted by the intricate 52ft Great Gravity Clock, Florida's largest kinetic-energy sculpture, this environmentally oriented **museum** (☎ 954-467-6637; www.mods.org; 401 SW 2nd St; adult/senior/child 2-12yr $15/14/12; ⊗ 10am-5pm Mon-Sat, noon-6pm Sun) is a treat for kids of all ages, with exhibits on rocket ships, Florida ecoscapes the Everglades restoration efforts. The admission price also includes one **IMAX 3D show**. Before leaving, check out the **parabolic display** across the street: two dishes face each other 60ft apart. Turn toward one dish and have a friend turn toward the other. Whisper into the dish and you'll hear each other perfectly.

HISTORIC HOMES

A fine example of Florida 'vernacular' design is also one of Florida's oldest homes, the landmark **Stranahan House** (☎ 954-524-4736; www.stranahanhouse.com; 335 SE 6th Ave; admission $12; ⊗ 9:30am-4:30pm Mon-Fri). Constructed from Dade County pine, the house has wide porches, tall windows and many original furnishings. It served as both home and store for Ohio transplant Frank Stranahan, who built a small empire trading with the Seminoles before committing suicide by jumping into the New River after real-estate and stock-market losses in the late 1920s.

Hugh Taylor Birch, after being blown ashore in a freak accident in 1893, believed this part of the world was where God wanted him. Subsequently, he purchased 3 miles of beachfront property (for $1 per acre) and developed it. Today, the picturesque **Bonnet House** (☎ 954-563-5393; www.bonnethouse.org; 900 N Birch Rd; adult/senior/child 6-18yr $20/18/16, grounds only $10; ⊗ 10am-4pm Tue-Sat, noon-4pm Sun) stands as a tribute to Birch and features 35 subtropical acres overflowing with native and imported plants, including a vast orchid collection. Seeing the art-filled house requires a guided tour (and 1¼ hours) but you're free to wander the grounds and nature trails on your own.

RIVERWALK & LAS OLAS RIVERFRONT

This meandering **pathway** (☎ 954-468-1541; www.goriverwalk.com), along the New River, runs from the Stranahan House to the Broward Center for the Performing Arts. Host to culinary tastings and other events, the walk connects a number of sights, restaurants and shops. **Las Olas Riverfront** (☎ 954-522-6556; cnr SW 1st Ave & Las Olas Blvd) is basically a giant alfresco shopping mall with stores, restaurants, a movie theater and live entertainment nightly; it's also the place to catch many river cruises (see p224).

FORT LAUDERDALE BEACH & PROMENADE

In the mid-1990s, this promenade received a $26 million renovation, and boy-oh-boy, does it show. A magnet for runners, rollerbladers, walkers and cyclists, the wide, brick, palm-tree-dotted pathway swoops along the beach, running parallel to A1A. You can also surf at Fort Lauderdale beach.

And what a beach it is, stretching from the southern edge of **South Beach Park** (where the cruise ships pass) north 7 miles to Lauderdale-by-the-Sea (see p228). Thirty public-parking facilities – expect to pay about a buck an hour, if you can find a meter – serve the smooth, white beaches here, recently declared among the nation's cleanest, safest and most accessible. The 27.5-acre **South Beach** is the most family friendly, regularly hosting basketball games, beach-volleyball tourneys and family reunions at the on-site grills and picnic tables. Further north, the stretch across from E Las Olas Blvd is less for recreation and more for, um, sightseeing. Expect olive-skinned, oiled-up saline queens and European guys in banana-hammocks strutting their stuff.

Even further north, dog-friendly **Canine Beach** (☎ 954-828-7275; cnr Sunrise Blvd & N Atlantic Blvd; ⊗ 3pm-7pm winter, 5pm-9pm summer; weekend permits $6) is the 100-yard swath running from E Sunrise Blvd to lifeguard station 5.

For beach conditions, call ☎ 954-828-4597.

HUGH TAYLOR BIRCH STATE RECREATION AREA

This state **park** (☎ 954-564-4521; 3109 E Sunrise Blvd; per vehicle/cyclist $4/1; ⊗ 8am-sunset), which recently enjoyed a major renovation of its trails, contains one of the last significant maritime hammocks in Broward County. There are mangroves and a freshwater-lagoon system (great for birding) and several endangered plants and animals (including the gopher tortoise and golden leather fern). You can fish, picnic, stroll the short Coastal Hammock

Trail or bike the 1.9-mile park drive. Canoe rentals, to be used on the half-mile trail, cost about $6 per hour.

WATER ACTIVITIES

If you're curious how mansions along Miracle Mile look from above, sign up for a trip with **Fort Lauderdale Parasail** (☎ 954-543-2938; 1005 Seabreeze Blvd; flights $70-95). Soar between 600ft and 1000ft above the waves while strapped securely to an enormous smiley-face parachute.

If you want to stay closer to Mother Earth, maybe a glass-bottom boat ride and snorkel excursion sounds about right. **Sea Experience** (☎ 954-467-6000; www.seaxp.com/departures.html; 801 Seabreeze Blvd; adult/child $35/21; ☺ 10:15am & 2:15pm daily) takes guests in a 40ft glass-bottom boat along the Intracoastal and into the ocean to visit a natural reef, thriving with marine life, in 10ft to 20ft of water.

For more vigorous exploration of the waterways, renting a boat is a good bet. **Best Boat Club** (☎ 954-779-3866; www.fortlauderdaleboatrentals .com; 801 Seabreeze Blvd; per vehicle/cyclist $4/1; ☺ 8am-sunset) rents everything from single-engine 21ft Bowriders to luxurious 27ft Crownlines. Renters must be 22 years or older and have boating experience (yes, you must prove

---

SWABBING THE DECKS, CHASING DOWN TIPS – LIVING THE YACHT-CREWING LIFE
Rick Starey

Among its other nicknames – Venice of America (for its waterways) and Liquordale (for obvious reasons) – Fort Lauderdale is known among the nautical set as the yachting capital of the world. It's home to thousands of luxury motor yachts and sailboats, and somebody's gotta make them run, right? Enter a water-loving workforce with varying experience, many of whom divide their time between Fort Lauderdale (winter) and places up north such as New England (summer).

For those who join this workforce, it means great coin, idyllic destinations, incredible cultures and the mystic beauty of the ocean. Combine that with scrubbing decks, polishing stainless steel, detailing acute and minute features and then scrubbing a few more decks. Reveling in a portion of the former and getting down and dirty in a lot of the latter is the life of a deckhand aboard a luxury yacht. Here's an industry where money is flaunted for fun, excess is paramount and bottom lines are ignored at all costs.

Boat destinations are mouthwatering. Megayachts roam the world's hotspots of culture, style and ecology. In the space of a few seasons you could soak up Rio de Janeiro's sexy samba, chill with the polar bears of Alaska, revel in Spain's rich traditions, carve up the Italian piazzas, sun up in the Caribbean and explore the ecological fantasy that is the Galapagos Islands.

These floating beauties have been designed to overwhelm, entertain and exude a lifestyle that's far beyond 99.9% of the world's population. Although the monetary value of these megayachts equals the national wealth of a small country, these pricey pieces of fiberglass are, in essence, just very big toys for rather loaded boys. So loaded, in fact, that the vast majority of megayachts run at a monumental loss – to the delight of the owners' accountants – year in, year out.

Life on board requires a certain type of individual, as close quarters, communal living and a stacked dictatorship come together to provide a unique atmosphere. Always present is a heavily regimented pecking order essential in any offshore activity. Another aspect is that you can't leave the office, meaning you are at the ship's beck and call 24/7. Even when you're nursing a nasty hangover.

The job of a 'decky' could best be described as a jack-of-all-trades gig. You become a world-class cleaner, meaning your chamois is not only your best mate but also your greatest tool. You'll learn a bit about engines, fiddle with radars, paint anchors, throw heaving lines, study weather patterns and maybe even learn to read a chart or two. But, above all, the quality of a deckhand is best judged in two simple departments: work ethic and an eye for detail.

Fort Lauderdale is the place to be for aspiring crewmen, as it's justifiably regarded as the world's center for luxury yachting where thousands of captains look for their next crew. The megayacht industry can be a postcard lifestyle: sailing off into another perfect sunset with tax-free cash, lifelong friends and crystal-clear memories. The yachting game at its best is almost unbeatable; at its worst, well, did I mention the decks?

Rick Starey is a Lonely Planet author as well as a deckhand on board a luxury yacht.

it). Rates start at $219 per day, plus fuel, oil, insurance and tax.

The waters off Fort Lauderdale are rich with marlin, sailfish, snapper, tarpon, wahoo and more. Naturally, there are plenty of fishing charters available, like **Fish Lauderdale** (☎ 954-764-8723; www.fishlauderdale.com; 801 Seabreeze Blvd; up to 6 people, per hour $125; ⏰ 8am-sunset), which has four boats to take you trolling for dinner.

Tours

Carrie B (☎ 954-768-9920; www.carriebcruises.com; tours adult/child under 12yr $17/10) is where locals take guests, so if you're alone, pick a family and join them. This narrated waterfront tour on a replica 19th-century riverboat lasts 90 minutes, and paddle-wheels past some of the biggest homes fronting the New River and the Intracoastal. Tours leave at 11am, 1pm and 3pm from Las Olas at SE 5th Ave.

Jungle Queen Riverboat (☎ 954-462-5596; www.junglequeen.com; 801 Seabreeze Blvd; adult/child $16.50/11.75) runs three-hour tours along the waterfront, Millionaires' Row and part of the Everglades on a Mississippi-style paddle-wheeler; four-hour evening excursions include all-you-can-eat shrimp or BBQ dinners and entertainment ($37).

Enjoy a narrated **Trolley Tour** (☎ 954-761-3543; www.suntrolley.com; adult/child $25/15) allowing you to hop on and off all day – past the cruise ship port, luxury yachts and homes, beaches and historic sites. Bottled water is provided; protection from corny trolley-driver jokes is not.

With over 300 miles of navigable inland waterways, Fort Lauderdale is known as 'the Venice of America.' For a peaceful, relaxing tour of the man-made finger lakes here, arrange for a **gondola ride** (☎ 877-926-2467; www.gondolaman.com; ride $125) during which an authentically dressed gondolier will share with you the history of gondolas and of Fort Lauderdale – or keep quiet and let you sip your champagne and soak it all in. Rides depart from the canal adjacent to 1109 E Las Olas Blvd.

Fort Lauderdale Ghost Tours (☎ 954-523-1501; www.flghosts.com; adult/child under 13yr $18/13) offers 90-minute lantern-led tours along the historic district on the banks of the New River. Tours depart from the Museum of Art (see p219).

Sleeping

The splashiest hotels are found along the beach. Of course, those places are also the priciest. Meander inland, and you'll discover some wonderful inns with Old-Florida charm, many of which exclusively welcome gay guests (these are noted below).

BUDGET

Beach Hostel (☎ 954-567-7275; www.fortlauderdalehostel.com; 2115 N Ocean Blvd; dm $20, r $45-55; **P** **□**) With 61 beds, three kitchens, two TV rooms and one prime location (a block from the sand and a mile from the main beach), this two-story motel-turned-bungalow provides something virtually no one else does: dirt-cheap accommodation in Fort Lauderdale.

Tropi Rock Resort (☎ 954-564-0523; www.tropirock.com; 2900 Belmar St; r summer $76-118, winter $107-180; **P** **□** **♨**) Close enough to the late-night strip for an easy walk home, but far enough to sleep in silence, this bright sanctuary offers a variety of clean rooms, a flower-ringed pool and hand-laid mosaics around each corner.

Seaside Motel (☎ 954-462-1352; www.floridaseasidemotel.com; 350 N Birch Rd; r $110-180; **P** **♨**) This clean, old-style motel (plus its sister property next door) offers low-frills rooms and efficiencies to delight any beachgoer – especially since the beach is less than a block away. There's a pool on-site and gas BBQs, too. Small pets are OK, but Spring Breakers are turned away.

MIDRANGE

Silver Seas Beach Club (☎ 954-467-2531; 101 N Atlantic Blvd; r $135-220) With its ziggurat stylings and Key lime paint job, this exquisitely landscaped time-share looks like it picked up and moved from Miami's art-deco district. Pros: a complete kitchen in each unit, a pool, a shuffleboard court, and ocean views. Cons: maid service is only provided with a week's rental and a three-night minimum stay is usually invoked.

Schubert Resort (☎ 866-763-7435, 954-763-7434; www.schubertresort.com; 855 NE 20th Ave; r summer $99-209, winter $159-309; **P** **□** **♨**) One of the area's many gay inns, this retro place – the recipient of a recent $2.5 million renovation – is housed in the shell of a 1953 motel but is thoroughly modern. Behind the neon sign out front you'll find sleek rooms with marble baths and boldly striped bedspreads, many of them surrounding the lovely (clothing-optional) pool area and 10-man Jacuzzi.

Riverside Hotel (☎ 954-467-0671, 800-325-3280; www.riversidehotel.com; 620 E Las Olas Blvd; r $139-469; **P** **□** **♨**) This 1936 hotel, smack in the middle of downtown and fronted by stately columns, oozes an old-fashioned, Old Florida charm. Although it was previously not among the most stylish sleeps in Lauderdale, a recent renovation added glass-enclosed showers and new carpet. Its Las Olas location is a huge plus.

TOP END

Pineapple Point (☎ 888-844-7295; www.pineapple point.com; 315 NE 16th Terrace; r $179-269, ste $279-679; **P ☐ ☑**) A supremely stylish gay guesthouse set in intimate, verdant surroundings, the Point boasts tasteful rooms with four-poster beds, sumptuous duvets, hardwood floors and sun porches. There's a clothing-optional pool, too, of course.

ourpick Lago Mar Resort (☎ 800-524-6627, 954-523-6511; www.lagomar.com; 1700 S Ocean Lane; r $180-560; **P ☐ ☑**) On the south end of South Beach, this wonderfully noncorporate resort has it all: a private beach, over-the-top grand lobby, massive island-style rooms, a full-service spa, on-site eateries and the personal touch of family ownership.

Pillars (☎ 954-467-9639, 800-800-7666; www.pillars hotel.com; 111 N Birch Rd; r $185-550; **P ☐ ☑**) This luxe Key West–style retreat features plantation-style rooms surrounding a courtyard pool, a private dock with outdoor dining, a beautiful lobby with hardwood floors and lushly landscaped grounds. It's a block from the beach, half a mile from E Las Olas Blvd and facing one of the best sunsets in town.

Pelican Grand Beach Resort (☎ 954-568-9431; www.pelicangrandresort.com; 2000 N Ocean Blvd; r $185-359; **P ☐ ☑**) Featuring cushy, oversized furniture, a wraparound veranda, private balconies with oceanfront views and a heated pool, this immaculate resort isn't just about elegance. It also screams fun, since it's home to Lauderdale's only lazy river water-ride.

Sheraton Yankee Clipper (☎ 1-800-325-3535; 1140 Seabreeze Blvd; r $199-349; **P ☐ ☑**) It smells like a Sheraton and has all the amenities of a Sheraton, but this sprawling, 500-room complex (one of the three nautical-themed buildings resembles a giant cruise ship) offers an unbeatable mix of comfort and convenience. Straddling both uberpopular South Beach and the 40 bus line, this behemoth is the hub for many of the area's beach-based expos.

St Regis Resort & Spa (☎ 954-465-2300; www .starwoodhotels.com; 1 N Fort Lauderdale Beach Blvd; r from $250; **P ☐ ☑**) Looking like a backdrop for a J Lo music video, this exclusive hotel has five stars, 24 stories and endless amenities,

including a prime beachfront location, an upscale restaurant, a 17,000-sq-ft full-service spa and large rooms blessed with both ocean and Intracoastal views.

Eating

BUDGET

Ciao Cafe (☎ 954-463-4054; 411 S Fort Lauderdale Beach Blvd; mains $3-7) You gotta pay for the fresh gelatos, salads and sandwiches here but the wi-fi's free.

Lester's Diner (☎ 954-525-5641; 250 SE 24th St; mains $4-17; ☹ 24hr) Hailed endearingly as a greasy spoon, campy Lester's Diner has been keeping folks happy since the late 1960s. Everyone makes their way here at some point, from business types on cell phones to clubbers to blue-haired ladies with third husbands.

Primanti Brothers (☎ 954-565-0605; www.primanti brothers.com; 901 N Fort Lauderdale Beach Blvd; mains $5.35-15.50; ☹ 24hr) Don't come here if you're (a) a prissy eater or (b) only sorta hungry. Primanti serves traditional Italian dishes, but what really makes famished diners salivate is the sandwiches. Served on Italian bread piled high with slaw, cheese, your choice of meat *and a mountain of steaming fries*, the whole thing's smashed flat and wrapped in butcher paper. This greasy double-fister is the perfect antidote to the hangover you're about to start nursing.

MIDRANGE

Stork's Bakery (☎ 954-522-4670; www.storkscafe.com; 1109 E Las Olas Blvd; mains $4-17; ☹ 8am-9pm Sun-Thu, to midnight Fri & Sat) Fresh breads, rich cheeses and crispy veggies load the sandwiches in this tastefully appointed, canal-fronting bakery-café, which also serves intriguing salads (like roasted sweet potato), exceptional soups, coffees and more sweets than you can handle.

Sublime (☎ 954-539-9000; www.sublimeveg.com; 1431 N Federal Hwy; mains $10-19; ☹ 5:30-10pm Tue-Sun) This modern vegan palace (which even carnivores will love!) boasts a massive menu, a take-out café and a boutique with cruelty-free products from chips to soaps. The menu changes daily but always reflects various world cuisines, with colorful options such as hydroponic arugula salad, gardein-and-black-bean enchiladas, portobello filet mignon, plus a slew of veggie sushi rolls.

TOP END

ourpick Casablanca Cafe (☎ 954-764-3500, www .casablancacafeonline.com; 3049 Alahambra St; lunch $10-22, dinner $13-38; 11:30am-1am Sun-Tue, 11:30am-2am Wed-Sat) On Wednesdays, Fridays and Saturdays, this sophisticated bar grooves with night-time entertainment, but the real attraction at this romantic, hibiscus-ringed café is the delightful Mediterranean-inspired dishes; try the twisted hummus or the fennel-infused steamed mussels. Order a sublime frozen mojito, head up to the oceanfront balcony and watch cruise ships inch along the horizon.

Timpano's (954-462-9119; www.timpanochophouse .net; 450 Las Olas Blvd; mains $14-36; lunch & dinner) Be sure to bring your tommy gun when you come to this Italian-flavored martini bar and chophouse. With its heavy velvet draperies, starched white tablecloths, oversized chandeliers and swooping, question-mark-shaped bar, you'll feel like you're in the mafia when you cut into your dry-aged hand-cut filet or bass *aqua pazza*.

Rustic Inn (954-584-1637; www.rusticinn.com; 4331 Ravenswood Rd; mains $14-73; lunch & dinner) Don't wear your Sunday best here – or bring a date you want to whisper sweet nothings to. Hungry locals at this messy, noisy crabhouse use wooden mallets at long, newspaper-covered tables to get at the good stuff served here. The house specialty is crabs – choose from Dungeness, blue or golden – drenched in garlic and a secret family recipe (think: butter). Not in a crabby mood? This hearty, happy family-style restaurant has schools of seafood and pasta options.

Canyon Southwest Café (954-765-1950; www .canyonfl.com; 1818 E Sunrise Blvd; mains $11-35) This popular eatery is Santa Fe–chic, specializing in tasty, southwestern fusion grub such as smoked-salmon tostadas and filet mignon with a rich poblano-pepper goat cheese. Don't miss the fine tequilas or the sweet prickly-pear margarita, which fuel the raucous din from late-night diners.

Seasons 52 (954-537-1052; www.seasons52.com; 2428 E Sunrise Blvd; mains $12-27; lunch & dinner) This sophisticated grill prepares market-fresh, seasonal meals – like sea scallops with roasted asparagus or grilled boneless trout with new potatoes – using natural cooking techniques to provide the best taste and the least guilt. In fact, every nutritionally balanced menu item has no more than 475 calories – including dessert. Plus, they have 140 kinds of wine. Wow.

Mai-Kai (954-563-3272; www.maikai.com; 3599 N Federal Hwy; mains $17-38; 5-10:30pm Mon-Thu, 5-11:30pm Fri-Sat) This old-school Polynesian joint is pure kitsch – with some good food and

amusing entertainment thrown in for grins. Las Vegas–style shows (additional $10.95) follow the meals, which range from Hawaiian chicken and seafood with noodles to the massive oak-roasted filet mignon Madagascar for two ($60). Don't miss the froofy cocktails, including the potent 'mystery drink.'

Shula's (954-355-4000; www.donshula.com; 321 N Fort Lauderdale Beach Blvd; mains from $35) Owned by former Miami Dolphins coach Don Shula, this elegant (if slightly stuffy) steakhouse is a must-visit if you're a fan of either the Dolphins or steak. Their thing is certified Angus beef, cut thick and seared fast – and they do it impeccably. They also serve seafood, but vegetarians may be wild-eyed at the shortage of options.

Drinking & Entertainment

Fort Lauderdale bars can stay open until 4am on weekends and 2am during the week. For gay and lesbian venues, see opposite.

Culture Room (954-564-1074; www.cultureroom .net; 3045 N Federal Hwy) An intimate spot to catch live music, from Broken Social Scene to the Robert Cray Band.

Poor House (954-522-5145; 110 SW 3rd Ave; 5pm-2am) Great brews, diverse live music (usually blues, funk, rock) and a multigenerational crowd.

Dicey Riley's (954-522-2202; 217 SW 2nd St) Your standard Irish pub, with traditional cuisine, draft Guinness and Bass and live Irish bands Tuesday to Saturday.

Lulu's Bait Shack (954-463-7425; 17 S Fort Lauderdale Beach Blvd, Suite 212) A great view of the beach can be seen over the rims of the fishbowl cocktails this place serves.

Elbo Room (954-463-4615; www.elboroom.com; 241 N Fort Lauderdale Beach Blvd) Open since 1938, this dive achieved immortality thanks to the '60s classic 'Where the Boys Are.' It hit its stride during the Spring Break years, but keeps going with drink specials and great music that attracts the young, beer-swilling, hip-shaking set.

Voodoo Lounge (954-522-0733; www.voodoolounge florida.com; 111 SW 2nd Ave; 10pm-4am Wed-Sun) Here you'll find 50,000 watts of booty-shaking sound, plus 'Rodman's Rehab,' a wing of the club designed by basketball player/madman Dennis Rodman.

Shooters (954-566-2855; www.shooterscafe.com; 3033 NE 32nd Ave; 11:30am-late) It's old-school Lauderdale raucousness here, with great live music, waterfront views and strong drinks.

Shopping

Fort Lauderdale Beach Blvd has a gaggle of T-shirt shops and sunglass huts.

Check it, bro: the flip-flop selection at **Maui Nix** (☎ 954-522-5255; 17 S Fort Lauderdale Beach Blvd) surf shop is totally boss, and the place crawls with bunnies.

Don't be surprised to see a bona-fide celeb cruising the pink showroom at the **World of Jimmy Star** (☎ 954-828-9979; www.worldofjimmystar.com; 1940 E Sunrise Blvd; 11am-9pm Mon-Thu, to 10pm Fri & Sat, to 6pm Sun), filled with one-of-a-kind 'art to wear' that's a provocative blend of '70s porn, '80s glam and '90s urban.

Next door, **Jezebel** (☎ 954-761-7881; http://www.myspace.com/jezebelchic; 1980 E Sunrise Blvd) offers racks of vintage clothes and accessories alongside new shoes, funky tees and Disney-esque handbags.

Getting There & Away

AIR

Fort Lauderdale-Hollywood International Airport (FLL; ☎ 954-359-1200; www.fll.net; 🖳) is easy to reach from I-95 or US 1 and sandwiched about halfway between Lauderdale and Hollywood. The airport is served by more than 35 airlines, including some with nonstop flights from Europe. There's also free wi-fi throughout the airport. In fact, FLL is so hassle-free and accessible that many Miami visitors choose to fly from here. From the airport, it's a short 20-minute drive to downtown, or a $20 cab ride.

BOAT

The **Port Everglades Authority** (☎ 954-523-3404) runs the enormous Port Everglades cruise port (the second busiest in the world after Miami). From the port, walk to SE 17th St and take bus 40 to the beach or to Broward Central Terminal.

If you're heading to Fort Lauderdale in your own boat (not that unlikely here), head for the **Radisson Bahia Mar Yacht Center** (☎ 800-755-9558).

BUS

The **Greyhound station** (☎ 954-764-6551; www.greyhound.com; 515 NE 3rd St at Federal Hwy) is about four blocks from Broward Central Terminal (p228), the central transfer point for buses in the area. Buses to Miami leave throughout the day (one-way $5, 30 to 60 minutes) but, depending on when you arrive, you might have to wait as long as 2½ hours for the next one.

TRAIN

Tri-Rail (☎ 800-874-7245; www.tri-rail.com) runs between Miami and Fort Lauderdale (round-trip $6.75, 45 minutes). A feeder system of buses has connections at no charge. Free parking is provided at most stations. Provide ample cushion for delays. **Amtrak** (☎ 800-872-7245, www.amtrak.com) also uses Tri-Rail tracks. **Fort Lauderdale Amtrak station** (200 SW 21st Tce) is just south of Broward Blvd and just west of I-95.

Getting Around

If you're driving here, I-95 and Florida's Turnpike run north–south. I-595, the major east–west artery, intersects I-95, Florida's Turnpike and the Sawgrass Expressway. It also feeds into I-75, which runs to Florida's west coast.

Once in town, driving provides the best way to access spread-out Lauderdale. But the flatness here makes it easy to get around by bike. Check with your hotel – many have bikes to loan or rent.

TMAX (☎ 954-761-3543), a free shuttle bus, runs every 15 minutes or so between downtown sights, between the beach and E Las Olas Blvd and the Riverfront, and between Tri-Rail and E Las Olas Blvd and the beaches. **Broward County Transit** (BCT; ☎ 954-831-4000; 200 W Broward Blvd) operates between downtown, the beach and Port Everglades. The fare is $1.25 for adults, 60¢ for seniors and children; an all-day pass is $3, or $2 for seniors and children. From **Broward Central Terminal** (☎ 954-357-8400), take bus 11 to upper Fort Lauderdale Beach and Lauderdale-by-the-Sea; bus 4 to Port Everglades; and bus 40 to 17th St and the beaches.

The fun, yellow **Water Taxi** (☎ 954-467-6677; www.watertaxi.com; 651 Seabreeze Blvd) travels the canals and waterways between 17th St to the south, Atlantic Blvd/Pompano Beach to the north, the Riverfront to the west and the Atlantic Ocean to the east. A $13 daily pass entitles you to unlimited rides.

LAUDERDALE-BY-THE-SEA & DEERFIELD BEACH

☎ 954 / Lauderdale-by-the-Sea pop 6000 / Deerfield Beach pop 76,000

If you're looking for a relatively quiet coastal community with an authentic beach vibe, keep reading. The main draws at these two sleepy seaside communities are spectacular sandy beaches and close-at-hand eating and drinking options; around here, it's easy to park your car and leave it for the duration.

Orientation & Information

Seven miles north of Fort Lauderdale, Lauderdale-by-the-Sea is a small but festive town centered on the intersection of

Commercial Blvd, running east to the ocean and El Mar Dr, a divided road running north–south with shops, bars and eateries.

Deerfield Beach is 9 miles north of Lauderdale-by-the-Sea (5 miles south of Boca Raton). You'll find most of the action here near the dog-legged intersection of E Hillsboro Blvd, running east to the Atlantic, and N Ocean Blvd, running parallel to it.

Deerfield Beach Chamber of Commerce (☎ 954-427-1050; www.deerfieldchamber.com; 1601 E Hillsboro Blvd)

Lauderdale-by-the-Sea Chamber of Commerce (☎ 954-776-1000; www.lbts.com; 4201 Ocean Dr) Info on businesses throughout the area.

Sights & Activities

Both Lauderdale-by-the-Sea and Deerfield Beach love their anglers. At Lauderdale-by-the-Sea's **Anglin's Pier** (☎ 954-491-9403; Commercial Blvd) you can score bait in a 24-hour tackle shop and rent a rod for $5. Lit for night fishing, the pier is an easy shuffle from the rest of town. Don't expect to hook a 300lb grouper here, though it has been done!

Further north, the **Deerfield Beach Fishing Pier** (☎ 954-426-9206; 200 NE 21st Ave) is known for large catches like king mackerel on west winds. Rods rent for $15.

No trip to Florida would be complete without a ride in a convertible. Deerfield's **Fun Rentals** (☎ 954-427-4647; 1985 A1A) rents roofless, three-wheeled, go-kartlike trigger scooters (one hour $50, 24 hours $150) plus bikes (one hour $10, 24 hours $30) and scooters (one hour $25, 24 hours $189).

Scuba diving off the coast here is popular because of the area's extensive artificial-reef program. Nearby Pompano Beach offers numerous options. At **South Florida Diving Headquarters** (☎ 954-783-2299; www.southfloridadiving.com; 101 N Riverside Dr, Pompano Beach) head out into the gorgeous glassy waters with an experienced guide. The HQ also has 45ft catamarans and glass-bottomed boats for those who want to see below without getting wet.

SKI RIXEN

Deerfield's Quiet Waters Park is home to **Ski Rixen** (☎ 954-429-0215; www.skirixen.com; 401 S Powerline Rd, Deerfield Beach; 60min/ful-day pass $18/38; ☽ 10am-7pm Tue-Sun), South Florida's only cable water-ski system. Using an innovative cabling system suspended from towers surrounding a half-mile course, water-skiers (and wake-boarders) are pulled over a wake-free water-course. Obstacles are available for advanced tricksters; otherwise, riders can perfect their water-skiing techniques without the hassle of a boat. Skiers under 18 must have a waiver form notarized and signed by their parents.

BUTTERFLY WORLD

The first indoor butterfly park in the US, **Butterfly World** (☎ 954-977-4400; 3600 W Sample Rd, Coconut Creek; www.butterflyworld.com; adult/child $21.95/16.95; ☯ 9am-5pm Mon-Sat, from 11am Sun) today is one of the largest butterfly exhibits anywhere, featuring thousands of live, exotic species, such as the bright blue morphos or camouflaged owl butterfly. Various exhibits, each highlighting different creatures – from butterflies to hummingbirds – make Butterfly World an excellent place to spend the better part of a day, especially with wide-eyed children or trigger-happy shutterbugs. Coming from I-95, exit at Sample Rd; head west.

Sleeping

Sunrider Beach Resort (☎ 954-427-7900; 100 NE 20th Tce, Deerfield Beach; r $129-289; P ☐ ☒) Sure, this fab hotel has a pool and hammocks, but who needs those when you're 70ft from the sand and 280ft from the water? Choose among the property's 18 efficiencies, suites and standard rooms. HBO, a continental breakfast and a chat with Deerfield's friendliest host are included.

Courtyard Villa (☎ 954-776-1164, 800-291-3560; www .courtyardvilla.com; 4312 El Mar Dr, Lauderdale-by-the-Sea; ste/apt $125/329; P ☐) This Mediterranean-style quartet of courtyard suites and apartments is infused with a breezy style with its ceiling fans, parquet floors and four-poster beds. Overnighters get free use of the bikes, grills, tennis courts and rooftop patio. It's no wonder rooms here go fast.

High Noon Resort (☎ 954-776-1121; www.highnoon resort.com; 4424 El Mar Dr, Lauderdale-by-the-Sea; r/cabana $173/387; P ☐ ☒) Spilling onto the beach, this ultraclean motel-resort includes two sister properties, the Sea Foam (apartment-styled stays) and the Nautilus (for those seeking seclusion). Guests can enjoy the property's seven tiki huts, two pools and shuffleboard court. Steps from bars and restaurants, nothing says Florida like relaxing under this property's numerous palm

trees and listening to the sea breeze rustle the leaves.

Eating & Drinking

Country Ham & Eggs (☎ 954-776-1666; www.country hamneggs.com; 4405 El-Mar Dr, Lauderdale-by-the-Sea; meals $5.25-10; ☯ 7am-2:30pm) Since 1968, this sociable place has been firing up the griddle to cook various Benedicts, 'rolled omelettes' and French wheels (thick French toast topped with eggs and sausage). Breakfast is served all day; lunch is stellar, too.

Rattlesnake Jake's (☎ 954-421-4481; 2060 NE 2nd St, Deerfield Beach; mains $8-17; ☯ 11:30am-10pm Sun-Thu, to 10:30pm Fri & Sat) More Tex than Mex, this laid-back *taqueria* has a prime view of Deerfield's main drag and a bar that demands to be sidled up to. The salsa's a tad bland, but bring your own fresh-caught fish and they'll spice it up for you.

Aruba Beach Cafe (☎ 954-776-0001; www.aruba beachcafe.com; 1 Commercial Blvd, Lauderdale-by-the-Sea; mains $10-26; ☯ 11am-11pm Mon-Sat, 9am-11pm Sun) The food isn't the only reason people flock here (though the conch fritters *are* divine). There's also live music nightly, daily drink specials served from three separate bars and only a bank of sliding glass doors separating you and the beach.

Village Pump (☎ 954-776-5840; www.villagegrille .com; 4404 El Mar Dr; lunch $6-15, dinner $6-20; ☯ 8am-2am) Serves full meals throughout the day and sturdy drinks into the night.

Getting There & Around

Tri-Rail (☎ 800-874-7245; www.tri-rail.com) heads north from Fort Lauderdale. If you're driving, try to take A1A (sometimes called Ocean Blvd): the drive's glorious.

BOCA RATON

☎ 561 / pop 74,800

The name Boca Raton may mean 'mouth of the rat,' but there's nothing ratty about this proud-to-be-posh coastal town. What began as a sleepy residential community was transformed in the mid-1920s by architect Addison Mizner, who relied on his love of Spanish architecture to build the place into a fancy-pants town. His fingerprints remain on numerous structures throughout the area, though his name is most often invoked when talking about the popular anchor of town – the alfresco mall, Mizner Park. The rest of

Boca is a mostly mainstream collection of hoity-toity chain stores and restaurants and, as you near the ocean, some peaceful beaches and parks. Most people don't come to Boca on vacation unless they have family here – and that suits residents just fine.

Bizarrely, pretty much everything outside Mizner Park closes on Sunday, so don't plan on much shopping then; even dining options are limited.

Orientation

The sprawling town has neighborhoods that spread from the ocean to far west of I-95 and Florida's Turnpike.

The city's main east–west drag is Palmetto Park Rd, bisected by north–south Old Dixie Hwy, often just called Dixie Hwy, (not to be confused with Hwy 1, here called Federal Hwy); these two roads divide city addresses into north, south, east and west. Avenues, courts and places run north and south, and streets run east and west. Hwy A1A, here called Ocean Blvd, is most conveniently accessible by the bridge at Palmetto Park Rd, as well as by bridges along Spanish River Blvd to the north and Camino Real Blvd to the south.

Boca's difficult to navigate compared to more-compact beach cities nearby, so if you plan to explore, pick up a copy of the custom-made Dolph map, available at the chamber of commerce.

Information

Boca Raton News (www.bocanews.com) is published daily.

Chamber of Commerce (☎ 561-395-4433; www .bocaratonchamber.com; 1800 N Dixie Hwy) Helpful, with racks of pamphlets and the best map in town.

Library (☎ 561-393-7852; 200 NW Boca Raton Blvd; ❧ 9am-9pm Mon-Thu, to 6pm Fri & Sat, noon-8pm Sun) Free internet access.

Post office (170 NE 2nd St)

Sights & Activities

GUMBO LIMBO NATURE CENTER

Boca's best asset is not its collection of retail, cultural or culinary treats, but this condo-free stretch of waterfront parkland. The crown jewel of the system is the **Gumbo Limbo Nature Center** (☎ 561-338-1473; www.gumbolimbo.org; 1801 N Ocean Blvd; admission free; ❧ 9am-4pm Mon-Sat, noon-4pm Sun), a wild preserve of tropical hammock and dunes ecosystems. Dedicated to educating the public about sea turtles and other local

fauna, the natural-history displays include fascinating saltwater tanks full of critters – fed with leftover seafood scraps donated by local businesses. Plus, it's one of 10 places in the US where you can (legally) observe sea turtles nesting, 9pm to 11pm every Monday and Thursday between May 20 and July 11 ($5).

The preserve also has a number of secluded hikes along elevated boardwalks through tropical foliage and along an artificial mangrove wetland, reclaimed using filtered wastewater from the city. A native-flower garden attracts a slew of gemstone-colored butterflies.

BEACHES

Thanks to a unique outcrop of rock and reef just offshore, **Red Reef Beach** (☎ 561-393-7815; 1 N Ocean Blvd; per vehicle Mon-Fri $10, Sat & Sun $12; ❧ 8am-sunset) is tops for water-lovers, offering lifeguards in swimming areas, and great shallow pools for beginner snorkelers. Above water, Red Reef Beach and neighboring **South Beach Park** together encompass some 60 acres of wild shores.

MIZNER PARK

This outdoor **shopping mall** (☎ 561-362-0606; www.miznerpark.org), bounded by Federal Hwy and Mizner Blvd north of NE 2nd St, and bookended on one side by the **Boca Raton Museum of Art** (☎ 561-392-2500; www.bocamuseum.org; 501 Plaza Real; adult/child $8/4, 5-9pm Wed free; ❧ 10am-5pm Tue, Thu & Fri, 10am-9pm Wed, noon-5pm Sat & Sun) offers free valet parking plus live music on Saturday nights. The lovely mall provides a nice breezy stroll, but the abundant chain stores squelch its uniqueness. A notable exception is **Kerzen Candles** (☎ 561-362-5968; www .kerzencandles.com; 443 Plaza Real), whose non-toxic, gourmet candles are fascinating displays of waxen art.

SPORTS IMMORTALS SHOWCASE MUSEUM

Founded by sports-memorabilia collector Joel Platt, this **museum** (☎ 561-997-2575; www .sportsimmortals.com; 6830 N Federal Hwy; adult/child $5/3; ❧ 10am-6pm Mon-Fri, 11am-5pm Sat) is a preview of his more ambitious project, the Sports Immortals Experience, 'in the works' for years. Today, you can view rotating exhibits featuring mementos from balls and helmets to plaques and artwork. The top floor features interactive displays, footage of outstanding feats and items like the 'death ball' that killed baseball player Ray Chapman in 1920.

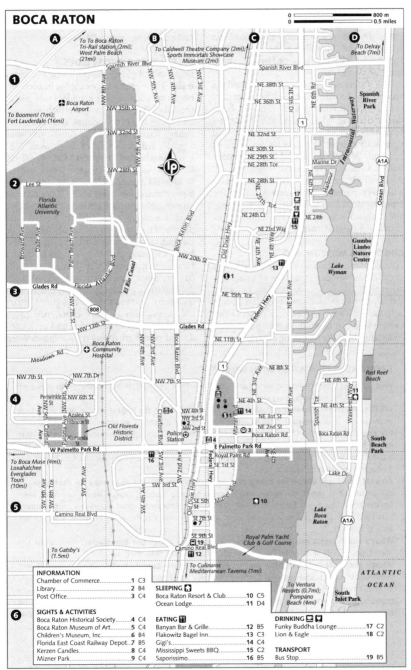

BOCA RATON

SOUTHEAST FLORIDA

BOCA RATON HISTORICAL SOCIETY

The main reason to visit this tiny **museum** (☎ 561-395-6766; www.bocahistory.org; 71 N Federal Hwy) is to check out the building, the former Boca Raton town hall (1927), topped by a glimmering gold dome.

The society runs a guided **trolley tour** on the second and fourth Thursdays from January through April (tickets $15). The 1½-hour docent-led trip takes you to the **Florida East Coast Railway Depot**, a Mediterranean Revival train station built in the 1930s for Flagler's railroad, as well as the **Old Floresta Historic District**, a 1920s-era residential neighborhood. Alternatively, take a guided **walking tour** ($12, Tuesdays, November through April) of the fabulous Boca Raton Resort & Club (opposite), a historic hotel from the 1920s by architect Addison Mizner.

CHILDREN'S MUSEUM, INC

Housed in the 1925 'Singing Pines' home, one of the oldest wooden structures in town, this **museum** (☎ 561-368-6875; www.cmboca.org; 498 Crawford Blvd; admission $3; ☺ noon-4pm Tue-Sat) has rooms with various themes, like Oscar's Post Office (where kids can make their own postcards), KidsCent's banking (featuring a working vault with prizes) and FACES Multicultural Room (with musical instruments, try-on clothing and crafts from around the world).

EVERGLADES AIRBOAT RIDES

Boca isn't all glossy development and glitzy malls. The western edge of town borders the northern reach of the Everglades (see p164), the only subtropical park in North America. To explore this time-fogotten area, filled with swamp ferns and nodding nixies, you need a guide. Ten miles west of downtown, Wild Lyle's **Loxahatchee Everglades Tours** (☎ 561-482-6107; www.evergladesairboattours.com; 15490 Loxahatchee Rd; adult/child under 12yr $32/16; ☺ 10am-5pm) offers hourly ecoexplorations of the Everglades on one of eight custom airboats (a boat using a fan instead of a propeller to push it over the water). Guests enjoy an adventure ride through swampy marsh, around papyrus and hurricane grass, past long-winged birds and turtles and gators sunning themselves. At the halfway point, Lyle stops the boat, discusses the importance of the Everglades and answers questions. You can't stump this guy. A crusty old bugger with 35 years' experience, Lyle's explored the area thoroughly and even conducted rescue missions recovering downed

---

EVERGLADES EDUCATION WITH WILD LYLE

Wild Lyle has been exploring the Glades for more than 35 years. Here, he shares his views on the marshes he works in every day.

What's important about the Everglades? The Everglades is the largest habitat area of its type in the world: approximately 2200 sq miles. The 'KEO,' as it's called, includes the Kissimmee area, the Everglades and the Okeechobee area. The water comes through a natural flow system from as far as Georgia's Okefenokee Swamp. Water's the most important ingredient, forming the habitat area for plants and animals. The area produces oxygen and promotes changes in weather through transpiration, making rain.

Airboat tours get abuse for being anti-environmental. What's your take on that? Most of the argument is about the noise, which seems to be a 'people thing.' Ordinances have been on the books for years for mufflers: all private and commercial boat operators must comply. However, airboating is a recreational sport for most – not a commercial business – so compliance is difficult.

What's the biggest misunderstanding people have about the Everglades? They think the Everglades is only west of Miami. It extends further north than that.

What's the most unusual thing you've ever seen in the Everglades? I've been involved with hundreds of search and rescues. Nothing surprises me. However…one Sunday morning I came around a trail to find a sunken airboat – seats barely above water. Two well-dressed ladies were standing on the seats. One man was sitting on one of the seats; one was on the cage of the boat, smoking. Beer cans floating in the water. There were two gators nearby; they moved away as I slowed down. I had 12 passengers on my boat – first tour of the day. We took the ladies back to the landing to their car. Came back for the guys.

planes. Kid-friendly but science-drenched, an airboat ride with Lyle is a great way to get to know a part of the world that most people don't understand. For more about Wild Lyle, see opposite.

From downtown, take W Palmetto Park Rd west to US 441, turn left (south) and then right (west) on Loxahatchee Rd. Follow it all the way to the end. If you drive into the swamp, you've gone too far.

Sleeping

Goodbye, independent hotels…hello chains. With few options that are cause for excitement (with the exception of the Boca Raton Resort & Club), your best bet is to bunk down in nearby Delray Beach.

Ocean Lodge (☎ 561-395-7772; www.oceanlodge florida.com; 531 N Ocean Blvd; r summer/winter $55/120; P 🖳 🕱) In each enormous, comfortable room there's a full granite kitchenette, a flat-screen TV and travertine bathroom. Like several similar motels along Ocean Blvd, it's across the street from South Beach Park.

Ventura Resorts (☎ 561-392-0375; www.ventura atboca.com; 2301 S Ocean Blvd; r summer $275-295, winter $375-395; P 🖳 🕱) Roomy two-story suites with tile floors, private balconies, satellite TV and full kitchens. The beach is right across the street.

Boca Raton Resort & Club (☎ 888-498-2622; www .bocaresort.com; 501 E Camino Real; r summer $195-450, winter $360-845; P 🖳 🕱) This Addison Mizner–built resort, a trio of opulent buildings, is as old-school glam as it gets. Its Mediterranean style is coupled with a modern collection of amenities, from two 18-hole golf courses and a 32-slip marina to a private beach and otherworldly spa. Add in the five pools, 10 restaurants and priceless historic vibe and you'll find you can stay a week and never leave the grounds.

Eating

BUDGET

Flakowitz Bagel Inn (☎ 561-368-0666; 1999 N Federal Hwy; mains $5; 🕑 7am-3pm) This New York–style deli always has a huge breakfast crowd thanks to its 20-something variety of bagels, enormous plates of eggs, pancakes and the usual. Lunch is a quality experience, too. The line moves fast.

Boca Muse (☎ 561-367-1133; 7136 Beracasa Way; mains $8-13; 🕑 11:30am-10pm Tue-Fri, 5-10pm Sat-Mon)

Equal parts classy bar, intimate dining space and secluded lounge, this oasis is as comfortable as a Roy Orbison song. Visitors are provided provocative coffee-table books to spark conversation while waiting for their food (tapas, salads and sandwiches), which is delightful.

MIDRANGE

our pick Mississippi Sweets BBQ (☎ 561-394-6779; 2399 N Federal Hwy; mains $8-18; 🕑 11am-9:30pm Mon-Fri, 4-10pm Sat) This tiny restaurant dishes up huge portions of sweet-sauced barbecued ribs and chicken, served with classic southern sides like deep-fried sweet potatoes.

Culinaros Mediterranean Taverna (☎ 561-338-3646; 6897 SW 18th St; mains $17-28; 🕑 dinner) A fine waterfront tavern with a heavy dose of Greek flavor. Specialties include grilled lamb chops, spanakopita and lemon-marinated chicken. Make reservations on weekends, when belly dancers prance and jingle.

TOP END

Banyan Bar & Grille (☎ 561-395-9335; www.theaddison .com; 2 E Camino Real; mains $19-65; 🕑 lunch & dinner) This historic house lavishes diners with a fancy, US bistro–style resplendency. Select from traditional fare with modern twists, such as blackened mahimahi with fruit salsa and lobster shepherd's pie.

Saporissimo (☎ 561-750-2333; 366 Palmetto Park Rd; mains $15-39; 🕑 noon-3pm Wed-Sun, 5:30-11pm Tue-Sun) Translating as 'extremely delicious,' this Italian restaurant is simultaneously romantic and shabby-chic, unlike many of its frou-frou neighbors. Choose from unusual Tuscan treats –wild boar, truffles, rabbit and elk – or more traditional options like ravioli or veal.

GiGi's (☎ 561-368-4488; www.gigis.com; 346 Plaza Real; mains $15-45; 🕑 11:30am-11pm Sun-Thu, to 11:30pm Fri & Sat) Beneath this tavern's soaring 24ft ceilings are a huge stage, two bars and a whole lot of lacquered, chocolate paneling that can't decide if it's vintage or modern. Great oyster bar – plus several tasty chicken, steak and seafood options.

Drinking & Entertainment

Lion & Eagle (☎ 561-394-3190; 2401 N Federal Hwy) A British pub with Guinness, Fullers and other British brews on tap, plus bangers and mash on the menu.

Gatsby's (☎ 561-393-3900; www.gatsbysfl.com; 5970 SW 18th St) It's a step up from your standard singles bar: cocktails, beers and cruising, but with a well-coiffed crowd, cigar room, sushi room and about a dozen pool tables.

Funky Buddha Lounge (☎ 561-368-4643; www .myspace.com/thefunkybuddhalounge; 2621 N Federal Hwy) Choose from over 90 microbrews, dozens of organic wines and teas, fair-trade coffees and over 40 shisha flavors to smoke in the on-site hookahs.

Caldwell Theatre Company (☎ 561-241-7432; www .caldwelltheatre.com; 7901 N Federal Hwy; tickets $40-55) It may be in a strip mall, but this theater, a couple of miles north of town, turns out high-quality dramas, classics and off-beat hits for a sophisticated audience.

Boomers! (☎ 561-347-1888; 3100 Airport Rd) A perfect place to keep your little ones occupied for an hour or five, this indoor–outdoor fun park has go-karts, bumper boats, and endlessly flashing and buzzing arcade games.

Getting There & Around

Boca Raton is about 50 miles north of Miami and sprawls several miles east and west of I-95.

You can also get there from points north and south on Hwy A1A or US 1. The town is more or less equidistant to Fort Lauderdale-Hollywood International Airport (FLL; p227) and Palm Beach International Airport (PBI; p251).

The Boca Raton **Tri-Rail station** (☎ 800 874-7245; 680 Yamato Rd) is near the Yamato Rd exit of I-95 and provides shuttle services to both airports. PalmTran bus 94 connects downtown Boca with the Tri-Rail station.

PalmTran (☎ 561-841-4287; www.palmtran.org) serves southeast Florida from North Palm Beach to Boca Raton. It costs $1.25 to ride (60¢ if you're over 65 or have a student ID), and transfers are free; be sure to have exact change. From the Tri-Rail station, bus 2 takes you to PBI and bus 94 to FAU, where you can transfer to bus 91 to Mizner Park. From Mizner Park, take bus 92 to South Beach Park.

Metro Taxi (☎ 561-276-2230) serves the area.

DELRAY BEACH
☎ 561 / pop 60,000

Founded by Seminole Indians, and further settled by newly freed slaves and Japanese agriculturists, this melting pot retooled itself for

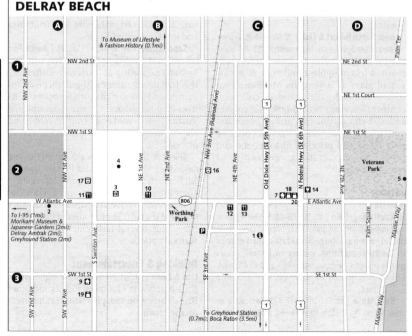

the tourist trade when the railroads chugged through Delray Beach, and never looked back. Local hotels and clubs turned a blind eye to prohibition laws and accommodated everyone. Perhaps this eclectic mix of early residents – from the industrious to the lawless – is why Delray today so effortlessly juggles a casual seaside vibe and a suave urban sophistication. Look for cute beachy shops, high-end antiquaries, thoughtful cultural attractions and wide-ranging restaurant options. Also, there's a dynamite farmers market on Saturdays in Worthing Park (SE 2nd Ave at Atlantic Ave).

Orientation

Downtown's main drag is Atlantic Ave, which runs from Hwy A1A (Ocean Blvd), across the Intracoastal Waterway and west past I-95. US Hwy 1 splits into northbound Federal Hwy and southbound Old Dixie Hwy through the city center.

Information

Chamber of Commerce (☎ 561-278-0424; www .delraybeach.com; 64 SE 5th Ave) For maps, guides and local advice.

Library (☎ 561-266-0194; 100 W Atlantic Ave; ☺ 9am-8pm Mon-Wed, to 5pm Thu-Sat, 1-5pm Sun) Free internet access in this brand new facility.

Sights & Activities

MORIKAMI MUSEUM & JAPANESE GARDENS

West of the beach, away from the hubbub downtown, is this serene **cultural landmark** (☎ 561-495-0233; www.morikami.org; 4000 Morikami Park Rd; adult/child $10/6; ☺ 10am-5pm Tue-Sun). The initial aim of the so-called Yamato settlement was to attract Japanese families to Florida, where they would introduce new and profitable agricultural techniques to the region. There was one big problem when it opened in 1905: only single Japanese men came; the stable families that founders had hoped for were uninterested. The group soon disbanded, though one settler, Sukjei 'George' Morikami, stuck around and planted some gardens.

Today his plantings skirt the edge of the 200-acre property – with more than a mile of trails – highlighting traditional Japanese landscaping techniques from intricate bonsai to authentic koi-filled ponds, all with monuments favored by Japanese gardeners

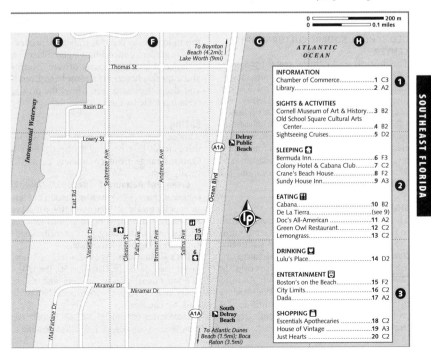

INFORMATION
Chamber of Commerce...................1 C3
Library...2 A2

SIGHTS & ACTIVITIES
Cornell Museum of Art & History....3 B2
Old School Square Cultural Arts
    Center......................................4 B2
Sightseeing Cruises.........................5 D2

SLEEPING
Bermuda Inn...................................6 F3
Colony Hotel & Cabana Club...........7 C3
Crane's Beach House........................8 F2
Sundy House Inn.............................9 A3

EATING
Cabana..10 B2
De La Tierra...........................(see 9)
Doc's All-American........................11 A2
Green Owl Restaurant....................12 C2
Lemongrass....................................13 C2

DRINKING
Lulu's Place...................................14 D2

ENTERTAINMENT
Boston's on the Beach....................15 F2
City Limits.....................................16 C2
Dada..17 A2

SHOPPING
Escentials Apothecaries 18 C2
House of Vintage 19 A3
Just Hearts 20 C2

of various eras. The outstanding Morikami Museum has a collection of 5000 Japanese antiques and objects, including textiles, tea-ceremony items and works of fine art. There are tea ceremonies in the **Seishin-An teahouse** on the third Saturday of the month.

BEACHES

Among the best sandy spits are the **Atlantic Dunes Beach** (1600 Ocean Blvd), with 7 acres of shorefront sporting clean restroom facilities, volleyball courts and picnic areas, and the **public beach** (Ocean Blvd at Atlantic), a hip gathering spot for young locals and visitors, with excellent surf for swimming. Coin-operated meters charge $1 per hour.

MUSEUM OF LIFESTYLE & FASHION HISTORY

This new-ish **museum** (☎ 561-495-8785; www .mlfhmuseum.org; 322 NE 2nd Ave; admission $5; ⏱ 10am-5pm Tue-Sat, 1-5pm Sun), housed in a former five-and-dime shop in the Pineapple Grove Shops plaza, displays exhibits on topics from lifestyle and architecture to fashion trends and toys. Plus, it organizes 105-minute **historic bus tours** (☎ 561-243-2662; tours $10) of Delray Beach on the fourth Saturday of each month.

OLD SCHOOL SQUARE CULTURAL ARTS CENTER

This historic and cultural **center** (☎ 561-243-7922; www.oldschool.org; 51 N Swinton Ave), a collection of preserved buildings on 4 acres, injects a dose of culture into Delray. For example, the **Cornell Museum of Art & History** (☎ 561-243-7922; 51 N Swinton Ave; adult/child under 13yr $6/free; ⏱ 10:30am-4:30pm Tue-Sat), a restored 1913 elementary-school building with four galleries, shows rotating exhibits of masters and locals and also houses a tea room and the Delray Historical Archives.

SIGHTSEEING CRUISES

The Intracoastal from Delray Beach south to Boca Raton is pretty swanky. Get to know the area better with a narrated **sightseeing cruise** (☎ 561-243-0686; www.delraybeachcruises.com; launching from 777 Atlantic Plaza; adult/children under 12yr $20/17) aboard the 105ft luxury *Lady Atlantic*. Choose from chipper day trips (Wednesdays to Sundays at 1:30pm) or romantic sunset cruises (Saturdays only, 7pm to 9pm). Departs from the canal side of Veterans Park.

Sleeping

our pick Bermuda Inn (☎ 561-276-5288; www.theber mudainn.com; 64 S Ocean Blvd; r summer/winter $85-189/202-249; ⓟ 🖵 🕿) Spotless rooms, overlooking the ocean and one block from Atlantic Ave, make this one of the easiest choices around.

Colony Hotel & Cabana Club (☎ 561-276-4123, 800-552-2363; www.thecolonyhotel.com; 525 Atlantic Ave; r $100-200; ⓟ 🕿) Built in 1926, this place offers fabulously renovated, charming rooms with gleaming wooden floors, white-draped beds and lots of light. The hotel's in the center of everything, and the private oceanfront beach club is just 2 miles away. Committed to ecological preservation, management uses native species in garden design, provides nontoxic, biodegradable bath products and tastefully distributes recycling bins around the property.

Crane's Beach House (☎ 561-278-1700; www.cranes beachhouse.com; 82 Gleason St; r & ste $130-400; ⓟ 🖵 🕿) Wooden floors, 27 light-filled rooms and pastel beach decor that makes you feel like you're in Florida, this pet-friendly boutique is a great choice for laying your head. There's a lovely pool and a short walk to the beach.

Sundy House Inn (☎ 561-272-5678; www.sundyhouse .com; 106 S Swinton Ave; r summer $145-575, winter $275-650; ⓟ 🖵 🕿) The most romantic option by far, this hidden-away gem has it all: an acre of exquisite gardens concealing a lagoonlike pool, a choice of lavish rooms or private cottages and a quirky, luxurious atmosphere. Even if you sleep elsewhere, don't miss the on-site restaurant, De La Tierra (opposite).

Eating

Almost everywhere you turn there's something fresh just begging to be devoured. Options range from completely casual to totally posh.

Green Owl Restaurant (☎ 561-272-7766; 330 E Atlantic Ave; mains $4-7; ⏱ breakfast & lunch) The classic spot for breakfast – big omelettes, pancakes and such – also turns out delicious lunches and dinners such as burgers, tuna melts, salads and refreshing pink lemonade.

Doc's All-American (☎ 561-278-3627; 10 N Swinton Ave; mains $6-15; ⏱ 11am-11pm Sun-Thu, to 1am Fri & Sat) Great, greasy burgers and thick, frosty shakes from an open-aired '50s-style walk-up counter.

Lemongrass (☎ 561-247-7077; 420 E Atlantic Ave; mains $8-25; ⏱ noon-3pm & 5:30-10:30pm Mon-Thu, to

11:30pm Fri & Sat, to 10pm Sun) Buddhist art, soothing earth tones and sleek, calming lines in this modern Asian bistro almost make up for the absolute always-totally-packed franticness of it all. The food, though, is divine; hence, the always-totally-packed franticness. Authentic Thai curries, one-off sushi creations (like Sex on the Moon) and Vietnamese noodles are some of the many offerings here.

Cabana (☎ 561-274-9090; 105 E Atlantic Ave; mains $9-26; lunch & dinner) The only thing splashier than the multicolored walls in this slick Latin restaurant is the to-die-for Latin food. Serving attractive meals emphasizing fresh seafood and spicy meats, this place is a surefire winner if you want something flavor-packed for dinner.

De La Tierra (☎ 561-272-5678; 106 S Swinton Ave; mains $27-37; dinner & weekend brunch), Dine inside the refined 1902 Victorian mansion or at tables scattered throughout the tropical gardens – certainly, the most romantic spot in town.

Entertainment

Most hipsters head to West Palm to party, but there are a few places worth haunting right here in town.

City Limits (☎ 561-967-4573; www.newcitylimits.com; 19 NE 3rd Ave) Dunno what's cooler about this music venue: the blond parquet flooring, dual glass-block bars and friendly feel of the stage or the dynamite bands that fill it – national rockers like John Ralston and Toots and the Maytals and local stars like Summer Blanket and The Heavy Pets.

Dada (☎ 561-330-3232; 52 N Swinton Ave) Join the cool cats lounging in this two-story bungalow to sip cocktails, hear poetry readings or live bands and nibble on fare like ravioli, salads and hummus. The front porch, outdoor lanterns and boho vibe all add to the romantic charm.

Boston's on the Beach (☎ 561-278-3364; www.bostonsonthebeach.com; 40 S Ocean Blvd; 7:30am-2am) This beachfront gem serves good (predictable) US grub. It's got a bustling bar scene thanks to two patios overlooking the sea (upstairs is the best view in Delray), plus live music nightly.

Shopping

Atlantic Ave and the arteries leading from it are filled with boutiques aching for exploration.

Escentials Apothecaries (☎ 561-276-7070; 533 E Atlantic Ave) All things bath and body (some organic), for both the two-legged and the four-legged.

Just Hearts (☎ 561-265-7277; www.justhearts.biz; 537 E Atlantic Ave) Jewelry, handbags, stained glass, art and more, all centered on a single theme.

House of Vintage (☎ 561-276-7477; www.myhouseofvintage.com; 123 S Swinton Ave; 11am-6pm Tue-Sat) Hand-selected pieces presented in themed rooms (the Walk-In Closet Room features dresses). Men will adore the House of Sweets (aka the kitchen), loaded with cupcakes.

Getting There & Around

Delray Beach is about 20 miles south of West Palm Beach and 45 miles north of Miami on I-95, US Hwy 1 or Hwy A1A.

The **Greyhound station** (☎ 561-272-6447; 402 SE 6th Ave) is served by PalmTran. Bus 2 takes you to PBI or Boca Raton; bus 81 services the Tri-Rail station, Amtrak and downtown Delray.

Amtrak (☎ 800-872-2745; 345 S Congress Ave), half a mile south of Atlantic Ave, shares a station with **Tri-Rail** (☎ 800-874-7245; www.tri-rail.com).

LAKE WORTH
☎ 561 / pop 36,300

Billing itself as 'Where the tropics begin,' this bohemian community sits further east than any place in South Florida. Meanwhile, just offshore, the Gulf Stream flows further west than anywhere along the coast. This geographical good fortune means Lake Worth has warm weather year-round – but also enjoys near-constant breezes, especially at night. Don't misunderstand: in August, it's still hot!

With a distinct artsy vibe, this down-to-earth, ragtag beach town boasts a cool collection of eateries and nightspots – not to mention a robust local music scene. Take a stroll along Lake Ave and you'll see a healthy mix of unpretentious visitors and locals milling about; cross over the causeway and you'll find a spectacular sliver of public-access beachfront.

Orientation

Lake Worth is 8 miles south of West Palm Beach. The small downtown lies on the mainland, straddling two one-way streets: eastbound Lake Ave and westbound Lucerne Ave. Lake Ave leads to the bridge and Lake Worth's beautiful beach, and divides addresses into north and south. US Hwy 1 is called Dixie

Hwy 1; other north–south streets are lettered from west to east.

Information

Chamber of Commerce (☎ 561-582-4401; www .lwchamber.com; 501 Lake Ave)

Post office (Lucerne Ave btwn J & K Sts)

Public library (☎ 561-533-7354; 15 N M St) Free internet access.

Sights & Activities

MUSEUM OF THE CITY OF LAKE WORTH

This tidy historical **museum** (☎ 561-586-1700; 414 Lake Ave; admission free; ☒ 9am-1pm & 2-4:30pm Tue-Fri) is packed with obscurities and ephemera, such as early-20th-century 'special occasion dresses' (that look unimaginably hot) and a life-sized photo of local farmer Erwin Smith, whose beard reached 7.5ft in 1832. In the same building, the **Lake Worth Art League Gallery** (☎ 561-586-1700; admission free; ☒ noon-4pm Mon-Fri) features local artists.

LAKE WORTH BEACH

This stretch of sand is universally agreed to be the finest beach between Fort Lauderdale and Daytona. Surfers come from miles to tame the waves; everyone else comes to enjoy the fine, white sand. If you're looking for a laid-back place to get sunburned – er…to relax on the beach – this is a great place to do it.

BIKING

For a relaxing route, head east along Lake Ave to **Bryant Park**. From there, follow S Lakeside

Dr south, past the Birthday Cake house (you'll know it when you see it) to S 18th St, go one block west and follow S Palmway north, back to the park. Total trip: 3 miles. **Fat Cat Bicycles** (☎ 561-547-1396; 702 Lucerne Ave; ☒ 10am-6pm Mon-Fri, to 5pm Sat), rents cruisers for $15 per day.

WATER SPORTS

Thanks to its unspoiled beaches and tranquil waters, Lake Worth enjoys some excellent snorkeling and diving opportunities. Head to nearby (unfortunately named) **Wet Pleasures** (☎ 561-547-4343; www.wetpleasuresfla.com; 312 W Lantana Rd) for lessons, equipment and advice. For a safety-conscious, super-friendly dive crew, give **Mermaid Charters** (☎ 561-596-2594; www.mermaid divecharters.com) a ring.

If you're looking for some deep-sea fishing, grab a seat aboard the **Lady K** (☎ 561-588-7612; www.b-love.com; 314 E Ocean Ave; adult/child under 12yr $35/22). Launching from nearby Lantana Marina at 8am, 1pm and 7pm, the crew provides rods, baits your hook and fillets any fish you catch. BYO drinks.

To explore the Intracoastal, rent **wave runners** (☎ 561-735-0612; 700 Casa Loma Blvd; per hour $95) from nearby Boynton Beach's Two Georges Marina. Head south for mangroves and a scenic view of area homes. Head north for a wide lagoon, ideal for making donuts in the water…uh…very responsible, safe donuts, of course.

Massive **Nomad Surf & Sport** (☎ 561-272-2882; www.nomadsurfsport.com; 4655 N Ocean Blvd, Boynton Beach) has a great selection of surf gear.

TOP SUNRISE SPOTS

Florida has some of the most magical sunrises anywhere. Those pale pinks, lavenders and blues can really invigorate and set the tone for the entire day. When preparing for a sunrise, be sure to set out a few things the night before. The more prepared you are, the easier it'll be to drag yourself out of bed. Be sure to bring warm clothes (early mornings can be surprisingly cool) and bug spray, especially if you are near mangroves. You might also consider packing your camera, sunglasses, a chair or blanket to sit on – and a chilled bottle of champagne and a jug of Florida OJ, for fun.

Almost any spot will do, as long as it faces east. Here's a short list to get the brain working:

- Overlooking the inlet at Fort Lauderdale's South Beach (p222)
- Palm Beach's public beach, just off Barton Ave (p242)
- Your Peanut Island campsite (p248)
- Blowing Rocks Preserve (p253)
- Wide, peaceful – and dog-friendly! – Juno Beach (p254)
- Any of the sandy, empty beaches on Hutchinson Island (p256)

Sleeping

Hummingbird Hotel (☎ 561-582-3224; www.humming birdhotel.com; 631 Lucerne Ave; r $47-165, ste $300; ☐) Built in 1921, this old-fashioned hotel is equal parts B&B and youth hostel. The recently renovated charmer has eight frilly rooms (not all of which have private baths, so clarify when booking), a cute lobby, a full kitchen and continental breakfast on weekends. The location can't be beat.

Mango Inn (☎ 561-533-6900; www.mangoinn.com; 128 N Lakeside Dr; r summer $120-150, winter $155-275; ☐ ☒) All three buildings comprising the Mango Inn were built between 1915 and 1920 in a residential area. As a result, this lushly landscaped inn today boasts one of the most secluded settings around. Only three blocks from town and a 15-minute walk to the beach, accommodation ranges from single rooms (many with private entrances) to an adorable cottage with French doors opening onto the heated pool.

Eating

ourpick Pelican (☎ 561-582-4992; 610 Lake Ave; mains $3-10; ☉ 6:30am-2pm) This early-risers' place offers hearty portions of perfectly prepared breakfast, plus a carnival of vegetarian-friendly specials, many with Mediterranean or Middle Eastern flavors (the owners are Pakistani). They also offer divine Indian dinners on Fridays from 6pm to 10pm with a range of potent curries and masalas.

Soma Center (☎ 561-296-9949; www.thesomacenter .com; 609 Lake Ave; mains $4.50-15.75; ☉ 11am-8pm Tue-Thu, to 9pm Fri & Sat, 11am-4pm Sun; ☐) This hybrid health food/fitness center serves organic salads and smoothies, handmade vegan baked goods (like zesty flax crackers and homemade granola) and raw vegan specials. Eat surrounded by art inside or under a bougainvillea canopy out back. The studio offers daily yoga, dance and fitness classes for all levels.

Cottage (☎ 561-586-0080; 522 Lucerne Ave; mains $7-11; ☉ 11am-2am) The prettiest spot in Lake Worth, the Cottage offers unique small plates and a dynamic bar featuring local and regional microbrews and wines. Dine alfresco under a twinkling canopy, surrounded by thick weeping figs and in sight of the projector screening classic films, or inside by the light of candles and the one-of-a-kind rainbow-splashed stained-glass bar back.

Prime 707 (☎ 561-533-0000; www.prime707steak house.com; 707 Lake Ave; mains $17-40; ☉ lunch & dinner) This classy steakhouse has exposed brick walls, cozy curved banquettes and a perfect people-watching perch, right on the main drag. But the real attractions are the delicious, expertly prepared cuts of beef – filet mignon, New York strip, even knockout burgers – plus fresh fish and flavorful pasta dishes. Pair it all with a martini or fine bottle of wine, end it with a stroll downtown, and you've got yourself a perfect night in Lake Worth.

Drinking & Entertainment

Evening on the Avenues (Cultural Plaza) On the first and third Friday of the month, Lake Worth throws a downtown street party with live music, street food and local crafts.

Brogue's Irish Pub (☎ 561-585-1885; 621 Lake Ave; ☉ 11:30am-2am) An authentic pub appealing to all ages: the Banshee Room in back hosts youthful alt-rock bands on Friday nights, while Monday's trivia night attracts an older crowd.

South Shores (☎ 561-547-7656; www.southshores tavern.com; cnr Lucerne Ave & M St) Out back, this place offers the most exotic music venue in town.

Havana Hideout (☎ 561-585-8444; www.havanahide out.com; 509 Lake Ave) The newest, funnest place in town, open-aired, palm-fringed Havana has live music most nights, a thoughtful draft-beer selection and an on-site *taqueria* that fills countless stomachs on Taco Tuesdays, when tacos are a buck apiece.

Bamboo Room (☎ 561-585-2583; www.bambooroom .com; 25 S J St) This favorite spot with an intimate roadhouse feel features regional and internationally known blues, rockabilly, alt-country and jam bands, drawing music-lovers from miles around.

Lake Worth Playhouse (☎ 561-586-6410; www.lake worthplayhouse.org; 713 Lake Ave; tickets $15-22) Housed in a restored 1924 vaudeville venue, this intimate spot stages classic community theater. The attached Stonzek Studio Theatre screens independent films (tickets $6 to $8).

Lake Worth Drive-In (☎ 561-965-4517; 3438 Lake Worth Rd) When was the last time you went to the drive-in?! Screening first-run movies under the stars seven nights a week, drive in, tune in and sit back. Coolers are welcome; dogs are not.

Getting There & Around

The **Tri-Rail Station** (1703 Lake Worth Rd) is at the intersection of A St. PalmTran bus 61 connects the station to downtown.

Lolly the Trolley (☎ 561-586-1600; ☉ 9am-5pm Mon-Sat), a fleet of red San Francisco–style trolleys, has three lines originating near city hall, at the corner of Lake Ave and H St (adult/child $1/50¢). You can flag them down anywhere on their route. Pick up a system map at the chamber of commerce.

PALM BEACH
☎ 561 / pop 10,500

Similar to the Hamptons but with fewer palm trees and comparatively little nightlife, this playground for the rich and famous revolves around benefit bashes, second houses (read: hulking mansions), elegant dining and Beverly Hills–style shopping. With its wide streets and alfresco cafés, though, you should feel welcome to explore. A stroll along the truly gold Gold Coast beach is stunning and a bike ride past the massive gated compounds or down ritzy Worth Ave is jaw-droppingly good fun.

Orientation

The long, narrow island of Palm Beach sits between the Intracoastal Waterway, here called Lake Worth (or just 'The Lake'), and the Atlantic Ocean. It's just east of West Palm Beach and the other communities south of West Palm. The main north–south artery is S County Rd (Hwy A1A), and two major bridges link downtown to the mainland: Flagler Memorial Bridge (Royal Poinciana Way) and Royal Park Bridge (Royal Palm Way). Further south, Southern Blvd and Lake Ave both provide access to the island.

Downtown stretches from Royal Poinciana Way to Worth Ave, with most major sights scattered between. Prices tend to rise as you head southward. Ocean Blvd runs from the southern edge of the Breakers (p243) to the southern tip of the island; most of the mansions worth ogling are below Worth Ave.

Information

Note that many shops and restaurants are only open during high season, roughly Thanksgiving to Easter. For 'normal' needs, such as internet cafés and laundries, head to West Palm Beach.

Chamber of Commerce (☎ 561-655-3282; www .palmbeachchamber.com; 400 Royal Palm Way) Excellent maps, racks of pamphlets and several gratis glossy magazines, including *Worth Avenue*, *Palm Beach Illustrated*, *Palm Beach Society* and *Vive*, all of which offer convincing arguments for indulgence at every level.

Post office Two on the island, at 95 N County Rd and at 401 S County Rd.

Sights
FLAGLER MUSEUM

The only true **museum** (☎ 561-655-2833; www.flagler .org; 1 Whitehall Way; adult/child $15/8; ☺ 10am-5pm Tue-Sat, noon-5pm Sun) on Palm Beach is probably the county's most fascinating. Housed in the spectacular 1902 mansion built by Henry Flagler as a gift for his bride, Mary Lily Keenan, the Beaux Arts–styled Whitehall Mansion is beyond belief. Built in 18 months, the elaborate 55-room palace was the first residential home to feature both a heating system and an air-con system; features pink aluminum-leaf wallpaper (more expensive, at the time, than gold); impresses with a 4750-sq-ft Grand Hall, the largest single room of any Gilded Age private residence; and sports a drool-worthy billiards room. Don't expect many details about Flagler the Railroad Mogul, however, as the emphasis here is on the couple's opulent lifestyle. Gruesome tip: Flagler died as a result

---

THE MOST EXPENSIVE HOME IN PALM BEACH COUNTY

In May 2008, real-estate tycoon Donald Trump signed a contract to sell a Palm Beach mansion to an unidentified foreign purchaser for $100 million, a record in the county and only $3 million shy of the most expensive home ever sold.

Trump purchased the property in 2004 for $41.35 million, sunk $25 million in renovations into it and listed it for $125 million. The oceanfront home has nine bedrooms, a ballroom, an art gallery and a conservatory. It also has 475ft of private beach. Factor in two guesthouses and a 50-car garage and the square footage of the property totals 81,738.

If you want to see this property for yourself, head to Palm Beach and go north on N County Rd to 515, on your right. The property is just after Miraflores Dr (on your left). With that huge hedge, you're more likely to see it from the water – it's 0.6 miles south of the southern edge of Palm Beach Country Club. It's the one with the enormous, white, arched windows in the gently swooping rotunda.

PALM BEACH

0 ─────── 400 m
0 ─────── 0.2 miles

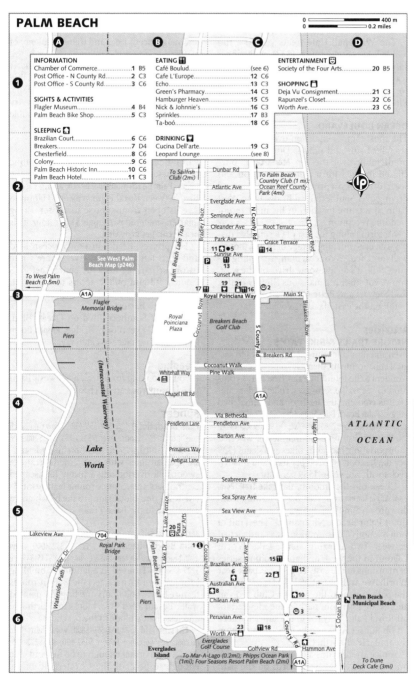

INFORMATION
Chamber of Commerce................**1** B5
Post Office - N County Rd.............**2** C3
Post Office - S County Rd.............**3** C6

SIGHTS & ACTIVITIES
Flagler Museum...........................**4** B4
Palm Beach Bike Shop.................**5** C3

SLEEPING 🏠
Brazilian Court............................**6** C6
Breakers.....................................**7** D4
Chesterfield................................**8** C6
Colony..**9** C6
Palm Beach Historic Inn..............**10** C6
Palm Beach Hotel.......................**11** C3

EATING 🍴
Café Boulud.............................(see 6)
Cafe L'Europe...........................**12** C6
Echo...**13** C3
Green's Pharmacy......................**14** C5
Hamburger Heaven....................**15** C5
Nick & Johnnie's........................**16** C5
Sprinkles...................................**17** B3
Ta-boó......................................**18** C6

DRINKING 🍷
Cucina Dell'arte.........................**19** C3
Leopard Lounge......................(see 8)

ENTERTAINMENT 🎭
Society of the Four Arts...............**20** B5

SHOPPING 🛍
Deja Vu Consignment.................**21** C3
Rapunzel's Closet......................**22** C6
Worth Ave................................**23** C6

SOUTHEAST FLORIDA

of injuries sustained from tumbling down the Grand Staircase, so watch your step.

The Whitehall Café treats you to a full 'Gilded Age–Style' lunch ($33), with finger sandwiches, scones and custom-blended teas. It's served 11:30am to 2:30pm Tuesday to Saturday, noon to 3pm on Sunday. Pinkies out!

OCEAN BOULEVARD

The most famous mansion overlooking this stretch of surf and sand is Donald Trump's predictably over-the-top **Mar-a-Lago**, purchased in 1985 for a paltry $8 million and soon turned into a private club. Best glimpsed driving over Southern Blvd Bridge from West Palm, it was the location of his most recent wedding reception.

Motoring along the rest of Ocean Blvd displays an eye-widening parade of riches, though walls and hedges conceal many sprawling estates. Still, it's an awesome drive: on the west, you've got stunning mansions (Jimmy Buffet, Rod Stewart and Bette Midler all own homes here); on the east, dazzling cobalt vistas.

Activities

NATURE TRAILS & BIKE PATHS

Even among all the man-made luxuries and surgical enhancements, there are some truly natural wonders to be found in Palm Beach. It's common to see walkers, joggers, rollerbladers and cyclists enjoying the fresh air and unmatched views. **Palm Beach Bike Shop** (☎ 561-659-4583; www .palmbeachbicycle.com; 223 Sunrise Ave; ◷ 9am-5:30pm Mon-Sat, 10am-5pm Sun) rents all manner of wheeled transportation, including bikes and skates ($39 per day), scooters ($100 per day) and quadricycles with sun visors ($39 per hour).

Check out the smooth, flat **Lake Trail** (Royal Palm Way at the Intracoastal Waterway), running from downtown almost all the way to the northern tip of Palm Beach. Nicknamed 'The Trail of Conspicuous Consumption,' it's sandwiched between two amazing views: Lake Worth Lagoon to the west, and an unending series of mansions to the east. To get here, park near Worth Ave, walk west to S Lake Dr and follow the path north to the Sailfish Club. For an abbreviated version, park in the metered lot off Royal Palm Way (or in the supermarket's lot on Sunset Ave) and head west to pick up the trail. Head north. Gawk.

A nice stretch runs along **N County Rd**. Park on Sunset Ave and head north on the path

running to Palm Beach Country Club. At just under 2 miles, the route is lined with houses and magnificent trees and there are plenty of exotic side streets to explore.

You can also head south and park at **Phipps Ocean Park**. Stroll the path paralleling the Intracoastal and terminating at Lantana, approximately 3 miles south. On the way, try to guess how much the yachts cost. Double that figure; you're still low.

PUBLIC BEACHES

Palm Beach boasts two beautiful public beaches, kept pleasantly seaweed-free by the town. **Palm Beach municipal beach**, along Ocean Blvd between Royal Palm Way and Hammon Ave, is open from sunrise to sunset. Bring quarters: metered parking is $1 per hour. This beach can get crowded.

For privacy, head north on S Ocean Blvd and turn left on Barton Ave. There's free two-hour parking near the church before S County Rd and public access to the beach across from Clarke Ave, one block before you turned onto Barton.

South of Southern Blvd on Ocean Blvd, before the Lake Worth Bridge, **Phipps Ocean Park** is another place to catch rays.

Sleeping

If you're looking for a deal, head west. Palm Beach properties aren't cheap.

BUDGET

Palm Beach Hotel (☎ 561-655-4580; www.palmbeach hotelfl.com; 235 Sunrise Ave; r $125-285, ste $200-335; P ☆) Built in 1926, this hotel blends classic Spanish lines with exotic Mediterranean swoops all overlooking a lushly landscaped central pool area. Simple rooms feature kitchenettes, a one-block jaunt to the beach and a 300ft hike to the Lake Trail.

MIDRANGE

Palm Beach Historic Inn (☎ 561-832-4009; www .palmbeachhistoricinn.com; 365 S County Rd; r $145-345, ste $225-395; P) Housed in a landmark building brimming with character, the well-lit rooms feature hardwood floors and brightly painted walls. Best of all: it's two blocks to Worth Ave and less than a block to the beach.

Chesterfield (☎ 561-659-5800; www.chesterfield pb.com; 363 Cocoanut Row; r $152-520, ste $222-945; P ☐ ☆) Formal enough to be fun and chic enough to be cool, the Chesterfield offers deluxe rooms and suites in floral patterns. The rooms skew to the cramped side, but you can stretch your legs in the terrific pool, during the traditional afternoon tea, or in the garish-but-festive Leopard Lounge.

Colony (☎ 561-655-5430; www.thecolonypalmbeach .com; 155 Hammon Ave; r $190-525, ste $270-700; P 🖳 🐆) Like much of Palm Beach, this 90-room hotel recently received a facelift. Super-stylish – as it should be, towering over Worth Ave – the pale yellow and hunter-green rooms have hosted the likes of President Clinton and Zsa Zsa Gabor. The beach is a block away, which can be tricky, considering how alluring the alfresco poolside court is.

TOP END

Brazilian Court (☎ 561-655-7740; 301 Australian Ave; www.thebraziliancourt.com; r $200-370, ste $450-2500; P 🖳 🐆) Built in 1926, this swanky resort is an excellent choice for those who want pampering but not obsequiousness. Trendy but timeless, it's got a lovely Mediterranean style, a romantic courtyard and fashionable, recently renovated suites effortlessly blending sleek lines and soft comfort. The on-site Frédéric Fekkai salon and renowned (and ultraromantic) French Café Boulud are major draws, too.

Four Seasons Resort Palm Beach (☎ 561-582-2800; www.fourseasons.com/palmbeach/; 2800 S Ocean Blvd; r & ste $359-3900; P 🖳 🐆) Snuggled among the high-rise condos lining the shores south of the mansion region, this resort has everything you'd expect from a Four Seasons: classy, spacious rooms and suites with to-die-for views; full spa services; tennis courts, golf courses, a fitness facility and a pool; a kids' program; and three serious dining spots.

Breakers (☎ 561-655-6611, 888-273-2537; www .thebreakers.com; 1 S County Rd; r $350-1250, ste $550-5500; P 🖳 🐆) Originally built by Henry Flagler (in 1904 rooms ran $4 per night, including meals), today this 550-room resort sprawls across 140 acres and boasts a staff of 2300 fluent in 56 languages. Just feet from the county's best snorkeling, this palace has two 18-hole golf courses, a mile of semiprivate beach, four pools, two croquet courts and the best brunch around (see p244). For opulence, elegance and Old World charm, there's no other choice.

Eating

Dining out in Palm Beach is pretty much a high-end affair, though there is a pleasant selection of budget bites. After all, just because you can afford to eat foie gras and kobe beef every night doesn't mean you never crave a big, greasy burger with fries, right? Right?

BUDGET

Sprinkles (☎ 561-659-1140; 279 Royal Poinciana Way; mains $4-10; 🕙 9am-10pm Sun-Thu, to 11pm Fri & Sat) In this fashionable yet laid-back place, beach bums sit shoulder-to-shoulder with heiresses and enjoy the sandwiches, soups and knock-out gelato.

Green's Pharmacy (☎ 561-832-4443; 151 N County Rd; mains $4-13; 🕙 breakfast & lunch) This place, housed inside a working pharmacy, hasn't changed since John F Kennedy, looking to slip away from the Secret Service, would stroll across the mint-green linoleum and grab a bite. Choose between a table or a stool at the Formica counter and order from the paper menu just like everyone else, from the trust-fund babies slumming it to the college girls headed to the beach.

Dune Deck Cafe (☎ 561-582-0472; www.dunedeckcafe .com; 100 N Ocean Blvd, Manalapan; mains $4-13; 🕙 breakfast & lunch) Adjacent to the Ritz-Carlton (but worlds away), this breezy, friendly outdoor spot is right on the beach – fie on the sea grape for obscuring the ocean views! Offering omelettes, burgers and fresh salads, it's a great place to head when all you feel like pulling on is flip-flops and beachwear. Beware: the Deck is cash only and there's no ATM on-site.

Hamburger Heaven (☎ 561-655-5277; 314 S County Rd; mains $6-14; 🕙 7am-3pm Mon-Sat) Delightfully frills-free, this bright diner is a locals-magnet. Slip into a vinyl booth and order a burger the way you like it; you may just spot a makeup-free, baseball-hat-hidden celeb while you're chewing.

MIDRANGE

Nick & Johnnie's (☎ 561-655-3319; www.nickandjohnnies .com; 207 Royal Poinciana Way; mains $10-40; 🕙 11am-3am Mon-Sat, from 7am Sun) The newest spot in town, this elegant California-inspired restaurant serves everything from kosher hot dogs to lemon panko yellowtail. With its robin's-egg-blue and chocolate walls, abundant mirrors, endless black bar and travel photos by local shooter Tony Arruza, this gargantuan see-and-be-seen spot nails sophisticated fun.

TOP END

Ta-boó (☎ 561-835-3500; www.taboorestaurant.com; 221 Worth Ave; mains $13-42; 🕙 11:30am-10pm Mon-Fri, to 11pm Fri & Sat) If you believe the legend, the Bloody Mary was invented here, mixed to soothe the hangover of Woolworth heiress Barbara Hutton. Today, with the most coveted window seats on Worth Ave, competition is as stiff as her drinks from the previous night. But get past the intricate woodwork and you'll enjoy a well-executed US bistro meal.

Echo (☎ 561-802-4222; www.echopalmbeach.com; 230A Sunrise Ave; mains $20-38; ⓥ 5:30-9:30pm Wed, Thu & Sun, to 10pm Fri & Sat) This ultramodern Asian restaurant, simultaneously slick and inviting, offers dishes grouped according to the five elements: wind (small plates), fire (the wok), water (sushi, seafood, shellfish), earth (meat, game, poultry, produce) and – since the options in this last 'element' are, indeed, heavenly – flavor (desserts).

Cafe L'Europe (☎ 561-655-4020; 331 S County Rd; mains $25-49; ⓥ 11am-2:30pm Tue-Sat, 5-10pm Tue-Sun) Reservations are essential if you hope to sample the fab caviar, poached salmon, lamb chops or snapper. The dining room is transcendent, the owners friendly.

ourpick Breakers (☎ 561-659-8440, 888-273-2537; www.thebreakers.com; 1 S County Rd; per person, including tax & tip, $110; ⓥ 11am-2:30pm Sun) Sure, it's steep, but it'll certainly rank among the most amazing brunches you'll ever enjoy. Beneath soaring 30ft frescoed ceilings, surrounded by ocean views and entertained by a roving harpsichordist, guests begin their feast at the breakfast bar, featuring homemade donuts, tropical fruits and an on-demand omelette chef. Next, swing through the carving station, past the cheese table brimming with exotic goat cheeses and more, and make your way to the 4ft-tall ice sculpture standing vigil over the seafood bank overflowing with tiger shrimp, king-crab legs and mussels. Hit the hot-foods banquette and as you weave back to your seat, grab a treat from the caviar station (featuring both American sturgeon and salmon). Gorge. Repeat. Top off the fine repast with one (or more) of the 40 ever-rotating, single-serving desserts on display. Strong coffee and festive mimosas are included; bottled water is not.

Drinking & Entertainment

Society of the Four Arts (☎ 561-655-7226; www.four arts.org; 2 Four Arts Plaza) The concert series here includes cabaret, the Palm Beach Symphony, chamber orchestras, string quartets and piano performances. There's also a Friday and Sunday film series, screening everything from foreign flicks to hard-hitting documentaries

Cucina Dell'arte (☎ 561-655-0770; 257 Royal Poinciana Way; mains $15-55; ⓥ 7am-3am) Reminiscent of a Florentine cafe, this high-end eatery overflows with warm colors, art and some of the finest glitterati in Palm Beach. Around 10pm, they shove the tables out of the way and blast the music. Expect to see dancing botox queens, beautiful visiting fashionistas, desperate old guys and totally normal people soaking it all in. Pretentious enough to be fun, if you arrive wearing a serious face, you'll be sorry.

Leopard Lounge (☎ 561-659-5800; www.chesterfield pb.com/dining/bar/; 363 Cocoanut Row; ⓥ 6:30pm-1am) Under a hand-painted fresco covered by seductive half-naked provocateurs, naughty cherubs and leering satyrs, this retro jungle-themed place attracts a mature crowd and the occasional celeb (neither photos nor autograph-hounds are allowed). Live music nightly.

Shopping

The quarter-mile, palm-tree-lined strip along **Worth Avenue** (www.worth-avenue.com) is Florida's answer to Rodeo Drive. You can trace its history to the 1920s, when the now-defunct Everglades Club staged weekly fashion shows and launched the careers of designers from Bonwit Teller to Elizabeth Arden. Today you'll find more than 200 shops, representing every exclusive brand known: Cartier, Armani, Gucci, Chanel, Dior, Jimmy Choo, Ann Gish, Loro Piana, Emilo Pucci and Hermes are just the beginning. Half the shops close for summer, but it's fun to stroll and window shop (and celeb-spot), whether you want to lay down your plastic or not. If you're looking for deals, keep moving to…

Rapunzel's Closet (☎ 561-659-3436; www.shop rapunzels.com; 326 S County Rd; ⓥ 10am-6pm Mon-Sat, noon-5pm Sun) Owner Randy Evans travels the country looking for stylish jeans and tees, sexy dresses and skirts and reasonably priced shoes and bags for her hip, young clientele.

Deja Vu Consignment (☎ 561-833-6624; 219 Royal Poinciana Way; ⓥ 10am-6pm Mon-Sat, noon-5pm Sun) Palm Beachers don't like to be seen multiple times in the same outfit so this immaculate secondhand store overflows with very gently used clothes. Most of the items are grandma-friendly, but a little digging can yield fantastic results. Prices can still soar into the thousands for the likes of Armani suits.

SOUTHEAST FLORIDA

Getting There & Around

Palmtran (☎ 561-841-4287; www.palmtran.org) bus 41 covers the bulk of the island, from Lantana Rd to Sunrise Ave; transfer to bus 1 at Publix to go north or south along US 1. To get to Palm Beach International Airport in West Palm Beach, take bus 41 to the downtown transfer and hop on bus 44.

Though it's a fairly compact city, the two major downtown neighborhoods, centered on Royal Poinciana Way and Worth Ave, are a fair hike apart.

WEST PALM BEACH

☎ 561 / pop 107,000

When Henry Flagler decided to develop what is now West Palm Beach, he knew precisely what it would become: a working-class community for the labor force that would support his glittering resort town across the causeway. And so the fraternal twins were born – Palm Beach, considered the fairer of the two; and West Palm Beach, working hard, playing harder, and simply being cooler.

West Palm is a groovy place to explore, despite the seemingly never-ending condo construction going on downtown and along the waterfront. It's a community with a surprisingly diverse collection of restaurants, friendly inhabitants (including a strong gay community) and a gorgeous waterway that always seems to reflect the perfect amount of starlight. If you ask most people where to go, they'll send you to CityPlace – the massive alfresco mall that's practically taken over town – so be sure to ask where *else* you should go. CityPlace is cool, but this city has much more to offer.

Orientation

West Palm Beach sprawls along the west bank of Lake Worth (the Intracoastal Waterway), separating it from Palm Beach. It's a planned community with a fairly straightforward grid. The main north–south routes are I-95 and US Hwy 1, which splits into S Dixie Hwy (southbound) and Olive Ave (northbound) through downtown. Flagler Dr also runs north–south, hugging the water and making for a prettier and more relaxed drive. Major east–west roads are Okeechobee Blvd (which crosses the causeway to Palm Beach), Belvedere Rd and Southern Blvd. Downtown centers around Clematis St and CityPlace (running along Rosemary Ave). There's fantastic public transportation throughout the immediate area.

Information

The *Palm Beach Post* (www.palmbeachpost .com) is the largest paper, but the *Palm Beach Daily News* (www.palmbeachdailynews.com) has more human-interest stories. Weeklies *New Times* (www.browardpalmbeach.com) and *City Link* (www.southflorida.metromix .com) are saucy and free, though *Closer* (www .closermagazine.com) is hipper. The local chamber of commerce publishes both the annual *Guide to the Palm Beaches* and the *Palm Beach County Guide*.

Radio stations here are terrible. The best of a bad lot include FM's 88.5 (local alternative bands), 90.7 (public radio), 95.5 (pop) and 98.7 (classic rock).

Chamber of Commerce (☎ 561-833-3711; www .palmbeaches.org; 401 N Flagler Dr) Geared toward businesspeople, though there's some basic info on cultural attractions and local accommodations.

Clematis St Newsstand & Café (☎ 561-832-2302; 206 Clematis St; 🖳) A great selection of international magazines and newspapers, books, gifts and a tidy café. Internet access is $8 per hour.

Library (☎ 561-659-8010; 100 Clematis St; 🖳) Offers free internet access.

Main post office (640 Clematis St) Conveniently located.

Sights & Activities

NORTON MUSEUM OF ART

The largest museum in Florida, the **Norton** (☎ 561-832-5196; www.norton.org; 1451 S Olive Ave; adult/child $8/3; 🕑 10am-5pm Mon-Sat, 1-5pm Sun, closed Mon May-Oct) opened in 1941 to display the enormous art collection of industrialist Ralph Hubbard Norton and his wife Elizabeth. The Norton's permanent collection of more than 5000 pieces (including works by Matisse, Warhol and O'Keefe) is displayed alongside important Chinese, pre-Columbian Mexican and US Southwestern artifacts, plus some wonderful contemporary photography and regular traveling exhibitions. Don't miss the Nessel Wing, consisting of an oval atrium, 14 galleries and a colorful crowd pleaser: a ceiling made from nearly 700 pieces of handblown glass by Dale Chihuly. Lie back on one of the corner's couches and get lost in his magical creation.

ANN NORTON SCULPTURE GARDEN

This serene collection of **sculptures** (☎ 561-832-5328; 253 Barcelona Rd; admission $5; 🕑 11am-4pm Wed-Sat)

SOUTHEAST FLORIDA

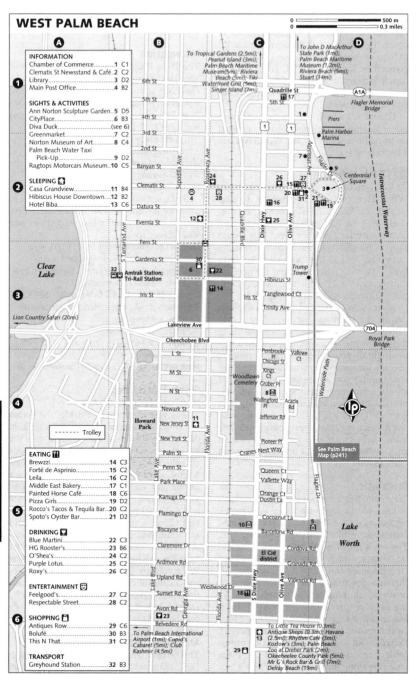

WEST PALM BEACH

0 ────── 500 m
0 ────── 0.3 miles

To Tropical Gardens (2.5mi);
Peanut Island (3mi);
Palm Beach Maritime
Museum(5mi); Riviera
Beach (5mi); Tiki
Waterfront Grill (5mi);
Singer Island (7mi)

To John D MacArthur
State Park (1mi);
Palm Beach Maritime
Museum (1.2mi);
Riviera Beach (5mi);
Stuart (34mi)

6th St
5th St
4th St
3rd St
2nd St

Banyan St
Clematis St
Datura St
Evernia St
Fern St
Gardenia St

Quadrille St
5th St

Flagler Memorial
Bridge

Piers
Palm Harbor
Marina

Centennial
Square

Intracoastal Waterway

**Clear
Lake**

Amtrak Station;
Tri-Rail Station

Iris St

Lakeview Ave

Okeechobee Blvd

Lion Country Safari (20mi)

Trolley

**Howard
Park**

L St
M St
N St
Newark St
New Jersey St
New York St
Palm St
Penn St
Park Place
Kanuga Dr
Flamingo Dr
Biscayne Dr
Claremore Dr
Ardmore Rd
Upland Rd
Sunset Ave
Avon Rd
Belvedere Rd

Pembrooke
Pl
Chicago St
Kings
Ct
Gruber Pl
Wallingford
Pl
Jefferson Rd
Pioneer Pl
Cranes Nest Way

**Woodlawn
Cemetery**

Trump
Tower

Hibiscus St
Tanglewood Ct
Trinity Ave

Royal Park
Bridge

Yallowe
Ct
Acacia
Rd
Queens Ct
Vallette Way
Orange Ct
Dustin La
Cocoanut La
Barcelona Rd
Cordova Rd
Granada Rd
Valencia Rd

**El Cid
district**

**Lake
Worth**

See Palm Beach
Map (p241)

To Palm Beach International
Airport (1mi); Cupid's
Cabaret (5mi); Club
Kashmir (4.5mi)

Westwood Dr

To Little Tea House (0.3mi);
Antique Shops (0.3mi); Havana
(2.5mi); Rhythm Café (3mi);
Kozlow's (3mi); Palm Beach
Zoo at Dreher Park (2mi);
Okeeheelee County Park (5mi);
Mr G's Rock Bar & Grill (7mi);
Delray Beach (19mi)

SOUTHEAST FLORIDA

is a real West Palm gem. The historic house, verdant grounds and enormous sculptures are all the work of Ralph Norton's second wife, Ann. After establishing herself as an artist in New York in the mid-1930s, she became the first sculpture teacher at the Norton School of Art in West Palm and soon married Ralph. When creating the garden, she intended to create a soothing environment for the public to relax. She succeeded.

After poking through Norton's historic, but simple, antique-filled home, you can wander the grounds and uncover her soaring feats of granite, brick, marble and bronze. Perhaps most awe-inspiring is the 1965 *Cluster*, a collection of seven burka-clad Islamic women done in pink granite. Before leaving, be sure to peek into Norton's light-filled studio, where unfinished pieces and dusty tools lie just as she left them.

CITYPLACE

This massive outdoor **shopping and entertainment center** (☎ 561-366-1000; www.cityplace.com; 701 S Rosemary Ave) is the crown jewel of West Palm Beach's urban-renewal initiative; locals love telling visitors how this area was formerly filled with crack houses. A mix of boutiques and chain stores, CityPlace is a one-stop destination for diners, moviegoers, trendy-shop shoppers and anyone who wants a reason to take a stroll. Its 600,000 sq ft comprise a slew of stores, about a dozen restaurants, a 20-screen movie theater, the Harriet Himmel Theater and 570 private residences – not to mention free concerts in the outdoor plaza. Beautiful but vaguely sterile, CityPlace has nevertheless been immensely successful in bringing all types together in one spot, from tourist families looking for fun on a rainy day to clutches of local ladies out for a day of shopping – and everyone in between.

CLEMATIS STREET

Long before CityPlace came along, there was Clematis St, a hip, bohemian strip bustling with locals doing their shopping, diners looking for a foodie scene, and scads of bar-hoppers come nightfall. In short, this stretch is the most eclectic strip in town – and much of it's also a historic district with a jumbled collection of architecture – Greek Revival, Venetian Revival, Mediterranean Revival and art deco.

Every Thursday night, Clematis plays host West Palm's signature event: Clematis

by Night (p251. On Saturday mornings, just north of the plaza at 2nd St and Narcissus Ave (where local school kids frolic in the fountains on hot afternoons) there's a delightful **Greenmarket**, where you'll find treats ranging from locally grown avocados and orchids to organic coffees and dog treats.

LION COUNTRY SAFARI

The first cageless drive-through safari in the country, this incredible **animal park** (☎ 561-793-1084; www.lioncountrysafari.com; 2003 Lion Country Safari Rd; adult/child $23/18; 9:30am-5:30pm) puts you in the cage (ie your car) as 800 creatures roam freely, staring at *you*. Equal parts conservation area and safari, the park's 500 acres are home to bison, zebra, white rhinos, chimpanzees and, of course, lions. You tour the safari section in your car (unless it's a convertible; short-term rentals are available), driving slowly, hoping the animals approach the vehicle. The best time to go is when it rains, because the animals are more active when it's cool.

After experiencing this backward-zoo, you can enjoy the aviaries, reptile exhibits, petting zoo, water park and daily educational presentations. The safari is an official rehabilitation facility, taking in injured animals and nursing them back to health before returning them either to the wild or to a more appropriate (less touristy) home. It's a surreal combo of tacky tourism gone wild and animal-loving kindness – but for many people, this is as close as they'll come to seeing wild animals 'in the wild.'

PALM BEACH ZOO AT DREHER PARK

The highlight of this compact **zoo** (☎ 561-547-9453; www.palmbeachzoo.com; 1301 Summit Blvd; adult/child $12.95/8.95; 9am-5pm) is the Tropics of the Americas exhibit, a 3-acre recreation of a rainforest, stocked with jaguars, monkeys, snakes, macaws and other tropical creatures. Gator feedings occur regularly and are advertised. The zoo's also home to a few of the last remaining Florida panthers, North America's rarest mammal. Other unusual residents include Komodo dragons (the largest lizard in the world), capybaras (the largest rodent in the world) and red kangaroos, which can hop at speeds of up to 40mph.

RAGTOPS MOTORCARS MUSEUM

This spot was originally a classic-car dealership with three convertible Mercedes, Ty Houck's incredible **automobile collection**

(☎ 561-655-2836; www.ragtopsmotorcars.com; 2119 S Dixie Hwy; admission $8; ⊙ 10am-5pm Mon-Sat) grew quickly, compelling area automotive enthusiasts to stop by for a look-see. Today, you can test-drive many of the vehicles on display, though it helps to have serious intent to buy. Otherwise, you're free to browse the rarities displayed, including an amphibious 1967 Triumph, a regal 1935 Bentley and a 1959 Edsel station wagon.

PEANUT ISLAND

Plopped right off the northeastern corner of West Palm, **Peanut Island** (☎ 561-845-4445; www .pbcgov.com/parks/peanutisland) was created in 1918 by dredging projects. Originally named Inlet Island, the spit was renamed for a peanut oil-shipping operation that failed in 1946. It has long been a popular spot for boaters to moor and party by day, and in 2005 the county plunked $13 million into island rehabilitation resulting in Peanut Island Park, which includes a pier, a man-made reef and some pretty sweet campsites (right).

The island also features a blast shelter built in secret for President John F Kennedy shortly after his 1960 election. Kennedy never used the facility – other than as a jumping-off point for water-skiing – but today, the **Palm Beach Maritime Museum** (☎ 561-832-7428; www.pbmm .org; admission $10; ⊙ 11:30am-4:30pm) offers guided tours of the red-roofed facility.

There are no roads to the island. Visitors must either have their own boats or take the water taxi (see right).

BIKING, BLADING & WALKING

You'll find several parks around town, many equipped with paved trails suitable for biking, blading or running. Five miles south of town, **Okeeheelee County Park** (☎ 561-966-6600; 7715 Forest Hill Blvd) has a 6-mile paved path – not to mention a BMX track, golf course, water-ski park, nature center and equestrian trail.

The most scenic walk – a smooth, waterside path wide enough for all sorts of active folk – is the one that edges the Intracoastal Waterway along **Flagler Dr**. From Okeechobee Blvd heading north, notable waymarkers include aging but impressive Trump Tower and secluded Palm Harbor Marina.

Heading south from Okeechobee, you'll enter the historic **El Cid district**, a lovely neighborhood packed with multimillion-dollar homes – ranging from Mediterranean Revival to classic Florida bungalow – offering numerous tantalizingly distracting side streets.

Tours

Palm Beach Water Taxi (☎ 561-683-8294; www .watertaxi.homestead.com; 98 Lake Dr, Singer Island) runs a water taxi between downtown West Palm and Singer Island (one-way/round-trip $7/12), as well as a water taxi to Peanut Island (round-trip $7) leaving from the Singer Island. Additionally, they offer guided tours along the Intracoastal, including 90-minute narrated tours of Palm Beach mansions ($24), 60-minute sunset cruises ($20) and seasonal manatee tours ($21). The pickup location in West Palm Beach is at the intersection of Banyan St and Flagler Dr.

The hybrid bus-boat **Diva Duck** (☎ 561-844-4418; www.divaduck.com; adult/child $25/15) gives quacky 75-minute narrated tours of downtown's historic district, CityPlace, the surrounding waterways and the shores of Peanut Island. Yes, the bus really does float on the water. Tours start at CityPlace.

Sleeping

Skip the depressing chain hotels near the airport and try one of these cool spots.

Peanut Island (☎ 561-845-4445; www.pbcgov .com/parks/camping/peanutisland/; sites $18.40) This tiny island has 20 developed campsites by reservation only and a host of primitive sites right on the sand on a first-come, first-served basis. There are some restrictions, so call or hit the website.

our pick Hotel Biba (☎ 561-832-0094; www.hotel biba.com; 320 Belvedere Rd; r summer/winter $109/150; P 🖳 🖳) West Palm has a smattering of cool sleeping options, but the funky, retro Hotel Biba beats them all. This groovy art-deco spot has lots going for it – spare-chic decor in vibrantly colored rooms; a leafy little courtyard with hidden-away pool; and a hip, sexy bar where you'll find the complimentary continental breakfast (featuring local Cuban pastries) in the morning and a thriving lounge scene at night. A block from the Intracoastal, the Biba is perched on the edge of the beautiful El Cid district. It's a three-minute drive to CityPlace or Clematis, five to the airport.

Tropical Gardens (☎ 561-841-7210; www.tropical gardenbandb.com; 419 32nd St; r low season $135-155, high season $145-175; 🖳 🖳) Located in historic Old Northwood, north of town, this small yet progressive B&B uses natural bath products and cleaning and pool supplies; serves organic breakfasts (including vegetarian and vegan options); and has its own tiki bar overlooking the pool. There are two clean guestrooms inside, but angle for one of the cottages out back and you'll be happier.

Hibiscus House Downtown (☎ 561-833-8171; www .hibiscushousedowntown.com; 213 S Rosemary Ave; r $120-240, ste $140-280; 🖵) Fabulously located, this pair of 1917 homes has four-poster beds, floral prints, abundant light and a cool front porch with wicker chairs. Take a load off and watch the world – including the city trolley, which stops out front – roll by. Renowned for its fab bar, it's worth a visit even if you're not staying here.

Casa Grandview (☎ 561-313-9695; www.casa grandview.com; 1410 Georgia Ave; per week $750-2200; P 🖵 🐾) This pet-friendly dual-pooled compound in historic Grandview Heights is just different. There are no rooms; guests get their own cottage. There aren't any daily rentals; cottages rent by the week. This isn't your grandmother's B&B; with bold colors and suave, contemporary decor, this place straddles classic elegance and modern design better than the vast majority of resorts.

Eating

The food scene here is an eclectic affair – ethnic eats mixed with quirky spaces and quaint tearooms – and lots of affordable options. Here's where you'll find the antidotes to the fancy fest across the waterway.

BUDGET

Little Tea House (☎ 561-832-5683; www.thelittle teahouse.com; 3627 1/2 S Dixie Hwy; mains & tea $6-11; ⏰ 9am-2pm Mon-Sat) Tucked down a tiny alley, this pocket of calm consists of several small seating areas, outdoor dining deck and teashop. Choose from big fresh salads, quiche, sandwiches and, of course, tea service, complete with fresh scones, clotted cream and finger sandwiches.

Pizza Girls (☎ 561-833-4004; www.pizzagirls.com; 205 Clematis St; slice/pizza $4/21; ⏰ 11am-10pm Mon-Wed, to 11pm Thu-Sat, noon-9pm Sun) Pizza Girls' huge, innovative pizzas named mostly after the Big Apple (the New Yorker sports portobellos, roasted peppers, spinach, onion and toasted goat cheese) are slices of heaven in earthly downtown West Palm. There are only five tables inside, so order a slice, trot to the Intracoastal and watch the water lap at your feet.

Middle East Bakery (☎ 561-659-7322; www .salloumfoods.com; 327 5th St; mains $6-9) In an unassuming little building, Adib Salloum and his gang prepare fresh Moroccan, Lebanese and Mediterranean cuisine. Even if you just come to browse their olive barrels and hummus selection, this place's warm, spicy aroma will compel you to grab one of their takeout options, like falafel sandwiches or shistawooks.

Tiki Waterfront Grill (☎ 561-845-5532; 200 E 13th St; mains $8-15; ⏰ 11am-10pm Mon-Fri, from 8am Sat & Sun) Nestled inside the Riviera Beach Marina, this hidden gem is pure Florida. Open-aired, thatch-roofed and right on the water, it has a rowdy but friendly feel and live music Thursday through Sunday. In addition to hearty pre-boat-ride breakfasts on weekends, this divine dive dishes up the best Buffalo shrimp and Baja-styled fish tacos on the east coast.

From downtown, take US 1 (here called Olive Ave) north over the bridge to E 13th St; go right.

MIDRANGE

our pick **Rocco's Tacos & Tequila Bar** (☎ 561-650-1001; www.roccostacos.com; 24 Clematis St; lunch $9-16, dinner $12-19; ⏰ 11:30am-1am Sun & Mon, to midnight Tue & Wed, to 1am Thu-Sat) This brand Nuevo Mexican restaurant, in the heart of West Palm's Clematis St, is not your typical *taqueria*. Under the warm twinkle of cool chandeliers enjoy guacamole prepared tableside, one of 175 different kinds of tequila from a long wooden bar and flavorful barbicoas, fresh-made ceviches or fruity spinach tostadas. Choose from a range of tacos, too, from the typical meat-stuffed to mushroom or grilled cactus paddle. Classy, tasteful and romantic, Rocco's Tacos also manages to be loads of fun, serving as both a great place to meet before going out, or as a hip, enjoyable destination all on its own.

Havana (☎ 561-547-9799; 6801 S Dixie Hwy; dinner $11-16; ⏰ 11am-11pm Sun-Thu, to 1am Fri & Sat) Biting into this Cuban restaurant's tender *ropa vieja* (shredded beef in a spicy sauce) is like stepping into Cuba, c 1955. Added bonus: the walk-up window, serving the full menu, is open round the clock. When you need a pick-me-up, nothing works faster or tastes better than the steaming *café con leche* here.

Brewzzi (☎ 561-366-9753; www.brewzzi.com; 700 S Rosemary Ave, Suite 212; mains $14-25; ⏰ 11:30am-10:30pm Mon-Thu, to 11:30 Fri & Sat, to 10pm Sun)

SOUTHEAST FLORIDA

Three things: first, the award-winning on-site brewery crafts half a dozen fine brews. Second, the outside bar overlooks CityPlace's promenade, providing one of the finest people-watching spots in town, especially after dark, when CityPlace is all a-twinkle. Third, the pizza? Heavenly.

Leila (☎ 561-659-7373; www.leilawpb.com; 120 S Dixie Hwy; mains $17-38; ☺ 11:30am-2:30pm Mon-Fri, dinner from 5:30pm nightly) Cobalt walls, gauzy scrims and iridescent sconces transport you to another place; after one bite you realize that place is heaven. Translating as 'exotic night,' cosmopolitan Leila offers mouthwatering starters like grilled Syrian cheeses; main dishes include zesty plates of lamb, beef or veggies. Cap dinner with a muscular Turkish coffee or a post-meal puff from a hookah. (Also cool: each month, the owners donate a percentage of profits to charity.)

TOP END

Spoto's Oyster Bar (☎ 561-835-1828; 125 Datura St; mains $14-28; ☺ lunch Mon-Fri, dinner daily) Featuring freshly shucked, cold-water Blue Point oysters, steamed littleneck clams from Cape Cod and a rotating oyster special, this stalwart has been a fixture in downtown West Palm forever, it seems. Jammed with a chatty lunch crew and filled with a romantic evening crowd, Spoto's is the snazziest raw bar in town.

Rhythm Café (☎ 561-833-3406; www.rhythmcafe.cc; 3800 S Dixie Hwy; mains $15-33; ☺ dinner Mon-Sat) Housed in a former pharmacy, this cozy bistro in the heart of West Palm's antique district sports a super-fun, super-unpretentious atmosphere and delicious, eclectic eats. Owner-chef Ken Rzab unveils new, seasonal dishes daily, heaping on the flavor and morphing old standbys into novel creations (hog snapper with a tropical-fruit compote,

ginger and rum). Aside from the vintage lunch counter, there are only 10 tables, so call for reservations.

Painted Horse Café (☎ 561-833-1490; 2417 S Dixie Hwy; mains $19-27; ☺ dinner Mon-Sat) An unassuming little gem right on the highway, the Painted Horse is elegant and earthy all at once. You'll find a well-mixed crowd of older Palm Beach types and well-coiffed young folks; a classy menu featuring grilled salmon, seared tuna and New York strip steak, and an extensive wine list.

Forté de Asprinio (☎ 561-833-3936; www.fortepalmbeach.com; 225 Clematis St; mains $18-35; ☺ 5pm-1am Mon-Sat) Launched by wunderkind Stephen Asprinio, a contender on the first season of *Top Chef*, Forté is a sleek, *Jetsons*-esque palette of whites and pinks and lavenders featuring a carnival of rotating Italian-ish menu items, ranging from the mostly traditional (butternut squash mezzaluna) to the curiously exotic (pasta with braised rabbit). With its emphatically South Beach vibe – nearly more nightclub than restaurant – it's almost too cool for Clematis.

Drinking

Clematis and CityPlace have a revolving door of ultrachic bar-lounges and late-night dance clubs; they're also home to a couple of great, casual, stalwart hangouts.

O'Shea's (☎ 561-833-3865; www.osheaspub.com; 531 Clematis St; ☺ 11am-3am Sun-Thu, to 4am Fri & Sat) A quality Irish pub with good draught beer, live music most nights and – clichéd but true – lots of homesick Irish people at the bar.

Roxy's (☎ 561-296-7699; www.roxyspub.com; 309 Clematis St; ☺ 11:30am-3am Sun-Thu, to 4am Fri & Sat) Home to the county's first liquor license, this joint has changed hands (and locations) several times, but the 42ft mahogany and brass Brunswick Bar has remained since 1935.

GAY WEST PALM BEACH

Recently, some worn-out Miamians and Lauderdalians have been escaping the 'rat race' of those communities, cashing in and heading north to West Palm Beach. The website **www.outinwest palmbeach.com** is a great illustration of how extensive the LGBT scene has become here – especially when it comes to nightlife. Mellow hangouts include **HG Rooster's** (☎ 561-832-9119; www.hgroosters.com; 823 Belvedere Rd), **Kozlow's** (☎ 561-533-5355; 6205 Georgia Ave) and **Lulu's Place** (☎ 561-278-4004; 640 E Atlantic Ave, Delray Beach). For straight-up, in-your-face booty, men should make a beeline for **Cupid's Cabaret** (☎ 561-642-5557; 4430 Forest Hill Blvd), where constant go-go boys and monthly porn-star visits are pleasant distractions. **Club Kashmir** (☎ 561-649-5557; 1651 S Congress Ave) is another lively dance club. For up-to-date club info, navigate to www.jumponmarkslist.com or www.floridagayclubs.com/WestPalmBeach.html.

With 55 beers on tap, a great pub menu and frequent live music, the recently renovated Roxy's is one of West Palm's newest hotspots. Again.

Blue Martini (☎ 561-835-8601; www.bluemartini lounge.com; 550 S Rosemary Ave; ☺ 4pm-3am Sun-Thu, to 4am Fri & Sat) This chic CityPlace lounge, known to attract its share of celebs, has three full bars, an extensive martini menu and live music nightly. Dress to impress – it's required.

Purple Lotus (☎ 561-337-4610; www.myspace.com/purple_lotus_kava; 312 S Dixie Hwy; ☺ 7pm-midnight) Surrounded by tiki torches, tribal masks and mellow music, guests can enjoy a coconut bowl of kava, a legal intoxicant that's near the intersection of Beer and Valium. Consumed throughout the South Pacific, the bitter drink increases relaxation without disrupting mental clarity; a trip here promises a laid-back night.

Entertainment
CLUBS
Respectable Street (☎ 561-832-9999; www.respectable street.com; 518 Clematis St) Respectables has kept South Florida jamming to great bands for two decades; they also organize October's MoonFest, the city's best block party. Great DJs, strong drinks and a breezy chill-out patio are added bonuses. See if you can find the hole that the Red Hot Chili Peppers' Anthony Kiedis punched in the wall when they played here.

Mr G's Rock Bar & Grill (☎ 561-434-9917; www.mrgslive.com; 2650 S Military Trail) During the week, there's Beer Pong (Tuesdays, also Biker Night), open mic (Wednesdays) and college night (Thursdays). Weekends rage with live rock blasting among a sea of pool tables. The menu features music-themed dishes (Phish dip), but don't arrive too early: the party doesn't get going till the dancers show up after work.

Feelgood's (☎ 561-833-6500; www.drfeelgoodsbar .com; 219 Clematis St) Co-owned by Motley Crue frontman Vince Neil, this 8500-sq-ft rock bar/dance club has shiny choppers, rock memorabilia and a mammoth snake slithering into the rafters. Heads up: the place is packed with girls, from bartenders in skimpy outfits, to dancers on the poles, to customers coming to get wild – some visitors will love it and some will loathe it; bypass this place if you are of the latter variety. Not enough big '80s hair, but it's still good, cheesy fun.

PERFORMING ARTS
Florida's largest waterfront music and art festival, **SunFest** (☎ 561-659-5980; www.sunfest .com) rawks for five days in early May, attracting more than 250,000 visitors and raising money for scholarships for art students. In addition to giving up-and-comers a stage, international acts have ranged from Sheryl Crow to Ziggy Marley.

Every Thursday from 6pm to 9:30pm, the city shuts down the eastern terminus of Clematis St, brings in food carts and crafts vendors and stages a free outdoor music festival under the stars. The kid- and dog-friendly **Clematis by Night** (☎ 561-822-1515; www.clematisby night.net) spotlights great local and national acts playing everything from rock to swing. Drink up: proceeds from the beer truck are split between the city and the nonprofit group pouring drinks that night.

On Fridays and Saturdays, CityPlace hosts **free outdoor concerts** (☎ 561-366-1000; www.cityplace .com) from 6pm to 10pm in front of the gorgeous CityPlace Fountain. Bands stick to familiar rock, R&B and occasionally country sounds.

Shopping
Just south of town is a peerless **antiques row** (S Dixie Hwy). With more than 50 antiquaries, you're sure to unearth an incredible find from a Palm Beach estate.

Slick **Bolufé** (☎ 561-366-8620; www.shopbolufe .com; 700 S Rosemary Ave) tantalizes with plenty of fashion-forward, celeb-approved threads, like Rawyalty, 1921 and Z Brand.

This N That (☎ 561-833-5223; 216 Clematis St; ☺ 11am-2pm & 4pm-7pm Tue, Wed & Fri, to 10pm Thu, 9am-6pm Sat, 10am-3pm Sun) is a funky consignment shop with stuff that's more modern (or at least less musty) than most vintage shops. Expect edgy art and all manner of hodge-podgery.

Getting There & Around
Palm Beach International Airport (PBI; ☎ 561-471-7420; www.pbia.org) is the king of medium-sized airports. Small, hassle-free, conveniently located, parking a-plenty and best of all, free wi-fi throughout the entire 560,000-sq-ft facility, PBI is served by most major airlines and car-rental companies. It's about a mile west of I-95 on Belvedere Rd. **PalmTran** (☎ 561-841-4287; www.palmtran.org) bus 44 runs between the airport, the train station and downtown ($1.25).

SOUTHEAST FLORIDA

DETOUR: SINGER ISLAND

To reach Singer from West Palm Beach, take Olive Ave north over the bridge (where it's called Broadway) until you hit Blue Heron Blvd; cross the causeway, turn right on Lake Dr and follow it to the **Sailfish Marina** (☎ 561-42-8449; www.sailfishmarina.com; 98 Lake Dr), which serves brunch on weekends between 8am and 1pm ($17 for adults, $12 for kids). Grab a seat close to the water, slowly chew your smoked salmon, tropical fruit or fresh Belgian waffles and watch the resident pelicans paddle around the yachts, searching for their own breakfast.

Full? Good. Get in the car and head east to S Ocean Ave, then head north to Beach Rd and scoot into the parking lot. Park and head past the surf shop and gently rolling dunes. You're probably thinking, 'Where are all the people?' Yup, that's why we're here. Pick a spot, spread your towel, lie down and let breakfast digest. Read a magazine. Stroll the beach. Take a dip.

Holy cow, where did the time go? If you're thirsty, nearby Tiki Waterfront Grill (p249), a dive teeming with sunburned boaters, has a loud, fun bar, great fish tacos and regular live music. To get there, head back along Blue Heron to Broadway, turn left (south) and then left on E 13th St. The Tiki Grill is at the end of the street. Enjoy your tacos; dance awhile. You're in Florida.

In a brilliant display of civil engineering, **Greyhound** (☎ 561-833-9636; 215 S Tamarind Ave), **Tri-Rail** (☎ 800-875-7245; 203 S Tamarind Ave) and **Amtrak** (☎ 561-832-6169; 201 S Tamarind Ave) share the same building, the historic Seaboard Train Station. The surprisingly beautiful Spanish-Mediterranean complex started seeing action in 1925, when Henry Flagler's *Orange Blossom Express* made its first run southward. PalmTran serves the station with bus 44 (from the airport).

Once you're settled, driving and parking is a cinch, plus a cute and convenient (and free!) trolley runs between Clematis St and CityPlace starting at 11am.

TREASURE COAST

If you ask people to describe Florida, many would probably mention Miami's art-deco scene, Fort Lauderdale's party scene, Palm Beach's mansion scene…and skip straight to Disney. While the area north of West Palm – dubbed the Treasure Coast – doesn't have many party strips or flashy mansions, it does have much to offer.

The Treasure Coast gets its name from the same source that the Gold Coast gets its moniker from – for being the site of numerous treasure-laden shipwrecks over the years. In fact, today the Treasure Coast is where you'll find Florida's true jewels, in the form of unspoiled paradise.

Industrialist billionaire and philanthropist John D MacArthur once owned almost eve-rything from Palm Beach Gardens to Stuart, and he kept it mostly pristine during his life. Over time, he grew concerned that Florida's real-estate bonanza would compromise – or destroy – what he considered paradise. Therefore, in his will, he stated that thousands of acres would be kept wild, and the rest would be deeded out incrementally, in order to save the oceanfront property from Miami's fate. And you know what? His plan worked.

There are several urban attractions on this stretch – Stuart's the highlight – but even it can't compare with a moonlight kayak trip through St Lucie Inlet State Park or a stroll along one of the many people-free miles of beach on Hutchinson Island.

JOHN D MACARTHUR STATE PARK

While this **state park** (☎ 561-624-6950; www.macarthurbeach.org; 10900 Jack Nicklaus Dr; per car with up to 8 passengers/pedestrian $4/1; ◷ 8am-sunset) is one of the smallest in the region, it has among the best turtle-watching programs around, as loggerhead, green and leatherback turtles nest along the beach in June and July. It's home to several aquariums and a spectacular 1600ft boardwalk spanning the mangroves of Lake Worth Cove. The on-site nature center offers guided (single/double $20/35) and unguided (single/double $10 to $15 per hour) **kayak trips**.

On alternate Thursday mornings, the park offers yoga on the beach, and on full-moon weekends, it offers moonlight concerts and bluegrass shows. Free, guided nature walks are offered daily at 10am.

JUPITER & JUPITER ISLAND

☎ 561 / Jupiter pop 50,028 / Jupiter Island
pop 653

Jupiter is largely ritzy-residential, but it does have some good parks and a few nice joints for hanging out with friends.

Orientation & Information

Just about a half hour north of West Palm is the otherworldly Jupiter, home to pristine beaches and a couple of stars (such as Burt Reynolds). For the best regional information, hit the **visitor information center** (☎ 561-575-4656; www.jupiterfloridausa.com; 8020 Indiantown Rd; ☿ 8:30am-5:30pm Mon-Fri) on your way into town.

Sights & Activities

JONATHAN DICKINSON STATE PARK

With almost 11,500 acres to explore, this is an excellent **state park** (☎ 561-546-2771; 16450 SE Federal Hwy; per car with up to 8 passengers/pedestrian $4/1; ☿ 8am-sunset) between US Hwy 1 and the Loxahatchee River. There's no ocean access in the park, but its attraction lies in its several habitats: pine flatwoods, cypress stands, swamp and increasingly endangered coastal sand-pine scrub. Ranger-led nature walks leave at 9am Sunday from the Cypress Creek Pavilion, and campfire programs are offered Saturday at dusk next to the Pine Grove campground.

You can rent canoes and kayaks from the **concession stand** (☎ 561-746-1466; www.floridaparktours.com; ☿ 9am-5pm). Canoes cost $16 for two hours; kayaks cost $15/20 for singles/doubles for two hours. You can also rent motorboats at $50 for two hours, but mind the manatees. Guided-tour boat rides of the Loxahatchee River are available throughout the day (adult/child $19/12).

There are also several short-loop **hiking and bicycle trails**, the most popular of which is the Kitching Creek Trail, just north of the boat landing, walkable in about 1½ hours. Visit www.clubscrub.org for details on biking options.

JUPITER INLET LIGHTHOUSE

Built in 1860, this historic **lighthouse** (☎ 561-747-8380; www.jupiterlighthouse.org; intersection Capt Armour's Way, US Hwy 1 & Beach Rd; ☿ 10am-5pm Tue-Sun) hasn't missed a night of work in more than 100 years and is among the oldest lighthouses on the Atlantic coast. Visitors can climb the 108 steps and see the surrounding area (including the

ocean). Tours to the lighthouse depart every half hour. There's some interesting Seminole and pioneer Florida memorabilia in the small (and woefully disorganized) museum.

HOBE SOUND NATIONAL WILDLIFE REFUGE

A 1035-acre federally protected nature sanctuary, **Hobe Sound National Wildlife Refuge** (☎ 561-546-6141) has two sections: a small slice on the mainland between Hobe Sound and US Hwy 1, opposite the Jonathan Dickinson State Park; and the main refuge grounds at the northern end of Jupiter Island.

The Jupiter Island section has 3½ miles of beach (it's a favorite sea-turtle nesting ground), mangroves and sand dunes, while the mainland section is a pine scrub forest. In June and July, nighttime turtle-watching walks occur on Tuesdays and Thursdays (reservations necessary), and birding trips can be arranged through the Hawley Education Center at Blowing Rocks Preserve. There's also a leafy bike path.

BLOWING ROCKS PRESERVE

This **preserve** (☎ 561-744-6668; admission $2; ☿ 9am-4:30pm) encompasses a mile-long limestone outcrop riddled with holes, cracks and fissures; when the tide is high and there's a strong easterly wind (call for conditions), water spews up as if from a geyser. Bring a tripod and an empty memory card. Even when seas are calm, you can hike through four coastal biomes: shifting dune, coastal strand, interior mangrove wetlands and tropical coastal hammock. Across the street, **Hawley Education Center** (☎ 561-744-6668; 574 S Beach Rd, Jupiter Island) has rotating art exhibits with nature themes, as well as two short nature trails and a butterfly garden.

Finding the refuge is a little tricky, as there's no signage: from US Hwy 1, take Bridge St (708 east) to Hobe Sound. Turn left on Beach St (707). Travel about 3 miles; the refuge is on your right.

MOROSO MOTORSPORTS PARK

Located on 200 acres of wooded property, **Moroso Motorsports Park** (☎ 561-622-1400; www.racemoroso.com; 17047 Bee Line Hwy) has a 2.25-mile 10-turn course and regular race events of all stripes. But the real fun here is the twice-weekly 'Test & Tune' on the NHRA-sanctioned 0.25-mile drag strip. Every

SOUTHEAST FLORIDA

Wednesday and Friday from 6pm to 11pm, you're allowed to race your beater against another vehicle on the track. Just slip on the helmet you brought (mandatory if you plan to drive over 13.99mph), stage and burn rubber. After your run, pick up your time slip to see how your vehicle performed. It's $20 to race, $13 to watch.

To get here from downtown, take Indiantown Rd west 11 miles to CR 711 (aka Pratt-Whitney Rd) and turn left. Drive south 3 miles and hang a right onto Bee Line Hwy. The Park is a mile up on the right.

BASEBALL AT ROGER DEAN STADIUM
It may not be a 'nature' activity, but an afternoon at this **stadium** (☎ 561-775-1818; www.roger deanstadium.com; 4751 Main St) will get you outdoors. This small but immaculate stadium is home to spring-training action for the Florida Marlins, the St Louis Cardinals and various minor-league teams. Ticket prices vary; call for details.

ACTIVE PURSUITS
Jupiter Outdoor Center (☎ 561-747-0063; www.jupiter outdoorcenter.com; 1000 Coastal A1A) rents kayaks (per hour/half-day/full day $25/$35/45) and organizes themed kayak trips in the area, like languid moonlight excursions and exploratory trips around Jupiter Inlet's mangroves.

You can get cycling information and rent your wheels from **Cycle Science of Jupiter Inc** (☎ 561-746-0585; 103 US 1), which has cruisers (day/week $15/75) and racing bikes ($45 per day) to use in this mostly flat, scenic region. The area parks are the best spots to find trails.

The county's only **dog-friendly beach** (☎ 561-748-0791; www.friendsofjupiterbeach.com) is in nearby

Juno Beach. To get there, follow Indiantown Rd east to A1A and turn right (south). The dog-friendly stretch begins across from Xanadu Lane and stretches two miles south, to Marcinski Rd. Good luck finding more delighted grins anywhere along the east coast.

Tours
Jupiter Island is more famous for its Forbes-magazine-confirmed status as the wealthiest community in the USA than for its natural wonders, but most mansions can't be seen from the road. Enter **Manatee Queen Tours** (☎ 561-744-2191; www.manateequeen.com; 1065 N Ocean Blvd), which offers two-hour afternoon tours and 1½-hour sunset tours (adult/child $24/15) on its 40ft catamaran. Voyeurs can peep at the homes of Burt Reynolds, Tiger Woods and more.

Water Taxi of the Palm Beaches (☎ 561-775-2628; www.water-taxi.com; adult/child $21/10) offers a two-hour tour around the emerald waters of Jupiter Inlet, which includes, of course, chances to gawk at the homes of the rich and famous.

Sleeping & Eating
Baron's Landing (☎ 561-746-8757; 18125 Ocean Blvd; r $120-150; ﹣) Calling all boaters: with dock rentals out back, these no-frills motel apartments overlook the Intracoastal and are an easy stroll to the ocean.

Jupiter Beach Resort (☎ 561-746-2511; www.jupiter beachresort.com; 5 N A1A; r $199-669; ﹣﹣) This elegant Key-lime-and-chocolate destination offers rooms (and over-the-top penthouse suites for $600 to $1500) sporting a cheerful, Caribbean style and million-dollar views. Inside, the floors are lined with Turkish

---

DETOUR: KAYAKING THE LOXAHATCHEE RIVER
One of two federally designated 'Wild and Scenic' rivers in the state, the free-flowing Loxahatchee River is home to a wide range of habitats, from tidal marsh riverines and dense mangrove communities to tidal flats and oyster bars. Translated as 'River of Turtles,' the coffee-colored river, which flows north, is home to countless shelled reptiles, as well as heron, osprey, otter, raccoon, the occasional bobcat – and lots of alligators. For a great day exploring the various aquatic preserves here, no one beats Riverbend Park's **Canoe Outfitters** (☎ 561-746-7053; www.canoeskayaks florida.com; 9060 W Indiantown Rd; 2-person canoes/single kayaks $50/40), which provides access to this lush waterway. From the launch, paddle to the right for thick, verdant waterways overhung with fallen branches and a small but thumping rapid; paddle to the left for open vistas and plentiful picnic areas. Canoes are good for families, but difficult to maneuver in this narrow waterway, so choose wisely. This terrific day out is gentle enough to be kid-friendly but eye-popping enough to appeal to the discerning adventurer.

marble; outside, the resort provides 1000ft of secluded beach, tennis courts and heated swimming pool with a poolside bar.

ourpick **Square Grouper** (☎ 561- 575-0252; 1111 Love St; snacks $1-7; ☺ noon-midnight Sun-Thu, to 1am Fri & Sat) If this Old Florida dive looks familiar, it's because the video for the Alan Jackson–Jimmy Buffet tune 'It's Five O'Clock Somewhere' was shot here. Perched on the water, with an ample (sandy) dance floor, this place is an ultracasual gem in an otherwise well-heeled town.

Reef Grill (☎ 561-624-9924; 12846 US Highway 1; mains $14-24) Thoroughly unpretentious but entirely drool-worthy, this casual, wood-paneled restaurant serves the best seafood dinners in the county. Featuring walls thick with fishing photos and taxidermied fish, this is the perfect place to try a Florida microbeer (Monk in the Trunk) and discover how locally caught grouper should be prepared.

If you would like to stay in the Jonathan Dickinson State Park there are two developed **campgrounds** (sites summer/winter $14/17) with hot showers, plus **cabins** (for 4 people per night $85), which have a minimum two-night stay at weekends. Sites have grills, and you can make campfires (no gathering wood in the park). Bring linens for the cabins. Two primitive riverside **sites** ($3) are also available; one is 5 miles from the ranger station, the other 10 miles. Both are accessible by boat.

Getting There & Around
Though I-95 is the quickest way through this area, do yourself a favor and get off the freeway. US Hwy 1 runs consistently up the coastline, and Hwy A1A jumps back and forth between the mainland (where it's the same as US Hwy 1) and various barrier islands.

STUART & AROUND
☎ 772 / pop 15,728
Often overlooked in favor of its more famous southern neighbors, Stuart has long been a hush-hush destination for sporty millionaires and their gleaming yachts. It wasn't until the late 1980s, however, that Stuart got its first exit off I-95, which is when the wave of rich folk, leaving places like Boca, started coming by in earnest.

Still, even though Stuart is posh, it's got a quiet, small-town feel and some stunning natural highlights. Fishing is tops here, too, which explains Stuart's nickname: 'Sailfish Capital of the World.'

Orientation & Information
Downtown Stuart, 20 miles north of Jupiter, was not designed for drivers: the unavoidable intersection – aka 'Confusion Corner' – of the city's major throughways, Colorado Ave, Flagler Ave, Dixie Hwy (A1A) and East and West Ocean Blvds confuses (and annoys) both locals and visitors.

The basic layout is this: Dixie Hwy slashes through the city from southeast to northwest. The town's two main drags, Flagler Ave and Osceola St, run parallel. East Ocean Blvd runs along the south side of downtown, connecting the mainland with Stuart Beach on Hutchinson Island. Sewell's Point is a spit of land between Stuart and Hutchinson Island, separating the St Lucie River from the Intracoastal Waterway.

The **chamber of commerce** (☎ 772-287-1088; www .goodnature.org; 1650 S Kanner Hwy; ☺ 8:30am-5pm Mon-Thu, to 4pm Fri) is about a mile south of town.

Sights & Activities
MARTIN COUNTY COUNCIL FOR THE ARTS
An umbrella organization for local cultural offerings, this **council** (☎ 772-287-6676; www .martinarts.org; 80 E Ocean Blvd; admission free; ☺ 10am-4pm Mon-Fri) is housed inside the 1937 WPA-built Martin County Courthouse. Its woefully underappreciated art gallery presents rotating exhibitions by local and regional artists, and also sponsors Artfest, an annual March event promoting local artists.

ST LUCIE INLET STATE PARK
Accessible only by boat, the main part of this park (☎ 772-219-1880; 4810 SE Cove Rd) protects 6 sq miles of reef in the Atlantic Ocean just off Jupiter Island. Twelve species of hard and soft coral inhabit the reef, so anchor on the sandy bottom. Snorkeling and scuba diving are permitted; depths range from 5ft to 35ft. Complementing the 2.7 miles of beaches are

> **SNOUT STOPPER**
> What's that smell in St Lucie Inlet State Park? It's the skunklike white stopper, a tropical tree. A major berry source for birds, the white stopper emits a lingering musky scent from the evaporation of volatile oils from its leathery leaves. Ironically, the leaves of this 'stink bush' have been used to treat diarrhea.

SOUTHEAST FLORIDA

toilets and running water, piers and hiking trails. From the mainland at the eastern end of Cove Rd, a 3300ft boardwalk runs from dock to beach.

If you want to explore the miles of tidal creek this park has to offer, rent a kayak from **Island Water Sports** (☎ 772-334-1999; 1504 NE Jensen Beach Blvd; ☻ 10am-6pm Mon-Sat, to 4pm Sun; singles/tandems per day $50/75, per weekend $75/90). In most cases, you can arrange delivery of their kayaks to your hotel, but if you're headed here, collect the boats yourself.

HUTCHINSON ISLAND

This long, skinny barrier island, which begins in Stuart and stretches north to Fort Pierce, features a stunning array of unspoiled **beaches**, all with free access, excellent for walking, swimming and even some snorkeling. Most of the access roads and parking lots are dirt, but barring a 40-day flood, you're unlikely to get stuck. The beaches get less touristed the further north you go.

If you've got your four-footed friends with you, be sure to head to the only dog-friendly beach in St Lucie County, **Walton Rocks**, across from the **St Lucie Power Plant** (6501 Hwy A1A).

Elliott Museum

If you need a break from the sun, stop at the **Elliott Museum** (☎ 407-225-1961; www.elliottmuseumfl .org; 825 NE Ocean Blvd, Hutchinson Island; adult/child $4/0.50; ☻ 10am-4pm), dedicated to inventor Harmon Elliott. In this eclectic collection of old Americana exhibits you'll see a fabulous miniature circus, recreations of old-time shops (an apothecary, a barber shop), a Victorian parlor and a typical 18th-century girl's bedroom. It's a strange and diverse collection that's a fun switch from the rest of town.

Florida Oceanographic Coastal Science Center

Right across from the Elliott Museum, this **center** (☎ 772-225-0505; www.floridaoceanographic.org; 890 NE Ocean Blvd; adult/child $8/4; ☻ 10am-5pm Mon-Sat, noon-4pm Sun) is great for kids, who'll be mesmerized by the four 300-gallon tropical-fish aquariums, a worm reef and touch tanks with crabs, sea cucumbers and starfish.

FISHING

Being the Sailfish Capital of the World, there are plenty of opportunities for fishing around these parts.

The **Safari I** (☎ 772-287-2500; www.safari1deep seafishing.com; 4307 SE Bayview St; adult/child $35/25; ☻ 8:30am-1pm, 1:30pm-6pm) will take you out, bait your hook, and clean and fillet any fish you catch. There are no guarantees of hooking dinner, but with 20 years of experience and frequent catches of snapper and porgies (which you can eat) and triggerfish and rays (which you probably don't want to), they know where to sink their lines.

If the thought of sharing a large boat with lots of other anglers is unappealing, charter a boat. **Hot Tuna Charters** (☎ 772-334-0401; www .hottunacharters.com; half-/full day $450/650), run by native Floridian Captain Wakeman – boasting over 20 years' experience and holding 10 world records on both fly and conventional tackle – will help you find and catch stuff that swims.

Finally, if you don't feel like leaving shore, check the fishing report at www.snooknook .net/Fishing_Reports.html, rent a rod from **Snook Nook** (☎ 772-334-2145; www.snooknook.net; 3595 NE Indian River Dr; ☻ 6am-8pm Mon-Sat, to 6pm Sun; per day $7.50) and head to the water.

Sleeping

Savannas Recreation Area (☎ 772-464-7855; www .co.st-lucie.fl.us/parks/savannah.htm; 1400 Midway Rd; per night $10-22) Covering 550 acres and five distinct biological communities – pine flatwoods, wet prairie, marsh, lake and scrub – the Savannas feature numerous camping options, from primitive to fully improved. Canoe and kayak rentals are available.

Inn Shepard's Bed & Breakfast (☎ 772-781-4244; 601 SW Ocean Blvd; www.innshepard.com; r $85-185; ☐) Overlooking a waterfront park and set an easy stroll away from downtown Stuart, this lovely white B&B has four comfortable rooms and a communal hot tub in the friendly back patio. A continental breakfast is served on the roomy porch, and bikes and a kayak are available to use at no extra cost.

our pick **River Palm Cottages & Fish Camp** (☎ 772-334-0401; www.riverpalmcottages.com; 2425 NE Indian River Dr, Jensen Beach; summer $89-299, winter $139-429; Ⓟ) Perched on Indian River, this paradisiacal complex has adorable cottages with kitchens, some with waterfront views and all sporting cool tile floors and a breezy, Caribbean style. The peaceful grounds are lush with grassy patches, palm trees and other flowering and fruit-bearing varieties, including guava and the exotic praying-hands banana tree. There's a private beach, a ping-pong table and a pier for watching sunsets. Pets are welcome, too.

On Hutchinson Island, you'll find mostly ritzy resorts; the **Marriott Beach Resort** (☎ 772-225-3700; 555 NE Ocean Blvd; $119-398; P ⊡ ⊠) is the pick of that litter. Stuart and Jensen Beach do a good job keeping the beach-vibe authentic.

Eating

BUDGET

Fredgie's Hot Dog Wagon (3595 NE Indian River Dr, Jensen Beach; lunch $2-4; ⊙ 11am-4pm Wed-Sun) This vending cart has been dishing dogs for 14 years.

Mary's Gourmet Kitchen (☎ 772-334-9488; 3310 Indian River Dr; breakfast $5-7, lunch $4-7; ⊙ 6am-2pm Tue-Sat, to 1pm Sun) Bamboo shades prevent a retina-burning sunrise from detracting from filling scrambles or megasized French toast. Takeout is available for the hearty sandwiches here, guaranteeing a great lunch. No credit cards and no ATM on site.

Key Lime Cafe (☎ 772-220-2400; 211 Colorado Ave; mains $6-9; ⊙ 10am-7pm Sun-Wed, to 9pm Thu-Sat; ⊡) Inside, among bold greens and lavenders, guests can grab a coffee or tea to go. Outside, there's casual outdoor dining, including yummy Build Your Own Burritos and Keys-inspired sandwiches, under fun tiki huts or near the Potsdam Garten's soothing pond.

MIDRANGE

Crawdaddy's N'Awlins Cafe (☎ 772-225-3444; 1949 NE Jensen Beach Blvd, Jensen Beach; lunch $7-12, dinner $11-20; ⊙ 11am-10pm Sun-Wed, to 11pm Thu-Sat) With a menu drenched in a Louisiana tradition – think: rum-soaked shrimp and the New Orleans picnic (for hungry seafood-lovers) – and a twinkling courtyard hosting live music on weekends, this place is a sliver of the French Quarter right near the beach.

Osceola Street Cafe (☎ 772-283-6116; www.osceola street.com; 26 SW Osceola St; breakfast $1-6, lunch $6-9, dinner $18-28; ⊙ 6am-10pm Mon-Fri, from 8am Sat) With fresh-baked breads, big, crispy salads and dinners emphasizing seafood, it's no wonder this place in historic downtown Stuart gets packed.

Conchy Joe's (☎ 772-334-1130; 3945 NE Indian River Dr, Jensen Beach; lunch $7-17, dinner $15-22; ⊙ 11:30am-10pm) Overlooking St Lucie River, drinks and pub grub at the palm-tree-filled bar are a surefire blast, especially when the band's jamming.

TOP END

11 Maple St (☎ 772-334-7714; 3224 NE Maple Ave, Jensen Beach; mains $13-39; ⊙ 6-10pm Wed-Sun) This romantic, sophisticated eatery – actually a series of rooms inside a converted cottage – straddles the dining intersections of Old Florida, New England and Nouveau French. Preparing organic, eclectic dishes ranging from small plates like panfried Caicos conch to entrees such as roasted baby barramundi, the menu changes daily, so you're never sure quite what'll delight tonight.

Shopping

Historic downtown Stuart overflows with cute shops and antique stores.

April Daze (☎ 772-221-1062; 308 Colorado Ave) Retro-inspired provisions for tropical living, loads of women's boutique clothes and an eclectic jewelry selection.

Rare Earth (☎ 772-287-7744; www.rareearthgallery .com; 41 SW Flagler Ave) Fantastic selection of locally thrown pottery, novel ceramics and colorful art.

Earthtones (☎ 772-288-1010; www.shopearthtones .com; 42 SW Osceola St) Get your own giant tiki head at this funky nature-themed shop.

Getting There & Away

Though I-95 is the quickest way to and from this area, if you've got some time, treat yourself and explore the local roads. South of Stuart, US Hwy 1 runs up the coastline and then jogs west, into and through town. If you're headed between Stuart and Fort Pierce, the best route is the slow-but-scenic NE Indian River Dr, with gorgeous waterfront homes to the west and the water to the east.

FORT PIERCE

☎ 772 / **pop 37,959**

Fort Pierce may not have as many millionaires as its neighbors, but it does have plenty to recommend it: a nice, sleepy feel, top sportfishing, some great beaches and a revitalized downtown.

Orientation & Information

Fort Pierce's main drag is 2nd St, which runs a block west of Indian River Dr. Here you'll find restaurants, the landmark Sunrise Theatre (1923) and old city hall. To get to Hutchinson Island, head north on 2nd St and then east on Seaway Dr, which deposits you at the northern terminus of Ocean Dr (Hwy A1A).

Seven Gables House (☎ 772-468-9152; 482 N Indian River Dr; ⊙ 9am-5pm Mon-Fri, 10am-4pm Sat) The visitors center in this historic building has loads of maps.

ISLAND HOPPING

Like so many of its residents, the Intracoastal Waterway isn't native. It 'moved' here – or rather, it was brought.

Between 1953 and 1961, the Intracoastal was created by dredging a 12ft-deep channel in the Indian River Lagoon. Happy by-products from the dredging, there are now 137 'spoil islands' throughout the 156 miles and four counties of the lagoon. Of those, the State of Florida owns 124 and most of those are publicly accessible.

Today, the islands are designated by use categories determined by accessibility, presence of native plants and animals, and historical human use. The four designations are 'active recreation' (ideal for picnicking, sunbathing, swimming and primitive camping); 'passive recreation' (only to be used for daytime recreation); and 'education' and 'conservation' (neither of which are to be used for camping or recreational activities).

What does this mean for you? It means that if you have a boat, you can cruise to any of the approved islands for free. For a list of the approved islands, log on to www.spoilislandproject .org/stlucie.htm and click either of the left-hand maps that highlight the Intracoastal. Check out any of the vendors at www.visitstluciefla.com/canoeing.html for kayak rental in Fort Pierce.

Sights & Activities

MANATEE OBSERVATION CENTER

Right downtown, this **center** (☎ 772-466-1600; www.manateecenter.com; 480 N Indian River Dr; admission $1; ☾ 10am-5pm Tue-Sat, noon-4pm Sun Oct-Jun, 10am-5pm Thu-Sat Jul-Sep) educates the public on the plight of the manatee. Videos, exhibits and even the gift shop teach boaters how to avoid hurting the creatures – and the rest of us how our lifestyle has indirectly eradicated most of the manatee population. Manatee sightings are common-ish in winter, however, when waters along the museum's observation deck, warmed by the nearby power plant, are home to between eight and 20 of the precious creatures.

FORT PIERCE INLET STATE RECREATION AREA

This 3400-acre **park** (☎ 772-468-3985; 905 Shorewinds Dr; per car with up to 8 passengers/pedestrians $4/1; ☾ 8am-sunset) has everything you'd want in a waterfront recreation spot: sandy shores, verdant trails, mangrove swamps with a beautiful park population and a family-friendly picnic area. It's also home to endangered beach stars, a low-lying sedge growing on the dunes and near the boardwalks, so stick to the sand, Bigfoot.

HEATHCOTE BOTANICAL GARDENS

Beginning as a Japanese-style garden in 1955, today this small but lovely **botanical garden** (☎ 772-464-4672; www.heathcotebotanicalgardens.org; 210 Savannah Rd; adult/child $4/2; ☾ 9am-5pm Tue-Sat year-round, 1-5pm Sun Nov-Apr) features a rainforest, a collection of palm trees from around

the world, a historic garden with century-old bonsai trees and shady trails through medicinal herb gardens decorated with fanciful yard-art.

UDT-SEAL MUSEUM

The world's only **museum** (☎ 772-595-5845; www.navysealmuseum.com; 3300 Ocean Blvd; adult/child $6/3; ☾ 10am-4pm Mon Jan-Apr only, 10am-4pm Tue-Sat, noon-4pm Sun) dedicated to the elite warriors of Naval Special Warfare, this Hutchinson Island exhibit features once-top-secret tools and weapons used by the most elite combat forces of the US. Located on the site where WWII Navy Frogmen (predecessors of the SEALs) trained, this place has videos and relics from US wars since 1945, including Granada, Panama, Vietnam and Desert Storm.

URCA DE LIMA

In 1715, a Spanish flotilla was decimated in a hurricane off the Florida coast. One of the ships, the **Urca de Lima** (☎ 850-245-6444; www.flheritage .com/archaeology/underwater/preserves/uwurca.cfm; admission free) went down (relatively) intact. Today, the wooden-hulled ship is partly exposed within snorkeling distance from the beach.

To get here, exit Ocean Blvd (Hwy A1A) at Pepper Park and walk north along the beach about 1000 yards from the park boundary. The wreck is about 200 yards from shore on the first offshore reef, under 10ft to 15ft of water.

DOLPHIN-WATCHING

Wild dolphins are spotted routinely in the Indian River Lagoon, occasionally from the riverbank. If you want to increase your chances of seeing them, you need to get on the water. **Florida Dolphin Watch** (☎ 772-466-4660; www.floridadolphinwatch.com; for 6 people $175) offers two-hour dolphin-spotting tours aboard their comfortable 25ft 'tri-toon.' With a cap of six passengers, the 15-mile charter comes complete with a wildlife library, binoculars, water and soda.

Sleeping & Eating

Stuart and Jensen Beach offer way more sleeping options, but there are a few worthy offerings in Fort Pierce.

Royal Inn (☎ 772-464-0405; www.royalinnbeach.com; 222 Hernando St; r & ste $79-109; 🖳) Only 20 minutes from the New York Mets Spring Training Complex, this tasteful, tropical inn offers unobstructed ocean and inlet views, and microwaves and fridges in all the rooms. It's within walking distance of the beach and restaurants.

ourpick Archie's Seabreeze (☎ 772-461-3352; 401 S Ocean Dr; mains $7-13; 🕑 10am-10pm Mon-Wed, to midnight Thu-Sun) This open-air biker-friendly bar has been partying since 1947. Look for big ol' picnic tables, raw-oyster shooters, pool tables ('Chicks with Sticks' tourneys are Tuesdays) and the coolest handmade floor ever.

Tiki Bar & Restaurant (☎ 772-461-0880; www.originaltikibar.com; 2 Ave A; mains $8-22; 🕑 11am-10pm; 🖳) Adjacent to the Fort Pierce Marina, a huge thatch roof covers two bars and dozens of tables. The waffle fries are supreme as are the 360-degree water views (look for dolphins and manatees cruising past). Dockage available.

Getting There & Around

From Stuart, take I-95 or US Hwy 1 (a gorgeous drive that's highly recommended as a trip unto itself!) about 25 miles north. To get downtown from I-95, take the Orange Ave exit east, crossing US Hwy 1 (here called N 4th St).

SOUTHEAST FLORIDA

Orlando & Walt Disney World

As neon lights lure sleepy travelers to diners and roadside motels, so Disney draws world-weary folks to Orlando. Come, it says: we promise you magic. Transformation. Regeneration. Let us take you away from deadlines and soccer matches, traffic jams and mortgages. Come into Walt Disney World, a better world. And folks come. By the thousands and millions, folks come to Orlando for Disney. Again and again, year after year, from all over the world. The city has grown to meet their needs, with endless chain motels, fast-food joints and shops with Mickey T-shirts, Mickey mugs, Mickey key chains.

Once here, however, some realize that maybe the flash and pizzazz of the happiest place on earth is not the elixir they're looking for. Sure, Disney is great, Universal Studios is pure unabashed fun, and animal shows at SeaWorld dazzle the spirit. But those who venture beyond Disney's gates discover that maybe Orlando's lakes, museums, sidewalk cafés and dripping cypress trees are as much a part of the magic as Cinderella's Castle. Orlando doesn't come prepackaged, and it doesn't always go down easy. It's a real city with ugly strips, seemingly endless road construction and an odd sense of incompleteness, as if it hasn't yet figured out who it is. It lives, quite literally, under the shadow of its theme parks – you can hear Disney's fireworks boom-boom-booming from miles away.

But Orlando has a raw spirit and a lovely demeanor quite distinct from its tourist face. So come for Disney. Come for Universal Orlando. But once here, take a few days to see Orlando's other side. Perhaps next time you'll come for Orlando.

HIGHLIGHTS

- Swimming with dolphins, snorkeling among tropical fish and floating on the lazy river through the bird aviary at **Discovery Cove** (p332)

- Hiking through **Nature's Conservancy's Disney's Wilderness Preserve** (p274) for a picnic on Lake Russell

- Paddling quietly past alligators and blue herons on Wekiwa River, **Wekiwa Springs State Park** (p274)

- Watching the elaborate twinkling floats and dancing Disney characters of Magic Kingdom's **SpectraMagic parade** and sticking around for Jiminy Cricket's **Wishes fireworks display** (p300) over Cinderella's Castle

- Strolling around the shops, poking through the art museums and lingering over wine at a sidewalk café in old Florida's **Winter Park** (p284)

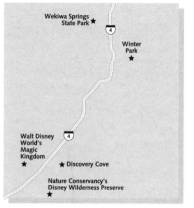

History
In 1824, three years after Florida became a US territory, swampy Mosquito County was established. The first US settlers arrived in 1837, and in 1838 the US military built Fort Gatlin as a base for the Seminole Indian Wars (p29). Upon Florida statehood in 1845, Mosquito County changed to the far more alluring Orange County. Orlando grew as a cow town, with lots of gamblin', fightin', and womanizin', and in 1875 the two-square-mile city (population 85) was officially incorporated. With the arrival of the railroad in 1880, Indian fighting and cows gave way to orange-growing and tourists. WWII brought air bases and missile building, but it was the 1971 opening of Walt Disney World's Magic Kingdom that paved the way to the city's contemporary reputation as the theme-park capital of the US.

Climate
Orlando's landlocked position makes for a warm city all year round. From October to May is generally the coolest time, while summers can be downright unbearable with temperatures nearing 100°F. June to September are the wettest months, hurricane season is from August through October, and thunderstorms with frequent lightning strikes are common all year. Hurricane season runs from May to October.

National, State & Regional Parks
State parks within easy driving distance from the city include **Lake Louisa State Park** (off Map p262; ☎ 352-394-3969; 7305 US Hwy 27, Clermont 34714; $4 per vehicle), **Rock Springs Run State Preserve** (Map p262; ☎ 407-884-2008; pedestrian/vehicle $1/2), three miles west of the Wekiva River bridge on SR 46, and **Lower Wekiva River Preserve State Park** (Map p262; ☎ 407-884-2008), whose southern entrance is nine miles west of Sanford on SR 46. For more information, go to www.floridastateparks.org.

See also boxed text Beyond the Pavement, p274.

Information
Official Orlando Visitors Center (☎ 407-363-5872; www.orlandoinfo.com)
Orlando Weekly (www.orlandoweekly.com)
Universal Studios (☎ 407-363-8000; www.universalorlando.com)
Walt Disney World (☎ 407-824-8000, 407-824-4321; www.disneyworld.com)

Getting There & Away
Orlando lies 285 miles from Miami; the fastest and most direct route is a 4½-hour road trip via the Florida Turnpike (toll). From Tampa it is an easy 62 miles along I-4. Both the Beachline Expressway and Hwy 50 will take you to the Space Coast; the expressway has frequent tolls, but is about an hour faster than Hwy 50. Orlando, serviced by Greyhound, Amtrak and hosts of domestic and international air carriers, is the region's transportation hub.

Getting Around
BUS
Lynx (☎ 407-841-8240 route info; www.golynx.com; single ride/day pass $1.75/4, transfers free) covers all of Orlando, with some buses running until the wee hours of the morning – timetables vary by route, so be sure to check before you hop on a bus that you can catch a return service. Lymmo is Lynx's free bus service, which circles downtown Orlando.

You can buy tickets, and get maps and specific route information from the information booth at the **Lynx Central Station** (Map p268; ☎ 407-841-2279; www.golynx.com; 455 Garland Ave; ⏱ 6:30am-7:30pm Mon-Fri, 8am-5:30pm Sat & Sun).

CAR & MOTORCYCLE
The major car rental companies (see P520) have offices at the airport, within Walt Disney World and at many hotels. If you have a motorcycle endorsement on your license or valid proof of a motorcycle license, you can rent a Harley from **Orlando Harley-Davidson** (Map pp264-5; ☎ 877-740-3770; www.orlandoharley.com; 3770 37th St; $100-140/day).

SHUTTLE
The biggest shuttle-bus service in the area is **Mears Transportation** (☎ 407-423-5566; www.mearstransportation.com; prices vary). Also try sedan and nine-passenger minivan shuttles at **Legacy Towncar of Orlando** (☎ 888-939-8227; www.legacytowncar.com; prices vary), whose prices include a convenient grocery-store stop on the way from the airport. Walt Disney World offers free regular shuttles to hotels and attractions within the resort, and from the airport to Walt Disney World hotels (see Walt Disney World, Getting There & Around, p318).

TAXI
Fares are $3.85 for the first mile plus $2.20 for each additional mile – and those miles can add

GREATER ORLANDO & THEME PARKS

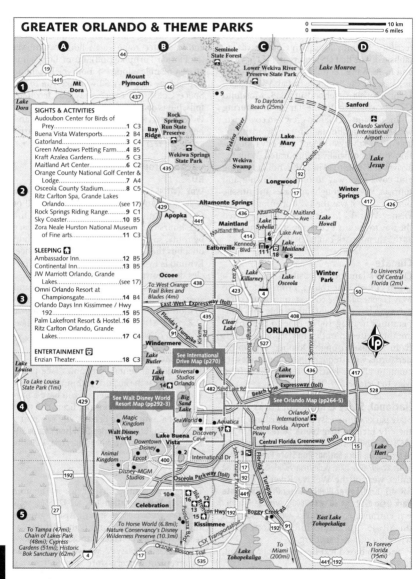

0 — 10 km
0 — 6 miles

SIGHTS & ACTIVITIES
Audoubon Center for Birds of Prey.................................**1** C3	
Buena Vista Watersports...........**2** B4	
Gatorland..................................**3** C4	
Green Meadows Petting Farm.....**4** B5	
Kraft Azalea Gardens.................**5** C3	
Maitland Art Center...................**6** C2	
Orange County National Golf Center & Lodge................................**7** A4	
Osceola County Stadium............**8** C5	
Ritz Carlton Spa, Grande Lakes Orlando..............................(see 17)	
Rock Springs Riding Range.........**9** C1	
Sky Coaster..............................**10** B5	
Zora Neale Hurston National Museum of Fine arts.........................**11** C3	

SLEEPING
Ambassador Inn.........................**12** B5	
Continental Inn..........................**13** B5	
JW Marriott Orlando, Grande Lakes.................................(see 17)	
Omni Orlando Resort at Championsgate....................**14** B4	
Orlando Days Inn Kissimmee / Hwy 192.................................**15** B5	
Palm Lakefront Resort & Hostel.**16** B5	
Ritz Carlton Orlando, Grande Lakes.................................**17** C4	

ENTERTAINMENT
Enzian Theater.........................**18** C3	

up! A ride from the Disney area to downtown Orlando, for example, costs roughly $50.

Cabs sit outside the theme parks, Downtown Disney, hotels and other tourist centers, but otherwise you'll need to call to arrange a pickup. Try **Yellow Cab** (☎ 407-422-5151, 407-699-9999).

WHEELCHAIR & SCOOTER

Orlando's theme parks rent wheelchairs and Electronic Convenience Vehicles (ECV), but they don't all take advance reservations. Reserve one in advance at Scooter Orlando (☎ 888-727-6837; www.scooterorlando.com) or Walker Medical and Mobility Products (☎ 888-727-6837;

www.walkermobility.com). Both offer free delivery and pickup.

ORLANDO & AROUND

ORLANDO

☎ 407 / pop 1.8 million

While it's quite easy to get caught up in the isolated worlds of Disney or Universal Orlando, squeezing in one more ride, one more parade, one more show and never venturing beyond their constructed environments (designed precisely to keep you there), Orlando has so much more.

Orlando's downtown area is in the process of a fundamental shift. The national housing slump and a general slowdown in the economy hit just when Orlando was poised to fast-track into the 21st century, and the city is struggling to find its way. Condo buildings sit half-finished, storefronts sit empty, new kids on the block try to make a go of things. There are, however, lovely pockets of up-and-coming treelined neighborhoods, established communities with an entrenched sense of history and community, and several fantastic gardens, parks and museums in and around the city. Orlando boasts a rich variety of performing arts, and in 2007 it initiated a sweeping green agenda whose aims include phasing out incandescent bulbs in stoplights, increasing the use of public transportation, developing public green space and transitioning city buses to biodiesel and other alternative fuels.

Even if you're coming to Orlando for the theme parks, take a few days to jump off their spinning wheels of adrenalin-pumped fantasy to explore the quieter, gentler side of Orlando. You may be surprised to find that you enjoy the theme parks all that much more because of the time you spend away from them.

Walt Disney World, Universal Orlando, and SeaWorld, Aquatica and Discovery Cove are detailed in their own sections in this chapter. See the boxed text What to Expect from the Parks (p288) for a synopsis of these parks.

Orientation

Highway I-4 is the main north–south connector, though it's labeled east–west: to go north, take the I-4 east (toward Daytona Beach); to go south, hop on the I-4 west (toward Tampa). Just about every place you'd want to go can be located through an I-4 exit number. From south to north, exit 62 through exit 87, you will find Disneyworld, Celebration and Lake Buena Vista; SeaWorld, Aquatica and Discovery Cove; International Drive; downtown Orlando; Loch Haven Park; and Winter Park.

The main east–west thoroughfares are Hwy 528 (Beach Line Expressway, formerly called Bee Line; toll road), which cuts east from I-4 toward the airport and connects Orlando to the Space Coast, and Hwy 408 (East-West Expressway; toll road), which bisects downtown Orlando. Hwy 417 (Central Florida Greeneway; toll road), heads east from I-4 at Celebration and veers north

Other major routes are Hwy 192 (also called Irlo Bronson Memorial Hwy and Vine Ave), International Drive (I-Drive) and Osceola Parkway. Hwy 192, a sprawling ribbon of concrete, motels, shopping malls, wannabe attractions and discount ticket stands of dubious reliability, has the cheapest motels and plenty of budget restaurants to go with them. International Drive roughly parallels I-4 south of downtown and north of Disney World. Universal Studios sits just west of its northern end, and SeaWorld, Aquatica and Discovery Cove sit on its southern end. In between you'll find Wet 'n' Wild and other tourist attractions, as well as many hotels and restaurants.

MAPS

Since the Orlando area is so spread out, good maps are essential, especially if you're driving in downtown, which is a one-way nightmare. Pick up a detailed nontourist map from any area gas station.

Information

BOOKSTORES

Barnes and Noble Bookstore (Map p270; ☎ 407-345-0900; Plaza Venezia, 7900 W Sand Lake Rd; ☻ 9am-10pm) Chain bookstore with a wide selection, conveniently located near theme parks and I-Drive. Call about character events and children's story hours.

Borders Books & Music (Map pp264-5; ☎ 407-647-3300; 600 N Orlando Ave; ☻ 9am-11pm) Best bookstore in Winter Park area.

Spiral Circle (Map pp264-5; ☎ 407-894-9854; 750 N Thornton Ave; ☻ 10am-6pm Mon-Thu & Sat, to 8pm Fri, noon-5pm Sun) More a spiritual destination than a

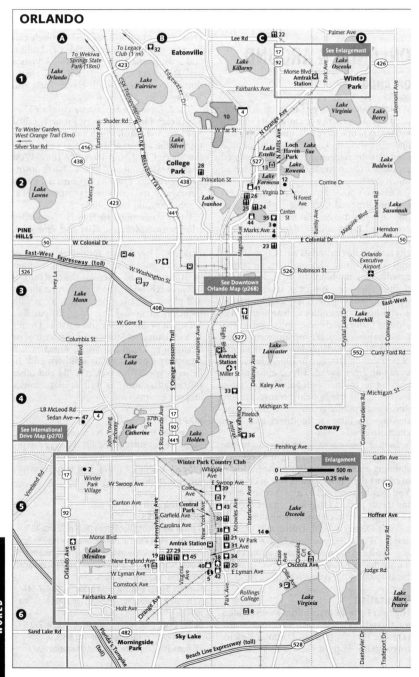

ORLANDO

See Enlargement

See Downtown
Orlando Map (p268)

See International
Drive Map (p270)

To Wekiwa
Springs State
Park (18mi)

To Legacy
Club (1 mi)

Eatonville

Lee Rd

Palmer Ave

Winter
Park

Lake
Orlando

Lake
Fairview

Lake
Killarny

Lake
Osceola

Lake
Virginia

Lake
Berry

To Winter Garden,
West Orange Trail (3mi)

Silver Star Rd

Shader Rd

W Par St

Lake
Silver

College
Park

Lake
Estelle

Loch
Haven
Park

Lake
Sue

Lake
Baldwin

Princeton St

Lake
Formosa

Corrine Dr

Lake
Lawne

Lake
Ivanhoe

Lake
Rowena

Lake
Susannah

Herndon
Ave

PINE
HILLS

W Colonial Dr

Marks Ave

E Colonial Dr

Orlando
Executive
Airport

East-West Expressway (toll)

W Washington St

Robinson St

Lake
Mann

W Gore St

Lake
Underhill

Columbia St

Clear
Lake

East-West

Amtrak
Station

Miller St

Lake
Lancaster

LB McLeod Rd

Sedan Ave

Lake
Catherine

Lake
Holden

Kaley Ave

Michigan St

Conway

Pershing Ave

Curry Ford Rd

Enlargement

Winter Park Country Club

Whipple
Ave

Gatlin Ave

0 —————— 500 m
0 —————— 0.25 mile

Winter
Park
Village

W Swoop Ave

E Swoop Ave

Coles
Ave

Lake
Osceola

Canton Ave

Central
Park

Garfield Ave

Carolina Ave

W Park
Ave

Hoffner Ave

Morse Blvd

Amtrak Station

Lake
Mendsen

New England Ave

W Lyman Ave

E Lyman Ave

Osceola Ave

Judge Rd

Comstock Ave

Rollins
College

Fairbanks Ave

Holt Ave

Lake
Virginia

Lake
Mare
Prairie

Sand Lake Rd

Morningside
Park

Sky Lake

Beach Line Expressway (toll)

INFORMATION
Arnold Palmer Hospital for
Children...**1** C4
Borders Books & Music..................**2** A5
Gay, Lesbian & Bisexual Community
Center..**3** C2
Spiral Circle....................................**4** C2
Winter Park Chamber of
Commerce.....................................**5** B6

SIGHTS & ACTIVITIES
Albin Polasek Museum & Sculpture
Garden..**6** C5
Charles Hosmer Morse Museum of
American Art..................................**7** C5
Cornell Fine Arts Museum.............**8** C6
Dinky Beach....................................**9** C6
Dubsdread Golf Course................**10** C1
Hannibal Square Heritage Center..**11** B6
Harry P Leu Gardens......................**12** C2
John & Rita Lowndes Shakespeare
Center...(see 13)
Loch Haven Park.............................**13** C2
Menello Museum of American Folk
Art..(see 13)
Orlando Museum of Art................(see 13)
Orlando Repertory Theater...........(see 13)
Orlando Science Center................(see 13)
Scenic Boat Tour............................**14** C5

SLEEPING
Best Western Mt Vernon Inn.........**15** A5
Courtyard at Lake Lucerne............**16** C3
Parliament House............................**17** B3
Plaza Hotel.....................................**18** C6

EATING
Ballard & Corum.............................**19** B5
Bistro 310 South............................**20** C6
Bosphorous Turkish Cuisine...........**21** C5
Bubbalou's Bodacious BBQ............**22** C1
Dandelion Communitea Café.........**23** C3
Ethos Vegan Kitchen......................**24** C2
Gargi's Lakeside.............................**25** C2
Greek Corner Restaurant...............**26** C2
Hot Olives......................................**27** B5
K Restaurant & Wine Bar................**28** B2
Market Café....................................**29** B5
Orchid...**30** C5

DRINKING
Eola Wine Company.......................**31** C5
Faces on Edgewater.......................**32** B1
Pulse...**33** C4
The Wine Room..............................**34** C5
Wally's Mill Ave Liquors.................**35** C2
Wylde's..**36** C4

ENTERTAINMENT
Parliament House.........................(see 17)
Citrus Bowl.....................................**37** B3

SHOPPING
Bullfish...**38** C5
Cida's Consignment.......................**39** C5
Farmers' Market.............................**40** B6
Hopscotch......................................**41** C2
NFX Apothecary.............................**42** C6
Ritzy Rags.....................................(see 3)
The Cheese Shop............................**43** C5
Tim's Wine Market.........................**44** C2
Tug Boat & the Bird.......................**45** B5

TRANSPORT
Greyhound bus station...................**46** B3
Orlando Harley-Davidson...............**47** A4

common bookstore, where you can tap into your hidden psychic abilities and connect with your angels before trading in used books.

Urban Think Bookstore (Map p268; ☎ 407-650-8004; www.urbanthinkorlando.com; 625 E Central Blvd; 11am-9pm Tue-Sat, to 6pm Sun & Mon) In Thornton Park, this decidedly contemporary little place is like curling up on your living-room couch, with an eccentric mishmash of artwork, readings and a children's story hour (Friday 1pm). Inside is Infusion Tea, an organic and vegetarian teahouse serving sandwiches and salads, and a bar with wine and beer.

CHILD CARE

All of the following provide 24-hour, in-hotel-room babysitting, as well as off-site babysitting to area theme parks, for children aged six weeks to 12 years. Caregivers are at least 18 years old and are certified in CPR and basic first aid. For feedback from parents who have used these services, do a web search of the company names and you'll find chat rooms with loads of stories about folks' individual experiences.

Walt Disney World, Universal Orlando, and most deluxe resorts have child-care centers (see p291 and p319).

All About Kids (☎ 407-812-9300; www.all-about-kids .com; credit card to reserve sitter, cash or traveler's checks only to pay sitter) Rates start at $13 per hour per child and each additional child is $2. There is a four-hour minimum and a $12 travel fee. It also rents equipment including strollers, car seats, backpack carriers and even rocking chairs.

Fairy Godmothers (☎ 407-277-3724) Rates start at $16 per hour for up to three children, with a four-hour minimum and a $12 travel fee. All caregivers are female and nonsmoking, and bring a variety of age-appropriate games with them. Family-owned; does not accept credit cards.

Kid's Nite Out (☎ 800-696-8105; www.kidsnite out.com; one/two/three/four children per hr from $14/16.50/19/21.50; 8am-9pm) Used by Walt Disney World Resort and Loews Hotels at Universal Studios. There is a four-hour minimum and a $10 travel fee charged. Credit cards only. You can make reservations up to three months in advance.

Delivery Services

Why lug all those diapers, wipes and jars of food through the airport when they can be waiting for you at your hotel room? These services do just that, and can also provide equipment rentals (booster seats, jogging strollers, bed rails, beach umbrellas and all

---

ORLANDO MUST HAVES

■ **Sunscreen and sunglasses** Central Florida's fabulous sunshine can be brutal on the skin and eyes.

■ **Water sandals** For jumping between roller coasters and water rides, canoeing and miles of walking. Try Keens or Chacos.

■ **Cell phone** Mom and three-year-old Susan, stuck in the Dumbo line, will be late meeting Dad and Joey for lunch. Be sure to put it on vibrate.

■ **Water bottle** Dehydration will knock the energy out of you faster than a gator can devour a Yankee.

■ **Road map** Orlando's crazy roads and confusing signs complicate efforts to get around.

---

kinds of things you didn't even know you needed). Place your order at least one week in advance of your trip.

Babies Away (☎ 877-835-2229; www.babysaway rentals.com; ☒ 24hr) Primarily rents gear.

Babies Travel Lite (☎ 888-450-5483; www.babies travellite.com) Incredibly comprehensive selection, including organic baby food, earth-friendly diapers and children's medicine.

Jet Set Babies (☎ 866-990-1811; www.jetsetbabies .com; ☒ 24hr) Standard selection of gear and supplies.

EMERGENCY

Call ☎ 911 in case of an emergency. For non-emergency police matters (eg reporting something stolen), call ☎ 321-235-5300. The main **police station** (Map p268; ☎ 407-246-2470; 100 S Hughey Ave) is downtown near Central Blvd.

INTERNET RESOURCES

City of Orlando (www.cityoforlando.net)
Downtown Orlando (www.downtownorlando.com)
Go2Orlando (www.go2orlando.com)
Orlando Restaurants (www.orlandoeats.com)
Visit Orlando (www.visitorlando.com)

LIBRARIES

The main **library** (Map p268; ☎ 407-835-7323; 101 E Central Blvd; ☒ 9am-9pm Mon-Thu, to 6pm Fri & Sat, 1-6pm Sun) offers internet access for $10 per week. Call for other library locations.

MEDIA

The most popular daily is the **Orlando Sentinel** (www.orlandosentinel.com). Its **Axis** (www.axismag.com) magazine covers the music, movie and bar scene. **Orlando Weekly** (www.orlandoweekly.com) and *Connections* are the major free weeklies.

There's alternative FM rock at 101.1; hip hop at 91.3; top 40 at 106.7; classic rock at 96.5; golden oldies at 100.3; and country at 92.3. National Public Radio (NPR) is at 90.7FM and 89.9FM. For children, go to Radio Disney at 990AM.

MEDICAL SERVICES

Arnold Palmer Hospital for Children (Map pp264-5 ☎ 407-649-9111; 92 W Miller St; ☒ 24hr) The city's primary children's hospital; connected to the Winnie Palmer Hospital for Women and Babies.

Centra Care Walk-In Medical (Map pp292-3; ☎ 407-934-2273; www.centracare.org; 12500 State Rd 535; ☒ 8am-midnight Mon-Fri, to 8pm Sat & Sun) A walk-in medical center offering adult and pediatric care. Located near Downtown Disney; see website or call for other locations.

Dr P Phillips Hospital (Map p270; ☎ 407-351-8500; 9400 Turkey Lake Rd; ☒ 24hr) Closest hospital to SeaWorld and International Drive.

Florida Hospital Celebration Health (Map pp292-3; ☎ 407-303-4000; 400 Celebration Pl; ☒ 24hr) Located in Celebration, this is the closest hospital to Walt Disney World.

Main St Physicians (Map p270; ☎ 407-370-4881; 8723 International Dr; ☒ 8am-8pm Mon-Thu, to 9pm Fri, 9am-9pm Sat, 9am-5pm Sun) A walk-in clinic, which costs $130 a visit. Call for other locations.

MONEY

You'll have no problem finding an ATM in Orlando, whether it's on the street, in your hotel or at the theme parks. The theme parks offer limited currency exchange.

American Express (Map p270; ☎ 407-264-0104; 7618 W Sand Lake Rd; ☒ 9:30am-5:30pm Mon-Sat) This full-service office is located close to International Drive.

Bank of America (Map p268; ☎ 407-244-7041; 390 N Orange Ave; ☒ 9am-4pm Mon-Thu, to 6pm Fri; drive-thru 8am-6pm Mon-Fri) Right downtown, but there are branches everywhere.

POST

FedEx Kinko's (Map p268; ☎ 407-839-5000; 47 E Robinson St; ☒ 6am-10pm Mon-Fri, 9am-6pm Sat & Sun) Has fax, internet access ($1/5 minutes), photocopier and desktop publishing services.

SCAMS

Unofficial 'tourist-information centers' line International Drive and Hwy 192 in Kissimmee. Most offer a hard sell on free or discounted tickets in exchange for looking at some pricey property; however, tours are tedious and tickets are often restricted or falsified. If you're promised free parking or the right to go to the front of lines, it's almost certainly a scam. Remember, you cannot use the remaining portion of someone else's multiday ticket. Disney scans your finger upon first entry to the park, and every time thereafter the ticket must match the finger scan to allow entry.

Post office (Map p268; ☎ 407-425-6464; 51 E Jefferson St; ⊗ 7am-5pm Mon-Fri) Located downtown.

TOURIST INFORMATION

Orlando's **Official Visitor Center** (Map p270; ☎ 407-363-5872, 800-551-0181; www.orlandoinfo.com; 8723 International Dr; ⊗ 8:30am-6:30pm) sells legitimate discount attraction tickets and there are racks and stacks of free coupon books and handouts.

You'll find a handful of walk-up tourist-information kiosks along International Drive, dozens of rinky-dink operations on Hwy 192, and plenty of information at your hotel.

UNIVERSITIES

The University of Central Florida (☎ 407-823-2000; 4000 Central Florida Blvd) sits northeast of downtown Orlando. The town of Winter Park (p284) is home to Rollins College (Map pp264–5), a small liberal-arts college with a lovely lakeside historic campus.

Sights

DOWNTOWN ORLANDO

The **Orange County Regional History Center** (Map p268; ☎ 407-836-8500; www.thehistorycenter.org; 65 E Central Blvd; adult/child 3-12/senior $10/3.50/6.50; ⊗ 10am-5pm Mon-Sat, from noon Sun) focuses on the history of central Florida. Permanent exhibits cover prehistoric Florida, European exploration and settlement, and citrus production, among other things. For a concentrated look at Orlando's rich African American history, head to the **Wells'Built Museum of African American History and Culture**

(Map p268; ☎ 407-245-7535; www.pastinc.org; 511 W South St; adult/child 4-14/senior $15/2/3; ⊗ 9am-5pm Mon-Fri). Dr Wells, one of Orlando's first black doctors, came to Orlando in 1917. In 1921 he built a hotel for African Americans barred from Florida's segregated hotels, and soon after he built South Street Casino, an entertainment venue for black entertainers. Together, they became a central icon of the African American music community. This small museum is housed in the original hotel. A mainstay of Orlando's emerging art scene, **City Arts Factory** (Map p268; ☎ 407-648-7060; www.cityartsfactory.com; 29 S Orange Ave) provides five handsome art galleries with changing exhibits. On the first floor of the historic **Rogers Building** (Map p268; 37 S Magnolia Ave), **Gallery at Avalon Island** (☎ 407-803-6670; www.galleryatavalonisland.com) showcases local artists. Upstairs, a small theater screens the annual Orlando Film Festival.

LAKE EOLA & THORNTON PARK

A gathering point for the downtown community, **Lake Eola** (Map p268; ☎ 407-246-2827; 195 N Rosalind Ave) provides a pretty, shaded backdrop on a hot day. A flat, paved sidewalk, about 1-mile long, circles the water, a pleasant **playground** sits on its eastern shore and you can toot around the lake on a **swan paddleboat** (per 30mins $10).

Fashionable **Thornton Park** (Map p268), an admirable example of urban revitalization, borders the lake to the northeast. Remodeled historic homes line its narrow brick streets, and giant Spanish oaks weave their gnarly branches into natural green canopies. Though it's a small area and there's a slight sense that the economic slump halted development just as it was hitting its stride, this neighborhood off the tourist track is where you'll find Orlando's best independent bookstore, Urban Think (p265), an excellent independent urban hotel, EO Inn & Spa (p276), several good restaurants and a handful of bars.

LOCH HAVEN PARK

Picturesque Loch Haven Park (Map pp264–5; ☎ 407-514-2000, 888-246-2287; 900 E Princeton St), with 45 acres of parks, huge shade trees and three lakes, is home to several museums and theaters concentrated within walking distance.

The **Orlando Science Center** (Map pp264–5; ☎ 407-514-2000, 888-672-4386; www.osc.org; 777 E Princeton St;

DOWNTOWN ORLANDO

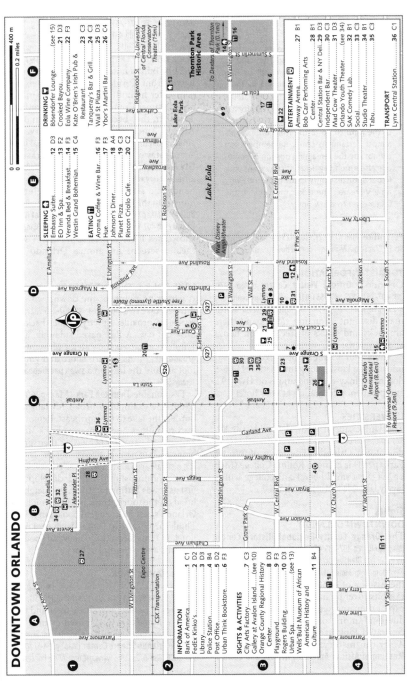

INFORMATION
Bank of America.........................1	C1
FedEx Kinko's..............................2	D2
Library..3	D3
Police Station.............................4	B4
Post Office...................................5	D2
Urban Think Bookstore............6	F3

SIGHTS & ACTIVITIES
City Arts Factory........................7	C3
Gallery at Avalon Island....(see 10)	
Orange County Regional History	
Center.......................................8	D3
Playground..................................9	F3
Rogers Building.......................10	D3
Urban Spa...........................(see 13)	
Wells'Built Museum of African	
American History and	
Culture....................................11	B4

SLEEPING
Embassy Suites..........................12	D3
EO Inn & Spa.............................13	F2
Veranda Bed & Breakfast.......14	F3
Westin Grand Bohemian.........15	C4

EATING
Aroma Coffee & Wine Bar......16	F3
Hue...17	F3
Johnson's Diner.........................18	A4
Planet Pizza...............................19	C3
Rincon Criollo Cafe..................20	C2

DRINKING
Bösendorfer Lounge...........(see 15)	
Crooked Bayou........................21	D3
Eola Wine Company................22	F3
Kate O'Brien's Irish Pub &	
Restaurant..............................23	C3
Tanqueray's Bar & Grill..........24	C3
Wall St Plaza.............................25	D3
Ybor's Martini Bar....................26	C4

ENTERTAINMENT
Amway Arena...........................27	B1
Bob Carr Performing Arts	
Center......................................28	B1
Central Station Bar & NY Deli..29	D3
Independent Bar.......................30	C3
Mad Cow Theater.....................31	D3
Orlando Youth Theater......(see 34)	
SAK Comedy Lab.......................32	B1
Social..33	C3
Studio Theater...........................34	B1
Tabu..35	C3

TRANSPORT
Lynx Central Station.................36	C1

adult/child 3-11 $15/10; ☺ 10am-6pm Sun-Thu, to 9pm Fri & Sat) is primarily a children's museum. It features changing exhibits on dinosaurs, the human body, the solar system and the like. Unfortunately, many are computer-generated and are too complicated to teach anything and too educational to be fun. The result is a lot of kids just running around punching buttons. One of the more successful exhibits is the sound wave machine, where you can speak into a microphone and see the waves your voice makes. There's also a small IMAX theater and a planetarium. Park for free in front of the museum, or pay $3 for the enclosed parking garage across the street.

Founded in 1924, the sprawling blindingly white and high-ceilinged **Orlando Museum of Art** (Map pp264-5; ☎ 407-896-4231; www.omart.org; 2416 N Mills Ave; adult/child 6-18 $8/5; ☺ 10am-4pm Tue-Fri, from noon Sat & Sun) has a great collection of modern and classic art and visiting exhibits that include Norman Rockwell and children's illustrators. On Thursday afternoons from 2pm to 3:30pm children can make an art project at the Creation Station, and on the first Saturday of every month the museum hosts a children's music, stories and activities program for three to five-year-olds ($5 per family). The tiny but excellent **Mennello Museum of American Folk Art** (Map pp264-5; ☎ 407-246-4278; www.mennellomuseum.org; 900 E Princeton St; adult/child under 12 $4/free; ☺ 10:30am-4:30pm Tue-Sat, from noon Sun) features the work of Earl Cunningham, whose brightly colored images, a fusion of pop and folk art, literally leap out from the canvas. The grassy lakeshore area next to the museum makes a particularly nice spot for a picnic.

The **John and Rita Lowndes Shakespeare Center** (Map pp264-5; www.orlandoshakes.org; 812 E Rollins St), home to the **Orlando Shakespeare Theater** (☎ 407-447-1700; tickets $20-35; ☺ Sep-May), holds performances of Shakespeare stand-bys like *Macbeth* and *As You Like It*, as well as classic theater, two children's shows a year, an annual theatrical premier, and holiday favorites – well, perhaps *A Tuna Christmas* isn't a favorite, but it's certainly an interesting holiday option. Across the way, the **Orlando Repertory Theater** (Map pp264-5; ☎ 407-896-7365; www.orlandorep.com; 1001 E Princeton St; tickets $10-25) offers theater for young audiences year-round. Local productions of national shows include *Charlie and the Chocolate Factory, A Year with Frog and Toad* and *Chronicles of Narnia*.

GATORLAND

With no fancy roller coasters or drenching water rides, this dusty mom-and-pop **park** (Map p262; ☎ 407-855-5496, 800-393-5297; www.gatorland.com; 14501 S Orange Blossom Trail; adult/child 3-12 $23/15; ☺ 9am-5pm) harkens back to Old Florida. It's small, it's silly, and it's kitschy with, you guessed it, plenty of gators. The park sometimes offers free admission to teachers – be sure to ask.

Allow time to see all the rather tongue-in-cheek shows, but don't expect to be wowed with special effects, dramatic music and spectacular light design. At the **Jumparoo Show** 10ft-long alligators leap almost entirely out of the water to grab whole chickens from the trainer, and after the **Gator Wrestling Show** you can go on down to get a photo of yourself sitting on a gator. The best is **Upclose Encounters**, where mysterious boxes hold animals the public has sent to the park. The trainers are too scared to open 'em, so they drag audience members down to help.

Sign up in advance for the recommended **Trainer for a Day** (incl park admission $125; 2hrs) program. After some safety demonstrations you may get to wrestle a gator, feed them chickens and hold one of the adorable babies. Every experience is different, and though kids must be at least 12 years old to participate, the little ones get a kick just from watching.

A splintery wooden boardwalk winds past the hundreds of alligators and crocodiles in the **breeding marsh**, and you can buy hot dogs to feed them. Kids enjoy the **Gatorland Express Train** ($2). Keep an eye out for staff walking around with cuddly lambs and the like as part of the park's **Critter on the Go**.

INTERNATIONAL DRIVE

I-Drive is packed with restaurants, hotels, elaborate miniature golf, dinner theaters and a handful of minor Orlando attractions. It parallels I-4 to its east, stretching from the Prime Outlets International (p284) to SeaWorld (p328). The couple miles between the convention center and Sand Lake Rd is a divided road, with palm trees, museums and a relatively pleasant walking district. From Sand Lake Rd north to the dead end at Prime Outlets International it's an unpleasant strip of asphalt, T-shirt shops and parking lots. Universal Orlando Resort (p319) lies west of International Drive on Universal Blvd just north of Wet 'n' Wild (p271).

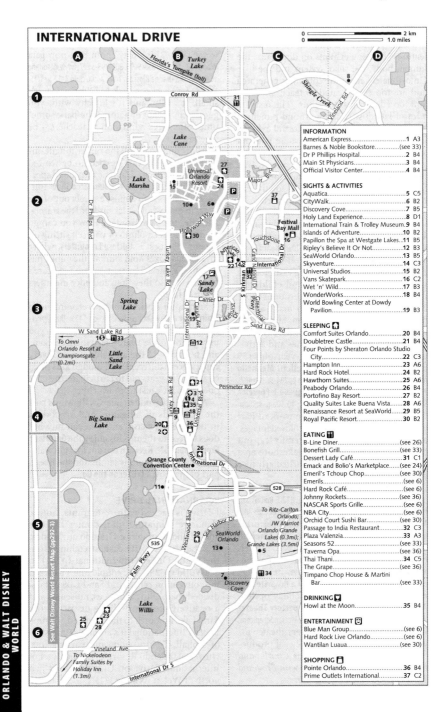

INTERNATIONAL DRIVE

INFORMATION	
American Express	**1** A3
Barnes & Noble Bookstore	(see 33)
Dr P Phillips Hospital	**2** B4
Main St Physicians	**3** B4
Official Visitor Center	**4** B4

SIGHTS & ACTIVITIES	
Aquatica	**5** C5
CityWalk	**6** B2
Discovery Cove	**7** B5
Holy Land Experience	**8** D1
International Train & Trolley Museum	**9** B4
Islands of Adventure	**10** B2
Papillon the Spa at Westgate Lakes	**11** B5
Ripley's Believe It Or Not	**12** B3
SeaWorld Orlando	**13** B5
Skyventure	**14** C3
Universal Studios	**15** B2
Vans Skatepark	**16** C2
Wet 'n' Wild	**17** B3
WonderWorks	**18** B4
World Bowling Center at Dowdy Pavilion	**19** B3

SLEEPING	
Comfort Suites Orlando	**20** B4
Doubletree Castle	**21** B4
Four Points by Sheraton Orlando Studio City	**22** C3
Hampton Inn	**23** A6
Hard Rock Hotel	**24** B2
Hawthorn Suites	**25** A6
Peabody Orlando	**26** B4
Portofino Bay Resort	**27** B2
Quality Suites Lake Buena Vista	**28** A6
Renaissance Resort at SeaWorld	**29** B5
Royal Pacific Resort	**30** B2

EATING	
B-Line Diner	(see 26)
Bonefish Grill	(see 33)
Dessert Lady Café	**31** C1
Emack and Bolio's Marketplace	(see 24)
Emeril's Tchoup Chop	(see 30)
Emerils	(see 6)
Hard Rock Café	(see 6)
Johnny Rockets	(see 36)
NASCAR Sports Grille	(see 6)
NBA City	(see 6)
Orchid Court Sushi Bar	(see 30)
Passage to India Restaurant	**32** C3
Plaza Valenzia	**33** A3
Seasons 52	(see 33)
Taverna Opa	(see 36)
Thai Thani	**34** C5
The Grape	(see 36)
Timpano Chop House & Martini Bar	(see 33)

DRINKING	
Howl at the Moon	**35** B4

ENTERTAINMENT	
Blue Man Group	(see 6)
Hard Rock Live Orlando	(see 6)
Wantilan Luaua	(see 30)

SHOPPING	
Pointe Orlando	**36** B4
Prime Outlets International	**37** C2

Traffic can be gridlocked and it's not unusual to be stuck in painfully frustrating traffic at 10pm. See Getting Around (p284) for information on the I-Ride Trolley that runs up and down I-Drive.

WonderWorks

Housed in a hard-to-miss, upside-down building, this bright, loud, frenetic museum (Map p270; ☎ 407-351-8800; www.wonderworksonline.com; 9067 International Dr; adult/child 4-12 $20/15; ☺ 9am-midnight) is a cross between a children's museum, a video arcade and an amusement park. It offers high-speed, multisensory education with several stories of wall-to-wall hands-on attractions and exhibits. You can lie on a bed of nails, sit inside a hurricane simulator, and measure how high you can jump. Younger children may find the pulse disorienting and frightening, but older ones will probably enjoy the cool stuff to do. Plus there's laser tag and the **Outta Control Magic Show** (dinner show adult/child $25/17; 9am-midnight), pairing dinner with illusions.

International Train & Trolley Museum

Home to the most extravagant model train set you can imagine, the **International Train & Trolley Museum** (Map p270; ☎ 407-363-9002; 8990 International Dr; adult/child 3-12 $8/6; ☺ 9:30am-7:30pm) features toy trains dating from the 1920s to the present day, all housed in a garden of waterfalls, trestles and 13ft mountains. Among the more impressive are a custom-made California trolley and an authentic Mason Bogey with two passenger cars.

Ripley's Believe It Or Not

The 1933 World's Fair in Chicago introduced Ripley's collection of 'oddities and unusual people' to the public. While it may today offend 21st-century politically correct sensibilities, this **museum** (Map p270; ☎ 407-363-4418; www.ripleysorlando.com; 8201 International Dr; adult/child 4-12 $19/12; ☺ 9am-1am, last entrance at midnight) embraces Ripley's vision with no holds barred. A short documentary film chronicles his search for the 'strange, exotic and incredible', and TVs throughout the museum screen footage of classic Ripley, including exotic food customs, the man with the 'strongest eyes in the world' and a snake slithering through a guy's nose and out his mouth. Exhibits range from the life-sized Rolls Royce made entirely from matchsticks to a shrunken skull to a model of the 1,069lb man who, as the story goes, gained so much weight because he burst a gland in the back of his neck during a bout of whooping cough at age three.

Wet 'n' Wild

Of the five water parks in and around Orlando, **Wet 'n' Wild** (Map p270; ☎ 407-351-1800, 800-992-9453; www.wetnwild.com; 6200 International Dr; adult/child 3-9 $34/28; ☺ vary year-round) caters primarily to teenagers who don't mind blaring music, bad food and stretching their towels out on pavement. Families with younger children should head to Disney's Typhoon Lagoon (p310) or SeaWorld's Aquatica (p332) instead.

While there is a small wave pool and a lazy river, this park is about high-speed thrills; if you can tolerate the lines, their dives, twists and turns won't disappoint. Attractions include the **Storm**, which dumps you into a huge whirlpool so you zoom around and around before dropping out the center into a pool below; **Mach 5**, a superslick mat ride; **Black Hole**, enclosed for maximum disorientation; and **Hydra Fighter**, which involves bungee cords and fire hoses in a two-person car.

Wet 'n' Wild participates in the Orlando FlexTicket program (see boxed text What to Expect from the Parks, p288). Parking is $6 per car and $7 per RV.

Skyventure

The closest you'll get to skydiving without getting into a plane, this ride (Map p270; ☎ 407-903-1150; 6805 Visitor's Circle; adult/child 3-12 $45/35; ☺ 10:30am-9pm Mon-Fri) simulates stomach-flopping, cheek-flappin' parachute drops inside the comfort of a high-energy wind tunnel. While the ride itself may be fun for some, the experience of being there is rather unpleasant as it sits squished between the parking lots and traffic of I-Drive across the street from Wet 'n' Wild.

DETOUR: STEAM ENGINES & THOMAS

Train buffs young and old will enjoy a ride on one of the many historic train tours offered through **Inland Lakes Railway** (☎ 352-589-4300; www.inlandlakesrailway.com). Departing from Mt Dora (Map p262) and other stations just north of Orlando, trips range in length from one hour to overnight, and vary according to season.

HOLY LAND EXPERIENCE

A self-proclaimed not-for-profit Christian organization, **Holy Land Experience** (Map p270; ☎ 407-367-2065, 866-872-4659; 4655 Vineland Rd; adult/child 6-12 $30/20, ☒ daily except for Thanksgiving Day & Christmas) is designed to look like Jerusalem c AD 33. Staff members wear flowing bedouin robes and hawk Middle Eastern food treats such as mint tea, tabbouleh and falafel, as well as Goliath burgers and chicken fajitas (that famous culinary delight from Jerusalem AD 33). Even more prevalent are the shops selling Holy Land Experience gear, carved wooden camels, Jesus-fish neckties, bibles and the like. Most of the attractions are proselytizing musical and dramatic live presentations, so if you want to cover the park you're going to need at least a half-day. Rules are strict: dress conservatively and don't smoke. Arrange tours for the deaf and blind in advance. Parking costs $5, and strollers can be rented for $5. To get to Holy Land Experience, follow the signs from the I-4 exit 78.

OLD TOWN

At this complex of rides, shopping, dining and live music, 'county fair' meets 'boardwalk', plopped among the exhaust, the neon lights and the treeless landscape of Hwy 192. Located on the Kissimmee strip, **Old Town** (Map pp292-3; ☎ 407-396-4888, 800-843-4202; www.old-town.com; 5770 W Irlo Bronson Memorial Hwy; free admission & parking, rides $1 each; ☒ 10am-11pm, rides & bars stay open later) offers classic rides like go-carts, a kiddie coaster, a Ferris wheel and a carousel, and is particularly fun for young children. There are car cruises Friday and Saturday, while Thursday is motorcycle night.

SKYCOASTER

The most adrenaline-pumping experience in central Florida is the **Skycoaster** (Map p262; ☎ 407-397-2509; www.skycoaster.cc; 2850 Florida Plaza Blvd; 1/2/3 people $40/70/90; ☒ 2pm-midnight Mon-Fri, from 10am Sat & Sun). Picture this: you and up to two other people are wrapped in an apron that's hooked onto a long rope, which pulls you more than 300ft straight up into the air. You dangle helplessly for a few moments, release and shoot down head first, 120ft free fall at speeds of up to 85mph. At the last second before impact, you're suddenly soaring over the water.

GREEN MEADOWS PETTING FARM

Take a day in the country at this farm (Map p262; ☎ 407-846-0770; www.greenmeadowsfarm.com; 1368 S Poinciana Blvd; adult/child over 2yr/senior/child 2yr & under $21/21/15/free; ☒ 9:30am-5:30pm) about a half-hour from Disney. You can pet the farm animals, milk a cow, ride a pony and ride the little train. It's certainly a pleasant spot with plenty of shade and grass, but unfortunately you can't just wander around – you must go on a two-hour tour. It's officially open until 5:30pm and has continuous tours until 4pm, but there's no regular tour schedule and if there aren't enough people, tours don't run. If you arrive after 4pm, you may not be allowed in. Call in advance.

MAITLAND ART CENTER

Since 1938, this **art center** (Map p262; ☎ 407-539-2181; www.maitlandartcenter.org; 231 W Packwood Ave; admission free; ☒ 9am-4:30pm Mon-Fri, from noon Sat & Sun) has provided classes and studio space to area artists, as well as galleries where they can display their work for the public. The

---

ONLY IN ORLANDO

▪ Waiting for an hour in line with a childless, middle-aged couple wearing Mickey Mouse ears and Disney World sweatshirts so your five-year-old can have her photo taken with a guy dressed as Piglet (p295).

▪ Drinking a Bud Light while bikini-clad women swing from ropes over the bar on a steamy night in downtown Orlando (p281).

▪ Wrestling an alligator and living to bring home the photo on a T-shirt (p269).

▪ Munching on Green Eggs & Ham as Spider-Man zooms up beside you on his motorcycle and leaps off into a dramatic crouch (p324).

▪ Catching an outdoor concert of Beatles look-alikes bopping to 'Twist and Shout' before riding through dinosaurland to learn about fossil fuels from Ellen DeGeneres' commentary (p304).

CYPRESS GARDENS

Before Disney and Universal, before rides became as much about the special effects and the narrative shtick as the thrill, there was **Cypress Gardens** (off Map p262; ☎ 863-324-2111; www .cypressgardens.com; adult/child 3-9 $40/35, second-day free if upgraded before leaving park; ☯ vary). This park, perched on the shores of Lake Eloise, opened as a botanical garden in 1936 and soon became world famous for its performance water-ski shows and carnival rides. It closed in 2003, but new owners updated and reopened the park in 2007. Today it is an enchanting mix of rides; bucolic gardens; live performances (including the now classic water-ski shows); animal displays, such as a butterfly house; and weekend concerts, blessedly free of loud music and sensory overload. And the Southern Belles walking around, straight out of *Gone With the Wind*, are as synonymous with Cypress Gardens as water skiing. Ask about them at the gate.

The rides are, quite simply, rides. No hoopla, no scary mermaids or mountain beasts, no creepy music and flashing lights. Best of all, the lines are often so short you can simply stay on for another go. Some of the kiddie rides at **Bugsville** are downright silly, the kind you'd expect at a county fair c 1957, but little ones love 'em. For more thrills, the park has three roller-coaster classics – including the **Starliner**, a restored 1962 wooden coaster, and **Swampthing**, where your feet dangle below – as well as **Thunderbolt** (Disney's Tower of Terror with all the thrills and none of the frills) and a handful of other familiar favorites. **Splash Island**, a water park, is open seasonally and is included in admission. Parking is $7 for a car and $9 for an RV.

For tasty barbecue, stop at the mom-and-pop café, **Schacks** (☎ 863-324-1537; 3000 Cypress Gardens Rd; mains $5-12; ☯ 6am-9pm), across from the Blockbuster just down the street from the park's entrance. Spend the night next door at the **Best Western Admirals Inn** (☎ 863-324-5950; www.bestwesternadmiralsinn.com; 5665 Cypress Gardens Blvd; r & ste $100-240; ☐ ☒) or continue the Old Florida theme and stay in an antique-furnished room at the oh-so-quirky, family-owned **Chalet Suzanne** (☎ 800-433-6011; www.chaletsuzanne.com; 3800 Chalet Suzanne Dr, Lake Wales; r & ste $130-250; restaurant ☯ breakfast, lunch, dinner, closed Mon; ☐ ☒). The restaurant makes and cans its own soup on site for national distribution, and has been serving up first-rate vittles since 1931.

Cypress Gardens is about a 50 miles from downtown Orlando. Take the I-4 west to exit 55 (Hwy 27). Turn right at the ramp, follow Hwy 27 for 18 miles and turn right onto Cypress Gardens Blvd. A visit to both Cypress Gardens and the Historic Bok Sanctuary (see boxed text Beyond the Pavement, p274) 10 minutes away makes an excellent day trip.

---

facilities, listed on the National Register of Historic Places, boast lovely gardens where live music, usually classical, is performed on an occasional basis.

Activities

BIKING

You can download six bike maps, including several lovely routes through historic districts, from the City of Orlando's **website** (www.cityofor lando.net). Most theme park resorts run their own cycling programs, including rentals and trails. One of the prettiest paths is between Disney's Boardwalk and Beach Club resorts, on a tandem candy-striped bike. Cyclists can also use select trails in Wekiwa Springs State Park (p274).

Rent gear from **West Orange Trail Bikes & Blades** (off Map p262; ☎ 407-877-0600; 17914 State Rd 438 Winter Garden; bikes hr/day/week $6-10/30-50/99-149;

☯ 11am-5pm Mon-Fri, 9am-5pm Sat & Sun). There is a $40 delivery/pickup charge, and rates include a car rack.

WATER SPORTS

Orlando may be landlocked, but its 300-plus lakes provide perfect water playgrounds. Inside Disney's Contemporary Resort is **Sammy Duvall's Water Sport's Centre** (Map pp292-3; ☎ 407-939-0754; www.sammyduvall.com; 4600 N World Dr; jet-ski rentals 30mins/1hr $75/125, water skiing & wakeboarding for up to 5 people $80/155, parasailing single/tandem 8-10min $195/160; ☯ 8am-5pm summer, from 10am rest of year) offers all sorts of water excursions, jet-ski rental and lessons. Make reservations up to two weeks in advance. Also try the **Buena Vista Watersports** (Map p262; ☎ 407-239-6939; www.bvwatersports.com; Lake Bryan; jet-ski rentals 30min/1hr $45/80, water skiing & wakeboarding $70/120, lessons $75; ☯ 9am-6:30pm).

BEYOND THE PAVEMENT

After a few days of rides and lines, fried food, loud music, traffic and shopping, a jaunt beyond the pavement can soothe and rejuvenate even the most harried of spirits.

Wekiwa Springs State Park

The best way to explore this **state park** (☎ 407-884-4311; www.floridastateparks.org/wekiwasprings; 1800 Wekiwa Circle; pedestrian/single driver/car up to 8 people $1/3/5) is by paddling along the tranquil, still waters of the Wekiva River, one of Florida's two federally designated 'Wild and Scenic Rivers'. You can take a two-and-a-half-hour guided **tour** (☎ 407-880-4110; www.canoewekiva.com; $35 per person, 4-person minimum). Alternatively, canoe or kayak about five hours to Katie's Landing (canoe 2/3 people $35/40, single/double kayak $30/40, children under six free) and hop a shuttle back (included in the trip price), or rent a boat (canoe $15 per two hours, single/double kayak $15/20 per two hours, two-hour minimum hire, $3 each additional hour) and simply toot around. To really get away from it all, book a campsite through the state park and spend a night or two in a primitive spot along the riverbank (two days and one night including canoe or kayak, tent, sleeping bags, stoves, lanterns and cooler $132). The park also has 13 miles of wooded hiking trails and a fantastic spring-fed swimming hole. Take I-4, exit 94 and follow the signs; it's about 45 minutes from downtown Orlando.

Kelly Park/Rock Springs

Children and adults alike head to this **park** (☎ 407-889-4179; 400 E Kelly Park Rd, Apopka; ☀ 9am-6pm summer, 8am-7pm winter; adults/children under 5 $1/free) to inner-tube down the shallow stream created by Rock Spring. The bucolic 1-mile stretch takes about 30 minutes to leisurely float down, and there are several spots where you can get out along the way. Rent an inner tube near the park entrance ($5). To get to the park, take I-4 north to the exit 101C, State Rd 46 (Sanford/Mt Dora), then head west just over 12 miles to Mt Plymouth Rd (County Rd 435). Turn left and drive 4 miles to Kelly Park Rd; make a left and take it 0.8 miles to the end. Campsites with water and electricity ($23) can be reserved up to 45 days in advance. There's a small concession in the park, and the nearby town of Apopka has several restaurants.

Historic Bok Sanctuary

Edward Bok, editor of the *Ladies' Home Journal* from 1888 to 1919, stood at the forefront of modern environmentalism and the promotion of progressive causes. Inspired by his grandmother's admonishment to 'make you the world a bit more beautiful and better because you have been in it,' he hired Frederick Law Olmstead Jr to design these **gardens** (☎ 863-376-1408; 1151 Tower

SURFING & SNORKELING

On Tuesday and Thursday, Disney's **Typhoon Lagoon** (p310) offers 2½ hour surf lessons ($140) before the park opens to the public. Make reservations on ☎ 407-939-7529.

You can snorkel with the manatee with **Fun 2 Dive Scuba and Snorkeling** (☎ 888-588-3483; www .fun2dive.com; 2-6 people 1 day $90) in Sanford, just north of Orlando.

FISHING

Central Florida is famous for its freshwater fishing (especially largemouth bass), and the canals and lakes in and around Orlando offer some of the best. For licenses, rules, tips and other info contact **Fish Orlando** (☎ 407-846-5191; www.floridafisheries.com/fishorlando). One of the best lakes for fishing, picnics and bird-watching

is **Lake Tohopekaliga** (Map p262) just south of Kissimmee.

Local guides include **Gator Rod Charters** (☎ 866-460-3474; www.centralfloridafishingguide.com), **Bass Pro Guides** (☎ 407-877-9676; www.probass guideservice.com) and **Lake Toho Fishing Guides and Charters** (☎ 407-928-4529; www.laketohotackle.com).

GOLF

Courses are least crowded from May to October, when you can pick your tee time and be confident that you can play as leisurely as you like. Also during those months, many private courses are available to the public. Ask about twilight discount rates, and be sure to check if your hotel offers special golf deals at select courses. The number of courses at your disposal in and around Orlando (more than

Blvd, Lake Wales; www.boksanctuary.org; adult/child 5-12 $10/3; 9am-6pm daily, last admission 5pm). In 1929 President Calvin Coolidge dedicated them to the US people. The centerpiece of the 250-acre property is the meticulously carved 205ft stone bell tower, and every afternoon the 60-bell carillon dongs its bells. Children enjoy looking for the iron rubbing posts, each with a different animal to rub onto special paper given upon entry, and there is plenty of room for running and playing in the grass and on the paths. Also on site is a small café, a museum and the beautiful 20-room Mediterranean-style **Pinewood Estates**, registered on the National Register of Historic Places; tours are offered several times daily. Sweet-smelling orange groves line the drive here, and a sense of calm, order and peace pervades the sanctuary. To get here, take I-4 west to exit 55. Proceed south on Hwy 27 for about 23 miles and follow the signs.

Nature Conservancy's Disney Wilderness Preserve
Hidden within Orlando's sprawl, this amazing and rarely visited 12,000-acre **preserve** (off Map p262; ☎ 407-935-0002; 2700 Scrub Jay Trail; adult/youth 6-17 $3/2; 9am-5pm Mon-Fri) is the result of wetland laws that required Walt Disney World to compensate for the company's impact on (and devastation of) wetlands and sensitive natural habitats. Home to gopher tortoises, bald eagles, sandhill cranes and hundreds of other wildlife species, the park features walking trails through the scrub, fields and woods. While the trails shift as a result of annual burns, the 1-mile loop trip to Lake Russell, one of central Florida's last remaining undeveloped lakes, and a longer 2.5-mile loop are generally open to visitors. The park is located about 15 minutes, or 15 to 25 miles, from Walt Disney World, just south of Kissimmee. Take Poinciana Blvd past Horse World several miles and turn right on Pleasant Hill Rd/Cypress Parkway. Drive 0.5 miles and turn right onto Old Pleasant Hill Rd for 0.7 miles. Look out for bird families on the drive in.

Harry P Leu Gardens
These lovely **gardens** (Map pp264-5; ☎ 407-246-2620; www.leugardens.org; 1920 N Forest Ave; adult/youth 18 & under $5/1; 9am-5pm, last admission 4pm) encompass 50 acres and include camellias (blooming October through March), desert plants, vegetables, wetlands and the largest formal rose garden in Florida. Twenty-minute tours of the **Leu House**, an 18th-century mansion listed on the National Register of Historic Places, are available every half-hour from 10am to 3:30pm. The gardens feature an outdoor movie the first Friday of every month from March to November (except July), storytelling every third Monday at 10am and occasional concerts. From I-4, take exit 85 to Princeton St and follow the signs.

150!) goes far beyond the scope of this book; to get the full spectrum go to www.golfing orlando.com. For details on Walt Disney World's six golf courses, call ☎ 407-939-4653 or go to www.disneyworldgolf.com.

Following are a few golfers' favorites.
Dubsread Golf Course (Map pp264-5; ☎ 407-246-2551; 549 W Par St; $15-30; 7am-5pm tee times) A bunker-happy course designed way back in 1923, which has seen the likes of legends Sam Snead, Ben Hogan and Claude Harmon.
Falcon's Fire Golf Club (Map pp292-3; ☎ 407-239-5445; www.falconsfire.com; 3200 Seralago Blvd; $50-110; 7am-5:00pm tee times) Flaunts a country-club atmosphere and a 6900yd, par-72 Rees Jones course.
Orange Country National Golf Center & Lodge (Map p262; ☎ 407-656-2626; www.ocngolf.com; 16301 Phil Ritson Way, Winter Garden; $60-105; 7am-5:45pm tee times) Offers excellent links-style play. Panther Lake is a rolling-hills 18-hole course, and Crooked Cat features Bermuda greens and some challenging par-3s.

BOWLING
With floating spacemen and surreal murals adorning the walls, the **World Bowling Center at Dowdy Pavilion** (Map p270; ☎ 407-352-2695; www.worldbowlingcenter.com; 7540 Canada Ave; adult/child $4/3, shoe rental $3; 12pm-11pm Mon-Sun, to 2am Fri & Sat) makes a fun place to hang out on hot or rainy days. On Friday and Saturday nights the lights go down and music cranks up for Moonlight Bowling.

SKATEBOARDING
Adrenaline junkies will love **Van's Skatepark** (Map p270; ☎ 407-351-3881; 5220 International Dr;

SADDLE UP

A day on the trails, far from the crowds and mayhem of the theme parks and tourist strips yet surprisingly accessible, can be a great way for the entire family to slow down, relax and unwind. For private English-saddle lessons ($30-100) head to the beautifully maintained formal stables at the lovely **Grand Cypress Equestrian Center** (☎ 407-957-9794; 4755 N Kenansville Rd, St Cloud 34773) just outside the gates of Walt Disney World. They also have pony rides for children aged three to seven (five minutes $10) and, from the resort down the road, private and group trail rides ($45-85). Disney's **Fort Wilderness Resort & Campground** (Map pp292-3; ☎ 407-939-7529) offers horse trail rides, pony rides and wagon rides, and **Forever Florida** (off Map p262; ☎ 407-957-9794; www.floridaeco-safaris.com; 4755 N Kenansville Rd, St Cloud) runs horseback safaris and overnight trips from their Crescent J Ranch. To get there, take exit 64 from I-4 and head east on Irlo Bronson Memorial Hwy/US 192, 36 miles to Holowpaw Rd/US 441. Turn south and drive about 8 miles. In Kissimmee, roam 750 acres at the low-key and no-frills **Horse World** (off Map p262; ☎ 407-847-4343; www.horseworldstables.com; 3705 S Poinciana Blvd; adult/child under 40lb riding with an adult 1hr $40/17). Advanced trail rides are also available.

North of Orlando, **Rock Springs Riding Ranch** (Map p262; ☎ 352-735-6266; www.rsrranch.com; 3700 County Rd 33, Sorrento) features one-, two- and three-hour and all-day rides through meadows, pine-scrub swampland and dense forests in the 14,000-acre Rock Springs Run State Reserve. Prices range from $37 for one hour to $157 for six hours, and children must be at least nine years old. A 45-minute wagon ride (adult/child 6-12yr $10/8) departs several times a day, and children must be at least six years old. Take the I-4 exit 101C. Head west, and it's about 8 miles on the left. Ask about the ranch's Hammock House B & B, which had not yet opened at the time of research.

Advanced reservations are required for all trail rides and lessons.

2hr session $12/15 weekday/weekend; ☺ 10am-10pm) inside Festival Bay Mall. You can rent a board ($5) and all the necessary safety equipment, right after you (or your legal guardian if you're under 18) sign a comprehensive waiver. An all-day pass, including gear rental, is $35 and sessions begin every two hours on the hour.

Sleeping

Rack rates vary according to demand, can change within the course of a day, and can sometimes be lowered by bargaining or as part of a package. As a general rule, rates are lower from June through September and higher from September through May. Rates quoted below are a general range during high season.

In addition to the following, you'll find every conceivable motel chain and plenty of cheap mom-and-pop motels.

DOWNTOWN
Midrange
Veranda Bed & Breakfast (Map p268; ☎ 407-849-0321; www.theverandabandb.com; 115 N Summerlin Ave; r & ste $99-189; ☐ ☒) Simple, friendly and low key, this cluster of four two-story buildings sits in the pleasant and leafy Thornton Park

neighborhood, within blocks of several restaurants, bars and a great bookstore. Rooms are spacious, with no frilly accoutrements, and there's a small pool in the shared courtyard. The Keylime Cottage has two bedrooms (each with a queen bed), two bathrooms, a pull-out couch and a full kitchen – perfect for families.

Courtyard at Lake Lucerne (Map pp264-5; ☎ 407-648-5188, 800-444-5289; www.orlandohistoricinn.com; 211 N Lucerne Circle; r & ste $99-225; ☐) This lovely historic inn (c 1883), with its enchanting gardens, romantic fountains and genteel breakfast, sits directly under two highway overpasses. The art-deco suites, housed in Orlando's first apartment building (built 1946) have small kitchens and plenty of room, there are handsome antiques throughout, and the staff is exceptionally friendly and helpful. But you can hear the trucks rumble overhead and it's an ugly walk to the restaurants and bars at Lake Eola and Thornton Park. Breakfast includes tasty pastries, cheese, hard-boiled eggs, bagels and fruit. In a better location, this place would be a favorite.

EO Inn & Spa (Map p268; ☎ 407-481-8485; www.eoinn.com; 227 N Eola Dr; r $139-229; ☐) A hip boutique hotel that wouldn't be out of place in South Beach. It sits right on the corner of

Lake Eola, and the soothing beige-and-white rooms evoke a sense of serenity that feels miles away from the hustle of the city. Complete the escape with a treatment at its on-site spa.

Embassy Suites (Map p268; ☎ 407-841-1000; www .embassysuites.com; 191 E Pine St; ste $140-414; ☐ ☒) In the heart of downtown, with a sunny indoor atrium and updated decor, it's not your average chain hotel. A solid choice for comfortable rooms within walking distance from attractions, restaurants and bars.

Top End

Westin Grand Bohemian (Map p268; ☎ 407-313-9000; www.grandbohemianhotel.com; 325 S Orange Ave; r & ste $199-450; ☐ ☒) Downtown's most luxurious and elegant option has a first-rate restaurant, impeccable linens and handsome urban rooms. Weekdays cost more than weekends.

INTERNATIONAL DRIVE & AROUND

Most of the following hotels offer shuttle service to Universal Studios, SeaWorld, Wet 'n' Wild and sometimes Walt Disney World. Always ask about shuttle details, including schedules, price and size.

Budget

Comfort Suites Orlando (Map p270; ☎ 407-351-5050; www.comfortsuitesorlando.com; 9350 Turkey Lake Rd; ste $90-150; ☐ ☒) Amid plenty of palm trees and greenery, the roomy suites are equipped with microwaves, refrigerators and comfortable beds – this is a great bargain among the glut of chains. There's a kiddie pool and a large swimming pool surrounded by an outdoor grille. Rates include a full breakfast. Shuttles to Disney cost $12; shuttles to Universal Orlando and SeaWorld are complimentary.

Midrange

Four Points by Sheraton Orlando Studio City (Map p270; ☎ 407-351-2100, 800-327-1366; www.sheratonstudiocity .com; 5905 International Dr; r & ste $125-350; ☐ ☒) The

---

> **VACATION HOME RENTAL**
>
> If you are keen to rent a home while you stay in Orlando, check out one of the following rental agencies.
>
> **All Star Vacation Homes** (www.allstar vacationhomes.com)
> **Disney Rents** (www.disneyrents.com)
> **Vacation Rental By Owner** (www.vrbo.com)

---

art-deco motif starts at the driveway arch and spills into the small checkerboard-floored and mirrored lobby of this tall, skinny building in the middle of International Drive mayhem. Nothing special, but it's conveniently located minutes from Universal Orlando.

Renaissance Resort at SeaWorld (Map p270; ☎ 407-351-5555, 800-327-6677; www.renaissanceseaworld.com; 6677 Sea Harbor Dr; r & ste $150-450; ☐ ☒) A beautiful koi-filled fountain and an enormous exotic birdcage dominate the atrium of this grand hotel. There is a Starbucks and a sushi bar in the lobby. It is located just across the street from SeaWorld and is equidistant to Universal Orlando and Walt Disney World.

our pick Doubletree Castle (Map p270; ☎ 407-345-1511, 800-952-2785; www.doubletreecastle.com; 8629 International Dr; r $90-300; ☐ ☒) You can't miss the castle exterior of this International Drive landmark, as distinctive inside as it is out. A whimsical purple 'castle creature' greets guests into the peach-walled lobby, which is adorned with gilt and chandeliers. The intimate breakfast room off the lobby serves tasty grab-and-go coffee, fruit, cereal and the like and a fish-shaped fountain spews from the center of the small pool. Take a picnic or a bottle of wine to the gardened rooftop terrace and catch Disney's distant fireworks. Small pets allowed.

Nickelodeon Family Suites by Holiday Inn (off Map p270; ☎ 407-387-5437, 866-462-6425; www.nickhotel.com; 14500 Continental Gateway; ste $200-400; ☐ ☒) With cartoon-themed suites, character breakfasts with Dora, SpongeBob and friends (adult/child $20/11), basketball, miniature golf, nightly shows, a Day-Glo water park swimming pool and even a kids' spa, this overloaded hotel is a kid's dream. All of the one-, two- and three-bedroom suites have kitchenettes, but that's where the attraction for parents ends. Perfect for folks who don't mind returning from a day of theme-park chaos to hotel chaos. Rates vary dramatically and can be as low as $150 or as high as $1000, depending on exact suite configurations, season and availability.

Top End

Gaylord Palms Resort & Convention Center (Map pp292-3; ☎ 407-586-2000; www.gaylordpalms.com; 6000 W Osceola Pkwy; r $160-350; ☐ ☒) More like a destination than a hotel. An enormous glass-topped atrium encompasses three sections of Florida: the Everglades, St Augustine and Key West, each with live plantings, piped-in insect sounds and running water. Balconies open into the atrium for bird's-eye views of all sections. This is, without a doubt, the most massive hotel in Orlando, and it's popular as a conference center (expect corporate banners hanging in the atrium's center) and a family resort. The pools are beginning to show their age.

JW Marriott Orlando, Grande Lakes (Map p262; ☎ 407-206-2300, 800-576-5750; www.grandelakes.com; 4040 Central Florida Pkwy; r & ste; $250-$475; ▢ ▣) A sister property to the neighboring Ritz Carlton

with shared facilities – the rooms are equally stunning rooms and often cost a bit less than those at the Ritz. It's peaceful and elegant, with plenty of greenery and the best lazy river pool in Orlando.

Peabody Orlando (Map p270; ☎ 407-352-4000, 800-732-2639; www.peabodyorlando.com; 9801 International Dr; r & ste $250-500; ▢ ▣) This first-rate hotel has all the amenities you'd expect at these prices, plus one famous extra: the March of the Peabody Ducks. At 11am a line of ducks waddles down a red carpet into the lobby fountain and at 5pm

DUCK MASTER DAVE

The general manager of the Peabody Memphis Hotel returned from a 1932 hunting trip in Arkansas and, as a prank, put duck decoys in the hotel fountain; in 1933 the hotel replaced the decoys with live ducks and in 1940 a bellman named Edward Pembroke taught them to march through the lobby. He worked as the Peabody's first duck master until 1991. The Peabody ducks have been featured on the *Tonight Show, Sesame Street* and the *Oprah Winfrey Show*.

In 1986, the Peabody Orlando hotel opened and the duck tradition continues in the sunshine state. We spoke with the Duck Master Dave.

'I answered the Peabody's newspaper ad and became duck master in March of 2007. What are my qualifications? When I was a boy growing up on an Indiana farm, folks used to dye baby ducklings as Easter gifts, but when they realized how messy they were they didn't want them anymore and they asked my dad to take them. The baby ducks would imprint on me and, thinking I was their mama, they'd follow me everywhere. Year after year, I loved the Easter duck rejects. I also had previous experience training animals as rat referee for rat (yes, live rat) basketball at the Indianapolis Children's Museum. Every time a rat would make a basket, I gave 'em a malt pellet. So I guess the Peabody figured I had the love of ducks and the knowledge of animal training they were looking for.

Our breeder chooses five ducks according to temperament when they are five months old. At 10 months old, they come to the Peabody and I begin the long and arduous process of training them. After a six-month 'tour of duty,' they return to the duck farm for six months' vacation. During break, the female ducks (hens) build nests, lay eggs, hatch their babies and watch them grow to adulthood (three months). After about four tours of duty, the ducks retire to a life of leisure at the farm. No, they are never sold for food and we don't serve duck or any kind of paté in our restaurants.

When not in the lobby fountain, the ducks live upstairs in their Duck Palace, decked out with an Italian black-marble pool, duck fountains and soft rubber matting for comfortable sleeping. Designed to look like a Japanese pagoda, it has glass walls and screens along the bottom and on parts of the roof so the ducks can feel the breeze and the rain. They eat water plants, lettuce and a mix of oats, cracked corn and millet. For a special treat, I sometimes give them mealworms from the pet store.

Every morning at 11am crowds gather to watch the ducks parade off the elevator, along the red carpet, and into the lobby fountain, and again when they march back up at 5pm. Anyone over four years old can be 'Honorary Duck Master' and assist in guiding the ducks on their parades, even if you're not a guest of the hotel. Call or email me at the hotel in advance, or sign up at the concierge desk. Kids in particular love to be duck master, but folks of all ages get a kick out of it. I give them a formal certificate and there's great pomp and circumstance.

I never get tired of talking about my ducks.'

David Robinson was born in Indiana and graduated from Franklin College there. He worked as a professional actor, and moved to Orlando in 1989.

they march back to their palatial nighttime digs (see the boxed text Duck Master Dave, opposite). Unlike its sister hotel in Memphis, this is a decidedly modern facility. Service is absolutely top-notch, beds are scrumptious, and the rooftop pool is a little hideaway of serenity and relaxation. No whistles blowing to announce scheduled kids' events, no water slides, no neon-painted palm trees.

Ritz Carlton Orlando, Grande Lakes (Map p262; ☎ 407-206-2400, 800-576-5760; www.grandelakes.com; 4012 Central Florida Pkwy; r & ste $275-475; ☐ ☒) The ultimate in luxury. Most rooms have balconies overlooking the free-form pool, the 18-hole golf course (which has won environment awards for conservative water use) and the theme-park fireworks beyond. Pay a little extra for club-level access, which has five daily servings of appetizer-size meals. The spa is divine, the service impeccable and the food outstanding. Excellent for honeymooners and families alike, this hotel is the rare gem that seamlessly combines child-friendly with adult-friendly. The Easter Brunch at the Vineyard Grill here is fantastic for families.

AROUND HIGHWAY 192
Budget
For a clean, decent and cheap room, try **Continental Inn** (Map p262; ☎ 407-396-1030; 4650 W Irlo Bronson Memorial Hwy, Kissimmee; r $30-40; ☒), **Ambassador Inn** (Map p262; ☎ 407-847-7171; 877-784-6835; www.ambassadorinnfl.com; 4107 W Vine, Kissimmee; r $60-90; ☐ ☒) or **Orlando-Days Inn Kissimmee /Hwy 192** (Map p262; ☎ 407-846-4714; 4104 W Hwy 192; r $40-50; ☐ ☒). If you want a hostel, the **Palm Lakefront Resort & Hostel** (Map p262; ☎ 407-396-1759; www.orlandohostels.com; 4840 W Hwy 192; dm & private rooms $15-20 per person; ☒) has six-bed dorms and private rooms that sleep two to five.

Top End
Omni Orlando Resort at Championsgate (Map p262; ☎ 407-390-6664, 800-843-6664; www.omnihotels.com; 1500 Masters Blvd; r & ste $200-450; ☐ ☒). Because the hotel is buffered from noise and congestion by two Greg Norman–designed golf courses, wetlands and plenty of green space, it's easy to forget you're so close to Orlando and the theme parks. The pool area is great, with a formal outdoor pool and a hot tub, as well as a family pool, waterslides and an 850ft lazy river with caves and fountains. Two- and three-bedroom villas sleeping six to eight people cost $560 to $750.

Eating
Save bundles by stocking up on snacks and drinks at the local Publix and Winn-Dixie supermarkets.

DOWNTOWN & THORNTON PARK
Lake Eola hosts the **Orlando Farmers Market** (☎ 321-202-5855; ☒ Sun 10am-4pm).

Budget
Grab a cheap bite or satisfy late-night munchies at **Planet Pizza** (Map p268; ☎ 407-650-8859; 14 W Washington St; slices $3, pizza $15-25; ☒ 5pm-3am).

Aroma Coffee & Wine Bar (Map p268; ☎ 407-426-8989; 712 E Washington St; mains $4-12; ☒ 7pm-10:30pm Tue-Thu, to 3pm Mon, until late Fri & Sat, 9am-3:30pm Sun) A neighborhood coffee shop and tiny wine-bar, this former house is a hangout for Thornton Park locals. There's a limited menu, with tasty toasted bread with prosciutto and cheese, mascarpone and jam croissants, pastries and egg sandwiches for breakfast and Italian-influenced salads, appetizers and toasted sandwiches for lunch and dinner.

Dandelion Communitea Café (Map pp264-5; ☎ 407-362-1864; 618 N Thornton Ave; mains $5-10; ☒ 8am-11pm Mon-Sat, to 9pm Sun) Unabashedly crunchy and definitively organic, this groovin' hotspot of the 'sprouts and tofu, green tea and soy milk' variety serves up creative vegetarian fare with vibe that invites you to sit down and hang out. The focus is on Florida-grown produce, and it is 100% green. If it all sounds too healthy, try a Fluffer Nutter (wheat bread with almond butter, bananas and ricemallow fluff), its nod to junk food. Call about art openings, poetry readings and music. Co-owner Chris Blank runs the Enzian (p286), Orlando's only indie theater.

Dessert Lady Café (Map p270; ☎ 407-822-8881; 4900 S Kirkman Rd; slices $3-6; ☒ 11:30am-11pm Mon-Sat, 1pm-9pm Sun) Ask Patti Schmidt how she became Orlando's first and only Dessert Lady and she'll tell you that it all started with a carrot cake. Now enjoy desserts from fruit cobbler to bourbon pecan pie over coffee or a glass of wine. And if you really must have a meal with your dessert, you can get a piece of quiche. But that's it.

Rincon Criollo Cafe (Map p268; ☎ 407-872-1128; 331 N Orange Ave; mains $5-9; ☒ 8am-3pm) Consistently wins as the hands-down local Cuban favorite. Take your pick from traditional black beans and rice to vegetarian cuisine like pressed veggie sandwiches smothered with fat Cuban bread.

Johnson's Diner (Map p268; ☎ 407-841-0717; 595 W Church St; mains $5-12; ⏰ 8am-7pm Mon-Thu, to 8pm Fri & Sat) Nobody does soul food better than this Orlando institution. Their calorie-busting meat-loaf sandwiches and homemade sweet-potato pie will have you loosening that belt quicker than you can say, 'More collard greens, please.'

Midrange

Hue (Map p268; ☎ 407-849-1800; 629 E Central Blvd; mains $12-20; ⏰ 4pm-11pm Sun-Wed, to midnight Thu-Sat, 11am-4pm Sun) Another favorite with the young Thornton Park crowd, this trendy spot serves eclectic North American cuisine in a decidedly urban setting. The name refers to hue of color, not the city in Vietnam.

Top End

K Restaurant & Wine Bar (Map pp264-5; ☎ 407-872-2332; 2401 Edgewater Dr; mains $12-25; ⏰ lunch, dinner) Deep-red walls, exposed brick and big windows give this little urban café an airy decor. The creative menu focuses on fresh,

seasonal ingredients and changes daily. For dinner on Mondays, the only option is the $35 prix-fixe meal.

INTERNATIONAL DRIVE
Budget

Johnny Rockets (Map p270; ☎ 407-903-1066; Pointe Orlando, 9101 International Dr; mains $6-10; ⏰ 11:30am-11pm Sun-Thu, to 2am Fri & Sat) Particularly good North American classics like burgers, fries and milkshakes served up in classic 1950s-diner surrounds. Straight out of *Happy Days*, with red vinyl seating, lots of chrome and flip-style juke boxes on the tables. The Fonz would feel right at home.

Midrange

B-Line Diner (Map p270; ☎ 407-352-4000; Peabody Orlando, 9801 International Dr; mains $8-20; ⏰ 24hrs) Excellent upscale diner food, including fish, pasta and steak, served up in a retro diner café. If nothing else, stop by for a late-night dessert and a glass of wine.

GAY & LESBIAN ORLANDO

The **Gay, Lesbian & Bisexual Community Center** (Map pp264-5; ☎ 407-228-8272; www.glbcc.org; 946 N Mills Ave; ⏰ 12pm-9pm Mon-Thu, to 5pm Fri & Sat) has a library and resource center, plus tips on local hotspots and social events.

Sleeping

Parliament House (Map pp264-5; ☎ 407-425-7571; www.parliamenthouse.com; 410 N Orange Blossom Trail; r $60-120, Gay Day $155; 🖥 🏊) is a gay resort and an Orlando institution. It sits on Rock Lake and features six clubs and bars, a restaurant and some of the best female impersonators this side of the Mississippi. There is a three-day minimum stay during Gay Days.

Drinking & Entertainment

Orlando's gay and lesbian scene is growing, and explodes during the weeks around **Gay Days Orlando** (see the boxed text, p306). Before you head out on the town, stop by **Ritzy Rags** (Map pp264-5; ☎ 407-897-2117; www.ritzyrags.com; 928 N Mills Ave; ⏰ 11am-6pm Tue-Thu, to 5pm Mon & Sat, to 7pm Sun), where owner and performer Leigh Shannon offers makeup and wardrobe tips for making the most of what you were born with. Wigs, dresses and size-14 pumps are also available.

Faces on Edgewater (Map pp264-5; ☎ 407-532-8442; 4910 Edgewater Dr; ⏰ 4pm-2am) A well-established lesbian bar that reopened in January '08 after its legendary owner Miss Sue Hannah passed away. It's just getting legs, so check that it's open.

Parliament House (Map pp264-5; ☎ 407-425-7571; 410 N Orange Blossom Trail) Legendary gay resort with cruisy country, piano and poolside bars, along with drag shows and other live entertainment.

Legacy Club (Map pp264-5; ☎ 407-521-2007; 3925 Clarcona-Ocoee Rd) Mostly for women, this has a pool table and dart boards as well as raucous bar bingo and dancing.

Pulse (Map pp264-5; ☎ 407-649-3888; www.pulseorlando.com; 1912 S Orange; $5; ⏰ 4pm-2am) Three nightclubs, each with its own distinct vibe but all ultramodern and sleek with high-tech lighting and sound. Check out college night.

Wylde's (Map pp264-5; ☎ 407-852-0612; 3557 S Orange Ave; ⏰ 5pm-2am) Small neighborhood bar with no glitz – the *Cheers* of Orlando's gay scene.

Passage to India Restaurant (Map p270; ☎ 407-351-3456; 5532 International Dr; mains $8-20; ☺ 11:30am-10pm) Heaven-sent for vegetarians needing a break from the salad bars. It's a little pricey, but worth it. Try the *bhaigan bharta* (baked eggplant).

The Grape (Map p270; ☎ 407-351-5815; Pointe Orlando; mains $7-17; ☺ 4pm-10pm Mon-Thu, 11am-midnight Fri & Sat, 4-9pm Sun) A sophisticated wine bar with a simple menu, plenty of windows and modern decor, the Grape attracts folks who just want to relax in relative quiet.

Taverna Opa (Map p270; ☎ 407-879-2481; Pointe Orlando; mains $9-18; ☺ 11am-midnight) The waitstaff at this high-ceilinged Greek eatery crush up fresh hummus table-side and serve it with warm pita rather than just plopping down a basket of bread. While it can get kind of crazy at night, when the belly dancer shimmers and shakes from table to table and it isn't unusual for folks to climb onto those solid tables and kick up their heels, the rest of the time it's a pleasant, simple place for solid and tasty Greek classics, including plenty of vegetarian options.

our pick **Thai Thani** (Map p270; ☎ 407-239-9733; 11025 International Dr; mains $9-22; ☺ 11:30am-11pm) Just past the gates to SeaWorld, Discovery Cove and Aquatica, this fantastic low-key Thai spot makes an ideal dinner choice after a day of dolphin shows and waterslides. It's friendly, cool and quiet, with gilded Thai decor and traditional Thai seating on the floor.

RESTAURANT ROW

The half-mile stretch of Sand Lake Rd just west of International Drive and I-4 (exit 74A) offers a concentration of diverse restaurants and upscale chains more popular with locals than tourists. Restaurants cluster in the Plaza Venezia (Map p270). Try **Bonefish Grill** (Map p270; ☎ 407-355-7707; 7488 W Sand Lake Rd; mains $12-21; ☺ 11am-10pm Mon-Wed, to 11pm Thu & Fri, 12pm-11pm Sat, to 10pm Sun), the recommended **Seasons 52** (Map p270; ☎ 407-354-5212; 7700 Sand Lake Rd; mains $12-25; ☺ lunch, dinner) and **Timpano Chop House & Martini Bar** (Map p270; ☎ 407-248-0429; 7488 W Sand Lake Rd; mains $13-40; ☺ 11am-11pm Sun-Wed, to 12pm Thu-Sat)

ANTIQUE ROW

Just north of downtown and off the tourist loop, this small stretch of interesting stores and restaurants makes a good stop on the way to museums at Loch Haven Park (p267) or Winter Park (p284).

Budget

Ethos Vegan Kitchen (Map pp264-5; ☎ 407-228-3898; 1235 N Orange Ave; mains $6-10; ☺ 11:00am-10pm Tue-Sat, 10am-3pm Sun) The 100% vegan menu includes pizzas with broccoli, banana peppers, zucchini and seitan, pecan encrusted eggplant, homemade soups and various sandwiches with names like A Fungus Among Us and the Hippie Wrap.

Greek Corner Restaurant (Map pp264-5; ☎ 407-228-0303; 1600 N Orange Ave; mains $6-14; ☺ 11:00am-10pm Tue-Sat, 10am-3pm Sun) A simple café with white walls and a small patio, this spot across from Lake Ivanhoe serves delicious gyros, moussaka and other Greek specialties.

Midrange

Gargi's Lakeside (Map pp264-5; ☎ 407-894-7907; 1414 N Orange; mains $10-20; ☺ 11:30am-10pm Mon-Thu, to 11pm Fri, 12pm-11pm Sat, 3-8pm Sun) While the food is very good, the best part about this restaurant is its quiet lakeside location next to a playground. Sit outside and watch the kids play while you relax over wine and a bowl of pasta. The menu offers several cold salad plates, like chicken curry salad plate, and panini, perfect for lunch.

LAKE BUENA VISTA

Three mom-and-pop restaurants in the Vista Center strip mall (Map pp292–3) offer decent food and make a good choice for folks looking for a quiet meal without any fanfare. Try **Havana's Café** (Map pp292-3; ☎ 407-238-5333; 8544 Palm Pkwy; mains $8-15; ☺ 11am-11:30pm), **India Palace** (Map pp292-3; ☎ 407-238-2322; 8530 Palm Pkwy; mains $7-14; ☺ 11am-11:30pm), or the kosher deli **Lower East Side** (Map pp292-3; ☎ 407-238-7755; 8548 Palm Pkwy; mains $5-12; ☺ 11am-11:30pm),

Perched above the Hyatt's resort pool, **Hemmingway's** (Map pp292-3; ☎ 407-239-1234; Hyatt Regency Grand Cypress, 1 Grand Cypress Blvd, Lake Buena Vista; mains $15-30; ☺ 11am-11:30pm) serves up crab cakes with big chunks of lump crab and very little filler, some of the best in Florida. Pare them with a salad and a glass of wine for a perfect little meal. Simple seafood dishes are clean, absolutely fresh and delicious. Ask to sit on the screened-in porch, nestled among the greenery and watched over by a bronze Buddha.

Drinking

The downtown Orlando drinking scene can be a crazy scene, like *Girls Gone Wild* meets Spring Break, particularly on the weekends, with thumping music blaring into the streets and burly bouncers manning the doors. Much of this action centers on **Wall St Plaza** (Map p268; ☎ 407-420-1515; www.wallstplaza.net; 25 Wall St Plaza), an eight-bar complex with live music, every imaginable kind of theme night and a joint block party every month. Most of the bars serve food and there's plenty of outdoor seating and mingling. See the website for details and special events. The significant police presence keeps drunken brawls and other unseemly behavior to a minimum.

For a neighborhood bar, head to tiny **Aroma Coffee & Wine Bar** (p279), **Dexters of Thornton Park** (off Map p268; ☎ 407-648-2777; 808 E Washington St; ⏱ 11am-10pm Mon-Thu, to 11pm Fri & Sat, 10am-10pm Sun) or **Eola Wine Company** (Map p268; ☎ 407-481-9100; 500 Central Blvd; ⏱ 12pm-midnight Mon-Thu, 4pm-2am Fri, 12pm-2am Sat, 12pm-midnight Sun) in Thornton Park.

Bösendorfer Lounge (Map p268; ☎ 407-313-9000; Westin Grand Bohemian, 325 S Orange; ⏱ 11am-midnight Sun-Wed, to 1am Thu, to 2am Fri & Sat) A hotel bar with all of the pomp and none of the attitude, this is a great place to come for a quiet drink. Popular with Orlando residents, who pop on over for an after-work drink, the lounge picks up with live jazz after hours. The name stems from the lounge's rare Bösendorfer piano.

Crooked Bayou (Map p268; ☎ 407-839-5852; 50 E Central Blvd; ⏱ 11am-2am Mon-Fri, 12pm-2am Sat, 7pm-2am Sun) A tiny dance floor and a fun menu with po' boy sandwiches and Cajun fries gives this little bar a New Orleans twist.

Howl at the Moon (Map p270; ☎ 407-354-5999; 8815 International Dr; $5-10 ⏱ 11:30am-2am Mon-Sat, 7pm-2am Sun) The audience sings along at the rock-and-roll dueling piano show. It's popular with tourists staying at the area's many hotels.

Kate O'Brien's Irish Pub & Restaurant (Map p268; ☎ 407-649-7646; 42 W Central Blvd; ⏱ 11:30am-2am Mon-Sat, 7pm-2am Sun) An Irish-style pub with live music Thursday to Saturday (no cover), lots of good beer on tap and standards like fish & chips on the menu.

Tanqueray's Bar & Grill (Map p268; ☎ 407-649-8540; 100 S Orange Ave; ⏱ 11am-2am Mon-Fri, 6pm-2am Sat & Sun) A former bank vault, this spot draws a more mature clientele, with folks just looking to hang out with friends over a beer. It has a smoky, low-key vibe, Guinness on tap and weekend bands, usually reggae or blues.

Ybor's Martini Bar (Map p268; ☎ 407-316-8006; 41 W Church St; ⏱ 5pm-2am Mon-Fri, 7pm-2am Sat) Removed from the high-energy clubbing mayhem, this bar hidden down an alley specializes in top-of-the-line martinis.

Wally's Mills Ave Liquors (Map pp264-5; ☎ 407-896-6875; 1001 N Mills Ave; ⏱ 11:30am-2am Mon-Sat, 7pm-2am Sun) Everyone seems to find their way to Orlando's favorite dive bar. It's been around since the early '50s, and while its peeling naked-women wallpaper could use some updating, it wouldn't be Wally's without it. Nothing flashy, nothing loud, just an Old Florida bar with a jukebox and cheap drinks. The adjacent store sells liquor, wine and beer.

Entertainment

Also see Universal's CityWalk (p327) and Disney's Pleasure Island (p311).

CLUBS & LIVE MUSIC

Central Station Bar & NY Deli (Map p268; ☎ 407-426-8336; 100 E Central Blvd; cover varies; ⏱ 11am-2am) With plenty of woodwork, brick walls and a small stage with sometimes unmiked drums, this reggae and rock venue smack in the center of downtown Orlando's bar-crawling madness attracts folks looking for something a bit more gentle and raw.

Social (Map p268; ☎ 407-246-1419; 54 N Orange Ave; cover varies; ⏱ 7pm-2am) Matchbox 20 got their start at this Orlando favorite for live music. Vaulted ceilings, an enormous bar and VIP lounges give it a South Beach flair.

Tabu (Map p268; ☎ 407-648-8363; 46 N Orange Ave; cover women/men from $5/10; ⏱ 9pm-3am) A mishmash of thumping hip-hop, dance and techno beats against three huge video walls and flashing lights. Expect masses of grooving bodies throwing back shots and clutching domestic beers.

Independent Bar (Map p268; ☎ 407-839-0457; 68 N Orange Ave; cover $10; ⏱ 10pm-3am Sun, Wed & Thu, from 9:30pm Fri & Sat) Hip, crowded and loud, with DJs spinning underground dance and alternative rock until the wee hours.

CINEMAS

Orlando has several massive Cineplex theaters, including AMC theaters in Pointe Orlando on I-Drive (Map p270), at Downtown Disney (Map pp292–3), and at Universal Studio's CityWalk (Map p270). For an old-fashioned movie experience, catch a flick in Celebration (p287). The easiest way to find out what's playing is to check the *Orlando Sentinel*.

Winter Park's Enzian Theater (p286) screens independent and foreign films.

DETOUR: ORLANDO TO MT DORA

Tiny Mt Dora (Map p262), a hamlet of B&Bs and giftshops, sits on Lake Dora, about 45 minutes drive northwest of Orlando. It's a bit fuddy duddy – the kind of place where cops have nothing better to do than ticket passersby who don't stop a full three seconds at a stop sign – but it makes a relaxing small-town getaway. There is a rambling historic hotel on the waterfront, a scenic boat tour and several little foodie gems. Simple and friendly, the **Mt Dora Historic Inn** (☎ 352-735-1212, 800-927-6344; www.mountdorahistoricinn.com; 221 E 4th St; r $125) offers four little rooms and serves a tasty full breakfast. Take I-4 east to Exit 101 BC and follow the signs.

The **Orlando Film Festival** (www.orlandofilmfest .com) takes place every fall in downtown's Rogers Building.

PERFORMING ARTS

Orlando boasts a sophisticated performing-arts scene, with a great opera, ballet and symphony as well as several stages showing classic and contemporary theater productions for children and adults. Indeed, little Orlando is coming into its own, kicking up its heels as if to scream to the world that yes indeed, there's more to Orlando than theme parks and techno-club hopping. The Dr Phillips Orlando Performing Arts Center, which will open in 2012. For more Orlando stages, see Loch Haven Park (p267), Disney's Cirque de Soleil (p317) and Universal Orlando's Blue Man Group (p327).

Mad Cow Theater (Map p268; ☎ 407-297-8788; www.madcowtheatre.com; 105 S Magnolia Ave) A model of quality local theater, this Orlando troupe earns rave reviews for its productions of classic and modern theater. Past performances include *The Laramie Project* and Chekhov's *The Cherry Orchard*.

Orlando Youth Theater (☎ 407-254-4930; www .orlandoyouththeater.com; 398 W Amelia St) Offering children's theater performed by children, they stage everything from *High School Musical* to *Les Misérables* at the **Studio Theater** (Map p268). Based in Studio Theater, **Orlando Youth Theater** (Map p268; ☎ 407-254-4930; www.orlandoyouththeater.com; Studio Theater, 398 W Amelia St), which is next to SAK Comedy Lab (right), has venues throughout the city. Check the website for information on special events (like monthly teen cabaret night), classes and audition schedules.

Orlando Venues (☎ 407-849-2000; www.orlando venues.net) This city-owned corporation supports Broadway shows, the Orlando Philharmonic Orchestra, Orlando Ballet, Orlando Opera, live music and sporting events at the **Bob Carr Performing Arts Center** (Map p268; ☎ 407-849-2577; 401 W Livingston St), **Amway Arena** (Map p268; 600 W Amelia St) and **Citrus Bowl** (Map pp264-5; 1610 W Church St).

SAK Comedy Lab (Map p268; ☎ 407-648-0001; 380 W Amelia St) Not your standard comedy act, the improv troupe here performs to packed crowds Tuesday through Saturday.

University of Central Florida Conservatory Theater (off Map p262; ☎ 407-823-1500; 4000 Central Florida Blvd; adult/student $10/6) Stages performances at the University of Central Florida and other area venues.

SPORTS

The National Basketball Association's **Orlando Magic** (☎ 407-896-2442; www.nba.com/magic) and the National Football League's **Orlando Predators** (☎ 407-447-7337; www.orlandopredators.com) play at Amway Arena (Map p268). Orlando's outdoor football arena, the Florida Citrus Bowl (Map pp264–5), hosts all kinds of sporting events, including wrestling, soccer and the New York's Day football classic, the Citrus Bowl. Go to www.orlandovenues.net for schedules and tickets. You can catch the **University of Southern Florida Bulls** (www.gousfbulls.com), which includes the gamut of men and women's teams, at the University of Southern Florida.

Even if you're not a baseball fan, **spring training baseball** in Orlando is a great way to wile away an afternoon or evening. Bring a blanket, grab the Cracker Jacks and watch baseball like it was meant to be. The **Atlanta Braves** play at **Disney's Wide World of Sports** (Map pp292-3; ☎ 407-939-4263); the **Cleveland Indians** play at **Chain of Lakes Park** (off Map p262; ☎ 863-293-3900; 500 Cletus Allen Dr, Winter Haven, I-4 west to exit 55) in Winter Haven, about 47 miles from downtown Orlando, near Cypress Gardens (p273); and the **Houston Astros** play at **Osceola County Stadium** (Map p262; ☎ 407-697-3200; 1000 Bill Beck Blvd) in Kissimmee. Ticket prices vary, but expect to pay about $20.

ORLANDO & WALT DISNEY WORLD DISNEY

Shopping

Pointe Orlando (Map p270; ☎ 407-248-2838; www.pointe
orlandofl.com; 9101 International Dr; ☻ 10am-10pm Mon-Sat,
11am-9pm Sun) Pleasant enough, with brick walkways and a fountain, this small outdoor shopping area features an odd assortment of shops
and several good restaurants (see p280). You'll
find the high end Keihl's and L'Occitane, cult
favorites for lotions and potions, as well as
Victoria's Secret, B Dalton Books and a huge
Cineplex movie theater (p282).

Prime Outlets International (Map p270; ☎ 407-354-
0126; 4949 International Dr; ☻ 10am-9pm Mon-Sat, to 6pm
Sun) Particularly popular with overseas travelers, this nondescript discount mall offers the
usual discount-mall suspects as well as a few
surprises, like the ultrachic Barneys.

Eli's Orange World (Map pp292-3; 407-239-6031, 800-
531-3182; www.orangeworld192.com; 5395 W Irlo Bronson
Memorial Hwy; ☻ 8am-10:45pm) When in Florida,
send an orange. In addition to fresh oranges,
tangelos and grapefruit, you can buy preserves
here and have them shipped anywhere.

ANTIQUE ROW

Quirky independent shops and antique stores
dot a 3-mile stretch of Orange Ave just south
of Loch Haven Park. Among the treasures
you'll find the great boutique children's store
Hopscotch (Map pp264-5; ☎ 407-898-5000; 1620 N Orange
Ave; ☻ 10am-5pm Mon-Sat) and the extensive wine
selection at **Tim's Wine Market** (Map pp264-5; ☎ 407-
895-9463; 1223 N Orange Ave; ☻ 10am-7pm Mon-Fri, to
5pm Sat).

Getting There & Around

For information on transport within Orlando,
see p261. See p261 for info on getting to and
from Orlando.

If you are sightseeing around International
Drive, you can use the **I-Ride Trolley** (☎ 407-
354-5656, 407-248-9590; www.iridetrolley.com; rides
adult/child under 12/senior $1/free/25¢, 1-/3-/5-/7-/14-day
pass $3/5/7/9/16), which runs two routes along
International Drive from 8am to 10:30pm.
Trolleys run every 20 to 30 minutes. You can
buy one-ride tickets on board (exact change
only) or a multiday pass at hotels and stores
along I-Drive.

WINTER PARK

Founded 1858, this cozy college town concentrates some of Orlando's best-kept secrets
into a few shaded, pedestrian-friendly streets.
Escape into small-town Old Florida.

Orientation & Information

Central Park, with a rose garden and fountains, is the centerpiece of the town; along
its west end runs Park Ave, with most of the
town's restaurants and shops. Just west of the
park's southern edge is Hannibal Square (not
a square at all) with a couple more blocks of
restaurants and shop.

For a schedule of events, contact the **chamber of commerce** (Map pp264-5; ☎ 407-644-8281;
www.winterpark.org; 151 W Lyman Ave; ☻ 8:30am-5pm
Mon-Fri).

Sights & Activities

In the summer, folks swim off **Dinky Beach** (Map
pp264-5). With the exception of the Audubon
Center for Birds of Prey and the Zora Neale
Hurston National Museum of Fine Arts, the
following sights are within walking distance
of downtown Winter Park or a short drive
through a pleasant residential district.

AUDUBON CENTER FOR BIRDS OF PREY

Housed in a cool old house and very much
off the beaten track, this lakeside **rehabilitation
center** (Map p262; ☎ 407-644-0190; www.adoptabird.org;
1101 Audubon Way; ☻ 10am-4pm Tue-Sun) for hawks,
bald eagles, screech owls and other talon-toed
feathered friends makes a fantastic outing. It's
small and low-key, with plenty of opportunities to see the birds up close, just hanging out
on the trainer's arms. Kids love it. The center is
located along Lake Sybelia in Maitland, immediately north of Winter Park (I-4, exit 88).

CHARLES HOSMER MORSE MUSEUM OF AMERICAN ART

Internationally famous for its comprehensive
collection of Tiffany leaded-glass lamps, windows, jewelry, blown glass, pottery and enamel,
this incredible **museum** (Map pp264-5; ☎ 407-645-
5311; 445 N Park Ave; adult/child under 12/student $3/free/1;
☻ 9:30am-4pm Tue-Thu, from 1pm Sun, 9:30am-9pm Fri Nov-
Apr, to 4pm Fri May-Oct), tucked into Park Ave, is one
of the best museums we've seen anywhere.
The centerpiece is the chapel interior Louis
Comfort Tiffany designed for the World's
Columbian Exposition in Chicago (1893). In
addition to Tiffany's work, you'll find a broad
selection of objects from the late-19th-century
Arts and Crafts movement and US paintings.
Absolutely beautiful, with gallery after gallery
of magnificently displayed masterpieces, this
is a must-see for anyone interested in US art
and design. Ask about the museum's free fam-

ily programs, with tours, activities and films designed for children aged five to 10.

CORNELL FINE ARTS MUSEUM

This tiny **museum** (Map pp264-5; ☎ 407-646-2526; Rollins College, 1000 Holt Ave; adult/child 2-11 $8/4; ☉ 10am-5pm Tue-Fri, from 1pm Sat & Sun) of primarily US art is worth a peek, but don't expect to go through inch by inch looking at a wealth of displays. Check out the giant cypress across the street, carefully held up with metal poles – an art installation in and of itself!

ALBIN POLASEK MUSEUM & SCULPTURE GARDENS

Scattered through the grounds of this stately home and serene **garden museum** (Map pp264-5; ☎ 407-647-6294; www.polesek.org; 633 Osceola Ave; adult/child under 12/senior $5/free/4; ☉ 10am-4pm Tue-Sat, from 1pm Sun) are the works of Czech sculptor Albin Polasek. The small yellow villa, listed on the National Register of Historic Places and perched on the shore of Lake Osceola, was the artist's home.

HANNIBAL SQUARE HERITAGE CENTER

As far back as 1881, Hannibal Square was home to African Americans employed as carpenters, farmers and household help in the Winter Park region. This **center** (Map pp264-5; ☎ 407-539-2680; 642 W New England Ave; adult/child 2-11 $8/4; ☉ 12am-4pm Tue-Thu, to 5pm Fri, 10am-2pm Sat) preserves the community's culture and history with a collection of photographic and oral histories, and is home to the *Heritage Collection: Photographs and Oral Histories of West Winter Park 1900–1980*.

SCENIC BOAT TOUR

This recommended one-hour **boat ride** (Map pp264-5; ☎ 407-644-4056; www.scenicboattours.com; 1 E Morse Blvd; adult/child 2-11 $8/4; tours every hr, ☉ 10am-4pm) floats through 12 miles of tropical canals and lakes. The enthusiastic tour guide talks about the mansions, Rollins College and other sites along the way. Boats are small pontoons, holding about 10 people each.

KRAFT AZALEA GARDEN

Particularly stunning January through March, when the azaleas burst into bloom, this 11-acre **garden** (Map p262; 1363 Alabama Dr, off Palmer Ave) on the shores of Lake Maitland promises tranquility. Stroll along the paths and relax by the water with a book.

ZORA NEALE HURSTON NATIONAL MUSEUM OF FINE ARTS

Novelist Zora Neale Hurston, a pillar of America's Harlem Renaissance and best known for her novel *Their Eyes Were Watching God*, was born in nearby Eatonville. This **museum** (Map p262; ☎ 407-647-3307; www.zoranealehurstonfestival .com; 227 E Kennedy Blvd, Eatonville; ☉ 9am-4pm) features changing exhibits of African American artists and hosts the annual **Zora Festival** (www .zoranealehurstonfestival.com) during the last week of January, a celebration featuring African American music, art, and culture.

Sleeping

ourpick **Plaza Hotel** (Map pp264-5; ☎ 407-647-1072, 800-228-7220; www.parkplazahotel.com; 307 S Park Ave; r & ste $180-320) Brick walls, cleanlined wood furniture, antiques and luscious white cotton bedding give every room at this historic two-story hotel a simple elegance and a distinct arts-and-crafts sensibility. Rooms lining Park Ave share a thin balcony, each with a private entrance and a few wicker chairs hidden from the street by hanging ferns, are well worth the extra money. Bring up a bottle of wine and cheese, and watch the Park Ave activity. Rates include homebaked muffins, coffee and juice. They do not allow children under five years old (not because they're snobby, but because of the thin walls – there's a small-building guarantee that every guest will hear a child's crying).

Best Western Mt Vernon Inn (Map pp264-5; ☎ 407-647-1166; www.bestwestern.com; 110 S Orlando Ave; r $100-175) A short drive from the village action, the Best Western offers less-expensive rooms and a far less memorable experience.

Eating & Drinking

Sidewalk cafés and wine bars, busy with a mixed crowd of established artists, lawyers, families and 30-somethings, line Park Ave. You won't find a sports bar or 50¢ tequila shots here, and there's no pounding music to lure you into a flashy club. Instead, folks linger late into the evening, chatting over wine and leisurely meals, strolling with ice cream or sitting quietly in the rose garden in Central Park.

BUDGET

Ballard & Corum (Map pp264-5; ☎ 407-539-1711; 535 W New England Ave; cookie or cake $1.24-4; ☉ 9am-5pm Mon-Sat) An old-fashioned bakery that's got a new-fashioned sensibility. Take away delicious cookies, cakes and cupcakes.

Market Café (Map pp264-5; ☎ 407-629-1029; 433 W New England Ave; mains $5-9; ☻ 8am-3pm Sun-Fri, from 9am Sat) Sister to Hot Olive, this fast-food sandwich shop features upscale delights and modern interpretations of classics. Try a mozzarella-and-basil, Cuban or meatloaf sandwich. For a picnic, call in advance to order a sandwich or salad platter, or a selection of eclectic cocktail appetizers (eg herb-coated goat cheese and coconut-shrimp spring rolls).

Bubbalou's Bodacious BBQ (Map pp264-5; ☎ 407-628-1212; 1471 Lee Rd; mains $5-15; ☻ 10am-9:30pm Mon-Fri, to 10:30pm Sat, 11am-8pm Sun) Casual and bustling, this friendly red house serves up brisket, pulled pork, ribs, fried catfish and other finger lickin' meat lovers' delights.

MIDRANGE

Orchid (Map pp264-5; ☎ 407-331-1400; 305 N Park Ave; mains $8-15; ☻ lunch, dinner) This excellent Thai café, with contemporary style and friendly service, offers a menu of classic dishes. Don't miss the delectable Golden Thai Doughnuts, dough balls fried with a sweet condensed-milk dressing and sprinkled with crushed peanuts.

our pick **Bosphorous Turkish Cuisine** (Map pp264-5; ☎ 407-644-8609; 108 S Park Ave; mains $8-21; ☻ 11:30am-10pm Mon-Thu, Sun, to 11pm Sat & Sun) Clean decor and excellent food make this a stand-out in a town of great restaurants. Try the *lahmacun* (Turkish pizza) or the Hunkar Begendi, an Ottoman dish with beef and eggplant. Kids love the chicken kebab. Turkish coffee and baklava perfect the meal, and smokers will want to try exotic tobacco in the long and elaborate hookah.

Hot Olives (Map pp264-5; ☎ 407-629-1030; 463 W New England Ave; mains $8-24; ☻ 11am-9:30pm Mon-Thu, to 10pm Fri & Sat) A breezy venue with fresh seafood. Ask for a table on the covered portico.

Bistro 310 South (Map pp264-5; ☎ 407-647-7277; 310 S Park Ave; mains $9-21; ☻ 8am-10pm Tue-Sat, to 3pm Sun) Serving solid and fresh contemporary North American food with few twists, this casual café is a favorite of Winter Park locals, who gather over baked Brie late into the night or relax with the paper and eggs on Sunday mornings.

Eola Wine Company (Map pp264-5; ☎ 407-647-9103; 136 S Park Ave; mains $8-14; ☻ from 4pm Mon-Fri, from 12pm Sat & Sun) This wine bar features a California-style menu of light foods designed to pair with wine or quirky independent-label beers.

How about a buffalo-chicken wrap with a bottle of Dogfishhead Ale, or roasted garlic with a flight of Take a Cab? You can also get a flight of beer or bubbly, and the cheese plate includes a choice from 16 Spanish, French, Italian and US cheeses.

The Wine Room (pp264-5; ☎ 407-696-9463; 270 S Park Ave; ☻ 10am-10pm Mon-Wed, to 11pm Thu, to 1:30am Fri & Sat, 12-7pm Sun) Purchase a wine card when you enter, and put as much money on it as you'd like. Then simply slide your card into the automated servers of whatever wine looks good, press the button for a taste or a full glass, and enjoy. Wines are organized according to region and type, and prices range upwards from $2.50 for a taste. You can purchase bottles to take away, but strangely, if you buy one to enjoy on the premise, there is a whopping $15 corking fee.

Entertainment

The clapboard-sided **Enzian Theater** (Map p262; ☎ 407-629-0054; www.enzian.org; 1300 South Orlando Ave; adult/child $7/5, weekend matinees $5; ☻ 5pm-midnight Tue-Fri, 12pm-midnight Sat & Sun) screens independent films and is home to **Florida's Film Festival** (www.floridafilmfestival.com; March). Sit on the small shaded patio under the giant cypress and enjoy a delicious veggie burger ($9) with a glass of wine or beer before settling onto a couch to watch the film. On the second Thursday of every month, the Enzian teams up with the city of Winter Park to present **Popcorn Flicks** (free), a series of classic movies like *Casablanca* screened outside at Central Park. Bring a picnic and a blanket, and kick back under the stars.

Shopping

Park Ave and Hannibal Square feature upscale chains like Williams Sonoma, Lily Pulitzer and Lucky Jeans, as well as all kinds of interesting independent stores. At **Bull Fish** (Map pp264-5; ☎ 407-644-2969; 102 N Park Ave; ☻ 10am-6pm Mon-Wed, to 7pm Thu-Sat, 12-5pm Sun) you'll find organic toys and stylish accoutrements for Fido, quirky wine accessories and gifts. Head to **NFX Apothecary** (Map ppp264-5; ☎ 407-622-1611; 327 S Park Ave; ☻ 10am-6pm Tue & Wed, to 8pm Thu-Sat, 11am-4pm Sun & Mon) for upscale bath supplies. Consignment-shop junkies will love the racks of vintage and designer fashions at overstuffed **Cida's Consignment** (Map pp264-5; ☎ 407-644-5635; N Park Ave; ☻ 10am-5:30pm Mon-Sat). Though expensive, the children's clothes, books and toys at **Tugboat and the Bird** (☎ 407-647-5437, 644-7296; 433

W New England Ave; 10am-7pm Tue-Sat, to 5pm Sun) are adorable and classy.

Specializing in traditional artisan cheeses, **The Cheese Shop** (Map pp264-5; ☎ 407-644-7296; 329 N Park Ave; 10am-7pm Tue-Sat, to 5pm Sun) is a great place to grab a bottle of wine and a snack for hors d'oeuvres on your balcony. Ask for a taste of their Guinness-infused cheddar; or, for something stronger, try the cheddar with whiskey. Many cheeses are locally produced and/or organic. The **farmers market** (Map pp264-5; ☎ 407-599-3358; at New England & New York Aves; 7am-1pm Sat) is housed in a former train station – hit it early for freshly baked croissants and local goodies.

Getting There & Away
Winter Park sits a few miles west of I-4, exit 87. It's about 40 minutes to the Disney area, more during rush hour. Lynx buses link downtown Orlando and Winter Park hourly, and Amtrak's 97 Silver Meteor from New York to Miami (see Transportation, p518) stops at Central Park.

CELEBRATION
Built from the swamps in 1994, the New Urbanism–style town of Celebration is small-town America like you imagine it may have once been...before David Lynch, *Desperate Housewives* and John Cheever introduced irony, before strip malls, before leaf blowers. You'd swear the town enforces a Must Be Friendly ordinance, as everyone – from the bellboy to the policeman, the waitress to the guy in his yard who gives you directions – is eerily friendly, polite and helpful. We could wonder what goes on behind closed doors, but why? Just let it go, and fall into the 21st century Beverly Cleary –*Father Knows Best* vibe that defines Celebration. Relax at a sidewalk café, enjoy a glass of wine, play in the fountain and watch the ducks. Sure, maybe it doesn't sound that exciting, but wasn't that day at Universal Studios exciting enough?

Several books offer an interesting glimpse into life in Celebration. *Celebration USA: Living in Disney's Brave New Town*, by Douglas Frantz and Catherine Collins, chronicles their years raising a family in the town. For the town's history, try *The Celebration Chronicles: Life, Liberty and the Pursuit of Property Value in Disney's New Town*, by Andrew Ross. Alternatively, read www.celebrationfl.blogspot.com.

And yes my friend, there really is a street called Wisteria Lane.

Orientation & Information
Celebration sits just south of Walt Disney World, to the east of I-4. Water St cuts south from Celebration Ave (south from the Central Florida Greeneway) and dead ends at Front St, which runs along the lake for a couple blocks. All the restaurants and shops are within a few blocks of this intersection. The town's website is www.celebrationfl.com.

Sights & Activities
While the town itself is a sight, there are also pleasant diversions for curious utopia seekers. The main attraction is the serene **lake**, with a perfectly manicured promenade circling its length and palm trees dotting the banks. Popular with the kids is the jumping **water fountain** on the lakeshore. There's also a small-town-style **movie theater** (☎ 407-298-4488; 651 Front St; adult/child $7/5) along the water, a little bookstore and several independent shops.

Sleeping & Eating
For something beyond the impersonality of a large resort and the chaos of bars, nightly entertainment and programmed children's activities, stay at ourpick **Celebration Hotel** (Map pp292-3; ☎ 407-566-6000, 888-499-3800; www.celebration hotel.com; 700 Bloom St; r & ste $170-350;). Quiet and genteel, with what has to be the city's smallest pool perched on the patio next to the lake, the town's only hotel offers excellent service and handsome rooms. Best of all, it's an easy drive to all the parks but feels years and miles away.

Celebration makes a great place to eat, if for no other reason than it's just so damn pleasant to sit outside and watch the comings and goings of small-town America. The handful of restaurants in town serve up a surprising variety of cuisine, and you'll be satisfied with any of them. They all face the water and have outdoor seating.

Market Street Cafe (Map pp292-3; ☎ 407-566-1144; 701 Front St; mains $8-16; 8am-10pm) has a home-cookin', middle-America café feel and an eclectic menu that includes everything from Cuban sandwiches to meat loaf to Asian shrimp pot stickers. At the modern **Seito Sushi** (Map pp292-3; ☎ 407-566-1889; 671 Front St; mains $8-23; 8am-10pm) you'll find the usual, including *yakisoba* (yellow egg noodles),

WHAT TO EXPECT FROM THE PARKS

In 1971 Walt Disney World opened the gates of Magic Kingdom; today, it includes 23 hotels, four theme parks (Magic Kingdom, Epcot, Hollywood Studios and Animal Kingdom), almost 100 restaurants, two water parks (Typhoon Lagoon and Blizzard Beach), a sports complex (Disney's Wide World of Sports), and two shopping and nightlife districts (Downtown Disney and Disney's Boardwalk), as well as six golf courses, three miniature golf courses and lagoons with water sports, all connected by a complicated system of free buses, boats and monorails. Just to get from one end of Disney to the other is a $25 cab ride!

In contrast, Universal Orlando is a pedestrian-friendly and intimate complex with two excellent theme parks (Universal Studios and Islands of Adventure), three first-rate resorts, and a carnival-like restaurant and nightlife district (CityWalk) connected by lovely gardened paths or a quiet wooden-boat shuttle. Located just about equidistant from both, you'll find the aquatic park SeaWorld, with fantastic animal shows, a handful of rides and animal-interaction programs; its water-park sister, Aquatica; and the worlds-away Discovery Cove, where a limited number of guests enjoy a day of lounging on a private beach, swimming with the dolphins and floating along the lazy river through the bird aviary. On top of these three biggies, there's Old Florida's Cypress Gardens, just south of town (p273), kitschy Gatorland (p269) and lesser attractions sprinkled throughout the city.

Planning a vacation to Orlando's theme parks can be overwhelming. Deciding when to go is a no-brainer. If US schools are in session, go; if they're on break, do not go. Do not go in June, July or August; Christmas Day through New Year's Day; Thanksgiving weekend; the weeks before and after Easter; and mid-March through April (Spring Break). September and October sees the smallest crowds, and the weather begins to lose that summer scorch. Other slow periods include Thanksgiving (except Thanksgiving weekend) to the week before Christmas and mid-January through February.

Now, where to stay? Simply put, follow the golden rule of real estate: location, location, location. Lake Buena Vista (particularly Palm Parkway) is a good choice for moderate-priced chains close to all the major theme parks. For el-cheapo, no frills, head to motels and chains on Hwy 192; if you want something close to the parks that isn't a chain or a resort, consider Celebration Hotel (p287) or the Perri House (p314). Disney and Universal Orlando offer perks to guests who stay on site.

Two mantras for a successful vacation to Orlando's theme parks: stay flexible and arrive early. If you get to a park when the doors open, you can ride the most popular rides and see the busiest attractions before the masses descend on them, and you'll be done in time for a late lunch and an afternoon at the pool. To save money and avoid time-consuming lines for mediocre food, stock up on lunch supplies and bring something simple with you.

The **Orlando Flex Ticket**, available online at teems of websites, gives 14-day unlimited entry to Universal Orlando's Universal Studios, Universal Orlando's Islands of Adventure, Wet 'n' Wild, SeaWorld and Aquatica (adult/child $235/195). Add Busch Gardens (p418) in Tampa Bay for about $45 more. Admission prices below are at the time of research; always check parks' websites for specials and ask about AAA, military and Florida-resident discounts. Note that park hours vary daily and seasonally.

For updated information on reliable Disney ticket discounts (as well as all things Disney), go to www.mousesavers.com and www.mouseplanet.com; for Disney as well as other parks, see www.undercovertourist.com and www.ticketmania.com. You'll find complete menus for restaurants throughout Walt Disney World and Universal Orlando at www.allearsnet.com.

Walt Disney World Resort

At **Disney World** (www.disneyworld.com) they sell a complicated **Magic Your Way Ticket**, a one- to 10-day ticket good for unlimited entry to any one of their four parks per day. Adult/child prices range from one-day $71/60, three days $203/171, seven days $219/182 and 10 days $225/187. Note that the per-day price becomes significantly cheaper the more days you purchase – the price difference between a three- and a ten-day ticket is negligible. To this base ticket, you can *add* options.

■ **Water Park Fun & More** ($5-50 per day) This gives a limited number of entries to the two water parks, DisneyQuest, Pleasure Island and Disney's Wide World of Sports, depending on the length of your base ticket.

■ **No Expiration** ($8-18 per day) All tickets expire 14 days after the first use, unless this option is purchased.

■ **Park Hopper** ($5-45 per day) Allows you to 'hop' between all four Walt Disney World parks within one day and for the length of your base ticket.

Peruse the Disney website for the dizzying array of packages that include park tickets, lodging and dining, as well as entertainment and recreation. For customized itinerary planning, premium dining and show reservations, consider the **Magic Your Way Platinum Package** and the **VIP Tour**. Note that if you buy a package, including something as simple as the money-saving dining plan (p291), you may not get a full refund if you need to cancel. If you only book accommodation, and buy park tickets and dining options at the last minute, you can cancel up to 48 hours in advance with no penalty. An **Annual Pass** (adult/child $448/395) allows admission to any of the four parks, any time, for 365 days from the date of purchase.

Disney hotels can get away with offering lower quality of accommodation, ambience and service for more money because they are Disney. Even the convenience of free buses, boats and monorails from your doorstep to the parks, however, doesn't mean easy access: Walt Disney World is a huge place, and the hotels and attractions are scattered throughout. Some hotels offer direct access to Magic Kingdom via a lovely and quiet wooden boat, while others require a 45-minute-plus ride in a bus reminiscent of midtown Manhattan. A big advantage of staying on site is 'extra magic hours' – every day, one park opens early and/or stays open late for guests at Disney hotels only.

For accommodation reservations at Disney hotels and a free trip-planning DVD, call ☎ 407-824-8000. For dining reservations, including character meals and dinner shows up to six months in advance, call ☎ 407-8939-3463. By mail, send requests for brochures or other information to **Walt Disney Guest Communications** (PO Box 10000, Lake Buena Vista, FL 32830-1000).

Universal Orlando

Both of **Universal Orlando's** (www.universalorlando.com) theme parks are shamelessly silly, snazzy and fun for the whole family. **Island of Adventure**, divided into clearly defined and masterfully designed sections, each with its own tone and vibe, has lots of great thrill and water rides as well as the fantastic Dr Seuss–themed area and, in 2009, the Wizarding World of Harry Potter section. **Universal Studios** is primarily movie- and TV-themed rides and scheduled shows, but it also has one of Orlando's best children's play areas and a sweet Barney show.

Universal Orlando sells an online-only two park, unlimited-admission ticket good for seven consecutive days for $82, a two parks/one day ticket for adult/child $77/67, and a one park/one day ticket for $71/60. If you stay at one of the three Universal Orlando resorts, you automatically receive an Express Plus pass (p319) to the parks.

SeaWorld, Discovery Cove & Aquatica

Owned by the same parent company, these three parks sit clustered together between Walt Disney World and Universal Orlando. With plenty of greenery and gardens, a focus on wildlife, decent food and fewer bells and whistles than the others, they offer a decidedly low-key ambience.

Online adult/child tickets cost $68/58 for one day to **SeaWorld** (www.SeaWorld.com) and a second visit within seven days is free; $39/33 for one-day admission to Aquatica; and $90/80 for seven-day unlimited admission to both SeaWorld and Aquatica. It costs between $169 and $189 (depending upon time of year) for one-day admission to Discovery Cove and a seven-day pass to SeaWorld or Bush Gardens, and $239 for a one-day admission to Discovery Cove and a 14-day pass to Aquatica, SeaWorld and Bush Gardens (add $100 to swim with the dolphins at Discovery Cove).

bento boxes and tempura. Seafood lovers will enjoy many fishy dishes, including the Sunomono Salad (shrimp, octopus and *kani* with cucumber).

For some delicious Italian, including tasty wood-oven pizza, try **Café D'Antonio** (Map pp292-3; ☎ 407-566-2233; 691 Front St; mains $12-24; ☑ 11:30am-10pm Mon-Sat, to 9pm Sun). At the spacious Cuban-Spanish **Columbia Restaurant** (☎ 407-566-1505; 649 Front St; mains $9-17; ☑ 11:30am-10pm Mon-Sat, to 9pm Sun) the food is solid and satisfying, but not fabulous.

After your meal, grab an ice cream from **Kilwin's Chocolates** (Map pp292-3; ☎ 407-566-8555; 671 Front St; ☑ 11am-10pm Sun-Thu, to 11pm Fri & Sat) and take a stroll along the water.

WALT DISNEY WORLD RESORT

Here in Florida, we have something special we never enjoyed at Disneyland…the blessing of size. There's enough land here to hold all the ideas and plans we can possibly imagine.

Walt Disney

Minutes before the Magic Kingdom opens, Alice in Wonderland, Cinderella, Donald Duck and other Disney Classics stand where all can see them, sing 'Zippidee Doo Dah' and throw sparkly Mickey Mouse confetti into the crowds. They dash off on open-windowed train, the gates open, and children, adults, honeymooners, grandparents and everyone in between enter the park, slowly snaking down the impeccably clean Main Street toward Cinderella's Castle. That iconic image is as American as the Grand Canyon, a place as loaded with myth and promises of hope as the Statue of Liberty. If only for these few minutes, this is indeed the Happiest Place on Earth.

Yes, there will be lines with seemingly endless waiting and sure, you'll spend more money than you intended on a Mickey Mouse sweatshirt that you wouldn't have dreamed of buying before you came. That Pirates of the Caribbean ride may not be everything everyone said it'd be, and you may get stuck behind the guy who spreads his shopping bags and empty stroller parallel to the curb so your kids can't sit down to see the parade ('I got here

first,' he growls). You'll return to the hotel exhausted and aching, vaguely dissatisfied with the day's meals, carrying your sleeping Belle, her face painted with now-smudging sparkles and her poofy yellow dress stained with ice cream, cotton candy and that green slushie so tantalizingly named Tinkerbell Twist. You swear that next time you'll take a real vacation… Until those last minutes before you fall asleep, when everything you need to do is done and you're finally relaxing in bed, your eyes closed. You see your child's face staring adoringly at Winnie the Pooh as he gives a big ol' bear hug, your child's arms reaching out to grab the Donald Duck that pops out from the 3-D movie. And it's OK. That beach vacation can wait.

Walt Disney World itself is like a child. One minute, you think you can't take another cafeteria-style restaurant serving fried food and bad coffee or another second in an overstuffed shuttle bus. There's no magic here, you mutter. And the next, she does something right – maybe it's the fireworks, maybe it's a particular turn in a particular ride, maybe it's the corny joke of the guy who drives the horse-drawn carriage down Main Street.

And all is forgiven.

History

When Disneyland opened in southern California, it took off in a huge way, fundamentally transforming the concept of theme parks. Walt Disney, however, was irritated at the hotels and concessions that were springing up in a manner that he felt was entirely parasitic. In 1965, after a secret four-year search, he bought 27,000 acres of swamp, field and woodland in central Florida. His vision was to create a family vacation destination and he wanted to control every aspect – hotels, restaurants, parking and transportation. Sadly, he would never see the realization of his dreams; in 1966, at age 65, Walt Disney died of lung cancer and his brother Roy took over responsibility for development. Walt Disney World's Magic Kingdom opened in 1971, and three months later Roy died of a brain hemorrhage. Epcot opened in 1982, Hollywood Studios in 1989 and Animal Kingdom in 1998.

Orientation

Walt Disney World sits about 15 miles south of downtown Orlando, just off I-4 (exits 64, 65 and 67). You can drive your own car within the resort (there's parking everywhere except at Magic Kingdom) or you can use Disney's complimentary transportation system of boats, buses and monorails (see p318). The Ticket and Transportation Center (TTC), with its enormous parking lot, serves as the park's central transportation hub.

MAPS
The free *Walt Disney World Resort Map*, available throughout the resort and at any Orlando visitor center, has a transportation-network chart. You'll get a free map of each individual park and a *Times Guide* with character greeting and show times when you enter each park – don't lose them because, strangely, they're not easily available anywhere but the entrance gate!

Information
See boxed text What to Expect From the Parks (p288) for general information including ticket details and prices.

CHILD CARE
Baby-care centers are located in every park. They're air-conditioned, packed with toys, and some run Disney cartoons. You can purchase diapers, formula, baby powder and over-the-counter medicine.

Several Disney resorts offer excellent drop-off child care centers (per hr per child incl dinner $11; ☺ 4:30pm-midnight) for children aged four to 12, with organized activities, toys, art supplies and a Disney movie to end the evening. This is particularly handy if you'd like to enjoy a quiet, upscale meal at a Disney resort, as you do not have to be a guest at the hotel to use the centers. All but Simba's Clubhouse require a two-hour minimum.

Camp Dolphin (Map pp292-3; ☎ 407-934-3000; Walt Disney World Dolphin Resort; $10 per hr, per child; ☺ from 5:30pm)

Cub's Den (Map pp292-3; ☎ 407-824-1083; Disney's Wilderness Lodge)

Harbor Club (Map pp292-3; ☎ 407-939-6301; Disney's Boardwalk Inn & Villas)

Mouse House (Map pp292-3; ☎ 407-824-2985; Disney's Grand Floridian Resort & Spa; ☺ from 4pm)

Mouseketeer Clubhouse (Map pp292-3; ☎ 407-824-1000; Contemporary Resort)

Neverland Club (Map pp292-3; ☎ 407-824-1639; Disney's Polynesian Resort; ☺ from 4pm)

Sandcastle Club (Map pp292-3; ☎ 407-939-3463; Disney's Yacht & Beach Club Resorts)

COFFEE-CHAT WITH MOMS
Take your morning coffee to the Mom's Panel at www.disneyworldforum.disney .go.com to learn from a panel of Disney-experienced moms. You can search the site for answers, or post a question of your own. It can be perversely addictive – be prepared for information overload.

Simba's Clubhouse (Map pp292-3; ☎ 407-938-4785; Disney's Animal Kingdom Lodge)

For private babysitting for kids under 12, see p265.

DINING PLAN & EATING
Disney offers an incredibly complicated but economical dining plan available to guests staying at a Disney resort. The plan allows you pay in advance for a designated number of 'quick service' meals, 'table service' meals and snacks purchased at over 90 restaurants on site at a significantly lower rate. You can also use your meals to pay for character dining, in-room dining and dinner shows. If you decide to purchase a dining plan, do not do so when you make your room reservation. You may not get a full refund of your dining plan if you need to cancel, and you can always add one at the last minute (though it cannot be added once you've checked into your hotel). Rates vary according to which plan you choose; see the website for details.

Expect lots of mediocre fast food, bad coffee, cafeteria cuisine and snacks at premium prices. Bringing your own food into the parks is officially not allowed, but no one checks too carefully. Rates given under Eating reviews are for dinner unless otherwise noted; expect prices at sit-down restaurants to be significantly less during lunch.

TRAVELERS WITH DISABILITIES
The *Guidebook for Guests with Disabilities*, available at Guest Services at each park and on Disney's website, has maps and ride-by-ride guides with information on closed captioning and accommodating wheelchairs and seeing-eye dogs. On many rides, folks in wheelchairs will be waved to the front of the line. You can borrow Braille guides and audiotape guides from Guest Services and rent manual ($10) and electric ($35) wheelchairs at

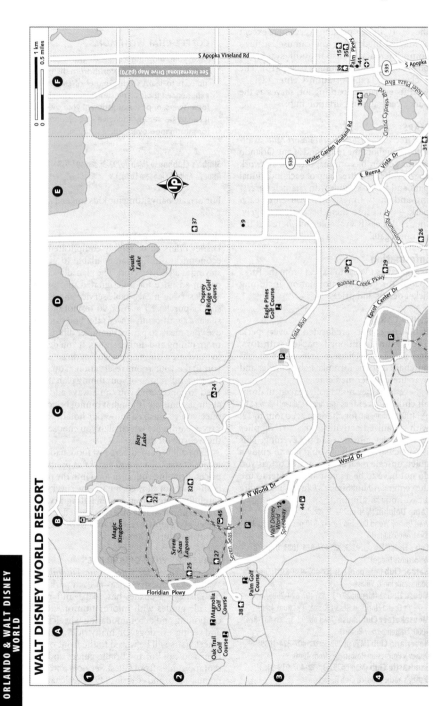

WALT DISNEY WORLD RESORT

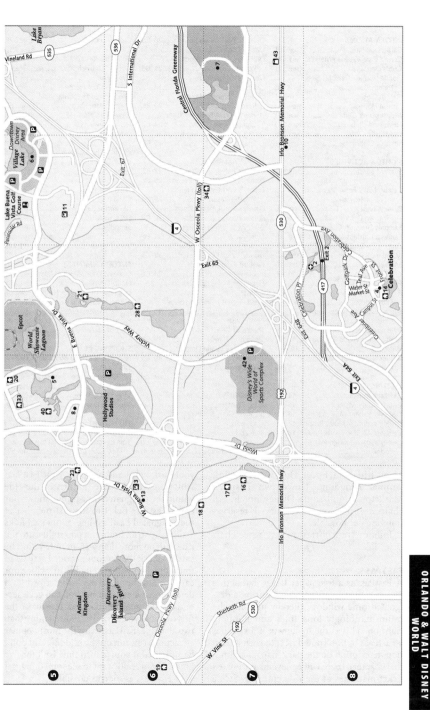

Magic Kingdom, Epcot, Hollywood Studios, Animal Kingdom, Downtown Disney's Marketplace and some Disney hotels. All chairs are first-come, first-served; reservations are not possible.

Public transportation is wheelchair accessible.

FASTPASS

A FastPass is a free paper ticket that allows you to return to an attraction during a designated time window, thereby jumping the mind-numbingly long lines and hopping right on. This is the lowdown: if a ride has a FastPass option (noted next to each attraction description on the park map and within this chapter), there will be several automated ticket machines at the ride entrance. Swipe your park ticket and out pops your FastPass with your return time. Return to the ride within the designated time frame, show your paper FastPass ticket to the cast member at the designated FastPass line, zoom past folks waiting up to an hour and pop right onto the ride with no more than a 15-minute wait. The catch? Check the bottom of your FastPass to find out when you are eligible to swipe your card for another FastPass – the crowd level determines whether or not you can get a second one before your allocated time to use the first one, and you are never allowed more than two at a time. FastPasses for the most popular attractions can run out by midday, and don't be surprised if your return time isn't for five hours. If you really want to see something, get your FastPass as soon as possible.

ORLANDO & WALT DISNEY WORLD

The FastPass system is a double-edged sword. On the one hand, it's fantastic that there is a way to bypass lines. On the other, to utilize its full benefits, you need to be rather systematic and anal about it, tackling a day at the park with a carefully executed strategy of attack that seems strangely unfitting for a day at the Happiest Place on Earth.

GUEST SERVICES
These are located just inside the ticket turnstiles of each theme park. Services include money changing (limited currencies for up to $50), ATMs, locker facilities ($6) and adjacent stroller rental (single/double $10/18, discounts for multiple days).

INTERNET ACCESS
Most Disney hotels offer internet access and USB cables. If you have wi-fi, you can connect to the internet in common areas of Disney's Boardwalk, Contemporary, Coronado Springs, Grand Floridian and Yacht and Beach Club resorts for a fee (one hour/24 hours $5/10).

KENNELS
Walt Disney World has five air-conditioned kennels ($9 per night). You must provide food and occasionally return to walk your pooch. Pets are allowed at the full-hookup campsites at Fort Wilderness, but are not welcome at any other Disney resort. See Universal Orlando (p320) for details on their three pet-friendly resorts.

LINES
Crowds can be amazing, especially in peak seasons. Approximate wait times are posted at the start of each line. Use Disney's FastPass (opposite) wisely to avoid lines. The best strategy

---

CHILD SWAP
Far too often frightened children are screaming and crying in the line, or are horrified during the ride, and that's just no fun. Universal Orlando and Walt Disney World's child-swap program eliminates the temptation to take children on rides that might scare them. One adult member of the party (eg one parent) can watch over the child (or children) while the other rides, and then you can swap.

---

is to get to the park early and get in line for the most popular rides first. Downpours and parades also tend to shorten lines considerably.

LOST & FOUND
Each park has its own Lost & Found, and items are sent to a central location at the end of each day.
Animal Kingdom ☎ 407-938-2785
Central ☎ 407-824-4245
Epcot ☎ 407-560-7500
Hollywood Studios ☎ 407-560-3720
Magic Kingdom ☎ 407-824-4521

MEDICAL SERVICES
There are several walk-in medical clinics and hospitals in and around Orlando (see p266). Medical facilities are located within each park; see park maps for locations.

PARKING
You will find parking lots (car/RV $8/9) at all the parks except for Magic Kingdom, and free parking at Downtown Disney. Parking tickets bought at one park are good all day for all Disney parks, so you can use the same one if you decide to visit more than one park in a day. Parking is free for guests at Disney resorts.

PHONE NUMBERS
Accommodation Reservations ☎ 407-824-8000
Central Switchboard ☎ 407-939-8170
Dining ☎ 407-939-3463
General Information ☎ 407-939-6244

Tours
Walt Disney World offers at least a dozen **guided tours** (☎ 407-939-8687). The five-hour **Keys to the Kingdom** ($60) takes you through the Magic Kingdom's underground tunnels (no children allowed, so as not to destroy the magic). Attendance is limited and prices vary widely; check the website for a full listing of tours.

Festivals & Events
Pull on your eye patch or your most sparkly princess dress for **Mickey's Pirate and Princess Party**, held several nights each month at Magic Kingdom. This limited admission event (adult/child $48/42) includes private access to the park from 7pm to midnight, a special parade and fireworks, pirate and princess events, and 'treasure' stations with beads and other trinkets. Because you do not need

MEETING DISNEY CHARACTERS

Folks of all ages pay a lot of money and spend a lot of time in line to get their photo taken with Winnie the Pooh, Snow White, Donald Duck and other Disney favorites. It doesn't make much sense on paper, but somehow, once at Disney, even the most hard-hearted swoon.

Free Meetings

Each park has specific places were characters hang out, and you can simply hop in line to meet them and have your photo taken. Check the *Times Guide* for details.

One of the best free character encounters in the parks is Magic Kingdom's **Storytime with Belle** (p298). Over at Fort Wilderness Campground, don't miss the intimate and low-key **Chip 'n' Dale Campfire Singalong** (🕑 winter/summer 7pm/8pm) followed by an outdoor screening of a Disney film (free). Purchase s'more supplies ($7) or bring your own – don't forget a blanket to stretch out on! Cars are not allowed in Fort Wilderness; park at the first left after the entry gate and catch a shuttle to the campfire.

Character Dining

Check the Disney website for a complete list of the many character-dining meals in the park and resorts, and call Walt Disney World Dining (☎ 407-939-3463) up to six months (yes, six!) in advance to guarantee a seat. Meals range from breakfast with Lilo and Stitch at Disney's Polynesian Resort to country-and-western singin' and stompin' and fried chicken at **Mickey's Backyard Barbecue** (Disney's Fort Wilderness Resort & Campground; adult/child $44-50/$27-30; 🕑 dinner). Disney's Grand Floridian features a buffet breakfast with Winnie the Pooh, Mary Poppins and Alice in Wonderland, as well as lunch or dinner with the princesses, and there's a jam-packed breakfast and dinner with Goofy and pals at Chef Mickey's in the Contemporary Resort. Probably the most coveted seat is one at **Cinderella's Royal Table** (adult/child $33-45/$24-28; 🕑 breakfast, lunch, dinner) inside Magic Kingdom's castle. Cinderella greets guests and sits for a formal portrait (included in the price), and a sit-down meal with the princesses is served upstairs. Character meals are not fine-dining experiences, nor are they intimate affairs – they can be rather loud and chaotic. Characters rotate around the room, stopping for a minute or so at each table to pose for a photograph.

One of the priciest, most elegant and intimate options is **My Disney Girl's Perfectly Princess Tea** (one adult & one child $250) at Disney's Grand Floridian. Enjoy high tea served in silver and a visit from Aurora; the price includes a princess bracelet, a doll and other goodies. Also at the Grand Floridian is the no-adults-allowed **Wonderland Tea Party** (ages 4-12 only; $43; 🕑 1:30-2:30pm Mon-Fri), where Alice in Wonderland characters help children decorate cupcakes.

Magical Experiences

For parties of eight or more (over three years old), Disney offers four **Grand Gathering Magical Experiences** (☎ 407-939-7526) with various characters. There is the **International Dinner and Illuminations Reception**, with food, dancing, storytelling and reserved seating at Epcot's Illuminations fireworks; the **Good Morning Character Breakfast** at Magic Kingdom; the **Magical Fireworks Voyage**, which includes a Magic Kingdom fireworks cruise hosted by Mr Smee and Captain Hook, songs, storytelling and a dock-greeting by Peter Pan; and the **Safari Celebration Dinner**, a post-park-closing Kilimanjaro Safari, a family-style character meal at Tusker House, and the chance to get up close to exotic wildlife. Each experience includes a FastPass pin that allows each individual unlimited access to FastPass lines throughout the park for one day. Prices vary and individual character details change. Note that you will be grouped with other parties.

a park pass to attend this event, and you can enter a few hours before the party begins, this makes a great way to start your trip. On select nights from September 5 through October 31, **Mickey's Not-So-Scary Halloween Party** (adult/child $49/43) features characters decked out in costumes, trick-or-treating and Halloween-inspired fireworks, parade and events.

The Disney topiary and garden displays at the annual **Epcot International Flower and Garden Festival** (March to June) are spectacular, and folks return annually for **Epcot's Food and Wine**

Festival (October). See website for specific dates, details and other special events.

MAGIC KINGDOM
When most people think of Disney World, they're thinking of the Magic Kingdom, home to that famous blue castle and classic rides like Peter Pan's Flight, It's a Small World and Pirates of the Caribbean.

Orientation & Information
The Magic Kingdom is divided into seven very different 'lands.' Enter the park under the railroad station and continue on to Main Street, USA and walk past the small-town America storefronts toward Cinderella's Castle. A horse-drawn carriage runs continuously from the castle to the park entrance; from a cul-de-sac in front of the castle, four roads branch off to Adventureland, Liberty Sq, Frontierland and Tomorrowland respectively. Walk straight through the castle (or around either side) into Fantasyland. To reach Mickey's Toontown, you need to walk through Fantasyland or Tomorrowland.

Immediately upon entering the park you will find Guest Services, Lost & Found, wheelchair and stroller rental, ATMs and storage lockers. At the end of Main St, on the left, there's an information board with the day's show and parade times, estimated ride waits and other helpful tips.

Attractions
MAIN STREET, USA
This is the welcoming area to the Magic Kingdom, with a variety of services, eateries and the mother lode of gift shops.

ADVENTURELAND
Swiss Family Treehouse
More than a yawn than an attraction, this replica treehouse of the shipwrecked family from the book and movie *The Swiss Family Robinson* shows how the Robinsons' skills turned their disaster-stricken lives into a paradisiacal wonderland. Be prepared for a slow train of people climbing the 116 steps.

Magic Carpets of Aladdin
Fly around and around, up and down on Aladdin's magic carpet, but be careful to avoid the waterstream of the spitting camel! Little ones love it, but the line rivals Dumbo so get here early.

Enchanted Tiki Room
Iago, the scurrilous parrot from Disney's *Aladdin,* and Zazu, the bossy hornbill from *The Lion King* sing 'In the tiki tiki tiki room…' and crack corny jokes in this two-bit attraction. It's a pleasant place to relax in the air-conditioning, but scary surprises like booming god and goddess voices and a lightning bolt might frighten little ones.

Jungle Cruise (FastPass)
With fake crocodiles, elephants and monkeys and a captain throwing out the cheesiest jokes in all of Disney World, this silly cruise through the jungle is low on thrills and high on kitsch. Folks love it or hate it.

Pirates of the Caribbean
Though showing its age, the slow-moving indoor boat tour through the dark and shadowy world of pirates remains one of the most popular at Disney. Drunken pirates sing pirate songs, sleep among the pigs and sneer over their empty bottles of whiskey, but unless you're scared of the dark or growling pirates, this whimsical ride is just silly fun. And that Jack Sparrow looks so incredibly lifelike that you'll swear it's Johnny Depp himself!

FRONTIERLAND
Splash Mountain (FastPass)
This ride, based on the movie *Song of the South,* depicts the misadventures of Brer Rabbit, Brer Bear and Brer Fox, complete with chatty frogs, singing ducks and other critters. The 40mph drop into the river makes for one of the biggest thrills in the park. You will get very, very wet!

Big Thunder Mountain Railroad (Fast-Pass)
The 'wildest ride in the wilderness' takes you through the desert mountain and a cave of bats, past cacti and hot-spring geysers. With no steep drops or loop-dee-loops, this mild runaway-train roller coaster is a great choice for little ones.

Tom Sawyer Island
Dubbed by many as a peaceful escape, this is a disappointment. People mill about, not sure what to do and wondering why they waited so long in line to take a boat out here. Some kids may enjoy exploring Injun Joe's Cave and the rustic (at best) playground, but most

seem as puzzled as the adults. If there aren't any crowds, it could be fun, but if the boat line is long, just walk away.

Country Bear Jamboree

In this odd and strangely dated theater attraction, stuffed bears emerge from the stage and sing corny country songs. Corny in an irritating way, not a kitschy-fun way. It is, however, air-conditioned and dark – duck in to cool down or nurse a baby. Shows run continuously, and you can enter and exit at your leisure.

LIBERTY SQUARE
Hall of Presidents

All sorts of presidential memorabilia, including a handwritten eighth-grade autobiography of Nixon, an impressionist portrait of Clinton and a bust of 'Dubya', decorate the waiting area. Folks are herded into a theater to watch a superpatriotic flick on US history. The finale has every single US president standing or sitting before you on stage.

Liberty Belle Riverboat

Perfect for getting away from the crowds or sitting to nurse an infant, a big paddle-wheel riverboat toots around Tom Sawyer Island and Fort Sam Clements.

The Haunted Mansion

Ride slowly past the haunted dining room, where apparitions dance across the stony floor, but beware of those hitchhiking ghosts – don't be surprised if they jump into your car uninvited! While mostly just silly ghosty fun, kids may be frightened by spooky pre-ride dramatics where everyone gathers in a small room with strange elongated paintings on the wall and an eerie voice warns guests that there are no doors, no windows and no escape.

FANTASYLAND

Quintessential Disney, Fantasyland is the highlight of any Disney trip for the seven-and-under crowd. Cool off at **Ariel's Grotto**, a small children's play area with squirting fountains and Ariel herself. Winnie the Pooh and his gang can sometimes be found outside the more spacious but water-free **Pooh's Playful Spot** play area.

It's a Small World

This sweet boat trip around the globe has captivated children since its debut at the 1964 New York World's Fair. It was transported to Disneyland in 1966, and is a cornerstone of Disney's Florida, Tokyo and Paris Magic Kingdoms. Small boats gently glide through country after country, each decked out floor to ceiling with elaborate and charmingly dated sets and inhabited by hundreds of animated dolls dressed in clothes appropriate to their country. They sing 'It's a Small World' as they dance and play in their native environments. While snide comments about how the song sticks irritatingly in your head for weeks have become a Disney cliché, we find something poignantly endearing, almost melancholy, in this simple ride. Little ones love it and the wait is rarely longer than 10 minutes.

Peter Pan's Flight (FastPass)

Board a pirate ship and fly through fog and stars over London to Never Neverland. Delightful, though some children may be afraid of the dark and the pirates.

Cinderella's Golden Carousel

A gilded carousel with plenty of horses to keep the lines from ever getting too long or too slow. Stop here when you need to get a little one on a ride and quick!

Mickey's PhilharMagic (FastPass)

Without a doubt the best 3-D show in Disney, this whimsical adventure takes Donald Duck through classic Disney songs and movies. Ride with him through the streets of Morocco on Aladdin's carpet and feel the champagne on your face when it pops open during Beauty and the Beast's *Be Our Guest*. Fun, silly and light-hearted, this is Disney at its best.

Dream Along With Mickey

With classic Disney style, this high-octane musical performance brings the villains, princesses, Mickey and Donald to the steps of Cinderella's castle for dancing and dramatic twists. See the *Times Guide* for show times.

Fairytale Garden

In a little stone grotto, Belle tells the story of *Beauty and the Beast* in a sugary-sweet voice befitting a Disney princess. Volunteers from the audience don silly costumes and become characters in the story, and afterwards you can line up for a photo with Belle. Show times are listed outside the garden and on the *Times Guide*.

Snow White's Scary Adventures
More about the witch than the sweet, animal-loving girl, this ride through *Snow White and the Seven Dwarfs* is often too scary for most of its target audience.

Dumbo the Flying Elephant
Jump on Dumbo and ride slowly around and around, up and down. Kids love to control how high they go. Go first thing in the morning as the slow-moving line quickly becomes long.

The Many Adventures of Winnie the Pooh (FastPass)
Who doesn't love Pooh Bear? Take a sweet journey through Hundred Acre Wood with all the beloved characters, including Tigger, Piglet, Roo, Eeyore and, of course, that Christopher Robin and his favorite bear Winnie.

Mad Tea Party
Wait until your last meal is well digested before venturing out on this barf-o-rama of a ride – especially if you think your kids have it in for you. It's a basic spinning ride, and you and others in the teacup get to decide just how much you'll be twirling.

MICKEY'S TOONTOWN FAIR
A dated homage to Mickey and Minnie, this is primarily a place to meet characters. Look for the elaborate and sparkling **face-painting** as you enter.

Mickey's & Minnie's Country Houses
That's right, houses, plural. They don't live together. Walk through their homes, climb on the furniture and see the botched job Goofy did on Mickey's kitchen. Lines to see Minnie outside in the gazebo wind through her house, and it's often packed and hot. If you're not picky about which mouse you see, head to the Judge's Tent (below) for Mickey instead.

Toontown Hall of Fame Tent
This character-meeting tent gives you a lot of bang for your buck. Wait in line just once to weave your way through a handful of princesses and other Disney characters.

Judge's Tent
There's nothing here but a chance to see Mickey Mouse. In contrast to the lines for

Minnie, however, you stand in a cool, dark room watching old Disney cartoons while you wait!

The Barnstormer at Goofy's Wiseacre Farm
Short and sweet and designed for small bodies, this roller coaster is a perfect initiation for those who've never ridden one before. Be warned that the unusually slow-moving queues are so much longer than the one-minute ride.

Donald's Boat & Toon Park
A rather tattered, worn and vaguely depressing water and play area next to the roller coaster. Somehow Walt Disney World, like Peter Pan, isn't supposed to grow old like this.

TOMORROWLAND
Tomorrowland Indy Speedway
Little ones' Speed Racer fantasies come to life when they can put the pedal to the metal on grand-prix-style cars around a huge figure-eight track. You can control the speed (up to what can best be described as a brisk 'poke,' about 7mph) but the cars themselves are affixed to the track. Note that kids must be 52in tall to drive on their own, which pretty much eliminates this ride's target audience. Strangely, plenty of childless adults wait in long lines to squish into an affixed car and toot around the track.

Space Mountain (FastPass)
The most popular ride in the Magic Kingdom hurtles you through the darkness of outer space.

Astro Orbiter
It's really not much to speak of – just a revolving rocket ride. You can get a nice view of Tomorrowland though.

Tomorrowland Transit Authority
Not exactly the most thrilling ride, this people mover makes a great break from the chaos of the park. Riders wind through Tomorrowland and take a detour through Space Mountain. The best time to ride this is when it's really hot or at night, when the area is lit up like a futuristic neon city.

Walt Disney's Carousel of Progress
This 20-minute audio-animatronic film celebrates the role of technology in everyday life.

Unless you're desperate to get out of the sun, you're better off celebrating elsewhere.

Buzz Lightyear's Space Ranger Spin (FastPass)

You're inside the film *Toy Story II* – actually the spin-off video game for the film – letting loose with your laser cannon at almost anything that moves. Steer your own Star Cruiser (in a 360° circle) as it races through space, with the Evil Emperor Zirg close behind.

Stitch's Great Escape (FastPass)

This 20-minute show is downright painful to sit through. The shtick is that audience members sit as prisoners on an alien spaceship, 'common criminals of the cosmos,' and the cute guy in the glass-enclosed tube in the center is imprisoned for 'jaywalking between the moons.' An awkward overhead harness unexpectedly slams folks into their seats, Stitch escapes, and all kinds of contrived chaos and mayhem ensue. Most of the time you have no idea what is going on, and you just have to sit uncomfortably and endure water spewing in your face, long periods of darkness, irritating smells, flashing lights and smoke.

Monster, Inc Laugh Floor

No longer interested in harnessing screams, the monsters of Monsters Inc now must capture human laughter. This hilarious interactive movie, different every time and incorporating audience members projected on the big screen, is all about trying to make you laugh and it's all just very silly in the very best sense of the word.

PARADES & FIREWORKS

Magic Kingdom has two parades, the daytime **Share a Dream Come True** and the after-dark **SpectroMagic**. Both feature incredible floats and all your favorite classic Disney characters dancing down the street, but the one at night has the added attraction of millions of sparkling lights. The **Electrical Water Pageant** (9pm) is a water parade with 14 lighted boats cruising the Seven Seas Lagoon. Jiminy Cricket narrates **Wishes**, the fireworks display over Cinderella's Castle.

Note that a separate and very different parade and fireworks display takes place on the nights when the park is open only to those with tickets to the Pirate and Princess Party (p295). Check the *Times Guide* for exact show times and parade schedules.

Eating

If you bring your lunch there aren't many quiet places to enjoy it. Try the tables at the end of the short dead-end streets halfway up Main Street, or the covered waterside pavilions just

---

TOP FIVE SPOTS TO WATCH MAGIC KINGDOM FIREWORKS

While nothing beats the classic Disney experience of heading to Magic Kingdom itself for the SpectroMagic Parade and the Wishes fireworks, there's something to be said for escaping the crowds and watching the sky from a distance. You can ride an elegant wooden boat from Magic Kingdom to the Polynesian and Grand Floridian, or hop on the monorail to the Contemporary.

- **Boat** Take a private **Specialty Fireworks Cruise** (☎ 407-939-7529, book up to 90-days in advance; 6-10 people $225-$300) on a pontoon or a 1930 mahogany reproduction Chris Craft. Rates include driver, snacks and nonalcoholic drinks. Dinner can be arranged in advance.

- **Contemporary Resort** Make advance reservations for a meal at the Contemporary's California Grill (p316), or just head up for a drink on its terrace.

- **Grand Floridian Resort & Spa** Grab a glass of wine at Narcoossee's and sit on the bench just outside the restaurant. For real seclusion, walk over to the grassy area in front of the lagoonside rooms.

- **Lagoon View Room** Snuggle into your PJs and watch from the luxury of your private balcony. Several deluxe Disney hotels, including the Grand Floridian and the Polynesian, offer rooms with a view of Magic Kingdom, and they don't cost much more than other views; always ask when making the reservation.

- **Polynesian Resort** Sip a pink umbrella drink on the beach.

off the bridge in front of Cinderella's Castle. Phone numbers are listed for those restaurants that take reservations.

For something beyond the usual chicken nuggets and hot dogs, **Tomorrowland Terrace Noodle Shop** (Tomorrowland; mains $7-10; lunch, dinner) serves up teriyaki chicken, beef and broccoli and noodle bowls in a shiny, bright cafeteria. Over at Liberty Sq, the **Columbia Harbour House** (Liberty Sq; mains $7-12; lunch, dinner) offers decent vegetarian chili and a Garden Galley Salad with mixed greens, chicken, pecans, pineapple and feta cheese. Enjoy standard North American cuisine (clam chowder, sandwiches, prime rib etc) in an early-American setting of wood and shiny brass at **Liberty Tree Tavern** (407-939-3463; Liberty Sq; mains $8-19; 11:30am-2:45pm & 4pm-8:50pm), The dinner buffet features Minnie Mouse, Goofy, Chip and Dale. An Italian bistro with a *Lady and the Tramp* theme, **Tony's Town Square Restaurant** (407-939-3463; Main St; mains $12-22; lunch, dinner) offers seafood and pasta dishes that are surprisingly good for theme-park food.

The best snack in the park is the individually made ice-cream sandwich with oozing vanilla ice cream squished between warm chocolate-chip cookies at **Sleepy Hollow** (Liberty Sq; 9am-park closing). Also try the tasty Mickey Mouse waffles sprinkled with powdered sugar.

Getting There & Around

See Walt Disney World Getting There & Around (p318) for information on Disney transportation to the Magic Kingdom. If you drive, you have to park at the Ticket & Transportation Center and then take the monorail or the ferry to the park.

The open-air **Walt Disney World Railroad** follows the perimeter of the park and stops at Main Street, USA, Frontierland and Mickey's Toontown Fair. A **horse-drawn carriage** carries folks back and forth down Main Street, USA, from the entrance gate to Cinderella's Castle; look for the sign.

HOLLYWOOD STUDIOS

The least charming of Walt Disney World's theme parks, Hollywood Studios has a few stand-out attractions in a sea of mediocrity and offers none of the nostalgic charm of Magic Kingdom, the kitschy fun of Animal Kingdom or the sophisticated delights of Epcot. *High School Musical* blares through the streets, Hannah Montana souvenirs line store shelves, and screams from the Tower of Terror echo through the park.

Befitting the tone of this park, an American Idol attraction is scheduled to open at the end of 2008. It will host daily auditions for guests 14 and older, and at the end of the day the winners will perform at a Grand Finale.

Orientation & Information

Enter on Hollywood Blvd, which is basically a cluster of movie-themed gift shops. Make a right onto Sunset Blvd to hit the big rides, and left toward New York for the movie-based attractions. The giant Sorcerer's Hat on Mickey Ave serves as the park's primary focal point.

Attractions
HOLLYWOOD BOULEVARD
Toy Story Mania
This interactive 3-D ride inspired by Pixar's *Toy Story* had not yet opened at the time of research.

The Great Movie Ride
Ride past soundstage sets for some of the world's most beloved movies, including *The Wizard of Oz, Casablanca* and *Raiders of the Lost Ark,* and their animatronic stars.

ECHO LAKE
Sounds Dangerous – Starring Drew Carey
With no interesting storyline, no funny twists and no special effects, this movie is undoubtedly the worst attraction in the park, perhaps in all of Disney. For a full seven minutes of the incredibly boring 30-minute show the audience sits in complete darkness listening on individual headphones as detective Drew Carey clumsily chases down bad guy Lefty Moreno.

Indiana Jones Epic Stunt Spectacular (FastPass)
In this huge outdoor theater, professional stunt people show the audience how stunts are created. Indiana Jones falls into a vat of steam and fire, is chased by a boulder and leaps out of tall buildings. Audience volunteers don costumes to become extras in the Cairo market scene.

Star Tours (FastPass)
Enter the StarSpeeder and ride, via a movie, with Star Wars' R2D2 and C-3PO at the speed

of light through falling meteorites and other intergalactic debris to the planet of Endor. Unfortunately the trip is nothing more than dramatic narrative and a shaking seat. Hardcore *Star Wars* fans might enjoy it.

STREETS OF AMERICA
Muppet Vision 3-D
The 3-D technology of this Muppet movie, helped along with animatronic hecklers in the audience, *becomes* rather than enhances the story. With no driving narrative and aging special effects, this is truly ho hum. Unless you're a huge fan of the Muppets, skip it.

Honey I Shrunk the Kids Movie Set Adventure
Kids climb, slide and crawl through the oversized corn, gigantic insects and mountainous weeds, and a huge garden hose serves as a sprinkler. The best part is that there is only one exit, so you can let the kids play without worrying that you'll lose them.

Lights, Motors, Action! Extreme Stunt Show (FastPass)
This massive 30-minute stunt show features cars, motorcycles and characters from the Pixar movie *Cars* engaged in all kinds of speeding, crashing and jumping. The auditorium seats more than 2500 people, so it's usually easy to get a seat. Check the *Times Guide* for performance times.

Studio Backlot Tour
The idea here is that you're taken behind the scenes to see how movies are made, but in practice it's all rather ho hum with a lot of waiting. Ride a tram through staff parking lots past the Mickey Mouse–eared water tower, planes used in *Pearl Harbor,* props from different movies and Walt Disney's private plane. The best part is the stop at Catastrophe Canyon, a movie set canyon where you see how they produce special effects for an out-of-control disaster. A gas tank explodes and 70,000 gallons of water come crashing through the canyon walls straight for the shuttle.

MICKEY AVENUE
Walt Disney: One Man's Dream
This is a biographical exhibit on the great dreamer himself, Walt Disney, with some technical animation exhibits thrown in for good measure. It's an interesting story, and

there's enough eye candy (TV monitors with cartoon clips and miniature set replicas) to keep little ones amused.

ANIMATION COURTYARD
Voyage of the Little Mermaid (FastPass)
Black lighting creates utter darkness so that the fluorescent sea critters (handled by puppeteers swathed in black) pop out in a brilliant flash of color. Bubbles descend from the ceiling to complete the underwater effect, and Ariel croons classic songs from the film. Unfortunately it's disappointingly short, with huge narrative holes that confuse even the most die-hard of *Little Mermaid* fans. We meet Ariel under the sea with her fish friends, we see her make a deal with the nefarious Sea Witch and then, next scene, Ariel is happily married to the prince!

The Magic of Disney Animation
See animation artists at work during this 35-minute tour bookended by two short films about the history of animation.

Playhouse Disney – Live on Stage
Familiar faces from Disney's Playhouse Disney TV channel sing and dance, and everyone is invited to help them plan Minnie's birthday party. It's a favorite with toddlers.

SUNSET BOULEVARD
Beauty and the Beast – Live on Stage
This simple and sweet outdoor theater performance of *Beauty and the Beast* follows the storyline, incorporates the classic songs, and doesn't fall back on any special effects or crazy shenanigans. Check the *Times Guide* for show times.

Rock 'n' Roller Coaster Starring Aerosmith (FastPass)
The shtick here is that you're hurrying off in a limo to catch the Aerosmith concert. 'Dude (Looks Like a Lady)' cranks through headrest speakers as the coaster twists and turns in darkness, but there are no steep drops that send your belly through your mouth. Some claim this is one of the best rides in Disney, but we say it's high on hoopla and short on thrill. Hugely popular – go first thing or get a FastPass.

The Twilight Zone Tower of Terror (FastPass)
Follow the screams to creepy Hollywood Tower Hotel, now eerily abandoned. The pre-ride spiel

explains how the hotel came to be so ramshackle and empty. And then, Rod Serling invites you into the…Twilight Zone. Enter an elevator and slowly climb up the old hotel, past the lurking ghosts. Clatter, clatter, clatter, until suddenly and without warning the elevator free falls down. Clatter up, crash down, again and again, all in total darkness. Every ride is different.

PARADES & FIREWORKS

The daily afternoon **Disney Stars and Motor Cars Parade** clogs Hollywood Blvd with characters galore. Don't miss the over-the-top light and music show **Fantasmic!** in which Mickey Mouse faces Disney's assembled dark side. Seating for the 25-minute show begins 90 minutes prior to the starting time. To guarantee a seat, book the **Fantasmic Dinner Package** (☎ 407-969-3463). Children may be frightened by the dramatic villains and the giant fire-breathing dragon.

Eating

ABC Commissary (New York St; mains $6-12; ☽ lunch, dinner) With surprisingly interesting choices like tabbouleh wraps, Cuban sandwiches and even a children's vegetable noodle stir-fry, this makes a great choice for anyone tired of the usual chicken nuggets and hamburgers.

Mama Melrose's Ristorante Italiano (☎ 407-969-3463; Sunset Blvd; mains $12-22; ☽ lunch, dinner) Tasty Italian food, including flatbread pizzas, risotto and pasta, all washed down with a carafe of sangria.

Sci-Fi Dine-In Theater (☎ 407-969-3463; Echo Lake; mains $11-21; ☽ lunch, dinner) A 'drive-in' where you eat in abbreviated Cadillacs and watch classic sci-fi flicks.

50's Prime Time Café (☎ 407-969-3463; Echo Lake; mains $13-21; ☽ lunch, dinner) Step into a quintessential 1950s home for a home-cooked meal, including Grandma's Chicken Pot Pie, Aunt Liz's Golden Fried Chicken and Mom's Old-Fashioned Pot Roast, served up on a Formica tabletop. Waitresses in pink plaid and white aprons banter playfully and admonish folks who don't finish their meals and put their elbows on the table with a sassy 'shame, shame, shame.'

Hollywood Brown Derby (☎ 407-969-3463; Sunset Blvd; mains $18-32; ☽ lunch, dinner) Gourmet eats and a great-looking Cobb salad in semi-upscale surroundings modeled after the LA original.

Getting There & Around

See Walt Disney World Getting There & Around (p318) for information on Disney transportation to the park. There is no transportation within the park.

EPCOT

With no roller coasters screeching overhead, no parades, no water rides, and plenty of greenery, things here run a bit slower, with a bit less va-voom, than in the rest of Walt Disney World. Slow down and enjoy. Smell the incense in Morocco, listen to the Beatles in the United Kingdom and eat sushi in Japan.

Orientation & Information

Epcot is divided into two sections. **Future World** is composed of eight pavilions, each holding rides and attractions and separated by grass, fountains and gardens. **World Showcase**, arranged country by country around the lagoon, offers shops, restaurants, a couple of movies and a live show about the US. Staff members from the nations represented come here on one-year contracts, and operate authentic-feeling villages that offer some of the most interesting shopping and food in Walt Disney World.

Though the park map shows only one entrance, there are two. The main entrance, next to the bus and monorail stations, sits at the landmark geodesic dome of Spaceship Earth in Future World. Guest Services is to your left as you enter the park. The back entrance, at International Gateway, brings visitors into the United Kingdom; from here, walk to the left and along the lake through United Kingdom and Canada to Future World, or cross the bridge on the right into France and walk left through World Showcase. From the back entrance you can catch a boat to Epcot resorts and Hollywood Studios (see Walt Disney World Getting There & Around, p318).

Both entrances have lockers, strollers and wheelchair rental.

Attractions

In addition to the following attractions, each nation in the World Showcase has live music, comedy, drumming or dancing shows; check your *Times Guide* for times. Little ones can cool off in the fountain just before the central bridge from Future World to World Showcase. The fountain is pictured on the map.

FUTURE WORLD

Spaceship Earth

This icon of Epcot, resembling a giant golf ball towering over the park, actually contains a kitschy ride narrated by Jeremy Irons where you'll see how communications have developed from prehistoric times through the Renaissance to the 19th century and today, and developments into the future.

Ellen's Energy Adventure

Arguably the oddest ride in Orlando, this 45-minute attraction begins with a movie during which Ellen DeGeneres dreams that she is playing Jeopardy with Jamie Lee Curtis. Determined to outsmart her know-it-all opponent, Ellen joins the Bill Nye the Science Guy on a trip through history to learn about energy sources. At this point, you enter a 96-passenger vehicle and lurch slowly through the darkness into the Cretaceous period (the root of today's fossil fuels). Giant dinosaurs stomp about menacingly and, in one particularly surreal display, a mannequin Ellen battles a particularly ferocious one. After this jaunt through dinosaurland, the movie discusses wind energy, hydro-energy and other alternative fuel sources, and concludes with Ellen's Jeopardy victory.

Mission: Space (FastPass)

Become an astronaut and ride a spaceship into the stratosphere. While this is not a high-speed ride, the special effects can be nauseating. There are two options, one with less intensity than the other.

Test Track (FastPass)

The rather disturbing shtick here is that you are a living crash-test dummy. Ride a General Motors car through heat, cold, speed, braking and crash tests – at one point a huge semi with blinding headlights heads right for you, its horn blaring. When testing the acceleration, the car speeds up to 60mph within a very short distance and while it's fast and fun, there are few turns and no ups and downs like a roller coaster. If you don't have a FastPass, take the line for solitary riders. At the exit, you can climb around a Hummer, a Saab convertible and other models, talk to a GM representative, and pick up that perfect Disney souvenir, a T-shirt with a pink-sequin Hummer.

Innoventions

A huge glass building divided into **Innoventions West** and **Innoventions East** by a pleasant courtyard, this attraction is for the most part company-sponsored interactive technology demos. Attractions here change, but expect hands-on computer games and displays, lots of teenagers excited to escape into the myriad Sega games, and frenetic littler ones simply running around pressing buttons.

Epcot Character Spot

Mickey Mouse, Minnie Mouse, Goofy and other Disney characters, each with an appropriate backdrop, line up so you can go through and catch them all in one stop. Perfect for filling those autograph books, and it's air-conditioned.

The Seas with Nemo and Friends

Ride a clamshell as you gently wind through the ocean looking for Nemo. If you like the movie, you'll like the ride, but if Bruce the shark scared your little ones on the screen, he'll scare 'em here. Like Peter Pan and Snow White's Scary Adventure in the Magic Kingdom, the darkness and special effects are the scariest part.

Turtle Talk with Crush

We don't know how they do it, but hey, that's the Disney magic. A small blue room with a large movie screen holds about 10 rows of benches with sitting room for kids in front. Crush talks to the children staring up at him, taking questions from the 'dude in the dark-blue shell' and cracking jokes about how sea grass gives him the bubbles. Dory shows up and gets squished against the screen by the whale. It's a fantastic and funny interactive show.

Soarin' (FastPass)

This fabulous experience simulates hang gliding over California. Soar up and down, hover and accelerate as the screen in front of you takes you over citrus groves, golf courses, mountains, coasts, rivers and cities. You smell the oranges and your feet almost touch those surfers below. FastPasses for this run out quickly, so head here first thing and ask for a front-row seat to avoid the distraction of people's dangling feet. While not at all scary in terms of speed or special effects, folks with agoraphobia may feel a bit uneasy.

Living with the Land (FastPass)

Ride a boat past laboratorylike greenhouses while a narrator talks about growing food in and under water. It's much more interesting than it sounds. Look for vegetables grown into Disney shapes.

The Circle of Life

This 13-minute film about the fragile relationship between the environment and the creatures that live within it features Simba and his buddies from *The Lion King*. It's a playful movie with a powerful message that, despite being rather corny, gets through to the audience.

Journey into Imagination with Figment

Figment the purple dragon takes you on a no-thrills ride showcasing how the imagination works. No biggie to miss.

Honey, I Shrunk the Audience (FastPass)

Without a doubt one of the worst attractions at Walt Disney World, this 3-D movie stars Rick Moranis as Dr Wayne Szalinski from the movie of the same name. The narrative premise is that Dr Szalinski is being honored with the Inventor of the Year Award. In demonstrating his incredible shrinking machine, things go awry. And this is where random and disconnected special effects kick in. Unless you're particularly hot and tired and just want to sit down in an air-conditioned theater, absolutely do not waste your time.

WORLD SHOWCASE

Who needs the hassle of a passport and jetlag when you can travel the world right here at Walt Disney World? Watch belly dancing in Morocco and buy personally engraved bottles of perfume in France before settling down to watch fireworks about world peace and harmony. Disney was right. It truly is a small world after all. Sure, this is quite a sanitized and stereotypical vision of the world, but so what? This is, after all, a theme park. The featured countries are Mexico, Norway, China, Germany, Italy, Japan, Morocco, France, the United Kingdom, Canada and the USA. Each section has architecture unique to that country, restaurants serving national cuisine and gift shops with country-specific merchandise.

Gran Fiesta Tour Starring the Three Caballeros

A boat takes you through Mexico with Donald Duck and his comrades from the 1994 Disney film *The Three Caballeros*.

Maelstrom (FastPass)

Tucked away in the Norway pavilion, this cute little boat ride meanders past Vikings, trolls and a couple of good waterfalls. Afterward, you'll watch a film put out by a Norway tourism company about the wonders of that Arctic land.

Reflections of China

A 20-minute film screened on a 360° screen focuses on China's stunning landscape and exotic cities. Unfortunately, the theater is standing room only.

The American Adventure

Benjamin Franklin and Mark Twain host a cacophony of audio-animatronic figures in this oversimplified interpretation of US history. From the Pilgrims to Charles Lindbergh, from Susan B Anthony to Magic Johnson, this show celebrates the US with plenty of dramatic music and special effects. Check the *Park Times Guide* for a performance schedule.

Impressions de France

This spectacularly beautiful, 18-minute film celebrates France's natural countryside. While it may sound boring, it's very lovely, and the sit-down theater is air-conditioned.

O'Canada

Give the Canadians the attention they deserve at this 10-minute film showcasing the beauty of the country in a 360° theater.

Fireworks

IllumiNations: Reflections of Earth, which takes place in the center of the park's lagoon, is one of the best things about Epcot. In typical Disney style, this interpretation of the history of the earth begins with the world's fiery emergence and concludes with a dramatic celebration of cultures. Because so much of this story revolves

QUIET SPOT

With views of the lagoon and the classic architecture of each country's buildings, the patio on the water just off the bridge from the United Kingdom to France makes a pleasant spot to escape the crowds. Grab a beer from the pub or a class of wine from France and just sit and relax.

around the massive globe in the center of the lagoon, the best place to watch is from anywhere along the water's edge. Remember that the park usually closes after the show so everyone is going to be leaving; if you're exiting via boat, watch the fireworks from the United Kingdom or France so you'll be close to the boat dock.

Eating & Drinking

Eating at Epcot is as much about the experience as the food, and many of the restaurants go overboard to create an atmosphere characteristic of their country. You can savor a glass of champagne in France, relaxing alongside the lagoon, or taste wine at the tavern in Germany, before heading to China for wonton soup. As one visitor said, perusing the McDonalds menu of a fast-food eatery in Future World, 'I'm gonna wait and try something exotic over in Morocco.' None of the food is going to knock your socks off, but it's a lot of fun and a great alternative to the usual theme-park offerings. Make reservations up to 180 days in advance (☎ 407-939-3463) for the midrange and top-end restaurants; stop by guest services for same-day reservations.

BUDGET

You'll find cafeteria-style restaurants in Future World and a handful of walk-up service booths with crepes and other food appropriate to each country along the lagoon. Next to the lavish temples of Japan and inside the pavilion is the counter-service **Yakitori House** (Japan; mains $4-8; ☺ 11am-park closing), offering miso soup, teriyaki chicken and sushi. Over in the United Kingdom, grab fish and chips with vinegar and a Bass to enjoy on the patio at **Yorkshire County Fish Shop** (United Kingdom; fish and chips $8; ☺ 11am-park closing).

MIDRANGE

Rose & Crown Pub & Dining Room (United Kingdom; mains $13-21; ☺ 11am-park closing) Housed in a classic British pub, this little spot serves up pub fare including ploughman's lunch, steak, fish and chips and a tasty vegetable curry. Wash it down with Bass on tap before heading across the path for a garden concert of the Fab Four (various times).

Teppan Edo (Japan; mains $16-29; ☺ 11am-park closing) Chefs toss the chicken, fling the chopsticks and chop frenetically at the veggies at this cook-in-front-of-you eatery next to Japan's lovely gardens. Kids love the showmanship of it all, and you might be surprised at how much they like the food too!

Chefs de France (France; mains $19-32; ☺ 11am-park closing) Bright and bustling, this French café features steak *frites* and other standards of a French bistro. The French Menu ($30), a set meal of appetizer, main and dessert, is available until 7pm.

Biergarten (Germany; buffet adult/child lunch $20/11, dinner $27/13; ☺ 11am-park closing) Satisfy a hearty appetite with a buffet of traditional German foods, and don't miss the pretzel bread. The restaurant interior is made to look like an old German village, with cobblestone, trees, and an oompah band in the evening.

TOP END

Le Cellier Steakhouse (Canada; mains $21-35 ☺ 11am-park closing) If you love meat, this place is for

---

GAY DAY AT WALT DISNEY WORLD

In 1991 Orlando gay activist Doug Swallow and a handful of friends encouraged gays and lesbians to 'wear red and be seen' when visiting the Magic Kingdom. Some 2500 made it. Ever since, an estimated 40,000 to 50,000 red-shirted gay and lesbian visitors descend on Cinderella's Castle on the first Saturday in June for what is now an entrenched Florida tradition.

Disney (whose record of fair treatment to gay and lesbian employees has been exemplary, going so far as to extend health-care benefits to same-sex partners) stresses very publicly that this is not an official Disney event. Still, it tolerates – even helps organize – Gay Day. At 1pm, bears (um, hirsute gentlemen) head to the Country Bear Jamboree to sing along with their animatronic friends. And at 3pm everyone gathers for the Main Street parade, where characters put on an especially enthusiastic show as they navigate a truly awesome sea of red.

The festivities have grown to encompass almost every attraction in Orlando, with the day at Magic Kingdom being but one day in the week-long Orlando Gay Days. Log on to www.gaydays.com for hotel information and a schedule of events ranging from pool parties to building a house for Habitat For Humanity; from a film festival to a day at Animal Kingdom.

you. Try the buffalo. Rather dark and cavernous, it makes a good spot to escape the heat, but the dense sauces and decadent desserts might not be the best fuel to get you through the day. Come here if your afternoon promises nothing more than lazing by the pool, or come for a hearty dinner.

Restaurant Marrakesh (Morocco; mains $21-36; 11am–park closing) Enjoy lamb kebabs and vegetable couscous while watching sparkling belly dancers shimmer and shake. Kids enjoy dancing along with them.

Tutto Italia Restorante (Italy; mains $24-36; 11am–park closing) If you can tolerate the hoity-toity attitude (this is Disney, for goodness sake, not Venice), the classic Italian fare is quite good. The only way to get a room outside in the piazza is if you wait in line for stand-by – all reservations are seated indoors.

Bistro de Paris (France; mains $29-43; dinner) The most upscale option in the park, this elegant 2nd-floor restaurant, decorated in muted earth tones and self-consciously fancy, serves up-market French food. A five-course meal with wine pairings costs $120 ($75 without wine). Reserve a window table (up to 30 days in advance) for an excellent view of the fireworks.

Getting There & Around
Epcot can be reached on Disney transportation via boat, bus and monorail. See Walt Disney World Getting There & Around (p318) for details. A **boat shuttle** departs from two boat docks at Showcase Plaza, just outside Future World, for Morocco and Germany.

ANIMAL KINGDOM
Set apart from the rest of Disney both in miles and in tone, Animal Kingdom attempts to blend theme park and zoo, carnival and African safari, all stirred together with a healthy dose of Disney characters, storytelling and transformative magic. The result is, at times, rather odd.

Orientation & Information
Enter the park at the Oasis and walk either direction toward the bridge to Discovery Island. Here, a road lined with food outlets and shops circles the landmark Tree of Life and four more bridges cross the water into Africa, Asia, DinoLand USA and Camp Minnie-Mickey. Raffi's Planet is accessible by train from Africa.

Attractions
OASIS
Lovely gardens hide all kinds of cool critters, but it's best to move along to other attractions before the lines get too long. Pause to enjoy on your way out.

DISCOVERY ISLAND
This is the park's hub, and like Cinderella Castle at Magic Kingdom and Spaceship Earth at Epcot, the huge, ornate **Tree of Life** serves as the best landmark for orienting yourself in Animal Kingdom. It's 14 stories tall and has over 325 animal images carved into its trunk.

It's Tough to Be a Bug! (FastPass)
This is awesome and a lot of fun, but if your kids are terrified of darkness or creepy crawlies keep them out of this 3-D extravaganza. Even though it's very cute much of the time, you will definitely hear children crying by the end. Be prepared for surprises!

Discovery Island Trails
As you walk around the island, there are little paths that lead to the water. Often quiet, these are a good spot for a picnic on the bench or a respite from the crowds. Keep your eye out for animals like tortoises and lemurs in and around the water.

CAMP MINNIE-MICKEY
Pocahontas and her Forest Friends
Pocahontas fans and animal-lovers will enjoy this short and rather quaint live show about nature preservation. Live animals, sometimes including a skunk and a snake, help the Disney princess tell her story. Word is that this show is to be replaced with something with more bells and whistles, so double-check your map.

Festival of the Lion King
One of the most overrated attractions at Disney, this 30-minute theater in the round features acrobats, dancing, singing and fire theatrics. The *Lion King* music is fun, and actors decked out in full African garb involve the audience in all kinds of silly animal sounds, but there's no narrative structure to hold it all together. The best part are the massive floats, each a different animal.

Greeting Trails
Four separate huts each house a Disney character, and you can wait in individual lines to

---

DISNEY DETAIL

Disney's attention to the tiniest of details of the Walt Disney World experience is perhaps best epitomized by the directive posted in every bathroom at the park: '1. Wash hands and apply soap. 2. Scrub hands and rinse. 3. Dry hands thoroughly using paper towels.'

---

get your photo taken with them individually. Mickey and Minnie (in safari garb) each have their own regular spot, but the other two huts could have anyone from Pluto to friends from *The Lion King* or *Jungle Book*.

AFRICA
Kilimanjaro Safaris (FastPass)
With live animals and that Disney touch, this could compete with just about any zoo in the country. Board a rickety jeep and ride through the African Sahara. But beware. Just as you're barreling down rutted roads, past zebras, lions and more, the driver gets word that poachers are on the loose! Local law enforcement can't do it alone, so you've got to help but, oh no! The bridge that's been causing so much trouble seems worse today and it might just give out on you. Unless your kids are scared of lions, there's nothing scary here at all.

Pagani Forest Exploration Trail
This lush path passes gorillas, hippos, a great bat display and a hive of naked mole rats.

RAFIKI'S PLANET WATCH
The **Wildlife Express Train** you take to get here might just be the best part of this Disney enigma. The **Habitat Habit** features a few adorable, fist-sized tamarinds, and the **Affection Section** is a pleasant enough petting zoo with sheep and goats. Veterinarians care for sick and injured animals at the **Conservation Station**, the park's veterinary and conservation headquarters. Sometimes they have live-animal interactions.

ASIA
Flights of Wonder
This bird show has some cheesy dialogue, but the animals are spectacular. Sit in the middle and watch them to fly over your head. Owls, peregrine falcons and others will dazzle you, and

afterward you can approach the trainers and their birds to ask questions and take photos.

Maharajah Jungle Trek
See Bengal tigers, huge fruit bats, Komodo dragons and other Asian critters lounging around on this self-guided walking tour. The habitats, designed to look like Angkor Wat, would convince even Indiana Jones he's not in the US of A anymore.

Kali River Rapids (FastPass)
This starts out pleasant enough, as you drift free-form on a circular 12-person raft through bamboo, rainforests and temple ruins. In fact, it's quite scenic (though some kids may be scared by the animal special effects). But this ain't no float trip – it's a ride through rapids, so be prepared for some sharp turns and other surprises. You will undoubtedly get wet.

Expedition Everest (FastPass)
Wait (and wait, and wait) in a reconstructed Nepalese village, made to make you feel that you are indeed about to take a train to the top of Mt Everest. Signs warn about a mysterious mountain creature, but you pay no attention as you board the steam train. It's only as you climb, up and up and up into the glaciers, that you begin to worry, Like so much of Disney the ride is as much about the narrative shtick and set design as the ride itself. This is a roller coaster. It goes backwards, it plummets at high speeds, it zooms around turns, but there are no loop-dee-loops. Everyone knows a train through the Himalayas doesn't do loop-dee-loops, silly!

DINOLAND USA
While this strange carnival-like area seems more like a local fair in rural Midwest America than part of Disney's magic – and it's a bit odd to plop the garish plastic dinosaurs of Dinoland right along with the live animals of Asia and Africa – there are some fun rides here.

The Boneyard
Kids can dig for mastodon skeletons or sit atop massive rib cages and other fossils. Unfortunately this sounds more fun than it actually is.

Fossil Fun Games
Typical midway games with the chance to win massive stuffed animals.

Finding Nemo – The Musical

Arguably the best show at Walt Disney World, this sophisticated theater performance in a large, air-conditioned theater wows children and adults alike. The show is directed by Peter Brosius, artistic director of the Children's Theater Company of Minneapolis, and the spectacular puppets were created by Michael Curry, who helped design the puppets for Broadway's *Lion King*. The music is fun, the acting is phenomenal, and the whole thing is an absolute pleasure from beginning to end. Masterful special effects add to, rather than become or overpower, the vision behind the production, and the narrative structure mirrors that of the movie. Unlike the Ariel show (p302) at Hollywood Studios, there are no gaping plot holes. Be prepared for huge puppets to walk along the aisle that separates lower from upper seating and for the bubbles drifting down from the ceiling.

Dinosaur (FastPass)

One of the most thrilling rides in the park takes you back in time to the Cretaceous period, where you've got to rescue a huge and scary dinosaur specimen before a meteor hits… This is definitely not for little kids, unless yours is tough as nails.

Primeval Whirl (FastPass)

Yeah, so it's a kid's coaster. It's still a whirlytwirly good time, but it's not superbarfy like a tea-cup ride (and you don't control the spins). The coaster on the left is identical to the one on the right.

PARADES

Very different from other Disney parades, the vaguely tribal **Mickey's Jammin' Jungle** features huge folk-art animal puppets, African dancing and Disney characters in safari motif. The parade runs during the day only.

Eating

There aren't many restaurants here, but plenty of quick, counter-service joints and what seems like an endless stream of McDonald's chains disguised behind African names. **Tusker House** (☎ 407-939-3463; buffet adult/child breakfast $19/11, lunch $20/11, dinner $27/13; ☷ breakfast, lunch, dinner) does a character breakfast (see boxed text p296) and there are plans to introduce a character-dining boat ride.

Getting There & Away

Disney **buses** stop at Animal Kingdom, but note that this park is pretty far away from everything else at the Walt Disney World so the ride here can be up to 45 minutes, maybe longer. The closest hotel is Animal Kingdom Lodge (p313). Rumor has it that Disney is going to expand the monorail system to include Animal Kingdom, but at time of publication there's nothing in the works.

OTHER DISNEY ATTRACTIONS

It would only take, oh, two weeks to experience (almost) everything in the four parks, but Disney would like you to stick around a little longer. So they've provided you with several other entertainment options, many of which are listed here. There are parasailing and surfing lessons, water skiing (p273) and more. Call Walt Disney World Recreation (☎ 407-939-7529) for details.

Sights & Activities

WATER PARKS

Disney's two water parks are included in the price of a Water Park Fun & More ticket (p289), but on their own, each costs $34 per adult and $28 for a child aged three to nine. Rentals include lockers (small/large $5/7) and towels ($1). Swimsuits with buckles or metal parts aren't allowed on the slides.

Of the two parks, Blizzard Beach boasts the better thrills and speed, but Typhoon Lagoon has the far superior wave pool and ambience. Families with small children will want to go to Typhoon Lagoon, as its lazy river and tots' play area are great, and there's plenty of room to just play on the beach and splash.

Be prepared to spend upwards of a half-hour in line for a ride that's over in less than a minute and take those wait times seriously – if it says the wait is 60 minutes, it's 60 minutes. Yes, 60 minutes for *one* slide. Come in the morning to beat the crowds, and head straight to the high-speed slides.

Hours vary by day and by season; from October through March, only one Disney water park is opened at a time. For other water parks in and around Orlando, see Wet 'n' Wild (p271), Aquatica (p332) and Cypress Gardens (p273).

Blizzard Beach

Though the newer of Disney's two water parks, **Blizzard Beach** (Map pp292–3; ☎ 407-560-3400) is the

1980s Vegas Strip hotel to Typhoon Lagoon's Bellagio. At its center sits the snowcapped **Mt Gushmore**, from which the waterslides burst forth. You can choose several options for your descent, but because the wooden-bench chairlift that transports riders to the top rarely works you'll have to huff it up before you can zoom down. But don't worry – the lines are usually so long you'll have plenty of time to relax on the way up! The fastest and craziest ride down is **Summit Plummet**, where you sit on the slide itself (no tube or toboggan) and fly more than 55mph down more than 360ft. Alternatively, try the slightly less intense **Slush Gusher** or hurtle headfirst down the eight-lane **Toboggan Runner**.

Butting against a thin slice of artificial beach is **Melt-away Bay**, a tame wave pool, and **Cross Country Creek**, a 'lazy' river with hidden geysers and sporadic ice-cold streams of water. There are two kids areas: **Ski Patrol Training Camp** for preteens, and **Tike's Peak** for the smaller ones.

Typhoon Lagoon

Perhaps the most beautiful water park in the country, **Typhoon Lagoon** (Map pp292-3; ☎ 407-560-4141) boasts an abundance of palm trees, a zero-entry pool with a white sandy beach, and the best **wave pool** in Orlando. Twice the size of a football field, the pool generates a massive 10ft wave every 90 seconds. First you hear the low rumble as the wave is generated, then the ripples of delighted anticipatory squeals as swimmers see the wave approach, and finally the laughing and screams of joy as everyone dives into and rides the wave. Again and again. And the best part is, no line. A few islands along the lagoon's shore break the waves and create a calm, shallow inlet for tots, and you can lay out in deck chairs right in the water.

The center point of the park is **Mt Mayday**, with a wrecked shrimp boat on its perch. Several slides emanate from the peak, including the ultrasteep crazy-fast **Humunga Kowabunga speed slides** and the **Mayday Falls tube plunge**. For more relaxing thrills, float through dense rainforest, rocky gorges and meticulously landscaped tropical flowers and foliage on **Castaway Creek**. The aptly named **Ketchakiddee Creek** attracts the little ones with a leaky tugboat, bubbly fountains, warm-water pools and family-friendly slides.

Typhoon Lagoon has two attractions that the other water parks do not have. First is the **Crush 'n' Gusher** water coaster – a combination log flume and roller coaster with jets of water that propel your tube up snaking hills and down through dark tunnels. It's fun, but as with every other ride the bore of the wait offsets the thrill of the 30-second ride. At **Shark Reef**, you can jump in and snorkel (free rentals) for an up-close look at rays, sharks and tropical fish. Sounds cool, but be warned that the water is very cold, you're not allowed to leave the surface or kick your feet, and the sharks are tiny and hang out down at the bottom. To spend more time with the fishes, take the **Surface Air Snorkeling (SAS) Adventure** (per 30mins $20, second person $15), which uses a regulator like in scuba diving; sign up at the kiosk.

DISNEY'S WIDE WORLD OF SPORTS

This huge **complex** (Map pp292-3; ☎ 407-828-3267; www.disneyworldsports.com; adult/child $10.75/8; ☺ hours vary according to event, call for schedule) is home to the **NFL Experience**, where you can take on the same obstacle courses and other fitness challenges as your favorite US football players. The massive complex also plays host to a mind-boggling array of professional and amateur sports events, including the Atlanta Braves' spring training games and the Harlem Globetrotters. Events tickets are not included in the price of admission.

WALT DISNEY WORLD SPEEDWAY

This is where you'll find the **Richard Petty Driving Experience** (Map pp292-3; ☎ 800-237-3889), where NASCAR wannabes can race Winston Cup–style cars around a real track. The Ride Along Program ($105) puts you shotgun in a stock car (riders must be at least 16) and three other options allow you to drive on your own.

DOWNTOWN DISNEY

Stretching along the water, this outdoor mall (Map pp292–3) lures tourists with three districts of chain restaurants, music venues, clubs, shops and a massive movie theater. It is accessible by boat from three Disney hotels (Port Orleans, Old Key West and Saratoga Springs) and by Disney buses. You can walk from one end to the other, or catch the boat shuttle that stops at each district.

For details on shopping and eating at Downtown Disney, see (p318 and p315).

West Side

With five dizzying floors of exhibits designed to indulge video-game addicts, **DisneyQuest** (adult/child 3-9 $36/30; 11:30am-11pm Sun-Thu, to midnight Fri & Sat) makes the perfect place to while away a rainy or hot afternoon. Virtual-reality rides, arcades, alien invasions, flight simulators and other technological delights (including designing your own roller coaster) will satisfy folks with even the most limited attention spans. Catch live music at **House of Blues** (☎ 407-934-2583; www.hob.com), or just stop in for some good ole southern cooking.

Pleasure Island
This small stretch of **nightclubs, bars and shops** (☎ 407-939-2648; all clubs/one club $22/11; shops 10:30am-1am, clubs 7pm-2am) is Disney's version of a happening downtown. Clubs include **BET SoundStage**, which spins hip-hop; **8Trax**, for disco; **Mannequins**, with a revolving dance floor and blaring techno; and **Motion**, for Top 40. The audience joins in the comedy acts at Pleasure Island's two improv-comedy clubs, **Adventurers Club** and **Comedy Warehouse**.

The 24-screen **AMC Pleasure Island** (☎ 407-298-4488; tickets $6-9) screens Hollywood blockbusters.

Marketplace
There are some pretty good shops and restaurants here, but that's about it. See Shopping (p318) and Eating (p315) for details.

DISNEY'S BOARDWALK
Less harried and crowded than Downtown Disney, this small area next to Epcot and along the lagoon echoes Disney's Boardwalks of turn-of-the-century New England seaside resorts. In the evening you may find a sidewalk magician, and there's a pleasant grassy area where little ones can run around. Sports fans will want to check out the **ESPN Club** (☎ 407-939-1177; 11:30am-1am Sun-Thu, to 2am Fri, Sat), with so many TVs screening the hottest game that even in the bathroom you won't miss a single play. At **Jellyrolls** (☎ 407-560-8770; admission $10; 7pm-2am), comedians tickle the keys of dueling pianos and encourage the audience to partake in all kinds of musical silliness. For a quiet drink, head to the **Belle Vue Room** (5pm-midnight) on the 2nd floor of Disney's Boardwalk Inn. It's more like a sitting room than a bar: you can relax and play a game, listen to classic radio shows like Lone Ranger, or simply take your drink to a rocking chair on the balcony and watch the comings and goings along Disney's Boardwalk.

GOLF
Walt Disney World has six **courses** (☎ 407-939-4653; www.disneyworldgolf.com; green fees vary, private lessons adult/child $80/55; 6:45am-dark) and two miniature golf courses. **Winter Summerland** (☎ 407-560-3000; adult/child 3-9 $12/10; 10am-11pm) is just outside Blizzard Beach and sweet **Fantasia Gardens** (☎ 407-560-4870; adult/child 3-9 $12/10; 10am-11pm) sits across from the Walt Disney World Dolphin. The latter is a welcome change from the bright, loud and over-the-top miniature golf endemic to Orlando.

TENNIS
Six resorts and Disney's Wide World of Sports offer hard courts and three offer clay. Bring your own racquet – there are no rentals except at Disney's Contemporary Resort (p313). Clinics and lessons are available (☎ 407-939-7529).

Sleeping
WALT DISNEY WORLD RESORTS
Disney resorts are divided according to price range (value, moderate, deluxe) and location (Epcot, Magic Kingdom, Animal Kingdom and Downtown Disney). Resorts below are organized by price; location and Disney-provided transportation to *that* location is indicated in the review. It is important to take note of what transport is available to/from your chosen resort when planning your trip. You can use Disney transportation to reach any attraction from any resort, but some resorts are accessible by bus only and not everything is directly connected (see Getting There & Around, p318).

Rates vary drastically according to season. See the website for a complete listing of accommodations and precise dates for 'value,' 'regular,' 'summer,' 'peak' and 'holiday' season. Moderate and deluxe resorts offer junior and multibedroom suites and villas.

Note that swimming off any resort beach is forbidden; they are strictly for lounging and playing in the sand. A Four Seasons resort is scheduled to open at Walt Disney World in 2010.

Camping
ourpick Disney's Fort Wilderness Resort & Campground (☎ 407-824-2900; campsites value $42-68, peak $70-100, cabins value/peak $255/360; Magic Kingdom;) Located in a huge shaded natural preserve, Fort Wilderness caters to kids and families

with hayrides, fishing and nightly campfire sing-alongs (p296). Cabins are hardly rustic, with cable TV and full kitchens, and while cars aren't allowed within the gates, you can rent a golf cart to get around. Campsites have at least partial hookup and those with full hookup have cable. Staff keeps a strict eye on after-hours noise, the grounds are meticulously maintained, and there's a wonderfully casual and friendly tone to the entire resort. Disney-provided transportation is by boat.

Value Resorts

The least expensive properties available, these have thousands of very small motel-style rooms, are garishly decorated according to the theme, connect to the parks by bus only and cater to families and traveling school groups (expect cheerleading teams practicing in the courtyard or a lobby of teenagers wearing matching jerseys). You will definitely feel the difference in price: instead of proper restaurants, there are only food courts and snack bars, and things are particularly hectic and loud.

Rates for a double room range from $82 to $110 during value season and from $119 to $150 during peak season. Disney-provided transportation to the following resorts is by bus only.

Disney's All-Star Movies Resort (☎ 407-939-7000; Animal Kingdom; 🖳 🛋)
Disney's All-Star Music Resort (☎ 407-939-6000, Animal Kingdom; 🖳 🛋)
Disney's All-Star Sports Resort (☎ 407-939-5000; Animal Kingdom; 🖳 🛋)
Disney's Pop Century Resort (☎ 407-939-6000; Animal Kingdom; 🖳 🛋)

Moderate

Standard double room rates at these full-service resorts range from $155 to $190 during value season and from $190 to $270 during peak season.

Disney's Caribbean Beach Resort (☎ 407-934-3400; Epcot; 🖳 🛋) A Disney taste of the islands means painted beds, pastel rooms and a food court that looks like a street festival during Carnival. The pool resembles ancient temple ruins and has a pretty cool water slide. Disney-provided transportation is by bus only.

our pick Disney's Coronado Springs Resort (☎ 407-939-1000; Epcot; 🖳 🛋) The Southwestern theme, evidenced in the warm pink-and-yellow guest rooms, the colored lights strung across the

Pepper Market and the adobe-colored buildings, creates a low-key tone that sets this resort apart from other Disney hotels. Several pleasantly landscaped two-story buildings, some with their own private and quiet pools, sit along a central lake. There's plenty of grass, and little beaches with hammocks hung between the palm trees sprinkle the shore. At the central pool, an open-air slide zooms down a Maya pyramid. Disney-provided transportation is by bus only.

Disney's Port Orleans French Quarter and Riverside Resorts (☎ 407-934-5000; Downtown Disney; 🖳 🛋) Lush Savannah-esque gardens and a jubilant Mardi Gras motif blend to create a Louisiana feel. These sister resorts, combined to create one of the largest at Walt Disney World, offer plenty of activities. There's a pool with a sea-serpent waterslide, several quiet pools, boat rental, fishing and evening horse-drawn-carriage rides. The simple rooms, some with rough-hewn beds, are showing their age; request one without a parking lot view. A boat shuttles guests between the two resorts (or it's a 15-minute walk) and to Downtown Disney, but it's an inconvenient bus ride to the parks.

Deluxe

While these upscale themed resorts are the best Disney has to offer, don't expect the same bang for your buck as you'd get elsewhere. They do, however, offer a wide array of services and room configurations (many with bunk-bed options), upscale restaurants, children's programs and incredibly easy access to at least one theme park. Epcot resorts offer easy walking access and boat transport to restaurants and entertainment at Disney's Boardwalk (p311) and Hollywood Studios. Rates for a double room range roughly from $250 to $500 during value season and from $350 to $650 during peak season. Add upwards of $100 for a suite.

Disney's Wilderness Lodge (☎ 407-824-3200; Magic Kingdom; 🖳 🛋) The handsome lobby's low-lit tepee chandeliers, hand-carved totem pole and dramatic 80ft fireplace echo national-park lodges of America's ole West. Though it's meant to feel as if you're in John Muir country, with its wooded surrounds and hidden lagoon-side location, the fake geyser and singing waiters in the lobby restaurant dispel the illusion mighty quick. Transportation is by boat.

Disney's Animal Kingdom Lodge (☎ 407-938-3000; Animal Kingdom; 🖳 🐾) Abutting the African Safari section of Animal Kingdom, an on-site 33-acre savannah parades a who's who of Noah's Ark past hotel windows and balconies. With park rangers standing ready to answer questions about the wildlife, a distinctly tribal decor and African-inspired food served at the recommended restaurants, this resort succeeds better than any other in creating a themed environment. Ask about intimate guided tours through the animal park and storytelling around the fire. Disney-provided transportation is by bus only.

Disney's Contemporary Resort (☎ 407-824-1000; Magic Kingdom; 🖳 🐾) The granddaddy of Disney resorts, the Contemporary's futuristic A-frame carries smoothly into the 21st century. Balcony rooms front Magic Kingdom, and an excellent top-floor restaurant lures folks with its excellent views of Disney's fireworks. Streamlined rooms with a decidedly modern vibe are some of the nicest in the park. Transportation is by boat and monorail.

Disney's Polynesian Resort (☎ 407-824-2000; Magic Kingdom; 🖳 🐾) With faux-bamboo decor, a jungle motif in the lobby, and coconut-shell cups and shell necklaces in the store, you may think you're in the South Pacific. The rounded lagoon-side pool features a slide, a zero entrance perfect for little ones and an excellent view of Cinderella's Castle. Transportation is by boat and monorail.

Disney's Yacht Club Resort and Disney's Beach Club Resort (Epcot; 🖳 🐾); Yacht Club (☎ 407-934-7000); Beach Club (☎ 407-934-8000) These handsome sister resorts, pleasantly located along the water, strive for old New England beachside charm. The pools earn rave reviews, but we found them cramped and in need of a face-lift. The resorts are accessible by boat and on foot.

Disney's Old Key West Resort (☎ 407-827-1198; Downtown Disney; 🖳 🐾) Victoriana oozes from every gingerbread-accented corner, palm-tree enclave and the azure-blue waters. This is an 'all villa' resort, meaning accommodation ranges from studio suites with a kitchenette that sleep four ($285-410), to 2375ft three-bedroom villas ($1170-1645). Transportation is by boat.

our pick Disney's Boardwalk Inn (☎ 407-939-5100; Epcot; 🖳 🐾) Located on the shores of Crescent Lake, this resort embodies the seaside charm of Atlantic City in its heyday, with a water-front the color of saltwater taffy, tandem bicycles with candy-striped awnings, and a splintery boardwalk that circles the entire resort. The lovely lobby features sea-green walls, hardwood floors and soft floral vintage seating areas. Elegant rooms have terraces or balconies. The resort is divided into two sections, the Inn and the Villas; the Inn, with cute picket-fenced suites, quiet pools and plenty of grass, is far nicer and subdued. The resort is accessible by boat and on foot.

Disney's Grand Floridian Resort & Spa (☎ 407-824-3000; Magic Kingdom; 🖳 🐾) Just one easy monorail stop from Magic Kingdom, the Grand Floridian rides on its reputation as the grandest, most elegant property in Disney World. The four-story lobby, with a grand piano, formal seating areas, and huge flower arrangements, has all the accoutrements of Old Florida class and style, but at its heart this is Disney. Sparkling princesses ballroom-dance across the oriental rugs, exhausted children sit entranced by classic Disney cartoons and babies cry. Transportation is by boat and monorail.

Walt Disney World Swan & Dolphin Resorts (Epcot; 🖳 🐾); Swan (☎ 407-934-3000); Dolphin (☎ 407-934-4000) These two hotels, which face each other on Disney property and share a gym and pool facilities, are actually owned by Sheraton. The cushy down feather beds at the Dolphin arguably offer the best night's sleep in town, and there's a full-size lap pool along the lagoon. Character breakfasts and other Disney perks are available at both. The resorts are accessible by boat and on foot.

Disney's Saratoga Springs Resort & Spa (☎ 407-934-7639; Downtown Disney; 🖳 🐾) Set on 16 acres and modeled on an upstate New York resort spa, this grassy complex of three- and four-story units attracts families looking for plenty of space. Studio, one- and two-bedroom villas surround a family-friendly zero-entry pool complete with a Donald Duck fountain play area, a pool that winds through boulders and tiny-tot slide. Boats run regularly to Downtown Disney, but you have to take a bus to all the parks.

Disney Vacation Club
Disney Vacation Club is Disney's version of a timeshare, and many of the properties above participate in the program. Go to www.disneyvacationclub.com for details.

Other
In a category all its own, **Shades of Green Resort** (☎ 407-824-3600; Magic Kingdom; r & ste $90-275; 🖳 🐾)

sits within Walt Disney World but is owned by the Armed Forces Recreation Center. Only active and retired members of the US Armed Services (including members of the National Guard) and their widows and widowers can stay here, and rates are determined according to rank. It has simple, spacious rooms, tennis courts and two pleasant pools surrounded by greenery. and is flanked by two golf courses. Disney-provided transportation is by bus only.

LAKE BUENA VISTA

These hotels are conveniently located just outside the entrance to Walt Disney World's northern entrance and minutes from Downtown Disney. Most offer complimentary and scheduled transportation to the parks. Motels on Palm Parkway sit on a quiet stretch with plenty of palm trees and grass, and are equidistant to Walt Disney World and SeaWorld. Also try the recommended **Courtyard by Marriott** (Map pp292-3 ☎ 407-239-6900; www.marriott.com; 8501 Palm Pkwy; r & ste $109-250; 🖳 🖭); **Hampton Inn** (Map p270; ☎ 407-465-8150; www.hamptoninn.com; 8150 Palm Pkwy; r & ste $105-260; 🖳 🖭); and **Quality Suites Lake Buena Vista** (Map p270; ☎ 407-465-8200; www.qualityinn.com; ste $140-225; 8200 Palm Pkwy; 🖳 🖭).

Midrange

our pick Perri House (Map pp292-3; ☎ 407-876-4830, 800-780-4830; www.perrihouse.com; 10417 Vista Oaks Court, Lake Buena Vista; r & ste $109-140; 🖳 🖭) No bellmen or room service, no organized children's games or winding slides into the pool, no pink cocktails with umbrellas or sushi in the lobby. Just a one-story house, with eight simple rooms that each open onto the grass and trees of the yard, boxes of cereal on the counter of the community kitchen, shelves of videos to watch in your room and a small pool in the back. Quiet, easy, personal and friendly, this charmingly informal bed and breakfast is like a home away from home and a welcomed change from the fancy resorts, boring chain motels and Botox-theme hotels that define accommodation in Orlando. Relax, make yourself comfortable, and help yourself to a peanut-butter-and-jelly sandwich while you do your laundry and the kids play in the yard. It's located about 3 miles from Downtown Disney and 5 miles from Magic Kingdom, and is an easy drive to both SeaWorld and Universal Orlando. But when you're sitting on

your patio, looking out at the fields and woods beyond and listening to the birds, you'd swear you were hours away from it all. The rooms with king-sized beds are the nicest; two rooms can accommodate a family of five, and a separate house ($229-250) sleeps six.

Hawthorn Suites Lake Buena Vista (Map pp292-3; ☎ 407-597-5000, 866-756-3778; www.hawthornlake buenavista.com; 8303 Palm Pkwy; ste $100-210; 🖳 🖭) Every suite includes a full kitchen, and the comfy beds don't have those cheesy polyester blankets. There's a small pool, a basketball court, and a complimentary beer and wine reception Monday through Thursday. Steps up from a standard chain motel.

Sheraton Safari Hotel (Map pp292-3; ☎ 407-239-0444; www.sheratonsafari.com; 12205 S Apopka Vineland Rd; r & ste $109-289; 🖳 🖭) The jungle motif here extends to the zebra-printed bed quilts. Nothing special, but a solid and reasonable option that won't disappoint.

Top End

Hyatt Regency Grand Cypress Resort (Map pp292-3; ☎ 407-239-1234, 800-233-1234; www.hyattgrandcypress .com; 1 Grand Cypress Blvd; r $169-350; 🖳 🖭) The villas here are some of the nicest accommodations in Orlando. Considering the proximity to Disney (just outside the gates) and SeaWorld,

---

BEST HOTEL POOLS

- **Portofino Bay Hotel** (p320) There's a pool with bells and whistles for kids and one surrounded by grass and palm for quiet.

- **Hyatt Regency Grand Cypress** (above) Two pools, each with a water slide, connected by a cavernous grotto.

- **JW Marriott Orlando, Grande Lakes** (p278) Looping lazy river pleasantly located with views of the golf course, and complimentary access to the pool at the Ritz.

- **Disney's Coronado Springs** (p312) Family pool with waterslide through Maya ruins as well as several discreet and quiet pools scattered throughout the grounds.

- **Peabody Orlando** (p278) A quiet rooftop pool with a canopied eating area and balmy breezes.

and the quality of the rooms, the service, the grounds and the amenities, this is one of the better-value top-end resorts in Orlando.

Eating & Drinking

While it's difficult to find a decent meal at Disney – and you certainly won't find it at the hotel cafeteria – there are a few standouts. See individual theme parks for eating within the park gates and the boxed text Meeting Characters (p296) for character meals. Call ☎ 407-939-3463 for priority seating up to 180 days in advance. Even if you're not sure of your plans, make reservations as far in advance as possible. You can usually cancel – see p291 for information about canceling pre-booked dining plans.

BOARDWALK

The walk-up bakery here serves up tasty coffee, doughnuts and cute lil' Mickey Mouse cakes.

Midrange

Big River Grille & Brewing Co (Map pp292-3; ☎ 407-560-0253; mains $10-25; 11:30am-11pm) Open-air microbrewery with outdoor seating offers hearty burgers, salads and simple North American fare. Try the Rocket Red Ale with your meat loaf.

Spoodles (Map pp292-3; ☎ 407-939-3463; mains $14-23; 7:30am-11am & 5pm-10pm) Grab a slice from the walk-up pizza window or settle in to the high-ceilinged dining room for Mediterranean-inspired cuisine like hummus, lamb kebabs and house-made gelato. For breakfast, try the fire-roasted vegetable and feta cheese frittata or the challah-bread French toast.

Top End

Flying Fish (Map pp292-3; ☎ 407-939-2359; mains $26-36; dinner) One of the best restaurants in Walt Disney World, this modern eatery along the water offers creative and deliciously fresh seafood as well as a handful of vegetarian and hearty meat dishes. The changing menu incorporates seasonal ingredients. Call in advance to arrange special dietary accommodations.

DOWNTOWN DISNEY

In the Marketplace, you'll find **Fulton's Crab House** (Map pp292-3; ☎ 407-939-3463; mains $22-40; 11:30am-3:30pm & 4-11pm) serving decent seafood on a replica paddleboat; the ever popular **Rainforest Café** (Map pp292-3; ☎ 407-827-8500; mains

$11-24; 11:30am-11pm, to 12pm Fri & Sat); **Ghiradelli Soda Fountain and Chocolate Shop** (Map pp292-3; ☎ 407-934-8855; 9:30am-11:30pm, to 12pm Fri & Sat) with Disney's best coffee, yummy ice cream and decadent concoctions involving entire chocolate bars blended into milkshakes. For surprisingly good toasted sandwiches, one of the better lunches at Disney, try **Earl of Sandwich** (Map pp292-3; sandwiches $5-8; 7:30am-10pm).

DISNEY HOTELS
Midrange

Citrico's (Map pp292-3; ☎ 407-939-3463, Disney's Grand Floridian Resort & Spa; mains $14-29; dinner) An extensive wine list and a northern California ambience sets this low-key spot apart from other Disney restaurants; it falls between the hectic family-style and the self-consciously upscale options, and serves up tasty and fresh eclectic North American fare.

Kona Café (Map pp292-3; ☎ 407-939-3463; Disney's Polynesian Resort; mains $16-25; 7:30-11:15am, lunch, dinner) An intimate South Pacific café offers pomegranate barbecue, coconut almond chicken and macadamia-crusted mahimahi. Ceiling fans and a carpet designed with huge Hawaiian flowers complete the Pacific Islands decor.

our pick 'OHana (Map pp292-3; ☎ 407-939-3463; Disney's Polynesian Resort; mains $15-30; character breakfast 7:30am-11am, 5pm-10pm) The Polynesian's signature restaurant evokes a South Pacific feel with rock-art graphics of lizards, octopuses, and other animals on the ceiling, a huge oak-burning grill cooking up massive kebabs of meat, and demonstrations of hula and limbo dancing, coconut racing and other Polynesian-themed shenanigans. Kids jump from their seats to join in the fun. The only thing on the menu is the all-you-can-eat family-style kebabs and veggies, slid off skewers directly onto the giant woklike platters on the table. Sit at the corner for views of Cinderella's Castle.

Boma (Map pp292-3; ☎ 407-939-3463; Disney's Animal Kingdom Lodge; buffet adult/child breakfast $17/10, dinner $27/13 7:30-11am & 4:30-10pm) Several steps above Disney's usual buffet options, this African-inspired eatery offers wood-roasted meats, interesting soups like coconut curried chicken and plenty of salads. Handsomely furnished with dark woods, decorated with African art and tapestries, and enclosed on one side with plate-glass windows overlooking the garden, Boma offers not only good food but unusually calming and pleasant surrounds.

Top End

California Grill (Map pp292-3; ☎ 407-939-3463, Disney's Contemporary Resort; mains $15-38; ⏰ dinner) Earning consistent rave reviews from locals and repeat Disney guests, the rooftop California Grill offers everything from quirky sushi like the Double Crunch Rainbow Roll or Snake in the Grass to chicken and dumplings; from triple-cheese flatbread to spinach ravioli. The kid's menu is blessedly chicken-nugget free. Window views for Magic Kingdom's fireworks are the most coveted seats at Walt Disney World.

Narcoossees (Map pp292-3; ☎ 407-939-3463; Disney's Grand Floridian Resort & Spa; mains $19-37; ⏰ dinner) On the shores of the Seven Seas Lagoon and an easy boat ride from Magic Kingdom, this muted dining room offers a pleasant respite from the theme-park mayhem. Expect primarily seafood options, though there's also duck, filet mignon and free-range chicken.

Artist Point (Map pp292-3; ☎ 407-939-3463; Disney's Wilderness Lodge; mains $21-43 ⏰ dinner) US Arts and Crafts decor and expertly prepared dishes with a hint of the American West.

ourpick Jiko (Map pp292-3; ☎ 407-939-3463, Disney's Animal Kingdom Lodge; mains $24-35; ⏰ dinner) Excellent food, with plenty of grains, vegetables and creative twists, a tiny bar and rich African surrounds make this low-key spot one of our favorites at Disney. For a less expensive option, enjoy an appetizer (the Taste of Africa features various dips and crackers) at the bar.

Blue Zoo (Map pp292-3; ☎ 407-934-1111; Walt Disney World Dolphin Resort; mains $28-34; ⏰ dinner) Floor-to-ceiling silver threads shimmer in columns at this flashy blue-infused seafood hotspot.

Victoria and Albert's (Map pp292-3; ☎ 407-939-3463, Disney's Grand Floridian Resort & Spa; prix fixe per person $125; ⏰ dinner) When Disney announced that children under 10 would no longer be allowed

ORLANDO THEME PARK ATTRACTIONS GUIDE

Attraction	What It's Like	Tips & Tricks	Location	Page
Caro-Seuss-El	Horton and the Grinch, Thing One and Thing Two, around and around	Allow time for several rounds: little ones will want to try all their favorites	Universal Orlando's Islands of Adventure	p326
Believe	Whale show spectacular starring Shamu	Arrive 45 minutes before the show – Seats fill quickly	SeaWorld	p330
Dreams Come True Parade	Quintessential Disney parade featuring classic characters and elaborate floats	Sit on the curb along Main Street to enjoy the wide street and the Cinderella Castle backdrop	Disney's Magic Kingdom	p300
Dudley Do-Right's Ripsaw Falls	Water ride with a crashing descent	Be prepared to get soaked	Universal Orlando's Islands of Adventure	p325
Expedition Everest – Legend of the Forbidden Mountain	Roller coaster with a Nepalese twist	Take advantage of FastPass	Disney's Animal Kingdom	p308
Finding Nemo – the Musical	Most sophisticated performance in the park – would be at home on Broadway	Don't miss – check show times when entering the park	Disney's Animal Kingdom	p309
Incredible Hulk	A hulkin' roller coaster inspires screams heard around the park	Head here first thing	Universal Orlando's Islands of Adventure	p325
It's a Small World	Sweet and gentle float through the continents; a Disney classic	Perfect break for little ones fed up with the heat and lines	Disney's Magic Kingdom	p298
Kilimanjaro Safaris	See lions, giraffes and elephants on African safari	Not worth the wait if lines are long; use a FastPass	Disney's Animal Kingdom	p308

at this crème de la crème of Orlando's dining scene, headlines roared with news of Disney's ban on children and the internet gaggle was nothing short of horrified indignation. But with almost 100 other restaurants to choose from, families should have no problem finding alternatives to this three-hour, seven-course meal (wine pairing costs an additional $60). Indulge yourself with exquisite food and top-notch (if self-conscious) service in the Victorian-inspired decor of earthy creams. Along with Cinderella's Table (p296), this place books up months in advance; make reservations the morning of the 180th day before you want to dine!

Entertainment

Disney offers three dinner theaters. At the South Pacific styled **Spirit of Aloha** (Disney's Polynesian Resort; adult $53-62, child 3-9 $27-32), there's lots of yelling and pounding on drums while hula-clad men and women leap around the stage, dance and play with fire. With vaguely western-themed costumes and decor, corny jokes, dancing, and music like 'Hokey Pokey' and 'My Darling Clementine', the **Hoop-Dee-Doo Revue** (Disney's Fort Wilderness Resort; adult $52-61, child 3-9 $27-40) is an incredibly popular goofy show. Despite three shows nightly, it's difficult to get a reservation. The third dinner theater is the character meal **Mickey's Backyard Barbecue** (p296). Call ☎ 407-824-1593 or ☎ 407-939-3463 for reservations up to six months in advance.

Disney's best live show is **Le Cirque du Soleil La Nouba** (☎ 407-939-7600; Downtown Disney's West Side; www.cirquedusoleil.com; adult $59-87, child 3-9 $44-65; ☻ 6pm & 9pm Tue-Sat), featuring absolutely mind-boggling acrobatic feats expertly fused to light, stage and costume design to create a cohesive

Attraction	What It's Like	Tips & Tricks	Location	Page
Kraken	Loop-dee-loop coaster with big-time thrills	Go immediately upon arrival as lines get long	SeaWorld	p329
Mickey's Philhar Magic	3-D movie with Donald Duck popping through classic Disney films	Nothing scary for kids makes this best 3-D for all ages	Disney's Magic Kingdom	p298
Revenge of the Mummy	Indoor roller coaster past mummies	Thrills and special effects combine for a high scare factor	Universal Orlando's Universal Studios	p323
Soarin'	Gently hang glide over California's coast, cities, orange groves and golf courses	Request a front row seat to avoid dangling feet in the periphery of your view	Disney's Epcot	p304
The Dueling Dragons	Double coaster	Ride the fire coaster for bigger thrills	Universal Orlando's Islands of Adventure	p326
Space Mountain	Disney's classic roller coaster	Expect a scary creature around the corner	Disney's Magic Kingdom	p299
The Mystic Fountain	Talking fountain banters with folks and sprays 'em with water	Look for people talking to a fountain, as there's no line or sign	Universal Orlando's Islands of Adventure	p326
Turtle Talk With Crush	Intimate interactive attraction featuring *Finding Nemo*'s most famous dude	Funny, sweet and air-conditioned	Disney's Epcot	p304
Twilight Zone Tower of Terror	Sit in dark elevator that unexpectedly plummets	If a child is scared during the pre-ride narrative, leave	Disney's Hollywood Studios	p302
Twister…Ride It Out	Stand on a small-town movie set as tornado whips closer and closer	Too scary for anyone with an existing fear of tornados	Universal Orlando's Universal Studios	p322

ORLANDO & WALT DISNEY WORLD

artistic vision. And of course, there's a silly Disney twist involving a princess and a frog.

For live music, clubs and bars, see Downtown Disney (p310) and Disney's Boardwalk (p311).

Shopping

While there are endless stores throughout Walt Disney World, don't expect to find the same things in all the parks and resorts. Most stores are thematically oriented, so after the Star Wars ride you'll find lots of Star Wars stuff, after the Winnie the Pooh ride you'll find lots of Winnie the Pooh stuff, and after the Indiana Jones ride you'll find, well, an Indiana Jones hat, of course.

At **Downtown Disney** (p310) there's the massive **World of Disney** (☎ 407-363-6200; Marketplace; ⊙ 9:30am-11pm) with any Disney product you could possibly want, the two-storied **Virgin Megastore** (☎ 407-828-0222; West Side; ⊙ 10:30am-11pm), filled with DVDs, books and CDs, and all kinds of shops selling everything from cigars to magnets. Check out the amazing life-size Lego creations and create your own masterpieces outside **LEGO Imagination Center** (☎ 407-828-0065; Marketplace; ⊙ 9:30am-11pm); inside, you'll find all things Lego, including a wall of individually priced Lego pieces. Next door, kids can design a personalized My Little Pony and create their own tiara at **Once Upon a Toy** (Marketplace; ⊙ 9:30am-11pm). Fairy godmothers at the **Bibbidee Bobbidee Boutique** (☎ 407-939-7895; Cinderella's Castle, Magic Kingdom & Marketplace, Downtown Disney) finalize your kid's transformation from shorts and T-shirt to bedazzling princess with fanciful hairstyling and makeup. Girls three and older can choose from the coach package (hair and makeup, $46), the crown package (hair, makeup and nails $50) or the Castle package (hair, makeup, nails, costume and photograph, $180). For just a plain ole hair cut, perhaps with some spiky green hair or a pink updo and Disney sequins ($10-20) go to the **Harmony Barber Shop** on Main Street, just as you walk into the Magic Kingdom.

Head to **Epcot's World Showcase** (p305) for an international twist to your Disney souvenir. Buy a belly-dancer kit (including a scarf, a hat, a CD and finger cymbals) in Morocco, tartan shawls and Mickey Mouse Shortbread cookies in the United Kingdom, and a pink be-jeweled wine stopper in France. Japan has a store filled with Hello Kitty stuff, and in Germany you can buy Steiff animals and make your own doll. The wine shop in France offers a pretty extensive selection; with three hours' notice they will have your bottles waiting for you to pick up at the park exit.

Note that if you are staying at a Disney hotel, shops throughout the park will send your purchases directly to your hotel at no extra charge. Just ask.

GETTING THERE & AROUND

If you're flying in to Orlando International Airport and staying at a Disney resort, and have no urge to visit Orlando or the surrounding area, you don't need to rent a car. Arrange in advance complimentary luxury bus transportation to and from the airport through **Magical Express Service** (☎ 866-599-0951). If you transfer from one Disney hotel to another in the middle of your stay, the resort will transfer your luggage while you're off for the day.

From Orlando's Lynx Central Station you can catch buses to the Disney parks, but it's a long ride. If driving, take the I-4 to well-signed exits 64, 65 or 67. At the **Disney Car Care Center** (Map pp292-3; ☎ 407-824-0976; 1000 W Car Care Drive; ⊙ 7am-7pm Mon-Fri, to 4pm Sat) there is a full-service garage and an Alamo car-rental desk. A second Alamo desk is inside the Walt Disney World Dolphin Resort (Map pp292-3).

The Disney transportation system utilizes boats, buses and a monorail to shuttle folks to hotels, theme parks and other attractions within the resort. The **Transportation and Ticket Center** (Map pp292-3) operates as the main hub of this system.

Monorail Loops between Magic Kingdom, Contemporary Resort, Grand Floridian Resort & Spa and Polynesian Resort. A second monorail route connects the Transportation & Ticket Center to Epcot.

Boat Loops between Contemporary Resort, Grand Floridian Resort & Spa, Polynesian Resort and Magic Kingdom. A second route connects Magic Kingdom to Fort Wilderness Resort & Campground and Wilderness Lodge. A third loop connects Epcot, Hollywood Studios, Boardwalk Inn & Villas Resort, Yacht Club and Beach Club Resorts, and Walt Disney World Swan and Dolphin Resorts. Ferryboats connect Magic Kingdom to the Transportation and Ticket Center.

Bus Most areas are accessible by bus (city-bus style) from other areas, including theme parks, water parks, Disney resorts and Downtown Disney. However, they do not provide direct service between all destinations so you may need to transfer. Magic Kingdom is not accessible by bus from the Grand Floridian Resort & Spa, Polynesian Resort or Contemporary Resort.

Note that it can take up to an hour to get from point A to point B using the Disney transportation system. Pick up a copy of the *Walt Disney World Transportation Guide/Map* at the resorts or from Guest Relations at the parks.

Taxicabs can usually be found at hotels, theme parks, Disney's Wide World of Sports and Downtown Disney. If you're stuck in lines for Disney's free shuttles, along with everyone else leaving the park after the fireworks, with tired kids holding melting ice cream and lugging the folded stroller, dinner leftovers and that Cinderella Castle play set, consider grabbing a cab. Piling into the air-conditioning and being home in minutes might just be worth that $10!

UNIVERSAL ORLANDO RESORT

Smaller, easier to navigate and pedestrian friendly, Universal Orlando is everything you wish Disney could be. Both resorts offer fantastic rides, excellent children's attractions and entertaining shows, but Universal does everything just a bit smarter, a bit funnier, a bit more smoothly. Instead of the seven dwarfs, there's the Simpsons. Instead of Donald Duck and Mickey Mouse, there's Spider-Man and Shrek. While Universal can never replace Disney, and it certainly lacks the sentimental charm of Snow White, Peter Pan and Winnie the Pooh, it offers pure, unabashed, adrenalin-pumped, full-speed-ahead fun for the entire family.

Universal's got spunk, it's got spirit, it's got attitude. And, like the class clown from junior high who is just too damned smart to take himself too seriously, Universal has a sense of humor about itself and you just can't help but laugh along with it.

Orientation

The Universal Orlando Resort consists of two theme parks – Islands of Adventure, with incredibly designed themed areas and the bulk of the thrill rides, and Universal Studios, with movie-based attractions and shows – one entertainment and dining district (CityWalk); and three deluxe resort hotels. All but one hotel are within an easy walking distance of the parks, and small wooden shuttle boats connect the entire resort.

Information

Contact **Universal Orlando Resort** (off Map p268; ☎ 407-224-4233, 407-363-8000; www.universalorlando .com; 1000 Universal Studios Plaza; ☺ 9am-varied) for ticket, theme park, dining and accommodation information. Ask for an **Official Studio Guide information packet**. For vacation packages, call ☎ 877-801-9720; for TDD, call ☎ 800-447-0672.

Pick up a free map and an *Attractions & Show Times* guide, with a schedule of events, show times and time and location of free character interactions, at each park entrance. You can rent single/double strollers ($12/16) and lockers ($5) at both parks.

See the boxed text What to Expect From the Parks (p288) for prices.

CHILD CARE

Nursing facilities and companion bathrooms are located at the Health Services and First Aid facilities in each park. A baby-bottle icon next to the select stores on the park map indicates which stores carry baby supplies (not on display). Gift shops at the resorts offer a wider selection.

Each resort has a drop-off child-care center, with DVDs, arts and crafts, organized activities and games for children aged four to 14 available to hotel guests only. Per hour prices vary and hours are limited. For private babysitting services, see p265.

TRAVELERS WITH DISABILITIES

The free *Rider Safety and Guests With Disabilities* guidebook is available at Guest Services, and includes attraction scripts and detailed ride requirements. See the park map for details on the wheelchair accessibility of each attraction. There are also sign language interpreting, closed captioning and assistive listening devices available at no extra charge, and large-print and Braille maps. TDD-equipped (Telecommunications Device for the Deaf) telephones are located throughout the park; an icon on the maps indicates location. Rent wheelchairs (per day $12) and Electric Convenience Vehicles (ECV; per day $40) at the entrance to each park.

EXPRESS PLUS

This pass allows you to avoid the lines at designated Express Plus rides (identified on the map and in this book) by flashing your pass at the separate Express Plus line. You can

ORLANDO & WALT DISNEY WORLD

go to any ride, any time you'd like. If you are staying at a Universal resort (right) you automatically receive an Express Plus pass; otherwise, a limited number of passes per day are available online or at the park gate. Prices vary according to season, but range from $26 to $60 for a one-day/two-park pass and from $20 to $46 for a one-day/one-park pass.

GUEST SERVICES

You will find a **Guest Services** (☎ 407-224-6350), with **Lost & Found** Universal Studios (☎ 407-224-4244); Islands of Adventure (☎ 407-224-4245), foreign language maps and brochures, a limited foreign-currency exchange and services for visitors with disabilities, at each park entrance. If you have any problems or questions, go here.

KENNELS

Day-boarding of pets is available at the Studio Kennel (☎ 407-224-9509; per pet per day $10) in the parking structure. You must provide food and occasionally return to walk your animal. The three Universal Orlando resorts welcome pets.

MEDICAL SERVICES

Each park has medical facilities; see park maps for locations. For area hospitals and clinics, see (p266).

PARKING

Parking is available inside a giant garage structure (car/RV $11/12); valet parking is $18.

Sights & Activities

Characters roaming the parks include Spider-Man, the Incredible Hulk, SpongeBob SquarePants, and characters from *The Simpsons, Madagascar* and Dr Seuss books.

The only character meal within the parks is Confisco Grille's **character breakfast** (☎ 407-224-4012; adult/child 3-10 $16/10; ☺ breakfast Thu-Sun) with Spider-Man and the Cat in the Hat. The three resorts offer **character dinners** (☎ 407-503-3463 for reservations up to 3 months in advance; ☺ dinner) with Scooby-Doo, Woody Woodpecker, Curious George, Shrek and others, on select nights.

In addition to the two theme parks and the entertainment complex detailed below, Universal Orlando offers **Golf Universal Orlando** (☎ 407-503-3097), which includes preferred tee times, complimentary transportation and club rental arrangements at several of Orlando's golf courses.

Tours

The **VIP Tour** (☎ 407-363-8295; $100-150) includes a personal escort through the park, priority entrance to rides and shows, and valet parking.

Festivals & Events

During the Christmas holiday season, Islands of Adventure hosts **Grinchmas**, featuring a live musical production of *How the Grinch Stole Christmas,* and Universal Studios hosts the **Macy's Holiday Parade**. See website for other events.

Sleeping

Universal Orlando boasts three excellent resorts. Generally less expensive than Disney's deluxe accommodation, they offer far superior service, food, decor, amenities and rooms. The *New York Times* is delivered to your door, the coffee has kick, and the spacious bathrooms offer luxurious towels and upscale toiletries. It's also a pleasant gardened walk or a quiet boat ride to the parks, kids get a free gift at check-in and the Loews Loves Pets program welcomes Fido as a VIP (Very Important Pet). Ask about kids' suites, including the new Jurassic Park–themed suites at Royal Pacific. For reservations and package deals, call ☎ 888-273-1311.

Royal Pacific Resort (Map p270; ☎ 407-503-3000; 6300 Hollywood Way; r & ste $300-600; ☐ ☒) The glass-enclosed Orchid Court, with its reflecting pool, Balinese fountains and carved stone elephants splashing in the water, sits at the center of the airy lobby at this friendly South Pacific–inspired resort. The grounds are lovely, with lots of grass, tropical plantings, flowers, bamboo and palm trees, and the on-site restaurants are excellent (see opposite). Unfortunately, the over-the-top, family-friendly pool, with an interactive play area, real sand, volleyball, shuffleboard and ping pong, is loud, chaotic and unsupervised.

Hard Rock Hotel (Map p270; ☎ 407-503-2000; 5800 Universal Blvd; r & ste $270-450; ☐ ☒) This place embodies the pure essence of rock and roll, from the shocking black-and-white bathrooms to the pumped-in underwater music in the pool and the lavish Graceland suite outfitted for the King himself. Families mingle harmoniously alongside a young party crowd, and there's even Camp Lil' Rock for your lil' rockers. Keep in mind that a loud live band could be playing in the lobby.

Portofino Bay Resort (Map p270; ☎ 407-503-1000; 5601 Universal Blvd; r & ste $345-600; ☐ ☒)

Sumptuous and elegant, with cobblestone streets and goose-down duvets, plenty of pillows and chenille throws in the earth-toned rooms, and sidewalk cafés around a central lagoon, this resort evokes the charm of seaside Italy. There are three pools, including a family pool and two quiet pools surrounded by grass, palm trees and a peaceful bocce court, the outstanding Mandara Spa (p333) and supervised children's activities.

Eating

Universal Orlando offers the all-you-can-eat **Universal Meal Deal** (adult/child under 9, one park/one day $20/10; two parks/one day $24/12), which allows you to eat as much as you'd like from participating restaurants at Islands of Adventure and Universal Studios. It's good only from lunch through dinner. See p296 for details on character meals and p327 for eating at Universal Orlando's shopping and entertainment district.

PARKS

In the parks themselves, the only sit-down restaurants that take reservations are Mythos Restaurant (p327) and Confisco Grille (p327) at Islands of Adventure and Finnegan's Bar and Grill (p324) and Lombard's Seafood Grille (p324) at Universal Studios. Call ☎ 407-224-9255 for reservations. Otherwise, there are several cafeteria-style options and snacks. Details are listed under the individual theme parks.

RESORTS

Each of the three resorts offers a range of restaurant options, and the food is surprisingly good at most of them.

Emack and Bolio's Marketplace (Map p270; Hard Rock Hotel; ice cream $3-8; ⏱ 6:30am-11pm) Originally from Boston, Emack and Bolio ice cream beats all the rest hands down. And of course, only at this bastion of rock and roll will you find Bye Bye Miss American Mud Pie.

Orchid Court Sushi Bar (Map p270; ☎ 407-503-3000; Royal Pacific Resort; sushi $4-8, mains $12-20; ⏱ lunch, dinner) Sip on a Cherry Blossom Saketini over first-rate sushi and sashimi. Located within the light and airy glass-enclosed lobby of the hotel, with cushioned couches and chairs for seating, this informal restaurant makes a great place to relax and people-watch.

Emeril's Tchoup Chop (Map p270; ☎ 407-503-2467; Royal Pacific Resort; mains $15-30; ⏱ lunch, dinner Mon

& Wed-Sun, dinner Tue) Excellent island-inspired food, including plenty of seafood and Asian accents, prepared with the freshest ingredients. Unfortunately, the service is painfully slow.

Entertainment

At the biweekly **Wantilan Luaua** (Map p270; ☎ 407-503-3463; Royal Pacific Resort; adult/child under 12 $52/29), fire dancers and Pacific Island dancers shimmer and shake on stage while guests enjoy a tasty buffet of roast suckling pig, guava barbecued short ribs and other Polynesian-influenced fare. The Maori warrior's roar can be rather scary and that fire might be a bit close for comfort in the eyes of little ones, but there's a pleasant grassy area next to the open-air dining theater where kids can putz about. The atmosphere is wonderfully casual and, like everything at Universal Orlando, this is simple unabashed silliness and fun. Audience members are cajoled on stage to strut their stuff, and the service is warm and friendly. Unlimited Mai Tais, beer and wine are included in the price.

Also see CityWalk (p327).

Getting There & Around

From the I-4, take exit 74B or 75A and follow the signs. From International Drive, turn west at Wet 'n' Wild onto Universal Blvd.

Water taxis, which leave each point about every 20 minutes, shuttle regularly between the resort and CityWalk, just outside the gates of the parks. Service begins at 8:30am and ends at 2:30am. Hard Rock Hotel and Portofino Bay are accessible by pedestrian walkways from CityWalk.

There is complimentary shuttle service to SeaWorld and Wet 'n' Wild for resort hotel guests. **Mears Shuttles** (☎ 407-423-5566; round-trip to Walt Disney World per person $16) can be arranged at least one day in advance for transport to and from Walt Disney World. See p261 for information on airport shuttles.

UNIVERSAL STUDIOS

This park is also a working movie studio, and it incorporates that theme into the park, from elaborate New York and San Francisco backdrops to motion-simulator rides and audience-participation shows. The silver screen inspired the majority of the rides here, including what may be Orlando's best roller coaster, Revenge of the Mummy, but adrenaline junkies should seek out the park's wilder sibling, Islands of Adventure (p324) for the thrill rides.

Orientation & Information

Less clearly defined by theme than other Orlando parks, Universal Studios consists of several geographical regions (eg New York and Hollywood) defined by region-specific architecture and ambience. Because many of the attractions here are live shows, be sure to check the *Attraction & Show Times Guide* as soon as you arrive. It's difficult to coordinate times so that you can cover it all in one day.

Attractions

PRODUCTION CENTRAL

Hollywood Rip, Ride, Rockit (Express Plus)

Scheduled to open in spring 2009, this multi-sensory roller coaster combines the thrill of the roller coaster with 21st-century special effects and Universal's trademark commitment to the interactive experience. You'll Rip up to 65mph, Ride 17 stories above the theme park and around a record-breaking loop-dee-loop, and Rockit to customized music (chosen before you strap in). At the time of research, this ride had not yet opened.

Jimmy Neutron's Nicktoon Blast (Express Plus)

The first part is a demonstration of Jimmy's newest rocket invention – one that lets the audience see what's happening elsewhere in the park. The second part is a motion simulator starring SpongeBob SquarePants, Rugrats, the Fairly OddParents and Arnold.

Shrek 4-D (Express)

This movie picks up where the movie *Shrek* left off, and it sends you zipping along with Shrek and Donkey in a desperate effort to save Princess Fiona from a fierce dragon. And that dragon is indeed fierce – it pops out at you from the screen with red eyes, spitting fire into your face. The dragon sneezes and you feel it, and your chair rocks when Shrek and the donkey chase the dragon. It's a lot of fun, but little ones will be scared.

HOLLYWOOD

Universal Horror Make-Up Show (Express Plus)

This attraction delivers, though if you're really into horror makeup it may be a little too short. It's humorous, full of silly antics and not really all that gross, although some optical illusions are performed that could freak out small children if they're not really clear from the get-go that it's not real.

Terminator 2: 3-D Battle Across Time (Express Plus)

CyberDyne headquarters showcases the creepy future of technology here, including fully operational examples of their brand-new, heavily armed cybernetic soldiers. Watch their informative presentation – oh wait – the signal's been interrupted! Linda Hamilton and Arnold Schwarzenegger, in glorious 3-D, want you out of the building now! It's not gory, but it's very loud and might be sensory overload for some children.

Lucy – A Tribute

Fans of the famous redhead Lucille Ball will particularly enjoy this biographical exhibit. Clips, costumes, photos and Lucy's letters are displayed, and there is a tough trivia quiz at the end.

NEW YORK

Twister...Ride It Out (Express Plus)

Just waiting in line for this ride is enough to frighten kids. Several TV screens show film clips from the movie *Twister*, including a child screaming as a tornado makes its way toward her home. Bill Paxton and Helen Hunt, the stars of the movie, talk in grave tones about the dangers of tornados and the perils of working on the film set, and they warn that this attraction will take you into the horror of their film-making experience. The attraction itself takes folks into a film set of a rather dilapidated, old-fashioned Midwest America town. There's a drive-in theater and an old gas station. A radio announces a severe storm warning, and slowly you see and feel the storm approach. A tornado develops in the distant sky, and it's coming, closer and closer, louder and louder...

Anyone who has felt the fear of living through a real tornado, or children who already wake up scared of them thanks to sirens, hours in the basement and the eerie blanket of tornado-breeding green skies, should seriously think twice before going to this attraction.

The Blues Brothers

Jake and Elwood sing and dance the blues on Delancy Street in New York City.

Revenge of the Mummy (Express Plus)

Delve into ancient Egyptian catacombs in near pitch black – whatever you do, don't anger Imhotep the mummy or…well, too late for that. Incur his wrath as he flings you past fire, water and more in-your-face special effects, making for one of the best thrilling coaster rides in Orlando. Watch out for those bugs and the twist at the end.

WOODY WOODPECKER'S KIDZONE

Animal Actors on Location! (Express Plus)

Live animals and their trainers, including a particularly spunky orangutan, engage in all kinds of silly shenanigans. Kids adore it.

A Day in the Park with Barney (Express Plus)

The intimate 360° theater, simple set design and gentle special effects make this Barney and friends sing-along show particularly special for tots. When they sing 'If All of the Raindrops Were Lemonade and Gumdrops' a slight mist drifts over the audience and during 'I Love You' mobiles with heart-shaped balloons hanging from them descend from the ceiling. It's a fun performance that splendidly follows the spirit and tone of the popular TV show.

Afterward everyone emerges for hugs and photos in **Barney's Backyard**, a great play area with pint-sized slides and plenty of climbing and crawling opportunities.

Curious George Goes to Town

A themed water-play area geared toward two- to five-year-olds. Children follow the poor misguided monkey's footsteps painted on the ground…as Curious George gets into more and more trouble, you get wetter and wetter. Of course, you don't have to play here in any particular order – there's plenty of opportunity to just splash around, but beware of the massive bucket of water that tips over regularly. It's enough to knock a little one right down!

Woody Woodpecker's Nuthouse Coaster (Express Plus)

This perfect starter coaster for future thrill seekers is good for everyone as it's not very fast and there are no scary special effects. Kids must be at least three years old and 36in tall.

Fievel's Playland

This kids' play area was inspired by the cartoon *An American Tail,* about a family of Russian mice that emigrates to the US. Climb and slide all over giant 'garbage' that really does give you a mouse's-eye view, toot down a small water slide with an inflatable boat, and crawl through tunnels.

ET Adventure (Express Plus)

There's a problem on ET's planet, and he's counting on you to get him back to help. Board a bike and ride through the woods, the police in hot pursuit, before rising safely into the sky and floating over the city and through outer space to ET's home planet. Here you'll find a magical, fanciful place of bright flowers and adorable ET creatures. There are a couple of spooky spots on this ride, including loud noises and steam, but like so much at Universal Orlando and Walt Disney World, it's the special effects and narrative premise more than spins, speeds and plummets that can be frightening for children.

SAN FRANCISCO/AMITY

Beetlejuice's Rock 'n' Roll Graveyard Revue (Express Plus)

Beetlejuice, the Werewolf, Dracula, Frankenstein and his Bride rock out in this unbelievably corny show. This is one of those rare cases, however, when it's so corny that it's somehow enjoyable. Be prepared for lots of booger jokes and spooky characters, and it's exceptionally loud.

Disaster (Express Plus)

The premise of this attraction is that you are the cast of a disaster movie entitled *Mutha Nature*. A fast-talking Hollywood casting agent chooses a handful of folks from the audience, gives the actors directions ('give me terror like Britney Spears is your babysitter'), and each volunteer is filmed for a second or so. Everyone then heads to the 'set' and boards

---

EAST GREEN

A fenced-in grassy area with shade trees, flowers and views across the lagoon sits just across from the entrance to Woody Woodpecker's Kidzone. Spread a picnic blanket for lunch, or simply chill-out for some down time. It makes an excellent meeting spot, and is a pleasant and quiet place to nurse an infant. The park map shows the park but does not label it.

a subway train in the incredibly authentic replica of a San Francisco BART (Bay Area Rapid Transit) station. Suddenly, the big one hits: tracks buckle, the place crumbles and general mayhem ensues. Hint: 65,000 gallons of water are released and recycled every six minutes, but you don't get wet. And yes, you do see the footage of those volunteers.

Fear Factor Live (Express Plus)
Like the TV show of the same name, preselected audience members compete to see who can best overcome their greatest fears. Think creepy-crawly bugs and jumps from high places.

Jaws (Express Plus)
Take off in a little boat off Nantucket for a scenic ride through the harbor. But beware. This is Jaws territory, and he just might be lurking below the surface. The boat driver does his best to keep everyone safe, with various weapons to stave off the great white beast, but it's no easy task. The great white lurches toward the boat, his huge mouth and sparkling teeth poised for attack, and gas tanks burst into flames.

WORLD EXPO
Men in Black Alien Attack (Express Plus)
Can you qualify for the most elite law-enforcement agency in the galaxy? Well, you'll have to prove it. Aim your lasers at aliens of every size and description while your car swings and spins through a danger-laden downtown.

Eating & Drinking
You'll find a plethora of snack and drink stands, most serving icy beer. Take one to the outdoor shows, or just settle back on the grass or a bench by the water and watch the crowds go by. Restaurants hours vary, but those below are usually open from 11am to park closing. The only restaurants in the park that take advanced reservations are Finnegan's Bar & Grill and Lombard's Seafood Grille.

BUDGET
Munch on wood-oven pizza, salad and pasta at the **Classic Monsters Cafe** (Production Central; mains $5-12), a mad scientist's laboratory complete with visiting monsters. For a sandwich and a milkshake, head to the quintessential ice-cream counter at **Schwab's Pharmacy** (Hollywood Blvd; mains $5-10). You half expect a roller-skating waitress to serve up that burger and fries at

Mel's Diner (Hollywood Blvd; mains $6-13), a quintessential '50s diner complete with classic cars and rockin' bands outside.

MIDRANGE
An Irish pub straight out of the streets of New York, **Finnegan's Bar & Grill** (☎ 407-224-9255; New York; mains $8-20) serves up Cornish pasties, shepherd's pie and even Scotch eggs, as well as Harp, Bass and Guinness on tap. Try the corned-beef sandwich served on a yummy pretzel roll and warm bread pudding.

TOP END
Head to **Lombard's Seafood Grille** (☎ 407-224-9255; San Francisco; mains $12-25) for seafood, burgers and stir-fry. You can sit outside on the pleasant little deck overlooking the water and listen to the jingle-jangle of the boats on their buoys.

ISLANDS OF ADVENTURE
This place is just plain fun. Scream-it-from-the-rooftops, no-holds-barred, laugh-out-loud kind of fun. Superheros zoom by on motorcycles, roller coasters whiz overhead, and plenty of rides will get you soaked. Some say there's not enough here for little kids, but don't listen. They'll love Seuss Land, and there are plenty of gentle and thrill rides alike.

Orientation & Information
Islands of Adventure is organized into five distinctly themed sections. A sixth section, the **Wizarding World of Harry Potter**, was scheduled to open in late 2009 at the time of research. Here you will be able to enter a fully realized world of JK Rowling's Harry Potter, complete with Hogwarts Castle, the Forbidden Forest and other iconic locations, food from the films and interactive attractions inspired by the stories. Academy Award–winning production designer Stuart Craig, who worked on the Harry Potter films, leads the creative design.

Attractions
MARVEL SUPER HERO ISLAND
Techno music blares from the fake facades of superhero covered buildings, the Incredible Hulk Coaster rumbles and roars overhead and superheroes speed through on motorcycles. Bright, loud and fast-moving, Marvel Super Hero Island is sensory overload and a thrill-lover's paradise. Comic-book characters patrol this area, so keep an eye out for your favorites.

The Amazing Adventures of Spider-Man (Express Plus)

Hop onto the combination roller coaster/motion simulator quickly – Spider-Man needs you now! Supervillains rendered in state-of-the-art 3-D are on the loose (jumping on your car and chasing you around with giant electrical plugs), and it's up to you and your favorite webslinger to stop them.

Doctor Doom's Fearfall (Express Plus)

This is less scary than it looks, which is great for timid folk but a bummer for adrenaline junkies. You'll be shot up in the air, which will take your breath away, and then dropped – but gently, and not very far.

Storm Force Accelatron (Express Plus)

Another barf-o-rama, this one's on par with Walt Disney World's Mad Tea Party – only in the dark.

Incredible Hulk Coaster (Express Plus)

One of those coasters with a surprise twist, which might turn you Hulk green if you've just eaten! You can hear the screams as soon as you walk into the crazy mayhem of Marvel Super Hero Island.

TOON LAGOON

Loud and bright, with lots of short buildings covered with primary colored cartoon classics, this sparkly, light-hearted spot aims to transport visitors to the days when lazy weekends included nothing more than watching *Popeye* and the *Rocky and Bullwinkle Show* on a Saturday morning and afternoons running under the sprinkler.

Dudley Do-Right's Ripsaw Falls (Express Plus)

A classic water ride, this one has a short but steep fall. You will get soaked.

Me Ship, the Olive

Kids crawl, climb, squirm and squirt other kids on Popeye's playground ship. Climb to the top of the tunnel waterslides for one of the best views anywhere of the park.

Popeye & Bluto's Bilge-Rat Barges (Express Plus)

Ripsaw Falls not wet enough for you? Head across the way, where Popeye, Bluto and Olive Oyl operate a somewhat tamer (little kids can go), though no less drenching, raft ride. You float, twist and bump along on a circular raft with 10 or so other folk.

JURASSIC PARK

Oddly quiet, with no screams or loud music, no neon colors or hawking vendors, this oasis of palm trees, greenery and ferns takes visitors back to the days of the dinosaurs. **Camp Jurassic** and the **Discovery Center** are a kids' playground and an interactive natural-history exhibit, respectively. Compared to the park's other play areas, however, these are a disappointment, with little to hold kids' or adults' attention.

Jurassic Park River Adventure (Express Plus)

A water ride with a prehistoric twist floats you past friendly, vegetarian dinosaurs. All seems well and good until, you guessed it, things go wrong and grass-munchin' cuties are replaced with the stuff of nightmares. To escape the looming teeth of the giant T. rex roaring down at you, you need to plunge in darkness 85ft to the water below. Prepare to get soaked. Children will be terrified by the creatures, the dark and the plunge.

Pteranodon Flyers

If you don't have a child 36in to 56in, you can't fly. They literally won't let you on without a munchkin, but chances are you wouldn't want to anyway. This ride floats gently over the lush landscape of Jurassic Park and all its robotic dinosaurs in a quiet hang glider assembly, but waits can be upwards of an hour for the 80-second ride! With no Express Plus option, you'll want to hit this first thing.

THE LOST CONTINENT

Magic and myth from across the seas and the pages of fantasy books inspire the rides and decor of this mystical corner of the park. Here you'll find dragons and unicorns, talking fountains and psychic readings, fortune-tellers and Dragon Scale Ale.

Poseidon's Fury (Express Plus)

Right up there with that Drew Carey movie over at Walt Disney World, this is one of the worst attractions in Orlando. Expect to be herded into and through a massive, dark structure for what seems like eternity and forced to watch some sort of strange nonsensical story with lots of banging and special effects, but no narrative spirit.

The Mystic Fountain

One of the best things at the park for kids, this very personalized and funny improvisational talking fountain throws little ones (and their adults) completely off kilter! No one expects a fountain to talk, much less talk directly to the little girl in blue, holding the cotton candy. The fountain banters sassily, soaking children with his waterspouts when they least expect it and engaging them in silly conversation. And no, no one hiding with a remote control. This is a talking fountain.

The Eighth Voyage of Sinbad (Express Plus)

Sinbad and his sidekick Kabob must rescue Princess Amoura from the terrible Miseria, and of course, Sinbad has to tumble and jump around to do it. There's lots of swashbuckling shenanigans, with corny jokes, the audience warning the clueless Sinbad of lurking danger and hissing for the bad guys. Water, flames and particularly evil-looking villains creeping around to ominous music might scare little ones.

The Dueling Dragons (Express Plus)

Get two roller coasters in one with these synchronized thrillers – sometimes you're so close to the other cars that you'll want to pull your dangling feet out of the way. The red coaster is the Fire Coaster, the blue is the Ice Coaster. Hardcore coaster fans say the front car on 'Fire' and the last car on 'Ice' are the best.

The Flying Unicorn (Express Plus)

This sweet wooden roller coaster is a good starter coaster for little ones.

SEUSS LANDING

Anyone who has fallen asleep to the reading of *Green Eggs and Ham* or learned to read with *Sam I Am* knows the world of Dr Seuss: the fanciful creatures, the lyrical names, the rhyming stories. Here, realized in magnificently designed three-dimensional form, is Dr Seuss' imagination. The Lorax guards his Truffula Trees, Thing One and Thing Two make trouble, and creatures from all kinds of Seuss favorites adorn the shops and the rides. Drink Moose Juice or Goose Juice, eat Green Eggs and Ham, and peruse shelves of Dr Seuss books before riding through *Cat in the Hat* or around and around on an elephant bird from *Horton Hears a Who*. Seuss Landing, one of the best places for little ones in all of Orlando's theme parks, brings the spirit and energy of Dr Seuss' vision to life. So come on in, walk into his world and take a spin on a fish.

If I Ran the Zoo

Here's another interactive play area with squirty triggers and lots of color and climbing apparatuses.

The Cat in the Hat (Express Plus)

Grab a couch and watch as Thing One and Thing Two instigate all sorts of mayhem. A narrator reads the story (edited down, of course) as you move along. The ride jerks and twists a bit, making this slightly crazier than similar theme rides through a story.

Caro-Seuss-El (Express Plus)

Even if you don't want to ride this, go check it out. This merry-go-round of fanciful Seussian characters is so awesome-looking that you might wonder if it will eventually end up in the Smithsonian.

One Fish, Two Fish, Red Fish, Blue Fish (Express Plus)

Like the ever popular Dumbo ride at Disney's Magic Kingdom, this attraction gives riders up and down controls. But instead of riding an elephant, you ride one of those silly Seussian fish. And there's the added thrill trying to avoid (or confront) streams of water.

The High in the Sky Seuss Trolley Train Ride (Express Plus)

A gentle train ride takes you above Seuss landing for a (low-flying) bird's eye view of its creatures and whimsy.

Eating & Drinking

All the usual fast-food suspects are sold at premium prices throughout the park, but with a commitment to theme that you don't see elsewhere. Sip a Predator Rocks ($8) in the lush foliage of the Cretaceous period at the **Watering Hole** in Jurassic Park, or grab a Dragon Scale Ale at the **Alchemy Bar** inside the same gnarled old tree as Enchanted Oak Tavern. Restaurant hours vary, but the following are generally open from 11am to park closing. The only restaurants at the park that take advanced reservations are Confisco Grill & Backwater Bar and Mythos.

Blondie's (Toon Lagoon; mains $6-13) Enjoy US classics like meat-loaf sandwich and 'the Dagwood,' with ham, salami, turkey, bologna, Swiss and US cheeses and tomato.

Confisco Grill & Backwater Bar (☎ 407-224-9255; Port of Entry; mains $6-22) Chase burgers and panini with a cold beer or other cold libation from the full bar.

Enchanted Oak Tavern (Lost Continent; mains $7-18) Housed in giant Oak Tree, you can sit outside at a single row of tables along the water or in the cool, dark interior and eat corn on the cob, turkey legs, barbecue and other meaty fare befitting an enchanted-oak tavern.

Mythos Restaurant (☎ 407-224-9255; The Lost Continent; mains $11-16) Housed in an incredible and ornate underwater grotto, this fun spot offers tasty basic fare like hamburgers, steak and risotto.

CITYWALK

Connecting both theme parks is **CityWalk** (Map p270; ☎ 407-224-2691; www.citywalkorlando.com; ☺ 11am-2am), a thin strip of pleasantly land-scaped pedestrian mall along the canal with restaurants, bars, a handful of shops, a carousel and a fountain for kids to play in. Clubs crank out live music, and it's packed with partying 20-somethings, families, teenagers and everyone in between. After 6pm parking is free.

Eating

Restaurants serving everything from pizza to Latin American fare, as well as several massive themed restaurants, draw crowds all day long. Options include **Hard Rock Café** (Map p270; ☎ 407-224-2155; CityWalk; ☺ 11am-varied) offering excellent burgers and a rock-and-roll theme; **NBA City** (Map p270; ☎ 407-363-5919; CityWalk; ☺ 11am-varied), with a giant basketball player out front and endless basketball games on screens throughout the restaurant; and **NASCAR Sports Grille** (Map p270; ☎ 407-224-2155; CityWalk; ☺ 11am-varied), featuring NASCAR simulators and games.

The creative Creole fare with an Asian twist at **Emeril's** (Map p270; ☎ 407-224-2424/2779; mains $18-35; ☺ lunch, dinner) provides respite from the beer-and-burger themed revelry just outside its doors. High ceilings with arched lighting fixtures, a stainless-steel bar, plenty of floor-to-ceiling windows and hardwood floors create a decidedly contemporary and sophisticated ambience. Try the seafood-and-andouille gumbo and the hickory-smoked lemongrass duck. Reservations recommended.

Many of the entertainment venues below also serve full menus for lunch and dinner. Call ☎ 407-224-2779 or ☎ 407-224-2155 for priority seating reservations at all restaurants in CityWalk except NBA City and Emeril's.

Entertainment

The **Blue Man Group** (Map p270; ☎ 407-258-3626, 407-224-2691; CityWalk; adult $59-74, child under 9 $49-64), which originally started as an off-Broadway phenomenon in 1991, features three bald men painted blue engaging in all kinds of craziness involving percussion 'instruments', paintballs, marshmallows and modern dancing. It's crazy, high-energy and multisensory fun that appeals to adults and children alike (though not recommended for children under three). You will be given rain gear to protect you from whatever may spew from the stage if you sit in the 'poncho section,' and think carefully before volunteering to participate on stage!

The hulking 3000-person capacity **Hard Rock Live Orlando** (Map p270; ☎ 407-351-5483; www.hardrock live.com; CityWalk; tickets $20-30; box office ☺ 10am-9pm) draws some fairly big rock-and-roll names and comedy acts through its doors.

Movies, music and mucho alcohol sums up the entertainment options clustered together at CityWalk – and that's just the way the tourists like it. Purchase a **CityWalk Party Pass** ($12, free with multiday theme-park admission ticket) for unlimited club access; for a movie and clubbing, buy the **CityWalk Party Pass and Movie Ticket** ($15).

AMC Universal Cineplex (☎ 407-354-5998; ☺ box office opens at 12:30pm) Twenty wall-to-wall screens and beer and wine at the concession stand. Call or stop by City-Walk Guest Services Ticket Window (☎ 407-224-2691) to purchase a Movie and Meal Deal ($22).

Bob Marley – A Tribute to Freedom (☎ 407-224-2155; cover after 8pm $5; ☺ 4:30pm-2am) Jamaica inspired food and music

CityWalk's Rising Star (☎ 407-224-2189; cover $7; ☺ 8pm-2am) Karaoke to live music and talent contests.

Groove (☎ 407-224-2165; cover $5; ☺ 9pm-2am) Dance club with sleek blue neon walls and blaring music from the 70's and 80's. Check website for select 'teen nights'.

Jimmy Buffet's Margaritaville (☎ 407-224-2155; cover after 10pm $5; ☺ 11:30am-2am) Three bars themed around Jimmy Buffet songs, a full-menu and live music after 10pm.

DATE NIGHT

After a day pushing strollers, spinning in teacups and negotiating melting ice cream, parents can use some time alone. So wash that cotton-candy outta your hair, ditch the diaper bag, hire a babysitter or drop the tots off at one of Disney's child-care centers (p265) and paint the town red.

If you're staying at Disney and don't want to venture too far from the kids, there's plenty of adult entertainment within the gates of Walt Disney World. Enjoy Magic Kingdom's fireworks and one of Disney's best meals from the rooftop California Grill (p316), dish out some serious bucks for elegant adult-only dining at Victoria and Albert's (p316) or feast on delicious seafood at Flying Fish (p315). Afterwards, head to Downtown Disney where you can take in live music at House of Blues (p311), treat yourself to Le Cirque de Soleil's La Nouba (p317), one of the best shows in town, or laugh out loud at the silly shenanigans at the Comedy Warehouse (p311). Over at Universal Orlando, catch the Blue Man Group (p321) or a show at Hard Rock (p321).

Beyond the theme parks, you'll find excellent theater at Loch Haven Park (p267), impromptu comedy at SAK Comedy Lab and world-class opera and symphony (p283). Sidewalk cafés and wine bars at Winter Park (p284) make for a relaxing evening, and there's an excellent independent movie theater just north of the town (see Enzian Theater, p286). On select nights, you can stretch out a blanket for an outdoor film at their Popcorn in the Park series (p286) or at Leu Gardens (p274).

But if you're like most parents after a day at Orlando's theme parks, perhaps all you'll have energy for is a couples massage at one of Orlando's sumptuous spas (p333) and glass of wine. Alone and quiet.

Pat O'Brien's (☎ 407-224-2106; cover $5; ☻ 6pm-2am) A homogenized slice of New Orleans with Cajun food and that strange Orlando obsession, dueling pianos.

Red Coconut Club (☎ 407-224-2425; cover $7; ☻ 8pm-2am Sun-Thu, from 6pm Fri & Sat) Live bands and rooftop balcony.

SEAWORLD, DISCOVERY COVE & AQUATICA

Though far more subdued than Disney or Universal, these animal-inspired theme parks strut a personal style that sets them apart from the rest of Orlando. SeaWorld is not only a stellar marine-animal facility, but boasts a few knuckle-whitening rides, an excellent kiddie-ride section and a full day's worth of outstanding animal shows. At the idyllic Discovery Cove you can swim with dolphins, feed exotic birds from the palm of your hand and enjoy the crowd-free atmosphere of a private beach and a winding lazy river nestled in a tropical Eden. It's quiet, relaxing and blissfully free of screams and loud music, roaming characters, long lines and flashy entertainment. Aquatica, which opened in 2008, is a water park.

The three theme parks, while owned by the same parent company and located next to each other, are not a self-contained resort like Walt Disney World and Universal Studios.

Public transportation to the parks includes Orlando's Lynx bus (p261) and the I-Ride Trolley (p284). There is a complimentary shuttle that runs regularly between SeaWorld and Aquatica.

SEAWORLD ORLANDO

Beyond the handful of rides and the excellent shows, SeaWorld offers opportunities to feed stingrays, sea lions and other critters, is pleasantly landscaped with plenty of greenery and flowers, and has decent food. If you're the sort of person who likes leaping dolphins, sliding sea lions and crashing whales, you're going to have an incredible time.

A percentage of each admission fee goes directly to the SeaWorld Orlando Animal Rescue Team, one of the most respected animal rescue organizations in the country.

Orientation & Information

Located at the southern end of International Drive, just north of Walt Disney World, **SeaWorld Orlando** (Map p270; ☎ 407-351-3600, 800-327-2424; www.seaworld.com; 7007 SeaWorld Orlando Dr; adult/child 3-9 $68/58; ☻ 9am-varied) is organized around a central lagoon. You will be given a map with show times upon entry; look at this carefully, take a few minutes to decide what shows you want to see and plan a day's schedule.

Guest Services, to the left as you enter the park, has an ATM, a Lost & Found, foreign-language guides, guides for visitors with disabilities, kennel services ($6 per day; you must bring your own food and return occasionally to walk your dog) and lockers ($8). All attractions are wheelchair accessible, and there are TDD phones and assistive listening devices sprinkled through the park. Single/double strollers ($10/17) and manual/electric wheelchairs ($10/38) can be reserved in advance online. SeaWorld participates in the FlexTicket program (see p289); see the website for hotel packages and special offers. Parking is $10 per car and $12 per RV.

To get here, Take I-4 exit 71 and bear right onto Central Florida Parkway. SeaWorld is a few blocks up on your left.

Attractions
ANIMAL INTERACTION
SeaWorld is, at its heart, devoted to the care and protection of sea animals. Several animal interaction experiences allow guests to see, touch and feed the animals up close. Make reservations online, or call ☎ 800-406-2244. Over at Discovery Cove (p332), you can swim with the dolphins in intimate groups of eight.

Beluga Interaction Program ($179; minimum age 10) There just aren't that many places where you can touch, feed and talk (via hand signals) to a beluga whale. Or any whale, for that matter.

Marine Mammal Keeper Experience ($399; minimum age 13) Just what it sounds like: participants prepare special meals, work with animal trainers and interact with marine life from beluga whales to sea lions. Includes lunch, a T-shirt and a seven-day pass to SeaWorld.

Shark's Deep Dive ($150; minimum age 10) Descend in a shark cage into a tank of sandtiger sharks, nurse sharks and schools of fish. You don't even need to know how to scuba dive, thanks to a 'water helmet'.

RIDES
Folks who have little ones in tow will want to count on spending a couple hours at Shamu's Happy Harbor and the rides surrounding it (see Family Rides, p330). Because SeaWorld does not have the equivalent of Disney's FastPass or Universal Orlando's Express Plus pass, the best way to avoid painfully long lines is to go first thing in the morning

and to take advantage of the single-rider line when available.

Kraken
Touted by aficionados as one of the most wicked coasters in Florida, this floorless steel whiplash ride of twists, turns, inversions and plunges is quintessential roller-coaster fun. There are times when you're literally lifted off your seat, and the screams from Kraken echo outside the park and down International Drive!

Journey to Atlantis
This coaster plunges 60ft into the water. It begins in darkness, moving gently through an underwater world of neon and fluorescent coral and fish. Things turn macabre when the creepy evil mermaid beckons you into her world and up you go, clackity-clack, through the steam. It doesn't twist upside down or too fast, but the special effects will frighten little ones.

Wild Arctic
An IMAX movie where viewers are traveling to Base Station Wild Arctic in an incredibly high-powered helicopter as a bad storm front moves in. The pilot brings you very close to some polar bears before setting down on thin ice. Of course, after hearing an awful rumbling sound, you fall through the ice, and it's touch and go for a while, but… Afterwards, see above- and below-water views of polar bears, walrus and other Arctic life.

Shamu's Happy Harbor
Not so much a ride as a kid's dream playground, this well-designed 3-acre space includes a ballroom, fountains and plenty of places to climb, crawl and jump. The focal point is a massive net system suspended from the sky where even the littlest can toot around (wear shoes – those ropes hurt bare feet). Across the path is water-spewing fun at **Water Works**.

BATHROOM LINES

The line of anxious kids hopping from one foot to the other at the bathrooms in Shamu's Happy Harbor can wind out the door. Instead, head to the bathroom inside the Baby Center (the cute house with rocking chairs on the porch) just next door.

Family Rides

Six eye-candy rides, perfect for little tots, surround Happy Harbor. Ride a dolphin or another creature of the sea on the **Sea Carousel**, twist yourself round and round on **Jazzy Jellies**, and board the **Shamu Express** for a gentle coaster thrill. Lines for everything but the carousel move incredibly slowly, and are particularly long just after lunch; this is one of those places where a cell phone comes in handy. One person can wait in line while the other watches the kids play at Happy Harbor.

SHOWS

This is why folks come to SeaWorld, and none of them disappoint. Note that shows change seasonally, and in the summer there are night shows that are not offered during the rest of the year. Check your park map when you arrive for current shows and show times.

Believe

Killer whales are the stars at SeaWorld, and this don't-miss show is where you watch them do their thing. It actually brings tears to some folks' eyes! The first 15 rows – sometimes more – of Shamu Stadium are the 'splash zone,' and both whales and trainers enjoy soaking the crowd with icy seawater.

Blue Horizons

More than a dolphin show (and thankfully lacking any of the preachy and condescending rhetoric about how we must protect the dolphin and our environment that is so common at most dolphin shows), this fantastic extravaganza of light, music, dolphins, birds and acrobats in spectacular costumes tells some sort of story of good and evil. But never mind the details of the narrative, as none of that matters. It's just a good ole show, with lots of splashing and drama.

Clyde & Seamore Take Pirate Island

Another must-see, this delightful show stars sea lion, otter and walrus 'comedians.' It's great for kids, who find it hilarious – and the humans in it are funny too.

Odyssea

A bit like Cirque du Soleil on a much pared-down level, this unusual 30-minute circus performance combines acrobats, elaborate costumes and a heap of special effects to recreate what it's like to move under the sea. The

gravity-defying stunts will have you holding your breath.

Pets Ahoy!

Featuring the talents of cats, birds, rats, potbellied pigs and others, this show tickles little ones' funny bones. Many of the stars were rescued from local animal shelters.

Elmo and the Bookaneers

Anyone with a Sesame Street fan in tow will want to catch this light-hearted performance along the lagoon.

Shamu Rocks

A seasonal nighttime extravaganza that fuses killer whales with killer rock and roll and incredible light design.

OTHER ATTRACTIONS
Skytower

The best view around is from SeaWorld's **landmark tower** ($3) in the middle of the park. Capsules take six minutes to slide up the 400ft pole, slowly rotating for a 360° panorama of the area, including points as far away as downtown Orlando.

Dolphin Nursery

Is there anything cuter than a bunch of baby dolphins playing? Red balls bounce around the water as the little tikes learn to earn their fins.

Key West at SeaWorld

Roughly defined by its somewhat Florida Keys vibe, this area sits immediately to the left after the entrance. For $7 you can purchase a box of fish to feed the dolphins (or just pet them for free) at **Dolphin Cove**, and you can do the same to stingrays at **Stingray Lagoon**. Don't get frustrated if the stingrays don't take your fish, as there's a trick: hold the food between your index and middle finger, and place your hand in the water palm-up, with the lil' fishies swaying enticingly in the water. When the rays go by, they vacuum it right up. Pet their backs as they glide past – it feels just like the white of a hard-boiled egg.

Pacific Point Preserve

California sea lions, fur seals and harbor seals make merry (and plenty of noise) in this area, created to look like the rugged Pacific coastline. There's underwater viewing as well.

Come at feeding time when these goofy little sweet-faced guys will surely make you giggle.

Shark Encounter
Menacing sharks, rays, barracudas, lionfish and skates swim all around the 60ft-long Plexiglas tube, which you're transported through on a conveyor belt.

Clydesdale Hamlet
Walk through the stables of these enormous and proud horses, which are the symbol of Anheuser-Busch products. Unless you really love horses or want to see a Clydesdale, there's not much reason to come here.

Manatees: the Last Generation?
The heroic SeaWorld Orlando Animal Rescue Team rescues injured and sick manatees, and this is where you'll see the recuperating sweeties. It begins with a heart-wrenching film and finishes with a fine view of manatees bearing the scars of human encroachment. As much as possible, the SeaWorld manatees are eventually released back into the wild.

Penguin Encounter
People movers take you past penguin tanks made to look like the Arctic, with manufactured snow and ice. If you want to stick around and watch these silly little guys waddle around, slide into the water, and swim around like munchkin torpedoes, you can step into a standing area. They're quite amusing.

Jewel of the Sea Aquarium
Nothing particularly exciting, this well-designed aquarium of brightly colored tropical fish next to Journey to Atlantis makes a nice place to keep busy with little ones while everyone else is on the ride.

Anheuser-Busch Hospitality Center
This 'educational' attraction teaches you a bit about the brewing of Anheuser-Busch products and a lot about the self-acclaimed greatness of the company (which owns SeaWorld). Afterward, you'll sample several to make sure they're OK. All in all, it feels like one big Budweiser ad. Yes, you get free beer.

Paddle Boats
Kids will want to toot around the lagoon on one of these enticing pink flamingos. Yes, they're cute, but in the end they're paddle boats and you have to work pretty hard to get them to move.

The Waterfront
An attempt at recreating an exotic waterfront port, but it's really just an area of shops and restaurants. However, the food is much better than traditional park offerings, and costumed performers roam the cobbled streets providing entertainment. The patio of the spectacular Spice Mill restaurant is a perfect base for watching the Mistify finale.

FIREWORKS
The park closes with **Mystify**, a fireworks, light and water show over the lagoon.

Tours
The seven-hour **Adventure Express** (☎ 800-406-2244; adult/child 3-9 $120/100) features premium reserved-seating at the whale show *Believe* and a second show, front-of-the-line access to Kraken, Journey to Atlantis and Wild Arctic, and the chance to touch a penguin. Parties are limited to 18; for private tours, sign up for the Elite version. Less elaborate tours focus on different animals and take about an hour; see the website for complete options. Make reservations by phone or online.

Eating & Drinking
You'll find plenty of fast-food options, and most have decent healthy alternatives and **Shamu Kids Meals** ($7), which consist of a peanut-butter-and-jelly sandwich, chips and a soda in a Shamu lunch box. The **Seafire Inn** (Waterfront; mains $8-14) serves up a blend of Mediterranean, Cajun and Caribbean flavors, and it's not unusual to see burgers flipped next to Mongolian woks. Head to **Voyager's** (Waterfront; mains $9-15) for tasty wood-fire pizza.

Two restaurants take advanced reservations. With a pleasant view of the harbor, creative appetizers, and live music, the **SandBar** (☎ 407-351-3600; Sky Tower; appetizers $5-13) makes a good spot for a beer or a specialty martini. Eat among the sharks at **Sharks Underwater Grill** (☎ 407-351-3600; shark area; mains $9-21), an underwater grotto with full-service dining.

PRIVATE DINING EVENTS
The park offers several specialty meal opportunities. Options include **Breakfast With Elmo and Friends** (adult/child 3-10 $34/18); dinner by the Shamu pool followed by reserved seating for

the Shamu show at **Shamu Rocks** (adult/child 3-10 $32/17); and a lunchtime **Backstage at Believe** (adult/child 3-10 $25/10). Prices do not included required park admission. Note that these are not particularly intimate affairs, as there could be 100 other guests at your 'private' event.

The recommended **All-You-Care-To-Eat Family Picnic** (adult/child 3-10 $14/8; ⊗ 12:30-2:30pm & 4-6pm) serves hamburgers, hot dogs, barbecue chicken, salads and dessert picnic-style. You can't beat the price, and the food is pretty tasty.

Call ☎ 407-351-3600 or go online to make the required advanced reservations.

DISCOVERY COVE

Walk into the Discovery Cove lobby, with its stone floor, turquoise dolphins suspended above, printed rattan furnishings and beamed ceiling, and you instantly feel that you're somewhere special. Inside, visitors spend the day in a tropical sanctuary of boldly colored flowers, white-sand beaches and warm pools surrounded by boulders. One of the most relaxing places in Orlando, this lovely hideaway feels worlds away from the other theme parks and the city's endless strip malls and traffic.

Schedule a day here between visits to other theme parks to give everyone some much needed downtime.

Orientation & Information

Adjacent to SeaWorld, **Discovery Cove** (Map p270; ☎ 407-370-1280, 877-434-7268; www.discoverycove.com; admission with dolphin swim $269-289, without dolphin swim $169-189; ⊗ 8:30am-5pm) allows only 1000 guests per day and you must make advanced reservations. Once you're in the park, everything from wetsuits to unlimited beer and snacks, from a family portrait to a buffet lunch, is included in the price.

During the summer, the park opens for **Twilight Discovery** ($269; ⊗ 3-9pm). Rates include a buffet dinner, music, dancing and wading with the dolphins. See website for details on the **Trainer for the Day** program (per person $468-488; ⊗ 8am-4pm); children aged six to 12 must be accompanied by a paying adult.

Attractions

DOLPHIN SWIM

This is the most popular reason to come to the park. You'll start with a brief orientation, then follow your instructors into the water with the dolphins. After some hands-on basic training, you perform a few tricks and hang on to the dolphin's fin for a short glide through the water. Cameras aren't allowed in this area – there's a professional photographer and videographer stationed in the water ready to capture all the action (for a hefty fee!).

RAY LAGOON

Though stingrays may look a little creepy, these guys have had their stingers removed. You can wade right into the chilly salt water and touch the velvety creatures as they glide past.

CORAL REEF

Explore an underwater world of crusty shipwrecks, submerged grottos and a tropical rainbow of exotic fish – luckily for swimmers, the sharks and barracuda cruise safely behind protective glass.

TROPICAL BIRD AVIARY

Don't be surprised if a colorful bird or two drops down onto your shoulder! Pick up a cup of food and watch them eat right out of your hand.

SWIMMING

A lazy river winds around the entire cove, including the aviary (ingeniously blocked from the rest of the park with two small but powerful waterfalls that you must pass under), and an enormous waterfall empties into a luxuriously warm swimming lagoon.

Eating & Drinking

Included in the cost of admission is an upscale cafeteria lunch, featuring roast chicken, hamburgers and seafood salad, served beachside on the patio from at 11am. Admission also includes unlimited snacks (such as ice cream, Oreos and pretzels), beer and sodas from snack huts sprinkled through the park.

AQUATICA

Orlando's latest water park opened with great fanfare in the spring of 2008, but for all intents and purposes, it's just another water park. It's newer and cleaner than the others, with better food, plenty of greenery, some cool animals to check out and little of the narrative shtick that defines Disney attractions. But in the end, come here to splash around in the water, laze in the sand, float along the lazy river and zoom down slides into water. That's what you do at water parks, and Aquatica is no different.

Orientation & Information

Aquatica (Map p270; ☎ 888-800-5447; www.aquaticaby seaworld.com; 5800 Water Play Way; adult/children 3-9 $39/33; ☯ 10am-varied, from 9am during peak season, closed select Mon & Tue Nov-Dec) This is located at the southern end of International Drive across from SeaWorld. Parking for cars costs $10 ($12 for RVs); guests visiting SeaWorld, Discovery Cove or Aquatica on the same day pay for parking only once. Guest Services, just inside the park doors, rents single/double strollers ($10/15) and wheelchairs/ECVs ($12/38). There are locker facilities ($12) and beach-towel rental ($4). See the park map for the location of ATMs, currency exchange, diaper-changing and nursing stations and first aid. Life vests can be checked out free of charge throughout the park, and you can rent a private cabana, stocked with 15 nonalcoholic sodas (all day for four people $150).

Attractions

Aquatica boasts that the **Dolphin Plunge** spits you through a glass-enclosed tube through a tank of Commerson's dolphins, and it does indeed do this; the problem, of course, is that perhaps a high-speed waterslide just isn't the best way to see dolphins. You zoom through so fast and the stretch through the tank is so short that you're lucky if you catch a passing glance at the black-and-white cuties. Check 'em out at the **Commerson's Dolphin Exhibit** instead. Other animal encounters include rafting **Loggerhead Lane** through the grotto of tropical fish, and meeting macaws, anteaters, turtles and other critters that roam the park with their trainers.

For high-speed thrills, try the **HooRoo Run**, a blessedly simple open-aired inner tube slide, and its enclosed sister ride the **Walhalla Wave**; **Tassie's Twisters**, where you speed around and around and are then dropped into a pool below; **Taumata Racer**, the multilane toboggan run; and **Whanau Way**, a twisting, enclosed inner-tube slide.

THE SPAAAH LIFE

Given the need for a dose of pampering in this activity-packed city, Orlando's proliferation of full-service spas is not surprising. The following spas offer the traditional menu of services and most offer on-site child care for a nominal fee.

Canyon Ranch Spa Club at Gaylord Palms (Map pp292-3; ☎ 407-586-1000; www.gaylordhotels.com; 6000 W Osceola Pkwy) Tucked inside the massive Gaylord Palms convention hotel. With 12 different kinds of massage, 'healing energy' experiences and body treatments with names like 'Ancient Waves Body Glow' and 'Hydrating Paradise Wrap,' you're bound to find something that will leave you rejuvenated and ready to tackle your vacation.

Ritz Carlton Spa, Grande Lakes Orlando (Map p262; ☎ 407-393-4200; www.grandelakes.com/the -ritz-carlton-spa-40.html; 4012 Central Florida Pkwy) Located in its own serene and beautifully appointed building, this spa features a private outdoor pool, a lovely café and a luxurious assortment of treatments. After a few days at the amusement parks, you may truly need that 'Volcanic Force Revitalizer' body treatment! For aspiring spa junkies, they offer teen massages and the 'Princess Fizzing Pedicure,' designed for ages two to 10. The child-care center at the Ritz is particularly nice – you can relax knowing your kids are having as good a time as you are!

Mandara Spa (Maps p270 & pp292-3; Portofino Bay Hotel ☎ 407-503-1244, Walt Disney World Dolphin ☎ 407- 934-4772; www.mandaraspa.com; inside Universal Orlando's Portofino Bay Hotel & inside Walt Disney World Dolphin) Sends guests to the South Pacific, with exotic themed massage rooms and treatments like the oh-so-decadent body-cleansing 'Javanese Lulur,' with turmeric, red rice and ylang-ylang. The Dolphin location oozes Balinese ambience, with temples, rattan and richly embroidered pillows. Both offer serene and peaceful surroundings in the best of spa traditions.

Papillon the Spa at Westgate Lakes (Map p270; ☎ 407-992-2938; www.papillon-spa.com; 9600 Turkey Lake Rd) Offers not only the usual spa menu but also airbrush tanning and hypnosis to help lose weight and stop smoking. Less expensive than some of the others in town, the Papillon is also less elegant.

Urban Spa (Map p268; ☎ 407-481-8485; www.eoinn.com; 227 N Eola Dr) The most intimate of the spas offers a couple's massage on the tiny patio, a Dead Sea mud wrap, detoxifying seaweed treatments and other delights.

The children's play areas here are excellent. At **Walkabout Waters** buckets of water dump regularly over all kinds of brightly colored climbing structures and fountains, while **Kookaburra Cove** offers tiny slides and shallow water perfect for toddlers.

Eating & Drinking

Food at the park's three restaurants is pretty good and far better than what you'll find at Orlando's other water parks. If you've built up an appetite from all that slippin' and slidin', your best options is the all-you-can-eat **Banana Beach Cookout** (all-day pass adult/child 3-9yrs $20/10, one-time meal $13/8; 10:30am-park closing). The buffet includes veggie burgers, barbecue chicken, corn on the cob, hot dogs and salads. Purchase tickets online in advance or at the park. At the **WaterStone Grill** (mains $6-12; 11am-park closing), you'll find heavier items like cheese-smothered steak sandwiches and Cuban pork as well as a few hearty salads. For something on the run, head to **Mango Market** (mains $5-13; park hours) for tasty wood-fired flat-bread pizza, grilled-chicken salad, veggie wraps and other grab-and-go options. You can also buy baby food here. The park sells Anheiser-Busch beer.

The Space Coast

The space shuttle is to the Space Coast what pastel hotels are to South Beach, and you'll be amazed, amused (and exhausted?) by the celestial themes swirling in every gas station, roadside café and hotel lobby within a meteorite's throw. C'mon, even the area code is 321! Not surprisingly, the Kennedy Space Center is both the largest attraction in the area (occupying more than 140,000 acres) and the biggest (more than 1.5 million visitors spin the turnstiles annually).

In contrast to the high-tech buildings and bad space puns, however, the area also boasts some of Florida's most deliciously undeveloped areas. The Space Center only uses about 10,000 acres for its purposes. The rest of the area is set aside as a federally protected wildlife refuge, so don't be surprised to see sunning alligators, soaring birds (including bald eagles), and rooting wild pigs, giving new meaning to the term 'government pork.'

Along the coast, you can find some of Florida's finest sea turtle observation programs and among the most pristine beaches in the state. For adventure-holics, the waves from Sebastian Inlet to Cocoa Beach offer the state's gnarliest surfing and just west of the barrier island, the lagoon is dotted with quiet, undeveloped islands, perfect for wiling away warm summer days.

However, if neither space ships nor surfing nor barren islands make your socks go up and down, then cruise on south to the quaint but cool sister cities of Melbourne and Indialantic, where you can savor small town friendliness peppered with an authentic beach vibe.

And for shoppers? Well...there's no shortage of places to browse – just hope you like surfwear!

HIGHLIGHTS

- Partying before (and after) a shuttle launch at **Kennedy Space Center** (p340), a once-in-a-lifetime experience – if the heavens align

- Watching a sublime sunset at Cocoa Beach's **Sunset Waterfront Grill & Bar** (p347)

- Paddling among lush mangroves and deserted islands at **Canaveral National Seashore** (p343), and finding a secluded, remote campsite near frolicking manatees

- Hanging ten on the gnarliest wave breaks in Florida at **Cocoa Beach** (p345) and getting lost in the legendary Ron Jon Surf Shop

- Having lunch at the remote **Mosquito Lagoon** (p343), where it's just you and several hundred deserted islands

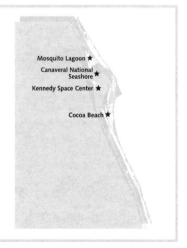

★ Mosquito Lagoon
★ Canaveral National Seashore
★ Kennedy Space Center

★ Cocoa Beach

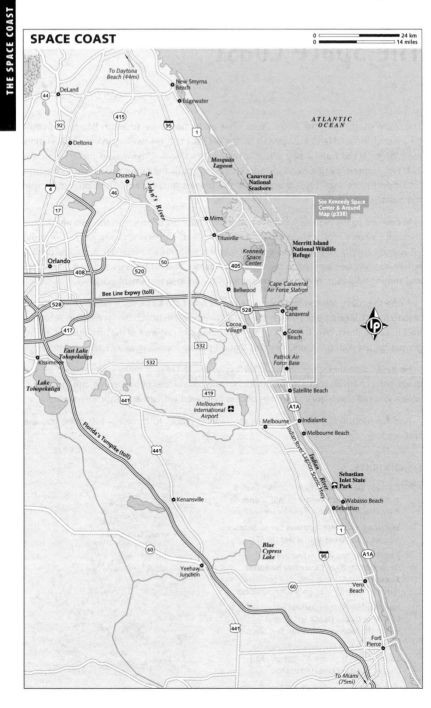

SPACE COAST

0 — 24 km
0 — 14 miles

History

Inhabited by humans for more than 12,000 years, this area was occupied by the Ais Indians when Juan Ponce de León came ashore in 1513. The Ais disappeared during the 18th century, and citrus farmers began to crop up the following century. In 1949, President Harry S Truman established the Joint Long Range Proving Grounds at Cape Canaveral for missile testing, and on October 1, 1958, NASA was born here.

Climate

The Space Coast's oceanfront location enjoys a mild climate, with winter temperatures around mid-60°F and summer temperatures around mid-80°F. Between June and September, beware of frequent thunderstorms with the possibility of severe lightning strikes. Florida holds the dubious honor of ranking first in the world for death by lightning.

National, State & Regional Parks

This part of Florida has some of the best, unspoiled parks with very low crowd factors. Among the more popular are Merritt Island National Wildlife Refuge (p343) and Canaveral National Seashore (p343).

Information

Cocoa Beach Area Chamber of Commerce (☎ 321-454-2022, 877-321-8474; www.visitcocoabeach.com; 400 Fortenberry Rd, Merritt Island 32952)

Florida's Space Coast Office of Tourism (☎ 877-572-3224; www.space-coast.com; 430 Brevard Ave, Suite 150, Cocoa Village 32922)

Melbourne-Palm Bay Area Chamber of Commerce (☎ 321-724-5400, 800-771-9922; www.melpb-chamber .org; 1005 E Strawbridge Ave, Melbourne 32901)

Getting There & Around

The Space Coast is accessible by land and air, though it can be tricky to get around without a car. **Melbourne International** (☎ 321-409-2093; www.mlbair.com) and **Orlando International Airport** (MCO; ☎ 407-825-2001; www.orlandoairports.net) are the main airport hubs. **Amtrak** (☎ 800-USA-RAIL; www .amtrak.com) trains run as far as Orlando, and the **Space Coast Area Transit** (SCAT; ☎ 321-633-1878; www.ridescat.com) operates a local bus service throughout the region.

KENNEDY SPACE CENTER

The National Aeronautics & Space Administration (NASA) was established July 29, 1958, at Cape Canaveral Air Force Base, and the following week, the neophyte agency announced Project Mercury. Its mission: manned space flight. Immediately, NASA threw 110 US test pilots at an unprecedented battery of physical and psychological tests. Seven made the cut – but none would be the first in space; Soviet cosmonaut Yury Gagarin took that honor on April 12, 1961. Though NASA was humiliated, a month later Alan Shepard completed a 15-minute suborbital flight. On May 25, 1961, President John F Kennedy announced that the US intended to land a man on the moon by the end of the decade, and a new facility on Merritt Island, just north of Cape Canaveral, opened nine months later. In February 1962, John Glenn completed a successful three-orbit mission around the earth. In 1963, after Kennedy's assassination, the new space facility was dubbed the Kennedy Space Center. Work continued frantically for the next few years, and on July 16, 1969 a *Saturn V* rocket left Kennedy Space Center; four days later, the Eagle module landed on the moon. As the world watched, Neil Armstrong rasped the immortal phrase: 'That's one small step for man, one giant leap for mankind.'

Today, not only is the **Kennedy Space Center** (KSC; ☎ 321-449-4444; www.kennedyspacecenter.com; adult/child 3-11yr $38/28; ◐ 9am-6pm, Hall of Fame to 7pm) among the most popular attractions in Florida, it's also a working spaceport operating missions year-round. However, because the Space Center hasn't been upgraded in a while (aside from the absolutely out-of-this-world Shuttle Launch Experience), some visitors may be underwhelmed at the sight of one of the world's most forward-thinking organizations in its humdrum environs. That said, if you're over the moon about space travel, this robot- and rocket-packed complex will be a bigger hit than Disney World and is certainly a worthwhile trip. Plan to spend an entire day seeing the massive launch apparatus; both films screening in the IMAX theater; and numerous stellar exhibits, including an enormous *Saturn V* rocket.

Orientation

The Kennedy Space Center takes up about 46,000 acres on Merritt Island. Some of it is used for NASA facilities, but the northern third of the island is wilderness area, comprising Merritt Island National Wildlife Refuge and Canaveral National Seashore.

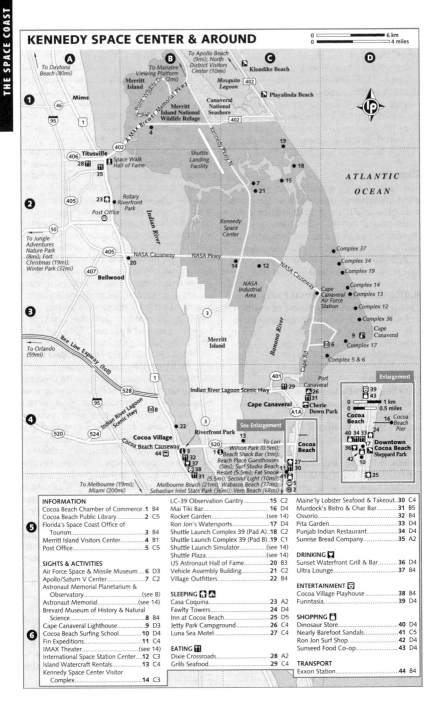

KENNEDY SPACE CENTER & AROUND

The Visitor Complex is located on the east side of the Intracoastal Waterway (here called Indian River), accessible from Titusville via Columbia Blvd (Hwy 405; NASA Parkway) and from Cocoa Beach and Orlando on Bee Line Expressway (Hwy 528). From either Titusville or Cocoa, plan on a 30-minute drive. The Banana River separates the KSC from Cape Canaveral Air Force Station.

All commercial maps of the facility are doctored to protect sensitive areas, but colorful handouts at the information desk are helpful for finding your way around. If you love to explore things on your own, you're out of luck: facilities outside the Visitor Complex are accessible by tour bus only.

Information

In addition to pamphlets and a friendly, multilingual staff, the **information desk** (☎ 321-449-4444; ☻ 9am-6pm) at the Visitor Complex offers lockers, kennels and audio guides in seven languages ($6 each). Guests with disabilities can call ☎ 321-449-4364 (voice) or ☎ 321-454-4198 (TDD) to arrange special tours in advance.

There are ATMs at the Visitor Complex, Apollo/Saturn V Center and, of course, the Space Shop, which has a constellation of hard-to-find books detailing NASA and space travel. NASA broadcasts countdowns and other space news on 920AM, available throughout the Space Coast. TV channel 15, also available throughout the Space Coast, has a constant video feed of NASA operations.

Security is heightened in this area, so expect to have your bag hand-searched. Large bags should be left at the hotel.

Sights & Activities

VISITOR COMPLEX

The **Visitor Complex** (☻ 9am-6pm) features several excellent exhibits accompanied by explanations geared for the average spaceaholic with a high-school education. For more technical discussions of events and hardware, visit the Space Shop bookstore. Prepare to be overwhelmed.

Tour buses to the LC-39 Observation Gantry, the Apollo/Saturn V Center and the International Space Station Center leave the Visitors Complex every 15 minutes from 10am to 2:45pm (see p341). To find the poorly marked departure gate, exit Information Central and make a gentle right.

Follow the path between the Space Shop and Robot Scouts.

Shuttle Launch Simulator

Taking a page out of the amusement park playbook, Kennedy Space Center recently unveiled the Shuttle Launch Simulator, a $60 million virtual ride demonstrating how bone rattling a shuttle launch is. Developed over three years with the help of astronauts, test pilots and NASA experts, the high-fidelity ride envelopes you, jostles you, and leaves you reeling.

After viewing a pre-launch briefing from astronaut Charlie Bolden, visitors are ushered into a 44-seat room and strapped into the 'cockpit.' The floor tilts back and – using intense sound, light and motion effects like seat compression systems – the simulator creates the impression of a vertical launch into orbit, allowing you to experience the tension of busting though Earth's gravitational pull, the shudder of jettisoning rocket boosters, and sweet relief of entering zero gravity. Near the end of the voyage, the shuttle's bay doors open to reveal a breathtaking view of the earth. Equal parts amusement and information, this is a highlight of any Space Center visit.

Rockets & Spacecraft

The **Rocket Garden**, visible from anywhere in the complex, is an inspiring collection of engine replicas and full-size Redstone, Atlas and Titan rockets, originally developed by the military to blow people up but adapted by NASA to send them into outer space. The 363ft *Apollo Saturn 1B* rocket is the exception, designed specifically to carry astronauts up, up and away. Free tours are given at 10:30am and 4pm daily.

Throughout the Visitor Complex are dozens more spacecraft and scale models, including the *Gemini 9* and a mock-up of the Apollo-Soyuz rendezvous (the Apollo capsule is real, the Soyuz is a full-scale model). Some vessels are covered with transparent plastic, allowing you to peer inside and wonder how astronauts could endure being cooped up in those things for so long. It also explains why astronauts don't eat beans.

The **Shuttle Plaza** features a full-size model of a space shuttle, dubbed *Explorer*. You can go inside and check out the (surprisingly small) cargo bay, refitted with a mock-up of the new payload arm. Outside, don't miss the steering

THE SPACE COAST

rockets or the custom-fitted heat tiles, which must be replaced after each reentry using an exacting process that would shoot Henry Ford into orbit.

Next to the Shuttle Plaza is the **Astronaut Memorial**. Featuring a shiny granite wall – reminiscent of the black obelisk from *2001* – the memorial is emblazoned with the names of those who have given their lives in the name of exploration. Thank heavens the wall has refreshingly few names.

IMAX Theater

The five-story-high screens of the complex's two IMAX theaters show films throughout the day. *Space Station 3D*, narrated by Tom Cruise, depicts the construction and operations of the International Space Station (ISS). The newest film, *Magnificent Desolation:*

Walking on the Moon 3D, is narrated by Tom Hanks and features rarely seen NASA footage woven together with live-action renditions of the lunar landscape. Show up early: seats fill fast.

Astronaut Encounter

With its auditorium seating and generic fireproof carpeting, at first blush you might wonder if you've flown back in time and landed in high school. However, the moment a real-life astronaut dressed in NASA blues graces the stage, your opinion sure will change. From the opening introduction to the end of the hour-long Q&A, this is your chance to ask an astronaut anything you like. Inevitable questions about bathroom breaks aside, it's interesting to hear tales of weightlessness and radiation from the people who've

---

LET'S DO LAUNCH

Shuttle launches from the Kennedy Space Center (KSC) are a real bang, but there is a universe of things to bear in mind for doing it right. Here are some things to help make your blast-off experience…a real blast.

- **Don't plan your vacation around a launch** Launches are often delayed; instead, fit a launch into your vacation. KSC launches several times a year, so there are plenty of chances for you to make it work. Call the NASA **launch hotline** (☎ 877-893-6272) or check the **KSC website** (www.kennedyspacecenter.com/launches/) for details on upcoming launches.

- **Don't ignore the rules** Launches viewed from the KSC involve gobs of policies, particularly concerning launch delays and what you can bring onto the property. Visit http://kennedyspacecenter.stores.yahoo.net/imlaunbrview.html to get the facts.

- **Don't worry** If you can't score tickets to KSC facilities, no sweat – there are lots of great places to see shuttles soar. Popular spots include the Astronaut Hall of Fame, Jetty Park Campground, Cherie Down Park, Rotary Riverfront Park, Space View Park, Cocoa Beach Pier, Bennet Causeway (aka Hwy 528) and the Brewer Parkway Bridge in Titusville. Additionally, many local outfitters offer shuttle-viewing excursions for kayakers. In truth, pretty much all of Brevard County has views of the launch – and feels the structural shuddering arising from it – so the most important thing is to pick a spot and make sure you're comfortable.

- **Be aware** Most area radio stations broadcast periodic launch updates, but tune to 920AM for up-to-the-minute reports and, five minutes before the big event, the countdown. Also, check the **NASA News Room** (☎ 321-867-4636) for an up-to-the-minute launch status throughout the day.

- **Be flexible** As mentioned, launches are often delayed. Make hotel reservations early, and plan to stay for a while.

- **Arrive early** There are lots of other people who won't be as organized as you. Don't fight with them. Get to your viewing site early.

- **Be prepared** Bring everything you need. You don't want to miss the launch because you're getting tissues. Items to be sure to pack: a camera, binoculars, sunscreen, an umbrella, food, soft-sided cooler, ice, beer – and extra beer. It's an international tailgate party no matter where you end up. Expect vendors to sell ice cream, soda and even mission-specific T-shirts (starting at $10, they make great souvenirs) so don't forget to bring cash, too.

experienced them. Encounters are included in the admission price. Check the 'Upcoming Events' section on the space center's website or call ☎ 321-449-4444 for the schedule of astronaut appearances.

Kennedy Space Center Tour

The Visitor Complex provides a great overview of the space program. However, to deepen your understanding, go on a bus tour of the facility (included in the price of admission).

The first stop is the **LC 39 Observation Gantry**, a 60ft observation tower with views of Shuttle Launch Complex 39 (Pads A and B), from which the space shuttle is hurled into space. Short films provide simplified explanations of how shuttles are loaded and prepped for flight once they've made it to the launch pad, and you can also get a look at a 14ft-long, 7000lb main engine from one of the shuttles.

During the tour, the bus winds through the launch facilities, an area filled with superlatives. For example, visitors get a look at the **Vehicle Assembly Building** (VAB), where Saturn rockets and shuttles are assembled and stored. With an 8-acre base, and a roof so large Yankee Stadium could fit on it, the 525ft-tall VAB is the largest one-story building in the world. Also be on the lookout for **Crawler Transporters**, which carry the shuttle at a mind-numbing 1mph from the VAB to the launch pad. Weighing 6 million lb, these are the world's heaviest vehicles.

The second stop on the tour is the **Apollo/Saturn V Center**, which blasts off with the **Firing Room Theater**. Using equipment from mission command as props, video footage on three screens and a sound-and-light show that approximates the moment of liftoff, this may be the most moving experience in the entire Space Center. After the multimedia show, pull out your wide-angle lens as you gape at a restored 363ft **Saturn V** rocket, one of the most complex pieces of machinery ever developed. Additionally, the center contains some of the most important relics of the space race, including the **Lunar Module** and **Command Service Module** from the Apollo program. There's an **AstroVan** on display, too. Kids will enjoy controlling a mock Mars Rover via joystick in one of the presentation halls, and the **Lunar Theater** attempts to dramatize Neil Armstrong's riveting moon landing. Though this film doesn't match the power of that in the Firing Room

Theater, don't miss the preview footage, showcasing Walter Cronkite's classic coverage of the event.

The final stop in the tour is the **International Space Station Center**. Not only can you witness actual components of the International Space Shuttle being constructed, but a high-tech observation deck shows the astronauts' cramped living space – claustrophobes beware.

US ASTRONAUT HALL OF FAME

Much of this museum is oriented toward kids, but it's definitely of interest to any space junkie. After passing a mural painted by astronaut Alan Bean and enduring a short film, you finally get to the good stuff: a room filled with spinning rides and motion simulators (obsolete for astronauts but still packing a 4G wallop). Visitors can also experience colorful, technologically impressive displays transforming physics problems into video games; inspect a life-sized model of the space shuttle; and view a tribute to the astronauts lost in the *Apollo I* disaster and the actual *Apollo 14* module.

Eating

Overpriced eateries are sprinkled throughout the Visitor Complex. The most exotic is the Moon Rock Café at the Apollo/Saturn V Center, which complements your dining experience with a chunk of Earth's oldest satellite.

If you don't feel like talking to the people you came to the KSC with, consider scheduling **Lunch with an Astronaut**, (☎ 321-449-4400; adult/child under 11 $23/16, in addition to general admission ticket). Held daily at 12:15pm, this is a great opportunity to get up close and personal with some of the world's most accomplished people. BYO Tang.

Kennedy Space Center for Children

Several exhibits at the Visitor Complex are designed to lure kids into the world of math and science, using the promise of potential space travel as bait. Pick up a free Interplanetary Passport at the gift shop, which kids can have stamped throughout the KSC. The **Kid's Play Dome** is for smaller children, who'll squeal over the climbable versions of the space shuttle and ISS, while **Exploration in the New Millennium** will entertain older kids with interactive displays and the opportunity to touch a rock from Mars. Don't miss **Robot Scouts**, which introduces young people to talkative 'trailblazers for human exploration'. Finally, Professor Pruvitt – along with his wacky colleagues, Kelvin and WD-4D – combine live action and computer animation to transform audience members into 'astronaut trainees' in **Mad Mission to Mars**.

Tours & Programs

In addition to the bus tour included with your admission, the KSC offers several other special tours and programs, all costing extra. You can order tickets by calling ☎ 321-249-2444 or logging on to www.ksctickets.com.

The **NASA Up Close** (adult/child $59/43) tour includes regular admission plus an expertly narrated two-hour tour that affords a much closer look at the launch pads and the VAB, as well as a peek at other 'restricted areas.' Expect to see numerous 'pad rats' (aka center employees) scurrying around; the world's largest private laundromat, used for washing and drying parachutes; and the runway where the shuttle lands. At 15,000ft, it's so long you can't see one end from the other end, due to the earth's curvature. It's well worth the upgrade if you want to see behind the scenes. Note that just prior to a launch, this tour is cut short.

The **Cape Canaveral Then & Now** (adult/child $59/43) tour tops off your visit with a look back at the life of NASA. The tour lasts about 2½ hours and includes a stop at the **Air Force Space & Missile Museum**, featuring restored hardware from the early days of space travel; NASA's Launch Complex 5/6, where Alan Shepard and John Glenn blasted off on their Mercury missions; and 'Hanger S,' where early astronauts lived and trained. A visit to the **Cape Canaveral Lighthouse** is included.

The **Astronaut Training Experience** (ATX; ☎ 321-449-4400; per person incl lunch & gear $250) is the closest you will ever come to being an astronaut without all that pesky schooling and training. This full-day experience puts you through the

---

TITUSVILLE, THE WORLD'S LARGEST ALLIGATOR, AND A PLACE WHERE IT'S CHRISTMAS 365 DAYS A YEAR

Titusville is the main gateway to the Kennedy Space Center. Overlooking the Indian River, Titusville's about 45 minutes north on US 1.

For breakfast, grab coffee and a muffin from **Sunrise Bread Company** (☎ 407-268-1009; 315 S Hopkins Ave; ☺ 6am-6pm Mon-Sat; ☐), an airy coffee shop/bakery the size of a barn.

After filling your stomach, go see the world's largest alligator. Big enough to let you stand inside his gaping maw, this reptile isn't real. Swampy, as he's affectionately known, is a 200ft alligator greeting visitors to **Jungle Adventures Nature Park** (☎ 407-568-2885, 1-877-4-A-GATOR; 26205 SR 50; adult/child 3-11yr $20/11; ☺ 9:30am-5:30pm). This quirky roadside attraction is home to rare Florida Panthers, black bears, gray wolves, tropical birds and more. Feeling brave? Take a jungle swamp cruise, where more than 200 alligators'll surround you. From Titusville, head west on SR 50. Eight miles after I-95, Swampy will appear on your right. Don't leave Jungle Adventures without grabbing a bite from the **Coffee Bus** parked outside. This retrofitted school bus has tasty sandwiches and outstanding bread pudding.

After lunch, head west 2.6 miles; when you spot the year-round holiday display on your right, you're in **Christmas, Florida**, where it's Christmas 365 days a year. Turn onto Fort Christmas Rd, and drive about a mile to **Fort Christmas Historical Park** (☎ 407-568-4149; 1300 Fort Christmas Rd; admission free; ☺ 8am-6pm in winter, to 8pm in summer), a beautiful oak-filled park draped with garlands of Spanish moss. Featuring a full-size replica of Fort Christmas and seven meticulously restored 'Cracker' homes dating to 1870, this is the best history lesson in the region.

After touring the Cracker homes, return to Titusville and grab dinner at **Dixie Crossroads** (☎ 321-268-5000; 1475 Garden St, Titusville; meals $9-35; ☺ 11am-9pm). This local institution – a riot of murals and sculptures, ponds and fountains – looks like grandma decorated it, but the locally caught rock shrimp make the pastels go down easy.

After dinner, bed down at the **Casa Coquina** (☎ 321-268-4653, 877-684-8341; www.casacoquina.com; 4010 Coquina Ave; $79-159; ☐ P ☎), an eclectic hodge-podge of a B&B. Featuring a garden stuffed with as many statues as the Louvre (plus a rockin' koi pond!), this elaborate three-story mansion from the 1920s oozes serenity. Inside, each room has a music station, and guests can enjoy the property's Jacuzzi, deluxe massage chair, and musical instruments in the British Pub Room.

astronaut wringers, including the one-sixth gravity chair and a mission-control countdown. You'll also have a Q&A with former astronauts plus exclusive tours of the shuttle launch pads, International Space Station Center and NASA's press site. Participants must be 14 years and up; those under 18 need to be accompanied by an adult. The program is extremely popular so book well in advance.

Getting There & Around

From the I-95, take the Beeline Expressway (528) east to Hwy 3 north and you'll run straight into the entrance.

Getting here without a car is difficult. Greyhound only has service to Cocoa and Titusville; from Orlando it's $18, but that doesn't include the taxi (about $20, one-way) from Cocoa to the KSC.

MERRITT ISLAND NATIONAL WILD-LIFE REFUGE

Merritt Island National Wildlife Refuge is home to 16 endangered and threatened species – including four kinds of turtles – more than any other refuge in the continental USA. The area around the KSC is federally protected wilderness area and is usually open to the public. Many of these areas are closed at least three days before a launch, so call ahead. You can camp on Apollo Beach, or – if you've got a canoe or kayak – on several super-remote islands within Canaveral National Seashore.

Orientation & Information

NASA uses only about 4% of its total landholdings for getting into space. In 1963 NASA turned management of its unused land over to the US Fish & Wildlife Service (USFWS), which then established this **refuge** (☎ 321-861-0667; admission free; ☾ 8am-4.30pm Mon-Fri, 9am-5pm Sat & Sun, closed Sun Apr-Oct). More than just an undeveloped patch of land, the refuge is home to seven distinct habitat types, including mangrove swamps, brackish marshes and hardwood hammocks. The Merritt Island visitors center, located 4 miles east of Titusville on SR 402 (exit 80 off I-95), has lots of informative pamphlets.

Sights & Activities

From the visitor's center, pick up a pamphlet detailing a self-guided tour around the refuge's most popular and easily accessible attraction, **Black Point Wildlife Drive**. This 6.1-mile loop is the best place to see wildlife on the refuge. To increase your chances of spotting critters, head out during the two hours after sunrise or two hours before sunset.

Feel like stretching your legs? **Boardwalk Trail** is a quarter-mile nature trail next to the center. Three other hiking trails begin about a mile east of the main visitors center: the half-mile **Oak Hammock Trail**; the 2-mile **Palm Hammock Trail**, winding through hardwood forest, with boardwalks above the open marsh; and the 5-mile **Cruickshank Trail**, beginning at stop 8 along the Black Point Wildlife Drive.

For a special treat, cross your fingers and head to the **manatee viewing platform**. While you're not guaranteed to spy a manatee, from this location as many as 42 of these lovable but endangered sea cows have been seen at once. To get here, go east on the SR 402, turn left (north) on SR 3, cross Haulover Canal Bridge, make the next right onto the dirt road, and follow it to the viewing platform.

If you want to feel truly alone, take a canoe trip through **Mosquito Lagoon**, located off the northeastern tip of Merritt Island refuge. Not only are there hundreds of deserted islands on which to have a quiet picnic, but manatees and dolphins are often spotted weaving through the lush mangroves.

It's best to visit the refuge from October to May, when the weather is mildest. This is the height of migratory bird season, too. Along with Canaveral National Seashore, Merritt Island is one of the best birding spots in the country, with 310 bird species identified so far. Serving as one stop along the Atlantic Flyway, a path birds follow traveling between North and South America, peak wintertime concentrations of waterfowl often exceed 100,000. Pick up a free bird-spotting guide at the visitors center.

CANAVERAL NATIONAL SEASHORE

The 24 miles of windswept beaches along this **seashore** (☎ 321-267-1110, recorded visitor information ☎ 407-867-0677; www.nps.gov/cana; admission $3; ☾ 6am-6pm Nov-Mar, to 8pm Apr-Oct) are the longest stretch of undeveloped dune on Florida's east coast. A favorite haunt of surfers, campers and nature lovers, the dune today looks like it did before Spaniards landed in Florida almost 500 years ago.

Orientation & Information

All the park's visitor programs and information services are handled by the **North District**

ENJOY THE SPOILS

The Spoil Island Project is a volunteer driven program spearheaded by the Florida Department of Environmental Protection Aquatic Preserve Offices, with support from other state and local agencies. We spoke to the East Central Aquatic preserve staff, who manage the spoil islands locally.

What are the spoil islands? The spoil islands are a series of 137 islands dotting the Indian River Lagoon, formed when engineers dredged the lagoon to a depth of between eight and 12ft. All the material they recovered – all the project's 'spoils' – were heaped into piles in the middle of the waterway, creating islands. There are some natural islands there but most are manmade.

How are they maintained? The only maintenance we perform is very basic island restoration like planting mangroves and other native vegetation. Though there's more dredging going on, they're not adding more spoils to the islands. The spoils are being sent elsewhere now.

What kinds of facilities are on the islands? There are several designation use categories: education, active or passive recreation and conservation. You're free to use any of the designated recreation islands. All we ask is that you don't approach those islands marked conservation, because they're for the rookeries. You'll know right away that it's a conservation island, because you'll see lots of birds flying… and it'll smell a little.

How can I learn which islands I can access? We have spoil islands booklets available in our offices explaining where the islands are located and the designated use for each. You can also visit www.spoilislandproject.org, click on 'interactive maps' and browse the islands. They're all labeled according to designation, so it's easy.

What can I do on the islands? Some have docks, kiosks, BBQ pits and picnic tables. Most are undeveloped. Mostly, you bring your own stuff and remove your own trash. It's first come first served and there's no charge. If you have any questions about use or facilities, just check the website. Ultimately, we want people to use the islands, to learn that humans and nature can be together, but please remember to keep away from any islands that have birds on them! It's their home.

If you have more questions about the spoil islands, please visit www.spoilislandproject.org or call ☎ 321-634-6148.

Visitors Center (☎ 321-267-1110), 7 miles south of New Smyrna Beach on Hwy A1A. From here, sea turtle watching programs take small groups (20 people, maximum) along the beach between June and July starting about 10:30pm. These book faster than turtles running, so call for reservations up to 11 months in advance.

On most Sundays, rangers lead two hour guided pontoon boat tours (per person $20), explaining the importance of barrier islands, describing the duties of dune plant communities and pointing out indigenous fauna. Reservations are required (☎ 386-428-3384) and space is limited.

Sights & Activities
BEACHES
Let's face it: this is the real reason you're here. **Apollo Beach**, to the north, is favored by families because of the calm surf (watch out for riptides, though). **Klondike Beach**, the 12-mile stretch between Apollo and Playalinda Beaches, is as pristine as it gets, without even a nature trail

to mar it. **Playalinda Beach**, at the southern end, is surfer headquarters, with decent breaks and lots of dudes named, um, Dude.

You can canoe or kayak through Mosquito Lagoon, though winds can get strong. Village Outfitters (p346) operates kayak tours through the area.

Sleeping
You can **camp** (☎ 386-428-3384; up to 6 people $10, 7 people or more $20) at two sites along Apollo Beach from November to late April. If you've got a boat, there are 12 primitive campsites scattered throughout the islands – many in manatee zones! – open year-round. Permits are required for both types of camping, and you'll need to pack in everything, including drinking water. Make reservations early and note that there is no camping during shuttle launches.

Getting There & Around
To enter through the North District, take I-95 to SR 44 (Exit 249). Head east on SR 44 to the

A1A, then go south on A1A nine miles to the park; for the South District take I-95 to SR 406 (Exit 220), then 406 east to 402 east and the entrance. There is no public transportation within the park.

COCOA VILLAGE & COCOA BEACH
☎ 321 / pop 17,000

Sandwiched between Cape Canaveral and Patrick Air Force Base is the lively but sprawling Cocoa Beach. As *I Dream of Jeannie* fans may suspect, it's basically a service town for NASA and the air force bases, albeit with a hard-packed sand beach strewn with partiers and surfers. Don't plan to be overrun by servicemen and women, however. Rather, expect plenty of condos, eateries and surf shops.

Historic Cocoa Village has upscale restaurants, niche stores and historic buildings; pick up a brochure with a self-guided tour at the welcome center.

Orientation
Cocoa Village is located due west across the causeway, about 7 miles from Cocoa Beach, which skirts the oceanfront.

Information
To find out what's going on, check out the bimonthly *Cocoa Village* paper.

Chamber of Commerce (☎ 321-454-2022; www .visitcocoabeach.com; 400 Fortenberry Rd; 🕘 9am-5pm Mon-Fri) Located on the Merritt Island side of the causeway, with plenty of free maps and pamphlets on the area.

Cocoa Beach Public Library (☎ 321-868-1104; 550 N Brevard Ave; 🕘 9am-9pm Mon-Wed, 9am-6pm Thu, 9am-5pm Fri & Sat, 1-5pm Sun) Wi-fi accessible 7am-10pm, even from the parking lot.

Post office (cnr 4th St & N Brevard Ave) One block west of Hwy A1A.

Sights & Activities
COCOA BEACH PIER
Built in 1962, this funky **pier** (☎ 321-783-7549; www.cocoabeachpier.com; 401 Meade Ave; fishing/walking $5/$1; 🅿) attracts more than a million visitors a year. Along its 800ft walk are one stage, two gift shops, four restaurants, five bars and countless speakers pumping out beachy tunes. You can rent a rod and reel for $10 (includes pier access) and buy bait for $3. At its tip, the fabulously weathered **Mai Tiki Bar** (🕘 noon-10pm Mon-Thu, to 11pm Fri-Sun) – decorated with rotting dollar bills and leathery bar flies – may be the finest spot in Cocoa Beach to view a launch.

BEACHES
Cocoa has three public beaches. **Sheppard Park**, at the end of Hwy 520, is more family oriented, while busy **Cocoa Beach**, by the pier, caters to space tourists and the surf crowd. **Downtown Cocoa Beach**, at the intersection of Minuteman Causeway and Hwy A1A, is geared toward adults, with a collection of cool bars and upscale restaurants abutting the sand.

ASTRONAUT MEMORIAL PLANETARIUM & OBSERVATORY
No need to eat your carrots; this excellent **center** (☎ 321-433-7373; www.brevard.cc.fl.us/planet; 1519 Clearlake Rd; show adult/child under 13yr $7/4, show & planetarium $11/9; 🕘 exhibit halls Wed 1.30-4.30pm, Fri & Sat 6.30-10.30pm; observatory Fri & Sat sunset-10pm) houses Florida's largest public telescope.

Planetarium shows start at 7pm and show off what's billed as the world's only tandem team of Digistar projectors and the USA's only Minolta Infinium star projector. At 8pm films screen in the IWERKS (like IMAX, but smaller) theater; laser shows start at 9pm. The planetarium is on the Broward Community College (BCC) campus, off Clearlake Rd between Michigan Ave and Rosetine St. From US Hwy 1 take Dixon Blvd west to Clearlake and turn north; the campus is on the left.

BREVARD MUSEUM OF HISTORY & NATURAL SCIENCE
This **museum** (☎ 321-632-1830; www.brevardmuseum .org; 2201 Michigan Ave; adult/child 5-16yr $6/4.50; 🕘 10am-4pm Mon-Sat) has a permanent collection including 7000-year-old Indian artifacts and exhibits on area wildlife. It also holds special exhibits on subjects as diverse as arachnids, powder horns and early-20th-century weaponry. A pleasant, shady trail around the lake links the museum and observatory.

DREAMING OF JEANNIE

Almost nothing in Cocoa Beach references the 1960s US sitcom *I Dream of Jeannie*, which was set in this idyllic beach town. The single tribute to the show can be found on US 1. About 1 mile north of Minutemen Causeway, the eagle-eyed can spot I Dream of Jeannie Lane leading east. Turn onto I Dream of Jeannie Lane, and you'll wind up in Lori Wilson Park, a beautiful spot with a dog park and beach access.

SURFING COCOA & BEYOND

A well-developed tourist infrastructure, endless coastline, and mild water and air temperatures attract surfers to Florida's Atlantic shore like sharks to a chum slick. While Florida is home to some worthy surf spots – storms tracking from Africa can produce offshore surf up to 10ft! – the entire state doesn't receive these bodacious waves. In fact, the Bahamas protects much of the southern portion of Florida from wave action. Consequently, most surfers consider Fort Pierce to be the southernmost spot for acceptable surfing, but the area from Sebastian to Cocoa Beach is tops. From south to north, here are some essential spots for hanging ten:

- **Sebastian Inlet** Just north of Wabasso Beach
- **Indialantic** Right off the boardwalk
- **Satellite Beach** North of Indialantic, near Satellite Senior High School
- **Second Light** East of Patrick Air Force Base
- **Downtown Cocoa Beach** Right off Minutemen Cswy
- **Cocoa Beach Pier** To get here, head north on Ocean Beach Blvd and turn right on Meade Ave

Thanks to those African storms, look for the most dependable breaks to occur from August to November (the only upside of having a hurricane season).

Don't know how to surf? Contact **Surf Guy's Surf School** (☎ 1-866-SURFGUY; www.surfguyssurf .com; Melbourne Beach; semiprivate/private lessons per hr $40/45, 4-day camps $200), and they'll get you started. The **Cocoa Beach Surfing School** (☎ 321-868-1980; www.cocoabeachsurfingschool.com; 3901 N Atlantic Ave; semiprivate/private lessons per hr $45/60) boasts members of the US National Surfing Team as instructors.

No doubt the biggest surfing event in Florida is the **Ron Jon Easter Surf Festival**. The country's second oldest surf competition, this clash of surfing titans overlaps with Spring Break. Look for 30,000-plus cool surfer dudes, tan beach bunnies, and sunburned college kids packing Cocoa's beach.

If you know how to surf, but want the surf report, Indialantic's **Longboard House** (☎ 321-953-0392) runs a surfing information hotline and **SurfGuru.com** offers a mobile surf report for the entire region. Direct your cell phone's browser to www.surfguru.com/mobile/and check conditions.

KAYAKING & WATER SPORTS

Village Outfitters (☎ 321-633-7245; www.villageout fitters.com; 229 Forrest Ave; tours single/double kayak $60/90; ☺ 10am-5pm Mon-Fri, to 4pm Sat), in Cocoa Village, runs half-day kayak tours to Merritt Island Refuge, Pine Island and elsewhere, including visits to wild beaches with jaw-dropping views of the shuttle launch. They'll also rent you kayaks ($30 for a single, $45 for a double) so you can explore some of the area's primitive spoil islands on your own (see p344).

Fin Expeditions (☎ 321-698-7233; www.finexpedit ions.com; Ramp Rd; per person $30) takes you kayaking with manatees.

Next to the Ron Jon Surf Shop, **Ron Jon's Watersports** (☎ 321-799-8888; 4151 N Atlantic Ave; ☺ 8am-8pm) rents just about anything water-related from fat-tired beach bikes ($15 daily) to surfboards ($30 daily).

Island Watercraft Rentals (☎ 321-454-7661; www .islandwatercraftrentals.com; 1872 E 520 Cswy) rents jet skis (per hour $80) and larger watercraft.

Sleeping

Cocoa Beach attracts surfers at Spring Break and space junkies during launches, so expect higher prices during those times.

BUDGET

Jetty Park Campground (☎ 321-783-7111; www .jettypark.org; 400 Jetty Rd; campsite $20-40, depending on utilities & season) In nearby Cape Canaveral, this has some of the best shuttle-launch views in the area.

Luna Sea Motel (☎ 321-783-0500, 1-800-586-2732; www.lunaseacocoabeach.com; 3185 N. Atlantic Ave; r $70-90; ☐ P ☒) As cheerful as the waving tiki idol greeting visitors, this centrally located motel offers spotless rooms and a complimentary cooked-to-order breakfast.

MIDRANGE

Fawlty Towers (☎ 321-784-3870; www.fawltytowers resort.com; 100 E Cocoa Beach Causeway; r $80-170; P ☒) Almost as gaudy as Ron Jon's, this pink compound nevertheless has nice rooms and a tropical-themed pool fronted by a tiki bar.

Surf Studio Beach Resort (☎ 321-783-7100; www .surf-studio.com; 1801 S Atlantic Ave; summer r $110-210, winter $95-170; **P** **R**) Away from the hubbub, this low-key surfer retreat – a converted motel, family-owned since 1948 – will rent you a surfboard for $35 per day and welcome your pet.

TOP END

Inn at Cocoa Beach (☎ 321-799-3460, 800-343-5307; www.theinnatcocoabeach.com; 4300 Ocean Beach Blvd; r $135-295; **□** **P** **R**) Well-situated and immaculately manicured, this beachfront complex has comfortable rooms, an overflowing honor bar, daily wine-and-cheese socials and (despite its size) an intimate feel.

Beach Place Guesthouses (☎ 321-783-4045; www .beachplaceguesthouses.com; 1445 S Atlantic Ave; ste $195-350; **□** **P** **R**) With lush gardens (concealing a very cool beach shower), tranquil ocean views and immaculate one- and two-bedroom suites, this is the place for a private getaway. Numerous restaurants are nearby, but each suite comes with a fully equipped kitchen, so why bother?

Eating

BUDGET

Maine'ly Lobster Seafood and Takeout (☎ 321-799-4700; www.mainelylobsterseafoodandtakeout.com; 210 N Orlando Ave; meals $4-16; 🕑 11am-7pm Sun-Wed, to 9pm Thu-Sat) For nearly 20 years, this family-run shack has provided New England and local seafood (yum…locally caught mahimahi) to locals. Recently, they added a seafood takeout window, so you can grab your crab cakes and bolt.

Ossorio (☎ 321-639-2423; 316 Brevard Ave; meals $7-9; 🕑 8am-8:30pm Mon-Sat, 9am-6pm Sun) Bright oranges, purples and greens complement the sublime sandwiches and wood-oven fired flatbread pizzas at this cheery café. Mouthwatering pastries, crisp salads and quirky ice creams (PB&J!) are all made from scratch in-store. No time to dine? Grab an iced coffee from the walk-up window and keep moving.

Murdock's Bistro & Char Bar (☎ 321-633-0600; www.murdockscocoavillage.com; 600 Brevard Ave; meals $7-13; 🕑 11am-10pm Mon-Thu, to 12.30am Fri, to midnight Sat & Sun) One look at the exposed rafters, antique gingerbreading and hulking colonnades with their curlicue detailing, and you know this place is special. Renowned for their burgers,

Murdoch's has a patio for drinking, dining and grooving to (almost) nightly live music.

MIDRANGE

Pita Garden (☎ 321-799-9933; www.pitagarden.com; 269 W Cocoa Beach Cswy; mains $7-15; 🕑 7am-10pm Sun-Thu, to 10:30pm Fri & Sat) Delicious Middle Eastern meals made fresh.

Punjab Indian Restaurant (☎ 321-799-4696; www .punjabindianrestaurant.net; 285 W Cocoa Beach Cswy; mains $9-15; 🕑 7am-10pm Sun-Thu, to 10:30pm Fri & Sat) If the sand isn't hot enough, you need some Indian food. Served under lavish tapestries, the Singh family offers plenty of 'Sabazi Bazar' options for visiting vegetarians.

Grills Seafood (☎ 321-868-2226; ww.visitgrills.com; 505 Glen Cheek Dr; meals $7-19; 🕑 7am-10pm Sun-Thu, to 10:30pm Fri & Sat) This Cape Canaveral spot has music on weekends and a marina-facing bar 24/7. Best time to come, however: breakfast. Order the massive fruit platter ($7.50) and cool it as the sun rises and the boats putter through the second-busiest cruise port in the world.

TOP END

our pick **Fat Snook** (☎ 321-784-1190; 2464 S Atlantic Ave; meals $17-40; 🕑 from 5:30pm Mon-Sat) Hidden inside an uninspired building on the south edge of town, the Fat Snook features a rotating blue crab appetizer, a thoughtfully assembled wine selection, and a whip-smart staff. The ten small tables inside the blue and green walls fill fast, so get reservations.

Drinking & Entertainment

Cocoa Village has a great community playhouse, and Cocoa Beach is where the Space Coast comes to party. Some bars are a typical beach scene, but others showcase great local music.

Sunset Waterfront Grill & Bar (☎ 321-783-8485; 500 W Cocoa Beach Cswy; meals $15-20; 🕑 11am-10pm) Sure, they serve food, but the main attraction is the sunset – you won't find a view this divine anywhere in Cocoa (maybe anywhere on Florida's east coast). Grab a seat on the deck, order a drink, and wait for the show to begin.

Beach Shack Bar (☎ 321-783-2250; www.beach shackbar.com; 1 Minutemen Cswy; 🕑 10am-2am) With wobbly chairs made of PVC and wood paneling that must be decades old, this is a true locals' bar. However, with two pool tables, an oceanfront patio, and live blues seven nights a week, this place rocks.

Ultra Lounge (☎ 321-690-0096; 407 Brevard Ave; ☽ 8am-midnight Mon-Fri, to 2am Sat) Slick, modern and comfortable, this place has premium wines and beers, a full coffee bar, gourmet appetizers and more pillows than a home store. Live jazz on the weekends.

Cocoa Village Playhouse (☎ 321-636-5050; www .cocoavillageplayhouse.com; 300 Brevard Ave; tickets $15-22) Stages locally produced plays on the site of the ornate Aladdin Theatre (1924). Has a ghost named Joe.

Funntasia (☎ 321-799-4856; 6355 N Atlantic Ave; adult/child $6.75/5.75; ☽ 10am-10pm Mon-Fri, to 11pm Sat, 12pm-10pm Sun) The waterfalls are fake, but the swinging good times are for real at this 36-hole minigolf course.

Shopping

Ron Jon Surf Shop (☎ 321-799-8888; www.ronjons.com; 4151 N Atlantic Ave; ☽ 24hr) Rising from the center of town like a pastel palace, the 52,000 sq ft Ron Jon is more than a store: live music (like Beach Boys cover bands), classic cars and a warehouse jammed with swimsuits, surfboards and more make visiting here an event.

Sunseed Food Co-op (☎ 321-784-0930; www.sun seedfoodcoop.com; 6615 N Atlantic Ave; ☽ 10am-6pm Mon-Wed & Sat, to 7pm Thu & Fri) Swing by this healthy oasis and grab some organic (and locally grown) fruits, veggies, wines and after-sun lotions. They also have an extensive micro-brew selection and yummy organic raw cocoa energy cubes.

Dinosaur Store (☎ 321-783-7300; www.dinosaurstore .com; 299 W Cocoa Beach Cswy; ☽ 10:30am-5pm Mon-Fri, to 7pm Sat) Filled with museum-quality specimens, this unusual store's offerings range from di-nosaur bone jewelry, to spiny trilobite fossils, to $5000 fossilized dinosaur eggs. No bones about it, the enormous dinosaur skulls inside are startling.

Nearly Barefoot Sandals (☎ 321-784-2244; www .nearlybarefoot.com; 350 N Atlantic Ave; ☽ 10am-6pm Mon-Sat, noon-6pm Sun) If the flip-flops at the surf shops don't make your heart stop, check out the quality footwear here.

Getting There & Around

Greyhound buses stop at the **Exxon station** (☎ 321-636-6531; 4301 Hwy 524). **SCAT** (☎ 321-633-1878; www.ridescat.com) buses serve Cocoa Beach Monday to Friday. Bus No 9 runs along Hwy A1A, connecting Cocoa Beach to Cape Canaveral. Fares are $1.25.

HOW TO AVOID A SHARK BITE

Florida is the 'shark bite capital of the world.' On average, one-third of the world's shark bites are recorded in the sunshine state, and in 2007, Florida recorded the most unprovoked shark bites in the country with 32. To avoid a shark bite, sink your teeth into these tips:

- Swim with a group of people (activity repels sharks).
- Don't enter the water with an open wound (blood attracts them).
- Don't swim at dawn or dusk (this is when they feed).
- Avoid wearing shiny jewelry (you'll look like a small fish).
- Stay out of murky water (this is where they prefer to hunt, and you're less likely to see them).

MELBOURNE & INDIALANTIC
☎ 321 / 76,000

Melbourne (to the west of the Intracoastal) and Indialantic (to the east) make a good base for turtle-watchers and affluent surfers sick of battling crowds at Cocoa Beach (a small but fairly consistent break can be spotted off the mini-boardwalk). The area is home to a handful of small colleges, yet the median age is 48. As a result, the area is packed with trendy surf shops and doily-filled antiquaries, pro-gressive yoga studios and pastel hair salons. Its dichotomy is part of its charm.

Information

Eau Gallie Public Library (☎ 321-255-4304; 1521 Pineapple Ave; ☽ 9am-9pm Mon-Thu, 9am-5pm Fri & Sat) Free internet access and a grand view of Indian River.

Melbourne-Palm Bay Area Chamber of Commerce (☎ 321-724-5400; www.melpb-chamber.org; 1005 E Strawbridge Ave; ☽ 9am-5pm Mon-Fri) Has information on local attractions.

Sights & Activities
DOWNTOWN MELBOURNE

The historic downtown area, along E New Haven Ave, right behind the chamber of commerce, offers a pleasant stroll among antique and clothing stores. Just two blocks west of the chamber, at **Crane Creek Manatee Sanctuary**, you can spot river turtles and catfish and, if you're lucky, manatees.

The small **Brevard Museum of Art & Science** (☎ 321-242-0737; www.brevardartmuseum.org; 1463 Highland Ave; adult/child $5/2, free on Thu; ☼ 10am-5pm Tue-Sat, from 1pm Sun) rotates through some interesting art collections, ranging from classic to pop.

The race-car-themed **Andretti Thrill Park** (☎ 321-956-6706; www.andrettithrillpark.com; 3960 S Babcock St; unlimited rides 2/4hr $25/35; ☼ hours vary) really gets the blood flowing with three go-cart tracks, bumper boats, laser tag, a massive arcade and an 18-hole miniature golf course.

BEACH & BOARDWALK

The area's main public beach and boardwalk, at the end of Hwy 192 in Indialantic, isn't expansive, but it sure feels homey. Further adding to its appeal is its great surfing, white sandy shores, and light tourist traffic. There are only a few restaurants and bars here, which reinforce the area's authentic beach vibe. Grab a massive slice of pizza from breezy **Bizarro Pizza** (☎ 321-724-4799; 4 Wavecrest Ave; ☼ 11am-9pm Mon-Thu, to 11pm Fri & Sat, noon-6pm Sun) and you'll be full the rest of the day.

Across the street, the **Longboard House** (☎ 321-951-0730; www.longboardhouse.com; 101 5th Ave; ☼ 9am-9pm Mon-Sat, to 6pm Sun) in Indialantic sells a huge selection of new and used surfboards;

it also rents longboards for $25 to $30 per day and bodyboards for $10 per day.

Take advantage of the beach's flat, scenic routes by renting a bike from **Beach Bicycle Works** (☎ 321-725-2500; 113 5th Ave; single-speed/multi-speed bikes per day $20/25).

Sleeping

Tuckaway Shores (☎ 321-723-3355; www.tuckaway shores.com; 1441 S A1A; ste $99-149; P 🖳 🕿) Surf-fish right from the property's back door and cook it in the fully furnished kitchen in your four-person suite. Also on-site: a convenient BBQ area, laundry facilities and lots of kids.

Crane Creek Inn (☎ 321-768-6416; www.crane creekinn.com; 907 E Melbourne Ave; r $100-199; P 🖳 🕿) Two short blocks from historic downtown Melbourne, this cheerful B&B sits right on Crane Creek, a tributary of Indian River. The Inn's five rooms are pleasant (if a bit frou-frou), but if you really want to relax, grab a cool drink, swim up to the property's in-pool table and watch the creek slowly trickle past. Pets are welcome. Children under 18 are not.

Windmere Inn By the Sea (☎ 321-728-9334, 800-224-6853; www.windmereinn.com; 815 Hwy A1A; r $149-262, ste $380-390; P 🖳 🕿) An immaculate ocean-front B&B with all the trimmings: English antiques, spas in a few of the rooms, afternoon

---

DETOUR: SEBASTIAN INLET STATE PARK

Sebastian Inlet is about 20 miles south of Indialantic on Hwy A1A. There are a few small museums here, but the main attractions are the fishing, surfing and camping opportunities at **Sebastian Inlet State Park** (☎ 321-984-4852; 9700 S A1A; pedestrian/car $1/5; ☼ 24hrs).

The park sits on a narrow stretch of the barrier-island chain and attracts all manner of salty, outdoorsy types. There's great surfing here and you can snorkel or scuba dive the remains of Spanish galleons (and perhaps find a doubloon of your own). If you feel motivated, try clam digging for your own dinner.

The Indian River and Atlantic Ocean also provide ample opportunities for boating; try the **Inlet Marina** (☎ 321-724-5424; www.sebastianinlet.com; 9502 S A1A; canoes per 2hr/day $18/35; kayaks s/d $38/45; ☼ 8am-6pm), if you don't have a boat of your own. The concession stand runs ranger-led, two-hour boat tours at 2pm ($35 per hour, plus rentals, minimum two hours) and serves cheap meals (under $10).

The small **Mclarty Treasure Museum** (☎ 772-589-2147; 13180 N A1A; adult/child under 6yr $1/free; ☼ 10am-4:30pm), within Sebastian Inlet State Park, displays Spanish treasures from 11 galleons that were destroyed in a hurricane just off the coast back in 1715. The exhibits are fascinating and silver-sparkly, but the best reason to come takes place during 'salvage season' (May through September). From the galleon-shaped pier behind the museum, you can watch divers and treasure hunters moored right offshore doing their thing.

Planning an overnight? Get one with nature at Sebastian's **campground** (☎ 321-984-4852; 9700 S Hwy A1A; sites $25), which offers 51 waterfront spots. Pets are welcome!

tea and a full breakfast. If you're coming as a group of four, try snagging the oceanfront suites: you'll get two huge bedrooms, a common room and a stunning sunrise.

Eating

our pick **905 Cafe** (☎ 321-952-1672; 905 E New Haven Ave; mains $3-10; ☺ 9am-5pm Mon-Sat) Don't be surprised to see grannies nibbling on Brie platters inside this shotgun shack of a restaurant while teens congregate outside chowing shrimp salad sandwiches on marble rye. Pink and pleasant, it also has great coffee.

City Tropics Bistro (☎ 321-723-1300; www.citytropics .com; 249 5th Ave; meals $8-20; ☺ 11am-10pm) Owned by local restaurateur Djon Pepaj (a former aerospace engineer), City Tropics features an extensive outdoor deck and a sprawling interior with a colorful island mood. In addition to great crab cakes, City Tropics boasts an onsite wine shop with more than 1000 bottles. Drink it here, or take it with you.

Chart House Restaurant (☎ 321-729-6558; www .chart-house.com; 2250 Front St; meals $19-36; ☺ 11am-10pm) With the marina on the starboard and Indian River on the bow, it's full-steam ahead to the Chart House for elegant waterfront dining. Try the crusted mahimahi or the prime rib.

Drinking & Entertainment

Friday Fest (☎ 321-724-1741; cnr E New Haven Ave & Waverly St; ☺ 6-9pm Fri) On the second Friday of the month, Friday Fest closes historic downtown Melbourne to traffic and brings in live music, carnival games, drinking in the streets and all manner of merrymaking.

Sun Shoppe Cafe (☎ 321-676-1438; 540 E New Haven Ave; ☺ 8am-12am Mon-Sat; ⌨) By day, The Sun Shoppe is a mild-mannered coffeehouse/eatery. At night, it transforms into a live-music venue showcasing American roots music. Equal parts bohemian café and mini-museum, this understated spot also boasts free wi-fi and a rotating art collection.

Meg O'Malley's (☎ 321-952-5510; www.megomalleys .com; 810 E New Haven Ave) Features 20 brews on tap, including its own Irish cider, and live music – usually Irish bands or local jazz and blues groups – every night around 8pm. It gets packed.

Foo Bar (☎ 321-728-7178; 816 E New Haven Ave; ☺ 4pm-2am Wed-Sat) A change of pace from the typical Florida beach bar, be sure to try this funky lounge's signature drink, the 'Snafoo.'

Getting There & Around

Melbourne International Airport (☎ 321-723-6227; www.mlbair.com) is a growing airport (the future site of the sorely needed Space Coast Amtrak station) served by Delta, Spirit, Comair and Atlantic Southeast Airlines, as well as a handful of rental-car companies and the SCAT bus No 21. There's also a **Greyhound bus station** (☎ 321-723-4329).

SCAT (☎ 321-633-1878, 952-4672; www.ridescat.com) also runs bus No 26 from the transfer point at Babcock and Hibiscus to serve Indialantic and the beaches ($1.25).

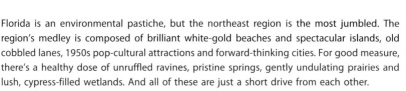

Northeast Florida

Florida is an environmental pastiche, but the northeast region is the most jumbled. The region's medley is composed of brilliant white-gold beaches and spectacular islands, old cobbled lanes, 1950s pop-cultural attractions and forward-thinking cities. For good measure, there's a healthy dose of unruffled ravines, pristine springs, gently undulating prairies and lush, cypress-filled wetlands. And all of these are just a short drive from each other.

Perched on the Atlantic Coast, Daytona Beach, the party king with a need for speed, is only 30 minutes from Flagler Beach's spartan coast. Further north, 400-year-old fortifications stand guard over wizened St Augustine, the country's oldest continuously occupied European settlement, with its jasmine-infused streets drenched in history and dotted with romantic restaurants and B&Bs. Spanning the languid St John's River, peppy Jacksonville boasts modern athletic facilities, a thriving performing-arts scene and funky shopping. Way up on the northern tip, Amelia Island, a true Southern Belle, graciously shares her Victorian architecture and silken beaches.

Inland, the vibrant college town, Gainesville, home to the nation's second-largest university, is a football's toss from Victorian gingerbread towns and a deluge of accessible natural attractions, including crystal-clear spring runs, and hiking and biking trails that crisscross the majestic Ocala National Forest.

Yep, northeast Florida has just about anything a traveler could want. But the best part? Even if you find yourself in an environment you're not totally stoked about, the next ecosystem is only about 20 minutes away. Hop in your car or on your bike and within a few minutes, you'll be far, far away.

HIGHLIGHTS

- Grab a great photo op in **Jacksonville** (p370) when the cobalt-blue Main St Bridge is reflected in St John's River and Jax Landing is illuminated in the background

- Walk the forlorn beach at **Big Talbot Island State Park** (p380) and discover an eerie driftwood graveyard set against a barren bluff

- Have a wacky science lesson in haunted **St Augustine** (p366) and use electromagnetic field meters and camera equipment to locate spirits haunting the town

- Down a few beers and check out a local band in **Gainesville** (p400), a college town with a thriving music scene

- Hike, camp and canoe your way through the wildlife-rich **Ocala National Forest** (p392)

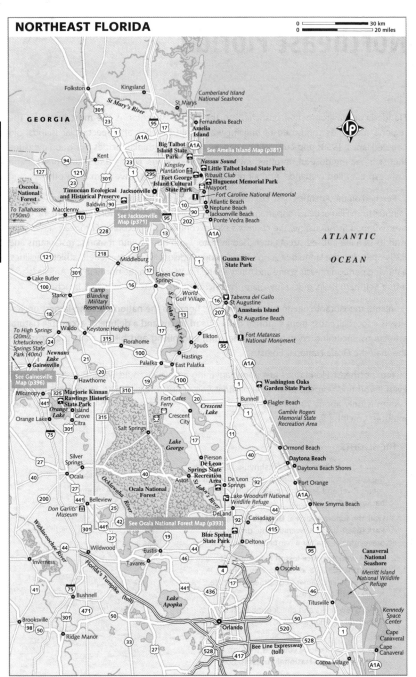

NORTHEAST FLORIDA

0   30 km
0   20 miles

History

Timucuan Indians first settled the area we call northeast Florida about 1000 BC. In 1513, Spanish explorer Juan Ponce de León sighted land, came ashore and claimed the so-called 'Land of Flowers' for Spain. In 1565, the Spanish established a military base – St Augustine – which has since become the oldest continuously occupied European settlement in the country. Roughly 250 years later and 40 miles north, two farmers donated land at a narrow point in the river and Jacksonville was born. Thirty years later, tourists started flocking to Amelia Island, and shortly thereafter, Henry Flagler laid railroad tracks along the coast and began developing the wild coast further and further south. Industrious American Indians, determined Spanish, clever farmers, curious tourists and visionary businessmen: all had a powerful hand in shaping this gorgeous land.

Climate

Northeast Florida's coast is mild and temperate year-round. Winter (around 55°F to 65°F) is generally off-season; if you're surfing, swimming or snorkeling, you'll want a full wetsuit. Inland winters can be chilly, but freezes are rare. Summers (around 80°F to upwards of 90°F) bring the region's peak rainfall.

National, State & Regional Parks

At the heart of Florida's northeastern region, the Ocala National Forest (p392) sprawls over 400,000 acres of clear natural springs, sand pine scrub, palmetto wilderness and subtropical forest, and is home to endangered flora and fauna. Northeast Florida also houses the 46,000-acre Timucuan Ecological and Historical Preserve (p375), which is the largest urban park system in the country, incorporating numerous areas of cultural and natural significance. There's also Blue Spring State Park (p386), one of the best places in the state to view manatees, Ichetucknee Springs State Park (p401), where you can leisurely float down the river on a raft or tube, or the dramatic Big Talbot Island State Park (p380), with polished live-oak driftwood strewn along its forlorn beach.

Information

Daytona Beach Area Convention & Visitors Bureau (☎ 386-255-0415; www.daytonabeach.com; 126 E Orange Ave; 🕙 9am-5pm Mon-Fri)
Historic Downtown Visitor's Center (☎ 904-261-3248, 800-226-3542; 102 Centre St; 🕙 11am-4pm Mon-Sat, noon-4pm Sun) Reams of useful information and maps in the old railroad depot. A fun stop in itself.
Jacksonville Landing visitor information (☎ 904-791-4305; 2 Independent Dr; 🕙 10am-7pm Mon-Sat, noon-5:30pm Sun) On the lower level.
St Augustine Visitor Information Center (☎ 904-825-1000; www.ci.st-augustine.fl.us; 10 Castillo Dr; 🕙 8:30am-5:30pm) Helpful, period-dressed staff sell tour tickets and answer questions.

Getting There & Around

Driving from the Space Coast, you can follow I-95 or US 1 north, or hug the coastline along the far more scenic Hwy A1A, all of which travel the length of Florida's Atlantic Coast. Hwy A1A terminates at Amelia Island; I-95 and US 1 continue over the state line to Georgia. Driving from Orlando, I-4 takes you northeast to Daytona Beach, while heading west on US 441 then north on Hwy 19 will bring you into the Ocala National Forest; continuing on US 441 takes you to the city of Ocala. See p516 for airport information.

ATLANTIC COAST

Leaving 'The World's Most Famous Beach,' Daytona Beach, zoom north along Florida's Atlantic Coast to historic St Augustine, buzzing Jacksonville and charming Amelia Island, with plenty of picturesque islands, parks and places to explore en route.

DAYTONA BEACH

☎ 386 / pop 65,000

Known for expansive beaches, '50s pop culture carnival attractions and Spring Break madness – all overlaid with pastels – Daytona Beach's strongest association, however, is with supercharged speed.

Anything but a wallflower, Daytona Beach has an overflowing dance card: it hosts one of the last Spring Breaks on the Atlantic Coast (tamer now than during its halcyon days); its population quintuples during Speed Weeks; and as many as half a million bikers roar into town for motorcycle events in spring and fall. There's also a tame side: Daytona is also home to a gentrified downtown, quality cultural attractions and nesting sea turtles.

Somehow, the thought of the racetrack and souped-up autos everywhere inspires drivers to push the pedal to the metal. Police know this, of course, and quickly curtail any need for speed.

NORTHEAST FLORIDA

NORTHEAST FLORIDA

DAYTONA BEACH

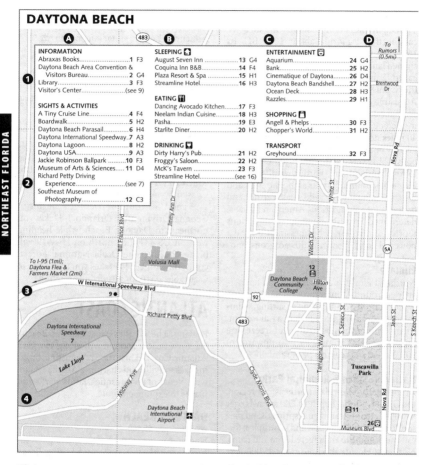

INFORMATION
Abraxas Books.............................1 F3
Daytona Beach Area Convention &
    Visitors Bureau.......................2 G4
Library...3 F3
Visitor's Center.......................(see 9)

SIGHTS & ACTIVITIES
A Tiny Cruise Line........................4 F3
Boardwalk....................................5 H2
Daytona Beach Parasail...............6 H4
Daytona International Speedway..7 A3
Daytona Lagoon..........................8 H2
Daytona USA...............................9 A3
Jackie Robinson Ballpark..........10 F3
Museum of Arts & Sciences.....11 D4
Richard Petty Driving
    Experience.........................(see 7)
Southeast Museum of
    Photography.......................12 C3

SLEEPING 🏠
August Seven Inn 13 G4
Coquina Inn B&B.......................14 F4
Plaza Resort & Spa 15 H1
Streamline Hotel........................16 H3

EATING 🍴
Dancing Avocado Kitchen.......17 F3
Neelam Indian Cuisine.............18 H3
Pasha...19 E3
Starlite Diner.............................20 H2

DRINKING 🍷
Dirty Harry's Pub......................21 H2
Froggy's Saloon.........................22 H2
McK's Tavern 23 F3
Streamline Hotel...................(see 16)

ENTERTAINMENT 🎭
Aquarium....................................24 G4
Bank..25 H2
Cinematique of Daytona..........26 D4
Daytona Beach Bandshell..........27 H2
Ocean Deck................................28 H3
Razzles.......................................29 H1

SHOPPING 🛍
Angell & Phelps 30 F3
Chopper's World........................31 H2

TRANSPORT
Greyhound..................................32 F3

To Rumors (0.5mi)

Brentwood Dr

Nova Rd

(5A)

To I-95 (1mi);
Daytona Flea &
Farmers Market (2mi)

Volusia Mall

Bill France Blvd

Jimmy Ann Dr

W International Speedway Blvd

9 ●

Daytona International
Speedway
7

Lake Lloyd

Midway Ave

Richard Petty Blvd

(483)

(92)

Clyde Morris Blvd

Daytona Beach
International
Airport

White St

Welch Dr

12
🏛

Daytona Beach
Community
College

Hilton
Ave

S Seneca St

Tarragona Way

Jean St

S Keech St

Tuscawilla
Park

Nova Rd

🏛 11

26 🎭
Museum Blvd

History

Europeans began arriving in the late 1700s and a century later, Matthias Day (the city's eponymous founder) constructed a hotel, drawing a few tourists. Soon after, Henry Flagler purchased the railroad chugging into the town and brought more folks. Today, an estimated 8 million people visit 'the world's most famous beach' annually.

In 1902 speed catapulted Daytona into the national psyche when playboy racecar drivers Ransom Olds (of Oldsmobile fame) and Alexander Winston waged a high-profile race along the unusually hard-packed sandy shore, reaching an unheard of 57mph. The Florida East Coast Automobile Association was founded in 1903, and the Winter Speed

Carnival (predecessor to today's Daytona 500) in 1904. For the next 30 years Daytona Beach was where speed records were made – and subsequently shattered. Stock-car racing came into vogue during the late 1930s; 'Race Weeks' packed beaches with fans. In 1947 Nascar was born here (see boxed text Nascar & the American South, p356). In 1959, racing was relocated from the beach to the Daytona International Speedway.

Orientation

Perched just northeast of the intersection of I-95 and I-4, Daytona Beach extends across the Halifax River (aka the Intracoastal Waterway, actually an estuary) to the Atlantic Ocean. The main east–west drag, International

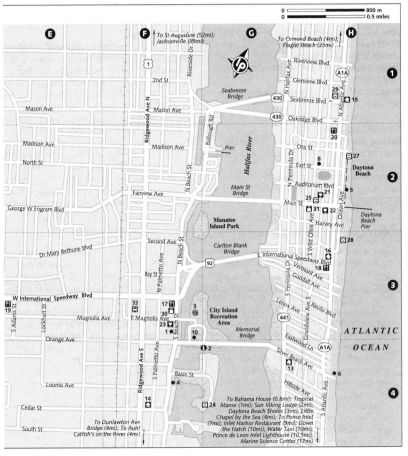

Speedway Blvd (US Hwy 92), connects the beaches with Daytona International Speedway, Daytona International Airport and I-95. The beaches are about a mile from historic downtown.

On the barrier island the main north–south road is Atlantic Ave (Hwy A1A); on the mainland, it's US Hwy 1 (also called Ridgewood Ave). Beach St runs parallel and is the main downtown drag. Mason Ave, Main St (the north–south divider), International Speedway Blvd and Orange Ave, as well as Dunlawton Ave to the south, all have bridges connecting the mainland with the beaches. Note that, confusingly, most road names change as the bridges fly over the water. Greater Daytona Beach also takes in Ormond Beach to the north, Daytona Beach proper, and Daytona Beach Shores to the south along A1A extending to Ponce Inlet.

Information

BOOKSTORES
Abraxas Books (☏ 386-258-8060; 256 S Beach St) Offering over 100,000 used books; located downtown.

INTERNET ACCESS
Library (☎ 386-257-6036; 105 E Magnolia Ave; ☑ 9am-7pm Mon-Thu, to 5pm Fri, to 3pm Sat, 1-5pm Sun) Two hours free internet access.

MEDIA
Backstage Pass (www.backpassmag.com) Details local entertainment.

Daytona Times (www.daytonatimes.com) Serves the African American community.

Dixie Biker (www.dixiebiker.com) For bikers, by bikers.

Gaydaytona (www.gaydaytona.com) News and entertainment for the gay and lesbian community.

National Public Radio (NPR) 90.7FM and 89.9FM; both out of Orlando.

News-Journal (www.news-journalonline.com) The big daily paper.

TOURIST INFORMATION

Daytona Beach Area Convention & Visitors Bureau (☎ 386-255-0415; www.daytonabeach.com; 126 E Orange Ave; ☺ 9am-5pm Mon-Fri)

Visitor's Center (☎ 386-253-8669; 1801 W International Speedway Blvd; ☺ 8:30am-7pm) In the lobby of Daytona USA.

Sights & Activities

DAYTONA INTERNATIONAL SPEEDWAY & DAYTONA USA

The 480-acre **Daytona International Speedway** (☎ 800-748-7467; www.daytonaintlspeedway.com; 1801 W International Speedway Blvd; tickets from $15) boasts a more diverse race schedule than any other track in the world, hence its billing itself as the 'World Center of Racing.' Event ticket prices accelerate sharply for big races, but if nothing is going on, you can wander through the gift shop and into the grandstands for free.

Adjacent to the speedway, **Daytona USA** (☎ 386-947-6800; www.daytonausa.com; adult/child $24/19; ☺ 9am-7pm, longer during peak times) is a superbly flashy shrine to the sport. In addition to stock cars driven by Nascar's biggest names, high-

---

NASCAR & THE AMERICAN SOUTH

During Prohibition, production of moonshine (corn liquor with a lightning-bolt kick) was integral to the Southern economy, and renegades with cars speedy enough to outrun cops handled distribution. During their time off, they raced each other; when Prohibition was repealed the races continued. The most alluring venue was Daytona's Beach St track, where driver Bill France began promoting 'Race Weeks' that attracted thousands.

The sport exploded, though some automotive enthusiasts dismissed it as rednecks racing cars any mechanic could build. France knew better and in 1947 set about transforming his obsession into a world-class sport. The result was Nascar, which succeeded beyond his wildest dreams.

The appeal of Nascar makes sense when you understand that dumping money at cars doesn't buy victory; winning relies on strategic driving skills and knowledge (when to pit, for example, or how many tires to change). Beneath those colorful product endorsements, the cars are everyday autos that conform to strict regulations to ensure the driver and pit crew – *not* the car – are tested.

Daytona hosts races throughout the year; premier events include July's Coke Zero 400; January's Rolex 24; and the pinnacle, February's Daytona 500. Check www.daytonainternationalspeedway. com for ticket information.

If you're lucky enough to score tickets to one of the events, don't forget to bring:

- a soft-sided cooler (6in x 6in x 12in) with water, canned soda or beer
- snacks
- earplugs
- binoculars
- camera
- seat cushion
- umbrella or rain poncho
- sunscreen
- cash
- scanners and headsets (diehard fans bring these to listen to race commentary).

If watching a race just isn't enough, strap in for the **Richard Petty Driving Experience** (☎ 800-BE-PETTY; www.daytona500experience.com; from $135; ☺ 9am-5pm), in which you ride shotgun with a professional driver around the speedway.

lights include the Pit-Stop Challenge (changing a tire in 16 seconds), a 30-minute tram tour of the track and pits, a 45-minute IMAX film screening throughout the day and a motion simulator ride based on the Daytona 500. The VIP Pass ($50) gets you an extended tour, lunch and vouchers for Acceleration Alley, which is an interactive racing experience.

THE BEACH

One look at this perfectly planar stretch of sand and you can see why it served as the city's raceway. Today you can drive sections of **Daytona Beach** (☎ 386-239-7873; per car $5; 🕙 8am-7pm May-Oct, sunrise-sunset Nov-Apr), tide permitting, to a strictly enforced top speed of 10mph. There are six well-signed beach entrances from Ormond Beach (Granada Blvd) to Ponce Inlet (Beach St); between Seabreeze Blvd and International Speedway Blvd it's traffic-free. Tired of your boring old ride? There are a few transport options from beach-side vendors: rent an ATV tricked out like a '58 Vette convertible from **Fun in the Sun** (☎ 386-547-2449; per hr $25-50) and cruise the beach; for those looking for a workout, **MYeTRIKE** (☎ 813-526-1118; per hr $15) has recumbent tricycles, while **Ducer Cruzer** (☎ 813-383-7433; 2 bikes day/week $35/100) delivers fat-tired two-wheeled beach cruisers to your hotel. If you're tired of wheels, beach-based vendors rent slick-bottomed boogie boards ($5 per hour) and 8ft surfboards ($10 per hour).

For an adrenaline rush that affords a bird's-eye view of the coast, try **Daytona Beach Parasail** (☎ 386-547-6067; www.daytonaparasailing.com; $65-100), on the beach to the left of the Silver Beach approach ramp.

Beyond the high-tide mark, looser sand creates a nesting environment for sea turtles to lay eggs at night from May to October. The eggs and hatchlings are monitored carefully by the Marine Science Center (see p358), which is a rehabilitation center for turtles.

BOARDWALK & DAYTONA BEACH PIER

Follow Main St E and you'll cross Daytona's sabal palm–lined, ocean-fronting **Boardwalk**. Look for ice-cream shops, arcade games and beachside patios where you can sip beer from plastic cups. It's good family fun with a side of sleaze to keep things hopping.

Follow Main St further east and you'll stumble onto coral-colored **Daytona Beach Pier** (☎ 386-253-1212; 1200 Main St; walk-on adult/child $1.50/1,

fishing with own pole/rental $6/14). Easy to spot for its iconic 180ft tower (which formerly zoomed sightseers heavenward for panoramic views, but now sits frustratingly impotent on the pier), two-person cabled gondolas carry you the length of the 1000ft pier and back for $7 per person. It is worth a gander, but the pier's vintage feel has somehow disappeared. Too bad: this pier – among the longest on the east coast – has been around over 100 years.

Alcohol is prohibited on the beach.

PONCE DE LEÓN INLET LIGHTHOUSE

Climb the 203 steps to the top of Florida's tallest working **lighthouse** (☎ 386-761-1821; 4931 S Peninsula Dr; adult/child $5/1.50; 🕙 summer to 9pm, winter 10am-5pm), then take your time checking out the museum and buildings dotting the grounds of what was once a remote, lonely outpost; displays include a restored 15ft, 10,000 Fresnel lens. The lighthouse is 10 miles south of Daytona; follow A1A to Beach St.

JACKIE ROBINSON BALLPARK

On an island in the Halifax River, **Jackie Robinson Ballpark** (☎ 386-257-3382; www.daytonacubs.com; 105 E Orange Ave; VIP/adult/child $12/7/6) is home to the Daytona Cubs, a Class A minor league affiliate of the Chicago Cubs. In 1946, the Montreal Royals, Jackie Robinson's team, was in Florida to play an exhibition against their parent club, the Brooklyn Dodgers. Other Florida cities refused to let the game proceed due to segregation laws, but Daytona Beach cried, 'Play ball!' and Robinson later went on to be the first African American baseball player in the majors. The ballpark, seating 4200 people, was renamed in his honor in 1990.

DAYTONA LAGOON

Kids can burn off energy at the **Daytona Lagoon** (☎ 386-254-5020; daytonalagoon.com; 601 Earl St; attractions $6-28), which has a tube float, tidal-wave pool and multilevel water playground, as well as arcade games, go-karts, laser tag, a climbing wall, an erupting volcano and a canon blaster firing foam balls.

MUSEUM OF ARTS & SCIENCES

Beat the heat at this diverse **museum** (☎ 386-255-0285; www.moas.org; 1040 Museum Blvd; adult/student $13/7; 🕙 9am-4pm Mon-Sat, 11am-5pm Sun), featuring cultural collections ranging from Cuban to African to Chinese. In the Museum of Arts & Sciences you'll find the noteworthy **Dow Gallery**

PARKING LOT PREACHING

Back in 1954, when the old Neptune Drive-in Theater closed, this car-obsessed town devised a novel solution for increasing church attendance: services people could attend while remaining in their cars.

Little Chapel by the Sea (3140 S Atlantic Ave; admission free; ��️ services 8:30am & 10am Sun; **P**) is a drive-in Christian church. Pull up, hook a speaker to your car (or do as the locals do and tune to 680AM or 88.5FM) and listen to the Rev preach. He and the choir hold service on a balcony overlooking the sea of cars. There's free coffee and donuts between services. Only in Daytona.

---

of American Art, showcasing early American paintings, and antique furniture and silver donated by a wealthy St Augustine benefactor. **Root Museum**, sponsored by the family that bottled Coca-Cola from day one, has a surreal assortment of relics from the soda's history, including ancient vending machines and 1920s delivery vans.

SOUTHEAST MUSEUM OF PHOTOGRAPHY

The only museum in Florida dedicated solely to photography, the vibrant **Southeast Museum of Photography** (☎ 386-254-4475; www.smponline.org; Daytona Beach Community College, 1200 W International Speedway Blvd, Bldg 37; admission free; ��️ 11am-5pm Tue, Thu & Fri, 1-5pm Sat & Sun) doesn't shy from provocative subjects like human rights in its rotating exhibitions. Some images can be confrontational – check before taking impressionable eyes.

MARINE SCIENCE CENTER

Despite the built-up environs at Daytona Beach, loggerheads, green turtles, Kemp Ridleys and occasionally leatherbacks are found in the area. A rehab center for injured sea turtles and birds, the **Marine Science Center** (☎ 386-304-5545; www.marinesciencecenter.com; 100 Lighthouse Dr; adult/child $5/2; ��️ 10am-4pm Tue-Sat, noon-4pm Sun) has a wet/dry lab, some great kid-friendly exhibits and a guided tour of the on-site turtle and seabird rehabilitation facilities (call ahead).

Tours

Cruising the waters of the Halifax River puts a completely different spin on this auto-oriented town.

A Tiny Cruise Line (☎ 386-226-2343; 425 S Beach St; adult $13-24, child $8-11) runs cruises up the Halifax throughout the day and at sunset. The two-hour Midday Waterway cruise offers dolphin-spotting opportunities; BYO lunch.

Festivals & Events

Speed Weeks In the first two weeks of February the Rolex 24 Hour Race and Daytona 500 are held, and 200,000 people accomplish a *lot* of partying.

Bike Week Over 10 days in early March, 500,000 bikers drool over each other's hogs and party round the clock. Locals run a 'death pool' predicting the number of casualties.

Spring Break Currently with one-fifth of the attendance of peak years, 100,000 breakers do keg stands in March. Most of the action's at the beach.

Black College Reunion Same as Spring Break, but for African American students. Held in March/April.

Coke Zero 400 Nascar fans fly the checkered flag at this 400-lap race during July 4 weekend.

Biketoberfest Same as Bike Week, but in mid-October. More drinking.

Sleeping

Accommodation here runs the gamut: you can find everything from filthy fleabaggers, to cute B&Bs, to luxury suites – with a range of price tags. Prices soar during events, so book well ahead if there is something on. The Daytona CVB (Convention and Visitors Bureau) has a *Superior Small Lodging* booklet; see also www.daytonalodging.com.

Streamline Hotel (☎ 386-258-6937; 140 S Atlantic Ave; r from $35) This seafoam deco building, the birthplace of Nascar, looks like it was picked up from Miami and dropped hard – real hard! – right here. Tattered, peeling and emphatically smoky, this is a great budget option, but not for the timid.

Tropical Manor (☎ 386-252-4920, 800-253-4920; 2237 S Atlantic Ave; r $65-225; **P** **🖥️** **🐕**) With enormous painted hibiscuses splashed across the walls, miniature horse statues hidden hither and thither, and beachfront umbrellas colored from the dye of candy hearts, staying here is like sleeping inside a game of Candy Land. If you can survive the pastel overload, this immaculate place offers everything from one-room efficiencies for two people, to three-bed and two-bath suites sleeping 11. Right on the ocean, there's a huge heated pool and more pink than in Barbie's wedding.

Sun Viking Lodge (☎ 386-252-6252, 800-874-4469; www.sunviking.com; 2411 S Atlantic Ave; r $77-285; **P** **🐕**) The comfy rooms here could use a renovation (or at least rust-free fridges), but the balcony views are divine. Moreover, the outdoor pool with a 60ft waterslide, the endless activities planned for kids, and the 2ft walk to the beach make the dated rooms seem like heaven. Oh, and there's shuffleboard!

Coquina Inn B&B (☎ 386-254-4969; www.coquina inndaytonabeach.com; 544 S Palmetto Ave; r $99-139; P ✗ ⌨) In this goldenrod B&B, look for made-to-order five-course breakfasts, fresh flowers in guestrooms and a spa. Bicycles are available to explore the surrounding historic district and pets are welcome (pending approval from Godiva, the owner's dog).

our pick **Bahama House** (☎ 386-248-2001; www .daytonabahamahouse.com; 2001 S Atlantic Ave; r $99-339; P ⌨ 🖭) This lemon-yellow gem offers spacious, sophisticated, spotless Caribbean-themed rooms with private balconies, full kitchens and ocean views. There are free cocktails at 5:30pm and a two-tiered sundeck overlooks the pool and beach.

The August Seven Inn (☎ 386-248-8420, 877-79S-EVEN; www.jpaugust.net; 1209 S Peninsula Dr; r $105-185; P ⌨ 🖭) Boasting seven luxurious rooms, most with whirlpool tubs, guests can opt for the full catastrophe or 'order à la carte' from a menu (high-end sheets, plush towels, bath robes?) to create the perfect package. Four blocks from the ocean, it's an easy stroll to the beach but eons from Spring Breakers.

The Plaza Resort & Spa (☎ 800-329-8662; www.plaza resortandspa.com; 600 N Atlantic Ave; r $139-600; P ⌨ 🖭) Built in 1908, this glossy resort recently received a $70-million renovation – and every penny shows. From the miles of honey-colored marble lining the lobby to the 42in plasma TVs and cloud-soft beds in the rooms, to the 15,000-sq-ft spa, this resort coos luxury.

Eating

our pick **Dancing Avocado Kitchen** (☎ 386-947-2022; www.avocadokitchen.net; 110 S Beach St; mains $3-10; 🕑 8am-4pm Mon-Sat) Fresh and healthful, a meal here makes you feel better…or is it just the fresh air flowing through the custom-made air filters? Yummy Mexican dishes like extreme burritos and quesadillas dominate the menu at this vegetarian-oriented café, but the signature dancing avocado melt is tops. There's a juice and smoothie bar on-site, the salsa is made from scratch, and once a month all tips go to charity.

Pasha (☎ 386-257-7753; 919 W International Speedway Blvd; mains $4-11; 🕑 10am-7pm Mon-Sat, noon-6pm Sun)

Virtually unchanged since it opened in the '70s, this place combines an Aladdin's cave deli of imported Middle Eastern goods and a café with authentic dishes like Armenian breaded cheese pie and platters served with the owner's grandma's pita bread.

Starlite Diner (☎ 386-255-9555; 401 N Atlantic Ave; mains $4-12; 🕑 7am-midnight Mon-Thu, to 1am Fri & Sat, to 10pm Sun) Straight outta *Happy Days*, this gleaming chrome diner serves giant good 'n' greasy portions under assorted '50s memorabilia. Hope that red vinyl booth is comfortable; service can be agonizingly slow.

Neelam Indian Cuisine (☎ 386-238-1022; www .neelamindianrestaurant.com; 318 S Atlantic Ave; lunch buffet $8, dinners $11-18; 🕑 11:30am-2pm & 5pm-10pm Tue-Sun) A great way to 'escape' Daytona, the spicy smells of Neelam's tandoori oven immediately transport you away from the beaches of Florida – all the way to the mountains of northern India.

Down the Hatch (☎ 386-761-4831; www.down-the -hatch-seafood.com; 4894 Front St; mains $7-30; 🕑 11am-9pm Mon-Fri, 8am-9pm Sat & Sun) Overlooking the gently lapping Halifax River and acres of pristine mangroves, this former fish camp appeals largely to Daytona's condo crowd, but it still nails the casual seafood-dive vibe thanks to live Floribbean music and unmatched sunset views.

Aunt Catfish's on the River (☎ 386-767-4768; www.auntcatfishontheriver.com; 4009 Halifax Dr; mains $6-39; 🕑 11:30am-9pm, 9am-2pm Sun) Emphasis on meat, butter and fat – even the green beans are stewed…and locals love it. This insanely popular place also has fried, grilled and Cajun-style catfish. Sunday's endless Blue Jean Brunch features a 27-year-old cinnamon roll family recipe.

Drinking

Daytona's diverse entertainment scene includes cultural performances, biker bars with rollicking live music (mostly along Main St), high-octane dance clubs (on or near Seabreeze Blvd), and some good kitschy retro places.

Froggy's Saloon (☎ 386-254-8808; 800 Main St; 🕑 7am-3am) Outside this train wreck of a bar, a bone chopper gleams in the window. Inside, a sign asks, 'Ain't drinking fun?' You better believe they mean it: opening at 7am, this is Party Central for bikers and others who want to go bonkers. Expect to see flashing chicks, smoky beards, orgasm contests and more leather than on an African safari.

NORTHEAST FLORIDA

McK's Tavern (☎ 386-238-3321; 218 S Beach St; meals $6-15; ☺ 11am-2am) This refreshingly un-Daytona-style pub has 28 draft beers and dozens more in the bottle, live music at 9pm on weekends and two new dartboards. A friendly staff serves extremely snackable bar food.

Streamline Hotel (☎ 386-258-6937; 140 S Atlantic Ave; ☺ 11am-3am) Two bars here. Just off the lobby, the Nascar Lounge (the sport's birthplace) offers live entertainment, DJs and a race-themed games room with pool tables. Upstairs, with a wraparound balcony and views over Atlantic's party strip, the Penthouse Lounge attracts an older gay male crowd. Both bars have drinks specials and can get rowdy.

Dirty Harry's Pub (☎ 386-252-9877; 705 Main St) Regular live music and an impressive collection of automatic weapons on the wall.

Entertainment

CLUBS

The Bank (☎ 386-257-9272; 701 Main St) Built in 1922, this former bank was converted to a blues club in the '70s and rages still. The original vault remains inside but now it holds goods more precious than money: beer and wine.

Aquarium (☎ 386-252-9877; 125 Basin St; ☺ 9pm-3am Wed-Sun) 'Tank' and 'Blue Lips' greet comers at this blue – very blue – restaurant and club. They're not doormen; they're the resident fish. Filled with aquaria and flat-panel TVs playing loops of swimming fish, the light show on the dance floor bounces and sparkles just like an undersea world.

Razzles (☎ 386-257-6236; 611 Seabreeze Blvd; cover $5-10; ☺ 8pm-3am) Nightclubs come and go, but this high-energy dance zone keeps on thumping. Twenty years after it opened, this cavernous warehouse features 10 bars, dazzling light shows, cutting-edge beats and more beads than Mardi Gras.

Rumors (☎ 386-252-3776; 1376 N Nova Rd; ☺ 2pm-2am) A gay hotspot (but all are welcome), with professional drag shows every Friday and Saturday night and up-and-coming drag artists on Wednesday nights.

Ocean Deck (☎ 386-253-5224; 127 S Ocean Ave) No woman? No cry! Live reggae nightly at this beachfront bar.

PERFORMING ARTS

Daytona Beach Bandshell (☎ 386-671-8250; www .daytonabandshell.com; 70 Boardwalk) Constructed in 1937 from coquina shell, this landmark beach-front venue stages a summer concert series.

Cinematique of Daytona (☎ 386-252-3778; www .cinematique.org; 410 S Nova Rd; matinee/evening tickets $6/8) Home to the Daytona Beach Film Festival, Cinematique screens independent and foreign films at noon on Wednesdays and 7pm on Fridays and Saturdays. On Fridays in summer they also show classics under the stars.

Shopping

Chopper's World (☎ 386-252-1922; www.choppersworld .com; 618 Main St; ☺ 9am-5:30pm Tue-Sat, from 1pm Sun) The best of the bike shops, browse brain buckets, deerskin dusters and studded saddlebags among more than 10,000 motorcycle parts.

Angell & Phelps (☎ 800-969-2634; www.angelland phelps.com; 154 S Beach St; ☺ 9:30am-5:30pm Mon-Fri, to 5pm Sat) Churning out chocolate since 1925, today this factory makes 100,000lb of 137 different kinds of candy each year, including white chocolates shaped like conch shells. Free factory tours on the hour from 10am to 4pm, excluding noon.

Daytona Flea & Farmers Market (☎ 386-253-3330; www.daytonafleamarket.com; 2987 Bellevue Ave; ☺ 9am-5pm Fri-Sun) With over 1000 booths and 600 vendors, it claims to be the world's biggest flea market. At the corner of US 92 at I-95, 1 mile west of the Speedway.

Getting There & Around

Daytona Beach International Airport (☎ 386-248-8030; www.flydaytonafirst.com; 700 Catalina Dr), just south of the Speedway, is served by AirTran, Continental, Delta and US Airways and all major car-rental companies.

The **Greyhound** (☎ 386-255-7076, 800-231-2222; 138 S Ridgewood Ave) bus station has multiple services to Miami.

Daytona is close to the intersection of two major interstates, I-95 and I-4. I-95 is the quickest way to Jacksonville (about 90 miles) and Miami (260 miles), though Hwy A1A and US Hwy 1 are more scenic. Beville Rd, an east–west thoroughfare south of Daytona proper, becomes I-4 after crossing I-95; it's the fastest route to Orlando (55 miles).

Votran (☎ 386-756-7496; www.votran.com) runs buses and trolleys (adult/child under 6 $1.25/ free) throughout the city.

Ride the **water taxi** (☎ 386-428-4828, 866-257-4828; www.watertaxi-nsb.com; one-way adult/child/family $12/7/30) to New Smyrna Beach. The taxi leaves Daytona from both **Down the Hatch** (p359) and **Inlet Harbor Restaurant** (☎ 386-767-5590; 133 Inlet Harbor Rd) several times daily.

FLAGLER BEACH & AROUND
☎ 386 / pop 5000

Just 30 miles north of Daytona, isolated Flagler Beach is far removed from the towering hotels, dizzying lights and tire-tracked sands of its rowdy neighbor. On a 6-mile stretch of beach, this string of modest residences and smattering of shops has a three-story cap on buildings, spectacular sunrises and an end-of-the-earth feel.

Right downtown, you can rent a rod for $8.50 from **Flagler Beach Pier** (☎ 386-439-2278; www.flaglerbeachpier.net; 215 S Hwy A1A; entry fishers/spectators $6/1.50; ☾ 6am-midnight) or a soft-top surfboard from **Z Wave Surf Shop** (☎ 386-439-9283; www.zwavesurfshop.com; 400 S Hwy A1A; per hr/day $5/20). A lovely place for a picnic or some fishing is the **Washington Oaks Gardens State Park** (☎ 386-446-6780; 6400 N Oceanshore Blvd; per carload/motorcycle/car & driver only $4/3/3) with resplendent camellia- and bird-of-paradise-filled gardens.

Of several inexpensive motels, the standout is the bright, pet-friendly **Topaz Motel** (☎ 386-439-3301; 1224 Hwy A1A; r $70-155; ☒ ☒). Upping the indulgence factor, intimate **Island Cottage Oceanfront** (☎ 386-439-0092; www.islandcottagevillas .com; 2316 S Hwy A1A; r $199-375; ☒ ☒) pampers its guests with sensuous spa options.

Camp beachside at **Gamble Rogers Memorial State Recreation Area** (☎ 386-517-2086; 3100 Hwy A1A; car/pedestrian/cyclist entry $4/1/1, sites $23), which straddles both sides of A1A; you can rent kayaks here from **Kayaks of Flagler Beach** (☎ 386-561-8509; from $15).

Local fave **High Tide at Snack Jacks** (☎ 386-439-3344; www.nackjacks.com; 2805 Hwy A1A; mains $5-15; ☾ 11am-11pm) has valet parking, but only to squeeze everyone in for their fried and grilled fish at this laid-back, open-air place. Cool off with a sundae from **Sally's Ice Cream** (☎ 904-439-4408; 401 N AIA; ice cream $2-8; ☾ 11am-10pm), a sherbet-pink shop with sweet ocean views.

To reach Flagler Beach take Hwy A1A 30 miles north of Daytona Beach.

FORT MATANZAS NATIONAL MONUMENT

This tiny, 1742-built **fort** (☎ 904-471-0116; www .nps.gov/foma; 8635 Hwy A1A; admission free; ☾ 9am-5:30pm) is located on Rattlesnake Island, near where Menendez de Avile executed hundreds of shipwrecked French soldiers and colonists when rations at St Augustine ran low. Today it makes a terrific excursion via a free five-minute ferry that launches every hour (at

half-past) from 9:30am to 4:30pm, weather permitting. Once there, the ranger provides an overview and lets you wander.

From Daytona, take I-95 north to exit 289. Exit right and follow Palm Coast Parkway (a toll road) until you reach Hwy A1A. Turn left and follow A1A north to the monument, which will be on your left. The trip should take just under one hour.

To catch the 35-person ferry to the monument – the last free thing in Florida – go through the visitor's center and out to the pier. The ferry ride lasts about 10 minutes.

ST AUGUSTINE
☎ 904 / pop 13,000

The oldest continuously occupied European settlement in the US, St Augustine was founded by the Spanish in 1565. Today, tourists flock here to saunter along cobbled roads, linger at cute cafés, browse endearing shops, learn about the city's rich history at countless museums – and cap it all off with snug dinners at lamp-lit restaurants and brews at quaint pubs. Meanwhile, horse-drawn carriages clip-clop past townsfolk dressed in period costume wandering this 144-block National Historic Landmark District.

It could all add up to a theme park–style experience at best – traveler hell at worst – but for the most part, St Augustine eclipses tourist trappings and retains charm and integrity. Why? Many reasons. First, unlike theme parks, these centuries-old buildings, monuments and narrow lanes are authentic. Second, the charming, one-off cafés and restaurants are the real deal, too: there's plenty of good eating in this small town. Third, even though they may not be required to, many people dress in period costume for work, emphasizing the town's historic character – some settle here purely for this lifestyle. And fourth, there are still many gems to discover off the well-trodden trail.

History

Timucuan Indians settled what is now St Augustine about 1000 BC. In 1513, Spanish explorer Juan Ponce de León sighted land, came ashore and claimed La Florida (Land of Flowers) for Spain. In 1565 his compatriot Don Pedro Menendez de Avilés arrived and established a military base against the French (who had established Fort Caroline near present-day Jacksonville). The French fleet did

DOWNTOWN ST AUGUSTINE

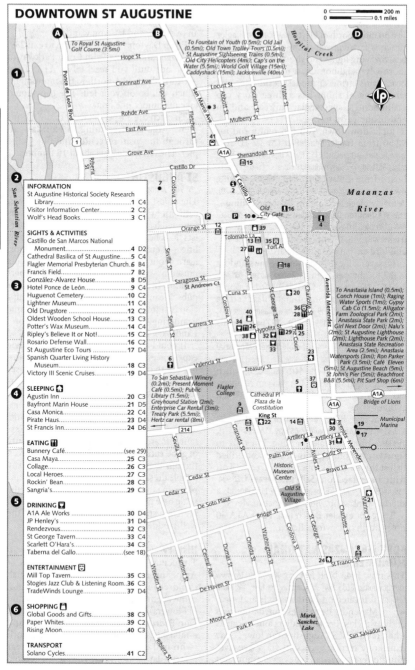

NORTHEAST FLORIDA

him the favor of getting stuck in a hurricane; Menendez' men butchered the survivors. By the time Spain ceded Florida to the US in 1821, St Augustine had been sacked, looted, burned and occupied by pirates and Spanish, British, Georgian and South Carolinian forces.

Today the coquina buildings, a DIY concrete made of sedimentary rock mixed with crushed shells, lend an enchanting quality to the slender streets, and the city's long and colorful history is palpable. Sadly, preserving the historical structures and countless buried artifacts is prohibitively expensive. For the city to acquire and sustain them all would take tens of millions of dollars, and this tiny town has an equally tiny property tax base. More than a third of the town's 6500 parcels, from churches to museums, is tax-exempt. Without revenue to fund preservation, an average of one historic structure is demolished every month. The city relies on museum admissions, gift-store sales, grants, donations, and, here's the kicker, rent from commercial property, effectively prioritizing commercial interests over historical. Tacky shops threaten to compromise the authenticity that visitors come to experience. For now, though, it's still here.

Orientation

St Augustine is 40 miles southeast of Jacksonville, served by both US Hwy 1, which runs through the city, and I-95, about 10 miles west. The compact historic district is downtown and roughly bordered by the Old City Gate (on Orange St) to the north, Bridge St to the south, Avenida Menendez and Matanzas River to the east, and Cordova St to the west. St George St is a pedestrian-only zone from Cathedral Pl at the south to Orange St at the north.

North of downtown, Avenida Menendez turns into San Marco Ave, which eventually intersects Ponce de León Blvd (US Hwy 1). King St connects US Hwy 1 and Hwy A1A (Beach Blvd) via the Bridge of Lions, becoming Anastasia Blvd on Anastasia Island, on the east side of Matanzas River. Both Anastasia State Park and St Augustine Beach are on Anastasia Island.

Information

BOOKSTORES
Wolf's Head Books (☎ 904-824-9357; www.wolfs headbooks.com; 48-50 San Marco Ave; ☼ 11am-7pm Mon-Fri, to 5pm Sat, 12:30-5pm Sun) A treasure trove of antiquarianism.

LIBRARIES
Public Library (☎ 904-827-6940; 1960 N Ponce de León Blvd; ☼ 10am-8pm Mon-Wed, to 6pm Thu & Fri, to 5pm Sat) Free internet access.
St Augustine Historical Society Research Library (☎ 904-825-2333; 6 Artillery Lane; ☼ 9am-4:30pm Tue-Fri) Delve into the area's history here.

THERE BE PIRATES

Notorious throughout the Caribbean and Americas, pirates routinely ransacked St Augustine, given its vulnerable seaside location. Laying in wait along the coast, pirates would pounce on silver- and gold-laden fleets returning to Europe from Mexico and South America. When ships weren't around, they'd simply raid the town (which was home to the Spanish Royal Treasurer for Florida, no less).

Among the many brutal attacks on St Augustine was Sir Francis Drake's raid in June 1586, when he and his cohort pillaged the township before burning it down. Perhaps even more violent was Jamaican pirate Robert Searle's attack in 1668. After capturing a Spanish ship, Searle and crew went on a plundering and killing spree. No one was safe: one of Searle's victims was a five-year-old girl, whose ghost, it's said, haunted him to madness and ultimately suicide.

Both these events are meticulously reenacted every year in St Augustine. Participants must conform to rigid requirements including no skull-and-crossbones emblems (they weren't used regularly by pirates until the early 1700s); no polyester or modern items of any kind, including eyeglasses and wristwatches; and no 'silly plumes.' If you're interested in participating, get thee to the St Augustine in March (to reenact Searle's raid) or June (for Drake's). For more information, log on to www.searlesbuccaneers.org.

Other local pirate activities include September's 'Talk Like a Pirate Day' (www.talklikeapirate.com), a global event that particularly shivers timbers in this place, and November's Saint Arrrgustine's Pirate Gathering (www.pirategathering.com).

MEDIA

The daily **St Augustine Record** (www.staugustine record.com) has good visitor information on its website. The free **Folio Weekly** (www.folioweekly .com) has events information, restaurant and bar listings every Tuesday.

Most radio stations originate in Jacksonville; St Augustine's own is 88.5FM, from Flagler College, plays lots of new music plus jazz, classical and world music.

TOURIST INFORMATION

Visitor Information Center (☎ 904-825-1000; www .ci.st-augustine.fl.us; 10 Castillo Dr; ☒ 8:30am-5:30pm) Helpful, period-dressed staff sell tour tickets (see p367). Between 9am and 4pm, you can watch a 45-minute film (single/family $1/3) of the town's history.

Sights & Activities

CASTILLO DE SAN MARCOS NATIONAL MONUMENT

Wandering from the clogged downtown streets onto the headland where this incred-ibly photogenic **fort** (☎ 904-829-6506; www.nps .gov/casa; adult/child $6/free; ☒ 8:45am-5:15pm, grounds closed midnight-5:30am) stands guard, amplifies its imposing scale. In 1672, after the British had burned the city around them one too many times, the Spanish began constructing this coquina citadel. Completed 23 years later, it's the oldest masonry fort in the continental US. Rangers wearing Spanish Colonial–era uniforms add to the medieval ambience and can answer questions as you take the fort's excellent self-guided tour. Cannons can be heard all over town when they're fired on the half hour (10:30am to 3:30pm, Friday to Sunday); cannons are not fired if less than four visitors are at the monument. The fort is located between San Marco Ave and Matanzas River.

SPANISH QUARTER LIVING HISTORY MUSEUM

Spanning 2 acres, this **living history museum** (☎ 904-825-6830; entry via 53 St George St; adult/student $7/4.50; ☒ 9am-5:30pm) is a recreation of 1740

PONCE DE LEÓN & THE FOUNTAIN OF YOUTH

Would you like to drink from the fountain of youth? An ancient discovery in St Augustine may quench your thirst.

Timucuan Indians – looming over 6ft and often ageing beyond their 60s – occupied present-day St Augustine from about 1000 BC. In 1513, seeking a fabled land of giants who lived to be ancient, or seeking gold (depending who you ask), a 4ft-something explorer called Juan Ponce de León sighted land, came ashore and claimed La Florida (Land of Flowers) for Spain.

Once ashore, the Timucuans showed him a freshwater spring, from which de León and his men drank. De León left a stone cross next to the spring to mark the spot. Juan Ponce de León miraculously lived to 61 – roughly twice as long as his contemporaries – and perished finally from a poison-tipped arrow. And so the myth of the fountain of youth began.

Fast forward to 1868, when HH Williams purchased a tract of land in St Augustine, on which he found a stone cross next to a spring. Then in 1900, Dr Louella Day MacConnell and her husband uncovered a parchment witnessing Ponce de León planting a cross next to the same spring. In 1934, workmen installing orange trees inadvertently exposed human bones at the same spot. They called the Smithsonian Institution, who identified an area 40ft by 80ft containing over 100 skeletons from both Christian and prehistoric burials, reaffirming the significance of this historic site. The spring on this site is said to be de León's fabled fountain.

Today, you can visit the **Fountain of Youth** (☎ 800-356-8222; www.fountainofyouthflorida.com; 11 Magnolia Ave; adult/child/senior $7.50/4.50/6.50; ☒ 9am-5pm) to drink from the curative trickle.

Forty-minute tours start with plastic cupfuls of the legendary liquid, collected in pewter jugs by staff. Treated before it's served, it tastes like regular Florida water, though it may take more than a shot to work. Surrounded by gaudy American Indian figurines, the well is still the original spring, just re-engineered due to changing water tables. After your drink, guides give an overview of de León's arrival, a short history of the Fountain's rediscovery, and encourage you on to the Planetarium and Discovery Globe, two sadly underwhelming exhibits that attempt to explain celestial navigation and to provide a concise overview of 100 years of Spanish exploration. Once finished, you can stroll the well-maintained grounds of the park. Just be careful to avoid the aggressive peacocks patrolling the area – or you may not live such a long life after all.

St Augustine. Walled off from the street, you're encouraged to wander the garrison's restored buildings and speak to the crafts-people (re-enactors) who use 18th-century technology to operate recreated 'storefronts': a blacksmith, a leather shop and a carpentry studio. Explanations of the centuries-old pro-cedures are in 21st-century vernacular, but the craftspeople live out their period roles, often camping for weeks in nearby wilderness areas using only materials available in the 1700s, road-testing the clothing and tools you see them make here.

LIGHTNER MUSEUM

This brilliantly eclectic **museum** (☎ 904-824-2874; www.lightnermuseum.org; 75 King St; adult/child $10/5; ☺ 9am-5pm) is in the restored Alcazar Hotel, one of Henry Flagler's two St Augustine re-sorts, which housed (at the time) the world's largest indoor pool. None of the exhibits seem to relate to each other, but that's part of the charm. Expect everything from antique mu-sical instruments (played at 11am and 2pm; amazing acoustics make this a must-hear), to a shrunken head, to Egyptian-themed art-deco sculpture.

Founder Otto C Lightner started his career writing about collections for a hobby maga-zine and then started buying them – buttons, match safes, Renaissance art – becoming, essentially, a collector of collections.

OTHER MUSEUMS & HISTORIC BUILDINGS

The nine homes in **Old St Augustine Village** (☎ 904-823-9722; www.old-staug-village.com; 149 Cordova St; admission $9; ☺ 9am-5pm Mon-Sat, 11am-4:30pm Sun) are Florida's largest collection of historic homes. Dating from 1790 to 1920, highlights include the delightfully crooked Carpenter's House; the crayon-colored windows of the Spear House; and the Murat House, which was the one-time home of Prince Achille Murat, Napoleon's nephew. Yes, *that* Napoleon.

Built from red cedar and cypress, the 200-year-old **Oldest Wooden School House** (☎ 888-653-7245; www.oldestwoodenschoolhouse.com; 14 St George St; adult/child $3/2; ☺ 10am-4:30pm Mon-Sat, 11am-4:30pm Sun) is peopled by animatronic teachers and students providing a glimpse into 18th-century life and education. Naughty kids may be frightened into civility when they see the Dungeon.

Named for its first owner, Tomás González, and its second, Gerónimo Alvarez, who later became the town's mayor under Spanish con-stitution, **González-Alvarez House** (☎ 904-824-2872; www.oldesthouse.com; 14 St Francis St; adult/student $8/4; ☺ 9am-5pm) claims continuous occupancy since the early 1600s (though the present structure dates from between 1703 and 1727).

Built in 1891, the **Old Jail** (☎ 904-829-3800; 167 San Marco Ave; adult/child $8.10/4.50; ☺ 8:30am-4:30pm) is the former town prison and residence of the town's first sheriff, Charles Joseph 'the terror' Perry (towering menacingly at 6ft, 6in tall and weighing 300lb). Today, costumed 'deputies' escort visitors through cellblocks and detail the site's arresting history.

Built in 1739, the **Old Drugstore** (☎ 800-332-9893; 31 Orange St; admission free; ☺ 9:30am-6pm) offers a unique collection of antique vials and tonics in sepia-colored bottles, as well as some other curiosities, like vintage suppository molds. Adjacent to the artifacts is an extensive assort-ment of herbal remedies for sale (from stevia leaf to lotus flowers) for homeopathic use.

An 80ft domed rotunda and stained glass crafted by Louis Comfort Tiffany are the hallmarks of the Spanish Renaissance Revival **Hotel Ponce de León** (☎ 904-823-3378; adult/child $6/1; 74 King St; ☺ tours 10am-3pm), Henry Flagler's flagship resort. Completed in 1888, it had to contend almost immediately with the vagar-ies of tourism: a yellow-fever epidemic and the worst freeze in Florida's history (1895). Nonetheless this architectural wonder, the first major poured concrete structure in the US, quickly became the country's most exclu-sive winter resort, before succumbing to a lack of guests in the 1960s, which led it to become part of the private Flagler College.

Opposite the Bridge of Lions, in the heart of downtown, the grassy **Plaza de la Constitution**, a former marketplace for food (and slaves), has a gazebo, some cannons and a Civil War memorial, as well as the remains of the town well.

Other historic remains include the **Old City Gate**, at the northern end of St George St, built in 1739 to defend the northern St Augustine line from British attacks; and the **Rosario Defense Wall** (opposite the **Huguenot Cemetery**), a recreation of the original Spanish-built earthen barrier – spiky yucca plants and prickly-pear cacti along the top successfully fended off the Brits.

For biting political satire, visit **Potter's Wax Museum** (☎ 800-584-4781; 17 King St; adult/child $9/6; ☺ 9am-5pm Sun-Thu, to 9:30pm Fri & Sat). At Potter's

HAUNTED ST AUGUSTINE

Many companies in St Augustine operate ghost tours. Equal parts campfire story, casual history lesson and guided tour, many of the outings smack of sensationalism.

For a more serious – and scientific – exploration of area hauntings, try **Haunted St Augustine** (☎ 904-823-9500; www.haunted-st-augustine.com; tours $25; ☾ 9pm daily, reservations required). After a careful explanation of the various types of spirits, Dr Harry Stafford provides each participant with an electromagnetic field meter to detect spikes in energy (caused by passing spirits...?). Then, for the next two hours, you'll tour the northern quadrant of town – circling the fort, passing darkened cemeteries, testing for electromagnetic spikes and trying to isolate floating orbs. Throughout the evening, Stafford entertains questions, debunks myths and encourages you to employ your senses and think critically about hauntings. Not designed to frighten – but rather to challenge what you know about hauntings and use science to test for them – this tour is a hair-raising evening out.

you can check out Dubya, sculpted by either a bitter Democrat or *Mad* magazine fan.

Ripley's Believe It or Not! (☎ 904-824-1606; 19 San Marco Ave; adult/child $15/8; ☾ 9am-7pm Sun-Thu, to 8pm Fri & Sat), inside the old (1887) Castle Warden, is the first and cornerstone of Ripley's monuments to the bizarre.

CHURCHES & SHRINES

Lording over the Plaza de la Constitution, the magnificent bell tower of the Spanish Mission–style **Cathedral Basilica of St Augustine** (☎ 904-824-2806; www.thefirstparish.com; 38 Cathedral Place; admission free) is likely the country's first Catholic house of worship.

Henry Flagler, his daughter and her stillborn child lie in the mausoleum at **Flagler Memorial Presbyterian Church** (☎ 904-829-6451; 32 Sevilla St; admission free; ☾ 9am-4pm Mon-Sat), Flagler's own, magnificent Venetian-Renaissance edifice. The floor is Sienna marble, the wood is Santo Domingo mahogany and the pipe organ (played 8:30am and 11am Sunday) is colossal.

ST AUGUSTINE BEACH

The 7-mile stretch of St Augustine Beach is a great place to soak up rays, and the road fronting it has fun hotels, family restaurants and boisterous bars.

Cross the Bridge of Lions and take Anastasia Blvd right out to the beach; there's a visitor's information booth at the foot of the **St John's Pier** (☎ 904-461-0119; 350 Hwy A1A; walk-on 50¢, fishing adult/child $3/1; ☾ 24hr), where you can rent a rod and reel ($3 for two hours, $1 for each additional hour).

About three blocks south of the pier, the end of A St has – as Florida goes – some fine waves. For late-breaking surf conditions, to rent or buy a board, or to sink into the comfy couch in the screening room for a free, inspirational surf film, stop at **Pit Surfshop** (☎ 904-471-4700; www.pitsurfshop.com; 18 A St; boards per day $16; ☾ 9am-8pm).

Raging Water Sports (☎ 904-829-5001; 57 Comares Ave) rents kayaks ($20 per hour), sailboats ($40 per hour), jet skis ($85 per hour) and motorboats (starting at $70 per hour).

ST AUGUSTINE LIGHTHOUSE

The light produced by this 1870s striped **lighthouse** (☎ 904-829-0745; www.staugustinelighthouse.com; 81 Lighthouse Ave; museum & tower adult/child $8/6, house & grounds only $6/4; ☾ 9am-6pm) beams all the way downtown. A great place to bring kids over six and more than 44in tall (since all climbers must be able to ascend and descend the tower under their own power), the lighthouse operates 'Dark of the Moon' paranormal tours on weekends at 8:30pm (adults/child $25/20).

ANASTASIA STATE RECREATION AREA

Escape the tourist hordes at Anastasia Island's **recreation area** (☎ 904-461-2033; 1340 Hwy A1A; pedestrian/car $1/5), boasting a stunning beach, vibrant dunes, bike trails, a tidal salt-marsh-fringed lagoon and a campground (see p368). Inside the park, **Anastasia Watersports** (☎ 904-460-9111; 850 Anastasia Park Rd) rents kayaks (one hour/four hours $15/40), Hobie cats (one hour/four hours $30/70) and windsurfers ($25 per hour).

SAN SEBASTIAN WINERY

Free hour-long tours at this **winery** (☎ 904-826-1594; www.sansebastianwinery.com; 157 King St; ☾ 10am-6pm Mon-Sat, 11am-6pm Sun) are capped with wine tastings and a video about Florida winemaking since the 1600s; there's wine and live jazz from 7pm to 11pm at the rooftop **Cellar Upstairs** (wine per glass $4-6; 4pm-midnight Fri, noon-midnight Sat & Sun). If you're around in August, join the squishy fun during the annual grape-stomping competitions.

ALLIGATOR FARM ZOOLOGICAL PARK
Maximo – a 1250lb, 15ft, 3in Australian saltwater crocodile – is the biggest of the reptiles at the **Alligator Farm Zoological Park** (904-824-3377; www.alligatorfarm.com; 999 Anastasia Blvd; adult/child $22/11; 9am-5pm, to 6pm in summer), the world's only facility with every species of crocodilian in residence. Look for albino alligators, freaky gharials and seven different species of endangered monkey, including the world's smallest, the pygmy marmoset (the size of a mouse). There are talks and shows throughout the day; catch hungry alligators snapping their jaws at feeding times (noon and 3pm).

WORLD GOLF VILLAGE
The ultimate monument to a good walk spoiled, the **World Golf Village** (904-221-0027, 800-948-4653; www.wgv.com; 1 World Golf Pl) is home to the World Golf Foundation (WGF) and PGA Productions, the media entity responsible for televising golf events.

Even non-fans will enjoy the **World Golf Hall of Fame** (adult/student $15/17; 10am-6pm Mon-Sat, noon-6pm Sun). Featuring 18 exhibits (get it?), the front nine cover golf's history while the back nine examine modern pro golf. Separating them is the Hall of Fame itself, with multimedia exhibits on inductees. Admission includes 18 holes on a putting green designed to PGA specifications and an IMAX film.

If you're keen to improve your swing, two- to five-day **PGA Tour Golf Academy** packages start from $635 and include accommodation at one of three on-site resorts. Private lessons start at $90 per hour.

Whether you're staying here or not, grab a burger from **Caddyshack** (904-940-3673; 455 S Legacy Trail; mains $7-14) restaurant and bar, named for the movie starring Bill Murray, who – along with his five brothers – owns it.

World Golf Village is just off I-95 via exit 323.

GOLF & TENNIS
The new **Royal St Augustine Golf Course** (904-829-0700; www.royalstaugustine.com; 301 Royal St) has undu-

lating fairways and well-placed bunkers and lakes – call for tee information and prices.

You can play a round at the World Golf Hall of Fame (World Golf Village) from $99 to $189 on one of two courses, including the King & Bear designed by its (nick)namesakes, Arnold Palmer and Jack Nicklaus.

You can play tennis for free at St Augustine's four public tennis facilities at Ron Parker Park, Treaty Park, Francis Field and Lighthouse Park – BYO racquets and balls.

Tours

Two tourist choo-choos chug through city streets. Hop on and off all day with tickets from **Old Town Trolley Tours** (904-829-3800; www.trolleytours.com; 167 San Marco Ave; adult/child $21/8). The trolley ticket includes travel on the Beach Bus, which takes passengers to and from St Augustine's beach. **St Augustine Sightseeing Trains** (904-829-6545; www.redtrains.com; 170 San Marco Ave; adult/child $19/6) get you around in distinctive fire-engine-red trains. You can get on and off as often as you like at any of 20 stops.

Old City Helicopters (904-824-5506; www.oldcityhelicopters.com; St Augustine Airport, 4900 US 1 N, Suite 400; from $65) whoosh you over downtown and beyond in the day or at sunset. They also offer after-hours flights from November through January, when the already-enchanting city glows with festive seasonal lights. Minimum two people.

The cityscape is magical from the water; tour options include **Victory III Scenic Cruises** (904-824-1806; www.scenic-cruise.com; adult/under 18yr/under 12yr $15.75/9.25/7.50; 11am, 1pm, 2:45pm, 4:30pm year-round, plus evening cruises spring-fall) offers narrated 1¼-hour waterfront cruises, leaving from the Municipal Marina, just south of the Bridge of Lions.

For some truly engaging time on the water, try **St Augustine Eco Tours** (904-377-7245; www.staugustineecotours.com; 111 Avenida Menendez; per person $45; mid-morning & dusk), which has certified naturalists who take kayakers on 3-mile ecology trips. If you don't feel like paddling, their 1½-hour boat tours explore the estuary and use hydrophones to search for bottlenose dolphins. A portion of profits go to environmental organizations.

Sleeping

The most atmospheric rooms are in historic downtown St Augustine, an area which boasts more than two-dozen elegant B&Bs;

check www.staugustineinns.com. The beach has some nice spots, too. St Augustine is a popular weekend escape for Florida residents so expect room rates to rise about 30% on Friday and Saturday; often there's a required minimum two-night stay. Summer rates tend to be higher than winter.

BUDGET

Inexpensive motels and chain hotels dot San Marco Ave, near where it meets US Hwy 1.

Pirate Haus (☎ 904-808-1999; www.piratehaus.com; 32 Treasury St; dm $18, r $50-85; P X 🖳) Famed for its free all-you-can-eat 'pirate pancake' breakfast, this family-friendly European-style guesthouse/hostel has light, bright rooms, a full kitchen, rooftop barbecue, bike rentals… all in what is arrrrgh-uably the best downtown location possible (parking is limited, however). Innkeeper 'Captain' Conrad is a wealth of local info, matey. Dig that staircase.

Anastasia State Recreation Area (☎ 800-326-3521; 1340 Hwy A1A; sites with electricity $25) Beautiful campgrounds, spotless facilities.

MIDRANGE

Conch House (☎ 904-829-8646; www.conch-house .com; 57 Comares Ave; r $95-275; P X ♨) Sixteen rooms, most facing the 200-slip marina, and the coolest hotel bar in town, make this a must-stay for boaters. Minutes from either downtown or the beach.

St Francis Inn (☎ 904-824-6068, 800-824-6062; www .stfrancisinn.com; 79 St George St; r $99-279; P X 🖳 ♨) Pets – and children – are welcome at this inn, the town's oldest, in continuous operation since 1791. It has toasty open fireplaces, a maze of antique-filled nooks and crannies, a lush courtyard, wheelchair access and an epicentral location.

Agustin Inn (☎ 904-823-9559; www.agustininn.com; 29 Cuna St; r $99-289; P X 🖳) In the heart of the historic district, this buttercup inn secrets an exotic garden, a bay view and some of the cleanest rooms in town. Plush robes come with each of the 18 elegant, individual rooms (17 of which have whirlpool tubs). Also expect: a lovely gourmet breakfast, plenty of porch space for cooling your walked-out feet and complimentary parking (almost unheard of here).

Beachfront B&B (☎ 904-461-8727, 800-233-2746; www .beachfrontbandb.com; 1 F St; r $149-289; P X 🖳) For people who like seasides more than cityscapes, this romantic place – with sumptuous linens,

rich pine floors and private heated pool – is perfect. Steps from the beach, most of the immaculate rooms have fireplaces and private entrances. All the rooms on the 2nd floor have beach views but the Surfside Suite is sweetest.

Bayfront Marin House (☎ 904-824-4301; www.bay frontmarinhouse.com; 142 Avenida Menendez; r $119-299; P X 🖳) Featuring a bi-level wraparound porch with a commanding view of Matanzas Bay, sunrises are born here. Most of the 15 spacious rooms have Jacuzzis and fireplaces; all are appointed with period antiques and Victorian decor. Homemade breakfasts in the gazebo are to peaceful what history is to St Augustine.

TOP END

Casa Monica (☎ 904-827-1888, 800-648-1888; www.casa monica.com; 95 Cordova St; r $179-779; P X 🖳 ♨) Built in 1888 and superbly restored in 1999, this colossal turreted landmark encompasses St Augustine's finest digs and is worth a stop even if you're not sleeping here. Through the grand carriage entrance are a spectacular lobby, expansive swimming pool, fountains, gourmet restaurants, shops…as well as richly appointed suites with wrought-iron beds, ceramic-tiled bathrooms, mahogany furnishings, imported feather duvets and every amenity you can imagine.

Eating

Many eateries in St Augustine are pleasantly inexpensive, and there are lots of quick bites in historic downtown.

BUDGET

Local Heroes (☎ 904-825-0060; 11 Spanish St; mains $3.50-8; ☽ 11am-5pm Tue, to 10pm Wed, to midnight Thu-Sat, noon-5pm Sun) This blue 1820s bungalow has hot sandwiches, frosty brews, a cool back porch shaded by a massive oak and an awesome Curtis Mayfield collection. A fun way to jump from the 1570s to the 1970s.

Bunnery Café (☎ 904-829-6166; 121 St George St; mains $4-7; ☽ 8am-6pm) The friendly staff at this bakery pour frosting on your cinnamon rolls to your specs.

Nalu's (☎ 904-501-9592; 1020 Anastasia Blvd; plates $5.25-7.25; ☽ 11am-6pm Mon-Sat, noon-6pm Sun) Can't mess with a taco stand outside a surf shop (p370). Dressed Baja style, they're perfect for taking to the beach.

Present Moment Café (☎ 904-827-4499; 224 W King St; meals $6-12; ☽ 11am-2pm & 5-9pm Tue-Sat, to

10pm Fri & Sat) Dishing up 'Kind Cuisine,' this folksy restaurant only serves vegetarian and vegan options. Its organic dishes burst with flavor, live enzymes and nutrients and won't leave you feeling bloated – unless you order a second chocolate marble torte with drunken banana.

Sangria's (☎ 904-827-1947; 35 Hypolita St; mains $7-12; ☼ noon-1am) On the 2nd floor overlooking the intersection of St George and Hypolita, the outside corner table is supreme for people-watching. Three kinds of sangria (the white Sangri-La is exquisite), a great tapas menu, and live music (mostly jazz) nightly. The kitchen closes around 9pm.

MIDRANGE

Casa Maya (☎ 904-823-1739; 17 Hypolita St; mains $6-18; ☼ 8:30am-3:30pm, 5:30-10pm) Snappy jazz wafts through the jasmine-shaded patio of this vegetarian-friendly Mayan (or Northern Central American) restaurant. The Mayan wrap features (oddly, but tastily) hummus and feta, and comes with organic chips. Most dishes incorporate local ingredients.

our pick Cap's on the Water (☎ 904-824-8794; www.capsonthewater.com; 4325 Myrtle St; mains $12-25; ☼ 11:30am-9:30pm) Overlooking the Matanzas River, the setting sun streaks through an unobscured sky offering the region's best sunset. Featuring new coastal cuisine (Southern dishes with Asian-European influences) in an Old Florida setting (this former fish camp was built in 1947), this restaurant has three seating areas (inside, waterfront, oyster bar). You'd think that'd be enough, but the wait often exceeds two hours. Arrive early or be prepared to linger.

Other recommendations include these:

Rockin' Bean (☎ 904-284-5198; www.rockinbean.com; 48 Charlotte St; ☼ 8:30am-10:30pm) Great coffee. Head upstairs for a warm, mellow vibe.

Gypsy Cab Co (☎ 904-824-8244; www.gypsycab.com; 828 Anastasia Blvd; mains $15.50-21; ☼ 4:30-10pm Sun-Thu, to 11pm Fri & Sat, lunch 11am-3pm Mon-Sat, brunch 10:30am-3pm Sun) The diverse menu of this local fave, with influences from German to Floribbean, is impossible to pigeonhole.

TOP END

Collage (☎ 904-829-0055; 60 Hypolita St; mains $24-36; ☼ 5:30pm-close) Inside the terracotta walls of this alluring place you're transported far from St Augustine's tourist commotion. The head chef, 24-year-old Melody, is a wizard in the kitchen, working her magic over (mainly)

seafood and steaks. There's a carefully assembled wine list and each course is separated by a homemade tropical sorbet as a palate cleanser. The wait staff can be a bit hovery, but service is impeccable.

Drinking

Taberna del Gallo (☎ 904-825-6830; 53 St George St; ☼ 2pm-9:30pm Thu-Sat, noon-7pm Sun) Sans electricity, only flickering candles light this 1736 tavern, which serves beer and wine to guests in the stone-walled interior and outdoor courtyard. On weekend nights the Bilge Rats sing sea shanties that get progressively bawdier.

A1A Ale Works (☎ 904-829-6824; www.a1aaleworks.com; 1 King St; ☼ 11am-11:30pm Sun-Thu, to midnight Fri & Sat) Sidle up to the copper bar and order a Bridge of Lions Brown Ale or A Strange Stout (named for the founder's granddad). Though it lacks the historical ambience that makes St Augustine special, the beers brewed here are spectacular.

JP Henley's (☎ 904-829-3337; www.jphenleys.com; 10 Marine St; ☼ 11am-1am) With 50 beers on tap, 120 more in the bottle and over 75 bottles of wine, this place will appeal to even the most discriminating beer or wine snob. Great music, too.

Scarlett O'Hara's (☎ 904-824-6535; www.scarlettoharas.net; 70 Hypolita St; ☼ 11am-1am) Good luck grabbing a rocking chair: the porch of this pine building is packed all day, every day. Built in 1879, today Scarlett's serves regulation pub grub (mains $5 to $14), but it's got the magic ingredients – hopping happy hour, live entertainment nightly, hard-working staff, funky bar – that draws folks like spirits to a séance.

Other recommendations include these:

St George Tavern (☎ 904-824-4204; 116 St George St; ☼ 11am-1am) Hoist a pint with period-dressed locals. Drinks are half-price on Tuesdays after 8pm.

Rendezvous (☎ 904-824-1090; 106 St George St, Suite H; ☼ 11am-6pm Mon-Thu, to 12:30am Fri-Sun) This bar cultivates a list about 180 varieties of beer from around the world, like Belzebuth (France), Layla Dirty Blonde (Isreal) and Cuzquena (Peru).

Entertainment

TradeWinds Lounge (☎ 904-829-9336; www.tradewindslounge.com; 124 Charlotte St; ☼ 11am-1am) Tiny bathrooms and big hairdos rule this nautical-themed dive. Smelling sweetly of stale beer, this classic bar's survived two locations and six decades. Crowds tumble out the door during happy hour, and there's live music – mostly Southern rock or 80s music – nightly.

Stogies Jazz Club & Listening Room (☎ 904-826-4008; www.stogiesjazz.com; 36 Charlotte St; ☽ 4pm-1am Mon-Fri, 2pm-1am Sat & Sun) A humidor housing over 100 brands of cigars, including Stogies' own; an exceptional wine list; chess sets at the tables; and plush couches and armchairs whisk you to the '20s. Live jazz from 8:30pm to 12:30am Tuesday to Sunday.

Mill Top Tavern (☎ 904-829-2329; www.milltop.com; 19½ St George St; ☽ 11:30am-1am) Located on the 2nd story of a 19th century mill that's hugged by a huge oak, grooving at the open-aired Mill Top is like hanging out in a treehouse – that has a full bar and kitchen. The Mill Top boasts live music nightly, unmatched views of the Castillo and a cooler vibe than any bar in town.

Café Eleven (☎ 904-460-9311; www.cafeeleven.com; 501 Hwy A1A; ☽ 7am-9pm) Decorated by an Ikea-ophile, this slick hangout is a full-service coffee shop/restaurant during the day. At night, the tables get shoved aside and it transmogrifies into a theater for some of indie rock's biggest names (recent acts include Vampire Weekend, Modest Mouse and the Walkmen). Super-intimate but roomy enough to avoid crazed dancers, it's simply the best small venue on the east coast to catch a live show.

Shopping
Meandering through the town's antique shops could take days; contact **Antique Dealers Association of St Augustine** (☎ 904-826-1524; www.adasta.org) for advice on collectibles.

The Rising Moon (☎ 904-829-0070; www.therisingmoon.com; 58 Spanish St; ☽ 10am-6pm Mon-Sat, noon-5pm Sun) Among soy candles and crystals, browse fair-trade products made from recycled banana tree fibers or car engines. The business supports craftsmen from Kenya to Thailand.

Global Goods and Gifts (☎ 904-829-0900; 62b Spanish St; ☽ 10am-6pm Mon-Sat, noon-5pm Sun) Three doors away, Global Goods sells handmade crafts and farmer-grown coffee, all processed and imported by fair trades-people.

Paper Whites (☎ 904-342-4114; 4 St George St; ☽ 10am-9pm) Delightful, handmade silver jewelry.

The Girl Next Door (☎ 904-461-1441; 1020 Anastasia Blvd; ☽ 9am-8pm Sun-Thu, to 9pm Fri & Sat) Stylish, practical surf-wear for women, kids and home.

Getting There & Around
Driving from the north, take I-95 exit 318 and head east past US Hwy 1 to San Marcos Ave;

turn right and you'll end up at the Old City Gate, just past the fort. Alternately, you can take Hwy A1A along the beach, which intersects with San Marco Ave, or US Hwy 1 south from Jacksonville. From the south, take exit 298, merge onto US 1 and follow it into town.

Cars are a nightmare downtown with one-way and pedestrian-only streets and severely limited parking; outside the city center, you'll need wheels. **Enterprise** (☎ 904-797-1697; 2140 S US 1) and **Hertz** (☎ 904-826-1374; 4900 US 1) will drop off and pick up your car anywhere in St Augustine.

If you're flying into Jacksonville, **Airport Express** (☎ 904-824-9400; www.airportexpresspickup.com) charges $65 to drop you at Ripley's museum. For an additional $20, they'll take you to your hotel. Reservations required.

The **Greyhound** (☎ 904-829-6401; 1711 Dobbs Rd) station is 2 miles southwest of town.

The **Sunshine Bus Company** (☎ 904-823-4816; www.oldcity.com/sites/sunshine) runs approximately 7am to 6pm and serves downtown, the beaches and the outlet malls, as well as many points between ($1 one-way, exact change only).

Checker Cabs (☎ 904-829-1111) has shiny new vehicles.

Rent bikes from Pit Surfshop (p366) for $18 for 24 hours.

Try **Solano Cycles** (☎ 904-825-6766; www.solanocycle.com; 32 San Marco Ave; per 2/24hr $8/18) for bikes downtown and scooters that cost $30/75 for 2/24 hours.

JACKSONVILLE
904 / pop 782,000
More than anything, the lazy St John's River has shaped Jacksonville. Originally an American Indian settlement, later used by Europeans and ultimately established by farmers who dubbed it Cowford – because it was an easy place for cows to 'ford' (cross) the river. In 1821 two plantation owners donated land on the river's north bank to establish a proper town. Renamed for the first military governor of Florida, General Andrew Jackson (who never visited the city), Jacksonville soon became an important shipping hub and vacation destination.

In 1901 a fire ravaged downtown – 2300 buildings, $15 million in damages – in less than eight hours. Much of the rebuilding was done by Henry Klutho (1873–1964), a student of Frank Lloyd Wright and the first to use skyscraper technology.

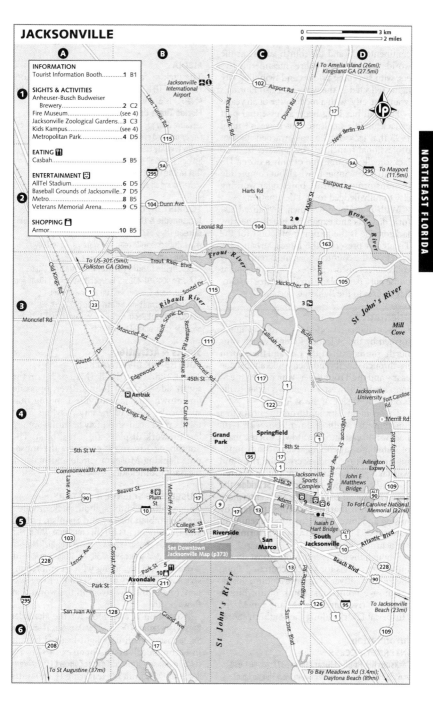

JACKSONVILLE

0 — 3 km
0 — 2 miles

NORTHEAST FLORIDA

Today, at a whopping 840 sq miles, Jacksonville is the largest city by area in the continental US and the fourth largest in the world. Sprawling along three meandering rivers, with sweeping bridges and twinkling city lights reflected in the water, it's also Florida's 'youngest' city, with a median age of 36 years.

Football has long been an essential part of Jacksonville's culture, but it wasn't until 1993 that Jacksonville was awarded its own professional franchise, the Jaguars. In 2005 Jacksonville became one of only a dozen US cities to host a Super Bowl, all but completing its transformation from blue-collar working city to fully fledged tourist destination.

With a buzzing downtown, revitalized historic districts and expansive beaches nearby, Jacksonville is the jumping-off point for the Timucuan preserve, the largest urban park system in the country, boasting a remarkable collection of historical sites. It's also a popular cruise port, particularly for short three- to five-day cruises to the Bahamas and the Keys.

Orientation

Jacksonville is trisected by a very rough T formed by the St John's River – which runs north–south, with a little east and then north jig, through the city and then banks almost due east – and the Trout River, which joins the St John's from the west. Downtown Jacksonville is on the west side of the St John's.

I-95 comes in straight from the north to a junction just south of downtown with I-10. Follow I-10 east into downtown, where a maze of state highways offers access to surrounding areas. Three bridges cross the river and will take you to San Marco: Fuller Warren (I-10), Acosta (Hwy 13) and **Main St Bridge**, the gorgeous cobalt-blue bridge and centerpiece of downtown that allows ships' passage by raising and lowering, rather than opening in halves. I-295 breaks off from I-95, forming a circle around the city.

Though the city is enormous, most sites of interest to the visitor are concentrated along the St John's River's narrowest point: downtown; Five Points, just south of downtown along the river; and the elegant San Marco Historical District along the southern shore.

Information
INTERNET ACCESS
Jacksonville Public Library (Map p373; ☎ 904-630-2665; 303 N Laura St; ☺ 9am-8pm Mon-Thu, to 6pm

Fri & Sat, 1-6pm Sun) This is the main branch, but free landline and wi-fi access is available at all locations.

MEDIA
The pick of commercial radio is old-school funk at 101.5FM. National Public Radio (NPR) is at 89.9FM.
Florida Times-Union (www.times-union.com) Conservative daily paper; Friday's *Weekend* magazine features family-oriented events listings.
Folio Weekly Free; with club, restaurant and events listings. Found all over town.
Out in the City Covers Jacksonville's gay and lesbian scene. Found all over town.

TOURIST INFORMATION
Jacksonville & the Beaches Convention & Visitors Bureau (Map p373; ☎ 904-798-9111, 800-733-2668; www.visitjacksonville.com; 550 Water St, Suite 1000; ☺ 8am-5pm Mon-Fri)
Jacksonville Landing visitor information (Map p373; ☎ 904-791-4305; 2 Independent Dr; ☺ 10am-7pm Mon-Sat, noon-5:30pm Sun) On the lower level.
Tourist information booth (Map p371; ☎ 904-741-3044; 14201 Pecan Park Rd; ☺ 9am-10pm) At the baggage-claim area of the airport.

Sights & Activities
SOUTHBANK RIVERWALK
This 1.2-mile boardwalk (Map p373) on the south side of the St John's River, opposite downtown and Jacksonville Landing, has spectacular views of the city's skyline. Most nights yield head-shakingly beautiful scenes, but firework displays are a real blast. The Southbank Riverwalk connects the museums flanking Museum Circle and makes a pleasant promenade.

MUSEUM OF SCIENCE & HISTORY
Enlightening exhibits about Jacksonville's pre-Columbian history and Spanish, French and US settlements fill this **museum** (MOSH; Map p373; ☎ 904-396-6674; www.themosh.org; 1025 Museum Circle; adult/child/senior $9/7/7.50; ☺ 10am-5pm Mon-Fri, to 6pm Sat, 1-6pm Sun), along with a comprehensive natural history of the St John's River system, one of the few rivers in the world that flows north.

Admission is also good for the **Alexander Brest Planetarium** (☺ shows 2pm Mon-Sun, 11am & 3pm Sat, 3pm Sun), which uses light-hearted humor in astronomical shows. For an extra $7 to $9, take in a laser-lighted **Cosmic Concert** (☺ concerts 8pm, 9pm, 10:30pm Fri & Sat), featuring 18,000 watts

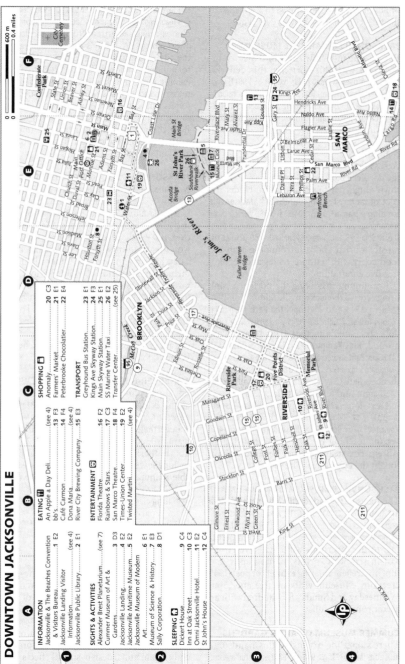

DOWNTOWN JACKSONVILLE

NORTHEAST FLORIDA

INFORMATION
Jacksonville & The Beaches Convention
& Visitors Bureau................................1 E2
Jacksonville Landing Visitor
Information..(see 4)
Jacksonville Public Library...................2 E1

SIGHTS & ACTIVITIES
Alexander Brest Planetarium...............(see 7)
Cummer Museum of Art &
Gardens...3 D3
Jacksonville Landing.............................4 E2
Jacksonville Maritime Museum............5 E2
Jacksonville Museum of Modern
Art..6 E1
Museum of Science & History...............7 E3
Sally Corporation..................................8 D1

SLEEPING
Dickert House..9 C4
Inn at Oak Street................................10 C3
Omni Jacksonville Hotel.....................11 E2
St John's House....................................12 C4

EATING
An Apple a Day Deli............................(see 4)
bb's..13 F3
Café Carmon.......................................14 F4
Dona Maria...(see 4)
River City Brewing Company...............15 E3

ENTERTAINMENT
Florida Theatre....................................16 F2
Rainbows & Stars................................17 C3
San Marco Theatre..............................18 F4
Times-Union Center............................19 E2
Twisted Martini...................................(see 4)

SHOPPING
Anomaly..20 C3
Farmers' Market..................................21 E1
Peterbrooke Chocolatier.....................22 E4

TRANSPORT
Greyhound Bus Station.......................23 E1
Kings Ave Skyway Station....................24 F3
Main Skyway Station...........................25 E1
SS Marine Water Taxi..........................26 E2
Transfer Center...................................(see 25)

of anything from '80s tunes, to Zeppelin, to the full score of Pink Floyd's *The Wall*.

JACKSONVILLE MARITIME MUSEUM

For insight into how maritime history intertwines with this port city, this densely-packed **museum** (Map p373; ☎ 904-398-9011; www .jaxmaritimemuseum.org; 1015 Museum Circle; admission by donation; 🕙 10:30am-3pm Mon-Fri, 1-4pm Sat & Sun) has an array of nautical artifacts, scale models and shipping logs.

NORTHBANK

Across the river from Southbank Riverwalk, the northern bank unfurls at the foot of downtown's high-rise business district. Under the roof of its most visible landmark, **Jacksonville Landing** (Map p373; ☎ 904-353-1188; www.jackson villelanding.com; 2 Independent Dr; 🕙 10am-8pm Mon-Thu, to 9pm Fri & Sat, noon-5:30pm Sun), are about 40 mostly touristy shops surrounding a tip-top food court with outdoor tables and regular, free live entertainment.

Continuing east along the northern bank brings you to the Jacksonville Sports Complex (Map p371) and **Metropolitan Park** (Map p371; ☎ 904-630-0837; Gator Bowl Blvd), a sprawling outdoor space adjoining the terrific 10-acre playground, **Kids Kampus** (Map p371; ☎ 904-630-5437; 1410 Gator Bowl Blvd; admission free; 🕙 8am-8pm Mon-Sat, 10am-8pm Sun). Here, tykes under six ride bikes through Safe City's 'streets' dotted with mini road signs and familiar city landmarks.

Next door is the kid-approved **Fire Museum** (Map p371; ☎ 904-630-0618; www.jacksonvillefiremuseum .com; 1408 Gator Bowl Blvd; admission free; 🕙 9am-4pm Mon-Fri), teaching fire safety and housing an Ahrens Fox steam pumper believed to have fought the city's Great Fire of 1901.

JACKSONVILLE MUSEUM OF MODERN ART

The focus of the **Jacksonville Museum of Modern Art** (Map p373; ☎ 904-366-6911; www.mocajacksonville .org; 333 N Laura St; adult/senior $8/5; 🕙 10am-4pm Tue-Sat, to 9pm Wed, noon-4pm Sun) extends beyond painting: in the cavernous white halls, you'll get lost in sculpture, prints, photography and film in excellent rotating exhibits of post-1945 creations. Museum visits are free after 5pm Wednesday and Sunday for children with an accompanying adult.

CUMMER MUSEUM OF ART & GARDENS

There's dazzling art inside this handsome **museum** (Map p373; ☎ 904-356-6857; www.cummer.org;

829 Riverside Ave; adult/student $10/6, 4-9pm Tue free; 🕙 10am-9pm Tue, to 5pm Wed-Sat, noon-5pm Sun), includes newly-acquired Norman Rockwells and George PA Healy's famous portrait of the city's namesake close to death. Also look for antiquities and a really fun interactive kids' exhibit. Draped with wisteria and shaded by a massive, mossy oak so large it needs supports for its limbs, the garden is a grand place to unwind after absorbing all the beauty inside. Both the museum and gardens are impressively accessible, including a number of braille and audio guides.

JACKSONVILLE ZOOLOGICAL GARDENS

Northeast Florida's only major **zoo** (Map p371; ☎ 904-757-4463; www.jacksonvillezoo.org; 370 Zoo Parkway; adult/child $12/7.50; 🕙 9am-5pm) opened in 1914 with one deer; today, it's home to over 100 exotic species. Jaguar football fans won't want to miss jaguars prowling replicated Mayan temple ruins. Other highlights include the wetlands of Wild Florida, with rare Florida panthers, and an elevated viewing platform that brings you face to nose with giraffes (you can even feed them!). There's also an animal-spotting train ride through the grounds (adult/child $4/2).

Take exit 358A from I-95 to Heckscher Dr E; the zoo's on your right.

ANHEUSER-BUSCH BUDWEISER BREWERY

Equal parts history and propaganda, a tour at the **brewery** (Map p371; ☎ 904-696-8373; www .budweisertours.com; 111 Busch Dr; 🕙 10am-4pm Mon-Sat) is nevertheless a fascinating look at how this plant produces 8.4 million barrels (or 2.7 trillion bottles!) of beer each year. Highlights include learning about the factory's sustainable manufacturing practices and (if you're over 21) sampling free Bud products while watching classic Bud commercials. Dude! Free tours depart on the half hour.

Take I-95 exit 360 at Busch Dr and follow the billboards.

SALLY CORPORATION

If you've ever wondered how theme-park rides like Universal Studios' 'ET Adventure' weave their robotic magic, a tour of **Sally Corporation** (Map p373; ☎ 904-355-7100; www.sally corp.com; 745 W Forsyth St; 🕙 tours hourly 9am-1pm Tue & Thu, excl Jul & Aug; 🅿), makers of animatronics and 'dark rides,' will demystify the process and explain initial design, special effects, sets, scenery, soundtracks, lighting systems and cooling technology. Free tours (reservation only) take you behind the scenes of the art and costuming, mechanical, pneumatics, and computer-programming departments.

FORT CAROLINE NATIONAL MEMORIAL

This **memorial** (Map p371; ☎ 904-641-7155; 12713 Fort Caroline Rd; ☺ 9am-5pm) is the administrative headquarters of the **Timucuan Ecological and Historical Preserve**, a confederation of federal, state and local parks – some located on Talbot and Fort George Islands (see p379). The confederation works with private landowners to maintain the St John's River ecosystem.

The memorial itself is a roughly two-thirds the size of the original fort built here in 1562, and was France's first attempt to stake a permanent claim in North America. The park also features several hundred acres of pristine wilderness fronting the St John's River.

To reach the main visitor's center from downtown, take Matthews Bridge (John E Matthews Bridge) to Atlantic Blvd Expressway (Hwy 10 E), then turn left onto Monument Rd; follow that to Fort Caroline Rd and turn right – the entrance is about half a mile ahead.

FISHING

Because of Jacksonville's unique riverfront and ocean-close location, opportunities for fishing abound. Anglers can choose to plumb the brackish waters along the mouth of the St John's or travel completely offshore in search of kingfish, tarpon, flounder, cobia, pompano and more. Alternatively, there are plenty of chances to hook freshwater swimmers like trout, bream, bass and bluegill along inland portions of the St John's River and beyond.

Dozens of **charter operations** between downtown and the ocean offer a wide range of packages, prices and promises. An excellent resource for researching charters is www.jacksonvillefishing.com, which lists operators by area, describes the services offered and provides contact information. Cost for charters range widely, depending on how many people join, where you want to go and how long you want to spend on the water. In general, plan to spend about $400 for a half-day trip or $600 for a full day.

For a mellower fishing experience, give **kayak fishing** – or yak fishing – a whirl. Sitting inside a kayak, fishing along spartina grass for mullet on a glassy tidal marsh is a postcard-perfect way to spend a day. The **Salty Feather** (☎ 904-645-8998; www.saltyfeather .com; 2683 St Johns Bluff Rd; half-day/day $375/525) runs half-day and day trips. To learn more about this slow-going, fast-growing sport, visit www.jaxkayakfishing.com.

GOLF

With 72 courses in the greater area, there are plenty of opportunities to tee off. You can browse course summaries by visiting www .visitjacksonville.com and following the links to 'visitors,' then 'golf.'

Sleeping

You'll find the cheapest rooms along I-95 and I-10, where the lower-priced chains congregate. Additional accommodation options, including camping, are available at the beaches (p378).

St John's House (Map p373; ☎ 904-384-3724; www .stjohnshouse.com; 1718 Osceola St; r $99-125; P ✗ 🖳) Surrounded by magnolias, citrus trees and a bird-feeding station, this B&B has two spacious rooms and a recently renovated carriage house – tiny but charming. Be sure to look down: the serpentine detail in the hardwood floors is mindblowing.

Dickert House (Map p373; ☎ 904-387-4762; www.dickert-house.net; 1804 Copeland St; r $99-139; P ✗ 🖳) Surrounded by fountains gurgling in jasmine-laced gardens, this 1914 prairie-style B&B has three two-room suites and a separate, roomy carriage house. Though the decor may be flowery, the water views and the pecan-pie-sweet Mrs Dickert – who prepares full, hot Southern breakfasts – make this place a gem.

our pick **Inn at Oak Street** (Map p373; ☎ 904-379-5525; www.innatoakstreet.com; 2114 Oak St; r $100-165; P ✗ 🖳) Bold colors and high-tech amenities (iPod-compatible clock radios, DVD and TVs in all rooms) put a contemporary twist on this restored 1902 B&B. Heart pine floors, gargantuan bathrooms, and fireplaces sprinkled throughout swank up the place. Cool packages include a Girls' Getaway with beauty treatments from the on-site spa, or an add-on English high tea served on the 70ft-long veranda.

Omni Jacksonville Hotel (Map p373; ☎ 904-355-6664; 245 Water St; r $89-199; P 🖳 🐾) Within sight of Jax Landing, this 354-room hotel has lavish, amenity-laden rooms (some with wheelchair access), acres of marble, a heated rooftop pool and, best of all, free video games – just perfect for decompressing. Small pets are allowed.

Eating

There are plenty of cheap eats at Jacksonville Landing (see p374).

An Apple a Day Deli (Map p373; ☎ 904-353-9191; Jacksonville Landing; mains $4-7; ⓧ 10am-8pm Mon-Thu, to 9pm Fri & Sat, noon-5:30pm Sun) Head here for healthy smoothies, salads and sandwiches.

ourpick Casbah (Map p371; www.thecasbahcafe.com; ☎ 904-981-9966; 3628 St Johns Ave; mains $4-14; ⓧ 11am-2am) Upon spying the swords, camels and Moorish lanterns lining the walls, you'll wonder if a passport is required for entry. Featuring authentic Middle Eastern dishes, beer, music and belly dancing, the café doubles as a hookah lounge with dozens of flavorful tobacco concoctions.

Dona Maria (Map p373; ☎ 904-598-2696; Jacksonville Landing; mains $7-15; ⓧ 11am-10pm) Great sunset views and the best ceviche in Jax Landing.

Café Carmon (Map p373; ☎ 904-399-4488; 1986 San Marco Blvd; mains $11-20; ⓧ 11am-10pm Mon-Thu, 11am-11pm Fri & Sat) Light and airy inside, the tables outside are best if you like people watching. Located across from the lions in the heart of fashionable San Marco, this cheery restaurant features creative pasta dishes and scrumptious salads.

River City Brewing Company (Map p373; ☎ 904-398-2299; 835 Museum Circle; mains $16-26; ⓧ 11am-3pm & 5-10pm Mon-Thu, to 11pm Fri & Sat, 10:30am-2:30pm Sun) Panoramic river views compete with first-rate fare at this restaurant/brewery. The dinner menu leans toward Southern-style seafood like ultratraditional jambalaya and gumbo. Sunday brunch (10:30am to 2:30pm) features hand-carved roasts. At night, the brewhouse draws an after-work crowd eager to unwind.

bb's (Map p373; ☎ 904-306-0100; 1019 Hendricks Ave; mains $20-33; ⓧ 10:30am-10:30pm Mon-Sat) With its molded concrete bar, clean, modern lines and daily cheese selection, this Euro-staurant may initially feel hipper-than-thou. But pull up a seat, chat with the staff and discover they're just like you – only dressed entirely in black. The chocolate ganache cake is worth the trip.

Entertainment

Many restaurants double as bars. Check www.downtownjacksonville.org for entertainment listings and events in the downtown area; for the greater Jacksonville area, go to www.jaxbars.com.

Times-Union Center (Map p373; ☎ 904-633-6110; 300 Water St; ⓧ box office 10am-4pm) hosts major performers, touring Broadway shows and the **Jacksonville Symphony Orchestra** (☎ 904-354-5547; www.jaxsymphony.org).

Florida Theatre (Map p373; ☎ 904-355-2787; 1128 E Forsyth St) Home to Elvis' first indoor concert in 1956, which a local judge endured to ensure Presley was not overly suggestive, this opulent 1927 venue is an intimate place to catch performances by BB King, Aretha Franklin and Wilco; it also hosts musicals, a summer movie classics series (Sundays at 2pm, $6) and other events. Ticket prices vary widely.

San Marco Theatre (Map p373; ☎ 904-396-4845; 1996 San Marco Blvd; adult/child $7/5) A landmark 1938 art-deco creation where you can order beer, wine, pizza and sandwiches while watching a flick; the theater screens classic midnight movies (like *Goonies*) on weekends.

Jacksonville Landing (see p374) often has free entertainment at the amphitheater, and many of the restaurants and bars also have live music. The **Twisted Martini** (☎ 904-353-8464; Jacksonville Landing; ⓧ 4pm-2am Wed-Sat) has live music from 7pm to 10pm Thursday to Saturday.

GAY & LESBIAN VENUES

A good resource for gay and lesbian listings of clubs, bars and community services is available at www.clubjax.com/info. Alternatively, swing by **Rainbows & Stars** (Map p373; ☎ 904-356-7702; 1046 Park St), in Five Points, and check out their community bulletin board.

Metro (Map p371; ☎ 904-388-8719; www.metrojax.com; 2929 Plum St) This gay-entertainment complex has a disco, a cruise bar, a piano bar, a games room with pinball machines, a smoke-free chill-out loft, a leathery boiler room and a show bar.

SPORTS

Completed in time for the 2005 Superbowl, Jacksonville Sports Complex (Map p371) encompasses the 82,000-capacity AllTel Stadium, home of the **Jacksonville Jaguars** (☎ 904-633-6100; www.jaguars.com). Outside the stadium, the Veterans Memorial Wall pays tribute to local soldiers.

Also at the complex is the 16,000-capacity Veterans Memorial Arena, home to the **Jacksonville Barracudas** (☎ 904-367-1423; www.jaxcudas.com) hockey team, and the Baseball Grounds of Jacksonville, where the minor-league **Jacksonville Suns** (☎ 904-358-2846; www.jaxsuns.com) play to a capacity crowd of 10,000.

BERRY PICKING

About 13 miles west of I-95 on Hwy 207, the town of Elkton offers peace and quiet and the chance to pick your own strawberries for $1 per quart ($2 if they're picked for you) at Tommy Howle's Vegetable Bin & Garden. Tommy Howle's is on the right-hand side of the road on the eastern end of town, across from the County Fairgrounds.

Shopping

Armor (Map p371; ☎ 904-388-8282; 3610 St Johns Ave; ⓨ 11am-7pm Tue-Sat, 12-5 Sat) This hip men's shop in Avondale features kickin' threads from the likes of Diesel, Ben Sherman and Caffeine. Sporting an excellent sales room, you're sure to leave looking like a runway model. Or at least like you…but way cooler.

Farmers' Market (Map p373; Hemming Plaza, 117 W Duval St; ⓨ 10am-2pm Fri) Head to Hemming Plaza, across from City Hall, for quirky jewelry and hand-carved flowers.

Anomaly (☎ 904-354-7002; www.anomalyfivepoints .com; 1021 Park St) Buying the jewelry, casual tops, or kids' beachwear in this lime-colored shop makes you feel warm inside: the goods sold here are created by local designers.

Peterbrooke Chocolatier (☎ 904-398-2489; www .peterbrooke.com; 1470 San Marco Blvd; ⓨ 10am-5pm Mon-Fri) Come here for chocolate-coated popcorn, pretzels and more. Reserve ahead for tours ($1 including samples), which run at 10am Monday to Friday. There's a great bench two blocks west. Munch away and watch the river roll past.

Getting There & Around

Offering free wi-fi, the sparkling **Jacksonville International Airport** (JAX; Map p371; ☎ 904-741-4902) is served by major and regional airlines as well as major car-rental companies. The airport's about 18 miles north of downtown on I-95, off the Airport Rd exit; a cab to downtown costs about $32.

The **Greyhound bus station** (Map p373; ☎ 904-356-9976; 10 Pearl St) is at the west end of downtown. The **Amtrak station** (Map p371; ☎ 904-766-5110; 3570 Clifford Lane) is 5 miles northwest of downtown. Jacksonville is at the intersection of I-10, which connects Jacksonville to Tallahassee and the Pacific Ocean, and I-95, a straight shot down the east coast to Miami. Hwy A1A is the slower, scenic route and runs north–south along the beaches; it connects directly to St

Augustine, to the south. If you're heading north on A1A you'll need to cross the St John's River on the **St John's River Ferry** (☎ 904-357-3006; car/RV $5/10; ⓨ 6am-8:30pm), also called the Mayport Ferry, which runs every half-hour.

The **Jacksonville Transportation Authority** (JTA; ☎ 904-630-3100; www.jtaonthemove.com) runs the bus service in town (fare 75¢) and to the beaches ($1.35). The main downtown **transfer center** (Map p373; 201 State St) is also the terminus of the scenic **Skyway** (☎ 904-743-3582; www.ridejta.net; ⓨ 6am-11pm Mon-Fri, 10am-11pm Sat) Main Station (Map p373; 201 State St); Kings Ave Station (Map p373; Kings Ave), which traverses the St John's River via an elevated monorail (35¢). The **trolley** (Map p373; ☎ 904-743-3582; www.ridejta .net; ⓨ 5:43am-7:23pm Mon-Fri, 8am-6pm Sat, 6:20am-7pm Sun) has 12 free stops throughout downtown's northern shore; the new Riverside Trolley (50¢) links downtown and Five Points, and runs from 10:30am to 2:30pm on weekdays.

Escape the traffic on an **SS Marine water taxi** (Map p373; ☎ 904-733-7782; www.jaxwatertaxi.com; round-trip/one-way $5/3; ⓨ 11am-9pm Sun-Thu, to 11pm Fri & Sat).

JACKSONVILLE AREA BEACHES
☎ 904 / pop 22,000

The stretches of beaches closest to Jacksonville are delightfully sparse. Moving from south to north, Ponte Vedra Beach is the posh home of the ATP and PGA tours, with golf resorts and courses. Urban Jacksonville Beach is where to go for a party, while cozy Neptune Beach is more subdued. And if you want some sand to yourself, Atlantic Beach, with several entrances off Seminole Beach Rd, is sublime.

Orientation

Referred to everywhere – including road signs – as 'Jax Beaches,' the Jacksonville area beaches are around 17 miles east of the city center.

Avenues run east–west and streets north–south. Coming from St Augustine, once you cross Butler Blvd you'll hit the 'south' streets. Beach Blvd is the divider.

Hwy A1A (3rd St) is the main north–south road along the beaches, jogging inland a bit along Hwy 10, then becoming Mayport Rd as it heads north to Hanna Park and the St John's River Ferry.

Information

The **Beaches Visitor Center** (☎ 904-242-0024; www .jacksonvillebeach.org; 403 Beach Blvd; ⓨ 10am-4:30pm Tue-Sat) has information about the beaches.

Sights & Activities

Most of the action is concentrated at Jacksonville Beach, which buzzes all summer (and most of the mild winter, too).

Constructed from removable planks, allowing it to be dismantled in the event of a hurricane, the 1300ft **pier** (☎ 904-241-1515; 503 N 1st St; walk-on/fishing $1/4; ☽ 6am-10pm) has a bait shop, concessions and fish-cleaning stations. Bring drinks, cast your line and wait for a nibble.

If the lure of the water is just too great, swing by **Atlantic Watersports** (☎ 904-270-0200; www.atlantic-watersports.com; 2327 Beach Blvd; all vessels 1/4/8hr $79/229/349), which rents 14ft fishing boats, 19ft bowriders, 24ft pontoon boats and three-person jet skis.

The roads are flat and the towns are small: why not rent a bike? In addition to various beach and water-sports equipment, **RentBeachStuff** (☎ 904-305-6472; www.rentbeachstuff .com) will deliver a 26in beach cruiser to your hotel for $30 per day.

Sleeping

Kathryn Abbey Hanna Park (☎ 904-249-4700; 500 Wonderwood Dr, Atlantic Beach; campsites with/without hookups $34/14.20, 4-person cabins $34) In Atlantic Beach, this place has a well-spaced, shady campground 200yd from the ocean with its own freshwater lake. Huguenot Memorial Park (p380) and Little Talbot Island State Park (p380) also have camping.

Sea Horse Inn (☎ 800-881-2330; www.seahorse oceanfrontinn.com; 120 Atlantic Blvd, Neptune Beach; r $109-199; **P** 🖳 🏊) Each room in this Pepto Bismol-colored refurbished motel has a view of both the kidney-shaped pool and the ocean. A seashell's throw from Pete's Bar – a smoky dive with 25¢ pool games – the Old Florida Sea Horse will make you feel decades from home.

Seawalk Hotel (☎ 904-249-9981; www.seawalkhotel .com; 117 1st Ave N, Jacksonville Beach; r $119-199; **P** 🖳) Forming a horseshoe around a courtyard thick with palms, the 25 rooms at the Seawalk are purely functional: tile floors, simple beds, a micro-fridge, tiny bathrooms. However, what this art deco–inspired hotel lacks in pizzazz it makes up for in location – it's a block from the sand.

Fig Tree B&B (☎ 904-246-8855; www.figtreeinn.com; 185 4th Ave, Jacksonville Beach; r $145-175; **P** 🐾 🖳) Constructed from cedar-shake shingles, this rustic, two-story 1915 cottage conceals six rooms, including the quirky Bird Room, with a handmade willow-frame queen-size bed and willow reading chair. In addition to breakfast (fully cooked on weekends, self-serve weekdays), it does an afternoon tea on the shady porch.

Casa Marina (☎ 904-270-0025; www.casamarinahotel .com; 691 N 1st St, Jacksonville Beach; r $159-229; **P** 🖳) Right on the beach, this restored 1925 building is a stunning example of Mediterranean architecture from the days when this stretch of coast was a playground for the rich (check the hallways' framed prints for proof). Dark timber furniture, airy bathrooms and feather-soft linens adorn the 25 rooms and parlor suites. The on-site restaurant includes an extensive tapas menu and a fantastic open-air dining courtyard.

Eating & Drinking

Beach Hut Café (☎ 904-249-3516; 1281 3rd St S; meals $3-8; ☽ 6am-2:30pm) Don't let its strip mall location deceive you: the food here is divine. Famous for its big, all-day Southern breakfasts, *huge* lines form outside – especially on weekends.

European Street (☎ 904-249-3009; 992 Beach Blvd; mains $5-12; ☽ 10am-10pm) Sneak away from the beaches at this combination chocolatier,

---

FREEBIRD LIVE

Fans of local-boys-done-good Lynyrd Skynyrd will want to pay homage at **Freebird Live** (☎ 904-246-2473; www.freebirdlive.com; 200 N 1st St; ☽ 8pm-2am Wed-Sat), a two-story music venue with wide verandas, owned by the Van Zant family. The band's founding lead singer Ronnie Van Zant and many of his band mates died in a 1977 plane crash; his younger brother Johnny took his place when the band reformed a decade later.

With two original members still in the lineup, Skynyrd rawks this joint when they're not touring; there's plenty of memorabilia, too. But the Freebird is way more than a shrine. With an intimate stage and great acoustics, it has carved out a reputation as one of the nation's best small music venues. In addition to giving local talent a stage, recent acts have included Willie Nelson, the Killers and George Clinton.

deli, bar (boasting 150 imported beers) and gourmet market.

Sun Dog (☎ 904-241-8221; 207 Atlantic Blvd; mains $7-10; 🕑 11am-2am Mon-Sat, 10am-12am Sun) The diner to visit if you miss your pooch. Above the 1950s-styled booths hang original artwork of…you guessed it…dogs. Not a dog-lover? No problem: there's plenty of outdoor seating for you.

Bukkets (☎ 904-246-7701; 222 N Oceanfront; mains $8-25; 🕑 11am-2am) Grab a seat on this bar's deck overlooking the boardwalk that fronts the beach, order a pitcher, and watch the people roll past. On weekend afternoons, enjoy live music while sucking down hot wings.

Shopping

Ukulele (☎ 904-246-1077; 38 Ocean Blvd, Neptune Beach) This self-proclaimed 'chick shop' offers pastel beachwear and sundresses.

Eco Organic Living (☎ 904-486-8598; 604 N 3rd Ave, Jacksonville Beach) If the yellow sun has made you red, check out this green store, featuring home decor, jewelry, and clothing all made from renewables.

Beachside (☎ 904-246-0248; 234 1st St N, Jacksonville Beach) In addition to $5 hats, this place has a bottomless supply of swimwear and ocean-inspired novelties.

Getting There & Around

Traveling by car from Jacksonville, follow I-10 to Atlantic Beach, and Hwy 90 (Beach Blvd) directly to Jacksonville Beach. Coming from St Augustine, you follow Hwy A1A due north.

Jacksonville Transportation Authority (☎ 904-630-3100; www.jtaonthemove.com) operates buses from Jacksonville to the beaches ($1.35).

TALBOT & FORT GEORGE ISLANDS
☎ 904

Between Jacksonville's beaches and Amelia Island, coastal Hwy A1A laces together the Talbot and Fort George Islands. Shaded by flourishing vegetation, it's a scenic drive even if you don't stop, but there are several reasons you'll want to: exceptional kayaking, distinctive state parks with natural and man-made wonders, and blissful beach and riverfront camping.

Orientation & Information

The islands are strung in a north–south chain. If you're heading north from Mayport via the St John's River Ferry (see p385), you'll drive off its decks directly onto Fort George Island.

From the ferry wharf, continue along A1A (here called Heckscher Dr). Fort George Rd – leading to the Fort George Island Cultural State Park, Ribault Club and Kingsley Plantation – is to your left, shortly followed by Huguenot Memorial Park on your right. Stay on A1A and you'll pass Little Talbot Island State Park, where the ranger station is located, then Big Talbot Island State Park. Continuing north takes you to Amelia Island.

Sights & Activities
FORT GEORGE ISLAND CULTURAL STATE PARK

Laden with history, this **state park** (☎ 904-251-2320; 12157 Heckscher Dr; 🕑 8am-sunset) is part of the Timucuan Ecological and Historic Preserve, which also includes Fort Caroline National Memorial (p375).

Enormous shell middens date the island's habitation by American Indians to over 5000 years ago. In 1736 British General James Oglethorpe (the founder of Georgia) erected a fort in the area, though it's long since vanished and its exact location is uncertain.

Fort George raged in the '20s when flappers flocked to the ritzy **Ribault Club** for Gatsby-esque bashes with lawn bowling and yachting. Built in 1928 on top of an indigenous shell mound, this bone-white mansion flaunts grand archways and three-dozen sets of cypress French doors. Meticulously restored, the club now hosts private events and houses a **visitor's center** (🕑 9am-5pm Wed-Sun). The island's 4.4-mile **Saturiwa loop trail**, which you can walk, bike or drive, begins and ends here. The visitor's center has first-rate historical trail guides, both printed and on CD, allowing you to undertake a self-guided tour at your own pace.

KINGSLEY PLANTATION

Zephaniah Kingsley moved to this former cotton and citrus **plantation** (☎ 904-251-3537; 🕑 9am-5pm) in 1814, managing it with his wife, Anna Jai, whom he originally purchased as a slave and later married in a traditional African ceremony, subsequently freeing both her and their children.

Ensuing tussles with the government over racial laws forced Kingsley to send his family to Haiti in 1835. He died in 1843, never having joined them. In 1860 Jai returned

NORTHEAST FLORIDA

to Florida in time to see the Emancipation Proclamation delivered.

Today, the main house is the oldest standing plantation house in Florida. While the main house is undergoing near-constant structural repairs necessitated by termites and humidity, you can tour portions of it as well as the remains of 23 tabby-construction slave cabins. Daily at 2pm, a ranger-led program discusses natural history, slavery and the Kingsleys' lives. It's a nice spot for a picnic.

HUGUENOT MEMORIAL PARK

Got a kiteboard? Come here to show off your skills. Just a landlubber? Drive over the dunes onto the beach at this lovely regional **park** (☎ 904-251-3335; 10980 Heckscher Dr; admission 50¢). Conditions vary significantly depending on tides and weather; if you're in a 2WD, avoid soft-looking sand.

The park's just past the turnoff to Fort George Rd on Hwy A1A.

LITTLE TALBOT ISLAND STATE PARK

This pristine **island** (☎ 904-251-2320; 12157 Heckscher Dr; pedestrian/car $1/4; ☼ 8am-sunset), the same size as Big Talbot Island, has 5 miles of unspoiled beaches, extraordinary wildlife (river otters, marsh rabbits, bobcats) and grand tidal fishing for mullet and sheepshead. Kayak Amelia (see below) rents kayaks and offers guided trips around the island.

BIG TALBOT ISLAND STATE PARK

Deposit your fee in the blue envelope and pull into the lone parking lot at this stark but lovely **park** (☎ 904-251-2320; pedestrian/car $1/2; ☼ 8am-sunset; ℗). Grab your camera and follow the short trail to Boneyard Beach, where the salt-washed skeletons of live oak and cedar trees litter the white sand, framed by a 20ft bluff of eroded coastline.

KAYAKING

Fort George Island Surf Shop (☎ 904-251-3483; 10030 Heckscher Dr; kayaks per day single/double $40/50; ☼ 9am-5pm) – hidden on the right of the road – rents kayaks and serves as the island's post office.

If you've never kayaked before, **Kayak Amelia** (☎ 904-251-0016, 888-305-2925; www.kayak amelia.com; 13300 Heckscher Dr; guided trips from $55, single/tandem/canoe rental per 4hr $30/45/45) doles out easy-to-follow instructions, moral support and home-baked chocolate chip cookies in equal measure.

Of their popular half-day trips, the standout – tide and current permitting – follows the former trade route of the Fort George River to the Kingsley Plantation, with time to wander the estate during a break from paddling. Feeling starry-eyed? Moonlight paddles through the silvered marsh are a magical way to experience meditative waters. Kids are welcome, but call in advance to make arrangements.

SEGWAY TOURS

Most people expect to tromp through parks on foot. However, **EcoMotion Tours** (☎ 904-251-9477; www.ecomotiontours.com; trips $55-85; ☼ 7am-8pm) offers a modern, 'green' spin on exploring Mother Nature. On the 4- and 5-mile low-impact tours, covering either Fort George or Little Talbot, Segway transporters roll you silently through the parks as you listen through headsets to certified guides detailing the area's flora, fauna and historical landmarks. No experience is necessary, but you must be over 13 years old (and under 250lb) to ride. Call for reservations.

Sleeping & Eating

There are two terrific camping options. **Huguenot Memorial Park** (unpowered sites interior/riverfront $6/8) is the best deal, but bring your earplugs on weekends when Jacksonville teens descend. Alternatively, wake up to the waves rolling in at **Little Talbot Island State Park** (beachfront sites with hookups $19).

Eating is limited to sandwiches and shrimp baskets from **Nicole's on the River** (☎ 904-251-9977; 9429 Heckscher Dr; meals $6-10; ☼ 6am-3pm) or the **Sandollar Restaurant & Marina** (☎ 904-251-2449; 9716 Heckscher Dr; mains $13-27; ☼ 11am-9pm Sun-Thu, to 10pm Fri & Sat), where you can dine on meat and seafood on a deck over the river.

The closest markets are near the ferry on Fort George Island or on Amelia Island.

AMELIA ISLAND

☎ 904 / pop 11,241

In 1857 the Florida Railroad Company platted this island, believing it would be a vital stop for transporting goods from Florida's Gulf Coast to the north. In the 1890s, as Henry Flagler tamed Florida's wild east coast and helped convert the area into a playground for the rich, Amelia began attracting wealthy snowbirds from the northeast, eager for warm weather. Soon after, enterprising fishermen began plying her rich waters.

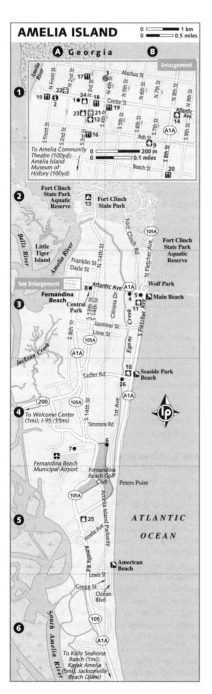

NORTHEAST FLORIDA

Amelia Island is a five-minute ferry ride from Jacksonville, followed by a glorious coastal drive. The island is home to Fernandina Beach, a charming shrimping village with 50 blocks of historic buildings, delightful eateries and unique B&Bs. Named for Princess Amelia, the daughter of England's King George II, Amelia today proudly displays the legacy of its 'Golden Age' – the late 19th and early 20th centuries – when hotels popped up to accommodate tourists. The same tourists deserted Amelia when Flagler's railroad and hotel empire funneled them further south. Dotting the island are swanky resorts, endless green fairways and miles of shark-tooth-covered shoreline, sealed by a commanding Civil War-era fort surrounded by a quintessentially Southern moss-draped state park.

Orientation
Just south of the Georgia border and 30 miles northeast of Jacksonville, Amelia is about 13 miles long – only 4 miles at its widest point –

and is Florida's northernmost barrier island. Most of the action takes place downtown, at the northwestern end. The township is laid out in a grid, with east–west streets given names and north–south streets numbers. Centre St (dig that European spelling) is the main drag and the north–south divider; it becomes Atlantic Ave east of 8th St.

When people speak of Fernandina Beach they usually mean the historic downtown area – not a specific stretch of sand. The island's most frequented beach is Main Beach, at the east end of Centre St. South of Centre St at the end of Sadler Rd is Seaside Park Beach, further south still is Peters Point; all of which, along with American Beach (see right), are lifeguard patrolled between Memorial Day and Labor Day. Vehicles can access the beach from Seaside Park and Peters Point, though you'll want a 4WD as sand can be deceptively soft.

Information

BOOKSTORES
Book Loft (☎ 904-277-7365; 214 Centre St; ☺ 10am-9pm Mon-Sat, noon-6pm Sun) Splendid, with lots of local books.

INTERNET ACCESS
Library (☎ 904-277-7365; 25 N 4th St; ☺ 10am-6pm Mon-Sat, to 8pm Mon & Thu) Free internet access.

TOURIST INFORMATION
Welcome Center (☎ 800-226-3542; www.amelia island.org; 961687 Gateway Blvd; ☺ 9am-5pm Mon-Sat) Coming from the west, it's your first right-hand turn once you cross the bridge to the island.
Historic Downtown Visitor's Center (☎ 904-261-3248, 800-226-3542; 102 Centre St; ☺ 11am-4pm Mon-Sat, noon-4pm Sun) Reams of useful information and maps in the old railroad depot. A fun stop in itself.

Sights & Activities
AMELIA ISLAND MUSEUM OF HISTORY
Housed in the former city jail (1879–1975), Florida's only oral-history **museum** (☎ 904-261-7383; www.ameliaislandmuseumofhistory.org; 233 S 3rd St; adult/student $7/4; ☺ 10am-4pm Mon-Sat, 1-4pm Sun) has tiny but informative exhibits exploring American Indian history, the Spanish Mission period, the Civil War and historic preservation. There's also a good overview of the history of water, timber and tourism in the county. Most fun of all is the eight flags tour, every day at 11am and 2pm, when guides provide lively interpretations of the island's intricate history: eight flags have flown over the island, starting with the French flag in 1562, followed by the Spanish, the English, the Spanish again, the Patriots, the Green Cross of Florida, the Mexican Rebels, the US, the Confederates, then the US again (1821 onward).

FORT CLINCH STATE PARK
The US Government began constructing **Fort Clinch** (☎ 904-277-7274; park pedestrian/car $1/5, fort adult/child $5/2; ☺ park 8am-sunset, fort 9am-5pm) in 1847. State-of-the-art at the time, rapid advancements in military technology rendered its masonry walls obsolete by the Civil War. A Confederate militia occupied the almost-complete fort early in the conflict but evacuated soon after. Federal troops again occupied the fort during WWII, when it served as a surveillance and communications station for the US Coast Guard.

Today, the park offers a variety of activities. In addition to a 0.5-mile long fishing pier, there are also serene beaches for shelling and 6 miles of peaceful, unpaved trails for hiking and biking.

On the first weekend of the month, authentically outfitted troops perform a reenactment of the Confederate evacuation that extends to cooking in the old kitchen's massive iron cauldron and sleeping on straw mats in the soldiers' barracks. A candlelight tour ($3) is a treat if you're here May to September; call for reservations.

Fort Clinch Rd is just west of Main Beach off Atlantic Ave.

AMERICAN BEACH
In 1901 AL Lewis (1865–1947) opened Florida's first insurance company, catering to his fellow African Americans. Business boomed and in 1935 Lewis, Florida's first black millionaire, bought land on Amelia Island and founded American Beach; the first African American beach along Florida's segregated shores.

In its heyday American Beach catered to throngs of African Americans who arrived by busload to enjoy the beaches and African American–owned motels, restaurants and nightclubs, where shows with Ray Charles, Louis Armstrong and others made for some of the biggest bills in Florida. In 1964, however, Hurricane Dora destroyed many homes and businesses; shortly thereafter desegregation allowed African Americans to stroll the beaches closer to their homes. Recently, golf courses and gated communities have encroached upon what's left of American Beach, though beach access is possible via Lewis St, off Hwy A1A.

SURFING
From fall through spring when nor'easters bluster through, surfable beach breaks can be common, especially at Main Beach. **Driftwood Surf Shop** (☎ 904-321-2188; 31 S Fletcher Ave; surfboard/bodyboard per day $25/10; ☼ 10am-7pm) gives lessons for $25 per hour. You'll want a full wetsuit and booties in winter.

HORSEBACK RIDING
Kelly Seahorse Ranch (☎ 904-491-5166; www.kellyranchinc .com; 1hr rides $60; ☼ 10am, noon, 2pm & 4pm) is a working ranch that also does beachside horseback riding tours; call in advance for longer trips. You don't need prior riding experience, but children must be at least 13 years old. The ranch is down the path that's the last left turn off Amelia Rd at the southern tip of the island.

TENNIS & GOLF
Free municipal tennis courts are located at the corner of Atlantic Ave and 13th St in Fernandina Beach. Get the key ($5 deposit) at the **Atlantic Ave Recreation Center** (☎ 904-277-7350; 2500 Atlantic Ave; ☼ 8am-8pm Mon-Fri, noon-8pm Sat, 2-4:30pm Sun).

Known for its expansive private golf courses, Amelia Island also has an outstanding public option, **Fernandina Beach Golf Club** (☎ 904-277-7370; 2800 Bill Melton Rd; 18 holes Mon-Fri $49, Sat & Sun $44, club rental per game $25; ☼ 7am-6pm).

Tours
Both the guided **Centre St Stroll** (adult/student $10/5; ☼ 3pm Fri & Sat Sep-Jun) and the atmospheric **Ghost Tour** (adult/student $10/5; ☼ 6pm Fri Sep-Jun) hit the highlights and last just over an hour. The Centre St Stroll departs from the Historic Downtown Visitor's Center; the Ghost Tour departs from the cemetery behind St Peter's Episcopal Church, corner 8th and Centre Streets.

Clip-clopping along historic streets on a half-hour horse-drawn carriage ride gives you time to soak it all in. Drivers with **Amelia Island Carriages** (☎ 904-556-2662; adult/child $15/7; ☼ 6pm-midnight/2pm-midnight summer/winter, weather permitting) linger patiently near the intersection of 2nd and Ash Sts.

Forty-minute tours swooping above the island in a Cessna 172 are available from

Island Aerial Tours (☎ 904-321-0904; tours $175) at Fernandina Beach Municipal Airport (take Hwy A1A to Amelia Island Parkway, then Airport Rd and follow the signs to the yellow hangar).

You can sail the islands, including Georgia's Cumberland Island (see p385), aboard a 100ft replica 19th-century gaffrigged packet schooner. **Voyager Ventures** (☎ 904-321-1244; adult/child $40/20) runs two-hour sunset cruises Wednesday to Sunday and Saturday afternoon cruises from 3pm to 5pm; BYO picnic dinner, wine and beer.

Sleeping
Room rates can rise by 50% during summer and special events.

BUDGET
Fort Clinch State Park (☎ 904-277-7274; sites $22) Despite 62 campsites in the park – the oak-and-moss protected Amelia River sites are far more private than the exposed beach sites – be sure to make reservations well in advance. Fires are in grills only, and you'll need to bring your own firewood; gathering it in the park is forbidden.

Amelia Hotel & Suites (☎ 904-206-5200; www .ameliahotelandsuites.com; 1997 S Fletcher Ave; r $99-179; P ✗ ▣ ▣) Only 86 steps from the sand, the rooms in this recently renovated coral-colored hotel are bright, airy and uncluttered; some are equipped for wheelchairs. It's a 10-minute drive to downtown, but when you've scored this kind of oceanfront view, inertia may keep you here.

MIDRANGE
Florida House Inn (☎ 904-261-3300, 800-258-3301; www .floridahouseinn.com; 20 & 22 S 3rd St; r $119-299; P ✗ ▣) Welcome to Florida's oldest hotel. Built by the Florida Railroad Company in 1857, these hardwood floors have hosted luminaries from President Ulysses S Grant to poet José Martí. Rooms are appointed with antiques and artwork; some have fireplaces. Guests receive four hours' use of two-person, two-stroke scooters; beyond that, rental (also available to non-guests) runs $30 for two hours. There's an on-site bar hosting local bands – come on Monday to savor the bluegrass open jam – and a boarding house–style restaurant.

ourpick The Addison (☎ 904-277-1606, 800-943-1604; www.addisononamelia.com; 614 Ash St; r $145-220; P ✗ ▣) Built in 1876, modern upgrades (whirlpool tubs, deluge showers, Turkish cotton towels and wi-fi) will trick you into thinking it was finished last week. While many B&Bs in Florida seem to have been decorated by grannies, this place manages to balance elegance, style and modernity better than most. Enjoy daily happy hours overlooking a delightful courtyard with the friendliest (and funniest) innkeepers on Amelia.

Hoyt House (☎ 904-277-4300, 800-432-2085; www .hoythouse.com; 804 Atlantic Ave; r $159-259; **P** ✗ ⬛ ⬛) This cheery B&B boasts an enchanting gazebo that begs time with a cool drink. Each of the 10 rooms is agreeably decorated (two have whirlpool tubs) and the hosts offer tasty breakfasts (think: blueberry caramel French toast). Beneath the weeping oaks in the back sits a cozy hot tub and pool. Small pets are welcome ($35), as are children over 12.

TOP END
Elizabeth Pointe Lodge (☎ 904-277-4851, 888-261-6161; www.elizabethpointelodge.com; 98 S Fletcher Ave; r $195-415; **P** ✗ ⬛) Expect fresh flowers, frequent snacks and abundant sunshine in this maritime-themed inn. Constructed in a 1890s Nantucket shingle style, the towering lodge is perched on the ocean, yet is only 2 miles from downtown. Rocking chair–lined porches hug the main floor and all the bedrooms have oversized tubs (some have Jacuzzis). The lodge offers buffet breakfast, bike rental and the best seats on the island for beholding a sunrise…if you can struggle out of bed.

Eating
Bright Mornings (☎ 904-491-1771; 105 S 3rd St; mains $4-8; ⏱ 7:30am-2pm Mon-Sun, closed Wed) Eating here is like eating at Grandma's: inspirational quotes, silk flowers and tablecloths decorated with flamingos adorn the place. Also like Grandma's, the big, delicious Southern breakfasts are made with love.

Carolyn's on Centre (☎ 904-277-6644; 316d Centre St; meals $8-15; ⏱ 11am-10pm) Out back, a jasmine-wrapped fence conceals a brick courtyard with twinkling lights and live music on Fridays and Sundays. Inside, the narrow bar has several microbrews on tap and dozens more in the bottle. Upstairs, a cozy dining area waits. Board games are available and the food is great.

our pick Espana (☎ 904-261-7700; 22 S 4th St; mains $19-27; ⏱ 5-10pm Mon-Sun) Decorated with Old World maps and Hispanic ceramics, this restaurant boasts a drool-worthy tapas menu.

An absolute must-visit, though kids may be unhappy with the unfamiliar offerings.

Brett's Waterway Café (☎ 904-261-2660; 1 S Front St; mains $16-33; ⏱ lunch 11:30am-2:30pm Mon-Sat, dinner from 5:50pm daily) Hard to get out of town without stopping here; after all, it's the only restaurant in town with sunset views over the marina. Specializing in steaks and seafood, Brett's also offers a divine spinach and artichoke dip.

The owners of Bright Mornings recently launched **Canopy Moon** in the same location for late night (⏱ 6pm-12am) 'light bites.' Order a $3 veggie pinwheel and watch the stars spin.

Other recommendations include these:

T-Ray's Burger Station (☎ 904-261-6310; 202 S 8th St; mains $3-6; ⏱ 7am-3pm Mon-Fri, 8am-1pm Sat) Hidden inside an Exxon station, this place looks more like an overflowing storage shed than a takeaway. The Big Breakfast, burgers and daily specials are revered by locals.

Café Karibo (☎ 904-277-5269; 27 N 3rd St; lunch/dinner $6-10/$14-20; ⏱ 11am-9pm Mon-Sat, 10:30am-2pm Sun) Creative dishes (Greek quesadillas), hot and fast. Relax under the oak and count how many stone birds you can spy in the garden.

Entertainment
Many of Amelia's restaurants double as bars. Most places open until 2am in summer but close earlier during off-season.

Palace Saloon (☎ 904-261-6320; 113-117 Centre St) Push through the swinging doors here, the oldest continuously-operated bar in Florida (c 1878), and the first thing you'll notice is the 40ft gas lamp–lit bar. Curiously appealing to both bikers and Shakespeare buffs, knock back the saloon's rum-laced Pirate's Punch in dark, velvet-draped surroundings.

Green Turtle (☎ 904-321-2324; 14 S 3rd St; ⏱ 3:30pm-2am) This long, skinny bar offers only wine and beer (12 on tap). Don't be surprised to bump into locals playing darts.

Amelia Community Theatre (☎ 904-261-6749; 209 Cedar St; tickets $5-18) A quirky, long-running local theater performing eight-ish productions a year.

The island hosts a fabulous four-day **book festival** (www.bookisland.org) in early October, attracting literary luminaries and bibliophiles from afar.

Shopping
Amelia Body & Soul (☎ 904-261-7723; 3 S 3rd St) What's that great smell? It's the scent of candles, massage oils and diffusers, made inhouse, from renewable soy-based oils.

DETOUR: CUMBERLAND ISLAND NATIONAL SEASHORE

The largest wilderness island in the US, **Cumberland Island** (☎ 912-882-4336; www.nps.gov/cuis) lies just over the Georgia state line. At 17.5 miles long and 3 miles wide, almost half of its 36,415 acres is marshland, mud flats and tidal creeks. Only 300 visitors are allowed on the island, accessible by a 45-minute ferry ride.

Ashore, rangers lead free one-hour tours concluding at the ruins of Thomas and Lucy Carnegie's 1884 mansion, Dungeness. Along the way rangers interpret the rich bird and animal life – including sandpipers, ospreys, painted buntings, nesting loggerhead turtles, armadillos and deer – and detail 4000 years of human history that spans Timucuan Indians, British colonists and Spanish missionaries.

After the Civil War, freed slaves purchased parcels of land at the island's northern end and founded the First African Baptist Church in 1893. Rebuilt in the 1930s, the late John Kennedy Jr and Carolyn Bessette married in this tiny, 11-pew, white-painted wooden church in 1996. It's open to the public, but it's a hefty 15-mile hike from the ferry drop through moss-draped thickets.

The historic village of **St Marys** (www.stmaryswelcome.com) is the island's charming gateway. Accommodation options on the island range widely, from an opulent mansion to rugged camping. Check the St Marys' website for details.

Ferries (round-trip adult/child $17/12) depart at 9am and 11:45am, returning at 10:15am and 4:45pm (an additional ferry runs at 2:45pm Wednesday through Saturday, March through November; no ferries run on Tuesdays or Wednesdays December through February). An additional $4 fee is charged per day for campers and day-trippers. Book ahead and arrive 45 minutes prior to departure for loading and briefing.

Be sure to come prepared: there are no shops on the island. Bring food, insect repellent and perhaps a camera…or maybe a canvas and paint palette.

From northern Florida, take I-95 north to St Marys Rd exit 1. Turn right onto GA-40/St Marys Rd E and follow it to the end.

Fantastic Fudge (☎ 904-277-4801; 218 Centre St; ☺ 10am-8pm, later on weekends & during summer) See all-natural fudge being made, or satisfy your sweet tooth with any of the other chocolate goodies, like divine peanut-butter cups.

At the intersection where Hwy A1A splits, hidden under an oak soaked with Spanish moss, is a rambling **fruit stand** selling boiled peanuts and locally grown fruits and veggies.

Getting There & Around

Hwy A1A splits in two directions on Amelia Island, one heading west toward I-95, and the other following the coast; both are well marked.

To get to Amelia the fastest route from the mainland is to take I-95 north to exit 373 and head east about 15 miles straight to the island.

Want a prettier route? Heading from Jacksonville Beach to the town of Mayport, catch the **St John's River Ferry** (☎ 904-357-3006; car/RV $5/10; ☺ 6am-8:30pm), which runs every 30 minutes to Fort George Island. After landfall, stay on Hwy A1A as it winds through Little

Talbot and Big Talbot Islands, turn left on Sadler Rd and go 2 miles.

Walking is your best bet downtown, but you'll need wheels to get around the island. **VIP Taxi** (☎ 904-225-8888) provides transportation throughout the island and to Jacksonville International Airport ($47).

Amelia Island's ideal for biking – flat and no major distances. **Pipeline Surfshop** (☎ 904-277-3717; 2022 1st Ave; ☺ 10am-6pm; bikes per hr/day $5/12) rents bikes, as does the Florida House Inn ($12 per four hours; see p383).

No public transportation serves the island.

NORTH CENTRAL FLORIDA

Upon escaping Orlando's northern clutches, you enter what might be a different state, one conversely more Southern than South Florida. Sprinkled between the thoroughbred horse studs, the sprawling forest of Ocala and the funky college town of Gainesville you'll find crystal-clear springs, meandering back roads and the small Victorian gingerbread towns that were the norm before mass tourism.

BLUE SPRING STATE PARK

The largest spring on the St John's River, Blue Spring maintains a constant 72°F and between November and March it serves as the winter refuge for between 25 and 50 West Indian manatees, though as many as 200 have been spotted here! The best time to see them is before 11am; there's a wheelchair-accessible path to the viewing platform. This tranquil **state park** (☎ 386-775-3663; 2100 W French Ave; admission pedestrian/car $1/5) is a revitalizing spot to swim (prohibited when manatees are present), snorkel or canoe. You can also spend two hours cruising the peaceful waters with **St Johns River Cruises**(☎ 386-917-0724; www.sjrivercruises.com; adult/

senior/child $20/18/14; ☺ tours at 10am & 1pm), whose nature tours offer thoughtful insight into this fragile ecosystem.

Certified divers can make their way through the narrow fissure at the source of the spring to 'cork rock,' a boulder suspended in the upwelling water. You can rent snorkeling equipment ($4/2 per first/subsequent hr) and canoes ($10/5 per first/subsequent hr) at concessions.

Hiking 4 miles through the wooded backcountry brings you to primitive campsites ($4 per night); if you prefer something less rustic, there's also a developed campground ($20 per night), and 6-person cabins ($85 per night).

The park is well signed, off French Ave at the northern end of Orange City.

CASSADAGA

In 1894 27-year-old New Yorker George Colby suffered from tuberculosis. Seneca, Colby's

---

SPIRITUALISM IN CASSADAGA

Ed Conklin holds a PhD in Religious Studies and teaches psychology, parapsychology and religion at university level. He began his study of mediumship in 1980 and is presently a SCSCMA Certified Medium working in Cassadaga.

What's special about Cassadaga? Founded by George Colby and other Spiritualists in the late 1800s, their main intention was to create a community of like-minded individuals capable of altered states of consciousness, including spirit communication. For residents today, Cassadaga remains a place to study and practice mediumship, but visitors come to Cassadaga for several reasons. Some come out of curiosity. Some come seeking evidence of an afterlife. Others come to be comforted: they want communication with deceased relatives or friends.

What's Spiritualism? The demonstration of the continuity of life and afterlife – and that communication can and does occur between them.

What's the difference between a psychic and a medium? A psychic is someone who uses their own mind and psychically or clairvoyantly picks up past or present or future impressions about an individual. A medium can be psychic, but they also have spirit communication. Most of their communication comes from spirits rather than their own mind.

What happens during a reading? A person comes in, sits down. I usually say a short prayer and have the person touch my hands, just to make contact. The person relaxes, then images, words, feelings come to me, and I describe what I see, hear or feel and I often give the meanings of these impressions. I don't like the individual to tell me lots of details. Basically, if I ask a question, they should just answer yes or no. For a successful reading, a person should be open – but also be skeptical. Be a little critical.

What would people be surprised to learn about Cassadaga? Skeptics would be surprised that there's real communication with deceased spirits. For those who accept this phenomenon, they'd be surprised to learn that mediums are humans with flaws. It's a beautiful gift they share, but they're still human. Also, Cassadaga is not unique, even though it has the oldest Spiritualist tradition in the US. Like other spiritual places, it forces one to consider the depths of existence. There's a depth to space. Science says it's 150 billion light years across – there's a very distant past and a very distant future. We're in the middle of that existence. And there's also a depth within us, as human potential. We're more than just body parts.

Ed Conklin works as a medium in Cassadaga, you can contact him for a reading on 386-216-8696 or sogowiththeflow@gmail.com.

American Indian spirit guide, told him to head south to a lake and found a spiritualist community, where he'd be healed. Colby did it, and Cassadaga (pronounced kassuh-*day*-guh) was born.

Today, Colby's camp – a collection of mainly 1920s Cracker cottages – is a registered historic district, the oldest active religious community in the US, and home to the **Southern Cassadaga Spiritualist Camp Meeting Association** (SCSCMA; ☎ 904-228-3171). The association believes in infinite intelligence, the precepts of prophecy and healing, and that communication with the dead is possible. It's said the area is one of 20 places in the world with an energy vortex where the spirit and earth planes are exceptionally close, creating a 'portal' between the two.

You wouldn't find Cassadaga if you weren't looking for it. Nestled about 2 miles off the main drag, the tiny camp doesn't have an ATM or gas station. Scattered throughout the camp are 30-some spiritual practitioners who offer readings – the main 'attraction' here – during which spirits gone from this plane speak through the practitioner, offering insight into your life. Readings start around $35 for 30 minutes (see opposite). Come prepared with questions, but don't expect to summon specific spirits.

Information about the camp is available in the **Cassadaga Camp Bookstore** (☎ 386-228-2880; www.cassadaga.org; 1112 Steven St; ☖ 10am-5pm Mon-Sat, 11.30am-5pm Sun), which sells New Age books, crystals and incense, and serves as the de facto visitor's center for the town. They also organize historical tours of the village (Saturday, 1pm and 3pm, $15) and orb tours (Saturday, 7pm, $25), where photographers shoot glowing balls of light – reportedly spirits from another world. A $1 donation gets you a camp directory, allowing you to make a pretty good self-guided tour. Mandatory stop: spooky, serene Spirit Lake, where residents scatter the ashes of the departed.

The original **Cassadaga Hotel** (☎ 386-228-2323; www.cassadagahotel.net; 355 Cassadaga Rd; standard r up to 2 people $50-80, deluxe r up to 6 people $75-150; P ☒) burned down in 1926. Today, ghosts reportedly lurk in the shadows (sniff for Jack's cigar-smoke, and listen for two girls terrorizing the upstairs halls) of the rebuilt hotel. Looking like a rejected set from *The Shining*, the hotel is appropriately creepy and creaky – on the atmosphere scale, this place is off the charts! –

but it's not terribly elegant. The musty **Lost in Time Café & Sports Bar** (mains $6-9; ☖ 11am-3pm Mon-Thu, to 9:30pm Fri & Sat, to 5pm Sun), serves salads, sandwiches and 'spirit burgers.'

There's no public transportation; by car, take I-4 to exit 54, head to the light, go east on CR 4101 for 0.25 miles, then turn right onto CR 4139. The camp is 2 miles down the road.

DELAND & AROUND
☎ 386 / pop 60,000

While much of Florida seems frantic to cover itself in neon and high rises, stoic DeLand shrugs that off as nonsense. Development is coming, but locals, intimate with the area and acutely aware of what's needed, are bringing it. The quaint, walkable Woodland Blvd, bisecting the east side of town from the west, is home to independent shops and restaurants – modern yet thoroughly small-town. Ancient oaks lean in to hug each other over city streets and Spanish moss dribbles from their branches. This is Old Town Florida, and it feels so cozy. Ironically, DeLand was the first town in Florida to enjoy electricity.

Despite all this hometown goodness, risk-taking flows through DeLand's blood. In the 1870s New York baking-soda magnate Henry DeLand traveled down the St John's River with a vision of founding the 'Athens of Florida.' That moniker has stuck, but these days, DeLand is most famous for skydiving – the tandem jump was invented here.

Orientation
Woodland Ave is 'Main Street,' with the historic district, museums and Stetson University located just north of the intersection with New York Ave.

To get here by car, take US Hwy 17 north from Orlando or south from Jacksonville; from Daytona, head west on Hwy 92. DeLand is not served by public transportation.

Information
Visitor information is available online at www.stjohnsrivercountry.com and at the town's **Welcome Center** (☎ 386-734-4331; www.delandchamber.org; 336 N Woodland Blvd; ☖ 8:30am-5pm Mon-Fri).

Sights & Activities
STETSON UNIVERSITY
DeLand was just beginning to profit from area citrus plantations when, in 1885, a

---

THE TAX BREAK WORKED TOO WELL

In 1886, residents of DeLand were allowed to deduct 50¢ from their taxes for each oak tree they planted along the right-of-way. So many people planted so many trees that DeLand couldn't pay the town marshal that year; the tax break was repealed in 1887. Today, however, the main drag is jammed with oaks.

---

severe freeze decimated the entire crop. It looked like the town's brand-new university would have to shut its doors when hat creator John Stetson intervened, renaming it **Stetson University** (☎ 386-822-7100; www.stetson.edu; 421 N Woodland Blvd).

Today, the nation's first private university remains one of its prettiest. Its entire 165-acre campus is listed on the National Register of Historic Places and features several significant buildings, ranging from 1884's Second Empire-styled **DeLand Hall** to the ultramodern **Lynn Business Center**, Florida's first 'green' building certified by the US Green Building Council.

DELAND HOUSE MUSEUM

Housed in a snow-white 1886 mansion, this **museum** (☎ 386-740-6813; 137 W Michigan Ave; admission free; ☻ noon-4pm Tue-Sat) overflows with antiques, period clothes and stained glass. Behind the museum is a gazebo built as a monument to Lue Gim Gong, the 'Citrus Wizard' who saved DeLand's, and by extension central Florida's, agricultural sector by cross-breeding frost-resistant oranges.

DELAND HOSPITAL MUSEUMS

Originally a hospital, today this quirky **museum** (☎ 386-740-5800; 230 N Stone St; admission free; ☻ 10am-3pm Wed-Sat) houses eight galleries and exhibits, ranging from a somewhat unsettling 1920s operating room to the Hawtense Conrad Elephant Fantasyland – a collection of more than 1000 elephants.

DE LEON SPRINGS STATE RECREATION AREA

A fantastic place to take kids, these **natural springs** (☎ 386-985-4212; pedestrian/cyclist/car $1/1/5; ☻ 8am-sunset) were used by American Indians 6000 years ago and have been developed into a huge swimming area.

Concessions provide canoes or kayaks for springs exploration ($10/21 hourly/half-day). The springs flow into the Lake Woodruff National Wildlife Refuge with 18,000 acres of lakes, creeks and marshes. Alternatively, Captain Frank takes passengers on 45- and 90-minute **ecohistory tours** (☎ 386-837-5537; www.foytours.com; tour $12-14) and discusses both the area's ecology and the likelihood that this area – and not the spring in St Augustine (see p364) – is the fabled Fountain of Youth.

Experienced hikers can attack the 4.2-mile Wild Persimmon Trail, meandering through oak hammocks, flood plains and open fields. Marked with blue blazes, this hike is robust.

Overlooking the manicured grounds, the **Old Spanish Sugar Mill Grill & Griddle House** (☎ 386-985-5644; mains $4-7; ☻ 9am-5pm Mon-Fri, 8am-5pm Sat & Sun) has a toasty open fireplace and great all-you-can-eat pancakes that you cook yourself on an electric griddle set into the center of the table.

The well-signed entrance is just off Hwy 17 on Ponce de León Blvd, about 6 miles north of DeLand.

SKYDIVING

If plummeting toward earth at speeds of 120mph sounds like a whiz-bang time, you're in the right place. A short briefing and a seasoned professional strapped to your back is all it takes to experience the least-boring two minutes of your life above some glorious countryside with **Skydive DeLand** (☎ 386-738-3539; www.skydivedeland.com; 1600 Flightline Blvd; jumps $174, freefall training & first jump $345). Experienced skydivers can jump solo or advance their skills at this first-rate facility. They also offer freefall training so you can learn to jump on your own.

From downtown, take Hwy 17 north to Hwy 92; head east and exit Lexington Ave to DeLand Municipal Airport. Continue to Flightline Blvd and make a right; Skydive Deland is at the end of the street.

Sleeping & Eating

Most of the cheap hotels are along Hwy 17 (Woodland Blvd), north of New York Ave. There's camping nearby in Ocala National Forest.

DeLand Artisan Inn (☎ 386-736-3484; www.delandartisaninn.com; 215 S Woodland Blvd; r $60; ☻ Ⓟ ✗ ☐) Atmospheric accommodation is available at this perfectly located 1924 Mediterranean Revival inn, with eight grand, three-room themed suites. Oh, and psst…room 4 is haunted.

Buttercup Bakery (☎ 386-736-4043; 197 E Church St; snacks $2-7; ☺ 7am-5pm Mon-Fri, 8am-3pm Sat) Perched on Sunflower Park, this exquisite bakery makes Willy Wonka seem bland. Outside, fanciful gingerbreading dances along the eaves. Inside, three women, using only pastel cooking equipment and all-natural ingredients, make luscious sweets: lemon curd bars, white chocolate apricot bars, chocolate-chip bread pudding, and more. They also serve organic coffee, tea and salad.

Gram's Kitchen (☎ 386-8736-9340; 844 E New York Ave; meals $4-8; ☺ 6am-3pm Sun, to 4pm Mon-Sat) Chuck your chaw at the door, fellas, this is a right nice place. This old-time diner – the kind of place where customers share their newspapers – has enormous portions, speedy service and painted saw blades on the walls. While you're waiting, count the Garfields inside.

Sweet Melissa's Raw Bar (☎ 386-736-4006; www.sweetmelissasrawbar.com; 1046 E New York Ave; mains $3-10; ☺ 11am-6pm Wed, to 11pm Thu-Sat, noon-8pm Sun) Most people come to this ramshackle dive for oysters or shrimp, but the homemade wings – dry-rubbed and roasted, not dripping with goopy sauce – rock harder than the Van Halen blasting on the radio.

The Abbey (☎ 386-734-4545; www.abbeydeland.com; 117 N Woodland Blvd; mains $7-10; ☺ 4pm-1am Mon-Thu, to 2am Fri & Sat) Enclosed with exposed brick and mustard walls, and filled with hightop tables and big, cushy sofas, this place has a varied, thoughtful beer selection (more than 100 kinds, from $4 to $65 a bottle, with an emphasis on Belgian brews), a robust wine collection (sold by the glass, flight, or bottle), and tasty sandwiches and salads. A visit here isn't about chugging beers. It's about sampling well-crafted beverages. Classy – but fun.

PALATKA
☎ 385 / pop 10,500

In its heyday, Palatka (pronounced puhl-*at-kuh*), about 30 miles west of St Augustine, was the furthest south you could travel by steamship and boasted more than 7000 hotel rooms for wealthy snowbirds, that is, until Henry Flagler's railroad diverted them further south. Today visitors are returning for sportfishing (welcome to the 'bass capital of the world'), Memorial Weekend's blue crab festival, and the only known Burger King with its own boat dock.

The main drag is Hwy 17, here called Reid St. Pamphlets with walking and driving tours of the town's historical sites are available from the **chamber of commerce** (☎ 386-328-1503; www.putnamcountychamber.org; 1100 Reid St; ☺ 8am-4:30pm Mon-Fri), next to the Amtrak station on 11th St. A drive along the St John's River is worth the time, but go slow: with the river on one side and exquisite historic homes on the other, keeping your eyes on the road is a challenge.

Sights

BRONSON-MULHOLLAND HOUSE

The former home of Judge Isaac Bronson, the green-shuttered 1854 **Bronson-Mulholland House** (☎ 904-329-0140; 100 Madison St; ☺ 2-5pm Tue, Thu & Sun), now serves as a historic museum; the on-site manager conducts 30-minute tours. Note the full-length glass doors opening onto the veranda: when the property was built, homes were taxed according to the number of windows, so many installed as French-style doors instead.

RAVINE STATE GARDENS

A pleasant 2-mile walkable road loops the inner boundary of this 182-acre **state park** (☎ 904-329-3721; pedestrian/car $1/4; ☺ 8am-sunset). A ravine, created millions of years ago by the St John's River, slices through the center of this pristine picnic spot. Some of the best views of this shallow gorge are from the swinging suspension footbridge – take the little path to the left of the Civic Center at the entrance. It's at its most spectacular between late February and early March when a riot of pink and red azaleas weave skeins through the deep-green foliage.

To get here, head east on Reid St to 3rd St. Turn right, and after 3rd becomes River St, cruise past some of the most elegant homes in Palatka. Turn left on S 15th St, right onto Twigg St and the park entrance is on the left.

Sleeping & Eating

Azalea House (☎ 386-325-4547; www.theazaleahouse.com; 220 Madison St; r $100-130; P ☒) This buttercup-yellow home with an intricate fretwork veranda is cross-stitch central but offers big rooms and gourmet breakfasts on weekends.

Floridian Resort (☎ 386-467-2181; 122 Floridian Club Rd, Welaka; www.floridiansportsclub.com; r $159-445; P ☒ ☒) Deep in the woods 18 miles south of town, you'll find luxuriously appointed motel-style rooms, a big communal lodge with

---

DETOUR: BARBERVILLE PRODUCE – KING OF THE ROADSIDE STANDS

On Route 40, plunked halfway between Ocala and Daytona and roughly one-third the way between DeLand and Palatka, nestled cozily beneath a Spanish moss canopy, sits the king of roadside stands, **Barberville Produce** (☎ 386-749-3562; Route 40 at Hwy 17, Barberville). Offering more than just fruits, veggies and honey, this open-air market fills three acres with mounds of fountains, wrought-iron furniture, gazing balls, ceramic drop-in sinks and old-fashioned peanut brittle. There's even an 8ft-tall aluminum rooster. Who doesn't need one of those?

---

open fireplace, and guided fishing tours – or you can just sit on the banks and dangle a line. Weekends at this fish camp require a two-night minimum stay.

River Adventures (☎ 1-866-OUR-BOAT; www.river adventures.com; 422 River St; from $1125, sleeps 10) An overnight in the marina is $50 per person (limit 4 people), but if you've got a large group, cruising the St John's River, hooking and cooking your own dinner aboard a fully equipped houseboat is the way to go.

Angel's Dining Car (☎ 386-325-3927; 209 Reid St; mains $2.50-8; ☟ 6am-8pm Sun-Thu, to midnight Fri) Looking like the spawn of a soda can and a subway car, honk your horn for curbside service or slide into a vinyl booth inside this diner for iconic menu items like Monnie (mini) burgers, black-bottom eggs (scrambled with hamburger meat) and Pusalow (pronounced puss-uh-loh): chocolate milk with vanilla syrup and crushed ice. Opened in 1932, it's Florida's oldest diner.

Cheyenne Saloon (☎ 386-328-9216; 337 S Hwy 17; mains $4-13; ☟ 8am-midnight Sun-Thu, to 2am Fri & Sat) The oldest bar in Putnam County, this biker hangout is quad-wheeled friendly. Drop in to shoot some stick or hear live music. If you're on the go, rumble through the drive-thru package store. Either way, expect lots of beards, leathers and hacking coughs.

OCALA
☎ 352 / pop 53,000

Greater Ocala is blanketed by velvety emerald paddocks that are hemmed by wooden post-and-rail fences, and sleek-limbed horses

neigh in the misty morning air. In short, the town's outskirts look like the (United States Department of Agriculture–certified) 'Horse Capital of the World' *should* look. There are about 1200 horse farms in Marion County, with more than 45 breeds represented.

Downtown Ocala, however, isn't as picture book pretty, though there's plenty of money in the historic properties southeast of town. The compact commercial district trots along at its own pace – there's a reason locals call it 'Slocala' – but live music at the local pub can spur things to a gallop. While you're navigating the area's tangle of one-way streets, be on the lookout for the 52, life-size fiberglass horses painted by local artists.

Anxious to get out of town? This rural city is surrounded by beautiful clear springs and the best backyard in Florida, Ocala National Forest.

Orientation

Ocala's main drag is Silver Springs Blvd (Hwy 40), which connects to Silver Springs and Ocala National Forest to the east. Silver Springs Blvd is bisected by Pine Ave (Hwy 441), which runs between Gainesville to the north and Orlando to the south. The two roads divide addresses into north, south, east and west, with the downtown square at their crossroads.

Information

Chamber of Commerce Visitors Center (☎ 352-629-8051; www.ocalacc.com; 110 E Silver Springs Blvd; ☟ 9am-5pm Mon-Fri, 10am-4pm Sat) Has free maps; ask for self-guided walking-tour brochures of the nearby Tuscawilla and Fort King St historic districts.

Sights & Activities
SILVER SPRINGS

Glass-bottomed boats were invented at this delightfully old-fashioned **nature theme park** (☎ 352-236-2121, 800-234-7458; www.silversprings.com; 5656 E Silver Springs Blvd; adult/child under 10yr $34/25; ☟ 10am-5pm; P) in 1878 to show visitors the natural springs and stunningly clear Silver River; they're still the main attraction here today.

Peer down as you slowly cruise over eel grass and spring formations, before the grand finale: a pass over Mammoth Spring, which is the world's largest artesian limestone spring and gushes 550 million gallons of 99.8% pure spring water per day.

Other attractions include the **Lost River Voyage**, transporting guests into untamed

Florida and winding among 500-year-old cypress stands; lofty views from the 80ft carousel-gondola **lighthouse ride** at the headwaters; plus snake- and bear-filled wildlife shows. Keep your eyes peeled for the 'Swamp Ghosts' – a pair of rare albino alligators.

Regular concerts held at **Twin Oaks Mansion** are included in admission; recent acts include Kenny Rogers, the Beach Boys and Bo Bice.

There are plenty of ice cream parlor- and café-dining options on-site. Parking costs $6.

WILD WATERS WATER PARK

Adjacent to Silver Springs, this **water park** (☎ 352-236-2121; www.wildwaterspark.com; 5656 E Silver Springs Blvd; adult/child $25/22; ☻ 10am-5pm daily mid-May–mid-Aug, Sat & Sun mid-Apr–mid-May & mid-Aug–mid-Sep, closed mid-Sep–mid-May; **P**) has a fan-shaped wave pool with 4ft waves, eight twisting water slides (zooming around giant oaks) and great play areas for kids. Parking costs $6.

BRICK CITY CENTER FOR THE ARTS

There's no better deal in the region for framed photography than in this roomy **gallery** (☎ 352-369-1500; www.mcaocala.com; 23 S Broadway;

☻ 10am-5pm Tue-Sat), part of the Ocala Visitors Bureau. Sure, the photographers are mostly locals honing their craft, but many of the dreamy Florida shots in here are worthy of *National Geographic*.

Tours

Ocala Carriage & Tours (☎ 352-867-8717, 877-WWOCALA; www.ocalacarriage.com; 2 people $75, 4-6 people $95) offers one-hour tours in carriages pulled by Clydesdales through the countryside, visiting various horse farms.

Most Marion County horse properties are working farms, closed to the public. For insurance reasons, unless you have your own horse, riding opportunities are limited. To see behind the scenes of one of these farms take a tour with **Youngs Paso Fino** (☎ 352-867-5305; www.youngspasofino .com; 8075 NW SR 326; tours $7.50; ☻ 9am-2pm Mon-Sat). For an additional $38 you can get an hour-long trail ride. From I-75 exit 326 to the west, travel about 3½ miles. Turn right on NW 80th Ave and look for the barn to your left.

Sleeping

There's a cluster of cheap lodgings just south of downtown Ocala on Hwy 441 (S Pine

---

DON GARLITS MUSEUMS

Fans will tell you straight up: Don 'Big Daddy' Garlits isn't just a legend of drag racing…Don Garlits *is* drag racing. Over four decades, his Swamp Rat series – 34 black, self-designed, hand-built racecars – saw him win 144 national events and 17 World Championship titles, shattering numerous records in his breakneck speedsters. One of them, his Swamp Rat XXX, is even enshrined in the Smithsonian.

Speaking of museums, Big Daddy, who doesn't do things by halves, has two of his own. Even if you're not into cars, the **Don Garlits Museums** (☎ 352-245-8661; www.garlits.com; 13700 SW 16th Ave; adult/child $15/6; ☻ 9am-5pm) are outstanding. If you like cars even a teeny bit, the museums are an essential pilgrimage.

First up: the **Museum of Drag Racing**, where you'll see engine collections and an impressive line-up of dragsters (about 150, arranged chronologically). Look for the 1969 Slingshot, the first dragster to successfully employ a planetary two-speed transmission. This car nearly cost Don his life. In 1970, Don lost part of his right foot in a freak explosion, but rather than let it get him down, he rebounded and developed rear engine cars that would go on to see even greater success.

Next door is a testament to Don's other great passion; the **Museum of Classic Cars** houses a phenomenal collection of more than 70 autos. Starting with a 1904 Orient Buckboard, there's a 1926 Model T, gleaming 1940s Studebakers, Don's red-and-white two-toned 1950 Mercury driven by the Fonz in *Happy Days*, and 1960s Mustangs and Chrysler Muscle Cars, some built to Nascar specifications. Now grandparents of five, Don and his wife Pat (who is a trophy-winning racer) live here.

Admission includes both museums; you'll want at least two hours to look around. Children under five must be hand-held, both for their safety and for the sake of Don's painstaking restoration of this impressive machinery.

The museums are about 10 minutes south of downtown Ocala on I-75; take exit 341 (CR 484) and turn left, then your first right – they're the first buildings on the right.

Ave) and more within walking distance of Silver Springs.

Silver River State Park (☎ 352-236-7148; 1425 NE 58th Ave; camping primitive/developed $4/21, cabins $100; P 🏊) Pets are welcome at any of the 59 campsites nestled among the woods at this 5,000-acre park. If you want something more sumptuous (but canine-free), try the park's fully equipped luxury cabins, which sleep up to six.

Seven Sisters Inn B&B (☎ 352-867-1170; www.seven sistersinn.com; 820 SE Fort King St; r $139-279; P 🏊 🖥) Really two B&Bs in one, the east building is a beautifully appointed (but fairly typical) B&B any grandma would love. The west building offers museum-quality themed rooms decorated from the owners' (both retired pilots) private collection from jaunts around the world. The Argentina room is the biggest, but the Egypt room is fit for a pharaoh.

Hilton Ocala (☎ 352-854-1400; www.hiltonocala.com; 3600 SW 36th Ave; r $129-349; P 🖥 🏊) Ocala's pad-dockside Hilton has its own Clydesdale horse, Buddy (and free horse cookies for you to feed him), who waits patiently to take guests on free carriage rides. There's a bi-weekly choco-late fountain and a jogging trail, too.

Eating & Drinking

Richard's Place (☎ 352-351-2233; 316 E Silver Springs Blvd; mains $3-7; 🕐 6am-2:30pm Mon-Fri, to 2pm Sat, 7am-2pm Sun) Evidently, hearty breakfasts make you live longer. At least, the clientele here seem to prove this theory. This homey place could use a good wipe-down, but Richard's has been serving country ham and red eye gravy for more than 20 years, so they're doing something right.

Genesis Juice Bar & Café (☎ 352-867-1654; www.find heaventhruhealth.com; 103 SE 1st Ave; mains $7-9; 🕐 10am-6pm Mon-Fri, noon-5pm Sat) Staffed by butt-busting employees, this healthy joint downtown has a smoothie/juice bar and numerous nutritious noshes (many vegetarian options).

Felix's Restaurant (☎ 352-629-0339; www.felixs ocala.com; 917 E Silver Springs Blvd; mains $8-49; 🕐 11am-2:30pm Tue-Fri & 4:30-10pm Tue-Sat) Renowned for its elegant 'comfort food with attitude,' this is Ocala's version of a tapas bar. Serving 'pe-tite entrées,' half the size of a regular entrée, Felix's encourages you to sample a number of dishes from its rotating menu. The pasta dishes are particularly tasty.

Tin Cup's Tavern (☎ 352-690-6902; 11 E Silver Springs Blvd; 🕐 3pm-close) The only real bar downtown, this place boasts a stained-glass and ham-mered-tin ceiling, an elegant wooden bar, live music most nights and people smoking all the time.

Getting There & Around

Greyhound (☎ 352-732-2677; 512 N Magnolia Ave) is in the Central Transfer Station, at the corner of NE 5th St, just a few blocks from downtown. The transfer station for **Amtrak** (☎ 352-629-9863; www.amtrak.com) is here, and so is **SunTran** (☎ 352-401-6999; www.suntran.com), whose buses can get you around town between roughly 6am and 7pm; bus trips $1.

By car from Gainesville, take either I-75 or Hwy 441 south to Silver Springs Blvd (Hwy 40), where Ocala is centered; go east to get to Silver Springs. From Orlando, take Florida's Turnpike to I-75, and that to Silver Springs Blvd.

OCALA NATIONAL FOREST
☎ 352

The oldest national forest east of the Mississippi River and the southernmost national forest in the continental US, the 400,000-acre Ocala National Forest is one of Florida's most important natural treasures. An incredible ecological web, the park is a tangle of springs, biomes (sand pine scrub, palmetto wilderness, subtropical forest) and endangered flora and fauna.

With 18 developed campgrounds and 24 primitive ones, 219 miles of trails and 600 lakes (30 for boating), there are endless op-portunities for swimming, hiking, biking, horseback riding, canoeing, bird- and wild-life-watching – or just meditating on how great it is that the government got here before the theme parks did.

Orientation
Two highways cross the region: Hwy 19 runs north–south and Hwy 40 runs east–west.

Information
Rangers serve most of the area and all camp-grounds have resident volunteers who are good sources of information. There's no sin-gle admission fee and no one number to call; day-use areas are generally open from 8am to 8pm. Pick up free literature and maps or buy a topographical version (around $7) at any of the visitor's centers, all open 8am to 5pm.

Ocklawaha Visitor Center (☎ 352-236-0288; 3199 NE Hwy 315) Your first stop if you're coming from Ocala and Silver Springs.

OCALA NATIONAL FOREST

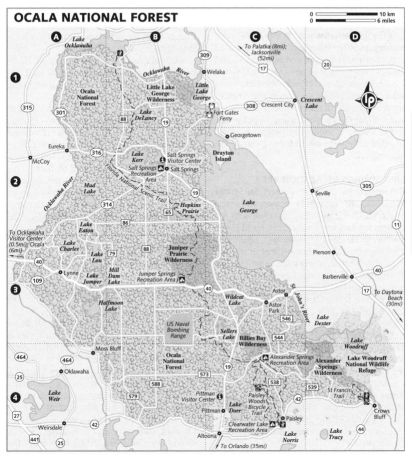

Pittman Visitor Center (☎ 352-669-7495; 45621 SR 19) On the major throughway from Orlando and Mt Dora.
Salt Springs Visitor Center (☎ 352-685-3070; 14100 N Hwy 19) In Salt Springs, accessible from Jacksonville and Palatka.

Sights & Activities
HIKING & BIKING TRAILS
Also referred to as the Ocala Trail, roughly 61 miles of the **Florida National Scenic Trail** spears the center of the forest north–south. Marked with orange blazes, pickup points include Juniper Springs, Alexander Springs and Clearwater Lake recreation areas. Outside hunting season, hikers can camp anywhere 200ft from the trail, but if you prefer to commune with others you'll find spur trails to

developed campgrounds about every 10 to 12 miles.

Passing through prairies and live-oak domes, the popular 22-mile **Paisley Woods Bicycle Trail** is yellow blazed. Its end points are Alexander Springs to the north and Clearwater Lake to the south, but it's shaped like a figure eight so you can do either half as a loop. Be sure to bring both a bike that can handle off-road conditions and plenty of water (none is available along the trail).

The 8.5-mile **St Francis Trail** (blue blazes) winds through riverine and bayhead swamp to the abandoned 1880s pioneer town of St Francis on the St John's River. No buildings remain, but you'll see the old logging railroad bed and levee built for rice growing.

JUNIPER SPRINGS RECREATION AREA

Developed in the mid-1930s, this is the forest's flagship **recreation area** (☎ 352-625-3147; admission/campsites $4/17; ⊙ 8am-8pm). Concessions sell groceries and firewood, and rent kayaks and canoes ($33.50, 8am to noon) for making the 7-mile, palmetto- and cypress-lined run down Juniper Creek. There's a pickup and a return shuttle at the end of the creek between 1:30pm and 4:40pm ($6 per person and $6 per boat).

Swimming is sublime at Juniper Springs. It's chilly, though: the water is a crisp 72°F year-round.

SALT SPRINGS RECREATION AREA

Rumored to have curative powers, **Salt Springs** (☎ 352-685-2048; admission $4, campsites with/without hookups $23/17; ⊙ 8am-8pm) is a favorite with RV owners for its lovely shady areas. Head to the **marina** (☎ 352-685-2255; ⊙ 7am-4pm), about half a mile south of the recreation area in front of the doctor's office, where you can rent vessels to cruise enormous Lake Kerr: canoes ($20), pontoon boats ($70 for four hours, $110 daily plus gas) or a 16ft Carolina skiff ($27.50 for four hours, $45 daily plus gas).

ALEXANDER SPRINGS RECREATION AREA

This picturesque **recreation area** (☎ 352-669-3522; admission/campsites $5/19; ⊙ 8am-8pm) has one of the last untouched subtropical forests left in Florida. The stunning sapphire-blue freshwater spring attracts wildlife, swimmers, scuba divers (extra $5 fee) and sunbathers. Canoe rental ($10.50/26 per two hours/daily) includes a welcome rehaul at the end of the 7-mile paddle.

Getting There & Away

SunTran (☎ 352-401-6999) runs between Ocala's Greyhound and Amtrak stations (see p392) and the western edge of the forest. Buses transport bikes for free, but remember that this is an enormous wilderness area – more than twice as big as Orlando – and once here, there's no public transportation.

All public roads are well maintained. Hard-packed dirt roads are generally OK for 2WD cars, but beware of soft sugar sand, stranding you faster than a freak downpour.

Several different entrances can be used to access Ocala National Forest. From Orlando take Hwy 441 north to the Eustis turnoff and continue north on Hwy 19 (about 40 miles); from Daytona take Hwy 92 west to DeLand, then head north on Hwy 17 to Barberville and west on SR 40 (about 30 miles); from Ocala take Silver Springs Blvd due west about 6 miles to the forest's main entry. For a scenic shortcut take the Fort Gates Ferry (see the boxed text, opposite).

GAINESVILLE

☎ 352 / pop 106,000

Originally a whistle-stop along the Florida Railroad Company's line chugging from Cedar Key to Fernandina Beach, Gainesville soon thrived as a citrus-producing community until repeated frosts in the 1890s drove orange-growers south. Today, Gainesville is an energetic, upbeat city, routinely ranked among the country's best places to live and play. It's also home to the nation's second largest university, the sprawling University of Florida (UF). The campus itself is 2 miles from downtown, but the student vibe infuses the entire city, with loads of economical eats, cool bars and fine galleries. The university also bequeathed Gatorade: the Science department developed it to counteract the onfield dehydration of its football team, the Fightin' Gators, which have a huge following here (just try getting a room on game weekends).

SPANISH MOSS

Not a moss at all, Spanish moss – aka Florida moss, long moss or graybeard – is an epiphytic plant, meaning it grows on other plants but doesn't rely on those plants for nutrients. Completely rootless, flowering Spanish moss uses its long, slender stems to cling to a host tree. Suspended thus, it uses its scaly leaves to harvest moisture and nutrients from the air. In dry spells, it becomes dormant until moisture returns.

In the past, Timucuan women wore Spanish moss as decoration. Later, settlers used it as stuffing for furniture and mattresses. It has also served as packing material, as mulch and been used in the floristry industry. Recently, the moss has been used to treat type II diabetes, heart disease and hemorrhoids.

DETOUR: FORT GATES FERRY

A little-known gateway exists between Ocala National Forest and Palatka. The **Fort Gates Ferry** (☎ 386-467-2411; one-way $10; ⊙ 7am-5:30pm Wed-Mon, closed during bad weather) is Florida's oldest ferry in continuous operation (since 1856). The ferry carries vehicles across the St John's River in 10 minutes.

Coming from Ocala National Forest, heading east on CR 316 brings you to Hwy 19. Instead of turning onto SR 19, travel straight down 7 miles of regularly graded sand road; it's accessible by 2WD vehicles, but check with rangers or ferry employees after heavy rain. The ferry runs on demand and waits on the opposite (eastern) bank; flash your headlights (or call from your cell phone) and it'll chug over to collect you.

The ferry dock is just below where Fort Gates (and before it, a trading post) once perched on the bluff. During the Seminole Indian War and the Civil War, hand-poled wooden barges traversed this one-mile stretch of river. These days, powered by a four-cylinder, 55-horsepower diesel engine, the present ferry combines a 21ft tug and a 40ft iron barge. Decked over and installed with a wheelhouse, the little tug was once a 1918 wooden sailboat. It can only carry two cars at once, but it has had some famous passengers: the ferry once starred alongside Paul Newman in a sports-car commercial.

On the eastern side, about 2 miles of graded sand road will bring you out on Hwy 309 into tiny Fruitland, roughly halfway between Georgetown (3 miles) to the south, and Welaka (4.4 miles). Following the 309 north connects you with Hwy 17, which runs you north to Palatka (22 miles).

Near the ferry dock is a real gem: the **Fort Gates Ferry Gateway Fish Camp** (☎ 386-467-2411; 229 Fort Gates Ferry Rd, Fruitland; cabins 2/3/4 people $35/40/50; P). Eight wooden cabins equipped with stoves, refrigerators and private bathrooms, as well as pots, pans and linen, provide a perfect base for some astounding fishing. You'll need to bring your own provisions as there aren't any stores. Nearby Kangaroo gas station on Hwy 309 sells basic supplies; for bait, head to **Welaka Bait & Tackle** (☎ 904-467-3845; 8002 Elm Street, Welaka). There's plenty of bream around and when the mullet runs, it's *running*.

Known for its thriving music scene, the most notable band to hail from Gainesville is Tom Petty and the Heartbreakers. Indie rock and punk rock rule clubs today, though audiophiles can find everything from bluegrass to hip-hop almost every night.

Gainesville is also a mecca for the outdoorsy. Surrounding the city are pristine wilderness areas and a succession of stunningly clear springs just aching to be tubed.

Orientation

Laid out on a grid system, Gainesville's avenues run east–west and streets run north–south. University Ave is the main drag as well as the north–south divider; its intersection with Main St, the east–west divider, is considered the town's epicenter. Downtown Gainesville is roughly bordered by 13th St to the west, 2nd St to the east, 2nd Ave to the north and 4th Ave to the south. The university is southwest of the center.

Addresses and streets are given a N, S, E, W or NE, SE, NW, SW prefix dependent upon their relation to the intersection of Main and University. It's confusing, even to locals, whose trick is the mnemonic device APRiL, which means: avenues, places, roads and lanes run east–west while everything else runs north–south.

Information
BOOKSTORES
Goerings Book Store (Map p396; ☎ 352-377-3703; www.goerings.com; 1717 NW 1st Ave; ⊙ 10am-9pm Mon-Sat, to 5pm Sun) Local books and more local books.

INTERNET ACCESS
You'll find free wi-fi coverage downtown around the Hippodrome.
Library (Map pp398-9; ☎ 352-334-3900; 401 E University Ave; ⊙ 9:30am-9pm Mon-Thu, to 6pm Fri, to 5pm Sat, 1-5pm Sun) Offers free internet access.

MEDIA
The daily paper is the **Gainesville Sun** (www.gainesvillesun.com) and Friday's 'Scene' section offers a thorough weekender run-down. Published

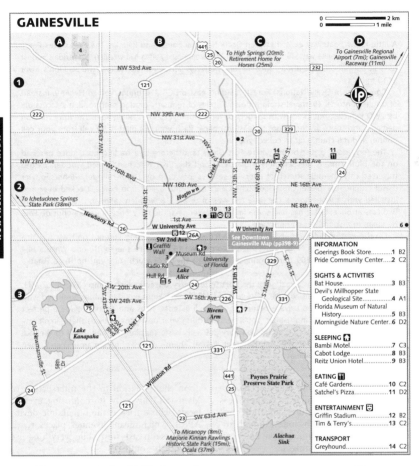

GAINESVILLE

monthly, Insite is the local bible for music reviews and entertainment listings. The daily political rag, **Independent Florida Alligator** (www .alligator.org), isn't officially associated with UF but is published by students attending the school.

Catch Bill Beckett's eclectic radio show – the Caravan, from 8pm to 9pm Saturdays on WUFT-FM Classic 89 (89.1FM; www .wuft.org), the home of NPR (National Public Radio).

TOURIST INFORMATION
Alachua County Visitors & Convention Bureau
(VCB; Map pp398-9; ☎ 352-374-5260, 866-778-5002; www.visitgainesville.net; 30 E University Ave; ☻ 9am-5pm Mon-Fri) East of Main St.

Pride Community Center (Map p396; ☎ 352-377-8915; www.pridecommunitycenter.org; 3131 NW 13th St; ☻ 3-7pm Mon-Fri, noon-4pm Sat) For gay and lesbian info.

Sights & Activities
UNIVERSITY OF FLORIDA
With more than 51,000 students and a 2000-acre campus, rambling **University of Florida** (UF; Map p396; www.ufl.edu; ☎ 352-392-3261) is the state's oldest university. Established in 1853 as the East Florida Seminary in Ocala, UF later relocated to Gainesville and in 1906 the first class of students, numbering a paltry 102, cracked the books. The Holland Law Center stands near the site of American Indian burial mounds, and archaeologists

have unearthed artifacts from pre-Columbian settlements here. For a campus map, visit http://campusmapufl.edu.

Griffin Stadium (also known as Florida Field) is home turf for the indomitable blue-and-orange Gators football team, winner of seven SEC (Southeastern Conference) titles and home to three Heisman Trophy Winners.

Note: the speed limit throughout the entire campus is a strongly policed 20mph.

FLORIDA MUSEUM OF NATURAL HISTORY

The highlight of this excellent natural history **museum** (Map p396; ☎ 352-846-2000; www.flmnh.ufl.edu; cnr SW 34th St & Hull Rd; adult/child $6/2, with Butterfly Rainforest $8.50/4.50; ☽ 10am-5pm Mon-Sat, 1-5pm Sun) is the expansive Butterfly Rainforest. Hundreds of butterflies from 55 to 65 species flutter freely in the soaring, screened vivarium. As you stroll among waterfalls and tropical foliage, peek at scientists preparing specimens in the rearing lab of this, the world's largest butterfly research facility.

DEVIL'S MILLHOPPER STATE GEOLOGICAL SITE

This **geological site** (Map p396; ☎ 352-955-2008; 4732 Millhopper Rd; pedestrian/car $1/2; ☽ 9am-5pm Wed-Sun) centers on a 120ft deep, 500ft wide funnel-shaped rainforest that's entered by descending a 232-step wooden staircase. Water trickles down the slopes from the surrounding springs; some of it flows into a natural drain and ultimately to the Gulf of Mexico. Rangers lead tours every Saturday at 10am.

To get there, take University Ave west to 441 and head north. Turn right on NW 53rd Ave, which becomes Millhopper Rd; the site is down to road to the right. The total trip is about 12 miles.

MORNINGSIDE NATURE CENTER

Only 3 miles from downtown, this 278-acre **nature center** (Map p396; ☎ 352-334-2170; www.kanapaha.org; 3540 E University Ave; ☽ 9am-5pm) boasts seven natural communities, including hydric flatwoods, depression marshes and savannahs of longleaf pines. In addition to a picnic basket and a camera, be sure to bring your walking shoes: the center offers 7 miles of trails.

From downtown, go east down University Ave and the center is on your left.

Sleeping

Prices soar during football games and graduations, when a minimum stay may be required and rooms fill rapidly. Many inexpensive motels are just east of UF, along SW 13th St or on approach roads.

Bambi Motel (Map p396; ☎ 352-376-2622; 2119 SW 13th St; r from $39; P ☒) Budget travelers rejoice! Many of the 34 clean, comfy rooms at this classic drive-up motel have kitchenettes; all have TVs; a pool is on-site.

Reitz Union Hotel (Map p396; ☎ 352-392-2151; Museum Rd, University of Florida; r $99-129; P ☒ ☐) Talk about 'centrally located.' This 36-room hotel occupies the 5th and 6th floors of the campus' Union building and offers dramatic treetop vistas. Shops, restaurants and Florida Field are within spitting distance and a buffet breakfast is part of the package.

Cabot Lodge (Map p396; ☎ 352-375-2400; www.cabotlodgegainesville.com; 3726 SW 40th Blvd; r $79-149; P ☐ ☒) One of a small chain of five in the southeast US, this business person–friendly establishment provides printers, scanners, copiers, free local calls, plus two hours of complimentary wine and cheese every evening. There's a gym, too, to get the blood flowing.

DETOUR: WINGED FURY AT THE BAT HOUSE

Across from Gainesville's little Lake Alice, adjacent to a student garden, stands what appears to be an oversized birdhouse. However, this gabled gray house on stilts is actually the **Bat House** (Map p396), home to a family of Mexican free-tailed bats. Built in 1991 after the flying mammals' poop began stinking up the campus, the population has since exploded to 60,000. Each night just after sundown, the bats drop from their roost – at the amazing rate of 100 bats per second! – and fly off to feed.

If you want to witness this winged fury for yourself, follow University Ave west to Gale Lamerand Dr, turn left and head south to Museum Rd. Turn right (west) and follow Museum Rd around a bend. The Bat House will be on your right. It's situated between two permitted lots, but at this time of day, you should be good. If anyone hassles you, just tell 'em you're a vampire coming to see your blood-brothers.

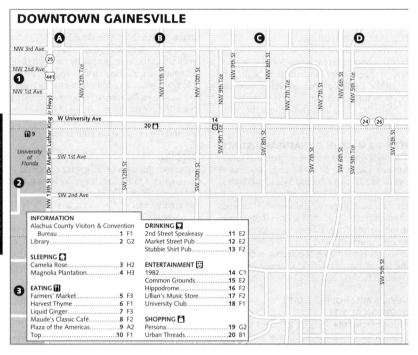

DOWNTOWN GAINESVILLE

INFORMATION
Alachua County Visitors & Convention
  Bureau.......................................**1** F1
Library..**2** G2

SLEEPING 🛏
Camelia Rose.................................**3** H2
Magnolia Plantation.......................**4** H3

EATING 🍴
Farmers' Market.............................**5** F3
Harvest Thyme **6** F1
Liquid Ginger.................................**7** F3
Maude's Classic Café......................**8** F2
Plaza of the Americas.....................**9** A2
Top..**10** F1

DRINKING 🍷
2nd Street Speakeasy **11** E2
Market Street Pub...........................**12** E2
Stubbie Shirt Pub............................**13** F2

ENTERTAINMENT 🎭
1982...**14** C1
Common Grounds............................**15** E2
Hippodrome....................................**16** F2
Lillian's Music Store........................**17** F2
University Club................................**18** F1

SHOPPING 🛍
Persona...**19** G2
Urban Threads.................................**20** B1

our pick **Magnolia Plantation** (Map pp398-9; ☎ 352-375-6653; www.magnoliabnb.com; 309 SE 7th St; r $120-155, cottages $200-380; P ✗ 💻) Lovingly restored, this French Second Empire–style mansion was unique to Gainesville when constructed by a woodworker in 1885. It's still unique today. The main house boasts five rooms, 10 fireplaces (check the detailing in those mantels!) and snacks around the clock. Outside, lush gazebo'ed gardens conceal six roomy (pet-friendly) cottages that are perfect for a private getaway.

Camellia Rose (Map pp398-9; ☎ 352-395-7673; www.camelliaroseinn.com; 205 SE 7th St; r $125-250; P ✗ 💻) Modern upgrades (like Jacuzzi tubs) integrate seamlessly with antique furniture (like tiger oak–panel beds) in this fabulously restored 1903 Victorian building. Featuring a wide, relaxing front porch, the Rose has the cleanest floors in Gainesville.

Eating

Harvest Thyme (Map pp398-9; ☎ 352-384-9497; www.harvestthymecafe.com; 2 W University Ave; mains $6-8; 🕐 8am-4pm Mon-Fri, 11:30am-3:30pm Sat) Too much

to drink last night? Refresh at this healthy pit stop serving organic coffees, fresh breakfast wraps, or if you slept late, deli sandwiches. Many veggie options and smoothies, too.

our pick **Satchel's Pizza** (Map p396; ☎ 352-335-7272; www.satchelspizza.com; 1800 NE 23rd Ave; mains $2.75-13; 🕐 11am-10pm Tue-Sat) Two miles east of downtown, this wacky place has the best pizza on Florida's east coast (and a darn good salad, to boot). Here, you can sit surrounded by funky outsider art and savor steaming build-your-own gourmet pies served on mismatched crockery. Grab a seat at a mosaic courtyard table or in the back of a gutted 1965 Ford Falcon. Most nights there's live music in the Back 40 Bar; there's bocce ball and a head-scratchingly eccentric junk museum featuring various bizarro collections. Satchel's doesn't take credit cards; the fees from the on-site ATM go to charity. Skip Satchel's and you miss Gainesville's soul.

Top (Map pp398-9; ☎ 352-376-1188; 15 N Main St; mains $6-20; 🕐 5pm-2am Tue-Sat, 11am-2:30pm & 5-10pm Sun) Combining 1950s kitsch, hunter lodge decor and giant owl art, this place is both hip and comfortable. Vegetarians will thrill at the op-

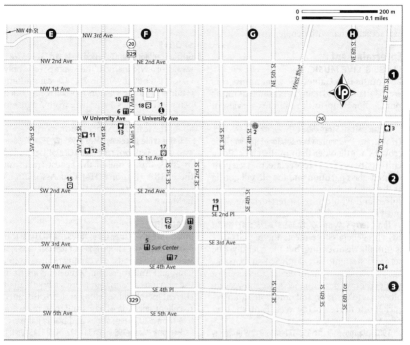

NORTHEAST FLORIDA

tions here and everyone will appreciate the working photo booth in the back ($2).

Liquid Ginger (Map pp398-9; ☎ 352-371-2323; 101 SE 2nd Pl, Suite 118; mains $7-21; ☺ 11:30am-3pm Mon-Fri, 5-10:30pm Mon-Sat, noon-10pm Sun) This Pan Asian restaurant is cute and cozy. The basil chicken is light but zesty, and the two-page tea menu offers intriguing options, like ginger tea.

Other recommendations include these:

Plaza of the Americas (Map pp398-9; lunch Mon-Fri) For the cheapest (and most spiritual) eats, head to UF's lunchtimes when Hare Krishnas play music and serve up vegetarian feasts on ecofriendly dishware for donations.

Maude's Classic Café (Map pp398-9; ☎ 352-335-1204; 101 SE 2nd Pl; mains $7-11; ☺ 7am-midnight Sun-Thu, to 2am Fri & Sat) Bohemian hangout, serving tea and coffee, as well as movie star–named sandwiches and salads ('When Harry Met Salad').

Café Gardens (Map p396; ☎ 352-376-2233; www .cafegardens.net; 1643 NW 1st Ave; mains $6.50-19; ☺ 11:30am-9pm Mon, to 10pm Tue-Sat, noon-9pm Sun) Since 1976 people have been scarfing up the homemade soups and salads served in its cozy courtyard.

Farmers' Market (Map pp398-9; Sun Center; ☺ 4-7pm Wed) Grab fresh produce at this weekly event.

Drinking

Stubbie Shirt Pub (Map pp398-9; ☎ 352-384-1261; www .stubbieshirtpub.com; 9 W University Ave; ☺ 5pm-2am) When Berkeley Hoflund visited Australia, she fell in love with the beer. Upon returning, she opened this very orange, very Aussie, very awesome pub serving 255 types of international 'stubbies and tinnies' (beer bottles and cans, mate), plus quirky T-shirts, custom-made while you wait. Don't try to outsmart the razor-sharp staff: they know waaaay more about beer than you. BYO food; they have games behind the bar.

Market Street Pub (Map pp398-9; ☎ 352-377-2929; 120 SW 1st Ave) Half of this 1908-built pub opens for concerts on big nights, but the main room, with pool and darts, always has something happening, like its 'double up for a dollar' nights on Wednesdays.

2nd Street Speakeasy (Map pp398-9; ☎ 352-271-7569; 21 SW 2nd St) If you're not paying attention, you'll cruise right past the dark door leading into Gainesville's chillest bar. Fringe-tipped crimson lamps, a mellow azure aquarium and cushy burgundy sofas are some of the cool features here. What's coolest though, is that the volume of the lounge music is set so you can actually chat with people.

Entertainment

CLUBS & LIVE MUSIC

Live music is to Gainesville what mouse ears are to Orlando, and many bars double as music venues. For an up-to-the-minute overview of local music, visit www.gainesvillebands.com.

Lillian's Music Store (Map pp398-9; ☎ 352-372-1010; 112 SE 1st Ave; ☼ 2pm-2am Mon-Sat, 3pm-11pm Sun) The crowd's a little older than in the clubs along University, so they appreciate that elegant stained-glass partition and the 3ft-tall gorilla at the entrance. The barbershop seats are in-spired and who can resist test-driving what must be the state's largest urinal?

Tim & Terry's (Map p396; ☎ 352-373-3786; 1417 NW 1st Ave) This general-store-meets-the-big-city dive is initially disorienting, but the friendly vibe sets you straight. Part sandwich shop, package store and instrument dealer, there's also a stripped-down performance space showcasing bluegrass (Tuesdays) and other folk-country-rock music the rest of the week. Fantastic beer selection. A hippie favorite.

1982 (Map pp398-9; ☎ 352-371-9836; 919 W University Ave) Cramped, dingy and musty, this sweet spot boasts both local and national bands, and a great beer selection. If the band sucks, you can play classic Nintendo games on one of four TVs behind the bar. Duck Hunt FTW!

Common Grounds (Map pp398-9; ☎ 352-372-7320; www.commongrounds.com; 210 SW 2nd Ave; 9pm-2am Mon-Wed, 7pm-2am Thu, 5pm-2am Fri, 9pm-2am Sat, 6pm-2am Sun) Delightfully retro, this cavernous venue offers punk, indie, hip-hop, rap – even the occasional stand-up comic. Come early and enjoy a frosty one on the Porch Bar.

University Club (Map pp398-9; ☎ 352-378-6814; www.ucclub.com; 18 E University Ave; 5pm-2am Mon-Fri, 9pm-2am Sat, 5-11pm Sun) Predominantly gay, but straight-friendly, this place is the hub of the local gay and lesbian scene and is famous for its drag shows. The entrance is around back. Free beer on Mondays.

PERFORMING ARTS

Hippodrome (Map pp398-9; ☎ 352-375-4477; http://the hipp.org; 25 SE 2nd Pl; independent films 7pm & 9pm Tue, Thu & Fri, 4:30pm, 7pm & 9pm Sat, 2:30pm, 5pm & 7pm Sun; documentaries Mon nights) In an imposing historic edifice (1911), the Hippodrome is the city's main cultural center, with a diverse theater and independent-cinema program.

SPORTS

Griffin Stadium (Map p396; Florida Field; ☎ 352-375-4683; www.ufl.edu) Nicknamed 'the swamp' (coz only Gators get out alive), this 88,548-seat stadium is home to the UF's Gators football team, which plays seven games a year here from August to November. Visit www.gatorzone.com for info about the team and other Gator sports.

Gainesville Raceway (Map p396; ☎ 352-377-0046; www.gainesvilleraceway.com; 1211 N CR 225) Upgraded in 2003, this is one of the fastest tracks on the NHRA (National Hot Rod Association) circuit and hosts the NHRA Gatornationals in March.

Shopping

Urban Threads (Map pp398-9; ☎ 352-384-1134; 1117 W University Ave; ☼ 11am-7pm Mon-Fri, to 6pm Sat, noon-5pm Sun) Urban Threads sells catalog returns from J Crew and Anthropologie. Some items are from the previous season, but there's a boatload of current merchandise selling at steep discounts. Excellent selection of pants and tops, many for less than $20. Also: shoes and boots galore!

Persona (Map pp398-9; ☎ 352-372-0455; 114 SE 2nd Pl; ☼ noon-6pm Mon, to 8pm Tue-Thu, to 10pm Fri & Sat, 1-5pm Sun) Vintage clothing for men and women, gobs of kitschy accessories and jewelry and some intriguing one-of-a-kind fashions.

Getting There & Around

By car, downtown Gainesville is about 3 miles east of I-75, between Orlando (114 miles) and Tallahassee (154 miles).

Gainesville Regional Airport (☎ 352-373-0249; www.gra-gnv.com), 10 miles northeast of down-town, is served by a handful of domestic car-riers. **Gainesville Cab** (☎ 352-375-8294) will run you into town for about $15.

The **Greyhound** (☎ 352-376-5252; 101 NE 23rd Ave) station has daily services to Miami, Orlando, Tallahassee, Atlanta and points north.

Gainesville Regional Transit System (RTS; ☎ 352-334-2600; www.go-rts.com; adult/student/day pass $1/0.50/2) services the city with buses.

AROUND GAINESVILLE

High Springs

☎ 352 / pop 3600

Quaint High Springs, the 'friendliest town in Florida,' is a hub for antiquers, bikers and locals seeking a getaway. Main St, dotted with shops, galleries and restaurants, is the major north–south divider. Intersecting it, Hwy 441 (here called 1st Ave) is the east–west throughway. There's no visitor's center; get info from www.highsprings.com.

Grady House Bed & Breakfast (☎ 386-454-2206; www.gradyhouse.com; 420 NW 1st Ave; r $100-185) has five rooms themed according to color: the Red Room has over 350 classic nudes gracing the walls; the Navy Room is styled nautically. **Floyd's Diner** (☎ 386-454-5775; 615 NW Santa Fe Blvd; mains $6-18; ☺ breakfast, lunch & dinner) is a 1950s diner with rockin' good US fare and an old-time soda fountain.

High Springs is the gateway to superb springs, including **Poe Springs** (☎ 352-454-1992; 28800 NW 182nd Ave; admission $5; ☺ 9am-sunset) off CR 340, 3 miles west and **Ginnie Springs** (☎ 386-454-7188; www.ginniespringsoutdoors.com; 7300 NE Ginnie Springs Rd; admission adult/child $12/3; ☺ 8am-7pm Mon-Thu summer, to 6pm winter; to 10pm Fri & Sat year-round; to 8pm Sun summer, to 7pm winter), 2 miles further west on CR 340. Kayaks/tubes per day $25/6 can be rented at Ginnie Springs, and there is camping (adult/child $18/6, hookups $7 daily) and some cottages ($175 for 4 people) available.

High Springs is about 20 miles northwest of Gainesville on Hwy 441 (NW 13th St), a straight shot from UF.

Ichetucknee Springs State Park

Relax in a tube and float the crystal-clear waters through unspoiled wilderness as otters swim alongside you.

The Ichetucknee River is fed by nine springs that together produce 233 million gallons of clear water daily, flowing downstream at about 1.25mph.

Various water sports are available here, but tubing is certainly the most popular. Floats last from 45 minutes to 3½ hours, with scattered launch points along the river. The **park** (☎ 386-497-4690; admission $5, canoes $5; ☺ 8am-sunset) runs regular trams bringing tubers to the river and also a free shuttle service (May to September) between the north and south entrances.

To minimize environmental impact, the number of tubers is limited to 750 a day; arrive early as capacity is often reached midmorning. Use the south entrance: the shuttle service takes you to the launch points, allowing you to float back down to your car.

You'll see farmers advertising tube rental as you approach the park along Hwy 238 and 47 (the park itself does not rent tubes). Tubes are $5 and one- or two-person rafts cost $10 to $15. At the end of the day, leave your gear at the tube drop at the southern end of the park; it'll be returned.

Ichetucknee Springs State Park is about 38 miles northwest of Gainesville, or 15 miles northwest of High Springs on Hwy 27.

Micanopy

☎ 352 / pop 652

The oldest inland settlement in Florida, Micanopy (pronounced mickuh-*noh*-pee) started as an Indian trading post. A hundred and ninety years later, it's still a trading post of sorts – for antique hunters. Known as 'the town that time forgot,' the nickname may seem trite, but it's jaw-droppingly accurate. Hulking oaks festooned with Spanish moss line wide roads that wind lazily past stoic brick buildings. Looking like a movie set, Hollywood has already come calling: *Doc Hollywood* was filmed here.

RETIREMENT HOME FOR HORSES

About 25 miles north of Gainesville is Mill Creek Farm's **Retirement Home for Horses** (☎ 386-462-1001; www.millcreekfarm.org; CR 235A Alachua; ☺ 11am-3pm Sat; Ⓟ), an equestrian sanctuary that Boxer from George Orwell's *Animal Farm* could only dream of. Under the care of Mary and Peter Gregory, elderly horses who've been serving in police work, circuses and other vocations are brought here to live out their final years moseying gentle pastures; Peter welcomes new retirees with a heartfelt speech dignifying their years of service.

Admission is two carrots; bagfuls are accepted. From Gainesville, turn right from US 441 to CR 235A at the traffic light immediately after Santa Fe High School. Follow it for about 3 miles to the Mill Creek Farm sign on your right, just beyond the I-75 overpass. Parking is adjacent to the picnic tables.

The 0.5-mile main drag, NE Cholokka Blvd, features half a dozen antique shops, the delightfully disheveled **O Brisky Books** (☎ 352-466-391; 114 Cholokka Blvd; 10am-5pm Tue-Sun) and the **Micanopy Historical Society Museum** (☎ 352-466-3200; crn Cholokka Blvd & Early St; admission $2; 1-4pm). Smack in the middle of it all, the **Chamber of Commerce** (☎ 352-466-9229; 207 Cholokka Blvd; 9am-5pm Mon-Fri) has as an art co-op.

Two miles north on Hwy 441, wild horses and bison roam the 21,000-acre **Paynes Prairie Preserve State Park** (☎ 352-466-3397; 100 Savannah Blvd; pedestrian or cyclist/car $1/4; 8am-sunset). This slightly eerie preserve's wet prairie, swamp, hammock and pine flatwoods have more than 34 trails, including the 16-mile Gainesville–Hawthorne Rail Trail, slicing through the northern section. The 3-mile La Chua Trail takes in the Alachua Sink and Alachua Lake, offering alligator- and sandhill crane–spotting opportunities. Just north of the **visitor's center** (9am-4pm), climb the 50ft observation tower for panoramas. Campsites cost $15, and include water and electricity.

Swing by the **Marjorie Kinnan Rawlings Historic State Park** (☎ 352-466-3672; 18700 S CR 325, Cross Creek; admission per car $2; 9am-5pm). Rawlings (1896–1953) was the author of the Pulitzer Prize–winning novel *The Yearling*, a coming-of-age story set in what's now Ocala National Forest. Her career flourished only after Max Perkins, Rawlings' (and also Ernest Hemingway's and F Scott Fitzgerald's) editor, told her that her letters about her friends and neighbors were more interesting than her gothic fiction, inspiring her to write *Cross Creek*, a book about her life in this area. Her former Cracker-style home is open for **tours** (adult/child $3/2; 10am-4pm Thu-Sun, closed Aug & Sep) on the hour (except noon). You can stroll the orange groves, farmhouse and barn on your own – pick up a self-guided walking brochure from the car park. The estate is just north of Orange Lake, off Hwy 325 between Island Grove and Micanopy.

For total stillness, Cross Creek's aptly named **Peace and Quiet Place** (☎ 352-466-3194; 17105 Hwy 325; canoes/pontoons per day $10/80) offers campsites ($20 per night) and simple cinderblock cabins with kitchens ($59 per night).

For pure luxury, nothing beats **Herlong Mansion** (☎ 352-466-3322, 800-437-5664; www.herlong.com; 402 NE Cholokka Blvd; $99-179), sitting on the northern edge Micanopy like a king surveying his fiefdom. Impeccably manicured, the mansion's 2nd floor boasts two endless porches, perfect for relaxing with a cool drink.

Blue Highway Pizzeria (☎ 352-466-0062; www.bluehighwaypizza.com; 204 NE Hwy 441; mains $6-13; 11:30am-9pm Mon-Sat, noon-8pm Sun) serves Neapolitan pies, tasty sandwiches and salads.

Cross Creek's cedar-shingled **Yearling Restaurant** (☎ 352-466-3999; www.yearlingrestaurant.net; 14531 Hwy 325; mains $6-13; 5pm-10pm Thu & Fri, noon-10pm Sat, noon-8:30pm Sun) serves 'Cracker cuisine' like gator tail, hushpuppies, catfish and sour orange pie, while roots music keeps things hopping.

Micanopy is about 11 miles south of Gainesville on Hwy 441.

Tampa Bay & Southwest Florida

If southwest Florida was a restaurant, it would specialize in tapas. Covering just 225 miles of coastline from Tampa to Naples, this region may be compact, but is far from lacking for diversity. Pearly sand dipped into turquoise-flecked seas, fiery red sunsets over the Gulf of Mexico, alligators, amusement parks, cigars, art and more than 100 barrier islands are just a few dishes on this eclectic menu.

If you've come for the beach, you're in luck. There are plenty of choices. Venice trumps in the laid-back department. Here life involves kicking back at the shrimp shack and sipping a frozen cocktail in the sand. If you need posh, you need Naples. Considered one of the best beaches in the US, streets are strewn with million-dollar mansions, fine restaurants and chic shops. For a good party, pay Fort Myers or St Pete Beach a visit. The college crowd adores both. To get back to nature, go to Sanibel Island; a haven for birders, reclusive millionaires and shell collectors.

Don't fill up entirely on beaches, though, because the menu here extends well beyond surf and sand. Ride an adrenaline-pumping roller coaster at Busch Gardens. Roll your own cigars in Tampa's historic and happening Ybor City. Discover Dali's surreal world in slightly gritty St Petersburg, which competes with Ybor City for the best bar scene. Go cultural in artsy Sarasota, the original circus town, where you can learn the story behind the 'Greatest Show on Earth.' Or take a boat out to Cabbage Key to grab a cheeseburger in paradise, just as Jimmy Buffet did. Who knows? Perhaps this region will inspire you to pen a classic tune as well.

TAMPA BAY & SOUTHWEST FLORIDA

HIGHLIGHTS

- Look for alligators as you canoe down the river at **Myakka River State Park** (p442)
- Take in the casual south-Florida beach-town vibe at **Venice** (p441), which boasts great sand, pretty water and front-row seats to those famous ruby-red gulf sunsets
- Roll your own cigars in **Ybor City** (p407), a historic Tampa neighborhood that also hosts the city's best bar scene
- Mingle with the rich and famous in picture-perfect and posh **Naples** (p454), the chicest beach town around
- Camp out in **Cayo Costa State Park** (p450) – this gulf-island jewel is accessible only by boat, has pristine beaches, and frequent manatee-sightings offshore

★ Ybor City

Myakka River
State Park ★

Venice ★

Cayo Costa
State Park ★

Naples ★

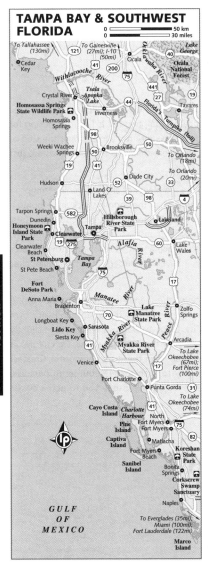

TAMPA BAY & SOUTHWEST FLORIDA

Fort Myers became a nationally recognized winter resort after the 1898 construction of the Royal Palm Hotel. The rich, famous and legendary were quick to snap up surrounding property – Thomas Edison and Henry Ford both spent winter in private mansions here. Today, the money has moved down the road to neighboring Naples. This wealthy town features multimillion-dollar mansions, luxury shopping and more Rolls Royces and Ferraris than Honda on its palm-lined streets.

On August 13, 2004 the region, with Fort Myers and Sanibel taking especially hard hits, was damaged heavily by Hurricane Charley, a Category 4 storm that made landfall just north of Fort Myers. Hurricane Wilma clobbered the area the following year, with the majority of the damage centered on Naples this time.

Climate

It's hard to complain. Like the rest of South Florida, west-coast temperatures hover around the 65°F in the winter (November to March). Summertime (June to September) is downright steamy, the mercury pegs about 90°F and there's a high probability of afternoon thunderstorms but the ocean breezes help. Spring and fall, perfectly pleasant, lie somewhere in between.

National, State & Regional Parks

The Bay Area and southwest Florida do not lack green space. Camping and canoeing are prime at the Hillsborough River State Park (p417), near Tampa, while the enormous Myakka River State Park (p442), near Sarasota, excels in hiking and river-boat touring.

Southwest Florida supports a rich ecosystem which in turn supports vibrant and varied bird species. They're best appreciated at Sanibel's JN 'Ding' Darling National Wildlife Refuge (p452), while the Chassahowitzka National Wildlife Refuge (p460) supports a sweet colony of endangered manatees. These gentle creatures also gather at Lee County Manatee Park (p451).

For great state-run, natural beach parks, Lover's Key (p447), Caladesi Island (p430) and Cayo Costa Island (p450) are definitely a tough trio to top.

Information

The tourist industry is well oiled. Each town has an active chamber of commerce and a visible visitors bureau; details can be found

History

This area's modern history began in the mid-1800s with the construction of the region's first highway, the Tamiami Trail, running between Tampa and Miami. During this time towns began to grow exponentially as the new highway brought in more settlers, and pushed more American Indians off their land.

throughout the chapter. Additionally, browse these newspapers' websites:
Fort Meyers News Press (www.news-press.com)
Naples Daily News (www.naplesnews.com)
St Petersburg Times (www.sptimes.com)
Sarasota Herald Tribune (www.heraldtribune.com)
Tampa Tribune (www.tampatrib.com)

Getting There & Around

Tampa, the unofficial regional capital, is a straight shot and 84 miles due west of Orlando via the I-4. It's also 130 miles due south of Gainesville via the I-75, another easy drive. From Florida's official capital, Tallahassee, it's 238 miles via US 19 and the connecting Seminole Parkway. From Miami it's 249 miles; take the I-95 north to the I-75 and head west across 'Alligator Alley' to Naples, then continue northward on the I-75.

Within the region, the I-75 skirts the eastern edge of Tampa Bay and the I-275 skirts the western edge through St Petersburg. The congested Alt US 19 connects barrier beach communities from St Pete Beach to Tarpon Springs. US 41 – full of traffic lights – connects major towns between Bradenton and Naples; it's also called the Tamiami Trail because it runs between those major destinations (hence the contracted name). Smaller roads linking the barrier beaches run west of US 41.

The interstate exits are not numbered sequentially; they're numbered according to how far they are from the end of the road (which is in the south).

Greyhound buses serve the area; see individual towns for details. The main airport is in Tampa (p416), but there are also airports in Clearwater, Sarasota and Fort Myers.

TAMPA BAY AREA

Set on a gorgeous deep-water blue bay, the state's largest metropolitan area is a buzzing place these days. Although staid looking from afar, stay around a while, and you'll find Tampa is more than office buildings and football. From the 35 miles of barrier beaches lining its western shores (stretching between St Pete Beach and Clearwater Beach) to a theme park opened before Disney World, the Tampa Bay area has a wildly diverse range of activities. Manatees outnumber mermaids in the northern reaches while boisterous bars outnumber cigar shops on the Tampa–

St Petersburg peninsula. From an aquarium where visitors can swim with the fish to a bike path that's the longest urban trail in the country, this bay area is the region's best undiscovered secret – even the airport is easy to negotiate.

TAMPA BAY

☎ 813 / pop 383,000

Tampa Bay may look big and imposing from the outside, but get off the freeway and you'll see its bark is a lot bigger than its bite. At heart, Tampa Bay goes back to its small-town roots. Just 84 miles west of Orlando, yet worlds apart, Tampa is a lively city that's both happening and historical. Downtown is compact (hence easy to negotiate), and even though it can feel a bit like the kind of place where people go to work during the day, in the evenings Tampa shakes off her suit and parties late into the night.

Ybor City is the place to go, day or night – and definitely where you should start and end your Tampa Bay experience. The center of the city's bustling (and ongoing) revitalization, Ybor City is a district of handsome brick warehouses that housed the old cigar industry. When the US embargo of Cuban products began in 1959, Tampa's fortunes fell, but when Ybor City was designated a National Historic Landmark District in 1990, it became a nightlife hub and kicked off a new round of development.

Plenty of other diversions have turned southwest Florida's oldest city, and the state's third largest, into a primo tourist stop. (It can be a traffic nightmare during rush hour.) Tampa boasts a hands-on science museum, an exceptional aquarium, a performing-arts center, a genteel residential district and a burgeoning cruise-ship terminal. And it all sits snuggly on and is divided by the tranquil Hillsborough River. Still, even with her attractions, Tampa Bay is really only a starting or ending point (and not the entire vacation) for most travelers; stay a night or two and then get on to southwest Florida's major selling point – beaches to the south.

Orientation

Tampa is crisscrossed by major highways and interstates. The US 41 (the Tamiami Trail) cuts straight through its center while the I-75 runs north–south and skirts its eastern edge. The I-275 also runs north–south and cuts through

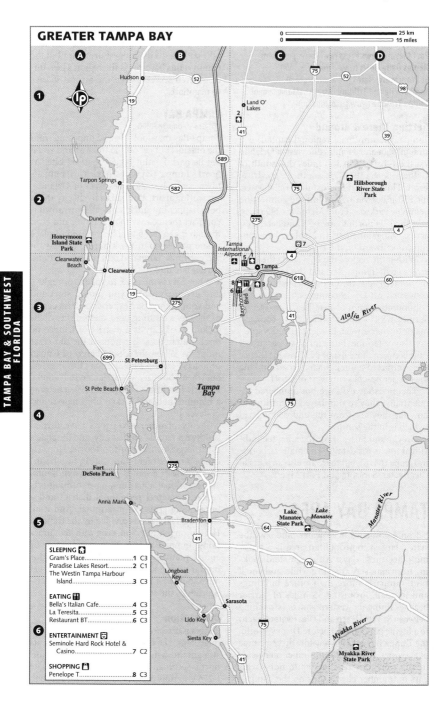

GREATER TAMPA BAY

0 — 25 km
0 — 15 miles

TAMPA BAY & SOUTHWEST FLORIDA

A B C D

1

Hudson

52

19

Land O' Lakes

2

41

589

39

98

75

52

2

Tarpon Springs

582

Dunedin

Honeymoon Island State Park

Clearwater Beach

Clearwater

19

275

Tampa International Airport

5

Tampa

4

618

I-275

I-75

Hillsborough River State Park

4

7

60

3

8

6 4 3

Bayshore Blvd

41

Alafia River

699

St Petersburg

St Pete Beach

Tampa Bay

75

4

Fort DeSoto Park

275

5

Anna Maria

Bradenton

41

64

Lake Manatee State Park

Lake Manatee

70

Manatee River

Longboat Key

Sarasota

Lido Key

75

Siesta Key

41

Myakka River

Myakka River State Park

SLEEPING ⌂
Gram's Place.............................1 C3
Paradise Lakes Resort.............2 C1
The Westin Tampa Harbour
  Island.....................................3 C3

EATING ⑪
Bella's Italian Cafe....................4 C3
La Teresita.................................5 C3
Restaurant BT...........................6 C3

ENTERTAINMENT ⊟
Seminole Hard Rock Hotel &
  Casino....................................7 C2

SHOPPING ⬚
Penelope T.................................8 C3

downtown before heading across the Howard Frankland Bridge through St Petersburg and south to Sarasota. The I-4 runs east and then northeast to Orlando and on to meet the I-95 on Florida's east coast. The Lee Roy Selmon Expressway (Hwy 618) cuts through downtown Tampa, running northeast to southwest to the airport.

Downtown Tampa is bordered by the I-275 at the north, the Hillsborough River at the west, the Garrison Channel at the south and Meridian Ave at the east. Franklin St is the center of the downtown pedestrian zone. Ybor City is just northeast of downtown; Channelside and the Port of Tampa are due east, just beyond the railroad tracks.

South Tampa is really old Tampa, the peninsula southwest of downtown (south of Kennedy Blvd), and is reached via the northeast–southwest Bayshore Blvd and the north–south S Dale Mabry Hwy. MacDill Air Force Base occupies the southern tip of this peninsula; Bay-to-Bay Blvd and Gandy Blvd (which heads over the bridge to St Petersburg) run east–west across it. North Tampa feels like the set of *The Truman Show*.

Information

BOOKSTORES
Old Tampa Book Co (Map p408; ☎ 813-209-2151; 507 N Tampa St; ⏲ 10am-5pm Mon-Fri, 11am-5pm Sat) This downtown shop has a huge selection and specializes in used books – a gem of a bookshop.

EMERGENCY
Tampa General Hospital (off Map p408; ☎ 813-251-7000; 2 Columbia Dr, Davis Island; ⏲ 24hr) South of downtown on Davis Island, this is the biggest local hospital.

INTERNET ACCESS
Federal Express Kinkos (Map p408; ☎ 813-632-3139; www.fedexkinkos.com; 400 N Tampa St; per hr $12; ⏲ 7am-8pm Mon-Fri, 9am-5pm Sat & Sun) Internet access.

LIBRARIES
Library Downtown (Map p408; ☎ 813-273-3652; 900 N Ashley Dr; ⏲ 9am-9pm Mon-Thu, to 6pm Fri, to 5pm Sat, 10am-6pm Sun); Ybor City (off Map p409; ☎ 813-272-5747; 1505 Nebraska Ave; ⏲ 10am-6pm Mon-Thu, to 5pm Fri & Sat) Both branches offer free internet access.

MEDIA
St Petersburg Times (www.sptimes.com) A big daily paper.

Tampa Tribune (www.tampatrib.com) Another big daily paper.
Watermark (www.watermarkonline.com) Biweekly listings for gays, lesbians and bisexuals.

MONEY
Amex (off Map p408; ☎ 813-273-0310; www.americanexpress.com; 4300 West Cypress St; ⏲ 8:30am-5:30pm Mon-Fri) Money-changing facilities near the Westshore Plaza Mall.
Bank of America (Map p408; ☎ 800-299-2265; www.bankofamerica.com; 101 E Kennedy Blvd) Branches are everywhere you want them to be.

POST
Post office (Map p408; ☎ 813-223-4225; 925 N Florida Ave; ⏲ 8:30am-5:30pm Mon-Fri)

TOURIST INFORMATION
Tampa Bay Convention & Visitors Bureau (Map p408; ☎ 813-223-1111, 800-826-8358; www.visittampabay.com; 615 Channelside Dr; ⏲ 9:30am-5:30pm Mon-Sat, 11am-5pm Sun) This visitors center has a free map that shows how all of Tampa's neighborhoods and interstates fit together. Pick up their self-guided tour of historic Tampa.
Ybor City Chamber of Commerce (Map p409; ☎ 813-248-3712; www.ybor.org; 1600 E 8th Ave; ⏲ 9am-5pm Mon-Fri, 10am-6pm Sat, noon-5pm Sun) This place, which also houses the Centro Ybor Museum, has information on this National Landmark Historic District and historical displays on the cigar connection. Pick up their excellent historic-walking-tour brochure, which illuminates Ybor City's former cultural and working heritage.

Sights & Activities

If you're traveling with kids and need distraction, Tampa is a child-friendly place to kick back for a few days. Many of the city's sights also double as activities – become part of the exhibit at the Florida Aquarium (see p410) after donning scuba gear and entering a 500,000-gallon faux-reef tank to swim with fish.

If you want a bit more hardcore exercise, head to Bayshore Blvd (p411). It's the best place within a 20-mile radius for walking, running or cycling. Visit at dawn or dusk for tranquility.

YBOR CITY
The coolest neighborhood in town is home to chic dining, chic nightlife and chic cigars. Once an iffy destination because of crime,

DOWNTOWN TAMPA

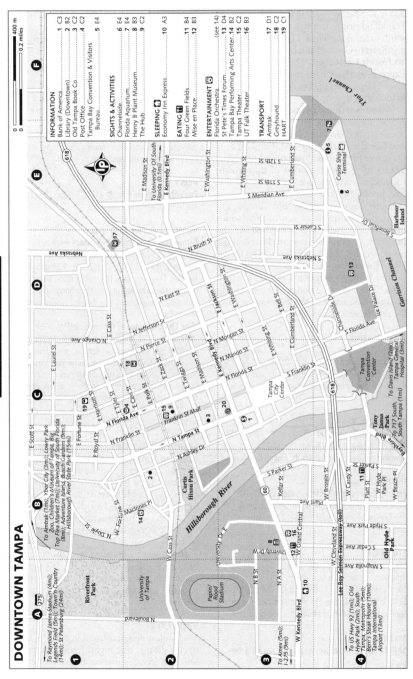

INFORMATION	
Bank of America...............................1	C3
Library (Downtown)..........................2	B2
Old Tampa Book Co............................3	C2
Post Office.......................................4	C2
Tampa Bay Convention & Visitors	
Bureau...5	E4

SIGHTS & ACTIVITIES	
Channelside......................................6	E4
Florida Aquarium..............................7	E4
Henry B Plant Museum.......................8	B3
The Hub...9	C2

SLEEPING	
Economy Inn Express........................10	A3

EATING	
Four Green Fields.............................11	B4
Mise en Place..................................12	B3

ENTERTAINMENT	
Florida Orchestra.........................(see 14)	
St Pete's Times Forum......................13	D4
Tampa Bay Performing Arts Center....14	B2
Tampa Theater................................15	C2
UT Falk Theater...............................16	B3

TRANSPORT	
Amtrak...17	D1
Greyhound......................................18	C2
HART..19	C1

today Ybor City has been revitalized, but not rebuilt. The cobblestone 19th-century historic district preserves a strong Cuban-Spanish heritage while embracing Tampa's hippest party scene. About two miles from downtown, Ybor (rhymes with Eeyore) City was established by the owner of a cigar factory who drew hundreds of Cuban, Spanish and Italian immigrant workers to the area, and that diversity has bestowed more charm on this area than the whole rest of Tampa put together. For young, urban professionals to 40-year-old party boys all looking for a good time, this area is a must simply for its after-dark energy and drink-till-you-drop potential – there are more than 60 bars and clubs packed into this small neighborhood. During the day wander palm-lined and brick-paved streets, past wrought-iron balconies à la New Orleans' Bourbon St, handsome former cigar factories and social clubs.

The main drag of Ybor City, 7th Ave (La Septima), is closed to cars on Friday and Saturday from about 9pm to 4am. The area is roughly bordered by 23rd St at the east, 13th St at the west, Palm Ave (between 10th and 11th Aves) at the north and the railroad tracks along 6th Ave at the south. 14th St is also called Avenida República de Cuba. The safest bet for parking (for ease and safety) is the garage on 7th Ave E at 16th St. Please note that although Ybor City is a lot safer than it used to be, crime isn't nonexistent and you should be careful walking outside of the main section of town mentioned above.

The **Fresh Market** (Map p409; ☎ 813-241-2442; cnr 8th Ave & 18th St; ☺ 9am-3pm Sat; P) is held at Centennial Park, and offers arts and crafts, fruits and veggies. Locals swear by it for fresh produce.

Ybor City State Museum
Covering about half a city block, this **museum** (Map p409; ☎ 813-247-6323; www.ybormuseum.org; 1818 9th Ave; admission $3; ☺ 9am-5pm) includes La Casita (a reconstructed 'shotgun'-style abode that housed immigrant cigar workers), the Ferlita Bakery (with its original brick ovens and exhibits on the bakery and cigar industry), cigar-rolling demonstrations (call for exact days and times) and fascinating photographs of the cigar factories and late-19th-century

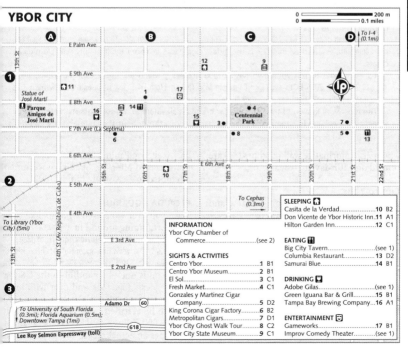

YBOR CITY

0 — 200 m
0 — 0.1 miles

To I-4 (0.1mi)

Statue of José Martí

Parque Amigos de José Martí

E Palm Ave
E 9th Ave
E 8th Ave
E 7th Ave (La Septima)
E 6th Ave
E 5th Ave
E 4th Ave
E 3rd Ave
E 2nd Ave

To Cephas (0.3mi)

To Library (Ybor City) (5mi)

Adamo Dr (60)

To University of South Florida (0.3mi); Florida Aquarium (0.5mi); Downtown Tampa (1mi)

Lee Roy Selmon Expressway (toll) (618)

ROLL YOUR OWN: YBOR CITY CIGARS

Tampa's revitalized historic cigar district has a rich heritage. But let's start further south. Due to its proximity to Cuba and its excellent tobacco, Key West (p199) had long been the cigar-making capital of the US. But when workers started organizing in Key West, the cigar barons figured that the only way to break the union's grip on their factories was to relocate them and the only direction in which they could head was north. In 1885, when Vicénte Martínez Ybor and Ignacio Haya moved their considerable cigar factories – the Principe de Gales (Prince of Wales) and La Flor de la Sanchez y Haya, respectively – to present-day Ybor City, it marked a turning point. And as if to send a message to Key West that its cigar-making days were over, a fire broke out there on April 1, 1886, destroying several cigar factories, including a branch of Ybor's Principe de Gales. Over the next 50 years, as more Cuban cigar-makers moved into Tampa en masse, Ybor City turned into the cigar capital of the USA. The cigar business never looked back.

To listen in on a thoroughly fascinating discussion of the merits of particular cigars and the paraphernalia that's necessary for their enjoyment, tune into *The Cigar General*, a radio talk show on Saturdays from noon to 2pm on 970AM. At first listen, there's a bit of a disconnect hearing someone light up when you can't see, taste or smell the after-effects. It begs the question: how well does that transfer to radio? Quite well – because of the passionate commentary and your ability to close your eyes and imagine. Perhaps afterwards you'll be able to answer this compelling variation of the ancient Zen koan: what is the sound of one man smoking?

There are a number of excellent places to pick up one of these famous cigars, and still see the master rollers hard at work. First up should be **Metropolitan Cigars** (Map p409; ☎ 813-248-3304; 2014 E 7th Ave; ⏰ 9:30am-8pm Mon-Fri, 10:30am-5:30pm Sat), one of the few places in the country that's actually set up as a humidor and by far the best cigar shop in Tampa Bay. It sells Arturo Fuente and Cuesta Rey cigars.

King Corona Cigar Factory (Map p409; ☎ 813-241-9109, 1523 E 7th Ave; ⏰ 10am-6pm Mon, to 10:30pm Tue, to 11pm Wed, to 1am Thu, to 2am Fri & Sat, noon-6pm Sun) is the largest cigar emporium in the city, complete with an old-fashioned cigar bar and even a barbershop. It carries Honduran and Dominican-made cigars.

El Sol (Map p409; ☎ 813-248-5905; 1728 E 7th Ave; ⏰ 9:30am-5pm Mon-Thu, to 9pm Fri, 10am-9pm Sat, noon-4pm Sun), established in 1929, is the oldest cigar store in Ybor City. It mainly sells Dominican cigars.

To learn how to roll your own, visit the **Gonzales y Martinez Cigar Company** (Map p409; ☎ 813-247-2469; 2025 E 7th Ave; ⏰ 10am-9pm Mon-Thu, to 11pm Fri & Sat, noon-6pm Sun), which has cigar-rolling demonstrations Monday through Saturday.

The most well known of the Tampa cigar brands is Havatampa, whose mass-marketed Tampa Sweets are available in supermarkets and tobacco shops throughout the state and the country.

Ybor City. Informative walking tours ($6) are offered on Saturday at 10:30am.

Centro Ybor

A dominating upscale shopping, dining and entertainment precinct, **Centro Ybor** (Map p409; www.centroybor.com; 1600 E 8th Ave) runs along 8th Ave between 15th and 17th Sts, but it also cuts through what would have been 16th St down to 7th Ave.

Friends of Martí Park

Parque Amigos de José Martí (Map p409; cnr 13th St & 8th Ave) contains an inaccurate but life-sized monument to Martí that was actually dedicated by Martí's son, actor Cesar Romero. The park is sited at Paulina Pedroso's house, where Martí stayed after the Spanish government attempted to assassinate him in 1892.

FLORIDA AQUARIUM

Have you ever wondered what its like to be a fish swimming around in a 500,000-gallon tank? Find out at the **Florida Aquarium** (Map p408 ☎ 813-273-4000; www.flaquarium.org; 701 Channelside Dr adult/child/senior $19/13/15; ⏰ 9:30am-5pm; 👤). The aquarium is one of a handful in the US that allows guests (aged six and over who know how to swim) to don scuba gear (you don't have to be certified) and plunge right into the 500,000-gallon Coral Reef Gallery tank. It simulates an actual reef in the Dry Tortugas near Key West, so you can get up close and personal with more than 2300 different types of fish and other marine creatures! The funniest part – you become the exhibit, as visitors get to check you out along with grouper, tarpon and moray eels, from a 42ft-high window on the dry side of the tank. This urban scuba experience is $80 for 30 minutes.

If you don't feel like getting wet, there are three floors of exhibits to see. These trace how water travels from its freshwater source to the open sea. Take the elevator to the top and start at the beginning with the Florida Wetlands, where you'll find itty-bitty fish, a limestone cavern, a mangrove forest and alligator hatchlings. In Bays & Beaches, indoor beach features dunes, waves, sea oats and live seabirds.

The aquarium also offers tours aboard a 64ft catamaran, the *Eco Tour,* that heads out into Tampa Bay looking for the 400 or so bottle-nosed dolphins that live here. Along the way you'll also see manatees and a bird island, too. Tickets for an adult/child/senior cost $20/15/19, but there are combo tickets with the aquarium, too, which will save you about $3 per person.

MUSEUM OF SCIENCE & INDUSTRY

This **museum** (MOSI; off Map p408; ☎ 813-987-6000; www.mosi.org; 4801 E Fowler Ave, University of South Florida; adult/child $21/19; ☼ 9am-5pm Mon-Fri, to 7pm Sat & Sun; ♿) is deservedly one of the biggest draws around, and it's definitely in contention for Florida's best hands-on science museum. With upwards of 450 'minds-on' activities, hyperactive kids will think they have walked into heaven. Look for traveling exhibits and a cool hot-air balloon exhibit, as well as ones on the human body and the amount of garbage the average North American generates annually. Enter a flight-avionics simulator or a Gulf Coast hurricane before taking the 1-mile trail within the on-site wetland preserve. Finish the day with an IMAX movie.

HENRY B PLANT MUSEUM

Railroad magnate Henry B Plant's Tampa Bay Hotel, which opened in 1891, was one of the most luxurious places imaginable in the early days of the city, when Tampa was about as remote as Miami. All 500 guestrooms had private bathrooms and electricity, and the extravagant hotel contained all the furniture, sculptures and mirrors Plant's wife had collected during their European and Oriental travels.

After the hotel failed in the early 20th century, the city of Tampa took over and today the National Historic Landmark is a **museum** (Map p408; ☎ 813-254-1891; www.plantmuseum.com; 401 W Kennedy Blvd; admission $4; ☼ 10am-4pm Tue-Sat, noon-4pm Sun) across the river from downtown on the University of Tampa campus. You can gawk at the luxury and tour the hotel's grand salon, guest room, solarium and lobby, among others. Even if you don't go in, admire the dramatic Moorish Revival architecture and silver minarets. The popular annual Victoria Christmas Stroll takes place from December 1 to 21, and it includes dramatizations of fairy tales by actors in period costume in different rooms of the hotel. Tickets for an adult/child cost $9/3.

ADVENTURE ISLAND

This 25-acre **water park** (off Map p408; ☎ 813-987-5600; www.adventureisland.com; 10001 McKinley Dr; adult/child $37/35, combination Busch Gardens & Adventure Island for 3 days $80/70, ☼ 10am-5pm Mon-Fri, 9:30am-6pm Sat & Sun in winter, 9am-7pm Mon-Fri, to 8pm Sat & Sun in summer; ♿), run by Anheuser-Busch, has 16 different areas, including Key West Rapids, on which rafters go down a six-story twist, ending in a 60ft-long pool. Other slide rides include the Aruba Tuba (some portions are in total darkness) and Rambling Bayou, where you go through weather 'effects' areas (some foggy, others have heavy rain). There's also a 9000-sq-ft swimming pool with waterfalls, diving platforms and tube slides. And don't forget the 76ft, free-fall body slide, Tampa Typhoon. Check online for discounts on both parks. Parking costs $5.

SOUTH TAMPA & HYDE PARK

Bayshore Blvd, the world's longest contiguous boardwalk, measuring a whopping 6.5 miles, is a great place to cycle, walk or run along the water. Visit during the early morning hours for fewer crowds, plus the early morning sunlight glosses the colorful mansions and mod metal sculptures with a special golden-pink hue. While you're in the area, drive or walk around **Old Hyde Park** (off Map p408; www.oldhyde park.com), a residential area with brick streets, gas lanterns and renovated Victorian-style architecture. It's the loveliest part of Tampa. Head up Rome, Dakota or Oregon Aves from Bayshore Blvd. You'll also find an upscale, outdoor retail and dining complex where these three roads intersect with Swann Ave. Keep an eye out for old-time fruit stands in South Tampa, too.

LOWRY PARK ZOO

This **zoo** (off Map p408; ☎ 813-935-8552; www.lowrypark zoo.com; 7530 North Blvd; adult/child/senior $19/14.50/18; ♿ 9:30am-5pm; 👶) has the great manatee encounter and aquatic center, and good exhibits on panthers, alligators, Komodo dragons, pandas, primates and bison. The Asian domain highlights a rare Indian rhinoceros, while families love the Wallaroo Station, an Australian-themed area with kangaroos and wallabies that kids can pet. They can also pet and feed stingrays elsewhere in the park. Before leaving, don't miss the 18,000-sq-ft, free-flight aviary. To reach the zoo from downtown, take the I-4 west to the I-275 north to exit 31; go west on Sligh Ave to North Blvd.

CHANNELSIDE

This huge entertainment **megaplex** (Map p408; ☎ 813-223-4250; www.channelside.com; Channelside Dr; ♿ 11am-7pm), directly on Ybor Channel, boasts a fun bar (Newk's Café with outdoor seating), an IMAX theater, a movie theater, lots of eateries, some clubs and open-air shops. You'll also find cruise ships pulling into the Port of Tampa here, as well as the Florida Aquarium (p410).

CHILDREN'S MUSEUM OF TAMPA

Located near Lowry Park Zoo and also known as **Kid City** (off Map p408; ☎ 813-935-8441; www.flachildrens museum.com; 7550 North Blvd; person over 2yr $5; ♿ 9am-2pm Mon, to 5pm Tue-Fri, 10am-5pm Sat, noon-5pm Sun; ♿), this place has interactive displays and a permanent, 45,000-sq-ft outdoor exhibition that kids love: child-size replicas of 13 buildings, each with activities. Care to try your hand as a judge in the courthouse or a reporter at a TV station?

DAVIS ISLAND

To glimpse another 'real' neighborhood in Tampa, head over to this little **village** (Map p408) straddling the roadside. Take Davis Island Blvd off Bayshore Blvd and then at the split, take E Davis Blvd. Grab a coffee and hang around or settle in with some chips and salsa at one of the sidewalk restaurants.

CONTEMPORARY ART MUSEUM

The University of South Florida's **museum** (CAM; off Map p408; ☎ 813-974-2849; www.usfcam.usf.edu; USF campus, 4202 E Fowler Ave; admission free; ♿ 10am-5pm

---

> **SPOOKY YBOR CITY**
>
> For something different from the usual vacation dinner-drinks-hotel routine, sign up for an evening **Ybor City Ghost Walk Tour** (Map p409; ☎ 813-241-8838; www.historic guides.com; 1805 E 7th Ave; tickets $10; ♿ 6pm Sat). Hosted by an actor in period costume telling tales of Ybor City's haunted past (it's not recommended for children under the age of seven), it provides exercise and entertainment. This way you won't feel bad about all those lemon-drop martinis you down at one of Ybor City's chic après dark lounges or the filet mignon you have for dinner at one of the neighborhood's storied restaurants. Reservations are highly recommended because tours can be cancelled for lack of interest.

Mon-Fri, 1-4pm Sat) mounts six to eight exhibitions by university students and alumni. Parking costs $3 Monday to Friday.

Festivals & Events

Florida State Fair (☎ 813-621-7821; www.florida statefair.com; Florida State Expo) For more than 100 years the fair, held in February, has rolled out the red carpet with rides, food and livestock.

Tampa Cigar Heritage Festival (☎ 813-247-1434) Pumped up with cultural presentations, ethnic food and music, this mid-November festival celebrates Ybor City's smoky history.

Victorian Christmas Stroll (☎ 813-258-7302; www .plantmuseum.com/events) Hosted by the Henry B Plant Museum, this event held in December harkens back to another time.

Sleeping

Tampa is not known for an abundance of interesting places to stay, but if you're just looking for a cheap bed, there are dozens of chains at every interstate exit in the area.

BUDGET & MIDRANGE

Gram's Place (Map p406; ☎ 813-221 0596; www.grams -inn-tampa.com; 3190 N Olna Ave; campsites $15; dm $23, r $25-70; ♿ 🖥) By far the coolest budget bet in Tampa, Gram's is a rocking hostel with great backpacker vibes (rare in this region), wi-fi, great music (the jukebox spins more than 400 CDs) and rooms themed by music genres. There's a BYO bar in the courtyard and a non-heated Jacuzzi to plunge into on stifling hot summer days. The airport shuttle will take you here for $12.

Paradise Lakes Resort (Map p406; ☎ 813-949-9327; www.paradiselakes.com; 2001 Brinson Rd, Land O' Lakes; r $75-150; P ☒) Want to walk around naked? Head to North America's largest 'clothing optional' resort, where you can get an all-over-tan. Its located 17 miles north of downtown Tampa on 80 secluded acres.

Tahitian Inn (off Map p408; ☎ 813-877-6721; www .tahitianinn.com; 601 S Dale Mabry Hwy, South Tampa; r $100-200; P ☐ ☒) Tired of chain motels? Try the very comfortable Tahitian, a landmark in South Tampa for over 50 years. It offers 79 rooms and suites on three floors, wi-fi, a full spa and a workout room. There is a Tiki theme throughout – check out the grass-roofed cabanas by the heated pool.

Don Vicente de Ybor Historic Inn (Map p409; ☎ 813-241-4545, 866-206-4545; www.donvicenteinn.com; 1915 Av República de Cuba; r from $139; P ☒) This charismatic 16-room boutique B&B was built in 1895 by the founder of Ybor City, and reeks of old-world elegance. Guest rooms feature canopy four-poster beds with fluffy down comforters and a smattering of antiques; the welcoming lobby boasts an impressive marble and gilt staircase. Breakfast is included.

Casita de la Verdad (Map p409; ☎ 813-654-6087; www.yborcityguesthouse.com; 1609 E 6th Ave; r $180-250; ♿) Right on the fringe of Ybor City, this place rents one lovingly restored 1908 cigarmaker's house with two colorful period bedrooms (check out the antique sleigh bed). The bathroom features an old claw-foot bathtub. This is a good place for a family, as it sleeps up to four people and has a full kitchen and BBQ grill at your disposal. The location, close to the party scene but not on top of it, is also a perk.

Also recommended:

Economy Inn Express (Map p408; ☎ 813-253-0851; 830 W Kennedy Blvd; r from $50; P) Located near the University of Tampa; good cheap chain choice.

Hilton Garden Inn (Map p409; ☎ 813-769-9267, 877-367-4458; www.hiltongardeninn.com; 1700 E 9th Ave; r from $100; ☐ ☒) Convenient and comfortable Hilton luxury in Ybor City. Wi-fi available.

TOP END

ourpick The Westin Tampa Harbour Island (Map p406; ☎ 813-229-5000; www.starwoodhotels.com; 725 S Harbour Island Blvd; r from $200; ☐ ☒ ♿ ♿) This Westin does a good job at convincing you not to leave the confines of its 177 acres – it's that relax-ing. Sitting on its own island in downtown Tampa it really is an urban oasis: stroll the private boardwalk to really appreciate your location. Rooms are supercomfortable, and come with bay views, pillow-top mattresses and soft white linens. The giant bathrooms were clearly designed with romance on the mind – check out the shower with duel showerheads. The waterfront Italian restaurant is popular and a good eating option. The Westin has wi-fi, is child-friendly and arranges babysitting. Parking costs $14 per day.

Eating

Ybor City has the largest concentration of restaurants in the Tampa Bay area, and is a good place to just walk around and browse for whatever you are craving. Also check out SoHo (South of Houstan Ave), a burgeoning dining area where new restaurants are opening everyday.

BUDGET

La Teresita (Map p406; ☎ 813-879-4909; 3246 W Columbus Ave; mains $5-7; ☉ 5am-midnight Mon-Thu, 24hr Fri & Sat, to 10pm Sun) Skip the restaurant and head for the horseshoe-shaped cafeteria counters to feast on stuffed plantains with yellow rice and black beans, plus Cuban bread and Cuban coffee. You'll be seated with locals from all walks of life, which only adds to this place's homey appeal.

Cephas (Map p409; ☎ 813-247-9022; 1701 E 4th Ave; mains $5-13; ☉ 11:30am-9pm Tue-Thu, to 3:30am Fri & Sat) This little eatery, a slice of Jamaica right in Ybor City, is run by Cephas Gilbert, who showed up in the US in 1982 with $37 in his pocket. Since then he's parlayed his small stake into a customer-friendly joint. Head here for huge plates of jerk chicken wings, curry goat or chicken and brown stew.

Bella's Italian Cafe (Map p406; ☎ 850-254-3355; 1413 S Tampa Ave; mains $7-20; ☉ lunch & dinner Mon-Fri, dinner Sat & Sun) Serving authentic Italian food to a loyal crowd of foodies, Bella's has been a Tampa institution for more than 20 years. It's not just the food that's soothing here, it's also the rustic ambience. Try one of the pizzas cooked in an oak-burning oven, or a delicious plate of thick, homemade spaghetti and your choice of freshly prepared sauce. Wash it down with the signature cocktail – the Bellarita – but beware, it's potent! This place stays open until 1:30am on Friday and Saturday nights.

MIDRANGE

Wine Exchange (off Map p408; ☎ 813-254-9463; 1611 W Swann Ave, Old Hyde Park; mains $10-25; ☺ lunch & dinner; ⓟ) When you care as much about pairing wine and food as you do enjoying them separately, this crowded Tampa Bay spot delivers the goods. Each component is heightened by the other. Order a sophisticated nightly specialty like encrusted salmon to take advantage. They also have good sandwiches and pizzas.

Columbia Restaurant (Map p409; ☎ 813-248-4961; 2117 E 7th Ave; lunch $9-22, dinner $15-22; ☺ lunch & dinner; ⓟ) Family-owned since it opened in 1920, gaudy and glitzy Columbia is a legitimate historical attraction. But don't write it off as a tourist trap – just go. The interior is gorgeous, with 13 dining rooms decorated lavishly with tiled scenes from *Don Quixote* and a central fountain. Salads and black-bean appetizers are excellent; paella à la Valenciana is a specialty; dinner is better than lunch. Consider catching the hot flamenco show (twice nightly except Sunday) for an extra $6. Or pop into the Cigar Bar for tapas and jazz (Thursday to Saturday).

ourpick Restaurant BT (Map p406; ☎ 813-258-1916; 1633 W Snow Ave; mains $16-24; ☺ lunch & dinner) Tampa's hottest restaurant is worth the hype. Serving gourmet French-Vietnamese fare in ultrachic environs, everything on the menu is fresh, delicious and authentic. If you like hot, you can't go wrong ordering hot pepper squid with chili paste and jasmine rice. Reservations are recommended – it's not unheard of for Floridians to drive five hours north from Miami just to try Chef Trina Nyugan-Batley's innovative creations.

Big City Tavern (Map p409; ☎ 813-247-3000; Centro Ybor, 1600 E 8th Ave, 2nd fl; mains $13-30; ☺ dinner) The Ybor City setting, complete with a spirited bar scene, couldn't be more dramatic: Big City Tavern is ensconced within an old ballroom with wrought-iron balconies and huge windows. As for the food, the high-falutin' creative cuisine is executed with just enough panache to get by.

Samurai Blue (Map p409; ☎ 813-242-6688; Centro Ybor, 1600 E 8th Ave; lunch $10-13, dinner $15-22; ☺ lunch & dinner Mon-Fri, dinner Sat & Sun) With cool architecture, Ybor City's Samurai Blue boasts a remarkable 30ft sushi bar, an unusual sake bar and an Asian fusion menu for the less adventurous.

Kojak's House of Ribs (off Map p408; ☎ 813-837-3774; 2808 W Gandy Blvd, South Tampa; mains $6-19; ☺ lunch & dinner Tue-Sun) One block west of Bayshore Blvd, this longtime South Tampa neighborhood favorite has outdoor porches and finger-lickin' ribs with all the sides. You'd never know you were in the city.

Four Green Fields (Map p408; ☎ 813-254-4444; 205 W Platt St; mains from $10; ☺ 11am-3am Mon-Sat, noon-3am Sun; ⓟ) This classic downtown restaurant looks like a traditional Irish cottage, and sure enough, it features traditional Irish cooking, thick brogues, Irish music, 30-weight Guinness, pints that pack a punch and friendly folk.

Mise en Place (Map p408; ☎ 813-254-5373; 442 W Kennedy Blvd; mains $16-27; ☺ dinner Tue-Sat; ⓟ) A longtime chef-owned SoHo bistro, Mise en Place is arguably Tampa's brightest culinary shooting star. The creative and seasonal menu, with Floribbean (blend of Caribbean and Floridian cuisines) twists, is decidedly eclectic and always a treat. Put on some trendy black and saunter over for mustard-and-pecan-crusted rack of lamb with a bourbon shallot demiglace.

TOP END

Bern's Steak House (Map p408; ☎ 813-251-2421; 1208 S Howard Ave; steaks $25-60; ☺ dinner; ⓟ) Tampa's landmark restaurant serves some of the best steaks east of the west, along with 26 types of caviar. Downstairs is heavy on the red velvet, gold leaf and statuary; upstairs, where patrons head for sweets in a cigar-friendly dessert room, the tables are made from redwood wine casks. Bern's wine list boasts more than 7000 labels and 1800 dessert wines, but the cellars stash upwards of a million bottles.

Drinking & Entertainment

For up-to-the-minute local events, check the **arts line** (☎ 813-229-2787; www.hillsboroughcounty .org/artscouncil) or cruise the web at www.ybor times.com. Or peruse the free *Weekly Planet* (www.weeklyplanet.com) on Wednesday; the Thursday pullout *Weekend* section of the *St Petersburg Times*; and on Friday the *Extra* section of the *Tampa Tribune*.

Gameworks (Map p409; ☎ 813-241-9675; 1600 E 8th Ave; ☺ 11am-11pm Sun-Wed, to midnight Thu, to 2am Fri & Sat) A high-tech play place with virtual-reality free-falling simulators and the like, Gameworks has plenty of decent eateries and bars to keep you entertained.

Seminole Hard Rock Hotel & Casino (Map p406; ☎ 813-621-1302, 800-282-7016; www.semtribe.com; 5223 N Orient Rd, East Tampa; ☺ 24hr; ⓟ) About 15 minutes from downtown Tampa off the I-4 (head east to Orient Rd and then head left), this casino sucks in those who love the thrill of winning big-time. But don't bet on it. Like a spider spinning a web with high-stakes bingo and stud poker, this place has it all and has designed on keeping it.

BARS & CLUBS

If the words 'party central' and 'bouncers' show up regularly in your conversations, Ybor City is your kind of place. Intense weekend crowds and partiers revel here into the wee hours. Show up early, get your hand stamped and come back later to push through the crowds like you're a celebrity. Since establishments come and go, check flyers on walls and lampposts – they're the most reliable source of up-to-date party, concert and nightclub information. Perhaps the easiest and best thing to do, though, is simply wander E 7th Ave, judge the crowds and music spilling out of each club, and head into the one that fits. Clubs tend to wear their clientele on their sleeves. Nightly drink specials and cover charges change more quickly than a leopard changes spots, so it's pointless to include them here (for the most part).

Adobe Gilas (Map p409; ☎ 813-241-8588; www .adobegilas.com; Centro Ybor, 1600 E 8th Ave; ☽ 11am-3am Mon-Sat, 1pm-3am Sun) The 2nd-floor balconies at this bar are a fabulous vantage point from which to take in the street scene below (and the bartenders also happen to mix fabulous margaritas). The Centro Ybor, where Adobe is located, is filled with plenty of other bars, should you tire of this one.

Tampa Bay Brewing Company (Map p409; ☎ 813-247-1422; 1812 N 15th St; ☽ 11:30am-midnight Mon & Tue, to 2am Wed-Sat) This fun brew-pub has a good selection of microbrews, $4 liters on Wednesday and weekday happy hours (4pm to 7pm).

717 South (off Map p408; ☎ 813-251-1616; 717 S Howard Ave; ☽ 11am-2am) Young professionals gather after work to mingle and sip martinis (there is a rainbow of flavors) in the posh lounge at one of Tampa's top spots to see and be seen. If you need something to eat after all the vodka, head to the restaurant dining room for imaginative takes on Italian classics served amid art-deco paintings, high ceilings and an open kitchen.

Hyde Park Café (off Map p408; ☎ 813-254-2233; www.thehydeparkcafe.com; 1806 W Platt St, Old Hyde Park; ☽ 8pm-3am Tue-Sat) This downtown late-night

indoor-outdoor café, pizza place (pizzas $9 to $15), and VIP club gets really packed on Tuesday nights with eclectic music. Patrons drop by on other nights to check out the DJ spinning tunes. Happy hour (with no cover) dominates from 8pm to 10pm, while silicone implants and South Beach slick attire pick up the slack after 10pm.

Green Iguana Bar & Grill (Map p409; ☎ 813-248-9555; www.greeniguana.net; 1708 E 7th Ave; ☽ 11am-2am) A cool, laid-back bar and restaurant by day (with Floribbean food, fish sandwiches and good burgers), by night the Green Iguana is actually two clubs in one. Head here for high-energy cover bands or DJ-driven dance music; $1 drinks on Wednesday.

Hub (Map p408; ☎ 813-229-1553; 719 N Franklin St; ☽ 10am-3am Mon-Sat, 1pm-3am Sun) This fun downtown hangout, complete with jukebox and cheap drinks, looks like a hole in the wall, but the bar gets packed on weekends with a Jack Daniels–and–Coke crowd. Be prepared to call a cab after ordering a few too many.

Metropolis (off Map p408; ☎ 813-871-2410; 3447 W Kennedy Blvd at Himes Ave, Central Tampa; ☽ noon-3am) This gay dance club with DJs draws more men than women (could that have anything to do with the strippers?), but girls are certainly welcome.

CINEMAS

Tampa Theatre (Map p408; ☎ 813-274-8286; www .tampatheatre.org; 711 N Franklin St; tickets $8.50; ☽ evenings & weekends) Built in 1926, this is an atmospheric theater, on the National Register of Historic Places, that screens independent and classic films and hosts concerts and other special events. Come early to hear the mighty Wurlitzer organ before every movie; it features sirens, boat horns, cymbals, sleigh bells and other wacky sounds. All the furniture (like old Broadway seats) in the 1446-seat theater is original, and, oh yes, the place is haunted by one Hank Fink, a projectionist here for 25 years who died in the late 1960s.

PERFORMING ARTS

Tampa Bay Performing Arts Center (Map p408; ☎ 813-229-7827, 800-955-1045; www.tbpac.org; 1010 MacInnes Pl; tickets $10-80) Beautifully sited on a riverside park, this is the largest performing-arts center south of the Kennedy Center in Washington, DC. It hosts major concerts, touring Broadway productions, plays, the Tampa Ballet and special events. The complex has five theaters:

Festival Hall (a 2500-seat venue where touring Broadway shows and headliners perform), Ferguson Hall (with 1000 seats), the Jaeb (a three-floor cabaret), the Teco (with 200 seats) and the 100-seat Shimberg Playhouse, a 'black box' venue for cutting-edge performances by local and national artists and groups. Free backstage guided tours are offered Wednesday and Saturday at 10am, by reservation.

UT Falk Theater (Map p408; ☎ 813-253-3333; www .ut.edu; 428 W Kennedy Blvd; tickets $10) This 900-seat theater is operated by the University of Tampa.

Florida Orchestra (Map p408; ☎ 813-286-2403, 800-662-7286; www.floridaorchestra.com; tickets $23-51) This 90-piece orchestra plays at the Performing Arts Center as well as venues in St Petersburg and Clearwater; look for free park concerts, too.

USF School of Music (off Map p408; ☎ 813-974-2311; www.usf.edu; USF campus, Fowler Ave; tickets $2-10; Sep-Mar; P) Also home to the USF Theater, this venue stages concerts and recitals open to the entire community. It's accessible from Fowler Ave exits on the I-275 and the I-75.

Sun Dome (off Map p408; ☎ 813-974-3111; www.sun dome.org; USF campus, 4202 E Fowler Ave; tickets $12-90) On the USF campus, the Sun Dome hosts rock, jazz, pop and other concerts – from Jimmy Buffet to Ludacris, from Luciano Pavarotti to the World Wrestling Federation (now there's some 'performing arts' for you!).

Improv Comedy Theater (Map p409; ☎ 813-864-4000; www.improvtampa.com; Centro Ybor, 1600 E 8th Ave; tickets $7-30; 6pm-1am Wed-Sun) In addition to hosting some national acts, this Improv joint mounts good doses of nightly comedic shtick.

SPORTS

The NFL's Tampa Bay Buccaneers play at **Raymond James Stadium** (off Map p408; ☎ 813-870-2700; www.buccaneers.com; 4201 N Dale Mabry Hwy; tickets from $30) from August (pre-season) to December, but you'll probably have to catch them on TV since season-ticket holders grab most stadium seats.

If you've never seen a US college football game, definitely don't miss the **Outback Bowl** (☎ 813-874-2695; www.outbackbowl.com; Raymond James Stadium; tickets $60), an NCAA (National College Athletic Association) football game on New Year's Day.

The **USF Bulls** (off Map p408; ☎ 813-974-2125, 800-462-8557; www.gousfbulls.com; USF campus, 4202 E Fowler

Ave; tickets from $10), a Division I-AA football team, play at Raymond James Stadium.

The New York Yankees play spring-training baseball games in March at **Legends Field** (off Map p408; ☎ 813-875-7753; www.legendsfieldtampa.com; 3802 ML King Jr Blvd at N Dale Mabry Hwy; tickets $13-19), the 10,000-seat stadium modeled after the 'House that Ruth Built' (ie Yankee Stadium in the Bronx, New York). The Yankees' minor-league team, the Tampa Yankees, plays at Legends Field from April to September (tickets $3 to $5).

The NHL's Tampa Bay Lightning play hockey at **St Pete's Times Forum** (Map p408; ☎ 813-301-6600; www.tampabaylightning.com; 401 Channelside Dr; tickets $8-99) from October to March. The forum also hosts basketball games, concerts and ice shows.

Shopping

Tampa has its share of malls, but the best street shopping is found in Ybor City, which is crammed with cool little places selling funky imports and retro shoes.

Penelope T (Map p406; ☎ 813-254-5740; 1413 S Howard Ave) For a new pair of fantastic jeans or the perfect little black dress, head to Tampa's favorite designer boutique for a little retail therapy in a shop designed for pampering. From Rebecca Taylor to Citizens of Humanity, Penelope T has all the midrange designers, along with quite a few lesser-known names (which come with lower price tags).

Big Top Flea Market (off Map p408; ☎ 813-986-4004; www.bigtopfleamarket.com; 9250 E Fowler Ave, Thonotosassa; 9am-4:30pm Sat & Sun; P) This market redefines 'bargain' with a capital 'B.' Forget retail when these 1000 enclosed and covered stalls can provide every essential and nonessential item ever produced. You gotta love it…or hate it.

Getting There & Around
AIR

The region's major airport, and the state's third-busiest airport, is **Tampa International Airport** (TPA; off Map p408; ☎ 813-870-8700; www.tampa airport.com; 5503 W Spruce St), about 13 miles west of downtown, off Hwy 589. It's an easy and pleasant airport to negotiate and there's free wi-fi should you have your laptop handy.

The No 30 Hillsborough Area Regional Transit (HART) bus picks up and drops off at the Red Arrival Desk on the lower level;

exact change is required. From the airport, buses make the 40-minute trip downtown (below) about every half hour from 5:30am to 8:30pm.

All major car agencies have desks at the airport. By car, take the I-275 to N Ashley Dr, turn right and you're in downtown. These days its always cheaper to book a car rental in advance online. At the time of research weekly economy rentals were going for about $15 per day through consolidators like www.priceline.com.

BUS
Tampa's **Greyhound bus station** (Map p408; ☎ 813-229-2112, 800-231-2222; www.greyhound.com; 610 Polk St) serves the region. The trip from Tampa to Miami takes seven to nine hours (one-way/round-trip $50/85); to Orlando, two to three hours ($31/48); to Sarasota, two hours ($23/34); and to Gainesville, three to 3½ hours ($36/58).

The **Uptown-Downtown Connector** (☎ 813-254-4278; www.hartline.org) is free and runs up and down Florida Ave, Tampa St and Franklin St every 15 minutes from 6:30am to 6:30pm Monday to Friday.

HART (Map p408; ☎ 813-254-4278; www.hartline.org; 1211 N Marion St) buses converge at the Marion Transit Center on Morgan St. Buses cost $1.30 one-way, $3 for an all-day pass. Check out these popular destinations by bus (all leave from the main terminal):

Destination	Bus	Departs
Ybor City	8, 46	30min
Busch Gardens & USF	5, 6	30min
Lowry Park Zoo	44, 45	30min
Henry Plant Museum	30	30min
Museum of Science & Industry	6 to University Transit Center*	30min

*Note there are two routes on bus 6, so check the destination.

CAR & MOTORCYCLE
To reach Tampa from Orlando, take the I-4 west. The fastest route to Miami is via the I-75 south which heads to Naples then due east to Fort Lauderdale where it connects to the I-95 south. Once you get to Naples, though, the more scenic route is via US 41 (Tamiami Trail) south to Everglades City and due east to Calle Ocho in Miami.

TRAIN
Amtrak (Map p408; ☎ 813-221-7600, 800-872-7245; www.amtrak.com; 601 Nebraska Ave) operates several daily shuttles between Tampa and Orlando.

TROLLEY
Old-fashioned, electric **TECO Line Street Cars** (☎ 813-254-4278; www.hartline.org; tickets $1.25; ⏰ 11am-10pm Mon-Thu, to 2am Fri, 9am-2am Sat, noon-8pm Sun) tootle around Ybor City from downtown and Channelside on a 2.3-mile route.

HILLSBOROUGH RIVER STATE PARK
Sick of the beach? Head to the woods. Just 12 miles north of Tampa, yet worlds away, this 3400-acre **state park** (☎ 813-987-6771; www.floridastateparks.org/hillsboroughriver; 15402 N US 301; per car $4; ⏰ 8am-sunset) is a favorite outdoor weekend escape for Tampa locals.

The park is home to 8 miles of hiking trails and a giant half-acre **swimming pool** (per person $2, campers free; ⏰ 10am-5pm Fri-Sun May-Sep, 10am-5pm Oct-Apr), but the most fun thing to do is get in a canoe. The river's current is not challenging and paddling allows ample opportunities for wildlife-viewing. The best time to canoe is early morning or around dusk, when the heat is less oppressive and the opportunity to spot animals is highest. Keep your eyes peeled for bobcats, white-tailed deer, opossums, raccoons, gray foxes, red-tailed hawks, ospreys, armadillos, water birds and alligators.

Canoe Escapes! (☎ 813-986-2067; www.canoeescape.com; 9335 E Fowler Ave; self-guided trips per person $22.50-32.50; ⏰ 9am-5pm), near the Hillsborough River in Thonotosassa, a half-mile east of the I-75, is the area's largest outfitter. Choose from one of six self-guided routes. Besides the canoe, these trips include transport to and from the river, and paddling instructions (if necessary). Boats can fit up to four people, and the company markets its trips to wildlife-watchers and families – this is not a party paddle. If you'd rather go with a guide, who will teach you about the ecosystem and help you spot wildlife, there are two guided trips per day (from $50).

Many people like to spend the night in this state park, and the 112 tent **campsites** ($20) are inexpensive and peaceful. Rates include the use of the pool, and each site has a fire ring, picnic table and a water source; there are also hot showers.

TASTING THE SERENGETI IN SOUTHWEST FLORIDA: VISITING BUSCH GARDENS

In a state known for its theme parks, **Busch Gardens** (☎ 813-987-5082, 866-353-8622; www.busch gardens.com; 10000 McKinley Dr; adult/child $65/55; ☺ 9:30am-7pm) stands out as a magical attraction; thrill-ing adults and children both with a taste of Africa and some of Florida's best roller coasters.

Orientation & Information

Busch Gardens is about 7 miles north of downtown Tampa and accessible from both the I-75 and I-275, both of which have Busch Blvd exits. Follow the signs – parking costs around $10.

The **Visitor Information Center** (☎ 813-985-3601; 3601 E Busch Blvd; ☺ 10am-5:30pm Mon-Sat, to 2pm Sun) across from the park sells discounted tickets. Also check the park's website for discounts of about $10.

Sights & Activities

From Timbuktu to Nairobi, the nine African regions featured in this park each have their own attractions.

Egypt The star of Egypt, Montu, is the southeast USA's largest inverted steel roller coaster. The three-minute killer ride features a 104ft vertical inverse loop. The coaster reaches speeds of 60mph, and the G-force hits a maximum of 3.85 – talk about speed!

Serengeti Plain The most authentic area at Busch Gardens, this 80-acre habitat is populated by about 500 animals. It can only be appreciated on the Serengeti Safari Tour (per person $30), which almost feels like you are on safari in Tanzania – look for zebras, giraffes, kudus, hippos, camels and even lions, all at close range.

Edge of Africa You can get nose-to-nose with lions, hyenas, ostriches, zebras, hippos and giraffes via a plate of glass separating the visitor from the animal habitat. Inquire about wildlife tours led by park zoologists.

Myombe Reserve The 3-acre reserve resembles the western lowlands of Africa, complete with gorillas, chimps, waterfalls and piped-in tropical fog. The Rhino Rally is the highlight here – you are a passenger in a 4WD-safari-vehicle race across 'the plains.'

Nairobi Nairobi is home to the Animal Nursery, a petting zoo and the kid-favorite Nocturnal Mountain, where nocturnal creatures are exposed (so to speak).

Reach Hillsborough River State Park from downtown Tampa via Fowler Ave east to US 301; head north for 9 miles.

ST PETERSBURG

☎ 727 / pop 248,100

Tampa's naughty little sister likes to party with a capital P. When it comes to night-life of all sorts, St Petersburg takes the cake. Not only does the town claim the dubi-ous honor of more all-nude strip clubs per capita than any other city in the US, it is also filled with hundreds of cool bars of the non-naked variety.

Downtown St Petersburg (not to be con-fused with St Pete Beach, which is the, well, beach, about 20 minutes drive west) is in the midst of a revival, but the city is still a bit edgy – be careful where you walk, there's no reason to go more than a block or two south of Central Ave. Crime is real here and you should stay in touristy areas to avoid problems.

Once you deal with this, however, you'll find St Petersburg is a sunny, spirited city, with a great historic downtown on the waterfront and a laid-back attitude – it's easily navigable and has a distinct small-town feel. From the lovely waterfront park, to the shops, galleries, bars and sidewalk bistros on Central Ave, St Petersburg is a happening place. Its rich arts scene buzzes under the weight of its offerings: the Salvador Dalí Museum holds the largest collection of the artist's works in the world; the St Petersburg Fine Arts Museum has one of Florida's finest collections and the Florida International Museum's blockbuster rotating exhibitions have brought national attention.

Orientation

St Petersburg is a typically sprawling Florida town. Downtown is about 10 miles northeast of St Pete Beach and about 20 miles southwest of Tampa across the bay. In the best of traffic, it's a good 25 minutes to the beach.

Timbuktu This area draws 'em in with the Scorpion – a 50mph ride with a 360-degree loop and 62ft drop. There are also kiddie rides, a video-game arcade and haunted lighthouse.

Congo Everyone goes to the Congo, one of the most popular areas in the park, to ride the formidable Kumba, one of the best roller coasters anywhere. It features a diving loop that plunges from 110ft, a camelback loop (spiraling 360 degrees and creating three seconds of weightlessness) and a 108ft vertical loop. The other roller-coaster ride here is the relatively tame (ha!) Python, a double-spiral corkscrew that hits speeds of 50mph.

Stanleyville Prepare to get wet. This African village features the Tanganyika Tidal Wave – a boat ride plunging over a 55ft waterfall, and Stanley Falls, a log-flume ride with a 40ft drop (height restriction 46in or with a guardian). The real attraction, though, is SheiKra, North America's first dive coaster. After a first fall that's almost 90-degrees straight down, the three-minute ride then plunges and rolls, mimicking the actions of an African Hawk.

Bird Gardens & Land of the Dragons Busch Gardens actually originated at the ever-so-humble Bird Gardens, which was merely a minor detour from the main action at the Anheuser-Busch Brewery tour: you'd guzzle some free beer and walk outside to see the birds. These days its home to Gwazi, a double, wooden roller coaster (the largest in southeast USA). You'll also want to check out the interactive Land of the Dragons, an enchanted forest with colorful dragons and kids' rides.

Sleeping & Eating

Busch Gardens is surrounded on all four sides by chain motels of every stripe and color. Check out the **Best Western All Suites** (☎ 813-971-8930, 800-786-7446; www.thatparrotplace.com; 3001 University Center Dr; r summer/winter $109/119; 🖳 🖳) for comfortable suites, perfect for the family. Each has two TVs, a refrigerator, a microwave, VCR, bedroom and living room. Breakfast is an all-you-can-eat hot buffet.

There are dozens of eating options in the park. Check out the casual **Crown Colony Restaurant** (mains $8 to $20) for North American fare with Serengeti views. Hit the family-friendly (there's a good kids menu) **Zagora Café** (mains from $5) for hot breakfast. Or visit the **Zambia Smokehouse** (mains $8 to $20) to eat yummy barbecue to soundtrack of screams from the thrill-seekers riding the US' first dive roller coaster located just out front.

The city is oriented on the ever-familiar grid: avenues run east–west and streets and boulevards run north–south. The north–south dividing line is Central Ave, and 34th St (US 19) is the east–west divider, though people usually ignore the east–west designation. The directional indicator is placed after the street. Avenues count upward away from Central Ave, so 1st Ave N is one block north of Central, and 1st Ave S is one block south.

Central Ave is the main street through downtown, and more or less the dividing line between safe and unsafe neighborhoods – the south side of town can be pretty rough. Most of the bars, hotels, restaurants and shops are on Central Ave between 16th St to the west and Bayshore Drive to the east. As a visitor, there's really no need to wander further south than 4th Ave S.

The best bargain for parking is at the Pier ($3 daily).

Information

BOOKSTORES

Haslam's Book Store (☎ 727-822-8616; 2025 Central Ave; ☑ 10am-6:30pm Mon-Sat) This incredible bookstore could be designated an attraction without raising any eyebrows. Founded in 1933, the shop needs half a block to house its 300,000 titles. It has a good Florida section, new and remaindered books and a core of used books.

Lighthouse Books (☎ 727-822-3278; 1735 1st Ave N; ☑ 10am-5pm Tue-Sat) This shop has good Florida and Caribbean sections; it also offers rare books, maps and prints.

LIBRARIES

Mirror Lake Library (☎ 727-893-7268; cnr 5th St & 2nd Ave N; ☑ 9am-6pm Mon-Sat) Free internet access.

MEDIA

St Petersburg Times (www.sptimes.com) Has a useful website.

Watermark (www.watermarkonline.com) Biweekly paper with up-to-date coverage of gay, lesbian and bisexual matters.

ST PETERSBURG

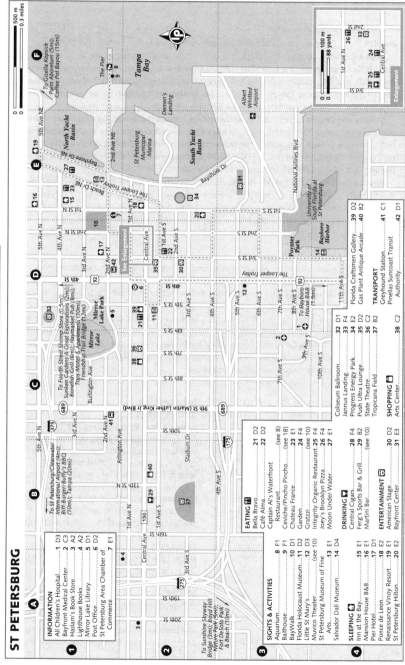

MEDICAL SERVICES

All Children's Hospital (☎ 727-898-7451; 6th St S, btwn 8th & 9th Aves; ⊕ 24hr) For medical emergencies, this is the area's largest hospital.

Bayfront Medical Center (☎ 727-823-1234; 701 6th St S; ⊕ 24hr)

POST

Post office (☎ 727-896-3901; 76 4th St N; ⊕ 8:30am-5pm Mon-Fri). This Mediterranean Revival building was the nation's first open-air post office, and it's a glorious thing, with a keystone-arched open front. It contains an itty-bitty display case in the rear with postal paraphernalia such as stamps, inkwells and a numbering device. Mailing letters has never been so educational.

TOURIST INFORMATION

Line of Tampa Bay (☎ 727-586-4297) This gay hotline has information on bars, restaurants and community events if you're willing to keep pressing keys on your Touch-Tone phone.

St Petersburg Area Chamber of Commerce (☎ 727-821-4715; www.stpete.com; 100 2nd Ave N; ⊕ 9am-5pm Mon-Fri, sporadic hr Sat & Sun) Head here for brochures, pamphlets and maps. The chamber produces a good downtown arts guide, a scenic driving guide and a general map with pullouts of different neighborhoods. They also have an information booth at the Pier (p422).

St Petersburg/Clearwater Area Convention & Visitors Bureau (☎ 727-464-7200, 877-352-3224; www.floridasbeach.com; 13805 58th St; ⊕ 8am-5pm Mon-Fri) Contact this office in advance for information since their location adjacent to the airport is inconvenient for drop-ins.

Sights & Activities

St Petersburg is more of a sight-centered city – other than watching sports, there aren't too may activities to participate in. However, just strolling down Central Ave, window shopping, then wandering over to the airport-control-meets-1980s-modern-art-styled pier for sunset counts as a little exercise, right? Especially if you walk all 16 blocks from 16th Street to the waterfront (Bayshore Dr).

SALVADOR DALÍ MUSEUM

Florida is surreal in so many ways, but this place – one of St Petersburg's top two attractions – takes the cake. Boasting the largest collection of Dalí's work outside Spain, the **Salvador Dalí Museum** (☎ 727-823-3767; www.salvadordalimuseum.org; 1000 3rd St S; adult/student/senior $15/10/13.50, half price after 5pm Thu; ⊕ 9:30am-5:30pm Mon-Wed, Fri & Sat, to 8pm Thu, noon-5:30pm Sun) is, quite simply, a must-see attraction. Although Dalí

was best known for his surrealist work, this $125-million collection covers his entire range: from early impressionism, cubism, still lifes and landscapes (1914–27), through his transitional period (1928), onto surrealism (1929-40) and back to classical works (1943–89)…not to mention the collection of masterworks include 18 major oil paintings produced between 1948 and 1970.

How the heck did all these paintings end up in little old St Petersburg? It's quite simple, actually. Industrialist A Reynolds Morse began collecting Dalí in the 1940s and when he was searching for a location that would be suitable, the town had the common sense to woo him.

ST PETERSBURG MUSEUM OF FINE ARTS

Recently renovated and doubled in size, this is one of Florida's best all-over **museums** (☎ 727-896-2667; www.fine-arts.org; 255 Beach Dr NE; adult/senior $12/6/10; ⊕ 10am-5pm Tue-Sat, 1-5pm Sun). Right on the waterfront, it has an enormous permanent collection that constitutes a very diverse and well-rounded history of art. Look for Asian, Indian and African art, pre-Columbian sculpture, photographic works, Cycladic sculpture from the 3rd century BC and North American and European paintings and sculpture.

FLORIDA HOLOCAUST MUSEUM

This **memorial** (☎ 727-820-0100; www.flholocaustmuseum.org; 55 5th St S; adult/child $12/6; ⊕ 10am-5pm Mon-Fri, noon-5pm Sat & Sun), one of the country's largest, is worth a visit not just for its Holocaust exhibits but also for those of Jewish life around the world. It also exhibits one of the three boxcars located in the USA used to transport prisoners to death camps in Poland. Visit the quiet meditation court before leaving and vow to make the museum's mission your own: promote tolerance today.

COFFEE POT BAYOU

This old northeast neighborhood, the heart of which is east of 4th St and between 19th and 30th Aves NE (but it's also very sweet around 9th Ave NE), was developed in the 1920s and is lined with brick streets and authentic period architecture. A 30-minute drive will reward you with an insider's view of St Petersburg beyond the museums and marinas. While you're in the area, drive over the Venetian-style Snell Isle Bridge (at Coffee Pot Blvd and 21st Ave NE) to appreciate some Mediterranean-style architecture. To reach the Coffee Pot Bayou, follow the waterfront north of downtown; take Bayshore Dr to North Shore Dr to Coffee Pot Blvd.

BOYD HILL NATURE PARK

A great 245-acre park, **Boyd Hill** (☎ 727-893-7326; www.stpete.org; 1101 Country Club Way S; adult/child $2/1; ☺ 9am-8pm Tue-Thu, to 6pm Fri & Sat, 11am-6pm Sun) is an oasis hidden in the midst of an urban area. Partly on the shores of Lake Maggiore, this natural butterfly habitat has about 3½ miles of nature trails and boardwalks that traverse scrubland, pine flatwoods, swamp woodlands and coastal willows. On Willow Marsh Trail you'll likely hear young alligators squeaking and see bald eagles, snowy egrets, box turtles and opossums among the oaks, cypresses and ferns. The friendly rangers here offer lots of good walks (check at the entrance when you arrive). Daily tram tours depart at 1pm; on Saturday there's an extra tour at 10am. There's a picnic area, playground and paths for bicycles.

From downtown take the I-275 south to exit 17, turn east onto 54th Ave S to Martin Luther King Jr Blvd S, then north to the first traffic light (Country Club Way S) and turn left (west).

THE PIER

Walk straight into the Gulf of Mexico, or so it feels when standing on the fishing platform at the edge of this old **railroad pier** (☎ 727-821-6164; www.stpetepier.com; 800 2nd Ave NE; ☺ 10am-9pm Mon-Thu, to 10pm Fri & Sat, 11am-9pm Sun) on the eastern edge of town. At the end of the long paved

---

INSIDER SCOOP: PEE (LEGALLY) ON A HISTORIC LANDMARK

At the very start of the pier – just after crossing Bayshore Drive – is **Little St Mary's** (515 4th St S; ☺ 9am-5pm), the coolest public toilet in the region, and probably the only toilet in all of Florida that is also a historic landmark. So how did this happen? Well the story begins with Henry Taylor, who was never paid for his design work at St Mary's Church. Out of spite he then built this Romanesque-revival miniature church and dubbed it Little St Mary's. The joke? When people showed up, they were greeted with a public toilet!

---

boardwalk is the pier's star attraction: a crazy looking, bright and blocky inverted pyramid structure that houses a five-story shopping mall, complete with three restaurants (which allow you to eat your seafood directly over the sea) and even a small **aquarium** (Mon-Sat adult/child $2/free, Sun free; ☺ 11am-7:30pm Mon-Sat, noon-6pm Sun). Walk to the fishing platform at the very edge of the pier around sunset for a fabulous natural-light show. A shuttle runs between the parking lots and the action. Parking costs $3.

You can feed resident pelicans (which are standing around waiting for you) with fish food from the **baithouse** (☎ 727-821-3750; 10 fish $5; ☺ 11am-7:30pm Mon-Sat, noon-6pm Sun). Or you can rent a fishing rod for $10 daily, which includes bait.

GREAT EXPLORATIONS

The term 'hands-on' reaches new heights at this fun **science museum** (☎ 727-821-8992; www.great explorations.org; 1925 4th Ave N; admission $4; ☺ 10am-8pm Mon-Sat, 11am-5pm Sun; ♿), adjacent to the Sunken Gardens. Kids get fired up with interactive computer games, chair pulleys, a harp made with lasers instead of strings and a tot area designed like a ship.

BAYWALK

The downtown revitalization continues with **BayWalk** (☎ 727-895-9277; www.baywalkstpete.com), an upscale shopping mall, bounded by 2nd and 3rd Aves N and 1st and 2nd Sts. The open-air emporium is pretty much just a mall, with lots of shops, eateries and a 20-screen theater. At night, however, it becomes one of Tampa's favorite restaurant and party zones, when loads of bars compete for your attention with various drink specials.

GIZELLA KOPSICK PALM ARBORETUM

This 2-acre **arboretum** (☎ 727-893-7335; www.stpete .org; cnr N Shore Dr & 10th Ave NE; admission free; ☺ sunrise-sunset) contains upwards of 300 different exotic and rare palms and cycads representing about 75 worldwide species. Follow the brick walkways to inspect the wildly diverse jelly palm, windmill palm and triangle palm, but don't overlook the garden-variety gru gru palm.

BIKING

The **Friendship Trail Bridge** (☎ 727-549-6099; 12020 Walsingham Rd; ☺ 7am-8pm), aka the old Gandy Bridge and US 92, is basically a 2.6-mile bik-

---

BIKING THE RAILS: THE PINELLAS TRAIL

This 47-mile paved bicycle trail, built on the abandoned CSX railway bed, runs from St Petersburg to Tarpon Springs. One of the top (and longest) urban trails in the country, it's one smooth ride – so much so that it caters to in-line and roller skaters almost as much as bikes.

There are lots of stops along the way, with cafés, pubs, bike shops, skate shops and fast-food places. As it's on the route of the old railway, the corridor cuts through widely varied terrain: sometimes you're in the middle of a town (Dunedin), sometimes along waterways, sometimes among orange groves (near Pinellas Park) and sometimes you're riding practically through people's backyards.

Head north over the causeway, and ride north on Fort Harrison Ave and east on Jones St for about three blocks. You'll pick up the southern end of the Clearwater to Tarpon Springs section of the path. It's 13.2 miles from Jones St to Tarpon Ave.

Contact the **Pinellas County Planning Department** (☎ 727-464-4751; www.co.pinellas.fl.us/mpo; 600 Cleveland St, Pinellas; ☺ 8am-5pm Mon-Fri) for their free guidebook listing rest stops and local attractions; it also has a mileage chart.

---

ing, walking and in-line skating path that runs alongside the Gandy Bridge, which connects St Petersburg and Tampa. Look for the trailhead on 34th St S near 8th Ave.

Festivals & Events

There is always something going on in St Petersburg.

International Folk Fair (Times Bayfront Arena) A three-day fair showcasing different cultures through traditional foods, crafts and folk dancing; in March.

Crawfish Festival (www.cajunconnection.org; Times Bayfront Arena) For a southern taste, check out this festival that features Cajun and Zydecko music and dancing; in March.

American Stage in the Park (☎ 727-822-8814; www.americanstage.org; tickets $5-25) A Shakespeare festival is mounted at 8pm Wednesday to Sunday from mid-April to mid-May.

Tampa Bay Blues Festival (www.tampabaybluesfest.com; Vinoy Park) Attracts blues fans from all around the country; in May.

Sleeping

The St Petersburg area has a higher concentration of B&Bs than most other towns in southwest Florida. Contact their local **Association of Bed & Breakfast Inns** (www.spaabbi.com).

BUDGET

Cheap motels of varying quality line 4th St N (which runs right into downtown) and 34th St N (which is just west of the I-275).

Tops Motel & Apartments (☎ 727-526-9071; 7141 4th St N, Gateway; r from $50; P ♿) Of the cheap motels on 4th St N, this place is the best of the bunch. It's in a safe neighborhood and has 18 clean rooms and apartments of varying size.

Fort DeSoto Park Campground (☎ 727-582-2267; www.pinellascounty.org/park; 3500 Pinellas Bayway S; tent/RV sites $34/40; P) Many of these prime 235 shaded tent and RV sites are waterside. There are two fishing piers – one over Tampa Bay, the other over the gulf – so you can catch your dinner. Should you not have luck, grab a cheeseburger from the snack shop with fabulous Gulf of Mexico views. Reserve in advance.

MIDRANGE & TOP END

`our pick` **Ponce de Leon** (☎ 727-550-9300; www.poncedeleonhotel.com; 95 Central Ave; r from $99; P ✗) The first structure to reach more than three stories in St Petersburg, this 1922 hotel is a boutique gem right in the heart of downtown. Rooms are big, and several have water views. All are eclectic and rather funky with new beds, fine European linens and soft white duvet coverlets. Walls are done in soothing mod colors and flat screen TVs come standard. The hardwood floors are a bonus, as are the cool blue sinks in some of the baths. We loved Room 217 – it's big, airy, bright and best of all, has a really cool Jacuzzi shower with tons of water-pressure settings and pulses to fool around with. Wi-fi is available.

Dickens House (☎ 727-822-8622; www.dickenshouse.com; 335 8th Ave NE, Coffee Pot Bayou; r $109-200; ✗ ▯) This lovely (and lovingly restored) arts-and-crafts-style bungalow in the historic Coffee Pot Bayou is just two blocks from the bay and within walking distance of downtown. Its five guest rooms are romantic charmers, complete with high-threadcount Egyptian cotton linens and baths with whirlpool tubs.

Eat breakfast on the porch. Rates vary dramatically based on season – check online. Wi-fi is available.

Pier Hotel (☎ 727-822-7500; www.thepierhotel.com; 253 2nd Ave N; r from $120; ✗ 🖳) Built in 1921, but renovated in 2001, this cotton-candy-colored (inside and out) hotel is a throw-back to old-world Europe, with claw-foot bathtubs, period woodwork and atmospheric public rooms with graceful archways and a lovely veranda. A breakfast buffet and free afternoon cocktails are included. It's a good deal.

Mansion House B&B (☎ 727-821-9391, 800-274-7520; www.mansionbandb.com; 105 5th Ave N; r from $135; ✗ 🅿 🖳 🕿) With a tranquil pool and courtyard garden, this B&B has 12 rooms and a suite in two wonderful old houses. You can expect antique and hand-painted furniture, wooden floors and nice bedding. Other features include gracious hosts, complimentary evening wine, full breakfast, heated pool and a great location. Check online for an array of discounts and theme packages.

Inn at the Bay (☎ 727-822-1700, 888-873-2122; www.innatthebay.com; 126 4th Ave N; r & ste $155-300; 🅿 ✗ 🖳) Painted a gorgeous pale yellow with green trim, this fabulous 1910 inn features 12 romantic guest rooms carved from an old neighborhood house. Perks include a full breakfast, four-poster feather beds, data ports and robes. Most bathrooms have two-person whirlpool tubs. The honeymoon suite is sweet. Stay a few nights to grab a generous discount.

Renaissance Vinoy Resort (☎ 727-894-1000, 800-468-3571; www.renaissancehotels.com; 501 5th Ave NE; r from $250; 🅿 ✗ 🖳 🕿) Stay here for in-your-face posh. Large, pink and flashy, the Vinoy is the grand dame of St Petersburg's hotels. Sitting in a prime bayside locale, it was built in 1925 and has hosted celebrities and politicians for its whole tenure. The National Historic Landmark boasts 360 richly furnished guest rooms, a day spa, huge fitness center, excellent golf and tennis facilities, and opulent dining and entertainment areas. Many rooms have bay views; rooms in the older section have standing-room-only balconies. Check online for deals.

Also recommended:

St Petersburg Hilton (☎ 727-894-5000, 800-774-1500; www.stpetehilton.com; 333 1st St S; r $99-165; 🖳 🕿) More than 300 rooms in a fine downtown location; plus restaurants, bars and a pool and fitness center. Good value.

Eating

BUDGET

Biff-Burger/Buffy's BBQ (☎ 727-527-5297; 3939 49th St N; mains $3-8; 🕓 breakfast, lunch & dinner; 🅿 🕿) The last remaining Biff-Burger (once a national burger chain) is a St Petersburg institution. It's no longer a fast-food drive-in, but instead a sit-down restaurant kitted out with the longest bar in town, two patios and 20 big-screen TVs tuned to sports. Come for eggs, pancakes and every other conceivable breakfast entrée in the morning, or stop by for live entertainment and a greasy cheeseburger or traditional Southern BBQ at night. Biff's attracts a biker crowd, especially on Saturday nights, and is proud to say so.

Joey's Brooklyn Pizza Place (☎ 727-822-6757; 210 1st Ave N; mains from $7; 🕓 11am-10pm Sun-Thu, 11am-3am Fri & Sat; 🕿) Big Apple transplants swear by the pizza at this small downtown restaurant – yep Joey's knows how to make New York–style pies just right. Dine alfresco under the date-palm trees or grab a take-away pizza to feast on in your hotel room. Joey's caters to the late-night crowd on weekends. Calzones, pasta and salads are also offered.

MIDRANGE & TOP END

our pick Ceviche\Pincho Pincho (☎ 727-209-2302; 95 Central Ave; lunch small plates $4-10, dinner small plates $7-15; 🕓 11am-2pm & 5pm-2am Tue-Sat) At one point it was the local morgue, but there's nothing dead about St Petersburg's most talked about restaurant today. Connected to the Ponce de Leon hotel, the dinner menu consists of more than 100 tapas (small plates), hailing mostly from Northern Spain and Catalan, in a romantic restaurant with a cavernous downstairs Flamenco bar. Lunch is served in Pincho Pincho, on the other side of the hotel. It's an intimate little wooden café barely big enough for its bar and a half-dozen tables. There's less choices than dinner, but the food is cheaper and equally good. The espresso drinks were some of the best we tasted in this part of Florida.

Moon Under Water (☎ 727-896-6160; 332 Beach Dr NE; mains $8-20; 🕓 lunch & dinner) Overlooking the park and bay (with a few outdoor tables), this British-style pub eschews tepid home-country fare for fiery dishes from India. Curry dishes beat anything you find in London. They also make a good burger and cheese steak and mix a good cocktail.

Captain Al's Waterfront Restaurant (☎ 727-898-5800; 800 2nd Ave NE; mains $8-20; 🕓 lunch & dinner)

Locals take their guests here to show off their city. Out at the end of the pier, it allows you to eat surrounded by water. Although the food is just average fried seafood and fish (although the crab appetizer is quite good), it is really enhanced by the killer views from outdoor tables. At least go for late afternoon cocktails.

Garden (☎ 727-896-3800; 217 Central Ave; lunch $5-10, dinner $12-22; ⏲ lunch & dinner, martini bar 9pm-2am Wed-Sat) The oldest restaurant in town hosts live jazz and makes a good salad Niçoise at lunchtime. Mediterranean-influenced dinner dishes might include grilled lamb chops or wild mushroom pasta. Or just sample a few dishes from the tapas menu. The Garden has indoor and outdoor seating, poetry readings, a martini bar and live jazz with the Buster Cooper Jazz Trio every Friday and Saturday from 9pm to 1:30am. On Salsa Nights (Thursdays), they dole out free dancing tips.

Bella Bravo (☎ 727-895-5515; 515 Central Ave; mains $10-27; ⏲ lunch & dinner Mon-Sat) Authentic northern Italian cooking, a 1000-bottle wine list and lots of atmosphere in a building, whose frontage sports bright-orange-and-yellow checkered tiles, all combine to make Bella Bravo a top Tampa eating experience. Whether you're indulging in thin-crust Roman pizza on the downstairs patio or house-made potato gnocchi on the upstairs balcony, you can bet that your nouveau Italian meal here will be delicious.

Café Alma (☎ 727-502-5002; 260 1st Ave S; mains $7-28; ⏲ 11am-10pm Mon-Wed, to midnight Thu & Fri, 10:30am-midnight Sat) This classy subterranean café gets high praise for its Parisian ambience and delicious food. The international menu includes creative sandwiches and salads, along with small plates and a few mains. After dinner the lights go down and the buzz goes up. Café Alma is a favorite late-night bar with the artsy and cultured crowd. DJs spin on weekends.

Gratzzi (☎ 727-822-7769; 199 2nd Ave N, BayWalk; lunch $7-12, dinner $11-29; ⏲ lunch Mon-Sat, dinner nightly) Within the BayWalk complex, locals consistently recommend this restaurant for stellar northern-Italian cooking. Slurp some fish soup, a deserving house specialty, or stick to the classics like osso buco.

Chateau France (☎ 727-894-7163; www.chateau francecuisine.com; 136 4th Ave N; mains $22-38; ⏲ dinner) French classics are paired with romance at Chef Antoine Louro's acclaimed restaurant in an early-20th-century Victorian house.

Everything is good, but the bouillabaisse, coq au vin, pâtés and filet mignon are superior. Save room for the decadent chocolate soufflé or bananas flambé. The wine list is exemplary.

Drinking

St Petersburg is party central these days, and if you're looking for a good night out, this is the place to do it. The vibe is lively and young, and the city is filled with tapas lounges, cigar bars, intimate clubs and lots of good old fashioned watering holes. A number of St Petersburg restaurants double as very popular bars come dark. **Café Alma**, **Garden** and **Ceviche** (listed on opposite) are three such places.

Central Cigars (☎ 727-898-2442; 273 Central Ave; ⏲ 10am-10pm Mon-Thu, to midnight Fri & Sat, noon-5pm Sun) In addition to an enormous selection of stogies and a full line of humidors and accessories, Central has a cigar bar (no cigarettes allowed) where you can sink into an overstuffed leather chair, sample some smokes, sip port and catch up on all your cigar-related reading.

Martini Bar (☎ 727-895-8558; 131 2nd Ave N, BayWalk; ⏲ 4pm-2am Tue-Sun) Step into your coolest black threads, slip on a sexy demeanor and head over to sip a trendy vermouth cocktail at this perennially popular and very slick martini lounge.

Ferg's Sports Bar & Grill (☎ 727-822-4562; 1320 Central Ave; ⏲ 11am-2am Mon-Sat, noon-11pm Sun; P) A friendly neighborhood place with an outdoor bar, and plenty of TVs to watch the football, Ferg's really gets hopping before and after big games. It's one of St Petersburg's favorite sports bars.

Haymarket Pub (☎ 727-577-9621; 8308 4th St N; ⏲ 2pm-2am) If you come to this casual and friendly gay bar more than once (and you just

---

DRINKING IN THE STREETS

St Petersburg celebrates the first Friday of every month with a big block party. From 5:30pm to 10pm, Central Ave between 2nd and 3rd Street is closed to traffic, vendors are set up, shops stay open late, bars are packed and there is live music on the street. The event, called 'Get Down Town,' is essentially a giant pub crawl – you can take your drink out onto the streets. It's one killer street party.

might), regulars will begin to recognize you and may start treating you like family.

Entertainment

Call the **hotline** (☎ 727-892-5700) for up-to-the-minute information and wander around the BayWalk (p422) complex on weekends (in particular) to see what's happening. If you want to see a movie, Baywalk also has a giant megaplex theater.

CLUBS & LIVE MUSIC

St Petersburg has a healthy nightlife scene, although clubs are always opening and closing. Check around at shops and bars for flyers of who is hosting what where.

Jannus Landing (☎ 727-896-1244; www.jannuslanding .net; 16 2nd St N; tickets $15-20; ☺ doors open at 7pm) The best place in the area to hear live music, Jannus Landing is St Petersburg's most revered live venue, with good reason. Set in a courtyard, it hosts several weekly concerts by local and national bands. It's a very casual place and all ages are admitted. Burgers, hot dogs and such are sold.

Push Ultra Lounge (☎ 727-871-7874; 128 3rd St S) DJs spin hip-hop and top 40 at this pulsating club that uses lots of colored lights and imagery to set the trippy mood at this popular club. Exposed brick walls and ultramod decor grace all three levels, and there's a rooftop bar if you need to get some air.

Coliseum Ballroom (☎ 727-892-5202; www.stpete .org/coliseum; 535 4th Ave N; tickets $5-50) Also called the Palace of Pleasure, this ballroom opened in 1924 and, over the years, big bands, classical orchestras and rock bands have all played here. In 1985, the Colliseum Ballroom made its film debut in *Cocoon* with an incredible ballroom scene. The red-oak dance floor is classic. If you're here on a Wednesday, big band Tea Dance sessions run from 1pm to 3:30pm (bring your own booze).

State Theatre (☎ 727-895-3045; www.statemedia.com; 687 Central Ave; tickets $5-12) This restored art-deco theater (built in 1927) has live music regularly – from acoustic acts and 'old wave' to new bands. Buy your tickets at the bar and head upstairs.

THEATER

American Stage (☎ 727-822-8814; www.americanstage .org; 211 3rd St S; tickets $22-32) The area's oldest professional theater ensemble stages shows ranging from American classics to Broadway shows.

Bayfront Center (☎ 727-892-5767; www.stpete.org/ arena; 400 1st St S; tickets $7-50) This venue houses the 8400-seat Times Bayfront Arena and the 2000-seat Mahaffey Theater, and hosts Broadway shows, concerts and some sporting events.

SPORTS

Tropicana Field (☎ 888-326-7297; www.devilrays.com; 1 Stadium Dr; tickets $5-25; ☺ 9am-5pm) is home to the major-league Tampa Bay Devil Rays, who play baseball from April to September. You'll find parking (about $7) around 10th St and 4th Ave S. The Devil Rays play spring-training games at **Progress Energy Park** (☎ 888-326-7297; 180 2nd Ave SE; tickets $7-20; ☺ 9am-5pm) in March.

Take a behind-the-scenes tour of Tropicana Field ($5 adults, $3 seniors and children) to check out the dugouts, press boxes, batting tunnels, weight rooms and the field. On nongame days, the 45- to 90-minute tours are given from 10am and 4pm weekdays; on home-game days, they're at 10am and noon weekdays.

Shopping

Antique stores litter downtown, especially on the north side of Central Ave between 6th and 11th Sts (it's a street waiting to happen, really), and along 4th St. The chamber of commerce publishes a complete brochure on antique stores. Central Ave is where to head if you want funky boutiques selling everything from vintage clothing to unique cards, lamps and other fun trinkets.

Gas Plant Antique Arcade (☎ 727-895-0368; 1246 Central Ave; ☺ 10am-5pm) For antiques, check out this great antique arcade with 150 dealers on four floors.

Florida Craftsmen Gallery (☎ 727-821-7391; www .floridacraftsmen.net; 501 Central Ave; ☺ 10am-5:30pm Mon-Sat) This retail and exhibition space features work from over 150 artists and craftspeople.

Arts Center (☎ 727-822-7872; www.theartscenter.com; 719 Central Ave; ☺ 10am-5pm Mon-Sat, noon-4pm Sun) This center has five galleries showing paintings, ceramics, printmaking, drawing and mixed media art.

Getting There & Around

AIR

St Petersburg-Clearwater International Airport (☎ 727-453-7800; www.fly2pie.com; Roosevelt Blvd & Hwy 686, Clearwater) St Petersburg is served by several major carriers, but if you're flying into the region, you'll probably land in Tampa (p416). If

---

SUNSHINE SKYWAY BRIDGE

OK, it's not exactly an 'attraction,' but it's impressive nonetheless: the 4-mile Sunshine Skyway Bridge ($1 toll) spans Tampa Bay south of St Petersburg. It's dramatic on approach and it's dramatic once you're on it. It's actually the continuation of the I-275, which meets up with the I-75 on the south side of the bay. Built to replace the old span, which was destroyed in 1980 when a boat, *Summit Venture*, rammed into its base, the Sunshine Skyway is a shimmering modern bridge. Each of its supports is surrounded by 'dolphins': gigantic shock absorbers capable of withstanding the force of an 87,000-ton vessel traveling at 10 knots (talk about shutting the barn door after the horse has bolted). The *Summit Venture* weighed 34,500 tons and was traveling at 8 knots when it struck the old bridge.

Much of the old bridge still stands, and has been converted into the world's largest fishing pier, spanning almost 2 miles. It's a great place to watch the sunset and fish.

---

you're looking for a quick jaunt to Key West, check for flights out of here.

BUS

Greyhound (☎ 727-898-1496; www.greyhound.com; 180 9th St N) has buses from St Petersburg to Miami, which take six to 10 hours (one-way from $44); to Orlando three to four hours (one-way from $25) and to Tampa half an hour to 1½ hours (one-way $10).

Pinellas Suncoast Transit Authority (PSTA; ☎ 727-530-9911; www.psta.net; 340 2nd Ave N; ☼ 5am-9pm Mon-Sat, 7am-5pm Sun) offers unlimited-ride Go Cards (day/week/month $3/12/40). It serves Clearwater and Tarpon Springs from St Petersburg; a good map is available from most chambers of commerce. Hourly departures from St Petersburg to St Pete Beach take about an hour on trolley 35 (fare $1.25, bills accepted).

The excellent **Looper** (☎ 727-821-5166; the pier; ☼ 10am-5pm Sun-Thu, 10am-midnight Fri & Sat) can be used as a 30-minute orientation tour since there is narration. It's a bargain since it stops at a dozen popular attractions around downtown; tickets cost 25¢ per ride.

PSTA bus 79 connects the airport to downtown. By car from the airport to downtown, take Roosevelt Blvd (Hwy 686) south across the jig on Ulmerton Rd to the I-275 south.

CAR

From Tampa, the best route to St Petersburg is the I-275 south, which runs right through downtown St Petersburg and continues across the Sunshine Skyway Bridge; it connects with the I-75 and US 41 (Tamiami Trail) on the south side of Tampa Bay. From Sarasota, take the I-75 north to the I-275 across the Sunshine Skyway. From Orlando, take the I-4 south to the I-75 and then take the I-275.

To Clearwater, take Roosevelt Blvd north to the Bayside Bridge (49th St) and go west on Causeway Blvd.

To get to St Pete Beach, take the I-275 to Hwy 682, which connects to the Pinellas County Parkway and head west to the beach. Or take Central Ave due west to the Treasure Island Causeway or turn south on 66th St to the Corey Causeway.

Getting around and parking in St Petersburg is a cinch. Just be sure to have a lot of quarters since you'll be feeding hungry meters. Consider parking at the pier and taking the Looper trolley.

ST PETE BEACH & AROUND
☎ 727 / pop 10,100

Just 20 minutes from downtown St Petersburg, yet worlds apart, is the funky little beach community of St Pete. Part of a long stretch of barrier beaches running from Fort DeSoto Park south to Honeymoon Island, St Pete and her sister beaches are the perfect antidote to city life, and make great day or overnight trips from the city. Whether you're lying on the sun-kissed sand, body-boarding in clear sapphire sea or drinking in a show-stopping sunset from a rooftop bar, this area is all about casual fun and lots of relaxation. The beach here seems to go on forever – Pass-a-Grille, a quiet residential suburb on the National Historic Register, is a good place to start. It sits at the southernmost tip of St Pete Beach and has the most authentic beach-community vibe, with sandy streets and little houses sitting next to weathered rooftop bars just off the water.

Orientation & Information

Part of a 30-mile-long string of barrier beaches west of St Petersburg, St Pete Beach is on

Long Key, about 10 miles west of downtown St Petersburg across the Corey Causeway or the Pinellas County Bayway. The island is long and narrow, and the main (and only) artery is Gulf Blvd (Hwy 699). Expect slow-moving traffic in high season (December to March). Barely indistinguishable beach towns blend into one another – from south to north: Pass-a-Grille, St Pete Beach, Madeira Beach, Redington Beach, Redington Shores, Indian Shores, Indian Rock Beach, Sand Key and onward to Clearwater.

The **Tampa Bay Beaches Chamber of Commerce** (☎ 727-360-6957, 800-944-1847; www.tampabaybeaches .com; 6990 Gulf Blvd; ☼ 9am-5pm Mon-Fri) has tons of pamphlets and coupons and an excellent beach map for free.

Sights & Activities
DON CESAR BEACH RESORT & SPA
This 277-room landmark **resort** (☎ 727-360-1883, 866-728-2206; www.doncesar.com; 3400 Gulf Blvd, St Pete Beach; r from $200; P X ☐ ☎) occupies a strategic stretch of prime beachfront. It'll probably be the first thing you notice when you pull into St Pete Beach. Built in 1928, this enormous pink palace was a hotspot for F Scott Fitzgerald, Clarence Darrow, Lou Gehrig and Al Capone. Since then it's gone through some changes: in 1942 it was turned into a US Army hospital and convalescent center for military personnel. Stripped of its splendor, the building was abandoned 25 years later by the Veterans Administration, which had taken it over after the war. It re-opened as a hotel in 1973 and was completely restored from 1985 to 1989. Today, the resort boasts a European-style spa, fine dining and an extensive kids' program. If you want an excuse to linger, have a drink at the poolside Beachcomber Bar or rent $14 beachfront chairs in front of the hotel.

SUNCOAST SEABIRD SANCTUARY
Founded in 1971, this **sanctuary** (☎ 727-391-6211; www.seabirdsanctuary.org; 18328 Gulf Blvd, Indian Shores; admission by donation; ☼ 9am-sunset) is the largest wild-bird hospital in North America (1½ acres). About 40 species of crippled birds have found a home here, and at any given time there are usually between 400 and 600 sea and land birds being treated and recuperating. Whenever possible, the birds are released back into the wild. When it's not possible, their offspring are released. Procreation doesn't

stop with recuperation. Tours take place Wednesday and Sunday at 2pm.

FORT DESOTO PARK & BEACH
Consistently ranked as one of the top beaches in the US by magazines, websites and even TV shows, this 1100-acre **county park** (☎ 727-582-2267; www.fortdesoto.com; 3500 Pinellas Bayway S; admission free; ☼ sunrise-sunset) draws the faithful. It offers camping (p423), 4 miles of self-guided nature and recreational trails (for biking, rollerblading, walking and hiking) and about 7 miles of swimmable and shallow shoreline. North Beach is on the Gulf side and has a concession stand while East Beach fronts Tampa Bay and both have lifeguards. There are also two fishing piers with bait shops and rod rentals, if you're so inclined. The fort was built during the Spanish-American War. To get here from St Petersburg, take the I-275 south to exit 4 and follow the signs. There is a $1 toll on the approach road.

BEACHES
Besides Fort DeSoto Park & Beach (left), the area's best is **Pass-a-Grille Beach** (Gulf Blvd), where you can watch boats coming through Pass-a-Grille Channel from the bay. Not surprisingly, the beach gets crowded but it still retains a neighborhood feel, although metered parking prevails. We'd recommend taking a drive along Gulf Blvd and checking out the various beaches – you'll come across at least half a dozen pullouts with metered parking where there's an organized beach of sorts. Some have more facilities than others. If you're looking for total quiet, drive to one of the lots not close to businesses.

JOHN'S PASS & WATER SPORTS
Off Gulf Blvd in Madeira Beach, John's Pass is a touristy former fishing village whose tin-roofed wooden buildings have been converted into souvenir shops. A boardwalk connects them to water-sports activities and boat rentals at appropriately named **John's Pass Watersports** (☎ 727-363-1881; www.johnspasswater sports.com; 209 Boardwalk Pl E). Roar around the gulf on a powerful jet ski (from $65 per hour) or float up to 1200ft above it under the canopy of a giant parasail ($45 to $75, depending on how high you want to go) hooked to a tow line off a motorboat. The company also runs popular morning snorkeling trips at the mouth of Tampa Bay – you get there via a

fun speedboat ride – and afternoon dolphin-swimming adventures. The two-hour trips (the morning one departs at 11:30am, the afternoon at 3:30pm) cost $21 for adults, and $15 for children – kids love both these trips. Call for opening hours.

There are plenty of other places along these beaches to go parasailing, dolphin-spotting or even on a shelling excursion. Check with the Tampa Bay Beaches Chamber of Commerce (p427) for more specifics on companies.

Festivals & Events

Music Fest on the Water (the pier) Rock out by the water on nearly every Sunday in March; the month-long festival hosts some decent live acts.

Grouper Fest & Arts Festival Find music, food, entertainment and arts and crafts; late October.

Sleeping

St Pete Beach is an easy day trip from St Petersburg (p423), but if you choose to stay overnight – which we recommend – there are a number of different options. Properties are spread out over many miles, so we've included the beach they are on in the listings' addresses. The two main roads we mention here and in the Eating section are Gulf Way and Gulf Blvd. Please note they are not the same road, but run parallel to each other – Gulf Way is on the opposite side of the peninsula from Gulf Blvd. For swank sleeping, don't forget the **Don Cesar Resort & Spa** (see p421).

Keystone Motel (☎ 727-360-1313; www.keystone motel.com; 801 Gulf Way, Pass-A-Grille Beach; r & apt $95-125; ✗ ⬚ ♿) Right across from the beach, and next to two popular rooftop restaurants, the Keystone offers good value in a great location. It's a small U-shaped motel with a Spanish-tiled roof that's built around a sparkling swimming pool with unobstructed gulf views. Rooms are motel standard issue but recently renovated; the deluxe apartment is really nice and at only $20 more than a basic motel room, even in high season, it's a steal.

Inn on the Beach (☎ 727-360-8844; www.innonbeach .com; 1401 Gulf Way, Pass-a-Grill Beach; r from $105, cottages from $175; ✗ ⬚) You can plop onto one of the hotel lounge chairs parked in the sand and watch the sun disappear over the Gulf of Mexico from the backyard of this charmingly casual hotel on Pass-a-Grille Beach. Rooms at the inn, along with three cabins (with alluring names like Love Shack and Shangri-La) come in a variety of sizes, shapes and styles, but all

are unique – we loved the striped bedspreads and bold colors found in some. For a laid-back beach shack at fair prices, it's hard to beat this inn. Wi-fi is available.

Alden Beach Resort (☎ 727-360-7081, 800-237-2530; www.aldenbeachresort.com; 5900 Gulf Blvd, St Pete Beach; r $130-270; ✗ ⬚ ♿) A step up from their neighbors, this family-owned resort has two pools, tennis courts, a Jacuzzi, bar, barbecue area and good service. The 143 waterfront rooms and one-bedroom suites are spread out over six stories. Check out the beachfront Cabana Bar, for a daiquiri in the sand at sunset.

Pasa Tiempo B&B (☎ 727-367-9907; www.pasa -tiempo.com; 7141 Bay St, St Pete Beach; r & ste summer $195-300; ✗ ⬚ ♿) Tranquility reigns at this upmarket B&B featuring eight individually decorated (one has an outdoor whirlpool, another a private terrace) units right on the water. Kick back on the private dock with a glass of wine and look for dolphins, take a dip in the gorgeous pool looking right into the surrounding bay or wander the lush, tropical gardens. Breakfast and evening wine hour are included in the rate. Wi-fi is available.

Also recommended:

Beach Haven (☎ 727-367-8642; www.beachhaven villas.com; 4980 Gulf Blvd, St Pete Beach; r summer $72-120; ⬚) Good value and location.

Palm Crest Motel (☎ 727-360-9327, 888-558-1247; www.palmcrest.com; 3848 Gulf Blvd, St Pete Beach; r $84-150; ✗ ⬚ ♿) Some units have kitchens.

Eating

Wharf (☎ 727-367-9469; 2001 Pass-a-grille Way, St Pete Beach; mains $5-15; ☺ lunch & dinner) When you're down at the marina and in need of some sustenance, follow the locals here for some pretty darn good seafood. Their clam chowder doesn't hold a candle to its New England cousin, but if you never tasted the latter, you'd love the former. Really, it's quite good.

Ted Peter's Famous Smoked Fish (☎ 727-381-7931; 1350 Pasadena Ave; mains $5-17; ☺ 11:30am-7:30pm Wed-Mon) On the way to St Pete Beach from St Petersburg, Ted Peter's has been smoking fish since the 1950s. It's an institution. Their salmon, mackerel and mullet, straight from the little smokehouse, are succulently fresh. Get takeout for the beach, or head next door where they serve more smoked seafood specialities and patrons drink lots of beer by the fireplace.

The Hurricane (☎ 727-360-9558; 807 Gulf Way, Pass-a-Grille; breakfast $4-8; lunch $6-15; dinner $10-30; ☺ lunch

---

DETOUR: HONEYMOON & CALADESI ISLANDS

Honeymoon Island State Recreation Area (☎ 727-469-5942; 1 Dunedin Causeway; per car $4; ☼ 8am-sunset) began life as a grand prize in a 1940s contest. Paramount newsreels and *Life* magazine were giving away all-expenses-paid honeymoons to newlyweds who'd stay in thatched huts lining the beach. A road connecting the island to the mainland was built in 1964 and the state bought the land in the early 1970s.

Today, the park offers diverse birdlife, good swimming and great shelling. Coastal plants include mangrove swamps, rare virgin slash pine, strand and salt marshes. There are also nature trails and bird-observation areas, as well as a ferry to Caladesi Island. Take Alt Hwy 19 north to the town of Dunedin and go west on Curlew Rd (Hwy 586), the Dunedin Causeway, which leads to the island.

Just south of Honeymoon Island, **Caladesi Island State Park** (☎ 727-469-5918; admission free; ☼ 8am-sunset) ranks at the top of national surveys for best natural beaches. Reach it by canoe or take a ferry from Honeymoon Island. In addition to nature trails and an unspoiled, palm-lined 3-mile beach, it's nice for picnicking, swimming and shelling. You might see armadillos, tortoises, raccoons, turtles and all manner of birds. Keep your eyes open and stay light on your feet.

Caladesi Connection (☎ 727-734-5263), at the western end of Curlew Rd (Hwy 586) in Honeymoon Island State Recreation Area, operates hourly weekday ferries to Caladesi. On weekends the 30-minute ferries run on the half hour, starting at 10am; the last departure from Caladesi is around 5:30pm. The round-trip fare is $9 for an adult and $5.50 for a child. One note: to manage passengers coming and going, you'll get a card stamped with your return-trip departure time (no more than four hours later). If you want to stay longer, you can, but other folks with that time will be taken first.

& dinner daily, breakfast Sat & Sun) In the Pass-a-Grille neighborhood, across from the beach, this popular seafood eatery has always been a local hangout. Even though the food can be inconsistent, you can't beat the sunset views – the restaurant broadcasts the exact time of sunset on a menu board out front. The Hurricane offers live entertainment and a cool rooftop deck area with bar.

The Brass Monkey Bar & Grille (☎ 727-367-7620; 709 Gulf Way, Pass-A-Grille Beach; mains $7-25; ☼ lunch & dinner) This place, located on the beach next to The Hurricane, has a giant North American menu, but specializes in Maryland-style crab-cakes (they will ship them anywhere in the country) and Buffalo chicken wings (there are six different flavors, including Maryland crab-cake). The upstairs patio bar has fans and views, views, views. It's a great spot to sip tropical cocktails and watch the sunset unfold.

Crabby Bill's (☎ 727-360-8858; 5100 Gulf Blvd; mains $8-35; ☼ lunch & dinner) Crabby Bill's serves a fried assortment of crustaceans, and of course very delicious crab. It's a casual place with picnic tables and water views that's been luring locals with fresh seafood for more than 20 years.

Salt Rock Grill (☎ 727-593-7625; 19325 Gulf Blvd, Indian Shores; mains $10-40; ☼ dinner) This oh-so-fashionable, upscale waterfront eatery has great views, a fun tiki-style bar and wood-grilled steaks cooked at a smoking hot 1200°F. Fish fanatics covet salmon prepared on a cedar plank, while seafood-lovers will dig all the lobster choices – from lobster and avocado salad and lobster pasta to good old-fashioned meaty, butter drawn lobster tail. Yum.

Lobster Pot (☎ 727-391-8592; 17814 Gulf Blvd, Redington Shores; mains $16-40; ☼ dinner) Without a doubt one of the area's best, the Lobster Pot is true to its origins and specializes in the tasty crustaceans cooked every which way. If someone at your table doesn't like lobster (gasp!), grouper and snapper are highly recommended.

Maritana Grille (☎ 727-360-1882; 3400 Gulf Blvd, St Pete Beach; mains $27-36; ☼ dinner) Serving creative North American cuisine with Caribbean overtones, Maritana in the Don Cesar Resort is easily one of the area's top restaurants. Try the lobster risotto with roasted beets and citrus vinaigrette.

Drinking

A number of the restaurants, including **The Hurricane** and the **Brass Monkey Bar & Grill**, (see p429) double as popular drinking venues come dark.

Undertow Bar (☎ 727-368-9000; 3850 Gulf Blvd) This glam beach bar attracts a bevy of young, tanned, bikini-clad revelers who come to sip tropical cocktails under thatched tiki huts and play volleyball in the sand. House specials include boozy frozen daiquiris, rum-runners and a light Bahamian beer called Kalik. A limited menu is served at the bar, and the wide deck is perfect for people-watching. There is live reggae on Sunday afternoons; DJs spin on other nights.

Getting There & Around
For information on how to get here by bus and car, see p426. Excellent PSTA Suncoast Beach Trolleys frequently ply Gulf Blvd, from Pass-a-Grille (just south of St Pete Beach) north to Sand Key, where you can connect with the Clearwater Beach Jolley Trolley.

CLEARWATER BEACH
☎ 727 / pop 108,000
If you're a follower of, or ever been curious about, the Church of Scientology, you'll want to visit Scientology's international spiritual headquarters. Otherwise, you might be rather disappointed by Clearwater's slightly tired 1950s-era downtown. Home to a few faded storefronts and dive bars, a pizza joint, beauty parlor, and… what will soon be the largest Scientology church in the world, the 'Super Power Building' – so big it covers a city block.

And even though there aren't many sights, Clearwater does host some fantastic white-sand beaches that tend to be less crowded than those in neighboring St Pete.

It's also a good area for kayaking, shelling and biking.

Orientation
This northernmost barrier island is about 22 miles north of St Pete Beach and 2 miles west of downtown Clearwater (a separate city on the mainland) over the Memorial Causeway (Hwy 60). From here the road south is S Gulfview Blvd and north is Mandalay Ave, Clearwater Beach's main drag. Pier 60 is right at the roundabout where these three roads meet. From St Petersburg, it's about a half-hour drive or a 1½-hour bus ride.

Although crowded, the scale of the island is humane (only 3.5-miles long) and it's easy to get around.

Information
Clearwater Beach Public Library (☎ 727-462-6890; 483 Mandalay Ave; ◷ 9am-5pm Mon-Wed & Fri, 11am-7pm Thu) Has free internet access limited to 30 minutes daily.
Clearwater Regional Chamber of Commerce (☎ 727-461-0011; www.clearwaterflorida.org; 1130 Cleveland St; ◷ 8:30am-5pm Mon-Fri) Contact for advance information (as it's inconveniently located for drop-ins).

Sights & Activities
SAND KEY PARK & BEACH
This 65-acre, family-friendly **beach park** (☎ 727-464-3347; 1060 Gulf Rd; admission free; ◷ 7am-sunset),

---

SCIENTOLOGY USA

For more than 30 years now Clearwater has served as the Church of Scientology's international spiritual headquarters and the mecca for this religion – that's been popularized by celebrity worshipers like Tom Cruise and John Travolta. Clearwater is home to the largest concentration of Scientologists outside of Los Angeles and what will be the biggest Scientology church in the world.

The Clearwater church, known as the Flag Land Base, was born in the late 1970s, when a Scientology-founded group calling itself the 'United Church of Florida' purchased the downtown Fort Harrison Hotel for a cool $3 million. As the group purchased the building anonymously, Clearwater residents and city-council members didn't realize the buyers were Scientologists until after approving the building's sale. They weren't happy. But the subsequent protests and rallies against the church's presence did little to keep it from establishing. And growing roots – today there are more than 8300 Scientologists living and working in the city.

The Flag Land Base itself has expanded exponentially in the last three decades, as the church has bought more property around Clearwater with each passing year. Its grandest endeavor is the Super Power Building, a giant, white Mediterranean Revival edifice that will take up an entire city block when finished (if ever, it's been under construction since 1998 at an estimated cost of well over $50 million). It will have 889 rooms over six floors, including an indoor sculpture garden, Scientology museum and, the most controversial addition of all, a two-story-high cross perched atop the building (already the tallest in town) that will be illuminated at night.

just south of the Clearwater Pass Bridge (or, depending on your perspective, at the northern end of a long barrier island in the Gulf of Mexico) is often voted in the top 20 beaches in the country. The half-mile-long beach is the widest in the area. It's also a great spot for watching dolphins, especially on the channel side, and a pretty good spot for shelling (best at low tide, especially during new and full moons and after storms). The Jolley Trolley (opposite) passes by; otherwise, it is an easy bicycle ride. Be prepared with some quarters to feed the parking meters.

CLEARWATER MARINE AQUARIUM

This nonprofit **aquarium** (☎ 727-447-0980, 888-239-9414; www.cmaquarium.org; 249 Windward Passage; adult/child $9/6.50; ☽ 9am-5pm Mon-Fri, 9am-4pm Sat, 11am-4pm Sun) is dedicated to educating the public and to rescuing and rehabilitating animals like dolphins, fish, sea otters and threatened loggerhead and endangered Kemp's ridley turtles. Presentations run during the day. Inquire about the two-hour Sea Life Safari with an onboard biologist (adult/child $20/13) and the dolphin-trainer-for-a-day program (per person $200). Between Clearwater and Clearwater Beach, off Memorial Causeway (Hwy 60), it's conveniently located since the Jolley Trolley stops here.

PIER 60

Sunset celebrations at Pier 60 are equivalent to those at Key West's Mallory Sq (p201). Jugglers and magicians perform, musicians play, and craftspeople and artists hawk their wares. Head down to the pier nightly, two hours before and after sunset. The pier is also a favorite spot for fishing.

WATER ACTIVITIES

The bay side of the beach, filled with mangrove islands, is prime for canoeing. The calm Gulf waters also promote easy paddling up to beautiful Caladesi Island (p430). **Cafe Honeymoon** (☎ 727-736-2132; Honeymoon State Park, 1 Causeway Blvd; per hr from $10, per day from $40; ☽ 9am-5pm) rents kayaks.

Just south of the rotary on Coronado Dr and across from the pier, activity booths hawk their trips and services, including fishing, water skiing and boating. This is also where you'll find **Parasail City** (☎ 727-449-0566; Clearwater Marina, Slip 2; ☽ 9am-5pm), which will get you up for $45 to $75, depending on how high you want to go.

Dolphin Encounter (☎ 727-442-7433; www.dolphin encounter.org; 25 Causeway Blvd, Slip 5; ☽ 11am-7pm Mon-Sat, 1-7pm Sun), opposite Pier 60, runs very good, frequent, daily, 80-minute dolphin-watching cruises into the Gulf of Mexico (adult/child $21/12) with free beer, wine and soda.

Festivals & Events

Fun N Sun Festival (☎ 727-562-4801) An annual festival including concerts, kids' activities and an illuminated night parade; early May.

Clearwater Celebrates An Independence Day festival with live music and fireworks right off the Intracoastal Waterway; July 3 & 4.

Sleeping

Koli-Bree Motel (☎ 727-461-6223; 440 E Shore Dr; apt from $70; ☆) Just a few blocks from the water, this is a good choice for families. Each of the 10 apartments in the two-story building are tidy and come with a range, microwave and fridge for cooking. Look for it northeast of the rotary.

Belleview Biltmore Resort & Spa (☎ 727-373-3000; www.belleviewbiltmore.com; 25 Belleview Blvd; r $89-200; ☒ ☒ ☐ ☒) This swanky and delightful 21-acre resort, off Hwy 60 on the mainland, was built in the 1890s by railroad magnate Henry B Plant and originally served as a retreat for wealthy northeasterners. These days, along with 241 elegant rooms and suites, guests can indulge in opulent spa services. Or play a game of golf on the hotel's 71-par championship Donald Ross–designed course. Guests have access to the hotel's private beach club on Sand Key Beach, which has an awesome oceanfront swimming pool. All this for as low as $90 in the off-season? That's a steal. Tip: visit the website for the best rates. Wi-fi is available.

Palm Pavilion Inn (☎ 727-446-6777; www.palm pavilioninn.com; 18 Bay Esplanade; r from $100; ☒ ☒) This hotel has 29 clean, spacious rooms just across from the beach. Its popular Beachside Bar & Grill (mains $7 to $16) serves beers in the sand, has live music nightly and lends a party atmosphere to the Palm. Light sleepers will be happier elsewhere, but backpackers will enjoy the congenial atmosphere at the alfresco bar.

Eating & Drinking

Frenchy's Original Cafe (☎ 727-446-3607; 41 Baymont; mains $8-12; ☽ lunch & dinner) A local hang-out since 1981, Frenchy's is a fantastic hole-in-the wall restaurant that wins awards for its grouper sandwiches, which are thick, juicy, fresh and ultratasty. The atmosphere is beach-bum casual at its best, complete with indoor and outdoor picnic tables. It's off Mandalay Ave north of the rotary.

Frenchy's Rockaway Grill on the Beach (☎ 727-446-4844; 7 Rockaway St; mains $10-20; ☾ lunch & dinner) Off Mandalay Ave north of the center of town, Frenchy's spin-off restaurant serves salads, excellent she-crab soup, burgers, seafood and a few Mexican and Jamaican dishes. Alternately, check out the live music on most nights, pool tables and happy hour (4pm to 7pm).

Island Way Grill (☎ 727-461-6617; 20 Island Way; mains $10-40; ☾ 4-10pm Sun-Thu, to 11pm Fri & Sat) This is not your ordinary beachfront seafood shack. Nope, Island Way is a slick glass-enclosed restaurant serving lusciously prepared Pan-Asian-influenced fresh fish dishes. After dinner, head out to the patio and outdoor bar, for an evening of champagne sipping and beautiful people-watching – owners and players of the Tampa Bay Buccaneers are among the regulars who hang out here.

Bobby's Bistro & Wine Bar (☎ 727-446-9463; 447 Mandalay Ave; mains $18-30; ☾ dinner) Behind its more conservative parent, Bob Heilman's Beachcomber, this upscale bistro dishes out jazz alongside gussied-up pork chops, fancy pizzas and grilled fish. The wine list, as you might imagine, is stellar.

Shephards (☎ 727-441-6875; 601 S Gulfview Blvd; cover $3-5; ☾ 11am-11pm) A beachfront tiki bar that has top-40 tunes and reggae music on weekend afternoons. Look for it on the Shephard's Beach Resort property.

Getting There & Around

Greyhound (☎ 727-796-7315; 2811 Gulf-to-Bay Blvd, Clearwater) runs about six buses daily that make the half-hour trip from Tampa to Clearwater (one-way from $10). Then to get to Clearwater Beach, take **PSTA** (☎ 727-530-9911; www.psta.net; 14840 49th Ave N) bus 60 from the stop across Causeway Blvd westbound to the Park St Bus Depot, and change there to bus 80 to Clearwater Beach. Buses run every 30 to 60 minutes. The PSTA's Suncoast Beach Trolley ($1.25) travels from downtown Clearwater to the beach.

From Tampa, take Hwy 60 (Courtney Campbell Causeway) through Clearwater and west out to the beach. From St Petersburg, take US 19 (34th St N) north to Hwy 60 and go west. From St Pete Beach, take Gulf Blvd north.

The **Jolley Trolley** (☎ 727-445-1200; www.jolleytrolley .com; 483 Mandalay Ave) runs around Clearwater Beach and onward to Sand Key (adult/child/senior $1/0.50/0.50) from 10am to 10pm daily; pick up maps at the trolley office. A second Jolley Trolley runs between the beach and Clearwater's Park St Station during the same time frame.

SOUTH OF TAMPA

The sun-kissed stretch of coastline south of Tampa is the kind of place where you'll want to linger. Cultured, sophisticated, wealthy, beautiful, natural, and there's no shortage of appealing things to see and do. So many in fact, you should dedicate at least a week to explore this region, if you want to really get into its meat. From Venice to Naples, the beaches here look as good as their names sound – a few are even called the best in the US. Towns like Sarasota dish up plenty of art and culture with their aqua waters, while islands like Sanibel fulfill your natural vacation fantasies. If looking for manatees, swimming with dolphins, hunting for shells and hanging out on some of the top 10 beaches in the US leaves you with an appetite, head to Cabbage Key for the original cheeseburger in paradise, à la Jimmy Buffet.

SARASOTA
☎ 941 / pop 55,500

Sophisticated Sarasota is an affluent yet welcoming place that serves as a bastion of the arts and the true cultural powerhouse of the region. John Ringling saw the city's potential: he chose Sarasota as the winter home of his circus. The Big Top may have made him famous, but he also gathered one fine art collection and today his museum-quality palace is a must-see for anyone passing through. You'll also want to save time for the Selby Botanical Gardens and Mote Aquarium, both top-drawer diversions. Sarasota has a rich dining scene and the vibrant downtown boasts an equally vibrant bookstore and café culture. When you're feeling ritzy head to St Armand's Circle for some window shopping and people-watching.

Lastly, but hardly leastly, Sarasota is also a county with upwards of 40 miles of barrier beaches, the kind of beaches that visitors fly across the country to hang out on. We like the beach at Siesta Key best – it's also the liveliest and most laid-back part of the Sarasota area.

Orientation

The Tamiami Trail (US 41) zooms north straight as a die from Venice to the southern end of Sarasota, then it follows the southwest curve of downtown and skirts the east coast of Sarasota Bay before slashing northwest toward Tampa. Within town, it's called N Tamiami Trail north of Gulf Stream Ave and S Tamiami Trail south of Bay Front Dr.

Downtown Sarasota streets and roads run east–west; avenues and boulevards run north–south. The main drag downtown is Main St while Pineapple Ave hosts a tiny but hip historic district near Burns Court.

From downtown, head east across the John Ringling Causeway to St Armand's Circle on Lido Key. Then head south to Lido Beach or north to Mote Marine Laboratory and Pelican Man's Bird Sanctuary. Continue northward to pricey Longboat Key and Anna Maria Island.

To reach residential Siesta Key from downtown, head south on US 41 and east on Siesta Dr. Midnight Pass Rd (Hwy 789) is the main thoroughfare, but Ocean Blvd skirts the northeastern portion of the key. The funkier Siesta Village, laid out along curvy canals, is wedged between Ocean Blvd and Midnight Pass Rd. Stickney Point Rd (Hwy 72), about halfway down the key, also takes you to US 41. To reach Longboat Key take US 41 to N Gulfstream Ave and travel about 10 miles north.

Information

BOOKSTORES

Sarasota is good book-hunting country.

Book Bazaar/Parker's Books (☎ 941-366-1373; 1488 Main St; ☉ 10am-5pm Mon-Sat) Sells used and out-of-print books.

Circle Books (☎ 941-388-2850; 478 John Ringling Blvd, St Armand's Circle; ☉ 10am-6pm Mon-Thu, to 9pm Fri, 9am-9pm Sat, to 5pm Sun) Very friendly bookstore.

Main Bookshop (☎ 941-366-7653; 1962 Main St; ☉ 9am-11pm) Four floors of new, remaindered and used books, lots of maps, a first-rate Florida section and a nice atmosphere.

EMERGENCIES

Sarasota Memorial Hospital (☎ 941-917-9000; 1700 S Tamiami Trail; ☉ 24hr) The biggest hospital in the area.

INTERNET ACCESS

Selby Public Library (☎ 941-861-1100; 1331 1st St; ☉ 9am-9pm Mon-Thu, to 5pm Fri & Sat, 1-5pm Sun) Fantastic library with dozens of computer terminals, free internet access and very helpful staff.

MEDIA

Sarasota Herald-Tribune (www.heraldtribune.com) The main daily owned by the *New York Times*.

POST

Post office (☎ 941-331-4221; 1661 Ringling Blvd; ☉ 8am-5:30pm Mon-Fri, 9am-noon Sat) At the corner of Ringling Blvd and Pine Pl.

TOURIST INFORMATION

Longboat Key Chamber of Commerce (☎ 941-383-2466; www.longboatkeychamber.com; 6960 Gulf of Mexico Dr, Longboat Key; ☉ 9am-5pm Mon-Fri) Has key-specific lodging and restaurant information.

Sarasota Arts Line (☎ 941-953-4636, ext 6000; www.sarasota-arts.org) Offers recorded information on music, dance, jazz and film festivals.

Sarasota Chamber of Commerce (☎ 941-955-8187, 800-522-9799; www.sarasotachamber.org; 1945 Fruitville Rd; ☉ 8am-5pm Mon-Fri) Hands out reams of information, including a detailed beach guide.

Sarasota Gay & Lesbian Information Line (☎ 941-923-4636) Has information on matters of interest to gay, lesbian and bisexual travelers. Look for the biweekly *Watermark* (www.watermarkonline.com), with up-to-date coverage.

Siesta Key Chamber of Commerce (☎ 941-349-3800; www.siestakeychamber.com; 5118 Ocean Blvd, Siesta Key; ☉ 9am-5pm Mon-Fri, to noon Sat) Has key-specific lodging and restaurant information.

Sights & Activities

RINGLING MUSEUM COMPLEX

Really, don't miss the 66-acre winter estate of railroad, real-estate and circus baron John Ringling and his wife, Mable. This excellent **museum complex** (☎ 941-351-1660; www.ringling.org; 5401 Bayshore Rd; adult/student/child $15/6/6; ☉ 10am-5:30pm), with exotic plantings and a rose garden, is easily worth at least a half-day of your holiday. Avid art collectors, over the years they amassed an exceptional collection of works by Rubens, Hals, Van Dyck and others. Ringling began work on a fine art museum in the early 1920s, which was donated to the state after his death in 1936. You can also tour Ringling's home, Cà d'Zan, and the enormous Circus Museum.

John & Mable Ringling Museum of Art

This enormous, imposing Venetian Gothic and Italian Renaissance building (1929) boasts a first-rate collection of 17th-century, late-medieval, Baroque and Renaissance French Dutch and Spanish paintings and tapestries.

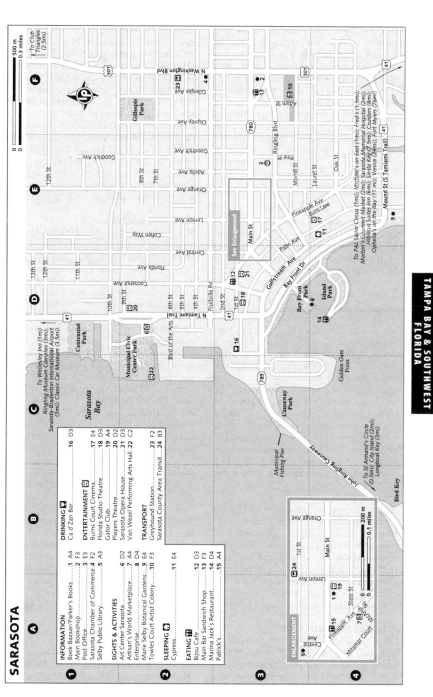

SARASOTA

Art works span 500 years, while the art-museum library has a whopping 60,000 books spanning all art periods. The sculpture garden contains bronze replicas of ancient Greek and Roman figures. You'll also find rotating modern exhibits and the **Asolo Theater**, a horseshoe-shaped, 300-seat theater that was originally built in the castle of Asolo, Italy, in 1798. After being dismantled in 1930 to make way for a movie theater, the theater was eventually bought by the museum from a Venetian antique dealer in 1950. Today, it's open for lectures, films and special events. Guided museum tours are offered on weekdays.

Cà d'Zan

Said to mean 'House of John' in Venetian dialect, Cà d'Zan (1924–26) was the grand winter home of the Ringlings. Fronting Sarasota Bay, it's a spectacular combination of Italian and French Renaissance, Baroque, Venetian Gothic and modern architecture. The lavish house has a ballroom, dining room, and taproom (with vaulted ceilings and stained-glass panels); the ballroom and playroom had their ceilings painted by Willy Pogany, a set designer for the Ziegfeld Follies. There's a catwalk around the 30ft-high court, or living room, with very fine tapestries throughout. In fact, the whole stupendous place is filled with eclectic and opulent decorative arts and furnishings. It exemplifies the lifestyles of the rich and famous, à la the Roaring Twenties. John's bedroom features an enormous ceiling painting, *Dawn Driving Away the Darkness* by Jacob de Wit. The bathroom contains such necessities as a bathtub hewn from a solid block of Siena marble, which also covers the walls.

Circus Museum

This fascinating place contains the wild Barlow Animated Miniature Circus, original and elaborately carved circus wagons, the cannon used to blast the Flying Zacchinis into low orbit, sequined costumes, calliopes and dozens of rare circus posters. Circus fans will be pleased to know that the spirit of the circus is still alive and kicking in Sarasota, though it's no longer the winter home of Ringling Bros Circus.

MOTE MARINE LABORATORY

One of the USA's premier organizations for shark study, this **laboratory** (☎ 941-388-4441; www.mote.org; 1600 Ken Thompson Pkwy, City Island; adult/child $17/12; 🕑 10am-5pm), just east of the drawbridge between Lido and Longboat Keys, operates the excellent and educational Mote Aquarium. Volunteers expertly guide you through the aquarium, where you'll see sea turtles, Florida lobsters, nurse sharks and a 135,000-gallon shark tank containing bull sharks, barracuda and groupers. Ever looked a shark in the eye and lived to talk about it? You can also learn all about the intricate Florida reef systems and check out sea horses, squid, octopuses and fireworms. Or check out the 25ft preserved giant squid. The enormous Contact Cove touch tank is filled with horseshoe crabs and stingrays. Check out the minimizing glass: when you look at the tank from above, everything gets bigger.

SARASOTA BEACHES

The area's excellent powdery, white-sand beaches are located on the barrier islands west of town; see p434. Parking is generally a snap; there are public lots, and public transport from the mainland. **Lido Key**, just west of St Armand's Circle (opposite), is divided into **North and South Lido Beaches**, the latter of which is huge and also shaded for picnicking. **Siesta Key Beach**, an absolutely deservedly famous strip of sand – its been rated one of the top 10 beaches in the US by magazines and TV networks alike. It has a great low-key beach vibe, with places to sleep and eat. Head south on Midnight Pass Rd to the end of Siesta Key for the quieter **Turtle Beach**. **Crescent Beach**, perfectly fine, is wedged in between those two. **Longboat Key**, north of St Armand's Circle, also has lovely beaches with lots of access points, many of which are backed by upscale condo developments.

MARIE SELBY BOTANICAL GARDENS

This 9-acre, indoor–outdoor **botanical oasis** (☎ 941-366-5730; www.selby.org; 811 S Palm Ave; adult/child $12/6; 🕑 10am-5pm) specializes in orchids (more than 6000 of them) but also has quite a selection of other botanicals. There's a hibiscus garden, cacti and succulent garden, a tropical house, bromeliad display, bamboo pavilion, koi pond, butterfly and waterfall gardens and tropical food gardens, where everything's edible. There's also a mangrove walkway. All in all, it's a great place to sit quietly and soak in the peaceful ambience.

SARASOTA BAYWALK

These shell paths and boardwalks circle a series of ponds surrounded by red, black and white mangroves. Though interesting, the

---

SARASOTA'S ART SCENE

The **Towles Court Artist Colony** (☎ 941-330-9817; www.towlescourt.com; Morrill & Adam Sts; 11am-4pm Tue-Sat) offers gallery hopping with a Sarasota twist. In this neighborhood, houses of fine art are set up in quirky bungalows and colorful cabins set among moss-draped oaks and lush sculpture gardens. Dozens of artists work out of this colony, and the studio-galleries feature everything from silver jewelry and mixed media installations to classic watercolors. When you tire of shopping, stop for a bite to eat at one of the restaurants mixed in between the galleries, or stop for an impromptu Tai-Chi class in the outdoor sculpture garden. Yes, Towles Court is that kind of place. On the third Friday of each month, galleries open their doors for an evening stroll (6pm to 10pm).

If you are short on time, but still want to scope out Sarasota's art scene, stop by the **Art Center Sarasota** (☎ 941-365-2032; www.artsarasota.org; 707 N Tamiami Trail; 10am-4pm Tue-Sat), originally founded in 1926 as the Sarasota Visual Art Center. It is a community gallery that serves as a good one-stop shopping experience.

Artisan's World Marketplace (☎ 941-365-5994; 128 S Pineapple Ave; 10am-5pm Mon-Fri, 9am-2pm Sat) is a nonprofit organization providing a retail outlet for artisans worldwide who live below the poverty level. For every $1200 worth of goods sold here, an artist in a developing country can work for one year and support a family of four.

---

lagoons were man-made and excavated by the Sarasota Bay Natural Estuary Program to different depths to attract different animals. The Baywalk is on City Island and is adjacent to the Mote, next to the bridge between Lido and Longboat Keys.

CLASSIC CAR MUSEUM

This sexy **museum** (☎ 941-355-6228; www.sarasota carmuseum.org; 5500 N Tamiami Trail; adult/child/senior $8.50/6/8; 9am-6pm), with hundreds of exotic and curvaceous cars, appeals to nostalgic travelers. Among the Rolls, you'll find a 1905 Rapid Depot Wagon, an '81 DeLorean, a 1932 Auburn speedster, a tiny 1958 Metropolitan, and that most sought-after transporter, a 1976 Plymouth Voyager Van. A small music room contains romantic radios, turntables and other ancient noisemakers. You can't miss it as you drive north on US 41 – look for the Flintstones' car outside.

ST ARMAND'S CIRCLE

John Ringling bought land on St Armand's Key from Charles St Amand with the intention of developing it into exactly what it is today: an upscale shopping center surrounded by posh residences. Then Ringling employed circus elephants to haul timber for the construction of the causeway between the mainland and key, and the area was opened to the public in 1926. Now, **St Armand's Circle** (☎ 941-388-1554; 9:30am-5:30pm summer, 9:30am-9pm winter) – yes, they misspelled St Amand's name for posterity –

is a fancy shopping center, surrounded by a traffic circle and packed with posh shops and cafés, that serves as the area's social hub. It's also a handy transfer point between buses to the beach (bus 4) and the Mote Aquarium and the Pelican Man's Bird Sanctuary (bus 18).

BIKING & KAYAKING

Siesta Sports Rentals (☎ 941-346-1797; www.siesta sportsrentals.com; 6551 Midnight Pass Rd, Siesta Key), on the south side of Stickney Point Bridge on Siesta Key, rents bikes (per day $15), kayaks (per day $45) and other water equipment. Guided kayak trips require advanced reservations and usually leave around 10am.

Tours

Sarasota Bay Explorers (☎ 941-388-4200; www.sarasota bayexplorers.com; 1600 Ken Thompson Pkwy, City Island; trips daily) operates Sea Life Encounter Cruises that depart from the Mote Aquarium daily at 11am, 1:30pm and 4pm. The 1¾-hour hands-on ecotours cost $26/22 per adult/child. While trawling under the supervision of marine biologists, you'll pick up and touch sponges, sea horses, puffers and cowfish. You'll also inspect rookeries and stop on an uninhabited island for a short nature walk. Maybe you'll even see manatees and dolphins; you never know what ocean mysteries will rear their heads. Guided three-hour kayak tours from the Mote cost $55/45 per adult/child.

Enterprise (☎ 941-951-1833, 888-232-7768; www .sarasotaboating.com; US 41 at Marina Jack's Marina) offers a two-hour afternoon sail and evening sunset sail (both for $45). It's a nice boat that holds only a dozen or so people, so you won't be crammed in like sardines.

Festivals & Events

Downtown after 5pm A showcase for live bands; second Friday March to June.

Classic Corvette Car Show Celebrates the auto at St Armand's Circle; in mid-May.

Oktoberfest (☎ 941-708-3456; Lakewood Ranch; tickets $7) For a taste of Germany in the Sunshine State, head to Lakewood Ranch for live entertainment, kids' activities and imported beer; early October.

Sleeping

Staying downtown (as opposed to the beaches) is always less expensive, but these beach options provide good value.

Captiva Beach Resort (☎ 941-349-4131; www .captivabeachresort.com; 6772 Sara Sea Circle, Siesta Key; r $115-300; ⊠ ❑ ☎ ☺) In the Stickney Point neighborhood of Siesta Key and just half a block from the beach, this older but pridefully maintained and value-laden motel offers units with kitchens and pillow-top mattresses.

Aloha Kai (☎ 941-349-5410; www.alohakai.net; 6020 Midnight Pass Rd, Siesta Key; r $150; ⊠ ☎ ☺) Dating back to 1963, these freestanding Siesta Key apartments, studios and motel rooms are all individually owned and have kitchens and screened-in porches. There are 68 units right on the award-winning beach. All are tidy with white walls, sheets and tiled floors that are cool on the feet.

Cypress (☎ 941-955-4683; www.cypressbb.com; 621 Gulfstream Ave S; r $150-289; ⊠) Sarasota's only B&B is a gem, lushly situated across the street from the bay and wedged between high rises. Each of the four guest rooms includes Victorian airs, Oriental carpets, antiques, nice linens and a full breakfast. Swing in the front yard of this sweet spot and watch the sunset.

Sunsets on the Key (☎ 941-312-9797; www.sunsets onthekey.com; 5203 Avenida Navarre, Siesta Key; apt $150-340; ⊠ ☎) Between Ocean Blvd and the beach, these studio, one- and two-bedroom units located off red-brick garden pathways offer some of the best value on Siesta Key. The hotel has a new giant 40ft heated pea-shaped swimming pool with a cascading waterfall and adjacent spa. Grab a fishing pole or boogie board and head out to the ocean for some free fun.

Longboat Key Club & Resort (☎ 941-383-8821, 800-237-8821; www.longboatkeyclub.com; 301 Gulf of Mexico Dr,

Longboat Key; r $200-425; ⊠ ❑ ☎) At the southern end of Longboat Key, this harborside golf and tennis resort has 232 stunning deluxe hotel rooms, all with balconies and oodles of services. Wi-fi is available.

Also recommended:

Hibiscus Inn (☎ 941-921-5797; www.hibiscus suites.com; 1735 Stickney Point Rd; r summer $119-159, winter $149-209; ❑ ☎) South of downtown and on the way to Siesta Key.

Wellesley Inn (☎ 941-366-5128; www.wellesleyonline .com; 1803 N Tamiami Trail; r summer/winter $69/109; ☎) Spotless downtown place with HBO; some have marina views.

Eating

For the most part, you needn't look further than Main St for a good place to eat.

BUDGET & MIDRANGE

Kilwin's (☎ 941-388-3200; 312 John Ringling Blvd, St Armand's Circle; ice cream from $3.50; ☺ 10am-11pm; ☺) This St Armand's Circle institution pumps out that overwhelmingly sweet smell that always pulls us in for homemade ice cream stuffed into authentic waffle cones.

Morton's Gourmet Market (☎ 941-955-9856; 1924 S Osprey Ave; mains $4-10; ☺ 8am-8pm Mon-Sat, 10am-6pm Sun) Purveyors of upscale picnic food (although they also have outdoor tables), this place has excellent sandwiches, pastries, salads and hot-food items. About 15 blocks south of downtown in the Southside Village area, Morton's is one of a few upscale places here and is frequented by neighborhood gourmands. Osprey Ave runs parallel to the Tamiami Trail, so this place is really on the way to Siesta Key from downtown.

Broken Egg (☎ 941-346-2750; 210 Avenida Madera, Siesta Key; mains $5-10; ☺ 7:30am-2:30pm) A charming Siesta Key breakfast place that serves the best hash browns in the world and a huge variety of Paul Bunyan–sized pancakes. Make sure to order a glass of fresh-squeezed Florida orange juice with your meal.

Blue Dolphin (☎ 941-388-3566; 470 John Ringling Blvd, St Armand's Circle; mains $6-14; ☺ breakfast & lunch) On St Armand's Circle, this friendly and casual diner is famed for breakfast (available throughout the day, thankfully). Try the lobster benedict or the savory and sweet peach and pecan pancakes. It also does a healthy lunch trade.

Main Bar Sandwich Shop (☎ 941-955-8733; 1944 Main St; sandwiches from $7; ☺ 10am-4pm Mon-Sat; ☺) Across from the multiplex, this Sarasota institution has been serving hot and cold sandwiches – from Italian to Cuban to kid-sized – to its guests since a couple of retiring circus performers opened it in 1958.

Patrick's (☎ 941-952-1170; 1400 Main St; mains $7-20; 11am-midnight) For all-American diner grub, you can't beat Patrick's. There are sports on the TV, super-sized burgers, sizzling steaks and potatoes cooked in all manner of styles. The atmosphere is just the right mix of low-key and downtown swank, the kind of spot where Sarasota's suit set comes after work for dirty martinis and networking. Patrick's stays open late.

Moore's Stone Crab (☎ 941-383-1748; 800 Broadway, Longboat Key; mains $10-25; lunch & dinner winter, dinner summer) This longtime bayfront eatery at the northern end of Longboat Key serves stone crabs in season from October through to March. Informal seafood dishes and sandwiches are served the rest of the year.

Bijou Cafe (☎ 941-366-8111; 1287 1st St; mains $10-30; lunch Mon-Fri, dinner Mon-Sat) A stylish chef-owned eatery with good service and an excellent wine list, this café offers substantial salads, steak frites, famously delectable *pommes au gratin* (a creamy potato and cheese concoction) and mains like spicy shrimp piri piri. It's a hands-down fave in the immediate area.

Lobster Pot (☎ 941-349-2323; 5157 Ocean Blvd, Siesta Key; mains $10-35; 11:30am-9pm Mon-Thu, to 9:30pm Fri & Sat, 5-9pm Sun only in winter) This Siesta Key institution is resort casual and worth stopping for a sandwich. It boasts enormous lobster rolls made with sweet Maine crustaceans.

Ophelia's on the Bay (☎ 941-349-2212; 9105 Midnight Pass Rd, Siesta Key; mains $18-25; dinner) Sarasota's winner for most romantic restaurant in town, Ophelia is perfectly situated on the southern tip of Siesta Key, overlooking a sweep of sparkling water and mangrove trees. Dine outside on a dockside patio, and savor the scent of the perfumed gardens around you. The food is as delicious as the surroundings. Ophelia's serves world-flavor-influenced haute couture North American cuisine, and has a lengthy wine and bubbly list.

ourpick Marina Jack's Restaurant (☎ 941-365-4232; 2 Marina Plaza; mains $16-30; lunch & dinner Mon, dinner only Tue-Sun) There are great panoramic views of the marina, downtown and Sarasota Bay at nearly every table here, thanks to theater-style seating and a location at the tip

of Island Park. The restaurant is divided in half – one side is an alfresco raw bar with covered patio seating, the other is an indoor dining room. The menu features lots of seafood, including Caribbean lobster tail (the house specialty), and chicken and steak staples. It has long been one of the top restaurants in the city.

TOP END

Fred's (☎ 941-364-5811; 1927 S Osprey Ave; lunch $7-22, dinner $16-45; lunch & dinner) A neighborhood bistro (in Southside Village) with swanky outdoor seating, Fred's draws an upscale young crowd to its happening setting. The Continental cuisine doesn't win any awards but it will satisfy your appetite. Friday nights are particularly fun here.

Michael's on East (☎ 941-366-0007; 1212 East Ave S, off US 41; lunch $8-15, dinner $24-40; lunch Mon-Fri, dinner Mon-Sat) Within the Midtown Plaza, Michael's serves exceptionally creative cuisine in elegant digs. The menu changes seasonally but patrons are loyal to Michael's throughout the year. To experience Michael's deservedly award-winning cuisine while still hanging on to your wallet, come for a fancy lunchtime sandwich or partake of the lighter bar menu.

Drinking

Besides the places listed here, check out **Fred's** (see above), a bistro that Sarasotans say serves one of the best martini lists in town – there are a number of exotic twists on the vodka or gin classic. Or **Patrick's** (left) for a low-key young-professional social scene.

ourpick Ca d'Zan Bar (☎ 941-309-2000; 1111 Ritz Carlton Dr) Inside the Ritz-Carlton, this swanky lounge serves the best chocolate martini in Sarasota – it's liquid dessert that gives you a buzz, and don't be surprised to find yourself licking the glass after the last heavenly sip. The atmosphere is old-world elegant, complete with jazz and dancing.

Old Salty Dog (☎ 941-388-4311; 1601 Ken Thompson Pkwy, City Island; mains $7-16; 11am-9:30pm or 10pm) Even if you're not visiting Mote Marine Laboratory (p436) on Longboat Key, this breezy outdoor restaurant and bar makes a great spot for an early evening beer.

Coasters (☎ 941-925-0300; 1500 Stickney Point Rd, the Boatyard; 11am-10pm) On the way to or from Siesta Key, Coasters is popular for its casual waterfront location, salads, sandwiches, wraps and two-for-one drinks. With a modicum of luck, you'll see dolphins frolicking in a waterway right near your table. This is a great place to catch the sunset and watch pleasure boats cruising by.

Siesta Key has a lively nightlife scene. Walk down Ocean Blvd and Beach Rd, and listen for the music. There are always new places opening, so follow your senses or just barhop until you find the right vibe.

The following places are recommended:

Daiquiri Deck (☎ 941-349-8697; 5250 Ocean Blvd, Siesta Key; ☺ 11am-2am) An after-beach happy-hour spot right on the water serving two-for-one drinks from 3pm to 7pm.

Siesta Key Oyster Bar (☎ 941-346-5443; 5238 Ocean Blvd, Siesta Key; ☺ 11am-midnight Sun-Thu, to 1:30am Fri & Sat)

Beach Club (☎ 941-349-6311; 5151 Ocean Blvd, Siesta Key; ☺ 11am-2am)

Entertainment

CINEMAS

In November, don't miss the annual 10-day CINE-World Film Festival of the **Sarasota Film Society** (☎ 941-364-8662; www.filmsociety.org), which screens over 40 of the year's best international films.

Burns Court Cinema (☎ 941-955-3456; 506 Burns Lane) In a sweet alleyway between Palm and Pineapple Aves, this happening cinema shows foreign and art films.

PERFORMING ARTS

FSU Center for the Performing Arts (☎ 941-351-8000; www.asolo.org; 5555 N Tamiami Trail, Ringling Estate; tick-

---

CIRCUS KIDS

Sarasota even celebrates its circus heritage in its school system. The **PAL Sailor Circus** (☎ 941-361-6350; www.sailorcircus.org; 2075 Bahia Vista St; tickets $10-15; ☺ late Dec & Mar-Apr; ⚥) is a truly unique circus experience – you don't have to worry about animal or human cruelty here – its troop is comprised entirely of Sarasota County students. The kids take 'circus' as an extracurricular school activity, and learn high-flying, tumbling and clowning, which they then perform under the big top. It's a wonderful experience that also supports positive after-school activities for children. Look for it tucked under the big blue-and-white circus tent east off S Tamiami Trail.

---

ets $15-50; ☺ Nov-Jun) On the Ringling Estate, this regional center hosts the Asolo Theater Company, visiting theater companies and the annual Asolo Theater Festival at its 19th-century Italian playhouse.

Van Wezel Performing Arts Hall (☎ 941-953-3368, 800-826-9303; www.vanwezel.org; 777 N Tamiami Trail; tickets $25-80; ☺ Nov-May) This city-run arts hall in a giant pink-and-purple building hosts some 200 events, from big band to easy-listening music, classical to pop, touring Broadway musicals and modern dance.

Players Theatre (☎ 941-365-2494; www.theplayers .org; 838 N Tamiami Trail; tickets from $18) A highly regarded nonprofit organization, this theater stages six well-known musicals, a couple of plays and summertime specials. Perhaps you'll discover the next Pee Wee Herman (who was actually discovered here).

Sarasota Opera House (☎ 941-953-7030; www.sarasota opera.org; 61 N Pineapple Ave; tickets $20-100; ☺ Feb-Mar) This elegant, 1000-seat Mediterranean Revival venue was built in 1926 and has served Sarasota opera well since the early 1960s. Don't understand Italian? No worries; English translations are projected above the stage.

LIVE MUSIC

Consult the free Wednesday *Weekly Planet* (www.weeklyplanet.com) for up-to-the-minute information.

Gator Club (☎ 941-366-5969; 1490 Main St; ☺ 11am-2am) Sarasota's most unique nightclub, the Gator offers live music seven nights a week – everything from Motown and salsa to reggae and alternative dance tunes. The vibe is comfortable and posh, reminiscent of an old upper-crust New York cigar club – think exposed brick walls, leaded glass mirrors and antique brass fixtures.

Blasé Café & Martini Bar (☎ 941-349-9822; 5253 Ocean Blvd, Siesta Key; ☺ 3pm-2am) This little Siesta Key place tucked into the Village Corner plaza (with outdoor tables basically in a parking lot) draws loyal locals because of great breakfasts, big casual lunches and much more gourmet dinners. (Think along the lines of pitch-perfect tuna.) Afterwards, hang out at the martini bar, which has live music on the weekends.

Getting There & Around

The **Sarasota-Bradenton International Airport** (SRQ; ☎ 941-359-2770; www.srq-airport.com; 6000 Airport Circle) is served by many major airlines. Driving from the airport, take University Parkway west to US 41, then head south straight into downtown.

Greyhound (☎ 941-955-5735; www.greyhound.com; 575 N Washington Blvd) plies the route between Sarasota and Miami (from $45, seven hours); Sarasota to Fort Myers (from $18, 2½ hours) and Tampa (from $15, two hours).

The **Sarasota County Area Transit** (SCAT; ☎ 941-861-1234; www.simplysiestakey.com; cnr 1st St & Lemon Ave; ☺ 6am-6:30pm Mon-Sat) operates area buses. There are no transfers or Sunday services.

Sarasota is roughly 60 miles south of Tampa and about 75 miles north of Fort Myers. The main roads into town are the Tamiami Trail (US 41) and the I-75. The most direct route from the I-75 is exit 39 to Hwy 780 west for about 8 miles; Hwy 780 turns into Fruitville Rd.

VENICE

☎ 941 / pop 20,100

Venice is our kind of beach town. Gorgeous, tidy, noncommercial and void of block-upon-block of cheesy hard-drinking beach bars and high-rise condos. It is less crowded and expensive than nearby Sarasota, and boasts a long sun-kissed stretch of golden sand, a fishing pier made for romantic sunset picnics and aqua surf with enough bumps to boogie board. There are also a few blocks of well-maintained pastel-hued buildings housing shark-tooth souvenir shops and sidewalk cafés.

Speaking of shark's teeth, did we mention Venice is the shark's tooth capital of Florida? Yep, shark's teeth have washed up on these shores for centuries due to coastal contours, and you can still find them if you're willing to walk with your head down and back hunched over. Head to the southern two-thirds of **Caspersen Beach**, south of town on Harbor Dr, to find the largest stash of teeth. If you have a bad back or would rather gaze out at the horizon, you can always buy bags of teeth in some tourist shops.

There is good **boogie boarding** to the right side off the **Venice Fishing pier** (follow the signs to the pier from Business 41). The pier itself is a great spot to watch the sunset. **Venice Main Beach** (again well signposted from the highway exits) is a long gorgeous sweep of sand. There are beach-volleyball courts and nightly pickup games, along with lifeguard stations. Grab a sandwich from the beachside **Food Shack** (it's on the right as you approach the beach and is open from early morning to about sunset)

and have a sundowner picnic on one of the wooden benches on the beach.

For something really different, check out the **Nokomis Beach Community Drum Circle** (www .nokomisdrumcircle.com) on nearby Nokomis Beach. The drumming starts an hour before sunset every Saturday. Attendance varies from several hundred to as many as several thousand depending on the month. There are between 25 and 100 regular drummers and belly dancers, and anyone with a positive attitude is invited to participate. Bring your own instrument, or join the spirited dancing inside the circle. As the sun sets, the beat becomes more frenetic until only the faintest hint of color remains in the sky – it is a beautiful experience. To get to Nokomis Beach take US 41 N to Albee Rd W.

The helpful **Venice Chamber of Commerce** (☎ 941-488-2236; www.venicechamber.com; 597 S Tamiami Trail; ☺ 8:30am-5pm Mon-Fri) can provide you with lots of tourist information.

Sleeping

A lot of places here close down during the off season – July to September. Check first, as Venice can become a bit of a ghost town during the hottest stormiest months.

Island Breeze Inn (☎ 941-488-4417; www.island breezeinn.com; 340 S Tamiami Trail; r from $60; ☒ ☒) This place offers 21 spotless and comfortable, welcoming rooms, a pool and a hefty Continental breakfast. It happens to be the oldest motel on the island, but it's also one of the best and quietest. If you have a laptop, there is high-speed internet available in the rooms.

Horse & Chaise Inn (☎ 941-488-2702, 877-803-3515; www.horseandchaiseinn.com; 317 Ponce de León; r $115-169; ☺ Oct-Jun; ☒ ☒) This two-story Mediterranean Revival inn, built in the mid-1920s and within easy walking distance of the little village, has eight guest rooms, each decorated to reflect some facet of Venice's history. There are plenty of places to relax, from the cozy common room to a porch that makes the most of cooling ocean breezes. Wi-fi is available and a full breakfast is included. Best of all it's pet friendly.

Inn at the Beach Resort (☎ 941-484-8471; www .innatthebeach.com; 725 W Venice Ave; r from $125; ☒ ☒) This low-rise motel looks a bit generic from the outside, but is really quite lovely once inside. Right on the beach, it has a tropical ambience and lush gardens. Rooms come in a variety of shapes, including ones with fabulous sunset views over the gulf from your private balcony, and others with money-saving kitchens. The staff are friendly, and there is a breakfast buffet included in the rate.

Banyan House (☎ 941-484-1385; www.banyan house.com; 519 S Harbor Drive; r from $139-189; ☒ closed Jul-Sep; ☒ ⊒ ⊒) This sprawling 1926 house boasts Venice's first swimming pool and a great climbing tree in its lushly shaded court-yard. A lovely B&B where full breakfasts are served on fine china, there is wi-fi, and all the rooms have private bathrooms and TVs; most have balconies.

Eating & Drinking

Snook Haven (☎ 941-485-7221; 5000 E Venice Ave; mains $6-14; ☒ lunch & dinner) Located at the end of a long dirt road, this Deep South landmark – a fishing camp and rustic restaurant on the banks of the Myakka River – served as the movie set for the earliest Tarzan flick. Come for fried sweet potatoes and a burger; stay for evening entertainment. On Thursday at noon, about 40 banjos gather to jam; it's a hoot. You can also arrange river trips here.

TJ Carney's Pub & Grille (☎ 941-480-9244 231; Venice Ave W; mains $8-15; ☒ lunch & dinner) This Venice institution has been dishing up home-cooked meals since the 1940s (though not under the same name). Locals return time and again for the cozy atmosphere and solid pub grub – think reuben sandwiches, juicy cheeseburgers and chicken wings. Sit inside the large dining room, or out on the patio to watch the action on the main street downtown.

ourpick Sharky's on the Pier (☎ 941-488-1456; 1600 Harbor Dr S; mains $10-25; ☒ lunch & dinner) Sharky's has a primo waterfront location at the Venice Fishing Pier and a fun-loving sunset crowd lingers at the tiki bar. Their seafood isn't going to rock your world, but their sunset views will. The food is fresh, it's just a little generic. Instead, come après beach frozen cocktails and appetizers on the deck.

Getting There & Around

Venice is best reached via private transport. To get here, follow US 41 south from Sarasota for about 25 miles and turn west to the beach (bear right) and Business 41. Parking at the beach is free.

Venice is a small place, and the three main areas – the Venice Fishing Pier, historic downtown and Venice Beach – are all neatly signposted.

MYAKKA RIVER STATE PARK

Florida's largest state park is well worth a visit. Comprised of dense woodlands, hammocks and prairies, the **wildlife preserve** (☎ 941-361-6511; www.myakkariver.org; 13207 State Rd 72; per car $5; ☒ 8am-sunset) weighs in (so to speak) at 47 sq miles. It offers great bird- and alligator-watching, 38 miles of boardwalks and trails and a few touring options. The airboat ride (on an enclosed, pontoon-type boat that remains in the upper lake area and doesn't damage wildlife but sure is loud) draws 'em in, but there is also a nature tram tour. Airboats depart at 10am, 11:30am, 1pm and 2:30pm (no 2:30pm tour in summer) and cost $8 for everyone over six years of age. Trams depart at 1pm and 2:30pm in winter only and cost the same.

The **Myakka Outpost** (☎ 941-923-1120; canoe rental from $20, bike rental from $15; ☒ 8:30am-5pm Jun-Sep, 10am-4pm Oct-May), within the park, rents canoes and bikes. Canoeing the Myakka River is a really cool experience. Or try renting a tandem bike (built for two) along one of the shady park trails.

Camping (sites $22, cabins from $60) is also primo here. There are five cabins with kitchens and linen and 76 RV and tent sites.

To reach the park from Sarasota, take US 41 south to Hwy 72 (Clark Rd) and head east for about 14 miles; the park is about 9 miles east of the I-75.

FORT MYERS

☎ 239 / pop 60,531

Dubbed the City of Palms for the 2000 royal palm trees that line McGregor Blvd, Fort Myers was a sleepy resort town in 1885 when Thomas Alva Edison decided to build a winter home and laboratory here. It was Edison who began planting the palms: he made a deal to plant them if the city agreed to maintain them after his death. He planted 543 as seedlings, and he imported another 270 from the Everglades, and these lined just the first mile of the avenue. Today McGregor Blvd is lined with palms for 14 miles. And you can visit Edison's estate, along with his next door neighbor's, Henry Ford.

Despite this illustrious connection, Fort Myers is known more for its urban sprawl, springtime baseball (p446), a ferry to Key West and a cypress slough than anything else. It's definitely more of the kind of city you live in, not visit. The beaches are about 30 minutes away and its downtown is a bit dowdy. If you've got kids, Fort Myers does have some diversions; while foodies may be interested in a few of the city's gourmand restaurants.

Orientation

The sprawling greater–Fort Myers area consumes the southwest corner of Florida. Fort Myers sits on the southern bank of the Caloosahatchee River; North Fort Myers on the north bank; Cape Coral sits to the west. To the southwest lie San Carlos and the Estero Islands (which include the *separate* city of Fort Myers Beach, see p447).

Distances in the Fort Myers area are expansive: for instance, Lee County Manatee Park, 8 miles northeast of downtown, is considered downtown Fort Myers. Anywhere you'll want to go beyond the immediate vicinity ends up being at least 40 minutes away by car. Stay at Fort Myers Beach if you're after sun and surf, but if you're primarily planning to canoe around the Matlacha Pass Aquatic Preserve (p449) or visit the Edison and Ford Winter Estates, you're in for a long drive.

Downtown is broken up by two intersecting grids. Streets in the historic district run kitty-corner to the standard east–west grid in the rest of the city. It's bounded on the south by Martin Luther King Jr Blvd, on the east by Evans Ave and the west by Cleveland Ave (US 41, the Tamiami Trail), which runs into the Caloosahatchee River Bridge and on to North Fort Myers. Downtown doesn't really have a main drag, but what action there is, is along 1st St, one block from the waterfront.

Information

Greater Fort Myers Chamber of Commerce (☎ 239-332-3624; www.fortmyers.org; cnr Lee St & Edwards Dr; 9am-4:30pm Mon-Fri) A helpful center that has the usual array of glossy tourist magazines and brochures, including one highlighting downtown public art.

Lee Memorial Hospital (☎ 239-332-1111; 2776 Cleveland Ave; 24hr) The area's largest hospital.

Library (☎ 239-338-3155; 2050 Central Ave; 9am-9pm Mon-Thu, to 6pm Fri & Sat) Has free web surfing on over 30 computers.

News-Press (www.news-press.com) The daily newspaper.

Post office (☎ 239-334-9159; cnr Bay St & Monroe Ave; 9am-5pm Mon-Fri) Located downtown.

Sights & Activities

EDISON & FORD WINTER ESTATES

The town's primary tourist attraction, this 14-acre **estate** (☎ 239-334-7419; www.edison-ford-estate.com; 2350 McGregor Blvd; adult/child/family $16/8.50/40; 9am-

4pm Mon-Sat, noon-4pm Sun) was the winter home of Thomas Edison from 1885 until his death in 1931. As you probably know, Edison was one of the most prolific inventors in the US, but unbeknownst to many he was also an avid botanist. As such, the grounds are lovely, brimming with more than 1000 varieties of plants. Check out the largest banyan tree in the US, which reaches more than 400ft. The interesting thing about the estate is the home is prefabricated – meaning it arrived in pieces and was constructed on site – but apparently the job was pretty sturdy, as it has withstood many a hurricane. The property also features the first in-ground swimming pool to be constructed in Florida.

Edison's laboratory here was mainly devoted to crossbreeding an American rubber tree at the behest of car and tire makers Ford and Firestone, who wanted to establish a reliable domestic supply. After experimenting with thousands of plants, Edison successfully created a hybrid goldenrod plant that grew to a height of almost 12ft in a season and contained 12% rubber – an unprecedented quantity. Unfortunately, the production process was too expensive and nothing commercial came of it. The remarkable laboratory has been kept pretty much as Edison left it – the array of gizmos is dizzying.

Adjacent to the laboratory (and included in the admission price of the estate), the **Edison Laboratory & Museum** contains a fascinating collection of hundreds of Edison's inventions and possessions. Look for his 1908 four-cylinder Cadillac coupe, tons of office equipment, movie projectors and kinescopes, Edison light bulbs, phonographs and the first three-wire generator system. Wander through the estate to the adjacent **Ford Winter Estate**, where the famed auto-maker and sometime philanderer resided. Ford and Edison were longtime friends, but didn't become neighbors until Ford built this genteel bungalow in 1916.

IMAGINARIUM HANDS ON MUSEUM

This excellent **science museum** (☎ 239-337-3332; www.cityftmyers.com/imaginarium; 2000 Cranford Ave; adult/child/senior $8/5/7; 10am-5pm Mon-Sat, noon-5pm Sun;), with over 60 exhibits, is favored by the wide-eyed kid in everyone. Don't miss the weather-forecasting exhibit, where kids can pretend they are meteorologists and present the weather using monitors. There is also a tornado machine and exhibits on ozone depletion and weather; touching a cloud is pretty

FORT MYERS

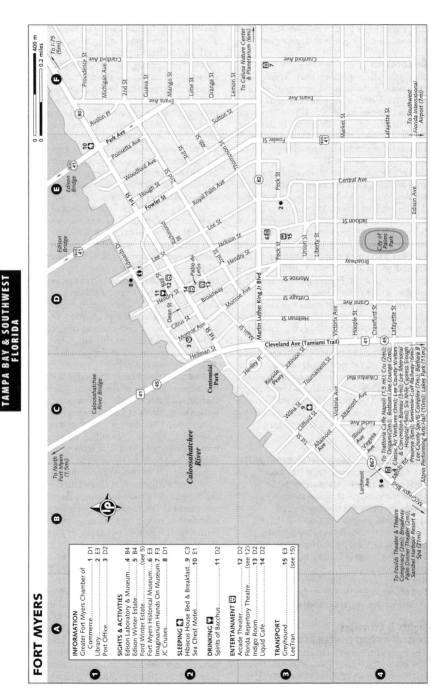

neat. A 3-D theater runs shows at 1pm and 3pm. Outside, a 'dig pit' lets kids look for fossils and shark teeth, while the lagoon teems with tons of freshwater fish and other Florida aquaculture. Check out the coral-reef tank, aquariums and reptile retreat.

SEMINOLE-GULF RAILWAY
Founded in 1888, this **railway** (☎ 239-275-8487, 800-736-4853; www.semgulf.com; Colonial Station, cnr Colonial Blvd & Metro Pkwy; tickets from $60; ☒ 6:30pm Wed-Sat, 5:30pm Sun) operated between Arcadia and Naples with a second line running between Bradenton, Sarasota and Venice. Today, it specializes 3½-hour, five-course, murder-mystery dinner tours on the line's restored trains among other day train excursions.

The station is near the intersection of Colonial Blvd and Metro Parkway; from downtown, take Cleveland Ave south to Colonial Blvd east until you think you'll run out of petrol; the terminal is on the left.

HIKING
A 2000-acre woodland and wetland, **Six Mile Cypress Slough Preserve** (☎ 239-432-2004; www.captiva .com/stateparks/sixmilecypress; 7751 Penzance Crossing; admission free, ☒ 8am-9pm) acts as a filter collecting runoff water during heavy rains. Before making its way out to the Estero Bay Aquatic Preserve, the water is filtered by the slough, where sediment and pollutants settle or are absorbed by the plants. It's an interesting place to visit during the wet season (June to October), when water up to 3ft deep flows through the area. The preserve also has an otter pond, a mile-long boardwalk lined with benches, free guided walks (call for times), a picnic area and an amphitheater used for flora and fauna talks. Parking costs $3.

From downtown Fort Myers, take Cleveland Ave south to Colonial Blvd (Hwy 884), east to Ortiz Ave and turn south; this road becomes Six Mile Cypress Parkway.

Tours
Classic Air Ventures (☎ 888-852-9226; 601 Danley Dr; per 2 people $150-350; ☒ 10am-5pm Thu-Sat Nov-Apr) At Page Field, off Cleveland Ave, just south of downtown Fort Myers, is flight-tour central. Among the outfits, Classic Air operates a restored 1940 open-cockpit biplane (that's right, goggles, leather helmet and all). It offers six different flights from 20 to 75 minutes in length.
JC Cruises (☎ 239-334-7474; www.jccruises.com; 2313 Edwards Dr; adult/child from $26/13; ☒ daily) Located at the Fort Myers Yacht Basin, JC offers two-hour and full day

lunch and dinner cruises, as well as manatee excursions (but only November to April), up and down the Caloosahatchee River and Intracoastal Waterway.

Festivals & Events
The annual **Edison Festival of Light** (☎ 239-334-2999; www.edisonfestival.org; 1300 Hendry St) is held between late January and Edison's birthday on February 11. There are dozens of mostly free events, block parties with live music ($5) and tons of food, high-school-band concerts, hymn sings, fashion shows and the Thomas A Edison Regional Science and Inventors Fair, which features more than 400 student finalists from the southwest-Florida school systems. It could be a blast – especially considering how Thomas himself blew up his railroad car and laboratory as a child. The fair culminates in the enormous Parade of Light, drawing up to 400,000 spectators.

Sleeping
Most visitors stay at Fort Myers Beach (p448) or 45 minutes away in lovely Naples (p454), but there are some downtown options if you have an early flight to catch.
Sea Chest Motel (☎ 239-332-1545; 2571 1st St; r from $55; ☒) On the river with a fishing pier, this motel has 32 cheap but perfectly adequate rooms and a heated pool.
Hibiscus House Bed & Breakfast (☎ 239-332-2651; www.thehibiscushouse.net; 2135 McGregor Blvd; r $100-200; ☒ ☐ ☒) Built in 1912, this nicely renovated and restored B&B has five quaint rooms – most feature white bedspreads and mosquito nets, setting a tropical vibe. A full breakfast is served, there is wi-fi and, unlike many B&Bs, children over five years of age are made welcome.
Sanibel Harbor Resort & Spa (☎ 239-466-4000; www.sanibel-resort.com; 17260 Harbor Pointe Rd; apt $220-550; ☒ ☐ ☒ ☒) Overlooking its namesake Sanibel Island, this resort of condo apartments is as luxurious as Fort Myers gets. Posh rooms have oversized beds, big picture windows and private sea-facing balconies. There are multiple pools and a fabulous spa. Kids are welcome, and there is babysitting available, along with a game room for teens. It runs free shuttles to area beaches.

Eating & Drinking
Considering its aging downtown, Fort Myers boasts a surprisingly large number of foodie-worthy restaurants.
Liquid Cafe (☎ 239-461-0444; 2236 1st St; mains from $4; ☒ 1-6pm Mon, 1pm-2am Tue-Sat) By day this cool

café has very good pies, specialty sandwiches, salads and coffee, as well as local art on the walls and funky chess chairs. By night, you can sample over 60 different bottled beers, check out the open mic on Tuesday and listen to bands on Friday and Saturday nights. Stop in and hang a while on the outdoor patio.

Spirits of Bacchus (☎ 239-689-2675; 1406 Hendry St; mains under $10; ⏰ 4pm–midnight) This wine and martini bar is a favorite Fort Myers watering hole. Appropriately named for the Greek god of drink, Bacchus serves excellent sandwiches and salads in a funky exposed-brick saloon. The wine list is lengthy.

Origami (☎ 239-482-2126; 13300 S Cleveland Ave; mains $5-20; ⏰ lunch & dinner) Despite a bland shopping-center setting, Origami is the local pick for excellent sushi. There are a variety of rolls and sashimi to choose from, all very fresh. Portions are large and prices very reasonable.

Cru (☎ 239-466-3663; 13499 S Cleveland Ave £241; mains $10-35; ⏰ lunch & dinner) Cru attracts a young, upbeat crowd who come for excellent steaks, Pacific Rim–flavored seafood (yes, the Daniel Boulud–trained chef is all about mixing and matching), strong drinks and a convivial atmosphere. For those looking more toward cocktails than dinner, there is a light tapas menu to keep your stomach from growling. Or come at lunch for similar dishes at much cheaper prices. Look for Cru in the Bell Tower shopping center south of town.

La Trattoria Caffe Napoli (☎ 239-931-0050; 12377 S Cleveland Ave; mains $17-25; ⏰ lunch & dinner) Run by the illustrious Gloria, this place fuses Cuban and Italian cooking with excellent results. Order the catch of the day – the fish special can be cooked in a spicy Cuban sauce or with Italian seasonings. Make sure to try the deep-fried plantains, they are loaded with garlic, and ultradelicious.

Entertainment

Consult www.downtownfortmyers.com for up-to-the-minute listings of what's up. The Patio de León laneway hosts an ever-changing lineup of nightclubs and cafés. Wander down and see what draws your attention.

Indigo Room (☎ 239-332-0014; 2219 Main St; ⏰ 11am-2am Tue-Sat, 7pm-2am Sun & Mon) This popular Patio de León pub-bar-club alternates between DJs and bands. In the contest for beer boasting rights, Indigo claims over 100 different brands.

Bottom Line Lounge (☎ 239-337-7292; www.clubtbl .com; 3090 Evans Ave; Fri & Sat cover from $5; ⏰ 2pm-2am)

Just north of Winkler Rd, Bottom Line has a predominantly gay crowd, with a good mix of lesbians, but all are welcome. Bar-top dancers gyrate and drag queens come out nightly except on Saturdays and Mondays. On Thursdays you can drink $5 mason jars of Long Island iced tea. Yowza.

Barbara B Mann Performing Arts Hall (☎ 239-481-4849; www.bbmannpah.com; Edison Community College, 13350 Edison Pkwy; tickets $22-64) The area's biggest performing-arts player hosts touring Broadway productions, classical and pops series and easy-listening singers.

Arcade Theater (☎ 239-332-4488; 2267 1st St; tickets $17-38) The beautifully renovated 1908 Arcade Theatre hosts popular comedies, dramas, musicals and ever-increasing local productions, including those by the year-round **Florida Repertory Theatre** (www.floridarep.org; 2267 1st St).

SPORTS

City of Palms Park (2201 Edison Ave), the spring-training field for baseball's hallowed **Boston Red Sox** (☎ 239-334-4700; www.redsox.com), is hopping in March. The **Minnesota Twins** (☎ 239-768-4270; www.mntwins.com) play at **Lee County Sports Complex** (☎ 239-461-7400; 14100 Six Mile Cypress Pkwy), just southwest of the intersection of Daniels Parkway and Six Mile Cypress Parkway. During the regular season, the Fort Myers Miracles (the Minnesota Twins minor-league baseball team) play here.

Getting There & Around

Southwest Florida International Airport (RSW; ☎ 239-768-1000; www.swfia.com; 16000 Chamberlin Pkwy) is east of the I-75 and off Daniels Parkway. It is served by about 15 airlines, and easy to get in and out of. It's also the main airport for nearby Naples.

Greyhound (☎ 239-334-1011; www.greyhound.com; 2250 Peck St) serves most places you'd want to go, including Miami (from $39, four hours), Orlando (from $45, three to six hours) and Tampa (from $35, three to six hours).

A decent public-transport system gets you around, albeit slowly. **LeeTran** (☎ 239-275-8726; www.rideleetran.com; 2250 Peck St) buses run throughout Lee County, but not to Sanibel or Captiva Islands, and they take a while (like an hour and a half from downtown Fort Myers to Fort Myers Beach). Fares are $1. From downtown, bus 20 runs (every 30 minutes) between the downtown station and the Edison and Ford Winter Estates.

KEY WEST EXPRESS

Kicking back on the **Key West Express** (☎ 239-765-0808, 800-273-4496; www.seakeywestexpress.com; Fisherman's Wharf & Salty Sam's Marina; round-trip/one-way adult $129/73, child $68/53; ⓨ daily) will save you 300 miles of driving and seven hours in the car. The high-speed ferry leaves Fort Myers Beach in the morning and arrives at Key West in the early afternoon; it arrives back in Fort Myers Beach at around 10pm. All in all you'll have about 5½ hours in Key West if you buy a return fare. If you just want to go and never come back, one-way tickets are now available. To reach the ferry, head south on San Carlos Blvd (Hwy 865) toward the Sky Bridge to Fort Myers Beach; just before the bridge, turn right on Main St and left on Fisherman's Wharf.

Because of sadistic distances between everything you'll want to see, a car is key. Downtown Fort Myers is about 40 minutes from Fort Myers Beach; the main connecting artery is Summerlin Rd (Hwy 869), which ends at Colonial Blvd. Another main connector between downtown and the beach is McGregor Blvd (Hwy 867), which forks away from Summerlin as it heads into downtown Fort Myers and becomes Martin Luther King Jr Blvd after it passes beneath US 41. Both Summerlin Rd and McGregor Blvd intersect with San Carlos Blvd, which continues to Fort Myers Beach and southward.

Fort Myers, between the I-75 and US 41, is about 140 miles from Miami and 123 miles from Tampa.

AROUND FORT MYERS

Some of southwest Florida's best natural attractions are around Fort Myers. From the excellent county parks and undeveloped splendor of Cayo Costa Island to the relatively undiscovered Pine Island and Matlacha Pass Aquatic Preserve, you can spend days soaking up nature, kayaking or canoeing, watching alligators, dolphins and manatees and really getting away from it all.

Or you can head over to Estero Island where Fort Myers Beach manages to be both a party town (at its Times Sq section) and a quiet beach resort (further south). Many people make this their base for exploring the area.

Fort Myers Beach

For a party atmosphere, especially during Spring Break, head to Fort Myers Beach. The town lines a pretty stretch of surf-and-sand – although the water can look a little polluted from the numerous jet skis and speedboats plying the waterfront. It is a bit faded, filled with high-rise condos and hotels next to pastel businesses all in varying shades of seaside decay – some are definitely looking one hurricane past their prime. That said, the sunsets here are phenomenal – think giant orange ball sinking straight into a blackening ocean. If you want an intense playground, head to the Times Sq party area. Although it's wishful thinking to invoke the famed New York City address, there are a number of lively bars and eateries here. Otherwise, prepare for sunning, drinking, parasailing and scootering around. And keep an eye out for frolicking dolphins in the bay.

Estero Island, a 7-mile-long sliver of thread, is about a 40-minute drive southwest from downtown Fort Myers. The main drag – actually the only drag – is Estero Blvd, which eventually leads across a bridge to Lover's Key State Park, Bonita Beach and US 41. Funky and hopping Times Sq is located at the intersection of Estero Blvd and San Carlos Blvd.

The **Greater Fort Myers Beach Chamber of Commerce** (☎ 239-454-7500; www.fmbchamber.com; 17200 San Carlos Blvd; ⓨ 8am-5pm Mon-Fri, 10am-5pm Sat, 11am-5pm Sun), about 3 miles north of the Sky Bridge, has all the requisite pamphlets and menus as well as a voluminous list of beachside condo rentals.

SIGHTS & ACTIVITIES

Between Fort Myers Beach and Bonita Beach, **Lover's Key State Park** (☎ 239-463-4588; 8700 Estero Blvd; per car $5, per pedestrian or cyclist $1; ⓨ sunrise-sunset) is quieter than Fort Myers Beach and offers very good shelling, 2.5 miles of good beaches and bird-watching. Canoe and kayak rentals are available.

Fort Myers beach is wall-to-wall sunbathers during the Spring Break, and draws a crowd even during the hot summer months. It's known for its party scene, and there are numerous beach bars, where booze is either served directly to your beach chair, or from the patio of a throbbing disco built right over the sand. It can be loud and rowdy, but the atmosphere is far from X-rated – Fort Myers is also popular with families. Many of the restaurants have children's menus and there are plenty of kids building sand castles on the beach (while listening to '80s rock pumping out of the beach bar next door).

The **boardwalk** is at the extreme north end of the beach, and is filled with hot-dog stands and T-shirt shops.

SLEEPING

Fort Myers Beach is really kid friendly. It's also a lot cheaper than Naples, which makes it appealing to those on a budget – you can go up to Naples or Sanibel for the day (Fort Myers Beach is less than an hour from both), but return here for better-value sleeping.

Island House Motel (☎ 239-463-9282; 701 Estero Blvd; r from $70; ✖ ♨) Just north of Matanzas Pass Bridge and within walking distance of the action, this very good old-Florida-style motel (built on stilts) has complimentary bikes and beach chairs, a pool and five units with kitchens just 300ft from the beach. The hosts are friendly, and the rooms are huge and modern.

Lighthouse Resort Inn & Suites (☎ 239-463-9392; www.lighthouseislandresort.com; 1051 5th St; r from $75; P ✖ ♨ 🏊) This multicolored hotel at the north end of town is across the main strip from the beach and quieter than its neighbors. It's a family-friendly place built around a pool and pirate-themed tiki bar with live entertainment – grab a room facing away from the pool to avoid noise. There is wi-fi and nine styles of rooms, including big family suites with kitchen. Beds are comfortable and loaded with pillows. Book through the website for the best deals.

Palm Terrace Apartments (☎ 239-765-5783, 800-320-5783; www.palm-terrace.com; 3333 Estero Blvd; apt $85-300; ✖ ♨ 🏊) Near the beach, Palm Terrace offers unique apartment rentals in varying sizes and views. Request a room on the highest floor to get unobstructed views of pelicans circling around the hotel. If you've got the family, grab a larger apartment facing the pool so the kids have easy access. Most apartments come with a deck or screened porch and kitchen. Staff are friendly and obliging – if you want a bag of microwave popcorn, just call down to the front desk and it will be arranged.

Outrigger Beach Resort (☎ 239-463-3131, 800-749-3131; www.outriggerfmb.com; 6200 Estero Blvd; r $110-160, apt $250; ✖ ♨ 🏊) With 144 rooms and apartments and a fun beachfront tiki bar with great sunset views, this beach resort is fairly priced – check online for mid-week room specials as low as $75. Families are well taken care of in efficiency apartments, with kitchens and multiple TVs.

EATING

Fresh seafood is a smart choice here, since 'daily catch' equates to truth-in-advertising: there's a sizable fishing port at Matanzas Pass.

Fish House (☎ 239-765-6766; 7225 Estero Blvd; sandwiches $7-10, mains $15-25; ✷ lunch & dinner; 🏊) At the Fish Tale Marina, this outdoor joint has killer grouper sandwiches; you know they're good when boat captains are chowing on 'em with a beer. Kids can choose from the children's menu.

Split Rail (☎ 239-466-3400; 17943 San Carlos Blvd; breakfast $2-6, lunch & dinner $7-15; ✷ breakfast, lunch & dinner; 🏊) A dependable breakfast source, this eclectic place has an unusual mix of Greek, Mexican (which predominates) and North American dishes (sandwiches and seafood). It's off the beach, about 1.5 miles back toward Fort Myers.

Beached Whale (☎ 239-463-5505; 1249 Estero Blvd; $7-15; ✷ lunch & dinner) Head upstairs to this rooftop restaurant and bar for southern specialities like barbecue ribs and tons of fried seafood – from shrimp to oysters. The food isn't spectacular, but it's good for inexpensive North American bar grub. Dining on the roof is breezy and popular, and comes with gulf views. Inside, it's cool and dark (a good option if you've had too much sun), with lots of wood decor and big TVs tuned to the game.

Matanzas Inn (☎ 239-463-3838; 416 Crescent St; lunch $6-15, dinner $15-25; ✷ lunch & dinner) You can watch fish being unloaded from the adjacent docks at this waterfront eatery, a casual option for fresh seafood (particularly stuffed grouper, mahimahi and beer-battered shrimp). It's hard to beat the dockside and deck dining.

Snug Harbor Seafood Restaurant (☎ 239-463-4343; 1131 1st St; mains $8-40; ✷ lunch & dinner) At the foot of Sky Bridge and popular among locals (who hang out at the dockside bar), Snug Harbor features Caesar salads, salmon cakes, sautéed grouper and blackened chicken breast. Freshly caught seafood specials are usually a good bet.

DRINKING & ENTERTAINMENT

Gulfshore Grill & the Cottage (☎ 239-765-5440; 1270 Estero Blvd; mains $8-20 ✷ lunch & dinner; 🏊)

You'll hear this super-popular beachfront bar's throbbing speakers from blocks away. Filled with a young party-hardy crowd, there is a giant tropical-drink menu along with daily drink specials and happy hour at the Gulfshore Grill, which has a huge, usually crowded, alfresco patio deck (from which the music blasts all day and night). Gulfshore serves a full menu, which features everything from burritos to wraps, salads, pasta and seafood dishes and even a kids' menu. The Cottage is the attached nightclub that features live entertainment every night except for Sunday. Acts range from karaoke to live guitar performances.

Top O'Mast Lounge (☎ 941-463-9424; 1028 Estero Blvd; ✆ 11am-2am) You can order a margarita and drink it right on your chair in the sand, at this true beach bar. Some people hate this bar, finding it noisy and full of drunk 20-somethings. Others love the flirty, hard-party atmosphere and the loud music blaring onto the surrounding beach. Live bands rock the place Thursday to Sunday nights. Guess you'll have to visit to decide.

Beach Pierside Grill (☎ 239-765-7800; 1000 Estero Blvd; ✆ 11am-11pm) Also in the happening Times Sq area, this hopping beachside bar has live music Wednesday to Sunday nights.

GETTING THERE & AROUND
From downtown Fort Myers, take McGregor Blvd to San Carlos Blvd and cross the Sky Bridge. From the south on US 41, turn west on Bonita Beach Rd at the southern end of Bonita Springs and head north.

A red **LeeTran trolley** (☎ 239-275-8726; www .rideleetran.com; 2250 Peck St; 25¢; ✆ every ½hr from about 7am-9pm) runs daily between the pier (opposite the Sky Bridge) and Bowditch Point Regional Park at the northwestern end of the island, all the way southeast to Villa Santini Plaza, where you can catch another tram that runs

south between Fort Myers Beach and Bonita Beach, past Lover's Key. In the summertime the tram runs from Summerlin Sq all the way to Bonita Springs.

Pine Island & Matlacha
The gorgeous barrier islands surrounding the pristine Matlacha (pronounced mat-la-shay) Pass Aquatic Preserve are perfect for kayak and canoe exploration. The preserve, along with the Pine Island Sound Aquatic Preserve, covers 90 sq miles and more than 70 miles of coastline, and it's made up of islands, mangrove swamps and shallow lagoons and bays.

Pine Island, at 17-miles long, is the area's largest, and while it's officially broken up into several communities, everyone calls the whole thing Pine Island. Fortunately, it's been spared development because of its location, and Florida height and density zoning limits. Communities include the tiny fishing village of Matlacha; Bokeelia (pronounced bow-keel-ya), at the northern tip, which is the commercial fishing center and home of the *Tropic Star* (p450); and Pine Island Center, the commercial district at the center of the island.

The volunteers at the **Greater Pine Island Chamber of Commerce** (☎ 239-283-0888; www.pine islandchamber.org; Pine Island Rd; ✆ 10am-4pm Mon-Fri, to 1pm Sat), just east of Matlacha, dispenses reliable information.

ACTIVITIES
At **Gulf Coast Kayak** (☎ 239-283-1125; www.gulf coastkayak.com; 4882 NW Pine Island Rd; ✆ 9am-2pm), on Little Palm Island, Matlacha, they offer several year-round wildlife and nature tours (per person $45) as well as kayak and canoe rentals (single/double $30/$45). Consider renting for several days since you could take camping trips to Cayo Costa State Park (p450). Reservations are recommended.

DETOUR: SWAMP ROMPING

Babcock Wilderness Adventures (☎ 800-500-5583; www.babcockwilderness.com; 8000 Hwy 31, Punta Gorda; adult/child $18/11; reservations required; ✆ 9am-3pm winter, 9am tour only in summer) runs super-popular ecofriendly swamp-buggy rides through the largest contiguous cattle ranch east of the mighty Mississippi River. These naturalist-led 90-minute tours cruise five different ecosystems on the enormous 90,000-acre Crescent B Ranch on the Telegraph Cypress Swamp. Look out for bison, quarter horses, Texas cougars, alligators, panther, deer, wild turkey and boar.

The ranch is about 10 miles northeast of Fort Myers; take the I-75 to exit 26 and take Hwy 78 east, then take Hwy 31 north for 6 miles.

SLEEPING

Bridge Water Inn (☎ 239-283-2423; www.bridgewater inn.com; 4331 Pine Island Rd; r summer $69-189; ✗ ⬚ ♿) Built on a pier, this great family-run place has three motel rooms and five large apartments. The two corner apartments have huge sliding-glass doors that look out onto the aquatic preserve and the waterfront. Dolphins and manatees swim by regularly.

Beach House Motel (☎ 239-283-4303; 7702 Bocilla Lane; r summer $90-125, winter $100-210; ✗) The motel, with its own pier, has three apartments and one simple room. If you're staying in the area for a while, this could make a decent base, as weekly rentals are quite affordable, ranging from $700 to $1200 per week depending on season and size.

EATING

A bunch of homey restaurants serving consistently reliable seafood and burgers are within walking distance of Pine Island Rd NW.

Matlacha Oyster House (☎ 239-283-2544; 3930 Pine Island Rd NW; mains $8-22; ☯ lunch & dinner) Try daily seafood specials like grouper fingers, seafood-stuffed flounder and poached salmon. On Friday and Saturday nights, there's live music out on the torch-lit porch.

Sandy Hook Restaurant (☎ 239-283-0113; 4875 Pine Island Rd; mains $12-18; ☯ dinner Tue-Sun, lunch Sun) This place offers excellent water views, good baby back ribs and combo platters with grouper and ribs.

GETTING THERE & AROUND

Pine Island is due west of North Fort Myers and is not accessible by public transporta-

tion. By car, take either US 41 north to Pine Island Rd (Hwy 78) or the I-75 north to exit 26 (Bayshore Rd, which becomes Pine Island Rd). Follow Pine Island Rd west until you get there; you'll pass Matlacha and Little Pine Island.

Cayo Costa Island

One of Florida's largest undeveloped barrier islands, Cayo Costa is the jewel of the gulf coast. It lies west of Pine Island and north of Captiva Island (opposite). The 2500-acre **state park** (☎ 941-964-0375, 800-326-3521; www.floridastateparks.org /cayocosta; campsites $18, 4-person cabins $30; ☯ 8am-sunset) offers great shelling, swimming, kayaking and canoeing. As if that wasn't enough, Atlantic bottle-nosed dolphins live around here and frolic just offshore. With white sand, palms, gumbo-limbo hammocks, clear water and cheap accommodations, this park offers arguably one of the best deals for enjoying Florida's sun and fun. There are three catches: you have to bring your own food (cooking and picnic facilities are available); you have to get there by boat; and there's no hot water or electricity in the cabins. Bring your own linen, utensils and, definitely, insect repellent. Reservations are required – check the website for details.

GETTING THERE & AROUND

The island is accessible only by boat. Park rangers run a tram between the island dock and the camping area, or you can walk the mile.

Gulf Coast Kayak (☎ 239-283-1125; 4530 Pine Island Rd; ☯ 9am-2pm), which rents kayaks and camping equipment, also runs guided tours that include everything you'll need except a tooth-

---

DETOUR: SCARFING A CHEESEBURGER IN PARADISE AT THE CABBAGE KEY INN

Everyone has slept at the **Cabbage Key Inn** (☎ 239-283-2278; www.cabbagekey.com; accessible only by boat, at MM 60; r from $90, cottages from $150; ☯ breakfast, lunch & dinner) including Ernest Hemingway, Julia Roberts, JFK Jr and of course Jimmy Buffet. As the story goes, Jimmy Buffet's song 'Cheeseburger in Paradise' was inspired by this 100-acre key and its hotel and restaurant. The home, constructed atop a Calusa shell mound by writer Mary Roberts Rinehart in 1938, has wacky wallpaper: 20,000 to 30,000 $1 bills festoon the walls. Supposedly, in the 1940s, commercial fishermen used to eat here, and when they were feeling flush, they autographed a dollar and stuck it to the wall. When they felt broke, they could always yank one down from the wall and buy themselves a bowl of chowder.

The inn's lunch menu – homey soups, burgers, large salads and the popular homemade smoked-salmon appetizer – is priced reasonably (mains $7 to $12). For a wonderfully romantic dinner of grouper with crabmeat, Gulf shrimp on angel-hair pasta or Szechuan salmon, count on spending about $30 per main (plus a water taxi, see above). If you do stay here, book early. There are only six rooms and seven cottages; the latter have kitchens. All are old-fashioned, wood-walled affairs.

brush and sleeping bag. Prices vary depending on the length of stay.

Tropic Star (☎ 239-283-0015; www.tropicstarcruises.com; 13921 Waterfront Dr; ☾ 9:30am & 2pm), departing from Knight's Landing in Bokeelia at the northern tip of Pine Island, cruises year-round to Cayo Costa. You can get off and camp here, or just bring lunch and beach gear for the day. Day trips cost $25 for adults, $17 for children. If you camp overnight it costs $30 for adults, $17 for children. You can also take the Tropic Star Nature Cruise, which continues up to the Cabbage Key Inn (see the boxed text, opposite), where you can buy lunch before enjoying two hours on Cayo Costa. Reservations are required.

The other option is a private water taxi. **Island Charters** (☎ 239-283-1113; www.islandcharters.com; 16499 Porto Bello St; ☾ daily) runs 25-minute water taxis (by reservation) from Bokeelia Marina to the Cabbage Key Inn for $45 per person.

Lee County Manatee Park

This Orange River **park** (☎ 239-432-2038, summer hotline 239-694-3537; www.leeparks.org; 10901 State Rd 80; admission free; ☾ park 8am-5pm year-round, visitors center 9am-4pm in winter, closed in summer) draws in the visitors with a manatee-viewing platform, picnic shelters, guided viewing programs, native plant habitats and an 'Eco-Torium' with manatee displays and info. Kayaks are available year-round (per hour/day $10/30), but in summer you must reserve them in advance online because the visitors center is closed. Remember, this is a noncaptive habitat and West Indian manatees only hang around when the water temperatures dip below 70°F (ie from December to March). The park is off Hwy 80, about 8 miles east of downtown Fort Myers and about 1.5 miles east of the I-75 exit 25. Parking costs $3.

SANIBEL & CAPTIVA ISLANDS

☎ 239 / Sanibel pop 6066 / Captiva pop 379

The beautiful barrier islands of Sanibel and Captiva offer the reclusive millionaire the perfect natural hideaway, while giving the tourist a chance to scout for seashells on glorious porcelain beaches, then dine on delicious fresh seafood at one of the chic beach-shack seafood joints lining the single road around the sand.

Although Sanibel has a reputation for being a bit on the snobby eccentric side – think retired hedge-fund managers and socialites – locals say this isn't true.

'Sanibel is for people who like seclusion. There is no pretentiousness. It is a very laid-back place. The people here have money, but they don't show it. There is a saying that Sanibel-informal equals covering your genitals. How informal is that?' says Lee Seidler, a longtime Sanibel resident and one of the founders of Bear Stearns & Co. 'Besides, Sanibel's a great place to visit. You can bike around the entire island. Even driving is easy – there isn't a single traffic light!'

Plus, development is limited, and high-rise blight has by-passed Sanibel – no resorts can stand higher than a palm tree. Captiva is even more undeveloped, secluded and idiosyncratic. At the end of the road, it feels like the ends of the earth, with most houses hidden behind a cloak of dense foliage.

The only downer is price – staying out here can be a bit expensive. If you're short on cash, still visit, but make it a day trip from Fort Myers or even Naples. Although Sanibel and Captiva are frequently whacked by hurricanes. Hurricane Charley made the last direct hit, and both islands lost a lot of trees. Sanibel has completely recovered but Captiva is still struggling a bit, and the extreme north edge of the island has never completely recovered.

Information

The **Sanibel & Captiva Islands Chamber of Commerce** (☎ 239-472-1080; www.sanibel-captiva.org; 1159 Causeway Rd, Sanibel; ☾ 9am-7pm Mon-Sat, 10am-5pm Sun in winter, 9am-6pm Mon-Fri, 9am-5pm Sat & Sun in summer) has mountains of tourist information.

Sights & Activities

Peolple come to Sanibel for the **sea shells** – the 'Sanibel Stoop' is a local phrase that was coined for the way people's backs stoop from shell hunting. Thanks to a quirk of currents, that deposits large amounts of shells on the shores, the shelling here is the country's best. To learn your shells, stop by **Bailey's Supermarket** (2477 Periwinkle Way) and grab one of their shell-bags. Pictures of the different varieties of seashells are printed on the front so you can collect and recognize. Look out for Sanibel's prize shell, the Juninia, a round shell with speckles – finding one will merit a photo of you and it in the local paper.

BEACHES

They're fabulous here, absolutely fabulous. The main beaches (where parking costs $2 hourly) are **Bowman's Beach** (long and private), **Sanibel Lighthouse Beach** (with a nature trail and fishing pier), **Turner Beach** (with limited parking but great for catching sunsets) and **Gulfside Park Beach**. East, Middle and West Gulf Drives provide gulf beach access.

You can't enter the wooden **Sanibel Island Lighthouse**, a working lighthouse that dates to 1884 and is located at the eastern end of Periwinkle Way. But it is lovely to look at, and there's plenty of adjacent parking surrounded by beach access.

JN 'DING' DARLING NATIONAL WILDLIFE REFUGE

Named for cartoonist Jay Norwood 'Ding' Darling, an environmentalist who helped establish more than 300 sanctuaries across the USA, this fascinating 6300-acre **refuge** (☎ 239-472-1100, 888-679-6450; www.dingdarling.fws.gov; Sanibel-Captiva Rd at MM 2, Sanibel; per car $5, per pedestrian or cyclist $1; ⏰ visitors center 9am-4pm May-Dec, 9am-5pm Jan-Apr, refuge sunrise-sunset Sun-Thu), at the northern end of Sanibel, is home to a huge variety of fish and wildlife. You'll see alligators, green-backed and night herons, red-shouldered hawks, spotted sandpipers, roseate spoonbills, pelicans and anhinga. The refuge also has canoe trails, an outstanding educational center and exhibition space, a 5-mile Wildlife Drive, alligator-observation platforms and walking trails. Shelling is strictly prohibited here. The best time to visit is low tide, when birds are feeding. The Bailey Trail, off Tarpon Bay Rd, is accessible on Fridays when the rest of the park isn't.

Excellent naturalist-narrated **Wildlife Drive tram tours** (☎ 239-472-8900; www.tarponbayexplorers.com; 900 Tarpon Bay; adult/child $10/7; ⏰ Sat-Thu) depart from the visitors'-center parking lot; call for departure times.

BAILEY MATTHEWS SHELL MUSEUM

This **museum** (☎ 239-395-2233, 888-679-6450; www.shellmuseum.org; 3075 Sanibel-Captiva Rd, Sanibel; adult/child $7/4; ⏰ 10am-4pm) is dedicated to all things shell-related. With over 30 exhibits, the wide-reaching galleries will educate you about edible scallops of the world; shells in art; and medicinal (and poisonous) properties of mollusks. A giant globe indicates where in the world the shells originated from. Check out the cool sculpture – made from shells, of course – called *State Fair Made of Shells*. The library boasts everything from an environmental coloring book and *Synopsis Omnium Methodica Molluscorum Generum* to a computerized research center with an enormous conchological data bank and a 35mm slide collection.

SANIBEL HISTORICAL VILLAGE

When you're really searching for something to do, this little **museum** (☎ 239-472-4648; 950 Dunlop Rd, Sanibel; admission $4; ⏰ 10am-1pm Wed-Sat in summer, to 4pm Wed-Sat in winter), a collection of buildings that preserves Sanibel's past, includes a mid-1920s general store and cottage, an old post office, a tea house and a museum with historical photos and displays on Calusa Indians.

BIKING

With over 23 miles of dedicated paths (which are the very definition of flat), biking is an excellent way to get around; the chamber of commerce has a detailed bike map. Head to **Billy's Rentals** (☎ 239-472-5248; 1470 Periwinkle Way, Sanibel; ⏰ 8:30am-5pm) or the southern end of Sanibel. Bicycles cost about $10 per hour or $25 per day.

CANOEING & KAYAKING

The folks at **Tarpon Bay Explorers** (☎ 239-472-8900; www.tarponbayexplorers.com; 900 Tarpon Bay Rd, Sanibel; ⏰ 8am-2pm), within the refuge on Sanibel, rent canoes and kayaks for $25 for two hours. That's plenty of time to paddle around the marked mangrove waterways or join a guided ecotour (adult/child $40/25) and then paddle around on your own (no additional charge).

'Tween Waters Marina (☎ 239-472-5161; 15951 Captiva Rd, Captiva; ⏰ 7:30am-5:30pm), on Captiva north of the refuge at the 'Tween Waters Inn, rents canoes ($30 for two hours). Although it's close enough to the refuge to paddle from the marina, ask about the tides. Even if you're just paddling around the resort, you can zip across to Buck Key, which has two canoe trails. 'Tween also books two-hour guided kayak tours at Buck Key for $50.

Tours

If you're itching to get out on the water, head out with **Captiva Cruises** (☎ 239-472-5300; www.captivacruises.com; McCarthy's Marina, Andy Rosse Lane, Captiva; ⏰ daily), on a naturalist-accompanied dolphin-watching or wildlife-adventure tour (adult/child $20/12.50), a sunset tour where you'll be serenaded with live music (adult/child $17.50/10) or a sailing cruise ($95 per hour).

Festivals & Events

Sanibel Shell Fair An annual fair that has been going strong since the 1940s; in March.

Sanibel Music Festival (☎ 239-336-7999; www .sanibelmusicfestival.com) One of the most anticipated events of the year for fans of classical and chamber music, this festival sees international stars of the genre play concerts in the Congressional Church every Tuesday and Saturday during March. Check the website for more.

Sanibel Captiva Lions Arts & Crafts Fair Includes more than 150 fine arts and craft exhibitors; in early April.

'Ding' Darling Days (☎ 239-422-1100; www.ding darlingdays.com) Hosted by the National Wildlife Refuge, this festival includes a week of environmental speakers and photography workshops; in mid-October.

Sanibel Luminary Fest Lights up the town with over 3 miles of paper luminaries and celebrates music; in December.

Sleeping

It's pricey to sleep on these two islands. For a complete listing of charming motel alternatives, contact the **Sanibel-Captiva Small Inns and Cottages Association** (www.sanibelsmallinns.com); for vacation rentals contact **Sanibel Accommodations** (☎ 800-237-6004; www.sanibel-captiva.com).

Periwinkle Park & Campground (☎ 239-472-1433; www.sanibelcamping.com; 1119 Periwinkle Way, Sanibel; campsites $35-45) Only a 10-minute walk to excellent beaches, there's no cheaper place to lay your head than this sandy park. With only about 80 spaces for RVs and tents, this place gets booked solid from Christmas until late April.

Palm View & Sandpiper Motel (☎ 239-472-1606; www.palmviewsanibel.com; 706 Donax St, Sanibel; ste & apt $85-185) On a nicely landscaped lot, these suites and apartments are the most affordable option on Sanibel. They're also fairly large with a bit of character – from the alligator coffee table to the bold-rimson or midnight-blue wall.

Tarpon Tale Inn (☎ 239-472-0939, 888-345-0939; www.tarpontale.com; 367 Periwinkle Way, Sanibel; r $100-255; ✗) Charming, with lush gardens in an old neighborhood, Tarpon Tale has five fresh and contemporary units with whitewash wicker and rattan decor, along with some antique oak furnishings. There are beach chairs, barbecue grills, bicycles and a hot tub. Check online for multinight-stay discounts.

Sundial Beach & Gulf Resort (☎ 866-565-5093; www.sundialresort.com; 1455 Middle Gulf Dr, Sanibel; r $129-300; ✗ 🖳 🏊 🍴) Swanky, modern and lushly landscaped, this place is right on the beach, with five gorgeous pools and an assortment of soothing guestrooms done up in khaki, ivory and blues. All digs feature big windows, plush beds and kitchenettes. Golfers will dig playing at the Dunes, an 18-hole championship course with spectacular Gulf of Mexico views. Water sports, bike rentals and shelling outings can also be arranged. The hotel is kid friendly, running a children's camp so parents can escape for some R&R. Wi-fi is available. Check online for off-season and web-only specials.

Casa Ybel Resort (☎ 239-472-3145, 800-276-4753; www.casaybelresort.com; 2255 W Gulf Dr, Sanibel; r $270-400; 🏊) A refined condo community with one- and two-bedroom suites with kitchens, the excellent Casa Ybel enjoys great amenities such as a pool, beach, tennis and manicured grounds. It's the nicest ritzy hotel on the island.

Eating

BUDGET

Amy's Over Easy (☎ 239-472-2625; 630 Tarpon Rd, Sanibel; mains $5-10 ⏰ breakfast & lunch; 🏃) Breakfast done right. Locals recommend this neighborhood restaurant for loads of egg choices – from sunny-side up to over-stuffed omelettes, and good waffles. Portions are huge. At lunch there are reuben sandwiches, bowls of tomato bisque and '70s music on the stereo.

Sanibel Bean (☎ 239-395-1919; 2240 Periwinkle Way, Sanibel; mains $5-10; ⏰ 7am-8pm) Stepping up to the plate where the coffee chains don't venture, this groovy little café serves light breakfast bagels, lunchtime salads, panini and namesake coffee-bean drinks.

Sanibel Cafe (☎ 239-472-5323; 2007 Periwinkle Way, Sanibel; mains from $5-15; ⏰ breakfast, lunch & dinner) Can't get enough seashells? The tables here are basically shadow boxes filled with sandy specimens to look at. But patrons really come for delectable omelettes and eggs benedict at breakfast, healthy lunchtime salads and sandwiches, and comfort foods (and great grouper) at nightfall. Save room for the Key lime pie.

MIDRANGE & TOP END

Lazy Flamingo Captiva (☎ 239-472-5353; 6520 Pine Ave; mains $9-24; ⏰ lunch & dinner); Sanibel (☎ 239-472-6939; 1036 Periwinkle Way; mains $9-24; ⏰ lunch & dinner) Hard to beat, this casual option with a sports-bar atmosphere has great oysters, good smoked fish, mesquite-grilled grouper sandwiches and grilled chicken breasts. Their specialty is 'The Pot,' two-dozen oysters or clams steamed in beer and seasonings ($18). It's the local pick for Sanibel attitude and good food at reasonable (for Sanibel) prices. Don't miss the string-and-ring toss game – ask the bartender if no one is playing.

Bubble Room (☎ 239-472-5558; 15001 Captiva Dr, Captiva; mains $10-15; ☽ lunch & dinner; ♿) Amusing or bizarre, depending on your perspective, this Sanibel classic is packed with memorabilia from the 1930s and '40s, flashing lights, movie photos, bric-a-brac and doo-dads. It's a totally insane place (with service to match), worth a stop simply for some appetizers (large Gulf shrimp in garlic butter or she-crab soup made with cream) and a drink or two. The food is only mediocre, but the portions are absolutely massive.

Timbers (☎ 239-472-3128; 703 Tarpon Bay Rd, Sanibel; mains $15-25; ☽ dinner) One of Sanibel's best places for fish or grilled meat. It doesn't get much fresher than this. The pleasantly casual place also has an adjacent sports bar.

RC Otter (☎ 239-395-1142; Andy Rosse Lane, Captiva; mains $10-20; ☽ breakfast, lunch & dinner) Ensconced in an old wooden cottage, this casual place with indoor and outdoor dining offers everything from good sandwiches and burgers to excellent and creative breakfasts. It's the local choice for a relaxing dinner, and there is usually some sort of musical entertainment.

Jacaranda (☎ 239-472-1771; 1223 Periwinkle Way, Sanibel; mains $20-30; ☽ dinner) Working hard at being chic, Jacaranda specializes in fresh seafood, black Angus steaks and pastas. They also feature live music nightly, drawing a hip middle-aged crowd.

Ellington's (☎ 239-472-0494; 937 E Gulf Dr, Sanibel; mains $20-40; ☽ dinner) Ellington's serves nouvelle North American food along with fresh jazz. The menu – which features lots of Southern-influenced dishes and seafood – is filled with plenty of tasty flavors, such as Gulf crab–encrusted grouper served with paella rice and mango-butter sauce. The restaurant lounge draws acclaimed jazz acts most nights of the week. Check out the autographed Grand Piano that bears the signature of past performers including Sweet Georgia Brown and Dave Brubeck.

Chip's Sanibel Steakhouse (☎ 239-472-5700; 1473 Periwinkle Way, Sanibel; mains $20-45; ☽ dinner) When you just want a perfect hunk of beef, visit this restaurant that rivals New York City when it comes to steakhouses. The meat is cooked just right – seared at 1700°F to lock in the juices – and comes in a variety of cuts, including one

$70 Porterhouse. More than half a dozen sauces are offered. Pair your filet mignon with a lobster tail or one of the other seafood delights on the menu. The decor is steakhouse cool – think lots of masculine colors and wood. The only downer is having to pay an extra $5 to get a side of mashed potatoes or asparagus.

Getting There & Around

Unless you're coming by boat, private plane or helicopter, there's only one way to get here: the Sanibel Causeway (Hwy 867), which has a $6 toll for cars, $2 for motorcycles. Fare collectors get you coming but not going. At the end of the causeway, follow Periwinkle Way to its end at Tarpon Bay Rd (look for the post office), turn right, and then left onto Sanibel-Captiva Rd. The shell museum is on the left, the JN 'Ding' Darling Refuge on the right. It'll seem to take forever and you'll probably think you've missed it, but you won't have.

NAPLES

☎ 239 / pop 22,000

This Naples is on the beach, not in Italy, but it's chic enough to be in the latter. The Gulf Coast's answer to Palm Beach is a rich town, and not afraid to flaunt it. The houses lining the beachfront road are ornate, gigantic affairs, done up in pastel colors and set back on perfectly manicured lawns filled with pink and purple flowering bushes and a view of the long, white sandy coastline and turquoise gulf. Despite the elegant shops and fine restaurants (many Italian, ironically) housed in the perfectly maintained tangerine and lemon buildings on swanky 5th Ave downtown, Naples still manages to feel laid-back. Plus, the beaches are less crowded than others nearby (although the accommodation tends to be a bit more expensive), the restaurants are better and the tone more romantic.

Naples isn't exactly a hot town with the younger set, it caters more to the baby-boomer billionaire set, so don't come looking for nightlife – the entire city pretty much shuts down by 10pm. But if you're looking for a top romantic beach on the Gulf of Florida, it's pretty hard to beat this genteel beach town with its serene atmosphere, delicious seafood and amazing sunsets.

Orientation & Information

Downtown Naples is laid out in a grid: streets run north to south, avenues run east to west.

Old Naples (bounded by 10th Ave S at the north, 14th Ave S at the south, the Gulf of Mexico at the west and the Gordon River at the east) is the epicenter, and 5th Ave S is the central artery. Gulf Shore Blvd runs north–south along the beach, from the southern tip at Gordon Pass, where it becomes Gordon Dr, all the way north to Clam Pass. Note, there is a break in the shoreline north of Lowdermilk Park and you'll have to jog east on Mooring Line Dr to US 41 and back west again via Harbor Dr to Gulf Shore Blvd.

The **Greater Naples Chamber of Commerce** (☎ 239-262-6141; www.napleschamber.org; 895 5th Ave S; ☺ 9am-5pm Mon-Sat) offers maps and information on local attractions.

The **Outdoor Concierge Desk** (☎ 239-434-6533; www .thirdstreetsouth.com; 3rd St S, btwn Broad Ave & 13th Ave S; ☺ 10am-6pm Mon-Wed & Sat, to 9pm Thu & Fri, noon-5pm Sun in winter, 10am-5pm Mon-Sat in summer) is staffed by friendly and knowledgeable folks.

Sights & Activities

In keeping with the ethos of the rich, retired American stereotype, it won't shock you to learn that Naples is the golfing capital of the world – there are over 50 courses laid out here.

NAPLES BEACHES

Naples' beaches are wonderful. Because construction was forbidden close to the water, that all-too-familiar Florida condo cluster along the seashore doesn't exist here. As such, the downtown beach is arguably the finest city beach in Florida – spotless, white sand and very popular. Access it at the Gulf end of each avenue, and bring quarters for parking meters. At the western end of 12th Ave S, locals congregate at the pier, a center of fishing activity, especially on weekends. It's a great place to watch pelicans.

Lowdermilk Park (cnr Millionaire's Row & Gulf Shore Blvd), north of Old Naples, has restrooms, vending machines, picnicking places and volleyball courts showcasing some of the best players around. If you're a world-class player visiting from, say, Hawaii, you might be able to join them. Otherwise, just watch the buff bods. And again, bring quarters for the meters.

Clam Pass County Park (☎ 239-353-0404; end of Seagate Dr from US 41; ☺ 8am-sunset), north of Old Naples, has a three-quarter-mile boardwalk through a mangrove forest that leads out to a powdery white-sand beach. Parking costs

$4 and there's a free electric tram from the parking lot.

Delnor-Wiggins Pass State Recreation Area (☎ 239-597-6196; 11100 Gulf Shore Dr; per car $5, per pedestrian or cyclist $1; ☺ 8am-sunset), also north of Old Naples, boasts gorgeous, pristine white sands, food concessions, showers and every item you might need for a day in the sun for hire (chairs, umbrellas, snorkeling, kayaks, etc). There's great snorkeling at a reef just offshore.

OLD NAPLES

Parts of ritzy Old Naples are right up there with Rodeo Drive. Along 5th Ave S, between 3rd and 9th Sts S, you'll find a collection of shops, restaurants and cafés. Over on 3rd St S, at Broad Ave, another cluster lies in wait. Take a stroll down Gulfshore Blvd between Central Ave and 8th Ave N to see how the most elite of the elite live. Giant art-deco mansions with Spanish roofs, done up in pinks, terracotta and apricot, line the beachfront drive. Sitting on large lots right on the ocean, their grounds are strewn with wispy palms, lemon trees and flowering bougainvillea.

NAPLES NATURE CENTER

The environmental nonprofit Conservancy of Southwest Florida runs great nature centers, including this **center** (☎ 239-262-0304; www .conservancy.org; 14th Ave N; adult/child $7.50/2; ☺ 9am-4:30pm Mon-Sat), off Goodlette-Frank Rd. It has a museum of natural history, a wildlife rehabilitation center, a 3000-gallon marine aquarium, an aviary with bald eagles and trails, naturalist-led hiking tours (free) and boating tours. Canoe and kayak rentals ($13 for two hours) are offered 9:30am to noon Monday to Saturday.

CARIBBEAN GARDENS

Formerly a 52-acre botanical oasis, these **gardens** (☎ 239-262-5409; www.napleszoo.com; 1590 Goodlette-Frank Rd; adult/child $19/11; ☺ 9:30am-5:30pm) are now a junglelike home to exotic animals like Bengal tigers, zebras, panthers and huge snakes. You can take a narrated cruise to observe monkeys and apes living freely on an island habitat. And even though it's not the focus of the place, kids love the petting zoo and myriad daily animal presentations. All activities are included in the admission price. The zoo is a nonprofit organization, and admission revenues go toward protecting wildlife around the world.

TAMPA BAY & SOUTHWEST FLORIDA

NAPLES MUSEUM OF ART
Within the Philharmonic Center for the Arts and worth a visit simply for the stunning entryway glass sculpture and dramatic glass dome, this **museum** (☎ 239-597-1900; www.thephil .org; 5833 Pelican Bay Blvd; adult/student $8/4; ☼ 10am-4pm Tue-Sat, noon-4pm Sun) has exciting contemporary works alongside traveling shows.

PALM COTTAGE
East of the pier, the late-19th-century **Palm Cottage** (☎ 239-261-8164; www.napleshistoricalsociety .com; 137 12th Ave S; by donation $6; ☼ 1-4pm Tue-Sat in winter, 1-4pm Wed & Sat in summer), home to the Collier County Historical Society, offers tours of one of the last remaining 'tabby mortar' homes in southwest Florida. Tabby was a kind of paste made from burning shells.

Tours
Naples Trolley Tours (☎ 239-262-7300; www .nttdestination.com; 1010 6th Ave S; adult/child $20/8; ☼ 8:30am-3:30pm) Has anecdotal and historical narration and makes a 1¾-hour circuit through the city, stopping at many hotels and the chamber of commerce. You can ride all day and get on and off as often as you like.
Sweet Liberty (☎ 239-793-3525; www.sweetliberty .com; Naples City Dock, 880 12th Ave S; adult/child under 12yr $40/15; ☼ 9:30am-sunset) A quarter-mile east of Tin City (a waterfront shopping mall that surrounds the city docks at the eastern end of 12th Ave S) on the Gordon River, this company offers relaxing three-hour catamaran trips past luxe Naples Bay homes and on to Key Island, where you'll have about an hour to swim and collect shells. You'll probably see some dolphins along the way.

Festivals & Events
Festival of Lights Held on the Monday before Thanks-giving, includes a free parade, live music and 'snow' in the historic district.
Third Thursday of the Month on Third St Features free musical performances from 6pm to 9pm year-round.

Sleeping
Naples is seriously lacking in the budget-hotel department, although its midrange and top-end hotels are good value for cost (except during the winter holiday season). For the best value, visit between June and September when hotels slash their prices by almost half. It will be sticky and hot, but some of these hotels have excellent swimming pools. Plus, everyone comes to Naples for the beach and swimming anyway. The prices listed here

represent a range throughout the year, and include the summer rates. But check online to see if you can score anything cheaper – all these hotels generally offer some sort of web specials during the off-season.

Cove Inn (☎ 239-262-7161, 800-255-4365; www.cove innnaples.com; 900 Broad Ave S; r $75-350; ☐ ☒) Don't judge this hotel by its exterior. On the outside it looks a bit tatty, but its much nicer inside. Right on the marina – the boats and water are nearly close enough to touch from some of the rooms – this low-key motel is great value, especially in the low season. The maritime-themed rooms have personal touches like guest books and framed photos of the innkeeper's family.

Lemon Tree Inn (☎ 239-262-1414, 888-800-5366; www.lemontreeinn.com; 250 9th St S; r $90-200; ☐ ☒ ☐) This motel is conveniently situated, has friendly staff, free lemonade (really!) and 35 spotless, well-appointed rooms situated around a breakfast gazebo and gardens.

Inn on 5th (☎ 239-261-0901; www.innonfifth.com; 745 5th Ave S; r $150-220; ☐ ☒) This Mediterranean-inspired luxury boutique offers a classy sleep in the heart of downtown. From a state-of-the-art fitness center to an enticing swimming pool, there is no question the Inn has great amenities. Plush robes, pillow-top mattresses and deluxe toiletries are pluses in the spacious and elegant old-world rooms. Wi-fi is available.

Hotel Escalante (☎ 239-659-3466; www.hotel escalante.com; 290 5th Ave S; r $195-285, ste $300-500, villa $600-900; ☐ ☒) A villa-style hotel made to look like it's been there for a hundred years, Escalante boasts stunning tropical gardens – walk around even if you're not staying here. The 70 rooms are outfitted with luxurious linens and decadent showerheads; some have a patio. Linger over morning coffee around the pool and courtyard, complete with stucco walls and wrought iron. For relaxing, there's no better place. For true luxury stay in one of the two-bedroom private villas.

Naples Grand Resort (☎ 239-597-3232, 800-247-9810; www.naplesgrandresort.com; 475 Seagate Dr; r & ste $180-500; ☐ ☒ ☼) This luxury resort (formerly known as the Registry Resort) on Clam Pass Beach is a kid-friendly place, and a great deal if you visit in the off-season. The modern rooms are large and comfortable, done up in soothing beige and brown patterns. There is wi-fi, and golf can be arranged, as can a visit to the posh Golden Door Spa.

Eating

Below is just a sampling of Naples varied restaurants. There are plenty more, simply stroll down 5th Ave S or 3rd St S in Old Naples for everything from Japanese to Italian.

BUDGET & MIDRANGE

Bad Ass Coffee (☎ 239-262-4106; 1307 3rd St S; mains less than $5; ⚅ breakfast & lunch) If you need espresso to start your morning, head to Bad Ass. Serving the best lattes and frozen coffee drinks in Naples, Bad Ass also has free wi-fi should you have a laptop with you. Chill out by the faux volcano at this Hawaii import specializing in beans from the Big Island.

Cove Inn Coffeeshop (☎ 239-262-7161, 800-255-4365; 900 Broad Ave S; mains $4-8; ⚅ breakfast & lunch) Locals recommend the Cove Inn Coffeshop (on the grounds of the hotel) for breakfast. It cooks up the best pancakes in town, along with loads of yummy omelettes stuffed with veggies, meat and cheese. The atmosphere is old-school North American greasy spoon – the eggs are piled up behind the counter, waiting to be cracked and fried in the open kitchen. Lunch is diner fare. Prices are very reasonable. For drip coffee, some say the Cove's is the best in Naples.

Lindburgers (☎ 239-262-1127; 330 Tamiami Trail S; mains $5-10; ⚅ lunch & dinner Mon-Sat) Just a couple of blocks east of 5th Ave, Lindburgers boasts over 50 kinds of burgers, including vegetarian ones, as well as sandwiches, salads and soups. Their patties are topped with just about anything you can think of.

Wynn's on Fifth (☎ 239-261-0901; 745 5th Ave S; mains $4-12; ⚅ breakfast & lunch) A longtime fixture in town, Wynn's excels at gourmet takeaway food, European pastries and other baked goods. If you're renting a unit with a microwave, you'll come here at least once.

Jane's Café on 3rd (☎ 239-261-2253; 1209 3rd St S; mains $6-13; ⚅ breakfast & lunch) Jane's is popular for its fabulous breezy courtyard dining and reasonably priced sandwiches and wraps stuffed with fresh ingredients – we were addicted to the tuna and avocado wrap. The salad list is long and creative and can be paired with a cup of homemade soup. The breakfast menu features the usual assortment of egg dishes.

Old Naples Pub (☎ 239-649-8200; 255 13th Ave S; mains $7-15; ⚅ 11am-10pm Mon-Sat, noon-9pm Sun) This small US-style neighborhood pub has a wonderful front courtyard tucked behind the upscale shops. For the area, its nachos,

salads, grouper and chips, ribs, tuna Caesar salads and catch-of-the-day specials are great value. There is live entertainment most nights in high season, and on weekends in the summer.

Dock at Crayton Cove (☎ 239-263-9940; 845 12th Ave S; mains $7-25; ⚅ lunch & dinner) Serving fried seafood on the open-air city docks, this rustic place also has hefty sandwiches, good daily specials and some Caribbean-style dishes. The bar is quite popular with locals. Watch the boats cruise by and munch on some snacks and a refreshing drink.

TOP END

Campiello (☎ 239-435-1166; 1177 3rd St S; lunch $12-17, dinner $13-42; ⚅ lunch & dinner) Campiello is one of Naples' most popular Italian restaurants. Not only does it have a lively alfresco bar scene and patio seating, it also serves delicious food. The lunch menu features a lot of salads and sandwiches not offered at dinner, as well as pasta entrées for less than they cost come evening. At dinner, the menu features lots of spit-roasted meat and fish along with pasta staples. People on a budget who are looking to experience Campiello's fantastic ambience but can't afford to shell out $42 for a steak, should try one of the single-serving wood-oven pizzas. Priced at $14 or less per pie, they are excellent value for this caliber of restaurant. There is often live music.

The Boathouse (☎ 239-261-1221; 720 5th Ave S; mains $26-42; ⚅ dinner) Rated by Naples' residents as the most romantic spot for sunset cocktails, the Boathouse is an eclectic place right on the water. It has a fabulous deck, a long list of tropical cocktails and an interesting menu that includes elk, buffalo and local seafood. Eat between 4pm and 6pm and you'll get an entrée, appetizer and dessert for around $15. Singles congregate at the big bar for drinks and sunsets; dress to be seen.

Drinking & Entertainment

Naples pretty much shuts down by 10pm, so doesn't have much in the way of nightlife. Besides the Irish pub listed below, Campiello, the Boathouse and the Old Naples Pub all double as watering holes.

McCabe's Irish Pub (☎ 239-403-7170; 699 5th Ave S; ⚅ 8am-11:30pm) Like any self-respecting Irish pub, McCabes has Irish bands on weekends and good suds nightly. It's the most popular after-dark spot in town.

Shopping

Take a stroll through Old Naples on 3rd St S or wander down ritzy 5th Ave S for all sorts of upscale boutiques, unique paper stores and organic-cotton children's clothing. The type of shopping here mimics Naples' population: wealthy.

Sonja Benson (☎ 239-263-8042; www.sonjabenson .com; 1209 3rd St S) Men can wait on the yellow 'husband' bench out front while their wives peruse this delightful handbag boutique. The bold multicolored patterned bags are reminiscent of Pucci, but are made by Sonja Benson, a Naples-based designer. Each is a unique piece of art; prices are reasonable.

Marissa Collections (☎ 239-263-4333; 1167 3rd St S) Stuffed with designer duds and accessories, Marissa has the best collection of haute couture clothing in Naples (with prices to match). Gucci, Prada, Manolo Blahnik, if the name is hot, you'll find it here.

Getting There & Around

Greyhound (☎ 239-774-5660; www.greyhound.com; 2669 Davis Blvd; ☉ Mon-Sat) makes multiple daily runs to Miami (from $37, four hours), Orlando ($52, six hours) and Tampa ($48, 5½ hours).

Naples is about 40 miles southwest of Fort Myers via I-75, at the southwestern end of the Tamiami Trail (US 41), just northwest of Marco Island and the Everglades. Most people flying into the area arrive at Southwest Florida International Airport (p446) in Fort Myers.

CORKSCREW SWAMP SANCTUARY

The crown jewel in the **National Audubon Society's** (☎ 239-348-9151; www.corkscrew.audobon .org; adult/child/student $10/4/6; ☉ 7am-5:30pm Oct–mid-Apr, 7am-7:30pm mid-Apr–Sep) sanctuary collection, this property provides the opportunity to venture back 500 years and experience a pristine swamp and jungle forest. Be sure not to miss it, even if you've seen the Everglades. The 11,000-acre property teems with wildlife, including gators, otters, Florida black bears, red-bellied turtles, white-tailed deer and over 100 species of birds. Explore the world's largest subtropical bald-cypress forest via a 2.25-mile-long boardwalk that cuts right through the center of the action. (Bald cypresses, by the way, are relatives of redwoods and have a girth of 25ft and tower to 130ft.) It provides a cool respite from the heat and is virtually free of mosquitoes, thanks to the wee fish that eat the larvae.

The preserve is northeast of Naples and southeast of Fort Myers; take the I-75 to exit 17 and head east on Hwy 846; follow the signs. It's remote, so bring a lunch.

NORTH OF TAMPA

Although not nearly as interesting as its southern counterpart, the region north of Tampa Bay does hold a few attractions. Plus, if you're driving up to the Panhandle, you'll go right through this part of Florida.

The area north of Tampa is filled with some strange, kitschy sites that are just quirky enough to be entertaining. Tidy little Tarpon Springs. touted as an authentic Greek sponging village, is touristy but charming. Home to a talking mermaid, Weeki Wachee or the 'City of Mermaids,' is the birthplace of Florida kitsch, while Crystal River is a magical place to swim near manatees.

TARPON SPRINGS

☎ 727 / pop 21,500

Once upon a time, Tarpon Springs was indeed a sponging center, and attracted the Greek immigrants who made up so much of the town's culture from the early 1900s until the sponge died off in the 1940s. After new sponge beds were discovered in the 1980s, the sponge docks bustled again, although these days only a few boats head out. If you've never tried Greek appetizers, it may be interesting to sample some at the dozens of Greek restaurants and bakeries around the docks. If you've had baklava on Rhodes, though, you probably won't hang around long. Regardless, the sidewalks are as stuffed with trinkets as dolmades are with rice.

The seven-block **Downtown Historic District**, however, is a charming 19th-century area, with brick streets, lots of antique stores and the fabulous **St Nicholas Church** (☎ 727-937-3540; 18 Hibiscus St; ☉ 9am-5pm Mon-Fri). The Greek Orthodox beauty, built with 60 tons of Greek marble and featuring Czech stained glass, is the focal point of the annual Epiphany Day celebration on January 6.

Don't miss driving or walking along the riverfront **Spring Bayou** (off Tarpon Ave west of downtown), where manatees linger and big Victorian estates line the road.

The **Chamber of Commerce** (☎ 727-937-6109; www .tarponsprings.com; on the sponge docks; ☉ 8am-5pm Mon-Fri) has more details than you'll ever need.

The **Spring Bayou Inn B&B** (☎ 727-938-9333; www
.springbayouinn.com; 32 Tarpon Ave; r summer $69-119, winter
$79-129; ✗), an architectural beauty, has six
large and lovely rooms. Rates include a luscious full breakfast. Champagne and chocolates can be arranged for special occasions, as
can massage therapy.

Have a thick pizza pie at the **Greek Pizza
Kitchen** (☎ 727-945-7337; 150 E Tarpon Ave; pizzas $20-
25, mains $6-15; ☺ noon-9pm, closed Sun & Mon in sum-
mer) or other Greek dishes like gyros, salads
and souvlaki.

From Clearwater, Alt Hwy 19 heads straight
north to Tarpon Springs.

WEEKI WACHEE SPRINGS
☎ 352 / pop 1100

The 'City of Mermaids' is…hold it…mer-
maids? Yup. Since 1947, families and celebrities, such as Esther Williams, Danny Thomas
and Elvis Presley, have been coming here to
see the star attraction: an **underwater show**
(☎ 352-596-2062, 877-469-3354; www.weekiwachee.com;
6131 Commercial Way/US 19 at Hwy 50; adult/child $25/17;
☺ 10am-4pm) at the springs starring long-haired
women in mermaid costumes who swim in
the natural spring (there are also mermen).
Parking costs $3.

The spring has a constant temperature of
72°F, measures about 100ft across and produces about 170 million gallons of water a day;
it's the headwater of the Weeki Wachee River.
The mermaids perform in the spring, alongside fish, turtles, otters, snakes and eels.

The shows here are the height of kitsch, a
trip straight back to the 1950s. You watch the
mermaids perform their mainstay show, *The
Little Mermaid,* in an underwater theater –
the audience watches through glass panels,
making this the world's only underwater artesian spring theater. The theater was built in
1946 by Newton Perry, an ex-Navy frogman.
Remarkably, the mermaids swim about with
what appears to be the greatest of ease.

Don't be fooled, though, as performing
under the water requires incredible stamina,
and the breathing apparatus is tricky. There
are submerged air hoses on the sides of the
theater: the mermaids swim over, grab some
air, hold their breath while swimming around
performing and then zip back for more air –
for half an hour at a time! They train first on
land and then without the tail in the water. It
takes about six months to get the whole thing
to look as effortless as it does. If it looks easy,
you try lip-synching to music under water
next time you're snorkeling!

The park also has a river cruise, water park
and bird shows. To see them all, budget five
hours. You can also rent **canoes** (☎ 352-597-
0360; 6131 Commercial Way/US 19 at Hwy 50; ☺ 9am-5pm
Mon-Fri, 8am-5pm Sat & Sun, last launch at 11am on Sat &
Sun) on the river from the rear of the parking
lot. Take the crystal-clear 7-mile canoe trail,
which would take 2½ hours without stopping
(but you will stop to picnic, right?), and you'll
probably see manatees. Flowing at 4mph, the
twisting and turning river is one of the fastest

A MERMAID'S TALE

For more than 10 years Marcy Terry has delighted audiences with underwater mermaid performances at Weeki Wachee Springs. Marcy now holds the dual title of Underwater Theatre Manager
and Head Mermaid. We sat her down to answer a few questions:

What's your favorite thing about being a mermaid? I just love the environment. My office is
a beautiful underwater spring; I get to swim and get paid; I interact with children who believe
in mermaids and they're just so happy to be here.

How long does it take to become a mermaid? First we have to get scuba-certified, then we learn
to breathe through air hoses, which is different from regular scuba diving. Then we start learning
how to swim in a tail and how to do the choreography, so it takes three to six months.

Other than Weeki Wachee, what's your favorite Florida tourist attraction? I would have to
say Disney. I just love the magic there, and I have a (toddler) and she loves going there. I love
seeing her little eyes light up. Everybody's happy and all the little kids believe in all that stuff so
you can't help but feel that way also.

If you had visitors from out of state, where would you take them? First I would bring them
here. Then, the beaches are beautiful; we'd probably go to a beach. Of course we'd hit Disney.
And, I don't know, I think the small roadside attractions need all the tourists they can get, so
I'd probably do those.

Marcy Terry is the head mermaid at Weeki Wachee Springs.

in central Florida. Reservations are highly recommended. Double canoes and kayaks rent for $40, single kayaks for $30; rentals include a pickup service.

Most people come here as a day trip from the Clearwater/Tampa area, but there's a 122-room **Best Western** (☎ 352-596-2007, 800-490-8268; 6172 Commercial Way, US 19; r from $70; 🏊 ♿) across from the park entrance. It's nothing special, but will do especially if you want to make this a special night for the kids.

The springs are about 25 miles north of Tarpon Springs via US 19 and 80 miles northwest of Orlando via Hwy 50. If you're coming directly from Tampa, it takes about 45 minutes via the I-75 north to Hwy 50 west.

HOMOSASSA SPRINGS
☎ 352 / pop 12,500

Leave monotonous US 19 and head west toward Old Homosassa down a shady lane draped with palms and live oaks dripping with Spanish moss. Finally – Old Florida, where time stands still and you can breathe again.

Local residents come for peace and quiet and out-of-staters come to **Homosassa Springs State Wildlife Park** (☎ 352-628-2311; www.manatee cam.com; US 19; adult/child $9/5; 🕙 9am-5:30pm, last ticket sales at 4pm), in essence, the state's largest all-natural theme park. The headwaters of the Homosassa River are home to a 168-acre park made up of wetlands, hydric hammock and spring-run streams that bubble out of the 45ft-deep Homosassa Spring. The park showcases diverse and often rehabilitating wildlife – manatees, black bears, bobcats, white-tailed deer, alligators, American crocodiles and river otters. Interpretive programs include alligator and crocodile demonstrations, animal encounter programs on snakes or birds

of prey, and one on manatees. But best of all, you can also watch manatees and 10,000 fish within a floating underwater observatory. A pontoon boat will take you on an orientation tour, after which you're free to wander on the nature trails. Plan on spending a few hours here.

MacRae's (☎ 352-628-2602; 5300 Cherokee Way; r from $65) is a good sleeping option 3 miles from the park off W Yulee Rd past the old sugar mill. It's a fisherman's paradise of pseudo log cabins and has 22 rooms (some with kitchens) complete with front-porch rockers. MacRae's also operates the riverfront **Tiki Bar** (mains $4-10; 🕙 lunch & dinner), perfectly perched for exceptional afternoon drinks. You can come to MacRae's to do nothing but read, or you can arrange tarpon fishing trips, boat tours and kayak rentals from their marina.

The park is about 20 miles north of Weeki Wachee, 65 miles north of Clearwater and 75 miles north of Tampa; the US 19 north leads right to the park entrance.

CRYSTAL RIVER

No matter what time of year, Crystal River offers one of the surest bets for seeing endangered manatees. About 70 of them call this place home year-round, but in the winter there are 10 times that many frolicking in the warmth of the springs at **Chassahowitzka National Wildlife Refuge** (☎ 352-563-2088; 1502 SE Kings Bay Dr Way; 🕙 sunrise-sunset). You can swim and scuba dive in the spring, but the refuge is only accessible by boat; contact the **Crystal Lodge Dive Center** (☎ 352-795-6798; www.manatee -central.com; Best Western, 614 NW US 19, Crystal River; 🕙 8am-6pm), which offers boat tours ($15), a manatee snorkeling tour ($15) and a Rainbow River snorkeling and diving tour ($10).

The Panhandle

Gentle Southern charm, quiet bayous teeming with wildlife and roadhouses serving up red-hot blues may not be what most folks imagine when they think of Florida. But those are among the treasures you'll discover here, in the magnificent Panhandle, where country roads cut through thick, hushed forests and lead to charmingly historic downtowns filled with people who are truly sweet as pie.

Add to all that the truly gorgeous Gulf Coast beaches – boasting fine, soft-as-sugar sand and crystalline waters whose luscious aqua glow will make you think you've landed in the Caribbean – and you've got a seriously fine region for exploring, no matter where your interests lie. Love nature? Head to one of the area's freshwater springs, like Steinhatchee, or to the forested hiking trails of Apalachicola National Forest, or to the bird-filled quietude of St George Island State Park. Prefer urban-style culture? Then hit Tallahassee or Pensacola, where you can easily fill days by gallery hopping, dining on treats from fresh oysters to fried green tomatoes, bopping your head to excellent live music or simply strolling the wonderfully mellow city streets. You could also just kick back in the sand with an ice-cold brew and watch the small waves lap the shore.

The Panhandle may be the much-traveled state's least-traveled region, but don't spend too much time wondering why; just be glad it's true, and revel in the fact that you won't have to share its myriad of charms with too many others.

HIGHLIGHTS

- Follow the road sign to find the magnificent clay creations at **George Griffin Pottery** (p476), at the end of the sandy, oak-canopied dirt road in Sopchoppy

- **Grayton Beach State Park** (p488), with windswept dunes and luminous gulf waters, has the region's most picturesque beach

  Grayton Beach State Park ★
  Tallahassee ★
  Sopchoppy ★   Wakulla Springs State Park ★

- Get a wildlife thrill on a guided river cruise at **Wakulla Springs State Park** (p473), where mossy cypress trees and mangroves mingle with manatees, alligators and a slew of wading birds

- Enjoy the view from the top-floor lookout of Tallahassee's new **Florida State Capitol** (p465); the view spans the low-key city and then undisturbed green in all directions

- Discover the best blues at **Bradfordville Blues Club** (p470), just outside Tallahassee, down a torch-lit dirt road, with a blazing bonfire and sizzling music

THE PANHANDLE

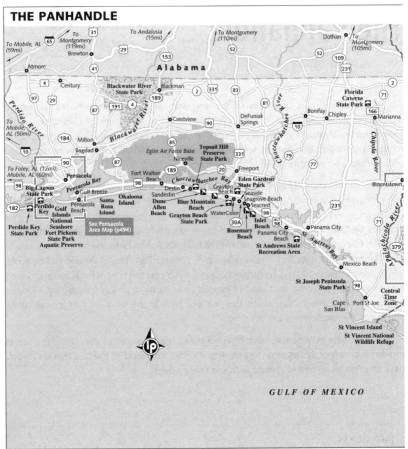

History

The area that would become Tallahassee (meaning 'abandoned fields') was first inhabited by the American Indians of the Apalachee tribes, who cleared out and were felled by disease after the region was settled by Spaniards in 1539, with explorer Hernando De Soto leading the way. After the US Territory of Florida was founded in 1821, Tallahassee was chosen as the state capitol; a plantation economy soon developed – as did the city's reckless reputation, with frequent knife and gun fights leading to the formation of the city's police department. A rail line linked Tallahassee with the gulf port in 1837, making it the commercial center of the region. And, by the late 1800s, cotton estates were snapped up by wealthy northerners, who turned them into hunting retreats. Eventually, environmentalists reacted against the man-versus-beast behavior of the hunters, which led to the establishment of groundbreaking ecological efforts in the region.

Climate

Unlike much of the rest of Florida, the Panhandle does have a distinct winter. From December to February temperatures drop to around the low 50s to low 60s (°F), though they still soar in summer, with temperatures averaging around the high 70s to mid-90s, on par with the rest of the state. The area can be prone to tornadoes, particularly in February and March, as well as hurricanes, which tend to hit the coast in late summer or early fall.

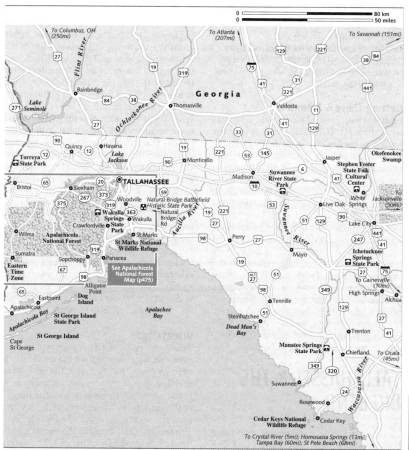

National, State & Regional Parks

Florida's largest forest, the Apalachicola National Forest (p474), covers 938 sq miles or roughly more than half a million acres. In the Panhandle it is located from just west of Tallahassee to the Apalachicola River and a snippet of coastline at Apalachicola Bay. The forest features wilderness swamps and hammocks especially near the Apalachicola River. Near Tallahassee, Wakulla Springs State Park (p473) is a wildlife haven with a huge 125ft spring. Northwest of here is the fascinating Florida Caverns State Park (p487), which allows visitors to trek underground. Along the Gulf Coast, state parks include the expansive St George Island (p483) and St Joseph Peninsula state parks. Florida's section of

the Gulf Islands National Seashore (which actually extends to Alabama and Mississippi) covers Perdido Key (p501), two sections of Santa Rosa Island (extending to the naval air station across the Fort Pickens State Park Aquatic Preserve) and a little section of coastline around Destin and Fort Walton Beach (p490).

Information
Emerald Coast Convention & Visitors Bureau
(☎ 850-651-7131, 800-322-3319; www.destin-fwb
.com; 1540 Miracle Strip Parkway; ☽ 8am-5pm Mon-Fri,
10am-4pm Sat & Sun)
Panama City Beach Convention & Visitors Bureau
(☎ 850-233-5070, 800-722-3224; www.thebeachloversbeach
.com; 17001 Panama City Beach Parkway; ☽ 8am-5pm)

THE PANHANDLE

Pensacola Visitors Information Center (Map p494; ☎ 850-434-1234, 800-874-1234; www.visitpensacola .com; 1401 E Gregory St; ⏱ 8am-5pm)
Tallahassee Area Convention & Visitors Bureau (Map p468; ☎ 850-413-9200, 800-628-2866; www.visit tallahassee.com; 106 E Jefferson St, Tallahassee; ⏱ 8am-5pm Mon-Fri, 9am-1pm Sat)

Getting There & Around

From the northeast of Florida, the I-10 runs west through Tallahassee and across the breadth of the Panhandle, continuing through Pensacola and into Alabama and beyond. From Perdido Key, the western extremity of the Panhandle, Hwy 182 continues directly into Alabama and travels along the Gulf Coast. Traveling from southwest Florida Hwy 98 or US 19 shadows the coast north from St Pete Beach to Homosassa Springs, Crystal River and heads around the Big Bend northwest into Tallahassee. Driving is the best way to see it all, although Greyhound does have bus stations in Pensacola, Tallahassee, Panama City, Fort Walton Beach and DeFuniak Springs. Tallahassee and Pensacola have regional airports, while Fort Walton Beach has a small one; meanwhile, the brand new Panama City-Bay County International Airport was scheduled to open at the time of publication.

TALLAHASSEE & THE BIG BEND

Florida's gracious state capital, blanketed by moss-draped live oaks and infused with a blend of historic and university cultures, sits inland at the edge of what's known as the Big Bend region – a little-traveled arc of the Florida coastline that curves around the Gulf of Mexico. Within it, you'll find remote fishing communities, freshwater springs, picturesque islands and the edges of the Apalachicola National Forest.

TALLAHASSEE

☎ 850 / pop 159,000

Florida's capital, cradled between gently rising hills and beneath tree-canopied roadways, is a calm and gracious city, far more Southern, culturally speaking, than the majority of the state it administrates. Geographically it's closer to Atlanta than it is to Miami, and culturally, like Jacksonville, its citizens consider themselves Southern, which is inversely the case the further south you travel.

Despite headquartering the state's major industry – tourism – Tallahassee is one of the least touristy towns in Florida; you'll notice, in fact, that its museums and other attractions, including the soaring capitol building, seem to have more locals than tourists milling about inside. It's a nice, communal feeling that leaves visitors with the sense that they've stumbled upon an important small town, rather than the city that it is. The pace here feels like that of molasses (for an urban center, at least). And the sweet scent that permeates the spring and summer air – a curious smoky-sweet smell, most likely a combination of flowering camellias, Japanese magnolias and controlled burning from surrounding rural areas – serves as a lovely reminder that you're really not far from the country after all. Tallahassee is home to two major universities, though, and its lively student body adds a nice dose of energy to the otherwise languorous city – as do government employees and lawmakers, who bring a buzz to downtown between March and May, when the state legislature is in session.

Orientation

Tallahassee's compact downtown is pleasantly strollable. Monroe St is the main north–south drag in town, which forms the east–west dividing line for addresses. Tennessee St is the north–south divider, and the northern boundary of downtown, with Cascade Park the southern border, the Florida State University (FSU) campus the western border and Magnolia Dr to the east. The major northeast thoroughfare, Thomasville Rd, forks to the right off Monroe St just north of Brevard St.

The city's lively Midtown section – home to many hoppin' cafés, bars and eateries –lies just north of downtown, off I-10, and is centered around Thomasville Rd.

Florida State University is about 0.75 miles west of Monroe St; massive Doak Campbell Stadium is at the southwest corner of campus. Florida Agricultural & Mechanical University (FAMU) is south of downtown, bordered by Orange Ave to the south, Famu Way to the north, Adams St to the east and Perry St to the west.

Tallahassee's canopy roads (covered almost completely by foliage), lovely for afternoon drives, include Old St Augustine Rd,

Centerville Rd, Meridian Rd, Miccosukee Rd and Old Bainbridge Rd.

Information

BOOKSTORES
Paperback Rack (Map p466; ☎ 850-244-3455; 105 N Monroe St) A favorite indie shop for new and used literature, fiction and travel books.

INTERNET ACCESS
Leroy Collins Leon County Public Library (Map p468; ☎ 850-487-2665; 200 W Park Ave; ◷ 10am-9pm Mon-Thu, to 6pm Fri, 10am-5pm Sat, 1-6pm Sun) Plenty of free online computers; enter the parking lot from Call St.

MEDIA
The *Tallahassee Democrat* (www.tallahassee .com) is the daily paper. WFSU (88.9FM) is the Florida State University radio station, broadcasting many National Public Radio shows.

MONEY
Bank of America (Map p468; ☎ 850-561-1876; 315 S Calhoun St) Downtown; change money here.
People's First Community Bank ATM (Map p468; ☎ 850-224-4117; 107 E College Ave) A conveniently located 24-hour ATM.

POST
Post office (Map p468; ☎ 800-275-8777; 216 W College Ave) Close to the center.

TOURIST INFORMATION
Florida Welcome Center (Map p468; ☎ 850-488-6167; www.flausa.com; cnr Pensacola St & Duval St; ◷ 8am-5pm Mon-Fri, 11am-3pm Sat) In the new Florida State Capitol, this is a must-visit resource.
Tallahassee Area Convention & Visitors Bureau (Map p468; ☎ 850-413-9200, 800-628-2866; www.visit tallahassee.com; 106 E Jefferson St; ◷ 8am-5pm Mon-Fri, 9am-1pm Sat) Runs the excellent Visitor Information Center, with brochures on walking and driving tours.

Sights & Activities

FLORIDA STATE CAPITOL & OLD CAPITOL
It's stark, ugly and massively imposing. But the 22-story **Florida State Capitol** (Map p468; New Capitol; ☎ 850-488-6167; cnr Pensacola St & Duval St; admission free; ◷ 8am-5pm Mon-Fri) still deserves your visit. That's mainly because of its top floor observation deck, which affords wonderful 360-degree views of the city and its edge of rolling green hills that stretch to the horizons. The building's walls hold a combination of local artwork and framed letters of historic correspondences between the city and national leaders. You can opt to just hang out up here, or go for the free half-hour tour, which includes a visit to the chambers. In session, the Capitol is a hive of activity, with politicians, staffers and lobby groups buzzing in and around its honeycombed corridors.

Next door, the 1902 **Historic Capitol** (Map p468; www.flhistoriccapitol.gov), adorned by candy-striped awnings and topped with a reproduction of the original glass dome, is as grand as its successor is uninviting. It now houses the **Florida Legislative Research Center and Museum** (Map p468; ☎ 850-487-1902; www.flrcm.com; 400 S Monroe St; admission free; ◷ 9am-4:30pm Mon-Fri, 10am-4:30pm Sat, noon-4:30pm Sun & holidays), including a restored House of Representatives chamber and governors' reception area, plenty of governors' portraits, and exhibits on immigration, state development and the infamous 2000 US presidential election, with displays such as the equally infamous butterfly ballot, now enclosed in glass.

Opposite the Historic Capitol, on S Monroe St, a huge US flag billows between two granite pillars of the **Vietnam Veterans Memorial** (Map p468), inscribed with the names of 1869 Floridians killed and 83 missing in action during the war.

MUSEUMS & HISTORIC BUILDINGS
Housed in a stark and off-putting modern building with no charm (it's a tie with the new Florida State Capitol for unattractiveness), the **Museum of Florida History** (Map p468; ☎ 850-245-6450; www.flheritage.com/museum; 500 S Bronough St; admission free; ◷ 9am-4:30pm Mon-Fri, 10am-4:30pm Sat, noon-4:30pm Sun) is filled with wonderful exhibits, tackling everything from Florida's Paleo-Indians, who inhabited these parts beginning at the end of the Ice Age, to Civil War times, Spanish shipwrecks in the Atlantic and the rise of 'Tin-Can Tourism,' when the middle-class traveler began hitting Florida in droves – driving south, camping out and eating dinner out of tin cans. You'll see a 1925 Model T, a 1911 Baker electric car, a reconstructed citrus packing house of the 1920s and the star attraction: a North American mastodon skeleton.

Great for kids is the Smithsonian-affiliated **Mary Brogan Museum of Art & Science** (Map p468; ☎ 850-513-0700; www.thebrogan.org; 350 S Duval St; adult/child $6/3.50; ◷ 10am-5pm Mon-Sat, 1-5pm Sun), which houses both a science center on the 1st and 2nd floors, and the Tallahassee art museum, mounting international exhibits, on the 3rd. It

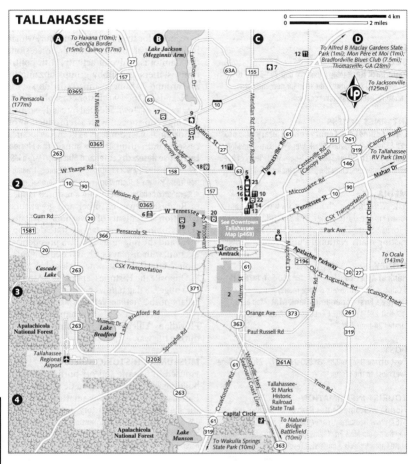

may seem like a strange marriage at first, but the museum does a great job of pointing out connections between left- and right-brained creations, with highlights including a living sea ecolab and a TV weather station, where kids can try their hands at forecasting.

Housed in a stately 1843 white column-fronted building, the **Knott House Museum** (Map p468; ☎ 850-922-2459; www.flheritage.com/museum/sites /knotthouse; 301 E Park Ave; admission free; ☼ gift shop 10am-4pm Mon-Sat, guided tours 1pm, 2pm & 3pm Wed-Fri, hourly 10am-3pm Sat) is a quirky attraction. Occupied during the Civil War by Confederate and then Union troops before the Emancipation Proclamation was read here in 1865, it's otherwise known as 'the house that rhymes.' That's because in 1928 it was

bought by politico William V Knott, whose poet wife, Luella, attached verses on the evils of drink to the many of the furnishings.

UNIVERSITIES
Tallahassee is first a capital, but its student population gathers in pockets that can make you feel like you've stumbled into a lively college town, especially on Saturday nights.

A liberal arts school of over 35,000 under-graduate and graduate students, **Florida State University** (Map p466; FSU; ☎ 850-644-2882; www.fsu .edu; Hendry St) specializes in sciences, comput-ing and performing arts (and football). From September to April, free campus tours depart from **Visitor Services** (☎ 850-644-3246; 100 S Woodward Ave) Monday to Friday. Call for a schedule.

Universally referred to by its acronym, FAMU (fam-you), **Florida Agricultural & Mechanical University** (Map p466; ☎ 850-599-3000; 1500 Wahnish Way) was founded in 1887 as the State Normal College for Colored Students, with 15 students and two instructors. Today it's home to a population of about 10,000 students of all races, as well as the **Southeastern Regional Black Archives Research Center & Museum** (Map p466; ☎ 850-599-3020; Carnegie Library, cnr Martin Luther King Jr Blvd & Gamble St; admission free; ☉ 8am-5pm Mon-Fri). A forerunner in research on African American influence on US history and culture, the center and museum holds one of the country's largest collections of African American and African artifacts as well as a huge collection of papers, photographs, paintings and documents pertaining to black American life.

MISSION SAN LUIS

In a lofty hilltop setting spanning 60 acres, the **Mission San Luis** (Map p466; ☎ 850-487-3711; www.missionsanluis.org; 2020 W Mission Rd; admission free; ☉ 10am-4pm Tue-Sun) is a trip back to the 17th century. The site of a Spanish and American Indian mission settlement from 1656–1704, it was at one time the provincial capital under Spanish rule and home to up to 1500 residents. The entire mission has been wonderfully reconstructed – including the dramatic, soaring council house of the Apalachee village, which stands like a towering, light-filled teepee on the bucolic land. Free tours, led by knowledgeable interpreters, are available at the excellent visitor center, which also screens a short film.

HIKING & BIKING

Biking trails wind through the **Alfred B Maclay Gardens State Park** (Map p466; ☎ 850-487-4556; www .floridastateparks.org/maclaygardens; 3540 Thomasville Rd; vehicle/pedestrian/cyclist $4/2/2; ☉ 8am-sunset), which peaks from January to April with more than 200 varieties of flowers. It's also the trailhead for the Lake Overstreet Trails, which circle the lake and wind through deer, gray fox and bobcat habitat. From I-10, take exit 30 to Thomasville Rd north and follow the signs – the entrance is on your left.

The ultimate treat for runners, skaters and cyclists is the **Tallahassee–St Marks Historic Railroad State Trail** (Map p466; ☎ 877-822-5208; admission free; ☉ 8am-sunset) – with 16 miles of smooth trails shooting due south to the gulf port town of St Marks and not a car or traffic light in sight. It's easy and flat for all riders, sitting on a coastal plain and shaded at many points by canopies of gracious live oaks. (More experienced riders may opt for forest trails, like the rugged 7.5-mile Munson Hills Loop trail, navigating sand dunes and a towering pine forest.) Though the rail trail begins 4.5 miles north of the main trailhead, the city section is not so scenic, and it's best to start at the main trailhead (with parking), 100yd south of the intersection of Capital Circle and Hwy 363. You'll find plenty of jumping on and off points with water and restrooms.

Note that the *only* place in Tallahassee that rents bikes is **Great Bicycle Shop** (Map p466; ☎ 850-224-1240; www.greatbicycle.com; 1909 Thomasville Rd; bikes per 24hr $25; ☉ 10am-6pm Mon-Fri, to 5pm Sat, noon-4pm Sun).

LAKE ELLA

Part of Tallahassee life for well over a century, **Lake Ella** (Map p466), east of N Monroe St to

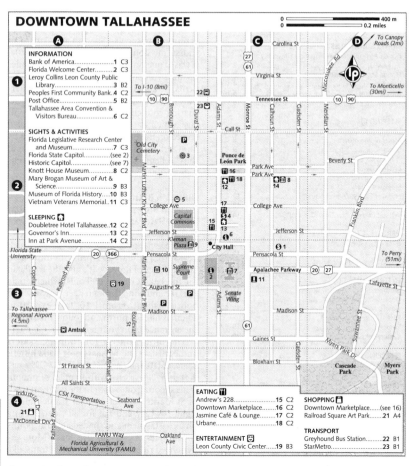

DOWNTOWN TALLAHASSEE

0 —————— 400 m
0 —————— 0.2 miles

To Canopy
Roads (2mi)

INFORMATION
Bank of America.....................**1** C3
Florida Welcome Center............**2** C3
Leroy Collins Leon County Public
  Library...............................**3** B2
Peoples First Community Bank.**4** C2
Post Office............................**5** B2
Tallahassee Area Convention &
  Visitors Bureau....................**6** C2

SIGHTS & ACTIVITIES
Florida Legislative Research Center
  and Museum..........................**7** C3
Florida State Capitol.............(see 2)
Historic Capitol...................(see 7)
Knott House Museum................**8** B3
Mary Brogan Museum of Art &
  Science...............................**9** B3
Museum of Florida History....**10** B3
Vietnam Veterans Memorial...**11** C3

SLEEPING
Doubletree Hotel Tallahassee..**12** C2
Governor's Inn.......................**13** C2
Inn at Park Avenue................**14** C2

EATING
Andrew's 228.........................**15** C2
Downtown Marketplace...........**16** C2
Jasmine Café & Lounge..........**17** C2
Urbane.................................**18** C2

ENTERTAINMENT
Leon County Civic Center.....**19** B3

SHOPPING
Downtown Marketplace......(see 16)
Railroad Square Art Park.......**21** A4

TRANSPORT
Greyhound Bus Station..........**22** B1
StarMetro.............................**23** B1

the south of W Tharpe St, is a much-loved urban park that's great for a run, blade or picnic. Originally known as Bull's Pond, in the 19th century this sylvan, spring-fed pool was renamed by planter Jabez Bull for his daughter. It has long been a swimming hole, baptismal site and picnic spot. It was here, in 1867, that more than 2000 newly freed slaves celebrated Emancipation Day. The 1920s made Lake Ella a playground for vacationers, with the addition of the 1924 Lakeside Motel; today the cottages, which lie on the east shore, house a jumble of boutiques and craft shops. Other reminders of the past include dozens of memorial plaques that edge the lake (generally war memorials), as well as a Huey UH-1 helicopter given to the city by France.

Today Lake Ella bustles with urbanites enjoying this patch of nature – as well as the Wednesday afternoon Grower's market and the mellow, communal Black Dog Café (see p470).

Sleeping

With just a couple of charming exceptions, you'll find that Tallahassee's hotels are mostly midrange chains, clumped at exits along I-10 or along Monroe St, between I-10 and downtown. Be sure to book well ahead during the legislative session and football games, when prices peak.

BUDGET

Motel 6 Downtown (Map p466; ☎ 800-466-8356; 1027 Apalachee Parkway; r $40-60; **P** **⊠**) One of the cheapest of the chains, this clean and basic motel is very close to the capitol area.

Super 8 (Map p466; ☎ 850-386-8286, 800-222-2222; 2801 N Monroe St; r $45-90; P ⊠) A pleasant surprise, this former Shoney's and brand-new Super 8 is a Mediterranean-style inn with bright, cheery rooms built around tree-shaded courtyards with trailing Spanish moss.

Little English Guesthouse (Map p466; ☎ 850-907-9777; www.littleenglishguesthouse.com; 737 Timberlane Rd; r $85-125; P ⊠ ⊡) Just two charming rooms – the London Room, with a winged leather reading chair, and the frilly, rose-colored Essex room, both with four-poster beds. This is an intimate, English-run place with imports like Radox bath relaxation gels for sale in the gift parlor. It's cozy, quiet and well run.

The closest camping is 10 minutes east of town at **Tallahassee RV Park** (Map p466; ☎ 850-878-7641; www.tallahasseervpark.com; 6504 Mahan Dr/Hwy 90; sites with hookups $38; P ⊠).

MIDRANGE & TOP END

Inn at Park Avenue (Map p468; ☎ 850-222-4024; 323 E Park Ave; r $139-199; P ⊠) This 1838 renovated Victorian, on the National Register of Historic Places, is a lovely spot with character – as well as 12ft ceilings, antique furniture, gleaming hardwood floors, and four intimate guest rooms, one equipped for visitors with wheelchairs.

Doubletree Hotel Tallahassee (Map p468; ☎ 850-224-5000; www.tallahassee.doubletree.com; 101 S Adams St; r $79-259; P ⊡ ⊠) You can stroll around downtown from this standard business-geared high-rise, which has 243 solid rooms, chocolate chip cookies at the efficient reception desk, and a retro-sophisticate feel. It's modern enough to have many energy-saving systems in place, from compact fluorescent bulbs and recycled paper products to highly efficient water pumps and air filters.

Governor's Inn (Map p468; ☎ 850-681-6855; www.thegovinn.com; 209 S Adams St; r & ste $139-229; P) Down the street from the Doubletree, and on par with its level of luxury (which is not grand, but not shabby, either), this is the nonchain option for classy travelers. It's got a lovely, intimate vibe, and a variety of room styles, including loft suites with a spacious downstairs bedroom connected by a spiral staircase to an upper-level sitting area with a fireplace, comfy couch, private bar and fridge, and French doors opening onto a balcony. There's a personable lobby scene,

where folks gather for glasses of wine and free newspapers, and there's valet parking and wi-fi.

Eating

BUDGET

Downtown Marketplace (Map p468; ☎ 850-297-3945; www.downtownmarketplace.com; Ponce de León Park; ⊗ 8am-2pm, Sat Mar-Nov) Gourmet food and farmers market produce, plus lots of great art and live music.

Whataburger (Map p466; ☎ 850-681-9202; 1101 Thomasville Rd; burgers $3-6; ⊗ 24hr) This kitschy A-frame, part of a popular Southern chain, packs 'em in at all hours (particularly after clubs close) for some of the cheapest and tastiest burgers around. Grab a red-vinyl booth and grab one with cheese – or opt for pancakes, grilled chicken or some hot apple pie.

Hopkin's Eatery (meals $6-10; ⊗ lunch, dinner Mon-Fri, lunch Sat) Lake Ella Plaza (Map p466; ☎ 850-386-4258; 1700 N Monroe St); Market Sq (Map p466; ☎ 850-668-0311; 1415 Market St) This popular, down-home lunch joint has cozy booths that get filled with locals chowing down on well-made, low-key sandwiches, from grilled Cubans to vegetarian subs.

MIDRANGE

Jasmine Café & Lounge (Map p468; ☎ 850-681-6868; 109 E College Ave; mains $10-15; ⊗ lunch Mon-Fri, dinner daily) Tallahassee's best sushi is at this cozy and casual eatery, popular with students, which also doles out excellent Asian stir fries, desserts and sakes.

Kool Beanz Café (Map p466; ☎ 850-224-2466; www.koolbeanz-café.com; 921 Thomasville Rd; mains $15-19; ⊗ lunch, dinner) It has got a corny name but a wonderfully eclectic and homey vibe – plus great, creative fare. The menu changes daily, but you can count on finding fresh salads and seafood dishes, as well as pork chops, duck breasts and delicious pastas studded with shrimp and fresh veggies. The kitchen will happily create vegetarian offerings, too.

Andrew's 228 (Map p468; ☎ 850-222-3444; www.andrewsdowntown.com; 228 S Adams St; mains $13-21; ⊗ lunch Mon-Thu, dinner daily) This upscale dining spot brings a hushed and glamorous Tuscany-meets-New York setting to town with a selection of fine pastas and steaks, along with excellent wines and 27 different martinis served in individual shakers. Spicy mussels arrabiata, toothsome lobster ravioli and rosemary flecked grilled lamb are among the tasty offerings.

Chez Pierre & 2 Chez (Map p466; ☎ 850-222-0936; www.chezpierre.com; 1215 Thomasville Rd; mains $17-25; ⏺ lunch & dinner) Southern charm meets French sophistication at Chez Pierre, a Midtown charmer located in a beautiful antebellum house and serving excellent, authentic dishes like beef bourguignonne, tuna nicoise and saffron-scented lobster ravioli. Its lower-priced, more casual adjoining 2 Chez, is a lovely outdoor café, specializing in raw-bar offerings, steamed mussels and burgers.

ourpick Urbane (Map p468; ☎ 850-422-2221; www.urbane-restaurant.com; 115 E Park Ave; mains $17-36; ⏺ dinner) A strikingly chic den near the center of downtown, this is by far the sleekest place going. Pop in for special, tasty fare ranging from eclectic individual pizzas (like shrimp with cilantro pesto) to plates of chili-glazed salmon or grilled elk chops. Just lazing over a cocktail at the lovely bar is a treat, too.

Drinking

Most of the frat bars are in and around Tennessee St between Copeland St and Dewey St. There are a few good options around town too.

Black Dog Café (Map p466; ☎ 850-224-2518; 229 Lake Ella Dr; ⏺ 7am-11pm Mon-Thu, 7am-midnight Fri, 8am-midnight Sat, 8am-11pm Sun) Wine and beer aren't served until 6pm, but this special spot, beloved by the city's creative community, is always happening, thanks to frequent poetry readings, open-mic music, chess boards and outdoor tables overlooking Lake Ella. If you want to eat here, mains are $2 to $7.

Leon Pub (Map p466; ☎ 850-425-4639; 215 E 6th Ave; ⏺ 5pm-midnight) This very local, dark and smoky place has a slew of beers from around the globe – more than 40 on tap and 250 in bottles. Prices are decent, and there's a juke-box and pool tables.

The Winery at the Red Bar (Map p466; ☎ 850-425-4639; www.thewinerytallahassee.com; 1122 Thomasville Rd; noon-5pm Mon, noon-midnight Tue & Wed, noon-2am Thu & Fri, 5pm-2am Sat) Located in the hip heart of Midtown, the sleek, low-lit Red Bar lounge features tons of wines by the glass, flight or bottle, plus a great selection of beers. Its winery, meanwhile, has homemade casks fermenting constantly, and offers a unique feature: you can speak with a wine crafter about your favorite *vino* qualities, and then wait six weeks for the vintage to be ready

for drinking; the wine is made available for purchase as your own private label!

Entertainment

Check the Friday 'Limelight' in the *Tallahassee Democrat* for theater and entertainment listings, or FSU's independent newspaper *FSView* (www.fsunews.com), published Monday and Thursday. For a comprehensive guide to cultural events in town, such as lectures and art exhibits, be sure to visit the handy online calendar at www.morethanyouthought.com.

CLUBS & LIVE MUSIC

Bradfordville Blues Club (Map p466; ☎ 850-906-0766; www.bradfordvilleblues.com; 7152 Moses Lane; tickets $15-20; ⏺ 8pm-2am Fri & Sat) Don't be creeped out by the long drive down a quiet dirt road. You'll be glad you braved it when you arrive at the famed cinderblock building, where friendly, old-time hippie hosts fired-up blues artists ranging from the known to the about-to-be. Torches and a raging bonfire light the yard, and the club's small tabletops bear painted portraits of blues greats from Bobby Rush to Gatemouth Brown. From the intersection of Thomasville Rd (Hwy 319) and I-10 (exit 301), head north on Thomasville Rd 4.5 miles; turn right onto Bradfordville Rd and follow it 3 miles then turn right onto Sam's Lane (there's a sign lit by a torch) and follow a bumpy, short dirt road. Veer left at the fork in the road; it's at the top of the hill.

Floyd's Music Store (Map p466; ☎ 850-222-3506; www.floydsmusicstore.com; 666 W Tennessee St) The only thing for sale at this warehouse-style venue is straight-up live rock and blues. Catch up-and-coming national acts like Falling at Will, Core and Egypt Central.

Tipper's (Map p466; ☎ 850-531-9787; 2698 N Monroe St; ⏺ 9:30pm-late) A raucous, smoky bar, with a funky-weird vibe where you can dance to live bands every night, or simply enjoy a cocktail with no door charge.

Brothers (Map p466; ☎ 850-386-2399; www.brothersnightclub.com; 926 W Tharpe St) Billed as 'Tallahassee's only pansexual playground,' this is the center of the gay and lesbian scene, featuring nightly DJs with a popular terrace bar and drag shows, poetry nights and '80s-themed soirees.

Waterworks (Map p466; ☎ 850-224-1887; 1133 Thomasville Rd) This popular gay nightclub in Midtown has a Polynesian tiki-bar theme, and packs 'em in with nights of live jazz and Latin salsa, as well as rotating DJs.

TALLAHASSEE BLUES

Gary Anton spoke to us about the local blues scene and the Bradfordville Blues Club.

How would you describe the local blues scene? Tallahassee has a modest but vibrant blues scene. A number of area bands are of national and international caliber – professional musicians who tour quite a bit. There are quite a few local blues bands, fueled in part by the two universities – Florida State and Florida A&M – with excellent music schools. The BBC is the only 'blues club,' though. Others have come and gone because the market won't support multiple clubs. In the meantime, we stick to our tried and true formula: bring national acts into the boondocks for weekend shows only, which has allowed us to develop a diverse and loyal customer base – the BBC 'irregulars' as they are known!

What are some of the show highlights from over the years? We've had a number of renowned acts at the club, including former Muddy Waters' sidemen James Cotton (harmonica), Pinetop Perkins (piano), Hubert Sumlin (guitar), Willie 'Big Eyes' Smith (drums) and Steady Rollin' Bob Margolin (guitar), all of whom have won numerous Blues Music Awards and front (or have fronted) their own bands. During one of James Cotton's recent shows, a massive oak tree next to the club fell just as James started to blow his harmonica! We now call it the 'James Cottonwood Tree.' The club was full, the parking lot packed and many people were walking around outside when the tree fell. The blues gods guided the tree down, because it missed everyone and everything – including two brand new cars by less than a foot! The tree provided us with fire wood for the entire winter.

What makes this place so special? It's a juke joint – an authentic juke joint – that's had a musical history to it for about 80 years. It draws a lot of people from all over the place because we're on the blues map. The older guys love it; this is where we cut our teeth. Of course there are other juke joints within about twenty minutes of here, but they don't have live music.

How old is this place anyway? Depends on who you talk to. It was first owned by the Henry family, who were slave descendents. I *can* tell you, though, that that oak tree there is 250 years old. It's on the national registry.

Are you a musician yourself? Not really. I went to Berklee College, where I studied jazz guitar, but that was a long time ago. I live it vicariously now.

Gary Anton is the owner of the Bradfordville Blues Club, Tallahassee.

PERFORMING ARTS

Leon County Civic Center (Map p468; ☎ 850-222-0400, 800-322-3602; 505 W Pensacola St) The city's major performance venue hosts everything from sporting events and touring theater productions to big-time music concerts.

FSU Theatre Department (Map p466; ☎ 850-644-6500; ✆ box office 11am-5:30pm Mon-Fri) The FSU Theatre Department has three venues. The Richard G Fallon Mainstage Theater in the Fine Arts Building, north of Call St on the campus, does large productions of plays and musicals. The Studio, in the Williams Building on campus, stages various free student productions. Off campus, at the corner of Lafayette St and Copeland St, the Lab does a range of works, from Shakespeare to musicals, in its 150-seat thrust-stage setting.

SPORTS

From September to November, the **FSU Seminoles** (☎ 850-644-1830, 888-378-6653; seminoles.cstv.com) football team plays to a crowd of over 80,000 at Doak Campbell Stadium on the FSU campus. FSU Seminoles baseball, meanwhile, steps up in the spring at Dick Howser Stadium, while Seminole men's and women's basketball heats up the court at the Leon County Civic Center.

The **FAMU Rattlers** (☎ 850-599-3141; www.thefamurattlers.collegesports.com) play football from August to November at Bragg Memorial Stadium.

Shopping

All sorts of eclectic art, antiques, clothing and artisan items can be found at galleries and studios around Tallahassee's burgeoning art district. **Railroad Square Art Park** (Map p466; ☎ 850-224-1308; www.railroadsquare.com; 567 Industrial Dr) hosts a festive First Fridays gallery hop monthly.

Another unique spot for one-stop shopping is the **Downtown Marketplace** (Map p468; ☎ 850-297-3945; www.downtownmarketplace.com; Ponce de León Park; ✆ 8am-2pm, Sat Mar-Nov) where you'll find artisans hawking fine arts and crafts along with booths of gourmet food.

THE PANHANDLE

Mon Pére et Moi (Map p466; ☎ 850-877-0343; 3534 Maclay Blvd; 🕒 lunch Tue-Sat, dinner Sat) sells exquisite ribbon-tied boxed handmade chocolates; there's also a café and pétanque games on Fridays from 5pm to 8pm.

Quarter Moon Imports (Map p466; ☎ 850-222-2254; www.quartermoonimports.com; 1641 N Monroe St; 🕒 10am-6:30pm Mon-Sat, noon-5pm Sun) is located in the cottages at Lake Ella. This eclectic shop offers fair-trade items from around the world – with handcrafted jewelry (of beads, silver, pressed flowers, amber or turquoise), ceramics, dresses from small-time designer labels and hemp wallets among the very cool offerings.

Getting There & Around

Tallahassee is 98 miles from Panama City Beach, 135 miles to Jacksonville, 192 miles from Pensacola, 120 miles from Gainesville and 470 miles to Miami. The main access road is I-10; to reach the Gulf Coast, follow Hwy 319 south to Hwy 98.

The tiny **Tallahassee Regional Airport** (Map p466; ☎ 850-891-7800, 800-610-1995) is served by a couple of major and several minor airlines. It's about 5 miles southwest of downtown, off Hwy 263. There's no public transport; some hotels have shuttles, but otherwise a taxi to downtown costs upwards of $20. Call **Yellow Cab** (☎ 850-580-8080).

The **Greyhound bus station** (Map p468; ☎ 850-222-4249, 800-231-2222; 112 W Tennessee St; 🕒 24hr) is at the corner of Duval, opposite the downtown StarMetro transfer center.

Amtrak (Map p468; ☎ 850-244-2779, 800-872-7245; 918½ Railroad Ave) travels to Orlando and cross country to Los Angeles.

StarMetro (Map p468; ☎ 850-891-5200), formerly TalTran, is the local bus service around the greater Tallahassee area and has a main transfer point downtown on Tennessee St at Adams St. Fares per adult/child cost $1/25¢ including free transfers. Routes and schedules are available online at www.talgov.com/starmetro.

AROUND TALLAHASSEE

You'll find historic sites, natural wonders and an abundance of antiquing opportunities in the fascinatingly diverse area surrounding Florida's capital.

Havana

☎ 850 / pop 1706

Before its decline in the late '70s and early '80s, Havana, named for the Cuban capital, boomed thanks to its cigar tobacco industry. But that all changed with the 1958 embargo, when the factories could no longer receive long leaf tobacco from Cuba, with which to wrap the outside of the cigars. Some clever locals turned the place around, though, by creating an antique shop district that has been luring visitors now for years.

Today Havana prospers as an antiquing town, with about 30 antique stores and galleries. Most are concentrated around 2nd St, such as **Planters Exchange** (☎ 850-539-6343; 204 NW 2nd St; 🕒 10am-6pm Wed-Sat, noon-5pm Sun), which houses 60 antiques dealers in a historic 1928 building.

Note that most shops are closed on Monday and Tuesday. A good online resource on shopping and events is www.havanaflorida.com. There are no accommodations in Havana but you can dine in cafés dotted around town, like the popular **Mockingbird Café** (☎ 850-539-2212; 211 NW 1st St; lunch Wed-Sun, dinner Fri & Sat), which serves everything from an authentic Cuban sandwich to grilled red snapper in its intimate dining room or lovely garden area. Owner Mike Henshaw also runs a great pottery gallery on the premises.

Havana is about 17 miles north of Tallahassee; Hwy 27 takes you directly there.

Quincy

☎ 850 / pop 6913

Nicknamed the 'Coca-Cola town,' Quincy residents' financial security was built on Coca-Cola shares thanks to the former president of the Quincy State Bank, Mark W Munroe, who believed in the power of Coke even in its fledgling days. He urged family, friends and bank patrons to save and invest in stock, and the gamble paid off, big-time. There's an original 1905 Coca-Cola billboard mural on E Jefferson St.

Today Quincy's entire downtown and surrounding area – 36 blocks – are listed on the National Register of Historic Places; you can pick up a walking tour brochure from the **chamber of commerce** (☎ 850-627-9231, 800-627-9231; www.gadsdencc.com; 221 N Madison St).

Also be sure to stop by the **Gadsden Arts Center** (☎ 850-875-4866; www.gadsdenarts.org; 13 N Madison St; adult/child $1/free; 🕒 10am-5pm Tue-Sat, 1-5pm Sun), where you'll find work by some standout local artists as well as quality traveling exhibitions. It's all housed in the old 1912 Bell & Bates hardware shop, transformed into a sleek light-filled space that's wheelchair accessible.

SLEEPING & EATING

Allison House Inn (☎ 888-904-2511; www.allison houseinn.com; 215 North Madison St; r $95-140; P ⊠ ◻) The former 1843 home of soldier and lawyer General AK Allison (who traveled to Washington to secure Florida's status as a state and was jailed for six months on charges of treason on his return) has six peaceful, antique-y rooms with brass or four-poster beds, and no shortage of flowered bedspreads. There are continental breakfasts daily, with full breakfasts on weekends, all featuring the signature homemade marmalade.

McFarlin House Bed & Breakfast Inn (☎ 850-875-2526; www.mcfarlinhouse.com; 305 E King St; r $90-200; P ⊠) The turreted 1895 Queen Anne home of tobacco planter John Lee McFarlin, who helped develop the shade tobacco process, offers nine museum-piece (if froofy) rooms. The King's View room is a gem, it is inside the turret and has a two-person spa.

An excellent dining option is between Havana and Quincy, 3 miles west of Havana at **Nicholson Farmhouse** (☎ 850-539-5931; 200 Coca-Cola Ave (SR 12), Havana; mains $14-30; ☽ 4-10pm Tue-Sat). The 1828-built restaurant is acclaimed for its steaks, especially the extra thick cut Delmonico, and for its delectably chocolaty Kentucky Derby pie. All meals begin with bowls of delicious boiled peanuts (a local delicacy). No alcohol is served but you can bring your own; set-ups for mixed drinks are $3, wine corkage is $2. It's a good idea to book ahead. The peaceful place is set amidst 50 acres of woods and horse pastures, and you can take an open-wagon hayride through its collection of old farmhouses and stores.

GETTING THERE & AWAY

Quincy is about 24 miles from Tallahassee; take Hwy 27 north, merge west onto I-10 for 7 miles, then Hwy 90 west for 12 miles and take exit 192 to Quincy.

From Havana, Quincy is about 12 miles; head southwest on 9th Ave, which becomes SR 12, and follow it all the way.

WAKULLA SPRINGS STATE PARK

Visit this 6000-acre **wildlife sanctuary** (☎ 850-922-3633; www.floridastateparks.org/wakullasprings; 550 Wakulla Park Dr; vehicle/pedestrian or cyclist $4/1), just a half-hour's drive from Tallahassee, and find a peaceful gem with plenty to see. Activities revolve around a cavernously deep and warm natural spring – which remains at a steady and delicious 69°F year-round and gushes 1.2 billion gallons of water daily. In 1850, scientist Sarah Smith discovered the bones of an ancient mastodon at the bottom of the spring; since then the remains of at least nine other Ice Age mammals have been found. Scenes from old Johnny Weismuller *Tarzan* movies were filmed here, as were parts of *The Creature from the Black Lagoon.* You'll actually feel as if you've stumbled onto some sort of an exotic set if you spend some time in these fascinating wilds.

If it's warm out, you can go for a swim in the deep waters. But don't miss the chance to take a 40-minute guided **river cruise** (adult/child $6/4; cruises 11am-3pm), which glide under moss-draped bald cypress trees and past an array of creatures, including precious manatees (usually in spring), massive alligators, tribes of red-bellied turtles and graceful wading birds, including anhingas, green herons and white ibises. On days when the spring is clear (and not after a storm, when the churned-up sludge ruins visibility), **glass-bottom boat tours** (adult/child $6/4; cruises 11am-3pm) allow you to peer down the spring's 125ft depths. There are also various nature trails for strolling. Pick up a guide from the rangers or Wakulla Springs Lodge.

Time has stood still at the faded 1937 **Wakulla Springs Lodge** (☎ 850-224-5950; r $85-105), an immense Spanish-style building with an enormous faux stone fireplace in the lobby, murals decorating 17ft heart cypress ceilings, a 70ft old-fashioned soda fountain in the adjoining gift shop, and honest-to-goodness Southern hospitality from warm, genuine staff. The 27 basic, slightly scruffy rooms have original marble floors, walk-in wardrobes and, blessedly, no TVs. The lodge is also ecofriendly, with low-flow toilets, energy-efficient lighting and landscaping that uses minimal water. The lodge's excellent **Ball Room Restaurant** (☎ 850-224-5950; mains $12-19; ☽ 7:30am-10am, 11:30am-2pm & 6-8pm), named for financier Edward Ball who built the lodge, is a favorite dining spot with Tallahassee locals – and a popular place for weddings.

The park is 15 miles south of Tallahassee, or, as described in the 1891 Florida guidebook *A Handbook of Florida* by CL Norton, it is '2½ hours by carriage from Tallahassee and 2 hours by rowboat from St Marks.' Take Hwy 319 south from Tallahassee to Hwy 61 south, and follow the signs; the entrance is on Hwy 267.

THE PANHANDLE

APALACHICOLA NATIONAL FOREST

☎ 850

The largest of Florida's three national forests, the **Apalachicola National Forest** (day-use areas $3; ☾ 8am-sunset) occupies almost 938 sq miles – more than half a million acres – of the Panhandle from just west of Tallahassee to the Apalachicola River. Made up of lowlands, pine, cypress hammocks and oaks, dozens of species call the area home including mink, gray and red foxes, coyotes, six bat species, beavers, red cockaded woodpeckers, alligators, Florida black bears and the elusive Florida panther. A total of 68.7 miles of the Florida National Scenic Trail extends through the forest, as well.

Orientation & Information

The Apalachicola National Forest is bisected by the Ochlockonee River, which flows south through its center. The forest is bounded by Hwy 20 to the north, Hwy 319 to the east and the Apalachicola River to the west, with the southern boundary in Franklin county – Forest Rd 125 is the closest southern access. Several highways traverse the forest, but otherwise all roads are gravel; 2WDs are fine to get to all of the developed campsites. You'll need maps to explore the area, available at either of the ranger stations.

The western half of the forest is controlled by the **Apalachicola Ranger Station** (☎ 850-643-2282; 11152 NW SR 20, Bristol), northwest of the forest near the intersection of Hwy 12 and 20, just south of Bristol. The eastern half is managed by the **Wakulla Ranger Station** (☎ 850-926-3561; 57 Taff Dr, Crawfordville), just off Hwy 319 behind the Winn Dixie in Crawfordville; the ranger stations operate together.

Sights & Activities

FORT GADSDEN HISTORIC SITE

In the west of the forest, the **Fort Gadsden Historic Site** is the former location of a 1814-built British fort armed by African American and American Indian soldiers, who the British armed and trained to defend against Spain's hold on Florida. The fort was blown to pieces two years later, killing more than 200 people, but its rebuilt fortification would later be used by Confederate troops. These days it's a green, serene picnic area, with an interpretive trail detailing its history. From Hwy 65, turn west on Forest Rd 129 then south on Forest Rd 129B.

HIKING, BIKING & HORSEBACK RIDING

On the eastern side of the forest is the 7.5-mile **Munson Hills Loop** bicycle trail, which spurs to the Tallahassee–St Marks Historic Railroad State Trail (p467). Experienced off-road cyclists can tackle this area made up of hammock, dunes, hills and brush, though its soft sand can make this a challenging route. If you run out of steam halfway through, take the Tall Pine Shortcut out of the trail roughly at the halfway point, for a total distance of 4.5 miles.

More than 6 miles of trails and boardwalks marked with interpretive signs wind past sinks and swamps in the **Leon Sinks Geological Area** ($3 per vehicle; ☾ 8am-sunset). Be sure to stay on the trails, as the karst (terrain affected by the underlying limestone bedrock dissolving) here is still evolving, and new sinkholes could appear anytime. One of the best viewing spots is the observation platform at Big Dismal Sink, where you'll see ferns, dogwoods and dozens of other lush plants descending its steep walls. The sinks are at the eastern end of the forest, just west of Hwy 319, about 10 miles south of Tallahassee.

Roughly 74 miles of the **Florida National Scenic Trail** (see p50) cuts a northwest–southeast swath through the forest. Prepare to get soaked if you opt for the Bradwell Bay Wilderness section, which involves some waist-deep swamp tramping. You can pick up the trail at the southeastern gateway, just east of Forest Rd 356 on Hwy 319; or the northwestern corner on Hwy 12.

The forest's trails are ideal for horseback riding; for rental horses contact **Conner Carriages and Occasions** (☎ 850-997-6803; www.connercarriages.com; 385 N Mulberry St, Monticello; 2 hr $32).

WATER SPORTS

You can sunbathe on the white sandy shores or swim in the waters of **Silver Lake** (close to Tallahassee in the northeast of the forest on Forest Rd 370), **Wright Lake** (Forest Rd 379 in the southwest of the forest) and **Camel Lake** (off Hwy 12 in the northwest of the forest), all of which have facilities and picnic areas.

There are also plentiful opportunities for canoeing along the forest's rivers and waterways. Information on canoeing in the area and canoe rental is available from either ranger station, or visit the excellent website for **Florida Greenways and Trails** (www.dep.state.fl.us/gwt/guide), which has maps and updated lists of outfitters

APALACHICOLA NATIONAL FOREST

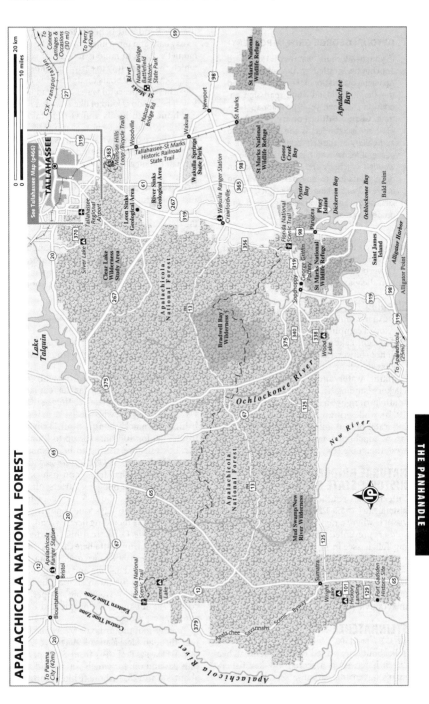

DETOUR: GEORGE GRIFFIN POTTERY

If you head south via Hwy 319 toward Sopchoppy, nestled at the edge of the Apalachicola National Forest, and heed the simple blue-and-white road sign announcing 'Pottery,' you'll be in for a serious treat. **George Griffin Pottery** (☎ 850-962-9311; 110 Suncat Ridge) is the home, studio and gallery of the self-taught Mr Griffin, a peaceful fellow who has created a unique, wooded sanctuary and, luckily, extends an open invitation to any passerby with an interest in checking out his pots, mugs, jars, plates and various other glazed and gorgeous creations.

---

in the surrounding towns. Canoe rental cost around $25 to $35 per day.

Powerboats are allowed on the rivers, but not on the glassy lakes.

Sleeping

None of the campgrounds have hookups. For developed camping ($8), head to Camel Lake and Wright Lake, which have full bathrooms with hot showers, shelters and picnic tables.

Less-developed campgrounds ($3) with drinking water and vault toilets include, Hickory Landing (from Sumatra, take Hwy 65 south; turn right on Forest Rd 101 and left on 101B), while primitive camping areas (drinking water but no toilets) include Wood Lake (from Sopchoppy, take Hwy 375 to Hwy 22 west, then take Hwy 340 south to Hwy 338).

NATURAL BRIDGE BATTLEFIELD HISTORIC STATE PARK

Fifteen miles southeast of Tallahassee, this **historic site** (☎ 850-922-6007; admission free; ⊙ 8am-sunset) is where a ragtag group of Confederate soldiers prevented Union troops from reaching Tallahassee in 1865. Today it's a peaceful picnic spot. In March costumed villagers and soldiers stage a battle reenactment, complete with a booming cannon. From Tallahassee, take Hwy 363 south to Natural Bridge Rd in Woodville.

STEINHATCHEE

☎ 352 / pop 1500

Talk about unexpected Florida! Steinhatchee (*steen*-hatch-ie) is a secret, low-key fisherman's haven that sits in a secret crevice of

the Big Bend and beneath towering pines, mossy oaks and pink, juicy sunsets. The sleepy hamlet's claim to fame is its scallop season, which runs from July to early September and brings up to 1000 boats on its opening day to the otherwise peaceful waters of Dead Man's Bay. The season is kind of like a twisted Easter egg hunt, with locals and visitors taking a mesh bag, donning a snorkel and mask, and snatching up their own seafood as they swim. Locals will often clean your catch in exchange for half the meat.

Orientation & Information

Just a handful of shops, marinas and restaurants make up the town, which unfolds along the river's northern bank, 3 miles inland of the gulf. Hwy 51 connects to Hwy 361, here called Riverside Dr, the town's main thoroughfare. There's no visitor information center, but information is available online at www.steinhatchee.com, www.steinhatchee.info or from the marinas, motels and resort.

Activities
FISHING & WATER SPORTS

Depending on the season, cobia, sea trout, mackerel, tarpon and the famous scallops are plentiful.

For a guided fishing charter with locals who know the waters, try **Captain Tony Jackson** (☎ 386-294-2216) or **Captain Bob Morgan** (☎ 352-498-5652, 352-215-0806), who specialize in inshore fishing for mackerel and trout. Trips cost from $350 for 10 hours for up to four people. For offshore fishing to hook snapper, **Booger Charters** (☎ 352-498-2705; www.boogercharters.com) guarantee that trips land fish or you don't have to pay. Booger Charters' offshore charter rates are $750/995 for 10/14 hours and $1995 for two-days, one-night trips for up to six people including licenses, bait, rods, reels and tackle. Offshore fishing charters are also available from **Outta-Here Charters** (☎ 352-498-2493; www.outtaherecharters.com). Outta-Here daytrips depart at 6:45am and return at 5pm, and cost $1095 for up to six people; to get further out for the seriously big snapper, trips cost $1295 for up to six people and depart at 6am.

Twenty-foot motor boats are available for rent through **Ideal Marina & Motel** (☎ 352-498-3877; 114 Riverside Dr SE; P) from $125 per day plus gas and oil, for which you should allow about $14 to $28. Inshore fishing charters in and near the coastline cost $350 per day for four people, or for your best chance of hooking prized grouper, offshore trips for four people start from $600 per day.

River Haven Marina & Motel (☎ 352-498-0709; 1110 Riverside Dr) rents a variety of fishing boats from $125 per day and can put you in touch with fishing-charter guides. River Haven also rents kayaks (single/tandem per half-day $30/40, per day $50/60), including pickup and drop off, which are great for exploring the myriad waterways.

Sleeping & Eating

River Haven Marina & Motel (☎ 352-498-0709; 1110 Riverside Dr; r from $65) This four-room motel also has cottages and mobile homes. It was for sale at the time of writing, so please check that it's still in business before setting out.

Steinhatchee River Inn Motel (☎ 352-498-4049; 600 Riverside Dr; r winter $75, summer $95-105; P ⬛ ⬛) This classic motel-style inn has decent-sized rooms and is close to the marina. Some rooms have kitchens, and all have TVs, coffeemakers, wi-fi and refrigerators.

Roy's (☎ 352-498-5000; cnr Hwy 51 & Hwy 351; mains $10-20; ☺ 4-10pm Mon-Thu, 11am-10pm Fri-Sun) Since 1969, Roy's, which sits overlooking the gulf, has been a favorite for seafood. The standard style is fried, but if you ask they'll serve it spiced and broiled, nestled up to sides that include heaping portions of grits, fries, baked potatoes and hushpuppies.

Fiddler's (☎ 352-498-7427; 1306 SE Riverside Dr; mains $11-20; ☺ 4-10pm Mon-Thu, 11am-10pm Fri-Sun) Right on the water, this wood-paneled, nautical-themed favorite will cook your catch for you. Mains are served with salad, potatoes, black beans and rice or grits, and the peanut butter 'moose pie' is perennially popular for desert.

Getting There & Away

Coming from either the north or south, take Hwy 19 (also called Hwy 19/27 and Hwy 19/98) to the crossroads with a blinking light, then drive west on Hwy 51 to the end, about 12 miles.

MANATEE SPRINGS STATE PARK

Between Cedar Key and Steinhatchee, this **park** (☎ 352-493-6072, 800-326-3521; www.floridastateparks.org /manatesprings; 11650 NW 115th St; vehicle/pedestrian/cyclist $4/1/1; ☺ 8am-sundown) is worth a stop, especially for a dip into the 72°F crystalline waters of the beautiful spring.

You can also scuba dive ($10 plus gear; certification and dive buddy required) at the spring-head, which gushes 117 million gallons of water per day, or canoe or kayak along the spring run (boat rentals $8 to $10 hourly). Scuba diving, canoeing and kayaking can be organized through the park office. On dry land – which

---

DETOUR: UPON THE SUWANNEE RIVER

Flowing 207 miles, the Suwannee River is immortalized by Stephen Foster in Florida's state song, 'Old Folks at Home.' Foster himself never set eyes on the river, but thought 'Suwannee' (or 'Swannee,' as his map apparently stated, hence his corruption of the spelling) sounded suitably Southern. As it happened he was right; the river winds through wild Spanish moss–draped countryside from the far north of the state to the Gulf of Mexico in the curve of the Big Bend. See it for yourself along the **Suwannee River Wilderness Trail** (☎ 800-868-9914; www.suwanneeriver .com), which covers 169 miles of the river to the gulf, with nine 'hubs' – cabins – spaced one day's paddle apart. All are now open, though heavily booked, so reserve as early as possible. River camps along the banks of the trail are also in the pipeline.

The trail starts at the **Stephen Foster State Folk Cultural Center** (☎ 386-397-2733, 800-326-3521; vehicle/pedestrian/cyclist $4/3/3, campsites $16, cabins $90; ☺ park 8am-sunset, museum & carillon 9am-5pm), north of White Springs. With lush green hills and monolithic live oak trees, the park has a museum of Florida history that you'd swear is a 19th-century plantation. Next door to the park, canoe rentals are available from **American Canoe Adventures** (☎ 386-397-1309; www.aca1.com; 10610 Bridge St, White Springs), which offers daytrips of 3 miles ($30), 6 to 8 miles ($50) and 10 miles ($60), where you're transported upstream, then paddle down. Overnight canoe rentals are $30.

The **Suwannee River State Park** (☎ 386-362-2746; 20185 CR 132, Live Oak; admission car/person $4/2, tent/RV sites $4/15, cabins $90), at the confluence of the Withlacoochee and Suwannee rivers, has Civil War fortifications. The five cabins sleep up to six people. The park is 13 miles west of Live Oak, just off US 90 – follow the signs.

is a uniquely spongy combo of sand and limestone shaded by tupelo, cypress and pine trees – there's an 8.5-mile-long hiking/biking trail, the North End Trail, on your right as you enter the park. **Camping** ($16 for tent or RV) is also available at 94 shady sites with picnic tables and ground grills. A highlight is the wheelchair accessible raised timber boardwalk that traces the narrow spring down to the Suwannee River as it flows to the gulf and out to sea.

Ranger programs include guided canoe journeys, moonlight hikes, nature walks and occasional covered-wagon rides. Contact the park office for details.

The park is at the end of Hwy 320, off Hwy 98, 6 miles west of Chiefland.

CEDAR KEY
☎ 352 / pop 979

The windswept and isolated island of Cedar Key, jutting 3 miles into the Gulf of Mexico, is an enchanting ensemble of historic buildings, bird-inhabited bayous and a fishing boat–filled harbor. The otherworldly landscape sings with marshes that reflect candy-colored sunsets, and tiny 'peaks' (for Florida) of 37ft, affording the best views of your surroundings. Cedar Key is just one of 100 islands (13 of which are part of the Cedar Keys National Wildlife Refuge) that make up this coastal community, which is gloriously abundant with wildlife and friendly, small-town vibes.

As the western terminus of the trans-Florida railroad in the late 1800s, Cedar Key was one of Florida's largest towns, second only to St Augustine. Its primary industry was wood (for Faber pencils), which eventually deforested the islands; a 1896 hurricane destroyed what was left. Consequently, the trees here are less than 100 years old. Aquaculture has recently revived the town's economy: spurred by government subsidies when net fishing was banned, it's now the largest clam farming region in the country.

Orientation & Information
Cedar Key is at the southwestern end of Hwy 24, 58 miles southwest of Gainesville. Hwy 24 turns into D St in town; the main shopping strip is 2nd St, less than half a mile north of the docks. In mid-October the streets of this sleepy village thrum with live music and jump with hundreds of stall-holders during the Seafood Festival.

The **Cedar Keys Chamber of Commerce** (☎ 352-543-5600; www.cedarkey.org; 525 2nd St; ☾ 10am-1pm Mon, Wed & Fri) offers local information. Across the street is the **post office** (☎ 352-543-5477; 518 2nd St; ☾ 9am-5pm Mon-Fri, to 1pm Sat) and the **library** (☎ 352-543-5777; 460 2nd St; ☾ 10am-4pm Mon, Wed & Thu, 4-8pm Tue, 10am-1pm Sat), which offers free internet access.

Sights & Activities
MUSEUMS
The eclectic **Cedar Key Museum State Park** (☎ 352-543-5350; 12231 SW 166th St; admission $1; ☾ 9am-5pm Thu-Mon, tours 1pm to 4pm) features the historic house, remodeled to its 1902 state, of St Clair Whitman. A main player in both the pencil factory and the local fiber mill, he arrived in the area in 1882 and started collecting everything he saw: insects, butterflies, glass, sea glass, bottles and infinite varieties of seashells. Take a tour for some true insight into the holdings, and afterward, enjoy a bucolic walk on the surrounding nature trails.

Staffed by friendly volunteers, the **Cedar Key Museum** (☎ 352-543-5549; www.cedarkeymuseum.org; 609 2nd St; adult/child $1/50¢; ☾ 1-4pm Sun-Fri, 11am-5pm Sat), run by Cedar Key Historical Society, is worth a peek to check out its exhibits of American Indian, Civil War and seafood industry artifacts, and especially for its extensive collection of Cedar Key historic photographs.

CEDAR KEYS NATIONAL WILDLIFE REFUGE
Home to 250 species of bird (including ibises, pelicans, egrets, herons and double-crested cormorants), 10 species of reptile and one romantic lighthouse, the 13 islands in this **refuge** (☎ 352-493-0238; www.fws.gov/cedarkeys) can only be reached by boat. The islands' interiors are generally closed to the public, but during daylight hours you can access most of the white-sand beaches, which provide great opportunities for both fishing and manatee viewing. Skiffs and pontoon boats are available for hire from **Island Hopper** (☎ 352-543-5904; www.cedarkeyislandhopper.com; City Marina) from $90 for four hours. Time your trip (and speak to the Hopper folks for advice) to avoid getting stranded on mudflats during low tide. Island Hopper also runs one-hour sunset cruises from $20.

KAYAKING
The waterways and estuaries in and around the refuge make for superb kayaking. Several

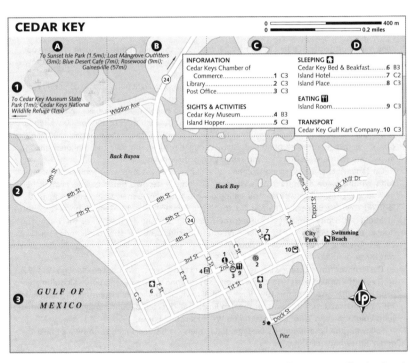

CEDAR KEY

INFORMATION		
Cedar Keys Chamber of		
Commerce	1	C3
Library	2	C3
Post Office	3	C3

SIGHTS & ACTIVITIES		
Cedar Key Museum	4	B3
Island Hopper	5	C3

SLEEPING		
Cedar Key Bed & Breakfast	6	B3
Island Hotel	7	C2
Island Place	8	C3

EATING		
Island Room	9	C3

TRANSPORT		
Cedar Key Gulf Kart Company	10	C3

companies operate ecotours, including **Lost Mangrove Outfitters** (☎ 352-477-0222; www.lost mangrove.com; 11850 SW SR 24; tours from $60), which also rents kayaks (from $30/50 per three hours/day) and can arrange to take you to offshore clam beds.

Sleeping & Eating

Sunset Isle Park (☎ 352-543-5375; www.cedarkeyrv.com; 11850 SW SR 24; tent sites $16, RV sites $38-42; P ✗) Options at this waterfront 'RV B&B' include primitive camping and RV sites, with perks including amazing sunsets, a buzzing clubhouse and frequent clamfests, open to the whole town, thrown by owner Denise. Coming from the mainland, it's on the right (north) side of Hwy 24 a mile past the first bridge.

Island Hotel (☎ 352-543-5111, 800-432-4640; www .islandhotel-cedarkey.com; 224 2nd St at B St; r $80-135; P ✗) A night in this old-fashioned, 1859 tabby shell and oak building will relax you for sure. Listed on the National Register of Historic Places, it has 10 simple and romantic rooms with original hand-cut wooden walls, a wraparound balcony with rocking chairs, a history of notable guests including John

Muir and President Grover Cleveland and, by all reports, as many as 13 resident ghosts. It's also home to the island's finest restaurant, specializing in baked and sautéed fresh-caught seafood. Mains are $16 to $27 and they are open Tuesday to Sunday.

Cedar Key Bed & Breakfast (☎ 352-543-9000; www .cedarkeybandb.com; cnr 3rd St & F St; r $99-225; P ✗) This beautiful 1880s home has rooms (some wheelchair accessible) furnished with brass, rattan and lace, but somehow manages to not be overly frilly. The back veranda is a calming place to sit after a day of touring, and the copious breakfasts a great way to start the day. Wi-fi is available.

The Island Place (☎ 352-543-5307, 800-780-6522; www.islandplace-ck.com; cnr 1st St & C St; r $105-190; P) This well-run complex features one- and two-bedroom condominiums with water views and a Caribbean feel. Each has full kitchen, a balcony, ceiling fans and floral-print couches.

Blue Desert Cafe (☎ 352-543-9111; 12815 SR 24; mains $8-18; ⏲ dinner Tue-Sat) Duck into this funky little pink house, where the eclectic offerings – such as seafood pizza topped with shrimp,

---

ROSEWOOD

Nine miles northeast of Cedar Key on Hwy 24, you'll pass the once flourishing town of Rosewood. Named for the red cedars in the area, all that's here today are overgrown remains of the town and of a tragic historical chapter.

This community of about 355 predominantly African American families was razed during racial riots that erupted when, on January 1, 1923, a 22-year-old white housewife, Fanny Taylor, from the neighboring town of Sumner, claimed that she had been raped by a black man (evidence suggests that she was in fact raped by her white lover). A lynch mob of 200 to 300 white vigilantes descended on the town, torching buildings and killing those they caught; the sheriff's office, meanwhile, turned a blind eye. Parents sought to hide and save their children, though many were murdered as the fires and rampage raged for days.

On January 6, some surviving women and children were rescued when white store owner, John Wright, made a contract with William and John Bryce, two brothers who owned their own logging train. The women and children were taken to Archer, Gainesville, and to the logging town of Bryceville (named for the Bryce family), near the Georgia border. A mob of about 150 white vigilantes returned the following day and torched all of the remaining houses except one, belonging to John Wright, the store owner. It still stands today on Hwy 24, a two-story, white veranda-ed house that you'll see from the road. The rest of the town was never rebuilt.

The Rosewood massacre was largely obscured until two survivors, Minnie Lee Langley (1914–95) and Lee Ruth Bradley Davis (1915–93), were offered pro-bono legal representation, which ultimately resulted in the passing of the 1994 Rosewood Bill, which offered the victims compensation. In 1997 the massacre was the basis for the film *Rosewood*, directed by John Singleton and starring John Voight as John Wright, and featuring Wright's actual house.

Following the Rosewood Bill's passage, today there's a historical marker on Hwy 24 near the green 'Rosewood' road sign.

Guided tours (☎ 800-250-4645; adult/child $35/25) departing from Gainesville provide historical context and background on the events, and visit key sights. Seat availability may not be confirmed until a few days prior to departure.

---

salmon, scallops and oysters – are prepared from scratch. An excellent selection of brews keep you sated till your food arrives.

The Island Room (☎ 352-543-6520; 192 E 2nd St; meals $20-30; ☾ dinner) Grab a nice gulf-view table in this elegant dining room, where chef Peter Stefani uses the bounty of local ingredients to create seafood and meat dishes like linguini with clams, pecan-crusted fish and succulent steak au poivre.

Getting There & Around

There's no public transport to Cedar Key, but driving is easy: take Hwy 19/98 or I-75 to Hwy 24 and follow it southwest to the end.

You'll see locals zipping around in golf ('gulf') carts, which are perfect for traversing the little island; try **Cedar Key Gulf Kart Company** (☎ 352-543-5300; www.gulfcart.com; cnr 1st St & A St; 2-person/4-person carts per 2hr $20/30; ☾ 8am-6:30pm). All-day rental rates are available, as are bicycles ($2.50/10 per hour/day).

GULF COAST

Dubbed the 'Forgotten Coast' along its eastern half, the name is apt to describe the entire shoreline here – unless you're from the region and are already happily familiar with the Gulf Coast's magical beauty. That's not to say the beaches are always desolate (though they certainly are in the off-season), just that most folks tend to think of the southern portion of the state when conjuring images of Florida's famed beaches. But these northern, gulf-side spits are spectacular: with sand that's soft and white as sugar, rolling dunes that resemble polished marble sculptures and clear, turquoise waters that'll make you wonder why you haven't been spending summers here all your life. Alongside all the natural beauty are towns that burst with Southern charm – from the lure of Apalachicola's historic district to the odd perfection of the lovely planned community of Seaside, along with some insanely over-developed Spring Break destinations that may be best avoided, depending on your constitution. But whatever you're looking for, you will find your place in the sun.

APALACHICOLA
☎ 850 / pop 2331

Slow and mellow and perfectly preserved, like a mini St Augustine minus the mobs, Apalachicola retains an old-world feel and incredible collection of romantic B&Bs, mint-condition historic homes and churches, and eclectic boutiques and eateries, all infused with the refreshing air that permeates the place, thanks to the oyster-rich Apalachicola Bay.

That glistening body of water, declared a world biosphere by the UN and among the cleanest and most productive in the country, is fed more than 16 billion gallons of freshwater daily from the Chattahoochee, Flint and Apalachicola Rivers. The bay's oyster-studded bottom has made the town famous, supports 'tongers' (formerly known as oystermen) who harvest the tasty morsels, and draws plenty of seafood-lovin' travelers, who make a date with a raw bar part of their peaceful stay in this lovely, historic town.

Orientation

About halfway between Tallahassee and Panama City Beach, Apalachicola is at the southernmost point on the Panhandle mainland, south of the Apalachicola National Forest. Hwy 98 runs from the west through the center of town and east toward St George Island (see p483). From the Gorrie Bridge (Hwy 98), downtown Apalachicola and the Apalachicola Historic District are on the eastern end of the spit. Streets run on a grid that's on a 45-degree angle to compass points. Market St is the southeast–northwest thoroughfare; west of here streets are numbered, beginning with 4th St. Bisecting the streets are avenues, lettered beginning with Ave B, one block northwest of Bay Ave at the waterline. Ave E is the main drag and the continuation of Hwy 98, running at a 90-degree angle from Market St all the way out of town to the west.

Information

Apalachicola Bay Chamber of Commerce (☎ 850-653-9419; www.apalachicolabay.org; 122 Commerce St; ☺ 9am-5pm Mon-Fri) Offers loads of tourist information and helpful advice.

Downtown Books (☎ 850-653-1290; 67 Commerce St) Lots of Floridiana books, along with tomes on gardening and cooking; it's also a yarn and knitting shop.
Municipal library (☎ 850-653-8436; 76 6th St; ☺ 10am-5pm Mon, to noon & 2-5pm Tue, Thu & Fri, to noon Wed) Free internet access.

Sights & Activities

The sights below – and 35 in total – are well marked on a chamber of commerce Historic Walking Tour guide and map, available free from the chamber office and most B&Bs. For a look inside many of the historic private homes, plan to be here for the annual spring house tour, held in mid-May.

MUSEUMS & HISTORIC BUILDINGS

The 1838 Southern plantation-style **Raney House** (☎ 850-653-9749; 46 Ave F; tour free; ☺ 1-4pm Sat), behind a white-picket fence and a facade of grand columns, was the home of Harriet and David Raney, the latter a two-time mayor of the city. A small museum has some historical exhibits on the town, and behind the building is the 1835 guest cottage – thought to be the town's oldest structure and now available to rent for overnight or weekly stays, see p482.

Just a few blocks away is the tiny **Gorrie House Museum** (☎ 850-653-9347; 46 6th St; admission $1; ☺ 9am-5pm Thu-Sun), former home to Dr John Gorrie (1803–55), who was mayor, postmaster, treasurer, councilor, bank director and founder of the Trinity Episcopal Church. He was also one of the pioneers of refrigeration, developing an ice-making machine to keep yellow fever patients cool. His patent was granted in 1851, but he was unable to market it, and died unaware of how his invention laid the groundwork for modern refrigeration and air-con. Displays include a model of Dr Gorrie's invention as well as exhibits on the local (and long-defunct) sponging and cotton-storage industries here.

The **Trinity Episcopal Church** (79 6th St), just across the street, was built in New York State and cut into sections, which were shipped down the Atlantic coast and around the Keys before making their way to this spot where the church was reassembled in 1836. Today it attracts a full and lively flock of locals, who enjoy live violinists with their worship services and are summoned to prayer by a couple of volunteers who ring the church's massive bell by tugging its thick rope by hand.

THE PANHANDLE

GRADY BUILDING

Built in the late 1880s and rebuilt after a fire in 1900, this hulking brick space was originally a ship's chandlery and general store, as well as the home of a French consulate installed to look after French nationals working in the shipping industry. Now it encompasses the **Grady Market** (☎ 850-653-4099; 76 Water St; ☺ 10am-5:30pm Mon-Sat), a collection of antiques traders and local artists' galleries, including creative textile designs, funky clothing and works of sculpture, painting and nautical-type crafts.

RICHARD BICKEL PHOTOGRAPHY

Don't miss a chance to get a close-up view of the captivating work at **Richard Bickel Photography** (☎ 850-653-3900; 81 Market St; www .richardbickelphotography.com), the gallery of a very talented, internationally acclaimed photojournalist who lives and works in the town, preserving the waterfront around him in images. His B&W photo books, *The Last Great Bay* and *Apalachicola River,* offer a moving portrait of the historic way of life here – and remind folks that, sadly, depending on the economy and environmental situation, it may not be long for this world.

BOATING & FISHING TOURS

Numerous companies offer wildlife-spotting tours, where alligators, wading birds and willowy trees are the main attractions. **Backwater Guide Service** (☎ 850-653-2820; www.backwaterguide service.com; $175-300) and **Brownie's Guide Service** (☎ 850-653-5529; www.apalachicolaguide.com) both offer such sightseeing tours, which include easy hikes along nature trails, as well as fishing charters including bait, tackle and licenses, and the promise of snagging your own red fish or speckled trout for grilling. Call Brownie's for their current tour prices.

Sleeping & Eating

Raney House Guest Cottage (☎ 850-653-9749; 46 Ave F; r $125; P ⊠) A great option for families, this historic white-painted cottage with hardwood floors has two bedrooms and two bathrooms, as well as a separate dining room and a fully equipped kitchen. Two gas fireplaces and central heating keep it cozy in winter; in summer there's a breezy screened back porch. All linens are included.

House of Tartts (☎ 850-653-4687; 50 Ave F; r $105-130, carriage house $195; P ⊠) This reasonably priced, elegant 1886 guesthouse has three antiques-rich rooms, a grand wraparound porch, a DIY-breakfast room with cereals and juices, and a newly restored carriage house, which has a decidedly more modern aesthetic, plus a large whirlpool for soaking after a day of sightseeing.

Gibson Inn (☎ 850-653-2191; www.gibsoninn.com; 51 Ave C; r $105-250; P ⊠) The first landmark you'll see if you're approaching town from the east on Hwy 98 is this grand and gracious duck-egg blue timber inn (c 1907), which dominates the little township. Listed on the National Register of Historic Places, ask for one of the sweeping 2nd-floor rooms that open onto the sprawling veranda. If you're game, request room 309, reputedly haunted by Captain Woods, who had a romantic liaison with one of the Gibson sisters. The inn also hosts several highly atmospheric murder mystery weekends a year.

our pick **Coombs House Inn** (☎ 850-653-9199; www .coombshouseinn.com; 80 6th St; r $119-229; P ⊠ ⬛) This stunning yellow Victorian inn was built in 1905 by lumber entrepreneur James N Coombs, a friend of Theodore Roosevelt who turned down both the vice presidency and the governorship of Florida. He probably didn't want to leave his elegant house, featuring black cypress wall paneling, nine fireplaces, a carved oak staircase, leaded glass windows and beadboard ceilings. The place was left vacant in the 1960s, when it spent years deteriorating until luxury-hotel designer Lynn Wilson and her airline executive husband Bill Spohrer discovered the property in the '80s, purchased it from surviving family members and brought it back to spectacular life. Settle into one of the fabulous rooms and be sure to join the other guests for nightly wine socials in the dining room, where a lavish breakfast is served each morning.

Café con Leche (☎ 850-653-2233; 32 Ave D; sandwiches $6-8; ☺ 7am-9pm Mon-Sat) This funky little storefront with a cool bohemian feel offers live music in the evenings, computer access ($13 per hour) and free wi-fi, plus good strong coffee drinks and tasty sandwiches, like grilled eggplant and a well-executed *cubano* (Cuban sandwich).

Papa Joe's Oyster Bar & Grill (☎ 850-653-1189; 301b Market St; mains $8-15; ☺ lunch & dinner) Hunker down at this locals' favorite to sample daily harvested oysters that are shucked to order and served on the half shell, in po' boys (in bread), steamed or baked and then topped with savories from butter and parmesan cheese, to capers and feta. The menu is also stocked with seafood treasures like crab cakes, popcorn shrimp and stuffed flounder, not to mention steaks and pasta creations.

Tamara's Café Floridita (☎ 850-653-4111; 17 Ave E; mains $15-28; ☙ lunch & dinner) In the heart of the historic district, Tamara's is the hottest table in town, especially on Wednesday tapas night. Spices influenced by Tamara's native Venezuela pack a punch in dishes like grilled herb pork chop with shrimp and scallops in creamy tomato-tarragon sauce. Her margarita chicken, sautéed in honey, tequila and lime glaze with scallops, is inspired.

Getting There & Around

Hwy 98 (which becomes Market Street) brings you into town from either direction. Downtown is easily strollable, but you'll need a car to explore the greater area.

ST VINCENT ISLAND & AROUND

You'll probably be itching to get into an interrupted stretch of nature after seeing it on the fringes of your travel so often through this region, and you'll find it at its most pristine on St Vincent Island. On Scipio Creek near Apalachicola's shrimping boat docks, the **St Vincent National Wildlife Refuge headquarters and visitors center** (☎ 850-653-8808; www.fws.gov/saint vincent/; north end of Market St; admission free; ☙ 8am-4:30pm Mon-Fri) has interactive exhibits and information about **St Vincent Island**, located a quarter-mile offshore at the west end of Apalachicola Bay, west of Cape St George and only accessible by boat. An afternoon of lollygagging here showcases dune ridges revealing 5000-year-old geological records and endangered species including red wolves, sea turtles, bald eagles and peregrine falcons. Fishing's permitted on lakes except when bald eagles are nesting. To get to the island, hop aboard the **St Vincent Shuttle Services** (☎ 850-229-1065; www.stvincentisland.com; adult/child $10/7), which can also take your bike (including fare $20), or rent you one of theirs (including fare $25).

Opposite the St Vincent National Wildlife Refuge headquarters, the **Apalachicola National Estuarine Research Reserve** (☎ 850-653-8063; 261 7th St; admission free; ☙ 8am-5pm Mon-Fri) provides a great overview of its research site which encompasses over 246,000 acres in Apalachicola Bay, with giant aquariums here simulating different habitats. A half-mile boardwalk leads down to the river where you'll find a free telescope on a turret.

ST GEORGE ISLAND

☎ 850 / pop 300

Located just over a 4-mile causeway from Apalachicola's neighbor of Eastpoint, this 28-mile-long barrier island is home to white sandy beaches, bay forests, salt marshes and an inoffensive mix of summer homes and condos. It's a great place for shelling, kayaking, sailing or swimming. At the end of every street on the island you'll find public beach access and, generally, plentiful parking. St George Island State Park sits at the island's northeastern point; Little St George Island lies southwest.

The brand new 79ft St George Lighthouse – the rebuilt 1852 structure that collapsed from erosion in 2005 – was expected to open just after the time of writing. The lighthouse is at the intersection of State Rd 300 and Gulf Beach Dr.

Sights & Activities

ST GEORGE ISLAND STATE PARK

The island at its undeveloped best is found here, in the 9 miles of glorious beach and sand dunes that make up this pristine **park** (☎ 850-927-2111, 800-326-3521; www.floridastateparks .org/stgeorgeisland; vehicle/pedestrian/cyclist $5/1/1; eastend access $6, camping $19). There is a 2.5-mile nature trail that offers exceptional birding, as willet, least terns, snowy plovers and black skimmers regularly nest here. Throughout the park, boardwalks lead to shell-sprinkled beaches, where the shallow waters are perfect for canoeing and kayaking, as well as fishing for flounder and whiting. You can camp here, too, at one of the 60 campsites on grounds featuring hookups and a playground, or at the Gap Point primitive campsites, accessible by boat or by hiking a 2.5-mile nature trail through pine forests and coastal scrub. Catch the amazing loggerhead sea turtles beginning in May, when they come ashore to dig nests and lay their eggs, yielding hatchlings that race into the gulf.

WATER SPORTS

Jeanni's Journeys (☎ 850-927-3259; www.sgislandjourneys .com; 240 E 3rd St) leads boat and kayak tours, and also rents kayaks ($60 daily), sailboats ($100 daily) and catamarans ($275 daily), all ideal ways to make the voyage to Cape St George.

Sleeping & Eating

Buccaneer Inn (☎ 850-927-2585, 800-847-2091; 160 W Gorrie Dr; r winter $60-115, summer $90-155; ⓟ ⌧ ⌘)

THE PANHANDLE

Right on the gulf, rooms here are like those of a basic, design-challenged motel. But all are surprisingly spacious with natural light, and some have kitchenettes.

St George Inn (☎ 850-927-2903, 800-322-5196; www .stgeorgeinn.com; 135 Franklin Blvd; r $119-169; P ✕ ♨) Spartan, motel-like quarters overlook a heated pool and have tiers of wraparound porches that afford peaceful views of the bay.

Blue Parrot Oceanfront Café (☎ 850-927-2987; 68 W Gorrie Dr; mains $17-30; ☯ lunch & dinner) Out the back of this relaxed and breezy gulf-front café, locals sip rumrunners and down oversized po' boys or delicious crab crakes.

Getting There & Around

From the dock-lined town of Eastpoint on Hwy 98, 7 miles east of Apalachicola, follow the 4-mile-long causeway onto the island until Gulf Beach Dr, also known as Front Beach Dr, at the end. Turning left brings you to the state park; a right turn takes you toward Government Cut, which separates Little St George Island.

If you want to ditch the car, **Island Adventures** (☎ 850-927-3655; Gulf Beach Dr E) rents bikes for just $10 a day.

CAPE SAN BLAS & PORT ST JOE
☎ 850 / pop 3644

Delicate Cape San Blas curls around St Joseph Bay at the southwestern end of the bulge in the Panhandle, starting on the mainland at Port St Joe and ending at its undeveloped, 10-mile-long tip with **St Joseph Peninsula State Park** (☎ 850-227-1327; 8899 Cape San Blas Rd; vehicle/pedestrian/cyclist $4/1/1; primitive camping $4, RVs & developed camping $20, cabins $80; ☯ 8am-sunset). The sugar-sand beaches stretch for 2516 acres along grassy, undulating dunes, edging wilderness trails and the 13-mile Loggerhead Run Bike Path, named for the turtles that inhabit the island, which is perfect for cyclists, joggers or bladers.

The state park is one of the most prized camping spots along the Gulf Coast, home to 119 sites in two separate developed grounds. You can stay in seclusion in just-renovated loft-style timber cabins with queen beds and walkways leading from your back door to the water (bring your own towels). At the peninsula's northern extremity, primitive camping is allowed in designated areas of the wilderness preserve in the park, a sojourning point for migratory birds and butterflies. You'll need to bring everything, including water and

a camp stove, as no fires are allowed. Pets are not permitted anywhere in the park.

To reach St Joseph Peninsula State Park directly from Apalachicola, veer left (northwest) at the fork of Hwy 98 and Hwy 30A, following 30A as it turns onto Cape San Blas and becomes Hwy 30E, which leads directly into the park. On the way through the developed portion of Cape San Blas, you'll see endless options for vacation rentals – everything from houses on stilts that sit right in the sand to not-so-pretty condo complexes. There is a lovely place to picnic right at the start of the cape, though – **Salinas Park** (Cape San Blas Rd), where you can stroll an over-dunes boardwalk, take a dip in the gulf or just sit and enjoy the waterfront breezes before continuing on with your journey.

Across the bay, which has gentle rip- and current-free swimming, the town of **Port St Joe** was once known as 'sin city' for the casinos and bordellos that greeted seafarers. The Florida Constitution was originally drafted here in 1838, but scarlet fever and hurricanes combined to stymie its progression as one of Florida's boom towns. These days it's in something of a transitional mode as industry, particularly paper mills, gives way to tourism, with a small historic district showing fledgling signs of renewal. It also became a favorite stop on the presidential campaign trail before the last election.

A really pleasant Panhandle overnight stop is the **Port Inn** (☎ 850-229-7678; www.portinnfl.com; 501 Monument Ave (Hwy 98); r $65-165; P ✕ 🖳 ♨), with front-row seats of the sunsets over the bay. A timber porch with rocking chairs runs the full length of this lovely inn, which has bay-view rooms with sisal carpet, wicker furniture and sparkling bathrooms. The Thirsty Goat lounge bar is a nice, mellow spot to wind up your evening with a cold brew.

Port St Joe is located on Hwy 98, 20 miles west of Apalachicola and 41 miles east of Panama City Beach.

PANAMA CITY BEACH
☎ 850 / pop 13,565

While much of the Panhandle's charms rely on its mellow 'Old Florida' roots, don't expect to find any of those vibes in Panama City Beach – an insanely overdeveloped gulf-front pocket that's in love with its recent transformation from an old-school resort to a mind numbing, over-commercialized mob scene of condo-mania. New, architecturally dire high-rises – one less interesting than the next – now line the waterfront, with more outdoor malls, chain hotels and restaurants crowding in at every turn. And, from March to May, the place goes absolutely bonkers as a Spring Break destination, when students from 150 colleges east of the Mississippi roar into town to drink in the sun till they puke (a phenomenon recently immortalized by the US TV reality show, *Ocean Force: Panama City Beach*).

Luckily, despite the build-up in town, the beaches themselves are quite dazzling, with powder-fine sand and cerulean, crystal-clear waters that beckon fans of swimming, fishing and diving. The area is renowned as a wreck-diving site with dozens of natural, historic and artificial reefs attracting spectacular marine life. And the ticky-tacky family atmosphere that usually prevails (with the exception of Spring Break time) may make it a natural destination – for better or worse – for those traveling with young, hard-to-entertain kids.

Orientation

Panama City Beach sprawls on a 27-mile barrier island roughly 10 miles west of and across St Andrews Bay from the entirely separate Panama City, an industrial and military town tied to Tyndall Air Force Base, linked by the Hathaway Bridge and notable for its constant highway sprawl.

Hwy 98, the main southern coastal road, splits at the northeastern end of Panama City Beach and becomes Hwy 98 in the north and Hwy 98A along the beach. The upper road is Panama City Beach Parkway (often still called, Back Beach Rd), the lower is Front Beach Rd, sometimes referred to as Alternative Hwy 98, with its main 6-mile or so stretch known as 'the strip.' Between Panama City Beach Parkway and Front Beach Rd, Hutchison Blvd (formerly Middle Beach Rd) picks up at the center of the beach at the corner of Lantana St and bends east to parallel the two. Thomas Dr runs two sides of a triangle: from Panama City Beach Parkway over Grand Lagoon and along the oceanfront to St Andrews State Recreation Area in the east, and doglegging to Front Beach Rd in the west.

The Spring Break action concentrates along the beachfront between Joan Ave and Hills Rd, and pickup trucks and crammed cars cruising the strip cause traffic to crawl; you may want to take an inland road.

Information

The **Panama City Beach Convention & Visitors Bureau** (☎ 850-233-5070, 800-722-3224; www.thebeachloversbeach .com; 17001 Panama City Beach Parkway; ☻ 8am-5pm) has maps, as well as loads of information about the new developments in town. Another great source is the brand new information office run by the **Panama City Beach Chamber of Commerce** (☎ 850-235-1159; www.pcbeach.org; 309 Beckrich Rd; ☻ 9am-5pm Sun-Thu, 9am-9pm Fri & Sat), which has touch-screen kiosks with information on where to sleep, shop and play. The **Panama City Beach Public Library** (☎ 850-233-5055; 110 Arnold Rd; ☻ 10am-8pm Mon, to 5pm Tue-Fri, to 4pm Sat) provides free internet access. The most convenient post office is at 420 Churchwell Dr.

Sights & Activities

ST ANDREWS STATE RECREATION AREA

A haven from the hurdy-gurdy of activity, this peaceful **recreation area** (☎ 850-233-5140; 4607 State Park Lane; vehicle/pedestrian/cyclist $5/1/1) spans 1260 acres graced with nature trails, swimming beaches, and wildlife including foxes, coyotes, snakes, alligators and seabirds. One of the best places to swim with children is the kiddie pool's 4ft-deep water near the jetties area. There's also excellent year-round waterfront camping, for both tents and RVs, which costs $24 nightly. You can still see the circular cannon platforms from when this area was used as a military reservation during WWII; look for them on the beach near the jetties.

The Camp Store (the first store you'll see as you enter the park) has an ATM and rents kayaks for $20 per half-day.

Just offshore, Shell Island has fantastic snorkeling. Buy tickets for the **Shell Island Shuttle** (round-trip adult/child $11.50/5.50, snorkel package incl gear & transportation $19; ☻ 9am-5pm, every half hr in summer, reduced schedule in winter) at the Pier Marketplace; there's a trolley service to the boat. Be aware that there are no facilities on the island, and no shade: wear a hat and plenty of sunscreen.

The park is at the eastern end of the island. From the beach, take Front Beach Rd onto Thomas Dr and follow it to the end.

FAMILY ATTRACTIONS

The brand-new **Circus by the Sea** (☎ 850-249-1101; Frank Brown Park; www.circusbythesea.com; adult/child $24/16; Jun-Aug) is a seasonal adventure that brings the Florida State University High Flying Circus and its trapeze pros to an air-conditioned big top.

THE PANHANDLE

Another new hotspot – perhaps more for adults than the little ones – is **Pier Park** (☎ 850-236-9974; www.simon.com; Front Beach Rd; ☽ 10am-9pm Mon-Sat, noon-6pm Sun), a sprawling outdoor mall with endless chain stores for clothing, accessories and snack foods.

The **Museum of Man in the Sea** (☎ 850-235-4101; 17314 Panama City Beach Parkway; adult/child $5/2.50; ☽ 9am-5pm), owned by the Institute of Diving, takes a close look at the sport. Interactive exhibits let you crank up a Siebe pump, climb into a Beaver Mark IV submersible, check out models of the underwater laboratory Sealab III, and find out how diving bells really work. There's also a cool collection of old diving suits and a sea life–filled aquarium.

The **Gulf World Marine Park** (☎ 850-234-5271; www.gulfworldmarinepark.com; 15412 Front Beach Rd; adult/child $22/15.50; ☽ 9am, last entry 2pm), meanwhile, is a good way to get up close to marine animals through its myriad of shows and activities, like a stingray-petting pool, swim-with-dolphins program and California sea lion show.

DIVING

Opportunities for **wreck diving** are excellent here; the area has earned its 'Wreck Capital of the South' nickname with more than a dozen boats offshore including a 441ft WWII Liberty ship and numerous tugs. There are more than 50 artificial reefs made from bridge spans, barges and a host of other sunken structures, as well as natural coral reefs. Visibility varies from 10ft to 80ft, averaging around 40ft. In winter, the average water temperature is 60°F, rising to 87°F in summer. Numerous dive companies offer packages; try **Dive Locker** (☎ 850-230-8006; 106 Thomas Dr; ☽ 8am-6pm Mon-Sat). Two-tank, four-hour dives start at $68, with gear rental costing extra. Certification classes cost $285.

Sleeping

There are endless places to lay your head here – just don't expect to find small, tranquil places brimming with character (though many of the motels are family-owned). Note also that rates vary dramatically between the quieter winter months and super-busy summers, and spike at various (and variable) times, such as Spring Break (March to May). For a complete guide to hotels and resorts, visit www.pcbeach.org.

Beachbreak by the Sea (☎ 850-234-3870, 800-346-4709; www.beachbreakbythesea.com; 15405 Front Beach Rd; d $89-169; P ☂) A refreshing four-story spot

in a sea of highrises, this place offers basic motel-style rooms, a central beachfront location and continental breakfast, not to mention reasonable rates.

Beach Tower Resort Motel (☎ 800-466-8694; www.beachtowermotel.com; 12001 Front Beach Rd; r $62-189; P ☂) This basic, family-owned inn on the beach has a great gulf-front pool (heated in cooler months) and pool bar, plus private balconies fronting the comfortable but nothing-special rooms. Extremely kid-friendly.

Marriott Bay Point Resort & Spa (☎ 850-236-6000; www.marriottbaypoint.com; 4200 Marriott Dr; r $139-409; P ☒ ☐ ☂) One of the most luxurious bases in PCB is the newly renovated Marriott-run resort, featuring views of St Andrews Bay, two golf courses, wave runner and kayak rentals, a lovely pool, four on-site restaurants and a full-service spa. Rooms are cushy, modern and airy.

Eating

Pineapple Willy's (☎ 850-235-0928; 9875 S Thomas Dr; mains $15-22; ☽ 11am-late) This kitschy, casual place features its own sheltered wooden pier jutting over the sand, gulf-view dining and a fun bar. It's famed for its house special – slo' cooked Jack Daniels BBQ ribs by the pound and pound-and-a-half bucket load. The frozen margaritas and special Pineapple Willy cocktail – a potent potion of Myer's rum, pineapple juice and cream of coconut – are pretty popular, too.

Treasure Ship (☎ 850-234-8881; 3605 Thomas Dr; ☽ closed Nov-Feb) A landmark since the '70s, this trip of a place houses three separate restaurants over three levels of a full-scale replica of Sir Francis Drake's 17th-century *Golden Hind* galleon. Hook's Grille & Grog, at dock level, serves Caribbean cuisine (mains $11 to $24), and is open for lunch and dinner. On the 2nd level, the Main Dining Room is open at dinner, and serves steaks, seafood and huge salads (mains $16 to $30). Opening onto an open-air deck, the 3rd level contains Captain Crabby's, with all-you-can-eat dinners of crab legs, shrimp and ribs (buffet $20 to $30), and cocktails served at the Deck Bar overlooking Grand Lagoon.

Captain Anderson's Restaurant (☎ 850-234-2225; 5551 North Lagoon Dr; mains $12-40; ☽ 4:30-10pm Mon-Fri, 4-10pm Sat) Widely regarded as Panama City Beach's top restaurant – as well as a dining tradition here – the Captain has an outstanding selection of seafood including market-price Greek-style open hearth broiled fish, as well as pasta and top-grade steaks. If you dine early, you'll see the day's catch being unloaded at the adjoining marina.

Firefly (☎ 850-249-3359; www.fireflypcb.com; Beckrich Rd; mains $18-39; dinner nightly) A new hotspot that created a big buzz from the get-go, this uber-atmospheric, low-lit fine dining establishment beckons diners with clever seafood dishes – salmon with merlot reduction and tempura-fried twin lobster tails – as well as meals of pasta, pork, lamb and beef. A cool lounge bar, designed to look like a fancy library, doles out tasty flavored martinis.

Getting There & Around

The **Panama City-Bay County International Airport** (☎ 850-763-6751; www.pcairport.com), here since 1948, is served by Delta Connection, Northwest and American. At the time of this writing, though, it was due to close and relocate all operations to its sparkling new location – the first brand-new airport to be built in the US since September 11, 2001.

Greyhound has a flag stop in Panama City Beach at the Hwy 98/Hwy 79 stoplight (meaning you'll need to book ahead); there's also a **Greyhound bus station** (☎ 850-785-6111; 917 Harrison Ave) in Panama City.

By car, Panama City Beach is almost halfway between Tallahassee (about 130 miles) and Pensacola (95 miles). Coming along the coast, Hwy 98 takes you into town; from I-10 take either Hwy 231 or Hwy 79 south.

The **Bay Town Trolley** (☎ 850-769-0557) runs in Panama City Beach. The service continues to add stops to its coverage, but its schedule is still limited to Monday to Friday between 6am and 8pm ($1.25).

California Cycles (☎ 850-233-1391; 10624 Front Beach Rd) rents the single/double yellow scooters that you'll see buzzing around like bees from $12/20 per hour (if you pay for two hours you'll get another two free), and bicycles from $15 daily.

INLAND PANHANDLE

Though most of the attractions around here are indeed on the gulf, there are a couple of spots inland that are worth going out of your way for.

Florida Caverns State Park

Three miles north of Marianna, on Hwy 166, is **Florida Caverns State Park** (☎ 850-482-1228, 850-482-9598, camping reservations 800-326-3521; 3345 Caverns Rd; vehicle/pedestrian/cyclist $4/1/1; cave tours adult/child $6/3), a

1300-acre park on the Chipola River with fascinating caves that are unique to Florida. Eerie stalactites, stalagmites and flowstone (formed by water flowing over rock) fill the lighted caves, along with calcified shapes formed over the centuries as calcite has bubbled through the stone. You can take a 45-minute guided tour, available from 9am to 4pm daily, with a volunteer – who will surely mention the quirky (and slightly ridiculous) names they've come up with to describe the various formations, from 'wedding cake' to 'bacon.'

The caverns are equidistant – 69 miles – from Tallahassee and Panama City Beach. If you're coming from Quincy (p472) it's about 51 miles; pick up I-10 and take exit 136 for Marianna and follow the signs. If you're coming from Panama City Beach, head north on US 231 then take I-10 east for 6 miles, take exit 136 to Marianna and follow the signs.

DeFuniak Springs

Switzerland has one, and the Florida Panhandle has the other: the Walton County seat of DeFuniak Springs is home to one of just two almost perfectly round lakes in the world (the other is near Zurich). It's popularly thought that the lake was created by a meteorite crashing to Earth eons ago, but there's no final scientific word on its formation. Ringing the lake's approximately mile-long circumference along Circle Dr is the town's historic district, with 39 splendid Victorian buildings. Besides driving around for the sheer oddity of it – as well as to gaze at the beautiful old homes and the 1880s **Walton DeFuniak Library** (☎ 850-892-3624; 3 Circle Dr; 9am-5pm Mon & Wed-Fri, to 8pm Tue, 3pm Sat), Florida's oldest library – there is not a lot going on in this dusty ol' town. But if it's time in your travels for a rest, you may want to check into the 1920s **Hotel DeFuniak** (☎ 850-892-4383, 877-333-8642; www.hoteldefuniak.com; 400 Nelson Ave; r/ste from $80/100), with 12 atmospheric rooms and suites. Its charming restaurant, **Club Zoots** (mains $14-26; dinner Mon-Sat) has a backdrop of jazz and swing.

DeFuniak Springs is 50 miles west of the Florida Caverns and Marianna along I-10; or 47 miles north of Destin on US 331.

SOUTH WALTON COUNTY BEACHES
☎ 850

This collection of unincorporated communities between Inlet Beach to Sandestin make up what is collectively known as Santa Rosa

Beach, or the Beaches of South Walton. They are precious, well-planned, idyllic places that lie along Scenic Highway 30A and an incredibly gorgeous stretch of gulf front that's been dubbed the Emerald Coast. Though most of what you'll see from the car is an endless row of beautiful, wealthy homes that prevent too many sweeping water vistas, there are, blessedly, no high-rises here. And simply getting out of your vehicle and strolling between buildings onto the beach affords spellbinding views of the aquamarine waters and white-as-snow beaches, which glow a surreal pink at sunset. Walk the other way – into any of the settlements along here – and you'll find treasures of a different sort: impressive art galleries, boutiques and restaurants, all with friendly vibes.

Orientation

South Walton County's beaches begin around 17 miles west of Panama City Beach. From Hwy 98, Hwy 30A travels 18.5 miles, with 9.4 miles of connector roads providing access north to Hwy 98 and across Choctawhatchee Bay. A total of 26 miles scoops up all of the Beaches of South Walton.

The region is made up of 13 mostly new, some elite, individual hamlets. Running east to west you'll travel through Inlet Beach, at the start of Scenic Hwy 30A; wild rosemary-swept Rosemary Beach; Seacrest, home to the idyllic Deer Lake State Park; the residential Seagrove Beach; the picture-perfect village of Seaside (see right); the whimsically named community of WaterColor; century-old Grayton Beach, with paradisiacal camping; the gulf's highest point, Blue Mountain Beach, which conceals some artists' retreats; and Dune Allen Beach. Scenic Hwy 30A then curves its way past Topsail Hill Preserve State Park and joins onto Hwy 98 (here it is called Emerald Coast Parkway), where you'll find the resort township of Sandestin, encompassing the waterside Baytowne Village, Miramar Beach and Seascape.

Though it's a relatively short distance, allow at least a 1½ hours to drive, even if you're not planning to stop, as speed limits are low, kids and cars plentiful and some views mesmerizing.

Information

The **Beaches of South Walton Tourist Center** (☎ 800-822-6877; www.beachesofsouthwalton.com; cnr Hwy 331 &

Hwy 98; ☼ 8am-6pm) is inland, between SR 283 and SR 83. There's also a bulletin board with tourist brochures on the eastern end of Seaside Town Sq.

A great web resource is www.discover30A .com, which is a constantly updated guide to beaches, shops, inns and eateries.

Sights & Activities

SEASIDE

Spending an afternoon or night – or even a half hour – in this perfect, Necco wafer–colored tiny town will make you feel like you've stumbled onto a movie set. Which, in fact, you will have done, as Seaside served as the on-location set for the 1998 movie *The Truman Show,* which was about an unwitting star in a popular reality TV show who lived in an annoyingly perfect place. And though the real place is pretty ideal – with street names like Cinderella Circle and Dreamland Heights – it's really not annoying. Famed and lauded as the country's first planned community, it was created in 1981 with input from a range of accomplished architects, and has been hailed as a model for New Urbanism. But instead of taking off as a year-round place to live, it has become an almost totally seasonal community, providing the second, summer homes for folks who live in other parts of the South.

If you come in the off-season (before April), it'll seem even more surreal than usual – especially if you spend a night in the local B&B, the Inn By the Sea, Vera Bradley (see opposite) and go for an evening stroll, when you may be the only one on the streets. In season, though, folks will be out in force, and really are incredibly friendly – in a genuine way. There's a hip book-and-music shop **Sundog Books** (☎ 850-231-5481; 89 Central Sq; ☼ 9am-9pm), carrying great literature and very cool tracks, plus a handful of excellent eateries, art galleries and an absolutely gorgeous beach. Its grassy town square is the site of the popular annual Seaside Jazz Festival, held in May, and is also a great spot to just sit and people watch.

GRAYTON BEACH STATE PARK

You'll be blown away by the beauty of **Grayton Beach State Park** (☎ 850-231-4210; 357 Main Park Rd, Santa Rosa Beach; vehicle/pedestrian/cyclist $4/1/1), a 1133-acre stretch of marble-colored dunes rolling down to the water's edge. The park sits nestled against the wealthy but down-to-earth community of Grayton Beach, home to the famed Red

Bar (see right) and to the quirky Dog Wall – a mural on which locals paint portraits of their dogs. The park also contains the Grayton Beach Nature Trail (get a self-guiding tour at the gate), which runs from the east side of the parking lot through the dunes, magnolias and pine flatwoods and onto a boardwalk to a return trail along the beach. Locals flock here for nightly sunsets, and to wakeboard on the unique coastal dune lakes that shimmer across the sand from the gulf; you can even spend the night in the wilds, as you can camp in tents or cabins here.

EDEN GARDENS STATE PARK
Located inland from 30A, on the northern coast of the little peninsula that juts out to form Walton County and on the shore of Choctawhatchee Bay, is the unique **Eden Gardens State Park** (☎ 850-231-4214; 181 Eden Garden Rd; entrance fee $3), a sprawling garden and lawn with moss-draped live oaks fronting the 1800s estate home of the Wesleys, a wealthy Florida timber family. The white-columned house was purchased and renovated in 1963 by Lois Maxon, who turned it into a mint-condition showcase for Louis XVI furniture and many other heirlooms and antiques. Today you can enjoy guided tours Monday to Thursday from 10am to 3pm for $3, or simply relax on the grounds.

BIKING
You can explore the area along the 19-mile paved Timpoochee trail, which parallels scenic Hwy 30A; the 8-mile Longleaf Pine Greenway hiking and biking trail, paralleling Hwy 30A inland from just east of SR 395 to just before SR 393; and the Eastern Lake trail, which starts in Deer Lake State Park and links up with the western end of the Longleaf Pine Greenway, and also offers numerous loops. You can find a virtual bicycle tour, complete with maps and photos, on www.discover30A.com.

Simply biking up and down the peaceful streets of each village is also a pleasant afternoon activity.

Big Daddy's (☎ 850-622-1165; www.bigdaddysrentals .com; Blue Mountain Beach) and **30-A Bike Rentals** (☎ 850-865-7433; www.30Abikerentals.net; Seagrove Beach) rent and deliver bikes starting at $20 a day.

Sleeping & Eating
Hibiscus Coffee & Guesthouse (☎ 850-231-2733; www.hibiscusflorida.com; 85 Defuniak St, Grayton Beach;

r $120-180 Oct-Feb, $140-275 Mar-Sep; **P** ✖ 🖳) This cool and cleverly-designed retro inn, run by a patchouli-scented owner who doles out wonderful hugs, is tucked into a tree-studded corner of the oldest of the area's townships. Anyone can enjoy breakfast at the on-site vegetarian café (mains $4.25 to $6.50; open 7:30am to 11:30am), but its included in the price for guests. The café serves creative morning fare like multigrain pancakes, home-baked biscuits topped with 'soysage' gravy, and waffles topped with treats like chunky peanut butter, fresh fruit, coconut, pecans or drizzled honey.

Pensione (☎ 850-231-1790; www.cottagerentalagency .com; 78 Main St, Rosemary Beach; r $165-225; **P** ✖ 🖳) This recently remodeled red stucco inn is studded with very stylish, compact and boutique hotel–like rooms, featuring tasteful colors, local artwork and simple furnishings. Spilling out to an alfresco terrace at street level is the attached Northern Italian restaurant, Onano, with accomplished pastas, seafood and other authentic dishes (mains $18 to $30).

Inn by the Sea, Vera Bradley (☎ 800-277-8696; www.cottagerentalagency.com/innbythesea; 38 Seaside Ave, Seaside; r $400; **P** ✖ 🖳) Formerly Josephine's, this white colonnaded, faux Georgian-style plantation recently changed hands and received an impeccable makeover by famed luggage and tote-bag designer Vera Bradley, known for using bright colors, quilted fabrics and paisley- and floral-strewn patterns. Now the nine rooms here all reflect that style, and the outcome is surprisingly stunning, if a bit precious (just try leaving the yellow-and-white checked carpeting in Sunnybrook as clean as you found it!). The place features deliciously comfortable beds, deep bathtubs, flat-screen TVs, wi-fi and big fat porches, plus yummy gourmet breakfasts.

Bud & Alley's Taco Bar (☎ 850-231-5900; Cinderella Circle, Seaside; tacos $3-6; ⏱ lunch & dinner) A new and welcome addition to Seaside, this colorful, open-air joint, just steps from the water, presents authentic meat, seafood and veggie tacos, with all the fixings you'd find at a great roadside stand on the other side of the border.

Red Bar (☎ 850-231-1008; 70 Hotz Ave, Grayton Beach; dinner mains $13-21; ⏱ breakfast & dinner) There's live jazz most nights at this funky, homey local's favorite, housed in the old general store and bringing in the friendly mobs, who either hunker down for beers or tuck into a small selection of well-prepared dishes, like crab cakes or shrimp-stuffed eggplant. A new breakfast menu livens up the morning with omelets, waffles and steak 'n' eggs.

Basmati's Asian Cuisine (☎ 850-267-3028; Hwy 30A, Blue Mountain Beach; mains $15-30; ☺ lunch & dinner) Soothing atmosphere, Asian-fusion dishes and a full-on sake bar make for a refreshing option along the stretch of 30A that is traditionally dedicated to seafood.

Bud & Alley's Restaurant (☎ 850-231-5900; www .budandalleys.com; Cinderella Circle, Seaside; mains $20-30, music cover $5; ☺ lunch & dinner) This landmark seafood restaurant, with dining room and rooftop tables that overlook the gulf, is a seriously happening place to be – especially at sunset, when locals and visitors gather to cheer on the sky while enjoying cold beers and some of the excellent dishes, from seared halibut to grilled shrimp and grits. Weekends brings live world, jazz and funk music.

DESTIN & FORT WALTON BEACH
☎ 850 / Destin pop 12,745 / Fort Walton Beach pop 19,339

These twin resort towns – slightly calmer, smaller and less developed than Panama City Beach, but still more on the party-hearty and high-rise end of the scale than the Beaches of South Walton – offer more luminous waters and sugar-white sands, plus plenty of happenin' spots to eat, drink and be merry. Bountiful deep-sea fishing is also an entrenched part of the area's tradition, with an offshore shelf dropping to depths of 100ft 10 miles off Destin's east pass, engendering its endearing claim as the 'world's luckiest fishing village' (back when it was still actually a village, and not the high-rise skyscape it has become since development took root). The area has a rich American Indian history, a historic downtown, and beaches and family attractions punctuating its adjoining barrier island, Okaloosa Island.

Between the pair of towns, which bend around Choctawhatchee Bay like two crab claws, lies pristine beachfront owned by the US Air Force, whose largest base, Eglin, is in Fort Walton Beach.

Orientation & Information
Destin sits at the western edge of a hammer-shaped peninsula, with Panama City Beach at its eastern end, and the South Walton County beaches in the middle.

Destin and Okaloosa Island are linked by Hwy 98 (known as Emerald Coast Parkway on the Destin side to the east, and Miracle Strip Parkway on the Fort Walton Beach side to the west), via the Destin Bridge. Hwy 98 carries on over Santa Rosa Sound via Brooks Bridge north to Fort Walton Beach's historic downtown district on the mainland; from here it's about 7 miles to Destin.

Servicing the area is the **Emerald Coast Visitors Welcome Center** (☎ 850-651-7131, 800-322-3319; www .destin-fwb.com; 1540 Miracle Strip Parkway; ☺ 8am-5pm Mon-Fri, 10am-4pm Sat & Sun). Additional info can be found online at the Destin Area Chamber of Commerce website www.destinchamber .com, and at www.destin-ation.com.

Sights & Activities
INDIAN TEMPLE MOUND & MUSEUM
One of the most sacred sites for local American Indian culture to this day, the 17ft tall, 223ft wide ceremonial and political **temple mound** (admission free) here, built with 500,000 basket loads of earth and representing what is probably the largest prehistoric earthwork on the Gulf Coast, dates back to somewhere between AD 800 and 1500. On top of the mound you'll find a recreated temple housing a small exhibition center. Next door, the **museum** (☎ 850-833-9595; 139 Miracle Strip Parkway; adult/child $5/3; ☺ 10am-4:30pm Mon-Sat) offers an extensive overview of 12,000 years of American Indian history, and houses flutes, ceramics and artifacts fashioned from stone, bone and shells, as well as a comprehensive research library.

GULFARIUM
This **marine show aquarium** (☎ 850-244-5169, 800-247-8575; www.gulfarium.com; 1010 Miracle Strip Parkway; adult/child $17.50/10.50; ☺ 9am-4pm winter, 9am-6pm summer, last admission 2hr prior to closing) is more than 50 years old, making it the oldest attraction of its kind in the world. But it still inspires fresh excitement through its dolphin and sea-lion shows, in addition to its program that lets you swim with a friendly dolphin named Kiwi for $150.

US AIR FORCE ARMAMENT MUSEUM
As you approach this **museum** (☎ 850-882-4062; 100 Museum Dr, Eglin Air Force Base; admission free; ☺ 9:30am-4:30pm), you'll see the aircrafts – which include an A-10A Warthog, an F-16A, a cool B-17 Flying Fortress and the SR-71A Blackbird reconnaissance (viz spy) plane – on

THE PANHANDLE

the lawn outside the base's west gate. The exterior appears small, but inside are tons of weapons, a Warthog simulator and a terrifying F-105 Thunderchief missile, plus a detailed history of Eglin. Don't miss the airborne battlefield command center, with worn leather seats that look as if the occupants had just been there a moment ago.

The museum is about 9 miles northeast of Fort Walton Beach; take Eglin Parkway (Hwy 85), and turn right on Nomad Way, which after 1.5 miles becomes Museum Dr – the museum is on your left.

FISHING & DOLPHIN-WATCHING

A quarter of a mile east of the Destin Bridge is AJ's Seafood & Oyster Bar restaurant, which is ground zero for October's **Destin Fishing Rodeo** (www.destinfishingrodeo.org), a big deal fishing tournament for sea creatures so massive you can almost ride 'em. It's free to enter if you're aboard any registered boat, or you can just join the cheering crowds as the catches are weighed each day on whopping scales and scores are tallied on a huge board.

You'll find plenty of operators at the marinas offering fishing trips and charters, or try **Moody's** (☎ 850-837-1293; www.moodysinc.com; 194 Hwy 98 E, Destin), with half-day deep-sea fishing expeditions starting from $35, including fish cleaning and charter trips by arrangement.

The **Okaloosa Island pier** (☎ 850-244-1023; 1030 Miracle Strip Parkway E, Fort Walton Beach; walk-on $1; fishing adult/child $6.50/3.50; 24hr) is lit for night fishing and has rental gear available.

Bottlenose dolphins live year-round in the temperate waters; dolphin cruises are offered by many companies including **Southern Star** (☎ 850-837-7741; www.dolphin-sstar.com; Harborwalk Marina; adult/child $27/13.50; 4 tours per day Mon-Sat Jun-Aug). The welcoming owner-operators will take you out on a two-hour cruise in a 76ft glass-bottom boat. Call for schedules in other months.

WATER SPORTS

Take advantage of the region's great diving with **ScubaTech** (☎ 850-837-2822; www.scubatechnwfl .com; 301 Hwy 98 E), where competent dive staff know the entire area from the bottom up. A four-hour, two-tank, 58ft to 90ft dive is $80 per person; a complete gear package including fins, mask and snorkel costs $55. ScubaTech also offers two-hour snorkel trips for $30 per person including gear and wetsuit.

Waverunners, parasailing and boat rentals are plentiful, and you'll often find specials. **Just Chute Me** (☎ 850-200-2260; www.parasaildestin.com; 404 Harbor Blvd, Destin) specializes in parasailing, with flights from $45 to $65. **Luther's Pontoon and Jet Ski Rentals** (☎ 850-650-8733; 202B Hwy 98) rents all the fun and noisy stuff at reasonable rates.

Sleeping

Fred Gannon Rocky Bayou State Park (☎ 850-833-9144; 4281 SR 20; sites $12, day use $4) Inland, on the banks of Rocky Bayou, is this excellent foresty paradise for tent camping.

Henderson Beach State Park (☎ 850-837-7550; 17000 Emerald Coast Parkway/Hwy 98; sites $21, day use $4) This coastal paradise has 60 very private sites and good restrooms amid twisted scrub pines, with a 0.75 mile nature walk through the dune system, though it's better suited to RVs than tents.

Aunt Martha's Bed & Breakfast (☎ 850-243-6702; www.auntmarthasbedandbreakfast.com; 315 Shell Ave SE, Fort Walton Beach; r $105-115;) A stroll down and the beach, this charming inn was built to look like a Victorian relic. Inside, rooms have water views and big brass beds, and the lovely common area has a baby grand piano, well-stocked library and French doors that open onto a breezy veranda. Martha's Southern breakfasts – crawfish quiche, ham and cheese grits, stuffed French toast, you name it – are a veritable feast.

Henderson Park Inn (☎ 866-398-4432; www.hend ersonparkinn.com; 2700 Hwy 98, Destin; r spring & summer $239-509, winter & fall $189-419;) This classy waterfront B&B is tucked at the end of a quiet road on the edge of peaceful Henderson State Park. Overlooking the Gulf of Mexico is a grand veranda and the well-designed rooms, which feature sleek furnishings, firm beds and French doors that open onto private terraces.

Eating & Drinking

Boathouse Oyster Bar (☎ 850-837-3645; 228 Hwy 98 E; mains $3-13; 11am-late) What looks like a waterfront shed (because it is – there aren't even any restrooms inside) is the most happening little place in Destin, with live music from country to jazz and phenomenal Apalachicola oysters, crawfish and seafood gumbo.

Kinfolks Bar-B-Q (☎ 850-863-5166; 333 Racetrack Rd NW; mains $6-15; lunch & dinner) It's off-the-beaten-track and a bit scruffy looking from the outside, but locals hail the ribs, pulled pork, chicken and stew for its rich and zingy mustard-based sauce, and for being the best Texas-style barbecue in the region – if not Florida itself.

Seoul Garden Korean Restaurant (☎ 850-243-0195; 234 Miracle Strip Parkway SW; mains $10-20; ⏰ lunch & dinner) Short on atmosphere but long on flavor, this nondescript spot on the highway is a nice ethnic surprise in this land of seafood and burgers. You'll find all the traditional Korean favorites, like bibimbop studded with fresh veggies and beef, kimchi fried rice and beef, chicken or pork bulgogi, with red pepper paste and red garlic. If you can't deal with the low-key ambience, then order takeout and enjoy it on your gulf-front terrace back at the hotel.

Staff's Seafood Restaurant (☎ 850-243-3482; 24 Miracle Strip Parkway SE; mains $15-30; ⏰ 5-10pm) Right near Aunt Martha's Bed & Breakfast (p491), this character-laden 1913 warehouse with pressed metal ceilings and quirky antiques has been in Martha's (from Aunt Martha's Bed & Breakfast) family for over 90 years. It's renowned for its elegant home cooking – of seafood, veggies and home-baked bread – and for the free dessert you get with every full meal.

Getting There & Around

Destin is about 45 miles west of Panama City Beach and about 47 miles east of Pensacola, along Hwy 98. The **Okaloosa Regional Airport** (www.flyvps.com) serves the Destin-Fort Walton area with direct services to many US cities, including Chicago and Tampa, with American Eagle, Delta and Continental.

Okaloosa County Transit (☎ 850-833-9168; www .rideoct.org) runs a shuttle service four times daily from 8am to 7pm Monday to Saturday in winter, and eight times daily from 8am to 10pm in summer (fares per sector 50¢ including one transfer).

PENSACOLA & PENSACOLA BEACH

☎ 850 / pop 53,248

A strong history, gentle gulf-front beauty and renovated downtown districts that feel like a series of small towns, Pensacola and Pensacola Beach are Deep South kind of places that are just fascinating to explore. The locals are not only warm and friendly, but fortified with an impressive sense of perseverance, formed out of necessity by the two influences that have shaped the city over the past several centuries: hurricanes and the military. The last

devastating storms to blow through here were Dennis and Katrina, both in 2005, and most of the damage had been repaired at the time of writing – with an effort to not only make up for what was lost but expand (several new hotels are on the horizon), but locals still live with the sense that their lives could be blown wide open, even destroyed, when the next one tears through.

But hurricanes are a part of this area's history. The Spanish (accompanied by some 100 African slaves) tried to colonize this stretch of the far western Panhandle in 1559, but the hurricane-plagued settlement was abandoned after two years, leaving St Augustine, founded by the Spanish in 1565, to claim the title of longest continuous European settlement.

Since Pensacola's permanent settlement was established in 1698, flags belonging to Spain, France, Britain, the Confederacy and the US have flown over the city, often more than once – legacies of which remain today. All 60 acres of waterfront land south of Main St are actually reclaimed, built on top of ships' ballast.

The town's navy flight instruction school trained thousands of US and foreign pilots in WWII, and the Pensacola Naval Air Station today is an intrinsic part of the city's population.

Orientation

Pensacola's historic districts and waterfront are quite walkable, but you'll definitely need a car outside the downtown area, and to travel freely between there and Pensacola Beach. Interstate Hwy I-110, a thoroughfare to chain motels away from the downtown, starts near the city center and shoots north to I-10.

Palafox St (called Palafox Pl south of Garden St), is the east–west divider, Garden St the north–south. The North Hill Preservation District, just northwest of downtown, is bordered by Palafox St to the east, Reus St to the west, Blount St to the north and Wright St to the south.

The Palafox Historic District, a collection of smaller districts making up one large preservation area that covers most of the eastern downtown area, is bounded by Cervantes St to the north, the waterfront to the south, Florida Blanca St to the east and Spring St to the west. Within the Palafox district is Historic Pensacola Village, with Government St to the north, Main St to the south, Palafox Pl to the

THE PANHANDLE

PENSACOLA POST–HURRICANE IVAN

Six months after Hurricane Ivan unleashed havoc on the far western Panhandle on September 16, 2004, an Atlanta newspaper ran a front-page article about Spring Breakers arriving at Pensacola Beach to discover the wreckage was worse than they'd expected; with one Breaker quoted as saying they 'forgot' about the hurricane. The headline: 'Spring Broke.'

But while visitors were understandably disappointed, this full-blown natural disaster had claimed numerous lives, pulverized homes and livelihoods, and flattened businesses with 120mph winds and a storm surge of 16ft. Families lived for months in hotels, major bridges and roads were cut for months, and rubble and debris littered the area. The reduction of tourists hurt businesses that did survive – the primary tourist draw, the beach, was by far the worst affected area. Though the region is no stranger to hurricanes: Hurricane Opal gave it a whack in 1995, and Hurricane Eloise in 1975, Ivan hit harder.

Before making landfall close by, near Gulf Shores in neighboring Alabama, Ivan had blazed a trail of death and destruction through Grenada, Barbados, the Dominican Republic, Venezuela, the Netherlands Antilles, Jamaica, the Cayman Islands and Cuba. The Florida Keys were evacuated, but the evacuation was lifted three days later as Ivan headed for the gulf instead.

By the time you read this, the Pensacola area's restoration and rebuilding will have continued to progress and all roads should be accessible. You'll still see some damage if you visit, as well as construction. But the welcome from locals is warm; there are plenty of accommodation and dining options open, and more opening all the time; and the beaches are still a sensational place to spend time in the sun.

west and Alcaniz St to the east. The Naval Air Station (NAS) is southwest of the city, toward Perdido Key.

Pensacola Beach is on Santa Rosa Island, southeast of Pensacola and Gulf Breeze. Gulf Breeze is connected to Pensacola by the Pensacola Bay Bridge (Three Mile Bridge) and to Pensacola Beach by the Bob Sikes Bridge (toll $1).

The Pensacola Visitors Information Center has various free maps covering both of the historic districts and the area at large, plus endless brochures on where to sleep, eat and play.

Information

BOOKSTORES
Subterranean Books (Map p496; ☎ 850-434-3456; 9 E Gregory St; ☼ 10am-6pm Mon-Sat, noon-4pm Sun) Fantastic used books in a cool, funky setting.

INTERNET ACCESS
Public Library (Map p496; ☎ 850-435-1760; 200 W Gregory St; ☼ 9am-8pm Tue-Thu, 9am-5pm Fri & Sat) Has free internet.

MEDIA
The daily is the *Pensacola News Journal*. There's also the *New American Press*, offering regional African American news. National Public Radio (NPR) is at 88.1FM.

TOURIST INFORMATION
Pensacola Beach Visitors Information Center (Map p494; ☎ 850-932-1500; www.visitpensacola beach.com; 735 Pensacola Beach Blvd) On the right as soon as you enter Pensacola Beach; this is a small place with some useful maps and brochures about goings on, road closures (due to storms) and anything else beach oriented.

Pensacola Visitors Information Center (Map p494; ☎ 850-434-1234, 800-874-1234; www.visitpensacola .com; 1401 E Gregory St; ☼ 8am-5pm) At the foot of the Pensacola Bay Bridge, has a bounty of tourist information, knowledgeable staff and a free internet kiosk.

Sights & Activities

PENSACOLA
Historic Pensacola Village
This well preserved little **village** (Map p496; ☎ 850-595-5985; www.historicpensacola.org; adult/child $6/2.50; ☼ 10am-4pm, tours 11am, 1pm & 2:30pm) encompasses a collection of 19th-century buildings housing museums with both indoor and outdoor exhibits. Admission includes a two-hour walking tour, leaving from **Tivoli House** (Map p496; 205 E Zaragoza St) and led by a period-costumed guide. You'll take in many district buildings such as, **Lavalle House** (Map p496; 205 E Church St) and **Julee Cottage** (Map p496; 210 E Zaragoza St), the former home of freed slave Julee Paton. Included in Historic Pensacola Village are the **Museum of Commerce** (Map p496; 201

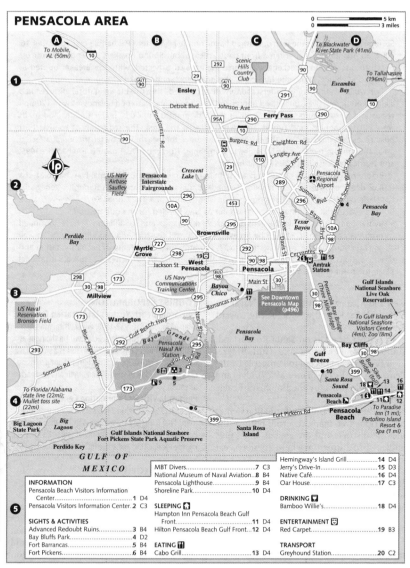

PENSACOLA AREA

THE PANHANDLE

E Zaragoza St), the **Museum of Industry** (Map p496; 200 E Zaragoza St), which was closed for renovations at the time of writing, and the **TT Wentworth Museum** (Map p496; ☎ 850-595-5990; 330 S Jefferson St; free; ☺ 10am-4pm), an elaborate 1907 yellow-brick Renaissance Revival building that was the original Pensacola City Hall. Across from the Plaza Ferdinand (where Florida was

admitted into the US), the museum dominates the block with its wide eaves, red-tile roof and deep 2nd-story arcade. Quirky displays include a Coca-Cola room and one on the 'City of Five Flags,' as Pensacola is historically known because of its being Spanish, French, British, Confederate and North American during its early history.

Pensacola Museum of Art

Interestingly housed in the city's old jail (1908), this **museum** (Map p496; ☎ 850-432-6247; www.pensacolamuseumofart.org; 407 S Jefferson St; adult/child $5/free; ☻ 10am-5pm Tue-Fri, noon-5pm Sat & Sun), features nearly 20 exhibits a year – anything from Rodin sculptures to the pop-art work of Jasper Johns. Its impressively growing collection, shown on a rotating basis, includes major 20th- and 21st-century artists across genres including cubism, realism, pop art and folk art.

Pensacola Scenic Bluffs Highway & Bay Bluffs Park

This 11-mile stretch of road, which winds around the precipice of the highest point along Florida's coastline, makes for a peaceful drive or (slightly difficult) bike ride. You'll see stunning views of Escambia Bay, and pass a notable crumbling brick chimney – part of the steam-power plant for the Hyer-Knowles lumber mill in the 1850s, which is the only remnant of what was the first major industrial belt on the Gulf Coast. Also along here is beautiful **Bay Bluffs Park** (Map p494; Scenic Hwy), a 32-acre oasis of wooden boardwalks that lead you down along the side of the steep bluffs, through clutches of live oaks, pines, Florida rosemary and holly down to the empty beach below.

Pensacola Naval Air Station & National Naval Aviation Museum

Every US WWII pilot was trained at this **naval air station** (Map p494; NAS; ☎ 850-452-0111), and now on any given day, there are some 6000 aviators-in-training here.

Take Hwy 295 to the NAS entrance, south of the bridge at the end of Navy Blvd, across Bayou Grande. You'll be stopped at the gate for a security check of your car, so be sure to bring photo ID. Once you're cleared, enter the base on Navy Blvd, which becomes Duncan Rd. Turn right at the second light onto Taylor Rd, which runs toward the **Advanced Redoubt ruins** (Map p494; ☻ noon-2pm Sat & Sun, tours 11am Sat summer) and **Fort Barrancas** (Map p494; ☎ 850-455-5167; admission free; ☻ 8:30am-4pm summer, 9:30am-5pm daily winter, tours 10am & 2:30pm summer, 2pm winter); the fort sits on a dramatic bluff overlooking Pensacola Bay, and is now part of the national park system. The ruins and fort were variously built, destroyed, remodeled and occupied by Spanish, French, British, Confederate and US forces since 1698.

Also accessed from the NAS are the 160ft, 1859-built **Pensacola Lighthouse** (Map p494; ☎ 850-455-2354; admission & tour free; ☻ noon-4pm Sun May-Oct or by appointment), which is in use today, and the **National Museum of Naval Aviation** (Map p494; ☎ 850-453-3604, 800-327-5002; www.navalaviationmuseum.org; 1750 Radford Blvd; admission free; ☻ 9am-5pm),

---

BLUE ANGELS

To maintain its profile after WWII, and to reinforce its recruitment drive, the US Navy gathered some of its most elite pilots to form the **Blue Angels** (☎ 850-452-4784; www.blueangels.navy.mil), a flight demonstration squadron traveling to air shows around the country. The name caught on during the original team's trip to New York in 1946, when one of the pilots saw the name of the city's Blue Angel nightclub in the *New Yorker*.

These days performing for about 15 million people yearly, 'the Blues' (never 'the Angels'), their C130 Hercules support aircraft named Fat Albert and their all-Marine support crew, visit about 35 show sites a year. Six jets execute precision maneuvers, including death-defying rolls and loops, and two F/A-18s undertake solo flights; culminating in all six planes flying in trademark Delta formation.

Each of the Blues does a two-year tour of duty, staggered to rotate every two years. In addition to the six pilots (which always includes one Marine) is a narrator, who'll then move up through the ranks, and an events coordinator.

The Blues practice frequently (as would you if you were doing 500mph stunts in a quarter of a million dollars worth of aircraft): you can see take-off (a jet-assisted, near-vertical incline by way of rocket propellant) on Tuesday and Wednesday at 8:30am between March and November (weather permitting); Wednesday sessions are followed by pilot autographs. It's best to arrive between 7:30am and 8am. Bleachers are available for the first 1000 spectators; BYO coffee and lawn chairs. The viewing area is behind the National Museum of Naval Aviation parking lot.

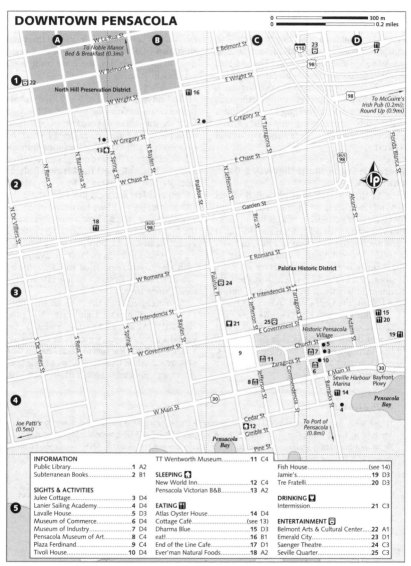

DOWNTOWN PENSACOLA

INFORMATION
Public Library.................................1 A2
Subterranean Books..........................2 B1

SIGHTS & ACTIVITIES
Julee Cottage...................................3 D4
Lanier Sailing Academy....................4 D4
Lavalle House...................................5 D3
Museum of Commerce......................6 D4
Museum of Industry..........................7 D4
Pensacola Museum of Art..................8 C4
Plaza Ferdinand................................9 C4
Tivoli House...................................10 D4

TT Wentworth Museum...............11 C4

SLEEPING
New World Inn.............................12 C4
Pensacola Victorian B&B................13 A2

EATING
Atlas Oyster House.......................14 D4
Cottage Café..............................(see 13)
Dharma Blue...............................15 D3
eat!..16 B1
End of the Line Cafe....................17 D1
Ever'man Natural Foods................18 A2

Fish House..................................(see 14)
Jamie's.......................................19 D3
Tre Fratelli.................................20 D3

DRINKING
Intermission................................21 C3

ENTERTAINMENT
Belmont Arts & Cultural Center.....22 A1
Emerald City...............................23 D1
Saenger Theatre..........................24 C3
Seville Quarter............................25 C3

which, at 291,000 sq ft, is one of the world's largest aviation museums.

In the entry foyer of the National Museum of Naval Aviation, the bronze *Spirit of Naval Aviation* monument depicts the same pilot in different wartime uniforms interacting with his self of other eras, symbolizing the constancy of the 'greater mission.' Above

him, original aircraft from each era are suspended from the ceiling. Then move into the atrium, to find four suspended A-4 Skyhawk jets retired by the Blue Angels when they upgraded to F/A-18s. The Blue Angels are a flight demonstration squadron, formed by the navy's most elite pilots after WWII, who now traveling to air shows around the country.

You can meet and watch the Blue Angels at the NAS, see p495 for more information. The Blue Angels' aircrafts are surrounded by exhibits, including motion-based flight simulators, cockpit trainers, a replicated carrier flight deck and 170 vintage aircraft. Finally, a walk through the POW exhibit is a somber reminder of the purpose and history of these machines.

Between March and mid-November, 1½ hour to 1¾ hour guided tours depart between 9:30am and 2:30pm, led by retired naval aviators, most of whom have served in some capacity and regale visitors with first-hand experiences of various aircrafts.

You can also hop on a shuttle for a free 20-minute tour of the flightline; buses to the tarmac leave twice hourly (check at the front desk of the museum for exact times and a boarding pass). You can take a tour that includes the restoration hangar, where dedicated volunteers refurbish historic aircraft for later exhibits, or check out the IMAX cinema (adult/child/senior/military $8/7.50/7.50/7.50), which screens films hourly from 10am to 4pm, launching you every second hour (starting at 10am) on *The Magic of Flight*, an audiovisual skyward journey. A rotating film screens every other hour from 11am.

Finally, you can take a break at the Cubi Bar Cafe in the museum, a precise recreation of the famous officers' club at Cubi Point in the Philippines, with over 1000 hand-carved Vietnam War–era squadron plaques brought over from the original venue. The Cubi serves perfectly good hot dogs, warm pita pilot wraps and salads (meals $5.50 to $6), but is really just as much an exhibit as the rest of the museum. Cubi opens 10:30am to 3:30pm daily.

The Zoo

When Hurricane Ivan hit years ago, many of the staff at the **Zoo** (off Map p494; ☎ 850-932-2229; www.thezoonorthwestflorida.org; 5701 Gulf Breeze Parkway/Hwy 98; adult/child $11.50/8.25; ☉ 9am-4pm), about 10 miles east of Gulf Breeze, risked their own safety to stay and look after the animals that had nowhere else to go. And today their personal attachment is still evident through this zoo, which is worth a visit especially if you're traveling with kids.

There are more than 1200 animals including leopards, tigers, giraffes, hippos and antelopes, many of which you'll see best on a 15-minute open-carriage train ride ($3), which loops through the animals roaming freely in 30 acres of wildlife habitat. There's a tower to handfeed the giraffes from, and a window to get a behind-the-scenes look at the animals' food being prepared.

PENSACOLA BEACH

Distinctly separate from Pensacola itself, Pensacola Beach (Map p494) – known fondly by Southern visitors as the 'Redneck Riviera' – is a paradise of powdery white sand, gentle warm waters and a string of mellow beachfront hotels. The beach occupies nearly 8 miles of the 40-mile-long Santa Rosa barrier island, surrounded by the Santa Rosa Sound and Gulf of Mexico to the north and south, and by the federally protected Gulf Islands National Seashore on either side. Though determined residents have protected much of the barrier island from development, there is change afoot, as several high-rise condos have recently created a bit of a Gulf Coast skyline.

The area is a major hub for local entertainment and special events, including Mardi Gras celebrations, a triathlon, wine tastings, a summer music series, parades and the annual Blue Angels air show in July, which is a local institution.

Gulf Islands National Seashore

Stretching 150 miles between West Ship Island, Mississippi, and Santa Rosa Island, Florida's section of the **national seashore** (Map p494; ☎ 850-934-2600; www.nps.gov/guis; 7-day pedestrian or cyclist admission $3, vehicle $8; ☉ sunrise-sunset) covers Perdido Key, two sections of Santa Rosa Island (extending to the NAS across the Fort Pickens State Park Aquatic Preserve) and a clip of coastline around Destin and Fort Walton Beach (p490).

The seashore's headquarters and main visitors' stop is **Gulf Islands National Seashore Visitors Center** (Map p494; ☎ 850-934-2600; 1801 Gulf Breeze Parkway; admission free; ☉ 9am-4:30pm) in these parts, at Naval Live Oaks, about 6 miles east of Gulf Breeze. There are a couple of lovely waterfront nature trails that wind through the sand-floored forests here.

One of the seashore's highlights is the pentagonal brick **Fort Pickens** (Map p494), begun in 1829, completed in 1834 and used until around the end of WWII. It sustained major damage during Hurricane Ivan in 2004, and though it was open at the time of research, the road was still impassable for cars, so the fort

THE PANHANDLE

remained strictly a place to reach by foot, bike or boat. Check with the visitors' information center for updates.

Diving & Sailing

The Oriskany CV/CVA 34 aircraft carrier, at approximately 900ft long and 150ft tall, was the largest vessel ever sunk as an artificial reef when it was submerged in 2007 off Pensacola Beach. Plenty of outfitters will gear you up and show you the way out, including **MBT Divers** (Map p494; ☎ 850-455-7702; www.mbtdivers.com; 3920 Barrancas Ave), offering two-tank Oriskany dives for $150, plus various other charters.

Conditions at Pensacola Bay are perfect for sailing. Beginners can take part in various sailing courses with **Lanier Sailing Academy** (Map p496; ☎ 850-432-3199; www.laniersail.com; 600 S Barracks St, Seville Harbour Marina, slip number N1), or rent a Capri 22 for $215 daily and take to the waters yourself.

UFO Spotting

Maybe it's activity from the nearby Pensacola Naval Air Station, but this stretch of the gulf has apparently had hundreds of UFO sightings in the past few decades; **Shoreline Park** (Map p494; 700 Shoreline Dr) in Gulf Breeze is a particular hotspot, where you're likely to find local skywatchers (including members of the Mutual UFO Network, which meets here regularly) with binoculars and lawn chairs. Sightings have been reported right along the coast – it's as good a reason as any to spread out a picnic or beach blanket and gaze up at the stars.

Sleeping

PENSACOLA

Pensacola Victorian B&B (Map p496; ☎ 850-434-2818, 800-370-8354; www.pensacolavictorian.com; 203 W Gregory St; r $85-125; ⓟ ✗) This stately 1892 Queen Anne building was built for a ship's captain whose son so loved entertaining musicians that the Pensacola Philharmonic Orchestra (now the Pensacola Symphony) was founded as a result. Today the warm and in-the-know owners, Chuck and Barbara, lovingly maintain four restful guestrooms – one larger and more gracious than the next – and offer home-baked treats and breakfasts. They also run the cozy Cottage Café, right next door, see opposite.

New World Inn (Map p496; ☎ 850-432-4111; www.newworldlanding.com; 600 S Palafox Pl; r $95-145; ⓟ ✗ ⚏) Well located between downtown and the waterfront, the historic inn's 15 rooms,

which were recently renovated to create a modern boutique-hotel feel, are earth-toned, tasteful and comfortable, if in need of a bit of tweaking from a feng shui expert. There's also a lovely outdoor courtyard.

Noble Manor Bed & Breakfast (off Map p496; ☎ 877-598-4634; www.noblemanor.com; 110 W Strong St; r $105-135; ⓟ ✗) Another period-piece, this one right in the heart of the North Hill Historic District, the Noble Manor offers five stately and romantic quarters, all in different styles (try the Osaka Room, with warm, wood floors, a king bed and a refreshingly modern vibe). The Tudor Revival house, completed in 1905, is filled with antiques and fine arts, and a small pool out back offers a great way to soak off a day of sightseeing.

PENSACOLA BEACH

Paradise Inn (off Map p494; ☎ 850-932-2319; www.paradise inn-pb.com; 21 Via de Luna Dr; r $110-205 spring/summer, $69-150 winter/fall; ⓟ ⚏ ⚏) Just across the road from the beach, this is the only nonchain hotel along the strip – and a refreshingly attractive and affordable one at that! The Paradise has adorable, spic-and-span rooms with cheerfully colored bedspreads, plus an on-site café serving po' boys and fried fish, a small pool, and a dock on the gentle Santa Rosa Sound.

Hilton Pensacola Beach Gulf Front (Map p494; ☎ 850-916-2999; www.hilton.com; 12 Via de Luna Dr; r $119-460; ⓟ ⚏ ⚏) The most luxurious digs along the main hotel strip here, the Hilton has beautifully modern rooms with terraces; a colossal pool and great pool bar; light-filled, airy colonnaded public areas; efficient, personable staff; and some excellent eateries, including a top-notch sushi spot, right in its lobby.

Hampton Inn Pensacola Beach Gulf Front (Map p494; ☎ 850-932-6800; www.hamptonbeachresort.com; 2 Via de Luna Dr; r $129-$570; ⓟ ⚏ ⚏) Right on the water, the neat rooms are spacious and have small fridges and white-duvet-topped comfy beds. Choose a room on the waterside for a bit more cash and you'll enjoy a private beachfront terrace. There's a small pool and bar edging the beach, and complimentary buffet breakfast in the lobby each morning. Just beware of Spring Break season, as this place is popular with partiers.

Portofino Island Resort & Spa (off Map p494; ☎ 877-484-3405; 10 Portofino Dr; $200-450; ⓟ ⚏ ⚏) The newest hotel in Pensacola is a spiffy foursome of luxury highrises, with homey two- and three-bedrooms that have fabulous water views, plus a bevy of perks, including a full-service spa, two restaurants, clay tennis courts and bike paths – not to mention the fantasy island–like private gulf beach.

Eating
PENSACOLA
Budget
End of the Line Cafe (Map p496; ☎ 850-429-0336; 610 E Wright St; mains $2.50-7, internet access per hr $8; ⏰ 10am-10pm Tue-Sat, 11am-5pm Sun) A funky, fair-trade café with velour and vinyl lounges, this is the place for casual vegan fare – like tempeh reubens and tofu BLTs – as well as regular cultural events, like Friday's open-mike night.

Ever'man Natural Foods (Map p496; ☎ 850-438-0402; 315 W Garden St; mains $4-6; ⏰ 7am-7pm Mon-Sat, 11am-4pm Sun) This co-op grocery welcomes the public to shop in its aisles of healthy foods and at its deli counter, which offers fresh salads, sandwiches and hot-food concoctions to be taken out or eaten at its few instore tables.

Cottage Café (☎ 850-437-0730; 203 W Gregory St; mains $6-8; ⏰ 11am-2pm Mon-Fri) Next door to Pensacola Victorian B&B, serving homemade sandwiches, quiches and desserts.

Joe Patti's (Map p496; ☎ 850-432-3315; www.joepattis .com; 534 South B St at Main St; ⏰ 7am-6pm Mon-Thu & Sat, to 7pm Fri) Don't leave Pensacola without a visit to this vibrant, bustling seafood market, where you can not only watch the catch come off the boat, and have it deboned and filleted at long stainless steel tables, but also stock up on fresh and delicious items for picnicking, from shrimp salad to clam chowder. To complete the meal you can grab wine and cheese from the connected emporium.

Jerry's Drive-In (Map p494; ☎ 850-433-9910; 2815 E Cervantes St; mains $7-12; ⏰ 10am-10pm Mon-Fri, 7am-10pm Sat) Look for the pig sign outside of this roadhouse-meets-diner (not a drive-in, though it was when it opened in 1939), serving up fat omelets, juicy burgers, milkshakes and plenty of daily specials under the kitschy neon signs. You'll rub elbows with serious regulars – the kind that get greeted by first name – especially at lunchtime, when the place gets packed.

our pick Dharma Blue (Map p496; ☎ 850-433-1275; 300 S Alcaniz St; mains $9-12; ⏰ lunch & dinner) A cheerfully pink house perched at the edge of a peaceful park, this quirky, friendly, very-Southern-style eatery is a local treasure. Choose a seat either outside on the fat porch – cooled by ceiling fans, marble-slab tables and plenty of hanging plants – or in the expansive dining room that is hung with bright local artwork, and order any of the delightful dishes. Lunch brings fried green tomato sandwiches, veggie stir-fry and daily quiches, while dinner dips into sushi, crab cake and duck breast territory. Free wi-fi will make you want to linger on the porch for hours.

Midrange & Top End
The Oar House (Map p494; ☎ 850-549-4444; 1901 Cypress St; mains $9-20; ⏰ lunch & dinner daily) This tucked-away haven, right on Bayou Chico at the edge of a marina, is an alfresco dining spot with tables under a huge palapa roof. Between the sand volleyball court and wispy palmetto trees, you'll feel like you're really on holiday – but it's especially true when you taste the food at this festive spot: seriously fresh oyster baskets, crab cakes, blackened fish sandwiches and fish tacos, paired with sides like black-eyed peas or garlic green beans. It's a special, friendly kind of place.

Tre Fratelli (Map p496; ☎ 850-438-4663; 304 S Alcaniz St; mains $12-18; ⏰ lunch & dinner) A traditional and romantic Italian restaurant tucked into a historic house, Tre Fratelli offers delicious pastas, pizzas and other favorites, like eggplant parmesan, in a truly unique setting.

Atlas Oyster House (Map p496; ☎ 850-437-1961; 600 S Barracks St; mains $12-20; ⏰ dinner Mon-Fri, lunch & dinner Sat & Sun) This new and instant favorite – paired, right on a breezy dock, with the slightly more upscale Fish House (mains $15 to $25) – is packed nightly with a range of locals who come for the outdoor seating, live blues and fresh-from-the-sea menu featuring everything from burgers and oysters on the half shell, to gulf shrimp and fish of the day served in a variety of ways, including pecan encrusted. The Fish House is known for its signature dish: World Famous Grits Ya Ya, which serves spicy gulf shrimp, bacon and garlicky veggies over steaming gouda-cheese grits.

eat! (Map p496; ☎ 850-433-6905; 286 N Palafox St; mains $15-27; ⏰ lunch & dinner Tue-Fri, dinner Sat, brunch Sun) This stylish place in downtown has been wowing them since it opened its doors. The modern take on Southern cuisine includes fried green tomatoes in brown butter and feta, peppercorn-crusted elk, rosemary-lemon lamb chops and carrot cake with goat-cheese crème fraiche.

Jamie's (Map p496; ☎ 850-434-2911; 424 E Zaragoza St; mains $29-39; ⏰ dinner) Housed in an 1880s

Victorian cottage and tucked on a quiet, residential stretch of the historic district, Jamie's wows big-spending guests with provincial French favorites, including simply prepared fish, filet mignon and lamb. Working fireplaces and a bevy of antiques heighten the glorious ambience.

PENSACOLA BEACH

Native Café (Map p494; ☎ 850-934-4848; 45a Via de Luna Dr; mains $4-7; ☺ breakfast, lunch & dinner) This brand-new budget spot, 'owned and operated by friendly natives,' is a welcome addition to the fried-fish stretch. Try a shrimp po' boy, grilled chicken sandwich, fish tacos, rice and beans or seafood gumbo – or, for a cheap morning jumpstart, eggs benedict or pancakes.

Cabo Grill (Map p494; ☎ 850-916-2226; 400 Quietwater Beach Rd; mains $8-15; ☺ lunch & dinner) Right on the Portofino Boardwalk, this festive Mexican spot serves all the usual favorites – tacos, quesadillas, enchiladas and, of course, huge and potent margaritas to sip at sunset.

Hemingway's Island Grill (Map p494; ☎ 850-934-4747; 400 Quietwater Beach Rd; mains $14-22; ☺ lunch & dinner) Also at the beach, Hemingway's serves wonderfully Key Westy cuisine on two levels of outdoor decking.

Drinking & Entertainment

Check the *Pensacola News Journal*'s Friday 'Weekender' section for listings. Or if you're looking for something to entertain everyone, try the **Seville Quarter** (Map p496; ☎ 850-434-6211; 130 E Government St; ☺ from 11am) in the historic district. This fun themed entertainment/restaurant complex houses several establishments, offering billiards at Fast Eddie's, music at Rosie O'Grady's and karaoke in Lili Marlene's.

BARS

McGuire's Irish Pub (off Map p496; ☎ 850-433-6789; 600 E Gregory St; ☺ from 11am) Signed dollar bills cover the walls and ceiling at this fun place. Happy hour is 4pm to 6pm; live music starts at 9pm. If you don't sing along, you'll find yourself up the ladder to kiss the moose.

Intermission (Map p496; ☎ 850-433-6208; 214 S Palafox Pl) A hip, smoky venue known for its super-strong cocktails, the bar is housed in a lovely old building, and draws a mixed crowd that expands exponentially on Friday and Saturday nights.

Bamboo Willie's (Map p494; ☎ 850-916-9888; 400 Quietwater Beach Rd; ☺ 11am-11pm) An open-air bar right on the boardwalk in Pensacola Beach, this is the spot to get twisted in a variety of ways, with signature frozen cocktails from the Bushwacker to the 190 Octane (don't ask – just drink).

PERFORMING ARTS

Belmont Arts & Cultural Center (Map p496; ☎ 850-429-1222; www.belmontartscenter.org; 401 N Reus St) Holds open-mic nights every Thursday from 7:30pm to 10pm (all performers welcome) and variously houses other arts, crafts and creativity workshops.

The Spanish-Baroque beauty, **Saenger Theatre** (Map p496; ☎ 850-444-7686; www.pensacolasaenger.com; 118 S Palafox Pl), was reconstructed in 1925 using bricks from the Pensacola Opera House, which was destroyed in a 1916 hurricane. Closed for a major renovation project at the time of research, this is home to a popular Broadway series as well as the **Pensacola Symphony Orchestra** (☎ 850-435-2533; www.pensacolasymphony.com) and **Pensacola Opera** (☎ 850-433-6737; www.pensacolaopera.com).

GAY & LESBIAN VENUES

The big annual gay event occurs on Memorial Day, when a veritable gay event circuit party brings gays and lesbians together for a wonderfully mixed, debauched bash that spreads its tentacles – DJ soirees, concerts, dances, all-night beach parties, drag-queen shows, you name it – all over town (quite a feat in a place that's not particularly gay-loving). Check out www.gaypensacola.com.

Emerald City (Map p496; ☎ 850-433-9491; 406 E Wright St; ☺ 5pm-3am Wed-Sun, 9pm-3am Mon) Pulling in a mixed crowd (heavy on the men Saturday), Emerald City features drag shows and plenty of other entertainment. Cover charges vary.

Red Carpet (Map p494; ☎ 850-453-9918; 937 N New Warrington Rd; ☺ 5pm-2:30am) This popular lesbian bar has special themes nightly.

Round Up (off Map p496; ☎ 850-433-8482; 706 E Gregory; ☺ 2pm-3am) The men gather here to cruise and drink, spilling onto the patio on weekends.

Getting There & Around

Pensacola Regional Airport (Map p494; ☎ 850-436-5005, 850-436-5000; www.flypensacola.com) is served by many major airlines; it's 4 miles northeast of downtown off 9th Ave on Airport Blvd. A taxi costs about $15 to downtown and $28 to the beach. Try **Yellow Cab** (☎ 850-433-3333).

INTERSTATE MULLET TOSS

Every year in April, locals gather on both sides of the Florida/Alabama state line for a time-honored tradition: the mullet toss. The idea – apart from a very fine excuse for a party – is to see who can throw their (dead) mullet the furthest across the border from Florida into Alabama. People have developed their own techniques: tail first, head first, or breaking its spine and bending it in half for better aerodynamics.

The mullet toss is organized by the **Flora-Bama Lounge & Package Store** (www.florabama.com). Out-there events are a hallmark of the Flora-Bama, they also host the annual Polar Bear Dip (a free drink if you brave the winter seas). They've tried to get mullet tossing into the *Guinness Book of World Records,* but its time hasn't come, yet.

Hurricane Ivan sadly did a number on the Flora-Bama, and at the time of research it was no longer. It once straddled the state line, and inside this legendary bar there were pay phones within arm's reach of each other, yet a long-distance phone call apart. True to the spirit of the Flora-Bama, they held an appropriate wake, the No Tears in the Beer demolition and rebuild party, which saw locals gather to watch bulldozers raze what Ivan hadn't…and toast the impending arrival of the new Flora-Bama. But even while the rebuilding takes place, the Mullet Toss goes on.

The **Greyhound station** (Map p494; ☎ 850-476-4800; 505 W Burgess Rd at Pensacola Blvd) is located north of the downtown area; the **Amtrak station** (Map p494; ☎ 850-433-4966; 980 E Heinberg St at 15th Ave) is just north of the Pensacola Visitors Information Center. **Escambia County Transit** (ECAT; ☎ 850-595-3228; www.goecat.com) has a limited bus service around Pensacola ($1.75 base fare), but none to the beach. The I-10 is the major east–west thoroughfare to catch the bus from; a number of buses pass down Palafox St.

PERDIDO KEY

About 12 miles southwest of Pensacola, off Hwy 292 (which becomes Hwy 182), the easternmost Florida piece of the Gulf Islands National Seashore (see p497) spans Perdido Key's crystalline waters. These dunes are home to the endangered Perdido Key beach mouse, which blends in well with the white-quartz sands here. There are two coastal state parks in the area: **Perdido Key State Park** (☎ 850-492-1595; 12301 Gulf Beach Hwy; admission $2; ☺ 8am-sunset) and,

on the northern side of the lagoon, between Perdido Key and the mainland, **Big Lagoon State Park** (☎ 850-492-1595; 12301 Gulf Beach Hwy; admission $4; ☺ 8am-sunset), with great crabbing in the lagoon's shallows. You'll find several free beach areas along the stretch of town, too.

The town of Perdido Key is centered not on hotels but condo resorts – with more on the way at the time of research – all requiring multi-night stays. There are also a handful of seafood spots along the main drag. The **Perdido Key Area Chamber of Commerce** (☎ 850-492-4660, 800-328-0107; 15500 Perdido Key Dr) has plenty of information about the area and can give advice on nearby overnight lodging, including places 3 miles west in Orange Beach, Alabama.

Perdido Key runs right to the state line, which is the site of the Interstate Mullet Toss, when locals throw dead fish over the state line, see above. From here, you can follow Hwy 182 straight into Alabama and take Hwy 59/US 90 north to connect with I-10.

If you're arriving in Perdido Key on Hwy 182 from the west, welcome to Florida.

THE PANHANDLE

Directory

CONTENTS

PRACTICALITIES

- Florida has three major daily newspapers: *Miami Herald* (in Spanish, *El Nuevo Herald*), *Orlando Sentinel* and *St Petersburg Times*.

- National Public Radio (NPR) is an excellent source of balanced news coverage. Florida receives all the major US TV and cable networks. Florida Smart (www .floridasmart.com/news) lists them all by region.

- Video systems use the NTSC color TV standard, not compatible with the PAL system.

- Electrical voltage is 110/120V, 60 cycles.

- Distances are measured in feet, yards and miles; weights are tallied in ounces, pounds and tons.

ACCOMMODATIONS

Our reviews indicate rates for single occupancy (s), double (d) or simply the room (r), when there's no appreciable difference in the rate for one or two people. Unless otherwise noted, breakfast is not included, bathrooms are private and all lodging is open year-round. Rates don't include taxes, which vary considerably between towns (see p511); in fact, hotels almost never include taxes and fees in their rate quotes, so always ask for the *total rate with tax*.

Throughout the book, hotel rates are usually 'high season' rates, unless rates are distinguished as winter/summer or high/low season. Note that 'high season' can mean summer *or* winter depending on the region; we note high seasons in the text, and for more general advice, see p13.

Our rate categories are for standard double rooms: 'budget' costs $125 or less, 'midrange' costs $125 to $250 and 'top end' rooms start at $250. Miami top end starts at $270 a night. Disney resorts are divided according to Disney price ranges ('value,' 'moderate,' 'deluxe'). In Disney resorts value accommodations range from $82 to $110 during value season and from $119 to $150 during peak season. A moderate room rate at a full-service resort ranges from $155 to $190 during value season and from $190 to $270 during peak season. Deluxe rates range roughly from $250 to $500 during value season and from $350 to $650 during peak season.

Holidays (p508) always command premium prices. When demand peaks (during special events no matter the time of year, see p17), lodgings book out well in advance.

As for icons (see inside front cover), city properties with on-site parking are identified in this book with the parking icon (**P**);

BOOK YOUR STAY ONLINE

For more accommodation reviews and recommendations by Lonely Planet authors, check out the online booking service at www.lonelyplanet.com/hotels. You'll find the true, insider lowdown on the best places to stay. Reviews are thorough and independent. Best of all, you can book online.

when hotels charge for parking, rates are noted in reviews. The internet icon (🖳) appears where establishments offer a dedicated internet terminal for guest use. Most Florida hotels have internet access (whether plug-in or wireless) for those who bring their own computers.

For more on discounts, see p507. For last-minute deals, check the following websites:

- www.expedia.com
- www.hotels.com
- www.hotwire.com
- www.orbitz.com
- www.priceline.com
- www.travelocity.com

B&Bs & Inns

These accommodations vary from small, comfy houses with shared bathrooms (least expensive) to sophisticated mansions with private baths and opulent antique-filled decor (most expensive). Most aim to create a more intimate and romantic atmosphere, and some may discourage young children from staying. Also, inns and B&Bs often require a minimum stay of two or three days on weekends and advance reservations. Always call ahead to confirm policies (regarding kids, pets, smoking) and bathroom arrangements.

Camping

Three types of campsites are available: undeveloped ($10 per night), public ($15) and privately owned ($25 and up). In general, Florida campgrounds are quite safe. While undeveloped campgrounds are just that (undeveloped), most public campgrounds have toilets and drinking water. Reserve state park sites by calling ☎ 800-326-3521 or visiting www.floridaparks.com.

Most privately owned campgrounds are geared to RVs (motor homes) but will also have a small section available that caters for campers. Expect tons of amenities, like swimming pools, laundry facilities, convenience stores and bars. **Kampgrounds of America** (KOA; ☎ 406-248-7444; www.koa.com) is a national network of private campgrounds; their Kamping Kabins have air-con and kitchens.

Hostels

In most hostels, group dorms are segregated by sex and you'll be sharing a bathroom; occasionally alcohol is banned. About half the hostels throughout Florida are affiliated with **Hostelling International USA** (HI-USA; ☎ 301-495-1240; www.hiusa.org; 8401 Colesville Rd, Suite 600, Silver Spring, MD 20910). You don't have to be a member to stay, but you pay a slightly higher rate; you can join HI by phone, online or at most youth hostels. From the US, you can book many HI hostels through its toll-free **reservations service** (☎ 888-464-4872).

Florida has many independent hostels (www.hostels.com); most have comparable rates and conditions to HI hostels, and some are better.

Hotels

We have tried to highlight independently owned hotels in this guide, but in some towns, chain hotels are the best and sometimes the only option. The calling-card of chain hotels is reliability: if you've stayed at one, you can usually depend on getting the same amenities and level of service at all the others in the chain. That said, a recent trend, most evident in Miami and beach resorts, is chain-owned hotels striving for upscale uniqueness in decor and feel.

High-end hotels – Ritz-Carlton in particular – overwhelm guests with services: valet parking, room service, newspaper delivery, dry cleaning, laundry, pools, health clubs, bars and other niceties. You'll find plenty of boutique and specialty hotels in places like Miami's South Beach and Palm Beach. While all large chain hotels have toll-free reservation numbers, you may find better savings by calling the hotel directly.

Chain-owned hotels include the following:

Hilton (☎ 800-445-8667; www.hilton.com)
Holiday Inn (☎ 888-465-4329; www.holidayinn.com)
Marriott (☎ 888-236-2427; www.marriott.com)
Radisson (☎ 888-201-1718; www.radisson.com)
Ritz-Carlton (☎ 800-542-8680; www.ritzcarlton.com)
Sheraton (☎ 800-325-3535; www.starwoodhotels .com/sheraton)

Motels

In the 1950s, motels thrived as drive-up rooms surrounding a parking lot and located near highway exits or along a town's main road. They remain quite prevalent throughout Florida. Most are budget or midrange places. Some are painfully unkempt and dirty, but others are nice, clean places to stay: it all depends on management. As a rule, they won't be as uniformly clean or have the same level of amenities as chain hotels, and rooms can vary a lot within the motel, so always ask to see your room first. Single travelers may feel safer staying in hotels with interior corridors.

A motel's 'rack rates' may be more open to haggling than at a hotel, too. If you simply ask about any specials, the price might drop; it doesn't always, and sometimes that's because that night demand's high all over town.

Resorts

Florida resorts, much like Disney World, aim to be so enticing, all-encompassing and luxurious you'll never want to leave. Depending on your agenda, that could be perfect: a round of golf, some tennis, a massage, swimming, sunbathing on the beach, a nice meal, a cold drink. They might be on to something. Many also have on-site babysitting services, as a further enticement to parents.

ACTIVITIES

For an introduction to all the places you can hike, bike, swim, surf, snorkel, dive, kayak, fish and camp in Florida, turn to Florida Outdoors (p49). This section focuses on the resources, websites, magazines and organizations that help you do all those things.

For more information on Florida's national and state parks, see Environment (p80), which lists websites for the various governing bodies. A great resource for ecologically minded activities of all kinds is **EcoFlorida** (www .ecofloridamag.com). Or check out *30 Eco-Trips in Florida* (2005) by Holly Ambrose, a loving and detailed resource covering the full gamut of Florida landscapes and the best ways to explore them.

Biking

Note that the state organizations listed under Hiking also discuss biking trails. Florida law requires that all cyclists under 16 must wear a helmet (under 18 in national parks).

Adventure Cycling Association (www.adventure cycling.org) Organizes tours, sells bike route maps (only a few for Florida) and publishes *Adventure Cyclist*.
Bicycling (www.bicycling.com)
Bike Florida (www.bikeflorida.com) Nonprofit organization that promotes safe cycling.
Florida Bicycle Association (www.floridabicycle .org) Advocacy organization provides tons of advice, a statewide list of cycling clubs, and links to off-road cycling organizations and to racing clubs, a touring calendar and more. Have a question? They probably have the answer.
League of American Bicyclists (LAB; www.bike league.org) National advocacy group publishes *American Bicyclist*.

Canoeing & Kayaking

Note that water-trail and kayaking information is also provided by the Florida state park and the Greenways & Trails websites under Hiking. There are a lot of Florida paddling guides to choose from. For the full monty, see *A Paddler's Guide to the Sunshine State* (2001) by Sandy Huff. Here are more resources:

American Canoe Association (ACA; www.american canoe.org) ACA publishes a newsletter, has a water-trails database and organizes courses.
Canoe & Kayak (www.canoekayak.com) Online magazine has Florida trail descriptions.
Florida Professional Paddlesports Association (www.paddleflausa.com) Provides list of affiliated member kayak outfitters.
Kayak Online (www.kayakonline.com) Good resource for kayak gear; links to Florida outfitters.
Paddler (www.paddlermagazine.com)

If boaters and backcountry kayakers need navigation charts, and can't find them, order them from the **National Oceanic and Atmospheric Association** (NOAA; http://chartmaker.ncd.noaa.gov).

Diving

Ocean diving in Florida requires an Open Water I certificate, and Florida has plenty of certification programs (with good weather, they take three days). To dive in freshwater springs, you need a separate cave-diving certification, and this is also offered throughout the state.

National Association for Underwater Instruction (NAUI; www.naui.org) Information on dive certifications and a list of NAUI-certified Florida dive instructors.
Professional Diving Instructors Corporation (PDIC; www.pdic-intl.com) Similar to NAUI, with its own list of PDIC-certified Florida dive instructors.

Scuba Diving (www.scubadiving.com) Lots of Florida-specific travel advice.

Sport Diver (www.sportdiver.com)

Fishing

Note that all nonresidents 16 and over need a fishing license to fish, and Florida offers several short-term licenses. There are lots of regulations about what and how much you can catch where; locals can give you details, but it doesn't hurt to review the Florida Fish & Wildlife Conservation Commission (FWC) website.

Florida Fish & Wildlife Conservation Commission (FWC; www.myfwc.com) The official source for all fishing regulations and licenses (purchase online or by phone). Also has boating and hunting information.

Florida Fishing (www.floridafishing.com) Fish reports and lists of charters.

Florida Fishing Capital of the World (www.fishingcapital.com) State-run all-purpose fishing advice and information.

Florida Sportsman (www.floridasportsman.com) Get the lowdown on sport fishing, tournaments, charters, gear and detailed regional advice.

Hiking & Camping

For advice on low-impact hiking and camping, see boxed text Tread Lightly, Explore Safely, p56 and visit Leave No Trace (www.lnt.org). *A Hiker's Guide to the Sunshine State* (2005) by Sandra Friend is packed with nitty-gritty details, and Friend's companion website (www.floridahikes.com) provides an equally rich introduction to Florida trails. A great book to take tramping, *Florida's Birds: A Handbook and Reference* outlines the calls, seasons and habitats of over 325 Florida bird species.

Florida Greenways & Trails (www.dep.state.fl.us/gwt) The Florida Department of Environmental Protection has downloadable hiking, biking and kayaking trail descriptions.

Florida State Parks (www.floridastateparks.org) Comprehensive state-park information and all cabin and camping reservations.

Florida Trail Association (www.floridatrail.org) Maintains the Florida National Scenic Trail (FNST); a wealth of online advice, descriptions and maps.

Florida Trails Network (www.floridatrailsnetwork.com) The state's main database of current and future trails.

Rails-to-Trails Conservancy (www.railtrails.org) Converts abandoned railroad corridors into public biking

and hiking trails; has a Florida chapter and reviews trails at www.traillink.com.

Recreation.gov (www.recreation.gov) Reserve camping at all national parks and forests.

For short hikes in national, state or regional parks, the free park maps are perfectly adequate. For long hikes and backpacking, good topographical (topo) maps can be invaluable; most outdoor stores and ranger stations sell them. You can also order them directly from the source: the **US Geological Survey** (USGS; ☎ 888-275-8747; http://store.usgs.gov). Or, create custom, downloadable topo maps at **Trails.com** (www.trails.com) and **National Geographic** (www.nationalgeographic.com), whose online store also has GPS maps.

Surfing

Looking for lessons, surf reports, competitions? Here you go:

Florida Surfing (www.floridasurfing.com) Instructors, contests, webcams, weather, equipment, history: it's all here.

Florida Surfing Association (FSA; www.floridasurfingassociation.org) Manages Florida's surf competitions; also runs the surf school at Jacksonville Beach.

Surfer (www.surfmag.com) *Surfer's* travel reports cover Florida and just about every break in the USA.

Surf Guru (www.surfguru.com) East Coast Florida surf reports.

BUSINESS HOURS

Unless otherwise noted the standard business hours in this guide are as follows:

Banks 9am or 10am to 5pm or 6pm Monday to Friday; some open Saturday mornings.

Bars & clubs 4pm to 2am; some clubs open later on weekends.

Businesses 9am to 5pm Monday to Friday.

Post offices 8am to 4pm or 5:30pm Monday to Friday; some open Saturday mornings.

Restaurants Breakfast 6:30am to 11am; lunch 11am to 2:30pm; dinner 5pm to 10pm.

Shops 9am or 10am to 6pm Monday to Saturday; some also open noon to 5pm Sunday; many open until 9pm in tourist areas and malls. Some supermarkets open 24 hours.

CLIMATE CHARTS

For general advice on seasonal travel, see Getting Started (p13). Each Florida chapter also has a Climate section discussing regional variations. In general, expect mild dry winters

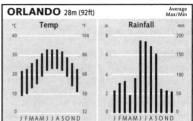

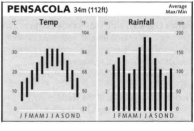

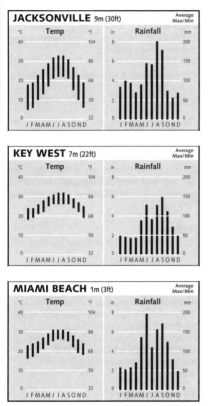

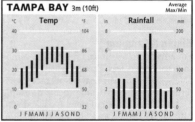

and wet humid summers. For hurricane advice, see opposite.

COURSES

The best place to find a fun course while on vacation is Miami, which offers visitors a range of salsa, Spanish language and cooking classes (p126).

If you're looking to learn a sport, nearly every place where sport is popular will have outfitters eager to teach you what to do and perfect your technique. See Activities (p504) and see Florida Outdoors (p49) for some general ideas, and see the destination chapters for specific places.

CUSTOMS REGULATIONS

For a complete, up-to-date list of customs regulations, visit the website of **US Customs and Border Protection** (www.cbp.gov). Each visitor is allowed to bring into the US duty-free

1L of liquor (if you're 21 or older) and 200 cigarettes (if you're 18 or older). US citizens can also import, duty-free, up to $800 in gifts and purchases; non–US citizens are permitted $100 worth.

Because of Miami's infamous popularity as a drug-smuggling gateway, customs officers here are known to be thorough in their examination of travelers who may fit the profile of someone ferrying narcotics. They may not be very polite – but you should be, and you should dress neatly and carry lots of traveler's checks and credit cards, or show other signs of prosperity lest they think you're here to work illegally.

DANGERS & ANNOYANCES

When it comes to crime, there is Miami, and then there is the rest of Florida. As a rule, Miami suffers the same urban problems facing other major US cities such as New York and Los Angeles, but it is no worse than others. If travelers remember their street smarts, they should be fine. The rest of Florida, even the large cities, tend to have lower crime rates than the rest of the nation. That said, any tourist town is a magnet for petty theft and car break-ins.

Here are the three essential, simple safety tips:

▪ Lock your car doors and don't leave any valuables visible.
▪ Avoid walking alone on empty streets or in parks at night.
▪ Use ATMs only in well-trafficked areas.

If you need any kind of emergency assistance, such as police, ambulance or firefighters, call ☎ 911. This is a free call from any phone. For health matters see p524.

Florida also has a range of dangers and annoyances that *aren't* encountered everywhere else. These include hurricanes, biting insects, venomous snakes, alligators and sharks. As for hurricanes, see boxed text The Mighty Winds, below. For advice on insects, snakes and alligators, see p525. And for sharks, see boxed text How to Avoid a Shark Bite, p348.

DISCOUNTS

Have we got a deal for you. Well, actually, *we* don't, but many, many Florida hotels and businesses specialize in discounts, price breaks, reduced-rate packages and on and on.

THE MIGHTY WINDS

Florida hurricane season extends from June through November, but the peak is September and October. As storms brew over the Atlantic Ocean and the Gulf of Mexico, a few gather enough strength to become hurricanes, and some of these aim for Florida.

A hurricane is a concentrated system of very strong thunderstorms with high circulation. The 74mph to 160mph winds created by a hurricane can extend for hundreds of miles around the eye (center) of a hurricane system. In addition to the damage caused by high winds and rain-caused flash floods, hurricanes can cause a 'storm surge' that forces the level of the ocean to rise between 4ft and 18ft above normal. An unfortunately placed storm surge can devastate coastal towns and cities.

Hurricanes are generally sighted well in advance, and there's time to prepare. When a hurricane threatens, listen to radio and TV news reports. Rumors can sometimes run rampant, so take **National Weather Service** (www.nws.noaa.gov) forecasts seriously. There's a **hurricane hotline** (☎ 800-342-3557), which will give you information about approaching storms, warnings, and estimated time till touchdown.

There are two distinct stages of alert: a 'hurricane watch' is given when a hurricane *may* strike the area within the next 36 to 48 hours; a 'hurricane warning' is given when a hurricane *is likely* to strike the area. Hurricane warnings may be followed by evacuation orders for the areas in the most danger. Hotels generally follow these orders and ask guests to leave. If this happens during your stay, you will likely be sent to a Red Cross–operated hurricane shelter, but they're just that – shelter. You must bring your own food, first-aid kit, and blanket or sleeping bag. And you might as well bring a book. Your hotel will have information about the logistics of evacuation.

If, for one reason or another, you must sit out a hurricane warning, have the following items:

▪ flashlight
▪ as much fresh drinking water as possible (storms knock out the water supply)
▪ butane lighter and candles
▪ canned food, nonperishable food, powdered or UHT (ultrapasteurized, long-life) milk
▪ cash (ATMs might not function)
▪ portable, battery-powered radio

When the hurricane hits, stay in a closet or other windowless room. Cover yourself with a mattress to prevent injury from flying glass. Taping windows does not stop them from breaking, but it does reduce shatter. State telephone directories provide a full list of preparedness tips.

You'll find scads of clippable tourist magazines throughout Florida; most of the time they're worthless unless you already want what they offer. But folks who dedicate time to internet browsing ahead of their trip can usually scare up good deals that fit their itinerary. Two places to start are **Roomsavers** (www.roomsavers.com) and **Mousesavers** (www.mousesavers.com). Then, if you don't find what you want, just ask. It's amazing what a little charming persistence can get you if you appeal directly to the business in question; Florida, after all, has a *very* competitive tourist industry.

Being a member of certain groups also gives access to discounts. Auto-club memberships (p520) are honored at many hotels, museums and the like with 10% discounts. Others offer discounts to ID-carrying seniors (generally those 65 and older, but sometimes those 60 and older); joining the **American Association of Retired Persons** (AARP; ☎ 888-687-2277; www.aarp.org; 601 E St NW, Washington, DC, 20049) gives access to more travel bargains. Students also get discounts at many places; generally, any student ID is honored, but international students might fair better with an **International Student Identity Card** (ISIC; www.isiccard.com).

EMBASSIES & CONSULATES

To find a US embassy in another country, visit the **US Department of State website** (www.usembassy.gov). For foreign embassies in the US, note that most nations have their main consulates in Washington, DC, but some have representation in Miami (and Coral Gables). Look under 'consulates' in the telephone book for diplomatic representation. Citizens of Australia and New Zealand may contact the British or Canadian consulates for emergency assistance, as neither country maintains consular offices in Miami.

Consulates include the following:

Brazil (Map pp92-3; ☎ 305-285-6200; www.brazilmiami.org; 80 SW 8th St, Suite 2600, Miami)
Canada (Map pp92-3; ☎ 305-579-1600; http://geo.international.gc.ca/can%2Dam/miami; 200 S Biscayne Blvd, Suite 1600, Miami)
France (Map pp92-3; ☎ 305-403-4150; www.consulfrance-miami.org; 1395 Brickell Ave, Suite 1050, Miami)
Germany (Map pp92-3; ☎ 305-358-0290; www.miami.diplo.de; 100 N Biscayne Blvd, Suite 2200, Miami)
Italy (Map p95; ☎ 305-374-6322; www.consmiami.esteri.it/Consolato_Miami; 4000 Ponce de León, Suite 590, Coral Gables)
Mexico (☎ 786-268-4900; www.mexicomiami.org; 5975 SW 72nd St, Suite 302, Miami)

Netherlands (Map pp92-3; ☎ 877-388-2443; www.cgmiami.org; 701 Brickell Ave, 5th fl, Miami)
UK (Map pp92-3; ☎ 305-374-3500; www.britainusa.com/miami; 1001 Brickell Bay Dr, Suite 2800, Miami)

FOOD

Eating sections are broken down into three price categories: budget (with mains costing $12 or less), midrange (with most mains costing $12 to $25) and top end ($25 and up). These price estimates do not include taxes, tips or beverages.

For information about Florida cuisine, see the Food & Drink chapter (p57).

GAY & LESBIAN TRAVELERS

Florida is not uniformly anything, so it's not uniformly embracing of gay life. It is largely tolerant, particularly in major tourist destinations, beaches and cities, but this tolerance does not always extend into the more rural and Southern areas of northern Florida. However, where Florida does embrace gay life, it does so with one big flamboyant bear hug of a squeeze. Miami (p151) and South Beach (p103) are as out as it's possible to be, with hot beaches, hot nightclubs and some massive gay festivals. Fort Lauderdale (p227), West Palm Beach (p250), and Key West (p212) have long supported vibrant gay communities and host some major parties. But notable gay scenes and communities also exist in Orlando (p280), Jacksonville (p376), and Pensacola (p500), and to lesser degrees in Daytona Beach, Tampa, and Sarasota.

Damron (☎ 415-255-0404, 800-462-6654; www.damron.com) publishes popular national guidebooks, including *Women's Traveller, Men's Travel Guide*, and *Damron Accommodations*. Other good gay and lesbian resources include the following:

Advocate (www.advocate.com)
Gay.com (www.gay.com) Comprehensive resource; lots of travel information.
Gay Yellow Network (☎ 800-697-2812; www.gayyellow.com) City-based yellow-page listings include six Florida cities.
Out Traveler (www.outtraveler.com)
Purple Roofs (www.purpleroofs.com) Lists queer accommodations, travel agencies and tours worldwide.

HOLIDAYS

For festivals and events, see the Events Calendar (p17). On the following national public holidays, banks, schools and government offices (including post offices) are closed, and transportation, museums and other services operate on a Sunday schedule. Many stores, however, maintain regular business hours. Holidays falling on a weekend are usually observed the following Monday. Keep in mind that prices will be a bit higher over holidays. Just as important, though, is that rooms fill faster than at other times, so make reservations as early as possible.

New Year's Day 1 January
Martin Luther King Jr Day Third Monday in January
Presidents Day Third Monday in February
Easter March or April
Memorial Day Last Monday in May
Independence Day 4 July
Labor Day First Monday in September
Columbus Day Second Monday in October
Veterans Day 11 November
Thanksgiving Fourth Thursday in November
Christmas Day 25 December

INSURANCE

It's expensive to get sick, crash a car or have things stolen from you in the US. For car insurance see p521 and for health insurance see p524. To insure yourself for items that may be stolen from your car, consult your homeowner's (or renter's) insurance policy before leaving home or consider investing in travel insurance.

Worldwide travel insurance is available at www.lonelyplanet.com/travel_services. You can buy, extend and claim online anytime – even if you're already on the road.

INTERNET ACCESS

If you usually access your email through your office or school, you'll find it easier to open a free account with **Yahoo!** (www.yahoo.com) or **Hotmail** (www.hotmail.com).

If you're traveling with a laptop or hand-held computer, be aware that your modem may not work once you leave your home country. The safest option is to buy a reputable 'global' modem before you leave home, or buy a local PC-card modem if you're spending an extended time in any one country. For more information on traveling with a portable computer, see www.teleadapt.com.

Cyber cafés and business centers such as Kinko's offer inexpensive online computer access. When hostels or other lodgings provide terminals for guests, this is noted with ▢. These days nearly every hotel from midrange

up has in-room dial-up or high-speed access for connecting your own equipment to, and an increasing number of budget hotels provide this too. Ask when reserving. Additionally, many hotels and cities offer wi-fi hot spots. See the relevant Internet Access sections (under Information) in individual chapters.

It's always safest to get local-access dial-up numbers from your internet service provider (eg Earthlink, AOL) before leaving home. In lots of places in the Southeast, dial-up access numbers require long-distance toll calls, which can be problematic for those traveling with a computer.

LEGAL MATTERS

In everyday matters, if you are stopped by the police, note that there is no system for paying traffic tickets or other fines on the spot. The patrol officer will explain your options to you; there is usually a 30-day period to pay fines by mail.

If you're arrested for a serious offence, you are allowed to remain silent (though never walk away from an officer), you are entitled to have an attorney present during any interrogation and you are presumed innocent until proven guilty. You have the right to an attorney from the moment you are arrested. If you can't afford one, the state must provide one for free. All persons who are arrested have the right to make one phone call. If you don't have a lawyer or family member to help you, call your embassy or consulate (see opposite). Federal laws are applicable to the postal service, US government property and many interstate activities.

Drinking

Despite what you might see, it's technically illegal to walk with an open alcoholic drink – including beer – on the street. More importantly, don't drive with an 'open container'; any liquor in a car must be unopened or else stored in the trunk of the car. If you're stopped while driving with an open container, police will treat you as if you were drinking and driving, no matter who is holding the bottle; to be caught and convicted of driving under the influence of alcohol or drugs is a serious offense, subject to stiff fines and even imprisonment.

The minimum age for drinking alcoholic beverages is 21, and you'll need a photo ID (such as a passport or US driver's license) to purchase alcohol.

DIRECTORY

MAPS

The most detailed state highway maps are those distributed free by state governments. Order them from state tourism offices in advance (see p512), or pick up maps at highway tourist-information offices when you enter a state on a major highway. The **Delorme Mapping Company** (www.delorme.com) and **Rand McNally** (www.randmcnally.com) publish good road atlases of the state.

For topographical or nautical maps for outdoor activities, see Canoeing & Kayaking on p504 or Hiking & Camping on p505.

MONEY

The dollar is divided into 100 cents. Coins come in denominations of one cent (penny), five cents (nickel), 10 cents (dime), 25 cents (quarter) and the rare 50-cent piece (half dollar). Notes come in one, five, 10, 20, 50 and 100 dollar denominations.

See the inside front cover for exchange rates and p13 for general information on costs.

ATMs

ATMs are everywhere: at grocery stores, malls, convenience stores, gas stations and even at banks. Being able to get as much cash as you want whenever you want eliminates the need for traveler's checks, but watch out for surcharges. Most banks in Florida charge around $1.50 per withdrawal, and ATMs not affiliated with a bank or major networks such as Cirrus and Plus may add even more fees.

Credit Cards

Major credit cards are widely accepted throughout Florida, but occasionally B&Bs and some smaller restaurants do not accept credit cards. Report lost or stolen cards on the following numbers:

American Express (☎ 800-528-4800; www.americanexpress.com)

Diners Club (☎ 800-234-6377; www.dinersclub.com)

Discover (☎ 800-347-2683; www.discovercard.com)

MasterCard (☎ 800-622-7747; www.mastercard.com)

Visa (☎ 800-847-2911; www.visa.com)

Currency Exchange

Banks in outlying areas don't always exchange major foreign currencies, so you should exchange your money in larger cities. Thomas Cook and American Express exchange windows in international airports offer exchange.

Tipping

Never tip in fast-food, takeout or buffet-style restaurants. In hotels, leave a few dollars in the room for the housekeeping staff for each day of your stay when you check out. Tip taxi drivers 15% of the fare and waiters 15% to 20% of the bill. Baggage carriers are usually tipped $1 to $2 per bag and bartenders $1 per drink.

Traveler's Checks

Traveler's checks provide protection from theft and loss. For refunds on lost or stolen traveler's checks, call the issuer, for example **American Express** (☎ 800-992-3404; www.americanexpress.com) or **Thomas Cook** (☎ 800-287-7362; www.thomascook.com). Keeping a record of the check numbers and those you have used is vital for replacing lost checks, so keep this information separate from the checks themselves. Foreign visitors will find life infinitely easier if the checks are in US dollars. Traveler's checks are readily accepted in major tourist destinations and can be used in lieu of cash.

PHOTOGRAPHY

Airport security X-ray machines will damage undeveloped film, so don't pack film into checked luggage or carry-on bags. Instead, carry your film in a clear plastic bag to show separately to airport security officials (ask for a hand check). Remember, finish the film in your camera and take it out, or those photos may end up foggy.

Both print and slide film are readily available, and it's prudent to develop film while in Florida. High heat and humidity can deteriorate exposed film quickly. Chain drugstores and supermarkets are the cheapest places: typically, regular service for a roll costs $7 to $8, while one-hour service might be $12 to $15.

If you have a digital camera – and who doesn't? – a great website with comprehensive advice to keep your pixels poppin' is www.malektips.com. Digital camera memory cards are available nearly everywhere film is now, plus stores like Circuit City; keep two on hand. It's also a good idea to burn your pics to CD as you fill up your memory cards – then you don't need to keep buying memory cards, and it backs up your photos, you know, just in case the memory card gets damaged. Walgreens and Wal-Mart are two major chains that do this (for around $5 to $7). Also, don't leave home without your battery charger.

For more picture-taking advice, consult Lonely Planet's *Travel Photography.* But here are some basic tips: when shooting people, get close up and out of direct sun, to avoid the dreaded 'who are those squinting strangers in the distance' shots; when shooting nature and landscapes, the best light is at dusk and dawn; vary your angle (get low and shoot up or get high and shoot down); and include people or foreground objects to add perspective. If you've never worked with a polarizing filter, overbright Florida is a good place to start.

POST

The **US Postal Service** (☎ 800-275-8777; www.usps .com) provides great service for the price. For 1st-class mail within the US, postage rates are 42¢ for letters up to 1oz (17¢ for each additional ounce) and 27¢ for standard-sized postcards. To find local post offices, see the Information sections under major towns.

International airmail rates for postcards and letters up to 1oz are 72¢ to Canada or Mexico, 94¢ to other countries.

You can have mail sent to you c/o General Delivery at most large post offices in Florida. General delivery mail is usually held for up to 30 days and you'll need to show identification when you pick it up. Most hotels will also hold mail for incoming guests.

Call private shippers like **United Parcel Service** (UPS; ☎ 800-742-5877; www.ups.com) and **Federal Express** (FedEx; ☎ 800-463-3339; www.fedex.com) for more important or larger items.

SHOPPING

Tacky souvenirs are a Florida staple; they are obscenely abundant nearly everywhere you go. If you find it hard to choose, consider one the fabulous items listed in the boxed text Tackiest Souvenirs, p15.

There are few handicrafts that are particular to the state, though visiting the Seminole reservation and some of the Cracker towns of north Florida will yield unique treasures. The ethnic enclaves of Miami offer numerous unusual shops, like Haitian *botanicas,* and the city has fashion and art boutiques out the wazoo. Another popular item is Florida citrus: numerous places will send a crate home for you. It's a delicious reminder of your trip.

If you're concerned about everyday shopping, don't be. Malls are also everywhere. They may be the death of culture, but they also have air-con.

SOLO TRAVELERS

There are no particular problems or difficulties traveling alone in Florida.

Many hotels offer lower rates for a single person, but not all do. Single rooms tend to be small and badly located, so if you want more comfort, make a reservation for a double. Similarly, restaurants often shunt single diners to cramped corners. To avoid this, make a reservation for two, and after being seated for a while, look disappointed that your friend isn't coming and order your meal; more than likely, the waitstaff will become extra helpful because of your plight. Or, if you want to meet people, eat at the bar if that is available.

Some issues of safety are slightly different for women than they are for men; women should see p515 for more specific advice. For anyone, hitchhiking is always risky and not recommended, especially hitchhiking alone. And don't pick up hitchhikers when driving.

In general, don't advertise where you are staying, or even that you are traveling alone, if someone strikes you as suspicious. Floridians tend to be friendly and eager to help and may even take in solo travelers; this is one of the pluses of traveling this way. However, don't take all offers at face value. If someone who seems trustworthy invites you to his or her home, let someone know where you're going (even your hotel manager). This advice also applies if you go for a hike by yourself. If something happens and you don't return as expected, you want to know that someone will notice and know where to begin looking for you.

TAXES

Florida's sales tax is 6%, but some communities also tack on a bit more for their fair share. States, cities and towns also usually levy taxes on hotel rooms and restaurant meals; in Orlando resorts especially, all sorts of taxes and extra charges can be added to your bill. When hotels quote prices, it almost never includes the tax, even though (or perhaps because) they may increase your final bill by as much as 10% to 12%.

TELEPHONE

In many areas, local calls have moved to a 10-digit calling system. This means you need to dial the area code even when making a local call – just start with ☎ 305 (or whatever the local area code is) and then the number you wish to reach.

With the prevalence of cell phones, pay phones aren't as ubiquitous as they used to be, but most shopping centers, gas stations and major city streets still have them. You just have to look harder to find them. Calls made within town are local and cost 25¢ to 50¢.

To make international calls direct, dial ☎ 011 + country code + area code + number. (An exception is to Canada, where you dial ☎ 1 + area code + number. International rates apply to Canada.)

For international operator assistance, dial ☎ 0. The operator can provide specific rate information and tell you which time periods are the cheapest for calling.

If you're calling Florida from abroad, the international country code for the US is ☎ 1. All calls to the Southeast are then followed by the area code and the seven-digit local number.

Cell Phones

In the USA cell phones use GSM 1900 or CDMA 800, operating on different frequencies from systems in other countries. The only foreign phones that will work in the USA are triband models, operating on GSM 1900 as well as other frequencies. If you have a GSM triband phone, check with your service provider about using it in the USA. Make sure to ask if roaming charges apply; these will turn even local US calls into pricey international calls.

You may be able to take the SIM card from your usual cell phone, install it in a rented mobile phone that's compatible with the US systems, and use the rental phone as if it were your own phone – same number, same billing basis. Ask your mobile-phone company about this. You can rent a phone for about $45 per week, but rates vary.

You can also rent a GSM 1900–compatible phone with a set amount of prepaid call time. **T-Mobile** (www.t-mobile.com) is one US company that provides this service, but it ain't cheap.

Finally, rural Florida gets spotty service. Make sure your provider covers your route.

Phone Cards

Phone cards are now almost essential for travelers using the US phone system. There are two basic types.

A phone credit card bills calls to your home phone number. Some cards issued by foreign phone companies will work in the USA – inquire before you leave home.

A prepaid phone card is a good alternative for travelers and widely available in big cities and from major retailers. Always check the card's connection fees (see if it has a toll-free access number from pay phones) in addition to the rate. AT&T sells a reliable phone card that's available at many retailers.

TIME

Except for the western section of the Panhandle, Florida is in the US eastern time zone, three hours ahead of San Francisco, and five hours behind GMT/UTC. West of the Apalachicola River, the Panhandle is in the US central time zone, one hour behind the rest of the state, two hours ahead of San Francisco, and six hours behind GMT/UTC. Daylight-saving time takes place from early March to early November: clocks 'spring forward' one hour in March and 'fall back' one hour in November.

TOURIST INFORMATION

Most Florida towns have some sort of tourist-information center that provides local information; be aware that chambers of commerce typically only list chamber members, not all the town's hotels and businesses. This guide provides visitor-center information throughout.

To order a packet of Florida information prior to coming, contact **Visit Florida** (☎ 850-488-5607, 888-735-2872; www.visitflorida.com; 661 E Jefferson St, Suite 300, Tallahassee, FL 32301), and also see the list of websites in Getting Started (p16).

TRAVELERS WITH DISABILITIES

Because of the high number of senior residents in Florida, most public buildings are wheelchair accessible and have appropriate restroom facilities. Transportation services are generally accessible to all, and telephone companies provide relay operators for the hearing impaired. Many banks provide ATM instructions in Braille, curb ramps are common and many busy intersections have audible crossing signals.

A number of organizations specialize in the needs of disabled travelers:

Access-Able Travel Source (☎ 303-232-2979; www .access-able.com; PO Box 1796, Wheat Ridge, CO 80034) An excellent website with many links.

Flying Wheels Travel (☎ 507-451-5005; www.flying wheelstravel.com; 143 W Bridge St, Owatonna, MN 55060) A full-service travel agency specializing in disabled travel.

Mobility International USA (☎ 541-343-1284; www .miusa.org; 132 E Broadway, Suite 343, Eugene, OR 97401)

Advises disabled travelers on mobility issues and runs an educational exchange program.

Travelin' Talk Network (www.travelintalk.net) Run by the same people as Access-Able Travel Source; a global network of service providers.

VISAS

After several years of evolution and upheaval, US entry requirements have become pretty well established again. However, all travelers should double-check current visa and passport regulations *before* coming to the USA.

The main portal for US visa information is www.unitedstatesvisas.gov; you can also get visa information at www.usa.gov. Both link to the **US State Department** (www.travel.state .gov), which maintains the most comprehensive information, providing downloadable forms, lists of US consulates abroad and even visa wait times calculated by country. The website maintained by the **United States Citizenship and Immigration Service** (USCIS; www.uscis.gov) focuses on immigrants, not temporary visitors.

Visa Applications

Apart from Canadians and those entering under the Visa Waiver Program (see p514), foreign visitors need to obtain a visa from a US consulate or embassy. In most countries, you must now schedule a personal interview, to which you must bring all your documentation and proof of fee payment. Afterward, barring problems, visa issuance takes from a few days to a few weeks.

Your passport must be valid for at least six months longer than your intended stay in the USA (some countries have exemptions from this), and you'll need to submit a recent photo (2in by 2in) with the application; there is a $100 processing fee, and in a few cases an additional visa issuance reciprocity fee (check the State Department website for details). In addition to the main nonimmigrant visa application form (DS-156), all men aged 16 to 45 must complete an additional form (DS-157) that details their travel plans.

Visa applicants are required to show documents of financial stability (or evidence that a US resident will provide financial support), a round-trip or onward ticket and 'binding obligations' that will ensure their return home, such as family ties, a home or a job.

There are numerous grounds for exclusion; see the State Department website for a full list. The most important concern is whether you have a criminal record or a communicable disease. If you are tempted to fudge the truth here, don't. US officials tend to grant exceptions to applicants who admit upfront to minor offenses, but they can deal harshly with those they feel are trying to mislead them, even on small points.

Because of these requirements, those planning to travel through other countries before arriving in the USA are generally better off applying for a US visa while they are still in their home country, rather than while on the road.

The most common visa is a nonimmigrant visitors visa, type B1 for business purposes, B2 for tourism or visiting friends and relatives. A visitors visa is good for multiple entries over one or five years, and specifically prohibits the visitor from taking paid employment in the USA. The validity period depends on what country you are from. The length of time you'll be allowed to stay in the USA is determined by US immigration at the port of entry.

If you're coming to work or study, you will need a different type of visa, and the company or institution to which you are going should make the arrangements. Other categories of nonimmigrant visas include those for people on visitor-exchange programs, the fiancés or fiancées of US citizens, and those undergoing intracompany transfers.

Entering the USA

If you have a non-US passport, you must complete an arrival/departure record (form I-94) before you reach the immigration desk. It's usually handed out on the plane along with the customs declaration. For the question, 'Address While in the United States,' give the address where you will spend the first night (a hotel address is fine).

No matter what your visa says, US immigration officers have an absolute authority to refuse admission to the USA or to impose conditions on admission. They will ask about your plans and whether you have sufficient funds; it's a good idea to list an itinerary, produce an onward or round-trip ticket and have at least one major credit card. Showing that you have over $400 per week of your stay should be enough. Don't make too much of having friends, relatives or business contacts in the USA; the immigration official may decide that this will make you more likely to overstay. It also helps to be neatly dressed and polite. If they think you're OK, a six-month entry is usually approved.

REGISTRATION

The Department of Homeland Security's registration program – called **US-VISIT** (www.dhs .gov/us-visit) – is essentially phased in. It includes every port of entry and every foreign visitor to the USA.

For most visitors, registration consists of having your photo taken and having electronic (inkless) fingerprints made; the process takes less than a minute.

A 'special registration' called NSEERS (the National Security Entry/Exit Registration System) applies to citizens of certain countries that have been deemed particular risks. These countries are mainly in the Middle East and Africa; visit www.travel.state.gov for a complete list. Registration in these cases also includes a short interview in a separate room and computer verification of all personal information supplied on travel documents. US officials can require this separate interview of any traveler.

Visa Extensions

If you want to stay in the USA longer than the date stamped on your passport, go to the local USCIS office (call ☎ 800-375-5283 or look in the local white-pages telephone directory under 'US Government') to apply for an extension well *before* the stamped date. If the date has passed, your best chance will be to bring a US citizen with you to vouch for your character, and to produce lots of other verification that you are not trying to work illegally and have enough money to support yourself. However, if you've overstayed, the most likely scenario is that you will be deported.

Visa Waiver Program

Under the Visa Waiver Program, citizens of certain countries may enter the USA without a US visa for stays of 90 days or less; no extensions are allowed. Currently, 27 countries are included: Andorra, Australia, Austria, Belgium, Brunei, Denmark, Finland, France, Germany, Iceland, Ireland, Italy, Japan, Liechtenstein, Luxembourg, Monaco, the Netherlands, New Zealand, Norway, Portugal, San Marino, Singapore, Slovenia, Spain, Sweden, Switzerland and the UK.

Under this program, visitors must produce all the same evidence as for a nonimmigrant visa application: they must demonstrate that the trip is for a limited time, and that they have a round-trip or onward ticket, adequate funds to cover the trip and binding obligations abroad. Passports issued before 2005 must be 'machine readable'; those issued after 2006 must be e-Passports, which have digital photos and embedded computer chips with 'biometric data.' Confirm with your passport-issuing agency that your passport meets current US standards. You'll be turned back if it doesn't.

In addition, the same 'grounds for exclusion' apply, except that you will have no opportunity to appeal or apply for an exemption. If you are denied under the Visa Waiver Program at a US point of entry, you will have to use your onward or return ticket on the next available flight.

It is mandatory for VWP travelers to apply electronically before leaving their home country; check the websites listed at the start of the Visas section on p513 for details.

Short-Term Departures & Reentry

It's quite easy to make trips to other countries (to Mexico or to the Caribbean, Cuba excepted), but upon return to the USA, those who are not North Americans will be subject to the full immigration procedure. Always take your passport with you. If your immigration card still has plenty of time on it, you will probably be able to reenter using the same one, but if it has nearly expired, you will have to apply for a new card, and border control may want to see your onward air ticket, sufficient funds and so on.

Traditionally, a quick trip across the Mexican (or Canadian) border has been a way to extend your stay in the USA without applying for an extension at a USCIS office. This can still be done, but don't assume it will work. First, make sure you hand in your old immigration card to the immigration authorities when you leave the USA, and when you return make sure you have all the necessary application documentation described above. US immigration will be very suspicious of anyone who leaves for a few days and returns immediately hoping for a new six-month stay; expect to be questioned closely.

VOLUNTEERING

Volunteer opportunities abound in Florida. They can be a great way to break up a long trip, and they provide memorable opportunities to interact with locals and the land in ways you never would when just passing through.

Volunteer Florida (www.volunteerflorida.org), the primary state-run organization, coordinates volunteer centers across the state. Though it's aimed at Floridians, casual visitors can find situations that match their time and interests.

Florida's state parks would not function without volunteers. Each park coordinates its own volunteers, and most also have the support of an all-volunteer 'friends' organization (officially called Citizen Support Organizations). Links and contact information for all are on the main **state park website** (www.floridastateparks.org/volunteers).

Finally, **Habitat for Humanity** (www.habitat.org) does a ton of work in Florida, building homes and helping the homeless.

WOMEN TRAVELERS

Women traveling by themselves or in a group should encounter no particular problems unique to Florida. Indeed, there are a number of excellent resources to help traveling women.

The community website www.journeywoman.com helps women talk to each other, and it has links to other sites. As for guides, try the inspirational *A Journey of One's Own* (1992) by Thalia Zepatos; the pocket-size expertise of *Gutsy Women: Travel Tips and Wisdom for the Road* (1996) by Marybeth Bond; or the irreverent, equally portable *The Bad Girl's Guide to the Open Road* (1999) by Cameron Tuttle.

These two national advocacy groups might also be helpful:

National Organization for Women (NOW; ☎ 202-628-8669; www.now.org; 1100 H St NW, 3rd fl, Washington, DC 20005)

Planned Parenthood (☎ 800-230-7526; www.plannedparenthood.org) Offers referrals to medical clinics throughout the country.

In terms of safety issues, single women need to exhibit the same street smarts and city savvy as any solo traveler (p511), but they can often be the target of unwanted attention or harassment. In particular, avoid being alone on beaches after dark. Some women like to carry a whistle, mace or cayenne-pepper spray in case of assault. These sprays are legal to carry and use in Florida, but only in self-defense. Federal law prohibits them being carried on planes.

If you are assaulted, the best course of action is often to call a rape-crisis hotline; contact numbers for these are normally listed in the telephone directory or contact **Rape, Abuse**

& Incest National Network (☎ 800-656-4673; www.rainn.org), a 24-hour hotline. Rape-crisis staff act as a link between medical, legal and social-service systems, advocating on behalf of survivors to ensure their rights are respected and needs are addressed. In rural areas, you can go directly to the nearest hospital for help, then decide later whether or not to call the police.

WORK

If you are a foreigner in the USA with a standard nonimmigrant visitors visa, you are expressly forbidden to take paid work in the USA and will be deported if you're caught working illegally. In addition, employers are required to establish the bona fides of their employees or face fines, making it much tougher for a foreigner to get work than it once was.

To work legally, foreigners need to apply for a work visa before leaving home. A J1 visa, for exchange visitors, is issued to young people (age limits vary) for study, student vacation employment, work in summer camps and short-term traineeships with a specific employer. The following organizations will help arrange student exchanges, placements and J1 visas:

American Institute for Foreign Study (AIFS; ☎ 866-906-2437; www.aifs.com; River Plaza, 9 West Broad St, Stamford, CT 06902-3788)

BUNAC (☎ 020-7251-3472; www.bunac.org; 16 Bowling Green Lane, London EC1R 0QH)

Camp America (☎ 020-7581-7373; www.campamerica.co.uk; 37A Queens Gate, London SW7 5HR)

Council on International Educational Exchange (CIEE; ☎ 800-407-8839; www.ciee.org; 7 Custom House St, 3rd fl, Portland, ME 04101)

InterExchange (☎ 212-924-0446; www.interexchange.org; 161 Sixth Ave, NY, NY 10013) Camp and au-pair programs.

International Exchange Programs (IEP) Australia (☎ 1300-300-912; www.iep.org.au; Level 3, 362 La Trobe St, Melbourne, VIC 3000; Level 3, 333 George St, Sydney, NSW 2000); New Zealand (☎ 0800-443-769; www.iep.co.nz; Level 10, 220 Queen St, Auckland)

For US citizens, seasonal work sometimes goes begging in theme parks and tourist areas, but know that these are low-paying service jobs.

Of course, Florida, and Miami in particular, is home to many foreigners and refugees who are working illegally in this country. Immigration officers know this, and they are as vigilant and frequent in their enforcement of these laws as anywhere in the country.

Transportation

(sidebar) TRANSPORTATION

GETTING THERE & AWAY

Most travelers to Florida arrive by air and car, with the bus service running a distant third option and the train service an even more distant fourth. Major regional hubs in Florida include Miami (p160), Fort Lauderdale (p227), Orlando (p284) and Tampa (p416).

Flights, tours and rail tickets can be booked online at www.lonelyplanet.com /travel_services.

ENTERING THE REGION

When arriving from outside North America, you must complete customs and immigration formalities at the airport at which you first land. Your luggage may be inspected at this point. The **Transportation Security Administration** (TSA; www.tsa.gov) keeps an ever-changing list of prohibited items that cannot be brought through security checkpoints. For more information see the Directory, p513.

Passport

All visitors arriving from other countries must have a passport, including US citizens. Most foreign visitors also need a US visa (see p513).

AIR

Unless you live in or near Florida, flying to the region and then renting a car is the most time-efficient option.

Airports & Airlines

Whether you're coming from within the US or from abroad, the entire state is well-served by air.

Major airports:

Fort Lauderdale-Hollywood International Airport (FLL; ☎ 954-359-1200; www.broward.org/airport) Serves metro Fort Lauderdale and Broward County. It's about 30 miles north of Miami and is frequently a less expensive alternative to Miami. See p227 for more information.

Miami International Airport (MIA; ☎ 305-876-7000; www.miami-airport.com) One of the state's two busiest international airports. It serves metro Miami, the Everglades and the Keys, and serves as a hub for American, Delta and US Airways. See p161 for more information.

Orlando International Airport (MCO; ☎ 407-825-2001; www.orlandoairports.net) Handles more passengers than any other airport in Florida. Serves WDW, the Space Coast and the Orlando area.

Tampa International Airport (TPA; ☎ 813-870-8700; www.tampaairport.com) Serves the Tampa Bay and St Petersburg metro area. See p416 for more information.

Other airports with increased international traffic include Daytona Beach (DAB) and Jacksonville (JAX).

Most cities have airports and offer services to other US cities; these include Palm Beach (PBI; it's actually in West Palm Beach), Sarasota (SRQ), Tallahassee (TLH), Gainesville (GNV), Fort Myers (RSW), Pensacola (PNS) and Key West (EYW).

The following domestic airlines service Florida:

Air Tran (FL; ☎ 800-247-8726; www.airtran.com)
American (AA; ☎ 800-433-7300; www.aa.com)

THINGS CHANGE...

The information in this chapter is particularly vulnerable to change. Check directly with the airline or a travel agent to make sure you understand how a fare (and ticket you may buy) works and be aware of the security requirements for international travel. Shop carefully. The details given in this chapter should be regarded as pointers and are not a substitute for your own careful, up-to-date research.

Cape Air (9K; ☎ 800-352-0714; www.flycapeair.com)
Continental (CO; ☎ 800-523-3273; www.continental.com)
Delta (DL; ☎ 800-221-1212; www.delta.com)
Frontier (F9; ☎ 800-432-1359; www.frontierairlines.com)
Jetblue (JB; ☎ 800-538-2583; www.jetblue.com)
Northwest-KLM (NW; ☎ 800-225-2525; www.nwa.com)
Southwest (SW; ☎ 800-435-9792; www.southwest.com)
Spirit (NK; ☎ 800-772-7117; www.spiritair.com)
United (UA; ☎ 800-864-8331; www.united.com)
US Airways (US; ☎ 800-428-4322; www.usairways.com)

The following international airlines service Florida:

Aerolineas Argentinas (AR; ☎ 800-333-0276; www .aerolineas.com.ar) Hub: Buenos Aires.
AeroMexico (AM; ☎ 800-237-6639; www.aeromexico .com) Hub: Mexico City.
Air Canada (AC; ☎ 888-247-2262; www.aircanada.com) Hub: Toronto.
Air France (AF; ☎ 800-237-2747; www.airfrance.com) Hub: Paris.
Air Jamaica (JM; ☎ 800-523-5585; www.airjamaica .com) Hub: Montego Bay.
Air New Zealand (NZ; ☎ 800-262-1234; www.airnew zealand.com) Hub: Auckland.
Alitalia (AZ; ☎ 800-223-5730; www.alitalia.com) Hub: Milan.
Bahamas Air (UP; ☎ 800-222-4262; http:// up.bahamasair.com) Hub: Nassau.
British Airways (BA; ☎ 800-247-9297; www.british airways.com) Hub: London.
Cayman Airways (KX; ☎ 800 422-9626; www.cayman airways.com) Hub: Grand Cayman.
El Al (LY; ☎ 800-223-6700; www.elal.com) Hub: Tel Aviv.
Iberia (IB; ☎ 800-772-4642; www.iberia.com) Hub: Madrid.
Lan Chile (LA; ☎ 866-435-9526; www.lan.com) Hub: Santiago.
Lan Peru (LP; ☎ 866-435-9526; www.lan.com) Hub: Lima.
Lufthansa (LH; ☎ 800-399-5838; www.lufthansa.com) Hub: Frankfurt.
Mexicana (MX; ☎ 800-531-7921; www.mexicana.com) Hub: Mexico City.
Northwest-KLM (NW; ☎ 800-225-2525; www.nwa .com) Hub: Amsterdam.
Qantas (QF; ☎ 800-227-4500; www.quantas.com.au) Hub: Sydney.
Sun Country (SY; ☎ 800-359-6786; www.suncountry .com) Hub: Minneapolis.
Swiss International Airlines (LX; ☎ 877-359-7947; www.swiss.com) Hub: Zurich.
Varig Brazilian Airlines (RG; ☎ 800-468-2744; www .varig.com) Hub: Sao Paulo.

Virgin Atlantic (VS; ☎ 800-821-5438; www.virgin -atlantic.com) Hub: London.

Tickets

Airfares to the US and Florida range from incredibly low to obscenely high. **STA Travel** (☎ 800-781-4040; www.statravel.com) offers online booking and has offices in cities nation- and worldwide. In major Canadian cities, check with **Travel CUTS** (☎ 800-592-2887; www .travelcuts.com). A good agent for cheap tick- ets in London is **Trailfinders** (☎ 0845-058-5858; www.trailfinders.com/usa).

For one-way flights, budget airlines such as Jetblue, Southwest, and Frontier are the place to look.

Many domestic carriers offer special fares to non-US citizens. Typically, you must pur- chase a booklet of coupons in conjunction with a US-bound flight from a foreign country (a country other than Canada or Mexico). In addition to other restrictions, these coupons typically must be used within a limited period of time.

Round-the-world (RTW) tickets can be a great deal if you want to visit other regions on your way to Florida. Often they are the same price – or just a tad more expensive – than a simple round-trip ticket to the US. The two main airline alliances are the **Star Alliance** (www .staralliance.com) and **One World** (www.oneworld.com).

Searching websites for good or discounted fares can be complicated. For an overview, visit **Airinfo** (www.airinfo.aero), then visit these:
Cheap Tickets (www.cheaptickets.com)
Expedia (www.expedia.com)
Kayak (www.kayak.com)
Mobissimo (www.mobissimo.com)
Orbitz (www.orbitz.com)
Sidestep (www.sidestep.com)
Travelocity (www.travelocity.com)
Travelzoo (www.travelzoo.com)

LAND
Bus

For bus trips, **Greyhound** (☎ 800-231-2222; www .greyhound.com) is the main long-distance operator in the US, and it can get you to Florida from most major cities. It also has the only scheduled statewide service (for more on Greyhound's service around Florida, see p520).

Long-distance fares can be relatively high: bargain airfares can undercut buses on long- distance routes; on shorter routes, renting a car can be cheaper. Nonetheless, long-distance

TRANSPORTATION

bus trips are often available at bargain prices by purchasing or reserving tickets three to seven days in advance. Then, once you've arrived at your destination, you can rent a car to get around (see p521). Inquire about multiday passes.

Sample seven-day-advance-purchase fares (one-way/round-trip) between Miami and some major US cities:

City	Fare	Time	Daily
Atlanta	$107/214	16-18hr	7-10
New Orleans	$130/242	22-25hr	3
New York City	$160/258	30-33hr	8-9
Washington, DC	$153/246	25-27hr	5-6

Car & Motorcycle

Driving to Florida in your own car certainly saves you renting a car while you're here, but if you can do without a car for a portion of your Florida trip, you might save money and time by flying here and then renting a car only for when you need it. (For information on rentals, see p521.) Lots of people come on their motorcycles, but use caution if you haven't done long-distance riding before; it can take a lot out of you.

Florida is serviced by three main interstate highways that connect it with the north and the west of the country: I-95 is the main East Coast route, extending from Miami to Maine; I-10 extends from Jacksonville (where it intersects with I-95) west to Pensacola and onward all the way to Los Angeles, while the I-75 runs west from metro Miami across Alligator Alley and northward to Michigan. I-10 is a particularly rewarding drive to/from points west of Florida, passing near luscious Pensacola beaches as you cross the Florida Panhandle.

Sample distances and times from various points in the US to Miami:

City	Road distance	Time
Atlanta	658 miles	11½hr
Chicago	1394 miles	23½hr
Los Angeles	2754 miles	46hr
New York City	1282 miles	21½hr
Washington, DC	1064 miles	18hr

Train

If you're coming from the East Coast, **Amtrak** (☎ 800-872-7245; www.amtrak.com) makes a comfortable, affordable option for getting to Florida. Amtrak's *Silver Service* (which includes *Silver*

Meteor and *Silver Star* trains) runs between New York and Miami, with services that include Jacksonville, Orlando, Tampa, West Palm Beach and Fort Lauderdale, plus smaller Florida towns in between. Unfortunately, there is no longer any direct service to Florida from Los Angeles or New Orleans; nor is there direct service from Chicago and the Midwest. From these destinations, you need to take a train that connects to the *Silver Service* and transfer; it's not hard, but it adds a day or so to your travel time.

Another option is Amtrak's *Auto Train,* which is designed to take you and your car from the Washington, DC area and drop you off in the Orlando area; this saves you gas, the drive, and having to pay for a rental while here – not bad! The *Auto Train* leaves from Lorton, Virginia and goes only to Sanford, Florida; it runs daily and takes 18 hours, leaving late in the afternoon and arriving the next morning. On the *Auto Train,* you pay for your passage, cabin and car separately.

Book tickets in advance. Children, seniors and military personnel receive discounts.

Sample one-way fares and times from NYC to points in Florida:

From	To	Fare	Time
New York	Jacksonville	$113	19hr
New York	Miami	$115	28hr
New York	Orlando	$113	22hr
New York	Tampa	$113	26hr

SEA

Florida is nearly completely surrounded by the ocean, and is a major cruise-ship port. For more on cruises, see p520. Fort Lauderdale is the largest transatlantic harbor in the US, and adventurous types might be tempted to sign up as crew members for a chance to travel the high seas. For a taste of this life, and a little advice, see the boxed text, p223.

GETTING AROUND

Once you reach Florida, traveling by car is the best way of getting around – it allows you to reach areas not otherwise served by public transportation.

AIR

Flying is convenient for saving time but is more costly than driving. Most airlines within

---

CLIMATE CHANGE & TRAVEL

Climate change is a serious threat to the ecosystems that humans rely upon, and air travel is the fastest-growing contributor to the problem. Lonely Planet regards travel, overall, as a global benefit, but believes we all have a responsibility to limit our personal impact on global warming.

Flying & Climate Change

Pretty much every form of motor travel generates CO_2 (the main cause of human-induced climate change) but planes are far and away the worst offenders, not just because of the sheer distances they allow us to travel, but because they release greenhouse gases high into the atmosphere. The statistics are frightening: two people taking a return flight between Europe and the US will contribute as much to climate change as an average household's gas and electricity consumption over a whole year.

Carbon Offset Schemes

Climatecare.org and other websites use 'carbon calculators' that allow jetsetters to offset the greenhouse gases they are responsible for with contributions to energy-saving projects and other climate-friendly initiatives in the developing world – including projects in India, Honduras, Kazakhstan and Uganda.

Lonely Planet, together with Rough Guides and other concerned partners in the travel industry, supports the carbon offset scheme run by climatecare.org. Lonely Planet offsets all of its staff and author travel.

For more information check out our website: lonelyplanet.com.

Florida fly small commuter planes, so expect propellers and noisy flights!

There are air services between the major cities in Florida, including services between Pensacola and Tallahassee; Jacksonville and Daytona Beach; Gainesville and Orlando; Tampa, Sarasota, Fort Myers and Naples; Miami and Key West; and Fort Lauderdale and West Palm Beach. See individual city sections for specific information.

Airlines in Florida

Main domestic airlines operating in Florida:

American (AA; ☎ 800-433-7300; www.aa.com) Travels to virtually every city in Florida.

Cape Air (9K; ☎ 800-352-0714; www.flycapeair.com) Convenient between South Florida and the Keys.

Continental (CO; ☎ 800-523-3273; www.continental .com) Offers competitive service between 17 Florida cities.

Delta (DL; ☎ 800-221-1212; www.delta.com)

Southwest (SW; ☎ 800-435-9792; www.southwest .com) Major budget carrier flying to Fort Lauderdale, Tampa and Fort Myers.

BICYCLE

Florida has some great regions for cycle touring – like Panhandle beaches and the Florida Keys, for starters, but see Florida Outdoors, p55, for more on great trails and places to bike. But while Florida is flat, it can also get

obscenely hot and humid unless you time it right (for more, see p13). If you're new to cycle touring, get lots of Florida-specific advice from the organizations listed in the Directory (p504), and consider doing it with the support of a tour group. You also might consider the bicycle roadside-assistance program offered by Better World Club (p520).

Adults are not required to wear helmets under Florida law (but helmets are required for those 16 and under). Still, wear one. Florida drivers aren't used to seeing cyclists, nor are roads always cyclist-friendly. Renting a bicycle is easy; if you want to buy, that's easy too. Road rules follow auto rules; ride on the right-hand side of the road, with traffic, not on sidewalks.

Transporting your bike as checked luggage on major airlines has become much more expensive and difficult in recent years. Airlines change their policies at the drop of a hat. A few still do it for free (if the bike is properly boxed), while others charge fees in excess of $100. The **International Bicycle Fund** (www.ibike .org) has a very comprehensive overview of bike regulations by airline and lots of advice.

Bicycle theft is common, especially in Miami Beach; lock your bike and remove the front wheel (and the seat if it has a quick release). Use a sturdy U-type lock rather than a chain and padlock.

TRANSPORTATION

BOAT

Florida is a world center for two major types of boat transport: crewing aboard privately owned yachts, and the fast-growing cruise-ship industry; see the boxed text, p223.

Each coastal city has sightseeing boats that cruise harbors and coastlines. It really pays (in memories) to get out on the water. There's a water-taxi service in Fort Lauderdale (p228), which you should take as it's fun to see Fort Lauderdale from the Intracoastal Waterway.

Cruises

Florida is a huge destination and departure point for cruises of all kinds. Walt Disney World even runs its own **Disney Cruise Line** (☎ 800-951-3532; www.disneycruise.com), which has a number of three- to seven-night cruises throughout the Caribbean, including to Disney's own private island, Castaway Cay.

For specials on other multinight and multi-day cruises, see:

- www.cruise.com
- www.cruiseweb.com
- www.vacationstogo.com
- www.cruisesonly.com

Florida's ports:
Port Canaveral (☎ 321-783-7831; www.portcanaveral .org) Near Orlando and giving Miami a run for its money.
Port Everglades (☎ 954-523-3404; www.broward .org/port, www.fort-lauderdale-cruises.com) The third-busiest Florida port.
Port of Miami (☎ 305-347-4800; www.miamidade .gov/portofmiami) At the world's largest cruise-ship port, the most common trips offered are to the Bahamas, the Caribbean, Key West and Mexico.
Port of Tampa (☎ 813-905-7678, 800-741-2297; www .tampaport.com) Rapidly gaining a foothold in the market.

Major cruise companies:
Carnival Cruise Lines (☎ 888-227-6482; www .carnival.com)
Norwegian Cruise Line (☎ 866-234-0292; www .ncl.com)
Royal Caribbean (☎ 866-562-7625; www.royal caribbean.com)

BUS

Florida's bus network is fairly extensive and reliable and it can get you from one major destination to another, but it's not really worth the extra time involved. And it probably won't get you to the smaller, more interesting places.

Greyhound (☎ 800-231-2222; www.greyhound.com) offers bus services between all major Florida cities. Individual city sections in this book usually include the local address for the Greyhound station. Because the permutations for itinerary planning with regards to bus routes are almost infinite, call Greyhound for specific information. It's always a bit cheaper to take the bus during the week than on the weekend. Also, fares for children are usually about half the adult fare.

To get you started, here are some round-trip fares and travel times around Florida:

From	To	Fare	Time
Daytona Beach	St Augustine	$42	1hr
Fort Lauderdale	Melbourne	$86	4hr
Jacksonville	Tallahassee	$79	3hr
Melbourne	Daytona Beach	$57	3½hr
Miami	Key West	$86	4½hr
Miami	Naples	$65	3hr
Miami	Fort Lauderdale	$12	1hr
Naples	Sarasota	$76	3½hr
Panama City	Pensacola	$56	3hr
St Augustine	Jacksonville	$24	1hr
Sarasota	Tampa	$33	2-2½hr
Tampa	Orlando	$47	2-2½hr
Tallahassee	Panama City	$46	2½hr

CAR & MOTORCYCLE

By far the most convenient and popular way to travel around Florida is by car. In fact, in many Floridian cities it's nearly impossible to get by without one. Even if you're visiting a smaller town such as St Augustine, getting to a supermarket will require a car or a very expensive taxi. Motorcycles are also popular in Florida, and with the exception of the rain in the summer, conditions are perfect for them: good flat roads and warm weather.

Automobile Associations

Until recently, the only US auto club was the **American Automobile Association** (AAA; ☎ 800-874-7532; www.aaa.com), which has reciprocal agreements with automobile associations in other countries; bring your membership card from your country of origin. However, an ecofriendly alternative has emerged: the **Better World Club** (☎ 866-238-1137; www.betterworldclub.com). In both organizations, the central member benefit is 24-hour emergency roadside assistance anywhere in the USA. Both clubs also offer trip planning and free maps, travel-agency services, car insurance and a range of discounts (car rentals, hotels etc).

The differences are that Better World donates 1% of earnings to assist environmental cleanup, it offers ecologically sensitive choices for every service and it advocates politically for environmental causes. Better World also has a roadside-assistance program for bicycles. AAA, on the other hand, offers travel insurance, its popular tour books, diagnostic centers for used-car buyers and a greater number of regional offices (such as in Orlando, Miami and Tampa, plus smaller cities), and it advocates politically for the auto industry.

Driver's License

An international driver's license, obtained before you leave home, is only necessary if your country of origin is non-English-speaking.

Fuel & Spare Parts

Gas stations are ubiquitous and many are open 24 hours a day. Small-town stations may be open only from 7am to 8pm or 9pm. At some stations you must pay before you pump; at others, you may pump before you pay. The more modern pumps have credit- or debit-card terminals built into them, so you can pay with plastic right at the pump. At more expensive, 'full service' stations, an attendant will pump your gas for you; no tip is expected. Fuel prices have been soaring recently, topping $4 per US gallon at the time of research.

Insurance

Liability insurance covers people and property that you might hit; if you have US auto insurance on your vehicle at home, it probably extends its liability coverage while you're in a rental car, but check. However, your personal auto insurance rarely covers damage to the rental vehicle itself. Rental-car companies offer a range of insurance options (and coverage levels). To cover damage to the rental car, they offer a collision damage waiver (CDW) for about $15 a day. However, some credit cards offer reimbursement coverage for collision damages if you rent the car with that credit card; again, check before departing. Most credit-card coverage isn't valid for rentals of more than 15 days or for exotic models, Jeeps, vans or SUVs.

Rental

CAR

Rental cars are readily available at all airport locations and many downtown city locations. With advance reservations for a small car, the daily rate with unlimited mileage is about $25 to $45, while typical weekly rates are $150 to $200, plus a myriad taxes and fees. (Rates for mid-sized cars are often only a tad higher.) If you can manage it, consider renting at a nonairport location, as you'll save the exorbitant airport fees. Because deals abound and the business is competitive, it always pays to shop around between rental companies. You can often snag great last-minute deals via the internet; train reservations made in conjunction with an airplane ticket often yield better rates, too.

Having a major credit card greatly simplifies the rental process. Without one, most companies simply will not rent vehicles, while others require prepayment, a deposit of $200 per week, pay stubs, proof of round-trip airfare and more.

In addition to local agencies mentioned in this guide, here are the larger car-rental companies:

Alamo (☎ 800-462-5266; www.alamo.com)
Avis (☎ 800-331-1212; www.avis.com)
Budget (☎ 800-527-0700; www.budget.com)
Dollar (☎ 800-800-4000; www.dollar.com)
Enterprise (☎ 800-261-7331; www.enterprise.com)
Hertz (☎ 800-654-3131; www.hertz.com)
National (☎ 800-227-7368; www.nationalcar.com)
Rent-a-Wreck (☎ 800-944-7501; www.rent-a-wreck.com)
Thrifty (☎ 800-847-4389; www.thrifty.com)

MOTORCYCLE

If you dream of straddling a Harley across Florida, and many do, **EagleRider** (☎ 888-900-9901; www.eaglerider.com) has offices in Daytona Beach, Fort Lauderdale, Miami and Orlando. They offer a wide range of models, which run from $170 a day and $760 a week (depending on what you choose), plus liability insurance. Adult riders (over 21) are not required by Florida law to wear a helmet, but considering that motorcycle fatalities sharply increased after Florida's helmet law was repealed in 2000, it's a good idea to put one on.

MOTORHOME (RV)

Touring Florida by recreational vehicle can be as low-key or as over-the-top as you are.

Rentals range from ultraefficient VW campers to plush land yachts that resemble suites at the Bellagio in Las Vegas. Whatever mode you choose, you're actually buying freedom (except when you venture to big cities, when freedom's just another word for parking nightmare.)

After settling on the vehicle's size, consider the impact of gas prices, gas mileage, additional mileage costs, insurance and refundable deposits; these can add up quickly. It pays to shop around and read the fine print. Given the many rental choices, it's incredibly hard to generalize, but weekly rentals can start as low as $700 and go up from there. Typically, they don't come with unlimited mileage, so it pays to calculate how far you'll drive and what the per-mile fee will add to the cost of the rental. **CruiseAmerica** (☎ 800-671-8042; www .cruiseamerica.com) is the largest and best known of the national RV-rental firms, and **Adventures on Wheels** (☎ 800-943-3579; www.adventuresonwheels .com) has an office in Miami.

If you've never rented an RV before, check out the website of the **Recreational Vehicle Rental Association** (RVRA; ☎ 703-591-7130; www.rvra.org; 3930 University Dr, Fairfax, VA 22030), which is a great resource for RV information and advice.

Road Rules
The maximum speed limit on interstates is 75mph, but that drops to 65mph and 55mph in urban areas; pay attention to the posted signs. On undivided highways, the speed limit will vary from 30mph in populated areas to 65mph on empty stretches. Speed limits in the city are between 15mph and 45mph. Be especially careful on causeways, which are limited to no more than 45mph.

Florida police officers are merciless when it comes to speed-limit enforcement. Speeding tickets are outrageous: for example, if you're clocked at 50mph in a 40mph zone, the fine is about $150. However, in-car radar detectors are legal in Florida.

As in the rest of the US, drive on the right-hand side of the road. You are supposed to pass on the left-hand side of the road, but in Florida, you'll find that cars pass on both sides! Right turns on a red light are permitted after a full stop. At four-way stop signs, the car that reaches the intersection first has right of way. If it's a tie, the car on the right has right of way. Flashing yellow lights mean caution; flashing red lights mean stop.

All passengers in a car must wear seat belts; the fine for not wearing a seat belt can be as high as $100. All children under three must be in a child safety seat (rental-car companies will provide one if you reserve them in advance).

In cities, parking is often a challenge, especially in Miami neighborhoods, St Augustine, Ybor City in Tampa and Key West. Look for metered parking or, if none is available, head for city or private parking lots. In city lots, parking is generally about $1 to $2 an hour; private lots can charge a lot more, especially during special events.

Remember, it's illegal to drink and drive.

HITCHHIKING
Hitchhiking is never entirely safe in any country, and we don't recommend it. Travelers who decide to hitch should understand that they are taking a small but serious risk. You may not be able to identify the local rapist or murderer before you get into the vehicle. People who do choose to hitch will be safer if they go in pairs and let someone know where they are planning to go. Be sure to ask the driver where he or she is going rather than telling the person where you want to go.

LOCAL TRANSPORTATION
Bus
Local bus services are available only in larger cities; fares are between 75¢ and $1.25. Exact change upon boarding is usually required, though some buses take $1 bills. Transfers – slips of paper that will allow you to change buses – range from free to 25¢. Hours of operation differ from city to city, but generally buses run from approximately 6am to 10pm.

Train
The **Amtrak** (☎ 800-872-7245; www.amtrak.com) trains run between a number of Florida cities. Within Florida, to rely solely on the train to get around, your travel must be very limited, but the train can make a great way to go between two points – ones where you will then rent a car, or where a car isn't necessary (perhaps Miami or an Orlando theme park).

There is twice daily service from Miami to Orlando and Jacksonville on both the *Silver Star* and *Silver Meteor* lines. The *Silver Star* stops in more towns, splitting off to reach Tampa. There is also thruway motorcoach (or bus) service that gets Amtrak passengers to Daytona Beach, St Petersburg and Fort Myers.

Here are some sample one-way fares:

From	To	Fare	Time
Miami	Jacksonville	$55-70	8½-11hr
Miami	Tampa	$35	5½hr
Miami	Orlando	$35	5-7½hr
Orlando	Jacksonville	$22	3hr

Tri-Rail (☎ 800-874-7245; www.tri-rail.com), the commuter rail system, runs between three Florida east-coast counties: Dade, Broward and Palm Beach (see p163 and p227 for more information). The double-decker trains are a marvel of cleanliness and can be quite cheap; fares are calculated on a six-zone basis. However, lengthier trips (such as from Palm Beach to Miami) take about four times longer than driving.

Health

CONTENTS

Because of the high level of hygiene here, infectious diseases are not generally a significant concern for most travelers – it's likely you'd experience nothing worse than a little diarrhea or a mild respiratory infection. Mostly, travelers to Florida need only be concerned about sunburns and mosquito bites.

BEFORE YOU GO

INSURANCE

The United States offers possibly the finest health care in the world. The problem is that, unless you have good insurance, it can be prohibitively expensive. It's essential to purchase travel health insurance if your policy doesn't cover you when you're abroad.

Bring any medications you may need in their original containers, clearly labeled. A signed, dated letter from your physician that describes all of your medical conditions and medications (including generic names) is also a good idea.

If your health insurance does not cover you for medical expenses abroad, consider obtaining supplemental health or travel insurance. Find out in advance whether your insurance plan will make payments directly to the providers or if they will reimburse you later for any overseas health expenditures.

RECOMMENDED VACCINATIONS

No special vaccines are required or recommended for travel to the United States. All travelers should be up to date on routine immunizations, tetanus-diphtheria, measles, chicken pox and influenza.

MEDICAL CHECKLIST

- acetaminophen (Tylenol) or aspirin
- anti-inflammatory drugs (eg ibuprofen)
- antihistamines (for hay fever and allergic reactions)
- antibacterial ointment (eg Bactroban) for cuts and abrasions
- steroid cream or cortisone (for poison ivy and other allergic rashes)
- bandages, gauze, gauze rolls
- adhesive or paper tape
- scissors, safety pins, tweezers
- thermometer
- pocket knife
- DEET-containing insect repellent
- permethrin-containing insect spray for clothing, tents and bed nets
- sunblock

INTERNET RESOURCES

There is a vast wealth of travel health advice on the internet. The World Health Organization publishes a superb book called *International Travel and Health,* which is revised annually and is available online at no cost at www.who .int/ith/. Another website of general interest is MD Travel Health at www.mdtravelhealth. com, which provides complete travel health recommendations for every country, updated daily, also at no cost.

It's usually a good idea to consult your government's travel health website before departure, if one is available:

Australia (www.dfat.gov.au/travel/)
Canada (www.hc-sc.gc.ca/english/index.html)
UK (www.doh.gov.uk/traveladvice/index.htm)
United States (www.cdc.gov/travel/)

IN FLORIDA

AVAILABILITY & COST OF HEALTH CARE

In general, if you have a medical emergency your best bet is to find the nearest hospital and go to its emergency room. If the problem isn't urgent, you can call a nearby hospital and ask for a referral to a local physician, which is usually cheaper than a trip to the emergency room. You should avoid stand-alone, for-profit urgent-care centers, which tend to perform large numbers of expensive tests, even for minor illnesses.

Pharmacies are abundantly supplied, but you may find that some medications that are available over the counter in your home country require a prescription in the US, and, if you don't have insurance to cover the cost of prescriptions, they can be shockingly expensive.

INFECTIOUS DISEASES

In addition to more-common ailments, there are several infectious diseases that are un-known or uncommon outside North America. Most are acquired by mosquito or tick bites.

HIV/AIDS

As with most parts of the world, HIV infection occurs in the US. You should not assume, on the basis of someone's background or appear-ance, that they're free of this or other sexually transmitted diseases. Be sure to use a condom for all sexual encounters.

Lyme Disease

This disease has been reported from many states, but most documented cases occur in the northeastern part of the country, espe-cially New York, New Jersey, Connecticut and Massachusetts. A smaller number of cases occur in the northern Midwest and in the northern Pacific coastal regions, in-cluding northern California. Lyme disease is transmitted by deer ticks, which are only 1mm to 2mm long. Most cases occur in the late spring and summer. The Center for Disease Control (CDC) has an informative, if slightly scary, web page on Lyme disease (www.cdc.gov/ncid od/dvbid/lyme/).

The first symptom is usually an expand-ing red rash that is often pale in the center, known as a bull's-eye rash. However, in many cases, no rash is observed. Flulike symptoms are common, including fever, headache, joint pains, body aches and malaise. When the infection is treated promptly with an ap-propriate antibiotic, usually doxycycline or amoxicillin, the cure rate is high. Luckily, since the tick must be attached for 36 hours or more to transmit Lyme disease, most cases can be prevented by performing a thorough tick check after you've been outdoors – see Tick Bites, p526 for details.

Rabies

Rabies is a viral infection of the brain and spinal cord that is almost always fatal. The virus is carried in the saliva of infected ani-mals and is transmitted through an animal bite, though contamination of any break in the skin with infected saliva may result in rabies. In the US, most cases of human rabies are related to exposure to bats. Rabies may be contracted from raccoons, skunks, foxes and unvaccinated cats and dogs.

If there is any possibility, however small, that you have been exposed to rabies, you should seek preventative treatment. This consists of rabies immune globulin and ra-bies vaccine and is quite safe. Any contact with a bat should be discussed with health authorities, because bats have small teeth and may not leave obvious bite marks and a rabies prophylaxis may be necessary.

West Nile Virus

These infections were unknown in the US until a few years ago, but have now been re-ported in almost all states. The virus is trans-mitted by culex mosquitoes, which are active in late summer and early fall and generally bite after dusk. Most infections are mild or asymptomatic, but the virus may infect the central nervous system, leading to fever, head-ache, confusion, lethargy, coma and some-times death. There is no treatment for West Nile virus. For the latest update on the areas affected by West Nile, go to the **US Geological Survey** (http://westnilemaps.usgs.gov/) website.

TRAVELER'S DIARRHEA
Giardiasis

This parasitic infection of the small intes-tine occurs throughout the world. Symptoms may include nausea, bloating, cramps and diarrhea, and may last for weeks. To protect yourself from giardia, you should avoid drink-ing directly from lakes, ponds, streams and rivers, which may be contaminated by animal or human feces. The infection can also be transmitted from person to person if proper hand washing is not performed. Giardiasis is easily diagnosed by a stool test and is readily treated with antibiotics.

ENVIRONMENTAL HAZARDS
Alligators

Alligators generally only eat when they're hungry – unless they think they're being attacked. They've been known to munch on small animals or things that look like them, such as small children or people crouching down low to snap a photo. Fairly common in suburban and rural lakes, alligators move around but generally mind their own business. 'Nuisance alligators' – those that eat pets or livestock – become the bailiwick of the police (call ☎ 911 if you see an alligator in a city). Generally speaking, the best thing to do with an alligator is stay away from it completely.

Bites & Stings

Common-sense approaches to these concerns are the most effective: wear boots when hiking to protect against snakes, and wear long sleeves and pants to protect against ticks and mosquitoes.

ANIMAL BITES

Do not attempt to pet, handle or feed any animal, with the exception of domestic animals known to be free of infectious diseases. Most injuries from animals are related to a person's attempt to touch or feed an animal.

Any bite or scratch by a mammal, including bats, should be promptly and thoroughly cleansed with soap and water, followed by the application of an antiseptic such as iodine or alcohol. The local health authorities should be contacted immediately for possible post-exposure rabies treatment, whether or not you've been immunized against rabies. It's also advisable to start an antibiotic, as wounds caused by animal bites and scratches frequently become infected.

JELLYFISH STINGS

Take a peek into the water before you plunge in to make certain it's not jellyfish territory. These gelatinous creatures with saclike bodies and stinging tentacles are fairly common in Florida's Atlantic coast. They're most often found drifting near the shore or washed up on the beach. The sting of a jellyfish varies from mild to severe, depending on the type of jellyfish. But unless you have an allergic reaction to jellyfish venom, the stings are not generally dangerous.

The Portuguese man-of-war is the worst type to encounter. Not technically a jellyfish, the man-of-war is a colonial hydrozoan, or a colony of coelenterates, rather than a solitary coelenterate like a true jellyfish. Its body consists of a translucent, bluish bladderlike float,

which generally grows to about 4in to 5in in length. A man-of-war sting is very painful, similar to a bad bee sting, except that you're likely to be stung more than once from clusters of its incredibly long tentacles, containing hundreds of stinging cells. Even touching a man-of-war a few hours after it's washed up on shore can result in burning stings.

If you do get stung, quickly remove the tentacles and apply vinegar or a meat tenderizer containing papain (derived from papaya), which neutralizes the toxins. For serious reactions, including chest pains or difficulty in breathing, seek medical attention.

MOSQUITO BITES

When traveling in areas where West Nile or other mosquito-borne illnesses have been reported, keep yourself covered (wear long sleeves, long pants, hats and shoes rather than sandals) and apply a good insect repellent, preferably one containing DEET, to exposed skin and clothing. In general, adults and children over 12 should use preparations containing 25% to 35% DEET, which usually lasts about six hours. Children between two and 12 years of age should use preparations containing no more than 10% DEET, applied sparingly, which will usually last about three hours. Neurologic toxicity has been reported from DEET, especially in children, but appears to be extremely uncommon and generally related to overuse. DEET-containing compounds should not be used on children under the age of two.

Insect repellents containing certain botanical products, including eucalyptus oil and soybean oil, are effective but last only 1½ to two hours. Citronella-based products are not effective.

Visit the CDC's West Nile webpage (www.cdc.gov/ncidod/dvbid/westnile/prevention_info.htm) for prevention information.

TICK BITES

Ticks are parasitic arachnids that may be present in brush, forest and grasslands. Hikers often get them on their legs or in their boots. Adult ticks suck blood from hosts by burrowing into the skin, and can carry infections such as Lyme disease.

Always check your body for ticks after walking through high grass or a thickly forested area. If ticks are found unattached, they can simply be brushed off. If a tick is found attached, use tweezers to push down the skin surrounding the tick, then grab the head and gently pull upwards – do not twist it. (If no tweezers are available, use your fingers, but protect them from contamination with a piece of tissue or paper.) Do not rub oil, alcohol or petroleum jelly on it. If you become sick in the next couple of weeks, consult a doctor.

SNAKEBITES

There are several varieties of venomous snakes in the US, but they do not cause instantaneous death, and antivenins are available. First aid is to place a light constricting bandage over the bite, to keep the wounded part below the level of the heart and to move the wound as little as possible. Stay calm and get to a medical facility as soon as possible. Bring the dead snake for identification if you can, but don't risk being bitten again. Do not use the 'cut an X and suck out the venom' trick; this causes more damage to snakebite victims than the bites do themselves.

SPIDER BITES

Although there are many species of spiders in the US, the only ones that cause significant illness are the black widow and the brown recluse spiders. The black widow is black or brown in color, measuring about 15mm in body length, with a shiny top, fat body, and distinctive red or orange hourglass figure on its underside. It's found throughout the US, usually in barns, woodpiles, sheds, harvested crops and outdoor toilets. The brown recluse or hobo spider is brown in color, usually 10mm in body length, with a dark violin-shaped mark on the top of the upper section of the body. It's usually found in the south and in the southern Midwest, but has spread to other parts of the country in recent years. The brown recluse is active mostly at night, lives in dark sheltered areas such as under porches and in woodpiles, and typically bites when trapped.

If bitten by a black widow, you should apply ice or cold packs and go immediately to the nearest emergency room. Complications of a black widow bite may include muscle spasms,

breathing difficulties and high blood pressure. The bite of a brown recluse typically causes a large, inflamed wound, sometimes associated with fever and chills (the bite of a hobo spider produces milder symptoms than that of a brown recluse spider). If bitten, apply ice and see a physician.

Dehydration

Visitors to coastal areas may not realize how much water they're losing, as sweat evaporates almost immediately and increased urination (to help the blood process oxygen more efficiently) can go unnoticed. The prudent tourist will make sure to drink more water than usual – think a gallon a day if you're active. Parents can carry fruit and fruit juices to help keep kids hydrated.

Severe dehydration can easily cause disorientation and confusion, and even day hikers have gotten lost and died because they ignored their thirst. So bring plenty of water, even on short hikes, and drink it!

Heat Exhaustion & Heat Stroke

Dehydration or salt deficiency can cause heat exhaustion. Take time to acclimatize to high temperatures and make sure you get enough liquid. Symptoms of salt deficiency are fatigue, lethargy, headaches, giddiness and cramps. Salt tablets may help. Vomiting or diarrhea can deplete your liquid and salt levels. Anhydrotic heat exhaustion, caused by the inability to sweat, is rare. Unlike other forms of heat exhaustion, it may strike people who have been in the heat for a while, rather than newcomers. Always use water bottles on long trips. One gallon of water per person per day is recommended if hiking.

Long, continuous exposure to high temperatures can lead to the sometimes-fatal condition of heat stroke, which occurs when the body's heat-regulating mechanism breaks down and body temperature rises to dangerous levels. Hospitalization is essential for extreme cases, but meanwhile get out of the sun, remove clothing, cover the body with a wet sheet or towel and fan continually.

HEALTH

The Authors

JEFF CAMPBELL
Coordinating Author

Jeff Campbell is the great-grandson of Florida pioneers who cleared the pines, mined the phosphate and paved the roads in central Florida. As a child, he remembers winter nights driving with his grandfather through the orange groves to 'light the pots,' searching for alligators in the local lake and riding Space Mountain the year it opened. As an adult, he's been a travel writer for Lonely Planet since 2000. He's been the coordinating author of *USA* three times, and also of *Southwest USA, Zion & Bryce National Parks Guide* and *Hawaii*.

BECCA BLOND
Tampa Bay & Southwest Florida

Becca first visited Florida on an 8th-grade class trip. Since then she has returned on holiday more than a couple of times – she has family in Tampa and Sanibel Island, and friends in Naples. She has been writing for Lonely Planet for the last five years, and has authored more than 25 guides covering five continents. When not on the road she lives in Boulder, Colorado, with her fiancé, Aaron, and their oversized bulldog, Duke. Beach-bumming is one of her favorite activities, so she was super excited to hit the road and research Florida's southwest coast.

JENNIFER DENNISTON
Orlando & Walt Disney World

Jennifer caught the travel bug at age nine, when her parents took the family on a 10-week trip through Europe; by the time she was 21, she had traveled independently across five continents. She earned a Masters degree in American Studies, taught writing at the University of Iowa and has written for Lonely Planet's *Southwest USA, USA, Arizona* and *Grand Canyon National Parks,* specializing in writing about traveling with children. She, her husband Rhawn and their girls Anna (eight years old) and Harper (five years old) spend summers road-tripping through the US and every winter escape icy Iowa for a couple of weeks in Florida. Jennifer's children, who accompanied her to Orlando and Walt Disney World, offered critical insight for this book.

THE AUTHORS

LONELY PLANET AUTHORS

Why is our travel information the best in the world? It's simple: our authors are passionate, dedicated travelers. They don't take freebies in exchange for positive coverage so you can be sure the advice you're given is impartial. They travel widely to all the popular spots, and off the beaten track. They don't research using just the internet or phone. They discover new places not included in any other guidebook. They personally visit thousands of hotels, restaurants, palaces, trails, galleries, temples and more. They speak with dozens of locals every day to make sure you get the kind of insider knowledge only a local could tell you. They take pride in getting all the details right, and in telling it how it is. Think you can do it? Find out how at **lonelyplanet.com**.

BETH GREENFIELD · The Panhandle

Beth, a New Jersey native, made her first pilgrimage to Florida as a toddler to visit her snowbird grandparents, but it's only as an adult that she has explored, with great joy and fascination, beyond the Miami area. Working as a journalist for nearly 15 years, she has written about everything from local politics to worldwide travel, and is currently a contributor to the *New York Times* and *Time Out New York*. A Lonely Planet author since 2002, Beth has contributed to the *Mexico, Florida, New York City* and *USA* guides. She is currently working on a memoir, due for 2010 publication, and lives in New York City.

ADAM KARLIN · Miami, The Everglades, Florida Keys & Key West

Adam visited Florida as a grandson for much of his childhood and later worked there as a reporter for the *Key West Citizen*. During his time covering Monroe County and its assorted trailer-park evictions, FEMA troubles and *Days of our Lives*-esque local politics, he passed Lonely Planet's writing test. He was perfectly happy to go back to the weird and wonderful Sunshine State on assignment. He is the author of Lonely Planet's *Miami & the Keys*.

WILLY VOLK · Southeast Florida, The Space Coast, Northeast Florida

Willy decided he liked traveling when his family moved from Iowa to Egypt when he was 10. Always one to wander down dark alleys, he soon found himself in college in Sarasota, Florida. After graduation, he suffered an acute case of wanderlust, so he bolted for Zambia, where he served as a Peace Corps volunteer for three years and explored the southern half of Africa with his friends. After returning to the US, Willy settled in South Florida, where he works from home, visits the beach as often as he can and is always in search of a better basket of conch fritters, a bigger slice of Key lime pie and a more glorious spot to watch the sun set with his sweet, sweet wife, Jodie.

Behind the Scenes

THIS BOOK

This 5th edition of Lonely Planet's *Florida* was written and updated by Jeff Campbell (coordinating author), Becca Blond, Jennifer Denniston, Beth Greenfield, Adam Karlin and Willy Volk. The 4th edition of Florida was written by Kim Grant (coordinating author), Loretta Chilcoat, Beth Greenfield and Catherine Le Nevez. The 3rd edition was written by Kim Grant, Elaine Merrill and Paige Penland. The 1st and 2nd editions were cowritten by Nick and Corinna Selby. This guidebook was commissioned in Lonely Planet's Oakland office and produced by the following:

Commissioning Editors Jay Cooke, Jennye Garibaldi
Coordinating Editor Anna Metcalfe
Coordinating Cartographer Sam Sayer
Coordinating Layout Designer Carol Jackson
Managing Editor Bruce Evans
Managing Cartographer Shahara Ahmed
Managing Layout Designer Celia Wood
Assisting Editors Melissa Faulkner, Laura Gibb, Penelope Goodes, Helen Koehne, Alison Ridgway, Kate Whitfield
Assisting Cartographers Peter Shields
Cover Designer Pepi Bluck
Project Manager Chris Love

Thanks to Eoin Dunlevy, Lisa Knights, Alison Lyall, Wayne Murphy, Raphael Richards, Michael Ruff

THANKS
JEFF CAMPBELL

My heartfelt thanks go to my coauthors who were, to a person, fantastic. In particular, Jennifer's kid-tested Orlando advice was invaluable for the Florida for Kids chapter. I thank Lonely Planet's commissioning editor Jay Cooke for putting wind in our sails and Lonely Planet's commissioning editor Jennye Garibaldi for bringing us in. Finally, I dedicate my work to my grandparents, who loved Florida completely, heart and soul.

BECCA BLOND

Huge, huge thanks to Dale Meck in Naples, for all the awesome advice and the hospitality. I loved your place the first time I saw it, now I just love it more! Also big hugs to my cousin Eric, his fiancée Denise and their daughter Khalia in the Tampa/St Pete area. It was great catching up. You guys are the best. Khalia: I hope to hunt down more pirates and treasure with you soon! In Sanibel, I have to give thanks to Lee and Gene Seidler, for showing

THE LONELY PLANET STORY

Fresh from an epic journey across Europe, Asia and Australia in 1972, Tony and Maureen Wheeler sat at their kitchen table stapling together notes. The first Lonely Planet guidebook, *Across Asia on the Cheap,* was born.

Travelers snapped up the guides. Inspired by their success, the Wheelers began publishing books to Southeast Asia, India and beyond. Demand was prodigious, and the Wheelers expanded the business rapidly to keep up. Over the years, Lonely Planet extended its coverage to every country and into the virtual world via lonelyplanet.com and the Thorn Tree message board.

As Lonely Planet became a globally loved brand, Tony and Maureen received several offers for the company. But it wasn't until 2007 that they found a partner whom they trusted to remain true to the company's principles of traveling widely, treading lightly and giving sustainably. In October of that year, BBC Worldwide acquired a 75% share in the company, pledging to uphold Lonely Planet's commitment to independent travel, trustworthy advice and editorial independence.

Today, Lonely Planet has offices in Melbourne, London and Oakland, with over 500 staff members and 300 authors. Tony and Maureen are still actively involved with Lonely Planet. They're traveling more often than ever, and they're devoting their spare time to charitable projects. And the company is still driven by the philosophy of *Across Asia on the Cheap*: 'All you've got to do is decide to go and the hardest part is over. So go!'

me the island and the wonderful dinner and conversation (and quotes!). At home, my undying gratitude is extended to my family and friends: Aaron, Duke, Mom, Dad, Jessica, G-Ma Vera. This book is dedicated to my grandma Jennie, who died in November at the ripe age of 95. She has always been my inspiration, and her motto: 'Life is an attitude and age is a number,' will always be my inspiration. At Lonely Planet, love to Jay, Jennye and the wonderful authors on the Florida team! XX B.

JENNIFER DENNISTON
Thanks to my commissioning editors Jay Cooke and Jennye Garibaldi, coauthor Jeff, cartographer Alison Lyall, Disney expert Kate Showalter and Orlando local Javier Restrepo. Special thanks to my girls Anna and Harper, Marj and Wes Whitley, my parents Joy and Rudy Rasin, and my husband Rhawn. I couldn't do this without you.

BETH GREENFIELD
Many thanks to the helpful folks at the Pensacola Visitors Center, the Tallahassee Visitors Center and at Sundog Books in Seaside, as well as to Gary Anton at Bradfordville Blues Club, Penny Vinotti at the Florida Caverns State Park, George (for your Pensacola excitement), Jeff Campbell, Jennye Garibaldi, Mom and Dad and, of course, Kiki.

ADAM KARLIN
Thanks to the Paquet family, Florida friends (especially the ex-Orlando Sentinel gang in DC), the Marathon crew, particularly Aaron, Jen and Mary, and anyone and everyone else who helped me on the road. Big ups to underpaid NPS rangers and serving staff in hotels, restaurants, bars etc in the Keys. And Mom and Dad, of course.

WILLY VOLK
Willy would like to thank his wife for her support and patience; Rob and Elizabeth for their suggestions and humor; Brian for helping explore Daytona; his parents for their encouragement; and his dogs for their sweet kisses upon his every homecoming. Thanks also goes to Jay, Jennye, Jeff, Brad, Wild Lyle, Ed Conklin, the East Central Aquatic preserve staff and every unassuming

SEND US YOUR FEEDBACK
We love to hear from travelers – your comments keep us on our toes and help make our books better. Our well-traveled team reads every word on what you loved or loathed about this book. Although we cannot reply individually to postal submissions, we always guarantee that your feedback goes straight to the appropriate authors, in time for the next edition. Each person who sends us information is thanked in the next edition – and the most useful submissions are rewarded with a free book.

To send us your updates – and find out about Lonely Planet events, newsletters and travel news – visit our award-winning website: **lonelyplanet.com/contact**.

Note: we may edit, reproduce and incorporate your comments in Lonely Planet products such as guidebooks, websites and digital products, so let us know if you don't want your comments reproduced or your name acknowledged. For a copy of our privacy policy visit lonelyplanet.com/privacy.

Floridian Willy wheedled tips from without their knowledge.

OUR READERS
Many thanks to the travelers who used the last edition and wrote to us with helpful hints, useful advice and interesting anecdotes:
Ted Adams, David Andrews, Didier Autard, Hilary Briegal, Romelle Castle, Nancy Collins, Frances and Terry Daniel, Annique De Haas, Sandie Deane, Jean-Louis Delaye, Denny Ebert, Mark Felton, Gila Goldstein, Annette Griffiths, Heather Harris, Ina Hensel, Tom Hunter, Hendrica Kock, Yvonne Laport, Graham Lowe, Jacco Maan, Peter and Delia Milner, Philip Milton, Jenny Mitcham, Elisabeth Mitter, Tara Porter, Eileen Roberts, Richard Samuelson, Berna Schuurman, Erin Taylor, Samuel Taylor, Denise Travailleur, Jean Williams.

ACKNOWLEDGMENTS
Many thanks to the following for the use of their content:
Globe on title page ©Mountain High Maps 1993 Digital Wisdom, Inc.

Index

GreenDex

To help our readers 'go green,' Lonely Planet has compiled this GreenDex. The following Florida businesses and organizations were selected by this guide's authors because they demonstrated active sustainable-tourism policies. There is no cut-and-dried criteria for inclusion. Some are involved in conservation or environmental education, while others are owned by local or native peoples and aim to preserve regional and traditional cultures. For more information on the specific ecological and sustainability issues confronting Florida, visit the website of the state's **Department of Environmental Protection** (DEP; www.dep.state.fl.us). DEP also runs a **Green Lodging Program** (www.dep.state.fl.us/greenlodging) that certifies ecofriendly Florida hotels. For an overview of how to lessen the impact of outdoor activities in Florida, see the boxed text, A Kinder, Gentler Wilderness Encounter (p75).

We want to keep developing our sustainable-tourism content. If you think we've omitted someone who should be listed here, or if you disagree with our choices, email us at talk2us@lonelyplanet.com.au. For more information about sustainable tourism and Lonely Planet, see www.lonelyplanet.com/responsibletravel.

MAP LEGEND

ROUTES

Tollway	Mall/Steps
Freeway	Tunnel
Primary	Pedestrian Overpass
Secondary	Walking Tour
Tertiary	Walking Trail
Lane	Walking Path
Under Construction	Track
Unsealed Road	One-Way Street

TRANSPORT

Ferry	Rail
Metro	Rail (Underground)
Monorail	Tram

HYDROGRAPHY

River, Creek	Canal
Intermittent River	Water
Swamp	Lake (Dry)
Reef	Mudflats

BOUNDARIES

State, Provincial	Regional, Suburb
Marine Park	Ancient Wall

AREA FEATURES

Airport	Land
Area of Interest	Mall
Beach, Desert	Market
Building	Park
Campus	Reservation
Cemetery, Christian	Sports
Forest	Urban

POPULATION

◎	**CAPITAL (NATIONAL)**	◉ **CAPITAL (STATE)**
●	**Large City**	○ **Medium City**
○	Small City	○ Town, Village

SYMBOLS

Sights/Activities	Drinking	Information
Beach	Drinking	Bank, ATM
Buddhist	Café	Embassy/Consulate
Canoeing, Kayaking	**Entertainment**	Hospital, Medical
Castle, Fortress	Entertainment	Information
Christian	**Shopping**	Internet Facilities
Diving, Snorkeling	Shopping	Police Station
Jewish	**Sleeping**	Post Office, GPO
Monument	Sleeping	Telephone
Museum, Gallery	Camping	Toilets
Point of Interest	**Transport**	**Geographic**
Pool	Airport, Airfield	Lighthouse
Ruin	Border Crossing	Lookout
Snorkeling	Bus Station	Mountain
Surfing, Surf Beach	Cycling, Bicycle Path	National Park
Winery, Vineyard	General Transport	Picnic Area
Zoo, Bird Sanctuary	Parking Area	Waterfall
Eating	Petrol Station	
Eating	Taxi Rank	

LONELY PLANET OFFICES

Australia
Head Office
Locked Bag 1, Footscray, Victoria 3011
☎ 03 8379 8000, fax 03 8379 8111
talk2us@lonelyplanet.com.au

USA
150 Linden St, Oakland, CA 94607
☎ 510 250 6400, toll free 800 275 8555
fax 510 893 8572
info@lonelyplanet.com

UK
2nd fl, 186 City Rd,
London EC1V 2NT
☎ 020 7106 2100, fax 020 7106 2101
go@lonelyplanet.co.uk

Published by Lonely Planet Publications Pty Ltd
ABN 36 005 607 983

© Lonely Planet Publications Pty Ltd 2009

© photographers as indicated 2009

Cover photograph: Pink Flamingo Decoration on Tropical Beach © Don Hammond/Design Pics/Corbis. Many of the images in this guide are available for licensing from Lonely Planet Images: www.lonely planetimages.com.